from
PEOPLES
into
NATIONS

from

PEOPLES

into

NATIONS

A History of Eastern Europe

JOHN CONNELLY

PRINCETON UNIVERSITY PRESS

PRINCETON & OXFORD

Copyright © 2020 by Princeton University Press

Requests for permission to reproduce material from this work
should be sent to permissions@press.princeton.edu

Published by Princeton University Press
41 William Street, Princeton, New Jersey 08540
6 Oxford Street, Woodstock, Oxfordshire OX20 1TR

press.princeton.edu

ISBN (e-book) 9780691189185

Library of Congress Cataloging-in-Publication Data

Names: Connelly, John, author.
Title: From peoples into nations : a history of Eastern Europe / John Connelly.
Description: Princeton : Princeton University Press, [2020] | Includes bibliographical
    references and index.
Identifiers: LCCN 2019021312 | ISBN 9780691167121 (hardback)
Subjects: LCSH: Nationalism—Europe, Eastern—History. | Europe, Eastern—History. |
    Europe, Eastern—History—Autonomy and independence movements. | Europe,
    Eastern—Politics and government.
Classification: LCC DJK38 .C64 2020 | DDC 943.7—dc23
    LC record available at https://lccn.loc.gov/2019021312

British Library Cataloging-in-Publication Data is available

Editorial: Eric Crahan, Thalia Leaf, and Pamela Weidman
Production Editorial: Nathan Carr
Jacket/Cover Credit: Blaha Lujza Square, Budapest, 1956
Production: Merli Guerra and Brigid Ackerman
Publicity: Maria Whelan, James Schneider, and Kate Farquhar-Thomson
Copyeditor: Cyd Westmoreland

This book has been composed in Arno

Printed on acid-free paper. ∞

Printed in the United States of America

10 9 8 7 6 5 4 3 2 1

To Nico, Irena, and Charlotte

CONTENTS

from
PEOPLES
into
NATIONS

Introduction

War broke out in Europe in 1914 because of a deed carried out in the name of a people no one had previously heard of.

That June, after years of internecine turmoil and armed conflict in southeastern Europe, a Bosnian Serb named Gavrilo Princip shot and killed Franz Ferdinand, heir to the Habsburg throne, in Sarajevo. The assassin said he was acting to defend the interests of the *Yugoslavs*, or South Slavs, who were seeking independence from the Austro-Hungarian monarchy.

The ensuing conflict was not only "Great" but also total, with states, economies, and armies aiming to organize themselves and destroy one another in ever more effective ways. When the war ended in 1918, statesmen and revolutionary activists made a new Europe, drawing on the impulse that had taken hold of Gavrilo Princip and his friends: that peoples should govern themselves. Clothed in the words *national self-determination*, this impulse was raised as a high political standard by both Bolshevik leader Vladimir I. Lenin and US President Woodrow Wilson, denoting socialism for the first, liberal democracy for the second.

The United States now got into the business of democratization, but it also fostered the first stages in Eurasia of *decolonization*, replacing imperial states like Austria-Hungary and the Ottoman Empire with dozens of supposed nation-states, several of which, like Czechoslovakia and Princip's Yugoslavia, constituted revolutionary acts on the old map of Europe. Yet democratization turned out to be trickier than anyone imagined, and during the Depression of the early 1930s, words emerged to describe new movements led by haters of democracy: fascism, corporatism, Nazism, totalitarianism.

Late in the decade, Nazi aggression exploded into war on Czechoslovakia and Poland and began spawning more new vocabulary, some of which made its way into English (for example, blitzkrieg). Specialists know about the Nazi plan to resettle Eastern Europe with Germans and create an imperial space extending to Moscow and the Crimea, the infamous *Generalplan Ost*, and most grade school graduates know translations directly from the German for crimes committed along the way: "final solution," "ethnic cleansing."[1] The word "genocide" was originally formulated in Polish (*ludobójstwo*) to denote the new crime of massacring an entire people.

At war's end, the disruption continued, with "population exchanges" and re-settlements of "displaced persons," phrases no one alive in 1914 would have understood. New regimes arose called "people's democracies," featuring dictatorships of the proletariat that used five-year plans to end the uncertainties of capitalism. A new age had supposedly emerged of human equality. Yet roughly since 1947, this period in which millions suffered deprivations, internal surveillance, and prison camps, has been called the Cold War, a time when the world divided into two hostile camps and seemed to stand on the verge of real war.

In 1953 Joseph Stalin died, and a system named after him plunged into crisis. Young *reform Communists* sent the clock forward by going backward. They dusted off ideas from eighteenth-century liberal philosophy, like "division of powers" and the rights to vote and assemble and speak, and they attempted to implement them in a process known as the "Prague Spring" of 1968. Yet in the miserable summer that followed, Soviet tanks restored Communist orthodoxy, and Soviet leader Leonid Brezhnev announced an eponymous doctrine, according to which socialism could lead only to Communism, and any reform toward pluralism would trigger fraternal assistance by the socialist community of states.

Because both the North Atlantic Treaty Organization (NATO) and the Warsaw Pact believed the intervention had stabilized Soviet rule in Eastern Europe, the two sides negotiated measures to reduce the dangers of armed conflict during the era of détente. At the 1975 Helsinki Conference, they reaffirmed their commitment to a principle enunciated soon after World War II: human rights. Yet just two years later, Communist authorities in Prague arrested a rock band called Plastic People of the Universe solely because they did not like its message. That caused Czech dissident intellectuals, mostly former Communists, to remind the regime of the accord it had just signed. The document they circulated became known as Charter 77. One of them, the playwright Václav Havel, also coined an ideal for citizens faced with pressures of self-censorship that would have caused people in 1914 to scratch their heads: living in truth.

Historians explored everyday life under Communism more directly after 1989, when Brezhnev's doctrine was scrapped, along with an edifice dividing Germany's former capital called the "Berlin Wall," except for a half-kilometer strip meant to edify tourists. The supposedly evident bankruptcy of this repressive system caused some to talk of an "end of history," because all countries were destined for free-market liberalism.

Now Eastern Europe was connected not only to its own interrupted history but also to the West. As after World War I, ideas and advisors made landfall, often not knowing anything about the region and its complexities, including native traditions of rights and democracy. This was a second wave of democratization, but like the first, it did not turn out as planned, spawning a batch of neologisms: Srebrenica, neopopulism, neoliberalism, and *illiberal democracy*, the last coined by Hungary's Viktor Orbán, an erstwhile grave digger of Communist authoritarianism who rescued himself from oblivion in democracy's free for all by becoming a nationalist authoritarian.

* * *

What unites this dramatic and unsettling history is a band of countries that runs from the Baltic Sea down to the Adriatic and Black Seas, between the much larger, historically imperial Russia and Turkey in the east, and Prussian and Austrian Germany in the west. These small countries constitute East Central Europe, a space where more of the twentieth century happened—for good and for bad—than anywhere else on the planet.

If one seeks a simple explanation for the energies that caused this area to produce so much drama and so many new concepts, a glance at the map suggests nationalism: no other region has witnessed such frequent, radical, and violent changing of borders to make nations fit states.[2] Two maps, one from 1800, one from 2000, tell the basic story: a shift from simplicity to complexity, from one small and three large multinational powers to more than twenty national states.

The story was carried forward by the demands of East European nationalists to control territory, demands that triggered resistance, because they contested imperial power and the European order. Since the 1820s, the work of nationalists has brought independent states into being in three stages: the first in 1878, when the Congress of Berlin produced Serbia, Romania, Bulgaria, and Montenegro; the second, in 1919, when revolution and peace making generated Czechoslovakia, Yugoslavia, and Poland; and most recently, in the 1990s, when Czechoslovakia broke peacefully into the Czech Republic and Slovakia, and Yugoslavia fragmented violently into Slovenia, Croatia, Serbia, two entities in Bosnia, Macedonia, Montenegro, and Kosovo. Hungary became de facto independent in 1867, when the Austrian Empire divided into Austria-Hungary; after 1920, it emerged much reduced from World War I, two-thirds of its territory going to its neighbors.

What can be debated is whether the degree of violence, especially in World War I, was necessary to break loose the nation-states that now constitute the map of Eastern Europe. Austria-Hungary was more resilient than critics gave it credit for and only began unraveling in the final year of a war that had been costly beyond any expectations. And there was little relation between intention and outcome: World War I did not begin as a war of national liberation. Yet by 1917, as the causality lists soared and any relation between intention and outcome was lost, it was interpreted to be one. It was a war for democracy—for Wilson's national self-determination—and that helped spawn the new nation-states.

At the same time, without the cause Gavrilo Princip claimed to represent (that South Slavs should live in one state), there would have been no assassination, no Habsburg ultimatum to Serbia (which had trained Princip and supplied him with his pistol) in July 1914, and no war. Seen in rational terms, the Habsburgs' belief that Serbia, a state of three million, represented a challenge requiring a full-scale military assault launched from their state of fifty-two million, seems one of history's great overreactions. But Princip, the frail eighteen-year-old rejected from the Serb army for his small stature, embodied the challenge of an idea, the idea of ethnic nationalism, and the Habsburg monarchy had no response other than naked force.

* * *

The Habsburgs were far from alone in believing that nationalism was a force that eluded rational discussion. At the height of the Munich crisis in 1938, British Prime Minister Neville Chamberlain called Czechoslovakia "far away lands of which we know nothing." Bohemia with its population of Germans and Czechs was supposedly governed by passions and not reason. In the 1990s, a well-read US president threw up his hands over the prospects of ending genocidal killing in southeastern Europe, portraying the peoples there as governed by "ancient hatreds"; until they "stopped killing each other, bad things will continue to happen."[3]

But nationalists are no more resistant to understanding than any other actors in history. They are guided by motives that are open to reconstruction and analysis. What seemed rational to one side of a nationality dispute usually seemed irrational to the other, and in fact their deeds confound any attempt to divide reason from unreason.[4]

Take Gavrilo Princip. On one hand, his act is easy to understand. When Austrian authorities apprehended him, he said he knew "what was happening in the villages." Thanks to education provided by the Austrian regime, which had ruled Bosnia since 1878, he knew that Austria had done little to alter traditional patterns in the countryside according to which poor Christian sharecroppers—like his parents—worked on properties owned by Muslims and were condemned to second-class lives. He was one of nine children, but five of his siblings had died in infancy. His father worked several jobs, one of which was lugging heavy bundles of mail up and down mountains, even at an advanced age. For Princip, the shots he fired at the Archduke promised to end this social injustice.

Yet on the other hand, the next step in his thinking is less easy to fit into cold categories of self-interest. He and his friends took for granted that a South Slav state would miraculously do away with all injustice. It would be a place where his parents and other peasants would no longer be a despised underclass, but instead human beings, living no longer under the condescending eyes of imperial authorities, whether Turkish or Austro-German or Hungarian. They would be fully respected in a world of their own culture and language, a world where everyone knew the stories of ancient Serbian heroes that they loved. It was a place where justice would be national and social, because nation and society would be one; all would be secure and fulfilled, working not too much and not too little; a place whose color and contours stretched the imagination but was well worth dying for, because it promised rebirth for everyone.

The question is: where did the idea come from that salvation would flow from a state of the South Slavs? Such a thing had never existed in history.

* * *

The answer lies in philosophy: German philosophy. In the early 1800s, when the grandparents of the Archduke's assassins were children living in Ottoman Bosnia, politically involved intellectuals in Germany and Eastern Europe shared a common predicament: they wanted a nation where they and others like them could live in justice, but they had no idea of what their nation's boundaries would be. The Germans knew what it was to live under the condescending gaze of a foreigner: French forces controlled most of the German lands from the early 1790s until 1813.

Yet before that, German intellectuals had lived in the shadow of French greatness for generations as veritable second-class Europeans. The pain was especially acute during obligatory study tours of Paris, where the young Germans from Stuttgart or Würzburg came to admire French fashions and ideas: only rarely was their curiosity reciprocated by their French hosts, for whom German music and literature were primitive and German statecraft was even worse. They parodied the Holy Roman Empire of the German nation as not holy or Roman or an empire. It consisted of an endless array of free cities, principalities, bishoprics, and a few kingdoms but could summon no forces to defend itself. When Napoleon declared it defunct in 1806, hardly anyone noticed, at least not immediately.

A reaction set in beginning in the 1770s, with the Germans discovering traditions and qualities in their own world that made it possible to stand aside the French, the English, or any other great nation. Germans did not have a state, but they had something that was uniquely theirs: the German language. The French, distracted by enthusiasm for systems and universal principles, had failed to notice the unique beauty and importance of a people's tongue; in contrast to the idea of French *philosophes* that languages were interchangeable, each one being an endless variety of the same thing, German thinkers held that every language gave expression to a people's soul, placing it in direct relation to God.

In the early nineteenth century, a cult of German language and culture grew in the Thuringian city of Weimar that was associated with the poets who made their home there, above all Friedrich Schiller and Johann Wolfgang von Goethe. But the cult's prophet was their friend Johann Gottfried Herder, a Protestant pastor, universal historian, and thinker about nationhood whose ideas became so popular among Germans that Goethe later said people forgot the origins of these ideas, assuming they constituted eternal wisdom.

After Napoleon's defeat in 1815, the university at Jena—an afternoon's walk from Weimar—became a hotbed for the new romantic nationalism among German students. Their ritualistic celebrations of the old German empire's supposed medieval glory—at the Wartburg castle and elsewhere—are the stuff of legend. Less known is that dozens of Slavic students from the Austrian Empire arrived at Jena in these years to learn Protestant theology from the university's luminaries, and many of them became disciples of the new nation cult as well. They came from humble circumstances, some from Bohemia but mostly from what we now call Slovakia, from farms not much different from that of Gavrilo Princip's parents, with many siblings, and landlords who spoke a different language than they did (usually Hungarian) and treated them and their parents as second-class human beings.

Herder himself came from a small German town in the far east, where Germany gradually became Poland, and he knew about the presence of Slavic speakers strewn across the map of central and Eastern Europe, many millions who, in his view, would be the strongest nation (or nations) in Europe if they could ever realize their existence in some kind of state.

MAP INTRO-1. East Central Europe, ca. 1818

So the young Slovak and Czech-speaking theologians shared the problem that also bothered their German friends in Jena and differed from anything that concerned French students at that time: where was their nation? Whether France was a kingdom or a republic, no one questioned where it was. It fell within borders that had shifted only slightly over the centuries and was an established fact on the map of Europe, questioned by no one. The same was true of England, Russia, or Spain. But what was the nation of the Germans in Central Europe or of the Slavs living in the Austrian Empire?

The answer seemed easier for Germans. It was the Holy Roman Empire. Yet that proved superficial on closer inspection. If a nation was made by language, what about the millions of German speakers who lived outside the old empire, like Herder's family in East Prussia? By what right should they be excluded? The answer given by the philosopher Johann Gottlieb Fichte was that Germany was wherever the German tongue could be heard. The German national hymn later proclaimed that the nation stretched from the Maas to the Memel: rivers mainly in other countries.

But the problem for Slavic intellectuals was degrees greater: unlike the Germans, they were not even sure what their language was. At that point, there were no dictionaries of Czech or Slovak or the South Slavic languages. The Slavic speakers in Bohemia and Slovakia spoke a series of dialects, and there was no agreement even about simple words; over the centuries, many Germanisms had crept into daily usage, and no one could say whether the Slavic dialects of Northern Hungary and Bohemia were two or more languages or variants of one. If language made a people, yet the language had no name, who were the people?

One of those students from Northern Hungary, the poet Jan Kollár, had an irrepressible feeling of belonging to a great nation and was determined to find answers. Beyond the teachings of Herder, he learned two things in Jena. Just a few centuries earlier, Slavic speakers had dominated that very part of Germany, but they had gradually disappeared. Remnants of the language remained in the names of geographical features and towns—for instance, "Jena" and "Weimar" were Slavic words. A bit farther east, north of Dresden, in Lusatia, villages still had sprinklings of Slavic speakers who called themselves Sorbs. Because he understood the Sorbs, Kollár considered them parts of "his" people, yet he also saw they were remnants on the verge of extinction. If he and his friends did not act soon, people speaking Slavic languages in Northern Hungary and Bohemia might likewise die out by being absorbed into the dominant Hungarian and German cultures.

The other thing he learned was how diverse the German language was: when Swabians spoke their dialect, fellow students from Brandenburg could not understand them. Kollár discovered that the Slovak he spoke was closer to dialects spoken in Bohemia than these German dialects were to each other. If Germans from the Black Forest and the sands of Pomerania could be one nation, so could Slavic speakers from northern Hungary and Bohemia. There is much more to this story—told in the following chapters—but the word he and his friends gradually arrived at was "Czecho-Slav" to describe this people. By the early twentieth century, people were calling them "Czechoslovaks."

When Kollár finished his studies and took a position as pastor to Slovak Lutherans in Pest (the eastern half of today's Budapest), he made the acquaintance of a younger but similarly earnest, imaginative, and gifted theologian who came from the south of the Hungarian kingdom—from Zagreb, the capital of Croatia. This man, Ljudevit Gaj, was well acquainted with the thought of Herder and had become aware that people from Croatia could understand people living in Serbia, Montenegro, and Macedonia. In fact, there was no border in language going from what we now call Slovenia all the way to the Black Sea. He concluded that the individuals living in this great space were one people, but they had to be awakened to their identity. That became his personal calling. He called this people Illyrians; later generations, including Gavrilo Princip and his friends, called them Yugoslavs.

An influential book tells us that nations are imagined communities.[5] Here we have two men who liked to discuss deep questions on paths in the hills above the Danube in the 1830s, who imagined two nations that politicians in Paris, including Woodrow Wilson, brought to life as states in 1919. We also know that neither state survived the twentieth century. Humans imagine nations, but not all the nations that they imagine have the coherence to stay together. Like unstable chemical compounds, some come apart; occasionally they explode.

* * *

The East European states fashioned in Paris after World War I had problems that Wilson, a political scientist from Virginia, understood poorly. He and the peacemakers intended Czechoslovakia and Yugoslavia to be national states—of the sorts that Princip or Kollár or Gaj dreamed of—but they wound up becoming miniature Habsburg empires, with numerous peoples within their boundaries. Before he arrived in France in December 1918, Wilson imagined that the "peoples" of Austria-Hungary might be easily separated. But by the time he left, he despaired of the new peoples visiting him "every day," demanding the very same real estate. His fault lay not in complete ignorance. As a young academic, he had written a detailed chapter on the Habsburg monarchy in a book on the world's governments, and he had not anticipated a problem. Nor had any of the dozens of advisors who accompanied him to Paris. In fact, there had been only one sign in recent history of the ultimate problems of realizing the ideas of Kollár or Gaj. It had flared briefly during the revolutions of 1848, and in the enthusiasm for creating a new world in 1919, its lessons were ignored.

The early months of 1848 were the first time that Europeans living in the vast space from the Atlantic Ocean eastward up to the Russian and Ottoman lands could organize and speak freely in public. From late March, German- and Czech-speaking democrats in Bohemia worked together on a constitution. But after a few weeks, they noticed they had differing ideas about what country they hoped to live in: Bohemia had been the heart of the Holy Roman Empire (and then the German Confederation), and so Germans assumed it would at the heart of democratic Germany.[6] Yet Czechs considered Bohemia to be their homeland, and the word for Bohemia in their language strengthened the idea. It was *Čechy*, and the kingdom of Bohemia was the *Královec český*. The very ground beneath their feet was by nature Czech.

If for German patriots it seemed axiomatic that Germany was at least the territory of the Holy Roman Empire, for Czech patriots their nation was at least the Czech kingdom. Rather than become part of Germany, these patriots thought that Bohemia, the land of the Czechs, should become an autonomous province of the Austrian Empire. By the time a Habsburg general bombarded Prague in June 1848 to restore dynastic order, there had been no resolution of this dispute. No one could draw a line on the map of Bohemia separating the larger Czech from the smaller German population, but every organization that emerged became divided by ethnicity.

To the east, in the first days of freedom and uncertainty, the Austrian Emperor Ferdinand had accorded a constitution to Hungary's nobility. He would be a constitutional monarch. Because the nobles were liberals, they went about making the kingdom into a uniform state: one and indivisible, just as France was. There would be one language and culture across the realm. The kingdom's population, however, was mostly non-Magyar, and when Hungarian officials and soldiers entered Serb- and Romanian-dominated regions to the south and east, they met armed resistance. Within weeks, a civil war erupted that cost some forty thousand lives and witnessed the first mass ethnic cleansing in the history of modern East Central Europe. The Jewish-Hungarian-Austrian writer Max

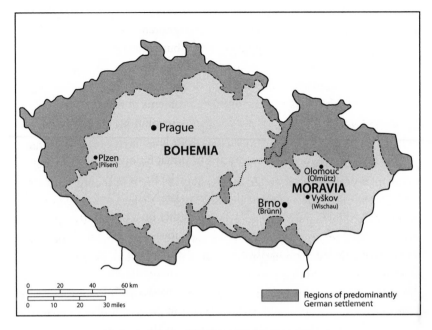

MAP INTRO-2. Kingdom of Bohemia, ca. 1860

Schlesinger wrote: "No revolution of modern times—the great French Revolution not excepted—is blackened with such horrible atrocities." An "old, long-restrained hate" had burst out among Serbs and Romanians, and Schlesinger compared their deeds to those of "Hurons and Makis of the American forests."[7] Other observers recorded the defiling of corpses, the burning alive of women and children, the executing of prisoners, and other acts of wanton cruelty that became more gruesome with each telling.

Farther north, Central Europe's great uniter and excluder, Otto von Bismarck, saw the usefulness of similar atrocity stories for focusing Germans' hatred on Poles in the Prussian east. In the spring, a civil war had raged briefly between Germans and Poles in the mostly Polish areas of Poznania, but in the end, the Polish side was crushed. Bismarck, an arch-conservative discerned but one guilty party. Berlin's "naive" democrats had let Polish rebels out of prison, he claimed, the result being that the Poles had gone back home to Poznania and formed bands that "ravaged the German inhabitants of a Prussian province with plunder and murder, slaughter and barbaric mutilation of women and children."[8]

The failed revolutions of 1848/1849 thus gave evidence of the ambivalent functions of nationalism: in the beginning, it seemed a force for liberating peoples from the rule of kings and princes in the name of self-government, but by the spring of 1849, the king of Prussia and the emperor of Austria were claiming to defend peoples from each other.

* * *

Assisted by a Russian army, Austrian Emperor Francis Joseph restored order to multiethnic Bohemia and Hungary and attempted to rule alone. Within a decade, he had lost a war to France and was almost broke. He decided that he had to involve some representatives of society in joint rule, if only the aristocracy. That meant overtures to the Hungarian nobility, which was refusing to pay taxes. In 1867, the two sides worked out a compromise dividing the empire in two, Austria-Hungary. In their half, Magyar elites, mostly noble landowners, undertook their state-making project peacefully and gradually: attempting to make everyone, including Slovaks and Romanians, into Hungarians, chiefly through schooling. Yet they had little more than contempt for the ethnic Hungarian peasantry, who worked the lords' lands but had little of their own. The result was to plant the first seeds of fascism, a force that would haunt their children's generation. Fascism grew when ostensibly nationalist politicians of the center—usually liberals—neglected the social needs of the nation. But that outcome would become clear only a generation later.

The other half of the former Austrian Empire had no proper name; it was more than just Austria and included Bohemia, parts of today's Slovenia, Italy, and Poland. People came to call it Cisleithania, lands on Austria's side of the Leitha river. All that united these diverse lands was the crown and the government in Vienna, with its proud and professional bureaucracy. But due to mass agitation in growing towns, emperor and noble elite had to give way to demands for increased suffrage, and as they did, political parties proliferated along ethnic lines, including the Marxian Social Democrats. Parliament had been housed in a magnificent neoclassical structure since 1883, but within a decade, it could not be governed by a majority, chiefly because of the continuing inability of Germans and Czechs to agree on how to rule Bohemia. The German minority there feared that any compromise, especially one making Czech and German equal languages in the land, would the first step to their own extinction as a people.

Bismarck had united Germany in 1871, leaving the Germans of Bohemia and Austria outside. In these lands, a political movement emerged that claimed to defend them in both a national and social sense: the National Socialist German Workers Party, otherwise known as the Nazi Party. The pattern was the same as in Hungary: lower class Germans felt the mainstream national movement, represented by German liberals in Vienna, had nothing for them but contempt.

At the same time, the Czechs in Bohemia created numerous parties, of which none became fascist, not even a party calling itself "national socialist." There the national movement maintained a sense not only of incorporating the desires of many Czech-speakers to use their own language—and be respected when doing so—but also of being a channel for upward social mobility. It built schools that permitted Czech-speakers to thrive in business, the trades, and scholarship using knowledge gained in their own language, and it provided savings banks where Czechs could save their money, free of German capital. In addition, the movement had a virtual philosopher king in Professor Tomáš G. Masaryk, who argued in Herder's terms that the Czechs indeed had a mission to humankind. It was, he claimed, to be democratic and humane. Supporting him in this belief was his American wife Charlotte, of German Huguenot and Yankee background, who learned perfect Czech and became a Czech Social Democrat.

Like the Czech patriots of 1848, Masaryk believed that the Habsburg monarchy could serve the Czech cause, but only if broken into federal units, like a united states of Central Europe. Yet both German and Hungarian politicians, who in effect controlled the monarchy's fortunes, refused to discuss such plans, because such a federation would diminish their relative power (in Bohemia and in Hungary). Soon after the Sarajevo assassination of 1914, Masaryk witnessed Austrian authorities arresting fellow Slavs who criticized war on Serbia and executing some of them. He escaped to Switzerland and then France, and set up a lobbying group to realize the dream of the early nationalists, calling it the "Czechoslovak committee." At the same time, both Yugoslav émigrés and Polish émigrés were setting up their own committees in Paris, also agitating for independent states.

But it was Professor Masaryk who spread the message of Herder to Professor Wilson, disguising it in language that made sense to an American liberal. He helped Wilson think that just as Americans were a people, so were Czechoslovaks, and they deserved to break from their king—the Habsburg Francis Joseph—just as Americans had broken from theirs, and determine their fate freely in a constitution of their own making. The idea was also a poorly disguised utopia, claiming to solve more problems than political institutions usually do.

MAP INTRO-3. East Central Europe, 1921–1939

The self-governing Czechoslovaks would combine with other democratically governed peoples in a League of Nations and ensure lasting peace among nations, because peoples who ruled themselves had no interest in war.

Masaryk did not tell Wilson about the Germans in Bohemia (more than 2.5 million of them), nor did he not enlighten the US president about the differing understandings of "people" in the United States and in Czechoslovakia—and that if Czechoslovaks existed at all, it was as a people united by language and tribal identity. The lone academic authority on East Central Europe in the US delegation to Paris, the Czech-American Robert J. Kerner (Harvard PhD, 1914), had portrayed Czechoslovaks as a "scientific fact," and the borders of Bohemia as sacrosanct, though slight adjustments would have permitted hundreds of thousands of Germans to live in Germany or Austria.

With that fact in mind, Bohemia's Germans demonstrated for inclusion in Austria and Germany, until on March 4, 1919, Czech soldiers and gendarmes killed fifty-four and wounded another eighty-four while dispersing a rally in Reichenberg/Liberec.[9] Within a few months, leading Slovak politicians were asking whether in fact Czechoslovaks were a people. They found the attitude of Czech bureaucrats condescending—reminiscent of German feelings about Napoleon's administrators a century earlier. The same was true of Croats who found the Serb administrators in Royal Yugoslavia to be overbearing, corrupt, and far from being "brothers." By the mid-1920s, separatist movements had emerged among Slovaks and Croats that would have shocked Jan Kollár or Ljudevit Gaj: the same language—indeed, even the same dialect—was not enough to make a people.

Still, the East European predicament of being small peoples lodged between larger ones militated for cooperation. Yugoslavia protected the Croats from Hungary on one side and from Italy on the other; the "miniature Habsburg Empire" had this same virtue as the real thing. Thus, when a Montenegrin deputy shot Croat leader Stjepan Radić on the floor of the parliament in Belgrade in 1928, Yugoslav King Alexander—of the Serb ruling house—offered to let Croatia go. Before succumbing to his wounds, Radić rejected the idea. By itself Croatia was an impossibility. And further north, if many Slovaks felt alienated by their supposed Czech brethren, others worked to keep the Czechoslovak state functioning as a democracy in the 1930s. Czechoslovakia had halted the gradual Magyarization of Slovak-speakers by creating Slovak institutions, like the University of Bratislava.

But in contrast to Masaryk's Czechoslovakia, the other supposedly self-ruling mini-nations succumbed to one form or another of authoritarianism. By 1938, democratization was revealed as a fiasco (though the lessons were lost on policy makers in later decades). Still, Czechoslovakia proved that multiethnicity alone did not condemn democracy: it was the most complex state in the region. And contrary to the opinion of some Nobel laureates of our day, the region, left to its own devices, was not destined for fascism.[10] Fascism did emerge as a mass movement in Romania and Hungary, yet came to power nowhere; in most of the region—in Poland, Czechoslovakia, Yugoslavia, and Bulgaria—it remained a marginal phenomenon, never above a few percentage points of popularity. Eastern European fascism failed because it seemed at odds with being Polish, Serb, or Czech: to march in black uniforms and raise one's arm in a fascist salute in Warsaw or Prague brought to mind not national salvation and rebirth, but death and historical oblivion.

Yet if the countries of the region hated fascism, they did not hold together when threatened by fascism's most extreme form: Nazism. The reason can be sought in the consuming concern to redeem national territory, no matter how tiny. Throughout the interwar years Czechoslovakia and Poland failed to ally because of a microscopic piece of land where the population was 40 percent Polish: the Silesian district of Teschen/Těšín/Cieszyn. The Czechs had seized this area in 1919 because of a rail line linking Bohemia to Slovakia that went through it. Poland did not forget, and instead of standing by Czechoslovakia when Germany threatened in the fall of 1938, Warsaw used the occasion to send its troops across the border and assert Polish sovereignty.

The following year, despite this implicit alliance with Germany, Poland became the first state anywhere to say no to Hitler, bringing down on itself a hecatomb of conquest and occupation. Prior to that point, Hitler had courted Poland as an ally against the Soviet Union; he had made Poland's leaders— whom he admired for their anti-Communism—what he thought was a decent offer. They would become Germany's ally, permit Germany to build an extraterritorial highway connecting Pomerania to East Prussia, and render to Germany territory Poland did not even possess (the city of Danzig). Poland said no, because subordination to Germany would make a mockery of its claims to national sovereignty. Poles had lived under foreign rule from 1795 to 1918, and no Polish leader could dilute independence. Besides that, Polish elites counted on effective support of the countries that claimed to be its allies: Britain and France. Instead, those countries watched passively as Poland succumbed to attack from four sides in September 1939, by Hitler and his new ally, Stalin.

* * *

What Hitler, the "Bohemian corporal" (he was actually Austrian) achieved through his war was to make northern parts of Eastern Europe much simpler. With the aid of local collaborators, his regime segregated and then killed the overwhelming majority of East European Jews.[11] But when the Red Army drove the Wehrmacht back to Vienna and Berlin in 1945, millions of Germans fled Eastern Europe as well, never to return. At the war's conclusion, as a result of allied decisions, Polish and Czech authorities placed the remainder of Germans from Bohemia and eastern Germany in railway cars and deported them to a Germany that was much smaller than Bismarck's Reich, let alone the Holy Roman Empire.

The most avid ethnic cleansers among the East Europeans were Polish and Czech Communists, and indeed, Communists everywhere proved enthusiastic nationalists. This is astounding for two reasons. First, Karl Marx and Friedrich Engels had little concern for national identity: workers had no fatherland. Nationhood was not a lasting site of human subjectivity but something ephemeral, which diminished in importance as capitalism advanced.[12] They had little but derision for East Europeans wanting to create their own nation-states. Engels called the small peoples to Germany's east "relics."[13] Czechs were destined to be "absorbed as integral portions into one or the other of those more powerful nations whose greater vitality enabled them to overcome greater obstacles." Other "remnants of bygone Slavonian peoples" slotted for assimilation included Serbs, Croats, and Slovaks. In 1852, Engels blithely predicted that the next world war would cause entire reactionary peoples to "disappear from the face of the earth."[14]

Second, when the world divided into two camps, appearances suggested that there was little room for East European nationalism. By 1949, every state in the region seemed to be a miniature USSR, with the same sort of ruling Communist Party, five-year plan, economy based on heavy industry, collectivized agriculture, and socialist realism. Few Poles or Hungarians, even within the Party, doubted that the annual pageant in red of May Day reflected doctrines and practices whose nerve center was in Moscow. For the first time, millions of East Europeans learned Russian, and many became as proficient in copying Soviet reality as they could. Hundreds of thousands became "self-Sovietizers," even holding their cigarettes the Russian way, or dressing in the militaristic style of the Bolshevik party. The Yugoslav Communists, with red stars on their caps, went so far that the Soviets tried to hold them back.

But these states were not Soviet replicas, nor were they (unlike Ukraine, the Baltic states, and Belorussia) actual parts of the Soviet Union.[15] Beyond the

MAP INTRO-4. East Central Europe, 1949–1990

façades of May Day processions in Warsaw in 1949, one saw banners in Polish, not Russian, and placards honoring Polish heroes. A few blocks from the parade route the Polish socialist state, governed by a Marxian party, was lovingly resurrecting old Warsaw, razed by the Nazis in 1944. This included rebuilding many of its churches, according to plans from the eighteenth century, with attention to the details of a saint's halo. Bookstores across the state socialist world stocked romantic authors like Jan Kollár, but also the Polish, Hungarian, or Romanian national bards Adam Mickiewicz, Sándor Petofi, and Vasile Alecsandri; the philologists Ljudevit Gaj and Vuk Karadžić; and the ethnographer Pavel Šafárik, who had studied theology with Kollár in Jena.[16] In Poland's west, the state fostered the destruction of all signs of the German past, including cemeteries, and proclaimed the new territories Polish to the core, though they had been German for centuries.

Though they imitated Stalin in slavish ways and built socialism before Moscow demanded it, Yugoslavia's Communists became the first to break with the USSR in 1948. They did so because Stalin demanded complete subordination of their national interests to those of his country. In a public speech, Josip Broz Tito reflected on his sudden heresy as a Marxist-Leninist: One can love the motherland of socialism, he said, but not love one's own country less. He did not mean Croatia or Serbia, Slovenia or Montenegro: Communist Yugoslavia was a second attempt to revive Ljudevit Gaj's old program, this time as national liberation for all peoples in Yugoslavia. Tito's Partisan movement had begun as a miniature Habsburg empire during the war, protecting Serbs, Jews, and others from fascist genocide, in the name of brotherhood and unity, a formula that succeeded until Tito's death in 1980.

If it had joined the newest version of the Habsburg Empire—the European Union (EU)—Yugoslavia might have survived. But fighting broke out in Croatia in 1991 before the EU had opened toward the east. Today Eastern Europe's leaders gain political capital by claiming that the EU, despite its generous funding of national infrastructures, education, and agriculture, somehow threatens their countries' existence. In June 2018, Hungarian president Viktor Orbán said that at stake in the election of an anti-EU candidate in Slovenia was the "survival of the Slovenian nation."[17]

* * *

The one certainty connecting these many periods from the early nineteenth century to the present has been this: as soon as patriots created national languages, nationalism itself became the language of politics, and no one who wanted power could avoid speaking it, whether they called themselves liberal, fascist, or Communist. This central argument of this book sets it at odds with other recent work on the region. Specialists on Habsburg Europe have portrayed the region's path to nation-states as just one of several possible choices. But for the efforts of the nationalists, East Central Europe might have continued in multinational states with no boundaries between peoples and large populations that remained indifferent to nationalism. One eloquent advocate of this approach urges his readers to liberate themselves from the "unnecessary discursive prison that nationalists around us continue to re-create."[18]

This newer work is inspired by an ethical motive that is unimpeachable. The misdeeds and crimes of nation-states—from institutionalized chauvinism to ethnic cleansing and genocide—seem a logical consequence of the principles of ethnic exclusion on which they are built. Czechoslovakia was a state for the Czechoslovaks, Poland for the Poles, and so forth. Furthermore, we know that national identity is learned and not natural and that borders are lines drawn on soil by human beings and not by God. Because nations are communities that humans have imagined, historians have looked back to the imaginings of actors more benign than the nationalists: imperial authorities who wanted to contain (other peoples') nationalism; socialists; and above all, tens of thousands of individuals in Eastern Europe who opted for no nationality at all: called by census takers "nationally indifferent." Had things gone differently, humans might have imagined no national communities at all.[19]

This newer literature has made exceptional cases seem as if they might have become the rule. Officials registered national indifference in border areas, where one language group fades into another. In those areas—Upper Silesia, part of the Bohemian Forest, Carinthia, eastern Poland, Bosnia—people speaking two or more languages had the freedom to use one nationality or another, depending on opportunity. For instance, the small-town populations in Upper Silesia, between German areas extending for hundreds of miles to the west and Polish areas extending for hundreds of miles to the east, spoke a Polish dialect at home and learned German in schools. And when state officials came, some of them would claim not to know what their identity was: that gave them the greatest leverage.

But on the background of the entire region, extending from the Baltic down to the Adriatic, such people were numerically insignificant. In central Poland, much of Hungary, Romania, most of the Serb and Croat lands, Bulgaria, and in large parts of Slovakia and Bohemia, the rule was for monolingual people to be sucked into the projects of nationalists and of nation-states, usually through schools teaching the standardized native language, but also through political mobilization and induction into national armies.[20] This is the pattern one sees beginning in the late eighteenth century with the slow emergence of nationalism, like the gradual movement of the sun across terrain, illuminating high ground, then valleys, and leaving few spots unexposed by the time its work is done. If the heat made nationalism thrive, it also caused alternatives to wither.

But there is a deeper conceptual problem connected to the insight that nations are constructed by humans. To paraphrase Karl Marx: humans make their own nations, but not just as they choose. They live in communities and speak languages that they help shape but have not manufactured. Nations never began as simple figments of imagination; instead, nationalists used building blocks of existing national chronicles and tales, interpreted to be sure, but never entirely invented. They made new words but built on existing syntaxes; they used ideas popular among rural folk about who they were, and about who their enemy was (usually an imperial power).[21] Some of the nations imagined by intellectuals never took root; Czechoslovakia and Yugoslavia were just two cases. Habsburg Bosnia was another.

As people made nations, so nations made people. That is, nations formed the spaces in which people made decisions about what was valuable—indeed, what was worth living for. People could debate where they stood on the idea of nations, but they could not deny that the debate matters. Take one of our time's great controversies: whether Polish gentiles could have done more to rescue Jews during the Holocaust. Being a Polish national does not impose a particular view: some say Nazi terror made aid to Jews impossible, while others say greater solidarity with Jews would have saved lives despite the terror. But the force of this question permits no one who calls himself or herself Polish to say: "I don't care about the answer." In that sense, Poland is an undeniable reality and has been for a very long time, including many decades when it was not on any map.

The power of nationalist arguments to drive political imagination—indeed to create the space in which politics happens—is repeated in country after country, yet its importance is not fully apparent in studies that focus on border regions within limited time frames.[22] It was not apparent to the patriots themselves, who emphasized their personal role in "imagining" their communities into existence. In the 1870s, the Czech patriot František Palacký remarked that if a roof had collapsed on the room where he and his fellow patriots were meeting a generation earlier, that would have been curtains for the nation. But during the same period in Zagreb or in Budapest, one found the same sort of patriotic activity among similar groups of zealots. Ukrainian patriots a generation later even told an analogous story: if the train they were traveling in had derailed, that would have been the end of the Ukrainian nation. At the opposite end of the Habsburg lands, Prague Zionists were applying Palacký's story to themselves.

The historian Pieter Judson has written that nationalism was "hard work," but we see in all these cases that plenty of people were willing to do it. A train derailed might have stopped some nationalists, but many others quickly found a different way of moving forward. Nationalism emerged and grew in Bohemia in the 1770s among Czech speakers who understood that the German elite—dominant in culture, politics, and business—considered their language a language of rude peasants. When the Habsburg state closed Czech high schools in the 1780s to make Czech speakers into German speakers, that painful sense of condescension was transformed into a fear that Czechs as a people would disappear: such fear became a regional syndrome, visible in Serbia, Hungary, parts of Romania, and Poland. When Prussia, Austria, and Russia wiped Poland off the map in 1795, they agreed to "abolish everything which could revive the memory of the existence of the Kingdom of Poland." Now that its "annihilation" had been effected, the kingdom's very name was to be suppressed "forever."[23]

This wording was so evidently repugnant that it was kept secret, and for decades, imperial censorship acted to suppress public expression of concern. But as soon as it lifted, metaphors poured forth. In April 1848, Czech journalist Karel Havlíček Borovský wrote "wherever your speech, your nationality, does not dominate [nepanuje], you are oppressed, even in the freest of countries." Because Czech speakers seemed to be the helpless subjects of foreign lords, he equated their lot to that of slaves in the United States. "Of what use to negroes," he asked, "is even the most liberal administration. . . . If we want to be free as a people, we must first have nationality." In these months, writers from Austria, Poland, Croatia, and Romania repeated precisely these words: without freedom for their nations, they could not be free as human beings.[24]

This ferocious language would have surprised Havlíček had he heard it a few years earlier. But a few years earlier, he had yet to taste the rancor of a public dispute carried out in a democracy. Particularly bitter was his quarrel with Bohemian German liberal Franz Schuselka, who as the name suggests, came from an originally Slavic family. Schuselka called Czechs wanting to use their language in public "Czechomaniacs." Austria's Slavs had produced no literature of account, he wrote, and had no universities or even high schools; their destiny was to become German. Slavs had once settled core German lands around Berlin and Leipzig, going as far west as Hamburg, yet over generations, they had been absorbed into the "irresistible" German culture. "They Germanized," Schuselka wrote, "because it is the moral duty of all human beings to improve and perfect themselves."[25] Other German democrats depicted Czechs as helots, a slave people, destined to work in the fields and kitchens, the "ruins" of a nation, having no history and no future. Any Czech of substance would "naturally" become a German.[26]

After imperial troops crushed the democratic revolutions, Habsburg authorities reintroduced censorship, but Havlíček continued to cause trouble. In 1851, they sent him into exile in northern Italy and permitted him to return to Prague four years later, only to learn that his wife had just died. He succumbed to tuberculosis a year later in the same sheets his wife had died in. At a funeral attended by all the early patriots, Božena Němcova, the first great Czech novelist, placed a crown of thorns in his coffin.

Over the decades that followed, Czech public life expanded into numerous associations and parties, and no Czech politician could afford to ignore the pain caused by the condescension that Havlíček expressed in his dispute with Schuselka. German opponents did not let them. We hear the same outrage that tormented Havlíček in the Bohemian parliament of the 1890s, when German deputies said that Czechs remained a people of kitchen help and field hands. Politicians of that time and place did not run on a platform of "indifference"; non-national identity was not a conviction, let alone a passion: it failed to spur sacrifice or activism, and it failed to make history. Or to make the point in Habsburg terms: no Czech or German party ran as "imperial" or "Austrian."[27] And when border identities between emerging nations grew in strength, as in Silesia, Bosnia, and Macedonia, they became new kinds of national identities. In other words, when nationally indifferent people became political, they became national, and they worried about what East Europeans worry about: oblivion.

Superficially, Eastern Europe's nationalism may seem like nationalism everywhere: occasionally flaring to incandescent passion, but normally, in everyday life, just one aspect of people's sense of self, and not the most important. Even in regions of mixed ethnicity where space has been hotly contested for generations, national identity is far from an everyday concern: people think of themselves in terms of age, or gender, or village, or profession. Yet nationalism remains a "crisis frame" of reference that politicians can appeal to when opportune, for example, in the enduring economic crisis of the 1930s, when radio stations in Germany spewed hate-filled messages to Germans living in Czechoslovakia, or during the hyperinflation that wracked Serbia in the 1980s when the banker Slobodan Milošević discovered the nationalist in himself and rose to power by resurrecting fears that Serbs faced "extinction."[28]

This crisis frame is not something one finds in Western European or Russian nationalism. During the worst days of World War II, few worried that the Dutch, French, or Russian peoples would become extinct. Yet this fear was very much alive among Serbs, Poles, Czechs, and East European Jews. The Polish-Jewish lawyer Raphael Lemkin drew from the wells of the region's anxieties when he fashioned the word "genocide." After the war, the region's poets attributed to themselves special intuitions about history's vicissitudes. Walking in Poland's capital in 1944, Czesław Miłosz felt that the pavement and streets were like liquid and could escape the temporary form given in stone or asphalt.

The fear of oblivion persisted after the war. In 1967, the Czech author Milan Kundera endangered his ability to publish anything at all by condemning state censorship in public. He said that without novels and essays and poems—without language—there would be no Czechs, and to show he meant what he said, Kundera forbade authorities from altering even a minor mark of punctuation in what he wrote.[29] In 1977, he emigrated to Paris and ruminated gloomily about his country's fate: Europe forgot that Czechs even existed. In defiance he rejected the term "Eastern Europe" as words signaling collusion in that ignominious act of forgetting and simply called the region "Central Europe." After all, Prague is to the west of Vienna, and Poland and Hungary were connected to the west in a way that Russia was not.

* * *

Today, many follow Kundera's call, using the words "Central Europe" to avoid the stereotype of seeming to be a different and inferior Europe, one that is "backward" and given to nationalist passion. But there is a problem with calling the region "Central Europe." Though Germany, as Václav Havel once said, has one leg in Central Europe, Germany does not belong to the region. The sensibility there is different. Even as he planned to destroy Germany's infrastructure in 1945, Adolf Hitler did not imagine the German people would cease to exist. More to the point: no one ever needed to argue that Germany, however constituted politically, should exist. That sort of rhetorical compulsion was reserved for places like Czechia, Slovenia, or Macedonia. Their existence was not secure unless someone made an argument and then devoted massive efforts to promoting it. No accomplishment of the Czech national movement—not a trade school, museum, library, theater, or university—was achieved without a struggle of words followed by deeds.

But Kundera's concern was not to describe a region; it was to defend its existence. His strategy was to say that Czechoslovakia, Poland, Croatia, or Hungary were qualitatively different from Russia. And he ascribed to them a higher virtue, a proximity to Western Europe that Russia would never reach, a host of positive legacies like liberalism, enlightenment, and division of powers (deriving from the investiture conflict). Central Europe constituted a region of the greatest difference over the smallest space, whereas Russia followed the opposite principle: the smallest difference over the greatest space.

This book ascribes no stereotypes to Eastern Europe beyond saying that it is an anti-imperial space of small peoples. In the corners of its political nightmares dwells this indistinct fear of being absorbed into larger powers. The anti-imperial struggle kept ethnic cultures alive, but it also promoted ideologies of exclusion that can become racist. The old empires, especially the Habsburg empire, inspire nostalgia, because they protected human rights and indeed nations and peoples better than did many nation-states that came later.

This book uses "Eastern Europe" interchangeably with "East Central Europe" to cut down verbiage, but also because both terms are understood to refer to a band of countries that were Soviet satellites not in control of their own destinies.[30] It denotes not so much a space on the map as shared experience, such that peoples from opposite ends of the region, despite all cultural or linguistic differences, employ a common narrative about the past. When he made his odd invocation of national survival, Viktor Orbán used words that would resonate not only in Hungary and Slovenia but also in Poland, the Czech Republic, or Serbia.

The former western republics of the Soviet Union—the Baltic states, Ukraine, and Belarus—are not included, because they formed a separate story throughout much of the period studied, subject to Sovietization that tested local cultures to a degree not seen in East Central Europe. For the same reason, the German Democratic Republic (GDR) is included: this small country shared the destiny of being controlled by a superpower without being absorbed into it.[31] But the GDR was also special. The East German regime eagerly took part in efforts to crush dissent in Czechoslovakia in 1968 and Poland in 1980, home to small-time co-imperialists with enough hubris to tell the Motherland of socialism what socialism was really about.

The inclusion of the GDR underscores the fact that Germans cannot be thought to be outside East Central Europe, and not only because millions have lived in this space for centuries. The question of how Germany would form a nation-state after the Holy Roman Empire became defunct in 1806 has shaped the region's fortunes and misfortunes. Bismarck's supposed resolution of the question in the "second empire" of 1871 only exacerbated the German question by provoking a sense of abandonment among the Habsburg Germans, one in three of the total number. It was no coincidence that the original Nazi Party was founded in Bohemia in 1903. What happened when German nationalism entered Eastern European space in a time of imperial decline—first of the Holy Roman Empire, then of the Habsburg monarchy—was that it gradually moved from the old practice of absorbing Slavs into German culture to a new one of displacing them from a vast supposedly German space.

* * *

What follows is not a simple heroic story of self-assertion: the anti-imperial struggle often made national movements imperialist, and the fight against oblivion involved complicity in driving others—during World War II, the region's Jews—into oblivion. Nationalism asserted itself beyond innumerable obstacles, from the wars of 1849 to the compromise between the Habsburgs and Hungary in 1867 and the sudden proliferation of new states in 1918. Up to and beyond 1945, it swallowed liberalism whole, sidetracked socialism, begat fascism, colonized Communism, and is currently doing things to democracy for which the word "populism" may be a weak placeholder waiting for some more chilling descriptor. If the region has produced indelible works of literature—the writings of Kundera and Miłosz are examples—that have given witness to suffering that is not *exclusive* to Eastern Europe, it still belongs to an experience that defies the imaginations of people in the West.

But anti-imperial East Central Europe is not an island. Much of global history has been concentrated here. If East Europeans have experienced modern times with special intensity, that is because they are part of our time and their stories are many people's stories, whether of democratization and decolonization, five-year plans and show trials, antifascist resistance or ethnic cleansing, civil society and illiberal democracy, all overshadowed by the fear of becoming *foreign in their own land,* traitors to their heritage. East Europeans are accused of being obsessed with the past, but that is because they have wanted to break from it. Occasionally, they have signaled paths to the future. Still, memory ineluctably shapes the present, even for those who claim superior knowledge of history.[32]

Above all the Marxist-Leninists. Because they seemed to represent foreign interests, followers of Marx and Lenin became more obsessed with memory than anyone, reconstructing bombed-out cities in national shapes and colors, producing freight cars full of national plays and poetry, and lavishly celebrating national holidays, for example, the 1,000-year anniversary of the founding of the Polish state in 1966. Poland's Communists orchestrated a huge festival and promised to build 1,000 schools in rural areas deprived of modern education.

As it happened, this anniversary coincided with the introduction into Poland of Christendom in 966 AD, and Poland's Catholic hierarchy grasped its own national symbol, the Virgin Mary, proclaimed queen of Poland in 1652 by King Jan Kazimierz for protecting Polish forces in the besieged town of Częstochowa. In 1957, Polish Cardinal Primate Wyszyński ordered a substitute made of the "black Madonna" portrait held at the monastery Częstochowa, complete with original scorch marks. It was blessed in Rome and then carried by the faithful in pilgrimages around Poland, on a schedule that would make sure every Pole could see and venerate the portrait at least once in the coming decade.

By 1965 the state's patience had run out, and authorities ordered the copy taken back to join the original in Częstochowa. Locals joked that the Virgin had been kidnapped. Yet now, instead of carrying a portrait of the Black Madonna, Poles carried an empty frame where she used to be. Everyone knew what it signified. But what did Poles see when they looked at the blank canvas? They claimed to see something that was theirs only, a vital image of a people endangered for a millennium.

Extend this empty frame to the entire region, and you see this book's purpose: it displays Eastern Europe as a region with a particular sensitivity about identity, gained over generations, and because it was vested in local language, this identity was untranslatable and resisted direct communication. That is what ethnic nationalism is: having something of one's own that does not go beyond ostensible boundaries, be it the family hearth, the nation-state, or an empty picture frame.

This book is not an encyclopedia. It does not recount histories of fixed numbers of peoples. It is not about any particular people or peoples. Nor is it a geography of lands marked by boundaries in the landscape. Rather, it tells of the predicament that engendered that particular sensitivity, of living in a space between empires; of stories told about and by peoples who have lived there. The common message is of absorbing existential threats and yet surviving. The point is not whether that perception is accurate but how it became a common mind-set, one that comes alive with little prodding, beyond the fall of empires, whether Holy Roman, Habsburg, Ottoman, Nazi, or Soviet. The predicament seems eternal and necessary. In fact, it is historical and very modern, just over two centuries in the making.

PART I

The Emergence of National Movements

CHAPTER 1

Peoples of East Central Europe

———— ❧ ————

When Westerners discuss Eastern Europe, they stress its complexity. It seems a place where an endless array of different peoples lay claim to the same spaces— so many, and so different, that the region seems to resist historical understanding. Yugoslavia alone consisted of some ten ethnicities, and there are subgroups and minorities (for example, the Muslims of southern Serbia, in the Sanjak of Novi Pazar, or the Hungarians to the north in Vojvodina). Interwar Czechoslovakia had five major nationalities, and the Habsburg Empire contained many more. As I write, three ethnic groups are making claims on parts of tiny Bosnia. Furthermore, the boundaries have changed so often and rapidly in the past two hundred years that it seems impossible to relate nationality to statehood. Poles lived in three states just over a century ago, and currently, Hungarians live in five; while Albanians live in Albania, they also populate Kosovo and parts of Montenegro and Macedonia (and are of three religions).

But on a global background, Eastern Europe appears not so different from much of Africa and Asia, where numerous ethnic groups are settled across smaller regions and where, in certain periods of history, colonial empires have ruled many groups simultaneously, drawing administrative borders with little concern for ethnic homelands. Take a map of Africa around 1900. West European powers had seized huge stretches of diverse territory, and political maps suggested a simplicity at odds with ethnic diversity, for example in German Southwest Africa, French Equatorial Africa, or the Belgian Congo.

In 1800, the peoples of East Central Europe lived in just four states: the Russian and Ottoman Empires, the Kingdom of Prussia, and the lands of the House of Habsburg (officially known as the Austrian Empire from 1804 to 1867). Within these lands, one could identify older political divisions, but if one simplifies a bit, one sees a map that is not difficult to grasp. In the north were the lands of the Polish-Lithuanian Commonwealth, defunct from 1795, when Austria, Prussia, and Russia divided the Commonwealth's lands among themselves. Farther south we find the Hungarian and Bohemian kingdoms, possessions of the Habsburg monarchy from 1526. Hungary comprised the kingdom of Croatia as well as the principality of Transylvania. The Ottoman Empire

MAP 1.1. East Central Europe, ca. 1795

included the principalities of Wallachia and Moldavia—the future heartlands of Romania—as vassal states, but it ruled directly the provinces (*eyelets*) of Bosna, Rumeli, and Silistre (which would become Bosnia-Herzegovina, Serbia, Albania, Macedonia, and Bulgaria) and contained the lands of the defunct medieval Bulgarian, Serb, and Bosnian kingdoms. Though nominally under Turkish rule, Montenegro maintained de facto independence because of its location in rugged mountain terrain.[1] Finally, the Ottomans occupied much of central Hungary from 1526 to the 1680s, using it as a launching ground for campaigns of aggression on Habsburg lands farther north.

As in any imperial space, the political borders imposed by foreign powers belied the linguistic, religious, and ethnic diversity that had resulted from the settlement and mixing of diverse tribes centuries earlier. Much of this region had been ruled from Rome and later Constantinople (for example, the provinces of Pannonia, Dalmatia, and Macedonia on the Balkan Peninsula) but some of it, especially north of the Danube, remained beyond Roman power, and the documentary record is scantier. Still, in broad terms, we know what transpired.

Around the time of Jesus of Nazareth, Celtic tribes dominated in Western, Central and parts of Eastern Europe. But beginning in the first century, they became displaced by Germanic tribes migrating from Scandinavia, so that by late antiquity, Celtic settlements had been pushed to Europe's peripheries: to Scotland, Ireland, Wales, Brittany, and Cornwall. From the fifth and sixth centuries, tribes of Slavic speakers began pressing on the Germans, some of whom had settled as far east as the Vistula river, and they came to populate the territories of present-day Poland, Slovakia, and the Czech Republic, as well as areas of what became Bulgaria and Yugoslavia.

Beyond the Celts, Slavic tribes also displaced, absorbed, or came to coexist with other groups, including ancestors of today's Albanians as well as speakers of Romance languages in areas of present-day Yugoslavia and Romania, thought by later nationalists to consist of descendants of Roman colonists and an earlier population of "Dacians."[2] But given the scarcity of documentation, all that seems certain is that the current Romanian language descended from Latin dialects spoken north of the "Jireček line," which separated Greek from Latin cultural influence in the Balkans.[3] Farther East, Slavic tribes came to inhabit areas between the southern Bug and Dnieper rivers in present-day Ukraine, and after the first century AD, some moved northward into what is now western Russia.

After the Slavic settlement was more or less complete, one non-Slavic— indeed, non-Indo European—group settled between the western and

MAP 1.2. Ethnolinguistic groups of East Central Europe, ca. 1880

Ethnolinguistic groups

- Germanic
- East Slavic
- West Slavic
- South Slavic
- Baltic
- Finno-Ugric
- Romance
- Greek
- Albanians
- Turco-Tataric

southern Slavic speakers: the Magyars, or Hungarians, tribes of nomadic warriors who came from Central Asia in about a twenty-year stretch around 890 AD.[4] The area known in Roman times as Pannonia was now transformed into the great Magyar-settled Hungarian plain. Like the Slavic tribes, the Magyars too were driven by pressure from other groups in Central Asia and now spent decades invading closer and farther regions to the west and seizing women with whom to help populate their lands. This continued until the Battle of Lechfeld in 955, when a German force under King Otto of Franconia defeated a Magyar army, killing several chieftains and halting the Magyar incursions for good. Now focused on peaceful settlement, the leaders of Hungarian tribes assimilated the existing populations of the lowlands. But people in the mountainous and hilly peripheries to the north, east, and south retained their cultures and languages, languages that over centuries evolved and were finally shaped into modern Slovak, Romanian, and Serbo-Croatian.[5]

Roughly speaking, three linguistic branches developed among Slavic speakers: western, eastern, and southern. To the north and northwest of Magyar settlement, the Polish, Czech, Sorb, and Slovak languages emerged and were shaped from among the western dialects; and to the south, Slovene developed along with Serbo-Croatian, Bulgarian, and Macedonian. To the east of what became the Polish and Hungarian states, Russian, Ukrainian, Belorussian evolved and were fashioned from the eastern Slavic dialects.

As we will see in detail, many nineteenth-century nationalists believed in Slavic political unity because Slavic speakers can learn one another's languages with little effort. Their languages have about 40 percent common vocabulary, and that percentage is much higher in the western, eastern, and southern subgroups. With careful study but little effort, a Czech can learn good Polish or a Serb good Bulgarian in half a year.

There are two important dialect continuums of Slavic languages in East Central Europe: one of South Slavic speakers extending downward from present-day Slovenia to the Black Sea; the other of West and East Slavic speakers going from West Bohemia and through today's Poland and Slovakia into Ukraine, Belarus, and beyond. People coming from either end of the continuum would hardly understand one another, but as one moved along the continuum, people in each neighboring village or town understood one another perfectly. These cases are similar to the dialect continuum of Germanic languages. Similarly, there was no break in linguistic continuity from Tirol in the south through Bavaria and Hessen northward into Saxony and Mecklenburg in the east and the Low Countries in the west.[6]

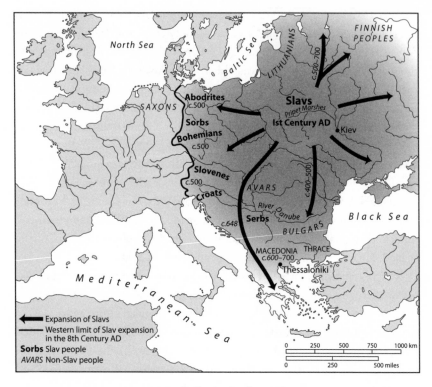

MAP 1.3. Settlement by Slavic tribes

If, in a later age when language was used to unify a political nation, intellectuals or politicians standardized a dialect somewhere between the ends of a dialect continuum, that could become a modern literary language understood by tens of millions of people. That in effect was what Martin Luther unwittingly accomplished by translating the Bible into a central German dialect. On this background, we see the epochal significance of the Magyars inserting themselves as a wedge between Slavic tribes: that event broke up the Slavic continuum and effectively hindered the emergence centuries later of some central and unifying dialect among Southern and Western Slavs.

From fragmentary documentary evidence, we know that around 1000 AD, speakers of Slavic languages, for example of the dialects that later became Polish or Bulgarian, sensed tribal and intertribal unities. In addition, proto-Croat and proto-Serb speakers who settled in what became Yugoslavia in the seventh century had a sense of being related as well as being distinct. From antiquity,

MAP 1.4. Dialect continua

these tribes had been in contact as they migrated through what is now Poland southward to present-day Croatia and Serbia. Similar to areas of Western Europe (for example, Castile, East Anglia, or Burgundy), strong rulers emerged in periods of intense feudal strife and managed to unite tribes into larger political entities, sometimes only for the rulers' lifetimes. From the early Middle Ages, we thus witness the rise of Polish, Bulgarian, Serb, Bosnian, Croat, and Hungarian kingdoms. The ninth century also saw a greater Moravian empire, in which West Slavic chieftains ruled over parts of the lands that would become the modern Czech and Slovak republics. (Moravia is now a region in the Czech Republic).

* * *

The populations of these kingdoms were not joined in a modern sense of nationhood: their subject status did not involve the belief that everyone was a member of a group united by language or citizenship, and these states did not attempt to inculcate such beliefs. The effort would have been pointless if it could have been imagined. Until well into the nineteenth century, nearly all Slavic speakers were illiterate. And but for vagaries of dynastic succession, entities might have emerged joining the western Slavic speakers in different combinations. For example, Poland might have looked quite different and included today's Bohemia and Slovakia if the descendants of King Bolesław Chrobry (992–1026) had been better able to hold his realm together. In that case, Prague might have been a provincial city in western Poland and Czech a west Polish dialect. In fact, the Polish state tended to expand eastward over time, into today's Ukraine, Belorussia, and Lithuania.

To bolster their pretensions to rule over people across vast spaces, the early kings fostered the spread of Christianity: they supported the emergent church hierarchy, and the church proclaimed their rule to be legitimate. We date the mass baptisms of Croats, Serbs, Poles, Czechs, Bulgarians, and Hungarians from the ninth and tenth centuries. In Europe, adherence to Christianity was essential if a ruling house was to be treated as an equal by other states. In the case of Poland, a close link to Rome also helped protect the kingdom from religious and political interference coming from Germany.[7] Yet a major fault line of Christianity ran right through East Central Europe after 1054, when the patriarch of Constantinople and the bishop of Rome excommunicated each other and Christendom divided into eastern and western churches.

Where eastern Christianity prevailed, the relation between throne and altar came to be especially close. The founder of the first Serb dynasty, Grand Prince Stefan Nemanja, was known for building churches and monasteries. The link between the Christian church and a specific people was far more direct in Serbia than in areas of western Christianity, meaning that religious and national identity became inseparable. This link also had consequences for the separation of powers: in the west, centuries of struggle ensued between secular and religious authority, leading to recognition of areas of respective autonomy, and thus *divisions of power*, whereas in the east, a relation between the two emerged that was "almost too harmonious."[8] In 1219, now leaning eastward, Sava, an archbishop and the younger brother of Stefan Nemanja, secured autocephaly (independence) from the Byzantine emperor for the Serb Church.

At his death in 1236, Archbishop Sava was declared a saint—as were his father and brother. Thus the Serbian royal family entered the church liturgy,

MAP 1.5. Western and eastern Christianity

"immortalized in frescoes that adorned the churches and monasteries" of their country.[9] Canonized kings are not unknown in the western tradition, but again the intimacy was distinct, as was their proportion among the communion of Serb saints: of fifty-eight Serb saints, eighteen are tsars, kings, queens, princes, and lords. A cult of royal saints told Serb people over many centuries of Ottoman rule that there had once been an independent kingdom, blessed by God with saints who could work miracles.[10]

The early Serb state declined after King Dušan died in 1355 and lapsed into dependence on and then suzerainty under the Ottoman Empire. In historical memory, the turning point was the battle of Kosovo polje of June 28, 1389, when Serb Prince Lazar lost a battle along with his life to a superior Ottoman force,

FIGURE 1.1. Herzegovinian sings and plays the
gusle (1823). *Source*: The History Collection/
Alamy Stock Photo.

and his son became a vassal of the sultan. Soon after, the Serb Orthodox church
made Lazar a saint for his martyrdom, and Patriarch Danilo proclaimed "if the
darkness of death comes to us, we accept it sweetly for Christ and for the godli-
ness of our homeland. It is better to die in battle than to live in shame."[11] Over
succeeding generations, myths emerged among the common people out of this
idea of virtuous death, explaining that Lazar had lost voluntarily, choosing a
heavenly over an earthly kingdom. One day Serbia would be resurrected. Despite the metaphysically ordained necessity of that scenario, the poetry also provided a Judas-like figure who had betrayed the Serb leaders to the Ottoman

usurpers. These stories were passed on over many generations in moving folk ballads sung in the privacy of people's homes to the accompaniment of the one-string gusle.

The ballads created a firm sense of identity among villagers who could not read or write, telling them they were Christian, Serb, and "virtuous," while the occupiers and local Islamicized Slavs, who spoke the same language as they did (still today called "Turks" by Serb nationalists) allegedly practiced deceit and lived off others' labor. Ottoman domination seemed unending but was portrayed as temporary because it was built on the basic injustice of rule by the foreigner; in the meantime, faithful Serbs persisted for the heavenly kingdom, while Turks feasted on the rewards of this life.[12] These stories left enduring impressions and were manipulated by generations of nationalists.[13]

National saints are special, and their numbers seem inexhaustible. In 1992, the Romanian Orthodox Church canonized Stephen of Romania (1433–1504), who defended his lands against Poland, Hungary, and the Ottoman Empire. Patriarch Teoctist said at the canonization ceremonies: "God has brought us together under the same skies, just as Stephen rallied us under the same flag in the past."[14] Five years later, Pope John Paul II traveled to Kraków to preside over the canonization of "King" Jadwiga, the most beloved Polish sovereign. A saint is a person whose salvation the church declares as secure. What had Jagwiga done? According to John Paul, she had undertaken "great works in the national and international sphere, and desired nothing for herself. . . . An expert in the art of diplomacy, she laid the foundations for Poland's greatness in the 15th century." Even more important was a cult that developed in the seventeenth century of our Lady of Częstochowa. In 1652, Polish troops had prevailed over the Swedes when all hope seemed lost after carrying a portrait of this "Black Madonna." That same year, King Jan Kazimierz declared Mary "queen of Poland," a title subsequently confirmed by Rome, and to this day, visitors to Kraków see her symbolic crown above the highest steeple of the old city.[15]

Memory fastened onto ancient saints or special cults because of the main fact of political life from the late Middle Ages. Regardless of whether peoples came under eastern or western Christianity, what united East Europeans, when no one imagined this area as a coherent region, was a precarious political existence. From the fourteenth to eighteenth centuries, Austrian, Turkish, and Russian empires conquered and subsumed the early medieval states, and what survived were legends, on which historians of later times could fashion narratives of their peoples belonging to a lasting political entity.[16] Jadwiga or Lazar were proof of

FIGURE 1.2. Crown on St. Mary's Basilica, Kraków. *Source*: Akos, via creativecommons.org.

divine favor for many generations when no other evidence was forthcoming. The Virgin's crown remained on the steeple at St. Mary's in Kraków under Austrian rule, while swarms of German-speaking troops and administrators ran the city below.

When Serbs in the Ottoman Pashalak of Belgrade rose up against misrule by local warlords (Janissaries) in 1804, they claimed to be fulfilling the legacy of Prince Lazar. They were almost entirely unable to read and write but had a distinct sense of their national identity and many centuries of shared history due to their oral tradition. After the Polish state was wiped off the map in 1795, in each succeeding generation, Polish patriots concocted political and military conspiracies, claiming they were resurrecting the old state and its mission of defending freedom and western Christendom. History "demanded" that this state reappear and that Poland again take its rightful place among European nations. As in Serbia, stories emerged telling Poles that the downfall of their powerful state was due to a traitor from within.

 But beyond legends, the early period also bequeathed legacies of linguistic and ethnic interweaving that made states of single peoples—nation-states— confoundingly difficult to create at a later date. People speaking different languages and practicing different faiths, with no sense of modern nationhood, had settled among one another everywhere in East Central Europe in the generations and centuries after the fall of the Roman Empire, so that they could not be divided by boundaries when anti-imperial movements demanding nation-states emerged many centuries later.

* * *

From the middle to late middle ages, three additional processes further complicated the East Central European map: the massive but very gradual migration of German settlers eastward, into areas of the Polish and Hungarian kingdoms; the movement of millions of Jews into Poland from central and Western Europe; and, farther south, conversions to Islam that took place in the Ottoman lands, with special intensity in Bulgaria, Bosnia, and the land between Serbia and Montenegro, which became known as the Sanjak of Novi Pazar.[17]

From the twelfth century, Germans began surging from crowded and increasingly prosperous western territories into more thinly populated areas farther east, into Transylvania and the Banat, which belonged to the Hungarian Crown, as well as the Silesian and Pomeranian territories under the rule of Polish kings. In exchange for settling territory and rendering feudal dues, they were given rights to work land, practice their own religions and their trades, and speak their language. Over time, German craftspeople also migrated into cities in much of the region, where their skills were prized. By the seventeenth century, the Lithuanian city of Wilno (Vilnius), for example, had Germans as well as Poles of several faiths, Ukrainians of two faiths, Jews, Lithuanians, Belorussians, and Muslims.[18] At the end of the eighteenth century, Zagreb, Budapest, and Prague were mostly German-speaking cities surrounded by villages populated by Croatian, Hungarian, and Czech-speaking peasants.

Later historians and publicists described the process of German settlement as "Drang nach Osten," that is, a persistent German push for territory in the east, which was interpreted by Polish and other nationalist schools as aggressive but by German scholars as the peaceful transport of a higher culture eastward. The stimulus for migration was really demographic, pressed by high birth rates in the west, including Dutch territories, and the desire of younger sons to have land to settle and plant. For their part, Eastern Europe's kings and princes simply wanted their lands populated.

Over time, German settlement in the east had the effect of moving eastward a language border between German and Slavic speakers, from a line extending from Lübeck, Berlin, and Dresden (1200) to one going from Danzig, Thorn,

MAP 1.6. Early states (ca. AD 1000)

Esthonians

Livonians

Lithuanians

•Novgorod

Baltic Sea

Gdańsk• Prussians

Bolgars

Mordvins

Smolensk•

•Minsk

POMERANIA

•Poznań

MAZOVIA

Pinsk•

KIEVAN RUS

DUCHY of
POLAND

CHROBATIA

Kiev•

•Cracow

SILESIA

D. of
MORAVIA
of
AUSTRIA

•Pressburg

K·I·N·G·D·O·M of

HUNGARY

TRANSYLVANIA

Zagreb•

P e t c h e n e g s

of
CROATIA

Belgrade•

DALMATIA

SERBIA

Ragusa•

Cherson•

THEME of
CHERSON

B l a c k   S e a

THEME of
LOMBARDY

THEME of
DYRRHACHIUM

BULGARIA

TH. of
HAEMIMONT

THEME
of the
STRYMON

TH. of
THRACE

Sinope•

THEME of CHALDIA

TH.of
PAPHLAGONIA

ARMENIAC
THEME

TH.of
COLONEA

BUCELLARIAN
THEME

TH.of
MESOPOTAMIA

SALERNO

Constantinople•

TH.of OPTIMATON

TH. of
THESSALONIKI

TH.of
MACEDONIA

TH.of
CHARSIANON

TH.of
SEBASTIA

THEME of
CALABRIA

•Thessaloniki

OPSICIAN
THEME

TH.of
LYCANDOS

B Y Z A N T I N E   E M P I R E

THEME of
HELLAS

TH. of
NICOPOLIS

ANATOLIC
THEME

TH.of
CAPPADOCIA

TH.of
CILICIA

TH.of
ANTIOCH

DOMINION of the HAMDANIDS

THRACESIAN
THEME

Tarsus•

•Athens

THEME of the CIBYRRAEOTS

THEME
TH.of
SELEUCIA

S Y R I A

TH. of
PELOPONNESUS

Sea

o TH. of CTRETE

TH. of CYPRUS

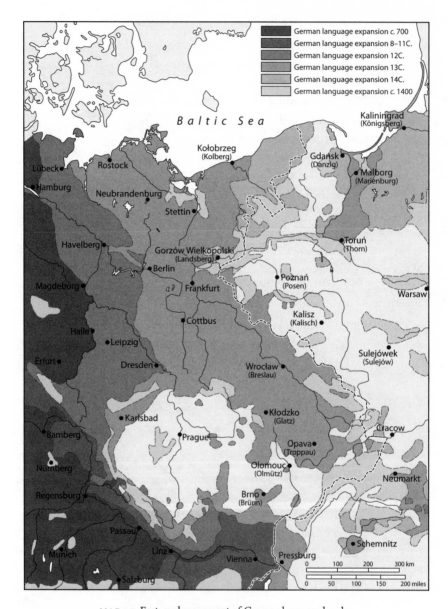

German language expansion c. 700
German language expansion 8–11C.
German language expansion 12C.
German language expansion 13C.
German language expansion 14C.
German language expansion c. 1400

Baltic Sea

Kaliningrad
(Königsberg)

Kołobrzeg
(Kolberg)

Gdańsk
(Danzig)

Lübeck   Rostock

Malborg
(Marienburg)

Hamburg

Neubrandenburg

Stettin

Havelberg

Gorzów Wielkopolski
(Landsberg)

Toruń
(Thorn)

Berlin

Poznań
(Posen)

Magdeburg

Frankfurt

Warsaw

Kalisz
(Kalisch)

Halle   Cottbus

Leipzig

Sulejówek
(Sulejów)

Erfurt   Dresden

Wrocław
(Breslau)

Karlsbad

Kłodzko
(Glatz)

Cracow

Bamberg   Prague

Opava
(Troppau)

Nürnberg

Olomouc
(Olmütz)

Neumarkt

Regensburg

Brno
(Brünn)

Passau

Schemnitz

Munich   Linz

Vienna   Pressburg

0   100   200   300 km

Salzburg

0   50   100   150   200 miles

MAP 1.7. Eastward movement of German language border

and Breslau (1400)—more than 200 miles.[19] In the course of this settlement, uncounted thousands of Slavic speakers were absorbed into German culture, and all that remained of once vibrant Slavic settlement were some ancient grave inscriptions, burial mounds, and place names, like Jena, Leipzig, and Potsdam. Awareness of the extent of Slavic settlement gave later generations of West Slav nationalists (notably Jan Kollár) a sense that they had to protect themselves from "Germanization." Yet in other places, the German settlers mingled and mixed into local populations, sometimes assimilating, sometimes creating "islands" of German language and culture, in Bohemia, Hungary, Transylvania, or later, in parts of the Russian empire.

But Germans were not the only group that Polish kings invited into their realm: beginning in the eleventh and accelerating in the sixteenth century, they also welcomed Jews, overwhelmingly Ashkenazi fleeing persecution in Germany, who brought with them the Germanic vernacular that we know as Yiddish. Poland became home to the largest community of Jews in the world. Smaller but significant Ladino-speaking Jewish communities entered southeastern Europe from the fifteenth century, after expulsion from Catholic Spain. Some mixed with Ashkenazi Jews after Austria-Hungary occupied Bosnia in 1878. By the twentieth century, one in seven inhabitants of Sarajevo was of Sephardic or Ashkenazi Jewish heritage, sharing the city with Muslims, Serb Orthodox, and Roman Catholics.[20]

The Polish kings had invited Jews to settle because they, like Germans, brought skills into thinly populated areas, and so their rights were mostly respected. Yet Poland was also part of Christendom and as such participated in the segregating of Jews into separate quarters of towns. Jews were not allowed to live in the countryside or own land there and were forced to wear special clothing and insignias. As in Western Europe, malicious myths were spread about supposed Jewish practices of ritual murder of Christian children or desecration of the sacred host. Rumors of the latter in 1399 in the Polish town of Poznań led to the arrest and cruel execution of a dozen Jewish leaders and their supposed Christian accomplice, and then a requirement that the Jewish community pay a tax to the church from which the communion host had supposedly been taken—for more than 300 years![21] Historians count some fifty local persecutions of Jews in Poland from the 1530s to the early seventeenth century, including the massacres perpetrated by Cossack forces and peasants rebelling against Polish rule in Ukrainian lands in 1648. Still, the Jewish community grew and flourished economically and culturally thanks to a relatively tolerant legal environment. Some rabbis even spoke of Poland as a paradise for the Jews.[22]

Looking across the region as a whole, Jews more than any other ethnic group were clearly identified: by language (usually Yiddish), by religion, by occupation, by dress, and by place of residence. Long before the age of nationalism, they were considered the ultimate "others," and in the nineteenth century continued to be targets of violence, especially during times of crisis and upheaval, no matter what their posture was to the new national movements. As we will

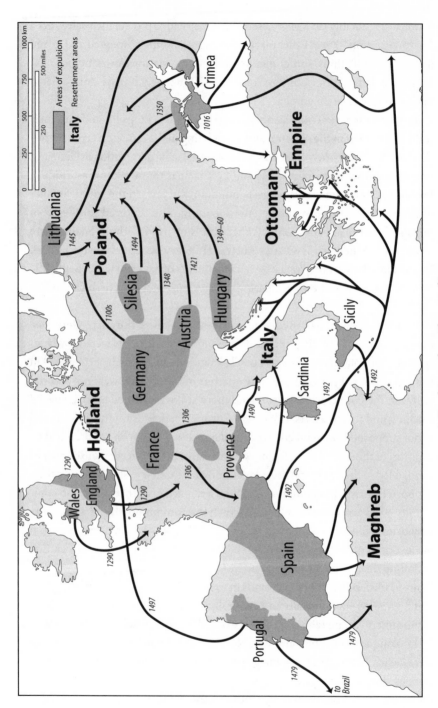

MAP 1.8. Expulsion and resettlement of Jews

Lithuania
Poland
Silesia
Germany
Austria
Hungary
Holland
England
Wales
France
Provence
Portugal
Spain
Italy
Sardinia
Sicily
Crimea
Ottoman Empire
Maghreb

1290
1290
1290
1306
1306
1490
1492
1492
1492
1492
1497
1479
1479
1479
to Brazil
1100s
1348
1421
1349–60
1494
1445
1350
1016

Areas of expulsion
Resettlement areas
Italy

0   250   500   750   1000 km
0   250   500   750 miles
0   250   500 miles

see, the rise of religious tolerance did not protect the Jews; it merely afforded the transfer of religious bias into secular bigotry, keeping alive the belief that Jews were destined to suffer for a crime in the deep past that nothing could expiate. This was the transition from Christian anti-Judaism to modern anti-Semitism.

But for the time being, the Polish kings did not care what religion their subjects practiced or language they spoke; like other monarchs, they often gained huge tracts of multiethnic, multireligious property through inheritance or marriage. Recently canonized Jadwiga of Poland had laid the foundations for Poland's early modern power by marrying Władysław Jagiełło in 1386 and joining the kingdom of Poland to the Grand Duchy of Lithuania. When his line died out in 1569, Polish and Lithuanian nobles agreed to transform the union into a commonwealth in which the king would be elected. That state lasted two more centuries, by which time Russia was paying nobles to vote for its candidates and subverting the commonwealth from within. Russia then subdued it from without in the three partitions of 1772, 1792, and 1795, which gradually made Poland disappear, adjoining its territories to Russia and its accomplices: Prussia and Austria.

The growth of the early modern Habsburg realm was even more spectacular. At a double wedding in 1517 at St. Stephen's Cathedral in Vienna, Louis Jagiełło, king of Bohemia and Hungary, married Habsburg princess Mary—they were both nine—and Louis's sister Anna wed the Habsburg emperor Maximilian. She was twelve and he fifty-six, but it was understood that the union could be transferred to Maximillian's grandson Ferdinand, whom she indeed wed in 1521 at Linz. In 1526 Ferdinand came into possession of the Bohemian and Hungarian crowns when his brother-in-law Louis died in action against the forces of Suleiman the Magnificent in the battle of Mohács. Some Hungarian nobles contested the Habsburg right to the Hungarian throne, but when the Ottomans were driven from all Hungarian territory a century and a half later, there was little question in Europe that this throne was hereditary through the male line of the House of Habsburg.

Louis's tragedy made the Habsburg monarchy: Bohemia included the lands of today's Czech Republic, but the Hungarian Kingdom was a vast space, comprising today's Hungary but also Slovakia, Transylvania, northern Serbia (Vojvodina), and parts of western Ukraine, Slovenia, and Austria. It also included Croatia, because the Croat nobles had elected the Hungarian king as their own (with obligations to protect their rights) in the twelfth century. Thus the head of the house of Habsburg was the king of Hungary as well as king of Croatia.

The Habsburgs had united with Louis in a desperate attempt to hold off the steady push up the Balkans of Ottoman forces, which had begun absorbing territory in the fourteenth century, usually by taking advantage of discord among Christian powers (for example, Hungary and Serbia). Before being repulsed at Vienna in 1683 and then gradually driven back, the Ottomans had conquered territories that later became Greece, Romania, Bulgaria, Albania, and Yugoslavia, as well as much of Hungary. They did not forcibly convert or make people learn the Turkish language, yet because non-Muslims could not own land or enter state service, over time hundreds of thousands converted from Christianity to Islam; many also did so because they were attracted to the religion, especially in the Bosnian sanjak, where by the seventeenth century, some 79 percent of the inhabitants were Muslims; the rest were Serb Orthodox, Roman Catholic, and Jewish.[23] Over the centuries, the Ottomans also forcibly wrested from Christian families some 200,000 boys, but after converting them to Islam and educating them, the Ottomans opened to them the highest positions in military and state service. The point of this blood tax was to maintain a constant inflow of fresh talent into the Ottoman state, of young men who were responsible and loyal to the central authorities; the system frustrated nepotism and patronage networks.[24]

Yet even before the Ottoman conquests, confession had divided the ethnic groups of Eastern Europe. The line between western and eastern Christianity went northward from Bosnia, separating Polish, Czech, Slovak, Slovene, and Serbo-Croatian Catholics from Bulgarian, Serbo-Croatian, Macedonian, Ukrainian, and Russian-speaking Orthodox populations. Romanians also were overwhelmingly Orthodox. Because its ruling house was Orthodox, Russia claimed affinity with the Orthodox populations in Eastern Europe, especially Serbs, Romanians, Greeks, and Bulgarians, and in the treaty of Kuchuk Kainarji of 1774, the Ottoman Empire recognized Russia's right to intervene on behalf of Orthodox Christians living in their territories. But Russia's interventions were not selfless: it supported Serb, Romanian, or Bulgarian independence when that meant extending its own dominance southward on the Balkan peninsula— either through client regimes or direct occupation of territory—ultimately hoping to control Istanbul and gain free access to the Mediterranean.[25]

Over the centuries, hundreds of thousands of Orthodox Christians left the Ottoman lands and migrated north, into areas just on the Habsburg side of the border, some in Croatia and others in southern Hungary, where they received land in exchange for service in border protection forces. As a result, the majority Orthodox Christian communities grew along the border to Bosnia in Croatia and Slavonia, and along the Danube east and just north of Belgrade. (The

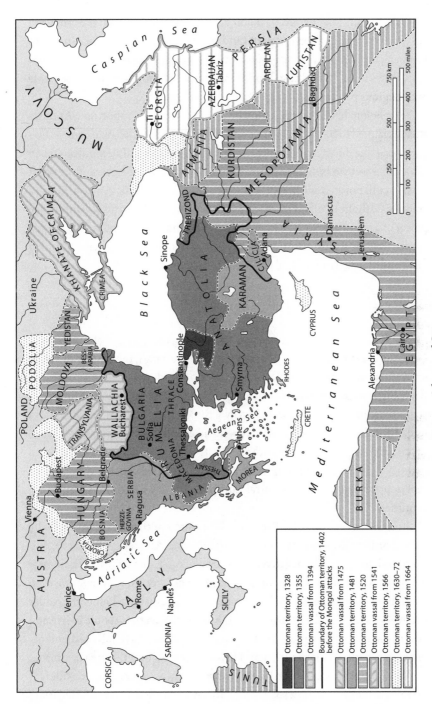

MAP 1.9. Advance of Ottoman power

German for this long defensive buffer zone that stretched around Bosnia and eastward on the northern edge of Ottoman Serbia is *Militärgrenze* [military frontier]; the Serbo-Croatian is *Vojna krajina.* See map 6.1.) Beyond land ownership, Serbs under Habsburg dominion received corporate rights of self-rule and religious practice.

Yet religion, like language, could be a tool, used when opportune. At times Russia claimed to be a supporter of oppressed Orthodox Christian Slavs in Bulgaria or Serbia, but it also happily worked with non-Orthodox countries when advantages were to be had. In the three partitions of the late eighteenth century, Russia collaborated with Protestant Prussia and Catholic Austria to wipe (mostly Catholic) Poland from the map. Now much of Poland was under the power of a religiously foreign power, a fact that tended to heighten Polish sense of identity—just as Muslim rule bolstered a separate sense of identity among Orthodox Christian South Slavs.

* * *

Few topics are as contentious as what to make of the heritage of centuries of Ottoman rule in southeastern Europe. For the most part, the empire did what states do: it guaranteed a modicum of order and presided over moderate growth. Arguably, it secured religious diversity more effectively than did West European states. Forced conversions were largely limited to the practice of taking boys into Ottoman state service, and there were no expulsions of Jews or Protestants of the sort that occurred in France and Austria. No witch trials took place, and heretics were not burned at the stake; there was nothing like the religious wars that depopulated much of Central Europe in the sixteenth and seventeenth centuries.

Still, the "memory" of Ottoman rule in much of the region—especially among historically Christian populations in Serbia, Montenegro, Greece, Bulgaria, and Hungary—is negative.[26] The local idiom to describe it is some variant of "slavery." There is no right or wrong in these stories. Whether one even cares about them depends on the ethnic perspective, that is, whether the reader believes it is of value for humanity for the Serb or Bulgarian people to live and advance in history, or for the South Pannonian plain to have solid settlements of ethnic Hungarians (the Ottoman-Habsburg contest over this area decimated the local Magyar population), or, most crucially, whether one considers it important for there to be a space on earth where the flourishing of Bulgarian, Hungarian, or Serb culture is protected by political boundaries.

For those who live in such narratives, the facts are simple and the conclusions clear. The early stages of Ottoman rule featured slaughter, pillage, and enslavement, the destruction and erosion of the native nobilities and merchant classes, leaving the ethnic Christian populations a vast underclass of peasant sharecroppers.[27] Works of art were destroyed, and the local cultures and languages stagnated; there was no schooling of any kind in the native language and no literature. To give a sense of the difference secure early modern statehood made, one can look at Poland, which maintained a native elite, and developed literature as well as high schools and universities, a native jurisdiction, a military, and political culture, remnants of which survive to this day.

As we have seen, peasant culture was by no means a vacuum in the South Slav region: a tradition of popular folk poetry persisted in private dwellings, which neither bothered nor interested the Ottoman overlords, and carried on the memory of the old Serb kingdom and Bulgarian Empire. Yet if there was progress in native high culture for South Slavs, it took place beyond Ottoman borders. Serb literature and scholarship, for instance, emerged in the southern Habsburg border areas where authorities had permitted refugees from the Ottoman territories to settle. Students from this area could travel to Italy and France and connect to modern trends in scholarship, science, or statecraft. In the late eighteenth century, a Serb enlightenment prospered in the Slavonian city of Sremski Karlovci (part of Habsburg Hungary); its guiding spirit, Dimitrije "Dositej" Obradović (1740–1811), popularized ideas of the French Enlightenment he had learned in Halle, Germany, especially in the form of moral tales and parables. In the early nineteenth century, when Serb insurgents carved out independent territory from the Ottomans, he went across the border to found a high school and help establish Serb educational institutions. Similarly, the Bulgarian enlightenment of the late eighteenth century and early nineteenth century grew and thrived largely beyond Bulgarian territory.[28]

Narratives emphasizing the costs of Ottoman rule note that while the economies began taking off in Western Europe, stimulated by advances in technology and science, southeastern Europe remained tied to an underproductive system that went into decline, economically and militarily, ironically and symptomatically, precisely as it stopped seizing boys for imperial service in the late seventeenth century. After that, pervasive corruption set into the local Ottoman ruling elites in southeastern Europe, giving rise to the insurgencies already mentioned that were launched in the Serb lands in 1804. At first the Sultan stood on the side of the revolutionaries, because he, too, wanted a functional political order and hoped to achieve it with their cooperation.

* * *

The word "nation" (*natio*) existed in the premodern period but did not have the meaning it has in our day.[29] The "nation" in the lands of Croatia, Hungary, or Poland was the hereditary elite, the gentry and nobles who enjoyed privileges that separated them from the "common" people. For example, nobles had a right to be tried by their peers and not imprisoned without charges, to raise soldiers, or to intermarry. In some cases, for example in Central Poland, the gentry were sizable, comprising up to one fourth of the population. The Hungarian gentry were about 6 percent; in France, by contrast, the nobility constituted less than 1 percent of the population.[30] In Poland and Hungary, the rights to self-rule became substantial and made the hereditary nobility more powerful than counterparts in France, not to mention in Russia. By the sixteenth century, the Polish gentry elected its kings; during the seventeenth century, a practice emerged in which passage of legislation in the Sejm (parliament) required unanimous consent, a practice called "liberum veto."

By the seventeenth century, the Polish nobility thus felt a strong sense of cohesion, politically and culturally, over a vast territory, and increasingly practiced Roman Catholicism, though the Protestant Reformation was at first popular and tolerated.[31] A myth emerged according to which Poland's nobles derived from "Sarmatians," an ancient Iranian people who had subjugated Slavic tribes during early Christendom. This had the function of tying the group together even more tightly against all others on Polish territory, reinforcing its sense of privilege, and tending to exclude all others from the idea of nation.[32]

But the cultural identity of noble nations was premodern. Polish or Hungarian poets wrote in their own tongues from the fifteenth century (native liturgical texts are much older), producing important literatures, but they did not make a cult of language. And unlike liberal-democratic patriots of the nineteenth century, early modern nobles did not believe that all those who happened to speak Polish or Hungarian constituted a Polish or Hungarian "nation." From the seventeenth century on, they tended to speak French or Latin among themselves and felt a cultural affinity with other European elites, with whom they shared tastes in architecture and music, and with whose sons their own mingled at universities in France and Italy.

Unlike modern nationalism, the idea of *natio* was therefore exclusive to a social group rather than insistently inclusive across a complex population ostensibly of one ethnicity. The early modern Polish or Croatian nobility did not think of Polish or Croatian-speaking peasants as part of their nation and often considered these peasants a lower form of humanity. The word for "peasant" was often synonymous with "slave," evoking coarseness and absence of all taste.[33] In decades when Western European peasants were being freed from the land and from compulsory services, a "second serfdom" was taking hold in much of Eastern Europe: those who worked the land became tied to it and could not leave without the master's permission. They were people whom he could whip and otherwise humiliate in dozens of ways. No clear line existed dividing Eastern from Western Europe in terms of agricultural regime, but as one traveled to the east, the freedoms of the peasants tended to decrease, as did the productivity of agriculture.[34]

When Polish or Hungarian nobles made claims to territory, it was therefore not in order to unite people of the same language or "blood."[35] They had no idea of including all people of their ethnicity in a particular state.[36] But this early modern noble national identity was also not ethnically exclusive in the sense of modern nationalism. Native Ukrainian-speaking nobles living in Galicia considered themselves part of the Polish noble nation, and many of them over time became culturally Polish with no questions asked. In the sixteenth and seventeenth centuries, the Vatican had supported arrangements permitting Orthodox believers in Ukraine (under Polish rule) and in Transylvania (under Habsburg rule) to be "reunited" with Rome while maintaining much of their own liturgy and practices, including married clergy. These churches of the Byzantine right that recognize papal authority are commonly known as "Uniate."

The importance of the older legacy of noble rights is that feelings of corporate identity and privileges survived in social groups even after political structures supporting them declined or disappeared altogether, and then were spread to other social groups, usually very slowly and unevenly. Thus the Polish, Hungarian, and Croatian gentries continued to insist on rights of self-rule and "freedom" after medieval and early modern statehood was crushed.[37] Among the Polish gentry, even after the destruction of the Polish state in the final partition in 1795, Poland continued as a community of ideas and practices—as a common culture—and was as present among the colony of émigré Polish writers in Paris in the 1840s as it was among Polish-speakers in Polish territories then part of Austria or Russia. The ideas of this "Great Parisian emigration"— that Poland had not perished and had a mission to humanity—made their way back to the Polish lands to inspire young people from other groups, including peasants, especially as Polish education became more widespread (often through the efforts of underground nationalist activists).

* * *

It would be wrong, however, to say that the less-privileged classes in towns or countryside had no sense of belonging to larger ethnic, cultural, or linguistic groups. After the Habsburgs decimated much of Bohemia's early modern elite (*natio*) at the Battle of White Mountain outside Prague in 1620 and promoted the ascent of a German-speaking elite, the Czech-speaking common people retained a special identity, though it did not yet involve a desire to create a state containing all other Czech speakers. This proto-national identity also did not lay exclusive claim to a person's loyalties and could seem irrelevant in day-to-day life. Still, Bohemian peasants passed down stories about the "good old days" under Czech kings and revered the traditions of their "fatherland." They considered the German-speaking ruling classes—in the nobility, civil and military services, or higher clergy—to be oppressors.[38] And though illiterate, they knew about very old traditions of native Protestantism, and how, centuries earlier, Czech military formations had arisen to defend the teachings of the Czech religious reformer Jan Hus. They also knew that the Catholic Habsburgs stood against this local heritage. Yet the sense of alienation was not entirely new. In their time, Hussite warriors had been fiercely anti-German, and Jan Hus (d. 1410) was a proto-patriot, who preached in Czech and helped modernize the language by introducing the "háček," a diacritical mark that greatly simplified writing (before that Czech was spelled like Polish).[39]

In Transylvania as well, shared religion overlapped with hereditary ethnic subordination to create a proto-national consciousness among Orthodox Romanian-speaking peasants against their Calvinist Magyar landlords.[40] In the late seventeenth century, the number of Romanian speakers approached half the population, yet not only did they not have title to land, but the Habsburg state also refused to recognize their existence as a community: only Magyars, Szeklers, and Saxons counted as "political nations" with rights.[41] But after 1700, the Habsburg state sent Uniate-rite priests for education to Western Europe, where they encountered Enlightenment texts that made them question their people's subordinate status. The result was a movement that demanded rights for Romanians.[42]

In one supposed scholarly account printed in Germany in the 1790s, Slovaks living on the March River appear as "lethargic, despondent, and soft," in contrast to the energetic Vlach hill people (Romanians).[43] Many Slovaks thought of Hungarians as "rogues," while Hungarians called Slovaks "good for nothings," and Romanians "poor devils."[44] These were not stereotypes about unknown foreigners but of neighbors in the next village, or in some towns, in adjoining houses and streets.

More than a feeling of what held them together, Romanians and other East European peoples therefore possessed a sense of distinction from other ethnic groups. Slovak or Slovene speakers knew they were not Hungarian or Italian, and early modern Croats called Serbs "Rascians" (those in Serbia) and "Vlachs" (those in Bosnia-Herzegovina). The literature of the Croatian Renaissance of the fifteenth and sixteenth centuries took on anti-Venetian and anti-Ottoman tones, and it castigated those who forsook the mother tongue.[45] Historians date a Polish couplet from the mid-sixteenth century: "as long as the world is the world, a German will never be a brother to a Pole."[46] As early as the twelfth century, Poland's elite felt superior to their neighbors and resented the Czechs and the still-pagan peoples to the north.

When Romanian peasants revolted in 1784 against arbitrary lord-subject relations, their animus focused on Catholic and foreign Hungarian "tyrants."[47] In the Serb lands, Muslims constituted the landowners as well as urban populations, and to be a peasant became synonymous with being a Serb.[48] Orthodox Serbs saw Slav Muslims as "neither Serbs, nor Turks, neither water nor wine, but as odious renegades." Churches dating back centuries featured images of severed Turk heads, and "warrior-saints" stabbing Turkish-looking soldiers.[49] People in border areas denoted wickedness in terms of Muslims: "worse than a Turk."[50]

In Bohemia, the land tenure system was more equitable, but travelers had no doubt that the Czech speakers constituted an underclass. The Prussian writer and adventurer Baron von Pöllnitz noted two things from his visit of the 1730s: first, there was no upper class on the planet more addicted to expensive living than that of Prague, and second, their noblesse obliged nothing at all. Bohemian noblemen rarely pursued careers in state service because "they are so used to be[ing] absolute masters at their estates where their *peasants are their slaves*, and to be paid homage like petty sovereigns by the burghers at Prague, that they don't care to reside at Vienna, and to be obliged like other subjects to pay their court to the sovereign and the ministers."[51] Bohemia was a land of spas and comforts, a playground for the wealthy.

When the British cleric George Gleig touched down there a century later, educated Czechs muttered resentment at the suppression of even the memory of Bohemian independence. Higher orders spoke indignantly of the ban on their beloved language and of the extinction of their privileges. "We shall never be content," they said, "until the laws are everywhere administered in a language which is intelligible to the people and we and they be permitted to exercise some control over our own affairs." Humbler folk concurred: "we are no longer a people. The *stranger* rules us, the shackles are on our wrists."[52] Not coincidentally, the sympathetic Gleig was Scottish, sensitive to the plight of subordinate peoples, and author of four volumes on British rule in India. Like his kin, Czechs wanted better management of their own affairs.

Etienne Balibar has written that "every modern nation is a product of colonization," emerging either from the experience of colonizing or being colonized: it was the latter that applied to the peoples of East Central Europe.[53] As in colonialism the world over, the levels of oppression came to intersect and reinforce one another: the cultural and linguistic, the administrative, the economic, and the social. In much of the region, the foreign (though native) landowner controlled his subjects' lives, and acted as an intermediary between them and the crown.[54] Popular resentment focused on suppression of culture and language, because it was here that the foreigner's condescension was most painful, insulting one's home, the world of one's parents and grandparents, that is, the original sources of identity and meaning. The basic goal of the Czech movement in the nineteenth century was for a political unit where the native language would be protected. Otherwise, wrote its foremost journalist, Karel Havlíček Borovský, one was a "slave" to someone else's language and culture. The language strikes us as hyperbolic, but he meant it literally.

* * *

The rulers in Vienna and Istanbul did not believe they were making colonies in the territories they took, whether in Poland, Bohemia, Hungary, or historic Serbia. But no matter what they intended for their realms, by uniting a huge space and permitting free traffic of ideas, wares, administrators, but above all of people, they succeed in making them marvelously and chaotically complex over many centuries. Thus the city of Vienna became like a mini-Chicago by the late nineteenth century, with "colonies" of Czechs, Poles, South Slavs, Jews, Italians, and Ukrainians. The Jewish community itself consisted of Czech and German Jews, but also Jews from small towns in eastern Poland. After 1878, the Habsburgs acquired Bosnia-Herzegovina, already a multiverse of religions and languages, now made even richer through an influx of Habsburg officials as well as businesspeople from all over the realm. By World War I, the Habsburg monarchy was perhaps the most religiously, ethnically, and linguistically diverse large space on earth, the quintessence of East Central Europe.

What made East Central Europe distinct from other areas was therefore not its position on the edge of the west, or beyond some boundary, on the other side of which was "Asia," to use the term employed by the chief Habsburg minister Metternich to describe everything east of Vienna. The line dividing the eastern and western Roman empires—and later, eastern and western Christianity—did not separate Eastern from Western Europe but ran right through the center of East Central Europe. East Central Europe was over-whelmingly rural, but it was not defined by "backwardness." The farther one traveled eastward from the English Channel, the fewer were the cities, the lower the productivity of farms, the fewer and poorer the roads, and the lower the literacy rate as well as life expectancy. But that descent occurred on a gradi-ent, with no clear boundaries. East Central Europe was an economically di-verse area somewhere between a highly developed western core and outer pe-riphery: low socioeconomic development did not define it. Areas farther east were even more rural.

East Central Europe was thus not so much an edge or periphery of the west as it was a space between east and west, and between north and south. "Crossroads" is too weak a word: the region was Grand Central Station and Times Square, with massive, hardly controlled movement from all directions at all times—migrations of Serbs from the south, Jews from the north, Germans from the west—drawing on influences from Anatolia but also from Russia and Italy as well as the Baltic Sea and central Germany. It was a place where the intellectual elite of the late nineteenth century routinely studied several semesters in St. Petersburg but then switched to universities in Vienna, Prague, or Paris; where a bright lawyer or doctor might grow up at the edge of Bohemia and make a career in today's Lithu-ania or in Trieste on the Adriatic; or where a Polish Jew, like Rosa Luxemburg, could study in Warsaw, Berlin, and Zurich and then become a commanding figure in Russian, Polish, and German Social Democracy simultaneously. Such move-ment of ideas and people was ceaseless, because where it lived and thrived as a society and culture, East Central Europe was virtually unbounded.

* * *

Still, East Central Europe was a definite place, ethnically, culturally, linguisti-cally, religiously, and economically. One noticed that when traveling from it east-ward or westward. When one no longer found multiple peoples living on the same square meter of land, appropriating history and imagination in radically different ways, one knew one was no longer in East Central Europe, but in

Moscow or Mannheim or Milan, Paris, or Lisbon, with one dominant governing language or culture, in a place where city flows into countryside rather
than seeming to be an alien civilization opposed to it.

History had shaped Western Europe differently, and it did not feature comparable ethnic complexity. The centuries after the collapse of Rome were a
time of movement of tribes, for example, the Franks in Gaul or the Normans
in England, but these strata were culturally absorbed over time. The same held
in the eastern marches of Germany, where millions of Slavic speakers became
culturally German over the centuries; or in the highlands of today's Austria and
Slovenia, where over many generations pockets of Romance language speakers
were absorbed into German and Slavic culture.

The few "foreign" linguistic groups that remained, like the Basques or Bretons, or the larger Catalan group, resided on the margins, and we find in all of
Western Europe, including Scandinavia and the Iberian Peninsula, little to equal
the complexity that was normal in Eastern Europe. For example, nothing resembled Wilno, where the language of the city was Polish, German, French,
Yiddish, and Russian, but that of the surrounding villages was Lithuanian and
Belorussian. There was no region in France, England, Spain, or Germany that
was like Transylvania or Bosnia, with their patchworks of ethnicity, rendering
the creation of a nation-state of the French sort—later taken as a model throughout Eastern Europe—impossible without applying great force.[55] For example,
the Magyar elite, when it gained control of the Hungarian Kingdom in 1867,
made learning a language other than Magyar difficult and expensive. By 1914,
there were no Slovak-language high schools to serve five million Slovaks in
Slovakia—an area Magyars called Northern Hungary. The only way to succeed
in life was to become Magyar.

The monarchies of France, Spain, England, Denmark, and Sweden built
strong states, supported local cultures and languages, and then transported them
abroad rather than desperately protecting them at home. They were colonizers
rather than colonized. Like its Magyar counterpart, the French state of the late
nineteenth century faced the challenge of making peasants into full members
of the nation, but its schools nationalized rather than de-nationalized. The standard French inculcated was a variant of the language most French citizens
spoke at home—their patois—and not something completely foreign in the
way that German or Magyar was for Czech and Slovak speakers. Rather than
contradict a sense of local identity, the French state built on preexisting foundations and reinforced them. The peasants and their ancestors had lived in
France from time immemorial and had no other memory to draw on.

The linguistic diversity that remained in France or the German lands ran along a dialect gradient and was not complicated by the deep religious divisions that characterize the Balkans, between Christianity and Islam, and within Christianity, between the eastern and western churches. Until 1871, Germany lacked a central state, but the multifarious Holy Roman Empire (and its successor, the German Confederation) nevertheless gave a sense of national unity. The Empire had had a coronation city and an emperor, a parliament, common laws and a central court, a history going back to Charlemagne, and a common high language, spread through publishing houses, reading societies, high schools, and universities. There were enduring disputes about precisely where Germany's boundaries ran, for example, between it and Denmark or it and France, and these "fine points" could and did lead to wars, but there was no question that France, Germany, and Denmark had existed for a very long time and should continue to exist.

* * *

As diverse and potentially tension-laden as it was, in the late 1700s, East Central Europe appeared stable, and the lives of its populations seemed mostly harmonious and orderly. Though an exploited underclass, Czech-speaking peasants peacefully tended their lords' fields or plied trades in villages and small towns, at the edge of European consciousness. They were not considered peoples comparable to the French, English, or Dutch.[56] As late as the 1840s, the "Slavonians," as they were known, hardly registered in the western mind.[57] As far as anyone knew, Bohemia was a province of the Holy Roman Empire (and then the German Confederation), in the heart of Germany, where the roads crossed between Breslau and Nuremberg, and Vienna and Berlin. Further east, even the word "Romanian" had yet to be coined; Slovakia or Slovenia appeared on no maps, and Poland was about to disappear. Infant morality was high, schools few, productivity low, small crafts abundant but industry almost nonexistent. But people knew no other reality. The elites lived from the labor of peasants forced to work on their properties, and they communicated with one another and with the distant court in Latin or French.

If there was strife and unrest, it resulted principally from the acts of foreign conquering armies: for centuries from Ottoman Turkey; in the 1600s, from Sweden and France; after 1740, from Frederick the Great's Prussia; and a few decades later, Catherine the Great's Russia. The acts of foreign armies, whether of declining Ottoman Turkey or the rising hegemons of Prussia or Russia, left the vast Habsburg realm no peace and created urgent pressures to organize a state that would produce wealth and taxes and fund armies. The halcyon surface of Hungarian or Bohemian villages was therefore deceiving: they existed in a Hobbesian East Central Europe, where states either defended themselves or disappeared.

This is where the challenges emerged for the deceptive stability of eighteenth century East Central Europe. Rather than admiring the rich complexity of the languages and cultures in their realm, Habsburg leaders after 1740, especially Joseph II (1780–1790) considered it a liability. He knew France and Russia and envied the ability of officials of those states to govern huge expanses of territory using one language. He decided to transfer this principle to his own diverse holdings, and the language he chose for rational governance was the language of the house of Habsburg: German. His enlightened program of state-building had an unintended effect, however: it planted fear in the hearts and minds of East Central Europeans, initially chiefly among sensitive intellectuals, that their peoples might become Germans and disappear from history.

Joseph would soon be swept from the stage; before dying, he said that everything he did was a failure. That was not true: the fear remained, and it grew, carried by schools, civil society, newspapers, and then political parties. Virtually every advance toward making East Central Europe a modern, literate, civil society of free expression and self-rule also produced forces that thrived on questioning, eroding, and then reducing the region's stunning complexity.

CHAPTER 2

Ethnicity on the Edge of Extinction

Few rulers have taken power under more catastrophic circumstances than the twenty-four-year-old Habsburg princess Maria Theresa (1740–1780). Within weeks of the death of her father, Charles VI, in October 1740, Prussia, Saxony, Sweden, Bavaria, and Spain, supported by France, were conspiring to seize as much territory as possible from the new queen's far-flung lands. In the Pragmatic Sanction of 1713, all but two states in Europe had promised Charles they would respect his daughter's rights as female heir to the Habsburg lands; now, however, opportunity was the only law, and no one dreamed that the princess—who loved drawing, dance, court festivities, and above all her husband but knew little of statehood and warfare—would rise to oppose her half-dozen enemies. This proved to be a serious miscalculation.

The first challenge came from cynical young Frederick II of Prussia. In exchange for Silesia, among Maria's wealthiest provinces, he offered to guarantee Habsburg possessions in Germany, as well as pay two million Thalers to the depleted Austrian treasury. Receiving a stern no, he sent his large and well-trained armies across the Habsburg frontier into Silesia in December 1740, where the Protestant population welcomed them. On January 3, 1741, Breslau, one of Germany's largest and richest cities, opened its gates wide to the blue-clad troops, and later that year, Bavarian and French forces occupied the rest of Habsburg Bohemia along with parts of Upper Austria and Tirol. (Silesia had been part of Bohemia.)[1]

In September, with French and Bavarian troops threatening Austria, Maria Theresa traveled down the Danube to Pozsony—today's Bratislava—capital of the Hungarian kingdom, a Habsburg possession since 1526. With her infant son Joseph on her arm, she addressed the nobles in Latin, Hungary's official language, and begged for protection. Reportedly impressed by her emotion and determination, they unsheathed their swords and pledged their "blood and lives," offering the queen shelter if foreign troops should take Vienna. Soon they had assembled an army of more than 50,000 men for the first use of Hungarian forces outside the kingdom.[2] This event has gone down as a turning point in the salvaging of the monarchy's fortunes.

FIGURE 2.1. Hungarian nobles swear "blood and lives" to Maria Theresa (1741).
Source: Historical Images Archive/Alamy Stock Photo.

But the arrangement was also a deal. Hungary's nobles supported the monarchy because it was the best guarantee of their continued control over the lands of the holy crown of St. Stephen. Only decades earlier, Habsburg troops had liberated Hungary from generations of back-and-forth warfare with the Ottoman Empire, which had ravaged much of southern Hungary, causing deforestation, economic decline, and the disappearance of many towns. Much of the ethnic Hungarian population had fled, died of disease, or was sent to the Ottoman lands as slaves. The repopulation was gradual and consisted mostly of other groups, often Serbs, but also Romanians, themselves fleeing Ottoman rule farther south and east. Therefore, Hungary's nobility was interested in stable governance of their lands and prevailed on Maria Theresa to respect their historic rights. Hungary's court treasury would handle revenues collected in Hungary, and Maria would strive to maintain the integrity all Hungarian territories, including Transylvania, as well as reside in Hungary at regular periods as the country's queen.[3]

Within two years, Austrian forces had retaken Upper Austria as well as Tirol and had driven the French and Bavarian forces from Bohemia, though the

Prussians retained control of most of Silesia. To protect herself from further threats, Maria made peace with Frederick in July 1742, sacrificing all but one-seventh of Silesia, including Liegnitz, Breslau, and Oppeln, thereby increasing Prussia's territory by one-third. Possession of this province permitted Prussia to become Austria's major rival for power in Germany, a contest settled in 1866 at the battle of Sadová (a village in northeastern Bohemia), after which Prussia ejected Austria from Germany. By then industrialists knew that Silesia also contained one of Europe's richest veins of hard coal.

The nobles of Bohemia reacted very differently to Maria Theresa's ascension to power than did those of Hungary. Like Hungary, Bohemia was a kingdom acquired by the Habsburgs (in 1526), and also like Hungary, it had ancient boundaries and a holy crown: the crown of St. Wenceslaus. Yet in spring 1743, during the French occupation, Bohemia's nobles met in Prague and quietly conceded to the Prussian king lands that had belonged to the Bohemian crownlands for four centuries, showing none of the cohesion and pride in their kingdom that animated their Hungarian counterparts.[4] Indeed, two years previously, under threat of losing their own properties and under pressure from the Archbishop of Prague (a native of the Rhineland), Bohemia's nobles had even elected the Bavarian duke Charles Albert as their king. Most treated Bohemia as if it were interchangeable with any province in Germany (that is, in the Holy Roman Empire of the German Nation), and a number would have preferred connecting their lands to Saxony in the north for the sake of trade along the Elbe.

Some noble families felt loyalty to the kingdom, but even they were not attached to Bohemia's crown of St. Wenceslaus in the way that Hungary's gentry felt attached to the crown of St. Stephen. The Bohemian nobility's patriotism was less coherent and focused, attached not to a well-defined territory but instead to the tradition and culture of their region, but without an absolute sense of boundaries. They lacked a clear sense of where their fatherland ran up against someone else's, or indeed what that fatherland was. Did they perhaps have two (for example, Germany and Bohemia, or Bohemia and Austria)?

* * *

The reason for these differing senses of identity among Hungarian and Bohemian nobles has to do with Maria Theresa's great grandfather, the hyper-devout Catholic Ferdinand II (1619–1637), who had provoked the mostly Protestant Bohemian nobility of his day by attempting to constrict their religious rights.

In 1620, in a battle at White Mountain just outside Prague, Ferdinand defeated these rebels and then had twenty-seven leaders of the revolt executed in Prague's Old Town Square and their property confiscated.

In succeeding decades, about half the estates changed hands, and some 150,000 Bohemians fled, including not only nobles but also leading intellectuals.[5] A host of newcomers took over vast properties, among them nobles and soldiers who had served the Habsburgs in the Thirty Years' War from as far away as Italy, Spain, and Ireland, but most were Catholics from elsewhere in Germany.[6] The elite now became ethnically foreign, and that explains the subsequent deterioration of the local language: Czech was no longer used in high society or in administration. The priests brought in to re-Catholicize the land were likewise overwhelmingly non-Bohemian, thus reinforcing the sense of the country being under foreign occupation (an occupation that in nationalist historiography lasted until October 1918). And even when the clergy had become fully native, the Catholic Church was perceived as somehow not fully Czech.

Ferdinand introduced a new local constitution, and the rebel province lost its ancient rights, and the rights it gained came to it by royal favor. The crown was now hereditary for the Habsburgs, and only the Catholic and Jewish religions were legal.[7] A Diet continued to exist but was rarely summoned, its competencies reduced to a few financial matters. Local autonomies faded, much in contrast to the situation in the Hungarian counties, where a century and a half of Ottoman rule had been less destructive of local traditions than the anti-Protestant vengeance enacted by the Habsburgs in Bohemia. Hungary never endured such wholesale replacement of the nobility, and therefore most Hungarian nobles continued to trace ancestry back to time immemorial and consider themselves the natural proprietors of their lands.[8]

Ferdinand had not extinguished a Bohemian sense of nationhood for eternity, however. Ensuring that Bohemia would return to European history as a nation was Maria Theresa and especially the infant son on her arm, Joseph, who was trained for rule from an early age and crowned Holy Roman Emperor in 1765 following the death of Maria's much-loved husband Stefan of Lorraine.

The existential threat of the wars of succession of the 1740s convinced the Habsburg rulers that if their realm was to survive, it had to be guided by a strong centralizing state. Maria Theresa and later Joseph saw that other powers of the time—England, France, and Russia—were relatively uniform, in contrast to their own hodgepodge of territories, some gained by conquest, some through inheritance and marriage, hopelessly fragmented by multiple legal codes, systems of land tenure, and rights of local estates, including those of the church.

The jumble of varying and competing competences meant that authorities in Vienna could not fully tap the mineral, agricultural, or human riches of their holdings. Land was tilled inefficiently because it was under the control of a gentry caste that had little incentive to improve it and was mostly protected from sale (and thus from markets and the pressures of competition from more rational farming). In most places, peasants could not leave the land. The gentry also controlled the draft of soldiers, thus restricting manpower available to Austria's military.

Maria Theresa introduced reforms in 1749 that began to make her assemblage of poorly connected territories into a state. She disbanded the Chancellery of Bohemia and combined it with that of Austria, thus integrating the Bohemian crown into her hereditary lands. Over the course of her reign, she increased the number of officials from 5,000 to 20,000, mostly concentrated in Vienna.[9] Part of the larger bureaucracy's job was to organize military contingents through networks of provincial and local governments responsible to a new *Directorium in Publicis et Cameralibus.* She and her advisors set up a council of state to rationalize central government and reform the state apparatus in the spirit of cameralism: it was to be the preserve of exquisitely trained professionals who would improve the realm in every way, from building health clinics, schools, and poor houses, to imposing work obligations and establishing precise numbers of workers per industry, to controlling the unbridled leisure activities of students. Rather than spend evenings drinking and in the company of women, young men were to take long walks in parks.[10]

In the countryside, the landowners ceased to be semi-sovereign in their domains, and measures were introduced to tax clergy and to better the lives of peasants so that they would become more productive. Maria and then her son Joseph used improved tax receipts to fund education, the building of roads, dredging of rivers, and further military reforms. They also began promoting the use of German in schooling and administration, but they spoke French, Italian, and Viennese dialects at court and were not German nationalists. When Joseph instructed his state council to awaken the "national spirit," he meant the whole population of the monarchy and not any particular ethnic group.[11] He did not discriminate by ethnicity in making appointments, and he and his mother viewed language primarily as a tool for communication. The more a particular language promoted this goal, the more useful it was. They supported the printing of practical journals and pamphlets in all their realm's languages, on topics ranging from bee-keeping, horticulture, and prevention of fires to military matters.[12]

Yet from his travels, Joseph had grown to admire a single, dominant language's ability to help unify Europe's strong states. "How many advantages would accrue to the general good," he wrote, "if only one language were used in the entire monarchy . . . how much closer would all parts of the monarchy be connected and the inhabitants joined in a stronger bonds of brotherly love. Everyone will understand this who looks at the examples of the French, English and Russians."[13]

German was the only possible candidate for uniting the Habsburg lands in a similar way. Neither Hungarian nor any Slavic language were spoken across the realm, and indeed, Czech and Hungarian had been reduced to peasant dialects after decades of neglect by the local elites.[14] Joseph hoped that civil servants united in German culture would become a cohesive force for transmitting his will in Austria, Bohemia, and the enormous Hungary of that time—including today's Slovakia, Croatia, and Transylvania—and would serve as the foundation for building the schools, administration, and judiciary of a modern state.[15]

The prime tool for inculcating language would be education. In 1777, mother and son oversaw a reform dividing schooling into primary school, middle school, and university. Students would start the lower grades in their native language, switching to German only in middle school. Children had to be literate in a language they understood before learning German, otherwise they would sit in befuddlement at the sounds of German words they could not understand.[16] But once pupils had learned to read their native Slavic tongue, it could be discarded, having served as a stepping stone to cultural unification of the realm through German.

In Bohemia, authorities therefore fostered primary education in Czech while closing the few Czech-language high schools that now lacked any practical use. No child could enter the remaining high schools without mastery of German, and German would become the exclusive language of local administration, driving out Latin and Czech. The elite throughout the Habsburg realm understood Latin, but Joseph regarded it as outmoded and a hindrance to progress. It would also yield to German in scholarship and science, and thereby make higher knowledge more accessible to the increasingly literate population.[17]

Accordingly, Joseph proclaimed that not only lectures at Prague's university—excepting those in theology—but also ordinances in Bohemia must be in German. Yet the power of Czech to teach skills to rural teachers (for example, animal husbandry) had not been exhausted, and therefore Joseph also created chairs in the Czech language at the universities in Vienna and Prague. By that point, a debased Czech was still used in official communications of the parliament (Diet) in Bohemia but in a subordinate status. Most Czech vocabulary seemed antiquated, and it had no proper expression for modern contrivances and ideas.

Reducing Czech to a tool for making unschooled Czechs into literate Germans was not the neutral act of state-building that Joseph had intended, however. He was signaling to Czech speakers that their language had no value and might as well be pushed into oblivion. At an individual level, there was nothing new to the Germanization he promoted. For generations Czech or Slovene speakers had been alienated from the culture of their families and villages as they moved up the social ladder and into towns, while completing schooling in Latin and German. What was different now was that entire cohorts of children were to be denationalized at the same time, thus raising the possibility that someone might notice. And that is precisely what happened. In a superb irony, just as Joseph was increasing the number of primary schools at which Czech-speaking children could learn to read in Czech, small groups of intellectuals were forming who produced pamphlets lamenting the disappearance of that language. Thanks to the gift of literacy provided by the Habsburg state, students could thus discover that this state considered the language of their parents and grandparents to be substandard, not fit for use above the sixth grade.

* * *

The groupuscles of intellectuals who now rose to defend Czech were devoted to Enlightenment principles: they wanted to use reason for bettering humankind. Czech had practical uses in this venture and they believed it deserved preservation and respect, yet most spoke the language poorly. Their concern to protect Czech was not a complete rupture with the past; over the generations since White Mountain there had been the odd priest or scholar who tried to defend and maintain the Slavic vernacular.[18] What was new was the intensity of concern: between 1773 and 1793, a dozen books appeared urging Czech speakers to use, esteem, and propagate their language.[19]

Most prominent among the authors was the noble general Franz Joseph Count Kinsky (1739–1805), a son of Maria Theresa's most trusted advisor Philipp (d. 1749), once Austrian ambassador to the United Kingdom and a friend of Joseph. His family owned huge estates in Bohemia with thousands of peasant subjects, but unlike most of Bohemia's nobility, Kinsky's was a very old family, which had survived the events of 1620 and considered itself both European and

FIGURE 2.2. Czech patriot Kinsky fights for the monarchy (Tourcoing, 1794).
Source: Charles Louis Mozin; Archivah/Alamy Stock Photo.

native. The count had commanded Habsburg armies in the war of Bavarian Succession (1778), reputedly having his horse shot out from under him at least three times. In 1773, now directing the Theresian Military Academy in Vienna, he published an anonymous pamphlet that signaled the dawn of modern ethnic nationhood in Bohemia.[20]

His compatriots should learn their native tongue from childhood, he wrote. Just as the French had a bias toward French, descendants of Slavs, like them, should favor their "mother" tongue. The land may have been bilingual, but Czech was its real language and possessed unique virtues. As an advocate of enlightenment, Kinsky stressed usefulness: Czech permitted lords to communicate effectively with peasants, and because of its many difficult sounds, it also prepared students for the classical languages. He knew that such ideas sounded strange in polite society, but that did not matter. Bohemians had special gifts. To see that, one had only to travel through its countryside: in German parts one found fewer people with musical talents than in areas that were "completely Bohemian."[21]

Kinsky's spirit was reasonable and measured, and the images he propagated of ancient virtues of Czech villagers were deeply conservative. Yet his tract was revolutionary because it implied that Bohemia's true language and culture were Czech. "German Bohemians" were less pure and would have to settle for lower status. Compared to Czech patriots of the following century, Kinsky was not intolerant, let alone chauvinist. He argued that Czechs' superiority lay not in blood but in the harmonic language they spoke. If Czechs should prefer their own history, that was because their heroes were close to them and so more likely to inspire great acts. But Bohemia was not a universal standard; otherwise it would be impossible to account for the worthy people one met outside Bohemia.[22]

While Kinsky was training troops and fighting battles, other pioneer-patriots explored questions of fatherland and mother tongue in books that posed as disinterested scholarship, with citations and sources. Deep down, they were driven by an enlightened fervor to discover all they could about their homelands. Some of these writers were clergymen of humble background whom the church had educated, and they wanted to be treated seriously as men of learning. The Catholic priest Gelasius Dobner (1719–1790) scoured ancient documents to write a history of his beloved land that would stand up to critical scrutiny, casting aside dusty fables that naively extolled the beauties of the Bohemian fatherland or claimed that Bohemia and Poland were founded by the brothers "Czech" and "Lech." "Truth should be the soul of all history," he wrote. "It is the foremost duty of the historian that out of love for fatherland and for knowledge he erase everything invented by later ages, and thus rescue his nation from the ridicule of foreigners."[23]

Dobner had numerous disciples, the best-known being František Martin Pelcl, a man of humble background educated in the church, who likewise dispensed with fables and relied on verifiable facts. He cited documents showing that Slavic tribes had settled in Bohemia around the year 534 and given themselves the name "Czechs." Still, the lessons of their history were mixed.[24] Some forefathers had been corrupted by pride or personal interest and betrayed their country, yet others personified righteousness, courage, and warm patriotism. His stories of ancient Czech villains and heroes were meant to inspire young noblemen who knew reams about France or England but almost nothing about their own land.

Mikuláš Adaukt Voigt, a second prominent member of Dobner's school, took the concerns about Bohemian history into the political realm, foreshadowing bitter battles over territory that would rise between Germans and Czechs in the late nineteenth century. According to him, Czechs had their own legal system, special and different from any other (whether German, Russian, or French), lodged deeply in the past of their land and deriving from their special character as Slavs. Though they had lived in close proximity with Germans for centuries, they had never merged because they had a different culture and sensitivity, expressed for example in an inborn love of freedom. He also said they had a natural disdain [*Widerwillen*] for Germans.

Yet despite the supposedly impenetrable barrier between them and Germans, Voigt and other early Czech patriots wrote and spoke almost exclusively in German. They were disciples of a new faith who could not abandon the old house of worship. According to one later commentator, for every nine German words that came to their minds, they could think of one in Czech. Pelcl craved respect for Czech and used an ancient orthography that was unpronounceable for Germans, writing "Jan Žižka" to depict a hero of the fifteenth century instead of the much easier "Johannes Schischka." In self-defense, he asked how a Frenchman would feel if a German wrote "Russo" instead of Rousseau. Yet he spelled his own name in German ("Pelzel") and not in Czech ("Pelcl").[25]

But in the 1790s, something began to change. Pelcl became the first professor of Czech literature at the university in Prague, and a growing sense of anxiety caused him to write historical studies in the Czech he spoke awkwardly. From research, he knew that millions of Western Slavs had once settled around Berlin and areas farther west, but they had been absorbed over the centuries into German culture. The last speaker of a Slavic dialect south of Hamburg had died just a generation earlier.[26] Would this be the fate of the Czechs? In 1794, F. X. Niemetschek, tutor to the sons of Wolfgang Amadeus Mozart, invoked the pain of a "genuine Czech" who saw that "in his fatherland every language is respected except his. Our language is finished, she must continue to decline and shrink because she is spoken on too small a patch of earth by too small a part of one people."[27]

But Pelcl and Niemetschek need not have worried as much as they did. Joseph II and his mother had created the schools that ensured that Czech would not go extinct, and out of these emerged a readership for the national history and literature, which they and other Czech patriots were producing. A second, much larger generation of scholars followed, who spent decades rescuing the Czech language from oblivion, inventing words and writing dictionaries, thus making sure the new history and literature were formulated in a language that was capable of the most intricate and sophisticated expression.

In the enlightened sprit of the time, Joseph and his mother had also encouraged critical approaches to history, and with that, an appreciation of the Bohemian Kingdom's past. From this spirit came pride but also feelings of inferiority. On one hand, the patriot linguist Josef Dobrovský wrote a friend in November 1790 of the glories of their homeland: Bohemia was handsome and had fostered many writers, largely from Prague, their "great capital." If given the chance, he wrote, Bohemians could surpass everyone. Yet on the other hand, everyone saw that was not yet the case. Gelasius Dobner felt he had to protect his land "from the ridicule of foreigners."[28]

The fascination with history "as it actually happened" also generated troubling questions, for example, why a language once used in the Bohemian court by Czech kings and preached in the land's finest churches (for example, Jan Hus's Bethlehem Chapel in Prague) was now a language of peasants. It would not be long before Czech patriots wondered why Bohemia was less respected than West European countries, and how the Habsburgs might be to blame.

As the new generation of patriot-intellectuals began focusing laserlike attention on such questions, the sense of loss became increasingly painful. Karel Ignaz Tham (1763–1816) was a brilliant linguist whose father worked as a cook and mother as a chambermaid for the noble Waldstein family.[29] Thanks to extraordinary intellectual gifts, he was able to attend high school and then university, but it bothered him that for these and other steps he took "upward" he had to abandon his native tongue.[30] While working as library cataloguer in Prague in the 1780s, he blew dust off tomes published generations earlier and was shocked to discover sophistication in the language now heard mainly in workshops, horse stalls, and kitchens. The library stacks were a treasure chest of forgotten books containing words long out of circulation; they showed indisputably that Czech could produce literature of worth.[31] The twenty-year-old Tham made a case for reviving the moribund language in his pamphlet *Defense of Czech*, directing special opprobrium at Bohemia's nobility for neglecting their sacred patrimony. His parents' boss, Waldstein, for example, had betrayed the fatherland by settling at a "better" address in the Rhineland, where he became known to history as a patron of Beethoven.

The more Tham investigated, the more painful discoveries he elicited, and the closer he got to the source of the problem: the house of Habsburg. During Bohemia's glory, King Charles IV (1316–1378), the Holy Roman Emperor of the Luxemburg family, had ordered the Prague town council to address him only in Czech, and that Czech be the language of law. Then came the catastrophe of 1620, when the old nobility lost its battle with Ferdinand Habsburg, who re-Catholicized the land, among other things by destroying books written in the Czech language. According to Tham, a Jesuit Counter-Reformation missionary had boasted of burning 60,000 Czech language books in an effort to root out heresies.[32] To burn books was to kill a people.

Invention of the word "genocide" lay generations in the future, but the sense of a new and ghastly kind of crime pervaded Tham's polemics. Those who tolerated this state of affairs did not love their country. He published dual-language dictionaries and became insistent about separating Czech from German. The culprits for the fact that German words had found their way into Czech were the Czechs themselves, Czechs who knew German well and became lazy, frivolously mixing words from that language into their daily speech. More passionately than Kinsky, Tham insisted on Czech's advantages. It dispensed with definite articles but had more letters and could render more sounds, and the Czechs, knowing more sounds, could learn foreign languages more easily than could Germans. Their language also produced sweeter sounds; one could say things in Czech more easily and naturally, more completely and precisely than in any foreign language.

The most compelling evidence for Tham's argument about Czech becoming a stranger in its own land was his own failure to find work at a Bohemian high school. Though multilingual, his specialty was Czech. After leaving Bohemia, he sought employment in Vienna with mixed success and feverishly continued writing. One of his books was aimed at compatriots who knew only German: *Learn Czech in Three Months*.[33] Perennially short of funds, Tham contracted tuberculosis, and only through generosity of another patriot—Josef Dobrovský—was he given a decent funeral.

Dobrovský, son of a soldier, was also a linguist of extraordinary talents. He published the first history of Czech literature (1792), the first serious Czech grammar (1809), and a general etymology of all Slavic languages.[34] Like Tham, he was driven by a painful sense of loss, and he wrote that the "Austrian government has robbed Bohemia of its freedom, religion, language, and most recently its silver."[35] Josef Jungmann, fellow patriot and likewise a brilliant and tireless linguist, came from a large shoemaker's family. He resented Bohemian Germans who refused to learn Czech and instead "barked and grunted" in their own language. Such Bohemians were betraying the legacy of their forebears.[36] Tham, Dobrovský, and Jungmann are names known to every educated Czech of our day: through their dictionaries and grammars, they resurrected Czech as a European language.

* * *

Because she had pledged to respect the Hungarian nobility's rights, Maria Theresa was careful not to take the language reforms into the vast Hungarian kingdom, but after her death in 1780, Joseph applied his reformist zeal to every inch of the Habsburg holdings. He viewed the realm's business as akin to a set of formulas, and his task was to calculate the most rational path forward. Where his mother learned from observation and broad consultation, Joseph trusted only his top advisor, Prince Wenzel Anton von Kaunitz. Thus, after Joseph took the reins of state, the Habsburg lands went from still semi-feudal, nonsystematic ideas of state-building to the regime of an ideologue aiming to move his realm to a higher level of development: European statehood.

Some of his measures remain celebrated, for example, his lifting of serfdom. An abiding concern for Habsburg monarchs was to utilize the agricultural land of their vast territories, whose productivity was hampered by a legal regime that bound peasants to their lords in a relation that not only limited yields of crops but also degraded the peasants' dignity. Lords not only owned land, but held peasants in hereditary servitude, in some places *"Leibeigenschaft"*: they owned peasants' bodies and lives. Without the lords' permission, peasants could not marry or move off their plots. Lords also upheld the law and could flog peasants publicly.

Joseph had enjoyed a superb education with French tutors and was conversant in Enlightenment principles. He considered such treatment of serfs to be an outrage to human dignity. He detested privilege enjoyed purely because of birth, writing that all we inherit from our parents is "animal life." He soon did away with slavelike relations in the countryside, with corporal punishment, and with torture. He also weakened censorship and promoted toleration of non-Catholics, including Jews; "the liberty innate in man should be accorded him as far as possible." Humans should kneel only before God, and therefore he forbade his subjects to kneel before him.[37] Yet the point was not only to accord humans the dignity they deserved, but also to cause them to serve the state better. Force used against human intellect and spirit was counterproductive.

In his mind, rational administration was not force but necessity, yet it was by imposing it on Hungary that he brought the land to the edge of rebellion, causing the noble nation, which had sworn life and blood to Maria, to consider seeking a non-Habsburg alternative to her son, for example Prussia. As in Bohemia, the catalyst for the new sentiment was language, yet here the language involved was not the native vernacular, at least not at first.

For centuries, communication in Hungary and between Hungary and Vienna had been conducted in Latin, which for Joseph was a dead language and an embarrassment to the state he hoped to form. He therefore decreed that German would now also be the official administrative language of Hungary. However, the situation was different than in Bohemia, where German was already in widespread use, and phasing out Latin generated no protest. Hungary was much more diverse, and because people spoke Romanian in the east, Slovak and Ruthenian in the north, Croatian and Serbian in the south, and everywhere German and Yiddish, Latin was not only traditional but also practical. And though it seemed moribund to Joseph, over many generations it had come to constitute a treasured lingua franca uniting the realm, employed even by people who knew only a few hundred words of the language and who rendered them in highly idiosyncratic accents. Virtually all official business in Hungary was recorded in Latin.[38]

Now officials had three years to learn German well enough for all transactions. Joseph also issued a supplementary directive making German the language of instruction in schools, permitting only religion to be taught in the native tongues. Unwisely, he added a political "reform" getting rid of the traditional counties, the *comitats*, which, like Latin, were treasured parts of a specifically Hungarian way of life.[39]

With these acts, Joseph unwittingly spawned a vigorous national movement, a fact that baffled him, because he wanted to supplant Latin and not Hungarian, a language the Hungarian nobility had not especially valued. Those who spoke it on a daily basis tended to use it with their servitors. But by threatening to make German the land's official language, Joseph raised the specter of Hungary becoming just one more German-speaking province in Central Europe. Petitions from all over Hungary deluged the court in Vienna. Inhabitants of one northern county evoked the fate of the ancient Etruscan city of Veii: who remembered them now? Like them, the Magyars would simply disappear from history. Joseph had "touched some deep nerve, bringing dormant feelings to the surface, ushering in a new phase of national development." Even more strongly than in Bohemia, people sensed a connection between language and identity, and petitioners wrote as if an attack had been launched on their own families.[40] Joseph replied as follows:

> Anyone asking me to change decisions I have already made must make his arguments through incontrovertible *evidence of reason*. But I see in the objections of your nation nothing of the sort. . . . The German language is the universal language of my empire. Why should I treat the laws and public business in a single province according to the national language of that province?[41]

In the following century, such worship of reason catalyzed the romantic cult of feeling, because reason failed to fully capture human experience. Yet in the 1780s, the Hungarian protesters also established a practical basis for rejecting

Joseph's well-reasoned reform. Latin was the language people understood throughout the diverse realm; it was much admired "by other nations" and cherished by Hungarians as a local prerogative going back centuries. Furthermore, leaders of Hungary's counties did not know German well enough to make the transition in three years. They feared an influx of upstarts from Germany who did not speak Hungary's languages or know its circumstances.[42] Joseph replied that many in Hungary already spoke German, and it was the best choice for administration. In any case, continued use of a dead language would reflect poorly on Hungarians' "cultural level."[43]

Hungarians feared that Joseph's goal was to make their land utterly subject to Austria, with German a tool of directing but also "reading" affairs of state. They feared becoming a colony, a concern that went back to Maria Theresa's practice of permitting Austrian manufactures to be sold in Hungary but imposing duties on the agricultural goods going from Hungary to Austria.[44] The changes reminded Hungarian nobles that their ancestors had once chosen a Habsburg as king, and the House of Austria had pledged to uphold the rights and customs of the Hungarian *natio* and not rule it like other provinces. "Woe to humankind," one noble wrote, "if the promises of princes were less binding than those of subjects." Customs like language changed not in three years but over the course of lifetimes, and people did not exist for the sake of the monarch, but rather the monarch for the people.[45]

Annoyance over the complaints from the Hungarian counties then caused Joseph simply to abolish them in 1785 and institute direct rule from Vienna. He reorganized Hungary and Croatia-Slavonia into ten districts, and he nominated men loyal to him as functionaries. This proved to be too much "reform" for the Hungarian nobility, however, and after war broke out with Ottoman Turkey in 1787, they began to court foreign military help and consider electing a foreign noble as their king. By decade's end, Joseph had fallen gravely ill, and shortly before dying wrote a letter to Hungarian counties revoking his reforms.[46]

Even though the centralizing measures had begun much earlier in Bohemia, resistance among nobles there had been largely verbal: murmurs and ostentatious use of Czech in the court in Vienna, a language they spoke to stable boys and not in good company. Next to their love of fatherland, the Bohemian nobility, most of whose families had risen due to Habsburg favor, also knew a pan-Austrian and German patriotism. When Joseph's brother Leopold took over in 1790, the reconciliation was rapid, with the king appearing in Prague to have the Bohemian crown placed on his head that his brother had stored away in Vienna.[47] Bohemia's largely German-speaking nobles also did not have the traditions of self-rule that Hungary's gentry had in their counties. They provided study spaces and funding for scholars like Dobrovský and Jungmann working on their land's history and language but did not make the cause one of personal honor; they evinced concerns over infringed privilege and growing centralization but made no demand for prerogatives to rule a nation.

But in both Bohemia and Hungary, the Habsburgs had made language an issue that was about more than language. By using German as part of their effort to control Hungary more effectively, they caused Hungarians to rally behind their own decayed vernacular as a means of self-defense. Language was not only vocabulary and syntax but also a symbol of a precious local way of being. Hungarian gentry may not have spoken Hungarian very well, but the prospect that they would become German made them fear losing their identity. This transformation, as consequential as any in the previous half millennium, was from a latent and vague sense of nationality to an active and soon very aggressive one: not everyone in Hungary, it would turn out, cared about Hungarian disappearing; not everyone in Hungary was Hungarian. That recognition proved intolerable to an increasingly modern sense of nationality.[48]

Leading patriots began arguing that Hungarian, though in a critical state, was not dead like Latin. It could return to life. Within a few years, they were insisting that the Hungarian language not only be revived but also be used by everyone in the realm. In contrast, the Czech movement never achieved that kind of exclusivity. If in Bohemia patriots hoped to recover language for an embattled ethnicity and place it on equal footing with German, here they wanted to displace German and all other languages, and use Hungarian in order to fully assert their nation's rights. It would be exclusive in Hungary the way French was in France. From the 1790s, even members of Hungary's high nobility began ostentatiously wearing native clothing and cultivating national traditions. A literary revival that, as in Bohemia, had ignited sparks of interest and devotion, grew and spread among the gentry rank and file. Joseph had coaxed Magyar and Czech nationalism to life not by intending to be an Austro-German nationalist, but by seeming to be one.[49]

* * *

In the minds of patriots, what the Habsburgs had done by denigrating the Bohemian and Hungarian nations offended more than single families or disparate regions somewhere between Germany and Russia; it was an injury to human history itself. Bohemia had once had a mission to Europe, and the task of patriots was to identify and recapture it. Whatever it was, it was not German or French; whatever it was, Austria might protect it, but it was not Austrian. It was Czech or Magyar. Now new ideas about nationhood would come from the west, first from revolutionary France. These ideas would then filter through German thought at German universities, where a third generation of Slavic patriots went to study just after the Napoleonic wars, a time known as "restoration," when it was difficult to propagate new ideas, especially about the rights of nations. The successors to Maria Theresa and her sons Joseph and Leopold also wanted a strong state and central control, but they did not have same faith in human reason. That gave rise to a standoff at the heart of the state: continued growth of ideas and industry, but a monarchy that wanted to freeze time while growing the bureaucracy.

The national ideas and projects differed in Hungary and Bohemia because of the differing identities of the patriots. In the former, the nascent movement was based on the nobility and strove to extend the ancient idea of nation to other groups. In contrast, in the latter, because of their humble origin, the patriots refashioned the idea of nationhood to claim that it had originally resided not among nobles but in the people, in everyone who spoke Czech. They claimed that it derived from a source older than medieval law and was vested in the descendants of the early Czech tribes who had claimed the Czech lands before they were a kingdom. Czechs were not German, but paradoxically, the idea that nations emerged from tribes united in language was one that came not from Czechs or any Slavs, but from the German thinkers Czechs and Slovaks encountered in Germany, above all in Jena in the circles of Johann Gottfried Herder.

CHAPTER 3

Linguistic Nationalism

Joseph II died just months after revolution broke out in France and was so worn out by resistance to his reforms in the Austrian Netherlands and Hungary, and the fiascos of his wars against Turkey, that he probably absorbed little of what was happening west of the Rhine. Perhaps he had sympathies with the revolution's assaults on the old order that had so bedeviled him at home. His brother and successor, Leopold II (1790–1792), at first welcomed news of the constitutional government and the undoing of noble and church privileges, and he urged the French king to reach accommodation with his subjects.[1] As the most gifted and fair-minded leader produced by the house of Habsburg, Leopold had already introduced constitutional rule in Tuscany, the province he ruled personally, and in 1786, he became the first monarch in Europe to abolish the death penalty. He also did away with torture and established homes for the handicapped. But then the French revolutionaries began acting in ways that horrified even progressives in Central Europe. One of Leopold's younger sisters was Marie Antoinette.

In the summer of 1791, she and her husband, Louis XVI, fled Paris hoping to inaugurate counterrevolution, but they were intercepted at Varennes and returned home in custody. Now Leopold's mood changed. In August he and Prussia's king issued a declaration at Pillnitz in Saxony threatening military action to protect legitimate rule in France.

The following month Leopold traveled to Prague to be crowned king of Bohemia, but political and intellectual turbulence left him no peace. He was celebrated at the Royal Bohemian Learned Society but also was challenged by the spirit of free discussion his brother had unleashed there. The scholar, priest, and Czech patriot Josef Dobrovský held a speech hailing Slavic culture and beseeching Leopold to safeguard the Czech language from "improper suppression and ill-considered persecution."[2]

On the second evening of their visit, Leopold and his court attended the premiere of what would be Mozart's last opera, *La Clemenza di Tito*, but here, too, politics left no time for simple entertainment. Mozart had employed artistic liberty to make the Roman Emperor Titus a figure who had grown in stature by showing tolerant clemency to his rebellious subjects. The royal company was not amused. Reportedly, empress Maria Luisa denounced the opera as a reckless celebration of the very problems that had just culminated in the virtual kidnapping of her sister-in-law.[3]

Within a few months, the empress and emperor, as well as Mozart, were all dead, victims of fast-acting illnesses for which the period's medicine had no remedies. Mozart's sons came under the care of philosopher F. X. Niemetschek, a Czech patriot who became a second father to them, while Habsburg power went to Leopold's narrow-minded son Francis, who would rule until 1835. Though a beneficiary of enlightened education, he fell into a panic at continuing news of excesses from France and spent his reign suppressing demands for constitutional rule and building a police state with copious censorship. Contemporaries remember him as colorless, having neither virtues nor vices, and no passion that might "stir him from his natural apathy."[4]

Within weeks of Francis's coronation, the Legislative Assembly of France declared war in response to his father's declaration at Pillnitz and expressed a desire to spread the revolution eastward. Austria and its Prussian ally acted first, however, thinking they would have an easy time asserting their will amidst the "chaos" reigning west of the Rhine. Their armies crossed French borders and began taking fortified positions, but they stirred alarm that caused the French government to tap a previously untested resource: the adult male population, which it conscripted, drilled, and sent into action, carried by the conviction that the revolution must be preserved.

By 1794 France's army numbered some 800,000, giving it a superiority of 2:1 in most engagements. After pushing intruders from French territory, French troops occupied the Low Countries and Germany west of the Rhine, areas they would hold until 1815.[5] During these years, most of Europe fought France through seven coalitions, aimed first at the Revolution, and after 1799 at the France of Napoleon Bonaparte, a brilliant military leader who by 1804 had created a "French Empire," consisting of an enlarged France with vassal states in Eastern and Central Europe. These states included a new Germany (Rhine Confederation), a new Poland (Duchy of Warsaw), and for the first time ever a state of South Slavs (Illyria).

Austria was a major force in the coalitions but lost decisive battles in 1805 at Austerlitz and 1809 at Wagram and had to cede territory. Still, it never endured direct French occupation, and thus its fate differed sharply from western German areas that were ruled from Paris and saw their traditional legal and social systems revolutionized. For the first time, thanks to Napoleon, everyone in

Hamburg, Bremen, and much of the Rhineland was equal before the law, peasants as well as townspeople, nobles, and churchmen, and Jews with Christians. All were free to do as they wished: to move about the map, marry, and buy or sell property. With feudal privileges abolished, for the first time these Germans, regardless of background, were citizens.

Napoleon also began revolutionizing the ancient Holy Roman Empire out of existence by compensating the moderately sized German states for territories lost to the new confederation west of the Rhine with ecclesiastical and free cities east of the Rhine. Within a few years, hundreds of tiny bishoprics, abbeys, and towns had been absorbed into Bavaria, Saxony, or Baden, a crucial step in the process of creating a simpler Germany, more susceptible to unification as a modern nation-state.

In the summer of 1804, responding to Napoleon's self-coronation as French emperor a few months earlier, Francis proclaimed himself emperor of Austria. As a Habsburg, he remained "Roman Emperor," but as the empire approached extinction, he wanted to ensure his status on the European stage against the Corsican upstart. The technical name for the Habsburg monarchy was now the "Austrian Empire," but the point was not to pursue an aggressive, self-confident imperial project of the sort that animated France, Britain, or Russia. The move was instead about *seeming* not to stand beneath a certain standard of dynastic prestige.

The self-coronation occurred not a moment too soon, as in August 1806 Napoleon declared the constitution of the Holy Roman Empire defunct, and several princes of his Rhine Confederation seceded on August 1. Five days later a proclamation was read from the balcony of the baroque Kirche am Hof in Vienna that the empire no longer existed. In fact, the empire had long been an ineffectual league of tiny entities, unable to defend the German lands. One practical consequence was that Austria's leadership in Germany came to an end, and indeed, Germany lost all definite political form. Though it had few effective powers of administration, the empire's constitution had balanced rights of cities and territories and in popular understanding had come to embody the nation in ways not fully tangible.

Reports from the summer of 1806 tell us that people across the German lands were outraged that a willful foreign usurper had simply disbanded the empire. The reports reveal a previously hidden emotional attachment, reminiscent of the indignation that arose in Hungary after Joseph replaced Latin with German. Like that supposedly dead language, the Holy Roman Empire provided a basic coordinate of identity. Johann Wolfgang Goethe's otherwise buoyant mother

Katharina wrote of deep unease, as if an old friend had succumbed to terminal illness. She sensed bitterness among the people of her home city of Frankfurt. For the first time in their lives—indeed for the first time in many centuries—the empire was omitted from prayers said at church, and subtle protests broke out across the German lands.[6] Was one now simply a Prussian or Bavarian? And if one was German, what did that mean?

Rhinelanders had welcomed Napoleon's rule because his legal code enhanced their freedoms, yet soon sympathies began to erode. The more territory France's emperor controlled, the less he was satisfied, and the more demands grew on his "allies" for money and soldiers. And west Germans felt humiliated by French victories over the large German states to the east. In 1806 Napoleon crushed the armies of Prussia at Jena and Auerstedt, then occupied Berlin. Two years later he forced Austria to join a continental blockade of England; and when Austria rose up the following year, he again smashed it down. The ill-fated *Grand Armée* that attacked Russia in 1812 was one-third German, and so were its casualties.[7]

Out of this sense of loss and humiliation grew a new and defiant movement of German patriots.[8] The French may have destroyed the old empire and occupied German lands, but they had not touched what made Germans German: their culture. In 1813, when armies from across Europe dealt Napoleon his first defeat at Leipzig, the poet Ernst Moritz Arndt asked "what is the Germans' fatherland?" It was absurd, he wrote, to link Germany to territory, for it transcended any that could be named: Prussia or Bavaria, let alone Tirol and Switzerland. Germany "must be greater than that" ran his refrain: it was everywhere that German was spoken. Yes, Germany had been the huge old empire, but it was also more, extending beyond Prussia's and Austria's eastern provinces, into today's Baltic states. And anything there that was not German would be expunged, especially if it was French:

> Where anger kills foreign trumpery
> Where every Frenchman is called the enemy
> Where every German is called Friend
> That it should be!
> The whole Germany shall it be.[9]

Urbane philosophers Friedrich Schlegel and Johann Gottlieb Fichte spoke of the need to "annihilate" the French, and the sensitive and tortured poet Heinrich von Kleist wrote simply "strike them dead, at judgment day no one will ask for reasons."[10]

* * *

But German nationalism was not exhausted in fits of rage; its ideas had been evolving for decades, also in direct response to challenges coming from France. Consider the now little-known mid-eighteenth-century thinker, Johann Georg Hamann, a pietistic Protestant close to Immanuel Kant. Hamann hated the way his compatriots bowed to trends from west of the Rhine, including the cult of reason. In his view, the French had become so rational as to be detached from what was really human. By positing that all experience could be reduced to abstraction, they had sacrificed what was particular and important in human affairs. He especially loathed the Enlightenment idea that languages were interchangeable variations on one set of expressions, essentially replicable, and not each unique in itself.

Hamann's pupil, the philosopher, theologian, and global historian Johann Gottfried Herder, took these inclinations several steps further. Herder had a celebrated career as preacher at the cathedral in Riga and the court in Weimar, where he became an intimate of Goethe and Schiller. But his origins were in Mohrungen, a humble town on the eastern reaches of Prussia, where German mixed with Polish, Yiddish, and Lithuanian in everyday life but where the high culture was francophone.[11] Through Hamann's influence, but also because of the rich complexity of cultures that sustained him as a young man, Herder was convinced of the importance of *specific* languages for human self-expression. Even in an unwritten form, the dialects spoken among peasants formed a sacred repository "of tradition, history, religion, and principles of life"; they were the tool through which the Almighty revealed his will for humanity. The soul of a people was its language.[12]

For that reason, states had the holy obligation to protect cultures and languages; they existed for the sake of peoples and not the other way around. "Just as God tolerates all the languages of the world," Herder wrote, "so should a ruler not only tolerate, but also honor the different languages of his people."[13] He opposed the idea that language was a tool for communication meant to strengthen the commonweal that could be dispensed with after it had served its purpose (for example, in Joseph II's plans to promote Czech only until it had helped make people literate in German).

Herder's ideas filtered into German thought, and within a generation had transformed notions about history and society, and not simply among nationalists like Fichte or Arndt.[14] Take Wilhelm von Humboldt, one of history's great philologists and anything but a poetic dreamer. Something unique existed among Germans, he wrote, a "commonality of habits, language, and literature, the memory of rights and freedoms enjoyed as a community, of fame attained and dangers overcome; remembrance of an intimate union, formed by the fathers, but alive only in the longing of the grandchildren."[15] In 1830 the elderly Goethe said "Herder's ideas have gone so deeply into mass consciousness that few who read them in our day will find them enlightening." His thoughts "had been borrowed so extensively by many thousands of others that they seemed commonsensical." Now that his *History of Humanity* had "done its job of educating the nation, it was as good as forgotten."[16]

The linguistic and cultural nationalism that Herder spawned had gotten a boost at the battle of nations at Leipzig in 1813, with Germans fighting on both sides, but some switching in the middle of the battle after turning their rifles on unsuspecting French soldiers. This was the beginning of Napoleon's rapid decline. The following year, Europe's powers came together at Vienna and returned the map to a semblance of order, restoring monarchies but also leaving the simplified Germany intact. Two things are clear in retrospect: linguistic nationalism had emerged as an irrepressible force in Central Europe, and Europe's monarchs would do all they could to keep this force from becoming politically destabilizing. Their methods included censorship and informants among students and faculty at German universities, above all at the university of Jena, where Fichte and Hegel had taught, and not far from Goethe's and Herder's Weimar.

* * *

Universities were a target because of the new nationalist fraternities, the *Burschenschaften*, where students, some veterans of the fighting at Leipzig, committed themselves to the German nation, sang the poetry of Arndt, and immersed themselves in the cult of the lost empire, meeting yearly in torchlight at the Wartburg, the medieval castle above Eisenach where Martin Luther had translated the Bible.

What is less known in this familiar story is that the participants of these events were not only German. Jena's faculty included Protestant theologians who attracted students from across Europe, including dozens from the Slavic lands of the Habsburg Empire. Yet these young speakers of Slovak and Czech proved receptive to Herder's ideas in a way that English or French intellectuals of that time were not. Indeed, Goethe had been shocked in the 1820s to learn that Herder's thought was all but unknown in France. The reason was partly practical: French intellectuals did not need linguistic nationalism. French kings had established the boundaries of France generations earlier, and there was no doubt about where France lay, who its subjects or citizens were, or what language they should speak. The national struggle was instead about whether kings or people would rule French territory. In England, the logic of nationalism was similar.[17]

But these Habsburg Slavs were even more insecure about their nations than were German intellectuals living in the shadow of France. Not only did they not live in national states, no names existed to describe their peoples. The thought of Herder proved more than irresistible: it was a compulsion. Aside from his message that nations truly lived through languages and not states, Herder had written of a great destiny for the Slavic peoples. His studies of history told him that the Slavic tribes that had settled Central and Eastern Europe centuries earlier had supposedly made territories fruitful that others had abandoned. Obedient and peaceful, Slavs disdained robbing and looting, but loved hosting strangers and spending time in merriment. Yet because of this openness, they had fallen victim to conquest by aggressive neighbors, in particular, Germans, who had committed "grave sins" against them.[18] Because they were so numerous, inhabiting the vast area between Berlin and Kamchatka, he believed that history had not heard the last word from the Slavs.

At Jena, the young Slavic theologians had arrived at the center of Herder's teaching. The patriotic historian Heinrich Luden, editor of Herder's *History of Humanity*, gave lectures so popular that students listened from ladders at open windows. He said that history, properly understood, should awaken active love for the fatherland. He also held that non-German peoples had a right to national development and, astoundingly, denounced the suppression of the Czechs after the battle of White Mountain.[19] Weimar, where Herder had lived and preached for decades and had many friends, was an easy afternoon's walk away, and the young theologians gained access to the deceased philosopher's personal circles.

Among their number, four became gifted poets, linguists, and historians, and they proved to be crucial for the history of East Central Europe: Ján Kollár, Ján Benedikti, Pavel Šafárik, and Juraj Palkovič. Kollár and Palkovič wrote poetry that is still read in Slovak schools, and Šafárik became one of the most influential geographers of the nineteenth century. All were of modest backgrounds: Palkovič and Kollár from farm families, Šafárik and Benedikti from the households of clergymen. Šafárik had upset his irascible father and was forced to live as beggar student, a "supplikant," who spent holidays soliciting money

FIGURE 3.1. Jan Kollár. *Source*: Via Wikicommons (from old postcard).

from a list of donors supplied by school authorities.[20] At first, none had a particular attachment to the national idea, and in keeping with the practices of the time, they enrolled in Jena according to the old sense of *natio*: they were "Hungarians." Of the thirty or so students from Northern Hungary, Kollár later recalled, only he and Benedikti initially showed any interest in Czecho-Slovak literature. Later, most of the cohort Magyarized completely.[21]

Goethe came to depend on Kollár for translations of Slavic folk poetry, which he believed gave him access to genuine folk spirit. Yet on walks to meet the great poet, Kollár and Benedikti could not help noting the un-German names of towns and villages. Jena had a Slavic name, indicating original settlement by Slavs, but so did other Thuringian towns—Gera, Lobeda, Apolda, Kahla, and Weimar. Where were the Slavs? The answer lay in Herder's description of

German treatment of Slavic peoples: they had fallen victims to centuries of aggression and been annihilated as a people. Much later Kollár recalled his melancholy sense in Jena of living amid a great cemetery of his kinfolk. Every town, hill, or river bearing a Slavic name was for him a gravestone.[22]

He reflected with alarm on the parts of Northern Hungary where he and his friends originated. The towns were German speaking, and he feared that Slavic speakers in the surrounding villages would share the fate of the tribes who once settled central Germany: they would disappear from the historical record.

Kollár sublimated his fears in the lyric-epic poem *Daughter of Slava*. The inspiration had come fortuitously. In April 1818 a "matron" knocked at his door and asked him to help her husband, George Friedrich Schmidt, pastor in nearby Lobeda, who had fallen ill and needed someone to deliver the Sunday sermon. Over evening coffee, Kollár discovered that the Schmidts were not German, but Sorbs, natives of Lusatia, just northeast of Dresden, where the hardy remnants of ancient Slavic settlers were holding their own against assimilation. Schmidt showed the enraptured student old prayer books in the Sorbian tongue and called Kollár his countryman.

Kollár's sermon the following morning drew from John 2:11, asking: what are the things for which Christ's followers will lay down their lives? Greatly moved, the congregation wanted Kollár made their permanent preacher, but he demurred, saying: I am Slovak and must lay down my life for my own despised people. What he did not reveal was that he had fallen in love with the pastor's daughter, Wilhelmine Frederike, who deep down, like the land itself, seemed to him Slavic.

In Kollár's five-canto *Daughter of Slava*, Wilhelmine was transformed into the Slavic goddess Mina, who acted as the muse to an unnamed singer in his wanderings of imagination above supposed Slavic lands—along the Saale, Elbe, and Danube rivers—now largely inhabited by German aggressors. The poem, suffused with romantic longing for a lost people, evoked the beauties of the Slavic countryside and summoned Czechs and other Slavs to their great mission. At its end, Mina accompanies the singer to Slavic heaven and to Slavic hell, where "special pain was reserved for the Germans because they spilled more Slavic blood than anyone else." The poem also chides the Slavic Danube for treasonously flowing into Ottoman lands.[23]

Kollár typified the contempt-laden defensiveness of the early Czech and Slovak nationalists, who were terrified of German culture but could not live without it. For years, Kollár had feared Wilhelmine—whom he called Mina—had died (thus the longing of his poem), but the two reconnected and married in 1835, moving to the German-speaking Hungarian city of Pest, where Kollár became pastor to Slovak Lutherans. Try as she might, Wilhelmine never learned proper Slovak, and the two conversed in German throughout their married life. But Kollár wrote poems and essays not in Slovak but in biblical Czech, suggesting a further set of mysteries: why were most early Czech nationalists Slovak, and why did these Slovaks write in Czech?[24]

The best answer returns to Kollár's metaphor of central Germany as a cemetery beneath which his own ancestors lay buried. What stirred his imagination were hints in history and geography that ancient Slavs were a great people spread over a vast space, stretching from Berlin down to the Adriatic, and then eastward to the Pacific, a space not yet charted. Pastor Schmidt called Kollár a countryman (*rodak*) because Slovaks understood the Lusatian Sorbs with ease. In Jena, Kollár had learned from German friends that a great people could be astoundingly diverse. The variants of German spoken in Baden, Thuringia, or Pomerania were hardly less different than the languages spoken by Czechs and Slovaks or Croats and Russians. Out of the pan-Germanism the "Hungarian" students witnessed among students from all over Germany in Jena grew their own pan-Slavism, most influentially in Kollár's friend Pavel Šafárik.[25]

* * *

In 1826 Šafárik published a pathbreaking study of the Slavic peoples and their speech, mixing his patriotic conviction with exhaustive scholarship. He took for granted that Slavs constituted one people, just as the Germans or Italians did. But he also investigated the Slavs' tremendous variety in studies of more than a dozen languages, displaying profound knowledge of linguistic development, laid out in innumerable grammatical tables. Yet he also simplified. According to him, there were not three but only two branches of Slavic languages: southeast, today's Slovene, Serbo-Croatian, and Bulgarian; and west, including Russian, Polish, and Czech.

Šafárik made anthropological observations that reproduced the rough stereotypes inherited from Johann Gottfried Herder. Slavs' excellent attributes—cheerfulness and warmth of perspective, broad interests and abilities, liveliness of feeling, and innocence—resulted not from education but "pure nature." These inborn traits explained why, from the Baltic to the Carpathians and down to the Adriatic, they had been a target for aggression. Huns, Goths, Avars, Franks, and Magyars had all fallen upon Slavic peoples as the latter peacefully planted their crops, and contempt for them found its way into countless writings of Germans and Hungarians.[26]

Šafárik was practicing an old art of imagining nations' characteristics, but he also raised Herder's implicit racialism to a higher level, for example, by imputing to Slavs as a whole an aptitude for music and dance, or to Serbs the inclination for adapting epic poetry to music.[27] Herder had rejected the word "race" because differences among humans were simply "shadings of one and the same great painting," but when considering the Chinese, he attributed their supposed failure to develop science and art to their "natural attributes."[28] Still, neither Herder nor Šafárik exhibited full-blown racism. Nations were facts of nature, and Šafárik considered the boundaries between them porous. He and Kollár lived in multinational environments and knew well the assimilation into Slavic peoples of Magyars, Germans, and many others.

Šafárik imagined a future in which Slavic peoples would coexist peacefully, enriching one another while growing closer, yet in the end remaining distinct. In *Slavic reciprocity*, a notion he originated in collaboration with Kollár, they would exchange words with one another: "all tribes and dialects remain unshaken in their old places, but foster through cross-fertilization and emulation, the flowering of a common national literature."[29] What this program might mean for a common political program was unclear, but the possibilities were tantalizing, especially for groups like the Czechs and Slovaks, who could communicate without needing translation.

Some patriots stressed the existence of the larger Slavic nation, others that of smaller tribes. Kollár believed in "one blood, one body, one people," consisting of tribes speaking four dialects: Russian, Polish, Czechoslovak, and Illyrian. This was the beginning of the Czechoslovak idea, or as he said, the Czechoslav idea: that the Slavic speakers of Bohemia, Moravia, Austrian Silesia, and the northern Hungarian areas were in fact one people. In his view, Slovak consisted of too many subgroupings to find general acceptance, and therefore he proposed adapting Czech and Slovak to each other, a "fusion on equal terms."[30] Though he hailed from northern Slovakia, Kollár selected words for his poems that could be understood by Czechs.

The problem for Kollár's plan was that the modernization of Czech was going apace with little concern for bringing it closer to Slovak, and that Czechs were less concerned about Slovak than the Slovaks, who knew Czech intimately, were about Czech. And there was still much uncertainty. People commonly made reference to regional groups like Silesians and Moravians, whom we now think of as speakers of dialects of Polish and Czech. But in the early nineteenth century, they seemed as distinct as Slovak-speakers, who, to make matters more complicated, were themselves regionally divided.

And all ideas of division or unification were matters of interpretation because even now, if one takes a journey from the western edge of Bohemia through Moravia and Slovakia, one encounters no break in language for hundreds of miles, and inhabitants of each village understand inhabitants of the next village perfectly. In fact, the continuum extends farther eastward into Ukrainian and Russian lands. This is a Slavic dialect continuum, precisely like the continuum that extends through German or Italian lands—south to north. Perhaps the Slavs, who lived on a much bigger patch of earth, could become more numerous and more powerful than the Germans and Italians. Šafárik's work had such success throughout the Slavic world that he received emissaries of Russia's tsar, though he and his friends remained loyal subjects of the Austrian crown.

Yet the crown was not loyal to them. In 1817 Šafárik was forced to leave Jena, partly for financial reasons, but partly because the Austrian government wanted to withdraw its "Hungarian" students from the liberal atmosphere of a German university. Before returning home, he made a pilgrimage to Prague, getting to know the linguists Josef Jungmann and Josef Dobrovský, as well as the later librarian of the Bohemian museum, Václav Hánka. Then he took teaching jobs in Hungary, first in a noble family in Pressburg (Bratislava), then as headmaster in a Serb Orthodox high school in southern Hungary, in Novi Sad, today's capital of the Serb province of Vojvodina. While in Pressburg, he became acquainted with a gifted young Protestant student from Moravia, František Palacký, a leader in the budding Czech national movement.

The ever-vigilant Austrian authorities stepped in a second time to frustrate Šafárik's career in 1832, when, hoping to curtail Slavic nationalism, they forbade Protestant Hungarians from teaching in Orthodox institutions of higher education. The police discovered that Šafárik was receiving money from Russian supporters.[31] After trying without success to find work in Russia, he looked to Prague, where Palacký was a famous man, editor of the *Časopis českého museum* [*Journal of the Bohemian Museum*], making the Czech movement a cause for thousands and then hundreds of thousands. Šafárik, father of eight children, was desperate for money, and Palacký threw him a lifeline, offering him work on projects of common interest, provided he wrote in Czech.

* * *

FIGURE 3.2. František Palacký (1843). *Source*: Art Collection 3/
Alamy Stock Photo.

Like other men of genius in the Czech and Slovak movements, Palacký was of
humble background. His father made a living as a tailor and produce-vendor,
and despite rudimentary education, was chosen by his community to direct the
town's Lutheran school. That was in the 1780s, when Joseph II became sole ruler
of the Habsburg realm, and Protestants could come out of hiding. From the time
of White Mountain in 1620, Palacký's family had secretly practiced the cult of
the Bohemian Brethren, keeping prayer books buried in the forest. Young
Palacký was the most gifted of eleven brothers and sisters, able to read the Bible
at age five.[32]

Wary of Catholic influences in Moravia, Palacký's father sent his talented son
across the border into the Slovak lands of northern Hungary, where Protestantism was more secure, and he received schooling in theology first at Trenčín

and then at the Lutheran Gymnasium in Pressburg, thus entering milieus where four and five languages were spoken routinely. He learned all of them. With the support of a solicitous noblewoman, he entered the circles of the Hungarian gentry and came to respect their single-minded determination to save a language from destruction.

Much later Palacký traced his turn to nationalism to a night spent with friends in the Slovak town Trenčín during the turbulent fall of 1813. The head of the house was interested in the Czech revival just across the border and asked Palacký for guidance on the language, assuming that as a Moravian, he knew Czech. Yet Palacký confessed ignorance of his native tongue. His first task on returning to Pressburg was to take Czech lessons from the Slovak scholar Juraj Palkovič. Through Palkovič, he became friendly with Kollár, Šafárik, and Jan Benedikti, all just arrived from Jena, and together the group plotted how to resurrect the Czech nation. They also gave Palacký letters of introduction to Josef Dobrovský as well as to the latter's noble benefactor Kaspar Sternberg in Prague.

When Palacký left for Prague in 1823, he had already been planning a popular history of Bohemia. His Slovak friends, with pretensions to wisdom common among recent university graduates, tried to dissuade him. Czechs could not have a great historian because they did not have a great history. Yet Palacký dispelled all doubt. "The glory of a nation," he said, "is not based on their number or physical strength: it lies in their life, their spirit . . . the spirit of a nation appears where it is ready to live and die for an idea."[33]

Indeed, without this conviction, he would have gotten nowhere in Prague, a city even more German in character than Pest. "Whoever wore a decent coat," Palacký later wrote, "did not venture so readily to speak Czech in public places."[34] Czech patriots there faltered in faith. During a dinner on Christmas 1825, Count Sternberg complained that his Bohemian Museum was attracting little attention. Palacký said he should make the building a centerpiece of a *Czech* cultural revival, but the count said it was too late. Young Palacký then castigated the great men for doing too little themselves. Dobrovský wrote in German because it was easy. Palacký swore that even if he were the last of a Gypsy clan, he would consider it a duty to ensure that honorable mention be made of it in the history of humankind. Sternberg offered him editorship of his museum's journal on the spot, and within a few years, it was turning a profit while reviving Czech culture. By contrast, the German edition of this journal dropped in sales and had to be discontinued.[35]

Palacký's optimistic defiance coincided with the growth of an audience of Czech readers happy to be "awakened" to the national idea. Herder had devoted but three pages to the Slavs in his universal history, and therefore it fell upon Palacký to document the greatness that patriots imagined in their people's past. His history was imbued with the spirit both of German idealism and enlightened scholarship, using more than seventy archives. This work also represented a new ideological quality, insisting on the pureness of national groups, with traits that persisted no matter how much mixing with others took place. He wrote that Czechs were the original owners of Bohemia because their tribes had arrived before the Germans.[36]

In the spirit of Hegel, Palacký projected Germans and Slavs as incorporating two opposing poles, out of which emerged a higher synthesis. The role assigned to the Slavs was virtuous: they were the hard-working, peace-loving inhabitants of a democratic state who continually fell victim to aggression.[37] After the fall of Rome, Germans had taken over as centralizing rulers, while Czechs quietly tilled the land. In the early middle ages, Germans had upset the Czechs' "democratic" order with feudalism; then they crushed the religious reform first of the Hussites (1400s) then of the Czech brethren (1620). Now the burgeoning Czech democratic movement formed the antithesis of Austro-German monarchical rule.[38]

For Palacký, this was not biased history, but history from which bias had been removed. Up to that point, chiefly monks and Jesuits had written about Czech history, though they could neither comprehend nor appreciate the "spirit of our ancestors." Palacký called on patriots to "banish the host of phantoms which their sectarianism had brought in, to give the plain truth to the friends of mankind to see." [39]

* * *

A problem in this self-serving interpretation was a dearth of documents about the early stages of the supposedly eternal Czech-German conflict. The oldest sources that Palacký found dated from the fourteenth century, Latin chronicles and Czech liturgical works that gave little insight into the people's spirit. But a few years earlier, a sensational discovery had been reported from two castles in Bohemia. In vaults allegedly undisturbed for centuries, patriots found documents celebrating Czech victories over the Poles and Tatars, and even more thrillingly, an account of the Czech court of the just and wise Queen Libuše. The latter supposedly dated from the ninth century and "proved" that early Czechs had their own "laws of holy statute brought in days of yore by our good fathers," that is, they were governed by Slavic laws brought during the original settlement from areas farther east in the sixth century. Supposedly Libuše had warned descendants not to borrow from Germans. To seek justice from them would be "indecent."[40]

From the beginning, doubts were voiced about these documents' authenticity. The linguists Dobrovský and Jedrej Kopitar considered them evident falsifications. But their opinions were the exception. The movement's mainstream was enthralled and treated the finds as if they were holy scripture. Palacký and Šafárik produced a German-language study with exhaustive analysis of both documents, including glossaries of the "old" words, as well as translations into German and Latin and scientific explanations of why the parchments had to be genuine.

Over the decades, doubts multiplied about the documents, but Palacký stuck by them, arguing that the unknown writing was a "special old school of Czech paleography" and claiming, falsely, that the historical data contained in them had been unknown until 1829.[41] He said that the objections only confirmed the documents' truthfulness, perhaps not in a paleographic sense, but in what the documents communicated. They showed that Germans would never accept Slavs as capable of culture and education. According to a German "doctrine," anything of value that the Slavs possessed had been borrowed.[42] And he predicted that German skepticism would only redound to the Czech movement's benefit, and in this he was right. Neither truth nor falsehood could stop its growth.

A quarter century later, in the mid-1880s, Palacký was dead, and the falsification all but indisputable. Evidence emerged showing that an early patriot, probably the Bohemian museum's librarian, Šafárik's friend Václav Hanka, had fabricated the parchments and sent them anonymously to a nobleman complete with "worm holes" to give the impression of antiquity. In the Czech movement, it took courage to admit this fact, but that is precisely what the second "father" of the Czech nation, philosopher and politician Tomáš Garrigue Masaryk (1850–1937), did. There was no other option. After all, the core teaching of Palacký's hero Jan Hus was "truth will prevail." Yet in debunking documents many considered holy, Masaryk also gave evidence to the cunning of nationalism. The virtuous practice of accepting uncomfortable truths was an even higher confirmation of Czech virtue.[43]

Therefore, Palacký and his friend Šafárik were the ultimate victors in this struggle. The Czech movement grew, believing in ancient and original Czech claims to land, law, language, and culture, always opposed to Germans. One patriot reflected in 1872 that the documents had "encouraged increased vigor in the defense of our inalienable national rights."[44] Masaryk rejected the forgeries, but he also avidly embraced their messages, and stuck with the idea that ethnic Czechs were the original settlers of Bohemia, and the Germans were latecomers, colonists, and "guests."[45]

Is the Czech case so unusual? The period counted numerous forgeries, such as those by Prosper Mérimée in France and those attributed to Ossian in Scotland. And were not nationalist myths as a rule built on fables? There were the stories of King Arthur in England and the Nibelungenlied in Germany. The Bohemian myths differed in two ways: first, Czech patriots created myths out of whole cloth. Even as fiction, they were false. But second, the myths were presented as facts and not fiction, facts based on the work of one of the period's foremost historians, who, like his great contemporary, Leopold Ranke in Germany, swore to write history "as it happened."

And what Palacký counted as fact had the odd fate of finding its way back into fiction, into literature, music, and art. The century's greater and lesser Czech composers wrote operas and songs based on the forged documents, and we still find sculptures and paintings of the fraudulent heroes in parks and museums across the Czech Republic, for example, statues of the valiant warriors Zaboj and Slavoj, perched in the national cemetery at Vyšehrad. Not far from them is the resting place of their probable creator, Václav Hanka, buried as the first great modern Czech in 1861, and later surrounded by figures like Antonín Dvořák and Bedřich Smetana—composers whose work was inspired by the history that arose from Hanka's imagination. The epitaph on the soaring monument dedicated to Hanka's memory reads: "peoples do not disappear as long as their language lives."[46]

Still, the Czech movement fits into broader patterns. Before Palacký lifted his pen, other Czech patriots were spreading disdainful sentiments about arrogant Germans just below the radar of censorship. The vitriol stemmed from the subordinate status of Czech speech in lands these patriots held to be Czech. Like mythologies everywhere, the movement responded to the popular need for meaning and a sense of belonging in an ostensible "homeland." As we have seen in Chapter 2, the linguist Jungmann said that inhabitants of Prague who refused Czech and instead "barked and grunted German" had betrayed the legacy of their "forebears."[47] Like nationalists everywhere, they felt the problem was not their own hatred, but the hatred that the despised "other" felt for them.

In the 1840s Jan Kollár traveled about Italy, but the German-Slavic contest left him no peace. Anything of value he attributed to deeper Slavic origins, for example, the ancient inscriptions in Avellino and Pompeii. He claimed that Latin was an ancient Slavic dialect. As he traveled farther north, crossing into Tirol (a "Slavic name"), his attention shifted to the Germans and their supposedly abiding hatred for Slavs. German faces were ugly; and the land they inhabited, the Austrian Alps, was less pleasing to the eye than the Slavic Tatra. Bavarians and Austrians did not speak their language but "groaned" it.[48] Soon he was attaching the "problem" to German bodies, distinguished by size, skin, hair color, skeletal build—and blood. Enabling all their other virtues was Slavs' biological superiority.

Though he wrote these reflections in Czech, Kollár preached in Slovak to his congregation in Budapest, in the shadow of more assertive efforts to assimilate them. The "hardworking and peaceful Slovaks" found themselves first in line for the "raging" efforts at Magyarization. "I long for air where I can be free and not a slave," he wrote to a friend in 1828. As the Germans wanted to Germanize, so the Hungarians wanted to Magyarize.[49]

* * *

But this empathy for Slovaks was unusual. By and large the early Czech and Slovak patriots (Palacký and Hanka, for instance) assumed that the pressure Slovaks faced from Hungarian culture was similar to what they faced from German culture. But they were misinformed. Of all the national movements in East Central Europe, none was more culturally aggressive than the Magyar, and in the 1840s the pressure Slovaks felt in every sphere—whether politics, economics, education, or even religion—caused the small leadership of a Slovak movement to adjust to the special threat by dividing itself from the Czechs.

A small coterie of Slovaks who came of age in this decade contributed to the growing Slovak nationalism, above all Ľudovít Štúr (1815–1856). Like the leading "awakeners" of the previous generation, Štúr was a student of the Pressburg lyceum. If Kollár felt air leaving the room in 1828, by the 1840s, Slovaks were attempting to survive in a bell jar. The simple fact of linguistic commonality, of the dialect continuum running from Bohemia and Moravia into Slovakia, was not enough to make a people. Slovakia lived under a Magyar and not an Austrian administration, and that government was denationalizing multitudes of Slovaks. Czechs and Slovaks in Prague like Palacký and Šafárik were living in a dream world. To halt the conversion of illiterate Slovaks into literate Magyars, one needed a language to rally around, and that could not be biblical Czech. Against the objections of the Czech patriots he looked up to in Prague, as well as Jan Kollár, Štúr fashioned a new standard Slovak from speech of mid-Slovakia, with an admixture of western Slovak elements.[50]

His practical struggle to secure a useful language had led Štúr to a path-breaking recognition: Kollár was wrong. Slavs were not one people. There were Czechs and Slovaks, just as there were Russians, Poles, and Serbs—brothers and sisters who should cooperate, but with different histories and different trajectories into the future. The fact of Czech and Slovak speakers having once inhabited a "Greater Moravian" empire, cited by František Palacký as a unifying experience, had no bearing on the lives of Slovaks a millennium later.

Ancient history no doubt was crucial. Like Tham or Palacký writing about Czech settlement of Bohemia, Štúr insisted that Slovaks had preceded all others in their own settlement area.[51] And he agreed that language was the expression of a people's spirit. Yet ultimately, the language was not decisive. Štúr was arguing, in a departure from Herder's linguistic nationalism, that language mediated a people's spirit, but the tangible evidence of this spirit was its history: its common trials, beliefs, values, and habits. When a people had a specific history, it also had a specific language as a unique common possession, even if many words of that language were shared with other groups of people.

Czechs, Moravians, and Slovaks all understood one another; no clear linguistic boundaries divided them at any point in the map. However, a political boundary ran between Slovakia and East Moravia, and on either side of it, the world presented itself in different ways, as the Kingdom of Hungary to Slovaks in the east, and the Kingdom of Bohemia to Czechs and Moravians in the west. A lot had happened since the fall of the Moravian Empire, the most important being the failure of the Reformation to shake the dominance of Catholicism in Slovakia.

That fact makes the position of the Protestant Slovaks as leaders of the early Slovak national movement all the more interesting. They represented a tiny minority in their own people, and if they sensed a commonality with Czechs, that was because they had more in common religiously with Czech patriots, whose national hero was the proto-Protestant Jan Hus. These Slovaks were closer to Czechs like the crypto-Protestant Palacký than to their own countrymen and women. That would change. If with Kollár, the early Slovak nationalists wore Lutheran collars, the leaders of Slovak nationalism two generations later wore Catholic gowns. (In 1939 one of them, Father Jozef Tiso, achieved an ostensibly independent Slovak state due to the graces of a "Bohemian corporal" named Adolf Hitler.)

Despite such early challenges, the idea of Czechoslovak unity survived for the time being; even Štúr insisted that much was to be gained through cooperation. A resonance remained on both sides, a vague idea, beyond all objections, that something vital linked Czechs (and Moravians and Slavic Silesians) with Slovaks that might make for a common future, perhaps in a federal state.[52] The ideas also remained attractive for practical reasons. Amid the large empires, an independent Bohemia seemed too small to be viable. Union with others speaking very similar West Slavic dialects gave each a power that was unthinkable if they lived in complete independence.

* * *

The aggressive Magyar nationalism that awakened in Štúr a sense of Slovak identity had grown from fear—not from strength. The influence of Herder on the budding nationalist intelligentsia was again crucial. Yet if he predicted a glorious future for the Slavs, he wrote in 1791 that in a few centuries, Hungarians would be engulfed in a sea of Slavs, Germans, and Romanians and would cease to exist.[53] When that view became widely known, nationalism that had interested small coteries of enthusiasts of language became a mass movement among the gentry determined to ensure that Hungarian became rooted in the population's daily use and so guarantee that Herder's prediction did not come true.[54]

The ideas of Kollár and Štúr had little resonance among the Slovak masses of the early nineteenth century, but they seemed to Hungarian nationalists like sparks flying into a parched field, preparing a conflagration of Slovak nationalism. And the problem was not limited to Slovak-speakers. The southern Hungarian lands were crowded with South Slavs, and in Transylvania to the east lived millions of Romanians. Serbs had immigrated centuries earlier and constituted majorities around the city of Novi Sad, where Pavel Šafárik taught in the 1820s, and much of southwestern Hungary comprised the kingdom of Croatia-Slavonia, united with Hungary for 700 years. The Croatian gentry spoke German, Latin, and demotic Croatian but had a firm sense of identity based in ancient political rights. Like Hungarians, they had a parliament, and like the Hungarians, they elected the Habsburgs as their kings.

Then there were the Germans. Like Czech counterparts, Hungary's patriots confronted dominant, self-confident German culture in virtually all the towns of their kingdom: the capital Pressburg (Bratislava), Odenburg (Sopron), Kaschau (Košice), Ofen (Buda), as well as Pest. In addition, there were German villagers, convinced of the superiority of their way of life. No one knew how to make them voluntarily assimilate into Magyardom. One German farmer told a patriot he wanted to live like a human being and not an animal. What did Hungary have to offer him as an economy and culture?[55] At that point, not much, his interlocutor agreed. In 1822 Vienna had twenty-six and Prague ten booksellers, yet in all the Hungarian kingdom there were only twelve.[56] The roads were poor, industry all but nonexistent, and poverty rampant.

The work of Hungary's nationalists in succeeding decades can be likened to the whipsaw of manic depression; first mad energies devoted to fantastic projects, and then exhaustion and a settling back into doubt about whether the effort had any chance; but then renewed conviction from the depths of resignation, and so on. The friction wore, and by late century, the gentry had settled into a retrenchment. They laid claim to state offices for themselves, and more than making a united, modern Magyar nation of equal citizens, they focused on keeping other nationalities from rising.

The mix of frantic energy and despair was more striking among Magyar than among Czech patriots because Slavs were a majority in Bohemia (and indeed in East Central Europe as a whole), whereas Magyars were a minority in their own county.[57] Czechs like Palacký could feel satisfaction at the steady conversion of Prague into a mostly Czech-speaking metropolis, propelled in part by processes of modernization. Budapest lost its German appearance at a similar speed, but in vast stretches of the north, east, and south, Magyarization advanced at an agonizingly slow pace among the majorities of ethnically "foreign elements."[58]

The conflict of Enlightenment universalism with nationalism was also much starker in Hungary because spreading Magyar meant denying other peoples' rights to education in and official use of their own languages. In Bohemia, the Czech and German movements never tried to fully to assimilate each other; the major object of the Czechs, and later the Germans, was to make people who spoke Czech and German at home identify with the respective national movements. In Hungary, by contrast, nationalists had a sense of either pushing back the foreign elements or being pushed back by them. The Hungarian language asserted itself, especially in the towns, but the fear of extinction never disappeared.[59]

Still, Hungarian patriots were by no means simply intolerant nationalists, but rather men and women devoted to reason and not force. Thus Ferenc Kazinczy, a philologist who did for Hungarian what Dobrovský and Jungmann did for Czech, called himself a cosmopolitan. Just as truth could be perceived through many religious confessions, it was also open to all nationalities. God forbid that his language's advancement would come at the destruction of another! Among his closest friends were German and Serb poets, and he insisted that a daughter who lived in Transylvania learn Romanian. His close friend Johann Kis sent his son to Pressburg/Pozsony to learn Slovak. Yet Kazinczy had barely succeeded in nurturing literary Hungarian back from the dead and wanted it protected. Especially troubling was the idea that a convert to Hungarian might remain German at heart: "I love the German German more than I do the Magyarized German," he explained in a letter.[60]

Rumors about growing Slavic power eroded tolerance for diversity because Hungarian intellectuals feared they would never live in a country that was securely their own. We get a sense of the clash between pessimism and optimism in the noble reformer István Széchenyi, outdone by no one in pouring energies into building a Hungarian nation. Like Kazinczy, he was also a man of moderation and reason, yet despair was never far away. In June 1829, Széchenyi confided to his diary: "Every day I see more clearly that Herder is right. Soon the Hungarian nation will cease to exist." Even he, perhaps the greatest patriot, had learned Hungarian as a foreign language and kept his diary in German. "I am waking up about Hungary," he wrote the following year, "She is stone dead. Drowned in German intelligence."[61]

To make matters worse, Slavs within Hungary's borders seemed in a league with Slavs everywhere, threatening to subvert Hungary from within and without.[62] Reports surfaced in the 1830s of Russian emissaries traveling through Eastern Europe to stimulate hopes for union with Russia as a core for a great Slavic empire: Slavs were brothers, and Tsar Nicholas their leader.[63]

They did not have to travel far to assemble evidence of the Slavic surge. The writer Gábor Döbrentei (1786–1851) visited Prague in 1806 and went to the Italian Theater. Yet "there is also a Czech one," he noted:

> This city is to Bohemia what Pest is to our fatherland. But it is a happier place. In Prague people speak Czech more than they do German. In Pest people mostly make German noises. And where is the Hungarian Theater! Foreigners will certainly inundate us if we do not show some effort. I revere native Germans, but whoever is unworthy of the dust of my fatherland, and only indulges himself and suppresses Hungarian culture—such a person I cannot love.[64]

Herderian ideology gave the basic structure of resentment a "higher meaning." One must live in a fatherland—where the bread, the dust, and even the

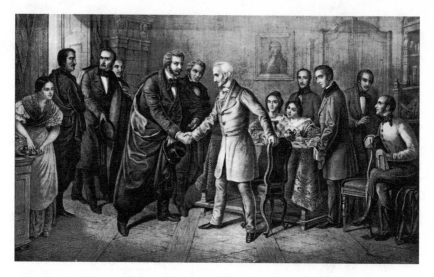

FIGURE 3.3. Meeting of Ferenc Kazinczy and Károly Kisfaludy (1828). *Source*: Based on painting by Soma Orlai Petrich / Petőfi Literary Museum, Budapest.

air are somehow one's own. But what sort of fatherland was this, where aliens governed the public spaces, freely and unapologetically made use of their language in business and in government offices? German speakers were the lords on the Hungarians' own property. In 1808 the poet Alexander (Sándor) Kisfaludy wrote to Ferenc Kazinczy: "For the good of the Hungarian language I am ready to become a henchman and repulse all those from my fatherland who live happily from Hungarian bread and air and do not want to learn Hungarian . . . it is so unfortunate to be Hungarian in Hungary, and I would be tempted to doubt my sanity if I did not feel this pain inside."[65]

Over the nineteenth century, homeland came to mean a place that was one's own in the deepest sense, where all non–fellow nationals, no matter when their ancestors settled, were newcomers who had to adjust to local habits. That fact pertained even to Croatia, whose nobles had entered the Magyar kingdom many centuries earlier based on reciprocity. In the 1820s, Hungarian patriots began arguing that their own forebears had taken Croats into Hungary's "bosom" as "guests" [hospites]: why was it a disgrace for them to use Hungarian, the language of the people from whom they had received law and freedom?[66] Croats of the eleventh century had supposedly taken for granted the superior position of Hungarian, and therefore not the Hungarians but the Croats were disturbing the peace by refusing to self-Magyarize.

In such arguments we witness a revolutionary change in language: the notion that "Magyars or national Hungarians" had some kind of priority in "their" country was among first appearances of the *ethnic idea* in Hungary. For the first time, people took for granted that the nation meant not simply nobility.[67] As in Bohemia, a national past was concocted with false and semi-true tales from the Middle Ages alleging an ancient antagonism between "natives" and others, especially Germans. Hungarian patriots said that Adam had been a Magyar, and some Czechoslav linguists claimed that Latin had Slavic roots.[68]

* * *

The genius of Herder was to project such obsessions with local and native prerogatives as universal, timeless, and in the interests of humanity. The Hungarians' desire for control of their supposed land was somehow transcendent.[69] At the same time, the nineteenth century was a golden age for forgers across Europe, and some patriots made lots of money for less than transcendent purposes. The Hungarians Kálmán Thaly and Sámuel Literáti Nemes sold for profit dozens of documents supposedly from the medieval period that seem so genuine as to confound historians even now.[70] Nemes's main purpose was not to alter understanding of the past but to amass a small fortune. Ultimately, bank vaults full of money were made on patriotism by those trading in national garb, native food and drink, or equipment for gymnastic societies to make ethnic bodies strong; by sellers of books and journals thick with propaganda; and by manufacturers of colorful cockades and banners, whose warehouses were bursting with kitsch.

But at its core, the early movement was not about material self-interest. Kazinczy or Palacký and Kollár could have saved themselves years of Sisyphean labors by doing what circumstances seemed to dictate: become German and fit into one of Europe's major cultures. For generations, entering the elite in Bohemia had meant cultural self-Germanization; the same was true of becoming Polish for Ukrainian and Belorussian speakers in eastern Poland. This seemed a small price for moving up the social ladder; in fact, for most, it was no price at all. Yet rather than portray themselves as sons and daughters of the culture that formed Goethe and Schiller, Bohemians who spoke better German than Czech struggled to produce their own Czech poetry, virtually from scratch, and endured ridicule for seeming to be cultish eccentrics obsessed with linguistic purity. Much of what they produced, like Kollár's sonnets, now seems utterly forgettable (except as historical curiosities).

It is difficult to generalize about the awakeners, but the appearance of "cult" gives hints as to what drove them. They called themselves "nationally conse-crated," shared priestly personalities with the urge to preach to others, guard what was holy, broadcast revelation, and redeem souls. Renouncing the "ben-efits" of upward mobility was not only reasonable but required, in keeping with a divine plan that only they fully understood and had pledged their lives to fulfilling. Šafárik wrote to a Czech friend in 1817: "a human being is human so that he can die for an idea." His task in life was to restore the fame of his ancestors.[71]

Patriots had been notable for their religious fervor before they became na-tionalists. Jungmann had wanted to be a priest but became an academic instead, and Dobrovský became a priest but wanted to be a missionary. Ján Kollár was a minister, and the later South Slav patriot Josip Juraj Strosmayer was a bishop. Ante Starčević, the founder of modern Croatian nationalism, would study the-ology in preparation for the priesthood.[72] Virtually all were intellectuals, and most came from modest backgrounds, born in stables to become saviors. Re-fusing to become German was not only unreasonable. It was also revolution-ary, an act meant to return history to its proper path.

The patriots came from areas where multiple languages were spoken, were linked to other ethnic groups by family backgrounds, and stood at the margins of their own groups. The Slovak and Polish populations tended to be Catholic, but Slovak awakeners Ján Kollár and Pavel Šafárik were Lutherans, as was the author of the first Polish dictionary (Samuel Linde) and the founder of the mod-ern Polish state (Józef Piłsudski). Linde hailed from the farthest western Pol-ish territories in Prussian Thorn/Toruń and Piłsudski from the eastern bound-ary of Lithuania. Frédéric Chopin had a French father and Polish mother, and the bard Adam Mickiewicz was born on the edges of Lithuania, a periphery of a periphery. Tomáš G. Masaryk's father was an illiterate Slovak coachman, his mother was a Moravian who taught him to pray in German, and he came to the world at the eastern edge of the Bohemian kingdom, on lands of a Jewish in-dustrialist who supported German culture. His wife was American. Two of the great Croat nationalists had German parents, while a third, the most anti-Serb, had a Serb Orthodox mother.[73]

It was also true that important thinking about the nation often took place not in the nation's "own" territory, but elsewhere: in Vienna, Budapest, and Paris. The ideas of Polish romanticism were "imagined" by men and women, often from Lithuanian and Ukrainian lands, who lived in Paris and operated in a French environment. To outsiders, the basic accomplishments of Slavic nationhood would have seemed the work of German scholars. Vuk Karadžić, Samuel Gottlieb Linde, and Josef Dobrovský produced their Serb, Polish, and Czech dictionaries in Vienna, where their circles intersected with those of the German elite (including Ranke, Goethe, the Grimm brothers), and they corresponded in German and French among themselves. Ljudevit Gaj and Jan Kollár were pastors who worked out in German their ideas for modern Yugoslavia and Czechoslovakia while taking walks through mostly German Buda and Pest.[74] František Palacký published the first volumes of his history of Bohemia in German, and even a generation later, Tomáš G. Masaryk was writing his early work exclusively in German.

Leading nationalist Polish poets of the 1830s constituted a "Ukrainian" school, deriving inspiration for the Polish cause from the history of their native Ukraine. A "whole army" of Lithuanian poets led by Mickiewicz (who called Lithuania his fatherland) wrote in Polish, including Ignacy Kraszewski, while central Poland failed to produce poetry of similar genius. Joachim Lelewel, Poland's leading romantic-era historian (akin to Palacký) also hailed from Lithuania, and he made a career in Polish-dominated Wilno (Vilnius), today's Lithuanian capital.[75]

The early nineteenth century was a time of excitement among like-minded missionary enthusiasts. We might call their networks "transnational," but most lived and worked in a single state: the Austrian Empire. Still, like good European intellectuals of their day, they moved easily across the map, traveling to Paris, Rome, or Moscow to satisfy their unbounded curiosities. Ironically it was these people thriving on complexity who ultimately promoted simplicity—indeed, uniformity. They were multilingual monolingualists who used many languages but insisted that people of their ostensible culture favor only one.[76]

Like many ardent believers, these patriots had thus not been born into their nations but had chosen them, after rebuffing all temptations. They portrayed their choice as natural and necessary, involving insight into their true identity, and spent the rest of their days in a mission to would-be fellow nationals. Yet they claimed that the issue was not choice. Czech speakers had nothing to choose. Instead it was recognition: recognition of their deeper identity. But only patriots could reveal this identity. Marginality had forced them to a keen awareness of nationhood that would not be felt by someone whose language, let alone identity, was never contested. They lived doubly alienated, and as outsiders (with foreign parents, or belonging to minority religion), they wanted to be part of the Croat or Czech-Slovak nations, a desire for which they were mocked, often by their own families.

The work involved self-sacrifice, but ultimately it was not selfless. The patriots discovered and "awakened" the people as a way back to themselves, as a
response to a dilemma nationalist intellectuals face across the globe: alienation
from the common people who spoke the language they had spoken at home,
as well as elites who did not. The national movements made the self whole. Discovering and modernizing languages permitted those who had grown distant
from their humble roots to reconnect, a fact that explains their love of collecting epic poetry as well as folk songs. At the same time, they assigned themselves
the role, or found a meaningful purpose, as custodians of the folk cultures they
had "rediscovered" as well as "created."[77]

* * *

At the heart of these national stories, ranging from the Baltic to the Adriatic,
were two: the Bohemian and Hungarian, both provoked by the language reforms of Joseph II, and both involving the intense work of scholars to "awaken
nations" that supposedly slumbered. The difference in Hungary was the insistence that soon emerged that everyone on the national territory should become
Hungarian in speech and culture.[78] People also said in a pre-racial sense that
Hungarians constituted a common "race." But the noble patriots were enlightened liberals who believed that everyone on Hungarian territory, regardless
what language they spoke or religion they practiced, could become Hungarian.
By contrast, Czech patriots always recognized that Bohemia was home to two
nationalities; what they required was that Czechs not be subordinate to
Germans.

What the two stories had in common was the claim that the nominal
nationalities—Czechs and Hungarians—were the original settlers of the land,
dating back to the arrival of Slavic and Magyar tribes in the seventh and ninth
centuries. This argument was aided in the Czech case by the linguistic coincidence that the native word to denote Bohemia: *Čechy* made Bohemia seem the
land of the Czechs. Bohemian Germans were quasi-guests because their ancestors had arrived later.

Two different social groups made these similar arguments. The Bohemian
nobility, mostly culturally German, failed to lead the movement for Czech rights,
leaving the cause of national salvation to others: people of peasant and small-
town backgrounds. The Czech movement was therefore also about redefining
upward social mobility. It aimed to gain respectability for Czech versus German speakers; in the Czech kingdom, there should be no position that an

ethnic Czech commoner could not hold, and within a few generations, the movement was tabulating the numbers of Czechs in the state administration and the percentages of Czechs holding property and bank savings. In Hungary, noble nationalists argued for their rights as a class that incorporated the nation and always had. The point for liberals among them was gradually to transfer the rights vested in this large group—some 10 percent of the population in the central Hungarian lands—to the rest of the adult male population of property holders. (By contrast, the Bohemian nobility constituted 1 or 2 percent of the population.)

Though the ideas of these movements radically challenged the framework of the Habsburg monarchy and would act to frustrate attempts to make it an efficiently functioning, purposeful modern state, the self-appointed patriots largely eschewed calls for secession. But calling the monarchy an "empire" misleads. When Francis christened his dominions the "Austrian Empire," the point was not to create an imperial entity that would rival the British, French, or even Russian empires: it was simply not to appear inferior in terms of dynastic vocabulary.[79] The Habsburgs never made "empire" a forceful or self-confident project. Instead they did their best to control the territory they possessed.

CHAPTER 4

Nationality Struggles:
From Idea to Movement

Hungarian and Czech patriots seeking to make their peoples great historical actors faced the same basic challenge: because nations lived through their speech, they had to resuscitate languages not used in high culture for generations. Despite their frantic efforts, progress was slow, especially in Bohemia. As late as the 1830s, the British traveler George Gleig found that "Bohemian" was a "dialect of which the use seems restricted to the very lowest and most despised of the peasantry." He noted with surprise that at the university "not a single lecture is delivered in the vernacular language of the country."[1]

If Gleig had taken the trouble to visit the university library or the Bohemian Museum across the river, he might have noticed a challenge emerging to his gloomy portrayal. A journal in the Czech language was published at the museum, and a few volumes of Palacký's history—in German, but full of patriotic sentiment—but most impressively, four volumes of a Czech-German dictionary, the necessary foundation for a nation based in language. It was the result of decades of labor by men who lived for words, many of which were their own creations.

Despite the school reforms of Joseph II, peasants and small-town people across Bohemia still spoke a degraded Czech that was laced with German words for basic ideas and lacked expressions for more sophisticated ones. The Jesuit Josef Dobrovský and his younger collaborator Josef Jungmann, authors of the new Czech language, had several responses. Frequently they went back into the old books that had fascinated Karel Ignaz Tham and simply dusted off forgotten words and placed them in their dictionary.[2] Yet they also adapted words from other Slavic languages for use in their own. The Czech of their day lacked words for "air" and "nature," and so they took the Russian *vozduch* and made the Czech *vzduch* and the Russian *priroda* to make the Czech *příroda*. Similarly, the Polish words for object and for science *podmiot* and *wiedza* became the Czech *podmět* and *věda*. Because they knew the other Slavic languages so well, they made the new words sound Czech, and the neologisms have stood the test of time. You can hear them on the streets of Prague today.

In Hungary, the Protestant nobleman and school inspector Ferenc Kazinczy played a similar role, likewise unearthing forgotten words from ancient texts, concocting new ones, and purging the native tongue of Latin while simplifying and standardizing its orthography and grammar. In all, he and his wordsmith friends made up 10,000 new expressions.[3] Kazinczy also translated foreign literature into Hungarian and sponsored the first productions of Shakespeare in the early 1790s. Yet in 1794, at the height of his productivity, Austrian authorities arrested Kazinczy as supposedly a participant of a Jacobin conspiracy inspired by revolutionary France. After hanging the leaders, they put him and his supposed accomplices in jail for seven years.[4] When he reemerged, Kazinczy redoubled his efforts to counteract the "mental inactivity and torpor that lay heavy upon the national body." Decades later, even critics admitted that without him, Hungarian literature would not have risen to a new blossoming. By 1814 his translations had appeared in nine volumes, and in addition he wrote scores of essays and poems. Authors of romantic poetry and historical novels joined him, taking inspiration from the past by glorifying the native tribes who once conquered Hungary but also rousing feelings against Germans.[5]

After the languages were manufactured, they had to be used, and here the stories of Bohemia and Hungary diverged. Bohemian patriots were of humble origin, mostly priests or pastors who became apostles of nationalism, but they had neither the money nor political power to advance their languages. Their counterparts in Hungary were nobles, who used their traditional diet to simply decree change. Because they as a class had threatened to defect to Prussia when Austria faced war in Turkey, Joseph abandoned his attempts to impose German on them. His brother Leopold kept up the conciliation and brought Hungary's crown back to Pressburg. In 1790 the diet reconvened, declaring the national language to be a concern of state, and two years later Hungarian became an ordinary subject in grammar schools.[6]

In the decades that followed, nobles in Pressburg/Pozsony but also in county assemblies acted to Magyarize all transactions, public spaces, and populations on Hungarian territory. Like Joseph, they saw Latin as a problem; if for him it hindered the formation of an Austrian state, for them it impeded the forging of a modern Hungarian nation. Beginning in 1805, counties could correspond with royal administration in Hungarian as well as Latin, and the use of Hungarian and Latin side by side entered the work of the diet. In 1830 Magyar was made obligatory for all holders of public office; in 1835 its use was extended to law courts as an alternative to Latin, and it was made an alternative language for all official documents. From 1839 the diet's addresses to the throne had to be drawn up in the native tongue, and the following year it superseded Latin as a language of government and parliament. Clergy had to learn Maygar, and all registers had to be compiled in it within three years—the same number of years Joseph had given Hungarians for learning German! In 1843 Magyar was made the exclusive language of government, parliament, administration, and public instruction, but in the counties, it had been language of administration and education long before that.[7]

Bohemia also had a parliament, the *Landtag*, and though the nobles, townsmen, and clergy who sat there called themselves Bohemian, few thought of themselves as Czech. Nobles were lukewarm about nationalism whether Czech or German. They spoke and wrote to one another in French and frequented institutions of culture and higher education that were German. They also had much less corporate identity or power than the Hungarian nobility. Despite demands by a few patriots that Vienna respect Bohemia's rights, the diet in Prague in the 1790s had settled for minor concessions from the Habsburgs, who, though weakened, continued to assert the central rule that Maria Theresa had imposed in 1749.[8]

The national museums founded in Pest in 1803 and Prague in 1820 highlight the differences in the two situations. In 1802 Count Ferenc Széchenyi donated his rich collection of art, maps, manuscripts, coins, and books "for the use and benefit of my dear homeland and people, irrevocably and forever," and five years later the Hungarian diet recognized the museum in Pest as an autonomous corporation, housing it in a former university building and soliciting donations from the Hungarian counties. Three decades later the diet voted funds to construct an impressive neoclassical structure that was in place by 1846. The Hungarian state had purchased the land in 1813.[9]

Counts Franz Anton Kolovrat and Kaspar Sternberg founded a Bohemian Museum in Prague in 1820 as a cultural bulwark from which to defend the identity of their homeland against the centralizing ambitions of Vienna. Themselves cosmopolitan, they supported Czech patriots because of a shared concern for Bohemian rights. Sternberg located the museum in his palace in Prague's small quarter, but in 1847 it went to another nobleman's palace and did not find its current home at the top of Wenceslaus Square above Prague's old town until the 1890s.

Recall that it was František Palacký who had suggested to Sternberg that the latter use the museum as a place to propagate Czech culture through its own scientific journal. Thus, from its early days the national movement latched onto this originally regional but non-nationalist institution. Only when it commenced publishing its journal in 1827 did the museum become the chief means of spreading knowledge to Czechs about their present and past. After 1831 the museum's board created a special foundation on the Serb model, the *Matice Česká*, to support the Czech language. Because this was a time of strict censorship, Palacký claimed its purpose was to publish "good Czech books of useful, scholarly, and belletristic kind." The museum also funded book awards, dictionaries, and an encyclopedia, and because it was supported by conservative nobles, Palacký managed to fend off suspicions that he was propagating nationalism, the cardinal political sin of the reactionary Metternich years.[10]

But unlike its Hungarian counterpart, the Bohemian Museum did not interest the country's diet, and funds came mostly from small donors, reflecting the broader, more "democratic" base of Czech nationalism. By 1840 it had 522 founding members and 1,735 small contributors, with about 40 percent of the support coming from the Catholic clergy, although the movement's message would grow increasingly anticlerical, in keeping with the centrality of the Hussite legacy for the Czech nationalist narrative. The Bohemian high nobility possessed enormous wealth but gave far less than Hungary's gentry. For example, in 1825 Széchenyi's son István had contributed 60,000 florins, a year's income, for a Hungarian Academy that would build on the scholarly work of the Hungarian Museum, and three of his noble friends gave an additional 58,000 florins. In Bohemia a small number of noble donors to the Museum in Prague gave between 100 and 1,000 florins.[11]

In general, Bohemia's nobles showed little interest in politics, national or otherwise. Political initiative, including the passing of laws on taxes for schools, lay with authorities in Vienna, and the Bohemian estates—nobility, clergy, and townspeople—accepted their decrees without contradiction. The mentally handicapped Habsburg Emperor Ferdinand I (1835–1848), was crowned Bohemian King in Prague in September 1836, and nobles began attending meetings of the diet more regularly, but they conspired to keep representatives of the towns or peasantry—who tended to be Czech—from having any say. In that sense they were antinational.[12]

* * *

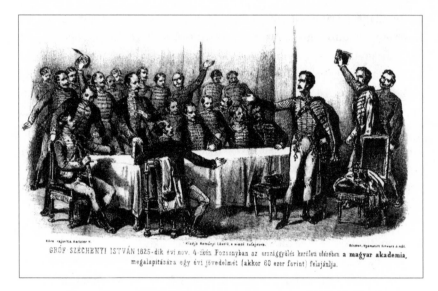

FIGURE 4.1. Count Széchényi donates a year's income to found the Hungarian Academy (1825). *Source*: Drawing by Vinzenz Katzler. Via Wikimedia Commons.

Nobles in the Hungarian parliament felt representative not simply of their class but of a European nation, and they wanted to extend their sense of nationhood to other social strata. Yet when they considered their land's international situation, two issues troubled them: first, that if they did not keep up intense efforts to promote the Magyar language and suffocate all competitors, Hungary would disappear as a nation. But second, if they did not do something about Hungary's wretched economic backwardness, the land would never stand as an equal to the great nations of Western Europe.

The nobles traveled to England and envied everything they saw, from the gentry and its affluent and self-confidant lifestyle, to the busy factories that could produce thousands of shoes in a day. In 1822 the patriot Baron Miklós Wesselényi described his impressions to a friend. "One glass factory, coal mine, and iron works next to the other," he wrote, "The entire area is covered by fire and smoke like the scenery of the last judgment." The West and East India Company docks, with hundreds of ships and warehouses, and the paved roads leading to the city, left him stunned. "I felt like a small-town tradesman in his Sunday suit," he complained, "ludicrously stiff and afraid to move."[13]

Like the Czech patriots, Hungary's noble activists endeavored to "awaken" the people to national life, but this word had a special resonance for them. If in Bohemia awakeners used literature and language to cause peasants and small-townspeople to embrace their identity as members of a great nation, in Hungary they did something more practical as well. When the great activist, polymath, and war hero Count István Széchenyi looked at the enormous Hungarian grain plantations, he saw tragically unproductive laborers and land. He proposed the obvious solutions of freeing peasants from forced labor, allowing land to be sold on the market, and giving both lords and peasants an interest in diversifying and increasing productivity. Making noble land salable would also permit the formation of credit markets, in which landowners could seek mortgages to finance improvements, and freeing peasants would unleash their labor. Széchenyi calculated that forced labor was only one-third as productive as labor given freely, whether for hire or on one's own property.[14]

Nothing that was related to Hungary's welfare failed to interest Széchenyi. During a sojourn abroad after university studies, he paid special attention to science and technology. In France for the coronation of Charles X in 1825, he took time to study the canal du Midi, which gave him the idea of regulating the Danube back home, an idea that led to a naval expedition down the river from Pest to Istanbul, after which he convinced the responsible Habsburg official—Palatine Joseph—of the project's worthiness and then formed a Danube Navigation Committee that completed its work in ten years. In England he noted how social clubs permitted the polite classes to come together for mutual enrichment, whether through reading, discussion, or business transactions; and in 1827 he founded a "casino" on their model in Pest. About a decade later the British traveler Julia Pardoe described her impression:

> The ball and billiard rooms are both extremely handsome; and the Casino known as the "National," for which only nobles or members of the learned professions are eligible, occupies the whole of the first floor; the one above being called the Kaufmännische Casino, and composed of merchants and respectable individuals connected with the commerce of the city; while the basement serves as a restaurant; said to be the best in Pest, whence dinners are provided in very good style all over the house.

The institution was duplicated throughout the Hungarian and then Bohemian lands as the professional classes expanded, and it was from casinos that political life emerged in both kingdoms.[15] By 1833 there were twenty-nine casinos and reading associations across Hungary, and by 1848 such societies had more than 10,000 members. Széchenyi's great rival in the national movement, Lajos Kossuth (1802–1894), said associations were a "mighty tool, strong and powerful like nothing else."[16]

As Pardoe's observation attests, associational life was limited to people of education and means who relied on German for ease of communication. Yet what astounds is how broadly based the patriotic movement had become by 1848, involving top aristocrats but also nobles of all stripes, as well as city folk, many from the free professions. All had been educated in Magyar institutions and became the prime audience for native-language plays, journals, and encyclopedias. By the 1860s Pest featured consumer and music societies; associations for physicians, geographers, and horse-betters; a club to promote artisanry and agriculture among Hungary's Israelites; associations for Catholic men and for those interested in supporting writers or children's day care. There were also women's associations in both Pest and Buda.[17]

Amazingly, not only were the nobles willing to mix with commoners as part of the same nation, but these nobles also advocated reforms that would upset their own protected worlds, opening them to the pressures of markets for land and labor. Such pressures injected risks into lifestyles that, as far as anyone knew, had never changed. But national ideology had taken such a hold of this group that it would forego privilege for the sake of a Hungary that had never existed.[18] Széchenyi shamed those who resisted, saying that noble privileges kept the fatherland weak, unable to grow or even defend itself.

Politically, the gentry mainstream consisted of more and less radical shades of liberalism, with a common vision of society based on legal equality, in which all had the same rights, for example, to move, to marry, and to buy and sell property. But they also had equal duties. Nobles as well as clergy would lose exemptions from taxation, and that would enhance the state's ability to dredge rivers; dig sewers; build roads, schools, and libraries; and finance scientific research. Yet the more such reform ideas became self-evident, the more a basic predicament grated on the noble imagination: their country had no state apparatus to carry out these reforms and duties. Despite the continued existence of the Hungarian diet with its two houses, as well as the nobility's control of administration in the counties, the final say about what happened in Hungary belonged to a foreign dynasty in a foreign city. For example, consider trade. For Hungarians, the kingdom's relation to Austria was like that of a colony to the center. In 1841, 27.4 million of Austria's 29 million florins' worth of industrial goods went to Hungary; yet industrial goods made up less than 2 percent of Austria's imports from Hungary, the rest being almost entirely agricultural products and raw materials.[19] That relation compounded Hungary's backwardness vis-à-vis Austria and Bohemia, which in turn were less prosperous than western and northern Germany. Hungary was somewhere in the middle of a developmental gradient that went downward from Western to Eastern Europe.

As a Catholic aristocrat and former Habsburg officer, Széchenyi was a moderate, hoping that Hungary and Austria could fine a modus vivendi. The aristocracy's political hegemony would guarantee a smooth transition to a more independent Hungary, he thought, precluding violent clashes between imperial authorities and the county nobility.[20] Széchenyi's challenger Lajos Kossuth was a lawyer and Lutheran from the impoverished gentry, who entered parliament at age thirty as a proxy for a widow whose estate he managed. He gained renown as a brilliant but dangerous political commentator and spent years behind bars for supposed subversion.

* * *

Despite profound differences in political style, Kossuth and Széchenyi agreed on the major questions of national politics. Each assumed that historic Hungary must be Hungarian politically and culturally, and each wanted liberation from the feudal regime that privileged nobility and clergy in order to create a nation of citizens, of "free land and free men," as Kossuth said. The understanding was also ethnic, as each thought it was nonsense to accord nationhood to unlettered peasants speaking dialects of Slovak or Romanian.[21]

Croatia was a separate case, a kingdom with a noble class ("natio") that had guaranteed rights dating back to its free accession to Hungary in 1106. But radicals among Hungary's liberals, including Kossuth, were willing at most to recognize Croatia's municipal rights. There is "but one nation here," he said in an 1847 address to the diet, "and I shall never but never recognize, under the Holy Crown of Hungary, more than one nation and nationality, the Magyar." Just a few years earlier, the diet had required Croatian officials to learn Magyar within three years.[22]

Széchenyi worried about the passions unleashed of one nationality against another in Hungary but also of poor against rich. He criticized Kossuth for incendiary rhetoric that might risk retaliation from Vienna, or even worse, cause it to play the other national groups in Hungary against the Magyars.[23] With a little reflection on history, Kossuth might have recalled that the enlightened Habsburg ruler Leopold had permitted the Serbs in southern Hungary to convene a national congress, where they demanded the separate status that Croatia enjoyed.[24] The current Habsburg leaders could (and, as we shall see, would) also play this game of divide and conquer to control Hungary.

But Joseph had provoked such fears among Hungary's gentry with his Germanization schemes that they became blind to such dangers. After de-Germanizing every cultural and educational institution in sight, they became obsessed with pan-Slavism, supposedly masterminded by Russia, and thus they inadvertently awakened and caused the spread of nationalism among the kingdom's Slavic groups.[25] In 1815 budding Slavic patriots from the Hungarian lands had still called themselves "Hungari," loyal subjects of the Kingdom of Hungary, but over the following decades, they began to identify as Serbs in the south and as Slovaks in the north.[26] In 1833 anonymous Croat authors complained that Pest had been transformed in six short years from what seemed a city in central Germany to a "Magyar Eldorado." People who spoke German for the sake of communication now faced contempt, and many were abandoning that language, because speaking Hungarian—and being Magyar—was chic. Those who insisted they could be good *Hungari* and speak a Slavic tongue were out of touch.[27]

Magyar loyalists were as deaf to the arguments of Slovaks or Croats as Joseph II had been to those of their grandparents. Did not inhabitants of France speak French? The argument was also about democracy: without a common language, citizens could not participate in the affairs of their common polity. Yet now the other nationalities argued (just as their grandparents had to Joseph) that languages were also an integral part of *their* heritage. Why not make Hungary multinational?[28]

In these years the Croat Ljudevit Gaj (1809–1872) arrived in Pest to commence his law studies and saw Magyar displacing German as well as the Slavic languages. He discerned a vital threat to his people that caused him to spend many hours in the national library taking notes from dusty old books on Croatia's deep past. To Hungarian jokes that he was preparing to conquer Hungary, Gaj retorted that he was simply defending Croatia. He penned a poem that warned compatriots not to let Magyars grind them into dust: "We shall rather die together, united, than let our language be taken from us."[29]

In 1830 Gaj met the Slovak Jan Kollár, sixteen years his senior, and they found an immediate mutual empathy, taking long walks and discussing how to prepare their peoples for the challenge of nationhood. Kollár taught Gaj about Slavic reciprocity: that all Slavs were one people of many tribes, and that each had to sacrifice something in order to share in the common greatness.[30] If Kollár wanted Slovaks to accept Czech words for the sake of a common national life, Gaj began thinking of ways that Croats might adapt their language for a state they would share with other South Slavs, especially the Serbs. To those claiming Hungarian was necessary for all Hungarian subjects, he issued an unsubtle taunt: "The Magyars are an island in a Slavic sea. I did not create this sea, but you should be careful that it does not close above you and swallow you."[31]

Czech and Slovak patriots called the larger people they sought to unite "Czecho-Slovak" or "Czecho-Slav," and Gaj called the South Slavs he hoped to bring together "Slavo-Croatian," or later, "Illyrian." "Illyria," an ancient word to describe western stretches of the Balkan Peninsula, had been used by Napoleon for the puppet regime that he created in 1809 with a capital at Ljubljana. This entity, where the French had promoted local cultures among Slovene, Croat, and Serb populations, suggested that South Slavs could live in single state.[32] Gaj took this general notion and married it to the Herderian idea that language makes a people.

The question he faced on returning to Zagreb—in our day a glittering Croat capital but then a provincial backwater—was what language the "Illyrian" people would use. He opted for a dialect spoken by most Croats and virtually all Serbs, so-called Štovkavian (based on the word used for "what": "što"). However, the choice was painful for Croats because it involved sacrificing the Zagreb variant with its own rich literary heritage, yet Gaj was willing to do so to attract other South Slavs—especially Serbs—to a common political life. The language he was proposing would be the standard Illyrian language, in the way that Martin Luther's German had become the common "high" language of the Germans.

Gaj's work for Illyrian unity drew strength from the agitation caused among Croats by forced Magyarization. By 1847, his journal *Danica* had more than 1,000 subscribers and the following year, "Illyrians" controlled Croatia's diet, the Sabor, where they replaced Latin with Croatian.[33] In Zagreb's main square, schoolchildren threw Hungarian textbooks into a huge bonfire. But given the resistance in Vienna to any restructuring of the empire, nothing could come of these plans for the time being. Still, the Illyrian idea had placed South Slav unity firmly on the table while ennobling the idea of Croatian self-sacrifice for the common good. The movement did not dream of upsetting the monarchy: even the most radical Illyrians assumed that the Habsburg monarchy would continue, and their program remained the preserve of intellectuals with little contact with the masses.[34] No one knew how people throughout the South Slav lands would respond to ideas of unity, especially those living under Ottoman rule.

It was from those lands that a competing idea emerged for South Slav unity, from the Serb philologist Vuk Karadžić, whom Gaj knew very well from scholarly circles in Vienna. Karadžić had standardized the Serb language decades earlier, also using the Štovkavian dialect. In the 1830s he wrote that all those who spoke this dialect, whether they were Muslim, Orthodox or Catholic, were in fact Serbs, and he projected a common future for them all, from Kosovo and Macedonia, Serbia, and Bosnia, as well as Croatia and other parts of Hungary inhabited by South Slavs. Before the revolutions of 1848, as we will see in greater detail in Chapter 5, a tension was thus emerging between Habsburg South Slavs in Croatia, Hungary, and Dalmatia and Ottoman South Slavs in Bosnia and Serbia to unify the same people *using the very same dialect*; the two tendencies would make the Yugoslavia of 1918 conceivable but also infernally difficult to govern.

* * *

The nationality struggle in Hungary went through three phases before the 1848 revolution. First, the patriots created Magyar cultural institutions in order to hinder Habsburg plans to Germanize them (1780s–1830s); second, they used political institutions to work out a national politics of economic development (1830s–1840s); and third, they unwittingly unleashed a reaction from the groups they attempted to Magyarize. By 1848 Croat, Slovak, Serb, and Romanian patriots were asserting their own cultural and political rights. The struggle in Bohemia was simpler: patriots demanded respect for the Czech language and by extension the Czech people. They defied the belief that Czechs wanting to be something better than a servant people had to become German. As in Hungary, the struggle was ignited by Habsburg attempts to centralize the land using German schools, but at no point did Czechs face denationalization equal to the Magyarization unleashed on Slovaks or Romanians in Hungary.

As we have seen, there were cultural institutions throughout the Bohemian lands, above all dense networks of schools, but also many theaters, the Bohemian Museum with a library, and the Royal Bohemian Learned Society. Yet the assumption was that these institutions, even if they used Czech, either created or served an audience that was culturally German. In response, Czech patriots, who were overwhelmingly of non-noble background, insinuated themselves into these institutions and expanded spaces in them for their culture and language. But they gained not an inch without fierce resistance.

Consider education. In the 1790s Hungary's parliament began dictating that schooling would be in the "national" language, and no force could contradict it. In Bohemia, primary education had grown steadily from the time of Maria Theresa. In 1787 there were 2,221 schools of all types, and by 1828 that number had grown to 3,252.[35] Though schools in Czech areas of Bohemia used Czech, their purpose remained the same: to make students literate in their own language in order to educate them in German. And the schools were run by the Catholic Church, an institution that taught fear of God and divinely ordained authorities rather than love for the Czech homeland. Before 1859 authorities forbade Czech secondary schools, and therefore patriots fought for minor increases in hours taught in Czech at existing schools, claiming that excellent Czech was needed to learn to spell German properly![36] They not only used existing state-sanctioned institutions but also state-sanctioned arguments for their own cause.

Though this was the heyday of romanticism, nothing was romantic about this uphill battle. Growing Czech urban populations wanted to educate young people aspiring to go into trades, and therefore patriots infiltrated the Union for the Encouragement of Industry in Bohemia (founded in 1833 by Bohemian nobles) and agitated for Czech trade schools. More than 2,000 tradesmen had made contributions before authorities closed down the operation in April 1847. But the guiding spirits of this campaign—A. P. Trojan (1815–1893) and F. L. Rieger (1818–1903)—gained experience in mobilizing patriots that they put to use as Czech politicians of the liberal period, from the 1860s on.[37]

After schooling, the most effective way of spreading patriotic messages was the theater. Theaters had traveled about Central Europe from time immemorial, making profits when they played in vernacular languages. But national movements wanted to control the stages of large towns. Joseph II gave an early boost by establishing theaters from west to east, from Baden and Graz to Lemberg (Lwów), Kassa (Košice), and Hermannstadt (Sibiu). Beginning in 1783, there was also an Estates (or Nostitz) Theater in Prague, opening in time to premiere Wolfgang Amadeus Mozart's opera *Don Giovanni*. As a hint of things to come, Czech-language productions played once a week there to sold-out audiences, but the building remained in German hands for two more generations. When the Czech players were expelled in 1787, they petitioned Joseph and were permitted to set up their own stage on today's Wenceslaus square, made of wood and therefore called simply the "hut." It closed after two years.

Like historian Palacký or the dictionary-writer Jungmann, the pioneers of Czech theater were of humble background, and their pioneer, Jan Nepomuk Štěpánek (1783–1844) had also trained for the church but then found a new calling: as an actor but also prompter, treasurer, manager, and then translator, writer, and producer. Štěpánek established a Czech theater in 1804 on Prague's small side, but it was banned five years later. In 1812 he and other enthusiasts founded an amateur stage that played patriotic themes to packed houses, but only on Sundays and holidays. From 1812 to 1823, Štěpánek sponsored sixty-nine Czech performances, before moving to the Nostitz Theater, where he directed more than 300 performances in Czech by 1834.[38]

Štěpánek took fire from priests of the movement like Jungmann for bringing lowbrow Viennese-style productions to Prague that failed to tap people's "moral energies" and doing little to develop tragedy.[39] But he was also a businessman, and he gave growing Czech audiences what they wanted: chivalrous robber plays and fairy tales that managed to be subversively humorous even when touching on German-Czech relations.[40] One of his comedies traced the misadventures of Germans unable to understand Czech, but in a "happy ending," the young Czech and German marry. Decades later, during a time of intense nationality struggle in Vienna, the idea of a mixed wedding caused rioting.

If his plays were comedic, Štěpánek acted as a serious community leader. He co-directed an institute providing for widows and orphans as well as a poor-relief association. He also founded a Prague orphanage. In 1821 he was made an honorary citizen of Prague and was accorded a royal decree. Friends celebrated his services with a cantata. But public life was inseparable from cultural production: while opposing stubborn attempts to expel Czech productions from the Nostitz Theater in the 1820s, he continued translating favorite operas from West European languages, including German.[41]

Students who had graduated from institutions of learning in Prague made sure the movement initiated by Štěpánek spread beyond the capital, building on very old traditions of traveling theaters. Despite censorship, light-hearted Czech plays were staged in towns up and down the Bohemian and Moravian countryside, featuring translations from Viennese comic opera but also gradually displacing German productions. Patriots felt optimistic: beneath the German cultural and bureaucratic elite, the audiences showed that a Czech middle class had survived since White Mountain; they were also consumers for the increasingly popular Czech periodicals of Prague's Bohemian museum.[42]

Many residents in these small-town communities knew German for the sake of public life, but it stirred no deeper sense of loyalty, whereas Czech was the language of the intimacy of the home. They flocked to spectacles that were extensions of their families' lives, a "traveling theater nation," where people sang together, instantly understood allusions, and nodded their heads about things that mattered, comedic or tragic. The punch lines came in rapid succession and served to define the community: Czechs were the people who got the jokes and laughed uncontrollably, while their "betters" stared in befuddlement.[43]

Still, the Czech movement advanced slowly against ideas of respectability and facts of ownership. All the established theaters in Bohemia and Moravia remained in German hands. A barrage of petitions moved imperial authorities to permit the building of a Czech theater at Prague, yet they allotted no money for it. Supporting a "nationalist" undertaking was out of the question, and the authorities wanted the two ethnicities to cooperate as they did in the Estates Theater in Prague, where the same actors appeared in German and Czech operas.[44] But ultimately, no force could stop the dividing of institutions in Bohemia. When Czech patriots got a chance, they separated from the Germans as soon as they could, first in theaters but then on every other stage, whether cultural, scientific, economic, religious, or political.

* * *

In the early nineteenth century, theaters also expanded in the Hungarian cities Pest and Pressburg, and Magyar-language productions rapidly displaced German. But by the 1830s, there was little to struggle about. If the Hungarian movement wanted Hungarian theater, the parliament simply decreed it. The gentry political elite that controlled this institution *was* the national movement, and its prime efforts had moved to the stage of public life: to the most recent speeches of Kossuth, or to debates about political reform between him and more moderate opponents that filled the newspapers.

By the 1830s the Hungarian movement was imagining how to take control of and build the institutions of a nation-state that might stand next to England or France, sharing a point of view that would emerge among Czech politicians only two or three generations later. At this juncture, the Hungarian and Czech movements each desired what the other took for granted. If Czech patriots looked with envy on the museums, high schools, casinos, and theaters sprouting up around the Kingdom of Hungary, Magyar activists looked jealously at the cities and industries, roads, bridges, and urban prosperity of Bohemia, the most economically advanced place in the monarchy.

Bohemia had long stood at the crossroads of commercial routes, and it possessed age-old industries, a diversified and intensive agriculture, and an educated workforce in its innumerable small towns and cities. From the time of Joseph II, we can trace a growth spike that made Bohemia unrecognizable within a generation. The number of linen looms in Moravia went from 8,769 in 1775 to 10,412 in 1780, and 14,349 in 1798. Workers in the Moravian textile industry increased from about 288,000 in 1780 to 504,000 in 1789. Glass, wool, cotton, and stationery manufacturing likewise improved in the late eighteenth century, and agricultural products became more abundant. Such increases in production then fostered the expansion of regional and transregional markets, which in turn promoted the communication and movement of people from villages to growing towns.[45]

At the same time, the transformation from rural to modern was achingly gradual in Hungary, noticeable in reforms accomplished through the strong will of a few workaholics like István Széchenyi, the most spectacular being the Chain Bridge connecting Buda and Pest in 1849, designed by Scottish engineers and financed by Greek capital. Yet Hungary's vaunted reform parliaments of the 1830s and 1840s did little to advance modernization beyond measures facilitating the litigation of commercial disputes; their major achievement was to firm up the use of Hungarian in the educational system.[46]

Hungary remained overwhelmingly and unproductively agricultural, facing tremendous legal barriers to even the thought of modernization. Seigniorial land could not be bought or sold, and peasants were not a labor force available to emergent industry but instead were bound servants of their lords. Széchenyi understood that agricultural land had to attract credit to prosper, but even after 1848, when seigniorial rights were abolished, Hungary did not bring in much foreign investment. Rather than put their money in the agricultural enterprise of an underdeveloped country, Western credit markets tended to fund transportation and industry in more prosperous regions.[47]

Hungarian parliamentarians had devoted hundreds of hours to drafting an Urbarial Act to revolutionize the relations between lord and peasant, but in the end, it was so diluted that individual lords decided for themselves whether they would redeem their peasants' feudal dues. In general, they tended not to be interested. By the 1830s the entrepreneurial spirit of the aristocracy was already waning, and nobles increased production not through capital intensification but through increased reliance on forced labor (*corvée* or *robot*). The reform process dragged because despite all patriotic feeling, at base it opposed the interests of the class for whom Kossuth, Széchenyi, or Ferenc Deák spoke. Kossuth, a stirring orator, tried to focus popular concern on the exploitative relations in the countryside, but before 1848, the only group he managed to mobilize in the diet was the impoverished "sandal" nobility. In 1843–1844 both chambers of parliament requested modification of internal tariffs separating Hungary from the rest of Habsburg lands, without success.[48]

At that time Hungary possessed one or two modern factories and a nascent industrial working class of about 30,000. Industrial production increased fourfold from what it had been under Joseph, but was only 7 percent of total Habsburg output, although Hungary constituted more than 40 percent of the monarchy's territory. And the Habsburg realm was far behind Western European countries like England or Belgium. Hungary's urban population numbered roughly 600,000, about the size as the nobility. But because industries tended to be in the hands of magnates, and most lucrative trade was in grain, the burgher class, associated with entrepreneurship and representative institutions, remained weak. Pest-Buda had grown to about 150,000 when it was declared the capital in 1848, but a sewer system was just being installed along with modern parks; at that point, only half the streets were paved and equipped with lighting.[49]

Perhaps the gaps in development between Bohemia and Hungary were most striking in education. By the 1840s more than 95 percent of school-age children in the Bohemian kingdom attended schools; so that by the 1850s, the problem of illiteracy had been eradicated. In Hungary in 1869, only 47.9 percent of school-age children actually went to school, and of the entire population, only 27.2 percent were literate.[50] But education played differing roles in the respective nationality struggles. Because they controlled state administration, the Hungarian elite continued to use their schools—though fewer in number—to Magyarize. Thus, the number of high schools teaching Slovak was reduced to zero by 1900. Because the administration in Bohemia favored German schooling, the Czech movement had to struggle for every new high school built. It did so with increasing passion and diminishing patience.

By the 1840s, literate Czechs were not satisfied watching Czech life take place on theater stages or in the pages of schoolbooks. They wanted to experience life as Czechs with no constraints, in the economy, in politics, and culture; there should be no café or club or casino where people looked at them strangely simply because they spoke the language of their forefathers. Not difficult to comprehend, this desire now spread beyond the apostles and martyrs through small-town elites and to the masses. Yet beyond the efforts of patriots, the movement was driven by the impersonal energies of modernization—in particular, the growth and development of towns. Or to put it another way: by the 1840s, Czech nationalists were riding a wave that had crested behind them, produced by forces beyond their control and comprehension.

For centuries, population and economic growth had been slow and steady, and cities and towns remained the preserves of elites speaking languages foreign to people in the surrounding countryside.[51] Under such conditions, young Czechs coming to Prague to learn a craft or enter state service picked up

German as the language of their new surroundings, and their families became German. The influx was gradual, and newcomers were readily absorbed. Cities worked not so much for the countryside around them (let alone for foreign markets) as for the feudal elite. This situation was not unique to Bohemia. Beyond its boundaries, one encountered German-dominated cities in Bratislava/Pressburg (among Slovaks), Llubljana/Laibach (among Slovenes), the Polish-dominated Wilno/Vilnius (among Lithuanians and Belorussians), or Lwów/Lviv (among Ukrainians).

Unusual in Bohemia was the growing density of urban settlement, and the measures taken in the 1820s and 1830s to connect towns to each other by firm-foundation roads, complete with new bridges. In addition, between 1827 and 1836, the second railroad on the European continent was established to connect Upper Austria with Southern Bohemia, and from there to river traffic leading northward through Prague. A train pulled by steam locomotive reached Brno from Vienna in 1836 and from Prague in 1840. Telegraph lines were built at the same time.[52]

As the feudal system declined and trade between city and countryside grew, the village became a client for middle-class traders and craftspersons from the cities. Urban areas grew, and the workers coming into them were soon too numerous to be easily absorbed. At the same time, as commerce expanded, craftspersons and traders who could communicate in Czech with people in nearby villages gained advantages over those speaking only German. The process now reversed: cities ceased Germanizing the rural population streaming in from the countryside; instead, as the numbers of these Czech-speakers became a torrent, the newcomers began to de-Germanize the city.

The political scientist Karl W. Deutsch, like other leading students of the subject originally from Bohemia, discussed this aspect of nationalism in terms of ease of communication. As society grew urban and modern, it became relatively more efficient and profitable to communicate with one large group of people than with another. *That people was a modern nation.* As urban populations grew that spoke a Slavic language on an everyday basis, institutions like schools, credit institutions, joint stock companies, and legal offices emerged to serve them and facilitate all sorts of transactions, from cultural and business and political to strictly social. Pressures to remove language as a barrier to communication also produced Czech pubs and restaurants, advertisements, shop windows, and street signs—in short, a Czech world.[53]

But this was not the whole story. Cities that gradually merged with the countryside became centers of cultural life where the national culture could revive and flourish. They provided not simply places to do business in an efficient way, but also platforms for the production and discovery of meaning in a setting where the pull of organized religion was waning. People seeking to make sense of their existence found answers in the nation emerging before their eyes: it became a source of value, a cardinal good from which others flowed. It became a structure that reformed religion, for example in the thought of T. G. Masaryk; a demand that could buttress every other demand, be it social, cultural, or gender related; a cause to live for and to die for.[54]

That was what the patriots had been preaching for decades, and now it caught on, but in a deeply ironic way. As the urban setting became increasingly modern, erasing signs of the past and putting three- and four-story structures in the place of centuries-old houses, Czech-speakers were told to think of their nation as ancient and rooted, original and essential. Just as traditional village life was being transformed beyond recognition, the national movement was creating the radically new image in Czechs' minds that they stood above history, in relation to people who had lived centuries earlier: knights, religious reformers, and heads of ancient clans.

The movement ingeniously smoothed over the contradictions. After mid-century, municipal authorities restored the façades of the old city gates in Prague, accentuating the Gothic forms and making them purer (in a sense "older") than the originals. This process of making the national past serve the nationalist present was not a self-evident one, however. First, Czech nationalists insisted that French rather than German Gothic models be used, yet then they invested energies in restoring Renaissance structures because these better reflected the times of Czech glory they wanted to recapture.[55]

From mid-century, nationalism grew rapidly in Bohemia because it responded to human needs at their most practical and impractical simultaneously, at moments of truth when people imagined the future in terms of money and career, but also when they sought meaning in ways that made money and career seem secondary. Herder's idea that suppressed peoples had providential destinies was spread through the expanding system of education, as well as the demand that state officials have good command of the Czech vernacular.[56] It was carried through the embers of shared grievance and blown into a hot fury by the poems, legends, and histories appearing in the books, pamphlets, and paintings of the national movement.

If the modernization that drove the nation-building forward was impersonal, the process was not automatic in a way that made the work of thousands of patriots immaterial. Identifiable leaders employed institutions in a quest for specific outcomes. The Czech historian Miroslav Hroch spoke of nation-building in small nations as occurring in three stages: the first of creating the intellectual resources; the second of molding a constituency among patriots; the third of spreading the idea in a mass movement. Crucial in stage two was the vigilance of school authorities. Before World War I, some 100,000 Czech-speakers lived in Vienna, and anxious German-language authorities used legal and financial means to suppress Czech schooling to prevent Vienna from becoming a Czech city.[57] Further north, Prague and Brno would not have become Czech if the Czech movement had not funded education. We see this sort of absorption in Southern and Eastern Slav lands as well, although slightly later: in 1900, only 5 percent of immigrants from Serbo-Croat areas to the Italian city of Trieste declared their everyday language to be Serbo-Croatian (the majority used Italian); and only 27 percent of people born in Ukrainian areas who had moved to Lwów spoke Ukrainian (the majority used Polish).[58]

National and social development reinforced each other in the Czech lands because of the neat overlapping of national and social oppression. For genera-tions, Czech-speakers had sensed a scorching injustice because those possess-ing status and wealth not only tended to be German-speaking but *had* to be German-speaking. Ambitious Czech-speakers striving for betterment readily embraced nationalism because its truths ennobled their cause, accounting for the unjust equation of the present through arguments from the past taken from František Palacký's prose and Ján Kollár's verse: that while Slavs had always been democratic and peaceful, Germans were not.

But the response was competition and not revolution. From the early de-cades of the nineteenth century, Czechs saved, pooled resources, and accumu-lated capital. By the late nineteenth century, they owned substantial sectors of Bohemian industry and commerce and on the eve of World War I had more than two billion crowns in banks and savings accounts (in all of Austria, there were 6.3 billion crowns in savings accounts).[59]

This campaign for economic equality accompanied the struggle for control of political and cultural institutions. In Prague there were German and Czech casinos, but from the 1850s, the latter came to overshadow the former.[60] In 1868 ground was finally broken for the Czech National Theater, but unlike the Hun-garian, it was built not with state money, but from donations of uncounted Czechs. A smaller provisional structure had emerged in 1862, but it was not until June 1881 that the neo-Renaissance edifice we know on banks of the Vltava

FIGURE 4.2. Laying Down the Foundation at the National Theatre in Prague (May 16, 1868).
Source: *Zlatá Praha* 33 (1908), 378. Via Wikimedia Commons.

opened to the music of Bedřich Smetana. Two months later, fire destroyed the interior, and now even more donations flowed in, so great that the organizers had to tell Czechs to stop sending money.[61]

* * *

At this point, Czech nationalism was the work of people from all walks of life who wanted simple respect when they used the language of their parents. During the theater's groundbreaking ceremony, František Palacký recounted to the huge crowd how different things had been forty years earlier. Patriots had joked that if the roof collapsed on the building where they were meeting, that would have been the end of the Czech nation. Now, he said, the sky would have to fall for that to happen (that would also destroy our enemies, he added). He was wrong. If it had not been his group of historians and philologists under that roof, it would have been another, also of common background: children of peasants, artisans, millers, and perhaps the odd teacher. Lower class status did not cause everyone to become a Czech patriot, but all the early Czech patriots experienced poverty.[62]

The social background of the Hungarian patriots could not have been more different. They were gentry who not only claimed the spaces in society that seemed rightfully theirs but also built or assumed control of institutions like schools, museums, and universities with no resistance whatsoever. They enjoyed implicit respect in their own country and strove from the 1780s to make it Magyar.

By the 1830s they had made Pest a "Magyar Eldorado" but were far from satisfied. If Czech nationalists wanted equality of status in Bohemia, Hungarians wanted respect in Europe. And it was not just the backwardness of their country that troubled them: the poor roads, dirt, the outdated farming methods. It was their inability to replicate the lifestyles of West European counterparts, above all the English gentry. From the 1840s, this was the driving force behind the policies of the Hungarian political class: the quest to consume the goods of life in similar volume and quality as West European counterparts.[63] That meant that after the revolutions of 1848/1849, Hungarian nationalism became socially exclusive. Rather than advance Hungarian-speaking peasants and on their quests for upward mobility, Hungary's political elite fought against commoners' rights to education, indeed to equality, and focused instead on achieving Hungarian self-rule with as little interference as possible from Vienna.

Thus, before 1848 we see differing trajectories in the Hungarian and Czech national movements. Hungary's gentry patriots could focus on practical questions of running a state, while Czechs struggled for equality for language and culture in order to appear as equals in their own society. Still, in both cases, the national leaderships subscribed to liberalism, the doctrine of freedom. The overlap of liberalism with ethnic nationalism was perfect, for it claimed to liberate human individuals where they could fully realize their personalities: in the nation.

The challenges of historical justification differed sharply in each case. The Hungarian nobility claimed that it was the actual proprietor of the Hungarian kingdom and its laws; it was the "nation." The challenge, which it failed to meet in the decades after 1848, was to extend this sense to other groups, ethnic and non-ethnic, living on the territory of the kingdom.

The Czech patriots faced different challenges. Bohemia belonged to historic Germany, they were not of noble background, and they possessed no political institution to rival the Hungarian Diet. A-national Bohemian nobles dominated the *Landtag* in Prague, and thus a robust set of ideas was needed to lift the movement into stable political orbit. The ideas were a mélange: of the supposed special virtues of Czech people, who had stood up for freedom centuries earlier and had once freely united with the Holy Roman Empire but might now find a different path. The minimal boundaries of a future Czech polity seemed clear: the Bohemian crown lands, which the movement called the Czech kingdom.

But did not the full nation also include people who spoke languages that were closely related to the Czech spoken in Bohemia: Silesians, Moravians, and perhaps Slovaks? There was no doubt that whatever nation the Czechs constituted should govern itself, if under nominal Habsburg sovereignty.[64]

To prosper, the Czech movement needed mass mobilization. The leaders may have had the typical liberal suspicions about universal suffrage, but they could not treat the lower classes with simple contempt: the Czech movement was nothing if not a movement of the common people. And thanks to modernization, the national cause spread rapidly across classes and therefore exemplified the process of nationalization more markedly than elsewhere. Beginning in the 1840s, the increasingly modern world became a stage for Czech life through a combination of factors, ideal and real: through an ideology of self-sacrifice and virtue as well as the tangible benefits of profit and employment that flowed from creating businesses and institutions that were Czech. Like all nations, the Czech one was a human creation, but the process had assumed a momentum that by now was as forceful and unstoppable as any movement in history.

CHAPTER 5

Insurgent Nationalism:
Serbia and Poland

Serbia is at the far south of East Central Europe and belongs to the Orthodox world, Poland at the far north and overwhelmingly Roman Catholic. The Serb state with its nobility disappeared after the Ottoman conquest in the late middle ages, and the landholding elite became Muslim, while the Polish state lasted until 1795, when Prussia, Russia, and Austria wiped it from the map—but its gentry class survived intact. Therefore, Serbs were overwhelmingly peasants, while Poland retained an important leading class, who controlled and possessed land, and for centuries dominated politics. One influential political scientist has said that Serbia and Poland belong to different civilizations, one eastern and one western, and few would imagine there was much value to putting them together in comparative perspective and seeing what each might tell about the other.[1]

Yet these two countries (or better, these two societies) possessed an extraordinary structural similarity from the beginnings of modern nationalism, from years when enthusiasm about language was gripping Czech and Hungarian scholars. Serbs and Poles also passionately promoted their national causes, and although some did so through scholarship, the most effective, dramatic, and widespread method was military. Tens of thousands of Serbs and Poles took up arms beginning in the late eighteenth century in efforts to throw off foreign rule. This reflects a political impulse: the conviction that nations not only had to build language and culture but also must seize territory and create an independent statehood. This conviction that was quite foreign to Czech or Hungarian patriots, who for generations endeavored to establish self-rule under the Habsburg dynasty.

Polish insurgents had advantages. The first generations came from a Polish professional army, formed in the independent Polish state before 1795, as well as the semiautonomous Duchy of Warsaw created by Napoleon in 1807, with its own officer corps, regimental traditions, and professional training. By contrast, Serb insurgents were a guerrilla army, whose cadres were trained by the

Austrians to be deployed in border wars against the Ottomans from the late 1600s. Whereas Polish insurrectionists faced three of Europe's strongest military powers, Serbs confronted the beleaguered and declining Ottoman Empire and were aided at various points not only by Austria but also by Russia.

What Poland and Serbia shared beyond all their differences were congruent and forceful national narratives that pulled the willing, unwilling, and indifferent into participation and judgment in terms of common assumptions: who is the hero, who the enemy, and who the traitor in one's own ranks. Both movements had proud traditions of literature, music, art, but the leading intellectuals laid down their pens to shoulder rifles for a duty that exempted no one. The narratives persisted into the twentieth century, and in the 1940s one finds prominent writers in the anti-Nazi resistance in both cases, who wrote verse taught in the schools of Poland and Serbia to this day but who also sacrificed their lives.

These narratives relied on a deeper similarity that defies influential theories of nationalism: that many Poles and Serbs were nationally conscious before the dawn of modern nationhood. The number in Poland in 1800 exceeded a million, but in the Ottoman lands stretching from Macedonia and Kosovo north and westward through the Serb lands and Bosnia up to the Croatian borders, the number of nationally conscious South Slavs was several times greater. Extraordinarily, these Orthodox Slavs were almost entirely illiterate. In Bohemia by contrast, despite the greater number of people who could read and write, those who were nationally conscious around 1800 comprised at best hundreds, perhaps thousands. The Polish and Serb cases challenge the idea that mass national consciousness had to wait for modernization, in particular the advent of print culture, but also the modern roads and infrastructure that supposedly make a modern nation possible among people who were strangers.[2]

The high degrees of national consciousness have differing roots. Because the Polish gentry (*szlachta*) remained a social formation after Polish statehood disappeared in 1795, so did its consciousness of having historic rights, reflected for example in the slogan "*nic o nas bez nas*" ["nothing about us without us"]. The Polish gentry tended to be literate, especially its upper reaches, who were also multilingual and fluent in European political and cultural trends.[3] In the following generations, many migrated to cities and evolved into Poland's intelligentsia, the nation's leading stratum with obligations of political loyalty that were understood to be deeply moral. Many nobles would have no choice but to work with the occupying powers, but they had to explain why their collaboration constituted greater service to the "nation" than support of armed conspiracy, and that made them less than fully reliable agents of Romanov or Habsburg imperialism.

The logic of Serb nationalism is more elusive. In 1800 Serb peasants living under Ottoman rule possessed rudimentary rights at best, and all living connections to the Serb nobility had long since ceased to exist.[4] These Serbs knew that hundreds of thousands of their compatriots just across the border from Belgrade in the Habsburg military region enjoyed corporate rights to land and self-rule, and these proved minimal aspirations for them when they rose up against Ottoman rule.[5] Yet the deeper sources of national identity for them and millions of other South Slavs lay elsewhere: in the continued existence of the Serb and Bulgarian Orthodox Churches as incubators of historic memory; and in the widespread practice of South Slav peasants (especially in Serbia) to spend evenings singing epic poems of ancient heroes, a practice that dated back centuries and told them who they were as a people. They did not wait for historians like Palacký to learn that their nation and its independence were worth living and dying for. That sort of message had been repeated generation after generation in folklore they knew by heart, and what happened in the 1790s is that men and women gained opportunities to act on it.

* * *

As far as Austria, Russia, and Prussia were concerned, the original sin of Poland was political, not military. After these powers' first seizure of the lands of a weakened Polish state in 1773, a Polish leadership rose to new life. And in a fascinating combination of Central and West European statecraft, this leadership passed a constitution eighteen years later that created a representative government with executive power in the hands of a king who was hereditary in the Wettin house of Saxony. For the previous century, Russia had been meddling in the election of Polish kings, and therefore a nonelected Polish king who would appoint his ministers signaled a reduction of Russian influence. The new legislature would pass laws by majority, thus putting an end to *liberum veto*, which had required unanimous consent of the noble nation for passage of any law, thus giving foreign powers able to buy votes—above all, Russia—the power to stall reform.[6]

The Polish constitution was the second in the world, and like its American counterpart, it introduced a separation of powers: executive, legislature, and judiciary each had their own functions. Its drafters hoped to make Poland a modern society, and placed peasants, who constituted more than 80 percent of the population and lived under the often-harsh jurisdiction of their lords, under the state's protection. Lords retained local sovereignty (*zwierzchność*) as well as land, and still held considerable power, yet the *szlachta*'s class privileges were reduced. The impoverished among them lost voting rights, and full citizenship was extended to property owners in town and country, thus expanding the nation to include potentially everyone, regardless of class or ethnicity.[7]

The constitution invoked nationalism's absolute claims to obedience: Poland's independence was "dearer than life and personal happiness."[8] But the spirit was also liberal, showing that modern statehood in East Central Europe did not necessitate absolutist rule. Poland would become a constitutional monarchy with significant powers left to society, and for that reason, the new document was celebrated by Thomas Paine and Edmund Burke, and by many in the new American republic.[9] The drafters were aware of the dangers of their neighborhood and hastily passed the constitution by acclamation on May 3, 1791, while many delegates were absent due to Easter vacation. Support for the document was strong among the moderately wealthy nobility and burghers who stood to gain from a more open, equitable society, but was much weaker among the poor as well as very rich *szlachta*—magnates—because it reduced their ancient status privileges. In the country as a whole, it met with overwhelming support: in meetings of local diets (*sejmiki*) in February 1792, all but one approved Poland's new basic law.[10]

Catherine II of Russia and King Friedrich Wilhelm of Prussia acted quickly to make sure the constitution's promise to strengthen Poland was never realized, however. In May 1792, more than 100,000 Russian soldiers invaded the country and were joined a few weeks later by forces from Prussia. As in the 1968 intervention that would stifle the Prague Spring, the Russian forces said they had been invited, and that was true. In April Polish magnates had contacted Catherine and signed an act of "confederation" in St. Petersburg, aiming to return to the status quo ante, and they publicized the confederation at Targowica in eastern Poland. The magnates wanted to keep the central Polish state weak, and they portrayed themselves as patriots defending the historic "liberties" of the noble Polish nation.[11]

The Polish army was small but was spurred on by a new kind of patriotism, similar to the French troops that would soon conquer much of Europe in the name of a nation that included everyone. Led by General Józef Poniatowski, it scored a remarkable victory on the Bug River on June 18, yet the general's cousin, King Stanisław August Poniatowski, decided on a hasty capitulation. His former lover Empress Catherine told him that only by surrendering the constitution could he preserve the kingdom in any form. The king signed onto the Targowica confederation, which now introduced censorship, ended postal privacy, and persecuted supporters of reform.[12]

Yet the compromises did not even protect territory. Prussia, wanting compensation for losses in land suffered against the troops of revolutionary France, prepared to carve off chunks of Poland, and Russia agreed to collaborate, claiming the country was spreading the virus of revolution. In a second partition of January 1793, the former seized 57,000 square kilometers (1 million people), and the latter 250,000 square kilometers (home to 3 million people), leaving Poland only 212,000 square kilometers and 4.4 million inhabitants. The Polish parliament was forced to express approval and accede to foreign occupation, yet some reforms survived, like the end to the *liberum veto*. Still, nothing of consequence could happen in Poland without the approval of the Russian ambassador.[13]

The severance of lands tore developing markets to pieces. That, combined with heavy charges demanded for the Russian occupying armies, unleashed an economic catastrophe, making Warsaw the most expensive city in Europe. At the same time, news was filtering through of radicalization in France as well as unrest in Prussian Breslau and the Sudeten mountains, causing Poles to think resistance might succeed as part of pan-European revolution. Warsaw was suddenly a breeding ground for secret societies that maintained contact with reformers who had taken refuge in neighboring Saxony, above all Hugo Kołłątaj and Ignacy Działyński. They hoped to connect to the masses.[14]

What finally triggered a country-wide insurgency were Russian plans to begin inducting Poles into their army.[15] General Antoni Madaliński defied his orders and moved troops to Kraków, where he was joined by Tadeusz Kościuszko, a hero of the American Revolution, who had been promoting the Polish cause in France and Italy. On March 24, 1794, Kościuszko took an oath as resistance leader before an enormous crowd on Kraków's central square, announced a general mobilization, and vowed to achieve three things: freedom for all (that is, the Polish nation one and indivisible, with no status distinctions), the integrity of Polish territory, and self-government by the people.[16]

At first, Polish forces scored victories, memorably at the battle at Racławice north of Kraków on April 4, where peasants with scythes captured Russian guns. Within weeks, Poles had risen up and liberated towns in Lithuania, central Poland, and finally western areas occupied by Prussia. Because of the weapons stored in its armory, Warsaw was crucial to the uprising's success, and the city's population rebelled on April 17, freeing the city after two days' heavy fighting. Through the spring and summer, Kościuszko worked to fortify the capital and

FIGURE 5.1. Hanging traitors in effigy (1794). *Source*: Jean-Pierre Norblin de la Gourdaine, National Museum, Warsaw. Via Wikimedia Commons.

created a National Governing Council, staffing it with moderates. However, radicals predominated in the city government, and they publicly hanged Poles suspected of assisting the partitioning powers.[17]

By June, Polish forces had engaged Russian, Prussian, and Austrian armies, but were falling back. First the Austrians took Kraków, Sandomierz, and Lublin; then Russian forces seized Wilno and placed Warsaw under siege, with Prince Poniatowski leading the defense. Poles in Prussian territories to the northwest provided relief by liberating towns and drawing away Prussian forces, but from the east, a new and huge Russian army descended, scoring a decisive victory south of Warsaw on October 10.

The battle pitted 7,000 Poles against 16,000 Russians, and Kościuszko was wounded and captured. In the city, Polish Jacobins organized resistance and held it until early November, when 30,000 Russian troops overwhelmed the 14,000 defenders. The Russians commenced slaughtering soldiers as well as civilians in vengeance for the treatment their forces had endured five months earlier, when Poles cut down Russian stragglers trying to surrender.[18] A Polish force of 30,000 escaped south and was partly captured and partly just dissolved into the countryside. After eight months, the Republic had gone down fighting, but the country had been remade.[19]

At least that was the legacy as described in future works of history, which emphasized support for political independence coming from all corners of Poland as well as all strata of society. On a broader canvas, the Kościuszko uprising was the earliest mass armed resistance to foreign rule in Europe, the first time a nation in the modern sense rose up to assert sovereignty against invading armies. It followed closely on the French *levée en masse* of 1792, which had revealed the powers of a national mobilization cutting across classes. About 140,000 Poles passed through the ranks of the reformed army, and some 100,000 served in the peasant battalions. Thousands more joined the municipal militias. Earlier in the century, when Poland effectively became a Russian protectorate, the army had been a nonentity. Now it seemed to embody popular demands for independence, and the infantry wore a distinctive uniform with a navy blue jacket and silver shoulder straps as well as white trousers and shoes "in the Hungarian style."[20]

The uprising also marked a vital political transformation. The head of state was not a king but the popular Kościuszko, who, while not elected, was chosen by leading conspirators and served as undisputed leader among all who wanted Poland to be free.[21] Observers called the political reforms a Polish revolution, but it was not violent. Polish Jacobins carried out executions not for class reasons, but against treason, and the reform movement relied on the gentry, especially the moderate forces that predominated in the countryside. The transformations were social as well as political: peasants gained personal freedom, security from expulsion from the land, and a reduction in compulsory labor (the robot) from between a quarter and a half.[22]

Still, one might ask whether Poland would not have been better off with no rebellion. The country was still large after the second partition, and it might have persisted if no one had fired a weapon in anger. But there is also evidence that nothing Poland did would forestall partition. The London *Times* was astounded to get news of the May 1791 constitution (it arrived by courier from Berlin about three weeks later) and predicted that it would "probably bring forward some very powerful confederation against it." In the end, Poland may "become the victim of its own patriotism."[23]

And so one is left with the paradox that patriotism seemed self-destructive. But it was also unstoppable. Despite the willingness of leading magnates and many of the gentry to work on behalf of foreign interests, by the 1780s, forces had welled up in Polish political life demanding a well-governed state. These forces lay in the hands of no single person or group and ultimately won over even the vacillating king, who had joined the Targowica conspiracy in a misguided effort to salvage reform. Similarly, Kościuszko and other leaders represented broadly held views, and they were moved to action because Russia was about to destroy Polish statehood. Moreover, they thought they could win. In early 1792, Prussia was still technically an ally, and Austria seemed preoccupied with events in France.[24]

Neither then nor later did Poles condemn the revolutionary activity of the early 1790s as inappropriate or foolhardy. The basic lesson was that Poland would not continue to exist as a nation without struggle. Still, with a glance toward other East European nations, one can ask whether the struggle had to be armed. Czechs or Slovenes did not rise repeatedly and yet maintained themselves as nations. But their situation was fundamentally different. They had little to no history of independent statehood, whereas in 1773, Poland was one of Europe's largest countries. Yet as the London *Times* noted, it was an "unfortunately situated country."[25] Unlike Spain, Sweden, and England, it was not protected by the sea but was surrounded by enemies.

The uprising went down in popular memory as an "armed act" that came close to succeeding, and it gave many Poles an exaggerated sense of what they might accomplish with military or paramilitary force. In Poland's future insurrections (in 1830, 1846, 1863, and 1944) as in the 1790s, the urge to act was driven by a sense of both possibility and necessity—of a great European nation asserting itself—but it was not tempered by purely rational calculation. To exist was to struggle. Other nations of East Central Europe (except Serbia) do not have an insurrectionary idea woven into their national narratives.

Still, support for reform and insurrection was far from universal. Despite Kościuszko's promise to grant peasants personal freedom, many in the countryside remained skeptical.[26] For most ethnic Poles, "Poland" meant little to nothing, and though Kościuszko tended to be popular, many rural dwellers looked on his efforts with indifference. The failure to connect massively to the common people would bedevil future uprisings, which were seen as events of and for the gentry and intellectual elites. In 1846 the estrangement was so great that Polish peasants defended Austrian rule when an armed insurrection broke out, going so far as to bring the severed heads of their masters to the Habsburg authorities as a sign of fealty. The German-speaking "occupiers" seemed less alien than the landowners of their own ethnicity.

* * *

After contentious negotiations that almost brought them to war with one another, Russia, Prussia, and Austria agreed on a division of their spoils. They undertook a third partition in 1795, erasing Poland from the map. In a separate article of the treaty, they pledged to "abolish everything which could revive the memory of the existence of the Kingdom of Poland." Now that its "annihilation" had been effected, the kingdom's very name was to be suppressed "forever." This article bore intentions so evidently repugnant that the powers agreed to keep it secret.[27]

They also felt a need for public justification that differed from declarations issued by conquering powers of more recent vintage. Unlike the German and Soviet states in 1939, they did not claim to be freeing ethnicities (Germans or Ukrainians) from Polish rule. The Prussian kingdom of 1795 was not a German nation-state. Beyond claiming to stifle Polish "Jacobinism," the powers made specious historical arguments that were twisted to serve their demands for territory. Russia was retaking lands that had once belonged to Kievan Rus, and Prussia reclaimed lands that the Polish commonwealth had supposedly usurped centuries earlier. Austria said it was retrieving territories in southern Poland once claimed by the Hungarian crown, held by the Habsburgs since 1526.[28]

That the powers had to hide their intention to obliterate all traces of Polish statehood shows concern over a new sense of propriety: Poland disappeared just as modern ideas were dawning, according to which nations should rule themselves. The London *Times* spoke of the third partition as a criminal act and lamented that Poles, who had "tasted and relished the sweets of liberty" were being driven back into the slavery of "despotism."[29] One French newspaper called the 1795 partition immoral, a "monstrous violation of all that is sacred."[30] The partitions of 1772 and 1792 had been justified as restoring the European balance of power by compensating Prussia and Austria for Russia's earlier gains in the Ottoman Empire, but this final partition destroyed an ancient kingdom, not in a faraway place where violence little troubled Europeans, but in the heart of their own continent. It spawned the "Polish question," a rallying point throughout the nineteenth century for Europeans advocating liberalism's promises of self-determination.[31]

Therefore this last partition not only offended conscience but also created it. After the next failed uprising of 1830/1831, Polish émigrés flooded into Paris, Brussels, and London. They embodied a new kind of European: a people without a country, deprived of homeland and freedom, and forced to dwell under foreign rule that became more brazen and self-confident as the century wore on. Some influential Austrians, often of Polish ethnicity, excoriated the Habsburg monarchy's participation in this "great crime of the age."[32] In the 1860s the Austrian foreign minister Count Johann Rechberg expressed regret over Austria's complicity and advocated Poland's restoration—of course in federal unity with the Habsburg lands. The only major state that refused to recognize Poland's disappearance was on the continent's periphery: Ottoman Turkey![33] According to a legend popular in Poland, in his yearly reception of ambassadors, the sultan would complain that the emissary from "Lechistan"—Poland—had not yet arrived.[34]

The eternal claim in German quarters was that Poland was a "chaotic" country incapable of development, and therefore administrators from Vienna or Berlin assumed it would submit easily to the order they imposed. But they got a surprise. Polish gentry were mostly willing to collaborate, but the transition was not smooth. Part of Poland's "chaos" stemmed from the gentry's traditions of self-rule, which had been realized on vast holdings in land but also through the gentry's right to form confederacies and to manage their affairs in regional diets (*seymiki*). Ironically, it was the "excessive" local freedom that Poland's reformers had hoped to curb that now bedeviled the new rulers. But Poland's peasants also had little to celebrate: especially in areas controlled by Russia, they found years of promises of land and freedom null and void.

The 1790s were a time of turbulence across the continent, and the three-power rule in Poland had little time to stabilize. Austria and Prussia fought almost ceaselessly against first revolutionary and then Napoleonic France, with diminishing returns, causing Polish patriots to hope the French would aid them in recovering sovereignty. Here too, in this decade, a long-lasting theme in Poland's quest for independence was consecrated. It was about rights to self-rule in Poland, but the struggle could go far beyond Poland. Just as some Polish leaders had left Poland to plot from the safety of Saxony in 1792, now Polish soldiers went abroad to join foreign armies, hoping to advance the Polish cause. The mission of revolutionary France was universal freedom, and that now became the spirit of the Polish struggle; Polish patriots claimed to fight for "your freedom and ours."

In 1797 Henryk Dąbrowski, a Polish general who had served with distinction in the 1792 and 1794 campaigns, established French army units consisting of Poles who had deserted Austrian formations. The idea caught on. Over the next five years, 25,000 men flooded into these "Polish legions," which saw action on many fronts, especially in Italy. A song written for these men—who wore the words "free people are brothers" on their epaulets—has become Poland's national anthem: "As long as we live, Poland has not perished."

However, unlike the heroes celebrated in verse, many never returned to their homeland. In 1802 Napoleon sent some 2,600 legionaries to crush a slave rebellion in Haiti, of whom only 300 survived.[35]

After his victories over Prussia and Austria later in the decade, Napoleon carved out a small state from their Polish territories, the Duchy of Warsaw (1807–1815), with its own administration and an army that fought for France in Spain and Russia. Its leader, Prince Józef Poniatowski, a hero of the 1792 campaign, had encouraged the French emperor to take a southern route to Moscow, advice that was spurned. Poles suffered above-average losses in the Great Army, but they remained with Napoleon through his crushing defeat in the Battle of Nations at Leipzig in 1813, in which Poniatowski drowned in the Elster River while preparing a new assault. But the legend of Poles' ability to fight for freedom only grew, even if the fight was for a foreign hegemon far from Polish territory. There was a moment in 1809 when Austria was attacking the Duchy of Warsaw while Polish armies were fighting in Spain (in 1944, Polish paratroopers were dropped in Holland while the city of Warsaw rose up against the Germans).

After Napoleon's defeat in 1815, the European powers gathered in Vienna and returned Polish territory to Russian, Prussian, and Austrian rule. Yet they also declared the central Polish lands with the capital in Warsaw a "kingdom" under Alexander I of Russia, who now bestowed a constitution on "his" realm.[36]

However, the Russian king of Poland incensed Polish patriots by failing to uphold the rights this document guaranteed, and soon complaints multiplied: about censorship, the crushing of institutions of self-rule, and arrests and deportations for those who simply recalled Polish liberties. For example, authorities punished students in Wilno for chalking on a wall: "long live the constitution of 1791."[37] Polish culture blossomed in these years, and as in Bohemia and Hungary, patriots perfected dictionaries and began writing histories. But the Poles' nationalism focused on rights they should enjoy in a Polish state. The poet Adam Mickiewicz even poked fun at the Czechs for their "obsessions" with language.

By 1830 his generation's patience had run out, and Polish military cadets launched an uprising against Russian rule that November. The consequences were disastrous. Rights that Poles possessed imperfectly were removed entirely, and many leading intellectuals, including Mickiewicz and Frédéric Chopin, now left Poland and formed the "Great Emigration" in Paris, which came to number some 10,000 individuals.[38] Afterward, the cause of Polish nationalism in the occupied lands was simple: nationally conscious Poles were those who could not accept the loss of sovereignty and demonstrated their "nationalist attitude" simply by maintaining their identities as Poles.[39] And as their political freedoms shrank, Polish nationalism became more and more a cultural cause.

In some ways, the task of nationalists was simpler than in Bohemia. Poland had been a European state until recently, and less effort was required to create legends from its past. It had not only a history as a state, with kings, administration, and armies, universities, and literature, it also had a tradition of writing about those things dating back centuries. In 1800 there were thick histories of Polish statehood and literature as well as an unbroken literary tradition featuring dozens of outstanding political, military, and cultural figures.[40] The state did not exist, but the Polish gentry did, meaning that a basic sense of national consciousness did not need to be crafted, and, as mentioned above, it extended to more than a million individuals in 1800, versus perhaps a few thousand nationally conscious Czechs.

If patriots in Prague were spreading ideas from very old Czech history to arouse a sense of national pride in their own time, in the Poland of that time, a mythology had grown before people's eyes, but it was as contradictory as it was undeniable. Yes, there had been massive resistance against three powers under heroic leaders, but Poland would not have gone down without the complicity of some Poles against others. More than a legacy, this heritage provided a script for Poles of the nineteenth century: those who collaborated with Austria, Russia, or Prussia inherited the mantle of traitors who had once brought down the republic. In 1876 one critic noted that "democrats" were so suspicious of other nobles that they routinely accused them of resurrecting Targowica. He coined the word "treasonmania." For example, during the revolution of 1848, Prince Adam Potocki saved old Kraków from senseless destruction by Austrian forces by negotiating with the commander, only immediately to hear accusations that he was heir to the old confederacy of traitors.[41] Yet not two years later, the Austrians arrested Potocki for participating in a conspiracy against them.

Regardless of the impossible standards for being a loyal Pole and the widespread distrust, Poles continued organizing compulsively, in the spirit of old freedoms, and every generation staged its own armed uprising, whether against Austrian (1846), Austrian and Prussian (1848), or Russian (1863) rule. In the late 1800s, Poland's great national leader Józef Piłsudski began his career as a revolutionary who terrorized Russian authorities, for example, knocking over a railroad train and stealing cash for weapons. Before long, rivals who were politically to his right accused Piłsudski of being irresponsible and therefore a traitor.[42] But they themselves were not innocent of more serious charges of collaboration: their leader, Roman Dmowski, sat in the Russian Duma. In most political cultures, exchanging calumnies is common practice because it promises accelerated access to power. But in few is as much at stake as for those accused of treason in Poland: they must refute charges of standing in a long tradition of internal enemies who threaten their country's very existence.

The uprisings ended in disaster, revealing in part the failure of the gentry organizers to connect to the broader masses and in part the impossibility of dislodging increasingly modern states with police forces, bureaucracies, and growing armies. The imperial regimes also had advantages in propaganda: in the Galician uprising, Austrian authorities posed as protectors of the peasants and encouraged them to rise up against their lords, many of whom were connected to the conspiracy. The Polish-speaking peasants had become so alienated from the proudly Polish lords whom they slaughtered that they seemed to be a different ethnicity. The rebels also provoked the question of whether squandering Poland's chances in a foolhardy struggle might be seen to incorporate the worst features of the old commonwealth. Such questions provoked further charges and countercharges of treason.

* * *

Beyond Poland, only Hungary possessed a large group of nationally conscious gentry. As in Poland, the challenge for the patriotic gentry was to extend its notions of national consciousness to a largely illiterate peasantry. But in contrast to Poland, a Hungarian political entity—the Hungarian kingdom—continued to exist, even if the king was Habsburg. Within that kingdom, institutions thrived that were controlled by the Hungarian gentry, above all a parliament and schools that inculcated in children a sense of duty to the Hungarian nation. The challenge was building even more schools in a largely agricultural country and spreading the message to areas where Hungarian was not spoken.

Yet Serb patriots faced challenges unknown to their neighbors. There had been no kingdom of Serbia for hundreds of years, and over the centuries, the Serb nobility had gradually faded away, either on the field of battle or through emigration, Islamicization, or simple reduction to poverty. In general, the Ottoman rulers did not impose Islam, but they encouraged conversion by reserving positions of influence and distributing land to their coreligionists. Landowners, administrators, and the wealthy tended to be Muslims, and Orthodox Christian peasants formed an underclass of sharecroppers.[43] It was unthinkable that a Christian could have a position of authority or command over a Muslim, whether in the economy or in the state. When a Serb national leadership emerged, it was from the more successful livestock farmers and village notables.

Regardless of wealth, Serbs possessed a sense of national identity. Percentagewise, probably more Serb-speakers were conscious of their identity as Serbs, than Polish-speakers were of their identity as Poles. This is a bit of a mystery. There were no Serb political institutions, and unlike Polish or Hungarian elites, even the wealthiest Serb peasants in Ottoman territories could not read and write. Still, Serb-speakers across a vast space, who might never meet one another, nevertheless felt they were linked.

That feeling partly had to do with the Serb Orthodox church, the one institution that the Ottomans permitted to survive, with separate legal jurisdiction for Orthodox believers as well as recognition of Serb identity (as opposed to Greek or Bulgarian). The Serb church assumed almost all civil authority of the defunct Serb state and kept that state's memory alive by canonizing Serbian kings. Humble worshipers were reminded day in and day out that people of their own language had once ruled them and should do so again. The Patriarchate of Peć, a self-governing Serbian branch of Orthodoxy under the Patriarch of Constantinople, referred to the territory under its jurisdiction as the "Serbian lands." From 1557 that territory included Kosovo as well as old Serbia and also areas farther north in Hungary.[44]

But equally important was a cultural form that no institution could control, the Serb practice of epic folk poetry, maintained from time immemorial, of Serbs gathering in small circles or in their homes and listening to poems sung to the accompaniment of a one-stringed instrument, the gusle. The songs, produced from memory, could last for hours and were passed down from generation to generation because they gave people consolation and a way to make sense of oppression. Best known is the dramatic "Kosovo cycle," which recounts the glories of medieval Serbia, up to a moment of heroic sacrifice at the battlefield of Kosovo, where a Serb force met a larger Turkish army on June 28, 1389.

A battle did take place on that date, one of several through which the Ottoman Empire expanded northward, into new territories. The historical facts are unglamorous. The Serb kingdom had been shrinking since death of its last great ruler, Dušan, in 1355. In June 1389, the vassals of the leading Serb prince Lazar met the armies of the sultan on Kosovo polje, the field of blackbirds, and both Lazar and the sultan were killed. The battle was not decisive. After the sultan's successor consolidated his position, he made Lazar's widow accept his authority. Her daughter Oliviera entered the sultan's harem, and her son Stefan fought for the sultan, for example in 1396 at Nicopolis against Hungary, where he saved the day for his brother-in-law. In the meantime, his father, Lazar, had been sanctified in the Serb church. During the following century, all Serbian lands gradually came under Ottoman domination as the empire spread its influence north and westward.[45]

The fact of foreign domination rankled in the local population, and within several generations, epic myths had arisen that gave comfort and hope. Lazar was not a failed potentate and victim, but a virtuous martyr who had freely accepted death. In a version of the cycle transcribed from local singers by the great linguist Vuk Karadžić in the early nineteenth century, a grey hawk had come from Jerusalem as emissary from the Mother of God, giving Lazar a choice: either the empire of heaven or of earth. If Lazar selected the latter, all the Turks would die. Yet he chose heaven, because an empire on earth is brief, whereas heaven is everlasting. He therefore died with his men. But the myth was incomplete: this virtuous choice could not fully account for the misery of a present when Orthodox Christians were an underclass, and so it was expanded to include the promise of redemption for Serbia in the future: redemption from the evils of foreign rule.

The Kosovo cycle was sustained by the Serbian Church. Lazar became a saint, and so did the sultan's assassin Miloš Obilić. The former's bones were kept by monks in a Kosovo monastery. The Ottoman state was aware of the myths' power and tried to control it, for example, by burning the bones and other relics of Serbia's patron St. Sava on the Vracar Hill at Belgrade in 1595.[46] (This event contributed to massive support for an uprising against Ottoman rule that lasted until 1597.) Turkish forces also had the habit of gouging out the eyes of saints on frescoes and icons, who in Serbia often represented medieval kings and queens. Peasants understood such practices as attempts to sever their links to the holy powers of their saints, and thus to cut them off from their identity as Christians and as Serbs.[47]

Yet the passing of the Kosovo story from generation to generation could not be stopped. The poetry sung in the home provided perhaps the most effective form of a nation's passive resistance known in European history. When linguist Vuk Karadžić traveled about the region collecting folk songs in the 1810s and 1820s, he reported that every Serb home had a gusle, and it was hard to find a man who could not play it. After they were written down, the stories were amplified and embroidered, departing even further from actual historical presonages or events; and though they served to foster Serb identity, they were never purely Serb. Central heroes figured in Macedonian and Bulgarian epic poetry and were used to form a sense of identity in the emerging national movments in those regions as well.[48]

The combination of epic poetry and the unbroken continuity of the Serb (but also Bulgarian) Orthodox church therefore meant that illiterate Serbs (and Bulgarians) knew about their national identity and did not need the revelations of national patriots or the ideology of Herder for basic information on who they were or who the national enemy was. And whatever the intention, destruction of a people's holy images had the effect of uniting many Serbs in a simmering rage that carries into the present. The Serb and Bulgarian states that emerged in the nineteenth century would discipline and control the memory of such things through schoolbooks, but the basic matrix of identity was set, and in the Serb case it extended across a significant territory, up to the edge of the Croat lands.[49]

Neither Serbia nor any of the Balkan national states would emerge peacefully. They would take shape in war, often with the involvement of a Russian state keen to see its sphere of influence expand at the cost of Ottoman power. However, Serbia also benefited from the involvement of a second imperial power: Austria. From the early sixteenth century, Austrian authorities had granted Serb refugees plots to farm in the Military Frontier (*Militärgrenze*) region in return for promises to defend the land against attack, yet they had also taken these "armed farmers" (*Wehrbauer*) along with regular military units in raids across the border.

In 1788 Maria Theresa's son Joseph II unwisely joined Russia in a campaign against the Ottomans, "seeking vengeance for humankind against the Turkish Barbarians," and recruited a corps of volunteers from the Ottoman lands that helped take Belgrade in 1789.[50] Yet Joseph, a micromanager with militarist inclinations, insisted on commanding the troops personally, and he soon suffered setbacks. By the time of his death the following year, he was facing rebellion from within Hungary as well as threatening moves by Prussia at his northern borders.

His successor, Leopold, made peace with the Porte and returned to the status quo ante. But Joseph had made a lasting contribution to the Serb cause: the 5,000 guerrilla fighters he trained formed a core of Serb fighters who rose up against the Ottomans in a rebellion that broke out in 1804 against chronic misrule by the Janissary class, once elite warriors, but by that time a deeply corrupt mercenary corps that lived on plunder and tax farming. Fighting had been provoked in January, when four Janissary renegades decided to nip resistance in the bud and executed up to 150 local Serb leaders, placing their heads on poles.[51] At first the Serbs, led by pig farmer Karadjordje Petrović, fought with the approval of the sultan against the corrupt local regime that he had lost control of.

Originally from Serb Šumadija, Karadjordje had fled across the border to Habsburg lands with his family in 1787. After receiving training in a Serb unit under Habsburg command, he advanced through the ranks, taking part in the campaign of 1788. With peace restored, he returned home and became a wealthy livestock dealer. As Jannissary rule grew harsher, Karadjordje bought ammunition and traveled throughout Šumadija, encouraging rebellion.[52] Once launched, the uprising scored quick successes, aided by forces the sultan sent from Bosnia. Yet the Ottoman-Serb cooperation broke down when the rebels made clear they were fighting for the reestablishment of a Serb state. Tradition told them that justice could be achieved only through independence, and they made common cause with Serbs elsewhere in the Ottoman Empire, extending into Montenegro. In August 1805 the rebels defeated an Ottoman army, and history might have taken a very different turn if Austria's rulers had heeded Karadjordje's plea to extend Habsburg sovereignty over the Christians of Serbia and tear them away from "Turkish slavery." But Austrian leaders were preoccupied with challenges coming from France and declined his request.[53]

In 1807 a Supreme Council emerged to govern the freed territory, and the following year it elected Karadjordje as its leader, using the hereditary title "Voivode."[54] Karadjordje thus originated the dynasty that would produce the first Yugoslav kings in the following century. In a speech in 1809, he sketched his larger vision with reference to the Kosovo myth. "Twice the hopes of Kosovo Christians were dashed that they would once again govern their own lands," he said. "But now that almost all Slavic lands of the Turkish Empire have been liberated, we hope that the hour of freedom will dawn for Kosovo as well." Yet with Serbia's supposed main patron Russia preoccupied in the pan-European conflict with Napoleon, Ottoman forces regained Serb territory, and Karadjordje fled to Austria in 1813.[55]

The territory was not pacified, however, because Serbs remained armed and unreconciled to Ottoman rule; the continued resistance elicited cruel acts of vengeance.[56] In 1814 almost 2,000 women and children were sold into slavery, and about 300 men subjected to torture and death, mostly by impalement, placed out for public display in Belgrade on long stakes. The dying went on for days, and some of the unfortunate tried to goad Turkish passersby into shooting them to end their misery. But soon the fury exhausted itself, and some of the refugees returned, including Miloš Obrenović, a commander who had fought with distinction as a voivode in the first uprising. He belonged to a group that opposed the increasingly authoritarian Karadjordje.[57]

Obrenović led a second uprising in July 1815, which soon freed much of central Serbia (the Ottoman pashalik of Belgrade).[58] Because of Napoleon's defeat, Russia again had a free hand, and conditions were ripe for Obrenović and the Turks to cut a deal. He received de facto autonomy, and was recognized as supreme leader, or *knez*, Prince of Serbia. A National Chancery of twelve notables was set up in Belgrade as the highest court of the land, and Serbian officials gained power to collect taxes and administer the territory's affairs. Janissaries were forbidden to own land, and Serbs gained full amnesty and could keep their weapons. Four years later, the Porte granted Serbia autonomy under its patronage as a "principality." In the meantime, Obrenović found out that his rival Karadjordje had slipped across the border from Hungary and ordered him hunted down and executed, sending his stuffed head to the sultan as a sign of fealty.[59]

Through skillful maneuvering, Obrenović achieved full autonomy by 1830, including the right to set up an army, though the state technically remained

FIGURE 5.2. Assassination of Karadjordje. *Source*: Than Mór, National Museum, Belgrade; Historical Collection/Alamy Stock Photo.

under Ottoman suzerainty until 1878.[60] Except for one brief span when Karadjordje's son Alexander held the throne, the Obrenović dynasty remained in power until 1903, when military officers, outraged over the weakness of Miloš's descendent Alexander and his choice of a bride of ill repute, butchered the royal couple and put the grandson of Karadjordje—from this point King Peter of Serbia—on the throne.

The apportioning of property in the new Serb state was resolutely ethnic. In the early 1830s Muslims lost their rights to own agrarian land, and within a year they had to sell real estate in the countryside and small towns to Serbs; they were permitted to live only in the six cities where the Ottomans kept garrisons.[61] This "de-Ottomanization" of property went hand-in-hand with the exodus of Muslims from Serb lands, mostly to other Ottoman territories, like Bosnia or Macedonia. The exodus extended back to the Austrian-Turkish wars of the eighteenth century and had accelerated in the uprisings of 1804 and 1815, when Serb forces expelled Muslims from territories they seized. The overall effect was to de-Islamize Serbia: from the turn of the century to 1874, the population of Muslims in the Serb Principality dropped from more than 50,000 to fewer than 5,000. The state was intended to be Serb and Christian: when its understanding of citizenship was formulated in the 1840s, Muslims were excluded.[62]

As Muslims were leaving the principality's territory, Orthodox Christians were streaming in. This trend also went back to the late 1700s, when Orthodox Christians, like Karadjordje's family, had moved from poorer areas of Herzegovina and Kosovo to the relatively fertile lands by the Danube and in the Sava and Morava river valleys. After it took power in Belgrade, the Obrenović regime fostered the migration of tens of thousands more Orthodox Christians from Ottoman-held lands, chiefly from Bosnia.[63] The effect was to make Bosnia more Muslim and Serbia almost entirely Orthodox. When the regime was distributing properties that had been held by Muslims, it did so relatively equitably, preventing the emergences of large estates, or a native landholding elite, in great contrast to Poland.

The ethnically cleansed principality was meant to form the cornerstone of a large and independent Serbia after centuries of foreign rule ("slavery"). In 1844 Obrenović's Interior Minister Ilija Garašanin, aided by exiled Polish nobleman Adam Jerzy Czartoryski, produced a memorandum known as the "Outline" (*Načertanije*) which envisioned the Serb state expanding into the territories once held by the medieval empire of Stefan Dušan (1331–1355), and therefore claiming substantial Ottoman territories because Dušan's realm had extended into Macedonia, Bosnia, and Albania. The Outline spoke of the "holy historic right" of the Serb people to constitute such a state, taking all good and useful material, stone for stone, out of Turkey to do so.[64]

Yet now the question emerged of who precisely the Serb people were. Serbs in the Belgrade pashalik had a highly developed national consciousness, and they knew very well that other Serbs had migrated generations earlier into neighboring Habsburg Hungary and Croatia. They knew of communities of Orthodox Christians living in Bosnia, and they believed that the Muslims there were descended from Christians who had converted to Islam over the centuries ("renegades"). They also knew about states in the distant past that were Serb. Their situation thus had parallels with that of the German or the Czech movement: they, too, believed that the farthest extent of some earlier political entity would represent the minimum of the new state's boundaries. The question was: what would be the maximum? Were those old boundaries sufficient? As was the case in Germany or Bohemia, the answer fell to linguists, the most prominent being Karadžić, the genius counterpart to the Czech Josef Jungmann, who corresponded with Goethe and also knew the Grimm brothers, as well as Leopold Ranke and the Croat Ljudevit Gaj, from common circles in Vienna. He reached conclusions that were both similar to but also very different from those of Gaj.

In his 1836 essay "Serbs All and Everywhere," Karadžić wrote that Serbs were those who spoke variants of a dialect of Eastern Herzegovina that he had made standard in a dictionary published two decades earlier. The decision was revolutionary for Serbs because it meant rejecting the most popular model for written language, namely, church texts used for centuries. Now people would write just as they spoke. The average Serb may not have needed Herder to tell them what their nation was, but by recognizing *Volk* language as the soul of his people, Karadžić was nevertheless revealing a debt of Serb nationalism to the German philosopher.

The dialect of Eastern Herzegovina was Štovkavian, spoken in regional variations by almost all Serbs in Serbia but also by populations in Montenegro, Bosnia, and most of Croatia.[65] It was the same dialect selected by Ljudevit Gaj in his plans for creating an Illyrian people, and thus from the start, Serb and Croat ideas of who were Serbs and who were Croats overlapped, including parts of Croatia, and more fatefully, much of Bosnia. Karadžić considered Catholic and Muslim speakers of Štovkavian to be Serbs whose ancestors had converted and could easily be won back. Supposedly Serbs "of the Turkish confession" had

MAP 5.1. Extent of Štokavian subdialects of Serbo-Croatian

been seen kissing the bones of the Serb king Stefan at the Studenica monastery, reading prayers to him as well as giving tribute.[66] These "Serb Muslims" supposedly shared with Christians the millenarian hope of redemption to be brought by the Saint's return.

Ilija Garašanin's secret *Načertanije* shared this understanding of the Serb people, and its general outline guided state policy up to and beyond World War I. As it was slowly resurrected, Serbia was supposed to fill a huge territory, including Dušan's old realm in Serbia, Kosovo, Bosnia, and Herzegovina, in Montenegro, but also Slavonia, Dalmatia, the Adriatic coastline up to Trieste, Croatia along the Turkish border, and much of southern Hungary. And those were only the areas that were considered to be indisputably the homelands of Serbs! There might be even more Serb lands in Albania and Macedonia.[67]

Like Ljudevit Gaj, Vuk Karadžić was above all a scholar who endeavored to understand what might unite people across territory, and he did not advocate forcible assimilation, let alone displacement or "ethnic cleansing."[68] Yet he did project his findings as based on reason, valid even if Croats speaking the Štokavian dialect did not think they were Serbs. Karadžić knew that Croat patriots did not share his interpretation, but he believed that over time, they would call themselves Serbs, because otherwise they would be people without a name. Germans and Hungarians after all practiced several religions but were unquestionably peoples; foreigners would ridicule "Serbs" (that is, Štokavian-speaking Croats and Muslims) who thought they were different peoples because they worshipped God in different ways.[69]

The major difference between Karadžić and Ljudevit Gaj was that the former's ideas were easier to understand, seeming to involve people as they described themselves, and the heritage of a state that had a name. No people called themselves Illyrian. Moreover, Croat intellectuals began to fear (especially as Hungary strengthened after 1867) that as Croats they would be subsumed, if not into Hungary, then into Serbia. The result from the 1860s was a separate Croat national movement that focused not on fanciful linguistic unities, but on actual Croat rights deriving from actual Croat history. Still, Illyrianism, later called "Yugoslavism," never disappeared entirely because it had practical advantages. Union with Serbia, in whatever form, promised Croats protection from Hungary, Austria, and Italy, all of which had designs on Croatian populations and territories.

* * *

The language of Serb nationalism shared basic assumptions with the Polish variant. There was no talk of "voluntary" inclusion in the alien ruling empire. Serbs had not chosen Ottomans, and Poles had not elected Moscovites, and rarely if ever did these foreign rulers respect local rights and traditions. In 1795 Poland's occupiers had vowed to destroy even the memory of Polish statehood. By that point, Turkish rulers had held Serb territory for more than four centuries, and the country no longer had a native nobility. But consciousness of local rights remained, and in both places, foreign occupiers were seen as just that: usurpers who had taken power through force and not right.

Still, the Poles adjusted. Over the generations of foreign rule, countless nobles, gentry, city folk, and commoners loyally served the new regimes as soldiers or officials. The partitioning powers kept order and especially in the case
of Prussia, contributed to economic development. But as in Serbia, when
chances emerged to assert native sovereignty (under Napoleon before 1815,
under Austria after 1867, or after the collapse of empires in 1917/1918), huge constituencies were immediately available, eager to create national institutions.
What the imperial powers had established appeared to be stable, regulated statehood, but in fact it was a truce.

The ideas came from different sources. For Poles of the early and mid-
nineteenth century, there had been a state in living memory, and the freedoms
it guaranteed (even if imperfectly) remained part of family lore among the
intelligentsia. Few could argue that it was not worth fighting for. In Serbia, a
tradition persisted of insurgencies against the injustices of foreign rule conducted by brigands (known as *hajduks* and *četniks*), later trained by Austria.
Independence for Serbia likewise became a practically unquestioned value, especially as the uprisings in Serbia (but also in Greece and later the Danubian
principalities of Wallachia and Moldavia) gained results.

Nationalists remade early histories to suit their demands for independence.
That was easy in Serbia because of the absence of written documents about the
states and leaders of the fourteenth century. But in Poland the massive literature went unexplored, and patriotic venom focused on the supposed absolute
betrayal of the Targowica conspirators, who in fact were a brand of Polish patriots, reactionaries who had been eager to protect local privileges threatened
by reforms that culminated in the May 3, 1791, constitution. The debates on
whether those reforms could have improved Poland's position continue to this
day. If Poles had been content to remain under the Russian protectorate created
earlier in the eighteenth century, perhaps there would have been no partitions.[70]
Still, what Targowica accomplished was to crush a Polish effort at self-rule embodied in the 1791 constitution, a document still celebrated in Poland's national holiday. In retrospect, the historiography highlights the uncompromising and disregards the circumstances in which people like King Stanisław August
Poniatowski attempted to navigate through treacherous alternatives to partial
and relative goods for their country.

In the Serb case, few question the rationale of the insurgencies. On one hand,
the independence movement seemed to emerge as a force of nature from the
common people, and if not led by one group (for example, the followers of

Karadjordje), it would be (and was) led by another (the Obrenovićs). On the other hand, the insurgencies' successes seemed unquestionable. The extortionate practices of those whom the Ottoman state had entrusted to rule Serb lands had only hastened its decline. Serbia grew, and as it did, it slowly became an obsessive concern to the Serbs' one-time patron, Austria.

What was similar in Poland and Serbia was that a widespread sense of injustice of being ruled by foreigners caused people to conspire and take up arms, in irregular and regular formations, and that legends were created that persisted over generations, into the twentieth century and World War II. The basic idea, from the 1790s Kościuszko uprising, was that the insurgents represented a higher form of legitimacy than those who wore uniforms of imperial states. Polish and Serb nationalisms were among the purest early forms of anticolonialism. Two generations later, Lord Acton said that Poland's 1791 constitution (and its suppression) had "awakened the theory of nationality in Europe."[71]

Religious ideas were invoked to support both causes (more easily in the Serb case, because the church was national), and they strengthened with the expansion of Serb secular power. The Catholic hierarchy in Poland cautioned against acts of violence directed against constituted authority. But both Christian traditions provided a language for imagining and demanding rebirth and resurrection: "messianism." Both involved syncretism, the mixing of national and theological images, easier in the Serb case because the pantheon of saints included Serb princes. The Poles would also celebrate the elevation of a queen and several princes to sainthood, and they made the mother of Jesus "their" queen and their greatest bard proclaimed that Poland was the Christ of nations.

That was a message to indicate that the Polish struggle was for the liberation of all humankind, and just as Poles died for other peoples' freedoms (in Italy and later in Hungary), so non-Poles should consider the Polish cause their own. The hopelessness that descended on Polish thinkers after the crushing of the 1830 uprising gave their nationalism an ethereal quality that was unusual against the broader European background.[72] Still, the basic demand for the restoration of Poland resonated beyond the Polish lands. Throughout the nineteenth and twentieth centuries, both Polish and Serb patriots rallied support in foreign capitals, in Paris and Moscow, among broad publics, but also in diplomats' chambers. Remarkable in both cases was how the determination to struggle for "national liberty" survived even when the country was cut off from effective aid

FIGURE 5.3. "In the Name of God, For Our Freedom and Yours" (banner from the 1830 uprising). *Source*: Polish Army Museum / GFDL CC-BY-SA 3.0 or CC BY 2.5.

from beyond its borders. The traditions of insurgent nationalism explain why, in 1939 and 1941, the Polish and Serb governments were backed massively by their respective populations, across deep political divides, when they decided to defy German power, against which there was no chance of success, at least not in rational terms. Struggle, more often in defeat than in victory, had made them who they were.

PART II

The Decline of Empire and the Rise of Modern Politics

CHAPTER 6

Cursed Were the Peacemakers: 1848 in East Central Europe

Never before or since have Europeans seen common hopes smashed so rapidly as in 1848, the year of democratic revolutions. In February and March, after a disguised King of France escaped the wrath of his people, populations across the continent rose up against princes and kings, unified as never before, seeming to act according to one script. Divisions of nation or religion that had caused countless wars no longer seemed to matter, and even terms like "east" and "west" became secondary. The watchword was self-rule. Crowds demanding rights and democracy forced divine-right rulers to retreat and negotiate, from Italy and France through central Germany and into Bohemia, Prussian as well as Austrian Poland, all of Hungary (including Transylvania), and even farther east, into the principalities of Wallachia and Moldavia (the heart of today's Romania), still under nominal Ottoman rule. Everywhere in this vast space, Europeans were telling the same story: they were leaving feudalism behind for better lives under democracy. If kings or princes survived, they would be bound to constitutions, as was the norm in Britain or the Netherlands.

But as early as April, the push for democracy was exposing divides among populations that few had imagined existed, and the stunned princes began surging back, making use of resources, some old (like a well-trained military), others new and unexpected. For the Habsburgs, virtually every national group turned out to be a potential ally against German and Magyar democrats, but they also exploited class divisions, playing peasants off against urban liberals, and urban liberals off against suburban proletarians. When pogroms broke out across Central Europe in 1848, the House of Habsburg also revealed itself as the defender of Jews and their property against urban mobs, who claimed that Jews stood with their ethnic enemies. That house was not only a bastion of the old order but also a defense of life and liberty against an emerging new order, of liberalism and national self-determination, but also of seemingly intractable interethnic feuding.

By the fall of 1848, the Habsburgs and other monarchs were rebounding, even if the final victories were not scored until the spring and summer of 1849, when imperial authorities closed down the elected parliament in Austria and crushed the democratic revolution in Hungary, with the assistance of Croat, Austro-German, Serb, and Romanian forces recruited from within Habsburg territories. The fighting between Hungary's democrats trying to establish their national state and these nationalities became so intense that the region became a staging ground for ethnic cleansing: Magyar, Serb, and Romanian forces staked claims for territory by expelling ethnic others and burning their villages.

The difficulties of making a transition from feudalism to freedom were shocking because Habsburg subjects had not known the full extent of the realm's complexity. The historian Joseph Redlich wrote much later that censorship and poor internal communications had kept the various parts of the monarchy ignorant of one another. There was little critical higher education, and for the elites, the "state almost completely coincided with German Austria," and they assumed it would govern from Vienna with no concern for the "nationally foreign" inhabitants of the Sudeten and Alpine countries. Little was known about Czechs and South Slavs, and few anticipated that people speaking in their names might demand independence.[1] Inhabitants of Central and Eastern European were neighbors who got to know one another only after they had to deal with one another as free human beings for the first time.

Liberal Revolution

The first spark of revolution in the Habsburg realm came from the east, from a place that Metternich had called "Asia," territories just down the Danube river from Vienna that are now in Slovakia but then were Hungarian. On March 3, Lajos Kossuth, among the age's great crowd-rousers, delivered a fiery speech in the Pozsony/Pressburg diet, proclaiming loyalty to the Habsburg monarchy but also excoriating the misrule that had driven the land to bankruptcy. He asserted that absolute rule must stop. The time had arrived for representative institutions throughout the empire, in which the Hungarian kingdom would have a separate and special place.[2]

Such language had never been heard in public and caused a sensation when word of it reached in Vienna. State finances were indeed a shambles, and because of crop failures, floods, and rapid population increase, there was neither enough affordable food nor available well-paying work to sustain workers and their families. The result had been food riots, which were put down with great force in 1846 and 1847.[3] In cities, the growing proletariat was clamoring for reform and representation, but found, like the peasants forced to do labor for their masters, that the feudal regime did little to promote rational and productive development.

On March 13, a bright early spring morning, the feudal diet of the Lower Austrian Estates assembled in Vienna for its regular meeting, with some of the liberal deputies determined to push for a free press, citizens' militia, and a united imperial parliament that would deal with urgent questions like the budget. From before dawn thousands of students and urban workers had been milling about the old town to press demands for democracy. The revolution began when authorities overreacted by calling in troops, who soon found themselves caught in the maze of narrow alleys and assaulted by stones flying from all directions. A single rifle discharged, leading to a hail of stones, many shots fired, and fatalities on both sides. Yet municipal authorities were unwilling to summon the full force needed to crush the protests, and the soldiers withdrew.

In the nearby Hofburg, Prince Metternich and archconservative general Prince Alfred Windischgrätz urged the weak-minded emperor to stamp out the embers of dissent, but Ferdinand and his advisors decided on a course of appeasement. Metternich fled for England wearing a disguise, and soon the Crown was lifting restrictions on public association and expression. For the first time ever, Austria's journalists could imagine reaching workers or intellectuals and not just their prime audience of state officials. Among the first democratic institutions were a National Guard (about 30,000) and an Academic legion (about 7,000).[4]

Ferdinand promised his subjects a constitution, and he appointed a caretaker government of liberals under the moderate Baron Franz von Pillersdorf. On March 16, the monarch paid a visit to a unit of the Academic legionnaires, exhilarated by their freedoms but clueless about the interests dividing them from other Austrians, let alone from one another. The following day, Anton Füster, a radical democrat and Catholic preacher at the University of Vienna, had the sad duty of burying five students who had fallen in the early skirmishes. He was joined by the Protestant Minister and Chief Rabbi of Vienna in a joint procession that would have seemed progressive even decades later. "The old and the new testament marched together under freedom's banner," he later wrote. It was a divine delight to see young revolutionaries, whether Germans, Italians, Poles, Bohemians, Illyrians, Dalmatians, Moravians, Magyars, or Croats, working in "fraternal, magnificent concord."[5]

FIGURE 6.1. Revolution in Vienna (May 1848). *Source*: F. Werner (lithographer).
Via Wikimedia Commons.

At the news of revolution in Vienna, Hungary's political class was becoming more assertive in its democratic rhetoric, mostly in gatherings at cafes and taverns of Pest, Buda, and Pozsony/Pressburg. On March 15, perhaps the most celebrated day in Hungarian history, a crowd of more than 20,000 gathered in front the Viceregal council in Buda—the supreme administrative authority in Hungary—and forced it to accept basic liberal demands, including abolition of censorship, a national guard, and a parliament elected by the people. The leaders were a small cadre of young intellectuals, at the head of which stood the twenty-five-year-old poet Sándor Petőfi, who electrified his followers with the lines: "we swear that we won't be slaves any longer!"

Two days later, emperor Ferdinand named the liberal landowner Lajos Batthyány as head of an independent Hungarian government, and it began work on a constitution on the Belgian model of 1831. What convinced imperial authorities to act was not so much the mass mobilization in Buda-Pest as rumors of a peasant army being assembled by Petőfi.[6] The completed draft featured an upper house of titled nobles and a lower one elected by propertied males, meaning that about 7–9 percent of male adults would be enfranchised (more than in the United Kingdom in 1832). Citizens would be equal before independent law courts, and the security of person and property guaranteed. All tax privileges and restrictions on the sale of land were to be abolished, and equality was proclaimed for Christian confessions, though not for Jews. Peasants were to attain personal freedom, and labor services to be abolished, as were all restrictions on residency. The laws maintained a link to Austria through the person of the king, who retained the power to make war, but they did not specify exactly how the two states would jointly organize defense and finances. When Ferdinand signed the laws on April 11, Hungary became the first constitutional monarchy east of the Rhine.[7]

The country's diet had gone a step further than Vienna's revolutionaries and indeed, all other pretenders to power in Central and Eastern Europe, including German liberals, who were preparing their own constitution in Frankfurt. Whereas elsewhere, democrats demanded a transformation of feudal into modern institutions, in Hungary, the feudal institution—the ancient diet—had transformed itself into a modern one. The nobles themselves had approved measures limiting their privileges, but they did so to head off greater unrest in the countryside. Everywhere in the Habsburg lands, peasants were no longer performing hereditary labor services, and rumors spread of violent attacks on manor houses.

The constitution that Emperor Ferdinand proposed for Austria at this point left him the right to veto legislation and featured indirect elections to parliament according to a franchise that favored nobles and the wealthy. The result was to further radicalize political opinion, and again students took to the streets, demanding an end to all class and status privileges. The Pillersdorf government then extended the vote to all except day laborers and domestic servants, provoking even larger demonstrations, after which it promised complete male suffrage.[8] The newly elected parliament was now a constitutional assembly, but this would prove a high-water mark of revolution in Vienna. The court, fearing mob violence, took refuge in pro-Habsburg, conservative Innsbruck.

Revolutionary forces in Vienna divided as radical republicans grew in strength and moderate elements receded. For example, the middle-class National Guard shrank to about 7,200, while the more extreme Academic legion remained strong. In the leadership, radical democrats prevailed, including the junior professors Dr. Josef Goldmark and Dr. Adolf Fischhof. Fischhof, a figure in Austrian politics for decades, would be the first person in the Viennese *Landtagshof* to demand freedom of education and press, trial by jury, and mutual settling of interests by Austria's nationalities. Students continued demonstrating to keep up pressure on the government, serenading by name those ministers who fell out of favor, and Fischof took control of a "Committee of Safety" to run the city's affairs, echoing Paris in the 1790s.[9]

The government's retreat continued before the radicalized citizens of Vienna but also before the nationalities. Besides the Magyars, the Czechs and Slovenes were clamoring for rights, and the Italian provinces of Lombardy and Veneto prepared to leave Austria for good as a movement for Italian unification spread across the peninsula, supported even by the recently elected Pius IX, who urged Ferdinand to release his Italian possessions and sent 16,000 troops to guard the Po border.[10] Revolutionaries, some carrying the pope's image, expelled Austrian troops from Milan and forced General Josef Graf Radetzky von Radetz, the empire's finest field commander, to withdraw to four isolated strongholds by March 23. His ethnically mixed forces held up well, though some Italians deserted.

Liberals in Vienna faced a quandary. On one hand, their political ideals favored unification of nations like Italy, yet on the other, they wondered what would happen to Austria if all the nationalities began acquiring independence. Surely the empire would slowly unravel. For conservatives like Radetzky, a Bohemian nobleman who liked to chat with soldiers in Czech, there was no question that Italy, like Bohemia or Hungary, was an integral part of the Habsburg domain and must remain so. Such views pervaded court circles who observed events with growing alarm. By the summer, a camarilla had emerged at the Innsbruck refuge that was determined to revert to absolute monarchical rule at the soonest possible date.

At its center stood the iron-willed Archduchess Sophia of Bavaria, spouse of Ferdinand's brother, Archduke Francis Charles, and reputedly the "only man" at court, who had been boundlessly humiliated by the emperor's concessions from earlier in the year. Later she told one general: "I could have born the loss of one of my children more easily than I can the ignominy of submitting to a mess of students."[11] Her own husband seemed indecisive, but she found support among military men like Radetzky and Windischgrätz, and among gifted monarchist officials interested in a strong, rationally governed state, especially Windischgrätz's brother-in-law, Count Schwarzenberg, but also the brilliant legal thinker Franz Stadion, Galician Governor Bach, and the Adjutant General Prince Lobkowitz.[12]

Besides the army and bureaucracy, two advantages helped these plotters reassert Habsburg power. One was Sophia's son, seventeen-year-old Francis

Joseph, whom she had groomed for the throne and trusted as loyal, principled, and reasonably talented. He had not been compromised by promises to the "mob" that Ferdinand had made in April 1848 and would fuse together the regions of the empire with his own will.

The second advantage was the empire's diversity. While students and the proletarian revolutionaries advanced ever more radical demands in the cities, Ferdinand had appeased the peasants by abolishing serfdom. But the realm's national divisions offered even greater promise. Magyar gentrymen had demanded autonomy, but Banat Serbs and Transylvanian Germans had traditions of self-rule, and from March 1848, Romanians and Slovaks (groups all but unknown to the Western European mind) likewise began clamoring to rule themselves. But most troublesome, and therefore hope-inspiring, was Croatia, a kingdom within Hungary, whose nobles knew their ancestors had freely entered a pact with Hungary in the eleventh century. Some were liberal, and many deeply conservative, but all were alarmed at the noises coming from the new Hungarian capital at Pest about making Hungary—including Croatia—"one and indivisible."

Hungary's leaders recognized the separate existence of civil Croatia but not of other parts of historic Hungary like Slavonia or the Military Frontier, areas with mixed Serb and Croatian populations. Their April laws said nothing about minority rights and established Magyar as the language of the land. Lajos Kossuth knew there were many "races" in Hungary, but he feared that recognizing any of them would generate a subdivision by cantons; in his mind, Serb, Slovak, Romanian, German, or Croat corporate rights were "harmful vestiges" of feudalism. He and fellow liberals aimed to centralize the state on the French model, so that everyone in Hungary was included in the Hungarian nation. Even political moderates among the Hungarians rejected concessions, and when realistic ideas did emerge to conciliate Croats Romanians, they came too late.[13]

In a stroke of luck for the Habsburgs, the position of viceroy (*Ban*) of Croatia became vacant in March, and after receiving advice from conservative Croatian nobles as well as the Illyrian patriot Ljudevit Gaj, Ferdinand chose as new Ban Josip Jelačić, an unmarried career officer who lived among and for his troops, elite guard units of the Military Frontier (*Grenzer*), a colorful mixture of Croats, Serbs, and Montenegrins.[14] In April Jelačić also became lieutenant field marshall and supreme commander of the Croatian segment of the Frontier. He was a Croatian nationalist whose statue adorns the central square of old Zagreb, but equally important, he was an Illyrian, and like his friend Gaj, he hoped to form a large South Slav state under Habsburg rule that would include

MAP 6.1. East Central Europe, ca. 1848/1849

Legend:
- Habsburg territory, 1848–49
- Ottoman territory, 1848–49
- Habsburg military frontier

RUSSIAN EMPIRE

GALICIA
- Tarnopol
- Lemberg
- Lublin
- Krakow

SILESIA
- Breslau

KINGDOM of SAXONY
- Leipzig
- Dresden

Bohemia
- Prague
- Regensburg

Moravia
- Brünn

KINGDOM of BAVARIA
- Ansbach
- Würzburg
- Munich
- Augsburg

Frankfurt
GRAND DUCHY of HESSE
GRAND DUCHY of BADEN
KINGDOM of WÜRTEMBERG
- Stuttgart

SWITZERLAND
- Zürich

Lower Austria
- Vienna
Upper Austria
- Linz
- Salzburg

Salzburg

Tyrol
- Innsbruck

Venetia
- Verona
- Mantua
- Venice

Lombardy
- Milan

KINGDOM of ITALY
PARMA
MODENA
PAPAL STATES

KINGDOM of HUNGARY
- Debrecen
- Buda
- Pest
- Arad
- Temesvar
- Pecs

Transylvania
- Brasov

Styria
- Graz
Carinthia
Carniola
- Ljubljana

Croatia
- Zagreb
Slavonia

Istria
- Trieste
- Fiume
- Zara
DALMATIA

Sremski Karlovci
Belgrade
Military Frontier

ROMANIA
- Bucharest
- Craiova

BULGARIA

SERBIA

BOSNIA
- Sarajevo

Adriatic Sea

Scale: 0 50 100 km
0 40 80 miles

Catholic Croats as well as Orthodox Serbs. Thus he threatened to disrupt Hungarian rule along the southern border, appealing to Croats to the west and Serbs to the east.

As early as March, Habsburg officials were planning to reimpose central rule on Hungary, but they maintained a veneer of loyalty to Hungary's constitutional government. Jelačić also played a double game. On one hand, he nodded when imperial officials reminded him that he was technically subordinate to Hungary's government, yet on the other, because of the growing power of the Camarilla around Archduchess Sophia, he understood that his value to the crown increased when he defied the Hungarian government. He thus refused to take a customary oath of allegiance and began purging Hungarian officials from Zagreb County.[15] Through a concerted campaign against all things Magyar, he gained support among diverse strata in Croatia: nobles, conservative and progressive intellectuals, and peasants.[16]

In March the assembly in Zagreb had tried to do for Croatia what the diet in Pozsony was doing for Hungary. It resolved to pursue its own foreign policy; created a national bank, army, and university; and passed a smattering of liberal and national rights, like equality of citizens before the law and the use of Croatian in the Catholic Church, schools, and the administration. Like their Hungarian counterparts, the drafters buttressed their demands in arguments about historic rights to territory. Elections based on indirect suffrage took place in May, with about 2.5 percent of the male population taking part. Even so, the Croatian parliament (*Sabor*) was different from the old noble-dominated body, and it voted in modern reforms, like taxes for the nobility and clergy and the abolition of serfdom.[17]

Croatia's lawmakers then directed their revolutionary gaze to the national question. Much more was at stake, Jelačić told the Sabor, than even culture and language: the time had come to connect with the empire's entire Slavic population. He was echoing demands from the streets. "Half the empire are Slavs but time and again we are squeezed and tortured like no other people," Zagreb's students complained. "Do you know what freedom is without nationality? A body without a soul."[18]

Farther to the east, Hungary's Serbs had been staging meetings from the first days of freedom. Their revolutionary council chose the young Habsburg officer Djordje Stratimirović to carry demands for political recognition to the Hungarian government at Pest. On being told that such recognition was out of the question, he swore to seek satisfaction elsewhere, causing Kossuth to quip: "in that case, we shall cross swords." What the Hungarian leader did not know was that Serbs in Hungary were receiving armed volunteers from the Serb principality across the border, with the knowledge and approval of the Austrian Consul in Belgrade.[19]

In May, the Habsburg Serbs staged a "National Congress" at Sremski Karlovci in the Miltiary Frontier under the leadership of Orthodox Metropolitan Josip Rajačić. They elected Stephen Šupljikac, a colonel of a frontier regiment, as their national leader (*Voivode*); thus the region's name: Vojvodina. The population was about one-third Serb, almost a quarter Hungarian, and a quarter German, with a sprinkling of Croats, Slovaks, and Romanians, yet Serbs claimed rights based on promises made centuries earlier by the Habsburgs, the most important being the right to elect the Voivode. Šupljikac vowed to draw up a constitution, and in June he traveled with other Serbs to Zagreb to form an alliance with the Croats.[20]

The mood was jubilant when they appeared in the Croatian capital, with the evident manifestations of pan-Slavic unity. On June 5, Serb Metropolitan Rajačić, accompanied by Catholic bishops, swore in Jelačić, calling on him to "protect the august house of Austria, our common good, sweet liberty, *our nationality*, the honor and glory of the Triune Kingdom."[21] The Croatian Diet worked out its own program for a greater Illyrian province, with all areas inhabited by Slavs to be given extensive home rule. This was the first mass display of Illyrianism (later called "Yugoslavism"), and from the start it succeeded best when the enemy was clearly identified. On his deathbed, Jelačić would recall that South Slavs expected him to liberate territory all the way to Istanbul.[22]

Following this meeting, Jelačić accompanied a delegation of Serbs and Croats to the Habsburg court at Innsbruck, from which members of the Hungarian government had just departed, assured of the court's continued respect for their April constitution.[23] The emperor even handed Hungarian Prime Minister Batthyány scraps of paper—"manifestos"—to allay his concerns: the first rejecting independence of the Germans and Romanians of Transylvania, the second charging his and not Croatia's government with defending the Military Frontier, and the third suspending Jelačić from his offices as Croatian Ban.

The final manifesto did not spoil Jelačić's visit because he was not told about it. While warning the Croat leader to desist from separatism, the emperor gave him an opportunity to speak at length. Reportedly Jelačić expressed his passion for Austria so fervently that the empress and Archduchess Sophia were moved to tears. It was only on his way home that word reached Jelačić at a provincial post station that he was no longer Ban; yet at the same time, he received confidential communications telling him the court continued to stand with him.

And its fortunes were improving. Field Marshall Radetzky had just taken the Venetian city of Vicenza and reestablished lines of supply, and he was planning to expand his offensive in northern Italy.[24]

The Hungarians got unwelcome surprises when they attempted to assert their control of the Military Frontier at Sremski Karlovci/Karlóca on June 10. After being repulsed, they saw to their amazement that the Serb forces firing on them flew the same imperial flag and wore the same uniforms as they did. They were led by 26-year-old Lieutenant Djordje Stratimirović, the man who had defied Kossuth. He was operating under direct orders of the Serb Main Council (*glavni odbor*) while his Hungarian opponent, General Janos Hrabovszky, commanded the garrison at Pétervárad. Both claimed to be asserting legality—the former Habsburg imperial, the latter Hungarian constitutional. Emperor Ferdinand prolonged his court's duplicity by confirming battlefield promotions on both sides.[25]

The fighting marked the first time that armed forces claimed territory in East Central Europe in the name of ethnicity, and it resulted in the region's earliest ethnic cleansing.[26] Tabulating casualties and damage was impossible. All that emerged with certainty were stories of atrocities on both sides: of the other acting first and committing unspeakable brutalities against women and old people, including the "disfiguring" of victims, and ritual acts aiming at ultimate humiliation. The cleansers left spaces so marked by horror that no one would think of returning, setting houses ablaze, throwing their living inhabitants into the flames, and then egging on bystanders to join in the violence.[27] The violence was all the more tragic as the area had been resettled after the devastating Turkish wars of the seventeenth century and become a dense mix of ethnicities, where Serbian, Romanian, German, Slovak, and Bulgarian settlers of the Catholic, Orthodox, and Protestant faiths lived together at peace. The ethnic cleansers also planned resettlements and population transfers; all that was lacking was time to carry them out.[28]

The revolution set loose pogroms in and beyond Hungary.[29] In Pest, crowds began attacking Jewish businesses in mid-April, but the police managed to restore control. Some observers said that the violence was triggered by a drive against paying rents to property owners, some of whom were Jews; but others claimed the middle classes had provoked the attacks to distract from radical social demands. For example, in March 1848, the message had gone out to mobs that property owners would lower rents, if only they did not face unfair competition from Jews. Jews were also associated with politics that the petite bourgeoisie did not like, for example, "ultra" republican rule. This was a harbinger of things to come in East Central Europe: perhaps for the first time, "red" politics was delegitimized by association with Jews.[30]

Farther north in Pozsony/Pressburg, ten Jews were killed and about forty wounded on April 24. The rioters were young and from the lower middle class, called "rabble" in period accounts, mostly apprentices and journeymen who felt threatened by the revolution's promise to emancipate the Jews. For example, before March 15, Jews could not work as night watchmen or cart pullers, but the following day, they were seen at city hall and doing service in the National Guard. Christian shoemakers thus felt a sudden advance and sudden decline in status: they had achieved the right to stand guard duty, only to share this honor with Jews. Batthyány and Kossuth responded by "excusing" Jews from this service and by ousting them from the Committee of Safety. Hoping to forestall further violence, some Jewish leaders retreated from demands for full emancipation.[31]

Seeing a liberal government yield to mobs caused many Jews to feel betrayed. Batthyány was willing to risk nothing for them, and simply repeated hackneyed phrases about Jewish usury and separatism as somehow justifying the popular hatred. But when Batthyány told Jewish committee members to give back their weapons, some refused. According to one eyewitness, "manly resistance" from Jews who had recently bowed to him annoyed the proud magnate. Within a few weeks, pogroms died down in Hungary but then spread to Bohemia and Germany, breaking out almost anywhere a suggestion was made that Jews would be emancipated.[32]

Bohemia

Just as General Hrabowski was preparing to storm Sremski Karlovci, the much better-known General Prince Alfred von Windischgrätz was launching a full-scale assault on the Bohemian capital, Prague, pitting soldiers against students, with Germans and Slavs on both sides. Yet the conflict was less violent than in Hungary, featuring few tales of atrocities. In all, some sixty-three persons were counted dead, including Windischgrätz's own wife, Eleonore, a sister of Count Schwarzenberg, who was killed by a stray bullet. The fact that the number could be tabulated precisely was reflective of restraint but also of the struggle's brevity: it lasted from June 11 to June 17. Yet for the fate of revolution in the Habsburg lands, this clash was decisive, marking the revolution's first setback as well as the first major sign that the regrouped absolutists were reasserting authority.

Windischgrätz's assault was a shocking coda to an experiment that had begun auspiciously in early March, when each day's mail coach brought news of an Italian potentate or German prince bowing out the day before. Secret political groups met irregularly in Prague's cafes and clamored for action, yet with Metternich still in power, there was no hope for a mass meeting. Therefore, a group group calling itself "Repeal" (after the Irish association) sent out invitations to "honest Czechs," to meet on Saturday, March 11, at the St. Václav baths, one of few secular spaces in the city that could hold a crowd.[33]

These early Bohemian democrats represented no political party because none yet existed; instead they stood for liberal and radical tendencies, of which the latter tended to predominate. None of the established and famous Czech patriots—such as František Palacký—appeared at the first meeting, where the demands were national and social: equality for the Czechs but also justice for workers. The thousand or so attendees were young and united in the will to break the chains of political absolutism. And they were courageous, acting in clear violation of the law, before revolution had prevailed in Vienna. The organizers included a roofer, inn-keeper, miller, several students, and a lawyer.[34]

The invitation to Czechs did not exclude Germans, yet because Prague was mostly Czech and those who attended were from the social margins, Czechs (especially upwardly mobile students) formed the core constituency. The Germans among the early revolutionary leaders tended to be radicals, who, for the sake of social change, were willing to support language rights for Czechs.[35]

A petition was formulated for the emperor that recognized two nations in Bohemia, yet only the Czech was "original and therefore had paramount right to the territory." The drafters demanded democracy for all lands of the "Czech crown": Bohemia, Moravia, and Austrian Silesia, thus making the earliest public call for "Bohemian state's rights," the demand that the Bohemian Kingdom in the borders of 1740 and its supposed legal integrity must serve as the basis of a nationally oriented political order.[36] In fact, as an administrative unit, the kingdom had ceased to exist with the Theresian reforms of 1749, and historically there had never been a central parliament for the three crown lands.

With this demand, Czech nationalists were advancing from romantic antiquarian enthusiasts to active political subjects. By referring to the rights of an ethnically Czech people, they were also moving beyond anything that could be traced to a legal document before or after 1740. No sovereign had ever made an agreement with Czechs. Yet the patriots traced Czech claims to Bohemia to a time before sovereigns, to west Slavic Czech and Moravian tribes' arrival in the seventh century. The argument hinged on the linguistic coincidence that the words for "Bohemian" and "Czech" are identical in the Czech language, thus naturalizing the idea that the Bohemian kingdom was Czech. Yet for those who spoke only German, the argument was incomprehensible; for them, it seemed equally axiomatic that *Böhmen* was a province in Germany and had been for hundreds of years.[37]

The petition was about more than national rights, however, and like documents drawn up by revolutionaries in Zagreb, Budapest, or Vienna, it also laid claim to civil liberties and social rights: freedom of the press, an independent judiciary, inviolability of the person, freedom of religious practice, the ending of feudal privileges of landowners, the lifting of hereditary serfdom and robot, equality before the law, and proper teacher training. Early drafts had featured more radical demands for publicly guaranteed wages and work, but these demands were missing in the final version: ironically, as the revolution succeeded and old authorities retreated, much more circumspect liberal forces gained courage to assert their views in public.[38]

On Sunday, March 19, a delegation took the petition to Vienna by special train, celebrated by crowds along the way, and Emperor Ferdinand committed himself to a unified government for the Bohemian crown lands and national equality in schools and in the administration, with the details to be worked out in a constitution.[39] The Bohemians knew that the Hungarian diet was drawing up a constitution for the Lands of St. Stephen at that very moment and were disappointed that Ferdinand did not approve convening a parliament in Prague. Still, they were heady about the possibilities for self-rule after decades of repression, and students as well as burghers set up militias to defend the new order, while newspapers proliferated, representing a diversifying political spectrum.

Yet for the moment, divisions of opinion on politics seemed not to matter, and Bohemia was awash in the colors of the land: parasols and bowties in red and white, in German as well as Czech districts. On March 18, the mostly German-speaking spa town Karlsbad was decked out in red and white, with women and children wearing cockades. Newspapers spoke of Czechs and Germans as "one body," united under a common king and history, jointly suffering for the same fatherland. Prague's Germans seemed sympathetic to the more evident presence of the Czech language in public affairs. Foremost was everyone's enthusiasm for the promises of democracy, celebrated in constitutional dances, hats, and croissants.[40] Manual workers, students, writers, but also innkeepers and farmers rushed to support a "National Committee" that had emerged during the early meeting at St. Václav baths, and patriotic processions included

Catholic priests as well as Protestant ministers and rabbis. On March 24, dozens of German and Czech writers in Prague said they felt elevated by the new freedoms, and that the promotion of equality for the Czech tongue would not disturb their unity.[41]

But beginning in late March, agitators, some from outside Bohemia, began arousing contrary hopes among Bohemian Germans: of their belonging to a great German state extending from the North Sea and the Baltic to the Alps and the Adriatic. Nothing in the vision of a "Bohemian kingdom" could compare. Those who asked about the rights of Czechs in a Bohemia were told that the new German state would be a federation recognizing the independence of individual lands, like a huge Switzerland. But fear as well as condescension began creeping into the German voices. How dare Czechs think that their numerical superiority in one German province might give them special status! The Bohemian German liberal Franz Schuselka pronounced his idea that Czechs would be absorbed into the higher culture.[42]

The problem for Bohemia was that, unlike in Switzerland, there was no way of dividing ethnic groups. Zurich was German and Geneva French, but the towns of central Bohemia had mixed populations. Small issues that no one thought of in March now took on huge import. What language would be spoken in the National Guard? No compromise could be found, and the Guard split into the German Concordia and the much larger Czech Svornost. Students divided into associations called Teutonia and Slavia, with Czechs dressed in old-style costumes and making use of supposedly ancient Slavic greetings. Any organization or fashion that could be was nationalized. Czechs refused to admit people to the National Committee who wore German cockades, and in response, Germans left the committee and created a "Constitutional Club," which, because it was perceived as pan-German, caused the Czechs to found their own pan-Slavic "Slavic Linden."[43]

The most charged question was what flag to fly because it signaled ethnic ownership of land. In early April, a student from Dresden recommended flying black-red-and-gold in Prague because he had seen the colors hoisted to the spire of St. Stephan's Cathedral in Vienna. (Czechs would not hear of it.) By contrast, Croats visiting Vienna had been horrified to see German national colors flying not only from the cathedral but also from the palace, making them feel alien in what they took to be their country's capital city. They liked the idea of Austrian patriotism, but what they were seeing among Austrian Germans was new and threatening to a national identity that they themselves were just growing to appreciate.

Germans were getting painful evidence of what democracy—power of the people—meant when applied to Bohemia. Prague, a city they had assumed was two-thirds German, had, in one of history's great transformations, come to seem like a Czech city. And the process had taken just a few weeks. With unseemly self-confidence, Czechs paraded and sang in their language, manifested Slavic identity, and made the privileged feel destabilized and alienated. As Czechs made Prague the key to their national existence, Germans became threatened by the status of a minority, a nightmarish existence from which liberalism offered no escape.[44]

The full extent of this problem became evident to liberals elsewhere in Germany in early April. In preparation for uniting their country, leaders of the Frankfurt pre-parliament sent invitations to political notables across German lands to help elect an assembly that would draft a constitution. In Bohemia, they turned to "Franz" Palacký, but he astounded them by replying that he was in fact a "Bohemian of Slavic origin," who had sworn eternal service to his small people. Historically, he wrote, Bohemia had been connected to Germany at the level of princes but not people, and the lands of the Bohemian Crown—*koruna Česká*—maintained an integrity that was not affected by the crown's historic association with the Holy Roman Empire. If the time had come for Germans to rule themselves, then they must recognize that Czechs also had rights to self-rule.

As a democrat, Palacký worried that German liberals would include Austria in the new Germany and destroy the Habsburg monarchy, leaving other small peoples of Eastern Europe on their own. Slavs, Romanians, Magyars, and Greeks as well as the remaining Germans, for example in Transylvania, would be at the mercy of a Russian colossus driven to become a "universal monarchy" by subjecting ever more peoples to despotic rule. As Europeans strode toward their democratic future, Austria would take on the mission of protecting the small peoples from the eastern mega-power. He now wrote his most famous words: "If it had not already existed, the Austrian imperial state would have to be created, in the interests of Europe, and of humanity."[45]

In a political program that crystalized from this sentiment, known as Austro-Slavism, Palacký included Germans and Magyars among those peoples threatened by Russia, but he also aspired to protect Slavs from German and Magyar hegemony. For years he had been fighting against German dominance in Bohemia, and from decades of close connections to Hungary, going back to his teen years, he knew that Hungarian liberals considered Slavs a people unworthy of nationhood, fit at best to be Magyarized. Now the prospect of German and Magyar nation-states made traditional German and Magyar condescension more dangerous than ever.

Therefore, Palacký supported plans that had emerged in Croatia and Poland for a congress to be held in Prague in which "Slavic" representatives from across East Central Europe would discuss how to strengthen Slavic unity. Enthusiasm for the congress had spread quickly among Prague activists, including the Slovak Pavel Šafárik, and it intensified in late April when a German committee from Vienna arrived to bully Czechs into supporting German unity. A shouting match erupted in Prague's National Committee, with the Austro-German Ernst Schilling taunting Czechs for wanting to destroy Austria. The following day, Karel Havlíček-Borovský's *Národní noviny* gave details on the proposed Slavic Congress, and soon contacts were established with politicians from Slovak, Serb, Polish, Slovene, and Croatian parts of the empire, and they agreed with the Czechs to hold the Congress in early June.

As that day approached, and Ukrainians, Serbs, and Croats arrived in Prague by the trainload, a German poet wrote that a once civilized city had been reduced to a "caravanserai," a "throng of strange shapes in queer costumes and un-European uniforms." In this transformation of Bohemia into unimagined exoticism, Germans could sense what awaited them if the Habsburg monarchy were ruled democratically from a parliament in Vienna. Germans would be a minority, condemned to gradual extinction through assimilation. But for Czechs, the feeling was the opposite: civil liberties and the promise of democracy made them feel free as never before. They no longer feared being looked down on for displaying Slavic identity, and Prague seemed increasingly their own.[46]

But the new feel and look did not happen automatically: being Czech was not a preference but a moral duty that grew out of the new freedoms. When Ferdinand announced his intention on March 15 to sanction constitutional rule in Bohemia, the journalist Havlíček-Borovský instructed Czech businesses to replace German signs with purely Czech ones. To German objections, Havlíček-Borovský wrote that he was appealing to justice, not hatred. He also said that he wanted to put an end to the idea that Prague was a German city. Czechs had slumbered for two centuries, but they had not perished. They were connected not to Germany but to Austria, where with their Slavic brothers, the Illyrians and Poles, they were guaranteed a numerical superiority.[47]

Such words unleashed fears among Germans which in retrospect appear excessive. Then and later, Poles, Czechs, and Croats were too divided to stand against the German and Hungarian establishments, not to mention the armed might of the Habsburg regime. The ethnically but also regionally complex

Bohemian kingdom wavered between dream and mirage. Just as Czechs did not want to belong to Germany, so, too, many Moravians and Silesians, whether they spoke German or Czech or Polish, did not want to belong to Bohemia. By early 1849 a Moravian diet worked out a liberal constitution proclaiming the equality of Czech and German and declaring Moravia an independent province.[48]

Yet regardless of where exactly they lived in the Bohemian kingdom, Czechs were united enough to resist all attempts to include them in Germany. On May 3, Czechs broke up a meeting of Germans hoping to prepare elections to the Frankfurt constitutional assembly, and clashes between Germans and Czechs spilled onto Prague's streets. Because they were identified with Germans, Jewish businesses became targets of mob violence. National agitators appealed to the masses, printing songs ridiculing Germans as colonizers of peaceful Czech lands and eternal oppressors. In the end, all the Czech-speaking districts in Bohemia abstained from the German parliamentary elections, so that deputies to Frankfurt came from only nineteen of its sixty-eight districts.[49]

Democratic freedoms had shown that Germans and Czechs imagined their political futures in incompatible ways, but that is not what caused the revolution in Bohemia to fail. The direct cause lay instead with a well-trained Austrian garrison near Prague under Bohemia's own General Windischgrätz, a Habsburg loyalist who embodied the old regime's will to survive. He was among the few who had urged Metternich to stay at the helm in March 1848, and at all points he urged violent suppression of the revolution. With Archduchess Sophia, he was disgusted by compromises with the "street," and increasingly felt he had been chosen to be the empire's savior.[50]

In Prague, Windischgrätz was already infamous for crushing a strike of cotton printers a few years earlier, and to nearly everyone's disappointment, he returned early from vacation in May 1848. Almost immediately his troops began disturbing the peace of the city streets with their incessant drilling and parading. Windischgrätz also brought in reinforcements, ostentatiously reviewed units in the town center, and placed artillery on hills above the city, which he refused to withdraw after a citizens' delegation objected. When told he seemed to preside over a foreign occupying army, the general said his only concern was to serve the emperor in Austria. Then he flatly dismissed a request to issue students 2,000 rifles and 80,000 rounds of ammunition. The students had lost touch with reality, he said.[51] On Sunday, June 11, the Czech student militia Svornost met to deliberate measures against the resurgence of "reaction."

The students resolved to summon supporters to an outdoor Catholic mass in central Prague the following day, celebrated by Father Jan Arnold, brother

FIGURE 6.2. Mass in Prague (June 12, 1848). *Source*: Interfoto/Alamy Stock Photo.

of a prominent patriot. The space is now called Václav Square, but then it was the Horse Market. As the crowd of 4,000 students and unemployed workers dispersed, clashes flared with soldiers patrolling near the Powder Tower.[52] As in Vienna three months earlier, rifles discharged, people fell dead or wounded, and insurgents began putting up barricades. Some 3,000 took up arms, mostly workers and students, but there were also shopkeepers, bureaucrats, and women. The university (*Clementinum*) became their command center.

Given Windischgrätz's determination, skill, and three-to-one advantage, the insurgency never stood a chance, and soon imperial troops were gaining ground and seizing routes of communication. On the second day, they took the university without a fight, and on June 17, hostilities ceased, yet not before the general, perhaps outraged by his wife's death, opened his batteries on insurgent positions from across the river.[53] Still, compared to the clashes in Paris and Milan or later in Vienna and Pest, the toll of forty-three killed and sixty-three wounded seemed moderate.

Windischgrätz shut down the Slavic Congress, even though the 400 delegates had taken pains not to offend the crown and were hopelessly divided. For example, Silesians wanted to be grouped with Poles (and not Czechs) to preserve their independence, and no one could figure out how to organize the

FIGURE 6.3. "Amazon on the Barricades, Prague, June 13, 1848." *Source*: Bedřich Anděl
(lithographer), courtesy of The City of Prague Museum

self-rule of Bohemia. In hours when Austrian gunners were training their
sights on targets in what the organizers billed as "ancient Slavic Prague," Palacký
was desperately working to smooth over differences. Slavs were an ancient
peace-loving people, held back by Germans, he said, but now, when "public
opinion makes itself heard as the very voice of God," the yoked Slav was rising
up. Austria would be transformed into a "federation of nations, all enjoying
equal rights."[54]

Some Germans understood that Windischgrätz's salvos were crushing
Prague's democratic experiment and rendered assistance to the insurgents, but
they were a minority; most thanked the general for saving them from the Slavic
peril. Parliamentarians in Frankfurt even asked the governments of Prussia, Bavaria, and Saxony to prepare troops to defend Bohemia's Germans, and Czechs
began to worry that a new democratic Germany would attach Bohemia to it by
force.[55]

Authorities in Prague proclaimed martial law, and the Habsburg regime
seemed to continue its upward swing, untethered to a constitution from the
people. The governor, Baron Thun, scion of an old Bohemian family, was a moderate who had tried to mediate in June, only to be imprisoned by the

insurgents. (A direct appeal from Palacký had secured his release.) He shut down the National Committee in Prague and purged the national guards but failed in attempts to create a Bohemian provisional government that would be independent of Vienna. Still, elections to an Austrian diet took place in August, and the delegates set to work on a constitution for the Habsburg lands outside Hungary, first in Vienna, then when things got dangerous in the fall months, in the Moravian town Kremsier/Kroměříž.

Reaction Triumphant: Austria and Hungary

In late July, the eighty-two-year-old Marshall Radetzky vanquished Piedmontese forces in northern Italy, and on August 6, he made a triumphant entry into Milan. Rather than lament these blows to democracy, the citizens of Vienna rejoiced. Balls were held, and Johann Strauss composed a march for Radetzky, an unofficial Austrian hymn still played at Vienna's New Year's concert. Austria's poet Franz Grillparzer celebrated the field marshall as a savior, and its foremost comic dramatist Johann Nestroy poked fun at the revolutionaries' naiveté in *Freiheit im Krähwinkel* [Freedom in a Crow's Corner]. Austrian Germans not only wanted to be part of Germany but also enjoyed acting as an imperial people, in a state that lorded over many provinces and peoples and extended to them the supposed benefits of its higher culture. But Croats, Serbs, and Romanians also happily supported the imperial cause as it moved to crush the pretensions of Magyar liberals to forming their own nation-state.[56]

After the Habsburg triumphs in Bohemia and now in Italy, the court returned to Vienna, with leading figures eager to get back to ruling. The unrest in the realm was mostly limited to urban areas and had not touched the sinews of power; because the revolutionaries were committed to constitutional monarchy, they had left the court in control of ministerial appointments, which tended to be conservative. State institutions remained intact, including the council of ministers and the bureaucracy, and throughout the crisis, only one Austrian military unit mutinied.[57] Even the supposedly revolutionary National Guard was often a dependable force for order, especially as the middle classes became concerned about attacks on their property.

As the Habsburgs pulled the reins tighter, a violent contest with Hungary became unavoidable. The April laws had linked it with Austria in the person of the emperor in his role as king of Hungary. But these laws did not specify how Hungary and Austria would share responsibility for defense and finances, the two matters that the Pragmatic Sanction of 1713—to which the Hungarian estates were contractually bound—had made a joint concern. How would a dual monarchy raise new troops? Hungary's government showed no concern for paying down the huge state debt, and because it simply created its own ministries of defense and finance, with no concern for matters of the monarchy as a whole, the Austrian government wrote on August 31 that Hungary was in violation of the Pragmatic Sanction, and therefore the April laws were null and void. It forbade Hungarian military activities against Serbs and Croats and ordered the Military Frontier to be subordinated to the defense ministry in Vienna.[58]

Five days later the emperor reinstated Hungary's nemesis Josip Jelačić as Ban of Croatia, and with quiet support from the Viennese court, including arms, he took thirty-thousand troops into Hungary a week later. Having no authority to declare war, he claimed he was putting an end to "rebellion."[59] Despite Jelačić's magnetic personality, his talents as field commander were less than first-rate, and the Hungarians routed his troops 40 kilometers southwest of Buda on September 29.

Meanwhile, events of even greater import were playing out in the Hungarian capital. On September 25, Ferdinand had named Hungarian Magnate Count Ferenc Lamberg head of Habsburg armies in Hungary. Lamberg was not hostile to the Hungarian cause and might have been able to separate hostile camps as commander in chief. Prime Minister Batthyány was eager to talk. Lajos Kossuth, however, denounced Lamberg as an intruder and traitor, and on September 27, ordered Hungarian forces not to follow his orders. (Kossuth headed a Committee of National Defense, created on September 21.) As Lamberg made his way to meet Batthyány in civilian clothes on September 28, a mob recognized him, stopped his carriage, and hacked him to death, distributing among themselves pieces of his bloody clothing. Now Ferdinand issued a manifesto dismissing the Hungarian parliament, subjecting Hungary to military rule, and making Jelačić head of Habsburg armies in Hungary. Whoever sided with Hungary after that was treated as a rebel against his majesty.[60]

These Habsburg attempts to overturn the Hungarian government now provoked Vienna's revolutionaries because they considered Hungary an allied bulwark of democracy and because Austro-Germans in general supported Hungarian efforts to discipline the Slavs. In early October, Hungarian forces pushed Jelačić across the border to Austria, and as he fell back on Vienna, Habsburg Minister of War Latour sent imperial troops in support. One of his officers, Hugo von Bredy, moved to clear a train station held by revolutionary students, but his troops fell back when they met with a hail of gunfire. In the fighting, the students managed to seize two cannons as well as Bredy's sabre and hat. Determined to keep imperial forces from aiding Jelačić, mobs with axes, picks, and iron bars proceeded to attack government ministries, and Latour was battered to death, his head caved in with a hammer, and his mangled body left dangling from a lamppost for fourteen hours, as passersby dipped their handkerchiefs in his blood and bedaubed their weapons and clothing with it. Crowds seized muskets from the arsenal but also pilfered medieval helmets and historical artifacts, including Turkish scimitars.[61]

The court again escaped Vienna, this time for Olomouc in Moravia, accompanied by members of parliament, including all the Czech deputies, a fact that only intensified suspicion among Germans that Czechs were two-faced. (On October 22, the parliament reconvened at the Moravian town of Kroměříž/Kremsier.) Imperial forces left Vienna to the revolutionaries, where the mood turned sharply radical, causing tens of thousands of property owners to flee the city.[62]

On October 16, Ferdinand turned over command of the army encircling Vienna to Windischgrätz, and his sappers promptly cut off water and gas. After an ultimatum to surrender expired, he launched a bombardment as well as full-scale ground assault. Jelačić joined the attack from the east; among his border troops were Montenegrins, wrapped in fiery red cloaks, who captured some thirty barricades in hand-to-hand fighting. Windischgrätz's forces cleared the industrial suburbs of resistance and bombed the inner city through the night of October 27/28. As they did, lookouts in the spire of St. Stephen's could make out 25,000 Hungarians approaching from the east. What they could not see was that Jelačić intercepted the would-be saviors in the suburbs. Windischgrätz finally stormed the inner city on October 31 in a frenzy of bloody terror, claiming that the Viennese—momentarily buoyed by the prospect of connecting to the Hungarians—had reneged on the terms of an earlier surrender.[63]

Windischgrätz disbanded the National Guard and Academic Legion, reintroduced censorship, and had 2,000 revolutionaries arrested, twenty-five of whom he had executed. Among them was Robert Blum, a revered democratic politician visiting from Frankfurt. As a German parliamentarian, Blum should have enjoyed immunity, and the death sentence against him for treason stirred lasting outrage against the House of Habsburg. The general's brother-in-law, Prince Schwarzenberg, formed a new government in November, but he was not a reactionary and permitted the parliament at Kroměříž/Kremsier to continue work on a constitution. In the sprit of Joseph II, Schwarzenberg supported centralized reforms that would strengthen the monarchy, with German language and culture as tools.[64] In December, he fulfilled Archduchess Sophia's wish and persuaded Ferdinand to abdicate in favor of his nephew—and her son—the barely eighteen-year-old Francis Joseph, who had made no commitments to rule by constitution. The lesson Francis Joseph would draw from the protracted turbulence was that his power depended on a loyal army.

* * *

In the winter of 1848/1849, Jelačić took his South Slavic Frontier troops back into Hungary, where they joined other forces opposed to Hungarian rule, including units of the imperial army but also irregulars, especially in the multiethnic southern, eastern, and northern regions: Croats; Serbs; Romanians; Germans; and in smaller numbers, Slovaks.

As in Bohemia, Hungary's ethnic groups had at first worked together to create new institutions, yet before long, differences began cropping up. On March 21, Romanian intellectuals demanded their people be treated as a national body with equal rights. Until that time, the feudal regime in Transylvania had recognized only Germans, Magyars, and Szeklers, though Romanians numbered more than 1.3 million and formed the largest ethnic group.[65] Now Romanians clashed with Hungarian activists, who looked on them as subjects of Hungary, but they also had disputes with Germans over control of the city of Brașov/Kronstadt, and with Serbs over privileges in the Orthodox Church (Serbs and the majority of Romanians were Orthodox). For the time being, Romanians, Germans, and Serbs rose jointly against the newly formed Hungarian state.

The Romanian movement startled onlookers the most because it emerged seemingly from nowhere. Suddenly a previously unheard-of nation was staging mass meetings, for example, at Blaj during May 3–15, 1848, attracting 25,000–40,000 supporters, despite all attempts by Hungarian authorities to stop them. The meeting attracted people from all walks of life and all parts of Transylvania, but also from Ottoman Moldavia and Wallachia (Țara Românească); it concluded with demands for an end to serfdom and independence for the Romanian nation. Observers, German and Hungarian, were impressed by the discipline of a crowd that size, which resembled a huge military encampment in the shape of a star, from whose center paths led out like rays through the dense throngs.[66]

Likewise in May, Slovak intellectuals convened a mass assembly that demanded recognition of their people's rights to govern themselves and use their own language; they proposed that the Kingdom of Hungary be transformed into a country of nations with equal rights. They also assembled armed units of volunteers that were smaller than in Serb or Romanian areas, in part because Slovak activists tended to be Lutheran while the Slovak-speaking peasants were mostly Catholic, with weakly developed national consciousness. Especially in eastern Slovakia, peasants were much more concerned about the abolition of feudal subjection than about Slovak political autonomy. Still, Hungary's leaders rejected negotiations with Slovak or any other national representatives, no matter how strong their movements.[67]

In September, authorities attempted to enlist Romanians into the Hungarian army, and the disparate quarrels exploded into civil war. In one town, thirteen people died while resisting forced recruitment. At the same time, imperial forces were encouraging resistance to the Hungarians among Romanians and Germans, and they were disarming Hungarian National Guard units in Transylvania to keep them from exterminating Romanians and Germans. Imperial forces also inducted thousands into new Romanian border guard infantry regiments, and soon these outfits were themselves uprooting and annihilating Hungarian townsfolk in the foothills of the Carpathians, committing atrocities so grisly that observers likened them to Tatar invasions in the thirteenth century.[68]

The emotion that propelled the violence was fear of extinction, fed by unverifiable and uncontrollable rumors: of rampant mistreatment of civilians by supposed forces of order, of slaughter of Romanians by Hungarian troops, and of Hungarian landowners by Romanian peasants.[69] The marauders set homes alight and butchered captured soldiers, along with civilians who ran across their paths, claiming that they themselves were the victims, and any aggression on their part was in fact self-defense. Heroic-seeming, charismatic leaders emerged who were willing to lead the ethnic cleansers in the escalating slaughter, knowing that even more radical figures waited in the wings if they did not take command.

Citizens living in contested regions faced dilemmas for which nothing in their experience had given them the slightest preparation. They were bound to heed the orders of imperial authorities who occupied a given town, but if Hungarian units took that town the next day, they found themselves accused of high treason. Heroes of one side were butchers to the other, and the rhetoric became so heated that punishments less than total seemed treasonous.

Take László Csányi, a minister in Hungary's government and governor in Transylvania, executed by imperial Austrian forces when they finally stamped out the last embers of revolution in the fall of 1849. In Hungarian accounts, Csányi figures as hero and martyr, a man who embodied liberal principles and the triumph of civilian over military rule. Yet Csányi opposed compromises and set up tribunals that pronounced summary executions of Germans who were simply asserting rights their communities had enjoyed from time immemorial. Especially painful for German Transylvanians was the case of Dr. Stephan Ludwig Roth, a Lutheran pastor and educator of renown, who obeyed Austrian orders to set up a government for thirteen villages near his hometown of Meschen. Roth was not a nationalist. In 1842, he had written an exposé advocating multicultural existence. In his view, Hungary's Germans, Magyars, Romanians, Jews, Armenians, and Gypsies benefited from living in one fatherland, each a "tree" in the Hungarian woods with its own purpose. But he did worry about the survival of Germans in Transylvania, and to Magyar nationalists' horror, he encouraged Germans to migrate there from western Germany.

When Hungarian forces took Meschen from the Austrians, they arrested Roth and condemned him to death, despite a guarantee of safety he held from General Józef Bem, a Pole who commanded a Hungarian army. A pastor friend attempted intervention, but was told by Csányi, in the typically inflated language of ethnic cleansing, that Roth deserved ten deaths for having worked for the "extinction of the Hungarian nation." When Csányi was hanged in October he denied none of his deeds, all of which he performed "for the patria."[70]

The Romanian nobleman Ioan Dragoş was a moderate like Roth, and loyally sat in the Hungarian Parliament. He had agreed to carry peace terms from Kossuth to the Romanian National Committee, hoping for a compromise that might appease the Hungarians but secure cultural rights for the Romanians. Yet Kossuth failed to order Hungarian units to respect the ceasefire that Dragoş secured to conduct negotiations with the Romanian leadership at Abrud Banya, a mining town of mixed Romanian, German, and Hungarian ethnicity, and when a Hungarian unit launched a surprise attack on the town, Dragoş was suspected of double-dealing and lynched. In the following days, Hungarian units apprehended and executed the Romanian leaders who had spoken with Dragoş, and though they possessed promises of safe conduct, hoping to negotiate peace with Kossuth at his headquarters in Debrecen, they were executed for no other reason than that peacemakers were easy targets for vengeance. (The Hungarian units in Abrud Banya also carried out a frenzied rage against the Romanian civilian population "plundering, robbing and raping with no concern for age or sex.")[71] The events alienated thousands of Hungarians and Romanians whose ancestors had lived in peace for generations, but now became convinced that any efforts at reconciliation by the other side were a trap.

The toll of the ethnic war in Transylvania was some 40,000 dead and 100 villages razed; the population of the Serb Vojvodina was so decimated that it took thirty years to recover. The killing ended only when Emperor Francis Joseph, literally on his hands and knees, begged Tsar Nicholas I for troops during a meeting the two had in Moravia. A large Russian force poured across Hungary's borders in May and June, more than doubling the fighting strength of the forces arrayed against the Hungarian government, compelling the last Hungarian units to surrender at the village of Vilagos in July. Imperial authorities then undertook retribution, infamously executing thirteen Hungarian generals, four of whom were not ethnic Magyars, and several of whom spoke imperfect Hungarian. They made a scapegoat of Prime Minister Batthyány, who was executed on October 6, himself giving the order to fire in three languages. Scores more

FIGURE 6.4. Slovak volunteers and their children. *Source*: F. Werner (lithographer). *Domová pokladnica* 5 (1851), 241. Via Wikimedia Commons.

were hanged and shot, and hundreds imprisoned. The punishment was disproportionate and alienated the Magyar population from Austria's rulers for years
to come.[72]

But the war itself had alienated virtually every group in Hungary: from the
Magyar elites to Romanians and Germans in Transylvania, to Croats and Serbs
in the south. Within a generation, scholars were applying a description to the
internecine conflict that did not exist before that time: *racial war*, a war between
peoples, involving not only ethnic cleansing but also the mutual killing of townsfolk on a mass scale. The Hungarians had executed 168 Slovaks by hanging
them from trees, but for those who died, their only crime had been fighting for
their country.[73]

* * *

Yet after it restored a semblance of order to Hungary, the House of Habsburg
did nothing to reward the nationalities without which it would not have survived. Instead, young Francis Joseph reimposed autocratic rule from Vienna and
rejected any talk of autonomy for Croats, Serbs, Romanians, or Slovaks.[74] He
also threw out the constitution drafted by the democratically elected Kroměříž
assembly for Austria, and then he imposed one drawn up by the gifted conservative reformer Franz Stadion. Yet on further reflection, even that document
struck him as ceding too much of his power, and he abrogated it as well and
endeavored to reassert the centralized rule that had prevailed before the revolution. Transylvania, Croatia, and the Military Frontier were separated from
Hungary, and new administrative districts were created to subordinate the entire realm directly to Vienna. The official language of the Hungarian kingdom,
frustrating decades of struggle to advance the vernacular, was once again German, and legions of German and Czech administrators streamed into the subdued crown of St. Stephen. The customs barrier that had protected Hungary
was lifted, and the population had to pay an enormous tax.

As we will see, this solution by compulsion in Hungary was at best temporary, as it proved impossible to rule the huge monarchy against the wishes and
interests of over half the realm. The revolutions of 1848/1849 had brought problems to the surface that would require a response more sophisticated than
simple military and bureaucratic force.

One dimension of the problem was social: most Habsburg subjects worked
the land, but most of them did not own land. They were unproductively employed sharecroppers and had little chance of developing or making use of their

skills in farming or in any other profession. Here the house of Habsburg had shown some shrewdness in March 1848 in a move that sucked much of the energy out of the revolution. Fearful of mass violence in the countryside, Emperor Ferdinand had abolished robot, the traditional system whereby peasants contributed forced labor each week for their lords. He thereby temporarily neutralized the peasantry as a political force while reinforcing the old idea that the Habsburgs protected the tillers of the land. As in the 1780s, measures to ameliorate peasants' lives had come not from local elites but from the crown.

For their part, liberals, including the Czech Palacký, were suspicious of peasants as well as of the urban proletariat and opposed including them in representative bodies. Lacking property, they were supposedly incapable of self-government. The result was that peasants in much of the Habsburg realm celebrated the triumphs of Austrian armies, beginning in the summer of 1848, because to them, revolution seemed an urban concern supported by intellectuals and nobles, which brought no benefits to the countryside. And because the army was largely peasants in uniform, this loyal, culturally conservative majority provided needed stability for the regime until the end.[75] Still, the land problem remained largely untouched because even peasants free of robot owned no land, and this problem would act as a drag on modernization for decades to come, in many places until the Communist upheaval of the 1940s.

The problem for which neither crown nor liberal revolutionaries found any solution, however, was the nationality conflict, which had fully revealed itself for the first time. Europeans had known of unrest in Poland and Serbia before 1848, in both cases directed against foreign imperial rule, but there had been little appreciation for the ethnic complexity of Habsburg Bohemia and Hungary and the disputes it might generate.[76] Evident now was the intermingling across vast territories of populations with irreconcilable visions of the future. Nothing in the events of 1848/1849 had altered the conviction in the Hungarian political class that Hungary must be a unitary Magyar state, with no special status accorded to any nationality; likewise, Germans and Czechs in Bohemia imagined their futures in ways that seemed impossible to bridge. Nothing would convince German nationalists, in or outside Austria, that the Austro-Germans' destiny was to stand as one among the small peoples of federal Austria. And federal Austria was the central plank in the Czech platform from 1848 to World War I.

Admittedly, the bulk of the populations living in East Central Europe was little concerned with these irreconcilables, and those who were tended to be town dwellers and politically engaged intellectuals. Yet at this stage, we can observe a trend in this group, which would become a perennial problem. Moderates who might have acted to unite German and Czech Bohemians, or Hungarian and Romanian Transylvanians, did not prevail. Instead the new institutions of democracy gave advantages to radicals who mobilized fear by arguing that their ethnicity was mortally imperiled. In Prague, each step of splintering the united citizenries of March 1848 involved stirring anxieties: of Czechs becoming a minority in Germany; of Germans becoming one in Bohemia. History seemed to teach that the fate of minorities was to be absorbed and disappear. Even non-readers had basic biblical literacy and knew that many ancient nations had survived in name only.

Ironically, when violence leading to fatalities broke out in Bohemia, it had nothing to do with ethnicity but was a joint effort of young Czech and German democrats to resist General Windischgrätz's provocations. But from the moment order was restored, the episode was remembered, especially on the German side, as having everything to do with ethnicity, signaling an irreconcilable conflict between Germans and Slavs. In memory, Czechs died at the hands of Germans, and Germans died in efforts to halt the construction of a Slavic empire.[77] The Slavic Congress in Prague, in fact powerless, only reinforced the idea that Slavs were moving to active aggression and unless stopped would establish a state stretching from Bohemia to the Black Sea and beyond, engulfing and smothering Germans, Magyars, and other non-Slavic groups. Such images were perpetuated in countless descriptions, setting a pattern for Czech-German relations lasting into the twentieth century.[78]

The Slavic Congress also held a place of pride in post-1848 stories about the perfidies of Slavs as egotists, enemies of freedom, and defiers of enlightenment. German and Hungarian sources published just after hostilities portrayed "Pan-Slavic" Czechs as anti-German and anti-Magyar, opportunists who would never admit their true identity, wearing one mask at one point and a different one at another. The liberal student pastor Anton Füster wrote that Czechs had acted German when in German Bohemia, but dropped the disguise as soon as they entered Czech areas.[79] For decades, many in the Hungarian elite had sensed a Slavic threat, and the 1848/49 revolution only gave it new intensity; after holding off challenges of Serbs, Slovaks, and Croats, their revolution had been crushed by armies from Russia. A common sense of endangerment by an enemy that was both intimate but also distant and exotic would form the basis for Austro-German-Hungarian understanding and reconciliation in the 1860s, an event unimaginable in the fall of 1849.

CHAPTER 7

The Reform That Made the Monarchy Unreformable: The 1867 Compromise

In 1867, after months of negotiations between Hungarian politicians and his own trustees, Emperor Francis Joseph endorsed a compromise between Austria and Hungary that divided the Habsburg monarchy into western and eastern halves ruled respectively from Vienna and Budapest. The former had no unified character, consisting of German-, Slavic-, and Italian-populated territories that came to be known as "Cisleithania"—the lands west of the Leitha River. The eastern area was also complicated ethnically, consisting of Magyars, Romanians, and a variety of Slavs, but for Hungary's elite, it was their historic kingdom, which they were now determined to convert into a modern national state.

The "Compromise" was perhaps the most spectacular reversal ever of a nation's fortune. Less than two decades earlier, imperial forces had subdued Hungary's armies, executed generals and politicians, and then reduced the land to a province ruled by Viennese ministers who scoffed at historical rights. In the Habsburg mind, Hungary as a realm with separate traditions and rights had ceased to exist, and Austria extended its civil code as well as rigorous censorship beyond the Leitha. Nobles associated with the "revolt" lost their estates, sometimes permanently. The ostentatiously exacted punishment was meant to be an enduring lesson about Austrian power; in the end, however, Francis Joseph proved to be the pupil and learned a lesson in humility.

In 1848/1849, imperial armies had subdued revolution in Budapest, but also in Milan, Prague, and Vienna, and so the young emperor believed that force had returned his realm to a preeminent position in European politics, and force would suffice to govern it. The order he imposed in the 1850s is often called *neo*-absolutist, however, because the reversion to Metternich's time was not total. Equality under law remained, as did the undoing of hereditary serfdom. Still, Habsburg subjects, including the nobility, were denied all hope of participation in politics, and Francis Joseph governed with a small coterie of advisors. As he did, the position of Austria declined, along with its ability to generate revenue.

The Way to Constitutionalism

The ingenuous emperor was especially keen to micromanage foreign policy, and he selected top state officials based on social background rather than on competence. But his self-assurance combined with habitual vacillation to produce diplomatic isolation and military disaster. The isolation resulted from Francis's inept handling of the Crimean War, which erupted in 1854 after Russia had sent its armies into the Danube principalities of Moldavia and Wallachia, claiming to protect Christian populations there, and then destroyed a Turkish fleet, with huge loss of life. Britain and France sent military forces to the Crimea, hoping to check Russian expansion, and a bloody conflict ensued that lasted for two years, featuring massive use of modern technologies, like telegraph and railroads. Tsar Nicholas had rescued Habsburg power in Hungary just five years previously, and at the very least he hoped for benevolence on the part of Francis Joseph. Instead, he received news that Francis had sent his own armies into Moldavia and Wallachia, hoping to annex them. Now France and Britain checked Austria. If Russia could not become bloated at Ottoman expense, neither could Austria. Yet rather than ally with France and Britain, Francis Joseph maintained a stance of armed neutrality, in effect alienating Austria from everyone, above all Russia.[1]

One power that gained from the conflict was tiny Piedmont-Sardinia, the catalyst for Italian unification, whose armies had lost disastrous campaigns in 1848/1849 in an effort to wrest Lombardy and Venetia from Habsburg control. Now its shrewd foreign minister, Count Camillo Benso di Cavour, threw his state's meager resources into the fight against Russia. Afterward Cavour met secretly with France's Louis Napoleon, and they agreed to provoke an Austrian attack on Piedmont. Then, France would act in support of its new ally, and together they would drive the Habsburgs out of northern Italy. The scheme worked as planned in April 1859. Piedmont mobilized troops along the Austrian border, Austria demanded a withdrawal, and after being rebuffed, declared war.

In two savage battles, Piedmont and France overwhelmed the Habsburg armies. The carnage at Solferino was so shocking that the traveling Swiss businessman Henry Dunant felt impelled to launch an international campaign to protect wounded soldiers, originating the Red Cross. Also galled by the bloodshed but concerned by the too-sudden rise of Italy, Napoleon stopped short of a complete rout and came to terms with Francis, forcing Austria to cede Lombardy but permitting it to keep Veneto.

Francis had commanded the troops at Solferino and understood that the fiasco was his personal doing. He was learning that he could not run the empire assisted only by a few top officials. Compounding his problems was Austria's failure to recover from the bankruptcy he had inherited in 1849. Between then and 1866, Austria's national debt had trebled, and as it became more dependent on money markets in Paris and London, creditors wanted to see evidence of government made accountable through representative institutions. Even Austria's non-policy of armed neutrality had been costly, forcing it to sell railways at bargain prices to foreign bankers. State finances had almost collapsed when the government attempted to raise funds for the 1859 war.[2] The emperor decided he had no option but to involve other forces in running the state.

But he had no intention of sharing power and did not permit his advisors even to use the word "constitution."[3] Instead, his plan was to invite notables, large landowners, aristocrats, and wealthy bourgeois for consultations that would make the realm produce more revenue. Despite the reorganization launched a century earlier, the Habsburg lands were still a highly diverse assemblage of properties, with several different legal regimes. The fundamental question was how the lands would be structured. Seven years of negotiations now commenced in which the emperor vacillated between acknowledging the realm's diversity through some kind of federalism, and the old Josephine idea of centrally directing rule through the Viennese bureaucracy. The former was supported by conservative elites (especially the Bohemian and Polish magnates), the latter by Austro-German liberals. Hungary's gentry fell in between: they were largely of liberal sentiment and wanted central rule for Hungary within Hungary and would reject all attempts to rule Hungary from Vienna, even through the most liberal institutions.

Reforming began modestly in the spring of 1860. After hand-selecting thirty-eight noblemen and high bourgeois from every corner of the realm for an "enlarged" Imperial Council, Francis chose as his first prime minister the Polish magnate Agenor Romuald Gołuchowski, Galician governor since 1849 and owner of vast territories in western Ukraine.

In Vienna, Gołuchowski displayed the attributes of a loyal and astute Habsburg statesman: he was supranational, tolerant, and conscientious. Yet as governor in Galicia he had proved a canny promoter of Polish interests who kept the nascent Ukrainian movement under wraps, refusing to divide the land into Polish and Ukrainian districts. While insisting that the bureaucracy use German in public, he had quietly replaced Austrian and Czech officials with Poles. The university in Lemberg (Lwów) remained heavily German because it was founded by the Austrian state, but Gołuchowski permitted Jagiellonian University in Kraków to become a fully Polish institution once more.[4] Because Gołuchowski publically identified as Austrian, "true" Polish patriots derided him as a traitor. But like members of his class, he never gave up on an independent Poland, and his planting of Polish officials prepared the way for Polish self-rule in Galicia later in the decade. He later told Galicia's diet that abandoning hopes for independence was not in the Poles' nature.[5] Still, a generation later, his son Agenor Maria served as the top diplomat of the Habsburg state, helping embroil it in a conflict with Serbia.

The initial charges Francis gave the Imperial Council in March 1860 were to determine the budget, examine closed accounts, and collect data on the state debt. But its discussions soon went further because questions of finance could not be divorced from questions of governance. As a conservative, Gołuchowski believed in devolving power from the center and permitting each kingdom or province to develop its own personality within historic boundaries. However, he did not think all nations were equal and assumed there would be a hierarchy: the culturally superior Poles, Germans, Hungarians, Czechs, and Croats would stand above the Slovenes, Slovaks, Serbs, and Ruthenians.[6]

Gołuchowski quickly found common ground with men of his class from Hungary. Their role was crucial. Hungary occupied more than half the space of the realm, and so its representatives were a large group, six in number versus three from Bohemia. But they also had an unusually strong sense of national identity and refused to parrot the Austrian state's rhetoric of "grants and decrees," insisting instead on Hungary's "laws and rights." Though conservative to the core, they expected nothing less than restoration of the Hungarian constitution. To some in Hungary, these magnates seemed dreamers, but they managed to win over counterparts from Austria and Bohemia to a common defense of "historical and political individualities."[7]

But they also intuited the deeper challenges that faced the monarchy. In a speech to the Imperial Council, Hungarian Count György Majláth, a conservative whose family of scholars and judges could trace its lineage to the ninth century, reflected on the task of implanting a sense of patriotism across the Habsburg lands, with the diverse institutions, customs, and intellectual and material possessions that had developed over centuries. "Fatherland cannot be decreed," he said. Anyone hoping to forge unity had to build on existing foundations, convincing subjects in each of the realm's parts that nothing could be superior to their association with the House of Habsburg. Then "patriotism for the state as a whole" would obtain naturally. But he and other Hungarian magnates also used more extreme arguments, warning that revolution could break out if their modest proposals were not accepted.[8]

In April 1860, Francis restored the administration of inner Hungary through a national diet at Budapest, and he also revived the country's counties along with most of their rights to self-government. Hungary was a recognized political reality once more. That summer, under Gołuchowski's leadership, the nobles drafted a document that Francis Joseph would release in the fall called the "October Diploma," providing for a parliament in Vienna with delegates appointed by the provincial diets (*Landtage*). The emperor would share with this parliament legislative powers and the right to impose taxes and raise loans. The Diploma expressed regard for the empire's component parts, promising to transfer to the *Landtage* all competencies that did not reside in the center. Francis Joseph was pleased. He wrote his mother that Austria now had a "little parliament," yet power remained firmly in his hands.[9]

In fact, the few dozen nobles of the Imperial Council had scored a victory for representative government that the emperor could not undo. Anticipating the full-fledged dualism that would come in 1867, the resurrected Hungarian kingdom again featured the system of local gentry self-rule in the traditional counties, with Hungarian restored as the language of administration. Non-Magyar bureaucrats were sent packing, and timeworn institutions of the kingdom, such as the "tavernicus" in Budapest, as well the native organs of justice (Judex curiae) came back to life. Hungary's system of government differed so clearly from that of the non-Hungarian lands that people began talking of lands on this and that side of the Leitha River, Cisleithania and Transleithania, roughly speaking, Austria and Hungary. The imperial parliament in Vienna affirmed the distinction by recognizing a sphere of competence for the western half and regarding itself as a partner for the Hungarian diet.[10]

But for Hungarians, this was far from sufficient. They overwhelmingly wanted the rights to self-government restored that had been contained in the April 1848 constitution. The six magnates along with Gołuchowski may have broken Habsburg absolutism and put Hungary back on the map, but rather than feting the nobles, Hungarian society denounced them for collaboration. As a British liberal wrote in 1861, "no effort was spared to induce such men as Apponyi, Majláth, and the rest to abstain from the first manifestation of public life in Austria." Even moderate liberals like József Eötvös and Ferenc Deák took no part in the new arrangements.[11]

Yet the new constitution also failed to pacify the realm beyond Hungary. German liberals claimed that the new provincial statutes relied on "reactionary" feudal principles, giving disproportionate powers to large landholders. They further detested the continued privileges that the Catholic Church enjoyed in education, taxation, and family law, and their indignation mounted when they contrasted Austria with other German states. For instance, Prussia had a parliament and a firm secular order that made Austria, supposedly the leading state in Germany, seem backward. And after the fiasco of Solferino, the Habsburgs were no longer a relevant force in Italy.[12]

The emperor's response was to replace Gołuchowski with Anton von Schmerling, a popular liberal connected to the high bureaucracy who favored limited representation in a state centrally run from Vienna.[13] In February 1861, Schmerling released an "imperial constitution" that built on the October 1860 Diploma, expanding the Imperial Council (*Reichsrat*) into a bicameral legislature, with an upper chamber appointed by the emperor and a lower one elected by the *Landtage*.

The system still fell far short of German liberals' aspirations. The new legislature had no right to call ministers to account, nor could it approve the state budget, and neither freedom of press nor religion was guaranteed. What they didn't know was that such shortcomings were part of the system's original intent. Francis wanted the *Reichsrat* to be an advisory body with certain representative features that would not get in the way of government business, and everything was calculated to ensure the control by great landholders of regional diets and the chamber of deputies (the second house).[14]

For their part, non-Germans chaffed at the constitution's inbuilt ethnic discrimination. The electoral boundaries favored German voters over Slavs, and authorities took steps to make sure it stayed that way. Czech-speakers made up two-thirds of Bohemia's population, yet thanks to manipulation of electoral boundaries and pressure from Vienna on the nationally agnostic (but culturally German) nobles, Bohemia delivered comfortable majorities of German delegates into the 1870s.[15] In 1863 Czechs and Poles withdrew their support, and the Bohemian, Moravian, Silesian, and Galician diets stopped sending representatives to the *Reichsrat*. Croats followed. But theirs was nothing compared to the indignation felt in Hungary, where the problem was not simply ethnic discrimination but a pervasive sense that Vienna disrespected Hungarian institutions.

A certain laxness had set into the neo-absolutist Habsburg police state in the late 1850s, and public dissent became common among Hungarians, reflected for instance in the ostentatious wearing of Magyar garb. Historical commemorations, like the hundredth birthday of Ferenc Kazinczy, now triggered minor demonstrations. Kazinczy had died largely forgotten in the 1830s but was now seen as the first modern Hungarian literary hero, and people flocked to celebrations of his life. These quasi-religious events were staged in more than 120 locales in 1859, usually centering on a bust of the poet and featuring national hymns conducted by officials known colloquially as "priests."[16]

The following year, on March 15, students in Pest commemorated the 1848 revolution and treasonously celebrated the defiance of Habsburg power in their day of crowds in Tuscany and Modena. After a student protester was shot in early April, about one-fourth of Budapest's population turned out for his funeral. Later that month, an estimated 80,000 attended the burial of István Széchenyi, whom, it was said, the Austrian regime had driven to suicide. Public demonstrations continued into the fall against the October Diploma, going beyond students to include the propertied nobility, middle classes, urban proletariat, and much of the peasantry. By the early 1860s, passive resistance was a way of life in Hungary, expressed most effectively in tax evasion.[17]

Local authorities had permitted elections to the Hungarian diet in the spring of 1861 but then refused to send delegates to the *Reichsrat* in Vienna. Their undisputed leader, the moderate yet tough wise man Ferenc Deák, denounced the October Diploma as well as the February Constitution as acts of "absolute power." The Schmerling government was treating Hungary as if it were a mere Austrian province, and Hungary's political elite, from left to right, demanded restoration of the constitution, not as a "gift, but founded on mutual agreement . . . [and] in law and justice." They did not need legal historians to tell them that Hungary had entered into a contract when it accepted the Pragmatic Sanction in 1723. In return for recognizing succession by his daughter Maria Theresa, Charles VI had promised to preserve all rights, liberties, privileges, customs, and laws of Hungary and its estates.[18] If Francis Joseph wanted Hungary to recognize his rule as legitimate, he had to abide by the spirit of that agreement.

The emperor responded by dissolving the Hungarian diet and attempting to return the land to military rule. He was trusting Schmerling's promises that Hungary would relent, promises that turned out to be very wrong. Thanks to the October Diploma, political life had become legal, and elections to the traditional organs of county rule and the Hungarian diet were awakening the political spectrum from right to left. Numerous "movements" pressed for constitutional rule, and soon Hungary had emerged as by far the monarchy's greatest problem. Because of Hungary's size relative to the rest of the monarchy, Magyar abstention made the *Reichsrat* dysfunctional; when it opened in

April 1861, only 203 of 343 delegates were in attendance. Meanwhile Magyar radicals were soliciting weapons from France and Italy and were in touch with Hungarian émigré circles; in turn these circles were encouraging Cavour and Napoleon III to resolve the stalemate with force.[19]

But now the Hungarians got support from unexpected quarters: the German "constitutional party" of Austria, a liberal grouping which saw appeasement of Hungary as the best guarantee that Slavs would not gain predominance in the monarchy. They had been watching with alarm as the monarch gave way to demands for popular representation, knowing that as the electorate expanded, so would the position of Slavs. Beginning in 1863, a majority of German deputies claimed it was necessary to reach an understanding with Budapest in order to secure constitutionalism in their own lands, and thenceforth the anti-Slav agenda formed the bedrock for cooperation of German and Hungarian political elites.[20]

* * *

The pressures on German liberals to seek allies within the monarchy were all the greater now that Prussia was gradually pushing Austria out of Germany. In 1863 the new Prussian chancellor Otto von Bismarck had outwitted Francis Joseph when the latter attempted a promising overture in German politics. Francis had the idea of creating a German federal state under Habsburg leadership, and he summoned the other German princes to Frankfurt to discuss the proposal. Bismarck believed either Prussia or Austria would dominate Germany— one either yielded or was forced to yield, he said—and he prevailed on the Prussian king to boycott the meeting. Smaller German states like Bavaria or Baden knew they could not act without Prussia (which by that time was in control of the wealthy Rhineland), and Bismarck's disruptive act had stifled the Habsburg initiative before it got off the ground.

This was a turning point in the fortunes of German and Central Europe that grew out of Bismarck's will. William of Prussia believed deeply in legitimacy derived from precedent and history, and had it not been for Bismarck's almost obsessive cajoling, William would have attended the Frankfurt meeting, and some looser form of German unity might have been achieved, far different from the one that emerged after 1871. The German princes favored a transformation of the German lands toward closer affiliation and opposed centralization. King William had felt so drawn to the meeting that his failure to board the train to Frankfurt brought him to the verge of a nervous breakdown.

By late 1864, Francis Joseph's patience with his own chief minister was running thin. Schmerling had failed to improve the country's finances, and concerns about Hungary clouded his thoughts of the future. In the emperor's mind, his realm could survive without peripheral territories like Veneto or Galicia—he called them *Ausland*—but the same was not true of Hungary. The dynasty's problems had to be solved with and not in spite of the Magyars. In December 1864, Francis Joseph contacted Ferenc Deák through intermediaries to learn the Hungarians' conditions for negotiations.[21]

Now Deák came under pressure to prevail against the majority in his camp, who thought the only relation between Hungary and Austria could be through the person of the ruler, and that otherwise they must constitute two states. Making things more difficult was the consuming hatred Hungarians felt for a potentate who had presided over the execution of generals and politicians guilty of doing nothing worse than defending a constitution guaranteed by Ferdinand Habsburg-Lothringen in April 1848. Széchenyi, whom even his rival Kossuth called the greatest of Hungarians, had said that Francis Joseph "reeked of human blood."[22]

When he visited Budapest in 1857, Francis Joseph was surprised at the barely suppressed contempt everywhere he turned. He had expected to be greeted as a wise sovereign. The situation was much worse than he imagined: the embarrassed Budapest city council had asked the moderate nobleman József Eötvös what kind of celebration they might arrange for the royal visit: he suggested hanging the police chief from the mast of the celebrated chain bridge. That would impress the visitor, please the Hungarians, and not cost much money. When Francis's daughter Sophia succumbed to an illness and died during this visit, there was no sympathy. People whispered that the little girl was only the first person close to the monarch who would have to die for the generals hanged in 1849. But they did pity the mother, the originally Bavarian Empress Elisabeth, who for her part took a fancy to the "free-spirited and independent" Hungarian nobles. She admired them so greatly that she determined to learn Hungarian.

But if Ferenc Deák had now yielded completely to his free-spirited fellow noblemen, he would have had no negotiations at all. The idea that Austria and Hungary could be connected only in the person of the emperor was a nonstarter in Vienna. Yet for their part, his interlocutors in Vienna had to transcend their expectations that the monarchy must be a proper empire, with no part essentially different from any other. The word *Reich* had a powerful and extraordinarily deep resonance in the German political mind that was difficult to relinquish, yet effective reform seemed to necessitate division of the realm into smaller units.[23]

What gave the two sides courage to venture into political no-man's land was fear of the alternatives. Czechs were agitating for an autonomous Bohemia that would have made the Germans there a minority, and Croats and Serbs desired autonomous spaces in Hungary that would have compromised the integrity of the Hungarian kingdom. Elites in Vienna and Budapest feared Slav power outside the empire as well. Russia had just crushed a Polish uprising and was increasingly assertive in the Balkans, stoking fears of a growing Slavic empire that might lay claim to spaces in the Habsburg monarchy. More clearly than ever, Hungarian elites shared common anxieties and therefore common interests with their German counterparts in Cisleithania.[24]

Still, opposition remained potent, and Deák took the reasonable step of telling the emperor that Hungary would recognize the Pragmatic Sanction that had been accepted by the Hungarian Diet in 1723 as a basis of negotiations. The Habsburgs were bound to respect this document, as it had established the unity and integrity of their holdings internationally and had been signed by the major European powers; from Vienna's perspective, it had the advantage of connecting Austria with Hungary in common concerns for defense, foreign policy, and therefore finance. But it also obliged Francis Joseph to accept coronation and defend Hungary's ancient institutions.[25]

By 1865 the two sides had reached the outlines of an understanding. In an important "Easter" article published anonymously in Budapest, Deák proclaimed the empire's integrity a paramount good, and said he would support modifications of the 1848 constitution to maintain it.[26] That summer Francis appointed new leaders in Hungary, including György Majláth, co-author of the October Diploma, who became chancellor. Schmerling, who had not even been consulted, read the handwriting on the wall and resigned. The emperor was signaling a move away from centralization, but he had no clear destination in sight.

The new head of government in Vienna, Count Richard Belcredi, an aristocrat of Italian descent from Moravia and a conservative, counted as a federalist. The emperor dissolved the *Reichsrat* and suspended its operations. In Hungary, he restored the parliament as well as the traditional system of gentry rule in the historic counties. Deák found he had a huge majority when Hungary's lawmakers met in December: 180 of his party—the "Addressers"—faced 21 old conservatives and 94 opponents of any deal.[27]

But what about Belcredi's Moravia, and the rest of the Bohemian kingdom? Czech nationalists said they also should have traditional rights restored, just like the Hungarians. Yet in contrast to Hungarian counterparts, Bohemia's hereditary elite—that is, its nobles—had no cohesive organization. Most were culturally German and considered Bohemia a Habsburg province, whereas leading Czech politicians, commoners like Palacký and his son-in-law František Ladislav, were insisting on what they called Bohemian state's rights. Although the Bohemian kingdom's boundaries had changed, most recently in 1740, they said it possessed an ancient historical integrity that the Habsburgs had to respect. What broke the logjam about Bohemia's status—and as it turned out, the fate of the monarchy as a whole—was a battle the Habsburgs happened to fight in Bohemia in the summer of 1866. The instigator was Otto von Bismarck.

Though deeply conservative, Bismarck believed it was impossible simply to suppress popular desires for German unity in and beyond Prussia. Nationalism had become an unstoppable force in Germany, but he endeavored to channel it into the creation of a national state dominated by Prussia. For the sake of cohesion, he wanted this state to be primarily Protestant, and that meant excluding Austria, where the population and dynasty were Catholic. Austria would then take the role of an aligned Central European state carrying on the old mission of extending German culture to the Slavic east.[28] That had been a goal of German liberals, in and outside Austria, and Bismarck supported it. But the first step was expelling Austria from the German Confederation.

In 1864 the Prussian chancellor lured Austria into a joint military campaign that wrested the principalities of Schleswig and Holstein from Denmark; and having achieved that, he used the question of succession in those provinces to provoke a war with Austria two years later near the eastern Bohemian town Sadová/Königgrätz. Prussia's better-trained and equipped armies revealed the limits of Austria's modernization. Austria had been unable to procure rapid-fire rifles, and so while its soldiers stood and reloaded their rifles after each shot, Prussian troops tore them to pieces from protected positions with accurate breech-loading rifles. For every Prussian casualty, there were three Austrians. The defeat was a further sign of Francis Joseph's incompetence in defense policy: thanks to his indecision, much of the Austrian army was held up in northern Italy, a strategically far less important area.

Austria's inability to match Prussia in military technology could also be traced to the sorry state of the former's finances.[29] The country was rich in people and natural resources, but the centrally directed pseudo-liberal regime under

Schmerling had not managed to extract revenue adequate to the needs of an imperial state. Compounding Vienna's problems was the sense among creditors that Austria was ruled by a semi-competent sovereign who presided over a regime rife with corruption and favoritism. Emperor emeritus Ferdinand, watching from the sidelines, said he could have done as well as his supposedly more able nephew.

Hungarian and German Liberals versus Slavs

The German liberal leadership in Vienna did not immediately understand how radically their country's position had declined, from the supposed leading power in Germany to outsider.[30] Their country would not be a large liberal Germany that included Austria and Bohemia, but at best a liberal Austria outside of Bismarck's small Germany. But how to maintain German dominance in the multiethnic monarchy? And what exactly was Austria? History provided no definitive answers, but what seemed clear was that it did not include Hungary, and that Austrian and Bohemian Germans had a community of interests with Hungary's elites in asserting joint cultural dominance over the various Slavic groups in the monarchy. The question was how to justify the containment of Slavs with liberal principles.

The contradiction seemed irresolvable. On one hand, liberalism involved expanding rights of self-rule to educated, property-owning men capable of rational decision making, regardless of ethnicity. On the other hand, no matter how these rights expanded, whether in separate crown lands or in a united monarchy, Germans would be in a shrinking minority. The dangers had been heralded in 1848 in the sudden Slavization of the "German city" of Prague, but now, almost two decades later, they appeared in a different guise. Czechs were not exotic Slavic nationalists, but among the best liberals in the monarchy, respectable bourgeois gentlemen, who spoke eloquent German but annoyingly insisted they were a different people.

Czech nationalists had no choice but to be liberal, because without arguments for self-government, they had no cause. A handful of nobles supported the Czech cause but otherwise, the movement's leaders were sons of peasants and millers who made the revolutionary claim that their nation's rights had been vested in a *people*—people descended from tribes that had come into possession of Bohemia many centuries earlier. (A synonym in this region for people was of course "nation.") So when Czech politicians talked endlessly of Bohemian state's rights, what they really meant were the rights of ethnic Czechs to

Bohemian territory. They therefore were radical liberals, favoring the stretching of suffrage to every male adult, advocating national self-determination decades before Woodrow Wilson entered the scene, because in Bohemia, they would always outvote the Germans.

The arguments of Viennese liberals against Czech rights to self-government therefore had to be cultural and imperialist: about protecting civilization against a deadly challenge. They portrayed Czechs as unreasoning nationalists and claimed to be following in the footsteps of Joseph II: uniting a realm behind a higher culture that happened to be German. Yet that old agenda was now overlaid with newer idioms of racism. Take Karl Ludwig Bruck, finance minister in revolutionary 1848 and a liberal of sterling credentials. He said Austria's destiny was to become the center of "all questions of civilized behavior [*Gesittung*]" in the Danube basin, and the local tongues—Romanian, Serbian, Ukrainian, and Slovak—were simply tools to educate [*durchbilden*] the eastern tribes in German ideas and opinions. This agenda logically went beyond Habsburg lands: Austria would win Romania and Serbia for Germandom "through just and reasoned action."[31]

Liberal Anton Schmerling's friend and coauthor of the February 1861 constitution, Johann Ritter von Perthaler (1816–1862) called Slavs "little peoples." "The Austrian knows," he wrote, "how vital the German element is for the empire, and if his politics are European, he still strives to strengthen the German peoples, because here the empire has its strongest core and the healthiest and highest energies, which can invigorate the rest of the body." Authorities engaged artist Hanns Gasser to create twelve statues celebrating the "peoples of the empire," for Vienna's Bank and Stock Exchange building (the ground floor is the Café Central), and he identified Slovenia as a "half-nation."[32]

But this liberal imperialism also involved damming a flood of dangers. As Austria had once defended Christendom against the Turks, it now secured civilization against "Muscovite barbarism." Works of fiction and scholarship portrayed German culture as enlightened and the Slavic peoples as exotics, given to drinking and slacking off; colonial subjects to be restrained and disciplined. In contrast to the inhabitants of Algeria or India, however, Czechs or Slovenes occupied lands considered integral to the metropole.[33]

Yet far from a united surging threat, these "Slavs" were hopelessly divided. In August 1866, the Moravian Belcredi summoned a second, much smaller, Slavic Congress to Vienna, inviting the Pole Gołuchowski as well as the Croat Bishop Strossmayer, whom the British liberal William Gladstone called one of the three most impressive people he had known. Also in attendance were Czech liberal nationalists František Ladislav Rieger and his father-in-law, František Palacký.[34] One reasonable method for reforming the monarchy that emerged among these Slavic spokespersons—who really only spoke for themselves—was to divide it in five pieces: two units in the Alpine lands, then the Bohemian Crown (Bohemia-Moravia-Silesia), the Kingdom of Galicia, and Hungary-Croatia. Yet they could not agree on this or any other proposal. The Poles thought they could do better in one-to-one negotiations with Vienna, and that would prove to be correct. To gain control over multiethnic Galicia, in 1867 Polish representatives in Vienna would support the Habsburg Compromise with Hungary—blithely forgetting Croat demands for autonomy. Poland's elites would allow the Magyars to lord it over Croats in Hungary so that they could lord it over Ukrainians in Galicia. The Slovenes also rejected the proposal, believing their needs were not sufficiently addressed.[35] That left the Czechs as the only supporters of federalism.

Despite this disarray, Viennese newspapers continued to refer to the "Slavs" as if they were a united hostile bloc. "Blinded" by nationalism, liberal Czechs had allegedly boycotted the *Reichsrat* in the 1860s rather than take democratic responsibility, and hypocritically allied with feudal counts and princes of the Bohemian aristocracy to frustrate (liberal German) progress. Yet for Czech liberals, their path seemed reasonable. They staged their boycott after seeing what the Hungarians had achieved through passive resistance, and if they grouped with Bohemia's nobles, they did so because the franchise favored nobles, and given the hostility of the German liberals to Czech rights, they had nowhere else to turn.[36] Vienna's press was revealing a characteristic contradiction in anti-Slavism: Slavs had deep, unspecified powers, ready to be unleashed against Germans through alliances with foreign states, but at the same time, Slavic delegates had been too emotional and chaotic to work out a serious program. It was not in their "nature" to organize anything.

Sensing the combined condescension and fear among Vienna's liberals, Hungary's liberal elite worded their appeals for control of Hungary to Francis Joseph in evocative anti-Slavic language. Take Gyula Andrássy, who was after Ferenc Deák the most important politician in Hungary, a military commander in 1848/1849 who had evaded a death sentence by escaping to France, where his noble background gained him access to elite circles. Because Habsburg officials hanged the dashing nobleman in effigy in 1849, women in Paris salons took to calling him *le beau pendu*—the beautiful hanged one. He shared the disdain for Slavs, accusing them of achieving an "artificial majority" in the monarchy, though in fact they constituted more than half the population.[37] In 1858 Andrássy took advantage of an amnesty to return to Hungary, and, with his

FIGURE 7.1. Gyula Andrássy. *Source*: GL Archive/Alamy Stock Photo.

charisma, wit, and natural political skills, soon became Deák's trusted lieutenant and the most important force in negotiations with the House of Habsburg
in 1866–1867.

Hailing from today's Slovakia, Andrássy saw federalization of the monarchy
as a step toward Slavic domination. He portrayed Bohemian state rights as a
fiction, because the Bohemian crown had been abrogated in 1627 and became
a nonentity based on Maria Theresa's reform of the Bohemian state chancellery in 1749 at the latest. In a memo to the emperor, Andrássy wrote that the
1620 Czech defeat at White Mountain had been regrettable, but one could not
recreate the conditions that existed beforehand.[38]

In a long career in which he rose to Habsburg foreign minister, Andrássy went
to extraordinary pains to keep Slavic groups from coming together, rejecting

not just federalization of the monarchy but also any federal settlement in non-Hungarian Cisleithania. First came the legal, then the cultural argument. The founding document of the state, the Pragmatic Sanction, was something Hungary had agreed to with Austria, not with its component parts. But to sacrifice the Pragmatic Sanction would not only alienate Hungary; it would also rob the monarchy of its strongest foundation, the Germans, who would lose their historical mission, their imperial task of bettering peoples on lower rungs of culture. If Austria ceased realizing this purpose, Andrássy wrote, it would be expelled not only from Germany, but also from civilized Europe.[39] And the result would be cries of pain from the Austro-German provinces and from Berlin and Munich as well.

Andrássy was adroitly echoing the logic of Austrian German nationalism. Moritz von Kaiserfeld, an important German liberal from Styria, wrote to a Hungarian deputy in 1866 of the dangers of a parliament responsible for the whole empire: it would remain a "battleground for national hegemony; there could be no purely political majority in such an institution." What he meant by "political" was ostensibly non-national, that is, German or Magyar. Slavic nationalism—concern with language rights—was not politics but an irrational obsession. If given a chance, he wrote, geographically and politically disparate Slavs would use such a *Reichsrat* as a "means to unite and establish their own hegemony over the empire." A Vienna newspaper representing German liberal opinion wrote that the Slavs, though located in the heart of Europe, "remain alien to it and don't offer any noteworthy contribution to any creation of art, science, industry, trade or intelligence."[40]

Hungarians, until recently exotic easterners in the eyes of Germans, could now become their partners. Austria-Hungary would be not simply two political halves but two mirror battlegrounds over culture, German against Czechs and Slovenes in one, Magyars against Romanians, Slovaks, and the South Slavs in the other. Andrássy summed up the rationale for dualism as follows: "you look after your Slavs and we will look after ours." There was an elegant political structure to match these inelegant words. Except Galicia and Dalmatia, most of Cisleithania belonged to historic Germany and was German dominated, essentially constituting Germany minus Bismarck's Reich, still an enormous space. Even Galicia was strongly German culturally, with universities at Czernowitz and Lwow/Lemberg that were Austro-German foundations. For its part Hungary had boundaries that seemed immutable because they extended back centuries—to the holy crown of St. Stephen—and a highly self-confident and united ruling group. And German middle-class liberals felt an attraction to the cohesion, pride, and "noble feeling" of Hungarian gentry liberals. Hungary had shown Austria's Germans that a people united in will could prevail despite a chain of setbacks and misfortunes.[41]

Uncertain Compromise

Still, nothing in this logic of common Austro-Hungarian interests made the 1867 Compromise that divided the realm inevitable. The decision rested with Francis Joseph, and influential figures at court, including his mother, were warning him about deals with any people. The empire must remain one. Yet from the summer of 1866, two fortuitous and highly personal factors intervened in favor of the deal between Austria and Hungary: one from Germany, the other from the emperor's own house.

After Königgrätz, Francis Joseph remained uncertain of whether he would submit to Prussia's verdict or seek to restore Habsburg power in Germany, perhaps in league with France. He appointed a foreign minister who knew much about Germany but little about Austria: the Dresden liberal Count Friedrich Ferdinand von Beust, minister to the Saxon king for decades, an enthusiast of British constitutional forms, and (unlike other Austrian leaders) a Protestant. Beust had broad horizons gained from decades of experience at embassies in Berlin to Paris and London, and precisely his ignorance of Austria allowed him to see simple solutions through the thickets of detail that eluded those who knew more. The essential fact was that Hungary had nearly wrecked the monarchy in 1848/1849 and had to be accommodated.[42]

Beust did not lead Austria back to Germany; given Austria's parlous finances, that was unworkable. But he did promote German ethnic ascendancy within the Habsburg Empire, and he recognized that this could not happen without the cooperation of the Hungarians. His liberal temperament brought him closer to Deák and Andrássy than to the Czech liberals allied with feudal elites in Bohemia, and soon he had taken on board the concerns about a "Slavic problem" that pervaded political classes in Vienna and Budapest. A showdown with the Moravian Belcredi, the head of government, took place in an extraordinary imperial council meeting called by Francis Joseph for January and early February 1867.

Belcredi had wanted to make Austria more Slav and federalist by calling an extraordinary *Reichsrat* freely elected by diets, a move that would have produced a legislative body controlled by Slavs. Indeed, by that time, delegates to diets in Slovenia, Croatia, Bohemia, and Poland were using their own languages, although the Germans present often could not understand them. In Beust's view, such a plan threatened the empire's substance because it failed to take into account the zero-sum nature of the national question. Any restructuring would favor one group over another, and the most important group for the monarchy's fortunes was the Germans, the primary force in the bureaucracy as well as the army, and holders of the greatest wealth and industry, even in Bohemia, where they were a minority. It would be much less costly to alienate the Slavs. And since the government could not satisfy all peoples, it had to rely on those who possessed the greatest vitality [*Lebenskraft*], and other than the Germans, that left the Magyars.[43]

Now Francis Joseph gave the all-clear for an arrangement with Hungary. The breakthrough did not come easily: he accepted Belcredi's resignation with tears in his eyes. Belcredi worried that an arrangement assuming the dominance of Germans and Hungarians—a minority in both halves of the empire—would make constitutional life in Austria an illusion (*Scheinleben*). But Francis Joseph could not delay any longer. The monarchy was unable to pay the indemnity of 30 million Gulden that Prussia levied after the defeat at Königgrätz, and the international money markets were making credit dependent on a constitutional reorganization. Austrian bonds were being traded at a discount of 45 percent below parity, an all-time low.[44]

* * *

The dogged Gyula Andrássy, a man Francis Joseph had once condemned to hang, probably had the greatest role in persuading the emperor of the merits of dualism. He put Francis's mind to rest on whether he would maintain a say over army and foreign policy, and he and other Hungarian leaders satisfied the emperor that Hungary would not subvert the monarchy. Still there was the question of how Andrássy could gain ready access to an emperor who would have preferred to have nothing to do with him. The answer lay with the empress.

Before marrying Francis Joseph in 1854, Elisabeth had been tutored in Austrian history by the nobleman Janos Majláth, a scion of the family we have already encountered and an émigré living in Munich, who regaled her with stories of Hungary's heroic struggle to survive over many centuries. After the couple's tragic sojourn in Budapest in 1857, she had astounded her husband by demanding to learn Hungarian, and he refused permission, saying it was too difficult. She proceeded anyway. When the imperial pair visited Budapest in the spring of 1866, to everyone's amazement the empress addressed the Hungarian

Cardinal Primate, then the diet, in eloquent Hungarian sentences and full paragraphs.

We know that she did not learn Hungarian only from books. Two years earlier, for unknown reasons, Elisabeth had taken an unknown, warm-hearted country girl named Ida Ferenczy into her service as lady-in-waiting. Ferenczy gained the empress's confidence, and the two conversed from morning to evening in Hungarian, greatly annoying the court, especially Elisabeth's detested mother-in-law, Sophia, who supposedly favored the Czechs. After Königgrätz, Elisabeth personally tended to wounded Hungarian soldiers, and when complimented on her accent-free Hungarian, she said she owed it to Ida. Ida made sure letters from Elisabeth found their way to Andrássy, Deák, and other noblemen whose cause she supported, for reasons that are not entirely clear. Her identification with Hungary eclipsed concerns for all other nationalities; when her husband's affairs went poorly in Italy, she told Andrássy that it pained her, but when they failed in Hungary, it killed her.[45]

Without Elisabeth's personal involvement, the crisis would have produced some resolution, but not the Compromise of 1867, a turning point in Habsburg fortunes and misfortunes. In the decisive summer and fall months of 1866, she was a "fanatical tool" of the Hungarian elite, making the fate of the monarchy seem to depend on appeasing Hungary.[46] She also held out the prospect of conjugal intimacy should Francis Joseph show favor to Hungary. In June 1867, Andrássy and the Cardinal Primate at long last placed the crown of St. Stephen on Francis Joseph's head in an elaborate ceremony in Budapest, and nine months later, their last child, Marie Valerie, was born.

After eighteen years, the illegal interregnum was over, and a living connection reestablished to the Pragmatic Sanction. As queen and king, Elisabeth and Francis Joseph spent several weeks each year in Hungary, she even more, making sure her children learned the country's history and culture. She told her lunch guests—all from Hungary, none from Cisleithania—that if possible, she and her husband would be the first to bring the Hungarian soldiers and politicians executed in 1849 back to life.[47] After the Compromise, a portrait of Deák hung above her bed, where it stayed to the end of her life; her public display of grief at his funeral a decade later caused a minor scandal.

The Compromise resulted in two centrally ruled halves of the monarchy, with common ministries of foreign policy, defense, and finance. Matters of joint interest (including state debt, tariffs, currency, and some indirect taxes) were subject to negotiation every ten years in delegations of sixty representatives from each parliament. In Hungary, the constitution was restored, with parliament and

FIGURE 7.2. Crowning of Francis Joseph and Elisabeth in Budapest (June 1867).
Source: Edmund Tull (painter). Via Wikimedia Commons.

cabinet appointed, and Gyula Andrássy made head of government. Hungary had to commit 30 percent to the empire's joint finances, and though the quota was renegotiated every ten years, it did not change much until 1918. Hungarian émigré circles blasted this or any arrangement with the Habsburgs as shameful, but over time, it proved an excellent deal: by the empire's twilight years, Transleithania was producing 35.4 percent of national income; Cisleithania 64.6 percent.[48]

The terms of the Compromise won approval in Hungary's parliament in March, but what would happen in Vienna was unclear. A smaller parliament had convened after state minister Beust dissolved the Bohemian and Moravian diets and called for a reelection to guarantee a German majority.[49] In October the government brought legislation to enact the Compromise before the *Reichsrat*, the economic arrangements having been settled in August and September between deputations from the two parliaments.

Now came the question of a constitution for Cisleithania as the final act of the restructuring launched in 1859. The German liberals used their leverage to press reforms on the emperor that he had not remotely envisaged seven years earlier. The result, the "December Constitution," established sanctity of property and person; privacy of the post; equality before the law; and freedom of speech, assembly, and conscience. A law on judicial power secured separation of powers, an Imperial Court was formed to protect individual rights, and the *Reichsrat* became a real parliament with legislative initiative.[50] A major limit to its power was the emperor's continued control over the army and foreign policy. Habsburg Austria became a constitutional monarchy but never evolved into a democracy.

* * *

The Compromise provided a stable legal platform for state consolidation and steady economic progress in both halves of the monarchy. From 1867 to 1914, the national income tripled, with a yearly rate of growth between 2.6 and 2.8 percent. In Hungary, agricultural exports grew and industrialization accelerated, though it lagged behind Bohemia and Austria. Still, its advance was remarkable. In the 1850s, an average of 250 kilometers of railroad were built each year, and after 1867, the total jumped to 600. The assets in Hungarian banks more than tripled between 1866 and 1873.[51]

The Compromise would have continued to provide a basis for law and order in the Habsburg lands beyond 1918 had World War I not intervened. But the new arrangement was also marked by tension from the start. Hungarians were never satisfied with junior partner or even partner status, and they hoped that the center of gravity in the monarchy would be Budapest, not Vienna.

In 1867 the monarchy's majority was Slavic, and in both halves Slavic politicians became deeply alienated.[52] Czechs, Croats, Serbs, and Slovaks said their nations had come to the Habsburgs' rescue in 1848/1849 but were now abandoned; the latter three had been placed at the mercy of the amnestied rebels! In Hungary, only Croats received any recognition, and that was due to the historic integrity of the Croatian kingdom. The others were simply "nationalities" to be subsumed in the "indivisible Hungarian nation." Rights applied not to national groups but exclusively to individual citizens, and there was no appreciation of the need to protect local vernaculars.[53] The Cisleithanian constitution respected German sensitivities above all others, not officially establishing the German language, but also not permitting it to be challenged as the dominant language of state. All ethnic groups (*Volksstämme*) had equal rights to nationality and language, but what constituted a *Volksstamm*, or how the state might protect it, was not specified.

In neither half of the monarchy did the new arrangement come close to satisfying the desires of the nationalities' political elites for self-government and legally binding protection of their cultures. The difference between the two halves was that the Hungarian state actively sought to make its subjects into Magyars, while the Austrian government was for the most part nationally agnostic. It even passed a school law in 1869 that gave each nationality the right to a school if forty of its children lived within 4 kilometers of a given locale. Yet once this provision passed, Czechs took it for granted rather than crediting it to the Austrian government, and as the percentage of literate Czechs reached among the top rates in Europe, so did the dissatisfiaction of Czech elites with the fact that they had no national autonomy comparable to the that of the Hungarians.[54] The Czech leader Rieger called the Compromise "unnatural injustice," and in general, Czechs referred to the December Constitution as "artificial."

Czech passive resistance dated back to 1863 with the partial boycotting of the Vienna *Reichsrat*, but full-scale abstention by Czech deputies began in 1868 from Vienna and extended to the Bohemian and Moravian diets. It was accompanied by public protests so severe in October 1868 that the government imposed a state of siege in Prague and surrounding communities. Czech politics became what would later be called "extraparliamentary opposition." Between 1868 and 1871, the movement staged more than a hundred mass meetings, called *tabory*, or camps, in the countryside, with between 1 and 1.5 million participants. The protesters called for Bohemian state rights, suffrage, education, and Slav solidarity. Authorities in Vienna tried to suppress the agitation through arrests and confiscsations of newspapers, measures that were in clear violation of the freshly printed constitution.[55] As we will see in Chapter 9, promising attempts to placate the Czechs were worked out in 1871 and supported by Francis Joseph, but they came to nothing because of Austro-German Magyar opposition. Magyar politicians feared that any concessions to nationalities in the west— "Cisleithania"—would encourage demands from the nationalities in Hungary.

The Compromise kept the monarchy afloat but ended any pretense that it might call itself an empire. The monarchy had no "imperial center" and no effective control over more than half the realm in the east, which was becoming a nation-state, while Cisleithania became a partly decentralized territorial conglomeration. Yet if Austria-Hungary was no empire, it was propelled by imperialist energies, based in the joint desires of German and Magyar elites to subjugate Slavs and convert them to the "higher" culture. The combination of condescension and fear led the monarchy forward—and also downward. In 1878, Austria-Hungary took the odd step of occupying Bosnia-Herzegovina, and taking charge of even more Slavs. In the background lay the conviction that it was bringing civilization to yet one more benighted region. In the foreground lay the simple determination to deny this land to a growing Serbia. Yet there was no chance of making Bosnians into Austrians or Hungarians. As the monarchy reformed, it made itself less reformable; as it grew in size, it shrank in self-confidence; and as it entered the imperial age, it was less an empire than ever before.

CHAPTER 8

The 1878 Berlin Congress: Europe's New Ethno-Nation-States

The idea of a "long" nineteenth century has grown fashionable in recent decades, and it is said to extend from the French Revolution to World War I. An adjunct to it is a "short" twentieth century from 1918 to 1989. The problem is that this short twentieth century has little coherence other than two convulsions of violence and the rise and fall of two totalitarian empires. The implication is that after the twentieth century ended, Europe could return to whatever development was interrupted by World War I. But we still do not know the ultimate destination of the twentieth century. Wherever that is, it would seem to involve a reassertion of the national state, driven by politicians willing to exploit populist nationalism. Perhaps, then, it makes more sense to tell the story of Europe's twentieth century in terms of struggles over national self-determination, recalling that not only liberals like Giuseppe Mazzini and Woodrow Wilson, but also fascists (Adolf Hitler, Corneliu Codreanu) and Communists (V. I. Lenin) invoked this term. If the twentieth century is (was) about national self-determination, then a good argument can be made for it really getting started in 1878 and lasting well into our own time.

In 1878, representatives of Europe's major powers convened in the capital of the new German nation-state for negotiations that bear all the hallmarks of the more famous effort in decolonization and democratization that transpired at Paris after World War I. At Berlin in 1878, statesmen determined the boundaries, constitutions, sovereigns, and even citizenship of four national states, which like Poland or Czechoslovakia in 1919, had to be created in the wake of imperial decline so as to secure Europe's balance of power. We date the independence of modern Bulgaria, Montenegro, Romania, and Serbia from July 1878.

But in the interests of balance, the statesmen in Berlin traduced the spirit of nationalism by denying to Serbia territory where a plurality of the inhabitants was Orthodox South Slavs. That was Bosnia-Herzegovina, a quilt of ethnicities, which Austria-Hungary was permitted to occupy in 1878 with no purpose other than making sure it did not go to Serbia. Politicians in Vienna and Budapest viewed the prospect of a "great South Slav state" with horror, all the more so as it promised to be a close ally of Russia.

Some have called this frustrated Serb determination to expand "irredentist," and that is both correct and misleading.[1] The characterization is correct because Serbia felt there were Serbs beyond its boundaries who had to be included, but it is also misleading in suggesting that this agenda was unusual. In fact, every new state, beginning with Italy (where the word "irredentism" originated) and Germany, was irredentist in the sense that it "redeemed" national territory. Piedmont-Sardinia had not been Italy, nor was Prussia Germany. Without irredentism, there would be no Serbia, or any other new East European state, whether created in 1878 or 1919. Therefore, it is not hard to understand the tremendous affront that many Serbs, in and outside Serbia, felt after 1878.

But where Austria-Hungary was concerned, it was not only an affront but also the bizarre act of a troubled imperial state, now taking millions more Slavs under its rule, just a decade after dividing into Austria-Hungary precisely to keep a lid on the empire's Slavs. But even more intriguingly and confoundingly, the man who negotiated the inclusion of more Serbs and Croats, as well as millions of Bosnian Muslims, was the beautiful hanged man, Count Gyula Andrássy, who became the Austro-Hungarian foreign minister in 1871, and whose own Hungary was trying to make loyal Magyars out of millions of Slovaks, Serbs, Ruthenes, and Croats. Before the Compromise of 1867, Magyar politicians had assured representatives of those groups that their rights would be legally guaranteed. Afterward, those promises were forgotten, and demands for national autonomy were treated as seditious.[2] Austria was not Germanizing its population, but German liberals were deeply concerned about the growing numerical superiority of Slavs. Now Vienna and Budapest took responsibility for 3 million more. How could they possibly make them into loyal citizens?

This story takes place in three acts. The first is the last major uprising of a Christian people against Ottoman rule in Europe, the Herzegovinian rebellion of 1875. The acts of Herzegovinian and then Bosnian peasants generated the pressures leading to the Berlin Congress. The second is the sanguineous military campaigns of Serbia, Montenegro, and Russia against the Ottoman Empire from 1876 to 1878, whose success triggered concern among the European powers about the growth of Russian and the decline of Ottoman power. The third is the Berlin Congress itself and how the European powers rescued peace as well as Austria-Hungary, largely by extending their blessings to four new states, each of which considered itself not an end product but rather a toehold from which the respective ethnic nation would expand.

Uprisings and the End of Ottoman
Rule in Bosnia-Herzegovina

The uprisings in Herzegovina in 1875 have much in common with those of 1848 because suddenly ethnic identities were forced to the surface that had rested peacefully beneath the surface of a feudal regime, largely unnoticed by West Europeans. If what provoked sudden and massive ethnic agitation in 1848 was the promise of political and civic rights, in Herzegovina in 1875, the cause was at first an agrarian dispute.

The trouble began in Nevesinje, a village that had just suffered a poor harvest. In normal times, the government's tax take was one-eighth, but now because of a deep fiscal crisis of the Ottoman state, surcharges were added, in some cases going up to half of production. Christian peasants saw their families starving while what little they produced was taken by Muslim landlords and the men who had leased the rights to collect taxes from Ottoman authorities, some of whom were Bosnian Christian merchants.[3]

Yet in 1874/1875, peasants in Herzegovina were kept even from harvesting at first, because the tax farmers failed to show up, and much of the grape and tobacco crop rotted. When the collectors finally appeared, they demanded more than the harvest was worth, and some peasants in Nevesinje refused to pay. In response, authorities unleashed the police (*zaptiehs*), who robbed, beat, and imprisoned the recalcitrant.[4] This led to a massive flight into the hills but also across the nearby borders to Montenegro, an autonomous principality under Ottoman suzerainty, as well as to Dalmatia, a Habsburg possession. Francis Joseph happened to be visiting, and some Catholics from Ottoman Herzegovina used the occasion put forward their grievances to him. Montenegro as well as Dalmatia were home to South Slav populations, whom Herzegovinians considered their ethnic kin. Within a few months, the refugee populations just beyond Ottoman borders had swelled to tens of thousands, and authorities in both places were organizing relief efforts.

The British geographer Arthur Evans wrote that Christians under Ottoman rule suffered from a "double disability," social and religious: the "*kmet*' or tiller of the soil, is worse off than many a serf in our darkest ages, and lies as completely at the mercy of the Mahometan owner of the soil as if he were a slave."[5] Christians as a class were share-croppers who could not attain personal freedom or own land; whereas the few Muslim peasants (less than 5 percent) could attain freedom as well as land.[6] Garrisons of an army that was almost exclusively Muslim kept order, and Christians could not count on any constituted

FIGURE 8.1. Refugees from unrest in Herzegovina. *Source*: Uroš Predić (painter).
Via Wikimedia Commons.

authority to enforce their rights. Evans told of an Albanian regiment on the
march through Bosnia that shot at Catholic peasants with impunity. The Ottoman regime in Bosnia-Herzegovina was hundreds of years old, but Christian
Slavs saw its authorities as foreign in a way that Muslim Slavs did not.[7]

Alarmed at the prospect of spreading violence, Bosnia's Ottoman governor
arranged for safe passage of refugee leaders from Montenegro back to Herzegovina, yet he was unable to control local officials. Border guards harassed the
returnees, and when they arrived home, several were murdered by local *zaptiehs*.
Fearful of full-scale rebellion, a high-ranking commission (Mustafa-*paša*, the
mutasarrıf of Herzegovina, and Selim Pasha [*Selim-paša*] military commander in
the sanjak) arrived in mid-summer to meet with elected Orthodox village elders
and made suggestions for reform, including an administrative regime that would
feature Christian border guards, perhaps as a first stage to limited self-rule. They
also promised to remedy the excesses of local tax farmers and gendarmes.[8]

Whether these officials could have reformed the local tax-gathering regime
or altered the centuries-old economically and culturally subordinate position

of Christian farmers is open to question. There was the long history of Ottoman dignitaries promising to correct abuses of local officials and finding themselves unable to do so: over time, corruption itself had become the system.
Attempts had been made in recent years to permit Christians to own land, but
local Muslim *begs* had simply seized it with no regard for higher authority. A
more pertinent question was whether promises of reform could compete with
the heroic Kosovo narrative told among Orthodox rebels. According to that narrative, those who treated with Ottoman authorities were traitors. Then there
was public opinion in Montenegro and Serbia, stirred up by local jingoistic
presses, which was well aware of the history of the preceding decades, in which
armed uprisings had gradually pushed Ottoman power ever farther down the
Balkan Peninsula.

But Nevsinje was not just any hamlet. As in many revolts, the outbreak occurred amid extreme manifestations of a general problem. That part of Ottoman Herzegovina was a "limestone desert," a karstic mountain area where the
population desperately struggled to get by even in good times.[9] Other areas of
the province were more productive and generated enough income for the state
but also for the local population. We get a sense of the desperation from the petition made by village leaders in their meeting with the arbitration commission
Ottoman authorities sent to Nevesinje. They demanded:

1. Christian girls and women should no longer be molested,
2. Churches should no longer be desecrated,
3. Christians should have equal rights with Turks before the law,
4. They should be protected from the violence of the *zaptiehs*,
5. Tithe farmers should not take more than that to which they were
    entitled, and
6. No forced labor should be demanded by the government, but all labor
    when needed should be paid for "as was the case all over the world."[10]

Still, the petitioners acted as loyal subjects of the sultan without a whiff of
nationalist fervor; there was no talk of unity with Serbia or Montenegro or any
hint of "pan-Slavism." Right before the uprising, Muslim landowners and Christian traders in Mostar had made complaints to the sultan about the finance
administration: their hope was to reform and not replace the existing system.
And according to a local Orthodox chronicler, the seriousness of the high commission had made a deep impression on the Orthodox leaders who knew that
a full-scale uprising would bring down a holocaust of suffering on their impoverished region.[11]

Yet other forces considered violence a rational tool for pursuit of their interests. *Agas* and *begs* employed *zaptiehs* to crush even suggestions that their privileges might be curtailed, and the hills gave shelter to bandit gangs (some local, others from Montenegro, Dalmatia, and Serbia), who lived on plunder and benefited from the disruption of authority. They enjoyed favor in the local population for their reputations of stealing from the wealthy and protecting the Christian *kmets* [serfs] from abuse. In July one band staged a brutal attack on a caravan from Mostar to Nevesinje, killing five Muslim traders, and at that stage, officials in Istanbul decided that all resistance must be crushed before there could be any talk of reform.

Bosnia's governor assembled an army, and the *begs* organized their own irregular troops, *bashi-bazouks*, all of which terrorized the peasant population: burning villages, hanging leaders, raping women, and enslaving children. At least 5,000 peasants were killed, and refugees fleeing Bosnia-Herzegovina by the end of 1876 numbered at least 100,000, perhaps as many as 250,000. The destruction went in both directions. In the district of Bihać, for example, 41 of 198 Muslim villages were burned down, while of 298 Christian villages, 223 were destroyed.[12] Each side dealt mercilessly with prisoners and also took trophies from the dead.

What had begun as a local agrarian revolt had now become not just a civil war, but an ethnic one. The rebel leadership came from the nationally and politically conscious Bosnian Christian middle classes—teachers, merchants, priests—and formed a "Bosnian national parliament." These self-described members of the Bosnian nation were of Serb nationality, similar to how Moravians might feel Czech while retaining a sense of regional identity. By October 1877, a Provisional National Bosnian Government consisting of ten Serbs, three Croats, and one Russian had emerged, wanting to unite with other Serbian lands.[13]

Despite efforts by the Serb and Montenegrin governments to stop them, thousands more South Slavs joined in the fighting, including tribes from Montenegro and men already "armed to the teeth" from Habsburg Dalmatia. Not much propaganda was needed to awaken ethnic solidarity; simple tales of atrocity sufficed, and they were abundant. The prince of Montenegro, Nicholas, told an Ottoman representative that the sultan could not expect him to hold back Montenegrins from intervening in the "struggle for freedom" of their Herzegovinian brothers (he was secretly arming them).[14] Volunteers also streamed in from Serbia and from Slovenia and Russia, believing that an awakening was about to take place among the South Slavs. Among their number were soldiers of fortune and even criminals.

The net effect was to cause Slavs from outside Bosnia-Herzegovina to see Christian Slavs from inside as their kinfolk, while Christians and Muslims from inside saw each other as strangers more than ever before, though of the same "ethnic stock."[15] Ottoman authorities inadvertently spread "Serb" consciousness among Orthodox Christians by targeting them for expulsion and sending in troops to hunt them down, while by contrast, local Muslims aided in suppressing the uprising because they feared changes to the status quo as well as violence at the hands of Christian neighbors. Soon there was little space for neutrality: the rebels persecuted Christians who refused to support them, and both sides drew the rational conclusion that it was safer to stand with one's ethnicity than outside it.[16]

Austro-Hungarian leaders tried to hold back Dalmatian Serbs and Croats from joining the rebellion because they were horrified at the prospect of national states being carved out of Ottoman territory. Foreign Minister Andrássy wrote in January 1875 that

> Turkey possesses a utility almost providential for Austria-Hungary. For Turkey maintains the status quo of the small Balkan states and impedes their national aspirations. If it were not for Turkey, all those aspirations would fall on our heads. . . . If Bosnia-Herzegovina should go to Serbia or Montenegro or if a new state should be formed there which we cannot prevent, then we should be ruined and should ourselves assume the role of the "sick man."[17]

Andrássy's statement reflects extraordinary insecurity on the part of a leader of a state that was better organized, wealthier, and stronger than the beleaguered Ottoman Empire. The insecurity reflected an immobilizing fear of Slavic nationalism that pervaded the Austro-Hungarian elite. The reference to a "sick man" suggests he thought that the dual monarchy might become a "victim" like the Ottoman Empire, with other powers (Russia) chipping off bits to serve their clients. His worry that tiny Serbia might seize the Dalmatian coast was not a rational concern, unless one imagined a huge anti-Austrian alliance forming and the other powers standing by. But his fears accord with the rising influence of social Darwinism. States that were passive—or as he said, "abstinent"—would decline, and therefore Austria-Hungary had to do something to seem virile and relevant. He knew that the monarchy could not call upon "national enthusiasm," and therefore would do better in a defensive position, if need be calling on its subjects to defend the "common fatherland."[18]

In a view common among the Magyar elite, Andrássy also believed that Russia and Germany aimed to make Hungary disappear. He took for granted that Russia's support of pan-Slavism was to blame for the unrest in Herzegovina, though of course Russia had not created the Ottoman state debt that made efforts to wring revenue from the barren earth so desperate. It was, however, true that news of the atrocities among Orthodox Slavs inflamed Russian opinion after the uprising began and helped drive Russia toward involvement. A traveler to the Dalmatian coast in 1876 witnessed a distinctly twentieth-century scene: desperate refugee populations, out of which foreign consuls, prominently the Russian, were recruiting mercenaries to fight against Turkey.

Encouraged by disarray in the Ottoman leadership, the Montenegrin and Serbian governments themselves attacked Turkish positions in July 1876. To their great surprise, the armies of the decrepit empire drove them back. Still, the rebellion against Ottoman authority spread, next to Bulgaria, where the repression was savage, with atrocities against civilians that (again) beggar description, unleashing a public outcry in Western Europe as well as in Russia. In December, Russia, Austria-Hungary, and Britain held a conference in Istanbul urging effective reforms, and the new Sultan Abdulhamid II made promises that he either would not or could not keep.[19]

In April 1877, Russia finally attacked the Ottoman Empire, sending troops south through the Danubian principalities, and now war was raging across the Balkan peninsula. Like the Serbs and Montenegrins, the Russians encountered

FIGURE 8.2. Serb military camp during Serbo-Turkish War (1876). *Source*: Military Museum, Belgrade. Via Wikimedia Commons.

unexpectedly stubborn resistance and were held up for six months at the fortress Plevna in Bulgaria, 32 kilometers south of their crossing point on the Danube, but then they renewed their advance, and in January 1878 Turkey called for a cessation of hostilities. Two months later, Russia and Turkey concluded a peace in a suburb of Istanbul called San Stefano, which satisfied Russia as well as a new Bulgarian state, but no one else.

San Stefano created a Bulgaria under a "Christian government" that was as large as could be imagined, stretching from the Danube in the north to Rhodopes in the South, from the Black Sea in the east to the Morava river and the Vardar in the west. It included some territories desired by Serbia and others desired by Greece. This Bulgarian mega-state was seen by Austria-Hungary and the other powers as a Russian client with a strategically vital position on the Balkan peninsula, opening the way to Istanbul and leaving St. Petersburg a step away from controlling the Dardanelles.[20]

San Stefano did propose a promising solution to the interethnic conflict in Bosnia, however, making the territory autonomous in the Ottoman Empire with a parliament where two-fifths of the seats would be held by the Orthodox, two-fifths by Muslims, and one-fifth by Catholics.[21] This approximated the arrangement made to share power and keep peace among religious groups in the nineteenth-century Netherlands (three "pillars"), but unfortunately, it was not resurrected when the other powers insisted that the San Stefano treaty must be revised. Its provisions had seemed especially threatening to Austria-Hungary, which was desperately concerned to keep Serbia and Montenegro from expanding up toward the Croatian borders and then appealing for unity with the Habsburg South Slavs on the other side. To Serbia and Montenegro, such expansion seemed a logical next step; after all, they had gone to war with the express hope of dividing Bosnia-Herzegovina between them.[22]

Yet a war between Austria-Hungary and Serbia would quickly have involved Russia and provoked a broader European conflagration. In particular, the German Chancellor Bismarck feared that any conflict, especially one involving Russia, would threaten his efforts to consolidate the new German nation-state. And because none of the other powers wanted war, yet all were unhappy with Russia's aggrandizement at San Stefano, they accepted his invitation to work out a new resolution at a congress in Berlin in June 1878.[23] This congress confirmed a reduction of Ottoman possessions in south Eastern Europe by about half, and it granted independence to Serbia, Montenegro, and the Danubian principalities—Romania—and made Bulgaria autonomous. But this Bulgaria was about two-thirds smaller than the San Stefano version, with Macedonia and

Budapest

RUSSIA

AUSTRIA-HUNGARY

Iasi

Moldavia

Arad

ROMANIA

Banja Luka
BOSNIA
Occupied by
Austria-Hungary 1878
annexed in 1908

Belgrade

Bucharest

DALMATIA

HERZEGOVINA

Sarajevo

SERBIA

Craiova

Nevesinje

Ragusa

MONTE
NEGRO

Podgorica

Nis

BULGARIA

So a

Turnovo

Varna

Dobrudja

Black Sea

Durazzo

ALBANIA

Skopje

Eastern Roumelia

Philippopolis

Adrianople

Roumelia

Constantinople

Bitola
Macedonia

Thessaloniki

EPIRUS

Corfu

Larissa
THESSALY

Ionian
Sea

Aegean
Sea

Lesbos

Euboea

Smyrna

OTTOMAN EMPIRE

Cephalonia

Patras

Athens

Mediterranean
Sea

Rhodes

——— Boundary of Bulgaria according to
the Treaty of San Stefano

- - - - - Boundaries according to the Treaty of Berlin 1878

Ottoman territory

Territory under Ottoman suzerainity

Territory ceded to Serbia

Territory ceded to Bulgaria

Territory ceded to Russia

Territory ceded to Montenegro

Crete

Adriatic Sea

ITALY

0   100   200   300   400 km

0   50   100   150   200 miles

MAP 8.1. Southeastern Europe, 1878

East Rumelia, the sites of the atrocities, reverting to Ottoman rule (the latter under a Christian governor).[24] Most fatefully, the Berlin Congress denied Bosnia-Herzegovina to Serbia and Montenegro by placing it under Austro-Hungarian occupation. Nominally the territory remained an Ottoman possession, but Austria-Hungary treated it as a colony from the start and began (illegally) conscripting troops there in 1881.

Though the Congress forestalled the next major conflict for more than thirty years, it left none of the new entities satisfied. Montenegro and Serbia continued to believe Bosnia-Herzegovina was rightfully theirs, and Serbia would quarrel with Bulgaria over Macedonia, which for the time being was returned to the Ottoman Empire. The new states justified their claims and counterclaims by what would later be called "national self-determination." Romania's goal was to expand into Romanian-inhabited parts of Hungary, but also to acquire districts of Bessarabia containing co-ethnics that Russia had received at Berlin. But for the time being, their arguments were not taken seriously. The British Foreign Minister Lord Salisbury said: "at Potsdam there are mosquitoes, here there are minor powers. I don't know which is worse." Bismarck likened Balkan politicians to "sheep thieves."[25]

The Berlin Congress had forced Russia to fulfill a promise the tsar had made to Francis Joseph in Moravia in 1876 and apparently forgotten, namely, not to create a large Slavic state out of Ottoman territories. But what was too large? Now that the Bulgaria of San Stefano had been put on and then taken off the map, Bulgarian foreign policy focused on getting the territories "back." The new state thus entered life with a "ready-made program for territorial expansion and a burning sense of the injustice meted out to it by the great powers."[26] But Bulgaria's problem struck at a core difficulty of the eastern question, that is, the gradual reduction of Ottoman power in Europe: if there was to be a South Slav state, what was its proper size? The Illyrians had imagined an entity going from Klagenfurt to the Black Sea.

Making Bosnians?

However large the South Slav state was, it exceeded what Austria-Hungary would tolerate because it would be an outpost of a pan-Slav, Russian superpower that Vienna and Budapest would face helplessly in terms of ideas and armed forces. So at Berlin, with the blessings of the other powers, Austria had halted what seemed the unstoppable momentum of Slavic power on its eastern and southern borders.

The occupation of Bosnia-Herzegovina was a temporary exception to the region-wide trend of pushing back multinational states in favor of nation-states. Instead of becoming part of Serbia, Bosnia-Herzegovina became an appendage of Austria-Hungary and was called a *Reichsland*, the one area that Vienna and Budapest ruled jointly. At the time, people said it was a colony, an outlet for the energies of would-be imperialists from the now defunct Austrian Empire, men and women who treated Bosnians as unfit for self-rule, like children who needed tutelage from the parent land.[27] But ultimately, this colony would not simply rebel and separate from the parent: the Bosnians' anti-imperial struggle turned out to be parricidal.

Technically, Austria-Hungary was supposed to occupy Bosnia-Herzegovina until "order" could be restored, and at the convention of Novi Pazar in April 1879, it recognized Turkish sovereignty and promised to protect the rights of Muslims. Effective rule went to the monarchy's imperial civil service, under a joint council (delegation) responsible for both halves. Therefore, the joint Austro-Hungarian minister of finance, the ambitious and well-traveled Hungarian nobleman Benjamin Kállay, became the land's governor.[28] Kállay was determined to leave a mark upon history and use Bosnia as a laboratory for fashioning a nation. Bohemia was becoming a perennial headache for the Habsburgs, and Hungary had been more difficult to corral than anyone had imagined, but in Bosnia-Herzegovina, officials could start from scratch: they would transform the inhabitants into "Bosnians," a people whose prime purpose was loyalty to the monarchy. Kállay's scheme was also an act of imperialist hubris: he wrote Francis Joseph that he and his officials were bringing the Bosnians the "blessings of culture," and would raise the land up to their own supposed level.[29]

The initial entry of imperial armies into Bosnia might have given Kállay pause; rather than being welcomed as liberators, they met violent resistance from Muslim and Orthodox militias who desired self-rule. The campaign took over two months and cost the Habsburg forces more than 946 dead. Still, the occupation seemed to offer a fresh chance. All Bosnians shared "history" with one another that went back centuries, whereas Bosnian Christians at best had religion in common with Serbs and Croats. Indeed, into the mid-nineteenth century, the differences among Bosnians were primarily thought of as confessional: they were *krstjani* (adherents of the western church) *hristjani* (eastern), and *musulmani*. There had been no economic or social reasons for hostility between Orthodox and Catholic populations, and the new regime established legal equality for all.[30]

FIGURE 8.3. Battle of Sarajevo (1878). *Source*: G. Durand (lithographer).
Chronicle/Alamy Stock Photo.

Yet to a careful observer, problems in forging Bosnian unity were evident from the start. Christians may have thought of themselves in religious terms, but they looked upon Muslims as ethnic foreigners, calling them "Turks," even though they were overwhelmingly of Slavic origin and spoke the same language as they did. This descriptor signals a deep barrier in perception; Muslims were identified as wrapped up in Turkish-Ottoman rule even after it had retreated.[31] As was often the case in East Central Europe, the national self relied on the "other" to come fully to life.

That sense of distinctiveness from Muslims in turn opened the Orthodox in Bosnia to the idea that they were not just brothers of Serbs in Hungary or Serbia: they were themselves Serbs, with a common history of living under "Turkish" oppression. And once Serb identity began advancing among Bosnia's Orthodox population, Habsburg authorities faced the kind of problem they had known in Italy, or more recently in Bohemia: nationalist agitators spread the message that people of one ethnicity should have their own state. The message coming from Serbia was that the Orthodox in Bosnia should belong to a state of South Slavs, whose center was Serbia.

Kállay, whose job it was to counteract this message, had excellent credentials for the job. He was born in 1839 to a very old Hungarian noble family and was fluent in many languages, including Turkish, Russian, Greek, and Serbian. On his mother's side of Serb origin, he had once run for office in Serb-inhabited parts of Hungary. He not only studied Serb history but also had published a book on it.[32] Kállay also knew a lot about Bosnia, having traveled from one end to the other in the summer of 1871. He even worked out a theory: Bosnians shared a deep national identity, going back to the early Middle Ages, which had been "overlaid by oriental deposits" in the centuries since. This deep sense of Bosnian consciousness had merely to be reawakened, and then it would displace pan-Croat and pan-Serb "fanciful dreams."

Yet he read the province through Hungarian lenses in a way that would prove self-defeating: he thought it possessed an ancient ruling stratum like Hungary's gentry, and he believed the Muslim landowning class, the *begs*, had an unbroken lineage dating back to the "Bogumil" medieval nobility, adherents of a mythical Christian sect controlled neither by Rome nor Constantinople, whose descendants had supposedly converted to Islam (after Ottoman conquest) to maintain their hold on the land. He thought the *begs* would return to Christianity if given the proper circumstances.[33]

He also had practical reasons to bank on Bosnia's Muslims: they felt a unique tie to the land. Unlike Catholics or Orthodox, they had no outside power to support their nationalism, and in fact shared a history of fighting for Bosnia's independence against the Ottomans. In 1831, Muslims under Husein-Kapetan Gradaševic had staged a revolt against attempts of Sultan Mahmud II (1808–1839) to enforce uniform rule from Istanbul. If there was to be a Bosnian nation, it had to start from this kind of feeling. Equally important, Muslims were the leading force in culture, administration, and the economy, and they were accustomed to ruling. Kállay was following in the footsteps of other colonial lords by ruling through a group whose authority was recognized. The alternative would have been social revolution.

With this group as his prime constituency, Kállay concocted a Bosnian identity with things that nationalists said made a nation—language, a common sense of history, and national symbols—using schools as the prime tool of inculcation. Under the Ottomans, education had been left to the separate religious communities, but Kállay promoted interconfessional schooling that celebrated regional identity, above all the legendary Bogumil Church, a supposedly ancient Bosnian heritage that predated the religious divisions that came later.[34]

He also advanced the local variant of Serbo-Croatian ("Bosnian," or *Bošnjak*), declaring it an official language in 1883 and having its grammar published in 1890, using both Cyrillic and Latin scripts. (Nationalists would reprint it in the 1990s.) Official rhetoric spoke of the population as Bosnians, a word whose meaning had been vague, sometimes used to denote the entire population, sometimes one of the groups. Orthodox rebels had used it to describe themselves in 1875.

By seeming both anti-Serb and anti-Croat, and by relying on the Muslim landholding elite, Kállay elicited the first flowerings of Bosnian identity among Muslim intellectuals attracted to the idea that they were derived from a feudal nobility and thus were "intrinsic" Bosnians.[35] For example, the mayor of Sarajevo wrote in 1886 that Bosniaks, "great Muslims," were the first patriots of the homeland, as shown in the 1831 uprising, in which the Bosnian Muslim leader Gradašević had defeated the grand vizier. As a communal politician, the mayor also bowed to the ethnic nationalism of the time and banished all suggestions that Muslims were "Turks" (that is, foreigners).

But the new Bosnian identity was not consistent in its use, even among early Bosnian Muslim nationalists. Sometimes they used *Bošnjak* to denote the entire population of Bosnia, sometimes just Muslim; sometimes they called their own group Muslims, sometimes Bosniaks. And the new identity also was not general among Muslims, who continued to think of themselves in religious terms, with some tending toward Serb, others toward Croat identity; others considered themselves Yugoslavs, and still others, probably the majority, had little concern for national identity.[36] But no matter how Muslims felt in the 1890s, Kállay had encouraged the first steps in a process of identity formation among Bosnian Muslims that would continue into the the following century, not fully crystalizing until the anti-Muslim genocide of the 1990s.

In the meantime, in the eyes of many Bosnian Christians, Muslims who opted for Serb or Croat identity did not count as fully Serb or Croat until they "returned" to Christianity. The predicament was similar to that of Jews living in Hungary, who in their neighbors' eyes could become fully Magyar only by converting to Christianity. Overwhelmingly, the Orthodox and Catholic populations did not embrace Kállay's ideas of Bosnian identity, and in 1907, four years after his death, they achieved recognition of the local language as Serbo-Croatian. Only for Muslims did "Bosnian" come to seem a distinct and separate language.[37]

For Orthodox and Catholic Bosnians, ethnic identity had begun taking root in the years just before the Austro-Hungarian occupation. A Turkish school reform of 1869 had been intended to spread Ottoman civic nationhood, but instead it caused fledgling Serb school and church communes to redouble their efforts to strengthen Serb consciousness. After the 1878 Austro-Hungarian occupation, Orthodox and Catholics took advantage of the freedoms of the new *Rechtstaat* to found separate political parties, magazines, and societies in order to refute the ideas of Bosnian identity. Serbs even printed books for their confessional schools that exhorted pupils to love the Serb fatherland. The borders were now open to Croatia and Serb-populated Hungary, and in flowed Orthodox clerics, imbued with romantic nationalism. These clerics helped with schooling, but they also set up a society to propagate the name "Serb" in Sarajevo, which then formed connections to Serb youth organizations in Hungary (for example, in Novi Sad).[38] Franciscan priests from Habsburg Croatia set up a parallel society for Catholics at Sarajevo.

As a young man, Kállay had translated John Stuart Mill's *On Liberty*, and the constitutional regime he presided over could hardly suppress discussions of Serb history or Croat nationhood, though there was harassment: in his first year of rule, more Serb schools closed than opened. His regime also employed the Habsburg monarchy's highly legalistic censorship, so that in the first half of 1906, the editor of the largest newspaper of Bosnia, *Srpska Riječ* (*The Serb Word*), had to appear twenty-two times before court for nationalist "excesses." Censors struck some 7,713 lines from his copy.[39]

The harassment was counterproductive, however, tending to further stimulate sympathies for Serbia, especially as the occupiers openly promoted their own Catholicism. The authorities built Catholic churches, including a cathedral at Sarajevo, and in the first six years of occupation, Sarajevo's Catholic population grew from 800 to 3,876.[40] Jesuits came in, and along with many Habsburg officials, they propagated Croat nationalism. Among the first acts of General Josip Filipović, a Croatian Catholic commander of the imperial occupation forces, was to pressure the Orthodox community to identify ringleaders of resistance, whom his men then apprehended and executed.

As late as 1902, almost 90 percent of the officials running the *Reichsland* came from the outside, and of the natives, Serbs were by far the smallest group. Even if Czech or Polish, Habsburg officials had perfect command of the local languages, and they submitted scores of reports on political attitudes, making Bosnians among the most closely watched populations on earth. The surveillance was especially close in Serb schools, but everywhere the Orthodox felt pursued by an army of spies, keen to record every word of those who "think and feel in a Serb way."[41] Urban planners and architects, many of them Czech, enhanced the sense among Bosnians of being subjects of a colonial power. Up went the ubiquitous stuccoed yellow Habsburg municipal structures on *Ringstrassen* and Kaiser Franz Joseph boulevards, and within a few decades, the centers of Bosnian towns were made to look like other provincial towns in the monarchy.[42] Roads and railways connected the *Reichsland* to Austria and Hungary, opening it to their manufactured goods and retarding the development of native industries.

The hallmark of a developed European society was education, and here Kállay's program revealed debilitating limitations. He managed to construct only 178 state schools and made hardly a dent in the region's illiteracy (still 87.4 percent in 1910, higher among Muslims). Only 0.7 percent of the annual budget in 1888, for example, went to primary education, and though authorities strongly encouraged parents to send their children to school, they did not require it. However, Kállay did invest in first-class secondary education, though only in very limited measure. During the occupation, Habsburg authorities built three high schools, a technical school, and a teacher training college.[43]

But here the project proved self-destructive. Schooling gave students the tools to learn about the actual achievements of Habsburg rule in Bosnia. They discovered that the occupiers had done little to correct the problems that had led to the great uprising in Herzegovina of 1875. Kállay's talk of Bosnians' common history meant little when his rule reaffirmed an order where 90 percent of the landholders were Muslim, and 95 percent of *kmets* [serfs] were Christian.[44] Serb opponents easily portrayed their national liberation struggle—of joining Bosnia to Serbia—as about freeing peasants from economic oppression based on ethnicity. Not until 1906, after Kállay's death, did authorities reform the practice of "tithing" farmers regardless of how little they had harvested, and instead calculated taxes based on a ten-year average of harvests.

There was real betterment in agriculture thanks to government measures, like draining the Bjelina lowlands, regulating the riverbed of the Narenta, encouraging the use of fertilizers, and creating a veterinary service. Agricultural production went from 545,000 tons in 1882 to 1,346,700 tons in 1898. But peasant lives remained miserable, and many fell behind on payments to their landlords. The state agreed to give them credits to help pay debts at 4.5 percent for a period of up to 50 years.[45] Yet this "reform," although doing little to better the lives of peasants, was seen by the landowning class as a threat and catalyzed the growth of Muslim political organizations, as well as national consciousness.

By seizing control of Bosnia-Herzegovina, Austria-Hungary had thus entered a lose-lose situation. If authorities wanted to promote order and development, they had to utilize the landowning class, the only significant potential proto-capitalists. They thus froze into place the social structure while attempting to advance development. But the few entrepreneurially minded Muslim landown-ers faced constraints from within the feudal regime that the authorities main-tained. The still-valid Ottoman laws gave peasants strong claims to the plots they farmed, including deciding what and how to plant. An additional constraint came from the fact that Hungary's conservatives were watching Bosnia very closely. They opposed any challenge to the rights of Bosnian landholders (for example, a reform that would make land available to the Christian sharecrop-pers), fearing the example that might be set for their own peasants in Hungary. And for that reason, the originally agricultural problems that had produced the explosion in 1875 went unaddressed.[46]

As in Bohemia, any human possession or organization that could be ethni-cized was ethnicized, confirming and extending the preexisting distinctions of religious and economic life, where to be a peasant meant to be a Christian. The Orthodox element grew economically at a rapid pace, within and often thanks to segregated institutions. By 1914, twenty-six Serb banks in Bosnia-Herzegovina had share capital of 10 million crowns; the ten Croat banks had three million; and eight Muslim banks held four million crowns. By 1912 there were 337 Serb associations, including 47 gymnastics societies, and a major cultural organ-ization (*Prosvjeta*) to support Serb students and help apprentices find work. It worked closely with Serb cultural organizations in Habsburg Novi Sad, Zagreb, and Ragusa as well as Serbian Belgrade.[47]

Over the years of occupation, tens of thousands of Muslims left the prov-ince, in part to avoid conscription, in part because they felt more at home in an increasingly Islamicized Ottoman Empire. Their overall share of the popula-tion in Bosnia declined from 39 to 32 percent (Catholics increased from 18 to 23 percent and Orthodox remained stable at 43 percent). By 1908 the Muslim National Organization (MNO) had emerged as the prime Muslim party, and there were 124 Muslim associations. Due to the Muslims' minority position, the MNO had to align itself either with Croat or Serb parties. The only thing that caused Serb political organizations to cooperate with Muslims before 1918 was the desire to form a common anti-Austrian front, and the basic demand was autonomy for Bosnia.[48]

Still, Kállay provided for interethnic comity in Bosnia as well as any regime did in the country's history; the state was about as neutral on ethnicity as one could find in all Eastern Europe. The US journalist W. E. Curtis, who visited in 1902, wrote "members of the different religious faiths mix with each other on amicable terms and show mutual respect and mutual toleration; the courts are wisely and honestly administered, justice is awarded to every citizen, regardless of his religion or social position."[49]

This outsider gave a keen appraisal of the surface realities of Bosnian society but failed to sense the deeper currents of nationalism and their power to command people's emotions. Muslims were declining in numbers and relative influence, yet Orthodox Christians still felt subordinate in Muslim-dominated society, and young people had grown impatient with foreign rule and were forming secret organizations (such as Young Bosnia) in order to put an end to it. Meanwhile, the Serb state was doing even less than Austria-Hungary for economic development, and illiteracy was even higher in Serbia, but to the Bosnian Orthodox, that state seemed to promise salvation. Modernization in Bosnia was thus self-destructive; as in other colonial settings, it exacerbated social inequalities and cultural and ethnic differences among locals rather than attenuating them.[50] Symptomatically, one of the few success stories—the rare gifted peasant child who became well educated—used the benefits of the Austrian system to become part of a conspiratorial network and shoot to death the system's figurehead. The student was Gavrilo Princip, and the victim Archduke Francis Ferdinand. Young Bosnian nationalists made the peasant question their cause célèbre because it powerfully fused the nationalist and social grievances against the monarchy, the entity held obviously responsible.

Europe's New Ethnic States

If Austria-Hungary intended to make Bosnia-Herzegovina a showcase for all Europe to admire, the powers at the Congress of Berlin wanted the newly created states to exemplify high European standards to the rest of the world. Chancellor Bismarck agreed with France's William Weddington, otherwise a sworn enemy, that the new states should secure the religious freedom as well as equality before the law for all their citizens. Their insistence was tied to the revolutionary character of these states: the statesmen at Berlin had justified their founding using the ethnic principle. The Bulgarian state, for instance, was to be a state of and for the Bulgarians (meaning Bulgarian Christians). The new states emerged at the expense of the Ottoman Empire, though Bulgaria remained under Ottoman suzerainty until Bulgaria's leaders unilaterally changed that status in 1908.[51]

The old order had been imperial, and an implicit favor had rested on the people of empire, a people not ethnically specific. Over the centuries, millions of Slavs had become loyal Ottoman, Habsburg, or Romanov subjects and even members of the ruling elites. Yet the new ruling peoples were imagined as groups no one could join: one was either born Bulgarian or Romanian, or one was not. Therefore, the old system through which the powers had claimed to protect the rights of Christians under Ottoman rule (inaugurated at Kuchuk Kainarji in 1774) was raised to a new level, and the Berlin Congress helped anchor the principles on which protection of minorities would be based in the twentieth century.[52] With the advance of racial understandings of ethnicity in the late nineteenth and early twentieth centuries, however, minority status under new ethno–nation-states became a far more fraught position than being Christian in the Ottoman Empire.

The powers had permitted the new states to emerge in order to maintain a difficult act of balancing power, and except for Russia, they would have preferred that these areas remain islets of the Ottoman Empire. The recognition of ethnicity as a basis for statehood thus implied no deep respect, and indeed, the politicians at Berlin expressed naked contempt for the upstarts: Disraeli thought of Serbs as a small half-barbarian people.[53] If the weakness of the Ottoman state had made it impossible to ignore the new nationalism, the powers did so warily and with safeguards. For one thing, they assigned their "wards" quasi-chaperones in the guise of legitimate princes of European houses. For another, they determined that the constitutions crafted by the local notables in Bulgaria or Romania must contain guarantees for the rights of non-ethnics. Any misbehavior on the part of the infant (though supposedly ancient) states would trigger intervention, a dangling threat that proved a source of lasting resentment.

Thus the Bulgarians were instructed to elect a prince from a European house, provided he was not a member of a reigning dynasty of a European power. The man chosen was the German Prince Alexander of Battenberg. Hundreds of thousands of non-Bulgarians (that is, Muslims) had fled the protracted and very bloody fighting in 1876/1877, and though Europe's powers did not require that the refugees return, they did not want them permanently excluded. Bulgaria's notables thus had to draw up a constitution (organic law), taking into consideration the interests of Turkish, Romanian, and Greek populations; no one could be kept from enjoying civil and political rights or from admission to public or private employment, including the professions. Freedom of religion was guaranteed, as were rights to hold property, even for Muslims who no longer lived in Bulgaria. The other new states had to agree to protect religious and ethnic minorities in similar ways.[54]

Bulgaria was a diminished client state still under Russian occupation and did not have the actual autonomy (until 1908) to protest. Its urgent concern, which would guide foreign policy for decades, was to make up for territory lost at Berlin. Serbia and Montenegro did not protest the new requirements, largely because their policies had made the lives of local Muslims so difficult over the decades that the great majority had already left. In the 1860s, authorities had expelled the Muslim population of Belgrade after a flare-up of fighting; in the course of the wars of 1876–1878, some 250,000 to 300,000 Muslims were killed, and 1.5 million fled deeper into the Ottoman Empire. For Serbia and Montenegro, those displacements were part of their own nation-building through exclusion. For its part, by 1878/1879, the Ottoman Empire had become a predominantly Muslim state (Muslims made up about 75–80 percent of the total), and over the next two decades, another million Muslims immigrated from the Balkans.[55]

Austria pledged to defend the rights of the communities in Bosnia-Herzegovina, and it did just that. As we have seen, it went so far in respecting the position of the Muslim elite that it wound up preserving the socioeconomic and legal structures of the old order. For Serb nationalists, the Austrians seemed to take the place of the Ottoman regime rather than redress the ills of Ottoman rule.[56]

However, Romania's political class violently objected to the requirement that it extend citizenship rights to all inhabitants of their territory. Perhaps they felt less secure about their claims to rule people and territory. Unlike Bulgaria, Serbia, or Montenegro, Romania had little history of independent statehood, and it constituted the earliest example of a state whose claim to existence was based on ethnicity. The ultimate origins of the people of state—the Romanians—seemed less clear than elsewhere and led to "over-anxiety" among Romanian intellectuals about their people's lineage.[57] Therefore, the precise meaning of the nominal nation and who got to define it seemed of an importance in Romania not seen elsewhere, and thanks to the ancient legacy of Christian anti-Judaism, the process took on a razor-sharp edge not felt elsewhere in the Balkans: the minority that Romania's founding fathers defined themselves against, along a supposedly clear boundary of selfhood, was not Muslim but Jewish.[58]

But for several fortuitous events, the state may not have emerged at all. The story stretches back to the spring of 1848, when the principalities of Wallachia and Moldavia were the lands farthest east in Europe to be touched by democratic revolution. Romanian students in France, mostly of local noble ("boyar") background, hurried home, and with members of the urban classes they briefly seized power in Bucharest and Iaşi. At seminars and salons in Paris, the boyars' sons had become romantic nationalists, and they demanded unification of the ethnically Romanian lands in an independent state with a constitutional government and civil rights. From this class of students educated abroad came Romania's national leadership.[59]

A liberal-seeming proto-constitution passed in Wallachia in June 1848, the "Islaz declaration," calling for equality of all citizens, a progressive income tax, freedom of the press, the abolition of forced labor services, an expanded school system with free education for everyone, and the election of the prince from any category of the population for five-year terms. Citizenship hinged on ethnicity and not social status, a provision that seemed progressive because it meant that peasants belonged to the nation equally with boyars and townspeople; yet ominously, it reflected agreement among the elites that Jews did not belong. But within weeks, the experiment was cut short by Russian and Ottoman intervention.[60]

After this failed revolution, the principalities of Wallachia and Moldavia, still under Ottoman rule, settled into a deal. Under conservative pressure, liberals agreed to scale back demands for social reform and focus on a common platform of national unification. From the standpoint of the nationalists, some improvements occurred in the 1850s. The Romanian language asserted itself in schools, the labor duties required of peasants were reduced (though not abolished), and a start was made on creating a national (Wallachian) army.

Fortuitously, a leader arose who would bring Wallachia and Moldavia together and devote his great energies to modernizing them. This was Alexander Cuza, scion of a lesser boyar family, who had enjoyed an interrupted education at the Sorbonne. In 1858, he became the compromise candidate of those for and against union after close elections in Moldavia, and the following year, boyar assemblies in both principalities elected him prince. This was a course of events no one had planned or anticipated, but in retrospect, it would appear to reflect an unstoppable momentum toward Romanian unification.[61]

Because it had its own Romanian population in Transylvania, Austria did not welcome the news arriving from the principalities, yet it faced military challenges in Italy and was powerless to intervene. The much stronger France was promoting a Romanian state as an eastern ally on Austria's Balkan flank, and in December 1861, Istanbul gave its technical consent for the principalities to be unified. Cuza formed a united government in Bucharest, bringing together the regional militias and centralizing the financial and judicial systems. But in the years that followed, reactionary boyars blocked his hopes to modernize the country with foreign loans and investments in railways.

Still, before falling in 1866, Cuza scored important successes. Against resistance from the Porte and from Russia, he expropriated church lands (mostly held by Greek monks), which amounted to one-quarter of the total area in Wallachia and one-third in Moldavia. In May 1864, Cuza carried out a coup d'état: against a "factitious oligarchy," he staged a popular vote on a constitution, and won by 682,621 to 1,307.[62] In August Cuza promulgated an agrarian law that settled peasants on holdings that varied in size by region (averaging four hectares per family), guaranteed them personal liberty, and swept away feudal dues and tithes. Two-thirds of the arable land was taken from landlords.[63] Given the haste of this reform, the results fell short of expectations. Peasants lost rights to grazing land and forests that became the property of boyars, and the plots they received tended to be of inferior quality. They also had to make annual payments for fifteen years to compensate former owners.

Consequently, the consumption of meat fell in the principalities during the following decades, and many peasants could hardly get by and were forced to hire themselves out to boyars. The agrarian law thus had the effect of strengthening the landholding class, which maintained large estates and took advantage of booming international markets for grain. With a supply of cheap labor that grew dramatically, the boyars had no incentive for modernization. Between 1859 and 1899, the Romanian population increased by 54 percent, and as it, did the tiny peasant plots were further subdivided. Romania would remain a country of large estates and depressed peasantry, in contrast to Serbia and Bulgaria where small peasant farms predominated.[64]

Although forceful and well motivated, Cuza doubted his own abilities and showed little interest in maintaining power. Though a patriot with a progressive agenda meant to benefit Romanians, he tolerated corruption and scandalized some by living with his wife as well as his mistress, Marie Obrenović (her son Milan would become the first king of Serbia). Cuza made enemies in virtually every quarter: in the church; among conservative landholders; among the great powers (especially Austria, Russia, and Turkey); and even among liberals, for whom he was too tame but also too autocratic. Cuza's supposed plans to be succeeded by the children of his mistress brought forth a "monstrous coalition" of liberals and conservatives who sent military officers to his private quarters in February 1866 and forced him at gunpoint to abdicate.[65]

A regency now emerged of liberal and conservative politicians that sought to find a prince for Romania from one of the ruling houses of the west. The choice fell on Charles of Hohenzollern-Sigmaringen of the Catholic branch of

Prussia's ruling family. A plebiscite—again suggesting limits in the propriety of the election regime of this time—approved this choice by 685,969 to 224.[66]

Among Cuza's final accomplishments was a civil code based in part on French models, according to which only Christians counted as citizens. This was the predominant understanding of the Romanian elite. Therefore, all Jews on Romanian territory, no matter how far back their lineage, were treated as foreigners. In July 1866, Prince Charles ratified a constitution carrying this provision, and lawmakers created a new category of criminal, the "vagabond Jew," who could be expelled from the country.[67]

What made Jews in Romania especially vulnerable was the fact that, in contrast to Polish Jews, they and their families had arrived relatively recently on the "native" soil and were easily portrayed as interlopers. Since the 1820s, the Jewish population in Moldavia and Wallachia had increased as the principalities produced more and more grain for demand abroad. The numbers of Moldavian Jews rose from 6,500 in 1774 to 19,000 in 1820, and to 125,000 in 1859, and they were especially notable in cities. For example, the Jewish population in Iaşi, the Moldavian capital, grew from about 3,000 in 1803, to 17,032 in 1831, and to 30,000 in 1839. By the end of the century, in the city and district of Iaşi there were 46,696 Jews among a total population of 191,828. In Wallachia, the increases were more moderate, so that in Bucharest, the Jewish population rose from about 5,000 in 1800 to 43,274 a century later. By 1899, the urban population in Romania was about 1,131,000, of which 215,000, or 19 percent, was Jewish.[68]

The Jews coming to Moldavia and Wallachia had fled misery and oppression in Russia and Galicia, and they brought with them skills that were rare among the principalities' largely illiterate population, as well as a willingness to pursue professions that Romanian elites found beneath their dignity (for example, in business and banking). Soon Jews occupied intermediary positions as innkeepers, moneychangers, grocers, rug merchants, peddlers, and artisans (such as tailors and glass makers). Jews' skills in such urban undertakings throughout East Central Europe had to do with measures taken historically to limit Jews' presence in the countryside.

What made these developments remarkable against the background of the other societies in the region was the rapidity with which Jews entered the country, becoming near majorities of some towns in less than a generation. Jews had lived in Poland for centuries, and even after the state disappeared, Polish patriots understood Poland's Jews to be part of the nation. To call them "foreign" was to deny an ancient history of cohabitation (and required the racist argumentation that came only in the late 1880s). But the Jews of Romania for the most part were evident newcomers, living in tight-knit family communities, fluent in accented Romanian but speaking Yiddish among themselves, with different customs and dress. And they had arrived precisely when ideas of Romanian identity were consolidating. Among Romanian elites, virtually no one disputed that Jews were an even older and separate people than Romanians, a different ethnicity, or as the liberal interior minister Kogălniceanu said in 1868, a "foreign nationality" by their origin, customs, and sentiment.[69]

The closer Romania inched toward full independence, the more the Jews became targets of a "cold pogrom" of systematic exclusion. Romania's most powerful politician, the liberal forty-eighter Ion Brătianu, called them a wound and a plague. Authorities restrained Jews' freedoms perhaps more severely than in any European space west of Russia: they could not live in the countryside, run taverns, own farms or vineyards; could not own homes or movable property in cities; were barred from pleading cases in courts; and could not become professors, lawyers, pharmacists, state doctors, or railroad employees.

After the fall of Cuza, the political establishment became even more determined that all differences must recede in the face of ethnic unity, including those of politics. Romania's independence had priority over economic and social reform, whether politicians called themselves liberal, national, or conservative.[70] The only way to justify the sudden appearance of Romania on the map of Europe was to assert the rights of an ancient community with a common origin in language and culture, and Jews who had arrived in the past generation or two were portrayed as evidently not belonging to this kind of community.

But Romania was too weak to take on the Ottoman Empire (of which it was still part) and required the intervention of Great Powers. In the years just before the Berlin Congress, a new discourse of humanitarian intervention was emerging on a global scale, meaning that new nation-states would be held up to standards of "decency" as a price for "joining Europe." Complaints had been pouring in from British and French Jews about mistreatment of Jews in Romania, and the president of the Alliance Israelite Universelle, Adolphe Crémieux, went to Bucharest in 1866 to plead the cause of Jewish equality, offering to raise a massive low-term loan in return for a clause in Romania's constitution guaranteeing that religion would not constitute an obstacle to naturalization.[71]

Yet word of Crémieux's offer leaked, feeding claims of local anti-Semites that Romania was the victim of an international conspiracy. Judaism had revealed itself, in the words of Mihai Eminescu, Romania's foremost poet, as a transterritorial nation, bound by religion as well as a sense of ethnic identity.[72] Jews were a "foreign people" who wanted to bend Romania to their will. A campaign unfolded against "selling Romania to the Jews," which culminated in the destruction of the Bucharest synagogue.

The discourse of the ethnic national movement unfortunately ruled out two obvious solutions: the first to promote Jewish cultural assimilation into Romanian society; the second to construct institutions that might make Christian peasants more skilled and competitive. It was much simpler to enhance anti-Jewish exclusions that had existed for centuries, especially those forbidding Jews to own certain kinds of property or practice certain professions. Anti-Semitism was a lazy habit that had started as a choice, but the group doing the choosing was so vast, its understandings so unquestioned, that it eluded simple objections that would have been logically devastating. For example, liberal politicians claimed that they had to stem a flood of Jewish immigration to avoid becoming "helots" in their own land, tied to Jewish creditors.[73] Yet in fact, liberals owned little agricultural land and were not dependent on loans.

Had the elite really wanted to strengthen Romania as a society, the simplest path would have been land reform, making mostly landless peasants into farmers with an interest in profit and productivity. But it was easier to ascribe Romania's socioeconomic backwardness to the supposedly harmful Jewish middlemen—tax collectors, merchants, money-changers—positions projected as exploitative, not productive, and allegedly proving that Jews could only "live from the fruits of labor of other peoples." By definition, the only "productive" class was the peasantry, while city populations consisted of mixed elements, some Romanian, some inassimilable "Yids." Though Jews were literate, skilled, urbane, and hard-working, they were projected as "less civilized" and "filthy and helpless."[74]

The tragedy of Romanian politics was that such views were espoused not merely by demagogues and rabble-rousers, but also by the pinnacle of Romania's literary establishment. The anti-Jewish polemicist Eminescu was also Romania's national "bard" and founder of the modern language; he is still commemorated in statues all over the country. In 1879 he wrote that Jews make a "race whose immediate aim was to get hold of Romania's real estate, and whose long-term goal was to get hold of this country." Such use of "race" was early for European standards, but it formed a logical extension of Eminescu's insistence that Jews differed essentially from Romanians. Jewishness existed in a realm beyond the senses, perhaps in shared blood, and it was therefore nonsense to speak of "native Jews" or "Romanian Israelites." Sentiments of this sort spread across the intellectual elite, including the poets Vasile Alecsandri and Ion

Heliade; scholars Bogdan Petriceicu Haşdeu, Dionisie Pop Marţian; and the liberal political leaders Ion Brătianu and Mihail Kogălniceanu. Brătianu originated the country's major political dynasty.[75]

Because of Romania's precarious position among many powers, Romanian nationalists believed they had more enemies than the Jews. In Transylvania, they fought for rights against Hungarians, Germans, and at times the Austrian government, while compatriots in Moldavia and Wallachia opposed Turkish political and Greek cultural control, first using and then resenting Russian "protection." There were also territorial disputes with Ukrainians, Poles, and Bulgarians, as well as resentments of Armenian merchants. But Jews attracted special opprobrium because they seemed to contest power within Romanian space, holding positions in the economy and professions that Romania's growing middle classes aspired to. They were portrayed as profiting from international capitalism while Romanian peasants suffered. "It is a moot point," writes Albert Lindemann, "whether anti-Semitism [in Romania] was the worst in Europe; certainly nowhere else did hatred of Jews become so prominently a part of national identity or one that so obsessed the intellectual classes."[76]

Before Romania's independence was recognized in 1878, the country had to accept Article 44 of the Berlin Treaty, requiring that Romania not allow creed or confession to exclude anyone from enjoying civil and political rights, or from being admitted to the professions or to public employment. The article was the fruit of lobbying by Central and West European Jewish organizations, but it also reflected German interests in Romanian railroads. Thus, Romania had to revise a constitution passed under Cuza in 1864 to include a provision that all parties in Bucharest rejected. When Romania's lawmakers refused to adopt the required revision, their German-born king simply dissolved the legislature and created an ad hoc body for the express purpose of revising the constitution. These men then revised Article 7 to permit naturalization of Jews on an individual basis after a very careful process of investigation. Each case required a special act of parliament. The foreign powers acceded to this compromise, yet not coincidentally, they did so directly after the Romanian government proposed a solution to the "railroad question" that seemed favorable in light of a financial crisis in Berlin. As a result of widespread collusion in the Romanian bureaucracy, in the following half-century only about 2,000 of Romania's more than 250,000 Jews were naturalized.[77]

The humanitarian intervention thus achieved little for Romania's Jews, while teaching its lawmakers that Western talk of religious freedom and rule of law could be a cover for other interests. What gave Britain or Germany the authority to judge Romania? Britain had accorded full rights to Jews in 1858, and Austria and Prussia only a decade later (in 1867 and 1869). Russia, another great power, refused to extend equal rights to Jews and indeed was the place from which Jews sought refuge in Wallachia and Moldavia. The German government could hardly pose as an exemplar of tolerance after arresting bishops and banning Jesuits from the country during a full-scale assault on Catholicism.[78]

Earlier than elsewhere, a skepticism set in among Romania's elites about the ambivalent blessings of liberalism—a skepticism bequeathed to children and grandchildren, leaving them little resistance to authoritarian and fascist rule in the 1930s. Romania had copied Western institutions under Western tutelage, and the result was hypocrisy and farce on a padding of corruption. Democracy required opposition, yet in a country that was mostly illiterate, citizens could scarcely inform themselves about basic political choices. Parties called themselves "liberal" and "conservative," but they represented the state machine, for whom it was far easier to continue to vilify Jews than to undertake reforms that would question its own privileges. A disgusted Mihai Eminescu called liberalism a system that "transformed Romania into a quagmire into which the social sewage of West and East is discharged." He and fellow writer Ioan Slavici said liberals were demagogues who took "Jewish money" to finance their own real estate interests and would sell Romania to whomever offered the most money.[79]

Yet liberals—above all Brătianu and his foreign minister Kogălniceanu—were in fact nationalists who were determined to restrict Jewish presence in Romanian life. Under Brătianu, Jewish noncitizens absorbed endless discriminatory measures of a sort unknown in Austria, the other Balkan states, Hungary, or Germany. Thus, in the 1880s the government decreed that Jews could not be druggists, could not "hawk" in rural districts, could not serve in chambers of commerce, could not send petitions to parliament, could not sell liquor in rural districts, could not act as money changers, could not serve as auditors in the national bank of Romania, and could not be more than one-third the workmen in a factory. The minister of the interior could eject a stranger from any place without giving a reason.[80] Jews were not exempted from military service but could not become officers. At any moment, even in the middle of productive careers as academics or businesspersons, Jews could be expelled from the country.[81]

* * *

Liberals like Gyula Andrássy gave nationalism a dynamism it did not need to have precisely through their almost mystical fear of its powers. The result was an inability to use nationalism in a rational manner. Critics noted that Austria-Hungary could have championed the South Slav patriots, joining Bosnia to Serbia or to federal units in the Habsburg monarchy and posing as liberators. The price would have been recognizing South Slavs as a nationality within Hungary and giving up the idea that Hungary must be a modern nation-state one and indivisible. The case of Otto von Bismarck shows that it was possible to adapt old structures to new realities. The German Empire he founded was a federated yet highly effective nation-state that respected age-old particularisms (for example, the Kingdoms of Bavaria and Saxony) while becoming something new.[82]

Instead, Hungarians, like German liberals in Bohemia, became willing to compromise only when they faced losing everything, and that came only in late 1918. Their respective communities had been "imagined" beyond all re-imagining: secular liberals were powerless to alter these realms' basic contours, and in neither case did the governing narrative allow for any option other than that of "ownership," attaching the nominal nation to its ostensible realm (in one case, to the lands of St. Stephen; in the other, the lands of St. Wenceslaus). Thoughts of Serbia frightened Andrássy because he knew Serbs—like Magyars and Czechs—also laid claims to territory. The difference was that no one could say exactly how much.

The distance he and his government had traveled in less than a year to their positions at the Berlin Congress of July 1878 was breathtaking.[83] Not long before, public opinion had opposed taking Bosnia-Herzegovina, and Andrássy had wanted to prop up Ottoman rule. Neither he nor others in the Hungarian elite had favored taking more Slavs into the monarchy. It was only at the news of the Serb and Montenegrin attack on Ottoman positions in 1876 that his government decided it must occupy Bosnia-Herzegovina to check Serb and Montenegrin ambitions.

Internationally, the Congress of Berlin was a major step toward the twentieth century, perhaps its inaugural event. The Congress took a principle implicit in the 1830 London Protocol founding modern Greece—that an ethnicity could be a source of sovereignty—and multiplied it by four. By implication, it also adumbrated the idea of minorities, people in the nation-state who did not belong to the nation and required protection.[84] The idea that ethnicity was the basis of the right to rule—a principle later called national self-determination—had been foreign to the Vienna system of 1815. Berlin was not just a halfway point; it was a rupture with that system. What changed in Paris in 1919 was to make the new principle not simply a result of grudging acceptance, but an explicit and valid—indeed, universal—method of organizing statehood.

For South East European peoples, the events of 1875–1878 had a meaning like that of 1848 in Bohemia: after initial uprisings, events soon cascaded in a way that forced choices about self-identification. In Bosnia-Herzegovina, the Orthodox still called themselves Bosnians but increasingly desired attachment to Montenegro or Serbia, while Catholics opted for Austria and more clearly than ever identified as Croats.[85] Religious identity was a starting place but not an endpoint; the participants in the 1875 uprising knew that they were united by religion against the "occupier" and were picking up a script from earlier in the century, when Christian populations in Serbia and Greece had likewise risen up and begun carving out autonomous zones from Ottoman territory. Yet the issue was not religion per se—the insurgents did not care about suppression of worship or doctrine—but a sense that religious belonging had condemned much of the population to subservience.

Did Bosnian identity ever stand a chance as a form of nationhood? "Of the basic criteria by which the Serb and Croat nations established themselves during this period, history, language, and religion," writes Noel Malcolm, "only religion could apply in Bosnia, a country which had its own separate history."[86] But in fact, history (that is, people's consciousness of the past) ignored the boundaries of Bosnia and focused instead on a past that Orthodox South Slavs in Bosnia believed they shared with Orthodox South Slavs in Serbia. According to epic poetry, the common history stretched back to the 1389 Kosovo battle and earlier.

In Bosnia, Orthodox and Muslims had separate imaginations: the former told stories in oral poetry of their coreligionists deceiving Turkish authorities; the latter of theirs outwitting the Austrians. And if advocates for Serb nationhood in Bosnia were inspired by the romantic nationalism that was popular at Central Europe's universities and understood language as a people's soul, they had to look no further than Vuk Karadžić, who had based his Serb dictionary on a dialect in Herzegovina. Against Karadžić, Benjamin Kállay had not stood a chance; probably ten times the number of schools he built would not have resulted in the Bosnian identity he intended.

If Bosnian identity amounted to anything, it was the beginning of a strategy for Muslims to oppose complete assimilation by Serb and Croat nationalism, each of which expected co-nationals to become Christian, at least nominally. What the Bosnian and Romanian stories share is a hint that twentieth-century

European nationalism was vigorously and exclusively Christian, even when its carriers were fiercely secular.

The Austrian occupation of Bosnia, considered necessary by Austria to rescue its regional position, put a huge question mark after the word "Bosnia-Herzegovina," because it purposely left its future open. That was not unique: the new states were all questions as much as answers. Serbia was a less than half-fulfilled nation-state. Bulgaria was cut down from the size agreed on at San Stefano, and it desperately wanted the lost territories restored. And Romania, perhaps the most "satisfied" of the new states looked across all of its borders and saw enemies as well as national territory waiting to be redeemed. The inherent contradiction of the Berlin Congress was to raise the new standard of national self-determination and to deny it at the same time.

In Austria, the occupation of Bosnia-Herzegovina divided German liberals into competing factions, including a German radical one, which would prove the origin point of Nazism.[87] By forcing the measures that legalized the occupation through parliament, Andrássy was in part to blame: most liberals came to believe he had misled them. But their opposition not only split liberalism, it also aggravated the emperor, a fact of dire consequence. Six months after imperial troops subdued Bosnia-Herzegovina at a cost of almost 1,000 dead, 112 liberals voted against the Berlin treaty, causing Francis Joseph to view them as unreliable. They opposed his prerogatives to direct foreign policy simply for the sake of high liberal principles.[88] He moved quickly to banish them from power, launching a crisis of identity and purpose from which Austro-German liberalism would not recover.

CHAPTER 9

The Origins of National Socialism: Fin de Siècle Hungary and Bohemia

Fascism was a European ideology of the twentieth century with multiple sources: French syndicalism and integralism, Italian irredentism, the paramilitary violence that ravaged Central and Eastern Europe after World War I, and the fear and loathing of socialism among much of Europe's middle classes. But the most powerful tributary leading to the fascist mainstream of the 1930s arose from the predicament of Germans who lived in Habsburg Austria and Bohemia in the late nineteenth century: in 1871 Bismarck created a German nation-state, and they were left out. Czechs self-confidently made Bohemia a place ever more Slavic in appearance, but German liberals, though in power in Vienna, did not have a clue about how to make their co-ethnics feel secure in what was supposedly an old German heartland. They carried on with routine politics, oblivious to the fact that by the 1880s, Czechs controlled 80 percent of the official positions in Bohemia and were gaining control of the University in Prague, one the oldest bastions of "German" culture in Central Europe. Nothing seemed able to stop them.

It was no coincidence that the future leader of the Third Reich, a state that claimed to represent Germans everywhere, came from just inside the Habsburg border along the River Inn, directly adjacent to the powerful new Germany. Each day offered the young Hitler occasion to admire and envy a state where a nation seemed in charge of its own fate. Like the worst humiliations, this one was self-enforced: his father Alois helped maintain the border to the new Germany as a Habsburg customs official. Of the 30 million Germans left out of the state fashioned by Otto von Bismarck, Austrian and Bohemian Germans knew most painfully that the German question was not settled. The sense went through all classes, deep into the Marxist-led workers movement, one of whose leaders, Karl Renner, expressed grudging but genuine satisfaction when Adolf Hitler joined his homeland to the German Empire in 1938.

An apologist for Austria's German liberals might have said they did their best for as long as they could. Soon after the 1867 compromise with Hungary, they disrupted a plan to strike a compromise between Czechs and Germans. In 1871 a ministry under the conservative Count Karl Hohenwart produced one draft law on nationality relations within Bohemia and another on Bohemia's constitutional position in the monarchy. The former foresaw an administration that would act bilingually at the provincial level and monolingually at the local level, with safeguards for minorities; the latter involved reinstating the autonomous Bohemian Chancellery that Maria Theresa had abolished in 1749. All issues not "common" to the monarchy—commerce, finance, citizenship—would be decided in the Bohemian diet in Prague. If this plan had worked, Bohemia would have achieved far-reaching autonomy, comparable to Hungary, and because it was mostly Czech, it would have become a Czech-controlled province.

In response, German deputies walked out of the diet in Prague, and the liberals in Vienna boycotted parliament. Violent rioting ensued. The newly crowned German Emperor Wilhelm warned that Bohemia's Germans might turn to him for support, and his chancellor Bismarck sounded the alarm at the prospect of a Slavic Austria gravitating toward Russia. Just a few years earlier, the tsar had lavished attention on a huge Czech delegation at an ethnographic exhibition at Moscow, telling them they were a "brother people" and should feel at home. For their part, the Czechs proclaimed Russia the "rising sun of the Slavs." The idea that a foreign potentate might support their cause further boosted Czech self-confidence, but it horrified many Germans and Hungarians. They portrayed any link among Slavic peoples as directed at the monarchy's destruction. Though Hohenwart's reform would have left Hungary untouched, the Magyar elite rejected it because they wanted to contain Slavic influence in the monarchy as a whole and feared that nationalities within Hungary might demand power-sharing like the Czechs.[1]

This was the last serious attempt to change the internal constitution of Cisleithania, although two more protracted efforts were made at resolving the relations between Germans and Czechs in Bohemia in 1890 and 1897, both of which failed. For the time being, Hohenwart fell, and was replaced, to the chagrin of the conservative emperor, by a government of German liberals led by Prince Adolf von Auersperg, a Bohemian great landowner of strongly anticlerical leanings.[2]

The Czech political class continued its boycott of the diet in Prague and parliament in Vienna that had started in 1863, while the German liberal ministers took no account of their demands, which was unfortunate because Czechs also advocated economic freedom and reducing the power of feudal elites as well as the Catholic Church. The two sets of liberals were identical in all but ethnicity, bearing the same political charge, and repelled each other. As Czech society became ever more urbane—resembling the society they themselves aspired to in all but language—Germans gave Czech leaders less respect and did what they could to curtail Czech political influence. The government in Vienna employed gerrymandering and limited the electorate by wealth to maintain the German majority against the Czechs.[3]

German liberals believed that the treasures of their higher way of life, if not forced on Slavs, would wean them from their supposed pan-Slavism. It was impossible for 8 million Germans simply to absorb 14 million Slavs, and therefore Adolf Fischhof, once a radical student leader, promoted the quiet advance of German culture through books printed in Slavic languages.[4] He was no chauvinist, and in fact belonged to the liberal minority that favored a federal solution for the empire. A second hopeful moment seemed to dawn in 1878, when Czech leader F. L. Rieger traveled to Fischhof's estate in Carinthia, accompanied by the editor of Vienna's liberal daily. These men represented huge majorities in the overall population, Germans as well as Czechs who wanted democratic rule and hoped politicians could cooperate in points of common interest, like advancing equality before the law and economic development.

They worked out a statement of principle and were planning to summon a high-level German-Czech conference when, out of the blue, German liberal leader Eduard Herbst scuttled the negotiations, supposedly because of an outrage committed by the Czechs. While vacationing in Budapest he had received news that Prague's city council had just christened a bridge honoring the recently deceased František Palacký rather than some obscure German notable. Contemporaries suspected Herbst had simply used this petty affront because any deal with the Czechs seemed too risky to contemplate.[5]

Herbst's act proved shortsighted. At that point the electorate comprised some 6 percent of males over 24 years old, and as it expanded, as liberals believed it had to, the power of Czechs would expand as well. Here had been a chance to make that expansion occur in mutual agreement, involving sacrifices as well as gains on both sides.

But if liberal Germans believed they had secured themselves against Czechs at this turn, they were undone by the South Slavs at the next, though for reasons beyond their control. When Habsburg diplomacy annexed Bosnia and Herzegovina in 1878, German liberals raised objections in joint delegations with Hungary. Their reasoning was straightforward: how, they asked, could the monarchy absorb more Slavs while maintaining German and Hungarian hegemony? And as liberals hoping to take full charge of government, they were even more bothered by the fact that the occupation burdened the state with huge new budgetary responsibilities that lacked parliamentary approval.

The following year, Minister President Auersperg, having lost support of members of his own party to support this policy, twice asked Francis Joseph to accept his resignation, and the second time the emperor said yes. For Francis Joseph, the crisis was a welcome excuse to drop the detested liberals. He especially resented their objections to the Bosnian occupation, his one "success" in foreign policy, and charged his boyhood friend Count Eduard Taaffe with forming a government. In the elections in June 1879, the German liberals (themselves divided over Bosnia) lost seats, and Taaffe cobbled together a government without them, consisting of conservatives, clericals and Slavs—including the Czechs! The combination wobbled but proved the longest-lasting government in Cisleithania: Taaffe said he maintained power by keeping the nationalities in a balanced state of mild dissatisfaction.[6] The Taaffe years were a nightmare for German liberals, who had "fought" for representative government for decades, only to be excluded by their enemies, some of whom had opposed the constitution as such.

Though hardly conservative and even less clerical, the Czechs now abandoned their boycott of government in return for promised concessions on the national question. Their representatives old and young operated as a disciplined club in Vienna's parliament and scored victories, above all the 1880 "Stremayr ordinance," which introduced Czech as an external language of administration in Bohemia (that is, as a language that had to be used with those who spoke Czech). A further achievement was the division of Prague's Karl-Ferdinand University into Czech and German halves in 1882, meaning that Czechs could be educated from the humblest to most advanced stages in their own language. They also got more high schools. But to achieve all this, the Czechs accepted conservative "reforms" that strengthened the church's role in education and marriage, moves at odds with their own liberal convictions, and not surprisingly, German liberals accused them of hypocrisy.[7]

After that, concessions had to be dragged out of Taaffe, about whom one Czech leader said he threw the Czechs "little crumbs, as if to poultry." Any progress for the Czech cause took place outside parliament through energies generated from below. As we have seen, when the Czech National Theater was damaged by fire just after opening in 1881, almost half the inhabitants of Prague contributed so that it could reopen two years later. In 1890 the Czechs founded and paid for their own Academy of Sciences and Arts, because the government had refused to support it.[8]

But Minister President Taaffe himself operated under pressure. German liberals were out of government, and Austria's ally in Berlin scrutinized what he did, protesting if anything seemed "pro-Slavic." Taaffe forbade a gymnastics festival called by the nationalist Sokol movement in Prague in 1887 because guests were expected from other Slavic lands.[9] This move in turn alienated the restive Young Czechs, the radical and growing wing of the Czech National Party, who formed a bloc within the Czech Club after 1888, calling for universal suffrage, local self-government, and getting the church out of schools. In accord with the ideology of Bohemian State's Rights, they insisted that the entire Bohemian kingdom was Czech property. In 1882 Taaffe had expanded the franchise by lowering the tax requirements for voting, and the number of Czech voters shot up in the parliamentary elections of 1885, while German liberals lost almost twenty seats.[10]

But if Taaffe left Czech politicians dissatisfied, he produced trauma among Germans. The division of the university in Prague, considered by Germans to be Germany's oldest, only aggravated fears that they were on a downward slope toward cultural obscurity. From then on, German professors treated Prague's university as a temporary way station, hoping for a call to a university outside Bohemia.[11] But much worse, Germans in Austria had to stand back and watch a modern state taking shape in Cisleithania without their input, a state that seemed increasingly Slavic.

Though the internal language of administration in Bohemia remained German, the Stremayr ordinance meant that even in solidly German districts, Czechs could now demand the use of their language and thereby "infiltrate" seventy-seven of the 216 judicial districts of Bohemia that were purely German. Czechs were already overrepresented in Bohemia's state administration and judiciary, and the requirement that officials speak both languages unleashed special anxieties because educated Czechs knew German, whereas Germans rarely knew Czech. After the Stremayr ordinance, Habsburg Germans felt they were not German Austrians but Austrian Germans.[12]

New forces emerged to do battle, with nationalists assiduously tabulating increases in those speaking their language at home and wealth owned on each side. Germans founded a *Deutscher Schulverein* to support private schools in areas with German minorities, and the Czechs an *ústřední matice školská* (Central School Foundation) to fund Czech education in German areas. By the mid-1880s, Czechs had also created four national unions (*národní jednoty*) to counter work of the German protective associations (*Schutzvereine*) and foster the "internal colonization" of Bohemia. Czechs also replicated the German nationalist gymnastics societies to strengthen the national body, and though led by bourgeois politicians, the movement spread through all social classes: about 30 percent of Czech gymnasts in 1887 gave their occupation as "worker."[13] Both sides also built their own agricultural associations.

Still there was a distinction. The language border in Bohemia was shifting to the Czechs' advantage. For example, in the German speaking "island" of Iglau/Jihlava (where Gustav Mahler attended school), the number of Czech-speaking immigrants had increased from 9 percent in 1846 to 44 percent in 1869. By 1900 the population of Bohemia as a whole was 62 percent Czech and 37 percent German.[14] A fear of dissolution before an advancing Czech tide spread across all classes of the German minority; industrial workers in the language islands feared that Czechs would accept lower wages to Czechify the region. Liberalism took on two different roles on either side of the ethnic divide. Within the Czech movement, the radical Young Czechs advanced, supported by organizations of civil society that a liberal state made possible, while Germans wondered whether any liberal organization could protect their *Volk* and its interests. Though the executive of state administration remained German throughout Cisleithania, the creeping gains by Czechs seemed to reflect a remorseless German decline.[15]

* * *

With horror scenarios looming, young German liberals gathered at Linz in 1882, proclaiming that the party had not done enough to defend the German people. The elders were evidently clueless about the national question, believing in their laissez-faire obliviousness that German would naturally assert itself over time. The party's top ranks were drawn from the administrative boards of powerful banks or rail corporations and had lost any link to the common people.[16] The rebels determined to follow the Czech model, supporting first the ethnic people and only after that the state. They understood the people in the new racist sense as a complete organism, including the socially weak and strong, and their politics was as much about social security as cultural identity, as much about political enfranchisement as about upward social mobility.

They drafted a statement of principle, known as the Linz Program, that sharply diverged from liberal orthodoxy by demanding protection from the caprices of early capitalism through pensions, accident insurance, an end to child labor, as well as nationalization of all "economic organizations important to the life of people." The aim was to shield the *Volk* from exploitation and to expunge moral rot, whether from among journalists who spread lies or among shady businessmen who grew rich on the backs of others. But the *Volk* not only needed to be protected; it had to be enabled to act, and for that, the Linz Program's authors wanted to extend voting rights to all "members of the German tribe" or *deutsche Stammesgenossen*. (Hitler would later speak of *deutsche Volksgenossen*.) Because expanding suffrage seemed progressive, this plank attracted the support of Viktor Adler, a later founder of Austrian Social Democracy.[17]

The social and ethnic demands fatefully came together in support for home industries and a ban on house-to-house peddling. These measures, directed against Jews, were inserted by the protofascist Georg von Schönerer and were meant to appeal to Viennese artisan associations. Three years later, he appended a further demand he considered indispensable for social reform: "the removal of Jewish influence from all sections of public life." But for the time being, Schönerer seemed to Adler (himself Jewish) to be a fellow nationalist likewise striving for a unitary *grossdeutsch* republic, the old ideal of democratic revolutionaries of 1848.[18] The Linz Program also called for freedoms of press and association, as well as separation of church and state.

The rebels' greatest lament was being left out of Germany, and the program envisioned much closer relations to Germany in an "international ethnic" community, including a customs union to complement the domestic safety net. To make Cisleithania as German as possible, the program accorded Bosnia-Herzegovina and Dalmatia to Hungary and proposed a looser union with Galicia and Bukovina. The remaining territory, including Austria's Italian, Czech, and Slovene lands, would be Germanized. Given liberalism's agnosticism in national questions, this was also both progressive and reactionary, advancing a German nation-state while driving back the "ever more unruly aggression of foreign language elements on old German lands." Germans in Austria and Bohemia would never forget, the program read, that "for a thousand years they had lived in political unity with other Germans."[19]

German students in Prague and Vienna saw a prophet in Schönerer, among them the later literary critic Hermann Bahr, by no means an inveterate hater, who was expelled from the University of Vienna in 1883 for deriding the monarchy's weak nationalism. His heart "throbbed," he later wrote, when recalling that "outside Austria Germans had [the 1870 victory at] Sedan, Bismarck, Richard Wagner, and what did we have? Where was the man among us who would do something about this? I heard only one name: Schönerer." Bahr's father called Schönerer's influence upon young people "demonic."[20]

But within a few years, the poorly organized, impractical, and quarrelsome Schönerer and his anti-Jewish Union of German Nationals (*Verband der Deutschnationalen*) had waned, and other new movements emerged from the ruins of Austrian liberalism, Adler's Social Democracy among them. There was also something new right of center: Christian Socialism, a mass movement crafted by the charismatic Karl Lueger, a liberal of lower-middle-class background who had been seeking a cause. If Adler appealed to the growing class of industrial labor, Lueger found a constituency among the threatened middle classes who were repelled by the anti-Catholicism of the Social Democrats and German nationalists. The Christian Socials were "Austrian" (that is, less interested in their role as German ethnics), and they rejected Schönerer's call to break up the Habsburg monarchy.[21]

But like Schönerer, Lueger, mayor of Vienna from 1897 until his death in 1910, stoked the anti-Semitism that was widespread in the middle and lower classes, stronger in Austria than in Bohemia. He was a rabble-rouser but also a gifted communal politician who transformed the imperial capital into a modern metropolis, with first-class public transportation, schools, and a sewer system. But he shamelessly employed hatred in mass rallies, claiming that Jews became wealthy by exploiting faithful and well-meaning Christians. Among his admirers was the young Adolf Hitler, who began his vagabond existence in Vienna in 1906. A Catholic priest led Christian Socialism in the 1920s, and the movement came to oppose Hitler's anticlerical Nationalist Socialist German Workers Party (NSDAP). But because Lueger had done so much to legitimize public vilification of Jews, many Christian Socialists found themselves celebrating Hitler's triumphs, culminating in the seizure of Austria in 1938.

But Slavs were also radicalizing, and Taaffe's coalition came apart in 1893, when patience ran out among the Young Czechs, who by that point had absolute control of the Czech Club in the parliament in Vienna. Nevertheless, Francis Joseph was keen to fashion a new majority in parliament because he anticipated a fight when the compromise with Hungary came up for its ten-year renewal in 1897. In the summer of 1895, he appointed as minister president the strong-willed Polish Count Kazimierz Badeni, who as governor in Galicia had managed to satisfy but also stall demands made by the Ukrainian national movement. When he arrived in Vienna, Badeni knew there would be no return to stable rule through parliamentary majority without resolution of the German-Czech dispute.[22]

He thus proposed a law to mollify the Czechs that went beyond the 1880 Stremayr ordinance by obliging the use of Czech in the *internal* correspondence of state administrators in Bohemia, in effect making the kingdom bilingual, even in areas where no Czech was spoken. When the law was announced in the spring of 1897, Germans staged violent rioting not seen in half a century: in Prague, Brno, Saaz, Teplitz, Reichenberg, and Eger, but also beyond Bohemia in Innsbruck, Vienna, Linz, Graz, and elsewhere. In Vienna, signs went up in restaurants: "Czechs, Jews, and dogs not welcome." German deputies practiced obstruction, and parliament closed on June 2, yet tumult resumed when it reopened in September. The sergeant at arms suspended unruly delegates for three sessions, but this only caused the unrest to spread further. On November 28, Francis Joseph accepted Badeni's resignation, and German students celebrated, some calling the fallen leader a "Polish pig." "The invasion of brutality into politics," the novelist Stefan Zweig later recalled, "thus chalked up its first success."[23] Badeni escaped Vienna in a closed cab.

With the language law's failure, it was the Czechs' turn to be outraged: in Prague, the reaction was so turbulent that the martial law retracted in 1895 had to be reintroduced. It was not safe to speak German, and numerous businesses, associations, and cafes were wrecked. In late November, police fired volleys into crowds of Czech demonstrators, killing several dozen.[24] The violence spread, focusing on Jewish property, because Jews, a minority of less than 2 percent, proved easy targets. Though acculturated and overwhelmingly bilingual, Bohemian Jews were hated by many Czech nationalists for being too "German," while German nationalists rejected culturally German Jews in and beyond Bohemia as racial "aliens."[25]

Czech and German politicians failed to understand the anger on the other side of the ethnic divide. Repeatedly, Czech leaders had failed to accept what Germans thought a sensible compromise: to divide the Bohemian kingdom into Czech, German, and mixed districts. Why did Germans need to know Czech in purely German districts, why not leave them in peace? Yet Czechs asked: would anyone chop up the French, Danish, or Spanish kingdoms? Yet the behavior of Germans rioting outside Bohemia was more baffling. They were under no direct threat. Writing after World War II, the historian Johann Albrecht von Reiswitz acknowledged that it was impossible from his day's perspective to see Badeni's language ordinances as inimical to German interests.[26] They might have served as a model for compromise in other dual-language areas. Czech is a difficult language, he admitted, but instead of rioting, why did Germans not ask for a five years' grace period? Would not learning a Slavic language have led to

FIGURE 9.1. Sketch of a "street battle" in Prague (ca. 1900). *Source*: Period postcard.
Via Wikimedia Commons.

a better understanding of one's fellow citizens?[27] And, what is so bad about enlightenment?

But for Germans, learning Czech was not enlightenment. The liberal Nobel laureate Theodor Mommsen called the Czechs "apostles of barbarism" who would engulf German achievements in the abyss of "*Unkultur*." Speaking from the floor of the Bohemian Parliament in Prague, the German Christian Socialist Rev. Ambros Opitz called Czech the language of the kitchen, while his nationalist colleague Karl Hermann Wolf compared Czechs to the "Eskimos and Zulus." Some German politicians spoke in gentler tones, saying their language was more precise for matters of administration, but the verdict was clear: Czech could never stand next to a world-class language.[28]

By this time, Czech had advanced far beyond kitchen and farm work, into secondary and higher education, museums, and theaters, and a twenty-eight-volume encyclopedia; soon Prague would feature exhibitions of Auguste Rodin and Edvard Munch with elaborate Czech commentary.[29] Dr. Alois Koldinský, later mayor of Prague-Smíchov as well as a playwright and theater director, expressed the pain of generations when he turned to German legislators just weeks after Badeni's resignation and told them in Czech:

Only we have reason for complaint in this diet of the Bohemian Crown. . . . *you* behave here as even enemies do not in enemy territory in time of war. You scorn everything that is Czech, and the poison of your contempt will turn this Bohemian Kingdom into a Czech graveyard . . . the hatred you nurture from generation to generation for the Czech nation is the very hatred you nurture against the Bohemian Kingdom—which for you is a mere province.[30]

He mocked the idea that Czech was insufficient for professional life and named a successful businessman in Hradec Králové who spoke no German at all. "We are not saying that we do not want to learn German," he said. "We learn not just German, but French and Russian—whereas you will not learn Czech or French or Russian . . . you don't even want your administrators to learn Czech!"[31]

For Czechs across the political spectrum, Badeni's language ordinances had been not a compromise but a minimal requirement for peace: if they were going to share their kingdom with a foreign people, that people should at least respect the local language. Hungarians and Galician Poles had secured their cultures after the erosion of absolutist rule in the 1860s, and Germans continued to dominate the top bureaucracy and the military as well as scholarship and the economy throughout Cisleithania. Only Czech existence continued to be endangered. Look at the bookshelves of any Czech city dweller, wrote the Young Czech Edvard Grégr, and you find one Czech book among a hundred German; open the doors of a German school in any Czech village and you will find it full of Czech children.[32]

Badeni's offending law was withdrawn in 1899, and German remained the internal language of administration in Bohemia. The monarch appointed heads of state who governed without parliamentary majorities, passing legislation when Czechs temporarily dropped their obstruction but also using the constitution's emergency clause when necessary. The dénouement was not the monarchy's end, but the end's beginning, reminiscent of Germany after 1930, when President Paul von Hindenburg appointed chancellors because the Reichstag could not produce a majority. Finally, in January 1933, Hindenburg appointed an Austrian immigrant who had grown up in the shadow of the Czech-German conflict, who called Georg von Schönerer a major inspiration.[33]

But a more direct bridge between Habsburg Vienna and Nazi Berlin was the radical nationalist Karl Hermann Wolf. He not only mocked the Czechs in Prague; he also shot Badeni in the arm during a duel in 1897. It was Wolf's popularity among Germans that helped the Schönerer party advance from eight to twenty-one seats in the elections of 1901. The following year, Wolf broke with Schönerer, partly for personal reasons, partly because he, as a Bohemian, cared far more about the Czech-German conflict and was willing to appeal to German-speaking Jews for support. In 1903 Wolf co-founded a party for Bohemian German workers who felt threatened by the Czech advances in culture and business, the German Workers Party, out of which later grew the NSDAP. He gave Badeni credit for unwittingly uniting Germans as never before.[34]

Before retiring in 1925, Wolf linked his "German National Party" to Austrian Nazis and received his party badge under the banner of the swastika. He and his small-trader wife fell on hard times during the Depression, but they got a boost from pensions supplied by the Nazi movement in the Sudetenland, and then the German state. When he died in 1941, Wolf was accorded state honors and a speech by Hitler Youth Leader Baldur von Schirach; a wreath sent from Berlin by Adolf Hitler honored him as a champion of the "great German idea."[35]

From the moment he emerged as a student leader in Prague in the 1880s, Wolf had preached that the *Volk* stood above dynasty. He understood with other advocates of Greater Germany that no existing state protected the German *Volk*: not Bohemia or Prussia, and certainly not Austria. Whatever the Austro-Hungarian monarchy was, it was not German.[36] But this protofascism was not only about belief; it was also about paramilitary political culture. The author Stefan Zweig, eyewitness to both the Badeni crisis and the rise of the Assault Division of Nazi Germany (S.A.) a generation later, wrote that Hitler

> took from the German Nationals the beginning of a ruthless storm troop that blindly struck out in all directions, and with it the principle of terroristic intimidation by a small group of a numerically superior but humanely more passive majority. What the S.A. men, who broke up meetings with rubber clubs, attacked their opponents by night and felled them to the ground, accomplished for the National Socialists was provided for the German Nationals by the Corps Students who, under cover of academic immunity, instituted an unparalleled campaign of violence, and who were organized as a militia to march in, at beck and call, upon every political action.[37]

Protofascism in East Central Europe

Bohemia's ethnic strife did not produce protofascism in Czech politics, and indeed, fascism would remain marginal in East Central Europe as a whole, emerging in strength in only German Bohemia, Hungary, and Romania. It flourished where national leaders, usually liberals, lost touch with the common people, thereby exposing themselves to accusations of treachery and contempt by forces further to the right. Like the Linz Program authors, these forces freely mixed socialism into their nationalism.

The liberal German leadership in Vienna, who "soft-pedalled their German-ism in the interest of a multi-national state," had alienated Bohemia's Germans by showing little concern for the nationality struggle in Bohemia.[38] Usually of high bourgeois background, these liberals considered lower-class supporters of Schönerer and Wolf unripe for the political process. We hear echoes of their social elitism in the words President Paul von Hindenburg later found for Adolf Hitler: he was a "Bohemian corporal." Hitler was not from Bohemia, but in Hin-denburg's mind, he fit the stereotype of a German ethnic of poorer quality. The 1882 Linz Program spoke for marginal people like Hitler and Wolf, in whom fears of national and social decline overlapped because they felt an urgent threat to a precarious status. They were being forced back down the social ladder be-fore they had reached the first rung of respectability.

Yet the situation differed markedly among Bohemia's Czechs. Their national leadership included few high bourgeois or large landholders, and the movement was about national as well as social upward mobility from the start, so that Czech politicians felt personally impugned when Germans said Czechs were a people of field hands and kitchen laborers. The directors of new institutions, political parties, scholarly organizations, and newspapers were one or two generations removed from small towns or the farm. Of the Czechs serving as deputies in the Austrian Parliament in 1900, 43.1 percent came from peasant and 36.5 percent from working-class backgrounds.[39]

This upward mobility was the consequence of institutions that Czechs them-selves had built, with some help from the Austrian state, to make the world around them one that seemed their own.[40] By 1850 Czech-language schooling was close to universal, and the Czech movement built on it with secondary and higher education. In the late nineteenth century, the wealthy architect Josef Hlávka put up hospitals as well as administrative offices for the new elites. The movement's ability to raise money for schools, hospitals, and museums reflected the wealth of a rising ethnic middle class, often pooled in Czech savings and loans associations.

The Czech middle classes rose in an economy that was already complex and well integrated with transregional commerce. Bohemia possessed one-third of the Habsburg monarchy's industry, with mining and textile production that went back generations; the land's agriculture was diversified and well capital-ized, and featured very old productive sectors, like fish farming. As capitalism grew and Czechs became wealthier, the abundance of social and material goods dulled the edge of class conflict, opening paths to cooperation across the political parties that had emerged by World War I, including the Marxist one. When Czechoslovakia was created in 1918, Czech parties continued to cooperate across the political spectrum.

Yet in the nationalist mind, the advance of capitalism also took place as a part of the struggle against German dominance. Though Czechs outnumbered Germans two to one in Bohemia, the relative share of wealth between the groups was almost the opposite. Czech nationalists therefore called for forming rural banks, joint-stock sugar factories, and a network of chambers of commerce where Czechs might vie for influence.[41] One patriot wrote that Czech civil society "emancipated wealth from the condition of being German."

By the 1890s, any organization that emerged to represent interests in an increasingly diverse civil society took on a national character, and no sphere remained in which Germans and Czechs could easily cooperate; increasingly, in the nationalist view of the world, ethnic coexistence seemed a barrier to ethnic development. The most efficient way to secure the Czech national life would be in a politically bounded state, and that growing realization made arguments for Bohemian "state's right" irresistible even on the Czech socialist left, just as it terrified Bohemia's Germans across lines of social class.[42]

An additional factor that boosted the Czech movement's claim to represent upward mobility was the kingdom's pattern of land holding. In contrast to Western Europe, but in common with most of East Central Europe outside of Bulgaria and Serbia, land was concentrated in relatively few hands: in Bohemia, 151 families owned 1.5 million of the province's 5.2 million hectares, and in Moravia, one-quarter of the land was held by seventy-three families.[43] Among the large landholders, even those who were of Czech ethnic heritage tended to identify with German and Habsburg culture, and that meant that the project of taking hold of Bohemia politically could be justified by making the "Czech lands" serve the Czech people.

But for Bohemia's Germans, the landholding pattern was yet another factor that alienated them from their national elite, though in truth, many of these culturally German Bohemian princes and barons who lived on enormous estates in drafty palaces had little concern for any form of nationalism. But Bohemia was not unique. We find similar landholding patterns in Hungary and Romania, which were also places that produced significant fascist movements a generation later. The rural economy in those countries consisted of big estates: 45 percent of the total in Hungary (91 percent in Hungarian hands), and 50 percent in Romania.[44] And here, too, the national elite had little more than contempt for the common people of their own ethnicity, intensifying the feeling among them that they were strangers in their own land: a complaint heard in populist rhetoric from then to now, universal in the extreme right-wing version of populism stoked by Hitler, Mussolini, and their East European cousins.

Elite and People in Hungary and Southeastern Europe

In Hungary, a gentry elite firmly dominated politics in the late nineteenth century, including the government in Budapest and all state administration, claiming privileges supposedly dating to time immemorial. Their ancestors were the "Scythians," an ethnically superior and foreign caste that had supposedly once led the Magyar people out of Asia and into the Pannonian plain of Central Europe, which they had staked and defended for the Hungarian nation that only they embodied. All others on the land were guests or hereditary servants who might or might not speak their language. It was therefore no surprise that Hungarian-speaking peasants saw nobles as alien: that was precisely what they were taught to believe.

Thus for most Hungarian nobles, all talk of land reform was nonsense: they were guarding a sacred and irrevocable patrimony, and though numbering only about 680,000 in a country of 12 million, shaped and used the political process in fulfillment of their historical mission.[45] Against the background of the rest of Europe, their vision seemed a bold one: it was to the keep the feudal hierarchy intact while making a modern nation-state. At the local level, this meant maintaining the continent's oldest estate institutions of self-government—the historic county (*comitat*)—so that single noble families often controlled the lives of families of commoners in one or more villages for centuries. At the national level, it meant that the monarch had not "given" Hungary a constitution in 1867; rather he had simply confirmed preexisting privileges. Even the Pragmatic Sanction was seen not as a contract but as a recognition by the Habsburgs of noble rights whose origins were lost in prehistory.

Though nobles had formed the backbone of the liberal revolution in 1848, in theory wanting to extend rights to everyone, after the 1867 Compromise, the elite by and large ceased caring for the Hungarian masses. Beyond its own general mythology of ethno-racial superiority, that was also due to the distillation of exalted social background we find in the political machine: from 1867 to 1918, 44 percent of members of the government in Budapest were aristocrats, and a third to half of ministerial officials came from the nobility.

The ruling party in Budapest still called itself "liberal," but it was a club of large landowners and industrialists, and it zigzagged between centralism and regional autonomy with no permanent program, membership, or central organization. It existed in order to govern and intervened in elections to guarantee itself majorities, employing forgery, intimidation, and the purchasing of votes. Its liberalism consisted of ideas about progress taken from the European Enlightenment but reshaped in an atmosphere of retrograde nationalism: the deeper color of noble social status thus bled through the cloth of liberal doctrines.[46]

Thus when the general situation favored economic liberalism, the Hungarian government's policies included the abolishment of guilds, the negotiation of labor contracts, or the removal of strictures on the sale of land. But when agricultural products fell through the floor with a 50 percent drop in prices in the late 1870s, the government protected the domestic economy and disciplined labor, beginning with a domestic farm and servants' act of 1878 that exempted masters from liability for "minor" acts of violence. This meant that workers could not sue for expressions of opinion about their conduct that would normally be regarded as offenses to "personal honor."[47] The state was simply putting its ideology into practice: lower-class Hungarians were beneath contempt.

By the 1890s, living standards were dropping in the Hungarian countryside, and as much of the country retreated to pre-capitalist modes of production, the law followed suit. Some ninety-two great "historic" families retreated to feudal legal arrangements, attaining from the crown protection of their properties from sale (*fidei commissa*). One-sixth of the arable land in Hungary was declared to reside in inalienable trusts, heritable through primogeniture. The growing Hungarian underclass, now reduced to neo-serfdom, ensured the neofeudal lords a reliable supply of labor, and the police colluded by returning workers to places of work if they breached seasonal contracts, and by forbidding union organization as "interference with work of others." Tillers of the land lapsed into semi-subsistence, with just 11 percent producing for the market, and the remainder consuming their own produce.[48]

Democracy shifted into reverse as well, as the percentage of male adults entitled to vote declined from more than 14 percent to 6.2 percent between the 1870s and 1905. In Austria, the electorate was growing steadily, and at the turn of the century, 27 percent of adult males could vote. (It rose to 100 percent in 1907. The figures in France and Britain were 28 percent and 16 percent, respectively.) Hungary's electoral districts were skewed to guarantee government party victories as well as the overrepresentation of Hungarians and underrepresentation of Romanians and Slovaks. To make the desired political outcomes even more certain, laws passed in the early twentieth century limited parliamentary debate, and lawmakers were left to discussing trivialities, skirting questions like land reform or working-class rights. When Hungary's "liberal" party finally lost in 1905, Francis Joseph refused to honor the election and appointed his own guard commander as prime minister. By now Hungary's liberalism was in fact a brand of feudal conservatism.[49]

The elite, however, considered themselves nationalist modernizers, and they did what they could to enhance production; industrial output increased sharply in two spurts, one in the 1860s, the other in the 1890s, the latter stimulated by foreign investment, and the percentage of population dependent on agriculture fell from 82 percent to 62.4 percent between 1890 and 1910. There was also improvement in agriculture; for example, more than 2.5 times as much wheat was produced between 1901 and 1910 as between 1871 and 1880. The gross national product went up five- to sixfold between 1867 and 1914, though the effects were very unevenly distributed. Still, Hungary was limited in what it could do to promote native industries; any use of tariffs against Austria was illegal. For political reasons, it was also difficult for the government to directly subsidize native industries, for example, textiles. The industry that did develop was highly concentrated in Budapest, and in relatively few branches and firms. In sum, although Hungary experienced dramatic growth after 1867, it remained a breadbasket for the dual monarchy and a society on Europe's semi-periphery.[50]

Rather than getting involved in risky commercial activity and taking on the role of a middle class as their liberalism demanded, for the most part Hungary's nobles turned to Jews, many from Galicia, who within a generation formed the backbone of the entrepreneurial and professional classes. In the process, they acculturated. If in 1880, 58.5 percent of Hungary's Jews claimed Magyar as their mother tongue, by 1910 that number had risen to 77.8 percent. Enjoying full legal equality, young Jews advanced through Hungarian educational and professional institutions and then excelled in urban pursuits in commerce, finance, and industry. They also took an important place in the agricultural economy, as landowning farmers, but also as tenants and salaried employees of large landowners, who valued Jews as efficient and rational producers.[51]

By World War I, Hungary's elite seemed to be opening up to Jews as well. In 1914, one-fifth of the large landholders were Jews, and over one-fifth of the deputies in parliament were of Jewish parentage.[52] Tens of thousands of upwardly mobile Jews also excelled in patriotism, and as teachers, journalists, and professionals went into Slovak and Romanian areas spreading Magyar culture. Numerically, Magyarized Jews made the culturally Magyar population just over half of the Hungarian kingdom. At the same time, the lower class Magyar Christian population, unable to adapt as quickly to the challenges of modernization, looked on the advance of Jews with skepticism and jealousy, becoming further alienated from the gentry elite.

In contrast to the Czech national elite, Hungary's gentry thus failed to provide perspectives for social and economic advancement for the land's village dwellers. Instead, it endeavored to use state resources to slowly Magyarize ethnic others.[53] Because of the property limitations on the electorate, and multiple forms of administrative chicanery, the spaces for opposition politics in Hungary, whether social or national, were severely constrained. A Hungarian Social Democratic party emerged but not a significant movement for Christian Socialism or agrarianism. The elite's suppression and neglect of the interests and rights of the local ethnicity virtually ensured a full outburst of radical nationalism when economic circumstances reached a nadir in the early 1930s.

The relations between elite and common folk were similar in Romania, but the extremes were greater. In 1912, 82 percent of Romanians still lived in the countryside. Some 2,000 families had owned 38 percent of arable land in 1864, and that percentage worsened: in 1905, some 5,000 families controlled 50 percent of all arable land. The share of medium-sized properties was negligible (10 percent), while 40 percent of all lands consisted of tiny plots between five and ten hectares. By 1905, there was probably no country in Europe where the disparity was so great between large- and smallholdings: a few thousand families held as much land as more than a million. Like its Hungarian counterpart, the elite was quasi-aristocratic, and through control of the local administrative apparatus, they became a law unto themselves, with little concern for the welfare of peasants.[54]

As in Hungary, professional bureaucrats of gentry (boyar) background dominated the state apparatus and acted as nationalist modernizers, focusing on development in a few large cities, but stopping short at the countryside, where grain and cereal were grown on huge estates, and asymmetrical social relations remained untouched.[55] Also similar to Hungary was the low level of overall development, with industrial output not exceeding 15 percent of national income before World War I.

Jews likewise had particular roles in the economy and society in Romania, but as we have seen, Romania's elite stalled on granting them citizenship rights—in defiance of the stipulations of the Congress of Berlin. Jews could not own land and therefore lived in cities, becoming artisans, traders, administrators, bankers, peddlers, tailors, and craftspeople. In 1900, less than 5 percent of Romania's population was Jewish, but it was almost entirely urban, constituting 50 percent of the inhabitants of Iaşi and one-third those of Bucharest. Jews were employed in the advanced sectors of economy, as in Hungary, and though enjoying far less official support, they still managed to develop the economy.[56]

The ethnic Romanian elite preferred city life and as a rule left the administration of their huge estates to middlemen, usually Greek, Armenian, Jewish, or German, who pressed as much from the peasants as possible in seasonal contracts. In Moldavia, the percentage of Jewish leaseholders approached 40 percent, and therefore in the eyes of peasants, Jews became identified as the outstretched hand of an exploitative system that extended from the remote and alien cities into their own rural homelands.[57]

The peasants either had no land or too little to make ends meet and tended to sharecrop on the large estates. As their numbers increased, so did their misery, and many fell victim to poor diets and pellagra (a disease caused by a chronic lack of niacin, often among people heavily dependent on maize for sustenance, reported cases of which rose between 1888 and 1906 from 10,626 to more than 100,000). A particular index of peasant poverty was the high mortality rate among children. Meanwhile, the government did little to protect peasants from exploitation by landowners and their middlemen, against whom the peasants had almost no bargaining power. In tough times, desperate need for money forced peasants to sell grain to speculators at below-market value. The loans on offer were extortionate, and state taxes could amount to 80 percent of the peasants' annual production.

Even if peasants had been literate and able to take full part in political life, the electoral system treated them as second-class citizens. It provided for nearly universal male suffrage, but the propertied classes selected 80 percent of the parliamentary deputies, while the peasantry and the lesser taxpayers chose the remaining 20 percent via delegates. The technique of generating electoral support differed from that used in Hungary. There, the "liberal" István Tisza regime (1903–1905, 1913–1917) mobilized massive pluralities of landless peasants to offset his weakness in rapidly developing urban areas. In Romania, by contrast, the "liberal" Ion I. C. Bratianu (1909–1910, 1914–1918) simply ignored sharecroppers, who were difficult to organize.[58] A generation later, they became a leading constituency for the fascist Iron Guard.

The great Romanian peasant rebellion of 1907 began with peasants employed by the Fischer family, leaseholders of Austrian-Jewish origin who controlled

FIGURE 9.2. Peasant unrest in Romania: Infantry escorting prisoners (1907).
Source: Hermanus Willem Koekkoek (lithographer), based on sketch of Rook Carnegie,
London Illustrated News, April 6, 1907. Via Wikimedia Commons.

most of the arable land in three counties of northern Moldavia (150,000 hectares in total). In February, peasant leaseholders there rose up after being told
their contracts would not be extended, and the protests quickly spread among
peasants who likewise feared being denied land to work. The government sent
in military units, but not enough to stifle the unrest. The movement spread
into Wallachia and became violent. Peasants looted stores and restaurants,
burned manor houses, and occasionally killed landowners and middlemen.
Everywhere the demand was simple: "*Vrem pamint!*" [We want land!]. Now a
government calling itself liberal replaced one that called itself conservative,
and the army fully mobilized, taking villages after artillery salvos, as if on a
proper military campaign. Some 9,000 peasants were killed before the uprising
was quashed.[59]

Modest reform efforts surfaced from the political class, for example, limiting rents that could be charged for land and fixing minimum salaries. Beginning in 1908, there was an Agrarian Credit Bank for those hoping to attain land.
Still, peasants remained dependent on landholders, and nothing fundamental
changed: the state administration kept an eye on villages through police and
army stations; peasants lacked the skills and knowledge to organize; and the
liberal governments promised change but never invested energy or manpower.

Thus, any reforms disappeared "without trace in the quicksand of Romanian public life." Politicians of all stripes thought of peasants as less than fully-fledged citizens, to be ignored or suppressed as the occasion required. For their part, peasants also placed faith in the king, unaware that he figured among the country's largest landholders.[60]

The 1907 uprising was the largest agrarian disturbance in Eastern Europe's recorded history and bears revealing similarities to the massive unrest of 1875 in Herzegovina that transformed Southeastern Europe. Both events emerged from the extremes of inequality, the earlier one of all Ottoman-dominated Europe, the latter of all Europe west of Russia. What was different was the ethnic dimension. In Herzegovina, the furor of Christian serfs turned almost immediately against Muslim landowners, and the alien regime of injustice they seemed to incorporate, while in Romania, the anger was class based. There was no effort to create a new state order, and the ethnic hatred—including anti-Semitism—did not fuel the violence because the leaseholders and land managers were of various ethnic backgrounds. In numerous places, peasants loyally petitioned Romanian authorities, only to be repulsed violently by police and army.[61]

A final similarity was that despite the violence, in neither place did much change: large landholders kept their properties intact, and the system of exploitation continued. The main difference was that the Romanian regime could distract peasants from their misery by claiming that an ultimate solution to all their problems would be achieved with the union of all Romanians in a greater Romanian state.[62] In Bosnia, by contrast, the ethnic argument now turned against Austria-Hungary, and its foreign, exploitative rule, hated by Orthodox and Muslims alike.

* * *

Though an underproductive agricultural regime also dominated the economies of Serbia and Bulgaria, a relation developed between elites and people in these countries that was more reminiscent of the Czech case, with national leaders drawn not from the gentry but rather from the common people; there was no native class of large landholders. Though like Romania, Serbia was a former Ottoman possession, where the overwhelming majority lived in the countryside, and socioeconomic development lagged, as in Bohemia, the medieval nobility had been destroyed. Also similar to the Czech areas of Bohemia, the emerging national elite was of peasant origin, and in the following generation, like the Czech lands, Serbia produced no significant native fascism.[63]

In Ottoman times, *spahis* had held the land and produce of peasants in return for service, and then came janissaries, who later degenerated into marauding raiders. But although the right to extract dues and tributes remained in Turkish hands, unlike rural populations in Hungary or Romania, Serb peasants were not enserfed. When the Serb principality took form in the decades after 1817, the Turkish landholders gradually left, and the Serb leader Miloš Obrenović refused to permit the emergence of large landed estates, fearing they might dilute his power (he became fabulously wealthy). Thus, he left Serb society mostly of one class, a highly undifferentiated peasantry. Besides him, none of the few power holders who emerged after the 1840s had more than a few hundred hectares of land, and no one was tempted to trace a grand lineage to noble or racially superior forebears.[64]

The Serb state at first seemed to rule by liberal principles. The constitution of 1868 provided for a legislature, and beginning in 1880, political parties developed. There were three centers of power: the bureaucracy, the politicians who had success in electoral politics, and the prince. Like Romania's king, the prince constantly interfered, preventing the emergence of a bona fide democracy. The most important political movement was the Serb Radicals, co-founded as a peasant party in 1881 by Nikola Pašić, a peasant's son who fell in with socialist circles during engineering studies in Zurich—a crossroads of East European Marxism—becoming Serbia's and then Yugoslavia's uncontested political leader until his death in 1926.[65]

But rather than act in the peasants' interest by promoting rural development, the Radicals evolved into an establishment political machine, advancing the state's power and wealth by focusing public resources on the army, bureaucracy, railroads, and diplomatic service, fostering virtually every civic project short of the needs of peasants. In 1908, the Ministry of Agriculture received only 3 percent of the annual budget, while 23 percent of that budget went directly to the military and 28 percent to debt services (mostly interest on loans for railroads and the army). The justification for these expenditures was to spread the Serb state into areas considered ethnically Serb.[66]

Yet because that agenda was broadly supported, the Serb Radical Party never sacrificed the loyalties of the peasantry, and indeed used the education system to stoke irredentist feeling. It helped that the per capita debt burden on the peasants decreased in the decades before World War I. But the Radicals also had good fortune in timing: they had claimed peasants' loyalty from the first days of independence, through the semi-populist program of Pašić's friend and mentor Svetozar Marković, Serbia's first socialist, who promised to lessen state intervention into peasants' lives. Although the Radicals were an establishment party, its intellectuals and professional politicians never lost contact with the villages, where they kept networks of supporters. When necessary, they could speak perfect peasant vernacular.[67] Society and government thus remained cohesive, even if the competing wings of the Radical party vigorously debated politics and went in and out of government from 1892 to 1900.

Bulgaria was similar in terms of the landholding regime. When the Bulgarian national renaissance began in the mid-nineteenth century, the country was almost completely rural, run by Turkish landlords. After independence in 1878, the Turkish landowners were ejected, leaving Bulgaria a place of smallholding peasants who produced for subsistence. The most coherent institution, as in Serbia, was the state, which grew beginning in the 1870s, becoming a kind of "class" in itself and filling a social vacuum.[68] But as we will see in Chapter 11, in contrast to Serbia, a major peasant movement emerged here—the Bulgarian Agrarian Union—with an original political philosophy that challenged the liberal state machine and irredentist nationalism as well as the monarch who pursued it.

Farther north in Habsburg lands, Slovene and Croat peasant movements emerged, calling themselves "peoples" parties. These parties claimed to represent the soul of nations on the front lines of struggle against German and Italian schooling; Magyar, German, and Italian capital; and Magyar and German administrative pressures. Slovene and Croat peasant leaders encouraged peasants to pool their savings in ethnic savings and loan associations while sidestepping German and Italian institutions, arguing that use of their vernaculars in financial transactions would lead to the formation of a "state within a state" and national liberation. The attitude is expressed well in a letter written by the Catholic priest and party leader Janez Krek, in 1905: "*only a cooperative movement of the Slovene peasants can stop the Germanization and Italianization of our territory.* . . . If the Slovene peasants already had their own loan institutions and savings banks, they would not have had to sell their land or borrow from foreign usurers."[69]

The difference between the Croatian and Slovene movements was the stronger role of the Catholic Church in the latter, which had grown directly out of a clerical party and prevented the splitting of the people's party into urban and rural variants (unlike Austria's Christian Socialism). Perhaps more than any other East European peasant party, Slovene populists took into account the ethnic needs among workers and farmers, against all German and Italian pressure. Through the force of his personality, Krek maintained links between the cultural elite and the common people, as well as the church. The Slovenes formed an alliance with two Croat parties in 1912, and later worked with Croat and Serb politicians to form a South Slav state as a bulwark against denationalization across the northern edges of South Slavic settlement.[70]

As we will see in detail, the Croat peasant movement under its tribune Stjepan Radić faced stronger pressures to orient itself toward a preexisting nationalism, which in Croatia had tended to neglect the peasantry and focus obsessively on the struggle against perceived enemies, above all Magyars and Serbs. Although Radić supported South Slav unity, after World War I, his party would evolve into a bulwark against the encroachment of Serb cultural and political domination in the new state of Yugoslavia.

What connected Slovene and Croatian peasant populism at this stage was the common challenge of small and medium-sized proprietors, as well as landless laborers, to assert themselves against a large-landholding class that was often of foreign ethnicity. Croatia was similar to Hungary in that much of the land (36.6 percent) was held in large estates. It was also similar to Bohemia in that the owners were often of foreign nationality: of the sixty-two largest landholders in Croatia-Slavonia, only thirty-three were Croatian or Serb.[71] Before World War I, because of limited franchise in Hungary (and Austria until 1907), the power of the Slovene and Croat people's movements was not yet evident. But as mass movements connecting the national leaderships to the peasantries, they, like the Serb Radicals and Bulgarian Agrarian Union, later helped keep fascism from developing in the countryside, where the great majority of the population lived.

* * *

Despite decades of scholarly attention, fascism eludes not only comprehension but also simple description. Was it a movement of the right or left? The Italian party sat at the far right of the country's lower house in 1921, but the movement never divested itself of socialism: it was national socialism. Some have described fascism as revolutionary conservative, but that is more an evocation of paradox than a description of practice. The apparently incongruent aspects of fascism made their earliest appearance in the 1882 Linz Program. Its protofascist authors wanted not the militant dictatorship we associate with fascism, but instead more democracy, more than liberals of their day would concede. They also wanted more social security, an end to corruption, and ethnic protection of

Germans. From the mid-1880s, one splinter identified Jews as enemies of the "people"—people understood as co-ethnics but also as the working people.

Fascism emerged from liberalism and from liberalism's agnosticism on the national question. But it also arose from failures in liberal economic policies and the laissez-faire doctrine that constrained state welfare policies. In the end, the strongest source of inspiration for fascism was simply liberals' neglect. Two generations earlier, liberal nationalism had sprouted in Eastern Europe out of the sense among patriot intellectuals that their peoples were victims of condescension by other ethnicities, above all Germans. A generation later, fascism would flourish in areas where the common people were treated with condescension by members of their own ethnicity. At least that would be the fascists' compelling argument.

But the Linz Program was not simply fascism's harbinger. What made it a pivot to the future, revealing the centrality of the German-Slavic dispute in Cisleithania, was that a program cooked up by dissenting intellectuals could grow into mass movements of the center right—into pan-Germanism and Christian Socialism—but also Marxian Social Democracy, in each case appealing to fears of decline in wide swaths of the population. The only solution that Habsburg leaders had for the fragmentation of the post-liberal landscape, and the challenges of forming governing coalitions in a mass of new parties, was to broaden the electorate in hopes of creating some whose appeal would stretch across ethnic lines. Yet as the electorate grew, political movements stoking fears of national and social decline only proliferated. Before 1918, no one had found a method for harnessing democracy in a way that might have permitted the multiethnic monarchy to cohere as a state.

CHAPTER 10

Liberalism's Heirs and Enemies: Socialism versus Nationalism

In 1848, liberals believed the future was theirs, because as monarchs retreated, the path seemed open to freedom. Through education and economic growth, they would shape societies where reasonable human beings governed their own affairs. Yet by the early 1900s, self-described liberals were fading from the scene, and the parties vying for power in Austria were Christian Socialist, Social Democratic, and variations on German nationalism. All rejected the liberal orthodoxies of free markets and a caretaker state, but they still participated in liberal politics by contesting elections, working in parliament, and recognizing the rule of law. With them in parliament sat a variety of national clubs from elsewhere in Cisleithania—Czech, Polish, Ruthene, Croat, and Slovene—each constituting a left-right spectrum of its own. By 1907, there was also a "Jewish club" in parliament. Vienna became the origin point of world Zionism, and Zionism itself began to fragment.[1]

Across the border in Transleithania, a Hungarian liberal party dominated parliament by fixing elections and limiting the electorate to weaken its many rivals: Romanians, Serbs, Croats, Slovaks, and Hungarian socialists, peasant activists, and others. Their luck ran out in 1905, when more determined Hungarian nationalists, dissatisfied with the 1867 Compromise, were voted into power. But little changed. This "1848 party" only intensified the determination to keep challengers to the Hungarian machine out of political life; among other things, it passed legislation to stunt the development of literacy among non-Hungarians. Hungarian politics was beset by deep tensions: on one hand, the elite still subscribed to principles of modernization and rule of law, but on the other, it fully recognized that only illiberal practices could help promote that "liberal" agenda in an ostensible nation-state that they sought to make uniformly Magyar.

Meanwhile, Czech liberals had long fragmented into the less and more radical Old Czechs and Young Czechs, and then, from the 1890s, into a right-left spectrum of nationalists, agrarians, and socialists, all of whom respected liberal practices but looked upon Hungary's elite with envy. Regardless of political stance, they wanted Bohemia to become Czech the way Hungary was becoming Magyar. Numerically their position was much stronger: Hungary was barely 51 percent Hungarian, whereas Bohemia was two-thirds Czech. Even progressive Czechs felt the German minority were "guests" in the Czech kingdom and therefore that assertion of Czech control was their right and duty.

Outside the Habsburg lands to the south and southeast, we encounter a mix of parties professing liberal principles while fixing elections to maintain power. In contrast to places farther west, liberalism's goal in Romania, Serbia, and Bulgaria was not laissez-faire economics or an assault on old social and political privileges. Instead, Balkan liberals translated liberal ideals of personal freedom and civic rights into the right of the nation to unimpeded development in its own state. Like counterparts in Hungary, liberals who ruled in these places rewarded their followers with jobs, but they also pursued foreign policies to redeem ostensible national territories that remained beyond the borders set by the Berlin Congress in 1878. In the eyes of their leaders, Romania, Serbia, and Bulgaria were not completed nation-states, but only halfway points to something bigger. But liberal and conservative establishments in these places were challenged by Marxian socialists and peasant parties, for example, the fascinatingly unorthodox Bulgarian Agrarian National Union (BANU), which organized labor in the countryside despite police repression and envisioned forms of social revolution that would set Bulgaria on a distinctive path involving respect for peasants and their way of life.[2]

Poland featured a welter of parties across the lands of three empires, but an unbridgeable divide emerged in the political center between Poland's Socialists and the right-wing "National Democrats" (or *Endeks*). The latter were one-time liberals who hated liberalism with the passion of Georg von Schönerer but were even more exclusive than his pan-Germans, denouncing all other would-be representatives of "their" nation as frauds. They presaged the rise of radical illiberalism in twentieth century Europe, though with greater ferocity than in France or Austria because they had to contend with the antidemocratic Russian state that controlled central Poland.

Among the factors eroding liberalism's popularity, three stand out. First, instead of becoming vehicles for growth and prosperity, economies went into depression after the crash of 1873, as production dropped, unemployment rose, and hopes dwindled for a better life for all citizens. Capitalism triumphed but did so in an expanding urban world of disease, dirt, and overcrowding; with workers spending long hours at factories, where only ingenuity learned on the job protected them from life-threatening accidents. (The misery in many rural areas was even worse.) Second, as the electorate expanded, new voters included laborers who had either tasted the ugliness of nascent capitalism in the towns or languished in the countryside with too little land. The well-dressed people they saw enjoying life in restaurants or on expensive vacations in spa towns seemed to owe their wealth to speculation and favoritism. For poorer Germans in Bohemia, such envies were coupled with fears of being displaced by Slavs willing to enter the labor market for lower wages. By the 1890s, only the wealthiest property owners—a dwindling fraction of the electorate—remained true to liberalism, and they looked on the new voters as driven by irrational urges.[3]

The third factor weakening liberal politics was science. The period's major trend, social Darwinism, refracted in Eastern Europe through the writings of Herbert Spencer, said that humans were products of conditioning, so that any ideas about politics—including liberalism—now seemed products of particular environments. Freedom, the heart of liberal doctrine, was an illusion created by those interested in preserving their own power and keeping laborers under control. If there was improvement in any field of human endeavor, it came from struggle.

At the same time, Darwinism suggested that differences among political groups, nations, or races could not be reconciled. In social or national conflicts, opponents were to be overwhelmed rather than met halfway, and reasoned discourse itself seemed compromised as anti-rational theories proliferated, some glorifying violence as the "rational" means of attaining improvements for the underprivileged.[4] Not coincidentally, one spokesman for this scientifically grounded politics of hatred was the French engineer Georges Sorel, another was the Polish biologist Roman Dmowski. He called Polish intellectuals who disagreed with him "half-Poles," akin to a wayward species of mutants.

Still, if liberalism had withered, it had not died. Not everyone lost faith in the power of intellect and free will to solve human problems; not everyone lost faith in the power of the franchise to achieve progress; and not everyone lost faith in the art of compromise, or the rule of law protecting civil society. Most people did not think that democracy was a sham. In a sense, liberalism's failure was liberalism's triumph: because basic civil liberties demanded in 1848 had been achieved, new parties grew up using liberal means to go beyond liberal agendas.[5]

Liberal forms and beliefs took special refuge among Social Democrats, most in the tradition of Marx, who believed that the future belonged to laborers. They sought to advance their interests in civil society through parties and trade unions, but also through educational associations, gymnastics, and women's clubs. More than anyone, Socialists pressed for direct, equal, and secret suffrage, and therefore also attracted people not of working-class background, including peasants.[6] Because it promised justice for all and a break with a despised past, Socialism also attracted leading intellectuals; indeed, few of its leaders were workers, and many were former liberals, like Viktor Adler, coauthor of the 1882 Linz Program.

Of the political movements that emerged late in the century, only socialism made sense to 1848ers who had entered politics with faith in reason, such as Austria's Adolf Fischhof or Hungary's Baron József Eötvös. The socialists' "rhetoric was rationalist," writes Carl Schorske, "their secularization militant, their faith in education virtually unlimited." Liberals may not have accepted socialists' demands for a welfare state, but they had a language in which to argue with them. They were liberals' heirs, and if they seemed unreasonable, they were not irrational.[7]

* * *

Austrian socialists fought to expand liberal democracy because they did not fear the power of the streets and stood to gain from enfranchising the poor, regardless of ethnicity. By contrast, German liberals sought to exclude workers and Slavs from the political process and colluded with feudal-conservative forces to keep the electorate below 10 percent of adult males. The Old and Young Czechs saw themselves as liberal, but German liberals viewed the Czechs as nationalists who had revealed themselves as unreasonable by refusing German culture.[8] Yet neither Germans nor Czechs could use liberal doctrine to support their nationalist arguments. How could reason "measure" the superiority of one culture over another? Though agnostics, liberal nationalists were akin to adherents of a religious cult whose teachings in fact gave no basis for their cherished beliefs: they claimed that reason favored their nation. But their heirs, the socialists, now raised reason itself to the status of a religion and became doctrinaire about nationalism (and many other things) in ways that would astound liberals.

Almost immediately, however, a national struggle presented itself for which the socialists' doctrines provided no answers: Poland. For generations, revolutionaries there demanded liberation from oppression and the reestablishment of a democratic Polish state, something socialists, like liberals, supported across Europe. But a splinter group in Poland focused on Marxism's call for *universal* revolution and rejected Polish nationalism as reactionary. For socialism to prevail, they argued, capitalism had to develop fully, and that could occur only in large states where the economies advanced without internal customs boundaries. In their view, socialists should support capitalist development in the space between Germany and the Pacific Ocean—which happened to be the Russian Empire—regardless of what language people spoke. This view's major advocate was Rosa Luxemburg, a Jew from eastern Poland, educated in Warsaw and Zurich in economics, and a major figure in Polish, Russian, and above all German Social Democracy until being assassinated by right-wing militants in Berlin in 1919.

Luxemburg's view was not popular in Poland, but it seemed faithful to the movement's founders, Karl Marx and Friedrich Engels, who wrote in 1848 that workers had no fatherland. For Marxists then and later, nationality was a secondary form of identity: nations rose with capitalism and would disappear when capitalism gave way to socialism. And even while they existed, nations had no value as such; nationhood was ephemeral and unsubstantial, not a lasting site of human identity.[9]

Still, Marx and Engels were not non-national; they were culturally German and despised the small peoples who hindered the consolidation of large, "historical" nations like France, Germany, and Italy. Marx ridiculed the idea that the insignificant Czechs, living at the heart of a dynamic Germany, could have a separate state, and Engels wrote that in every corner of Europe, one encountered the "ruins" of peoples, ready to side with reaction against "historical" peoples with their missions to humankind: Scots against English, Bretons against French, Basques against Spaniards, and most recently and tragically, the "barbarian" Czechs and South Slavs against Germans and Hungarians. But Engels had not lost faith. "The next world war," he wrote in January 1849, "will cause not only reactionary classes and dynasties, but also entire reactionary peoples, to disappear from the face of the earth. And that is also progress."[10]

As Engels aged, his fury tempered, but he never abandoned the notion that small peoples were "relics." It was misguided, he wrote in 1866, to think that the "Roumans of Wallachia, who never had a history, nor the energy required to have one, are of equal importance to the Italians who have a history of 2,000 years." The national movement continued to grow among Czechs, but he still considered them a nuisance, destined to be "absorbed as integral portions into one or the other of those more powerful nations whose greater vitality enabled them to overcome greater obstacles." Other "remnants of bygone Slavonian peoples" that he mentioned as destined to fade into greater peoples were the Serbs, Croats, Ukrainians, and Slovaks.[11]

The disdain for small peoples extended beyond Marx and Engels to the German socialist elite, to Ferdinand Lassalle, Johann Baptist von Schweitzer, Johann Phillip Becker, Wilhelm Liebknecht, and the left liberal Leopold Sonnemann. Liebknecht, co-founder of the Social Democratic Party of Germany (SPD), considered the workers' movement an "infallible tool to eliminate the nationalities question."[12] If humans saw their interests in material terms, in their ability to produce wealth and be properly rewarded, who cared what language they spoke? The imperial states were not racist and provided opportunities for Czechs or Poles who rose through education in the state bureaucracies as long as they used the imperial language. If one's interest was universal culture, why not just use German or Russian? Socialists found no justification in history for the heart of the East European nationalist project: rescuing local vernaculars from the edge of extinction.

Except for Ireland's James Connolly, no major West European socialist wrote about nationalism. The Second International failed to deal with the issue in its meetings in 1889 and 1896. Germany's most respected theoretician, Karl Kautsky, came from Prague, and was of Czech, Polish, Hungarian, and Italian origin, yet before 1907 his journal, *Die Neue Zeit*, did not even carry "nationalism" or "nation" in its subject index. There were, however, entries for "apothecaries" and "vegetarianism." In 1906 the second theoretician of German Social Democracy, Eduard Bernstein, wrote that socialism could support self-government of *Kulturvölker* only insofar as this was in keeping with the "common interests of all peoples." Yet globalization had already disqualified nine-tenths of entities calling themselves "national" as backward and contrary to the interests of civilization.[13]

Bohemia

The testing ground for socialist theory on nationalism was Bohemia, where heated nationality struggles accompanied rapid industrial growth. Contrary to the "orthodox" Marxist notion that workers would shed ethnicity as class-consciousness grew, national and class consciousness reinforced each other there because in Czech eyes, the wealthy were German. According to Czech socialists, after the battle of White Mountain in 1620, Austria had made the urban classes as well as the great landowners of Bohemia culturally German, leaving the poor classes Slavic. The battle for Czech power in the countryside and cities was therefore "progressive," and Czech Marxists came to favor not only the advance of Czech proletarians but also the struggle of the Czech over the German bourgeoisie.[14]

But this unorthodox view itself was a result of struggle, prevailing only after 1900. From the earliest days of the industrial working class in Bohemia, divisions were evident between workers who felt German and those who felt Czech. In 1848, Czech speakers identified with the revolution in Prague, while German-speaking counterparts placed their hopes with revolution in Vienna, imagining Bohemia as a province of a greater democratic Germany. Czech leaders operated freely in the world of German culture, but they looked to France for a deeper understanding of socialism. In the war of 1870/1871, workers in Czech quarters had quietly sided with France, while Bohemian German counterparts openly celebrated the victories of German arms.[15]

Thanks to the liberal constitution of 1867, an ethnically variegated workers movement could emerge in Cisleithania, yet Germans dominated the leadership and took for granted that society would advance toward socialism through their culture. Thus a manifesto of workers' representatives appeared in Vienna in May 1868 in German, Czech, Hungarian, Italian, Polish, Hungarian, and Romanian—only to declare that the working class had thrown all *prejudices* of ethnic difference over board: the "labor market does not recognize borders between national groups. Capitalism rules everywhere, expressed and measured in money, and it does not care about peoples' *supposed* ethnic background." Therefore, requests for representing people of *supposed* Slavic origin were portrayed as reactionary separatism, hindering the emancipation of laboring people everywhere.[16]

In late 1888, Viktor Adler united the socialist organizations of Cisleithania in the Austrian Social Democratic Party (SDAP) at Hainfeld in Lower Austria (the official founding date was January 1, 1889). Given his heritage in German liberalism Adler not surprisingly took the party on a centralist course, yet it was also democratic and did not suppress subgroups. The German section counted one member for every eighty Austrian Germans, while the Czech section had one member for every fifty Czechs, making the Cisleithanian party as a whole among the strongest Socialist organizations in Europe, behind only the SPD in Germany.[17] The French party had just one member per 740 inhabitants, and the Italian party one for every 1,200; the remaining socialist parties of Cisleithania—Polish, Italian, South Slav, and Ruthenian—were much smaller. In 1893, hoping to compete against the Young Czechs, Czech socialists changed their name from the "Social Democratic Czecho-Slavic party in Austria" to the "Czecho-Slavic Social Democratic worker party."

The Hainfeld Program said nothing about nationalism other than that the party opposed discrimination of every kind. But as the movement grew, the question could not be ignored, and the party's 1899 Brünn/Brno meeting addressed it to keep workers from drifting into nationalist parties. What had been shocking in the unrest following the Badeni decrees of 1897 was the behavior of otherwise tolerant Czech and German Social Democrats, who had demolished property they considered foreign, often Jewish. German Social Democrats were suspended from parliament for their furious obstructionism, and when they returned to their home districts, they and their ethnic comrades continued smashing property.[18]

In response, SDAP intellectuals Otto Bauer and Karl Renner came up with the notion of a "personal right" to nationality. People would indicate their national affiliation to state authorities, and then "belong" to their nations as they did to churches, intermixed in villages and neighborhoods but having specific group needs met by separate institutions. Just as there were central Catholic or Protestant hierarchies in Vienna, so, too, would there be "national chambers" in the capital to represent Czechs or Germans or Slovenes. When elections came, people would receive lists of politicians of their nationality to vote into these chambers regardless of where they resided, and the chambers would pass laws taking care of their national interests.[19] Germans from Galicia would thus be represented in Vienna as Germans, as would Germans from Austria or Dalmatia. The scheme thus bypassed the knotty issue of territory. If a given village featured three or four nationalities, each would send its own representatives to Vienna, without worrying about whether the village was part of Bohemia, Austria, or some other entity.

Bauer and Renner had studied nationality questions carefully and considered nationally indifferent or bi-national individuals too insignificant to merit representation: such people did not constitute groups and never produced leaders or organizations. The men complemented their scheme with a plan to divide the monarchy into self-governing areas in a "national federal state."

There began the difficulties. The borders of those areas were not specified and had already generated unending disputes. Would Bohemia be a district, as Czechs wanted, or would it divide into linguistic subregions to meet German preferences? A greater problem was the assumption that politicians could limit themselves to defending only the cultural rights of nations living in a multiethnic territory. Bauer thought nations were about language and culture, but after Czech politicians had achieved the proper supply of schools and textbooks in their language, how would his scheme aid them in addressing their nation's lower economic status (the *nationaler Besitzstand*)? In fact, from the start, the nationality battle had also been about material wealth.

In 1907, Czech Social Democrat Antonín Němec said that Czech workers were struggling for social but also civil and national equality. "Foreigners" (meaning Germans and Jews) dominated the state, and Czechs' employers were class as well as national enemies who exploited their labor power and told them to speak German.[20] His words represented crass hyperbole, because a Czech entrepreneurial class had been growing for generations; nevertheless, his speech fostered Czech nationalism among workers and thus served the socialist cause.

At the same time, Czech socialists were connecting to an older story of the survival of Czech ethnicity despite German efforts, with every gain achieved against massive resistance. The story was compelling because it had considerable truth. Germans were being whittled down in parliamentary representation, but as we have seen, they maintained advantages in ownership of capital and savings, and their attitudes of cultural superiority were untouched (indeed, they extended beyond the bourgeoisie and up into the leadership of Austrian Social Democracy). Otto Bauer had no concern about the expansion of German power and blithely recommended that Germans migrate to places like Ukraine, where the population would benefit from their higher civilization.[21] Along with such confidence, he shared the fears common to German liberals and remarked in 1910 that a Slavic "flood" endangered *Deutschtum*. Other Austrian Socialists threw contempt into the mix and accused Czechs of being spoiled and haughty because they opposed assimilation.

Bauer failed to specify how nations would lay claim to territory because he did not consider his scheme of nonterritorial nationalism a permanent solution. It would be an expedient while Germanization continued. As socialists in the tradition of Marx and Engels, he and Renner assumed that Slavs would be absorbed into the "historical" nations, as they had been doing for centuries. And when "natural" processes of capitalist development did not propel this process, schooling would help it along. Bauer opposed the establishment of Slavic schools in Vienna, where the booming economy had attracted more than 100,000 Czechs by the turn of the century. After all, Austria was "German." But in Bohemia, both he and Renner supported the maintenance of German schools because they worried about German speakers becoming Czech.[22]

Though Bauer was the odd German socialist who spoke Czech and reported on Czech affairs to Vienna, he had little concern for Czechs' feelings. He was also a strange Marxist in two senses. Against the quasi-dogmatic economistic approach of Karl Kautsky, for whom nationality reflected just a particular stage of capitalism, he had said that culture was always national in form and substance: it was "what is historical in us."[23] He thus rejected the Marxian idea that the history of regions like Croatia or Bohemia, would be transcended (*aufgehoben*) by world history. He had added the idea of community to the more common Marxian notion of society.

Yet while respecting nations' cultures and languages, Bauer seemed to forget Marxist tenets about the connections between economic and cultural power. Had national chambers emerged to secure peoples' cultural rights, richer nations would have continued to dominate advertising and the mass media, as well as the nationally specific architecture and music worlds—not to mention education and science. German nationalists understood the link. In negotiations about restructuring Bohemia, they insisted that national chambers draw upon the tax receipts of the respective national group. Because Germans were 37 percent of Bohemia's population but contributed 53 percent of taxes, they would have maintained greater power of all kinds. Not surprisingly the Czech side rejected this sort of "resolution."[24]

Czech politicians across the spectrum refused to consider nations as simply about culture and language because the history of Czech nation-building as well as the example of the Magyar state—with its clampdowns on Slavic cultures—showed that peoples without economic and political power faced decline. And such power was based on institutions within secure territory. Czech voters recognized these facts, and any party that denied "Bohemian state's right"—the demand that Czechs control all of Bohemia—courted oblivion. In 1897, five Czech Social Democrats dared to follow the party's "internationalist" party line by refusing to sign a "state's right" declaration of fellow Czech MPs, and they paid an immediate price: nationalist worker politicians formed a competing Czechoslovak National Socialist party that grew into a pillar of the Czech party system, accusing Social Democrats of being traitors to the nation. The result was that Czech Social Democrats lost ground in the 1901 elections, and never repeated that mistake again.

They held to the national line and rejected the national districts within Bohemia that German socialists desperately wanted in order to protect the German language from declining. This resolution seemed so common-sensical as to be advocated from afar by the editors of the *New York Times*. Even the much-admired leader Bohumil Šmeral, later founder of the Communist Party of Czechoslovakia, was unable to make his comrades support the ideas of Renner and Bauer. Yet as a result of their combined advocacy of workers' social and national rights, the Social Democrats became the strongest Czech party, with 38 percent of the votes among Czechs in 1907. Outside Scandinavia this was the best result for a workers party in Europe. Czech Social Democrats were "reformist" rather than revolutionary, and espoused gradual improvements in workers' lives in wages or working conditions and attracted Catholic workers as well by posing as a reform movement rooted in the working class.[25]

To objections that Czech socialists deviated from Marxist orthodoxy by adopting "bourgeois" positions on the national question, František Modráček, a former anarchist on the party's right wing, wrote that Marx and Engels had not had the time to fully develop their ideas on historical materialism, especially as regarded the cultural and linguistic differences that emerged in capitalism, and therefore the only option was to adjust policies to changing realities. That was true elsewhere as well: across Europe, social democracy accommodated nationalist demands that had no place in outdated Marxist schemes.[26] Though in cases of merciless exploitation, workers could see co-ethnic bosses as enemies, they rarely saw workers of other ethnicities as brothers and sisters.

The crown had consented to universal male suffrage in 1907 because it hoped that the influx of peasants and workers into the electorate would foster parties representing class interests across regional boundaries and thereby defuse the nationality conflicts. Yet the opposite occurred.[27] No single party reached across the visible regional and invisible ethnic boundaries of Cisleithania, and because of the one-man-one vote principle, politics became more local than ever before. Voters ended up choosing candidates from nationally defined parties: from the Czech Agrarians and the Slovene People's Party, the panoply of national variants of the Marxist movement (in 1911 the national subgroups of Social Democracy in Cisleithania divided into independent parties), or from the Pan-Germans, as well as new Jewish parties.

Shared ethnicity fostered cooperation transcending divisions of political and economic interest, producing remarkable cohesion across political spectrums, especially in the Czech lands, despite the increasing fragmentation of politics after 1890. There had been a "Czech Club" in parliament since 1879, which dissolved in 1890 and was reconstituted as a Czech National Council (*Česka národní rada*) in 1900, and then again as a Czech Club in 1907. Czech Social Democrats unofficially coordinated policies with this group but maintained an official aloofness until 1916, when the Habsburg leadership began making noises about federal rule. Similarly, there was a Polish club in Vienna that contained parties from Habsburg Galicia, and it grew tighter during the war as real opportunities emerged for national autonomy.[28]

For other Slavic groups—Slovenes, Slovaks, Croats, Serbs, and Ukrainians—the de-nationalizing pressure was so great that a full political spectrum had yet to develop, and the major political party, no matter what it called itself, was in essence a national party.[29] Not only was the new mass politics cohesive within national groups, it tended to foster cross-national cooperation when there was a sense of a shared threat. In 1905, the Serbs and Croats in Dalmatia formed a joint electoral alliance against Magyarization and Germanization, and from 1909, there was also a Slavic union in the Vienna Parliament bringing together the parties from the Slavic lands. The exception was Polish conservatives from Galicia, who used economic, cultural, and political predominance to keep the Ukrainians from advancing in these three domains.

In the meantime, no stable coalition emerged for a government in Vienna because Czechs and Germans refused to cooperate. Moderate Czechs and Germans continued talking to each other, hoping to reach an agreement, yet they were swimming against the stream: those who attempted compromise were vilified as traitors on both sides. Thousands of Czech and German entrepreneurs whose businesses suffered from the administrative deadlock complained to the government in Vienna to no avail.[30]

Poisoned Politics

Like their Slavic counterparts, the German political parties in the Viennese Parliament had a national club that coordinated their ethnic interests. Remarkable in the German case was a gap that opened in the 1880s in the center of the spectrum, dividing men who just a few years earlier had called themselves liberal. Within a decade, the opening had become unbridgeable, and Socialists on the left and Christian Socials and Pan-Germans on the right were separated not only by political preferences but also by views of the world so divergent that the delegates could hardly speak to one another, let alone cooperate. Indeed, they hardly recognized one another's right to exist.

There was no such gap dividing Slavic politics in Cisleithania, or in the political worlds of Serbia, Romania, and Bulgaria. In Hungary, the elite remained cohesive and in control of the political machine, and even after Hungarian "liberals" lost elections in 1905 to forces further to the right, no challenges emerged to the basic programs of modernization and Magyarization. The same political machine continued to run the country, divided in politics but not in policy.

Yet if we go beyond the northern boundaries of the Habsburg Empire, into areas of Poland seized a century earlier by Prussia and Russia, we see the same phenomenon as in German Austria: a gap suddenly emerging in the late 1880s among liberals, so deep that people on right and left considered each other not just rivals but traitors. As in Austria, the cleavages were driven by a younger generation, called in Poland the *niepokorni* ("the uncompromising ones"), young men sick of the half-measures of the older generation. Like the authors of the Linz Program, the *niepokorni* feared national decline, with the difference that in Poland, the decline was far more catastrophic. If Germans were losing their cultural and administrative presence in Bohemia, they still dominated the imperial state administration, military, high culture, and economy. In the Polish lands, however, two imperial states, Russia and Germany, were trying to make Poles disappear as a nation. How to respond provoked fierce debates that first divided liberals in the 1880s and then the *niepokorni* in the 1890s.

Polish liberals had come of age after the failed uprising that had spread across much of Russian-controlled Poland in 1863. Critics called the undertaking and the romantic philosophy behind it foolhardy because oppression had become more severe after the uprising was put down. Thousands were sent to Siberia, and many more emigrated to Austria, France, and beyond. In contrast to the southern Polish lands controlled by Austria—Galicia—in Russian Poland, political organizing was forbidden, and public education in the native language was reduced to almost nothing. Thus, if in Galicia, two Polish universities were thriving after 1867, north of the border in Russian-controlled areas even Polish high schools were closed, and secondary and higher education took place in Russian.

The reaction among Polish liberals of the 1860s and 1870s was "positivism": rather than focus on romantic dreams of independence or even on language and culture, Poles should take positive and verifiable measures to build the economy, in a reversal of the Austro-Marxist idea. If for Bauer and Renner the nation was about language and culture, for Poland's positivists its basis was economic, and they encouraged "organic work" at its material foundations to make the nation prosperous. The Russian state suppressed Polish culture, but it did nothing to stop Polish landowners from positive methods aimed at improving agricultural methods, nor did it stop Polish entrepreneurs from building factories, or Polish students from becoming first-class engineers and architects, even if they learned their crafts in Russian or German. An economically strong Polish element would be a fact to be reckoned with and could use its might to make demands in the realm of culture and politics.

Yet by the 1880s, positivism itself seemed foolhardy. The economy was growing, but Polish culture was fading from the scene. Warsaw increasingly appeared to be a Russian city, with Cyrillic business and street signs; Byzantine and "old Russian" style architecture; impressive Orthodox churches; monuments celebrating Russian triumphs; and Russian soldiers and police on the streets, who might shake down the unsuspecting passerby, looking for weapons or illegal books. Russian had been introduced into schooling in 1872, along with textbooks and teachers providing Russian interpretations of the Polish past. From 1885, all subjects except religion—but including Polish literature—had to be taught in Russian at all schools and all grade levels. It became illegal to speak Polish on school grounds.[31] Poles had been disabused of illusions that Russia was a state of law; lacking the freedom of association, which as the positivist Aleksander Świętochowski noted, was "such a powerful instrument in civilized nations," Poles struggled to maintain basic coherence culturally, but also politically and economically.

Nationally conscious Poles felt stifled but were not inactive: they passed on culture and language to the next generation in the privacy of their homes, and soon conspiratorial networks emerged to coordinate the efforts. According to data from the Russian police, 30 percent of Polish children in the old kingdom learned Polish in secret home schooling; the movement spread from the urban intelligentsia to village and working-class communities, especially as standards of living increased and people had more leisure time to explore alternative views of Polish history. In 1882, the teacher Jadwiga Dawidowa founded the "flying university," where women could receive higher education, sometimes secretly in public buildings, but always on the move to avoid detection, usually from apartment to apartment. At its height, the university, featuring numerous leading Polish scholars on its faculty, took 1,000 new enrollments yearly; among its graduates were Nobel Prize winner Marie Skłodowska Curie, the writer Zofia Nałkowska, and the educator Janusz Korczak (she did not exclude men).[32]

After the revolution of 1905, the tsarist regime entertained limited reforms and permitted Poles under its rule to create cultural and educational organizations, in part to combat high illiteracy; yet as retrenchment set in, the activities again had to move underground. Until 1915, when German armies ousted the Russian regime from central Poland, Poles had no way to ensure the survival of high culture in the institutions where it thrives: academies of science, political and social clubs, universities, foundations, theaters, and museums. Polish-language journals existed but were subjected to strict tsarist censorship.[33]

The plight of Poles in the western lands controlled by Germany was hardly better; there, too, authorities suppressed the free development of Polish education and political life. Cities like Poznań/Posen or Toruń/Thorn took on a German appearance, and schooling was German, and in the countryside, Bismarck's regime made land easily available to German settlers to reduce the

Polish share of the economy. The response of Polish society was cultural and economic self-defense: lending libraries with more than a thousand branches were established by 1890, from which parents could borrow books to teach their children the Polish language, history, and culture that were absent from the state schools; and Polish credit associations, land banks, agricultural circles, and trade unions were founded, through which Polish farmers and workers could pool savings, learn trades, and defend their interests.

The repression of Polish culture reached its early heights during Bismarck's Kulturkampf of the 1870s, but after that, it still remained onerous. In 1901, hundreds of students went on strike in Września when authorities forced German-language religious texts on them; several were beaten severely, and recalcitrant parents were arrested. (After 1873, religion and music had been the only subjects in Prussian schools that could be taught in Polish.)[34] At this moment, as we have seen, other Slavic nations were going in the opposite direction: beginning in 1878, Serbia and Bulgaria were full national states, and from 1879, Czechs sat in the government in Vienna and oversaw the growth of institutions in their own language, including a university.

FIGURE 10.1. Schoolchild strikers, Września (1901). *Source:* Via Wikimedia Commons.

The Poles' predicament more closely resembled that of Slovaks or Romanians under the denationalizing Hungarian regime, but even that repression was not as severe as in Russian Poland because the Hungarian state was still avowedly liberal. Authorities in Budapest discouraged but did not attempt to crush Slovak or Romanian political life, and therefore political parties could operate openly, despite various forms of semi-official chicanery. At the same time, the social forces pressing for modern politics were far stronger in Poland than in Slovakia or Transylvania, due to the huge politically conscious Polish gentry (*szlachta*). The 1864 land reform in the tsarist empire had taken property from this class without adequate compensation, leaving many no choice but to settle in towns, above all Warsaw, yet from their midst emerged the intelligentsia, men and women devoted to ideas and causes, aware of a very old heritage of political rights, and unreconciled to foreign rule. Their patriotism had grown more radical as repression grew more severe, gradually constricting the space for advocates of half-measures.

The *niepokorni* came largely from this class, and they shared a common organization and journal into the late 1880s, when they gradually split into a new left and new right over responses to the deepening oppression. As in Austria, left and right made populist appeals to the newly politicized masses who viewed old-style liberal politics as elitist. On the one side was socialism, emphasizing the old romantic insurrectionary tradition, and on the other "patriotism," soon called National Democracy (or *Endecja*), stressing organic work, and like Georg von Schönerer stirring fears among the Christian urban middle classes about Jewish competition.[35] Both socialists and National Democrats invoked self-sacrifice and idealism; both claimed to be realists; and both thought the other side's solutions were unacceptable because both were rooted in different and hostile conceptions of reality.

Like its Austrian counterpart, Polish socialism emerged from economic crises and the rapid growth of industry and population, but it was more clearly nationalist. The Austrian party was implicitly German, but the Polish was openly Polish, demanding an independent Polish republic in which Poland's proletariat could live in dignity. Because of strict prohibitions on political activity, numerous early leaders were executed and many more locked away in prison, along with hundreds of the rank and file.[36] Besides the native democratic insurrectionary tradition, the early movement drew on West European socialist ideas as well as Russian revolutionary practices, including efforts to agitate among the masses but also outright violent terror. Though led by the intelligentsia, it got a decisive impetus from workers in Lodz, who staged a great strike in May 1892 that was put down with 217 killed and wounded, and 350 arrested. Half a year later, socialist groups met in Paris and formed the Polish Socialist Party (PPS), which advocated the emancipation of *Polish* workers from the yoke of capitalism in an independent state returned to the boundaries of a century earlier.[37]

This demand raised questions of relations to other nationalities because the old commonwealth had contained ethnic groups that had nationalized in the preceding decades and were making political demands of their own: Ukrainians; Byelorussians; Lithuanians; and from the 1890s, Jews. As in the Habsburg lands, socialism in Russian Poland had divided into ethnic branches. Ukrainian Social Democrats strove to further their own language and culture, and in 1905, the Jewish "Bund" made demands for national-cultural autonomy for Jews but also sought the transformation of Russia into a federation of nations, relying on Renner's and Bauer's notions of individual cultural autonomy.[38]

Reminiscent of comrades in Austria, leading Polish socialists pledged to respect the rights of nationalities while assuming their own culture would be paramount in any new state. The old Polish commonwealth had not sought to reduce its many cultures, languages, and religions to one, even as it reformed, though its leading culture had been Polish. For the time being, the shared political oppression seemed to overshadow questions of ethnic rights: socialists of all nationalities had a common enemy in the tsarist regime, which kept workers from organizing while promoting Russification with the active assistance of the Russian Orthodox Church.

The chief intellectual and political force behind left-wing Polish nationalism, PPS leader Józef Piłsudski, came from an impoverished gentry family and was reared in the cult of the 1863 uprising. As a nationally conscious Pole from Lithuania (who later converted to Protestantism), he particularly treasured the traditions of the multireligious commonwealth. Piłsudski ardently advocated the underground struggle for Polish schooling and culture, and he wrote essays on politics and history. But he also insisted on active, violent work to undo Poland's oppression, no matter how unlikely the prospects of bringing down the partitioning powers. He felt that Poles were living lives of slavery, and the only response was terror. Employing Polish soldiers who had been trained in Paris by Japanese officers, he first schooled fighting units in Kraków, and because demand was so great, later surreptitiously on Russian territory. Using bombs and pistols, his militants staged hundreds of attacks; on a single day, August 15, 1906, they killed eighty Tsarist officials and Polish collaborators. Two years later, Piłsudski and a unit of fifteen men and four women—including his future wife,

Aleksandra—carried out their most famous attack on a Russian mail train near Wilno, seizing a small fortune (200,000 rubles) that was then used to purchase more weapons and finance paramilitary training.[39]

That was a year of rising antagonisms in the region because Austria-Hungary had annexed Bosnia-Herzegovina, enraging Serbia and aggravating Russia, and the Viennese government decided it would use Piłsudski as a card to be played in the likely event of conflict against Russia. By 1912 he had created a "Polish Military Treasury" and trained thousands of men in rifle brigades (later called "legions") for battle. Piłsudski's "revolutionary" Polish socialists became a state within a state.[40]

European socialists tended to favor Polish independence, but as mentioned, in Poland, a left splinter emerged in the 1890s under Rosa Luxemburg.[41] In a confrontation with Piłsudski at the Socialist International in London in 1896, she opposed Polish independence, arguing that the vast Russian empire provided better conditions for the development of capitalism and thus the social conflicts that would generate revolution. Yet Piłsudski, who had read Marx and Engels during his incarceration in Siberia in the 1880s, knew they had pleaded for restoration of Poland as a way to check Russia, the "dark Asiatic power" that threatened to undo progress in all Europe. Engels had added the caveat that Poland's territory was now multinational. The PPS thus advocated a federation of small nations, an idea that remained at the heart of Piłsudski's political program. Jews would be assimilated into Polish culture.[42]

Polish socialists' commitment to living in peace with other ethnicities made them seem enemies of the people to the National Democrats (*Endeks*) on their right, despite the fact that the leaders of both movements had ascended from the wreck of Polish liberalism.[43] If the Linz Program had demanded a German Austria, *Endeks* wanted a Polish Poland and condemned as absurd the romantic democrats of earlier times who had fought in Greece, Italy, or Hungary under the banner "for our freedom and yours." The only proper function of Polish politics was to make Poland strong. The movement's leader, natural scientist Roman Dmowski, came from western Poland and appealed to people like himself from the déclassé lower gentry, but also to the urban middle classes.

Dmowski understood the nation as a quasi-biological "living social organism," so that any talk of compassion was pointless. Poland's destiny was to fight other nations in a zero-sum contest, in a history without meaning, because human history was natural history. Any belief in progress lacked scientific foundations, and *Endeks* assumed the grim but necessary task of disciplining the

FIGURE 10.2. Rosa Luxemburg (1907 in Stuttgart). *Source*: Herbert Hoffmann
(photographer). Via Wikimedia Commons.

Polish national organism, uniting and coordinating its thoughts, desires, and
feelings. Like many liberals and former liberals, Dmowski was intensely anticlerical and claimed "national egotism" was morally superior to Christian
teaching because the command to "love one's neighbor" was actually rooted in
fears of revenge. Individual human beings owed everything to their nation, and
therefore the nation's interests had to stand above every other commitment.[44]

Dmowski rejected the notion that politics was about managing competing
interests: compromises signaled weakness and decline. This anti-liberal stance
was a break in Polish ideas, and indeed, along with Schönerer's pan-Germanism,
it heralded a new politics in the region as a whole. The nation should be of one
mind and empowered to make specific demands on all of its members, and it
was absurd to debate (let alone stipulate) such demands in any parliament.
Those who resisted this truth placed themselves outside the nation.[45] *Endeks*
thus raised to a new level trends that dated to the 1790s, according to which opponents were not just rivals but traitors. Zygmunt Balicki, a leading National
Democratic thinker, wrote that international class solidarity would alienate
workers from Poland and gravely damage "public morality."[46]

Unlike Georg von Schönerer, Dmowski was a savvy political entrepreneur who made his National Democratic Party the strongest right-of-center party. And while the Pan-Germans in Vienna sporadically waxed but mostly waned, *Endecja* grew and reached out via satellite organizations to young people (The Union of Polish Youth), and to the peasants (The Society for National Education), making radicalism—including racism—seem mainstream. Like Austria's Karl Lueger, Dmowski and his lieutenants did much to poison their country's politics.

But on the cobblestones of Poland's towns and in the mud of its villages, Poles tended to mix their allegiances to the two emergent political movements, simultaneously reading copies of the rival weeklies (*Robotnik* and *Czas*) that activists spread illegally. While the leaders of PPS and *Endecja* feuded in Warsaw or Paris, the everyday pressures of de-nationalization forced nationally conscious Polish men and women to collaborate in order to keep their culture alive, passing on proper orthography and a vibrant literary canon, but also the basic message that for people calling themselves Poles, independence was nonnegotiable.

In the Europe of that time, *Endecja* focused national egotism more strongly than other new right parties, even *Action française*, which was not as uncompromising in its chauvinism, because it did not match an unremittingly gloomy view of history with fears of a nation's extinction. National Democracy's mixing of frantic activity with consuming pessimism reflected the Darwinist imperative to strengthen the nation, but also the new radical secular view that nations grew and declined in a history where the race struggle was never concluded, but also never led to human betterment. Though its relations to Polish fascism are complex, *Endecja* gave a hint of new totalitarian movements to come. Certainties about political or economic development were broken, and it became necessary to arm the nation: "history itself had become delinquent."[47]

Anti-Semitism

The hatred *Endecja* stoked was a further watermark in ethnic nationalism's rise toward the intolerance and exclusivness that we know from more proximate times. The Herderian tradition had sought to protect a people's spirit, the *Volksseele*, but it did not question practices of assimilation dating back centuries. In the intellectual mood of the 1880s, however, a new question had emerged: if peoples were organisms, what happened when they absorbed foreign bodies?[48]

Science, history, and Christian theology colluded in portraying Jews as being of a different blood, from beyond Europe, members of a race cultivated in closed communities for centuries, with special and strange rituals. Dmowski believed Ukrainians or Lithuanians could be assimilated gradually, and that Russians were ethnic kinfolk. Jews, however, seemed to him a foreign element that had to be segregated and excised.

This mindset appealed to many déclassé gentrymen who had lost land after the March 1864 reforms in Russia, and to the Polish lower middle classes. Both groups found themselves poorly equipped to survive during the economic downturn of the 1880s. In previous generations, landowners had been able to rely on cheap labor and live lives of leisure, often not needing more than a third-grade education. But now, when younger sons were forced to leave the manor to seek their fortunes in Warsaw, Lodz, and other towns, they found commerce, finance, and industry already in the hands of "foreigners"—that is, of Polish Jews, even if Jews had been settled in Poland for many centuries. Rather than reflecting on a long history in which Jews were forbidden to live in the countryside, and therefore honed the skills valued in cities, these *szlachta* explained Jewish success through "inborn traits" of trickery and scheming. Many middle-class Poles embraced the *Endek* critique of the nobility's eastward expansion into Ukraine in the late middle ages; by relying on Jews for finance and commerce, these nobles had supposedly left the cities prey to Jewish and German domination and weakened Poland's ethnic core.[49]

This shift in ideas about assimilation can be seen in the history of a single family. The prominent economist Leopold Caro (1864–1939) descended from a Sephardic rabbinical family but had converted to Catholicism as a young man.[50] His father, Henryk, had fought in the 1863 uprising and was the first Jew buried in Kraków with Polish lettering on his gravestone. Although Poland, along with the rest of Europe, had an ancient tradition of anti-Judaism, which held Jews responsible for the death of Christ, into the 1860s, Jews and Poles had struggled together for the sake of Polish independence. Immortalized in poetry was the seventeen-year old Jewish student Michael Lande, who had lifted a cross from the hands of a wounded Catholic priest at a patriotic demonstration in Warsaw in April 1861 before being cut down by a Russian bullet. Priests, pastors, and rabbis presided at the funeral of Lande and four other martyrs for the Polish cause.[51]

But in the 1880s, Leopold Caro came of age in a transformed Poland, where positivism and Darwinism combined to raise a specter of the Polish nation—understood in racial terms—being overwhelmed by other peoples. Just a few decades earlier, he lamented, it was natural that Poles were Polish; yet more recently, the three occupying powers required that Poles "dissolve in the vast sea of German and Russian statehood." In response, a determination had grown among Polish nationalists aiming to make the "entire people Polish." They saw Jews as a foreign presence on Polish soil, and the only "cure" was that they cease being Jews. For Caro, this led to efforts to cleanse himself of his own Jewish past. He sided with *Endecja*, demanded a more "Polish" physiognomy in Polish cities, and urged Jews to convert as he had, opening themselves to a higher level of morality. According to Caro, Jews who had a warm heart for fellow human beings had already been pervaded by Christian morality, even if they did not know its source.[52] Soon Caro's "service" to Poland would not suffice for "native" *Endeks*, for whom even conversion could not solve the "Jewish problem." They suspected converts like Caro of insincerity, but more fundamentally, they believed that conversion could not undo Jews' alien racial characteristics.

Anti-Semitism grew across East Central Europe from the 1880s on, but in Poland, it had the unusual function of making many villagers into Poles, that is, making them feel a shared community of interests and perceptions with the nationally conscious Polish gentry and middle classes. In 1870, only 30–35 percent of Polish-speakers thought of themselves as members of the Polish nation, and the numbers were smallest in the countryside. That was not unusual. Smaller percentages of eighteenth-century French speakers had felt part of the French nation, but the French state inculcated in their descendants a sense of belonging through schooling.[53] In Poland, however, underground schooling fell short of including everyone, and even the occupiers' schools left most Polish villagers unable to read and write. For many, society was divided between manor and village, into lords and peasant subjects. The liberation of the peasants in Galicia and Prussia in 1848, and in Russia in 1864, had meant that Polish nobles were no longer feudal oppressors, yet they still seemed a foreign ethnicity. Most peasants were uninterested in Polish independence.

In much of East Central Europe, landowners or bosses were of a foreign nationality, and nationalists exploited a sense of economic oppression to spread national consciousness to the masses. For example, in the Czech lands, owners of factories or manors tended to be German, and the Czech movement accordingly defined Czech identity as anti-German.[54] In Bosnia, the landowner was Muslim; in Slovenia, German; and in much of Croatia, Hungarian. In 1800,

Prague and Brno, but also Budapest, Bratislava, Ljubljana, and Zagreb, were German-speaking cities. The German was an enemy against whom the self was clearly defined and who was then displaced from culture, business, politics, and all traces of the new standard version of the national language.

In central Poland, the landowners as well as peasants were Polish-speaking. The cities and towns, however, had mixed populations, mostly Polish, but there were also many Jews, who spoke their own language and pursued walks of life that were distinct: trade, commerce, money-lending, and small crafts. Jews often bought cattle and grain, made credit available to peasants, or ran the local inn. Nationalists thus had an opportunity: they could use anti-Semitism to convince village folk that Jews were foreign, and that as ethnic Poles, the villagers belonged to the same nation as Polish townspeople and gentry. They told poor villagers that their problem was not lack of land, education, or farming implements but the "alien" Jewish presence in nearby towns. As restrictions on Jewish ownership eased from the 1870s, Jewish families began competing with small farmers to buy up the land of impoverished gentry, and by 1912, they controlled 20 percent of the agricultural land in Galicia.[55] Arguments that presented these inroads as unfair Jewish advantages in the economy convinced peasants that they shared a common identity with Polish landlords.

Gradually the national idea caught on among peasants, even those who had been alienated from all talk of nation and felt that the court in Vienna was their protector. Beginning in the latter decades of the century, peasants participated more actively in local self-government and took a stronger role in national life, and that also meant heightened circulation among them of nationalist arguments.[56] Catholic priests contributed a debased and opportunistic reading of their faith to serve the cause. One wrote that a Pole who was not an anti-Semite "has no right to call himself a good Catholic or a good Pole, and cannot be a good patriot." The Polish national movement created "Christian" institutions to strengthen "Polish" ownership in the economy (the equivalent of the Bohemian *nationaler Besitzstand* was *polski stan posiadania*), and soon there were Christian shops, Christian lending institutions, and Christian pubs, all of which had the function of linking Poles across classes in village and city and promoting upward social mobility for co-ethnics.[57]

But even so, the inculcation of Polish nationalist narratives in the village was not easy. Before World War I, many peasants still uttered curses when the name Poland was mentioned because they associated Poland with the "lords." And when they embraced national consciousness, peasants and their political movements claimed to do so in a way all their own, saying that national culture was

unspoiled in the villages, in contrast to the towns, where the gentry had absorbed foreign ideas about states and laws.[58] In the early twentieth century,
leading Polish intellectuals bought those arguments and developed their own
cult for the genuine Polishness of villagers, even seeking peasant brides.

To be clear: where Poland stands out from its neighbors was not in a growing antipathy toward Jews. That was universal in nineteenth-century East Central Europe, though perhaps weaker in Hungary, where Jews were recruited to
tip the balance against the kingdom's many non-Magyar ethnicities. What was
unusual about Poland was not even the sense that Jews were like no other foreigner. Here the Christian world was clear about the Jews' otherness and their
irredeemability short of conversion (that is, the complete surrender of their
Jewishness). What was unusual in Poland was that all of these dimensions—
the religious, economic, cultural, professional, and racial—came together at a
time when the number of Jews was large and they could be portrayed as an alien
nation in Poland's midst.

The potential of anti-Semitism to fuse a gentile nation was matched only in
Romania, where liberal elites sought ways of connecting the often-indifferent
peasant classes to the national narrative, and made Jews to blame for the peasants' wretched status.[59] But in contrast to Romania, where the local Christian
church was ethnic (that is, Romanian Orthodox), the church in Poland was part
of an international institution that held conversion to be a method of becoming Christian regardless of ethnicity. Did the Roman Catholic Church not object to nationalism that portrayed baptized Jews as foreigners?

The answer is paradoxical. Despite the idea that to be a Pole was to be a Catholic (*Polak-Katholik*), the two strands of Polish nationalism—that of the PPS
and of National Democracy—emerged from intelligentsia groups that were anticlerical because they associated the church with conservatism. Indeed, the
papacy had condemned nationalism as a modern heresy, and many Catholic
prelates were lukewarm or hostile to Polish nationalism, for example Poznań's
archbishop Mieczysław Ledóchowski. Roman Dmowski claimed that his national egotism was higher than Christian ethics, but it was also separate from
it: the relation of the individual to the nation, let alone of nation to nation, lay
outside the church's legitimate concerns. Christian ethics was properly limited
to the individual in the collectivity of humanity.[60]

Yet over time, a synthesis occurred between National Democracy and elements of Polish Catholicism. *Endek* messages strongly appealed to much of the
lower clergy, and by the 1920s, Dmowski was proclaiming that Catholicism was
a vital component of Polish nationhood, while some Catholic priests were

saying that converts from Judaism were Catholics of a different race.[61] *Endecja* and the Catholic Church came to find each other useful; the former could be an ally of the church in combating liberalism, socialism, or cosmopolitanism (a codeword for Judaism), and the church could serve *Endecja* by strengthening a sense of duty to the nation through religious messages and imagery, falling back when opportune upon an ancient tradition of anti-Judaism.[62]

Jewish Responses: Zionism and Jewish Politics

For Jews, the scapegoating was not only unjust but cruel in its absurdity. They had emerged from centuries of second-class status just two decades earlier, and while some had done well in their urban pursuits, the overwhelming majority in Russian and Austrian Poland were desperately poor. Jews were not "foreign" but had lived in Poland from the eleventh century. Many young Jewish men, working long hours and helped by meager family savings, sought education and were fierce competitors for spaces in the professions and in entry-level positions in firms of all kinds. They succeeded despite official and unofficial restrictions at every level, from high school through university and chambers of commerce and the bar. State administration was largely closed to Jews, as were careers in the military, although Jews were inducted into all armies.[63]

But if *Endecja* found constituencies among Poles who preferred a narrative of victimization to the open competition of the modern economy, its growing popularity also encouraged an insistence among Jews that if there was a game, that it be played fairly, and Jews not suffer from quotas, boycotts, and violence. Yet conditions in the empire where most Jews lived inspired little hope. After the assassination of Tsar Alexander II, the liberator of the serfs, in 1881, pogroms were the order of business across the Russian countryside for three years, with dozens of fatalities. One Jewish response was to look beyond Europe for solutions: if East Central Europe produced the strongest tendencies to exclude Jews from national and civil life, it also fostered the self-defense known as Zionism, the idea that Jews also required territory to protect their national existence.

The crucial figure behind the emergence of Zionism was Theodor Herzl (1860–1904), a writer of Hungarian Jewish background, who arrived in Vienna to study law in 1878. He was a fervent German nationalist until he discovered that students in his fraternity would not accept him as one of them, no matter what he did.[64] They nicknamed him "Moses." Just as *Endecja* with its racist understanding of Polishness was making headway among young Polish intellectuals, so Schönerer's movement was making a brilliant career among

Austrian-German students who embraced the idea that Judaism was carried in the blood.

For Herzl, a moment of truth came when he personally encountered Vienna's mayor Karl Lueger, who supposedly represented a more "Christian" version of anti-Semitism than did Schönerer. In 1895, Herzl was on hand for Lueger's public appearance in Vienna just after his Christian Socialists had won elections for the Vienna city council; an impassioned bystander exclaimed: "that is our Führer!" "More than all the declamations and abuse," Herzl penned in his diary, "these few words told me how deeply anti-Semitism is rooted in the heart of the people." As a correspondent in Paris the previous year during the Dreyfus affair, he had heard crowds call for "death to the Jews," though the assimilation of Jews in France had supposedly succeeded.

Jews had lived under legal restrictions for centuries, enduring treatment as second-class subjects and citizens or worse. Yet whether in Austria or France, the liberation of Jews to civic equality had spawned a new kind of hatred, dressed in the language of racial science. If Jews assimilated, the insistence on seeing them as other became more insistent and deadly: they remained Jews even when they dressed and spoke like everyone else, and theories that were widely respected emerged to explain their success, because success for Jews was deemed unacceptable. Herzl concluded that nothing Jews could do would ensure for them a life of dignity and safety in European Christian societies.[65]

In 1896, Herzl published *The Jewish State*, and two years later, he organized the first Zionist congress in Basel, with 200 attendees in formal attire. Herzl was not the first to propose a Jewish return to Palestine, but he was indispensable as an organizer and propagator. During the few years remaining in his life, he traveled incessantly, raised funds, and met heads of state (including Emperor Wilhelm of Germany and the Ottoman sultan). His movement grew rapidly, from 117 associations in 1897 to 913 a year later, and when he died in 1904, Zionism was a fact of European politics, with hundreds of thousands of adherents and unstoppable energy.[66]

Zionism grew to particular strength in the Eastern European lands where Jews faced prejudice combined with poverty. Like other national movements, it divided into right and left wings, so that in Poland, in addition to Jewish Social Democrats, there were left and right Zionists. Herzl had imagined the Jewish state in Palestine as multilinguistic, with English boarding schools, French opera houses, and Viennese cafes, but the movement had other ideas. From the circles of Ahad Ha'am, a secular businessman and intellectual from a village near Kiev, came an insistence on Jewish culture, in particular, on teaching and propagating Hebrew, a language in which Ha'am was a superb stylist. His disciple, Chaim Weizman, later headed the World Zionist Organization that Herzl had founded and became first president of the State of Israel.

The movement had much in common with other East European nationalist movements: an intense concern with culture, history, and reviving a language; a sense of mission extending to messianism (something Herzl was accused of); the raising of national consciousness and its dissemination to the people; the fragmentation into factions advocating different solutions; and the determination to ensure the nation's survival. Early Zionists felt they stood apart from and above modern urban settings, where compromise and corruption were the norm. They by contrast exalted nobility of character and nurtured leaders who would embody higher virtue. The tiny Zionist circles in Bohemia opposed the materialist world around them with "new hearts and clean souls," and sought the end of the "exploitation of one class of the people by another." Jewish settlement in Palestine would redound to the good of the Arabs, but also of all humanity, whom Zionists would show how to build a state based on morality, on "justice and selfless love of every person for every other person." Such were the views of young enthusiasts in Prague, who liked to say that a sudden collapse of the roof in which they were meeting would be the end Bohemian Zionism, perhaps unaware that they were repeating words uttered by František Palacký to the Czech movement forty years earlier.[67]

What was exceptional against the background of European nationalism was Zionists' hope to found a national state in non-European territory. Other movements planned the settlement of foreign colonies—for example, a Czech outpost in Asia—but always maintained that the homeland was the supposed original ethnic settlement in Europe. For Zionists, the Jewish homeland was Palestine, *Eretz Yisrael*, and like Czech or Hungarian nationalists, they argued from historical sources about original ownership. But Zionists also faced the unique challenge of building the national organization where "their" nation was a small minority, in territory controlled first by Ottomans and then by the British, who consented to Jewish settlement during World War I, but at a gradual rate. Thus, a new Jewish homeland emerged slowly. By 1914, only some 85,000 Jews had put down roots in Palestine, where they lived under difficult conditions among 700,000 Arabs, who overwhelmingly opposed further Zionist settlement.[68] Therefore, from its emergence in the 1890s until after World War II, the heartland of Zionism remained East Central Europe.

* * *

Zionism responded to the general advance of a new kind of ethnic nationalism in the region, associated with Roman Dmowski and his fellow National Democrat Zygmunt Balicki. Yet the humane ideals of Zionism, but also of Polish insurrectionary socialism, show that ethnic nationalists could and did envision complex forms of coexistence with other groups. But what is also striking is how strong individuals could lend various movements their particular trajectories and valence.

Without Theodor Herzl and Karl Lueger, respectively, Zionism and Christian Socialism might not have emerged in Central Europe, and if they had, would likely have taken very different paths. Before Herzl, there had been vague calls for a return of Jews to the Promised Land, but no political movement. Herzl had gone through a complex evolution from German nationalist to advocate of mass conversion and finally to Zionist, and he was probably more sincere in his cause than was Lueger, who had worked productively with Jewish liberals before his sudden conversion to a new style of politics. Some portray Lueger as an opportunist who stumbled on anti-Semitism, almost inadvertently noting its power to gain mass sympathy.[69]

In founding Zionism, Theodor Herzl made direct reference to Lueger. Christian Socialist movements had emerged elsewhere in the nineteenth century, from the United States and the United Kingdom to France and Imperial Germany, but they hovered on the margins of politics. The same was true of Christian Socialism in Vienna in the late 1880s, before Lueger came on the scene, looking for a cause that he might make equal to his ambitions. Without Lueger, Christian Socialism would not have seized power in Vienna; there would have been no center-right movement that gathered and led much of the Catholic proletariat as well as clergy, beyond Vienna and into small towns and villages. Lueger gave form to demands that would have remained incoherent, and the early leadership saw in him a figure of providence. When Christian Socialism's intellectual father, Karl von Vogelsang, heard Lueger address a meeting in 1888, he exclaimed: "Now we have our leader!"[70] Lueger found his idea and brought it to life only when the movement found him.

Józef Piłsudski and Roman Dmowski were similarly indispensable for their own causes. They incorporated ideas thought to be mutually exclusive, but they also formed them in specific ways. We can ask whether without Dmowski and his programmatic *Thoughts of a Modern Pole* (1903), Polish middle-class nationalism would have turned so early toward racism. Yet we can also wonder whether without Piłsudski, the old romantic idea of interethnic cooperation would have taken a firm hold in modern Polish politics. Piłsudski succeeded because the socialist internationalist in him was always embedded in the conviction that Poland was destined to lead. He rose to prominence by competing effectively as a nationalist with other nationalists.

* * *

Pure internationalism or antisectarianism had no leader, a fact we see confirmed in the limited impact of the Austro-Marxists Otto Bauer and Karl Renner, as stimulating as their ideas seem in retrospect. In East Central Europe, they were always regarded as apostles of German culture. Similarly, East European socialism produced some great thinkers but no leader of ideas, acts, and charisma of the stature of Russia's V. I. Lenin. Still, none of East Central Europe's little-known socialist leaders left world historical wreckage on the scale of Lenin's, in part because Lenin proved willing not to be a bland multinational socialist, but instead to embrace nationalism, not just for Russians but for all peoples who opposed imperialism. Piłsudski, more faithful to Marxism's agnosticism on the national question, left the socialist movement during World War I, when he recognized that for him, the central goal of Polish nationalism—recreating statehood—was an end in itself.

In the hands of Lenin's successors, socialist internationalism evolved into a kind of imperialism that would extend to East Central Europe, portraying itself, as we will see, as a true nationalism. Yet at heart, it was afflicted with liberalism's original sin, of faith masquerading as reason, portraying other peoples' reason (for example, Polish desires for independence) as unreason. Yet what really opposed reason was a politics that neglected emotion and meaning that people sought in nonmaterial, noncalculable terms. What was irrational was for Germans and Russians to call Czech or Polish desires for national protection unreasonable—while taking for granted their own nation's right to territory, an assumption never exposed to reasonable doubt.

The alleged higher rationality of the antinational argument extends into our own day. Liberal historians close their eyes to the momentum in politics that has carried ideas of ethnic nationalism forward over generations, and they continue to imagine that completely a-national identities had realistic chances to assert themselves in a world where literacy was rising and with each decade, hundreds of thousands of people attained voting rights. The Czech story has drawn most attention among students of nationalism, because Czechs constituted the great internal problem of the Habsburg monarchy, and they did not even fit neatly into socialist proposals for solving national problem, because their insistence on Bohemian state's right made nonterritorial nationalism unacceptable.

Still, if they wanted autonomy in Bohemia, Czech politicians before the Great War were also very clear, from the nationalist Karel Kramář to the socialist Bohumír Šmeral, that the ending of the Habsburg monarchy would result in a nightmare, and it was this possibility that made Czech politicians fear the future. Šmeral wrote in December 1913 that if Austria-Hungary were divided after some future war, perhaps Bohemia would achieve the vaunted Bohemian state's right, but Czechs would be independent only temporarily—like Albania, booty for some victorious hegemon of the future. "If Austria-Hungary should not survive," he feared, "a new thirty years' war would come upon Europe, and, once again, as before the Peace of Westphalia, Bohemia would be the center point of the suffering."[71] No major politicians thought of leaving the dual monarchy, and the one Czech party advocating full independence got a single seat in the Reichsrat in 1911.[72]

CHAPTER 11

Peasant Utopias: Villages of Yesterday and Societies of Tomorrow

In 1939 the Austrian Jewish novelist Stefan Zweig began work on a nostalgic memoir, *The World of Yesterday*, about his youth in the Habsburg monarchy, an infinitely more civilized place than what came later, where law and order were respected, and where citizens of differing ethnicity lived in peace, freely traveling east to west as if boundaries did not exist. Dark forces of hatred were gathering but remained marginal. When the book appeared in Sweden in 1942, Zweig and his wife were no longer alive: they had ended their lives months earlier in Petropolis, a German community high above Rio de Janiero. Zweig's pained reminiscences created a persistent image of Austria-Hungary as a superior reality, now lost, behind the absolute temporal barrier of a first world war that made the second one possible and inaugurated a new century of previously unimaginable inhumanity.

Yet there was little nostalgia among writers from the Slavic lands and Romania for the pre-1914 world; for them, it had been a place where national and social oppression aggravated one another. In their minds the Great War, costly as it was, had made freedom possible from foreign rule: whether Turkish, Austrian, German, Hungarian, or Russian. Against all odds, Serbs, Poles, Czechs, and Romanians had enlarged kingdoms or created republics, all reflecting supposed historical justice. When these disappeared under Nazi rule, the idea only grew stronger that all remnants of Austria-Hungary had to be extinguished: the dual monarchy had been simply one manifestation of German rule, far less invasive and destructive than the Third Reich to be sure, but with the same basic purpose of stifling their lives as nations.

Behind these well-known narratives of nostalgia and heroic recovery dwell more mundane stories, all but forgotten in the war's aftermath. Before 1914, progressive political movements had attempted to deal with the time's great social problem: most people lived by farming land, but the land they farmed was too meager to permit them to lead lives of sufficiency and dignity. This chapter tries to capture some of their promise but does so in a particular way. It looks across the landscape for peasant politicians who transcended peasant politics: leaders who created movements that aimed at justice not just for the village, but also for the nation and the region.

"Ordinary" peasant politics, for example, in Serbia or Polish Galicia, tended to involve talented young men who left the villages for national politics, where they often rose to prominence, sometimes directing governments and fashioning coalitions. Though originally guided by enthusiasm for the peasant cause and backed by various kinds of "agrarianism"—a pragmatic ideology aimed at achieving improvement in peasants' lives—for the most part, peasant politicians became absorbed in urban political machines. They acted "peasant" in staged campaigns in the countryside during polling time, but otherwise reliably supported their governments' irredentist foreign politics (in Serbia or Romania) or made compacts with landholding elites to quell demands of a foreign ethnicity (like Ukrainians in Polish Galicia). In the end, little to nothing was done for the village.[1]

Yet in the decades before World War I, three charismatic and imaginative figures emerged from rural Moravia, Bulgaria, and Croatia who behaved very differently: T. G. Masaryk, Aleksandar Stamboliiski, and Stjepan Radić. After rising from poverty, they studied in Germany and France, became conversant in the European politics of their time, and made careers in cities. Yet they never forgot the dust, misery, and solidarity of the villages they left behind. None intended a career in politics, but after they stumbled into political life in the late nineteenth century, they did nothing the easy way, constantly taking stances that defied the sacred assumptions of the local national narratives. Remarkably, they prospered and won adherents. None of the three figures prominently in the history of ideas, but all showed the power of simple convictions when carried by people of charisma.

All three worked on the political left but avoided the blind spots that hampered Marxian Social Democrats in East Central Europe: the national and peasant questions. Rather than preach that progress demanded the disappearance of small nations and the fading of the peasantry into urban industries, they imagined a future with room for both: the prosperous medium-sized landholder peasant would be educated in his or her native culture, but would become part of a prosperous, peaceful, and cooperative Europe of nations. All three remind us of the infrequent ability of single individuals possessing vision, tenacity, and self-confidence to mold the views not just of a party cadre but also of hundreds of thousands of followers.

Their goals sound utopian but did not require the violence of Marxian or anarchist programs; rather than moving from ideas to complex realities—like

Otto Bauer—they proceeded from the realities of villages and towns to create programs that might unite both. All thought of themselves as realists, and they made their followers wary of taking the precise paths of West European societies. They had particular concern about people serving nation-states rather than the other way around, and as villagers, they argued for cooperation with people of other ethnicities, because they knew that in any conflict, it was people from the villages who did most of the dying.

Their plain speech carved out new political spaces but also generated plenty of opposition. Army officers apprehended and murdered Alexander Stamboliiski in 1923, and five years later, a disgruntled supporter of the Yugoslav government shot Stjepan Radić on the floor of parliament in Belgrade. Tomáš G. Masaryk (1850–1937) lived to a ripe age, but when he died, his Czechoslovak democracy was in the crosshairs of Europe's most violent politician, Adolf Hitler, who sent his troops into Prague a little over a year later.

Human beings never simply impose themselves on events. Without particular crises and much happenstance, Masaryk would have become a run-of-the-mill German professor, and Radić and Stamboliiski village elders or coffeehouse personalities. Something urgent in their time made leaders out of human beings otherwise content with the joys and challenges of professional and family life, similar to how the crises of the 1930s "made" Winston Churchill.[2] They adapted to history in order to change it, and in East Central Europe, that meant all appeals to multiethnic cooperation had to be phrased in the language of ethnicity, as national projects. Masaryk, the most influential among them, reinterpreted the Czech past to secure a Czech future in a world of free nations.

The circumstances of East Central Europe before World War I also show what happens when crisis fails to produce leaders of vision and purpose. A retrospective glance at people's everyday lives in halcyon Central Europe before 1914 may generate nostalgia, but a probing look into the deliberations of Austrian officials in those years yields little hope for reform that could have solved urgent problems. Instead we see fear, miscalculation, and dereliction of duty in the upper reaches of the Habsburg state. Grave social injustices in Bosnia-Herzegovina had triggered the wars that led the monarchy to occupy that land in 1878, and a generation later, it was the still-unaddressed problems of villages in this province that led to the unraveling of Habsburg power throughout Europe. The top men lacked the imagination that might have created new realities to save the old regime: when confronted with challenges, they could not see beyond their own fears of Slavic peoples, above all, the Serbs.

* * *

Tomáš Masaryk was born in 1850 in a small town in eastern Moravia; his father was a coachman of Slovak heritage, and his mother a cook whom he identified sometimes as German, sometimes as Moravian. (She taught him to pray in German.) He escaped an apprenticeship in Vienna at age fifteen and then worked for a time as a blacksmith in his home village of Hodonín. He then made his way to culturally German Brünn/Brno, where the city's police chief, impressed by Masaryk's gifts of mind, made him tutor to his sons and supported his education, first in the local German *Hochschule* and then in Vienna. In his courses at the university he studied philosophy in the broad sense that it was practiced in those days, comprising also sociology and literature.

After getting a doctorate on Plato, he continued studies in Leipzig, where he met Charlotte Garrigue of Brooklyn, a piano student descended from a Huguenot family that had fled to Germany in the seventeenth century. Her father, born in Denmark, ran a German bookstore in Manhattan and was a passionate member of the German society there as well as a faithful Unitarian. Though raised Catholic, Masaryk found the church's authority structures unjustified by reason and converted to Protestantism, taking it so seriously that he considered becoming a pastor.

In 1878, Tomáš and Charlotte married in a Unitarian ceremony at her father's house in Brooklyn, and he took Garrigue as his middle name, signaling his commitment to women's equality. Charlotte learned Czech quickly, took part in mass demonstrations for suffrage, helped her husband with his work, and was a vital companion until the end of her life. "She formed me," he later said. In 1881 he published a second dissertation (required even now for teaching positions in Central Europe) on suicide, an ultimate moral illness beginning to tear at the fabric of European societies, rising throughout Europe and reaching the alarming total of 50,000 yearly.[3] As a boy, he had seen a groom cut down from the rope on which he had hanged himself, and the horror never left him. Any worthwhile social order had to ensure that none of its members repeated what that desperate young man had done.

In 1882 the Masaryks decamped to Prague, the Bohemian capital that they knew not at all, and Tomáš became associate professor of philosophy at the newly opened Czech university. The call was fortuitous; had he taken a position at a German university (for example, in Freiburg im Breisgau or Austrian Czernowitz), he would have become just another German academic. Before the move to Prague, friends said he was nationally indifferent.

FIGURE 11.1. T. G. Masaryk and Charlotte Masaryk (1920).
Source: CTK/Alamy Stock Photo.

Yet in Prague, a person with political ambitions could not remain indifferent, because every pressing public concern somehow impinged on questions
of nationhood, and Masaryk soon stood at the center of controversies about
what it meant to be a good Czech. The first seemed to involve dry questions
of scholarship. For decades, the Czech national movement had based its ideas
of early Czech history on medieval documents supposedly discovered by the
librarian Václav Hanka in 1813 and 1817. They spoke of life at court of a virtuous
Czech queen "Libuše" before the year 1000, far earlier than previously known

Czech language sources, and patriots built ideas of Czech identity on these stories, in particular, the Czechs' supposed determination to live differently than Germans from time immemorial. The documents indeed seemed ancient, with wormholes and a version of Czech never before encountered, but doubts about their veracity swirled from the start. Based on "scientific" evidence, Masaryk sided with the doubters (the most prominent of whom were German), becoming persona non grata among Czechs who could not abandon the fabled ancient heroes. But Masaryk had his own version of Czech nationalism: a great people would accept truth, however painful. His support for science was therefore a moral choice, exemplifying courage and honesty.

Masaryk was not surprised about claims from the right that he was a traitor, but he was caught off guard by challenges that came from his own camp, from allies who also advocated reason and science. The writer Hubert Gordon Schauer, a supporter of Masaryk's realism who was of linguistically mixed background, restated the old challenge of German liberals: why did Czechs, if led by reason, not simply become German? Could a tiny nation manage to assemble the cultural and economic resources to stand by itself on the European stage? Was it worth all the effort?

Masaryk responded that history itself provided the answer. Czechs had always been animated by a higher calling, a dedication to "humanity," evident in the life of the early Protestant reformer Jan Hus, burned at the stake in 1420 for his witness to truth; the Czech brethren; and later the Bohemian renaissance, with its towering genius, the humanist intellectual Jan Amos Comenius, once invited to become president of Harvard. In Masaryk's view, this intrinsic mission had persisted through the dark ages of Catholic counterreformation after the battle of White Mountain to the second reformation of recent decades, guided by men like František Palacký and now him.

A generation later, when Hitler railed against his enemies, it was precisely against the value of "humanity": *Humanitätsduselei*. Still later, the Czech dissident human rights movement of the 1970s took Comenius and this enlightened heritage as a deep inspiration.[4] But in his day, critics said Masaryk's historical arguments added up to nonsense. *Scientific* historical study could not prove that a common "spirit" animated collectivities of people on the same territory over hundreds of years. At best, science could explore the causes of discreet events, and perhaps, if the sources were sufficient, tell people what it had been like to live in previous ages. But to say that a deeper impulse magically connected people of the 1390s and 1890s was to make a statement that was unreasonable. Masaryk was deeply hurt, but he did not waver in his effort to identify high causes of the past—like the freedom of conscience Jan Hus had died for—with his aspirations for the future.

Ironically, it was as a political "realist" that Masaryk would be proved right: his ideas about Czech history provided a foundation for state-building after World War I, while the positivist historians who opposed him produced tomes that collected dust.[5] In Masaryk's view, the nation did not serve science. Instead, the nation, acting from a quasi-divine mission, used science for its own higher ends of serving truth and humanity. His willingness to stand against the "sacred" but false documents cost him a promotion at the university for more than a decade.

This noncareerist approach to his academic career would have been impossible if Masaryk had not subordinated his ideas about scholarship to those higher ends. They had not derived from abstract theory but from Masaryk's work on suicide. Having himself been torn from the deeply religious environment of rural eastern Moravia, he regarded the causes of suicide's "immorality" as lying in the absence of guiding coordinates that could give meaning to people's lives. In particular, he worried about the dissolution in modern life of traditional Catholic beliefs—beliefs that in his view had governed people's lives in the Middle Ages. His thesis on suicide contained the following paean to Christ's role in history:

> Christ gave the new commandment of love, and that extended to one's enemies. In the possession of this love, the Christian knows how to arrange his life in a Godly manner: it is the bond that connects him with heaven and earth. Who could despair if he only had a spark of the love that Saint Paul describes in the unmatched hymn to the love of a Christian?[6]

Masaryk asserted that there was no going back to a time when Christianity shaped peoples' minds and gave their lives meaning. Still, if immorality derived from loss of faith, then modern people had to find a new faith, as he had, after encountering the probing questions of Protestantism, and more recently, those of the skeptic David Hume.[7] Masaryk remained a kind of Protestant (he said the only religious authority he trusted was Christ), but his real religion became Czech nationalism. He built on older Herderian notions that were popular in the Czech movement, that each nation had a destiny before God, but he gave the conventional readings a new inflection: the Czechs had the mission of showing humankind what "humanity" meant.

Masaryk's second public foray was even more daring, posing the question of whether a nation could hate in "self-defense." In 1899 a court condemned to death the Bohemian Jewish peddler Leopold Hilsner for the brutal slaying of the Christian Anežka Hrůzová. The Czech public quickly adopted the view from medieval Christianity that the girl had died in a ritual requiring Christian blood. The investigation had targeted Hilsner because he was reputedly an idler and a woman chaser. Putting aside academic tasks, Masaryk traveled to the place of the crime, and after interviewing forensic specialists, asked whether Hrůzová might have been killed by a family member. He also read widely and determined that no Jewish text called for a ritual of blood sacrifice, nor was there evidence that it was practiced in secret sects.[8]

Masaryk said the issue was science, but it was also the nation's moral character. Czechs propagating ideas about Jewish ritual murder assaulted "healthy reason and humanity," and showed they were stuck in an outdated mindset. Still, Masaryk maintained that such ignorance was not in their nature. Only the "Austrian" conditions under which Czechs lived—fostering superstition, unquestioned hierarchy, and subservience—had made such backwardness possible, even among judges, doctors, and journalists. Almost no one came to Masaryk's defense, and students in Prague kept him from speaking about the affair on campus. Though disappointed by "his" nation, he saved special opprobrium for Catholic authorities who had stood by the charges: he told parliament in 1907 that "no one who believes in Jesus can be an anti-Semite."[9] But by now he was so isolated that he considered settling in the United States with Charlotte and their five children.

Masaryk's achievement in this case was minimal: the emperor commuted Hilsner's death penalty but he was not released until 1918, and his sentence was never retracted. Yet Masaryk's profile was sharpened, making clear that those who stood with him had to argue in terms of evidence and humane ideals, and that anti-Semitism and ethnic hatred would not be tolerated among those who marched with him for Czech national rights. His message seemed to catch on. Czech intellectuals joined other Europeans in condemning a ritual murder trial that took place in Kiev in 1913.[10] Arguably Masaryk's efforts at transforming the national political culture were bearing fruit.

Where Bohemia's Jews were concerned, Masaryk was flexible, showing understanding for Jewish nationalism but also for cultural assimilation—the two major trends in the Jewish community. Perhaps because he took on the role of a teacher aiming to "regenerate" his own people, he was sympathetic to Zionism, though he believed that moral uplifting could occur anywhere Jews lived. For the time being, the colonization of Palestine seemed utopian. Later, as Czechoslovak President, Masaryk supported efforts of Jewish cultural societies on Czech territory, but he also considered cultural assimilation "justified and natural."[11]

Though his wife Charlotte became a Social Democrat, Masaryk rejected the existing options in Czech political life and in 1900 formed his own party, the Czech People's Party/Realists (*Česká strana lidová*), a name normally associated in the region with peasant politics. But he had greater ambitions than peasant politicians or other forces on the left. He supported Charlotte's progressive activism but rejected Marxian views of national and social development, in particular, the ideas that Czechs were bound to become Germans, and peasants to become city dwellers. The rural population, despite depletion, held up well in conditions of modern capitalism; contrary to Marxist predictions that medium-sized farms would disappear as large estates grew, in fact the former multiplied.[12] Moreover, small towns were so dense in Bohemia, in patterns going back to the Middle Ages, that industrialists built their factories in the countryside in order to attract labor, and much of the Czech working class was rural: Czech peasants could become modern industrial laborers without ever having to leave their traditional village and small-town settings.[13]

Masaryk welcomed this more gradual and gentle form of modernization: he far preferred the countryside to the town and spoke approvingly of "deurbanization," namely, the fact that Bohemia's excellent communications network permitted industries to sprout up beyond city limits. "Not even industry will be crowded into cities," he told Czech writer Karel Čapek in the 1930s, "and cities will be healthier. Even civilization can bring people close to nature." From the time they settled in Prague in the 1880s, he and his family spent as much time as they could in the countryside, close to both sides of his family, and he complained during the war years that incessant lobbying for the Czech cause kept him trapped in cities.[14]

The other Czech parties struck him as inadequate to the tasks facing the Czech people in their struggle for autonomy. He abhorred the Old Czechs' reliance on large landholders, dynasty, and the church, and he abandoned the Young Czechs in 1893, because they wanted suffrage limited by property and education. Despite his advocacy of rural life, the Czech Agrarians struck him as narrow. His visions for the future conformed to his understandings of the past: in their times of glory, the Czechs were united across all boundaries, whether of status or of town and village.[15] The Hussites of the fifteenth century had not even known a separate clerical class.

He changed his party's name to Czech Progressive Party in 1906 to reflect that deeper understanding: it became known popularly as the realists, advocating equal voting rights for men and women, and counting women among the party's leadership. Still, he did not idealize the masses; the willingness of Czechs to succumb to medieval prejudices in the Hilsner controversy caused him to demand strong and enlightened leadership (his own). Czechs should move into the future as he had, without leaving their past behind, avoiding the dislocations and despair that he had witnessed as a boy. Czechs would produce world-class work in science, education, and culture, yet like him and his family, never live far from the villages and small towns of their ancestors.

Masaryk's last stance before the war was not controversial for Czechs but was deeply disturbing for Habsburg officials, because it revealed dangerous rot at the upper levels of government in both Hungary and Austria. At issue was the treason trial of more than four dozen Habsburg Serbs at Zagreb in 1909, for which the penalty would have been death by hanging. The pretext for the trial drew on prejudices and fears that went back decades, to the crafting of the "dual monarchy" in 1867 to hold back a Slavic menace, and the 1878 Berlin Congress that had permitted the monarchy to occupy Bosnia-Herzegovina in order to deny it to Serbia. Despite these acts, the situation in southeastern Europe remained unstable. Austria-Hungary had treated Bosnia-Herzegovina as its own almost from the start, recruiting soldiers from the region and introducing its own institutions, but technically, the area remained Ottoman, and Serbia looked on it as an integral future province of the Serb kingdom.

For the Habsburg elite, the prospect of Bosnia becoming Serb continued to raise horror scenarios of a large and growing national state that would lay claim to Croat and Serb populations within the monarchy's borders who used the Štokavian dialect. The concerns only grew after 1903, when a group of military officers murdered Serb King Milan Obrenović and his bride and put in his place the more assertive Peter from the Karadjordje dynasty.

The murderers believed that the Serb national program had stagnated since 1878, and now the Serb government took a more assertive role in foreign policy, turning toward Russia. When a commercial treaty with Austria came up for renewal, Serbia allowed it to lapse, because its leaders no longer wanted to take Austria's industrial goods, and instead diversified (for example, by buying weapons from Russia's ally France). In response, Austria launched a trade war in 1906, refusing to take Serbia's livestock and hoping to bring Serbia to heal. It failed. France extended credits for slaughterhouses, permitting Serbia to export meat products rather than simply livestock, and giving Serbia an economic reason for coveting Bosnia in addition to the national one.[16] With connivance from within the Serb government and military, a secret society emerged called the "Black Hand" that supported bands of terrorists on Bosnian territory who endeavored to disrupt Austro-Hungarian rule.

In 1908 army officers seized power in the Ottoman capital Istanbul, promising to make Turkey a modern state under constitutional rule. Politicians in Vienna feared that a reformed Turkey would assert claims to Bosnia and Herzegovina, and therefore they proclaimed that the region was not simply occupied, but was now sovereign Habsburg territory, thus launching the "annexation crisis," humiliating Serbia, a client state of Russia, and damaging Russia's international reputation. At this time neither Turkey nor Russia was armed for confrontation, and no military challenge arose. But the event further destablized the region because Serbia, along with Greece, Bulgaria, and Romania, continued to view the status quo as temporary, and when the next conflict broke out between Austria-Hungary and Serbia, Russia would not stand by, believing that its status as a great power could not afford another humiliation.

The following year, allegations emerged from the Austrian Embassy at Belgrade that Serbia was operating a network of conspirators in Habsburg territory. On the basis of a list the embassy passed on, Hungarian authorities arrested fifty-three Serb politicians and charged them with treason. From the start, doubts were raised about the evidence, and after he had investigated the matter personally in Zagreb, Masaryk excoriated the trial as a final gasp of a corrupt monarchy delaying the irreversible path to democracy for the Slavic peoples:

> The [Habsburg] Court's aristocratic diplomacy and its delusion that a few powerful people and their helpers can decisively lead society and its development, have begun to decline. Domestic and foreign policy are subject to public debate and criticism; politics is becoming more democratic and scientific, and aristocratic absolutism and its diplomatic occultism are giving way to democracy and its critical, scientific public sphere.[17]

This time, Masaryk and other critics of Austria won: the "traitors" were acquitted, and the dual monarchy was subjected to derision across Europe. Especially humiliated was the historian Heinrich Friedjung, a moderate German nationalist who had been a major force behind the Linz Program of 1882 and vouched for the evidence. Yet soon Masaryk abandoned his residual hopes that the monarchy might be reformed in the direction of democracy. In 1914, war broke out after a terrorist supported by the Black Hand shot Habsburg Archduke Francis Ferdinand and his wife, and with a small entourage, Masaryk escaped to the West, now becoming a traitor to the monarchy and pursuing a mission which even bold Czech nationalists could hardly imagine achieving fruition: Czechoslovak independence. At home, the monarchy terrorized critics, including Masaryk's family; in 1916 Charlotte suffered a nervous breakdown.

Peasant Politics

During the same decades, the two other political figures mentioned earlier in the chapter emerged as national leaders in Eastern Europe. They also transformed the political landscape of their respective countries, creating movements from the ruins of liberal politics that elevated assumptions about the politically possible. Like Masaryk, they came from humble backgrounds, but unlike him, their vision for politics remained centered on the village. The first was Stjepan Radić, of Hungarian-controlled Croatia, and the second was Aleksandar Stamboliiski, who worked in Bulgaria, an autonomous state from 1878, and from 1909 an independent kingdom under the self-anointed "Tsar" Ferdinand.

These peasant politicians insisted that politics appeal to a nation's entire people, including villagers whom the urban intelligentsias that controlled politics held in contempt. Yet both were also united in a belief that concern for the peasantry ennobled the nation as a whole. Like Masaryk, they rose from rural poverty, thanks to the support of local teachers, and after leaving high school managed to study abroad. Radić took a degree in Paris after being ejected from Zagreb and then all the universities of Cisleithania for his uncontrollably subversive behavior; Stamboliiski studied agronomy in Halle before contracting tuberculosis and having to return home.

Both were physically robust and adept at invoking the right peasant metaphors before huge, usually adoring crowds. They made the revolutionary suggestion that peasants benefit from taxes as well as paying them, and they demanded the sane improvements to rural life that eluded state authorities: more and better schooling, enhanced farming methods, the provision of credit by the state, and the integration of villages into the nation through the provision of paved roads, electricity, and sanitation. Each envisioned a nation in which villagers could live in dignity and be recognized as a source of key values in culture and the economy. Unfortunately for the political left, vast gulfs separated peasant politicians from city-based Marxists, who largely disdained the "idiocy" of rural life and thought that peasant proprietors were selfish petty bourgeoisie, destined to be subsumed in agribusiness and then urbanized like everyone else.

Stamboliiski and Radić opposed violent revolution, and if they believed in a new politics, they were also republicans, imagining a future in which peasants would cooperate with other social groups. They thought change would come gradually and legally, though they were determined to use the law for the benefit of their supporters. Stamboliiski wanted a new kind of parliament consisting of interest groups representing various occupations, but it would reach decisions by compromise.

Without these two men, strong peasant movements may have never emerged in Croatia and Bulgaria, and peasants might have been more susceptible to right-wing national and social politics. Both men went on to national leadership after 1918, until they were cut down by assassins, Stamboliiski in 1923 and Radić in 1928. Yet they were men of peace, committed to a different kind of international politics that was based on cooperation with neighboring states rather than violent seizures of territory in the name of "national missions." (Before 1914, Masaryk believed in an Austria transformed into a federation of free peoples.) If Radić had succeeded, Croats would have lived in a vast South Slav state that respected the identities of each group while forming and fostering a common culture.

* * *

Politics in Croatia during the 1890s, when Radić got his start, took place on a tiny stage of one city—Zagreb—and was highly personalized. The political class mostly followed the Serb-hater Ante Starčević (1823–1896), founder of the Croatian party of right. Starčević's mother was Serb Orthodox. He had started as an adept of Ljudevit Gaj, but after 1849 became increasingly disenchanted as he witnessed unrelenting Magyarization at home—and scant interest among Serbs in Gaj's Illyrian ideas of South Slav cooperation. Serbs had their own kingdom and a scheme for unity that involved its extension to other territories. Starčević met the challenge of defending Croatian nationhood by recalling the tradition of Croatian state's rights: the rights vested for centuries in the Croatian nation.[18] He created a Party of Right that rejected all compromise with Austria and sought to pursue Croatian interests. Its visions of a future people of state were a mirror of the Great Serbian program, viewing Serbs as potential Croatians (and insisting that Bosnia-Herzegovina must belong to Croatia.)

Starčević believed in the nation but not in the immortality of the soul; in his view, the Catholic Church, though often taken to incorporate Croatian identity, had weakened Croatia by serving the Habsburgs. The papacy debased religion by using a dead language, annihilating any living contact between priests and believers. If the Church did any good at all, it was in defying the pope.[19]

A splinter formed to the right of his movement, driven by the racist Josip Frank, for whom Serbs were a different species. A generation later, the Croatian fascist Ante Pavelić would claim to be inspired by the ideas of Starčević and Frank, but his own support in Croat society never rose above a few percentage points, thanks in part to the alternative nationalism offered by Radić's movement.

As a young man, Radić had come to know both Starčević and Frank. He shared their concerns about the Magyarization of Croatian culture but was horrified by their idea that other South Slavs were irrevocably foreign and hostile. Radić knew they were wrong from his own experience: as a young man, he had liked to take long hikes from village to village, beyond Croatia, north into the Slovene lands, then eastward through Slavonia and Bosnia into Serbia. Rather than any clear borders, he discovered a continuum of language and custom, of people who understood one anther perfectly, village after village, but also a continuum of poverty and lost human potential. These rural toilers spoke dialects he understood, some called themselves Serbs, some Croats, and some practiced one sort of Christianity, some another. They all belonged to a great Slavic nation and had "one soul."[20]

Radić's budding Slavophilism became more passionate in the 1890s, when he began his university studies. After being ejected from Zagreb for excessive nationalism, he migrated with other Croat students to Prague and became fascinated by the politics of Czech nationalism and the teachings of T. G. Masaryk. From Masaryk he learned that a nation had to be based in realities of economy and culture and not in myths or dreams, let alone outright falsehoods. Nations were instructed and constructed from the hard work of enlightenment based on reason.

Yet this was a realism grounded in people's capacities to imagine and idealize. And just as Masaryk's politics would have been powerless without his unqualified love for its subject—the Czechs and their history—so Radić's would have been inert without a cult of the Croat people, the core of which was the peasantry. Radić never idealized the nation in a way that caused him to ignore the masses of unenlightened, poor, apathetic, rural dwellers; the perspective of the village remained his perspective. Even though he studied in Prague and Paris, becoming up to date in modern intellectual currents, Radić, like the villagers, had very little concern with differences of "race" or "religion" and was much more concerned with material well-being and basic dignity.

This broader view was not dampened by the vicissitudes of life after the encounter with Masaryk, which turned out to be brief. In Prague, Radić had fallen in with other South Slav nationalists, and when police broke up one of their meetings, Radić nearly threw an officer out of a window. For this he was placed in custody and forced to study abroad. After exploring Moscow, where he could not be accepted as a regular student, Radić enrolled at Sciences Po in Paris. There he took a demanding curriculum of sociology, diplomatic history, and finance, and finally received a degree in political science. In 1896 he was back in Zagreb, where, with his older and less impulsive brother Antun, he became a leading figure among young intellectuals, the *mladi*, many of whom were just returning from Prague.

In France, Radić had absorbed the lessons of Auguste Comte's positivism and, even later, he never succumbed to the Herderian temptation to think of the nation as an idea. Instead, nations were "complicated social organisms," and no component could be ignored. What annoyed him in Zagreb was the contempt that mainstream nationalists expressed for peasants. Leading patriots happily sang ballads about the homeland while ignoring the people who lived just beyond the city limits. Before his sojourn abroad, Radić had a decisive personal encounter with Ante Starčević. When told that his movement's message was incomprehensible to most peasants, who could not read and had no clue about "Croatian state rights," the old man had said: "Let the devil or God teach them, I will not!"[21] Other "gentlemen" in Zagreb whom Radić met looked on peasants as beings that were less than human.

Therefore, the ideas that Radić developed, in league with other young nationalists, broke with existing strains of Croat nationalism. The nation's unity remained of paramount value for them, but their ideal was the "social and political equality of the people, the 'common' people with the 'educated' gentlemen." Before looking toward union with other Slavs beyond Croatia, Croats had to work on themselves; nationalists worth their name had to make people literate, cultivated, productive, and fully European, but in a very particular sense: the *mladi* dedicated themselves to "instructing them by word, book and example . . . with love."[22]

Like Masaryk, Stjepan Radić synthesized existing politics, and rather than simply rejecting the "medieval" states' rights view, he made it part of his larger scheme. Croats would not disappear in a South Slav—or Yugoslav—sea, and Croatia would continue as an ancient European kingdom. Any South Slav state would thus be federal and not ruled from one city, featuring political and cultural autonomy for Croats and Serbs, as well as for Slovenes and Bulgars. For the time being, Croats and Serbs faced a common menace in the Magyar state: "our very national existence" was in danger, Radić wrote, and that necessitated political and economic work between Croats and Serbs at all levels, especially among peasants, who had to be organized economically and politically, and strengthened against Magyarization.[23]

The movement's ideas of Slavic unity went back to Ljudevit Gaj's Illyrianism, which Radić and his friends knew intimately. They also had living connections to this Yugoslav tradition in their patron Bishop Juraj Strossmayer (1815–1905) of Djakovo, a philanthropist and intellectual powerhouse, famous beyond Croatia as a man who sought closer Christian unity and questioned papal authority. Strossmayer was also known as a humane advocate of reconciliation with Orthodox Serbs and thus formed the opposite pole to Starčević, whom Strossmayer detested for his bigoted nationalism. The point of Croat nationalism should be to ensure that Croats would have the resources to become people of high character, not against but with other Slavs, tied in "reciprocity," producing their own "single strong culture." Rather than viewing eastern Orthodoxy as a foreign force, Radić, following Strossmayer, focused on common Christian principles that linked Croats with Slavs of the east. In fact, he thought that Croats themselves belonged to the east, and warned his co-nationals to be wary of what they took from the west.

In taking their rightful place in Europe, Croats should pay special attention to the Czechs and Russians. Radić knew about divisions between them and other Slavic peoples, but like Masaryk, he had an underlying belief that Slavs were united by character, tradition, and language to be "virtually one nation." The point was to approach the legacy critically. "Instead of blindly praising the Slavic people," Radić wrote, "we will study its character; instead of threatening others with 100 million Slavs, we will study Slavic languages." With his eye to the peasants who bore the costs of territorial disputes, he vowed to oppose the "the demons of tribal hatred" and believed that his ideas of Yugoslav unity would raise South Slavic politics to a new level, opening the way to an independent state in which concerns about Serb or Croat borders would lose meaning.[24]

Radić became a leading peasant politician, but at the start he had no intention of founding a movement. He led a "united opposition" to Magyar rule until 1904, when events suddenly imposed a trajectory he had not anticipated. Massive demonstrations had broken out for financial independence, which then fizzled out. Intellectuals had been caught by surprise, but the protests caused Radić to imagine a "magnificent national army" rising from the peasantry to become the core of the Croat movement. It needed leadership, and he would be its leader. He was alarmed by the anti-Serb agitation he witnessed among Zagreb nationalists, signaling where the movement might go if humane

FIGURE 11.2. Stjepan Radić (1920s). *Source*: Josip Horvat, *Politička povijest Hrvatske* (Zagreb, 1989). Via Wikimedia Commons.

leadership did not prevail. Other progressive Croats were content to let the anti-Serb violence take its course, but Radić intervened, personally stopping a mob from destroying a neighbor's property.[25] He told the rioters that not Serbs but Magyars were the enemy, and led them to the train station to tear down Magyar signs meant to denationalize the Croats. Yet again, authorities arrested him for disturbing the peace.

When he and his brother Antun founded their Peasant Party, few progressive colleagues followed, thinking the focus on the peasantry excessive. Some accused them of sentimentalizing the people and presuming some essential national soul and tradition, instead of holding them up to critical reflection.[26] But by idealizing the nation—as Masaryk did in Bohemia—Radić created a republican national movement that frustrated later attempts of Frankists or

Rightist nationalists to make inroads into the peasantry with the "realistic" messages of chauvinism.

The Peasant Party's huge growth after 1918 could hardly be sensed in 1904, when restrictions on the electorate kept it from gaining more than few seats in the Croatian parliament, the Sabor. But Radić's insight turned out to be correct. Croats were overwhelmingly peasants, and when universal manhood suffrage became a fact in 1918, they stood with him. Other Croat intellectuals, out of touch with popular sentiment, rushed into a bond with Serbia, without first settling questions of the new Yugoslav state's organization—in particular, whether it would be governed centrally from Belgrade or would permit local autonomy. It turned out to be the former. Radić had the courage to stand against this state as he had against the Magyar one; but he also took devotion to principle and personal impulsiveness to new extremes and would prove insensitive to reasonable compromise.

Aleksandar Stamboliiski of Bulgaria followed a path very much like that taken by Masaryk and Radić, from village poverty in a large family, through support by patrons, studies abroad, and then on to leadership of a powerful movement, all the while drawing on seemingly unlimited reservoirs of ideas and energy. Yet because Stamboliiski operated in a nation-state, questions of national and social oppression were much less urgent than in Bohemia or Croatia. When he came of age in the late 1890s, a Bulgarian elite controlled the state apparatus and the administration of culture, and it had driven Turkish landowners from the country, meaning that plots were smaller and spread relatively equitably. Only 618 farmers had more than one hundred hectares each, and some 550,000 had less than one hundred.[27]

But as in Croatia, the material situation of the rural population was often desperate, and the tiny urban elite had little concern for it. A bloated state apparatus exploited the peasants and promoted an aggressive irredentism, laying claims to territories disputed with Serbia, Turkey, and Greece, and above all Macedonia. Stamboliiski understood that dreams of expansion made no sense before the needs of people within current state boundaries were addressed. He knew that in any foreign adventure, peasant conscripts would be the prime victims.

As in Croatia, the peasant movement faced two problems: farms functioned unproductively; and, though the regime had copied a constitutional order complete with political parties from the West, villagers had no representation. Instead the would-be liberal state exploited them for taxes to support its version of national interests. Unlike Radić, Stamboliiski was not the first to organize his country's rural population. A Bulgarian peasant union (BANU) had emerged in 1898 from a first generation of agrarian enthusiasts, who, like Stamboliiski, were trained as village teachers. But when Stamboliiski became editor of the union's main journal a few years later, it was in decline, lacking a sense of purpose: its own "charter myth."[28] Along with charisma and indefatigable energy, purpose is what Stamboliiski provided, soon making BANU the strongest opposition movement in the country.

Marxists thought peasants would disappear as societies developed and urbanized, melting into an impoverished proletariat, but Stamboliiski believed that property owning was a human instinct and fact of life. As societies developed, they became not simpler (that is, not a huge army of proletarians against a tiny class of exploiters) but a complex mix of professional and trade groups, some urban, some rural.[29]

According to Stamboliiski, political parties in Bulgaria did not properly represent those groups. Instead, they had banded with the monarch against the people and had become "court parties," creating a regime that did not even govern according to the national constitution. In the 1880s, the strongman Stefan Stambalov had emerged as prime minister from the liberal ranks. But in 1894, agents of Bulgaria's Prince Ferdinand I Saxe-Coburg-Gotha assassinated Stambalov on the streets of Sofia and also made the point of cutting off his hands. Now the prince himself became the strongman, encouraging further fragmentation of the parties and cultivating the good will of the military. Ferdinand's ambition was to make Bulgaria the dominant power in the Balkans, and he doled out favors. Nearly every minister filled his pockets at public expense, and a class of functionaries who delivered votes at election time dominated the villages. Rather than represent their localities, mayors formed an extension of the royal dictatorship, using local agricultural banks and access to schools to reward followers and mounted police to control dissidents.[30]

Political parties thus revealed themselves as unable to deal with the problems of modern life. The political class governed through fraud and intimidation, squandering irreplaceable resources on weapons, while making workers, artisans, and peasants beasts of burden for the governing class's own pleasures. To help Bulgaria advance from this corrupt pseudo-democracy, Stamboliiski demanded an *economic parliament*, where occupational groups would be represented by corporate (*estatist*) organizations.[31] Whereas existing parties drew members from all walks of life and could not speak for anyone, the interest groups he proposed would emerge from society as it actually functioned and ensure democracy. Peasants would be the leading force. Stamboliiski believed that Bulgaria was already producing such corporate groups: besides BANU and peasant cooperatives, there were trade unions for industrial workers and guilds among the artisans.

As was true of Radić's schemes, this was a long-term vision rather than a precise plan to be implemented in the short run. But it gave Stamboliiski's supporters an alternative to cynicism and a cause to rally around, and it formed the moral and intellectual basis on which the movement grew. Beginning in 1904, BANU became more disciplined, and Stamboliiski made sure that its local branches (*druzhbi*) actually paid dues, and that their members did not defect to other parties. The *druzhbi* also became more focused on peasant needs, creating a life insurance fund, as well as financial support for the cooperative moment. By 1907 there were more than 400 *druzhbi*.

The 1908 elections showed that BANU, on the verge of disappearing before Stamboliiski asserted his leadership, was the largest opposition political organization in the country, netting more than 100,000 votes. A few years previously, Agrarian deputies were divided and had no clear program, but now they were a force that the regime could not ignore. The constitution made no provision for the prince to open the national assembly, but when he did so anyway, BANU deputies withheld their applause, and Stamboliiski rose to say that the peasantry would not tolerate a violation of the constitution.[32] This kind of direct affront was unheard of and announced the emergence of a force that could not be bought.

Like Radić, Stamboliiski thought that a gulf divided his country from the West, but he also urged caution in "catching up." Bulgaria's elite had been unproductively obsessed with aping foreign customs, creating a large diplomatic corps, army, and bureaucracy, all of which economically squeezed the peasantry.[33] Any transplanting of Western institutions had to take local conditions into account. The problem was not limited to Bulgaria, or even southeastern Europe. But if in Italy, liberals had failed to create a strong state through democratic institutions, in Bulgaria they had hardly created democratic institutions. To attempt liberal politics where illiteracy was high and the middle class meager was sheer fantasy. That is why Stamboliiski wanted a different kind of parliament attuned to local needs, promoting education and the development of Bulgarians as they actually lived, and not merely projecting their becoming like the French or British.

Prince Ferdinand, however, managed to use the rotten system that existed to his own ends, amassing public support at the polls and in the National Assembly with promises to make Bulgaria a regional power. In 1909, emboldened by Austria's aggressive stance in Bosnia and Turkey's acquiescence, he crowned himself tsar of Bulgaria. His immediate target for expansion was Macedonia, which Bulgaria had been forced to return to the Ottoman Empire at the Berlin Congress of 1878. Stamboliiski thought the drive to seize territory was madness. Serbia and Greece also laid claims to Macedonia, and seizure of any of it would only plunge Bulgaria and its overwhelmingly peasant population into deeper misery. No one could even say what parts of Macedonia were properly Bulgarian. In addition, the new constitutional government of the young Turks that governed Macedonia promised to end the religious and racial oppression of the Ottoman government, so there was no need to "liberate" this territory from foreign rulers. The program to free Macedonia, even if successful, would make Bulgaria a vassal of foreign banks. Stamboliiski's reasoned stance drew opprobrium upon his party. Vilified as traitorous, the party lost more than 30 percent of its seats in September 1911.[34]

The following year, Bulgaria allied with Serbia, Romania, and Greece and launched a war that all but expelled Turkey from European territory. But then they quarreled over the spoils (Macedonia in particular), and in the second Balkan War of 1913, Serbia, Greece, and Romania, joined by Turkey, prevailed over Bulgaria, which lost the territorial gains made in the previous year. Stamboliiski seemed a prophet, as we will see, not for the first time. Yet Ferdinand was undeterred, and in 1915 took his country into what some called the Third Balkan War, now known as World War I, on the side of Austria and Germany, hoping to retrieve Macedonia and other lost territory. The result was another fiasco, at the end of which Bulgaria lost Macedonia and territories along the Black Sea, as well as access to the Aegean. In October 1918, Ferdinand was forced to abdicate, and Stamboliiski formed the first government in European history to be led by a peasant party.

The Village Strikes Back

Ferdinand teamed with Austria-Hungary in World War I, even though he despised Francis Joseph, calling him an idiot and an "old dotard."[35] Among Austro-Hungarian decision makers, no one emerged with the charisma or the will to carry out strategically conceived ideas, and the monarchy's foreign policy became a chain reaction of reflexes generated by fear, which ultimately hastened the decline they were meant to counteract. These actions included moves Francis Joseph had made long before his dotage, from the 1850s onward, from his inept neutrality during the Crimean War and the wars lost to France and

Prussia, to the occupation and annexation of Bosnia, and finally the disastrous decisions of the summer of 1914.

Francis Joseph worked with a small coterie of advisors who aggravated his own weakness of vision, men who could dominate Habsburg foreign policy, because, as in Bulgaria or Romania, the government in Austria-Hungary was not accountable to the public through representative institutions. Manhood suffrage may have been universal in Cisleithania from 1907, and the monarchy by and large a state of laws (*Rechtsstaat*), but it was still far from a democracy, because diplomacy and defense remained beyond public scrutiny.

Unfortunately for the Habsburg state—and for the world of the twentieth century—the emperor's men operated in a hothouse of their own obsessions, and like the "architects" of the 1867 Compromise and the Austro-Hungarian position at Berlin in 1878, they seriously believed that Slavic peoples might overwhelm the monarchy. If, as Carl Schorske wrote, the 1890s marked the rise of irrational politics in Central Europe, that was true not just of the "rabble" who supported Karl Lueger in Vienna, but also of men wrapped in sashes and bedecked with medals that masked gargantuan insecurities. Ironically, their fears were given shape and substance by modern scientific disciplines: anthropology, nascent political science, and also geography. The bottom line was the belief that peoples either cleansed themselves in war or faced irreversible decline. Leopold von Berchtold, in charge of foreign policy, said that if the monarchy did not control tiny Serbia, that would be proof that the monarchy had been castrated.[36]

Berchtold sensed that Serbia made claims to the loyalty of Habsburg South Slavs that the monarchy could never match, regardless of its economic or military power, and he projected Serb nationalism as an unreasonable force, "bred in the soul of Serb priests, teachers and merchants," on both sides of the border. Only a war that Serbia could not wriggle out of would solve the problem.[37]

Like imperial rulers elsewhere, the Habsburgs shielded such insecurity in hubris. In 1901 foreign minister Agenor Gołuchowski said that Serbia was so disordered and weak that it would "always be dependent on us." Still, it was Austria that acted recklessly. Its 1908 annexation of Bosnia-Herzegovina was meant finally to "put Serbia in its place," but it had the opposite effect: national sentiment raged, especially among intellectuals and students, who felt Serbia had been cheated. Meanwhile the Austrian press was full of articles depicting Serbs as uncultivated "louse people," "prince killers," "thieving riffraff," and "donkey rustlers."[38]

When Serbia, with a strong army supported by an outsized military budget, joined Bulgaria and Greece in vanquishing Turkish forces in 1912, Habsburg Slavs flocked to the cause as volunteer soldiers, doctors, and nurses. Even the censored press in their language featured slogans such as "Balkans to the Balkan peoples," and "We are fed up with European controls."[39] A more conciliatory stance toward Serbia on the part of Austria-Hungary would have obviated all of this, but instead the escalation continued: Habsburg authorities responded to pro-Serb sentiments by denying passports to men of military age. Nowhere was sympathy for Belgrade stronger than in Bosnia, and nowhere else was the failure of Habsburg multinationalism more evident.

For more than a generation, the monarchy had modernized Bosnia, building bridges and railways, improving agriculture, making people literate, and introducing representative institutions while respecting eastern and western Christianity as well as Islam and Judaism. Never before had Bosnians been more enfranchised, politically as well as culturally. Scores of young men from humble families went off to universities in Graz, Prague, or Kraków and attained levels of education unimagined by their parents. Yet the more the Habsburg administration did "for Bosnia," the more it stoked an awareness that it had not touched the problems of inequality that occasioned the great unrest of 1875. In the countryside, Muslims held the land, and Christians were impoverished sharecroppers.

The assassin who killed Archduke Francis Ferdinand in June 1914, nineteen-year-old Gavrilo Princip, was the first in his family to attain literacy. After he was apprehended and could see the results of his deed—a war engulfing Europe—he said "I am the son of peasants and *I know what is happening in the villages*. That is why I wanted to take revenge, and I regret nothing."[40] Book learning had only intensified Princip's sense that the evils humiliating him and his family were rooted in foreign rule. He had superficial knowledge of the Serb state that supplied his pistol: in his mind, it was not foreign, and therefore not unjust. In contrast to Bulgaria, no Serb peasant movement had drawn attention to the failures of Serb leaders to invest in agriculture. The Serb Radical Party had started on the left and wound up firmly nationalist and irredentist, spending precious resources on the military.[41]

Some half-dozen co-conspirators joined Princip on June 28 in Sarajevo, but only happenstance permitted them to carry out their deed. When the motorcade arrived in the morning, one of the young men lost his nerve, and another tossed a bomb, which the archduke managed to deflect. In the early afternoon, Princip was standing idly by a delicatessen when suddenly the archduke's limousine was right in front of him. Inexplicably, the driver had taken a wrong turn after lunch at city hall, going right on Franz Josef Strasse instead of straight, as the protocol required. Getting the massive vehicle turned around on the small bridge required time. Princip fired two shots point blank, one striking the archduke in the neck, severing an artery, the other hitting his wife, Sophie von Chotek, a noblewoman from an old Bohemian family, in the stomach. Both were dead in minutes. Princip later said he deeply regretted hitting the "lady" (another co-assassin sent a letter of apology to the couple's three children: two responded, forgiving him).

Ironically, Princip and his friends had targeted Francis Ferdinand not because he hated Slavs. The truth was the opposite: the archduke and his wife spent much of their time in the company of Czech politicians and intellectuals at their castle south of Prague, and they wondered why Slavs should not have the same prerogatives as Germans and Magyars. They came to advocate federation of autonomous Slavic entities under Habsburg rule: Croats would gain control of Croat space, Czechs of Czech space, and so on.[42] Francis Ferdinand became so associated with advocacy of the Slavic cause that Slavic politicians routinely made appeals to him. For example, Slovenes argued that a stable "Yugoslav" entity in the monarchy would help protect it against Italian claims to Dalmatia, as well as the aspirations of a "greater Serbia."[43] But that was precisely the problem for patriots like Princip, who wanted Serbia and not Austria-Hungary to create a huge South Slav state. He called himself a Yugoslav patriot.

Had he lived, the archduke would have encountered severe difficulties in realizing his plans for breaking the monarchy into federal units. Magyar elites had opposed such ideas for decades because any increase in the power of Slavs would have reduced their relative strength. Instead of one-half of the dual monarchy, Hungary would make up one-third. A federal monarchy would have spelled the end of Hungary in their eyes; they were barely keeping the lid on as it was and feared any experimentation. For example, if there could be autonomy for South Slavs, why not for Romanians or Slovaks? Soon Hungary would be reduced to a tiny island surrounded by other groups.[44] After 1907, Croat deputies obstructed the parliament in Budapest, protesting language laws that forced young Croats to be educated primarily in Hungarian. The constitution of Croatia was suspended in 1912, and no resolution of Croatia's disputes with the Magyar elite was in sight when the war came.[45]

Yet even if Magyar politicians had given their assent, it was not clear how Habsburg territory would have been subdivided without creating even more aggrieved parties. Germans rioted when any concessions were made to the

FIGURE 11.3. Sarajevo trial (1914; Gavrilo Princip is third from left).
Source: Süddeutsche Zeitung Photo/Alamy Stock Photo.

Czechs. In Bohemia, already 80 percent of civil servants were Czech, but Czechs still wanted autonomy and kept the Bohemian diet (*Landtag*) in Prague (as well as the *Reichsrat* in Vienna) from functioning as intended. They hoped their obstruction would destabilize the monarchy so dramatically that the rulers would have no choice but to "compromise" with them as they had with the Hungarians.[46] In the meantime, Francis Joseph continued to appoint prime ministers to rule by decree and occasional consensus.

Still, we can easily imagine the monarchy continuing. Had the motorcade not taken its still unexplained wrong turn in Sarajevo on June 28, 1914, there would have been no major crisis in Europe that summer, and the Habsburgs would have carried on. Had the war broken out a year or two later, Russia would have been militarily stronger, and perhaps the Central Powers would have been forced to sue for peace much earlier. That might have saved Austria-Hungary. The Habsburgs had guaranteed the peaceful coexistence of more than a dozen peoples for generations, and their mostly honest administration would have continued settling people's quotidian concerns better than most states did. One sign of the monarchy's comparatively humane quality was that Gavrilo Princip was not executed, because he was a minor.[47]

The story of what actually happened is well known. Encouraged by Germany, a monarchical regime itself guided by a belief in an inevitable showdown between "Teuton and Slav," and concerns about proving its "manhood," Austria demanded that Habsburg officials conduct an inquiry into the assassination on Serb territory.[48] Serbia rejected this ultimatum as an infringement on its sovereignty; its patron Russia mobilized its armed forces, leading to a mobilization by Germany and threats and counterthreats. On August 4, a massive German invasion began of Belgium and France, aiming to knock France—Russia's ally—out of the war before Russia could attack from the east. Despite assaults undertaken from the fall of 1914, only in the summer of 1915—reinforced by German troops—did Austria-Hungary finally vanquish Serbia. By that time, Austro-Hungarian forces were engaged against Russian troops in Poland and Ukraine; in 1915, an additional front opened against Italy.

Habsburg reservists from all nationalities loyally entered their regiments and fought on these far-flung fronts. Still, there were differences: unlike troops from the German areas of Austria or Bohemia, or from Hungary, the Czech, Slovene, and Croat soldiers did not share the enthusiasm for "punishing" Serbia or protecting the monarchy and Europe from the "Slavic danger." In the late summer of 1914, a Czechoslovak delegation had visited the tsar in Moscow, who offered support for Slavic peoples under Habsburg rule. A Czech volunteer unit assembled on the Russian side, and when word of this seeped into Bohemia, the initiative encountered widespread enthusiasm.[49] Habsburg authorities brutally put down pro-Slavic demonstrations and incarcerated Czechs for critical remarks made in public places; several of those arrested for making treasonous remarks were put to death. In Bosnia and occupied Serbia, the authorities initiated a regime of terror against Serbs suspected of disloyalty, causing the Bohemian German writer Egon Erwin Kirsch to call the Habsburg reign "medieval." Women taken hostage for supposedly poisoning wells and fruit were summarily executed; in all some 30,000 persons are thought to have lost their lives in a punitive expedition meant to put Serbia in its place once and for all.[50]

Until the early fall of 1914, Tomáš G. Masaryk, like other Czech politicians, continued to work for the increasing democratization, federalization, and modernization of Austria-Hungary. He desired autonomy for Bohemia and understood that would involve power-sharing with the Germans. But when the war broke out, his views began to shift. By October, be became convinced that the monarchy would not survive, and he confided to the British publicist and historian R. W. Seton-Watson that he wanted to form an independent state with the Slovaks after the war. Masaryk made three trips to neutral Switzerland and

FIGURE 11.4. Execution of Serbs by Austro-Hungarian army (1916).
Source: Everett Collection Historical / Alamy Stock Photo.

Italy to begin sounding out Western opinion for support, and in February 1915, he decided not to return, having been warned that he would be arrested (that had been the fate of the nationalist Karel Kramář, who had hoped for liberation of Bohemia by Russian forces.)

In November 1915, Czechoslovak exiles, with Masaryk at their head, formed a Czechoslovak national committee in Paris. Earlier that year Habsburg South Slav politicians had set up their own Yugoslav Committee at Paris, hoping to create a greater south Slav state. They traveled to London and Washington, making their cases and connecting with political leaders as well as the huge émigré populations in the United States. When Russia left the war after the revolutions in 1917, the Entente powers took Habsburg Slavs and South Slavs seriously as a force that might counter Austrian and German power in the east. By now Czech forces were fighting in Russia in full legions, and the Serb army, locked down in Greece, was waiting for the anticipated collapse of Habsburg and Bulgarian forces on the Balkan peninsula.

Though it went unremarked at the time, there was something extraordinary about the founding of these two committees. Masaryk, his lieutenant Edvard Beneš, and dozens of men who conspired against the monarchy from Paris, as well as their ancestors going back hundreds of years, had known nothing other than Habsburg rule. Yet within months of the outbreak of a life-or-death struggle, the émigrés had thrown away that allegiance for the sake of states that were wistful musings, grown out of the minds of two intellectuals who liked to chat over politics in the still-German city of Pest in the 1830s: Jan Kollár and Ljudevit Gaj. Only time would tell whether the entities that emerged after the fighting—Czechoslovakia and Yugoslavia—would command more loyalty than the old monarchy.

Among Czechs, Habsburg loyalty had not translated into satisfaction, and any legitimacy they accorded the monarchy was provisional. It had secured moderate economic growth and significant cultural autonomy, but those things resulted from intense social and national struggle rather than the leaders' intentions let alone good will. From the 1820s, Czechs had extracted each advance in the cultural realm in the face of gratuitous condescension and at times severe opposition. They had only to look at Hungary to see how much more secure their existence would be if they controlled territory of their own, and that is why autonomy had been a non-negotiable demand for Czech parties from right to left for decades.[51]

No larger sense of community connected the Habsburg nationalities, even within the monarchy's regional components, such as Bohemia, or now, Bosnia. Historians have tried to personalize the blame for the failure. "In single-minded pursuit of [a] particular interest," writes William McCagg, the region's national elites "lamed and devoured the imperial power that still protected them."[52] But it's unfair to limit these accusations to nationalist elites: even those in the monarchy's leadership who stood proudly above nations were obsessed by the national question, from within and from without. The two dimensions were inseparable and were the source of their anxieties. Whatever the monarchy was, it was not a cause and was unable to tap the wells of commitment that sustained nationalism or socialism. The monarchy was like a landscape or a mood, a pleasing backdrop one might feel nostalgia for once it was gone; more practically, it was a regional peacekeeper, in Palacký's words, a state "that would have to be created if it did not exist," akin to a UN peacekeeping mission. It was something to kill for but not to die for, and the more dying it demanded, the more clearly its days were numbered.

PART III

Independent Eastern Europe

CHAPTER 12

1919: A New Europe and Its Old Problems

If the European revolutionaries of 1848/1849 aspired to break with an old world governed by monarchs, those of 1917/1918 actually succeeded. From Berlin and Vienna, Budapest and Warsaw, to Moscow and beyond, representatives of the "people" pushed aside the rule of kings, princes, and lords, and in a few months, the map of Eastern and Central Europe was populated by states never before seen. At the same time, however, a new kind of divide emerged on the political left to confound this first-ever mass experiment in democratization.

Two generations earlier, those favoring "rule of the people" had been liberals, with those on the left advocating full manhood suffrage, while those in the center wanted voting restricted to male adults with education and property. By now the landscape had shifted. Liberalism as an avowed form of political commitment had receded, and Central and Eastern Europe witnessed the proliferation of successors more and less dedicated to liberal principles. The largest were the social democrats, mostly in the tradition of Marx, but there were also national democrats; national socialists; Christian socialists; and a variety of peasant parties, called people's parties in some Catholic areas, Agrarians in Bohemia, Piast in Galicia, and Radicals in Serbia. At the end of World War I, a major divide in politics opened up in social democracy. Social democrats on the center and right advocated cooperation with other forces to build parliamentary democracy, but on the far left, forces emerged—called Communists— that wanted to seize power in the name of socialist revolution and smash the bourgeois state. The best-known theaters where forces on the two sides of this divide contested power were Russia and Germany.

In the spring of 1917, Russian women, and then workers and soldiers, crowded the streets of Petrograd to demand peace and bread. Despite police and army units shooting live ammunition and killing hundreds, the crowds grew, occupying the city center, and within days, the monarch abdicated, and liberal and socialist politicians created a provisional government that anticipated national elections. At the same time, workers and soldiers picked up organizational forms left from the 1905 Revolution, most fatefully, the grass-roots councils (soviets) movement, in which workers and soldiers elected their own representatives in factories, military units, and towns. Within Russian Social Democracy, the moderate forces (the Mensheviks) were the majority, but there was a radical left revolutionary group whose leader, Lenin, believed that the world war had pushed Europe to the verge of socialist revolution, and he would brook no cooperation with "bourgeois" forms of rule. His followers (the Bolsheviks) held majorities in several city soviets and were popular among soldiers and many peasants.

The Russian government, under pressure from its Entente allies, continued to prosecute an unwinnable war despite huge losses, and through the spring and summer of 1917, casualty lists grew and the supply situation in the cities worsened, so that the mood of the population continued to radicalize. In the fall, after an attempted coup from the right was put down by workers and soldiers, Lenin and his Bolsheviks found power "lying in the streets," and with left-wing peasant radicals, they seized power in the name of socialist revolution. In January 1918, they closed down the recently elected liberal constituent assembly, where they were a minority (yet by now Bolsheviks were a majority among Russian Social Democrats), consigning "bourgeois" parliamentary democracy to the "dustbin of history." Yet Russia was an agricultural county, with 85 percent of the population working the land, often by primitive methods, at far below the level of economic development Marxists considered necessary for the transition to socialism to succeed. Many from right to left believed the radical socialist revolution in Russia would fail if it did not connect to revolutions in the industrialized West.[1]

The German revolutions broke out in the fall of 1918, when civil war was in full force in Russia, with the Bolsheviks struggling to survive against white Russian and foreign armies. In October, against a regime that had been profligately sacrificing their lives for more than four years, German sailors and soldiers mutinied, and with workers, they began forming councils (*Räte*), forms of direct democracy like the soviets, meant to effect the transition from the old regime to democracy. In November, the monarch fled, and within hours, Social Democratic politicians Phillip Scheidemann and Karl Liebknecht proclaimed republics: one democratic and German, the other socialist. The former was meant to be a parliamentary democracy representing the will of the people and based on liberal institutions, the latter a socialist democracy that would break with the bourgeois order by smashing it. In December, representatives of the councils from across Germany met in Berlin and voted 400 to 50 for the former option.

The German working class was mostly not interested in a violent overthrow of the capitalist order. However, radicalized workers and soldiers in Berlin staged their own upheaval in January 1919, and the newly founded Communist Party of Germany, an offshoot from the far left of the Social Democratic Party, decided to support it. The mainstream Social Democrats were in charge of the caretaker government until elections could take place, and leaders Friedrich Ebert and Gustav Noske called on the army to quell the uprising, which it accomplished rapidly and brutally, using artillery and heavy machine guns. Their right-wing allies hunted down Communist leaders and executed the two most prominent, Rosa Luxemburg and Karl Liebknecht, in mid-January. For the time being, Bolshevik-style rule was banished from Germany, but German Communism remained a potent force, far from spent, and its supporters were deeply alienated from their one-time comrades among the Social Democrats.

By early 1919, the lands between Russia and Germany were engulfed in their own complex revolutionary transformations, which historians have underrated because these changes were republican, nationalist, mostly peaceful and based in liberal principles rather than communist and violent.[2] But they featured high drama, and for both Germany and Russia, and for Europe as a whole, the fates of revolution—whether liberal, communist, or otherwise—were decided here.

For Communists, the reason was obvious. Any bridge from their revolution in Russia to the workers' revolutions they expected in more developed Central and Western Europe would run through one of two places: the plains of Poland toward Berlin and Saxony, or the Hungarian basin toward Vienna and northern Italy. The Bolsheviks believed that radical socialist revolution would break out at any moment because the peoples of Poland and the Habsburg monarchy seemed to be following the script they themselves knew from Petrograd and Moscow: mass slaughter and starvation brought on by a pointless war followed by strikes and mutinies, then by the formation of workers' and soldiers' councils in places like Budapest or Vienna. At two moments in 1919 and 1920, the Red Army stood on the verge of connecting with radical left forces in Hungary as well as Poland, and it came close to military victory. In the summer of 1920, diplomats were evacuating Warsaw in anticipation of the storm of Red Cavalry that had descended on the city from Kiev and other points east.

Because of the return of hundreds of thousands of Austro-Hungarian and German soldiers who had been prisoners of war in Russia, Western observers for their part worried about the spread of Bolshevik ideas and practices into Central and Eastern Europe as a whole; it had been fear of Bolshevism and its violence and disorder that had caused the mainstream German social democrats under Ebert and Scheidemann to band with right-wing forces in the German military against their own Communists. In some ways, the fears seemed excessive, in others, not. Social democracy was the strongest political force in much of Eastern Europe, and the question was: would it generate the same split between center and left that we saw in Russia and Germany, and how strong would the new Communist parties become?

In Eastern Europe, the national question was of paramount importance, much stronger than in Russia, but it was the Bolshevik leader Vladimir I. Lenin who had best articulated the basic demand. In 1916 he stood up for the rights of oppressed nationalities to "self-determination."[3] Yet he did so to shatter the bourgeois order by drawing support from the many nationalities oppressed by the tsarist regime, and not from any attachment to nationalism, great Russian or otherwise. Indeed, at peace negotiations with the Central Powers at Brest-Litovsk in March 1918, he was willing to sacrifice vast expanses of land that had belonged to Russia for generations because he hoped to gain peace for the socialist revolution he had launched.

By invoking national self-determination, Lenin put pressure on the West to respond. In December 1917, Commissar for Foreign Affairs Leon Trotsky taunted Russia's allies, asking whether they, like the Bolsheviks, would promise self-rule to the peoples of Galicia, Poznania, Bohemia, and South Slavonia, as Russia had to the peoples of Finland and Ukraine.[4] The response was not long in coming. In early January, British Prime Minister David Lloyd George lambasted Austria for failing to recognize the autonomy of subject nationalities and emphasized that "government with the consent of the governed must be the basis of any territorial settlement in this war." The Austro-Hungarian "nationalities" must be guaranteed "genuine self-government," and an independent Poland must be created "comprising all those genuinely Polish elements who wish to form it." In his Fourteen Points speech delivered to the US Congress on January 8, Woodrow Wilson also demanded an independent Poland and advocated the autonomous development of the peoples of Austria-Hungary.

Wilson meant something very different from Lenin by "rule of the people." Wilson's nationalism was resolutely liberal, and his idea of national self-determination involved governance through parliament, rule of law, and free elections. He told Congress that "governments derive their just power from consent of the governed." But who were the governed?[5] This Wilson did not say, and though he had studied the problems of Habsburg politics as far back as the 1880s, the US president did not specify what "oppressed peoples" in East Central Europe he hoped to liberate, let alone what boundaries might be drawn to separate them into new national states.[6]

For both Lenin and Wilson, the promise of national self-determination was also tied to an ideology of international peace, though in different ways. Socialist revolution would efface the differences across peoples, ending the basic sources of human conflict by making the means of production social property. Wars were the result of capitalist conflict over markets. But liberal democracy, peoples governing themselves, would also make war unthinkable, because peoples had no interest in oppressing, let alone killing, one another. One peace activist, the Swedish diplomat August Schvan, expressed the point well in 1915: "With the principle of nationality—that is, the right of every nationality to govern itself as it thinks best—only those will quarrel who want to exert dominance over alien nationalities." In 1919 Wilson told the Paris Conference that if the peacemakers failed to satisfy peoples' wishes for self-rule, then no arrangement they made could guarantee the peace of the world.[7]

Eroding Habsburg Authority

Despite wartime censorship, the words *national self-determination* reverberated across Eastern Europe in 1917 and 1918, and with one exception, the hopes they awakened led to a victory of liberal over socialist revolution. Yet in that one exceptional case where socialist revolution briefly rose ascendant—in Hungary—it was because Lenin's radical socialism seemed to better embody the promise of nationalism than did Wilson's liberalism.

Wilson's promises were so well known that the German and Austro-Hungarian governments invoked them when suing for peace in the fall of 1918, even though still led by monarchs. Wilson had advocated peace without victors, meaning that everyone would have a place in the postwar settlement, and he had spoken of autonomous development of peoples in Austria-Hungary, which seemed to imply that the Habsburg monarchy might continue. But in his response of October 18, Wilson informed Austria-Hungary that events had shifted the playing field since his Fourteen Points speech to the US Congress in January. In the meantime, the US government had recognized a "Czecho-Slovak committee" as an allied government—its Czechoslovak legions were fighting for the Entente in Russia and France—and the United States had also advocated "the nationalistic aspirations of the Jugo-Slavs for freedom." Therefore, the representatives of these peoples had to be the judges "of what action on the part of the Austro-Hungarian Government will satisfy their aspirations and their conception of their rights and destiny as members of the family of nations."[8]

Wilson inspired Czechoslovak and Yugoslav nationalists, but he did not make them. The Czechoslovak National Council had commenced work in 1915, when Czech and Slovak politicians escaped the Habsburg lands and crossed into enemy territories, especially to France, in order to agitate for independence in Western capitals. Its leader was Tomáš G. Masaryk, who collaborated with Edvard Beneš, a professor of sociology and cunning diplomat, as well as the Slovak astronomer and fighter pilot Milan Štefánik (his life was cut short in a plane crash in May 1919). Also in 1915, Habsburg South Slavs established a lobby group of their own at Paris, the Yugoslav Committee. Their members, Croats and Serbs, had worked together against the denationalizing policies of Hungary and built on traditions of Illyrianism. The major figure was the capable editor Frano Supilo, who did not live to witness the new state's promises: he died in 1917 from a nervous breakdown suffered after years of struggle in Habsburg Croatia and fresh worries that the new Yugoslav state would be controlled by Belgrade.[9]

Polish émigrés also agitated for a national state, and like Yugoslav and Czechoslovak counterparts, they set up offices in Paris and made their case in Great Britain, the United States, and Japan. Prominent were the radical nationalist and author Roman Dmowski and the virtuoso pianist Ignacy Paderewski, a political moderate famed for his flowing hair and excellent connections to the political and social elites in the West. The *Endek* leader Dmowski, though brilliant and multilingual, never attempted to hide his ethnic fanaticism and made Western diplomats wary of Polish appetites for territory in the huge spaces between Germany and Russia that suddenly had no fixed borders.

No one had elected these men but themselves, yet they incorporated the basic desires for autonomy of the political classes back home, of Czechs in Bohemia, Serbs in Hungary, Croats in Dalmatia, and Poles in all three partition zones. If even the most radical among them—for example, the Czech Nationalist Karel Kramář—had failed to clamor for independence before 1914, that was because complete separation from the monarchy had seemed unrealistic, and Hungary demonstrated after 1867 that autonomy under Habsburg rule was possible.

But decisions of the Entente stretching back to early in the war, long before the pronouncements of Lloyd George and Woodrow Wilson, had gradually begun placing the monarchy and its integrity in jeopardy. British and French representatives had lured Italy (1915) and Romania (1916) over to their side with secret treaties promising tracts of Habsburg territory in Dalmatia, Istria, Trieste, the South Tirol, Bukovina, Transylvania, and the Banat of Temesvar.[10] In

December 1916, the Entente had expressed the desire for the liberation of "Slavs, Romanians and Czecho-Slovaks from foreign domination." Those words implied support for a radical reorganization of the monarchy because "Czecho-Slovaks" lived on two sides of the divide between Austria and Hungary. In the spring of 1918, the Entente, now including the United States, definitively pledged itself to Czechoslovak and Polish independence.[11]

Habsburg subjects were overwhelmingly loyal into that final year of the war. Direct enthusiasm for the war was greatest among Germans and Hungarians, but the death rates among some Slavic groups (for example, Slovenes and Croats) were well above average. From the late summer of 1914, numerous battles saw Poles from Austria facing Poles from Russia, or Serbs from Hungary opposing those of the Kingdom of Serbia. Some in the imperial army feared disloyalty and desertion of Habsburg Italian and Romanian troops when Italy and Romania joined the Entente in 1915 and 1916, but those who remained at the front proved as reliable as other troops.[12]

Yet the Entente's strategy was not simply military: it used a British naval blockade in the North Sea to cut off food supplies and starve the Central Powers into submission. In German-occupied Central Poland, the price index rose sevenfold during the war, and Poles, along with Slovaks and Czechs, saw their best foodstuffs sent to Germany.[13] They endured rationing from early in the war and after 1916 got little real bread due to a shortage of flour. In the winters, fruits and vegetables were almost impossible to come by.

By 1917 the collapse of living standards combined with unending casualty lists to raise questions that had once seemed theoretical: whose interest did Austria-Hungary serve? The war's purpose had been to crush Serbia, but that agenda had also generated anti-Slavic hysteria in the Habsburg lands, extending from Bosnia and Croatia into quiet Slovenia, and Bohemia, where police offices were flooded with denunciations of South Slavs, and authorities put national politicians behind bars under wartime emergency decrees for supposed sedition. During the war, Habsburg authorities had executed an estimated 50,000 Ukrainians, Czechs, Serbs, and Slovenes as "enemies of the state." Even harmless displays of national spirit, for example, the singing of Czech songs in army regiments, could bring the death penalty.[14] Whatever the war was about, it was not about furthering Czech or South Slav rights in any real sense of that term: obsessive fears of Slavic nationalism had led imperial authorities to trounce the civil liberties of citizens who happened to be Slavic. Neither Germans nor Hungarians were suspected of sabotage purely on the basis of their ethnicity.

FIGURE 12.1. Czech boys making ammunition for Austria-Hungary.
Source: Czech National Archive, Fotoarchiv Ústavu marxismu–leninismu
(NAD 1347), Inv. Nr. 13 882.

Francis Joseph died in 1916, and his successor, Charles, took a more moderate approach, releasing nationalist politicians from prison and relaxing censorship. He even entered secret negotiations through his Belgian brother-in-law to end the war. But he only succeeded in heightening expectations. In May 1917, a union of Czech parties in Bohemia called for a transformation of the monarchy into a federation because the dualist form of government had produced an unholy mixture of subject and dominant nationalities. In a little-noticed but revolutionary move, they based their demand not simply on the rights of the Bohemian crown, but also on the natural rights of nations to self-rule. Slovene representatives demanded the unification of all lands inhabited by Slovenes, Croats, and Serbs in the monarchy into one autonomous state, free from foreign domination but under the scepter of the Habsburg dynasty.[15]

Yet from the early months of 1918, hopes faded that the dynasty might be transformed into a free union of peoples. In April, the French government made public the efforts Charles had made for peace the previous year, forcing him to make a denial that no one believed, and then to offer a humiliating personal apology to William II in Berlin. The German grip on Austria-Hungary's fortunes, already tight, was now inescapable. To Slavic politicians, it was clear that victory for the Central powers would herald the rise of *Mitteleuropa*, a space from the Rhine to Russia and the Bosporus controlled by Berlin. A new sense of desperation opened them to more revolutionary thoughts. "The Slavic peoples," Austrian socialist Otto Bauer wrote in his *Austrian Revolution*, "bore a double burden of the sacrifices of blood and possessions brought on by the war. The sacrifices seemed for a foreign country, and a foreign cause. The longer the war lasted, the more the national revolutionary movement against Austria gained in strength." A dominant Austria now meant German domination, and in the historic memory of Czechs and Slovenes, that meant the power not just of German officials but also of German financiers and bosses.[16]

In the mass meetings and demonstrations that now gained strength, social and national demands became inseparable. On May 1, 1918, 100,000 people occupied central Prague, demanding national freedom and expropriation of capitalist property. In defiance of Austrian rule, representatives of "oppressed nations"—Czechs, Poles, Romanians, South Slavs, Slovaks, and Italians—met at Prague's National Theater and pledged that their peoples would "arise on the basis of national self-determination to new life in their own independent states." In Rome, a similar grouping declared the Habsburg monarchy an "instrument of Germanic domination and the fundamental obstacle to the realization of their aspirations and rights." Protesters in Slovakia demanded "unconditional recognition of the right to self-determination of all nations."[17]

From the beginning of the year, hundreds of thousands of workers in Austria had been demonstrating and striking for peace, and the unrest spilled over into Moravia and Hungary. The government sent in troops from the front to quash the protests, but increasingly, soldiers mutinied, from Austria and Hungary and into Poland as well as occupied Serbia, where on June 2, authorities had forty-four Slovak soldiers executed in one desperate display of repression. Such acts intensified the unrest, and the army continued to disintegrate. Numerous Polish units deserted, including a brigade under General Józef Haller, while attempts by Czech troops to evade service at the front were crushed in blood.[18]

In mid-June, Austria called off its last woeful offensive in Italy after only a week, with losses totaling 140,000 wounded and dead or missing, and by the late summer, Germany's armies were exhausted after a series of massive but pointless offensives in the west and were being pushed back to their own frontiers. Ten thousand US troops were landing in Europe every day, and the Central Powers could not win.

Yet the last leaders of Austria-Hungary carried on, refusing to consider autonomy for Slavic peoples. Minister President Ernst Seidler von Feuchtenegg said in July 1918 that the "the German people are today the backbone of this polymorphic state and they will remain so." He dusted off plans to create nationally homogeneous subdistricts in Bohemia that Czechs had rejected a generation earlier—just as he was releasing Czech nationalists from jail in efforts to appease the Czech movement. He tried to gain food from Ukraine by promising to place territories claimed by Poland (the Chełm region) under Ukrainian control, thereby unleashing massive protests in Polish towns.[19] Elites in Galicia withdrew their cooperation, making Habsburg rule in Poland untenable, and Polish patriots staged demonstrations across the map. Poles had patiently endured scarcity for years, but the prospect of sacrificing lands that had belonged to a long defunct Polish state—lands now ethnically Ukrainian—now brought them onto the streets. Seidler von Feuchtenegg was forced to resign.

The Magyar political boss István Tisza was saying as late as September that there would never be "trialism" in Austria Hungary; in other words, Magyar-German dualism would last forever with no representation for Slavs. In October, when the front was broken open by the Serb-French-Greek push in the south, Austria's last Minister President Hussarek von Heinlein presented a proposal for federalism limited to Cisleithania, that is, excluding Hungary (and with it, Slovakia). Nevertheless, Hungary's next-to-last premier Sándor Wekerle said such a reform would mean that Hungary was no longer bound to the 1867 compromise.[20]

The monarchy had long been beyond reform, and now it was beyond salvation. Therefore, it is misplaced to ask how and why the ancient Habsburg Empire suddenly "collapsed" in 1918. In fact, it self-destructed, unable to produce a structure that would satisfy its various components. It was replaced by entities that seemed to be based on living rather than on dead ideas.

New Liberal National States

Habsburg Emperor Charles promised autonomous development to the peoples of his realm on October 18, but few people were listening. The Balkan front no longer existed, and Entente troops were rushing north toward Croatia and Hungary. Political leaders in the Czech, Slovak, and Yugoslav lands began

FIGURE 12.2. Celebration of independence in Prague, October 28, 1918.
Source: Miroslav Honzík and Hana Honzíková, *Léta zkázy a naděje* (Prague, 1984), 187.
Via Wikimedia Commons.

establishing their own states, and peaceful handovers of power occurred in Kraków, Zagreb, Ljubljana, and Sarajevo. On October 28, Czech activists founded "Czechoslovakia" in Prague, and on November 10, the Polish leader Józef Piłsudski returned from imprisonment in Germany and assumed power in Warsaw the following day.[21] South Slav politicians from the Habsburg lands petitioned Serb King Peter for union, and on December 1, the Kingdom of Serbs, Croats, and Slovenes, later known as Yugoslavia, came into existence. That same day, Romanian delegates gathered in the Transylvanian city of Alba Iulia, and to mass acclamation, they voted to join the Romanian Kingdom, thus producing "Greater Romania." Earlier that year, Bessarabia and Bukovina, former Russian and Austrian areas with Romanian populations, had joined Romania.[22]

The Polish, Romanian, Czechoslovak, and Yugoslav Republics were new to the European political stage, but only the Czechs used the word "revolution" to describe what their activists were doing. They did not specify whether it was social or national, because it was both, realizing and contained within liberal principles. Suddenly Czech power dominated across Bohemia, freeing common people from the sense of bondage to German institutions and to the Austrian bureaucratic class. Karel Zmrhal (1888–1933), a moderate Czech Social Democrat, wrote that national [*národní*] revolution aimed at freedom from Habsburg absolutism as well as liberation from the "cruel oppression" of the German-Magyar capital. The Czechoslovak army was building a republic run by the people [*lidovlády*] and was mindful of demands for social justice.[23]

If they were related, social and national revolution moved at different speeds. The passage of social legislation took years, but in the meantime, there was much spadework being done for Czech culture. During a visit to Prague in 1868, Emperor Francis Josef had annoyed his hosts by saying the city had a German appearance, and over the following generation, Czech patriots tried to establish parity by massively settling in newer districts (Nusle) and placing bilingual signs in the city center. But that was not enough. The city had to be fully theirs. Now, as Habsburg power receded, Czechs reduced whatever was German to second-class status. An eyewitness described the scene in Prague on independence day, October 28: "All day long hundreds of people parade through the streets, and everywhere you see flags, banners, and standards, not only on the houses but also on people's hats, or the caps of the soldiers, even on the harnesses of the horses. They pulled the Austrian insignias from the caps of the officers, soldiers, letter carriers, and policemen. Some attempted to resist but quickly thought the better of it." Everywhere the Habsburg double eagle came down, and German words were painted over.[24]

Francis Josef had seen an early stage in evolution. What happened now was a breakthrough, a transformation as if from black and white to color, to Czech cultural domination, driven by sentiments that had proved stronger than bayonets. But the change was realized by the agents of administered revolution: uniformed police officers who had sworn loyalty to the emperor but now wore Czechoslovak insignias. Within hours of the declaration of Czechoslovak sovereignty, district "national committees" were taking power throughout the Czech lands in preparation for creation of a liberal Czechoslovak constitutional order.[25]

Ostensibly, that new order had deep roots. Masaryk and his followers had been propagating a cult of heroes from the deep past: the proto-Protestant Jan Hus, Czech enlighteners like Comenius. They claimed to summon the ancient

FIGURE 12.3. Symbolic funeral of the Habsburg monarchy in Czech town (1918).
Source: CTK/Alamy Stock Photo.

Czech heritage "of peace and freedom." Although the nationalist claim for Bohemian state's rights had attached political claims to the old Kingdom of Bohemia, Czech patriots of 1918 did not claim to be restoring a kingdom. *Czechoslovakia* of course included every inch of that old kingdom and claimed to embody all its positive legacies, but it was a republic, with the mission of moving Central Europe to a higher stage, from dark prejudice to popular self-determination. Yet it also included millions of Slovaks, whom no one had asked whether they wanted to belong. They had a new destiny: to become part of the people of the new state, the Czechoslovaks.

Among East European statesmen, T. G. Masaryk came closest to Wilson's liberal political idealism. The two men's faith in the upward development of humanity later caused the philosopher Karl Popper to criticize them for believing things that could not be demonstrated. But Masaryk also spoke in tune with Wilson because he knew the American scene from his Brooklyn-born wife; he was the only East European statesman to make knowledgeable references to US history. In Chicago, Pittsburgh, and other cities, he had assured audiences that the Czechoslovaks were simply replicating the principles on which the

American system was based. Wilson and Masaryk also harmonized as professors who spoke a reasoned language, and they patiently explained that rule by the people would guarantee peace.

Perhaps the word "revolution" seemed appropriate to the Czechs because the effect of reducing the national enemy was immediately obvious in a way not paralleled elsewhere. In Poland, Russian power had been political and cultural but not economic (that is, not clearly associated with the upper classes). And by the fall of 1918, Russian power was a distant memory because German armies had expelled the Russians from Central Poland three years earlier.

But those who witnessed events in Poland in those days could not help being impressed by the energies mobilized, even if they did not call them "revolutionary." On October 31, Polish troops took over military buildings in Kraków without loss of life, and within two days were raising red-white flags on state buildings throughout West Galicia. Farther north, on November 10, just as the Kaiser was fleeing Germany, Piłsudski's train pulled into Warsaw. Soberly appreciating the new balance of power, German storm troopers abandoned their posts and often left their weapons in the hands of high school students. Poles called these events "rebirth" or "regaining independence." With the props of injustice removed, Russia and Austria-Hungary "collapsed" and "dissolved." Imperial Germany was "crushed."[26] Yet the disappearance of a state that had ruled the Polish lands for generations usually involved one bureaucrat handing keys over to another.

Poles from several armies now became one and inducted new cohorts of young men. Within three days, the old Kingdom of Poland was cleared up to the Bug River.[27] Administrators followed, replacing German signs with Polish ones. Yet not all Polish-speakers were equally enthusiastic. The intelligentsia, artisans, and students supplied huge contingents for the new army, while in rural areas, whole villages held back their young men. To some on the far left, the revolutionary task of the new army seemed counterrevolutionary: it was to halt the Red Army as it advanced on Warsaw in the summer of 1920. Bolshevik revolutionaries in Moscow were astounded to learn that Polish workers, even socialists, placed national above international class solidarity.

Hungary's Failed Social-National Revolution

Yet by 1920, the most promising chance for radical socialist revolution to spread westward had already been squandered, thanks to the victory of counterrevolutionary forces in Hungary that were supported by Romania and the Entente.

As in Russia, developments there had started out more or less true to the expectations of Marxist theory. In February 1917, women, soldiers, and workers had ousted an autocrat in Petrograd, and in the fall of 1918, women, soldiers, and workers brought down the monarchical order in Budapest and created a republic. In both cases, history accelerated, and centrist governments hoping to create liberal order could not hold.

Hungarians called the peaceful transfer of power of October 1918 the "Chrysanthemum" revolution for the flowers worn by soldiers who joined citizens in the streets of Budapest to assert popular sovereignty. Plans were made for a new democratic constitution, and the liberal Mihály Károlyi, scion of one of Hungary's great aristocratic families, was appointed caretaker of the transition. Yet in March 1919, his government was handed a note ordering Hungarian troops to withdraw not simply from eastern and northern territories with Romanian or Slovak populations but also from areas on the eastern edge of the Hungarian plain with cohesive Magyar populations. The demand shattered faith in the good will of the Entente. Károlyi's liberal minister for nationalities said "we felt not only defeated, dejected, and debauched but—far worse—psychologically swindled, betrayed, and bamboozled." The Russian Red Army was making good progress in Ukraine in these days, approaching the Carpathian Mountains.[28] Now that Wilsonianism had failed them, Hungarians wondered whether an alliance with Russia might secure territory that seemed as vital to Hungary as Devon or Yorkshire did to England.

Károlyi and his prime minister resigned, and power was grasped by the tiny Socialist Party, a coalition of left Social Democrats and Communists, who created a "Hungarian Councils Republic" on the Bolshevik model.[29] Many leaders were Austro-Hungarian soldiers who had fallen into Russian captivity and then sided with the Bolsheviks in the Russian Revolution. The new head of government, Béla Kun, a journalist in civilian life, had known Lenin personally. His coalition's willingness to drive Czechoslovaks out of Felvidék (Hungarian for "Slovakia") caused it to become popular deep into the ranks of peasants but also among members of the urban middle classes, whether they were Catholic, Protestant, Jewish, or atheist.

Yet made reckless by early successes, Béla Kun overreached, failing to absorb lessons from the Bolsheviks about the need to placate peasants when vying for power in an agrarian society. Where Lenin had promised land and turned a blind eye as Russian or Ukrainian villagers seized it in 1917 and 1918, Kun first gave Hungary's peasants land, then took it away. In the spring of 1919, his agents were forcing peasants to join collective farms. Hungary's radical socialists further

FIGURE 12.4. Béla Kun speaks to workers (1919). *Source*: SPUTNIK/Alamy Stock Photo.

alienated often-pious peasants by closing churches and imprisoning priests. But Kun also estranged urban dwellers by outlawing nonsocialist parties, excluding the "bourgeoisie" from voting, and promoting terror against class enemies.[30] And he wasted revolutionary energies by regulating all manner of detail, for example, the number of shirts and underwear a citizen of the Soviet Republic was authorized to own.[31]

When Czech and Romanian troops with Allied reinforcements pushed from the north and east in the summer of 1919, Hungarian forces were routed. Béla Kun and his comrades fled to Vienna, leaving their supporters to face "white terror": an orgy of killings and arrests presided over by the conservative former Habsburg Admiral Miklós Horthy. His new right-wing regime arrested more than 70,000 people suspected of supporting the Hungarian Soviet Republic and had some 5,000 executed.[32]

Many leaders of that republic had been Jewish, and the counterrevolution took on anti-Semitic overtones, so that the great majority of Jews who had nothing to do with radical socialism fell victim to pogroms that were all the more shocking because in Hungary, violence against Jews had been almost unknown since the late 1840s.[33] Pogroms were not limited to Hungary in these years, however. Farther north, anti-Jewish violence raged through eastern Poland at a time when political order was weak and Christian peasant populations gave credence to stories of Jewish support for Bolshevism. For more than two years, the emerging Polish state did little to protect Jews and their property; the total dead in an estimated 279 anti-Jewish riots probably exceeded 500. Farther east, in future Soviet territories, between 50,000 and 200,000 Jews lost their lives in attacks by White, Ukrainian, and Red forces.[34]

Though Admiral Horthy and his Prime Minister István Bethlen eventually restored order and security for Jews and other Hungarians, the prewar gentry-Jewish alliance, in which Hungarian nationalists welcomed Jewish support in expanding Magyar culture throughout the Hungarian crown lands, yielded to bigotry and envy in a much smaller state. Jews were accused of having undue influence in commerce and the professions, and the practice of welcoming Jews to take part in Magyar state building gave way to a "closed, exclusive nationalism" that attracted the sympathies of much of the intellectual class.[35]

The national had asserted itself over the social before and during the Hungarian Socialist revolution. If Hungarian workers and peasants rallied around the Communist Kun, it was because he promised to recover territory. And when he pushed through measures of rapid social transformation, threatening private property and civil liberties, he alienated workers and peasants as well as the middle classes. In the years that followed, governments across Eastern Europe drew their own lessons, outlawing Communist parties as subversive everywhere besides Czechoslovakia. For its part, the radical left learned to be vigilant against "counterrevolution." Admiral Horthy had shown what happened when the organized working class sacrificed power: not only massive violence against socialists, but also the wheel of history spinning backward.

Revolution from Abroad?

As Serb, Czech, and Romanian armies seized land in former territories of the Hungarian Kingdom like Slovakia and Transylvania, the populations of these areas witnessed national revolution being imported by bayonet rather than making it themselves. In 1924 the Slovak poet Ján Smrek wrote "there was no true revolution here: no barricades, no blood supersaturated air." "Freedom came to us almost in secret," he wrote, "a covert operation of our people beyond our borders, and fell into our laps as a ripe apple."[36] That explained why in the new Yugoslavia, Croats and Slovenes (or in the new Greater Romania, Transylvanian Romanians) did not later recall these events as national liberation, let alone revolution. They had watched from the sidewalk cafes of their towns as troops and administrators poured in from Bohemia, Serbia, and Romania. The latter two had simply expanded their borders.

What is astounding is how quickly the recognition dawned that the new "Yugoslav" and "Czechoslovak" peoples were semi-fictions. Before 1918, even patriotic Croats or Slovaks thought of Serbs or Czechs as "brother" peoples, with whom they might build a common state. Gavrilo Princip, celebrated in our day as a Serb hero, called himself Yugoslav. Bosnian or Croat intellectuals likewise believed in Yugoslav unity. Scholars concurred—at least those favorable to the Slavic cause. Robert J. Kerner, a Harvard-trained historian who advised the US delegation at the Paris Peace Conference, said that the existence of a Yugoslav people was a "scientific" fact: "Croatia is virtually wholly Yugoslav," and the new state would be the fulfillment of the dreams of Croats, Serbs, and Bosnians. Kerner was a Chicago Czech, and his judgment as a scholar was colored by his encounters with T. G. Masaryk as a graduate student in Prague before the war.[37]

The Slovak nationalist Father Andrej Hlinka confessed to another member of the US delegation that he had told the Western Powers a few days after the Armistice, "we Slovaks are a part of the Czechoslovak race and we wished to live with them with equal rights in an independent state." Indeed, he had stumped for the new state from November 1918 to January 1919 and urged Catholic clergy to support it. But by the summer of 1919, witnessing the entry of Czech officials into Slovakia, he bitterly regretted his advocacy for Czechoslovakia. The "irreligious and free-thinking Czechs" were not the same people as his people. They were not even brothers. They regarded Slovakia "as a colony," he said, and treat "us as hewers of wood and drawers of water for their high mightiness of Prague." Hlinka's efforts in Paris to gain autonomy for Slovakia outraged Czech authorities, and on his return to Prague in October 1919, he was arrested. It was too late to alter the treaty of St. Germain, and Hlinka would be muzzled during the drafting of the Czechoslovak constitution, passed in 1920. On release from jail, he built a separatist movement that received more than a third of the votes of Slovaks in the 1925 election.[38]

A similar sobering was setting in among Habsburg South Slavs, who were discovering that they were not one people with the inhabitants of former Ottoman lands. In 1918, Serb forces had entered Bosnia, the once-Hungarian Bánát, Bačka, Syrmia (most of which they called "Vojvodina"), and Croatia, as well as Austrian Dalmatia and Slovenia. The Serbs called the campaign "unification" (*ujedinjenje*), the last stages of bringing all Serbs—that is, speakers of the Štovkavian dialect—into one kingdom. If Serbs tended not to speak of revolution that was because, like Poles, they were accomplishing a return to what was supposedly natural: the coming together of all Serbs, or, if one preferred,

"Yugoslavs." In the minds of Serb nationalists, those two words meant practically the same thing.

No one had asked Croats and Slovenes whether they wanted to belong to Yugoslavia. The Habsburg South Slav politicians who had traveled to Belgrade to ask admittance to the Serb Kingdom in December 1918 did not carry a popular mandate. They were intellectuals with little contact to the masses. There had never been proper suffrage in Hungarian-controlled Croatia, and no one knew how many Croats desired inclusion in Yugoslavia. As in Slovakia, enthusiasm gripped the population when Habsburg officials fled their posts in the fall of 1918. US diplomats reported in early 1919 that the "vast majority of Croatians" supported a united Yugoslavia.[39] But the mood quickly soured.

In March 1919, free and unfettered elections finally took place in Croatia, and Stjepan Radić's peasant party got a majority of the votes. He had been the one leader to caution Croat politicians eager to join Serbia, telling them before they went off to Belgrade in December 1918 that they were "rushing into the fog like drunken geese." After the March elections, Radić was arrested for publically demanding a republic.

What had gone wrong? Though the consummation of unity in the fall of 1918—made urgent by the collapse of Habsburg institutions—had indeed been rushed, Slavic intellectuals going back to Jan Kollár and his friend Ljudevit Gaj had been planning some kind of Czechoslovak and Yugoslav unity for generations, most recently in the committees created in Paris in 1915. Yet the men on these committees had not only debated and prepared the postwar orders, they also created facts on the ground, locking in decisions about state formation that bypassed the will of millions of East and Central Europeans. The members of these committees called themselves advocates of popular self-rule, in effect liberals, but they also feared that the new states might not stand a chance if their citizens were actually asked whether they wanted them.

And they also knew they could not form those states without the favor of the Allies. By July 1917, Russia had dropped out of the war, and the Entente wanted additional support in the east. It put pressure on the government of Serbia to receive a delegation of the Yugoslav Committee at Corfu, the Greek island where Serbia's king and his ministers had taken refuge after escaping the Austrian invasion of 1915. The Serb government had been keeping the Habsburg exiles at arm's length because it had its own ideas about the future, planning to expand Serbia's borders northward to embrace Bosnia and Herzegovina, but not Slovenia or areas of Croatia that were considered inassimilable (that is, beyond where the Štokavian dialect was spoken).

Now under pressure to act, above all from France, the Serb government and Habsburg South Slavs hastily agreed, on July 20, 1917, to form a Kingdom of Serbs, Croats, and Slovenes after the war. No one asked about the details of its organization. The Habsburg side favored decentralized rule, involving autonomy for Croatia, where the nobility had enjoyed special rights for centuries. But the Serb side imagined the expanded state as centrally organized because that was how one organized a strong, successful, modern state, the model being France.

Similarly, basic agreements were made about Czechoslovakia during the war years, far away from the would-be country's territory or population, by Czechs and Slovaks in exile, but also by Western statesmen. In 1915 representatives of Czechs and Slovaks in Cleveland agreed to form a common state, and in May 1918, Czechs, Slovaks, and Ruthenians gathered in Pittsburgh and agreed on the formation of the state of Czecho-Slovakia. The agreement said that Slovakia would have its own administration, parliament, and courts, and some Slovaks believed that implied autonomy. In October 1918, Tomáš G. Masaryk proclaimed Czechoslovakia's existence from Independence Hall in Philadelphia, and neither he nor his followers doubted that the state would be governed from Prague, just as France was governed from Paris.

Czech statesmen and their Slovak supporters were resolute on this point because they feared that anything short of unanimity might cost them support in Western capitals. They also worried about the dangerous examples that would be set by any talk of autonomy or regionalism. If Prague accorded the Slovaks self-rule, then demands for the same would pour in from Germans, Magyars, and Ruthenians.[40] Slovakia itself was highly heterogeneous, with Magyars dominating cities and the southern edge, and three large German "islands" in the west, center, and northeast. Some Slovak politicians hoped there might be a chance at a later date to negotiate the details of local rule, but in the meantime, they had to act to counter demands from Hungary. A new ideology of Czechoslovakism (of one people in two tribes) papered over doubts, and the constitution of 1920 referred to "a Czechoslovak" language. In practice, that meant that Czech administrators in Slovakia felt free to use Czech, which Slovaks understood almost perfectly. Yet by doing so they began grating on local sensitivities, creating a sense of differences that had never before existed, because the two peoples did not know each other.

Yet there was also a practical side to this "Czech imperialism." Because the Hungarian administration had stifled the development of Slovak elites for generations—in 1910, of 6,185 state officials at all levels in Slovakia, only 154 were Slovaks—educated and skilled Czechs were needed to build schools, create jobs, form the networks of cultural institutions, and simply run the state. For example, in the capital city of Bratislava (called Pozsony in Hungarian, Pressburg in German), as late as 1925 there were 420 Czechs to 281 Slovaks in the police directorate.[41] But the Czechs also exported condescension. Slovaks were a small population, foreign minister Beneš said, "insufficient to create a national culture on their own." Tomáš G. Masaryk, though his father was Slovak, insisted that

> there is no Slovak nation. That is the invention of Magyar propaganda. The Czechs and Slovaks are brothers. . . . Only cultural level separates them— the Czechs are more developed than the Slovaks, for the Magyars held them in systematic unawareness. We are founding Slovak schools.[42]

Uncomfortable facts were swept under the rug. Masaryk had attended the Pittsburgh agreement promising Slovaks some kind of autonomy, yet he failed to regard it as binding.[43] And when the constitution was drafted, representatives of the German, Polish, Magyar, and Ruthene communities—one-third of the new state's population—had no part in it. The Slovak delegates in the assembly were not elected but chosen by Vávro Šrobár, the Slovak chairman of the Czechoslovak National Council, a physician active in Slovak politics who happened to know Masaryk. Šrobár and the Slovak delegates came from the Protestant minority, which was more enthusiastic about union with the Czechs than was the Slovak Catholic majority. They assented to a centralized state because the largely illiterate Slovak population was not "mature" enough for local autonomy and also because the threat of a return of Magyar power seemed to necessitate close cooperation with the Czechs.[44]

Superficially, Transylvania had much in common with Slovakia and Croatia. Here, too, troops and administrators arrived from a neighboring kingdom (in this case, Romania) intent on swallowing new territories and including a population with whom they had never lived in a common state. But ultimately, the union succeeded without major problems.

Romanians in east and west shared the same language and alphabet, and for the most part, the same Orthodox religion, whereas beyond the basic Štokavian form of Serbo-Croatian which they happened to speak, most Croats and Serbs were separated by alphabet, religion, and regional language. Disputes lasted from the beginning to the end of Yugoslavia about whether Croat or Serb variants of the common tongue would be standard, and in our day, the separate states are cultivating what they call separate languages. In "Greater Romania," however, everyone took for granted that the standard Romanian language extended from Moldavia into Transylvania. And religion united rather than divided: in December 1919, Orthodox bishops from the old kingdom (the Regat) as well as Transylvania formed a common synod and elected the Transylvanian Miron Cristea as their leader. In 1925, he became the first Patriarch of the Romanian Orthodox Church.

Like counterparts elsewhere, the Romanian state-builders claimed that unity was natural; they were returning to the arrangement of 1600, when Michael the Brave acted as ruler of Transylvania, Wallachia, and Moldavia for several months. Their agenda of unity had been part of Romanian political discourse for generations, extending back to the 1840s, when one Transylvanian spoke of the stages in which transformation would be completed: democratic, social, and finally, national. Each stage depended on the others: without a social revolution in which they received land, peasants would remain slaves of a "few individuals." The new state responded quickly to this need by instituting the most radical land reform in Eastern Europe, aided by the convenient fact of land ownership by alien groups. In Transylvania, Romanian peasants got land that had belonged to Magyars and Germans.[45]

Romanianizing what had been Magyarized space proved the deepest source of common purpose for Romanians from the Regat and Transylvania. State administration as well as schools had to be made Romanian, and then schools had to be employed as vehicles of upward mobility for Transylvania's Romanian intelligentsia. A condition of becoming literate and professional was no longer becoming Magyar.

Yet a smoldering low-level dissatisfaction set in because the new state was ruled centrally from Bucharest. The December 1918 mass meeting at Alba Iulia had demanded inclusion in Romania but had also asked that Transylvania's rights be respected in a federal arrangement. Complaints soon multiplied that policy makers in Bucharest were not respecting this agreement, because, like counterparts in Belgrade, Prague, and Warsaw, they regarded the divisions of federalism as inadmissible.[46] Transylvanian Romanians felt in some ways they possessed a distinct and superior political culture, were proud of having drawn leaders from the common people and of supposedly belonging to a more honest and competent "Central European" civilization, whose practices stood in contrast to those of their theatrical and "Mediterranean" compatriots in the Regat. The Transylvanians also objected to the appointment of officials from across the border who had grade-school education at best, complained of acts of humiliation and persecution, and of previously unknown corruption. By the

1930s, the flooding of administrative posts with nonnatives caused locals to speak of "colonization."[47]

Still, these frictions were nothing compared to the alienation that Slovaks and Croats felt toward Czech and Serb supposed co-nationals. In addition to the fact that they combined regions that had never coexisted in common statehood, both Czechoslovakia and Yugoslavia were differentiated by wealth, with steep gradients running from east to west: in Czechoslovakia from largely illiterate Subcarpathian Ruthenia, through heavily Hungarian Košice and Bratislava, to wealthy and modern Brno and Prague; in Yugoslavia from poorer Kosovo, Bosnia, and Macedonia to richer Zagreb and still richer Ljubljana.

There were no easy solutions to the regional and ethnic disparities in wealth in the new states. Prague contributed mightily to Slovak educational infrastructure and other state institutions in Slovakia, yet Slovaks complained that foreign "colonial" exploitation kept them poor, thus demonstrating how subjective perceptions can overrule hard political and economic facts. Croats and Slovenes complained that their wealth was being diverted and drained to poorer sections of Yugoslavia and that it simply disappeared in a quagmire of corruption. Rather than encourage a national solidarity of sacrifice, economic differentiation helped prevent a broad national identity from forming in the first place. At the root of problems lay not wealth but perceptions of selfhood and foreignness, and the belief that "foreigners" were controlling one's own destiny. Yesterday it was the Magyars, today the Czechs (in Slovakia) or Serbs (in Croatia).

The persistence of differences in wealth by region reinforced existing stereotypes and contributed to new ones. Wealthier Czechs and Croats looked down on Slovaks and Serbs as indolent, while the latter saw the former as arrogant and soulless. Czech and Serb officials in the two states understood themselves as determined state builders from places where people got things done, improving on work done by previous generations in the now-victorious national movements.

Yet from the moment Serb officials entered Croatia, they gained a reputation for corruption and brutality. In a letter to his daughter from prison of May 17, 1919, Croat leader Stjepan Radić lamented the "beatings" carried out by Serb troops in areas liberated from Hungarian rule, and he said the corrupt system that was "shameful before the war is now catastrophic."[48] The "bashi bazouks" were doing to Croats what Hungarians had done to the Slovaks, but as supposed brothers of the Serbs, Croats could not complain. By contrast, what grated on Slovaks was not corruption but attitude: that Czechs did not treat them as equals, that Czechs decided on hiring, on staffing, and indeed on the structure of institutions created on Slovak territory. The result among Slovaks as well as Croats was a sense of not having a voice in their own affairs, and a creeping sense that democracy was not working; after all, democratic rule that was not for the nation was not self-determination, no matter how clean the institutional procedures. Many Slovaks and Croats became fodder for the right-wing populism of their day, having come to feel as strangers in their own land.[49]

Boundaries: Recasting Habsburg Europe

Czech and Serb state-builders did not draw the boundaries of their new states. For that they relied on the peacemakers in Paris, who imposed four treaties on the war's losers: the Treaty of Versailles for Germany, of Saint Germain-en-Laye for Austria, and Neuilly-sur-Seine for Bulgaria (all 1919), as well as Trianon for Hungary (1920). (These were named after the castles where the documents were signed.) Though never stated explicitly, the peacemakers settled boundaries using principles that were simple yet alien to Wilson's idealism: they rewarded victors and punished losers, using whatever superficial (yet supposedly profound) principle that could justify the decision at hand. Sometimes the principle was "historical," for example, that a particular region with a solid German majority had long belonged to the Czech crown. Sometimes it was ethnic: that the people of Transylvania "were" Romanian. But almost always, it was also strategic: Czechoslovakia, Poland, or Yugoslavia had to be large and strong as France's allies against Germany, even if that meant including foreign ethnics. By the same token, Germany, Hungary, Austria, and Bulgaria were to be weakened. As economist John Maynard Keynes noted, peacemakers became adept at conjuring high-sounding language to cover their real intentions. The Romanian Ion Brătianu, among the most profligate claimants of territories that were home to foreign nationals (usually Magyar), called the treaties "Wilsonian garlands around Napoleonic clauses."[50]

A special affront to ideals of national self-determination was the treatment of the rump of Austria after its supposedly Slavic and Italian lands had been shorn from it. What remained was an Alpine republic of 7 million people who considered themselves Germans and wanted to belong to the German national state. France vetoed the idea, because Germany could not grow as the result of a lost war. "Never has the substance of a treaty of peace so grossly betrayed the intentions which were said to have guided it," wrote an Austrian socialist newspaper, "every provision is permeated with ruthlessness and pitilessness, in which no breath of human sympathy can be detected." Yet instead of admitting that Austria was prohibited from uniting with Germany, article eighty of the Versailles treaty stated that "Germany acknowledges and will respect strictly the independence of Austria." This justification caused Keynes to call the treaty a product of the "subtlest sophisters and most hypocritical draftsmen."[51]

Where Habsburg Germans and Hungarians were concerned, the denial of self-determination was the rule rather than the exception and does much to explain why Adolf Hitler could successfully challenge the results of the peace treaties twenty years later, when he set his sights on destroying Czechoslovakia and Poland.

The major challenge in making the Czechoslovak borders was the German minority of almost 2.5 million in Bohemia. This group had been politically organized for generations, and its representatives voted for inclusion in German-Austria in the fall of 1918.[52] A glance at the map shows that most of these "Sudeten Germans" could easily have been included in a German state by simply moving the borders of Saxony, Bavaria, and Austria one or two dozen miles into Bohemian territory. (Such a resolution had been suggested as far back as the 1740s.) Yet various factors conspired against the Germans wanting to belong to Germany. Most prominent was the Czech insistence that Bohemia's crown lands retain their integrity as the quasi-divine realm of St. Wenceslaus. Although Czechoslovakia was a republic, the kingdom's ancient borders were beyond questioning. A more substantial reason was strategic: Bohemia's boundary areas coincided with hilly areas including the Sudeten Mountains and Bohemian Forest, and these areas provided a natural defensive shield. Czech diplomats further argued that Bohemia constituted a unit of production and commerce that had grown together over centuries and must be maintained for the sake of economic stability. That argument was made to seem less compelling when it came to the Habsburg monarchy, an enormous economic unit likewise of centuries' duration.

Masaryk and his secretary Edvard Beneš cagily added that it was in the Germans' own national interest that there be more rather than fewer of them in Czechoslovakia. If a simple border adjustment had been performed permitting two of the three million to go to the Reich, that would have increased the dangers of denationalization for the Germans who remained! Individual human beings had interests and rights, but these could be realized only within nations.

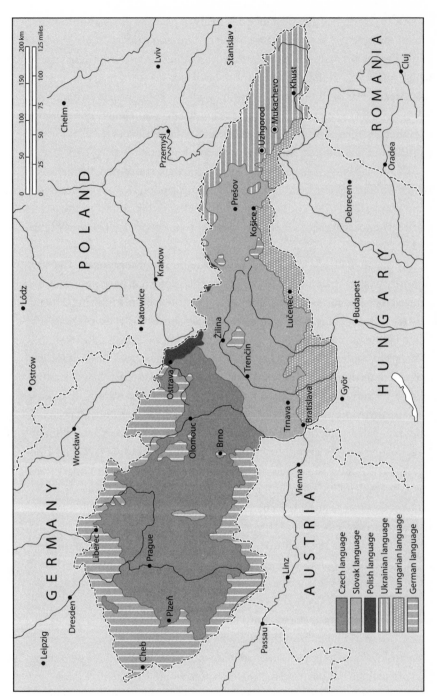

MAP 12.1. Interwar Czechoslovakia

Czech language

Slovak language

Polish language

Ukrainian language

Hungarian language

German language

When such arguments did not work, the new authorities used force: in March 1919, Czech soldiers shot dead fifty-two Germans demonstrating for the "autonomous development" that Woodrow Wilson had promised the "peoples of Austria Hungary" the previous year.[53]

The US delegation in Paris did little to oppose the Czechs' reasoning. Wilson had left his team in the dark about how to implement his vision, mystifying even Secretary of State Robert Lansing. "When the President talks of 'self-determination' what unit has he in mind? Does he mean a race, a territorial unit or a community," Lansing wondered.[54] Wilson's only recorded remarks on Bohemia's borders are irreducibly cryptic. On December 12, just before the USS Washington docked at Brest, France, escorted by ten battleships and twenty-eight destroyers, he said that "it would be too complicated to draw any new boundary in Bohemia, even though there is a clear line which could and should be drawn eliminating two million Germans from Czechoslovakia."[55] But why those borders should have seemed untouchable to Wilson at this point is unclear; as we will see, other ancient historical borders were vaporizing throughout the region, especially in Hungary.

What seems certain is that Wilson's own experts did little to apprise him of coming problems. Only one person on the 150-person fact-finding commission created by Wilson's advisor Edward M. House (the "Inquiry") knew Czech or anything about the Habsburg lands, and that was Robert J. Kerner. As we have seen, this later Berkeley professor was a Czech-American and hardly a neutral observer of Central European politics. When Masaryk went to lobby for the Czech cause at the Inquiry in 1918, he later recalled, Kerner was already working "on behalf of the Czechs." Kerner appears to have grossly underreported to his superiors the number of Germans living in Bohemia. When told their true number on the trip over to Europe, Wilson is reported to have exclaimed: "why, Masaryk never told me that!"[56]

In January 1919, the peacemakers created joint bodies of experts on the national question, and the chair on the Commission on Czechoslovak Affairs went to the skilled French diplomat, Jules Cambon, who was even more wedded to the inviolability of Bohemia's borders than were Masaryk, Beneš, or Kerner.[57] Beneš had been willing to consider corrections in favor of Germany, but Cambon feared that small adjustments might create a precedent for larger ones, and he gained assent that the basis for negotiation would be Bohemia's "historic boundaries." Even a single plebiscite in a "disputed fringe" would tempt German communities elsewhere in former Habsburg lands to demand one, and that would raise the specter of Germany being rewarded with territory despite its defeat.[58]

The trend of French policy was precisely the opposite: to weaken Germany and its former allies and make the new states of Eastern Europe strong bulwarks against the "Bolshevik poison." Thus, when setting borders farther east, in formerly Hungarian lands that now constituted Slovakia, French diplomats pressed for a boundary that went far to the south, as close as possible to a hilly region north of Budapest, deep into areas of solid Hungarian settlement. The following year, Czechoslovakia incorporated north Hungary down to the Danube, including a coherent block of 745,000 Magyars (more than 5 percent of the new state's population).[59] The French were more focused and consistent than US diplomats, who simply wanted the settlement to be "just." Indeed, if the ethnographic principle was already conceded to be malleable, why not make Czechoslovakia as big as possible?

A still larger group of Hungarians was lost to Hungary in 1918, when Romanian troops occupied Transylvania, territory promised to Bucharest in 1916 when it entered the war with the Entente. Like the Czechs, the Romanians took all they could get, incorporating territory to the west of the historic Transylvanian provincial boundary by simply occupying it. The Romanian liberal politician Ion I. C. Brătianu said his country needed the Tisza River as a protective boundary. Hungary was bound to lose hundreds of thousands in Transylvania proper in any case (it had a Romanian majority), but this relentless drive to push the boundary even farther into the Hungarian Plain again caused the sacrifice of large homogenous settlements of Hungarians.[60] The peace treaty imposed on Hungary in 1920 at Trianon left 3 million Hungarians outside their country, over half of whom lived in compact masses along the new borders.[61]

* * *

The Allies were deaf to all complaints. In the fall of 1918, the new Hungarian head of state, Mihaly Károlyi, had met with French General Louis Franchet d'Esperey, whose troops were helping secure the new boundaries. Franchet d'Esperey dashed all hopes of leniency, even when told that Károlyi represented a new, liberal Hungary. "I know your history," he said, "in your country you have oppressed those who are not Magyar. Now you have the Czechs, Slovaks, Romanians and Yugoslavs as enemies." Though Transylvania had been Hungarian since the eleventh century, no arguments prevailed against the ethnic one: Romanians claimed they had been in Transylvania even longer. It was the communication by the French in March 1919 that even areas with Magyar pre-dominance along a future border would be lost that caused Károlyi to resign, ceding power to the radical left, ultimately throwing back Hungarian democracy by decades and strengthening the Romanian hand at Paris, because Romanian forces served the Allied cause by crushing Kun's Soviet Republic. The French also allowed the Kingdom of Serbs, Croats, and Slovenes to take parts of the Banat with a heavy Hungarian presence as part of the province of Vojvodina.[62]

Only the Treaty of Versailles with Germany contained the obvious solution for dealing with contested territory: asking populations to which state they wanted to belong. The method was plebiscite, but even in the case of Germany it was employed only twice.[63]

In July 1920, inhabitants of much of East Prussia were asked whether they wanted to remain part of East Prussia, and more than 90 percent voted in the affirmative. Though a high percentage spoke a variant of Polish on an everyday basis, the territories had mostly not belonged to Poland since 1657.[64] The Polish side objected that Germans had great superiority in "propaganda," and, assuming Polish-speakers were Poles, said that the plebiscite contradicted the "nationality principle." Both sides admitted that Poland's fight with the Red Army near Warsaw at the time of the plebiscite caused voters to fear that the new Polish state would not last.

The situation was more complicated in Upper Silesia, an area that had not belonged to a Polish state since the fourteenth century; since then it had been under Czech, Habsburg, and Prussian/German rule. But the population, especially in the countryside, was Polish-speaking up to the borders of Lower Silesia (Brieg/Brzeg). The Polish side claimed the area based on nationality (language), but the region's majority (59.6 percent) voted on March 20, 1921, for Germany. Given strong Polish objections that the eastern zones were heavily Polish—backed up by three armed uprisings—the League did the reasonable thing and divided the territory (something permitted by the Versailles Treaty), giving the districts that had overwhelmingly voted for Poland to Poland. That was about a third of the total area. But the German side never became reconciled, arguing that the people's will had been violated, and that Germany had lost its second-strongest industrial region.

Polish foreign policy was in the hands of the onetime socialist Józef Piłsudski, who believed that borders in the east had to be settled by force of arms.[65] Yet, with the old Polish commonwealth in mind, he also thought that Poland needed to band with other nations to survive against German and Russian power.

FIGURE 12.5. Polish women's legion readying for the Bolshevik attack (August 1920).
Source: Agence Rol. Agence photographique 1920, from French National Library.

Therefore, in early 1920 he allied with the Ukrainian leader Symon Petliura and
led joint armies as far as Kiev, hoping to create a federation of nations—
Poland, Lithuania, Ukraine, and Belorussia. But he overextended his lines
and was hurled back upon Warsaw in the summer of 1920. Now it became
Piłsudski's turn to stage a rout, dispersing or destroying several Soviet armies
in a lightning-flanking maneuver. By September, the Bolsheviks sued for
peace, offering the Poles as much territory as they wanted in the east under
the condition that a halt to the fighting be called within ten days.[66]

In a peace conference at Riga the following year, Polish and Soviet negotiators divided territory, attaching eastern lands with the cities of Minsk and Kiev
to Soviet Belorussia and Ukraine, and making the remainder parts of Polish
voivodeships, including the east Galician city of Lwów/Lviv. Any hopes for federation with other nationalities in the east disappeared. Because the Polish
team was dominated by National Democrats, it applied a boundary desired by
Roman Dmowski and took much less territory than the Soviets made available,
for example, forgoing Minsk and abandoning Poland's Ukrainian ally Petliura.[67]
Yet Poland's eastern territories still contained millions of Belorussians and
Ukrainians, more than could be absorbed even by the most dedicated
Polonizers.

Ironically, Piłsudski had brought the kind of state into being that his rivals
desired: a Polish state by and for the Poles. The recognition troubled him; he
broke off his last conversation with Roman Dmowski in 1920 after the latter

taunted him: how can we take Lwów and occupy Eastern Galicia while at the same time claiming to support the desires of Ukrainians for a state that contains those very territories?[68] Similar contradictions in Piłsudski's actions applied to Lithuania. In October 1920, Polish general Lucjan Żeligowski seized the Lithuanian capital Wilno for Poland, thereby poisoning relations with Lithuania through the interwar years. But Żeligowski had acted with Piłsudski's unofficial blessing, even though Poland had promised the Allies to recognize Lithuanian sovereignty in Wilno.[69]

Thus the final outcome of this willy-nilly cooperation of supporters of Piłsudski and Dmowski was to create a Poland that frustrated both sides' ideas for Poland's development, whether domestically or internationally. Rather than form a regional alliance of small states, Poland stood alienated from neighbors small and large, within the boundaries of a miniature Habsburg Empire.[70] Boundary settling in the east had been a parade of illusion and deception. Piłsudski thought there could be a unity of small nations, never examining whether those nations agreed on the lines dividing their territories. When in doubt, he simply seized areas he regarded as Polish. Dmowski thought that a smaller Poland could absorb vast populations in the east, ignoring the fact that Austrian institutions had already provided for the spread of national consciousness among millions of Ukrainians in Galicia. And when the Soviet Union sued for peace, it was not sacrificing its long-term hope for global revolution; the Riga Treaty was never intended to be a permanent solution. It left Poland a "medium state situated between two giants"—Piłsudski's worst fear.[71]

The posters printed to stoke fears of the eastern menace used standard anti-Semitic images; some were directed at peasants otherwise hesitant to support the cause of Polish "lords." (That was the image used of Poland in Bolshevik propaganda). The Polish press was full of stories of Jews, especially in the east, siding with the Red Army, and of young Jewish men shirking service in Polish units. One rabbi was shot for supposedly telling the Bolsheviks about locations of Polish troops near Płock.[72] In fact, the attitudes of Poland's Jews toward the war varied as much as did attitudes of other groups in Poland. In central Poland, dozens of Jewish communities collected money for the defense of the country, and thousands of Jewish soldiers fought with Polish units until August 16, 1920, when the new Polish defense minister Sosnkowski ordered that all Jews be identified and removed from the ranks. Some 17,000 officers and men were interned at a camp in Jabłonna, and Jewish student volunteers were sent to labor battalions. This was the moment when the fortunes of battle were shifting in Poland's favor, and it was also a time when Polish soldiers were increasingly directing violence against Jews and their property. After peace and stability returned, Jews were again taken into the Polish army: in 1939, some 120,000 Jews fought with other Polish citizens against the German attack, about a fourth of whom lost their lives.[73]

On paper, the Allies supported the creation of a Ukrainian state. By the summer of 1919, Polish troops controlled most of Eastern Galicia.[74] The Allies knew that these territories had majority Ukrainian populations, and in June 1919, British Prime Minister Lloyd George and US President Wilson agreed that a plebiscite should be held; they referred the matter to the Council of Foreign Ministers, where opinions were divided. The French and Italians supported giving the territory to Poland; the British desired temporary Polish occupation followed by a plebiscite. The Americans suggested a compromise, granting Poland a mandate until the inhabitants could be asked what country they wanted to belong to.

Yet here again popular Polish opinion asserted itself, backed by the superior force of arms. Though the Polish representative, pianist Ignacy Jan Paderewski, accepted the American view, his countrymen were indignant about any reduction to Polish sovereignty; eastern Galicia was well within the Polish state that existed in 1772. In the end, the Allies agreed to grant Poland a twenty-five-year mandate, after which a plebiscite would be held. That, too, was unacceptable to the Poles, and in fact led to Paderewski's fall. (He resigned on December 9, 1919.) By that time, the US Senate had rejected the Treaty of Versailles, and the United States was no longer participating in the work of the conference. Less than two weeks later, the French and British suspended the decision on East Galicia, and it was never implemented.

The Ukrainians, the most numerous nationality between Germany and Russia, thus received no state at all. The Ukrainian national movement was much like the Czech one, aiming to create a modern nation representing a "nonhistoric" people that lived under foreign oppressors and had little history of statehood. The Ukrainians' national "awakening" took place about a generation after the Czech one. They also shared a problem with the Czechs: they occupied territory with other ethnic groups on it, above all, the Poles in Eastern Galicia. But they also faced the problem of living in lands claimed by Poland and Russia. West Ukrainian Lwów/Lviv was also an old Polish city (from 1349), while areas farther east counted as crucial to the early development of Russia. An old saying, repeated recently by Vladimir Putin, holds that Kiev is the "mother of Russian cities."[75]

Other large groups of Ukrainians (then known as Ruthenians) wound up in Czechoslovakia and Romania. The former ("sub-Carpathian Ruthenians") became Czechoslovak citizens because co-ethnics living in the United States had asked that all "Carpatho-Rusyns living South of the Carpathians" be adjoined to the Czechoslovak Republic, with guarantees of autonomy.[76] They were duly adjoined, but their autonomy was not respected.

* * *

The years after World War I witnessed the most momentous encounter between the New and Old Worlds going back to the fifteenth century. Stimulated by the French and German Enlightenment, but also by native concerns about subjugation by foreign powers, a series of national movements had emerged beginning in the late eighteenth century, all of which had one basic message: each nation should determine its own fate. In 1917, the US president, ignorant of these complex processes in lands distant from his own, began preaching what seemed to be the very same message to North Americans and Europeans: all civilized peoples should be free. He did not think his gospel would apply in the Middle East, Asia, or Africa.

Woodrow Wilson and his major ally in Eastern Europe, T. G. Masaryk, knew where their hopes and visions intersected, but the former had little inkling how the twinning of American ideas of people and East and Central European ideas of nation would produce explosive tension. Self-determination of the American people was not like the self-determination of the Czech or Czechoslovak people. The former implied equal citizenship for everyone in a given territory, the latter involved creating second-class citizenship for those on a given territory who did not belong to the ethnic "people." Czechoslovakia was for the Czechoslovaks, not the Germans. The latter were included only because they occupied territory that the Czechs wanted.

Despite guarantees of equality for all, Czechs and Slovaks could always use their language in state administration, no matter how weak their presence, yet Germans could insist on the use of German only when they had 20 percent or more in the smallest administrative district. Czech applicants were favored over German ones in the public sector.[77] In retrospect, we recognize that the Czech state accorded Sudeten Germans better treatment than any other ethnic minority in East Central Europe, but as the historian William John Rose noted at the time, they were still "far from enjoying the status they would have enjoyed on the right side of the frontier."[78] He might have added: and the superior status German-speakers had enjoyed in Bohemia for generations.

Of all the new leaders in the new East Central Europe, Masaryk was alone in pledging himself to higher principles of humanity, but in his mind those principles could only be realized through peoples, and in Bohemia, the Bohemians—the Czechs—were in charge. "We created our state," he said to the revolutionary national assembly in Prague in December 1918. "Thereby is determined the state-rights position of our Germans, who came to the country originally as emigrants and colonists." The "we" were Slavs, and the Germans were guests, to whom Masaryk assured "full equality." That was a gift, not a right. No matter how sincerely Masaryk invoked his noble principles, writes Roman Szporluk, "he never found a way to organize the new multinational state so that no one nationality had the ruling hand."[79]

In retrospect, federalism seemed the obvious solution for multinational Poland, Yugoslavia, Czechoslovakia, and perhaps Romania. Statehood, yes, but in flexible units that could take into account the interests of the nationalities concentrated in specific regions, such as the Ukrainians in Eastern Poland or the Germans in Western Bohemia. Give them say in matters of central concern: language, education, and culture. Don't let them feel at the mercy of the majority nation in economic and legal affairs. There were models for such arrangements in the plans for trialism that emerged in the late Habsburg empire, and in Bismarck's Germany, which had ceded significant rights to component parts, such as the Kingdoms of Saxony or Bavaria.

In the eyes of dominant nationalities, federalism seemed a scheme for strengthening national minorities, and inadvertently also national enemies. Understandably, newly constituted states wanted to be as strong as possible, and they eschewed the centrifugal forces of a decentralized government. Even liberals opposed federalism as compromising the power of democracy to transform polities.[80]

There were minority treaties, yet their object was to promote "gradual and painless assimilation."[81] But to speak of minorities is a bit misleading. An estimated 30–40 of 100 million Germans did not live in the German national state.[82] The numbers were imprecise and included non-European populations, but they signaled a problem: not only that many Germans considered Germany a *Volk ohne Raum*, but also that much of the *Volk* lived in foreign territory and acted as a force that corroded Europe's political architecture.

The problems that followed in the interwar years did not, however, derive from a Western imposition of ideas on the east; the postwar settlement was not a case of Wilson, the French, or the British imagining or inventing Eastern Europe. The East Europeans made their own revolutions, and they were everywhere of the national variety, and much like the new Germany, they featured liberal instiutions as well as a clear rejection of Bolshevism. The excesses of Bela Kun's revolution were embroidered and magnified, and every new state banned Communist parties, except one, Czechoslovakia, because banning Communism would have betrayed the state's commitment to liberal constitutional order.

Czechoslovakia's leaders, like counterparts elsewhere in the region, settled into adapting Wilson's (not Lenin's) ideas of national self-determination to their own needs, while telling Western leaders what they wanted to hear. The major problem the new nation states would face was the intermixing of the peoples they either purported to represent or whose existence they ignored. That was a general problem of the peace. In no case did the new states make arrangements for autonomous government for minorities, although devolved governance would have taken much of the sting out of living in a foreign state.

CHAPTER 13

The Failure of National
Self-Determination

The United States entered the Great War to make the world safe for democracy, and Western governments issued brochures hammering the message home: free self-government was the cause for which their young men were dying. But not much propaganda was needed to make the goal seem realistic. People everywhere assumed that once the oppression of the old kings and emperors was lifted, liberal democracy was the form of rule that would sprout up and thrive on its own.[1] Nations (meaning peoples) would finally rule themselves. The Allies told Germany and Austria there would be no negotiations to end the war until they became republics, yet the expectation was far more compelling for new states like Czechoslovakia, Poland, and Yugoslavia. Their only reason for existence was to realize self-rule for peoples who had never enjoyed this fundamental right.[2] They should have been hyperdemocracies, the most representative states ever seen.

A democratic order in the new states of Central and Eastern Europe, in turn, was tied to international peace. The oppressive Austro-Hungarian and German Empires had been led by potentates elected by no one, and they made secret treaties and launched wars that bore no relation to the interests of their peoples. Now, democratically elected states in Central and Eastern Europe would pursue peace because wars were not in the interests of any people; they would join an organized community of the responsibly governed nations of Western Europe as well as the rest of the global community.

The few western experts on the region foresaw no problems. One historian who stumped for the "new Central Europe" in London and Paris right after the war, the Canadian William John Rose, later professor at University College London, said that the old Danubian world had been a place of artificial loyalties and institutions. "The many peoples of Central Europe suffered the horrors of war unwillingly," he argued, "hating the things they had to fight and die for, all hoping and praying that the central empires would come down in ruin."[3] Rose had just managed to get out of Habsburg-controlled Silesia, where he had shared the hardships of the home front for three long war years. During that time, he had talked to dozens of Poles, Czechs, and Ukrainians, and he was sure of their desire for "freedom, the right to develop along the lines God meant for us."[4]

Democracy seemed the only option, and history knew no case where one had failed, because in 1919, democratization was an untried art. The spirit of the time stood against petty doubts. Carlton J. Hayes, later a leading historian of Europe at Columbia University, worked with Military Intelligence in the US General Staff during the Paris negotiations. From his many conversations with Europeans, he concluded that the human losses of the Great War had been "too prodigious" to allow the world to continue as it had been in 1914: it was "closing one era in human history and inaugurating another." The British-Belgian academic Charles Sarolea, a foremost authority on Europe and Asia, wrote that "after a thousand years of subjection the Slav today is at last coming into his racial inheritance." But among Romanians, too, enthusiasm for democracy ran high for the simple reason that two-thirds of the voters would now be peasants.[5] The new state simply had to be one that would agitate for the interests of most Romanians.

Sarolea, Rose, and Hayes knew there would be quarrels about borders, but these seemed trifles on the background of the world historical shift taking place. South Slavs desired unity, regardless of past differences; Czechs and Poles would "bury the hatchet" over disputes in Silesia; and Germans were supposedly reconciled to the new state of Czechoslovakia. In a vast region where the Habsburgs had ruled for centuries, few were shedding tears for the departing Austrian bureaucrats. The future was bright, with "malice toward none, with charity for all."[6] The war had taught Europeans that they must cooperate.

Rarely have hopes vested in political transformation been so thoroughly disappointed. After the appointment of Mussolini as prime minister of Italy in 1922, democracies began failing as if by a timetable. After Italy came Albania (1925); Poland and Lithuania (1926); Yugoslavia (1929); Germany and Austria (1933); Bulgaria, Estonia, and Latvia (1934); Greece (1935); and finally, Romania (1938). Hungary under Admiral Horthy had been a sham democracy since 1921, when lawmakers disenfranchised the rural population by imposing an open (rather than secret) ballot on the countryside and limiting the Social Democrats to urban areas. As a result, the government party ("Party of Unity" [1921–1932] and "Party of National Unity" [1932–1940]) never lost an election.[7] Democratic order survived longest in Czechoslovakia, up to September 1938, when Britain and France surrendered that country's fortified border regions to Hitler. When Hitler dispatched his troops to Prague the following

March, the failure of the postwar order was dramatically and catastrophically complete.

The major source of instability was the fact that several new states were not nation-states but miniature Habsburg empires: Poland, Czechoslovakia, Romania, and Yugoslavia all included millions of citizens who did not belong to the governing nation. That led to a proliferation of minority parties, which made stable coalition governments difficult to form, and it kept the region from cohering internationally. Rather than cooperate with neighbors, the new states tended to make claims on their territory. What united the "Little Entente" of Romania, Czechoslovakia, and Yugoslavia was joint defense against Hungary, whose government for its part endeavored to regain lands lost to these three countries at Trianon. Contrary to the hopes of French policy, no bloc of allies emerged among the new East European states, and in the 1930s, Germany deftly exploited the hypocrisies of the Paris peace order, in particular its denial of self-determination to Germans in Austria, Czechoslovakia, and Poland, in order to unmake those three states in a prelude to its genocidal programs of eastern colonization.

Still, Romanians, Czechs, and Poles still celebrate 1918 as launching national independence, and despite the failings of democratic rule, the postwar decade, before the Great Depression plunged Europe into deep economic crisis, marked the basic achievement of creating stable and mostly legal order in areas of great economic, legal, and cultural diversity.

And the region's experience of new nationhood was not uniform. Up and down we discern two patterns: on one hand, those miniature empires, Poland, Czechoslovakia, and Yugoslavia, all of which produced new constitutions and experimented with parliamentary rule, involving complex new peoples of state, with sets of political parties that had never before worked together. In Poland and Yugoslavia, the experiment was abandoned in 1926 and 1929, respectively, giving way to authoritarian rule, while in Czechoslovakia, it continued; the question is why these three cases differed. On the other hand, in Romania, Hungary, and Bulgaria, the basic constellations of government, including constitutions, were carried over from the pre-1918 period, and the nominally dominant "nation"—Romanians, Magyars, and Bulgarians—were far less threatened by challenges from minorities. The political spectrum was simpler, and so was the political story.

What united the entire region was the fact of much lower economic development than in Western Europe, reflected in low per capita income, high infant mortality, low rates of urbanization, and poor schooling. That last fact was especially problematic for state-builders because it was difficult to mobilize people who could not read or write. It caused the political scientist David Mitrany, originally from Romania, to point to the basic problem of transferring Western institutions to societies poorly prepared to receive them. The 1866 constitution in his native country was inspired by the liberal Belgian model, but it had failed to take into consideration the country's actual conditions. The bulk of Romanians, "being completely illiterate, could not realize the rights and duties imposed by the new organization. They had to rely for enlightenment upon the upper classes, and these did not fail to let the peasant know his duties, though conveniently omitting to explain his rights." Thus it was easy for the upper classes to manipulate elections to get the results they desired—despite a secret ballot. "The influence of the administration is so effective," Mitrany continued, "or the fear of it so great, that hardly any member of the Opposition would be elected at all but for the Government running no candidate in certain constituencies, so that it may not be deprived of a pro forma opposition."[8]

Still, these reflections, written in 1915, had not dampened Mitrany's enthusiasm for the postwar order, and for Romania's taking as much territory from Hungary as possible. Two years later he produced a brochure asserting Romanian claims to all the Habsburg and tsarist territories containing Romanians, with no concern about expanding a flawed political system to the new provinces. At stake was the very life of a weak European people, and he advised readers to consider the dangers that would accrue "from that misuse of power on the part of stronger peoples which results in the obstruction of the *natural* development of the weaker." By implication, non-Romanians in Transylvania did not belong there. What was unusual was not the view but its source: a founding thinker of internationalism, and of the idea that nation-state sovereignty should be limited in the name of human rights.[9]

Pseudo-Democracy

After World War I, East European states moved a huge step forward to complete manhood suffrage. Adult men received the right to vote everywhere (with the restrictions already mentioned in Hungary), and women in Poland, Czechoslovakia, and, for a time Hungary, received the ballot as well.[10] Yet little changed in the ability of the populations to exert their will on the political establishment, and little occurred to deal with festering social problems. Most people continued working the land, but had too little of it, and too little fertilizer, know-how, or access to affordable credit to make ends meet. Rather than concerning themselves with these basic impediments to economic and social development, governments focused on the needs of the cities and held the countryside in check. Occasionally they said that burning social problems had to wait until basic concerns of national interest were resolved. In Hungary, the loss of territory at Trianon was so grievous that the nation could not focus on any other issue—at least that was the government's self-serving propaganda.

Despite the "white terror" presided over by Admiral Miklós Horthy after the flight of Béla Kun and his collaborators to Vienna, as well as a boycott by the socialists, elections had taken place in Hungary in November 1919 to produce a national assembly. A governing coalition formed of the "Small Holder" (peasant) party and several right-wing parties, who undid the legislation of the liberal Károlyi and the Communist Kun regimes. Law I of 1920 returned Hungary to its traditional status as a kingdom, although the allies compelled Hungary to dethrone the Habsburgs.[11] The national assembly, meeting in a building used by army officers who had conducted the terror, elected as "regent" the strongman Horthy, former commander of the dual monarchy's navy as well as adjutant of Francis Joseph and a man of deeply conservative leanings.[12]

Hungary's Smallholder Party had been formed just before the war by István Szabó of Nagytad, a true peasant leader who stood for land reform, but the party leadership of the 1920s featured few actual members of the agricultural proletariat, and therefore the new government did not represent the urban or rural laboring classes.[13] But Hungary's middle classes also lived on the edge of desperation: many had placed savings in Austro-Hungarian war loans and lost everything. Their numbers were swelled by some 300,000–400,000 refugees from the successor states, mostly officials and their families. Many got by in lamentable conditions, living for a time in abandoned railway cars. They saw Marxists as their chief enemies and would become a pillar of the right-wing movements that emerged later in the decade.

Horthy's prime minister in the 1920s, the Calvinist Transylvanian nobleman Count István Bethlen, a staunch conservative and skilled diplomat, had been educated in Budapest, Vienna, and several universities in England. Bethlen exhibited little charisma in public, but he excelled in closed-door negotiations and proved a brilliantly effective representative of his own landowning class. Bethlen's goal was to return Hungary to the prewar system of limited enfranchisement, claiming the masses were not ready to take responsibility for their affairs. Governance could not be subjected to their blind rule, he said; any state not led by the intelligentsia would succumb to demagoguery and base sloganeering, inflated simultaneously by national and social resentments.[14]

Extraordinary for a member of his class, Bethlen first joined the Smallholders party, yet then employed tact and legal chicanery to merge them with other right-wing groups to create a Party of Unity, in effect, the government party.[15]

In 1922 he restored the prewar practice by which voters outside of towns cast an open ballot, meaning that when peasants voted, their landlords could detect dissenters and punish them through various kinds of administrative chicanery. The electorate was thus limited to about 28 percent, with further restrictions added for education and period of residence.[16] These and other tricks guaranteed control over the political system by Hungary's traditional elites—the gentry, landowners, the church, and the small capitalist class. A paltry land reform of August 1920 permitted about 7.5 percent of the country's total area to be taken from large estates for distribution, but landlords were given advance warning and parted with their least-valuable acreage.[17] At the same time, the Bethlen regime kept agricultural workers from organizing, meaning that when political agitators appeared in villages, they were promptly expelled by the gendarmes. Thus the old pseudo-feudal system continued with few changes, opening room for forces on the far right, who would claim to be true protectors of the ethnic people.[18]

Bethlen's scheme was to stimulate growth by attracting foreign investment and keeping wages low. A major achievement was to stabilize the currency. In 1927 he introduced the pengő based on gold, which proved to be among the soundest currencies in Europe; this, with massive foreign investment and loans, permitted a modest economic upswing, and the government undertook some social reform, including health as well as old age, widow, and disability insurance. A tariff provided shelter for native industries, and the number of factories increased by two-thirds from 1920 to 1929. Hungary's exports remained mostly agricultural, but for the time being, they found foreign markets and good prices, so that the value of foreign trade doubled. Yet the successful attraction of foreign capital also gave rise to complaints from the far right. Claiming that Hungary was becoming dependent on Jewish capital, former army officer Gyula Gömbös took six deputies of the Party of Unity and formed a racist Party of Hungarian Independence in 1923.[19]

Bethlen's Party of Unity guaranteed itself a majority in each election, but also tolerated opposition—knowing full well that it would never assume power.[20] He believed that industrial workers had to be an interest group in any modern society and permitted the functioning of trade unions.[21] In 1928 the (Marxist-inspired) Social Democrats returned to parliament after agreeing to refrain from strikes and from organizing voters in the countryside. Like elsewhere in

Eastern Europe (except in Czechoslovakia), the government outlawed Communists, yet otherwise mostly respected freedoms of the press, assembly, and speech. Political parties functioned from left to right, and it was possible to discuss philosophical and political ideas in newspapers and journals as long as the basic regime was not called into question. Until Germany deposed him in 1944, Horthy as a kinglike "regent" presided over this limited pluralism, choosing prime ministers and endeavoring (with diminishing success, as we will see) to keep Hungary independent.[22]

Though Romania benefited the most from the peace settlement, the situation there was similar to Hungary's in essential ways. The first elections of 1919 were by universal male suffrage (women would not gain the vote in municipal elections until the 1930s) and produced a majority for the peasant and national parties. Voters were punishing the liberal party for being unprepared for war and for chaotic administration in the years 1916–1918. A new coalition government set about planning socioeconomic reforms, investment in the villages, land expropriation, and most impressively, an administrative decentralization that would have respected the special character of the country's diverse regions and made Romania a model for other multiethnic states.[23]

But all this came to naught. Using a simple trick, King Ferdinand ousted this government in March 1920. The prime minister, the Transylvanian Alexandru Vaida-Voevod, had gone to Paris to negotiate the final borders of Transylvania and Bessarabia, and while he was away, acting Prime Minister Stefan C. Pop resigned along with his cabinet. This was a turning point with fatal repercussions for Romanian democracy. The elected parliamentary majority had been on the verge of consolidating popular rule behind the agrarian reforms of pro-peasant parties, combined with reconciliation with the "minorities." But the monarch and the liberal establishment considered such measures "treacherous," and for most of the interwar period conspired to frustrate the will of the electorate. After this time, as a rule, the government in power staged and also won elections.[24]

The pliant General Alexandru Averescu, a war hero of conservative leanings, was made premier, and elections were "organized" in May to give his eclectic People's Party an overwhelming if fraudulent majority. Standing for the rejection of social reform, anticommunism, anti-Semitism, anti-Magyarism, and Wallachian supremacy, Averescu imposed a rigid centralization on the country and formalized a politicized land reform that consisted of redistributing land from ethnic foreigners (usually Magyars and Germans) to Romanians. The reform did not create a strong and independent peasant proprietor class, yet it salvaged the position of the dispossessed landowners by planting them in the state bureaucracy and giving them directorships in commercial and industrial concerns owned by Jews and foreigners.[25] Having served his purpose, Averescu was let go, and the liberals organized elections in March 1922 that gave them a landslide victory.

They used their majority to rewrite the 1866 constitution, restricting rights of association in order to hamstring the organizing of workers and peasants, restricting land ownership to citizens, and confirming extensive royal powers while easing the declaration of martial law. The liberals felt confident that they could control King Ferdinand but were not sure about his son Carol, and therefore excluded him from succession through an act of January 4, 1926, allegedly because of irregularities in his marital life. When their pro-industrial and anti-agricultural policies became unpopular, they arranged the reappointment of General Averescu as premier, so that he could absorb the popular dissatisfaction. But when he became insufficiently reliable, elections were staged to bring the liberals back to power. In 1926, 1,366,160 voters cast ballots in favor of Averescu and only 192,399 for the liberals; but the following year, 1,704,435 voters chose the liberals over 53,371 who now supposedly voted for Averescu.

In theory, Romania's liberals faced two challenges: integrating hundreds of thousands of Hungarian ethnics into the body politic and improving the lives of peasants, who constituted the overwhelming majority of the population and to a large degree lived in premodern conditions. But the liberals stalled on both agendas by citing the primacy of national security, that is, fending off supposed threats coming from beyond Romania's borders. With Czechoslovakia and Yugoslavia, Romania belonged to the Little Entente, whose major purpose was protection against Hungarian irredentism. The rulers cited this imperative as ruling out any moderation in policies toward the huge Hungarian population. They said it was part of an "international conspiracy."

Liberals likewise portrayed Bolshevism as a threat creeping furtively across the eastern borders from the Soviet Union into Bessarabia and requiring constant vigilance. That vigilance extended to peasant activists who might come into Romanian villages from the towns to stir up "unrest," that is, to organize constituents. Fears of foreign infiltration thus served to frustrate any effective response to festering national and social problems.[26] The result was to radicalize forces to the left and right, among people of peasant background as well as the ethnic minorities, who filled the ranks of both the Communist Party and the fascist movement.

In 1927 King Ferdinand as well as liberal party leader Ion I. C. Brătianu (who had so shrewdly negotiated Romania's interests in Paris) died in quick succession. The following year, the second major party, the National Peasant party under the leadership of Transylvanian peasant politician Iuliu Maniu, stood for relatively fair elections and won 78 percent of the votes. It negotiated a foreign loan and managed to balance the budget and stabilize the currency. Tariffs were lowered to permit the import of farm implements and items of peasant consumption. Maniu also released restrictions on foreign investment, which his predecessors had limited by the nationality of the foreign investor.[27]

Yet the timing was bad, as agricultural prices were falling and credit drying up with the onset of the Depression. On June 6, 1930, Carol, a man who practically breathed corruption, returned to Bucharest, and two days later, parliament confirmed him as king Carol II by a vote of 485 to 1, reflecting a broad sentiment that the country required the continuity of dynastic order. Carol then appointed minsters and played politicians against one another, and when that did not work, fabricated coalitions, hoping to keep radicals at bay. His second wife, Helen of Greece, had divorced the free-living prince in 1928, and now he set up court with his mistress Magda Lupescu, a German-educated Catholic supposedly of Jewish background.[28] Maniu resigned in October, believing the king had betrayed him by failing to become reconciled to Helen, and conducting his life "in defiance of Christian morals."[29] His party faded after that, lacking leaders of his stature. Its one accomplishment was to bring about a genuine union of administration, central and provincial. But it was unable to shake a culture of corruption, bribery, and occasional police brutality.

In Bulgaria, the land problem was not as pressing because the country had a healthier property structure than any other state in Eastern Europe. Virtually the entire rural proletariat, and many city dwellers as well, owned some productive land, and the holdings, though small, were relatively evenly distributed. In addition, Bulgaria had the most advanced social security and insurance system in the Balkans.[30] In the early postwar years, Bulgaria was the East European country that came closest to testing peasant power as a form of rule. The reason lay in the series of disastrous wars (the Balkan wars and World War I) that created opportunities to form new majorities against the bourgeois parties who were responsible for these wars.

Aleksandar Stamboliiski, the founder of the strongest peasant moment in prewar Eastern Europe, surfaced in 1918 from three years of imprisonment for his opposition to the war. He argued that the regime's disastrous choices before and during World War I, leading to hundreds of thousands of pointless deaths,

FIGURE 13.1. King Boris and Prime Minister Stamboliiski (August 1920). *Source*: Library of
Congress, Prints & Photographs Division, American National Red Cross Collection.
Retrieved from http://www.loc.gov/pictures/item/2017677690/.

were not simply the result of the failures of politicians but of urban dwellers as
such, whose hatred of all things rural had brought misery to the entire country.
He did, however, begin taking nonpeasants into his Bulgarian Agrarian National
Union (BANU) if they promised to support the peasant program.[31]

Though Communists also benefited from the widespread disaffection among
Bulgarians, BANU became the strongest party, getting almost 40 percent of the
vote in the March 1920 elections. After invalidating the returns of thirteen deputies of left-wing parties (Communists and Social Democrats), Stamboliiski
fabricated a majority for his party. His goal was to create a peasant order, and
that involved not clean democratic methods but gradually displacing urban,
bourgeois influence from every institution, starting with the parliament and
ending with the city itself. He thought that people were not free unless they
owned land and planted crops. In a revolution not called revolutionary he would
transfer power from the parasitic town-dwellers—the "people-eaters"—to the
honest tillers of the soil.[32]

Before falling victim to assassins in the late spring of 1923, Stamboliiski
pushed through legislation meant to benefit that virtuous majority. A 1921 law

limited peasants to thirty-five hectares, and those who had more contributed to a fund for those without enough land to be viable. The effect was limited, as Bulgarian holdings were already small, but almost 65,000 families benefited, and the legislation was broadly popular, supported by all parties except the Communists, who derided it as petty-bourgeois. Stamboliiski created lower courts in the countryside where peasants could plead their cases before popularly elected judges, and he also instituted a progressive income tax. His government built more than 1,100 schools and made secondary education compulsory.

Yet favoring peasant proprietors meant reducing the urban sector. Stamboliiski also introduced legislation limiting all but the largest families to two rooms and a kitchen, and restricting office space. After a law passed in 1920 requiring males between twenty and forty to perform eight months of physical labor, between 14,500 and 29,000 young men were called up annually to build roads and lay railroad track, plant millions of seedlings, drain swamps, build dams, and string telephone wires. But the law was also a device to spread a sense of service and social solidarity, showing that no one was too good for manual work.[33] In accord with his belief that only artisans and tillers of the land possessed virtue, Stamboliiski exempted them from most taxation while placing severe levies on all capital; at the same time, he introduced price controls that kept manufactured goods cheap and made foodstuffs expensive.[34] He intimidated journalists and kept lawyers from holding office, accusing both groups of corrupting the political system with alien values.[35]

Unlike most peasant leaders, Stamboliiski also thought in broad regional terms. In his view, agrarian Eastern Europe should go a separate way between capitalism and Communism, and he hoped to form a union of the states that would rise above the conventional disputes over territory. The head of government in Belgrade, machine politician Nikola Pašić, did not understand his overtures and considered Bulgarians hereditary enemies. Still, Stamboliiski showed his sincere desire for regional cooperation by foreswearing irredentism, and he refused to recover territories lost to Romania. As a result, Bulgaria became the first defeated state admitted to the League of Nations. Yet he was uncompromising on territories claimed by Slavic Macedonians who aspired to independent statehood. Most of the space they claimed had fallen to Yugoslavia, but there were pockets of Macedonian settlement in southwestern Bulgaria, where armed units formed. Stamboliiski openly mocked them in words he would come to regret. "Since you've already taken Macedonia," he told journalists on a visit to Yugoslavia in late 1922, "why don't you take all the

Macedonians still in Bulgaria . . . take them all, and make them into human beings!"[36]

During this visit, Stamboliiski hammered out an agreement (signed in March 1923) by which Bulgaria and Yugoslavia agreed to cooperate in fighting Macedonian extremists. Soon the Bulgarian government banned all organizations suspected of terrorist activities, suppressed their newspapers, and placed their leaders in internment camps, thus further angering a potent enemy.[37] When Stamboliiski sent a peasant "Orange Army" to hunt down units of the Internal Macedonian Revolutionary Organization (IMRO), some 15,000 fighters simply disappeared into the mountains, and though he arrested Macedonian politicians, he could not clear the IMRO nests out of southwest Bulgaria because IMRO had sympathizers in the high ranks of the army.[38]

Here we have hints of the troubles that led to Stamboliiski's downfall: his life-and-death struggle against the urban establishment alienated the powerful while not attracting effective allies. Physicians feared being sent to remote villages, teachers resented purges of leftists from their ranks, professors disliked Stamboliiski's interference in academic autonomy, and the church objected to the purging of religion from school curricula. More consequentially, Stamboliiski estranged the state bureaucracy by flooding it with poorly prepared BANU devotees, alienated the Macedonians by crushing aspirations for self-rule, and alarmed the king by hinting at desires to form a republic. Corruption, which had been a nettlesome constant in Bulgarian life, grew to appalling proportions under Stamboliiski, especially among officials BANU appointed to village administration, who viewed their positions as a license for self-enrichment.[39]

Most short-sighted of all was Stamboliiski's dismissive attitude toward the armed forces, which he kept below even the reduced size of 20,000 stipulated by the Neuilly-sur-Seine treaty of 1919. Reserve officers cut from the army were forced to live on pittance pensions. In 1922, feeling humiliated and having no outlet for their frustrations, disaffected officers formed the conspiratorial Military League and soon joined forces with the Macedonian terrorists of IMRO as well the opposition bloc in parliament.[40] The conspirators were quietly abetted by the king, for whom the last straw was Stamboliiski's talk of a referendum on forming a republic after the elections of May 1923, in which BANU won 212 of 245 seats in the Sobranjie.

Military officers struck on June 9, seizing Sofia without bloodshed, and proceeding to the palace, where they easily induced the king to recognize them as the legitimate government. Stamboliiski had been vacationing but managed to organize a desperate resistance. It was of no use. A Macedonian unit took Stamboliiski captive, subjected him to a protracted and agonizing death, and then sent his head to Sofia.

The new regime was led by the flamboyant former leftist academic economist Aleksandur Tsankov, who liked to surround himself with bodyguards and German shepherds and would ultimately drift toward fascism after leaving office in 1926. He fashioned a "Democratic Alliance" that included all political forces except the Communists and peasants, and returned Bulgaria to the pre-1914 system, where a multitude of politicians looked for ways to feed at the government trough. Communists had polled a quarter of the votes in the 1919 elections and waited out the fighting, believing the rift in bourgeois forces would prepare the way for their own rule. Yet Tsankov crushed them brutally when they rose up in September 1923, and estimates run up to 30,000 killed. In November, he passed a defense of the realm act that gave the government power to "ban terrorism" and influence elections later that month.[41]

In April 1925, in a final desperate attempt to ignite revolution, Bulgaria's Communists bombed Sofia's cathedral during a funeral for General Georgiev, an adjutant of King Boris. The death toll topped 120, and Boris escaped only because he arrived late after his limousine's spark plugs failed. Tsankov's response was so vicious that it scandalized European opinion, leading to his fall and the assumption of power by the centrist Macedonian Andrei Lyapachev, a man lacking in a distinctive legislative program. The government drifted aimlessly. Lyapachev attempted to stabilize politics by copying a trick of the Romanian and Italian systems: whichever party got a plurality of votes received a majority of seats.

Strong Men Take Charge

Despite the bloodshed, Bulgaria weathered the tumult of the early 1920s with its constitution intact, and numerous parties, including the Communists and a new BANU, remained in parliament. The Communists even won the municipal elections in Sofia in 1931 and 1932. But the Great Depression transformed widespread poverty into abject misery, and in 1934, Bulgaria's King Boris seized power and then began ruling unchecked by the legislature. Four years later, his colleague in Romania, Carol II, did the same thing, suspending the constitution and introducing personal rule.

In Poland and Yugoslavia, strong men stepped in to suspend the constitution even before the Great Depression plunged the region into economic

darkness. These states had faced fragmentation unknown in Bulgaria and Romania. Yet ethnic complexity did not have to condemn them to political chaos.
Czechoslovakia was the region's most ethnically diverse state, with a mind-
numbing array of parties, but parliamentary democratic rule lasted until 1938,
when the great powers at Munich forced the country to abandon the fortified
border territories offering protection from Nazi Germany. But until then, the
Czechoslovak Republic was an oasis of tolerance for Czechs, Slovaks, Germans, Jews, Magyars, Ruthenians, and everyone else, coming closer to approxi-
mating ideals for multiethnic coexistence than the old Habsburg monarchy,
let alone the new Poland or Yugoslavia. We get some hints as to why by comparing Czechoslovakia to the latter, the state of the South Slavs. To observers at
the time, both states seemed to be bold experiments in Slavic self-determination,
yet the outcomes were quite different.

Like Czechoslovakia, Yugoslavia emerged in 1918 out of the conviction inherited from nineteenth-century nationalists that languages make nations.
Czech and Slovak, and Serbian and Croatian, were supposedly close enough
to permit related Slavic "tribes" to form cohesive nation-states. Yet in each case,
the ethnic group doing the uniting was numerically fragile: Czechs were just
over half the population of Czechoslovakia, and Serbs about 43 percent of Yugoslavia.[42] In both places, the challenges of making coherent states were huge;
in each case, the state apparatus united regions that had never coexisted. Croatia had been part of Hungary since the eleventh century, and Croats knew
virtually nothing about Serbs who lived beyond the once-Habsburg lands, let
alone the Montenegrins. Serb and Croat elites had shared a vague sense of the
need to unite South Slav territories for self-defense and mutual benefit, but Serbs
saw unity as part of the project of creating greater Serbia—even when the country was called Yugoslavia—while Croats, even if they were republicans,
imagined the continued political existence of the Croatian kingdom, with rights
of self-rule.

Despite the mythology of "Slavic" brotherhood uniting Czechs and Slovaks,
these two peoples also had starkly different histories. Magyarization had
brought the Slovaks to the edge of cultural extinction. As late as 1918, there were
no Slovak high schools and handfuls of Slovak civil servants. Sociologically,
the Slovaks were peasants, and they practiced a traditional Roman Catholicism (16 percent were Protestant).[43] Czechs by contrast had become one of
the most dynamic "young" nations in Europe, with a large and self-confident
middle class. Though most were nominally Catholic, their national mythology
heroized the Protestant Hussite movement that had been crushed during the

FIGURE 13.2. Prague's Marian Column, erected 1650
(ca. 1900). *Source*: Jindřich Eckert (photographer).
Via Wikimedia Commons.

Counter-Refomation. In 1918 Czech patriots across Bohemia destroyed statues
of the Virgin Mary that symbolized Austrian "tyranny"—acts that Slovaks,
whose folk Catholicism revered the Virgin, found incomprehensible. Among
the first manifestations of Slovak nationalism was a protest in Žilina in northwestern Slovakia against the toppling of the statue of Mary in Prague. Slovak
leader Father Andrej Hlinka, originally a supporter of unity, now portrayed
Czechs as a threat to his people's existence.[44]

Slovaks and Czechs understood each other linguistically, though their languages are distinct. In Yugoslavia, Croats and Serbs spoke the same language,
known for generations as Serbo-Croatian, but they wrote it in two different al-
phabets. The language's regional variations do not coincide with ethnic boundaries. The Serbs in Bosnia or Croatia speak the same dialects as Croats or

FIGURE 13.3. Marian Column destroyed by crowd (November 1918). *Source*: Cynthia Paces, *Radical History Review* (2001), 142. Via Wikimedia Commons.

Muslims in their vicinity, and not that of the Serbs living in central Serbia. In Czechoslovakia as well as Yugoslavia, the centralized state structure made for little flexibility, practically inviting Slovaks or Croats to blame problems on a far-away government controlled by the ethnic other.

In Czechoslovakia, the huge German minority of 3.2 million as well as that of Slovaks (2.3 million) and Magyars (692,000) came to feel that the state was Czech-centered, whereas in Yugoslavia, Croats believed the new country was a greater Serbia. Like the Germans in Czechoslovakia, they had not participated in drafting the state's constitution. Yet Czechoslovakia maintained political stability, whereas Yugoslavia was rocked by crises up to the imposition of royal dictatorship in 1929. Part of the explanation lies in Czechoslovakia's stronger economy, which permitted the state to maintain an ambitious social policy during the economic crisis of the 1930s, when the unemployment rate rose to a third. Yet Yugoslavia had failed as a democracy even before that point. Somehow the elites in Prague pulled off a feat of state-building that eluded counterparts in Belgrade. One place to look for explanations is the relative abilities of disgruntled nationalities to upset the new states.

The elections of 1919 produced stunning majorities in Croatia for the Croat Peasant Party, led by the mercurial, charismatic, popular, and erratic but

principled Stjepan Radić, who decided to boycott the meetings that drafted the
new state's constitution. He told other Croat politicians before they rushed off
to join the Serb Kingdom in 1918 that they were acting like "drunken geese in
fog," having learned nothing from the fall of Emperor Wilhelm in Germany
a few weeks earlier. Like the fallen emperor, they were in a hurry to impose
power on the people, rather than fostering self-governance by involving the
people. No one had asked Croats if they wanted to belong to the new state,
and that was an irrational, imprudent, and as time would show, self-defeating
act.[45]

Radić then led Croats in boycotting Yugoslav political institutions, and was
arrested frequently, once for seeking support for Croat independence in Moscow (an act considered seditious).[46] The other major political forces in
Yugoslavia—Serbs from the old kingdom (Radicals), Serbs from Habsburg
lands (Democrats), Muslims from Bosnia, and Slovene Catholics—thus ruled
the new state without the Croats. Things seemed to change for the better in 1925,
when Radić suddenly agreed to take a post as education minister and King Alexander made his first visit to Zagreb. Yet because of incompatibilities of the
leaders, this relative harmony only lasted for just over a year.

The differences between Serbs and Croats in political vision proved unbridg-
able. Croat leaders insisted that Croatia must be guaranteed local autonomy
in recognition of centuries of Croatian state's rights that had been respected even
under Hungarian rule. Yet Serbs had no tradition of federal rule. Having borne
the costs of liberating Yugoslav territory from the Austrians—while Croats
were fighting for Austria—Serbs claimed a moral right to rule the new state from
the center. The determination to rule was reflected in a stranglehold Serbs
established on institutions of state that lasted until 1941. Yet Serbs also argued
compellingly that Yugoslavia had not been a Serb idea in the first place, and
their political elite had acceded to unity in response to the urgent wishes of
Croat politicians, first at Corfu in 1917, then in Belgrade with the delegation
that appeared the following December. Without Serb backing, much of Croatia
would have been divided between Hungary and Italy.

Nikola Pašić, the respected leader of the Serb Radical Party, died in 1927, and
the parliamentary deputies in Belgrade sank into a routine of lobbing insults
across the lines of ethnicity. In June 1928, Radić called Montenegrin deputies
"apes," and the next day, the Serb Radical Puniša Račić shot Radić on the floor
of parliament along with two other Croat deputies. The two deputies died immediately, but Radić held on for several weeks, finally succumbing to compli-
cations from an operation in early August. The king reputedly offered to

separate Croatia from Yugoslavia, but Radić refused, perhaps anticipating the difficulties of separating Croats from Serbs in the old military frontier (*krajina*) in Croatia and fearing Italian domination of the rump state that would be left.[47]

In the end, Radić also acknowledged the basic need for a state that could secure the peaceful coexistence of the peoples on Yugoslav territory. Yet in contrast to Serb elites in Belgrade, his hope, and the hope of his deputy and successor Vladko Maček, was a federal Yugoslavia, perhaps even a Serb-Croat sharing of rule akin to the 1867 agreement between Austria and Hungary. One sign of hope was that since 1926, his Croatian Peasant Party worked in coalition with the Independent Democrats, a mostly Serb party from former Habsburg areas led by Svetozar Pribićević, also a target of the assassination in June 1928.[48]

But with Radić's death, the king felt a compulsion to act, and in January 1929, he declared a royal dictatorship, hoping simply to keep the state together. Parliament had proved a "hindrance to any fruitful work in the state" and to permit it to continue its work would expose Yugoslavia to the predations of its neighbors.[49] In a modernizing frenzy meant to force Yugoslavia to become a state, Alexander made historic borders irrelevant and divided the country into nine *banovine*, or districts, named after rivers and with little relation to any district that had ever existed. Bosnia and Croatia simply disappeared from the map. In the army he abolished all insignias and standards that were attached to historic Serbia, thus alienating many Serbs. The country was now officially Yugoslavia and no longer the Kingdom of Serbs, Croats, and Slovenes.

Perhaps the king's scheme was not so outlandish. After all, the very idea of a united South Slav state went against all prior history, and to some extent all interwar Eastern European politics involved creation of new units in disregard of old ones. And he was not a nationalist: far from a tool of the Serb bureaucracy, Alexander acted to reduce Serb predominance. (As we will see, like the region's other intemperate centralizer, Joseph II, he failed in almost everything he attempted.)

The founding of the Czechoslovak state also occurred without the participation of a group that, relatively speaking, was as large as the Croats in Yugoslavia: the Sudeten Germans, an ethnicity distributed across the new state's territory but living chiefly in border regions. Though this minority became more obstreperous and less loyal than the Croats, the Czechoslovak regime held and preserved democratic rule. If one focuses on political process, the differences become evident from an early point. The Yugoslav idea may have been a Croatian invention, but most Croats saw the new state as foreign, and a well-organized movement seeking autonomy guided them from the start. Ironically, the franchise of the Yugoslav state made it clear that the Yugoslav Committee that formed in Paris in 1915 had not spoken for the Croat people.

The idea of uniting Czechs and Slovaks may have originally been a dream of Slovak Protestants like Jan Kollár, but by 1918, it was owned by Czechs; decisive in holding the multiethnic Czechoslovak state together was the will of the Czech political elite, beyond all ideological distinctions.[50] Leaders of the Czech political parties, with key support from some Slovaks (mostly from the Protestant minority), were able to dominate Czechoslovakia in a way that the Serb elite could not dominate the more complex Yugoslavia, with its large, well-organized Croat opposition. The unity of the Czech elite went back to its origins in a single political context, Habsburg Bohemia, whereas Serb counterparts were divided between those of the former Ottoman and Habsburg lands.

Through the interwar years, five Czech and Slovak political parties—Agrarians, National Democrats, National Socialists, Social Democrats, and the Catholic People's Party—cohered in the center of a very broad spectrum, and their leaders worked out political deals behind closed doors in a "committee of five" (the *Pětka*), which guaranteed stable rule until the Munich catastrophe of 1938, though at times one party or another would drop out. Because their agreements were not open to public scrutiny (in fact, they kept no written records), compromises were possible that might have been politically destructive if debated openly in parliament. The nonconstitutional *Pětka* stabilized and probably saved the Czechoslovak democratic constitution, protecting the country from the bitter public disputes that made parliaments unworkable in Poland and Yugoslavia. At the same time, party leaders became quasi-dictators in their own organizations, expecting unquestioned support.

This was the price that Czechoslovak democracy had to pay for surviving the turbulent challenges of 1920 and 1921, when the Czech movement had become physically aggressive, going beyond what the new authorities sanctioned. In Prague, "patriots" seized German property, like newspapers, the German theater, and social club (*Kasino*), and riots broke out in predominantly German Teplice when Czech soldiers removed a statue of Joseph II, whom both sides recognized as a Germanizer. Masaryk was so disgusted at his fellow Czechs that he stopped going to Prague's Estates Theater, which Czech actors had usurped on November 16, 1920. For that he became a target of vicious rhetorical affronts.[51]

A practical success of early Czechoslovak policy was to stabilize the new currency, in 1919, the Czechoslovak crown, so that while Germany, Austria, and

Poland endured runaway inflation, the Czechoslovak economy enjoyed a decade of steady growth, further enriching Central Europe's most sophisticated industrial base. A reform in April 1920 did much to satisfy demand for land among Czech and Slovak peasants, providing for expropriation of estates with more than 150 hectares (many of which were Hungarian or German). The government also passed a Social Insurance Law in 1924, among the most progressive in the world, associating health insurance with invalidity and old age. The graceful modernist apartment houses and villas that went up in the hills of Prague or the suburbs of Brno in this period give testimony to the new state's defiant pride. Renegade Catholic priests formed a new Czechoslovak Church that was supposedly connected to old Hussite traditions, and here, too, left traces still visible to the tourist: modern houses of worship in clean, elegant structures replete with statues recalling heroes from the Czech past. However, as a cult, the new church never became dominant, and most Czechs remained non-churchgoing nominal Roman Catholics.[52]

Masaryk, though fully law-abiding, firmly used his authority to guide the work of Czech politics, protecting his country from the sorts of upheavals that shook other states.[53] He did not have to placate a recalcitrant social elite, because in contrast to Poland or Hungary, the local nobility was not dominant in the countryside, and the recent emergence of the Czech political leaders from villages and small towns militated in favor of popular rule and against conservatism. The state also could draw on an avowedly Czech democratic tradition that had grown in the incubator of Habsburg rule and was set off against the authoritarian "German" approach to politics. Before the onset of the Depression, the Czech establishment managed briefly to integrate German politicians into the new system, who felt they prospered from it.

Given that the "Slavic" states of Czechoslovakia and Poland both harbored German minorities and occupied lands desired by Germany, the two countries had every incentive to cooperate. Instead, they found themselves at odds over Těšín, a small town in formerly Austrian Silesia, which the Czechs seized in January 1919, claiming they needed a rail line that ran through Těšín connecting Prague to eastern Slovakia; without this junction they could not build their state. Though the town and the surrounding region (Cieszyn in Polish, Teschen in German) had a Polish majority, the allies sided with the Czechs and denied the Poles a plebiscite: Poland's seizing of ethnically Ukrainian lands in the east had weakened its claims on ethnically Polish areas in the west. Because the Poles were fighting for their state's survival in the east when the Czechs took Těšín, they never forgave the Czechs. Throughout the interwar years, Poland's leaders refused cooperation even on issues of mutual benefit like trade, and in October 1938, they "returned the favor" by seizing Těšín as the Czechs were absorbing crippling blows from Nazi Germany.[54]

Like Serbs, but unlike their Czech counterparts, Polish elites were divided because they had emerged in different states.[55] Take the Polish peasant movement. A united party might have pressed for effective land reform, benefiting the great majority of Poles who lived in the countryside. Instead, two competing peasant parties had emerged, one in former Austrian Galicia (*Piast*), the other from formerly Russian central Poland (*Wyzwolenie*). Reflecting local power structures, *Piast* tended to be conservative, willing to cooperate with the left and right, depending on opportunity, somewhat along the lines of parties in Italy or Romania. By contrast, *Wyzwolenie* was revolutionary, reflecting the desperate conditions of political life in tsarist Russia. *Piast*, under former Austrian Reichsrat deputy Wincenty Witos, became a center-right machine party that brokered most of the coalitions of the six years of Polish parliamentary rule. Because of the many Ukrainians in its home base of Galicia, the party did not support land reform that might weaken the "Polish element." *Wyzwolenie* by contrast favored radical land reform and sympathized with the interests of ethnic minorities. Until the Polish economic situation became dire in the 1930s, the two peasant parties did not cooperate.

These divisions among Poles, aggravated by ethnic complexity, resulted in political chaos. Though Poles made up almost 70 percent of the population (in contrast to Czechs, who were just half of the Czechoslovak population), they failed to cooperate across political divides, and from 1921 to 1926, Poland endured fourteen cabinets. Poland's journalists ascribed the parliament's failings to the self-destructive character of the political class, but arguably the deep gulf also reflected the ideological specifics of the two major political camps. The Czech representatives of National and Social Democracy may have despised each other—the latter were ousted from the governing coalition in 1926—but they did not perceive each other as representing dangerous existential alternatives. In Poland, by contrast, the National Democrat Roman Dmowski and former socialist Józef Piłsudski stood for well-articulated thought systems that had developed over decades, and though their practical policies in economy or society did not differ hugely, they would not even speak to each other. Czech elites may have differed over many questions, but ultimately, they cooperated on matters of common practical interest. Perhaps being surrounded by Germans on three sides, as well as possessing a huge minority within their own borders, gave them a more realistic sense of their fragile security. Many in the Polish elite were deluded into considering their country a power because of the Polish victory over the Red Army in 1920.

In the Czech lands, President Masaryk was almost universally admired, while his counterpart in Poland, Marshal Piłsudski, served as a target of criticism across much of the political landscape for reasons that are difficult to reconstruct. After all, Piłsudski had done more than anyone to resurrect Poland, and his unusual background—a sometime Catholic, native of Lithuania, and erstwhile revolutionary socialist—did not keep him from being recognized as Poland's preeminent first leader. But rather than causing Poles to rally around him, Piłsudski's achievements intensified the rage against him on the political right of center. His rivals quibbled over whether he or other military leaders had in fact brought about victory for Poland, and whether he had acted irresponsibly by attacking Kiev in early 1920, hoping to unite with independent Ukraine. Some called him a traitor.[56]

The Polish right believed in a strong leader, yet anticipating that Piłsudski would become president, a Constituent Assembly that it dominated drew up a constitution providing for a weak chief of state. In response, Piłsudski withdrew into seclusion, surrounded by his military collaborators (the "colonels"), saying that a president with a representative function should come from outside party life. The major achievement of this time, the stabilization of the Polish currency (złoty) in 1924 after it tumbled from 9.8 (December 1918) to 2,300,000 (November 1923) to the dollar was (perhaps characteristically) due to a supraparliamentary regime.[57] This success also taught a lesson: that ruling by decree was the way to achieve results.

Even if Polish political parties could not form stable ruling coalitions, they could agree to exclude non-Poles from local and state government. In 1923 the National Democrats, Peasant (Piast), and Christian Nationals drew up the Lanckorona Pact, stipulating that the "Polish national element" must be preserved and that any parliamentary coalition be based on Polish parties. A prime task of state was to Polonize the eastern territories. Through the interwar years, the ethnic Polish element maintained a stranglehold on state administration, while numbers of German and Ukrainian language schools declined, and Jewish students were gradually forced out of universities (the percentage of Jews at Polish universities declined from about one-quarter in 1923 to less than one-tenth in 1937).[58]

In December 1925, Germany launched a trade war to compel Poland to cede Upper Silesia. Thus, while finances stabilized in neighboring countries, the situation grew dire in Poland. The złoty could not be sustained, unemployment

FIGURE 13.4. Marshal Piłsudski during coup d'etat in Warsaw (May 1926).
Source: Marian Fuks (photographer), *Światowid*, June 1926.

rose to a third of the labor force, and voices from left to right called for what Piłsudski promised: "cleansing" the nation of the rot of politics.[59] The multiethnic parliament had revealed democracy to be an unworkable sham, and many in Poland feared catastrophe. As in Yugoslavia, the attempt to plant democracy in a fragmented political landscape now gave rise to calls for a strongman. In 1925, one mainstream newspaper wrote: "everywhere in the country one feels a longing for an iron hand that leads us away from the precipice."[60] In the first week of May 1926, the National Democrats, supported by the peasant leader Wincenty Witos of the centrist Piast party, appeared on the verge of forming a government that would rule against workers, with drastic budget cuts and a deflationary program. Instead, Piłsudski stepped in, and in a two-day coup (May 12–14) took power by force.

Piłsudski expected that the government would simply hand over power, but President Wojciechowski, a former socialist and an organizer of Poland's co-operative movement, resisted, and loyal army units supported him. Yet workers sympathetic to Piłsudski organized strikes and blocked the movement of troops and supplies to Warsaw, and ultimately he prevailed. The fighting had cost the lives of 215 soldiers and 164 civilians.[61] To avoid further bloodshed, President Wojciechowski and Prime Minister Witos resigned.

Piłsudski vowed to respect the constitution. He said that his goal was not dictatorship; supposedly a mass movement had compelled him to stage a "march on Warsaw" against the corruption, bribery, and misuse of state funds of the freshly installed Witos government. Though talk of a "march on Warsaw" brought to mind Mussolini's fascism, the labor movement, which was very anti-Witos, supported the coup, and some called it a "Polish revolution."[62] Secretly Piłsudski was alarmed by the growing threats to Poland's position: in 1922 Germany and Russia had come to an agreement at Rapallo, which soon led to secret military collaboration. And Germany had settled disagreements with the Western powers at Locarno three years later and was now focusing on revising its border with Poland.

Calling his regime *sanacja*, Piłsudski now pledged to "clean up" the mess left by parliament. He assembled a team of experts, ruling with temporary success because of a long strike in Britain that provided markets for Polish coal. Yet after 1930, the Polish economy rapidly declined, and he ruled increasingly by oppressive means, making a transition from a regime like that of Charles de Gaulle of the French 1960s to one more like that of Napoleon III Bonaparte a century before that.[63] Comparisons with Mussolini became more insistent: originally a man of the left, Piłsudski had crushed a parliamentary democracy and was becoming increasingly dictatorial.

Beneath the turmoil at top, the state administration was quietly achieving the historic feat of bringing Polish lands together in a state, but the demands were awesome. More than fifty Austrian and German railway lines had led to the Russian border but only ten continued, and they used different gauges. Only 8.2 percent of the trade of the three sections of Poland had been with another part of Poland; more than three-fourths (83.3 percent) had been with the respective partitioning power, Galicia for example was oriented toward Austria. Because Poland did not control the port of Danzig/Gdańsk, the industrial area of Silesia had to be connected to the sea through neighboring Gdynia, recently a village, but by the 1930s an impressive modern port city.[64] As in Yugoslavia, with its former Habsburg and former Ottoman Serbs, competing political traditions divided the purported people of state: Prussian Poles thought they incorporated "German" values like thrift, and because of the self-rule that had been permitted in Galicia, Austrian Poles tended to dominate the bureaucracy.

Poland, like Hungary and Czechoslovakia, built on preexisting social insurance legislation, some of which went back to Austria and Germany in the nineteenth century, with the goal of protecting workers against sickness, accidents, old age, and unemployment.[65] From 1920, for example, the Polish state required workers to carry health insurance, and workers as well as employers had to pay into it. In Poland as in Czechoslovakia, the eight-hour workday was introduced in 1918. As a Polish economic historian notes, the social legislation of Poland in that period was among the most progressive in Europe and represents an achievement still not reached in the much wealthier United States of our day.[66]

* * *

In interwar Eastern Europe, the predicament of multiethnicity in a hostile international environment combined with low social and economic development to frustrate the promises of liberal democracy. Or to put it differently: democracy, meaning rule of the people, promised to empower peasants, often ethnic others, who would have taken land and privileges from the wealthy and established elites. The elites therefore used their influence in the administration and army—staffed by members of their class—to frustrate democratic rule.

Romania and Bulgaria provided the early variations on this theme. In March 1920, the king had colluded with Romania's liberals to bring down a properly elected government led by the Romanian Peasant party, and thereafter, governments dragged their feet on measures that might benefit tillers of the soil. A bright moment seemed to dawn in 1928, when the National Peasant Party won free elections. Its leader, Iuliu Maniu, known for hard work and incorruptibility, realized that without far-reaching land reform, there could be no successful democracy: if it lacked a sound economic basis, the peasantry could have neither strength nor influence.[67] But Maniu had unusual concern for decorum among political leaders, gained from legal training in Vienna and a political career in pre–World War I Budapest (he was from Transylvania), where he was a doughty opponent of Magyar oppression. He acted as though what counted was the judgment of posterity.

Maniu resigned in October 1930 rather than work with a new king whom he considered flagrantly immoral. His party divided, the Depression plunged the country deeply into economic misery for which there were no solutions. As an index of desperation, at times even he considered working with the fascist Iron Guard (so did other members of the establishment).[68] But Maniu did not lose the civil courage to speak out for basic justice and rule of law. For example, in June 1935, he appeared before an assembly of 50,000 peasants in his native Transylvania to threaten consequences for any expansion of the king's powers. The farmers of Romania had started three revolutions in the past 120 years, he said, and were ready for another.[69] He did not say that these revolutions had achieved little and were crushed in blood. After World War II, Maniu figured among the few East European politicians whom the West celebrated for a commitment to democratic principles. But after a failed attempt at escape by a close associate, Communist authorities arrested him, and he died in prison in 1953.

The example of Maniu, a man committed to legality and moderation, gives us a better understanding for the vigorous measures undertaken by Bulgaria's Aleksandar Stamboliiski, whose methods violated the rule of law, yet who resolutely upended venal bourgeois politics to effect rule of, by, and for the people. Ultimately, his peasant revolution proved a setback. After the 1923 coup that cost Stamboliiski his life, the governing classes argued that any hint of social reform would lead back to the corruption and arbitrary suppression of civil liberties of his peasant regime—if not to the chaos of Bolshevism. Similarly, Hungary's and Poland's authoritarian rulers disqualified social reform as "bolshevization," the unspoken understanding being that such measures played into the hands of the (Russian) national enemy and weakened the paramount mission of securing the new nation-state.

In Poland, talk of land reform opened the question of whether a Polish state could place valuable acreage in the hands of Ukrainian and Belorussian peasants, while in Romania and Yugoslavia, land became available only when taken from ethnic others (Hungarians and Germans). But the problem of peasant politics in Yugoslavia went deeper than in Poland with its competing *Piast* and *Wyzwolenie* factions of south and north: the peasant movement was also divided by ethnicity, so much so that the avowed people's parties in Croatia and Slovenia became stand-ins for national parties and were supported by many non-peasants.

Some of the peasant parties also shed their peasant character, becoming associated with commercial and banking interests, like the Czech Agrarians. In Hungary, the Smallholders party also represented medium-sized landowners, while in Slovenia and Slovakia, the nationalist Catholic People's parties tended to muffle class demands altogether. Nevertheless, the region's peasant parties constituted a remarkable case of people in countryside making their will felt in national politics; one historian has said that such parties, more than anything else, defined East Central Europe as a region. They never spread south of the

Balkan range to Greece, and despite numerous attempts, similar political groups never scored successes in France, Bavaria, or Holland.[70]

After Stamboliiski's assassination, few among his lieutenants thought peasants might seriously threaten the wealthy classes, and theories were concocted (for example, by Hungary's Count István Bethlen), according to which the lower classes were unfit to rule themselves. But Marshall Piłsudski and King Alexander of Yugoslavia went a step further, wondering whether professional politicians could even maintain order. When they moved to establish personal rule, they argued in terms similar to those employed in 1933 by the well known Austrian strongman Engelbert Dollfuss: that parliament had "eliminated itself" through irresponsible bickering.

By the 1930s, the postwar enthusiasm for republicanism had spent itself virtually everywhere, especially among intellectuals. George Orwell wrote that the old slogan "war for democracy" had even taken on a sinister sound.[71] Whether democratic or authoritarian, governments battled unsuccessfully with problems of development, and the strongmen who succeeded Maniu and Stamboliiski failed to achieve breakthroughs. Either farms remained small and undercapitalized, as in Bulgaria and Serbia, or the agricultural sector remained in the hands of large landholders. In Poland in 1921, 47.3 percent of all estates were larger than 50 hectares, and the laborers recruited to work the land had little prospect of owning it. Despite a land reform requiring redistribution of 544,707 hectares in Hungary in 1920, in 1935 78 percent of holdings were larger than 57.5 hectares.[72]

In a time when democratic means could not achieve democracy and strongmen could not make strong states, one can understand the attraction East Europeans felt for the totalitarian regimes of Italy, Germany, and Russia with their programs of national unity and state-driven growth. The tools in the hands of Eastern Europe's politicians were limited. Even those who wore military uniforms could not simply mandate the massive pooling of resources and labor in the manner of a Soviet five-year plan. For fear of full-scale revolts, they dared not imitate Stalin and impose sacrifices on the peasantry that would benefit urban industries; the tariffs East Europe's governments used to protect native products had already alienated villagers now unable to afford imported agricultural machinery. Opposition from right to left remained a feature of life even after most states had transformed from democratic to authoritarian, and the illiberal rulers of Hungary, Poland, Bulgaria, Yugoslavia, and Romania humiliated and harassed dissenters without breaking them.[73]

Still, the Depression raised fresh challenges for managing dissent. Incomes spiraled downward, reducing consumption in parts of Poland and Yugoslavia to starvation levels. Fascism promised order, strength, and welfare, and its appeal could not be ignored. But it was revolutionary and threatening. Following the example of conservative elites in Italy and Germany, Admiral Horthy in Hungary and King Carol in Romania supported fascist politicians more and less openly hoping to use them. In 1932, Horthy even appointed an avowed national socialist whom we have already met, Gyula Gömbös, as prime minister, while Carol covertly financed the Iron Guard. In Yugoslavia and Poland, leaders imitated fascist rituals, spectacles, and politics of mass mobilization. Only the Czechoslovak elite resisted all overtures to illiberalism and racism; they became the first target of Hitler's aggression. Yet despite the wide popularity of extreme nationalism from the Baltic to the Adriatic, no fascist movement came to power in the region before being hoisted up by Adolf Hitler beginning in 1938.

CHAPTER 14

Fascism Takes Root: Iron Guard and Arrow Cross

The 1930s were the era of fascism. Extreme right-wing movements rose up across Europe, claiming that their nations had become decadent and needed racial cleansing and regeneration. Fascists said that only violence could break through bourgeois complacency and subdue national enemies, above all Jews and socialists. Yet despite a massive and protracted economic crisis, movements of national salvation seized power only in Italy and Germany. Farther west, in France and Spain, the Netherlands, England, and Belgium, fascist movements broke through the surface but never got more than a few percentage points of the vote. They seemed tiny knots of dangerous eccentrics.

The standard explanation for the success of fascists in Italy and Germany lies in these countries' rapid modernization after unification in 1870/1871, when much misery of social dislocation was compressed in a brief time: by the start of World War I, largely agricultural nations had become urban and industrial in a few short decades, as millions moved from the countryside to the cities and were suddenly cut off from the predictable and secure lives of village communities. These individuals sought higher wages and greater opportunity, but often encountered overcrowding, long hours, job insecurity, and few amenities. Alcohol and spouse abuse were rife, as was child labor. The result was trade unions and socialist parties committed to workers' rights, but they coexisted uneasily with representatives of the still-potent smallholding peasantries and an industrial-trade middle classes. After the spectacle of revolution in Russia, workers in those more traditional sectors felt embattled and feared extinction if socialism advanced unimpeded.[1] Though most European socialists were moderate, they were vilified as reds, indeed as Bolsheviks, and in the turmoil after World War I, fascist paramilitary squads emerged, promising to protect property and order. No other party could take action, or so they argued. Fascists were deeply illiberal, but liberal democracy was not firmly rooted in Italy or Germany, and during the social and economic turmoil of the early 1920s and early 1930s, conservative forces hoisted Mussolini and then Hitler to power, hoping for salvation from their decline in status and threats of dissolution.[2]

In the United Kingdom, the industrial economy had grown over time, spreading the pains of transformation over generations, and class anxieties were not as acute as in Central Europe. Although important industrialization had taken place in France, much of the country remained rural, and extreme nationalism failed to find adherents because conservative farmers dominated the countryside, leaving little space on the far right.[3] At the height of crisis in the mid-1930s, France's center and left united to keep the tiny fascist movements from growing, and forces of order kept discontent from spilling onto the streets. Economic distress was never as dire as in Germany, but above all, nationalism did not radicalize. France had no territories or oppressed minorities in other countries to reclaim and no damaged "honor" to recover.[4]

Similarly, Britain was a sated power with none of the irredentism that was so popular in Italy and Germany after World War I, and the social power of conservatism as a form of nationalism made fascists seem un-British.[5] In addition, France and Britain were places where strong national parties had taken on expanded administrative roles over generations. By contrast, Germany's political parties had yet to become accustomed to exercising power and were uncertain about how to integrate the socialist left without triggering civil war.[6] Italy's parties had little practice in representing clear constituencies, and they tended to meld into one great government machine, from which they doled out favors to party executives.

In this context, Eastern Europe does not make ready sense. Nowhere did a fascist movement take power unless aided by Nazi Germany: in March 1939 in Slovakia, April 1941 in Croatia, and October 1944 in Hungary. Romania's Iron Guard managed to share government in late 1940 but was ruthlessly purged by the less extreme and more dependably pro-German military in early 1941. Everywhere between Germany and the Soviet Union, fascism remained marginal, never above a few percentage points in popularity—everywhere, that is, except Romania and Hungary. In a vastly reduced Hungary, the Great War's greatest loser, but also in an enlarged Romania, major fascist movements emerged, called "Arrow Cross" and "Iron Guard," each numbering about 250,000 adherents by the late 1930s.

The primary reasons for fascism's impressive growth in Romania and Hungary had little to do with the crises of rapid development that plagued Germany or Italy. Both remained overwhelmingly agrarian countries, where relatively few individuals had suffered the pains of dislocation, and peasants lived in traditional environments, often illiterate and difficult to mobilize by fascists or anyone else. Romania and Hungary called to mind agrarian southern Italy, where fascism also made slow progress. As we have seen, men calling themselves peasant politicians in East Central Europe tended to serve bureaucratic machines, forgetting their past except during unavoidable but meaningless campaigning a few days a year, when they appeared "back home" in traditional costumes and put on a folksy style. If there was sustained modernization in Eastern Europe, it occurred in the Czech lands and western Poland, places that remained resistant to fascism.

As far as political life in general was concerned, the region tacked between the German and Italian variants: parties existed, but they tended to see their function as dominating the state bureaucracy rather than representing particular constituencies. As in Germany and Italy, the liberal orders had little experience in integrating the left, be it the socialist parties or the huge peasant movements. The response of the elites to gains made by left-wing parties, as we have seen, was to shut down parliament and construct governments consisting of their own favored politicians, usually in collusion with the king or regent.

In these regards, Romania and Hungary fit into general regional patterns. King Carol and Admiral Horthy chose ministers and otherwise stage-managed the political process. These two countries also fit the regional pattern of arrested development: the majority of citizens worked underproductively in the countryside, often as sharecroppers. The Depression ravaged the region's societies more or less equally, and greater misery in Romania or Hungary than elsewhere does not explain the success of fascist mobilization in these two countries. Irredentism was also not decisive. Whereas most Hungarians desperately wanted the return of territories lost at Trianon, Romania was a great winner that had seen all its territorial demands satisfied and then some.

What distinguishes these two places is the legacy of contempt by their liberal elites for the common people, a trend that can be dated to the 1870s, leaving huge spaces on the right for politicians claiming to represent "the people's" grievances in ethno-national as well as social terms. In both places, urban elites had shown particular condescension toward the rural masses and disingenuously claimed that social reform had to wait until the country had regained vast lost territories (Hungary) or successfully integrated vast new territories (Romania). In both places, the territories in question were mostly in Transylvania. And in both places, politicians derided the most basic need—land reform—as proto-Bolshevism, the first stage to collectivization.

These "liberal" arguments were so cynical and self-serving as to provoke a response on the right, and it would be characteristic of Romania and Hungary that fascist leaders were celebrated not so much for being strong and decisive (as in Italy or Germany) as for being honest and caring, and evidently distinct from the actual rulers. As in northern Italy or central Germany, their advance to mass popularity was not automatic; it required dogged work by activists, who had to contend with authoritarian rulers who used the police to suppress them. In Hungary, the regent Horthy tried to make use of the fascists' energies for his own purposes and learned that fascism could not be tamed. In Romania, King Carol more quietly abetted fascism, only likewise to conclude that fascists could not be used for his purposes. Yet despite severe measures of repression, neither country's leaders stopped fascism's advance, and Carol and his wife barely escaped assassination in 1940. Fascism remained a serious force in Hungary as well as Romania until Red Army troops crossed the borders in 1944/1945, bringing with them a revolution called antifascist and democratic.

Emergence of the Movements

In Hungary and Romania, radical nationalists argued almost from the moment the armistice was signed in 1918 that the war had set new standards for self-sacrifice, and that states must now defend national purity as never before. Experience soon showed that liberal politicians fell far short of the mark. When he took power, Hungary's Horthy had indeed staged a blood purge of socialist enemies and restricted the entry of Jews into business and professions by capping their numbers at universities, but under Count Bethlen, his prime minister through the 1920s, the political elite endeavored to return to "business as usual" with the Jewish community, stepped back from violence, and protected citizens' property and persons.[7] In Romania, the liberal regime committed the "sin" of extending full citizenship rights to Romania's Jews in 1922, and the country's first fascists were students who sought to hunt down the responsible politicians and kill them.

In both countries, radical rightists converted old stereotypes into tropes of their new racial ideology, portraying Jews as congenitally different, living off capital rather than working, and supporting subversive causes like Communism while shirking duties to the nation. These radicals selectively used data, claiming, for example, that 45 percent of the political leaders of the Hungarian Soviet Republic had been Jewish.[8] Ignored was the fact that Jews, often reserve officers, were overrepresented among holders of military decorations in all armies. Or that if Jews entered Communist parties, that was because they tended to live in urban areas from which Communists drew support; or that Communists radically opposed ethnic discrimination.[9] In fact, Communists were a small minority among Jews, who tended to support Zionist, moderate socialist, and traditional parties.

Upwardly mobile ethnic Romanians who aspired to urban careers believed that Jews unfairly usurped middle-class jobs: 80 percent of textile industry engineers, 51 percent of doctors in the Army Medical Corps, and 70 percent of journalists were Jews. The number of Jews in the professions, banking, or commerce in Hungary was similarly high. In addition, Jews were portrayed as favoring foreign nations and their cultures, whether Hungarian in Transylvania, or Russian and German in Bessarabia and Bukovina. The Romanian fascist Corneliu Codreanu, who began his career as a student radical in the Moldavian capital of Iaşi, called Jews an "army that comes into our land to conquer us," and said that if Communism prevailed, the Romanian people would be "mercilessly exterminated" and the land "colonized by Jewish masses."[10]

Like many fascists, Codreanu lacked military credentials because he had been too young to serve in World War I, but he made up for that by smashing the heads of workers and Communists in squadrons of strikebreakers who took to Iaşi's streets in the early postwar turmoil. His mentor Alexandru C. Cuza, a professor of political economy, was an extreme anti-Semite who formed the Radical Christian Union in 1922. Cuza used the swastika as his movement's symbol yet seemed tame to Codreanu and his friends because he foreswore militancy.[11]

In 1923 authorities arrested Codreanu for conspiracy to murder those responsible for granting Romanian citizenship to Jews. While in prison, he claimed to have experienced a vision of the Archangel Michael, urging him to dedicate his life to God, and four years later formed the "Legion of St. Michael" (also known as the Iron Guard), which preached national cleansing and the liberation of peasants, emphasizing "education" rather than economic reform. Codreanu, called the "Captain" by his followers, became a cult figure, especially among the young, yet never held office. Instead he led a crusade for moral rejuvenation against all who threatened to betray the Christian Romanian peasant.[12] He was hazy about politics, arguing that Romania needed "men" and not programs, and built on anti-Western traditions, according to which Romania had the special mission of shaping an economy rooted in the village and Christian values.

In Hungary, fascist thought first crystallized in 1919 among right-wing radicals in the southern Hungarian city Szeged (thus called the Szeged idea). Liberal democracy had led not to liberation but to rule by "enemies," above all by Jews, who were identified as an alien force with a lock on the ethnic nation's business, finance, and culture. Underneath the legality that had returned to Hungarian public life after the white terror of the early 1920s, secret societies devoted to the Szeged idea proliferated, for example, the Association of Awakening Hungarians, the Hungarian Scientific Race-Protecting Association, and the "X" association, which intended to resurrect the "spirit" of the Magyar tribes that had conquered the Carpathian Basin.[13]

Like fascist movements elsewhere, the Hungarian and Romanian variants originated in urban areas, among lower middle classes who felt threatened by modernization and were willing to believe that "foreigners" (that is, Jews) were to blame for their reduced salaries, difficulties getting jobs, or the competition threatening small businesses with extinction. But each place also had a distinctive character: Hungary's fascists tended to come from the army, Romania's from the universities.

After 1919 Hungary was flooded with some 300,000 refugees from the lost territories, mostly bureaucrats and army officers for whom there was not enough work in the truncated country. The Trianon Treaty had limited the army to 35,000 soldiers, and many unemployed former officers and civil servants streamed into the ultra-nationalist underworld. Right-wing leaders Gyula Gömbös and Ferenc Szálasi were professional military officers who also enjoyed support in the higher military echelons. Even though Szálasi's views were racist in the extreme, his Arrow Cross Party colonized the armed forces, drawing leaders from the officer corps throughout the party's existence.[14]

In their support for radicalism, Romanian universities fit into global patterns. In China and Russia, Anatolia and Europe, students agitated for social and national causes with greater passion than any other group, and in peripheral settings like Warsaw, Zagreb, Bucharest, the Baltic States, and Spain, universities became fascism factories, processing undergraduates who were discovering that the promises of middle-class comfort after graduation were an illusion.[15] Prominent among them were veterans shattered by the blatant insouciance of the well-heeled politicians who had sent thousands of young men to their deaths under the terrifying circumstances of mechanized war, yet now faced no consequences.

But in an age when students everywhere were flocking to radical movements, fascism's growth at Romanian universities was still extraordinary, traceable to immense disparities between city and countryside. Before World War II, nine urban centers had concentrated all Romanian industrial enterprises, while 80 percent of the population was rural. The few young people who made the transition to cities suffered wrenching dislocation, and the humiliation of low status combined with the hypocrisies of "decent" society to make the mix of national and social grievances traumatic in the extreme.[16] Professors and leading intellectuals encouraged young people's dissent, and together they sought to transform universities into bastions of ethnic Romanian learning. By the 1930s, a nationwide conspiracy had formed in Romanian higher education: right-wing students combed high schools seeking out young toughs and then presented these fledgling fascists' willingness to take part in attacks on Jews as a prime credential for university enrollment.[17]

Because of their country's obligations from the minority treaties imposed on Romania at Versailles in 1919 and the country's membership in the League of Nations, Romanian authorities did not directly limit Jewish access to higher education the way Hungarian counterparts did; still, anti-Semitic violence was a staple of interwar university life, and Jews were marginalized.[18] Compared to the population as a whole, Jews in Romania tended to be urban and literate, and at the outset they were well represented in higher education. If the number of Jews in the country was about 4.2 percent, among students the total was close to 14 percent in the late 1920s, higher in some faculties than in others. For example, between 1923 and 1936, Jews constituted around 40 percent of the students at the medical faculty at Iași and slightly less than a quarter of medical students in Bucharest. Yet because of thuggery and bureaucratic chicanery, the number of Jewish students dropped after the 1935/1936 school year, for example, from 14.8 to 7.9 percent in Bucharest, 23.1 to 16.1 percent in Iași, and 29.6 to 15.6 percent in Cernăuți.[19]

Like early nationalists throughout Eastern Europe, Iron Guard leaders were grandsons of peasants and children of shopkeepers or schoolteachers, and if fascist leaders tended to be young—Hitler was 44 in 1933—the Guard was even younger.[20] In 1931 the teacher's son Codreanu was thirty-two, and his lieutenants Motsa, Marin, and Stelescu were in their middle to late 20s. Of the Guard members forced into refuge in Germany between 1942 and 1944, just under half were young intellectuals.

The Guard's support of ultranationalism thus had the surface rationality of easing upward social mobility for ethnic Romanians caught in urban environments that seemed dominated by Jews, but also Turks, Hungarians, Germans, and Greeks. But the Guard's ideology was ultimately not rational. Its members

FIGURE 14.1. Memorial service for Iron Guard founder Corneliu
Codreanu (October 1940). *Source*: Süddeutsche Zeitung Photo/
Alamy Stock Photo.

swore oaths of blood loyalty, hunted supposed traitors in their own ranks, rejected urbanity, and yearned to return to the "people," a fictional entity consisting of all Romanians who had lived or ever would live. Ironically, the increasingly fascistic atmosphere of universities would socialize right-wing students
to reject all calculations for the "good life." The bourgeois world was foreign and
should remain so. Making the leaders' alienation even deeper was that many

were of mixed background and were as complexly foreign as the world they came to hate. Codreanu was of Polish and German, Gömbös of German, and Szálasi of Armenian and Magyar/Slovak descent.[21]

Because Hungarian students tended not to come from humble backgrounds, they did not share this profound sense of estrangement, and their latent anti-Semitism was mollified by the restrictions the regime placed on Jewish enrollment in the 1920s. As a whole, they tended to support the more conservative nationalism of the regime rather than fascism.[22]

Only after the Depression struck in 1929 did the Iron Guard and Arrow Cross become broadly popular, beyond their original constituencies at universities and in army barracks. The questions for the Romanian and Hungarian political establishments now became the same as in Berlin after the Nazis emerged as the second-strongest party in the fall of 1930: was it possible to use fascists to stabilize a system threatened by mass unrest, and if not, how could they be controlled? Ultimately, none of these groups found satisfactory answers, but they ended up at different kinds of dead ends.

Controlling Fascism?

Interwar Romanian politics mixed democratic procedure and rule of law with the corruption and duplicity common to much of the region. There were frequent elections and independent parties as well as many scrupulous and serious politicians who planned for cultural and economic progress. Yet the political classes also feared the common people and were willing to transgress democratic procedure to keep them under control. For example, Ion C. Duca, a courageous liberal antifascist who fell victim to a Guard assassination team in 1933, had colluded in manufacturing the electoral majority that brought him to office. And the Peasant party of the honest and charismatic Iuliu Maniu won the unrigged elections of 1928, but then stalled on promises to put more land in the hands of its supposed constituents and proved unable to alter the fundamental deficiencies of Romanian agriculture. The economy was poorly prepared for the crisis of the early 1930s, when Romania's grain exports collapsed, further constraining political options.[23]

The corrupt regime of King Carol II opened wide spaces on the right for "honest" men like Codreanu to profile their concern for fellow ethnics, above all in the countryside, whom Bucharest's elites held in contempt. Still, Codreanu was not openly subversive, called himself a monarchist, and enjoyed the king's secret financial support. Carol hoped to corrupt and use the Guard, but in the meantime, he set up his own paramilitary youth group *Straja Țării*: the guard of the country.[24]

In 1932 fascism vaulted suddenly to the pinnacle of Hungarian politics, when Regent Horthy appointed Gyula Gömbös as prime minister in the hope of containing explosive social unrest. Gömbös, a former captain in the Austro-Hungarian army, was, like Codreanu, a fierce chauvinist and organizer of counterrevolutionary squads. As minister of defense in the late 1920s, he had groomed himself on Mussolini's model and promised to rid Hungary of Jews and freemasons and to distribute land and jobs to peasants and workers.[25]

Yet once in power, Gömbös adapted to the system he claimed to detest, showing no appetite for total power; he neither abolished independent parties nor set himself up as dictator. He failed to sponsor the equivalent of Germany's Nuremberg laws, but instead "extended a friendly hand" to the Jews.[26] Even the Social Democrats and trade unions—in theory, archenemies of fascism— continued to exist, as did the workers' right to strike. Gömbös blocked Ferenc Szálasi's more radical Arrow Cross by keeping its supporters from voting, and indeed, he rigged the elections of April 1935 to ensure himself dominance in parliament with 43.6 percent of the vote.[27] He did little to promote land reform, and many peasants continued to live as they always had, in mud huts with stamped earthen floors and livestock under one roof.[28]

Nevertheless, Gömbös primed Hungary for fascism. He created a mass movement of 60,000 vanguard fighters for his Party of National Unity, and younger, more radical nationalists entered the state administration and army. In 1935 he assured an audience in Berlin that he would make Hungary into a one-party dictatorship, but he died of a kidney ailment the following year before fulfilling his pledge. By then his antics had frightened governing elites and caused them to unite with moderates to keep fascists out of power. Yet the rightward drift could not be stopped. His successor, the nationalist Kálmán Darányi, continued to harass the Arrow Cross by forbidding their meetings, yet he also attempted to placate an outraged right by sponsoring anti-Jewish laws in parliament, which passed despite opposition across much of the political spectrum. In a desperate move to dam up the far right, Darányi created his own fascist-seeming formation, the Ragged Guard (*Rongyos Gárda*), which staged raids into Slovakia and Ruthenia and harassed Jews in the northeastern counties.[29]

Under Gömbös and Darányi, Hungary was slowly pulled into Germany's orbit and ultimately became an ally in the campaign against the Soviet Union in 1941. The draw appeared irresistible for two reasons. First, taking advantage

FIGURE 14.2. Gyula Gömbös in Berlin (1935). *Source*: Süddeutsche Zeitung Photo/
Alamy Stock Photo.

of the inactivity of western states in the region, German government and private institutions concluded trade agreements to buy Hungary's agricultural products, paying not in exchangeable "hard" currency but in closed accounts in German banks and so forcing Hungary to buy German industrial goods, often of high quality. The percentage of Hungary's exports bought by Germany rose from 11 percent in 1930 to almost 50 percent in 1939; by that date, half of all foreign capital invested in Hungary was controlled from Germany.[30]

This pattern of creeping German economic control was repeated throughout southeastern Europe. In 1938 Yugoslavia contracted with the Krupp firm in Essen to construct a mill in Bosnia for manufacturing guns and artillery shells, and that same year, Berlin agreed to supply Bulgaria with 30 million marks' worth of armaments. From 1929 to 1939, Bulgaria's exports to the Reich rose from 29.9 percent to 67.8 percent. The Western powers never summoned the political will to halt the German advance.[31] Yugoslav officials had been disappointed that a loan negotiated with France in 1931 failed to help secure new markets, military supplies, or diplomatic support. A few years later, London denied Bulgaria a loan, but Germany quickly stepped in with credits of an additional 22 million marks.[32] For southeastern European elites, cooperation with Germany and Italy seemed not so much a gamble as a rational calculation to protect their economies from the ravages of the Depression.

But Hungary had a second, even stronger reason for turning to Germany: its population's determination to recover lost territory, stoked to a frenzy by government propaganda. A first reward for cooperation with Germany came in October 1938, after the Munich Conference, when a German-Italian arbitration committee returned the ethnically Hungarian areas of southern Slovakia to Hungary. Yet with its appetite properly whetted, the German government now required further evidence that Hungary was indeed part of the Nazi order: it had to become more authoritarian and more racist. And therefore, after Darányi's anti-Jewish laws followed three more, in 1939, 1941, and 1942, defining Jewishness ever more narrowly according to "race," forbidding marriage between Jews and gentiles, divesting Jews of their property, and excluding them from public life.[33] The supposed dividend came in 1940, with awards of territory in Transylvania, but the Nazi lust for Hungary's collaboration in its genocidal policies was unsated and would, as we will see in Chapter 17, ultimately cost the lives of 600,000 Hungarian Jewish men, women, and children.

Perhaps the drive to regain territory was unavoidable, given widely shared popular sentiments, but the elite's continued contempt for the common people, even after the scare generated by Gömbös, was not. The government might have redistributed land to promote a more diverse market economy in the countryside, but in 1936, Horthy declared that since there was not enough land for everyone, the nation's salvation lay in economic development.[34] How that would occur he did not specify, and the concentration of land and industry in the hands of ever fewer families continued unabated.[35] Developed sectors of the economy remained highly concentrated, with two Budapest banks controlling 60 percent of Hungary's industry. The general population's average daily earnings in 1938 had plummeted one third to a quarter below the level prior to the Depression. In Romania, there was also talk of advancing industry, but plans fell victim to favoritism and corruption and were not effectively implemented.[36]

In light of the Horthy regime's scorn for popular welfare, it was no surprise that the Arrow Cross remained popular, getting 750,000 of 2 million votes in the Hungarian parliamentary elections of May 1939. Aligned with four other national socialist factions, it captured one quarter of all ballots nationwide. The appeal extended from the disaffected to the ambitious and successful; from civil servants, employed and unemployed university graduates to the officer corps; and through the lower middle classes, workers and agricultural laborers, and then deep into the old middle class. In industrial Budapest, the fascists did far better than the Social Democrats, showing that workers in town and country accepted national socialist promises to deliver them from fear and desperation.[37]

Despite likewise operating under a sham democracy, with elections arranged by the interior minister of a government appointed by the king, Romania's Iron Guard managed to attract almost 16 percent of the vote (and 66 seats) in the Romanian elections of December 1937, becoming the third strongest party. In a sample taken of the Legionary rank and file in 1937 (about 272,000 members), 20.5 percent turned out to be unskilled workers, 17.5 percent peasants, and 14 percent skilled workers. But the leadership continued to consist of students and former students with a high percentage of lawyers.[38]

The main force alerting peasants and the working class to fascism's dangers were the illegal Communists, and hatred of Communism grew into an obsession among the Guardists, who associated it with Jews and Satan. The idea of class struggle seemed egregious to them because it implied divisions in the people, yet fascists also hated liberal democracy for being "alien" to the native soil. According to Guardist Vasile Marin, democracy produced the "universal, abstract, ideal man, always identical to himself, whereas we need men who are solidly rooted in our soil, in our history, and in our national consciousness."[39] The racist sociologist Traian Herseni added that no one besides the Legion represented "a political position that is valid and capable of electrifying the people. Beyond the Legion, there is only darkness and chaos." Against sham democracies, the Iron Guard and Arrow Cross promised action, and against "old boy" networks, they seemed to personify self-sacrifice for the sake of the poor.[40] But they did not impress through depth of thought. Ferenc Szálasi offered followers this retort to Marxism in his 1936 *Road and Goal*:

> Social Nationalism is life's only genuine physics and biology. The true individual forms matter within his soul; his hand is but an instrument. And since this is so, the formed matter is a value and not a ware. Social Nationalism is therefore the nation's biological physics and not its historical materialism.[41]

He thus attracted disciples not through well-considered political ideas but through evident honesty and sincerity, qualities that seemed rare in Hungarian public life. Like Hitler in Germany, Szálasi visited every corner of the country, charming followers by remembering their names; yet in contrast to the angry Führer, he tended to evoke love for his people rather than hatred of others. According to the British historian C. A. Macartney, a frequent visitor to Hungary in those years, Szálasi inspired devotion "such as no other Hungarian of his age could equal, and after his death [Hungarians] carried on a cult of him." Like Codreanu, Szálasi was a devout Christian, and like Codreanu, he considered Christ a local national patriot. In fact, he claimed that Christ was racially Hungarian (Turanian).[42]

In Romania as in Hungary, fascism's allure spread across classes, but in Romania, it extended to the most respected intellectuals, the most radical being the young. Even when they did not join the Guard, many among the younger urban intelligentsia in Bucharest or Iași propounded anti-Semitism and racism, demanding violent, ethnocentric revolution. Prominent thinkers espousing such views included the theater director Haig Acterian, the actor Marietta Sadova, the poet Dan Botta, and the later world-famous scholar of religion Mircea Eliade.[43]

After the war, some would accuse such established authorities of seducing them. In 1945 the playwright Eugéne Ionescu blamed the right-wing philosopher Nae Ionescu (no relation) for having led a generation of intellectuals astray, creating "a stupid, reactionary Romania."[44] But by the mid-1930s, the attraction to extremism was so widespread that it did not require special inducing. As in Spain, Austria, and Poland, the political center had vanished, and the young flocked to one extreme or the other. Intellectuals who resisted fascism in Romania opted for left-wing radicalism or different shades of ultranationalism. For example, the eminent historian Nicolae Iorga put on the uniform of King Carol II's fascist-imitation National Renaissance Front. For some, that was not radical enough. A year later, Iorga would fall victim to an Iron Guard hit squad.

A practical concern that drove Romanian intellectuals toward the extremes was the perceived difficulty of making Romania a modern nation. Sixty years had passed since the state's founding, and the bastions of national culture—high schools, universities, professions, commerce (indeed, major urban milieus)— seemed to remain in the hands of "foreigners," while Romanians were still mostly unlettered villagers, mired in poverty for which liberalism provided no solution. The ethnic understanding of who counted as Romanian had long ago morphed into an ethno-racial one, and multiple streams of agitators proposed ways of "de-jewifying" urban culture. Among them, the Guard was most popular because it seemed principled and determined to get results.

Outsiders think of fascist organizations like the Guard as constricting freedom, but intellectuals on the inside said it liberated them: from fear. "One joins the Legion because one is free," Mircea Eliade wrote in 1937, "because one has decided to overcome the limitations of biological determinism and of economic determinism.... those who join the Legion put on the shirt of death. This means that the Legionnaires feel so free that even death no longer frightens them." People released from fear of death could rise far above mundane concerns and dreamed of recreating a past when ethnic natives lived in harmony and fulfillment.[45]

Yet for the time being, the Romanian intelligentsia also shared the cultural pessimism that was gripping intellectuals across Europe. Consider the philosopher Emile Cioran (1911–1995), author of *The Trouble with Being Born* and *On the Heights of Despair*. Anxieties plagued Cioran when he pondered an uncaring universe with no higher laws, but they became unbearable when friends insisted that he commit himself to action: political engagement seemed unavoidable yet pointless.[46] The Legion promised release from such inner turmoil through its synthesis of national politics and local Christianity, attracting men and women eager to explore paths of self-sacrifice because they seemed ennobling. "We are fortunate," Mircea Eliade said in 1938, "to live in the days of the most significant change undergone by modern Romania: the emergence of a new aristocracy. The young Legionnaires, alongside other wonders achieved through sacrifice, dedication, and creative will, have also laid the foundations of a Romanian elite, the elite of the new man." "Let us all unite," Codreanu told villagers in a churchyard in 1929, "the hour of Romanian revival and salvation is drawing nigh. He who believes, he who will fight and suffer, will be rewarded and blessed by this nation."[47]

These appeals to Christian faith permitted the Legion to draw support from rural worlds that were still deeply religious. By contrast, Nazi leaders had treated Christianity as an opponent and developed their own rites of initiation, marriage, and burial, while promoting a cult of Germanic religion; after ultimate victory, they planned to abolish established confessions and convert churches into sites of Hitler worship.[48] In Romania the Guard mingled Christian rituals with its own, causing some to liken it to a religious revival, benefiting from antimaterialist sentiments that were widespread among disaffected youth, many of whom originated in villages. The Legionary press described in detail apparitions of the Blessed Virgin reported by a certain Maria Rusu, as well as mass pilgrimages to the field where the shepherd Petrache Lupu reported having spoken to God—in the guise of an old man calling himself "Mosa."[49]

In contrast to movements farther west, the Guard and the Arrow Cross renounced anticlericalism and pledged to protect church altars, and if Mussolini, Hitler, or Joseph Goebbels mocked and belittled priests (*Pfaffen*), Codreanu marched with them. It was unthinkable that a Legionary would follow the agnostic Benito Mussolini in challenging God to "strike him dead," or joke about a sexual affair between Jesus and Mary Magdalene. Nazism and Italian fascism did not function to reinforce Christian belief, yet in Romania, even for intellectuals no longer practicing Christianity, fascism could stimulate memories of a living faith that were "not far from the surface."[50]

Some have argued that the Guard's "Christian revolution" corrupted Christian faith with ancestor worship, xenophobia, and a cult of blood and soil.[51] Students symbolized unity by drinking their intermingled blood. But rather than quibble over proper interpretation, the Romanian Orthodox Church embraced the Guard, and its priests led legionary demonstrators with icons and religious flags while green-shirted young men brought up the rear. Priests were nearly a third of the 103 candidates put up by the "All for the Country" party in 1937. In their scuffles with Communists, legionaries said they were defending God's Son; an Iron Guard journalist even proclaimed, "God is a fascist."[52]

The Iron Guard did not simply draw on worlds of belief left behind in rural settings; legionaries took leaves of absence from studies or work and hiked out to the countryside, far beyond the railway network, avoiding gendarmes who might have curtailed their activities, to reach peasants no liberal politician would dare to visit. When they saw Guardists approaching, peasants often greeted them with lighted candles. "In the villages when we sang or spoke," Codreanu later wrote, "I felt that I penetrated into undefined depths of their souls, where the politicians with their *borrowed* programs had been unable to descend."[53] But the Guard did not simply preach. When Codreanu or his followers encountered peasants working in the fields, they stopped to pitch in, and afterward spent the evenings singing and talking in villages, impressing everyone with their eagerness to work for what they believed. Before moving on, they distributed icons of the leaders as well as holy cards portraying the movement's martyrs.

After exploring the terrain, the Guard chose sites suited for work camps, as well as agricultural cooperatives and farms. Hundreds of legionaries toiled for two summers to establish a work and vacation camp on the Black Sea that featured stone buildings, kitchens, roads, drainage canals, flower gardens, picnic tables, and a hen house.[54] In the camps, a new social world evolved, with its own rituals (such as weddings), planned leisure activities, songs, and folklore. The goal was to build a "new life by new men":

> who do not seek riches and gold squeezed out of the helpless worker, but who must be used to living only from hard and sober work. That is why the Captain of the Legionaries had filled the country with work camps where

churches are built, houses are erected for the poor, things are built for the public good. Because by working here arduously, intellectuals and city folk—the future leaders of a legionary country—will become used to another life, difficult and hard, and will no longer long for a life based on theft.[55]

Young legionaries would sweat out the last measure of corruption they had imbibed in the cities and then toil to efface distinctions between intellectual and worker, in a variety of enterprises they founded in town and countryside, including the camps, but also shops, small commercial businesses, sporting societies, kiosks, charity ventures, wine cellars, bars, and restaurants, all of which mixed social groups and encouraged voluntary, self-sacrificing labor.[56] During interrogations by Communist authorities after the war, legionaries recalled the pleasant surprise of customers who discovered that the wait staff in Guard-supported restaurants consisted of university graduates and that they refused to accept tips.[57]

The "new life" that legionaries were creating was not entirely new. They understood themselves as the most recent episode in a quest dating back to the 1830s to establish a world that was the Romanians' own, their romanticizing of village life built on efforts of earlier generations to imagine how Romania might bypass the misery, alienation, and fragmentation of modern city life. Yet their new world was much more than a village cooperative: it was a violent effort to replace traditional social ties with a disciplined hierarchy under a leader. "We have to make sure that the entire Romania becomes Legionnaire," said Codreanu, "the new Legionnaire spirit must reign. The whole country must be ruled according to the will of the Legionnaires." Historically mediated social ties would be recast into a "uniform, militarized way of life that would no longer be able to accommodate 'inefficiency,' or idle pastimes."[58] The Guard organized death squads to enforce discipline, targeting, for example, Mihai Stelescu, the movement's youngest deputy in parliament, who broke with Codreanu in 1935. The following year, ten legionaries (five of them theology students) tracked down the hospital where Stelescu was recovering from an appendectomy, shot him dozens of times, and then cut his body to pieces.[59] That same year, a student congress decided to form death squads to execute growing numbers of enemies, including other renegades.

In Hungary, by contrast, Horthy's regime kept the Arrow Cross under such tight control that it enacted no armed violence until brought to power by the Germans in 1944. Still, like the Iron Guard, Hungary's national socialists became popular through all strata of society because their cadres seemed to care when no one else did, making some urban workers finally feel that they were "organic parts" of the national community.[60]

The Legionary electoral success of December 1937—in which they had won almost 16 percent of the ballots—triggered a political crisis, because for the first time, the incumbent party failed to win, and despite manipulation, it could not form a majority.[61] Two months later, the king instituted a royal dictatorship and shut down all parties, including the Legion, along with its world of camps, restaurants, and businesses. Codreanu instructed followers to comply, evidently trusting in fate. Like his followers, the Captain seemed little concerned with death; in fact, the organization he led was a death cult. The standard practice of legionary hit squads was to surrender to authorities after carrying out their crimes.

King Carol had tacitly financed the Legion, which seemed to him an anti-Communist ally on the right. He had hoped it would serve him, because Codreanu respected the monarchy as a fundamental institution of the Romanian nation. Yet now Carol recognized that fascism was untamable and would subvert the existing order. In the fall, responding to a flare-up of unrest, he had Codreanu and several followers arrested and then executed, supposedly for trying to escape. In the summer of 1938, the Horthy regime put Hungary's charismatic fascist Ferenc Szálasi behind bars, where he remained for two years.[62] Neither movement took power until sponsored by Germany during the war; and in Romania, the Iron Guard's participation in government lasted only a few months (in 1940/1941), because their extremism endangered Romania's contributions to Germany's war efforts. Hitler preferred the radical nationalist general Antonescu to young fascist hotheads, and he extended his blessings when the general crushed the Iron Guard, even opening spaces at Dachau for Guardists who survived the blood purge.

* * *

The fascists of Romania and Hungary reveal what happens when a liberal national leadership permits space to open on the right by forces claiming to be both national and socialist, able to argue that the common people living in misery were victims of neglect by the comfortable establishment. Those in charge had no defense beyond force. These ethnic leaders had claimed to be nationalist but had done little to better national welfare; either they were uncaring and contemptuous, or weak. Fascists argued that liberal nationalists were both, and skillfully provoked the latent resentments of peasants and workers, telling them they were despised for who they were, intensifying pains felt at condescension that were very old but reached new potency in a time of recently attained mass literacy. The young fascists making appeals seemed honest and evidently driven by conviction, and they were fluent in the peasants' language, imbued with their concerns, and willing to listen as well as lend a hand.

Many fascists, for example in Germany, Austria, and Hungary, called themselves national socialists, and to many contemporaries, that is what they were. They said that social problems had national origins, caused by some foreigner, that the elites in state ministries claimed to be in the service of Admiral Horthy or the king but in fact were serving foreign capital. But at the same time, no one in Romania or Hungary could ignore the political show happening beyond the country's borders. By the late 1930s, Germany was not simply buying grain and propping up failing agricultural economies, it was poised to redraw the map of Europe. Romania and Hungary had to prepare themselves for a future that awaited everyone: the question was how other East European states would respond. How would they escape the pull of fascism—or would they ultimately succumb to its dubious allures? The story of fascism in Hungary and Romania showed that authoritarian regimes could enter the Nazi orbit while keeping native fascists in check, even suppressing them in a bloody purge. Indeed, that was what the German government itself preferred, because it meant their East European allies would be stable and supportive and not revolutionary—leaving the Germans a free hand to conduct their own revolution of the European and world order.

CHAPTER 15

Eastern Europe's Antifascism

In recent years, US newspapers have told their readers that Eastern Europe is on the verge of returning to the 1930s, when economic crises allegedly generated widespread xenophobia and fascism, propelling the continent into the genocidal war of the 1940s. One Nobel laureate among the op-ed writers believes that fascism was and is the "true historical path" for Eastern Europe—a fact supposedly evident in the rise of populism in today's Poland and Hungary, places where right-wing leaders fail to respect the separation of powers, routinely invoke nationalist rhetoric, and aspire to securing a permanent hold on power.

The national memory among most Poles, Czechs, and Serbs is very different: rather than producing fascism, they recall their countries standing in the first ranks of fascism's opponents. Poland's ambassador to the United States wrote that he could not accept claims that Poland was fascist, even as a "bad joke."[1] In fact, Poland was the first state to stand up against Hitler, and for doing so lost one in five of its citizens.

Despite their sensationalism, the opinion pieces do contain nuggets of truth. The Great Depression severely tested the ability of East European states to keep order. In some places—Poland especially—violence broke out against ethnic others: Jews in cities, Ukrainians in the countryside. But we have seen the Eastern European countries where fascism indeed sprouted—Hungary and Romania—and know its fate: to be trimmed down by authoritarian rulers each time it threatened to seize power. Horthy tossed fascists in prison; Carol had them executed. In direct contradiction to what our day's press asserts, East Central Europe was mostly barren ground for the seeds of fascism. In the countries whose stories follow, native hostility blew them away before they could properly take root.

There were to be sure nationalists, xenophobes, and anti-Semites in Poland, Bulgaria, Czechoslovakia, and Yugoslavia, but they don't live up to the name "fascist" because none of them assembled the revolutionary momentum that we saw in Romania's Iron Guard or Hungary's Arrow Cross; none proposed transcending the existing order to create a purified nation, shorn of all distinctions; none created uniformed paramilitary formations of the sort that went out into the Romanian countryside—and formed the core of fascism in Italy or Nazism in Germany.[2] None produced the sort of leader whom such formations revere.

Still, the story of East European antifascism is not a heroic one. What held back fascism in most of Eastern Europe were not regimes committed to fair play or human rights, nor strong institutions of liberalism or democracy. As in Hungary and Romania, in each place, a strong man acted to control the extremism of right and left and maintain order. And if fascist racism did not gain adherents in Poland, that was in part because established nationalists already preached racist exclusion, and that particular rhetorical space on the right was already occupied.

But in and beyond Poland, fascists also found that local nationalists stood opposed to their messages; the gap between national liberal elites and common people that grew so wide in Hungary and Romania was not replicated in Poland, Czechoslovakia, Bulgaria, or Yugoslavia. This does not mean that there were no privileged classes or exploited peasants or workers in these countries. The issue lies rather in the story repeated in our day by Poland's ambassador: that fascists could not be good Poles—or Czechoslovaks, or Yugoslavs. Fascists in these countries not only placed themselves at odds with the local national narrative: they seemed to be the nation's enemies. This was a story that made sense to elites as well as the masses, connecting them, and going from right to left. Germany and Italy, the countries that incorporated fascism, contested the very existence of Poland, Czechoslovakia, and Yugoslavia, and native fascists in these countries, by aping Mussolini's fascist salute and wearing Nazi-style uniforms, were seen to be the enemy's allies and stooges, not hypernational but anti-national.

Moreover, to many East Europeans, the "total rule," which Mussolini and Hitler personified, appeared deeply repugnant. According to core messages of local nationalists dating back to the nineteenth century, to be Polish or Czech or Serb was to favor liberty; the constitutions drawn up after World War I were not simple impositions by the West, but also reflected local traditions of self-rule. Even after the coups in Poland in 1926 and Yugoslavia in 1929, hundreds of thousands of Polish and Yugoslav citizens understood their countries' constitutions to represent valid national aspirations to freedom and rule of law.

Still, the region lived in the shadows of totalitarian states, and the temptations to go to the extremes of left or right pervaded the public imagination: the strong states of Germany and the Soviet Union had taken those countries on paths of dynamic growth, while the West remained mired in crisis. There was also a widespread fascination with state-led mass mobilization that leaders in nonfascist Poland or Yugoslavia tried to copy. The country that resisted such temptations altogether was the sole country to maintain adherence to democratic forms up to the moment that Nazi troops crossed its borders in 1938: Czechoslovakia. But even here we see a strongman presiding over the system—though not usually wearing a uniform—and if that country knew democracy, it was democracy managed from above.

Czechoslovakia: Managed Democracy

The Czech and Slovak strong man was T. G. Masaryk, the professor turned politician who agitated for Czechoslovak independence during the war years and became a virtually uncontested authority figure after 1918. His political "realism" had achieved statehood, and Czech parties quickly took hold of the administrative apparatus and used it to build a state for the sake of their national movement. That state adhered to its constitution and featured regular elections plus freedoms of speech and association, but because Czechs and their Slovak allies held a numerical majority, this new democracy was ethnic: rule by, for, and of the ostensible Czechoslovak people. It was a staged democracy held together by a rhetoric that made rule of the people an absolute value, with producer and director in the person of President Masaryk, who helped keep the democratic pieces in proper motion from his perch above party politics in Prague's Castle. Every Friday he invited trusted politicians for discussions; he encouraged them to work out deals and compromises, all safely beyond the scrutiny of Czechoslovakia's citizens, the ostensible demos.

Day-to-day management of government lay in the nonconstitutional Committee of Five (Pětka), which as we have seen in chapter 13, was established shortly after the war and consisted of Czech parties across the political spectrum, from the Social Democrats on the left through the National Socials, Agrarians, Catholics, and National Democrats on the right, with reliable support of parts of the Slovak political class. The Pětka was more coherent than ethnic parties in Poland, Serbia, or Romania, because the parties forming it had come together gradually over decades through combined efforts in the Austrian parliament in Vienna.[3] They had divisions like any spectrum, but given the neighborhood in which they operated, in which every border was contested, and the nation's ostensible enemies lived in strength both within and beyond the country's territory, the pressure to cooperate overwhelmed centrifugal forces. Unlike Poland's leaders, they could not delude themselves that they had won statehood by their own efforts. And democracy—or national self-determination—was the core justification for Czech and Slovak rule, and it found supposed sources in a humanitarian and progressive tradition of the Hussites. The old ideology of Bohemian state's rights both required and fulfilled demands for rule of the majority.

Nevertheless, in 1925 a tiny group did emerge espousing radical right-wing ideas, calling itself the "National Fascist Community." It performed abysmally in elections but tried to act from within the Czech Agrarian Party to promote cooperation with Nazi Germany.[4] In 1935, one of the Czechoslovak state's founders, National Democrat Karel Kramář, thought fascists might prove useful in stabilizing a Czech "national state" and merged with them.[5] Yet Masaryk had taken steps to crush this rising threat by demoting its leader, the daredevil military hero Rudolf Gajda, from general to private—while keeping him in the military—and then leveling more charges of treason against him than he could refute. In 1933 some seventy of his supporters attempted to seize weapons at a military barracks near Brno as the first steps in a march to power, but they retreated after a few shots were fired.[6] Only after the Munich Conference of late September 1938, when France and Great Britain permitted Germany to undermine Czechoslovak democracy, did Czech fascists assert themselves in Czech politics.[7]

A stronger challenge to democracy came from Czechoslovak Communists, who were dedicated to overthrowing the First Republic. They emerged late from a splintering of Czech Social Democracy (in 1921) and had been relatively moderate until 1929, when Stalinists purged rivals and proclaimed their intent to smash bourgeois rule. They campaigned in the 1934 presidential elections with the slogan: "Lenin not Masaryk!" and accused Czechoslovakia's president of using his authority to establish a fascist dictatorship.[8] Their major enemy was the moderate Social Democrats, whom Communists called "social fascists" for postponing the workers' revolution.[9] In the general elections of 1935, 10.3 percent of the electorate (849,495) cast their ballots for the Communist Party. Support was especially high in areas devastated by economic crisis, like Podcarpathian Ruthenia and the German-populated border areas of Bohemia, yet of all social groups, Communists' popularity was highest among leading intellectuals, though the party's leaders tended to be workers.[10] Fascism, by contrast, held little allure for educated Czechs.[11]

As disconcerting as political radicalism was in Czechoslovakia, it produced nothing like the destabilizing pressure seen in neighboring Germany, where in

1932, free elections yielded a majority against democracy, either for fascists (37.3 percent) or for Communists (14.3 percent). Germany's parliamentary center had been ground to bits, while the center held in Czechoslovakia, making use of a strong state, including the police, to do so.[12] Constituencies for radicalism were smaller in Czechoslovakia also because of the country's economic strength. In contrast to Austria, Germany, and Hungary, Czechoslovakia did not experience a hyperinflation after the war that wiped out both savings and trust in democracy among the middle classes.[13] Instead it featured a high gross domestic product, and the prosperity was palpable: major cities like Prague, Brno, and Plzeň grew, adding modern, sleek industrial buildings as well as residential structures, from villas to public housing, reflecting national pride and self-confidence.[14]

But the state also actively intervened in the economy with social policy to make sure that the hard times of the 1930s did not unravel the republican order: it was nationalist and socialist. When the Depression hit, an interventionist government under Agrarian Jan Malypetr instituted a Czech "New Deal," raising huge sums for public works, and issuing more than 240 decrees to inject life into the stalled economy.[15] A June 1933 bill gave the government the power to regulate the economy, and in 1934, Malypetr devalued the currency to stimulate exports. As a result, the economy turned the corner more quickly than in neighboring countries. Though Malypetr belonged to the right-leaning Agrarian Party, his economic policy derived from the plans of Czech socialists, highlighting the fact that Czech politicians cooperated across ostensibily thick political lines. And when National Democrats balked at policies they felt were hostile to business, the *Pětka* still managed to hold.[16] By contrast, the centrist Weimar coalition had fallen apart in 1930 over a dispute on financing unemployment benefits, opening the way for the electoral breakthrough of Nazism.

Yet if Malypetr's policy was democratic, it was not exactly liberal: under the growing shadow of Nazi Germany—and in the spirit of Masaryk's managed democracy—he also took steps to "protect" the Republic, passing laws curtailing freedom of the press and enabling his government to ban political parties. In 1933 two right-leaning German parties dissolved, preempting their expected prohibition by the Czechoslovak government after the Nazi seizure of power in Germany.

Yet despite all the strong guidance from the center, the new state failed to make the people of state—the Czechoslovaks—into a reality. A Slovak separatist movement grew despite occasional harassment, taking advantage of perceptions that Czechoslovakia was a Czech-directed mini-empire. The problem began at the top. In 1930, of 417 civil servants in the ministry of education in Prague, only four were Slovaks; in Bratislava, of 162 ministry employees, sixty-eight were Slovaks. Among 1,300 civil servants in the Ministry of Defense in Prague, six were Slovaks. The Czechoslovak Army had 139 active generals, but only one was Slovak. Among its 436 colonels, not one was Slovak. In the national railways' *Slovak* section, Czechs outnumbered Slovaks among the administrators, and only further down the hierarchy among the unskilled workers did one find natives. The interpretations varied: Slovak nationalists said this was evidence of colonialism, but Czechs argued that Slovakia did not yet possess educated cadres for administration.[17] The deeper reason was similar to an argument Serbs gave for sending administrators to Croatia: the governing nation could not trust the other ethnicities to behave responsibly.

But Czechoslovakia was not nationally oppressive. Czechs made possible the first Slovak institution of higher education in Bratislava and began creating Slovak professional elites, essentially rescuing the Slovak people from Magyarization. As a state respecting civil liberties, Czechoslovakia also protected German theaters and émigrés who had fled Hitler's Reich, like Ödön von Horvath, could stage their plays there in Prague, Brno, and Ostrava. German writers Thomas Mann and Heinrich Mann were granted asylum and passports permitting international travel while Austrian and German Social Democrats threatened with imprisonment in Vienna or Berlin moved their offices to Brno and Prague. After 1933, Czechoslovakia provided better conditions than any state in Europe—except Switzerland—for the flourishing of German culture and politics; an estimated sixty periodicals from all over the political spectrum were appearing in German before German troops marched into Prague in 1939.[18] Still, most Bohemian Germans and many Slovaks considered themselves "minorities" in Czechoslovakia, strangers in their own land, and thus became attracted to right-wing extremism.

In 1933, the Bohemian German schoolteacher Konrad Henlein formed the right-leaning but not openly fascist Sudeten German Party and soon attracted the interest of the Nazi party in Germany, which it supported with money and later weapons. Henlein then worked to sunder the "Sudetenland" from Czechoslovakia through massive and intimidating political mobilization among discontented Germans, but also by the formation of uniformed paramilitaries, who attacked institutions of the Czechoslovak state, like police stations and schools, as well as Jewish and Czech businesses. In 1935 Henlein's party won 15 percent of the vote, thanks to the support of more than two-thirds of German voters, more than the Nazis ever got in a free election in Germany or Austria, making them stronger than any other party in Czechoslovakia.[19]

The Slovak challenge to the Czechoslovak state came from the Slovak People's Party, founded in 1913 and led by the Catholic priests Andrej Hlinka and Jozef Tiso, which began demanding separation from the Czech lands in January 1938. In an autonomist bloc, the party got 30 percent of the vote in Slovakia in 1935, but only in the fall of 1938, when the Sudetenland was joined to Germany after the Munich agreement, did its extreme wing produce the "Hlinka Guard," consisting of uniformed units of supposedly racially pure fighters, similar to the Nazi paramilitary organizations SA and SS in Germany.[20] After complete severance from the Czech lands in March 1939, they shared power with more mainstream elements, making Slovakia an ally of Nazi Germany. Many Slovaks and Bohemian Germans had thus cooperated in Czechoslovakia's destruction from within nationalist separatist movements that had distinct fascist components.

Anti-Semitism was present in the Czech lands, but not so poisonously as elsewhere, perhaps because the economy was stronger and the perceived need to make scapegoats weaker. The Jewish community was also smaller. But the potential existed, as we see in the crisis of the early postwar years, when the Czech Agrarians and others propagated ideas of "Jewish Bolshevism" or supposed Jewish treason during the war. If the ideas did not get as far as in Poland or Romania, that was partly because the Czechs felt they were winners, and Bolshevism was not a direct threat. Though Zionism flourished in Czechoslovakia, Jews could also be integrated into Czech society and not seem to remain an "alien" nation. In other words, Jews were largely free to be who they wanted to be. "Nationalist hysteria," writes Blanka Soukupová, was "tempered by the joy at the birth of their own independent state."[21] As elsewhere, the most significant criticisms of anti-Semitism came from the left, from Social Democracy and Communism.

One might also credit native Communists with helping keep fascism tamped down: by channeling radical potential, especially among the young, fighting fascists in the streets, and publically refuting fascist positions, such as racism. Still, Communism had an ambivalent relation to fascism. In most places at most times, the Communists were the best-organized, most dedicated antifascist force, yet sometimes they frustrated antifascist cooperation across political camps (for example, in 1936 in Poland) when Moscow deemed that expedient. Thanks to Moscow, at times the Communists allied with fascists, most infamously from August 1939 to June 1941 during the Molotov-Ribbentrop Pact, an agreement that opened the way for Nazi Germany and the Soviet Union to destroy independent Poland.

Poland: Managed Authoritarianism

Poland differed in essential ways from Czechoslovakia: it was economically weaker and deeply divided politically, both between Poles and other ethnicities, and among the Poles themselves. An institution like the *Pětka* would have permitted ethnic Poles to control Poland, but the gap between Józef Piłsudski's center left and Roman Dmowski's center right was unbridgeable; the two men had their last personal conversation in 1920. Because of abiding chaos in parliament, Piłsudski had seized power in 1926 and ended Poland's democratic experiment. The country was similar to Czechoslovakia in the very tiny support that emerged for fascism, never growing above a few percentage points.

That had to do with the way fascism clashed with stories Poles told about Poland, and how those stories took shape in the rule of Poland's national elites. Piłsudski was a military strongman but also a Lithuanian native who considered himself heir of the multinational Polish commonwealth republic of centuries earlier, in which Protestant and Jewish communities had flourished. For decades he embodied the idea that Poland must cooperate actively with the nationalities of the region. Without his own forceful advocacy of alternatives, ethnic nationalism might have entirely eclipsed the heritage of the old commonwealth.

But he also represented a broad consensus on the virtues of the constitutional order that extended across the political spectrum. Piłsudski called himself a "democrat," but so did his enemies, the National Democrats, and together they connected to the venerable gentry tradition that nothing "about us should be decided without us" (*nic o nas bez nas*). No party supported the annihilation of parliament (the Sejm), which Poles understood to be an ancient institution of their own political culture.[22] The heritage of Polish democracy enjoyed support so deep that Piłsudski claimed he had seized power to protect it from its enemies.[23] And though he valued Poland's democratic traditions, he also knew that the veritable anarchy of early modern Poland, symbolized by the liberum veto, had left it open to dissolution and conquest.

Thus parliamentarianism was not simply an import, and in contrast to Germany, Russia, or Romania, no anti-Western ideologies took root among the intelligentsia; instead Poland claimed to have its own vital place in Europe, showing the continent its better side. The tiny groups of Polish fascists that nevertheless emerged evidently defied that heritage by transplanting German or Italian influences to Polish soil.[24]

Further constricting the space on which Poland's fascists operated was the embarrassing fact that they celebrated charismatic, militarist leadership, yet the only charismatic military leader on hand was Józef Piłsudski. Italian envoy Francesco Tommasini, who knew fascism from the inside, said in 1923 that Piłsudski was the only Pole who might have created a movement similar to Mussolini's.[25] At the moment Tommasini was writing, ideas about fascism were still crystalizing in European politics, and many considered Piłsudski to be Mussolini's twin. Both used nationalism to stir mass sentiment; both had a background on the left; and in 1926, Piłsudski seemed to further confirm the analogy by seizing power through a march on the nation's capital. Yet in contrast to fascists, Piłsudski's *Sanacja* regime at first allowed a fair amount of personal and political freedom. Apart from the Communists, political parties could continue, and the press was relatively free.[26]

And unlike Mussolini, Piłsudski failed to rally the masses, instead forming the colorless "Non-Party Bloc for Cooperation with the Government" (BBWR) in November 1927, which included conservatives, socialists, Catholics, peasants, and even ethnic minorities. Some of those who joined were stirred by conviction, but most by opportunism, fear, or resignation. Unlike fascist organizations, the BBWR sought passive acceptance and not absolute personal commitment.[27] Yet precisely because of his noninterventionist, laissez-faire approach to society and economy, Piłsudski's rule was less stable than Mussolini's. Mussolini had come from a humble background and knew the power of the left (in particular, the weapon of the general strike), and he intervened actively to maintain the economic and social bases of his power.[28] Piłsudski had been helped to power by striking workers but never felt a debt to them.

His distant style of rule worked reasonably well for a time, boosted by the British coal strike of 1926, which opened European markets for Silesian anthracite, but fortunes shifted with the onset of the Depression in 1930, after which social costs (such as unemployment, going as high as 40 percent of the labor force by 1935) forced harsh choices. Piłsudski ruled by decree, using rigged elections to win control of parliament in 1930. The economy stagnated, and none of his ministers took the bold moves that a crisis demanded.[29]

As a result, a center–left bloc emerged, which staged huge rallies in Kraków and other cities, demanding social legislation and a return to democracy. Piłsudski's response was to incarcerate some five dozen leaders at the great eastern fortress at Brest just before the 1930 elections; some were beaten and forced to do humiliating tasks, like clean latrines (and then not permitted to wash hands before eating). Eleven were convicted of planning a coup to remove the government by force, and five, including the prominent Peasant politician Wincenty Witos, chose to emigrate. In 1934, Piłsudski set up a detention camp at Bereza Kartuska in eastern Poland and had opponents sent there with the goal of breaking them psychologically.[30] Most were Communists, but there were also young fascists from the tiny Falanga movement as well as Ukrainian and Belorussian nationalists. The campaign against the Slavic minorities also degenerated into wanton destruction, with Polish army units ransacking Ukrainian villages and gutting cultural infrastructure and churches. In response, a Ukrainian underground carried out targeted assassinations of Polish officials.[31] Piłsudski had traveled quite a distance in a little over a decade: from envisioning a grand alliance of nations between the Baltic and the Black Sea, to squashing the aspirations to autonomy of fragments of nations on the territory of a would-be Polish nation state.[32]

Piłsudski did not have a profound understanding of party politics and expressed displeasure at the recourse to violence he himself had taken, saying that "force does not educate, it destroys."[33] He had assumed that society would

FIGURE 15.1. Center-left political rally in Warsaw (1930). *Source:* Jan Szeląg, *13 lat i 113 dni* (Warsaw, 1968), 221. Via Wikimedia Commons.

simply unite behind a vague national consensus, yet his sham constitutional rhetoric provoked a lethal mixture of cynicism as well as apathy. He might have done better by simply leveling with citizens about his methods and goals, arguing that crisis and chaos required a temporary resort to authoritarian rule.[34] Still, when he finally succumbed to cancer in 1935, Poles across classes and political divides mourned the old socialist and national revolutionary, and a quarter of a million people attended his funeral in Warsaw.

Poland descended deeper into social and economic crisis, but *Sanacja*'s opponents on the right did not exploit the growing unrest to seize power. The hold of Piłsudski's camp, mostly military officers, was too firm. Yet in an odd, indeed sinister way, his old enemies in National Democracy collaborated with *Sanacja* to keep right-wing extremism on Poland's political margins.

By the 1930s, fascism had crystalized into a definite substance on the European scene: it was about racism. The cornerstone of the Nazi order was the Nuremberg laws of 1935, which Italy reproduced in 1938, defining Jews by supposed shared blood. Yet in Poland, those attracted to racism did not need to become fascist. Racist anti-Semitism had a comfortable home among the *Endeks*. Since the 1890s, Dmowski and his followers had been obsessed by the "Jewish question." In their view, Jews constituted an "old" nation, which by holding crucial positions in the economy and professions was keeping the "young" Polish nation from thriving. In 1926 the *Endeks* had created the "Great Poland Camp," a nationalist mass organization with fighting units inspired by fascist models.[35] Poland's center right thus held back fascism by themselves embodying radical thought without any hint of social revolution. They were national socialists without the socialism.

But they were first-class chauvinists. Since the mid-1930s, explicit racism entered *Endek* thought, especially of its youth section, which rejected all talk of assimilation of Jews, even via baptism into the Catholic Church. *Endeks* demanded laws to eliminate Jews' rights, but like all in the grips of theories of biological destiny, they despaired: in their eyes, Jews were indestructible, and even severe repression would not weaken them.[36] It was out of the youth section that the tiny fascist group emerged called ONR-Falanga (National-Radical Camp-Falanga), which advocated expelling Jews from Poland as well as confiscating Jewish property.[37] Like fascists in Hungary and Romania, Falanga endured police repression and therefore could not assemble legally; still, historians estimate that it had 5,000 members by the late 1930s, about four-fifths of whom lived in Warsaw. As a movement of students, its ranks never stabilized, and it broke into numerous factions.[38]

Nevertheless, thanks to its flirtations with fascism, National Democracy remained an establishment party of the nationally minded middle classes, and though originally anticlerical, unlike many fascists, *Endecja* did not contest the cultural, religious, or economic establishment. Roman Dmowski called Catholicism Poland's religion, and his party boasted support from the clergy as well as the cultural elites and landed interests, all of which abhorred fascism, especially in its German embodiment. Dmowski, looking the part of a dour academic in suit and tie, never promoted a personality cult, but rather built his reputation as a writer and master of cabinet negotiations.[39]

Moreover, *Endeks* tended to support the idea of democracy. In May 1926, one National Democratic writer praised old strong old cultures, where respect for law caused the minority to respect the rights and convictions of opponents. The Polish left, he claimed, had not matured to that extent and lashed out with strikes and demonstrations when faced with a regime that represented the majority.[40] The Polish center-left and center-right thus quibbled over who was the true heir of Poland's democratic heritage as the country descended into economic crisis and the tightening grip of Piłsudski's authoritarian rule.

Yet after the Marshall's death, as war clouds darkened the horizon, the *Sanacja* left and *Endecja* right actually converged in their programs, from anti-Bolshevism and talk of social solidarity and corporatism to their reliance on Catholic tradition and willingness to use arbitrary executive powers.[41] Piłsudski's successors agreed upon the importance of ethnic Polish control of politics, culture, and the economy, and the *Sanacja* regime took on elements of National Democratic language. In 1937 they created a new mass organization (Camp of National Unification [OZON]) to replace the lifeless BBWR, with an emphasis on ethnic "self-defense."[42] In May 1938, OZON passed resolutions making the "Jewish question" a prime concern of public policy, calling the country's 3.5 million Jews an alien group that weakened the Polish state and that must leave.[43] There were also more extreme groups tied to *Sanacja*, like the Union of Young Nationalists, who demanded "work and bread for Poles" and expulsion of all Jews. Even the *Sanacja* left wing was not free of anti-Semitism; it shared the basic view that nationally foreign "Jewish" interests in the economy and in culture threatened the Polish state.[44]

In the mid- to late 1930s, some twenty Jews died and more than 2,000 were injured when anti-Semitic disturbances broke out across Poland. In addition, both the government and the Catholic Church supported boycotts of Jewish businesses that were organized by the radical right; the Primate August Cardinal Hlond even spoke of the need for Polish "self-love" and defense against

FIGURE 15.2. Women of Toruń "outed" for shopping in Jewish Stores (1937). *Source*: Daily "Pod Pręgierz." Via Wikimedia Commons.

Jews. Though discrimination at universities never became law, collusion of professors on university admissions committees caused the numbers of Jewish students to dwindle from more than 20 percent in the mid-1920s to 10 percent in 1939.[45] On campuses throughout Poland, nationalist students harassed Jewish classmates, forcing them to sit in designated areas of lecture halls ("ghetto benches"), and Jews who graduated were mostly refused entry into state administration, though they were inducted into the army.

The leadership of the PPS opposed discrimination and counted many people of Jewish origin in its ranks, yet by late in the decade, the mood in that party was shifting as well. "It is as if anti-Semitism constituted a kind of psychosis at the end of the Second Republic," writes the historian Jerzy Holzer, "disabling a healthy political sense and obscuring an awareness of the genuine threats to the life of the Polish state."[46] People across the political spectrum believed the protracted crisis had to with an economic structure in which Jews— "foreigners"—dominated trade and the professions. Such attitudes weakened efforts at recovery, though the Treasury Minister Eugeniusz Kwiatkowski (1935–1939) expanded the Polish mining, metallurgical, chemicals, and shipping industries, built an industrial region in central Poland, and made the north-coast village of Gdynia into an international seaport.

Despite Kwiatkowski's four-year investment plan, the number of unemployed remained high, and employers were reducing pay and violating agreements reached by collective bargaining. The result was 2,056 strikes in 1936, involving some 675,000 workers, the greatest number since 1923.[47] At times strikers were able to realize their demands, but more often the police crushed the protests, and workers lost jobs. A wave of factory occupation strikes engulfed Kraków in the spring of 1936. On March 23, reports that police had beaten women strikers provoked massive demonstrations, which police broke up using gunfire. A funeral for the eight workers killed that day brought tens of thousands to a procession that mixed Catholic with socialist symbolism: large silver crosses painted on black coffins and workers carrying burning torches and banners of the PPS. Despite the latent threats of police violence, the protests resumed, and by May, fifty-nine factories were again striking in Kraków.[48]

The antigovernment manifestations spread to the countryside, where the population was dispersed, illiterate, and difficult to organize but was mobilized nonetheless. In two famous manifestations, peasants leveraged national commemorations for the sake of democracy and socialism, claiming to have offered special services to Poland centuries earlier.

In June 1936, army inspector general Edward Śmigły-Rydz decided he would use celebrations of the battle of Nowosielec (1634), at which peasants had held off the Tatars with clubs and scythes, to show the unity of people with "its" army leader. In response, Peasant Party leaders decided they would use the general's visit to manifest their desire for a return to democracy. Peasants in regional garb greeted the general cordially with bread and salt, yet then began some unpleasant surprises. During breakfast, a local leader declared, "peasants have given their blood for Poland and will do so in the future, but we must be given back the rights that have been taken away in the last ten years." The crowd—some 150,000 in number—applauded enthusiastically. Later in the day, peasants broke through a security cordon and handed Śmigły-Rydz a note demanding that the government do more to earn the trust of the people (*lud*). There were also attempts of the extreme right Falanga youth to utilize the ceremonies for their propaganda, but local officials locked them in barns.[49]

The following year, the peasant movement summoned its followers to celebrations of the 143rd anniversary of the battle of Racławice, in which Tadeusz Kościuszko had led a force with scythes and clubs to victory over an army from Russia. The event turned bloody, however, when local police and army units seized the commemoration site; the crowds managed to eject them, with some police going over to their side, but troops then shot into the multitude as it returned home, killing two. Police arrested some 200 participants, and sixty received sentences from six months to two and a half years.[50]

The repression did not quell villagers' activism, however. In August 1937, peasants across Poland staged a ten-day strike, boycotting open markets and halting food deliveries to the cities. This was perhaps the most effective act of social protest witnessed in the region between the world wars. Organizers aimed to "liquidate" the *Sanacja* system and force the country to return to democratic practice. In the course of the protests, forty-two people died, and some 1,000 were arrested. Kraków's Cardinal Adam Sapieha asked whether the "horrible misery" that led to the bloody incidents was not a result of the unlimited desire to make profits.[51]

Repression at the hands of *Sanacja* had thus brought peasant politicians together as never before, but it also united factions of the democratic center—Polish socialists, peasant parties, and the Jewish socialists (the Bund). In many towns, the PPS organized single-day sympathy strikes, and at times ran on a common list with the Bund. The nationalists, however, did not weaken, and if Dmowski had not suffered a stroke in 1937, *Endecja* might have seized power. At the top, little changed. *Sanacja* remained a heterogeneous bloc with little real character or policy, and if one wing of the movement went too far, the other forced it back toward the center. Chemist and President (1926–1939) Ignacy Mościcki and the finance minister Eugeniusz Kwiatkowski acted for moderation, yet Colonel Adam Koc and Marshall Felicjan Sławoj-Składkowski were radicals. Some in the *Sanacja* camp broached ideas of electoral reform, but soon the threat of Nazi Germany smothered thoughts of anything else. In January 1939, the Peasant Party declared its support for the "unification of society around the defense of the state," and unity became the catchword after Poland rejected Germany's demands for alliance and territory in the spring.[52]

Yugoslavia and Bulgaria: Royal Dictatorship versus Fascism

In Yugoslavia, too, citizens rose up to demand a return to democracy through strikes, mass agitation, and an unruly press, and they also formed new kinds of alliances, many of them local, aiming to control what the authoritarian regime could not. In 1935 an opposition bloc emerged, joining Serb Democrats, Croat Peasants, antiregime Radicals, and Serb Agrarians. They wanted a new constitution approved by majorities of each of the ostensible peoples of state: Serbs, Slovenes, and also Croats. Despite police harassment, this group won 44.9 percent of the votes in December 1938 elections, with heavy majorities in Croatia (more than 80 percent).[53]

Yugoslavia had lived under dictatorship since 1929, when King Alexander took the reins, hoping to unite the country by force. To weld Yugoslavs into a nation, he redrew the map, creating nine provinces (*banovine*) that had never existed before and were named after rivers. Though they made up about 43 percent of the state's population, Serbs were a majority in six of the new entities, Croats in two, Slovenes in one, and Muslims in none.[54]

After the onset of the Depression, Alexander's rule foundered, and income fell while unemployment rose. He could not satisfy the expectations of all ethnic groups, and his unifying measures enraged virtually everyone while satisfying no one. For example, in December 1929, he disbanded the decades-old Sokol sport movement that had been the pride of Croatia, and ten months later, to show he was not playing favorites, he retired cherished and decades-old Serb army regimental flags. The new centralized state failed to bring any prestigious Croat or former Habsburg Serb into government, and Croats remained convinced that Yugoslav rule was disguised Serb rule. Of 656 ministers who served from the founding of the state to 1939, 452 were Serbs, and 137 were Croats. Of the latter group, 111 were regarded by the Radić's Peasant Party as "renegades," unrepresentative of Croat interests. On the eve of World War II, 161 of 165 Yugoslav generals were Serbs.[55]

Despite Alexander's pretenses of bringing order to the country, prominent Croat politicians could not be certain of their personal safety under his dictatorship. Some languished in prison, but several also fell victim to assassination. In 1931 the eminent Croatian historian Milan Šufflay was gunned down on the streets of Zagreb, an event so egregious as to catch attention even in the United States. (Albert Einstein and novelist Heinrich Mann drew up a letter of protest.) The killers were known police agents and were never brought to trial.[56]

In September 1931, the king issued a new constitution featuring universal manhood suffrage, yet instead of a secret ballot, it instituted a voice vote, permitting authorities to identify opponents precisely. The constitution was little more than a cover for one-man rule and was less popular, even among Serbs, than its predecessor of 1921. That same year, thanks to strong arm tactics by the police, government candidates won all 306 seats in the assembly. Many political leaders responded to the charade of democracy by emigrating.[57] One of these, the dangerous Croat radical nationalist Ante Pavelić, went to Italy and founded the fascist Ustasha movement ("Insurrection"), with the goal of achieving Croatian independence, by violence if necessary.[58] Under the protection of Benito Mussolini, Pavelić teamed with other anti-Yugoslav forces, including the Macedonian terror organization IMRO. In October 1934, while he was on a state visit to France, an IMRO terrorist caught up with King Alexander and fired a bullet into him at close range, also striking dead the French foreign minister. Hungary was also party to the conspiracy.

Because Alexander's son, Peter, was only eleven years old, a regency was established under his Western-educated cousin Prince Paul, a more practical man not dictatorial in temperament and interested in accommodation. He quickly released political prisoners, including opposition politicians, and relaxed police surveillance and censorship. Elections were still rigged, but political parties gained freedom of movement. Once more, they could represent ethnic interests, something that had been a taboo under Alexander. In June 1935, Paul appointed as prime minister the old Radical politician Milan Stojadinović, and his three years in office brought relative calm, continued relaxations of censorship as well as hopeful accommodation with the Croat leader Vladko Maček. Soon Muslim, Slovene, and even Croatian politicians were involved in the government.[59]

Meanwhile, a tiny Serb fascist movement had emerged under Dimitrije Ljotić, a lawyer from a prominent family, who had made a name for himself as a strike-breaker after World War I and as minister of justice from February to August 1931. During student days in Paris, Ljotić had come under the spell of the French integral nationalist Charles Maurras; he came to believe in the blood kinship of Serbs, Croats, and Slovenes, an unusual case of racism serving multiethnic cooperation. His ambition to reorganize Yugoslavia on a "corporatist" basis, mobilizing popular forces in nondemocratic structures, had caused King Alexander to sack him as justice minister. But in 1935, under the more lenient Regent Paul, Ljotić managed to unite several tiny Serb fascist parties into the Yugoslav National Movement (*Zbor*).[60]

Like other East European fascist movements, *Zbor* failed to build mass support and never got above 1 percent of the vote.[61] Not only did *Zbor* seem in league with Serbia's German and Italian enemies, but the causes it espoused—anti-socialism and nationalism—were already well represented in the conventional Yugoslav political spectrum: in a sense they were positions that were already "occupied." Moreover, constituencies for fascism were small in agricultural Serbia, where the general poltical culture was pro-Western and democratic.

Like counterparts elsewhere in the region, Yugoslavia's rulers did not hesitate to use the police to take fascists out of circulation, though their reasoning was unusual. The mostly secular Serb elite regarded Ljotić as a religious fanatic for the simple reason that he regularly attended church. Right before the 1938 elections, Stojadinović thus had him committed to a mental asylum. The prime minister also produced information showing that *Zbor* had been financed from Germany. Later, during Nazi occupation in World War II, Ljotić became a reliable collaborator, and his forces were complicit in genocide, for example, by helping round up Jews in 1941 in the early stages of the Nazi-led policy of extermination.[62]

Still, fascist tendencies did not leave Yugoslavia unscathed. Milan Stojadinović was not a democrat. Much like Poland's and Romania's rulers, he was impressed by the growing strength of fascist regimes, and like them created his own pseudofascist movement, the Yugoslav Radical Union. But Stojadinović went further, instituting fascist-style organizations, complete with green-shirted uniforms, an official salute, youth parades, and paramilitary guards. Crowds summoned for his public appearances chanted "Vodja, Vodja" ["leader, leader"], but he made them stop, because when the second and first syllables elide after repetition, the word "djavo" is produced, meaning "devil." This adulation seemed lifeless at best, ridiculous at worst, and true fascists, as well as the more numerous democrats, rejected it.[63]

Yet the question of whether Stojadinović was fascist tells us how the word's meaning has changed over the decades, not only on the left, where any authoritarian dictator was taken to be an exemplar (for example, Horthy or Piłsudski) but also in common parlance. After meeting Stojadinović in 1938, the Italian foreign minister Count Galeazzo Ciano said that the Yugoslav prime minister was fascist, "if not by virtue of an open declaration of party loyalty," then "certainly by virtue of his conception of authority, of the state, and of life."[64] Yet in fact Stojadinović was a cold and skillful politician, unable to rouse passions and lacking a fascist's charisma as well as inclination to take bold steps.[65] Like

Piłsudski or Horthy, Stojadinović was authoritarian and deeply anticommunist; he did not crush all political life and endeavored to abide by the country's constitution.

The real challenge for the Yugoslav regime came not from fascism but from the continuing sense among Croatians, one-fourth of the state's population, of living in someone else's country. The Munich crisis of September 1938 that led to the dismembering of Czechoslovakia alarmed the Regent Prince Paul because it demonstrated the fragility of multinational states like his own. Despite his strongman posturing, Milan Stojadinović had proved a disappointment.[66] Among his signature efforts was to open talks with the Vatican to regularize the position of Catholics in Yugoslavia by legalizing church schools and organizations like the "Catholic Action," hoping to give Croats a stronger stake in Yugoslavia. But before the agreement came up for a vote in the Skupština, a vigorous opposition had emerged among Serb Orthodox Church leaders, who worried about rivalry in dual-confession areas, and though the measure passed (by one vote), it was shelved. Reminiscent of King Alexander, Stojadinović had succeeded chiefly to aggravate both sides.

In February 1939, Regent Paul replaced him with the former Serb Radical Dragiša Cvetković hoping finally to placate the Croats. Cvetković knew something of the powers of nationalism, having himself organized fascist-style trade unions in the Yugoslav National Union. By August he had hammered out an agreement (*Sporazum*) giving Croats virtual autonomy in Yugoslavia, including control over agriculture, commerce and industry, social welfare, public health, education, and justice. The central government in Belgrade kept responsibility for foreign affairs, foreign trade, communications, and the army. Croatian territory (*banovina*) would include Croatia, Slavonia, Dalmatia, and some of Bosnia and Herzegovina, and Croats would have their own assembly as well as a chief executive officer appointed by the king. The Croatian Peasant Party leader Vladko Maček became vice-premier of Yugoslavia, and Ivan Šubašić, a moderate member of the party with good connections to Belgrade, was appointed the chief executive officer of Croatia.[67]

Like the Habsburgs in the Austro-Hungarian Compromise of 1867, Serb elites had "cut a deal" with the major discontented nation for the sake of the state's coherence. But just as Austria had more discontents than just the Hungarians, so Yugoslavia had more than just the Croats: the *Sporazum* did nothing for Bosnian Muslims, Albanians, Macedonians, or Slovenes. And many Serb nationalists griped at the inclusion in the Croatian *banovina* of majority Serb areas of the Krajina. The *Sporazum* was also a blow to a democratic movement that

Vladko Maček had been building since 1935 with Serb Democrats that had culminated in a visit to Belgrade in the summer of 1938. Tens of thousands of Serbs had turned out and celebrated him, also demonstrating their sympathy for Croats living under state oppression (the "terror of state gendarmes").[68] A Yugoslavia had seemed to be emerging united from below, yet now Maček simply abandoned his Serb allies and did not even appease the Croats.[69]

Still, radical nationalism remained a small minority option among Croats, mostly because Croat nationalism was well represented by the democratic Croatian Peasant party of Maček and its founders, the Radić brothers Antun and Stjepan. Unlike the Slovak people's party or the Sudeten German party, the Croatian Peasant Party did not produce a fascist splinter and resisted calls for cooperation with the far right. The main Croatian fascist, Ustasha leader Ante Pavelić, a lawyer by training, had been secretary of the Croatian Party of State Rights. He was inspired by the ideas of the old ethno-nationalist Serb-hater Ante Starčević, but in the shadow of the Peasant Party, his party had sunk into obscurity.[70]

With a membership of no more than a few hundred, the Ustasha cadre found conditions in Yugoslavia precarious, and along with Pavelić, took refuge in the early 1930s across the Adriatic in villages and camps in Sardinia, Sicily, and the Lipari islands, where the Italians held them as a bargaining chip for concessions that Mussolini might want from Yugoslavia.[71] When the Germans placed the Ustasha movement in power in Croatia after conquering Yugoslavia in April 1941, many of them spoke better Italian than Croatian. In other words, rather than reflect national self-assertion, these fascists seemed traitors to the nation, in alliance with Italy and out of touch with local traditions.

But pure racism was the only space available to Pavelić and his men in the politics of their country in the 1930s. To cut a profile that was distinct from Serb nationalism as well as mainstream Croat Catholicism, the Ustashas appealed to tribal unity, a deeper substance that Croats supposedly shared, making them superior to the despised "Slavo-Serbs" on one hand and Catholics on the other. The Church of Rome, with its mission to all nations, had "betrayed" the Croatian people. Yet blatant anticlericalism in pious Croatia, combined with the stifling presence of the much stronger Croatian Peasant Party and heavy state repression, condemned the Ustasha movement to insignificance through the 1930s.

Fascists in Bulgaria faced a distilled concentration of all the problems that handicapped counterparts in Yugoslavia or Poland: a native strongman, a native national movement that valued democracy, and an agricultural societal structure. In Bulgaria, fascism lacked the disorientated and enraged middle- and working-class constituencies that allowed it to flourish farther west. Still, like everywhere else, a native version did emerge, and it did so from the top of the political elite. After Stamboliiski's murder in 1923, the economics professor Aleksandar Tsankov became prime minister and vigorously suppressed the Bulgarian left. He fell from power in 1926 because his rule involved brutalities that shocked European opinion, causing London bankers to threaten the withholding of loans.[72] After that, a moderate government took office under the centrist Andrey Lyapchev (1866–1933), and the country again managed to secure international financing.

Tsankov did not fade from the scence entirely, however, and became increasingly attracted to fascist politics. In May 1934 he called for a rally ahead of Nazi leader Hermann Goering's visit to Sofia. Some 50,000 supporters were expected. Yet three days before Goering's visit, the Bulgarian military ("Military League") stepped in and seized power from a weak assemblage of mainstream parties. The army officers were supported by the civilian association *Zveno* ("The Link"), which held that Bulgaria must be modernized from above by the enlightened few because parliaments were a thing of the past. Under *Zveno*'s rule, Bulgaria conformed to regional patterns: increasing dependence on the German economy, nationalist chauvinism—reflected, for example, in the changing of Turkish to Bulgarian place names—and central rule. *Zveno* believed the state bureaucracy had to be streamlined and rationalized, and it reduced the ranks of the civil service by one-third.[73]

Zveno is yet another case of the terminological confusion of that period surrounding the word fascism. Although *Zveno* was not a paramilitary, radical nationalist, or a mass mobilization regime, the US newsweekly *Time* called it "fascist."[74] In fact *Zveno* was moderate in foreign policy and sought better relations with Belgrade rather than a violent seizure of disputed territory.[75] As in Marshall Piłsudski's *Sanacja*, prominent leaders were military men (Damyan Velchev, Pencho Zlatev, Kimon Georgiev), and like *Sanacja*, they vowed to undo the corruption of public life. Yet unlike Polish counterparts, they did not establish a government party (like BBWR) or mass movement (like OZON), although they did abolish the political parties.[76] The National Parliament (*subranie*) and local governments continued, but candidates had to run as individuals. Still, most successful candidates for office had belonged to the old parties and were recognized as such. *Subranie* elections in early 1938 netted the opposition one-third of the votes despite the sort of harassment and manipulation seen in Poland, Romania, Hungary, and Yugoslavia.

In early 1935, King Boris III, concerned about republican sentiment in the government, disbanded the Military League and appointed a civilian prime minister loyal to himself (he maintained the ban on parties).[77] From that moment until his death in 1943, the king controlled Bulgarian politics, appointing prime ministers as he saw fit, yet acting as a benign dictator, maintaining peace with totalitarian Germany and Russia while trying to associate Bulgaria with democratic France. As far as possible, he suppressed the terrorist IMRO. Calling himself a "democratic monarch," Boris stayed in touch with Bulgarians by touring the country in his own locomotive, occasionally stopping to visit with villagers, to whom he dispensed trinkets and other small gifts. Several right-wing associations emerged in the late 1930s that admired Nazism, but Boris kept them in check.[78]

Yet he also adopted certain popular fascist appearances. Given his impressive record as field commander in World War I, Boris wore a uniform with some justification, and his regime formed corporatist organizations like a state-run "patriotic" union, through which, one Communist asserted, the "fascists buried the class struggle." Again we see the period's flexible understanding of "fascist." For Communists, the authoritarian antisocialist regimes were fascist by definition. In 1936 *Zveno* created a "Bulgarian Workers' Union" that attempted to usurp the workers' cause in order to strengthen the state (again very reminiscent of Italy). May Day parades continued, but red flags were replaced by Bulgarian tricolors that were blessed by priests.[79] As we will see in Chapter 17, Boris supported the rescue of Bulgaria's Jews when they were threatened by Germany.

Like Hungarian and Romanian authoritarians, Boris suppressed fascism yet expended much less energy for similar results. His country, even more rural and with rampant illiteracy, featured few large towns in which people might be mobilized for fascist causes.[80] In addition, Bulgarian politics offered other options to absorb radical energies. There was Stamboliiski's mass agrarian movement in the 1920s as well as a potent military ultra-right, and there was IMRO, the Macedonian separatist movement, which featured a strong Bulgarian irredentist faction. All of this meant that Tsankov's followers had little chance in the urban spaces where fascism thrives. And much more successfully than Horthy or Carol, Boris III, a popular and uniformed war hero, appeared to embody the national cause. It was easy for his police to identify and arrest the relatively few fascists, especially at the universities, which served as hothouses for radical ideologies.

* * *

The 1930s were the height of the fascist age, yet fascism as a political movement remained marginal in Eastern Europe. Those areas that fell victim to the Nazi assault in 1939 and 1941—Poland and Yugoslavia—did so not by Nazi design, but by the determination of mainstream national politicians in Warsaw and Belgrade to oppose German actions, which aimed at reducing their states to puppet regimes. And the Nazis were not uniformly supportive of Eastern Europe's native fascism. After the Romanian army put down a putsch in January 1941, hundreds of Iron Guard leaders were interned at Dachau. Germany did nothing to court Poland's tiny fascist movement, whose members mostly became involved in the anti-Nazi resistance. Hitler considered Hungary's Nazis under Szálasi a reliable force, but he did not bring them to power until very late in the game, in October 1944, when Admiral Horthy attempted to make a separate peace with the West.

Still, fascism did not leave the region unscathed. Even if the East European regimes were not scheming to forge totalitarian states, the spread of right-wing nationalism caused observers to view several of them as watered-down versions: they were pseudofascist, half-fascist, or clerical fascist, but not nonfascist. As the decade wore on, leaders consciously and unconsciously imitated fascism (for example, OZON and Carol's youth organization, with their uniformed legions and fascist-style forms of greeting). During the fascist epoch, there were common forms of dictatorial and semi-dictatorial rule across borders, obsessions with purity, illiberalism, anti-Semitism, and admiration for the evident strength of men of the "deed" who ruled in Germany and Italy.[81] Also characteristic of this dark decade was the almost complete and unlamented disappearance of democracy and its proponents: a radical and extraordinary shift from the situation in 1919.

But fascism was not a stable quantity. Europe gradually learned this lesson as the 1930s progressed, and the instructors were in Berlin. The Nazis made themselves a fascist model through racist violence. If the model was impossible to emulate fully, non-German fascists did not criticize it: in that sense, there was a fascist unity. Some who considered themselves to be fascist in the early 1930s were revealed not to be fully so later in the decade. They adjusted, as Mussolini did, by becoming openly racist in 1938. Others continued to waffle, and some few became anti-Nazis: Austria's Kurt von Schuschnigg in 1938, Poland's *Sanacja* the following year, and Serb military officers who overthrew Prince Paul's regency in March 1941.

One factor that no theory accounts for is personality, and personality had the power to send fascism on unpredictable paths. Without a charismatic leader, there is no fascist movement, and without a leader dedicated to seizing power, there is no fascist regime. We saw this in Corneliu Codreanu, who preferred martyrdom to holding office. For the opposite we can look to Germany, where one man took hold of a fascist movement and shaped it according to his own peculiar visions, wielding such power that his followers struggled to anticipate what he might desire. They were constantly but somewhat blindly "working toward the Führer," as one of them put it.[82] It is in this man that fascism took on historical consequences for Eastern Europe.

As a former subject of the Habsburgs, Adolf Hitler was also not a stranger to the region; it was near the Bohemian borders and in the capital of Vienna that he honed his hatred for Slavs and Jews. But his ultimate visions transcended what anyone would have predicted for an Austrian or Reich German: they involved not only claiming all territories inhabited by Germans but also creating a colonial empire "in the East" that went far beyond Eastern Europe and deep into the Soviet Union. In this vision, territories in Bohemia, Poland, and east of Poland were slated to make way for German settlement, and every region of Europe was to support the needs of the emerging Third Reich. The first victim in this scheme was the region's sole surviving democracy: Czechoslovakia.

PART IV

Eastern Europe as Part of the Nazi and Soviet Empires

CHAPTER 16

Hitler's War and Its East European Enemies

The world into which Adolf Hitler was born could not have been more different from the one that survived him: the first the Austro-Hungarian monarchy, where there was constant, mostly peaceful, and often untidy interactions among people of many ethnicities; the second, Cold War Central Europe, where fortified borders separated people of differing ethnicities, but only after millions had been killed. Yet Hitler had absorbed his prejudices and obsessions from the complex Habsburg borderlands where he grew up, a region not far from Bohemia, where a nationalist movement emerged among Germans left out of Bismarck's Second Empire, who feared that Slavdom might grind them down into full insignificance. Like Hitler, these German ethnic extremists fiercely hated not only hated Slavs but also Jews and the Catholic Church.

Yet Hitler was also an original. Even if his ideas cannot be understood without reference to this upbringing, his ultimate visions went far beyond what anyone immersed in the Austrian-German subculture of the 1890s would have understood. When he rose as leader of the Nazi movement that had grown out of Bohemia, Hitler intended Germany to expand into and settle a vast colonial space, extending far beyond territories inhabited by ethnic Germans, deep into Ukraine and Russia. Inferior peoples would become slaves, and those who were dangerous—Jews above all—would disappear. Hitler chaotically mixed ideas and dreams of racists like Arthur de Gobineau, Jörg Lanz von Liebenfels, and Houston Stewart Chamberlain. In his view, nations either grew strong or they withered, and strong ones had to expand into the dimensions of an extensive space, which he called "Lebensraum" (living space), borrowing a word from the geographer Friedrich Ratzel.[1]

Hitler intended the nations of Central and Eastern Europe to play supporting roles in this violent enterprise of making Germany into a European empire, and in the beginning, he firmly imagined the destruction of only one state: Czechoslovakia. More accurately, he wanted to make Slovakia into an independent mini-state and to Germanize the Czech lands through expulsion and assimilation. Bohemia after all had once been a part of Germany for centuries. Yet beyond that, Poland and Yugoslavia, along with Hungary, Romania, and Bulgaria, would act as allies, supplying resources, labor, and in some cases soldiers for the massive assault on the Soviet Union. He believed that Britain, the sea power, would not interfere. In Hitler's mind, the Balkan Peninsula, including Yugoslavia, belonged to the Italian sphere of influence, and he had no intention of sending German troops there for any purpose.

As anyone with a basic knowledge of European history knows, events did not transpire as Hitler intended. World War II began in September 1939 not with Poland as Germany's ally, but with Poland as the target of a German surprise attack from land, sea, and air—and the Soviet Union as an ally. Not quite two years later, in the spring of 1941, Germany destroyed and occupied Yugoslavia just weeks before attacking the Soviet Union. Those assaults ushered in a new stage of the war, from wanton violence to genocide. Though this war would not have happened without Hitler's ideas and his will, he did not get the war he desired, largely because Poland and Yugoslavia refused to play according to his script.

* * *

In the mid-1930s, Hitler's intention to conquer and annex vast spaces in Ukraine and Russia was not well understood, and observers watched his gambles with astonishment, each changing the European chessboard to the Nazis' advantage. In 1935 Hitler reintroduced conscription, and every new soldier swore personal allegiance to Hitler. The following year he occupied the left bank of the Rhine, which Germany had pledged to keep demilitarized at Versailles in 1919. Before that point, France's armies could advance across the Rhine, a natural defense, and in a short time reach Berlin. The demilitarized Rhineland had made France's pledge to protect Eastern Europe credible. Yet now, with Germany's troops on both sides of the Rhine, France looked inward and sought security behind concrete fortifications running along the border to Germany, called the Maginot Line. Germany's challenges to Eastern and Central Europe in 1938 revealed France as unwilling to exert pressure: in March, French (and British) statesmen looked aside as Hitler seized Austria, which up to that point had been under an authoritarian Catholic dictatorship.

Now his attention turned to Czechoslovakia, the lonely democracy that he considered an implacable enemy. In preceding years, Germany had exploited the country's democratic institutions to prop up Konrad Henlein, and among

Sudeten Germans support for "unification" with Germany gradually grew, so that by the spring of 1938, some 90 percent of them voted for Henlein's party.[2] This was the greatest victory in free elections of any fascist movement at any time; extraordinarily, these Germans freely cast their ballots to exit a state that respected their civil and cultural rights in order to join a violent totalitarian dictatorship featuring judicial murder, concentration camps, and overt racism. This result confirms claims in recent historiography that the forms nationalism takes, especially its extreme varieties, rely on the agitation of nationalists. Without the active interference of the propaganda apparatus of the powerful Nazi state, in particular of its hatred-filled radio broadcasts, the marginal concerns of Czechoslovak Germans over language use would not have driven them to such outright rejection of Czechoslovakia.[3]

Meanwhile, Hitler was intimidating Czech leaders by massing armies on the Czech border. He had little to fear from the West. In November 1937, Britain's Lord Halifax had told Hitler that his government was not "necessarily concerned to stand for the status quo as today" in Austria, Danzig, or Czechoslovakia.[4] The German strongman claimed to be advocating Czechoslovak Germans' desire to return to Germany, but in reality, he intended to destroy Czechoslovakia as a viable power: the areas where Germans lived, the "Sudetenland," were also hilly and provided a natural defense. Without them Czechoslovakia would become a German puppet.

With broad support among the Czech and some of the Slovak population, the government of Edvard Beneš held firm, yet France and Britain were in no mood to risk war, in part because they recognized the hypocrisy of the Paris peace treaties, which had raised national self-determination to a general principle but then denied it to Bohemia's Germans, and in larger part because they wanted to avoid war at all costs. In late September, British diplomats informed the Czechs that Italy, Germany, Britain, and France had worked out an arrangement at Munich whereby the Sudeten areas would be surrendered to Germany according to schedule. Faced with the prospect of confronting Hitler alone, Beneš chose to comply, and then left his home country for Paris and then London, where he set up a government in exile. On October 1, German troops began occupying the Sudetenland, greeted as saviors by huge crowds of Bohemian Germans, in one town under the banner: "Your People Is Everything: You Are Nothing."[5]

A "second" Czecho-Slovak Republic now emerged on the remaining Czechoslovak territories (about two-thirds the original size), which attempted to placate Nazi Germany with censorship and racial laws. Hitler warned that if the

FIGURE 16.1. Women in the Sudetenland (Cheb) greeting German troops (October 1938).
Source: Scherl/Weltbild, Bundesarchiv, Bild 183-H13160.

country continued the policies of Beneš, he would settle its fate in 8 hours. The Agrarian Party's leader Rudolf Beran formed a reactionary-conservative government that included the tiny Czech Fascist Community, the parliament passed anti-Semitic legislation, and a wave of chauvinism swept the country. Streets and movie theaters were renamed to sound more "Czech." Mainstream journals openly vilified Jews as scapegoats for national humiliation, "outed" Jews in Czech public life, and claimed that Jews controlled the economy. One Czech right-wing nationalist not only dredged up the old stereotypes about Jews—as "dishonest," having a "beggar's" character or no character at all, as "intriguing and mendacious"—he also claimed their existence endangered Czechs as well: Jews had "infected" Czechs.[6]

This "republic" was no longer Masaryk's Czechoslovakia of a few months previously, a place where racist arguments had a distasteful sound and were not used in public life. The political spectrum had shifted sharply rightward, and if Czech nationalism turned so fiercely and single-mindedly against the Jews, that was because it could not be anti-German. The Czech government, consisting of many respected figures from the First Republic, even proclaimed that Jews were a problem to be "solved."

Yet such attempts to ape the Nazis' own language were to no avail. In March 1939, German forces occupied the rest of the Czech lands, creating a "Protectorate of Bohemia and Moravia," a semi-colonial entity with a Czech government and ministers under a German *Reichsprotektor* in the person of former foreign minister Konstantin von Neurath. (The Protectorate's borders did not correspond to those of the Bohemian kingdom; instead the territory was a rump shorn of majority-German districts.) The prime minister from April 1939 was Alois Eliáš, a general in the Czech army and an associate of Edvard Beneš. While attempting to appear loyal to the Germans, Eliáš secretly kept contacts to the Beneš's émigré government in London and supported the Czech resistance, for example by aiding Czech soldiers and airmen seeking to escape to the west (via Budapest) and serving pro-Nazi Czech journalists poisoned sandwiches (*chlebíčky*) at a lunch at Prague's castle in September 1941 (several got sick, and one died). Eliáš wanted to do everything he could to restore Czech sovereignty, but his activities became known to the Gestapo, and he was arrested in October 1941 and executed the following year. Much in the spirit of T. G. Masaryk, he had belonged to the "Truth prevails" masonic lodge.[7]

Though Eliáš technically headed a government, in fact he could not call his ministers together without the approval of German occupiers. And when they did meet, a representative of Konrad Henlein had to be present. The overlords enforced tight controls on intellectuals as a supposed national leadership—demonstrated in November 1939, when they arrested one in eight Czech students for participation in anti-Nazi protests—yet they treated industrial workers relatively well because Czech-produced armaments were crucial for the German military. Beyond relatively few, mostly intellectual opponents, and some 118,000 Czech Jews, the Protectorate was an island little affected by war, where the German leadership sent troops for rest, and the Czech population grew.[8] The Nazis permitted a small native radical nationalism (*vlajka*) to be directed against Jews, but most Czechs despised this regime with a quiet hatred, whose full ferocity became known only just after Germany lost the war—in May 1945.

In the east, the Nazis supported the creation of an "independent state" of Slovakia under control of the Slovak people's party, led by the Catholic Priest Monsignor Josef Tiso. Though himself not a fascist, Tiso abetted fascism in his regime, supported anti-Jewish racial legislation, and in 1942 oversaw the deportation of 52,000 Jews to Auschwitz, but only after the Slovak government agreed to pay the German Reichsbank 500 Marks for each Jew.[9]

* * *

After gutting Czechoslovak statehood in the fall of 1938, Hitler fixed his sights on Poland, and now his plans began to go awry. He and other Nazi brass respected Józef Piłsudski for defeating the Red Army in 1920; for Hitler personally, the admiration extended so far that it obscured broader notions of Polish racial inferiority that were common on the German right. In 1934 Hitler began courting Poland's military leadership, and the two countries concluded a non-aggression pact that West European countries found scandalous: but Poland's leaders thought it Poland's right and duty to go its own way, seeking balance between Germany and Russia, and they did not trust France (or for that matter, the League of Nations) to guarantee Poland's security. Germany also ended the trade war it had launched against Poland in 1925. In June 1935, despite protests of Zionist Youth, workers, and the Catholic church, the Polish government received Joseph Goebbels with full state honors, and each year thereafter until the outbreak of war, Hermann Goering came to Poland to hunt wolves and bears, accompanied by top officials like General Kazimierz Sosnkowski. In 1938 Poland teamed with Nazi Germany in putting pressure on Lithuania and Czechoslovakia, and even seized the mostly ethnically Polish territory near Těšín/Cieszyn that Czech armies had occupied in 1919.[10]

Hitler assumed that given the anti-Communism that ran through Polish society, Poland would be a natural ally in his campaign against the Soviet Union. He wanted it to join the anti-Comintern pact—an anti-Bolshevik alliance including Japan and Italy—and made two further demands that he considered generous: Poland should agree to Germany's control of Gdańsk/Danzig, a mostly ethnic German city that since 1920 had been a Free State under League of Nations protection (and not something Poland could have "granted" Hitler even if it had wanted to). And Poland should agree to German construction of an "extraterritorial highway" through the Polish "corridor," linking East Prussia to the main part of Germany.

Although this was the sole territorial demand, Poland refused, and in the spring of 1939, incurred Hitler's wrath by securing a British guarantee of its sovereignty; France was already bound by treaty to come to Poland's aid in the event of an attack. The German leader had misjudged Poland. For Poles, national sovereignty outweighed all other considerations. An alliance with Germany would have reduced Poland to vassal status, an intolerable humiliation, especially given the legacy of the struggles for Polish independence from the 1790s to 1918. As soon as Hitler was informed of Britain's pledge to do "everything possible" to protect Poland, he began planning that country's destruction, vowing to concoct a "devil's brew."[11]

Therefore, the furious German attack on Poland of the fall of 1939, and the genocidal policies that followed came not as a result of long-term plans but as a result of a decision by Poland's government, supported by its citizenry, to refuse Hitler's offer of alliance. The violence unleashed by Germany was unprecedented in European history. German tank columns and artillery barraged Polish hamlets and towns without warning, and the German air force machine-gunned escaping civilians and poured bombs on residential areas of cities. Tens of thousands of Polish noncombatants lost their lives: estimates are of 24,000 killed in mass executions in September alone. In the western towns, they overran in the first few days, German soldiers shot dozens of Poles, including many Catholic priests, simply for belonging to patriotic associations.[12] Polish armies fought valiantly, but the attack from three directions, including from Slovakia, left their undermechanized formations no chance.

To make matters much worse for the Poles, before ordering the attack, Hitler had concluded a nonaggression pact with the Soviet Union (the

FIGURE 16.2. Boy in ruins, seeking food for his family, Warsaw (September 1939).
Source: Julien Bryan (photographer). Via Wikimedia Commons.

MAP 16.1. East Central Europe under Nazi rule

Molotov-Ribbentrop Pact), with a secret clause that provided for a division of Polish territory as well as Soviet control of the Baltic States and parts of Romania. On September 17, when Polish forces were desperately countering the German advance coming from west, north, and south, the Red Army suddenly attacked from the east. Poland's Western allies—France and Britain—sat tight and did nothing to relieve Poland's predicament by challenging Germany in the west.

The Germans surrounded Warsaw two weeks into the attack, pulverizing the city with heavy ammunition, while the government and citizens built fortifications. When mayor Stefan Starzyński finally surrendered on September 25, the German overlords did not set up a Polish puppet regime, but instead created two zones of direct control: in the west, they annexed a band of territory directly to the Reich, while in Central Poland they established a *Generalgouvernement* for the Occupied Polish Territories (GG), using a French word evocative of colonial rule.[13]

In these two regions, German authorities subjected Poland's population to genocidal rule on two schedules: rapid in the west, because of the area's new status as German territory; but more gradual in the GG, which was slated to become fully Germanized in a generation. Thus, in the west, German officials immediately closed all Polish schooling, made public speaking of Polish a crime, and introduced compulsory labor from age fourteen for males and sixteen for females. Considering the educated classes a special enemy, the occupiers went about shooting tens of thousands in mass executions, and deporting hundreds thousands more to the GG after robbing them of their possessions. Ethnically Polish Catholic clergy they either shot, arrested, or deported; for example, of 681 priests of the diocese of Poznań, 461 were sent to concentration camps, the rest shipped to the GG.[14]

In contrast to parts of Western Europe they occupied, as well as the Czech Protectorate, Germany's leaders accorded the GG no native administration above the level of the village. The region was to be used as a "trash bin" in Heinrich Himmler's words, for ethnic "elements" unsuited to life in the Reich, above all Jews, Poles, and Gypsies, and would serve as a source for short-term economic exploitation before complete settlement with Germans. Over five long years of occupation, 1.3 million Poles were sent to Germany, and about 100,000 persons per year disappeared in concentration camps and other prisons, often for minor crimes, like theft. There were no high schools or universities; in Heinrich Himmler's words, Poles should be able to "count to 500, write their name, and know that it is God's commandment to be obedient to the Germans." They did not need to know how to read.[15]

People jokingly said GG meant *Gangstergau*, a Gangster colony, and like most jokes, it pointed to a truth: this was the place where the non-German population was placed beyond the law, at the whim of mobster-like local officials. A word entered discourse to describe these men and women: *Ostnieten*, eastern "losers," abject but ambitious Nazi flunkies who were useless in the Reich proper, to whom the word "administrator" did not apply; they were people suited primarily for underworld acts like extortion and murder. Some Polish economic organizations remained, like the cooperative Społem and the postal bank, and Poles remained at work on the railways and in the postal service, lower courts (for civil matters), and tax offices. Germany also maintained a Polish "blue" (for the color of their uniforms) police force of about 11,000–12,000 officers to aid its own formations.[16]

Eastern Poland fell under Soviet rule, and for almost two years, Soviet authorities acted as de facto allies of the Nazis, likewise carrying out policies meant to leave Poland a nation without native leadership. The gruesome low point was a decision taken in March 1940 by the Soviet politburo to execute some 22,000 Polish officers taken into captivity the previous year. Lavrenty Beria, chief of the Soviet Union's secret police (National Commissariat for Internal Affairs [NKVD]), said they were "sworn and incontrovertible enemies of the Soviet state." The captives were mostly reserve officers, and in civilian life worked as judges, writers, professors, doctors, teachers, and businessmen. The NKVD executed the men with shots in the back of the neck in forests near the prisoner-of-war camps, the most infamous site at Katyn in western Russia.[17]

About one-third of Poland's citizens lived in the areas that became Soviet (13.2 million vs. 21.8 million Polish citizens in German-controlled territory), but only about 40 percent of those were ethnically Polish. In October 1939, the Soviet authorities carried out rigged plebiscites in which more than 90 percent of the voters "requested" admission to the Soviet Ukrainian and Belorussian Republics (the Baltic populations followed suit the following summer). Thus, Stalin had retrieved for his country most of what the Russian Empire lost after 1917.

In the space of a few months, these territories passed through the social and political transformations that other parts of the Soviet Union had endured over two decades. Civil society disappeared as officials closed political parties, newspapers, associations (like the bar or chambers of commerce), and sporting or other clubs. They expropriated industrial and commercial assets, seized deposits in banks, and created state-run enterprises and collective farms. The poet Aleksander Wat who lived in Lwów, now part of Soviet Ukraine, said the most visible attribute of the new regime was that it left everything caked in mud. Schooling was transformed from Polish to Ukrainian, Belorussian, and Russian. Churches were closed, and priests and other suspected enemies arrested.

Still, this chokehold was not enough. In four deportations, Soviet authorities sent hundreds of thousands of Polish citizens—politically and socially "dangerous" elements, like state officials, teachers, and bankers—in cattle cars to Siberia and Central Asia and deposited them in collective farms, work camps, and villages, where they had to get by, usually at heavy labor (for example, harvesting timber). At least 5,000 died on the first deportation during midwinter.[18] The third deportation of some 80,000 (May–June 1940) focused on Jews (80 percent of the total), many of whom had escaped from German occupied areas.[19] Though the transports seemed an unfathomable tragedy at the time, they were in fact life-saving, because German forces massacred the Jews who had stayed behind in these territories in their assault on the Soviet Union of June 22, 1941.

The German divisions stormed across the partition line into eastern Poland in the early morning hours of that day, just after the last shipments of Soviet grain and other materials for the German economy had passed in the opposite direction. Within a week, Berlin had joined the eastern areas of Galicia (including Lwów) to the GG; the measures taken here against the Polish intelligentsia reached a new pitch of lethal intensity. In November 1939, German authorities had sent Kraków's professors to the concentration camp at Sachsenhausen, but mostly released them after international protests. Now, with no media present, SS execution squads simply abducted twenty-seven professors of Lwów University and shot them. The total executed in this "*Lemberger Professorenmord*" was forty-five. Along with former rector Longchamps de Berier, the Nazis murdered three of his sons, and they killed Professor Kazimierz Bartel, a former Polish prime minister. These special SS killing units (*Einsatzgruppen*) followed on the heels of the German army and also had orders to shoot Bolshevik political commissars. By late summer, they were also executing Jewish men, women, and children, inaugurating the Nazi genocide of Europe's Jews.

The SS drew up long-term plans for Poland and the western Soviet Union called the *Generalplan Ost* (General Plan East). Approximately 80–85 percent of Poles, 75 percent of the Belorussians, and 65 percent of Ukrainians would be removed from these territories and sent to Siberia; the remainder would be liquidated or Germanized. German authorities would settle the areas with healthy German ethnics, and war veterans would take priority as a supposed tough breed of fighting pioneers. Yet in only three places were the colonization

MAP 16.2. Generalplan Ost

schemes actually attempted during the war: in the Baltic area, the Zhitomir region of Ukraine, and around the renaissance town of Zamość in eastern Poland, where the Germans cleared some 300 villages, giving rise to resistance so massive that they had to delay further implementation. The SS planners don't seem to have wondered whether people from wealthier western Germany would want to move to the east in the first place.[20]

In the end, Nazi violence against "subhumans" in eastern Poland only served a losing cause: German armies encountered the Russian winter in the fall of 1941 and fell far short of their goal of annihilating Soviet resistance. In early December, their offensive (called Barbarossa) ground to a halt some 25 kilometers from Moscow after temperatures dropped below −35 degrees (German forward observers could make out the Kremlin in their field glasses).[21] Now Stalin threw in fresh Siberian divisions, who, unlike the German *Wehrmacht*, were prepared for winter war. Some German soldiers froze to their positions. After this point, Hitler inflicted massive damage on the Red Army in more than three years of desperate fighting, but he never came close to shaking the foundations of the Soviet state.

German soldiers were not prepared for the winter because Hitler's original plan was to strike on May 1 rather than in late June, permitting his armies to take Moscow in the summer, before fall rains and winter frost.[22] Yet the Germans had delayed the assault due to unanticipated trouble in the Balkans.

* * *

In October 1940, Benito Mussolini launched an invasion of Greece in an effort to establish Italy's hegemony in the eastern Mediterranean. Italian troops fared poorly, however, and Greek forces soon pushed them into Albania. From Hitler's perspective, this fiasco raised a prospect far worse than simply a humiliating blow to his major ally. Great Britain was obliged to defend Greek sovereignty, and Hitler feared the British would build airbases in Greece that might threaten his use of Romanian oil fields; indeed, he worried that Britain could establish a presence in the eastern Mediterranean from which to harass his assault on the Soviet Union. For that reason, Greece had to be crushed. Before that could happen, Germany needed guarantees of loyalty from Greece's Balkan neighbors, and Hitler sought their accession to the Tripartite Pact, the alliance of Italy, Germany, and Japan that had been established in Berlin two months earlier. Hungary and Romania signed on in November 1940, and Bulgaria joined on March 1, 1941.[23] That left Yugoslavia.

Despite urgent appeals by the German government, Prime Minister Dragiša Cvetković and the Regent Prince Paul resisted any agreement that might tie Yugoslavia to a country that many Serbs considered a mortal enemy. Yet on March 25, they finally gave in, signing the Pact, but with terms that to outsiders might appear moderate: Yugoslavia was not expected to participate in the attack on Greece or the Soviet Union, and it would gain access to the Greek port of Salonica. German troops would not cross Yugoslav territory on the way to subduing Greece, and Germany's intimate trade ties with Yugoslavia would continue, though to the exclusion of Britain.[24] What Germany wanted from Yugoslavia amounted to a guarantee of benevolent neutrality.[25]

Prince Paul signed because he feared dismemberment of his country at the hands of Germany and its allies, all of whom had designs on Yugoslav territory. He had received no hint that Western powers would assist him in any way. The failure of France and Britain to assist Poland stood as an object lesson. "You big nations are hard," the prince stated over dinner to the American ambassador Arthur Bliss Lane on March 20. "You talk of honor but are far away."[26] Though held in suspicion among Serbs for his aloof aristocratic manner, it would seem that Paul had worked out a reasonable basis for a small nation's survival in a hostile environment.

Yet this was not the perception in Belgrade. There, Paul appeared to have cozied up to Hitler. As soon as Yugoslavia's accession to the pact was announced, crowds formed in Belgrade's city center, and in the evening hours of March 26, a group of high army and air force officers, led by General Bora Mirković, staged a coup. That the Germans might retaliate did not enter their minds. They represented a consensus among Serb elites—from intelligentsia and leftist students, through the army and air force and the Orthodox clergy—that the signing of pact had betrayed old alliances and would doom Yugoslavia to dishonor.[27] The coup came off almost bloodlessly, and by 10 a.m. Yugoslav, British, and French flags were fluttering from the tallest buildings. Huge crowds sang and shouted slogans: *Bolje rat nego pakt, nema rata bez Srba, bolje grob nego rob* [Better war than the Pact; There is no War without Serbs; Better the grave than to be a slave]. The coup was "an emotional reaction," writes the historian Aleksa Djilas, "an outburst of anger against an alliance that went against Serbs' feelings, historical memories, and traditions," and represented the "quintessence of Serb history and Serb psychology." Even in those gloomy early war days, Serb elites were convinced that Hitler would lose and did not want to be penalized for being on the wrong side.[28]

FIGURE 16.3. Demonstrations against pact with Germany, Belgrade (March 1941).
Source: Celje weekly, (March 24, 1961). Via Wikimedia Commons.

Perhaps encouraged by British intelligence, General Mirković had planned
and initiated the coup, but support spread across Serb society.[29] To many, Paul
had seemed an authoritarian out of touch with popular sentiment, and with his
ouster, the political landscape began reviving. All parties, including the Croatian Peasants but excepting the outlawed Communists, were represented in the
new government. Beyond national honor, the mobilizing was about the recovery of self-rule, as reflected in the popular chants.

At the same time, the undertaking created a political situation that was not
sustainable, and the plotters knew it. Almost as soon as they ousted Paul—
causing, in Churchill's appraisal, "Yugoslavia to find its soul"—the new leaders
began signaling to Germany their intent to respect the pact that Paul had signed.
Yugoslavia would not threaten Germany. In the early afternoon of March 27, the
Yugoslav Foreign Minister assured German ambassador Heeren of "the continued cooperation with the Axis powers," particularly with Germany. The former government had suffered from limited popular support, but the new one
would have the "whole nation behind it." Now came the question of how Germany would react. If the Serb officers' coup laid bare the basic structures of

Serb political culture—as in Poland, the non-negotiability of national sovereignty, the hatred of fascism, and essential loyalty to western allies—it also once more revealed Hitler's inability to make rational calculations when faced with open defiance.[30]

The Führer ignored protestations of loyalty by the new government. Because of Yugoslavia's "nationality problems," he was unsure of the state's stability and said another coup could happen at any time. He even told Bulgarian Minister Draganov that the coup had brought relief; now the "everlasting uncertainty down there was over."[31] Furthermore, Germany could not risk British presence in Yugoslavia during its offensive against Greece to save Mussolini, or, more crucially, in the campaign after that against the Soviet Union. On March 27, he ordered an assault by land and air on Yugoslavia, predicting that the Croats would "take our side," in contrast to the Serbs and Slovenes, who "have never been pro-German." He also recognized the world historical import of the coup d'etat, telling his generals that it would delay the campaign against Russia by four weeks.[32]

On April 6, Luftwaffe bombers punished Belgrade as they had Warsaw a year and a half previously, and thousands of civilians lost their lives. The campaign against Yugoslavia also ended quickly as had the campaign against Poland. And, as had been the case in Czechoslovakia in the fall of 1938, the neighbors quickly moved in to claim spoils: Hungary, Italy, Bulgaria, and Germany itself all seized territory. There were, however, far fewer casualties in this campaign of eleven days than there had been in the month-long fighting in Poland: about 3,000 Yugoslavs and 200 Germans.[33]

What was different from Poland, and helps explain the swift defeat of a country with impressive geographical obstacles (Yugoslavia was mountainous, whereas Poland was flat), was the relative unity of the Poles. Despite desertions of some units, Croatian military units mostly fought loyally, but the Croat population welcomed Yugoslavia's fall. When German troops entered Zagreb on April 10, crowds lined the streets in jubilation, some raising their arms in the fascist salute. That same day the fascist Slavko Kvaternik, a former Habsburg general staff officer, acting under pressure from both Berlin and Rome, proclaimed the creation of an Independent State of Croatia in Zagreb. Germany had unsuccessfully courted the respected Croat Peasant Party leader Vladko Maček, but Maček now urged Croats to cooperate with the new Ustasha-controlled state. It was both more and less than Croatia: Italy took the Dalmatian coastline but the new state included Bosnia and Herzegovina. Though it was called independent, it had German and Italian zones of military occupation.

A vastly reduced Serbia, shorn of Macedonia and areas of Banat with Hungarian population, was placed under the collaborator regime of General Milan Nedić, former chief of the Yugoslav Army general staff, and kept under German military occupation.[34] Slovenia was divided between Germany and Italy.

Even after the *Sporazum* of 1939, which had accorded Croatia much autonomy, Croats, unlike the other peoples of Yugoslavia, had had little optimism about the country's future. If Serbs saw the coup of March 1941 as a hopeful sign of an opening political spectrum, Croats feared reassertion of central rule. They were not given the option of freely choosing the new "independent" state, but to many it would come to seem a platform for realizing the basic demands of the Croatian national movement. Many Croats admired Germany as a force for "order," whereas Serbs tended to see Germany as a nation bent on destroying their sovereignty.[35]

Resistance

By defying Hitler, Yugoslavia and Poland had triggered massive German land and air assaults that, in turn, called forth armed insurrections, in both cases resurrecting traditions dating back many generations. After the initial German incursions, violence spiraled upward in both places, giving populations no rational calculations of survival, and sending men, women, and children by the tens of thousands into a vast range of underground activities.[36] It was their "fanatical"—in German eyes—desires for independence that had caused the Polish and Serb politicians to oppose German overtures, and soon after defeat, people in both subdued countries began unearthing weapons, some that had not been fired in decades, as well as manufacturing their own. Because their conquest of Yugoslavia had proceeded so rapidly, the Germans had not been able to disarm all units of the Royal Army, and thus some light weapons became available to the underground resisters from its uncaptured stocks.

In both Yugoslavia and Poland, the German occupiers exacted reprisals that constrained underground operations, however, usually shooting 100 natives for each of their own soldiers killed. The *Wehrmacht* perpetrated executions in the fall of 1941 that were so traumatic for Serb resisters that they reconsidered how to continue their struggle. On October 21–22, 1941, in response to an attack in which nine Germans died and twenty-seven were wounded, German authorities shot some 2,800 male inhabitants of the industrial town Kragujevac. When the occupiers could not locate men in factories or offices, they had taken boys from schools. A few days earlier, the Germans had executed some 1,700

FIGURE 16.4. Kragujevac: Men being led to execution (October 21, 1941). *Source*: United
States Holocaust Memorial Museum, Photo #46726. Courtesy of
Muzej Revolucije Narodnosti Jugoslavije.

hostages in the Southern Serb city of Kraljevo. Serbs began to fear annihilation, specters of which seemed vivid after the Balkan wars and World War I, in
which 25 percent of the Serb population was lost to battle, disease, privation, and
mass execution.[37] In response, the Serb underground army—the Chetniks—
led by former Royal officers, worked out a strategy of biding time (that is, of
collecting weapons and engaging in acts of sabotage while waiting to launch an
uprising just ahead of Allied forces, coming, as they vainly hoped, from the
west). But Germans were not the only threat Serbs faced.

In territories of the Independent State of Croatia, the Ustashas had
launched a campaign of ethnic cleansing against Serbs in April 1941, just days
after assuming power. Accounts of the atrocities rivaled one another in their
brutality: in some places Serbs were burned alive in churches and barns, in
others they were butchered and thrown into rivers and ravines. The Croat
government's aim was to create ethnically pure territory (with the belief that
Bosniaks were "actually" Croats of Muslim faith) in the Independent State
of Croatia (NDH), and the methods included expulsion of Serbs to Serbia,
their forcible conversion to Roman Catholicism, and outright murder. The

number of Serbs expelled is estimated and at about 300,000; forcibly converted between 100,000 and 300,000; and murdered at between 320,000 and
340,000.[38]

This outburst of violence on Croatian soil came as a shock because there
was no ingrained animosity between the Serbs and Croats living there; domination of Croats by a Serb state had dated back just two decades. But it was
precisely the deep and peaceful integration of Serbs into Croat society that dis-
turbed the killers. They targeted those who blended in perfectly, above all local
leaders, for example, the lawyer Milan Vujičić, a Serb who had married into a
prominent Croat family in provincial Karlovac, entered the city's elite, and
courageously opposed the "Serb" dictatorship of Yugoslav King Alexander.
Such was the esteem for Vujičić that Croat Governor Ivan Šubašić had wanted
to appoint him a deputy after the Sporazum of 1939. Two years later, these facts
amounted to a death sentence. Vujičić and two other prominent Serbs of Karlovac were abducted on May 5 and were found in a shallow grave the next day.
The message was clear: under the Ustasha regime, there would be no compromise, especially with Serbs, whose ethnicity was suspect and therefore threatening. Vujičić, like his fathers and forefathers a native of Croatia, spoke not only
the same language as the Croats—Serbo-Croatian—but also the same local
dialect. Unlike Croats, his religious heritage was Eastern Orthodox, but it attracted little notice in the secular urban milieu where he and his friends lived
and thrived. He and the two other Serbs were murdered because their lives
defied the fiction of a pure Croat identity.[39]

The murderers were not native to Karlovac. They had been brought in by
truck from outside, representing ideas and concerns foreign to that area and to
most of Croatia, with the intention not only of ruthlessly separating Croats and
Serbs but also of involving others in the business of ethnic cleansing, usually
recruited from local underworlds of national radicals and criminals. A German
intelligence officer knew the type and reported in July that "the Ustasha movement has attracted many new adherents and since moral character was not an
issue, the worst rabble can be found in its ranks."[40]

The Ustashas, many of whom spoke better Italian than Croat, were a tiny
band of extremists making big facts for future Croat, Serb, and Serb Muslim relations; but as German observers also noted, the violence tended to reduce their
initial popularity in Croat society.[41] Unlike the Nazi Party in Germany, the
Ustashas had been marginal outsiders in the democratic period, performing
abysmally in free elections—0.5 percent in 1925—and unlike the Nazis, they
possessed a party apparatus far too small to staff state offices. In April 1941, just

before the German and Italian governments lifted them into power, there were only some 700 Ustasha militants holed up in Italian internment camps, and a further 900 sworn Ustasha supporters in the underground in Yugoslavia.[42]

Therefore, the origins of the killing have to be located in the ideas that animated these tiny groups of Croatian fascists; more perhaps than any other case of mass killing in World War II, the genocide that broke out in the NDH resulted from a basic ideological impulse. That impulse was strong precisely because the Ustashas knew they were weak. They had landed in Zagreb in their Italian-made uniforms in April 1941, with no traditional arguments to fall back on to justify staking the territory they had received thanks to Mussolini and Hitler. No historic Croatian territory had ever looked like the NDH, and even ethnic arguments could not explain Ustasha pretentions to ruling all of Bosnia-Herzegovina: not language (they shared that with Serbs), nor religion (Catholicism, though traditional in Croatia, was global).[43] So the Ustasha regime fell back on the radical Serb hatred concocted by Ante Starčević in the nineteenth century, adding to it the nihilism of fascism and the shoddy certainties of biological racism.

The murder of defenseless Serb villagers and townspeople caused violence to spiral beyond Ustasha control, however, and fortified armed resistance movements formed on NDH territory: first, Bosnian and Croatian units of the Serb Chetniks, and second, Communist resistance fighters called the "Partisans," both of which proceeded to conquer and hold much of the wooded and hilly countryside. By 1942, Ustasha rule was secure only in larger towns, where there were strong Croat and German garrisons.[44]

The Chetnik bands had risen up to protect Serb villagers against Ustasha marauders, but also against Muslims wearing uniforms of the Croatian state. (The fascists viewed Muslims as racially valuable, and the Nazis even formed an SS unit consisting of Muslims.)[45] Tales of the Chetnik counterattacks read much like the initial Ustasha assaults on Serbs. In the winter of 1941/1942 and summer of 1942, Chetnik fighters massacred thousands of Muslim civilians, including women and children, in eastern and southeastern Bosnia; in the town of Foča alone, some 2,000 Muslims were killed in August 1942.[46]

Like the Ustashas and the Nazis, the Chetniks were guided by ideologies of purity. They aspired to re-create Yugoslavia under Serb hegemony, and ethnic cleansing served that purpose.[47] One member of the Central National Committee of Chetniks, Bosnian Serb lawyer Stevan Moljević, proposed creating ethnically homogeneous entities in Yugoslavia, one of which, "homogenous Serbia," would include Bosnia-Herzegovina, much of Dalmatia, and other areas of Croatia. Chetnik ideology evoked historical memory more than the Ustasha counterpart, targeting Muslims as supposed carriers of ancient "Turkish" oppression. By contrast, the Ustasha ideology included anti-Serb images—Serbs as slaves, as incapable of order, and deeply corrupt—that were not embedded in ideas popular among Croats but were linked to the radical nationalist strand associated with Starčević and his follower Josip Frank.[48]

But the enemies of the Chetniks and Ustashas were not only ethnic. By late 1941, both opposed the Communist Partisans, which had arisen as an antifascist resistance force after June 22, 1941, the date of the German attack on the Soviet Union. The Partisans were a few thousand at first, with fewer experienced military men guiding them, but by 1944 had grown strong enough to govern a country of 18 million. Communists were initially weak in part because the royal government had outlawed them, but also because Yugoslavia had only three cities with more than 100,000 inhabitants and lacked the industrial working class that is typically attracted to a Marxist party.[49]

Yet the Communists would exploit other, latent sources of popularity in Yugoslav society. Before being outlawed in 1921, they had won 12.4 percent of the vote across territory of the new state, making them the fourth strongest party and the only one that could appeal beyond a single ethnic group. They were thus able to agitate successfully among alienated factory workers in Zagreb, landless peasants in Bosnia, or radicalized Serb intellectuals in Belgrade. The Communists were especially strong where national grievances and economic hardship reinforced one another, for example, among Hungarians in the Vojvodina, Albanians in Montenegro, or Macedonians in Macedonia (whom neither Bulgaria nor Yugoslavia recognized as an ethnicity).[50] And the more the Yugoslav state had treated opposition as Communist-inspired, the more those unsatisfied with royal dictatorship—especially young members of the intelligentsia—had come to sympathize with the Communist underground. Its leadership reflected the multiethnic character of the base: the chief, the charismatic Josip Broz Tito, was of mixed Croat and Slovene heritage; one major thinker, Edvard Kardelj, was Slovene; the other, Milovan Djilas, was a Montenegrin; and the security chief, Aleksandar Ranković, was a Serb.

At first the Partisans sought to cooperate with the Serb resisters; in fact, Tito met twice with the Chetnik leader Draža Mihailović, a colonel in the Yugoslav Royal Army, in the summer and fall of 1941. Yet differences soon emerged. If German reprisals had made Chetniks fear for the survival of the Serb people, the Partisans almost welcomed them, thinking not so much of the dead as of the survivors who fled German terror into the countryside, with nothing to lose and a thirst for vengeance, and thus natural reinforcements for Partisan units.

Furthermore, as Communists, the Partisans were internationalists, concerned not about the disappearance of any nation but with the strengthening of the motherland of socialism, which was fighting for its life. The German units tied down in Yugoslavia could not be deployed in the Soviet Union.

After 1941 the stories of Chetniks and Partisans diverged in spectacular ways. The Chetniks had weapons and training, and they fought for self-preservation yet declined. By contrast, the Partisans struggled for an ideal—socialism—best represented by a foreign power, and knew little about warfare, yet they steadily grew.

Initially Tito and his staff, hunted by German forces and their collaborators, fled to Eastern Bosnia, where they became popular among a population whose towns had been ethnically cleansed by the Ustashas and then by Chetniks. Their operation may have been small, but it was Leninist, and therefore disciplined and strictly hierarchical. The leadership purged the ranks from the start, so that when the Partisans grew, it was controlled growth. Yet the Partisans also had the advantage of flexibility. They were open to all nationalities and classes—workers, peasants, and intellectuals—and also included many thousands of women in their operations.[51] Partisan units were insistently mobile, never staying more than a night or two at any location until they had established solid control of territory. They therefore moved quickly, weaving in and out of often-savage terrain to evade the Germans, who were better armed but lacked intimate knowledge of the Yugoslav countryside.

By contrast, the Chetniks never possessed a coordinated command structure, and professorial-looking Draža Mihailović was unable to control units in Bosnia or Montenegro. A special problem was collaboration. In areas of Bosnia controlled by Italian forces, Chetnik units soon arranged truces with fascist army commanders, and occasionally even cooperated in operations against the Partisans, whom they came to view as the greatest long-term threat to their power. The Partisans, with their internationalist ideology, by contrast, largely avoided compromises with the enemy, a characteristic that slowly gained them support not only of the Soviets but also of the British.[52]

As the war and its gargantuan costs increasingly suggested to people across Europe that new realities had to emerge after the fighting, the Chetniks found themselves short of ideas. Unlike the Partisans, whose socialist order promised to transcend the many limits of Royalist Yugoslavia, the Chetniks stood for continuity of a Serb-dominated order. They had none of the Partisans' progressive social agenda that attracted women and also peasants and workers. The Partisans showed their long-term intentions for change even during the war.

After wresting territory from fascist control, Tito's followers organized it, setting up committees that coordinated education and land reform, often in areas that had seen little of either—illiteracy stood at more than 50 percent in much of Bosnia—as well as self-defense. The Partisans also built hospitals to care for the wounded, sometimes in caves and hidden dugouts.

This last fact gives a sense of the self-sacrifice involved in partisan warfare. The wounded begged to be left behind, but the leadership refused to make this a general policy (Tito ordered: "save the wounded at all costs"), and some units insisted on carrying hundreds of wounded through enemy lines to safety. During the fifth offensive of the Germans and their allies against the Partisans in 1943, some thirty doctors and two hundred nurses stayed with the wounded who could not be transported, and all suffered the same fate: massacre by Chetnik and German forces.[53] Such behavior of the fascists marked a total rupture with a code of Balkan guerilla warfare calling for the brotherhood of warriors. But the Partisans adapted, themselves at times refusing to take prisoners.[54]

Even after one has enumerated all the individual reasons for Partisan victory, there is still something breathtaking and not fully explicable about the ability of several thousand men and women having nothing but firm ideas in 1941 to build a mass movement that would take power three years later, outlasting and defeating German, Italian, Croatian fascist, and Serb nationalist forces, and creating a foundation from which to defy Stalin three years after that. More than perhaps any political or military organization during World War II, the Partisans saw their cause as a moral one. They were the first multiethnic group anywhere to subdue and then transcend ethnic nationalism—at its most vicious. And then by uniting Serbs, Croats, Slovenes, and many others in one state, they appeared to have succeeded where the Habsburgs had failed.

Yet the Partisans were not antinational. Instead, they played on the ambiguities of the word "nation." Their first government in 1943 was the "Antifascist Council for the *National* Liberation of Yugoslavia," evoking the old South Slav ideal of the Illyrians. But rather than suppress the ethnic identities of Serbs, Croats, or Slovenes, they worked to foster a broader unity that would make them secondary to Yugoslav identity. After all, the war seemed to show that none of these ethnicities could survive without the unity of all. That was precisely the Partisan cause: protecting Serbs or Muslims from complete destruction. They were Europe's first antigenocidal army, defying armed forces that strove for ethnic purity. At the same time, the Partisans were Communists, and the word "nation" always signified people in the social sense. For them, nation-building meant bettering the Yugoslav people's education, health, and social welfare.[55]

Because of the broadness of their attraction, the Partisans even absorbed local "national" traditions as their own, as long as they seemed revolutionary, for example, the insurrectionary traditions of the Serb and Montenegrin peoples. The internationalist Communist partisans did not hesitate to invoke the Kosovo stories of heroic self-sacrifice against foreign occupiers, in effect connecting antifascism to all previous battles against foreign oppression.[56] Decades later, Milovan Djilas described his encounter with some 400 peasants in Montenegro in the spring of 1942:

> I praised their heroism and self-sacrifice even above the heroism and self-sacrifice of their ancestors. We were no better equipped than the insurgents of olden times against the Turks, yet we had to face an enemy who fought with planes and tanks. I told them that we were their children, reminded them of their murdered relatives, brothers, sons and neighbors; our blood and lives could not be separated.[57]

Djilas wrote that in his own path to Communism, "party ideology was but the token and expression of traditional Montenegrin sentiment."[58] But neither he nor his comrades were opportunists who were simply using the word "nation" to fit the needs of the moment. If they failed to specify the precise meaning of *narod*, that was because they were Marxists, for whom ethnicity or nationhood were relevant if they advanced the revolution. For the time being, of paramount importance was unity against fascism and for socialism: for bringing about a world in which questions of language and ethnicity would recede into the background, and all humans could equally enjoy the fruits of their common labors in peace and security.

In his memoir, Djilas described the wartime struggle not chiefly in military terms: it was a popular uprising that happened to have a military aspect. That is why conviction spread so easily, from military and political leadership, downward, and outward across territory. The "revolution had to have its own army," Djilas wrote, and the revolutionaries operated not on a level playing field but on scorched earth abandoned by political rivals. Peasant politicians had failed to organize, and now the Partisans accepted virtually everyone, even renegade Ustashas or Chetniks: "When a civil war has permeated every pore of the nation," Djilas explained, "there can be no replenishing of units except with adherents of the opposite side." People entering the movement encountered men and women whose "concern for all did not yet reveal a desire to control everyone." Partisan officers listened to questions and did not indoctrinate.[59] Under the pragmatic leadership of Tito, the movement was also smart enough not to speak of the revolution's ultimate goals and how exactly they had been realized in the Soviet Union.

The story of revolution was thus also a story of redemption. The men who switched from Chetnik or Ustasha bands to Partisan ranks suddenly had a new past. In the midst of fighting in which brother slaughtered brother, and men, women and children fell to machine gun salvos without distinction, here was not just moral high ground, it was a place one could make a stand as a human being after the war, regardless of what crimes one had witnessed or perpetrated. By late 1943 the trend was easy to see and the Partisans grew, especially in Bosnia. Yet even in Serbia, the German occupiers were astounded to discover that conservative forces whose cooperation they had taken for granted, "preferred Bolshevism to the occupation."[60]

From the start, the Partisan-led mass revolution was inconceivable without its charismatic leader Tito, who through his own life story seemed to hold the Yugoslavs together. A member of the British military mission who dealt with Tito expected to find "a rigid doctrinaire, a fanatic, harshly molded by underground life, narrow in outlook." The truth was the opposite: Tito was a man "broadened by the experience of exile and prison, flexible in discussion, with a sharp and humorous wit, and of a wide curiosity." He was in a way reminiscent of Piłsudski, who had less support in society than his nationalist rival Roman Dmowski but was willing to take action, especially military action, to gain "tactical superiority" and create new facts.[61] Yet Tito also had something of Lenin: ultimately he was not limited but empowered by ideology, willing to do what was necessary while not abandoning principle.

* * *

In Poland, too, there was a competition among resistance armies: the Home Army (AK) (allied with the émigré government in London) fought the Germans alongside the Communist People's Army, and the radical nationalist National Armed Forces. The People's Army could never claim the popularity of Yugoslavia's Partisans because Poles tended to see Communists as threatening their national existence rather than embodying promises of any kind. Thus those who did become Communist in Poland, as was true of Yugoslavia, often came from persecuted ethnic minorities. Again we see the crucial but also unpredictable valence of nationalism: whereas the internationalism of Communists proved a trump card in Yugoslavia, because it protected nationalities from genocide, it was a liability in Poland. One of the slogans of the Polish

Communist Party, taken over by Communist underground organizations, was "Long Live the Soviet Polish Republic!" To most Poles, such words suggested the return to the "enslavement" of foreign rule. By contrast, the mainstream Home Army, by far the strongest underground force, evoked the causes of Poland's national as well as social liberation and kept the radicals of left and right at the margins. To give a sense of the relative strengths: in July 1944, the Home Army in Warsaw possessed approximately 40,000 fighters, while the National Armed Forces had 1,000 and the Communist People's Army about 800.[62]

The AK tended to husband resources, and like the Chetniks, limited itself to acts of sabotage and spectacular but rare acts of vengeance on leading figures in the Nazi apparatus of repression. The object was to make clear the possible consequences of ordering atrocities against civilians, and among the AK's pinpointed targets were SS Gruppenführer Friedrich Wilhelm Krüger, the Police General Franz Kutschera, and SS Obergruppenführer Wilhelm Koppe.[63] The AK also managed to free captives. In March 1943, one unit liberated twenty-five political prisoners being transferred from one Gestapo prison to another. But occasionally the AK launched an extended guerilla campaign to protect the Polish population, for example, in 1943 in the Lublin region, after the Germans ethnically cleansed more than 100,000 Poles to make room for German colonists. Battles raged for months and included raids on German settlers as well as German and Ukrainian military units. Even vicious measures of pacification did not break the defiance to this genocide in miniature, especially when word spread that thousands of children had been taken for "Germanization." In the end, the German command called the operation off, to be continued after its anticipated victory in the war.[64]

Like the Partisans, the Polish underground was not only a fighting army but also a political organization; yet by contrast it was not radical left but centrist, a "secret state" under the authority of the London Government that began functioning on Polish territory in 1940, carefully hidden from the Gestapo. It had twelve departments, including a Department of the Interior that gradually built up a new Polish administration, including an embryo police force, and was poised to assume the tasks of Polish statehood after liberation.[65]

Though denounced by Polish Communists, this hidden state was in fact progressive and would have introduced reforms similar to those of the postwar Communist regime had it come to power, including the nationalization of industry, redistribution of land (estates of more than 50 hectares of arable land were to be appropriated by the state), and expansion of state economic planning to promote growth and reduce unemployment. Unlike the extreme left, it pledged to achieve these goals through democratic governance. Social policy, evoking the aspirations of the young Marx, was meant to emancipate working people, strengthening their "will, fondness, and desire for work," and workers themselves would supervise production through trade unions and self-management. The new state would feature educational and cultural self-government, and in contrast to the Communists, the mainstream underground rejected "all attempts to impose on us a model of government from the east. Our distinctiveness from the Russian East and German barbarity is characterized by a thousand-year tradition of freedom and Christian culture."[66]

Though criticized by the right for insufficient attention to national interests, this mainstream Polish opposition rejected the Molotov-Ribbentrop boundaries. But when the front moved westward in 1943/44 into prewar Polish territories, the AK proved powerless to defend the lands that Hitler had accorded Stalin in 1939. In July 1944, AK units rose up in Wilno, hoping to cooperate with the Red Army in liberating the city from Nazi rule, only to be disarmed after the fighting was over. Some AK soldiers were integrated into a Soviet-controlled Polish Army under General Zygmunt Berling; others were arrested, often winding up in the Soviet system of political camps in Siberia.[67]

But the Soviet animus against the Home Army was not limited to disputes about Poland's eastern boundary. Soviet authorities also refused to fight alongside AK units in central Poland, most infamously during the Warsaw Uprising of August and September 1944. Anticipating imminent liberation of the capital by the Red Army, AK leaders ordered underground units to rise up and reassert Polish sovereignty against the German occupiers in late July. The idea was to seize the city just before the Soviets moved in.

Yet perhaps exhausted by their own rapid advance from deep in Ukraine, the Red Army stopped short of central Warsaw, and stood by across the Vistula in the city's eastern districts while the *Wehrmacht* regrouped and crushed the insurgency. German units, consisting largely of criminals (the Dirlewanger Brigade), and bolstered by former Red Army soldiers (who had a bad reputation even among the Germans), massacred some 30,000 to 40,000 Warsovians in the first days of August. More than a thousand civilians sought shelter in the hospital St. Lazarus, only to be murdered there along with the staff and patients. One German officer complained there were more captive men, women, and children than he had bullets to kill them.[68]

Fearing loss of labor, the German command ordered a halt to the full-scale slaughter and began funneling the captive population through holding centers to work camps. The AK fighters successively lost ground, having at best heavy machine guns against tanks and dive-bombers, but they did not surrender until October 1. In all, more than 200,000 Poles died, mostly civilians. After that, German sappers laid dynamite to most surviving buildings and systematically gutted them, leaving more than 85 percent of the city in ruins. By that time, German authorities had deported the remaining population to camps.

Some have criticized Home Army leaders for launching an uprising in an urban area, effectively condemning to death tens of thousands with no way of escape. But for most Poles, the enduring memory is of the heroism of Home Army units, including many women and teenagers, and of the Red Army standing by passively, permitting German units to kill both civilian noncombatants as well as much of Poland's military and intellectual elite. Soviet leaders did not even permit British and US aircraft to land in Soviet-controlled territory after they dropped aid to the Warsaw insurgents. The underlying problem with the AK for Stalin was not whether it was progressive or reactionary, but that it insisted on independence.

The Polish underground's ideas about the postwar order proliferated through a vast publishing network, including more than 1,500 newspapers and journals across the political spectrum. Despite the genocidal conditions of the Warsaw and other ghettos, the Jewish underground likewise managed to publish dozens of journals. The most popular AK publication was its Information Bulletin, which came out in 40,000 copies a week.[69] The underground also produced hundreds of books and brochures of high technical quality, hoping to combat the cultural degradation by occupiers who had closed down Polish publishing except for a few mass dailies featuring German propaganda and pornography.

In response to the shuttering of schools above grade six, Polish educators, professors, and students conducted classes in private spaces, usually conspiratorial apartments and homes. These initiatives arose spontaneously in 1939 but were ultimately organized and financed by the underground state's Department for Education and Culture, which issued thousands of diplomas for courses of study at all levels. By 1944 the number of illegal high school students in Warsaw reached the level of legal students in 1939.[70] In 1942 the underground state had a budget of some £400,000 for civilian purposes. Of this, 18 percent went to the conspiratorial schooling, 30 percent to social welfare, 15 percent to the bureaucracy of the civilian resistance, and 5 percent to protective measures against Gestapo infiltration. From 1942 to 1944, the civilian apparatus of the underground received about a third of the 27 million dollars that entered the country from abroad.[71]

All told, some 500,000 Poles engaged in some form of conspiratorial activity, and the number who were active occasionally or on a one-time basis was much greater. Opinions about the underground's impact vary. Some note that most Poles were passive. Even in Warsaw, the most densely organized arena of resistance, about two-thirds of the population took no part in the conspiracy. However, others emphasize that at least every fourth Warsovian was active, representing an "unusually high degree of mobilization and readiness to resist" on the background of Nazi-occupied Europe.[72] The presence of the Polish underground could be felt everywhere, even in concentration camps, where AK soldiers organized intelligence-gathering and mutual aid cells. Resistance cells multiplied among the hundreds of thousands of Poles deported to Germany as forced labor, as well as among the Polish police and administrative offices on Polish territory. "All social groups and strata," writes the historian Andrzej Paczkowski, "took up systematic conspiratorial activity, although cities offered the best conditions for it."[73]

* * *

By 1941, three zones of influence had emerged in Nazi-dominated East Central Europe. The first included areas where Germany destroyed states and left no native administration, itself taking rudimentary control. The second comprised areas where it destroyed states and replaced them with its own political entities, misleadingly called "independent states." In the third zone, states remained under control of native political elites, but they came under irresistible pressure to become German allies. Only Poland belonged to the first category.

The Protectorate of Bohemia and Moravia fit between the first and second zones: it was occupied and destined for absorption into Germany but valued as a place that produced high-quality industrial goods. Its population was thought to be racially valuable (50 percent of the Czechs were considered assimilable; only 10 percent of the Poles) and was permitted its own heavily supervised government, with a Czech cabinet and ministries, and even a tiny armed force. Serbia was similar, a rump, embodying nothing a Serb nationalist could be proud of, with a Serb head of state who had been a Royal Yugoslav general but was under direct Nazi oversight. As we have seen, in contrast to Bohemia, a desperate underground struggle raged, extending from Serbia across Yugoslav territory, pitting German, Italian, and Croat forces against Serb nationalists and Communist internationalists.

The second zone was made up of the "independent" states of Slovakia and Croatia, called into life by Berlin with the expectation they would be loyal, co-fascist regimes; and they matched expectations, to say the least. Their ultrana-tionalist leaders were eager to demonstrate—above all to themselves—their personal achievements for "the nation" by becoming even more racist than the state that had created them. In 1941, a Slovak newspaper boasted that the strict-est racial laws in Europe were Slovak; at the same time, the brutality of the Ustasha anti-Serb actions shocked even the SS.[74]

The final zone consisted of states that technically remained sovereign mem-bers of the international community, yet whose leaders could see from the fate of Yugoslavia and Poland the consequences of defiance. Still, unlike the pup-pets Croatia or Slovakia, the Hungarian, Bulgarian, and Romanian states did not owe their existence to Nazi Germany, and everything Germany wanted from them had to be negotiated.[75] The lever for Germany in gaining compliance was territory: though less rapacious than Nazi leaders, East European elites also hun-gered for *Lebensraum*. Bulgaria hoped to recover ground lost at Neuilly-sur-Seine and wrench away disputed lands from Greece and Yugoslavia. Hungary wanted back everything it had lost at Trianon. Romania desired the return of lands it had lost in 1940, when parts of northern Transylvania went to Hungary in the second Vienna award (at the insistence of Hitler and Mussolini), and Bessarabia and Bukovina fell to the Soviet Union. These three states knew that Germany as the regional hegemon could make their aspirations become a reality.

Yet from 1941, German diplomats increasingly insisted that the governments of East Central Europe must fulfill a prime wish of their state. They should iden-tify and segregate their Jewish populations, place them under racial laws, and deport them to German-controlled territories in Poland for a fate loosely de-scribed as "work in the east."

CHAPTER 17

What Dante Did Not See: The Holocaust in Eastern Europe

Hitler's regime was the most fanatically racist regime in history. Everything it did, whether in cultural or social policy, education, science, or war, was dictated by concern for the racially understood German people. At the same time, its policies were shot through with inconsistencies. Supposedly Nazism was anti-Slavic, yet Hitler allied with the Slavic states Slovakia and Croatia, while subjecting Slavic peoples like Ukrainians and Russians to genocide. Locating a long-standing ideological animus in Hitler's mind against Poles is impossible.[1]

Up to 1939, Hitler admired the regime of Józef Piłsudski and courted Poland for a campaign against the Soviet Union. If he had contempt for a Slavic group, it was the Czechs. Yet when the war was over, the Czech population had actually grown, and Czech towns were as picturesque as ever, while one in five Polish citizens had died, and many Polish towns and cities were in rubble.[2] The difference in treatment in these cases was due not to racial ideology but to the fact that the Polish government had defied Hitler, while its Czech counterpart had not. Defiance among Serbs also explains that ferocity of the German assault on Belgrade in April 1941: before Serb officers staged their coup days earlier, Hitler had no intention of attacking or bombing Yugoslavia, let alone provoking the guerrilla war that resulted in more than a million casualties.

Hitler considered the cause of Germany against the Soviet Union so holy that he would not permit captured Soviet soldiers to participate in it, though many, especially Ukrainians, would gladly have done so. He therefore permitted millions of Red Army prisoners to die of starvation and exposure in late 1941. They were not considered worthy of even slave labor for Germany. By 1943, the fortunes of war had shifted, and captured Soviet soldiers became useful. Hundreds of thousands received uniforms and weapons and fought for the Third Reich, though some turned against German forces right at the end, helping rescue the uprising that Czech patriots started in Prague on May 5, 1945.

These few examples suggest that racial ideology guided German policy only when it seemed politically opportune. When Slavs seemed useful, they were

465

courted as collaborators, and when they appeared defiant, they were annihilated. But that is not the whole story. If one looks at the central target of Nazi racism, the Jews, one sees a very different story. After a decision was reached in the Nazi leadership in 1941 that all Jews in Europe must be eliminated, there was no turning back, little deviation, and virtually no exceptions. Jews were considered useful for no purpose other than dying.[3]

Hitler could not simply impose his ideas; he found willing collaborators in and beyond German society. Still, this basic uncompromising attitude was his. In his mind, Jews were a human group, but something demonic and unholy attached to them, making them unlike any other human group. Hitler said that in killing Jews his regime was doing the work of "Providence." Genocide was in his eyes an act of great virtue. There could be no exceptions because he thought there was no end to the trouble that even a few Jews could cause. Shortly before Hitler died by his own hand in April 1945, having killed the overwhelming majority of Jews in the lands Germany occupied or was allied with, he continued to believe that an international Jewish conspiracy was advancing the fortunes of Germany's enemies. He told his secretary Martin Bormann that Jews were a "spiritual race."[4]

The Holocaust of the Jews was thus not a story that occurred alongside World War II. It was at the heart of Germany's struggle, a central theater of operations that opened in 1933, when Hitler's state developed its mechanisms of destruction: first legal definition, then expropriation, segregation, and finally, after the 1941 attack on the Soviet Union, physical annihilation.[5] These mechanisms were extended to wherever Germany controlled new territory, and for Hitler and his regime, nothing in Eastern Europe—not Romanian oil, Hungarian grain, or Slovak troops for the front—was more important than identifying, segregating, and then destroying Jews. This agenda overshadowed every other concern and was initiated from the moment German forces occupied Poland or Bohemia and maintained until the moment they fell back on Vienna or Berlin under the hail of Soviet rockets.

In only three allied states did the Nazi agenda coincide well with the mindsets of the governing elites: Romania, Croatia, and Slovakia. Not coincidentally, these were the places where nationalists were most insecure about their nationalism. The conundrums facing Romanian and Slovak elites were similar to those we have seen in Croatia: little to no history of statehood before the national era, none whatsoever within the boundaries drawn by Germany. On top of this, these countries faced multiple claimants on their territory. Their leaders therefore resorted to the strongest arguments for national territory, and those were racist. The nineteenth-century version stressing language and culture had become an old-fashioned curiosity; now those who wanted land for their ethnicity used arguments that were partly scientific, partly mystical. The Romanians' or Croats' precious "blood" justified the seizing of territory and making it and everyone on it "pure."

The war seemed to have supplied an opportunity for establishing a hold on territory that might never be repeated. In July 1941, Romania's General Antonescu said the war provided "the most favorable opportunity in our history . . . for cleansing our people of all the elements foreign to its soul. Therefore, without any formalities, and complete freedom, I take full legal responsibility, and tell you, there is no law."[6] A few months earlier, Adolf Hitler had told Croatia's Ante Pavelić: this is your opportunity. But the latter needed no cajoling. According to Milovan Djilas, Ustasha murderers listened calmly when Serbs told them the Red Army would liberate Yugoslavia. They may come, they replied, but when they do, you will be dead.[7]

Still, there was a difference between those states and Germany. No matter how racist, East European regimes modified their anti-Semitism according to how it served the overall goal of strengthening the nation. They were opportunistic and passed anti-Semitic legislation or deported Jews to Germany when that seemed to enhance their control of national territory, especially territory held by rivals. Yet later in the war, East European regimes also held Jews back from the German grasp when it seemed that Germany would lose, and the victors would exact retribution for crimes against humanity. And for none of them did the Jewish people come to represent a quasi-metaphysical evil as they did for Adolf Hitler.

That in a nutshell was the story of Romania, a state that killed Jews when Germany did not mandate it, but that later withheld Jews from death transports when Germany urgently desired it. For the Croat fascists, anti-Serbianism eclipsed anti-Semitism. For Nazi leaders, by contrast, the Jewish question was not a way of getting something else. Its "solution" through violence served no other goal, and no consideration of opportunity during the war or fear of punishment afterward could modify the killing plan once it existed. German officials were frustrated when they encountered Bulgarian or Hungarian nationalists who called themselves allies but seemed ignorant of the "dangers" posed by Jews in their midst and everywhere else.

* * *

For Gentiles who lived in East Central Europe during World War II, it made a world of difference whether they lived in places that had their own states (Hungary or Bulgaria), or in places that Germany ruled directly (occupied Poland) or semi-directly (the Protectorate of Bohemia-Moravia, Serbia). Occupied Poland was a place of unremitting terror, where any non-German native might be arrested and then murdered without any charges, let alone suspicions. The poet Czesław Miłosz once saw a couple out for a walk with their child; along came a German car, a man inside pointed his gun at the father, and he got in and they rolled off. He had done nothing other than displease a German official, perhaps by seeming to be enjoying his life.

But elsewhere, excepting parts of Yugoslavia where the underground struggle raged, life continued almost normally for non-Jews. In a typical Hungarian, Bulgarian, Czech, or Slovak town or village there were weddings, schooldays, and funerals; plantings, and harvestings, quotidian pleasures and pains. Some young men joined armies and fought for Germany but were called back when the losses were too grievous. In August 1944, Romanian soldiers suddenly turned their weapons on the Germans. For the majority of East Europeans, the war was something that intruded on their lives mainly through daily newspapers.

This was not how Jews in Eastern Europe experienced Hitler's war. Regardless of where they lived, the Nazi state, the supreme regional hegemon, wanted their lives to end, and as soon as that state controlled territory, their existence was transformed, and terror shaped waking moments as well as dreams. If for Slovak or Romanian peasants or Czech factory workers life went on, for Jews, it was supposed to stop in any form, and every moment, after late 1941, brought the possibility that it would. We know from nightmares the quintessentially modern terror of the "knock on the door," meaning an unspecified fate that could lead to death.

Now it was a reality for every person identified as Jewish, by the Nazis or whatever regime they helped prop up. The Lichtenstein family of Olomouc, a city in the Protectorate of Bohemia and Moravia, with father Vojtěch, mother Margareta, eleven-year old Filip, and nine-year old Alfred, lived their unremarkable lives just a block from one of Central Europe's great small town synagogues, until the Nazis gutted it in September 1939. Then came acts of discrimination, and rumors about killings and camps in the east, and finally a summons to pack suitcases. And in July 1942 came the knock on the door, with orders to evacuate from peaceful Olomouc, first to Theresienstadt and after that to "the East"—for reasons no one could have imagined let alone explained just a few months earlier.

FIGURE 17.1. Olomouc Synagogue: built 1897, destroyed 1939. *Source*: Jewish Community of Olomouc, used with permission.

Some Jews evaded the transports and went underground, but they became *vogelfrei*, human beings with no rights whatsoever, worse off than slaves and liable to be shot on sight.[8] If Jews left their hiding places for a breath of fresh air, any local Gentile they encountered might self-deputize and ask them to prove their Aryan credentials. The Polish Jewish writer Janina Bauman described how ruffians stripped a friend of hers naked on a tram in Warsaw in 1943. She was not wearing a star but they "sensed" she was Jewish. It was a beautiful spring day, and after many months of living in a closet, she had simply wanted to see and experience the world again.[9] We don't know whether this friend was shot at the end of the tram line or sent to a death camp.

The radical nationalism that desired the Jews' disappearance was not new, but the experience of terror was. It had no precedent and was precisely targeted, bypassing the Gentiles in the dwellings above and below the Lichtensteins in their Olomouc apartment house, or the school children who had sat in desks next to Alfred and Filip. They continued classes, as if nothing had happened, and had chances to live full lives.

What was distinctive about the Shoah therefore was not just its objective dimension—that it was the only continent-wide effort by a state to use its administrative power and technological prowess to kill one people—but also this subjective dimension, the power of the Nazi authorities and their helpers to instill naked fear, along with utter despair, loneliness, and feelings of abject failure, the worst being the inability to save one's children.

While this terror that Jews came to know was specific, other East Europeans also experienced fear: those who conspired to oppose the regime, like Communists or social democrats in the underground. If the Gestapo uncovered a conspiracy, there would also be a knock on the door. Sometimes the fates of these groups intertwined: many of those conspiring as Communists were Jewish. For example, an entire group of young Jews in Berlin, both friends and comrades were arrested and executed in 1942. If Jews joined the Communist Partisans in Yugoslavia, that was partly because they hoped they might be safe. Fear, as we have seen, was also the lot of Poles denied statehood from September 1939, though not in every waking moment nor with the same sense of deep dread.

Eastern Europe under German Control

Because Poland was home to the largest population of Jews in Europe, the Nazis moved quickly to solve the "Jewish problem" there, and within weeks of occupying Polish territory, authorities were implementing policies that had taken years to evolve in Germany itself. In November 1939, they required Jews to wear an identifying armband with a blue Star of David as a first step of segregating them from non-Jews. Next they began cordoning off areas in cities that Jews could leave only under penalty of death, sometimes with bricks, sometimes with barbed wire. They then made these "ghettos" into places where Jews would die out: through unsanitary conditions, absence of medical care, starvation rations, impressment into forced labor brigades, and painful overcrowding. The ghettos contained not just the Jews from a given town—say, Kraków—but also those from smaller communities in the vicinity, and families lived not just two to an apartment, but often two to a room. In Warsaw, a third of the city's inhabitants—some 338,000 Jews—were crammed into 2.4 percent of the city's territory. The destitution that the occupiers forced on the Jews in the ghettos created a world of misery and degradation that was shown on newsreels to audiences in the Reich to confirm the Nazis' images of the Jews, and to feed the preexisting hatred and disdain for them in the Gentile population.[10]

The genocide of the Jews entered a new phase in the summer of 1941 because the assault on the Soviet Union was a war of annihilation, aimed at destroying "Judeo-bolshevism." Following the regular army were four mobile killing squads of the SS (*Einsatzgruppen*), about 3,000 men in total, with orders to segregate the Bolshevik commissars from the captured Soviet troops and subject them to "special measures," that is, to shoot them. Soon they were including Jewish soldiers, and then Jewish male adults in the killing; by the late summer, they were rounding up Jewish men, but also women and children, and gunning them down in mass executions.[11]

German authorities endeavored to involve local Gentile populations and make their contributions to the violence seem spontaneous; in one town, Jedwabne in northeastern Poland, the Polish population undertook the killing of Jews with no German supervision, and after a day-long pogrom locked the Jewish inhabitants in a barn and set it ablaze. The death toll there was more than 1,000.[12] In Lwów, Ukrainians in German uniforms compelled the city's Jews to clear prisons of victims left by the NKVD—who had shot some 4,000 political prisoners shortly before the Germans entered the city—before staging a pogrom that killed hundreds of Jews.[13] By early 1942, the killing operations of the SS and local collaborators, on a front extending from the Baltic countries down to Romania, had cost the lives of at least half a million Jews.[14]

For the SS, killing by rifle power was not sufficiently systematic, and therefore it undertook experiments with poison gas from the late summer, using Soviet prisoners as subjects and victims at a concentration camp in eastern Silesia, Oświęcim in Polish, Auschwitz-Birkenau in German (it was on Polish territory appended to the Reich). They settled on a commercial pesticide, Zyklon B, that could be produced in pellets that vaporized into a poison gas at temperatures above 27 degrees Celsius. That same year, the SS constructed gas chambers and crematoria at Auschwitz and the Majdanek camp in eastern Poland, and the following year at additional killing camps near the Polish towns of Treblinka, Bełżec, and Sobibór.[15]

These camps became centers for killing Jews who came in by train from across Europe, according to a basic scheme laid out by officials from the SS and German government ministries at the Wannsee Conference near Berlin in January 1942. After that point, wherever they controlled territory, from the Channel Islands off France to strips of territory in the Caucasus that they held for a few weeks; from the Greek islands to villages in Norway above the Arctic Circle, German authorities attempted to identify, segregate, deport, and destroy every last Jew. They acted very quickly. If in March 1942, 75–80 percent of the Jews who would die in the Holocaust were still alive, by mid-February 1943, 75–80 percent of those who would die had been killed, mostly in killing camps on Polish territory.[16]

The killing of Polish Jews accelerated in the summer of 1942, when German police, often assisted by Ukrainian and Baltic collaborators, forced the

FIGURE 17.2. Column of Jews march down a main street in Kraków during liquidation of the ghetto. *Source*: United States Holocaust Memorial Museum Photo Archives #06694. Courtesy of Instytut Pamięci Narodowej. Copyright United States Holocaust Memorial Museum.

inhabitants of the larger ghettos to board freight trains, headed supposedly to labor in the "east," but in fact to the nearby death camps. In villages and the smaller towns of eastern Poland, the Jewish population was often not deported but were marched out of town and gunned down in mass executions. Those who evaded the killing and were found in their homes were simply shot there, in full view of the local Polish population—and often with its participation.

The experience for Jews in these areas was utter terror before and during the "action." For example, in the spring and summer of 1942, several hundred Jews of the small east Polish town Szczebrzeszyn received horrifying news on a daily basis, of train cars full of Jews from Bohemia and elsewhere going to nearby camps and returning empty, of round-ups and the murder of Jews on open streets in neighboring towns. The violence crept closer until on May 8, trucks of gendarmes arrived who drove people out of their homes with great brutality and then compelled them to walk to open pits beyond town, where they were executed. Many sought shelter, but the armed intruders hunted and then shot them "like ducks"—everyone, including small children. A Polish physician noted in his diary the growing panic in the days and hours before the killers arrived. "A real hell started," he wrote, "women were crying and tearing their clothes."[17]

An estimated 10 percent of Poland's Jews—about 250,000 persons—managed to evade deportations and executions like these, and they endeavored to survive among "Aryan" Poles until the Red Army came as liberators at some point between January 1944 and January 1945. However, the great majority did not survive, because members of the local Polish populations helped ferret out those Jews who attempted to hide.[18] This occurred in several ways.

Most immediately German police, in coordination with Polish village leadership, enlisted Polish peasants in manhunts that combed the forests, turning up the majority of Jews weeks and months after they had sought shelter beyond the ghettos. Those caught were executed on the spot, often by German but sometimes by Polish collaborator "blue" police. Then, in the months that followed, Polish and German authorities cooperated in periodic hunts in forests, especially when reports surfaced about Jews hiding in self-made bunkers and caves. In one region of southern Poland, the survival rate of Jews who escaped from ghettos and transports was about 15 percent: not because of a thick presence of Germans but because of the watchful eyes of Polish neighbors, who registered everything, including loaves of bread a family obtained that might be for Jews in hiding. In one case, a Polish family lost their lives when German police—called to the scene by Polish neighbors—found stores of food evidently meant for Jews they were protecting.

The Germans executed the entire family because that was the penalty for sheltering Jews: death for the shelterers, but also their families.[19] This uniquely severe penalty, not employed in Western Europe or the Protectorate, long served as an explanation for the high death rates of Polish Jews (over 90 percent) during the Holocaust. Yet in recent years, historians have noted that Germans also threatened those assisting the Polish underground with death, but Poles routinely sheltered members of the home army with no fear of being denounced by their neighbors. One Polish Jew who lived as an "Aryan" in Warsaw later reflected on the contrast: a taboo against denouncing other Poles, but not Jews:

> Living on the Aryan side in occupied Poland I could have told strangers without hesitation that my father worked for the underground or that he was engaged in sabotage of German military factories. The likelihood that these strangers would betray me to the Germans was quite low. However, telling a stranger or even an acquaintance [i.e., who might leak the information] that I was a Jew living on the Aryan side with false documents would simply mean committing suicide.[20]

The heroism of Poles who nevertheless aided Jews lay not so much in defiance of the occupiers, but in the fact that they vanquished fears of being betrayed by Polish neighbors.

Rarely has a society been more violently divided, Jews from Poles, but also Poles from other Poles. Janina Bauman escaped the Warsaw Ghetto with her mother and sister and lived among Polish Gentiles for two years. She recalled:

> Some time and several shelters passed, before I realized that for the people who sheltered us, our presence also meant more than great danger, nuisance, or extra income. Somehow it affected them, too. *It boosted what was noble in them, or what was base.* Sometimes it divided the family, at other times it brought the family together in a shared endeavor to help and survive.[21]

But that was not the whole story. Fears of retribution grew to fantastic proportions in the morally perverted world of the Nazi occupation, and in the eyes of many Poles, self-sacrificing efforts to rescue Jews were seen as selfish: rescuers were accused of endangering the lives of ethnic Poles. In one case, villagers breathed a sigh of relief when informed that a woman had drowned two Jewish children in her care (in fact she had not). Her behavior had supposedly jeopardized the entire village with possible German retribution.[22] At the same time, those engaging in criminal behavior—smuggling, stealing, practicing extortion—were held up as success stories. The Home Army tried to punish behavior beneath the dignity of Poles, but the "extortionists"—Poles demanding ransom from other Poles sheltering Jews—formed an underground beneath the underground, impossible to root out entirely.

Fear and privation were also a general experience of millions of Poles, and farther east, of millions of Ukrainians and Russians, who were allotted starvation rations, had no local government, and were placed outside effective law. The difference between their experiences and those of the Jews was one of circles in hell: Jews went to places that Dante had not visited, enduring Nazi occupation and knowing that discovery would bring instant death. Poles also knew they might be apprehended and sent away on any day of the occupation, or held as hostages, but death was not a certainty.[23] Those apprehended in a "round-up" by German police from a street in Warsaw might be executed as hostages, but they might also be sent as laborers to Germany, where conditions might be dreadful but the rule was survival.

Even the Jews who survived reached brinks of despair that Gentiles could hardly intuit. They hid in barns and attics where rats crawled across their faces at night, knowing that if they came out alive, their families would not. Other

words invoked to describe the Jews' predicament were loneliness and abandonment, utter dependence that had no precedent. Hell had descended on a world
that Jews felt part of, and they discovered that, instead of looking on them as
fellow citizens, neighbors generally saw them as outsiders, with sentiments ranging from hostility to indifference. Crouching in a hiding place, one man was
shocked to overhear his Polish "friend" say that he regretted not giving shelter
to thirty rich Jews, because if he had, he could kill them one at a time and take
from them what he wanted.[24] This was the most painful revelation about the
lethal admixture of ethnic nationalism and anti-Semitism that poisoned social
life in Eastern Europe ca. 1943: that it could exclude fellow citizens at the level
of basic human solidarity and seem natural.

By contrast, no matter how they suffered, Poles had hope: until arrested or
shot, they could conspire. We read of eleven-year-olds joining the underground
and becoming active, feeling free despite the danger. Jews in general were refused entry into the Polish underground. That is why young Jews in the Warsaw ghetto in the winter of 1942/1943 organized their own fighting units, which
managed to hold off heavily armed German forces for a month when they
came to clear out the ghetto in April 1943, using a handful of rifles and a few
dozen pistols, as well as homemade bombs. They had been transformed: no
longer condemned people waiting to die, but humans choosing their fate.
Rather than fight them directly, the SS set fire to the ghetto and smoked them
out. The few who survived fought in the general Warsaw Uprising of the summer of 1944.

* * *

After Czechoslovak President Edvard Beneš emigrated and formed an exile government in London, the old parties of the Czech lands were reduced to two:
a right-wing party of national unity and a workers' party. New officials took
charge of the ministries. Still, most politicians active before Munich remained
so. The new government began passing anti-Jewish laws, not because the German government required it to do so but because it wanted to curry favor, and,
as elsewhere, no matter how great their services to the local nation, Jews were
considered less than full co-ethnics who could be sacrificed to German authorities as a sign of "good will," to protect the supposed interests of the native
ethnic community.

Thus, forces that had been marginal and suppressed but were always present
now had their hour, and public discourse witnessed an anti-Semitism that had

FIGURE 17.3. Later leadership of Warsaw Ghetto uprising
(taken in 1938). The members of the Hashomer Hatzair socialist
Zionist youth movement are: Tzvi Braun, Shifra Sokolka, and
Mordechai Anielewicz (standing); Moshe Domb and Rachel
("Sarenka") Zilberberg (seated). *Source*: United States Holocaust
Memorial Museum Photo Archives #16499. Courtesy of
Leah Hammerstein Silverstein. Copyright
United States Holocaust
Memorial Museum.

last flourished in the time of the Hilsner affair of 1899, accompanied by a search
for scapegoats for the failure of Munich. Denunciations against Jewish doctors
and lawyers poured into newspaper offices, and on October 14, just two weeks
after the Munich Conference, professional associations demanded that Jews no
longer be able to practice. After Kristallnacht (as the pogroms enacted across

Germany in early November were called), the second Czechoslovak republic gave no refuge to Jews, even those from the Sudetenland who had been citizens just weeks earlier. In January 1939, the government of Prime Minister Rudolf Beran released all Jews from state service. In the press, second-rate intellectuals dusted off old stereotypes and adjusted them to pan-European tropes, offering a range of "explanations" about Jewish power in economy and politics, and alleging that Jews had been unwilling to speak proper Czech.[25] Yet even staunch liberals blamed Bohemian Jews for the loss of territory at Munich. The Prague German university, cultural institutions of both languages, and Czech sports clubs all purged themselves of Jews.[26] Only fears of the country's inability to secure credits from western banks kept the campaign from going further.

In March 1939, German troops occupied the "rump" Czech lands, creating the Protectorate of Bohemia and Moravia, and the Protectorate government under General Alois Eliáš tried to transfer Jewish wealth into Czech hands as quickly as possible. Yet after months of inconclusive talks, the German *Reichsprotektor* Konstantin von Neurath intervened, issuing a proclamation asserting the validity of the Nuremberg racial laws in the Protectorate and ensuring that the Jewish property now stolen by legalistic means, totaling about 20 billion crowns, would go into German and not Czech hands.[27]

Attitudes in the Czech population varied. Czech fascists burned down the synagogue at Jihlava and staged pogroms and attacks on Jews in Příbram and Brno, but many ordinary Czechs looked on the anti-Jewish measures with disgust. The prevalent attitude, however, as in the region as a whole, was indifference accompanied by a vague foreboding that the Gentile population might be next, a posture that encouraged compliance and reduced solidarity with Jews.[28] What most bothered many Czechs about Aryanization—the forced seizure of Jewish property—was how it went into German hands and promoted the Germanization of Bohemia.[29]

In the Reich, the German policy had been to encourage Jewish emigration, and that policy was now extended to the Protectorate through the work of SS Lieutenant Colonel Adolf Eichmann, who set up a branch of his Vienna offices in Prague.[30] Nazi authorities subjected Jews in the Protectorate to the same schedule of exclusion and destruction that they used in Germany and Austria; and when emigration was cut off for German and Austrian Jews in the fall of 1941, it ended in the Protectorate as well. An estimated 30,000 Czech Jews managed to get out, leaving behind some 80,000 mostly elderly Jews.

As they had done in the Reich, German authorities registered Jews and reduced their rights. From the fall of 1939, Czech Jews could not visit parks and other public places or stay outdoors after 8 p.m. After November 1940, the restrictions were extended to theaters, cafes, libraries, swimming pools, gymnasiums, and the sleeping and restaurant cars in trains (where Jews had to use the lowest class). Jews could shop only two hours a day and were not allowed to keep radios or pets. From September 1939, Jews could be fired without notice and enlisted for labor without their consent; Jewish children were forbidden from attending German schools in 1939, Czech ones in August 1940, and in 1941 from schools run by the Jewish community to teach trades. From September 1941, as in Austria and Germany, Jews in the Protectorate had to wear a yellow star with word "Jude" in the center.

Authorities were gradually shutting off the air for Czech Jews. After full-scale killing of Jews commenced in eastern Poland and parts of the Soviet Union in the summer of 1941, SS and other German authorities began making the Reich (including the Protectorate) "free of Jews." From October, they concocted plans for transferring Czech Jews to a single location in Bohemia and hit on the idea of using an old Habsburg fortress north of Prague at Theresienstadt/Terezin. Several hundred Jewish workers were sent there in October 1941 to prepare it for supposed settlement.

What Theresienstadt actually became was a halfway point to the killing camps in occupied Poland. Transports of Jews to Theresienstadt from Czech towns began in the spring and summer of 1942. In Olomouc, authorities summoned the Jews, including the parents and two boys of the Lichtenstein family, on July 8 to the town gymnasium. They were to bring 40 pounds of luggage. They then boarded trains that stopped a few miles outside the old fortress of Theresienstadt and had to complete the journey on foot with their bags. Many of the 660 Jews in this transport were beyond retirement age, and the trip itself pushed them up to and beyond their physical limits. After enduring weeks of malnourishment, crowding, and false hopes, on October 8, the Olomouc Jews boarded a second train of 1,000 people that made its way to the Polish town Treblinka, where German authorities had set up a death camp. Margareta Liechtensteinová was separated from her husband and sons, and all were immediately killed with carbon monoxide gas.

In Slovakia, anti-Jewish measures commenced almost immediately after the country obtained relative "autonomy" on October 6, 1938. The government was in the hands of nationalists drawn from the Hlinka People's Party under Father Josef Tiso, a veteran of Slovak nationalist politics and lieutenant to Father Hlinka.[31] The government's anti-Semitism had roots in Catholic anti-Judaism, in particular the old Christian belief that Jews were condemned to suffer for having killed God, but it also drew on nationalist and economic-social arguments. The basic message was straightforward: Jews are the eternal enemies of the Slovak people. In November 1938, Germany awarded much of southern Slovakia, with a solid Hungarian population, to Hungary, an inconceivable disaster for a regime claiming to have achieved "freedom" for Slovaks. The Slovak government responded by making Jews responsible and deporting some 7,500 into areas ceded to Hungary. The Jewish population in Slovakia had comprised 136,737 men, women, and children (4.11 percent of the population), but after November 1938, only 89,000 Jews remained.

When the Slovak state became nominally independent as a German puppet in March 1939, it quickly set about passing anti-Jewish legislation, aided by SS officer Dieter Wisleceny, sent to Bratislava as adviser on Jewish affairs. From April, the first definitions of Jewishness were passed, serving as a basis for exclusions from medicine, journalism, law, and the universities. Aryanization of property—seizing Jewish property and putting it in non-Jewish hands—was carried out based on law 113/1940 (the first Aryanization Act).[32] The Jewish code 198 passed in 1941 was one of harshest in Europe. It defined Jews racially; excluded them from secondary schools as well as social, cultural, and sporting events; instituted a morning and evening curfew; forbade Jews from assembling or traveling; and mandated the wearing of a six-sided star.

In early 1942, Germany requested 20,000 Jewish workers from Slovakia to be deployed "to the east." The Tiso government complied but offered to deport a large part of the remaining Jewish population as well. After dispatching eight trains full of able-bodied young men and women, in April it began detaining whole Jewish families and loading them onto trains. By June, 52,000 Jews had been transported, but then the process slowed. The brutality of the Hlinka guards had stirred disfavor in parts of the population, including in the regime itself, which was divided between hardline racists and more moderate figures. (Father Tiso stood somewhere in the middle.) At that time, Slovakia was the only state not directly occupied by Germany whose own officials identified and deported Jews.[33]

Some 30,000 Jews remained who were protected as valued laborers—for example, engineers and veterinarians—but many also escaped to Hungary or went into hiding. When German troops occupied Slovakia in the autumn of 1944—in the course of crushing an anti-Nazi uprising supported by the Slovak army—they carried out a second deportation of 13,000 Jews, and SS squads executed a further thousand. The non-Jewish Slovak population enjoyed a relatively high standard of living throughout the occupation, despite perennial supply problems.[34]

The process in Croatia was similar despite local variations. Soon after assuming power in April 1941, the Ante Pavelić regime mandated the wearing of Jewish badges (a six-pointed star as well as the letter Ž for "Židov"), required registration of Jewish property, and ordered Jews to pay levies. It made Jews do forced labor, and by decrees of June and November 1941, it gave a "legal" basis for mass arrests. It placed Jews in internment camps, including the notorious camp at Jasenovac, and the Ustashas murdered more than 200,000 victims, mostly Serbs, but also most of the 30,000 Jews in Croatia and Bosnia-Herzegovina. In the summer of 1942, Croatia's government deported 4,927 Jews to Auschwitz, where they were killed almost without exception. An unknown number found protection in Italian-occupied zones of Croatia, but when Italy dropped out of the war in 1943, German troops moved in and arrested many of those as well.[35]

For the Ustasha regime, the anti-Jewish policy was a derivative agenda, less important than anti-Serbianism. One of their chief ideological inspirations, Josip Frank (1844–1911), was born Jewish and was the father-in-law and grandfather of two leading Ustasha killers. But when, like their Italian fascist cousins, the Ustashas switched to an anti-Semitic agenda, they were uncompromisingly lethal: in 1943 their most charismatic youth leader, Vladko Singer, an enthusiastic hater of Serbs, was murdered in part because he was born Jewish.

Germany had more direct access to the likewise relatively small Jewish population of Serbia (about 12,000). Within a week of occupying Belgrade in April 1941, German occupation authorities began registering Jews and in May forced them to wear a badge. The puppet ruler General Nedić pronounced anti-Jewish decrees on May 31, compelling Jews to register their property and largely excluding them from economic life. After the Nazi attack on the Soviet Union, the repressive measures intensified. German authorities required the Jewish community to supply forty hostages daily, whom they shot almost daily in retaliation for Partisan attacks on German soldiers. In July, authorities began "Aryanizing" Jewish property, and the following month, they interned adult Jewish males, shooting some 5,000 of them over the following months, supposedly in response to continuing attacks on German soldiers. In December, German authorities interned Jewish women and children, and in the spring, the authorities executed them through asphyxiation in so-called "gas vans." The retaliatory measures extended to Serbs and Gypsies (some 1,000 of approximately 100,000 Gypsies in Serbia lost their lives.)[36]

The Fate of Jews in the Allied Balkan States

The most celebrated regional case of a state protecting Jews is Bulgaria, which has inappropriately been compared to Denmark, where the resistance, with much popular support, spirited some 8,000 Jews to safety in Sweden in October 1943. That same year, elements of Bulgarian society rose up to defend the Bulgarian Jewish population. Yet that occurred only after the Bulgarian state had diminished the status of Bulgarian Jews for years and delivered many thousands of Thracian and Macedonian Jews to German death camps. The delivery was part of an implicit bargain: Bulgaria had received Thrace from Greece and Macedonia from Yugoslavia in expectation that it would support German racial policy. Where Bulgaria differed from Germany was by interrupting the chain of destruction of Jews—definition through racial laws, expropriation, concentration in ghettos, and deportation to death camps—before it reached the final phase.[37] And even while the king and his government were enacting the early phases of destruction, they did so in a way that vexed the Nazis because it seemed unsystematic.

Bulgaria had entered the Nazi orbit in the mid-1930s, when Germany began absorbing increasing proportions of Bulgaria's exports: in 1932 Germany took 32 percent, but by 1939 that figure advanced to 67.8 percent.[38] Germany had stepped in to buy grain from desperate and depressed Romania, Yugoslavia, and Hungary as well, yet no other East European country had more trade with Germany than Bulgaria. Though he was irredentist, Boris's desire to gain territories did not cause him to fully cast his lot with Germany, even after Germany's awarding of Slovak territory to Hungary in 1938 made clear the benefits of cooperation. He feared being dragged into an alliance with a regime so evidently thirsting for war and believed Bulgaria's interests were best served through neutrality. He resisted temptations even when war broke out in September 1939, refusing to ally with the Soviet Union or the Balkan Entente.[39]

Given Boris's desire to maintain a certain aloofness, Germany moved in September 1940 to appease him, supervising an agreement between Romania and Bulgaria that took care of Bulgaria's major irredentist concern, and hoping to keep it from drifting into the Soviet orbit. Romania was made to cede South Dobrudja. The arrangement pleased much of the Bulgarian public, and the following spring, more gains in territory followed at the expense of recently subdued Greece and Yugoslavia: Thrace and Macedonia. Because of the German-Soviet alliance of this period, Bulgaria could continue its close relation with Germany while tightening bonds with the Soviet Union. A commercial treaty in early 1940 allowed the import of Soviet books, newspapers, and films, and in August 1940, a Soviet football team toured Bulgaria to widespread acclaim.[40] At the same time, Bulgaria began to approximate a fascist order, with a uniformed youth organization, compulsory labor service, the closing of popular masonic lodges, and increasing restrictions on Jews. From early February 1940, Petur Gabrovski, one of the few outspoken anti-Semites in the government, became Bulgaria's interior minister.

In November 1940, the Bulgarian government passed its first anti-Jewish law over voices of opposition in parliament, but it varied from the German one by considering baptized Jews and Jews married to Gentiles not to be Jews. The law also declared that people with one or two Jewish grandparents were not Jews.[41] Unlike Germany, but like Slovakia and Croatia, Bulgaria made special provisions for Jewish war veterans and their families, but also invalids and orphans, in all comprising about a tenth of the Jewish population. But otherwise the legislation was meant to exclude Jews from Bulgarian life, restricting Jewish employment, property ownership, and access to education, as well as forbidding the marriage of Jews with ethnic Bulgarians and their use of Bulgarian names. It required Jews to serve in labor batallions and to pay special "taxes" that had the goal of transferring their property to the state.[42] The laws were meant to remove Jews from Bulgarian life, but they figured in a broader policy of national cleansing: marriages were also forbidden between Christians and Muslims.[43]

Like Yugoslavia, Bulgaria signed the Tripartite Pact with Germany, Italy, and Japan in early 1941; yet unlike Serbs, Bulgarians generally did not see the accession as treasonous, because Bulgaria had been Germany's ally in World War I. Before the signing, three dozen German staff officers had landed in Sofia for secret discussions, and within two months, Bulgaria had consented to building a pontoon bridge across the Danube for German troops to cross into Greece. Yet Bulgaria waited until after Pearl Harbor in December 1941 to declare war on the Western powers. King Boris struggled mightily with the decision. After finally assenting to the declaration of war, he disappeared from sight and was found hours later praying in a remote corner of Aleksandar Nevski Cathedral in Sofia.[44]

Once Bulgaria had gained Thrace and Macedonia as spoils from the obliteration of Greek and Yugoslav statehood, German representatives pressed for further restrictions on the Jews, and Bulgaria's government complied. In 1942, it created a Commissariat for the Jewish Question, deported Jews from Sofia and other major cities, and required that all Jews wear the Star of David. Jewish families of two were limited to one room of an apartment, families of four to two rooms.[45] A further 20 percent levy was exacted on Jewish property, most Jewish organizations were disbanded, and Jews were forced to sell businesses.

The measures were so unpopular that the press was forbidden to report on them. As a result of continuing pressure from the German legate in Sofia (the former storm trooper Adolf Beckerle), the parliament (*subranie*) passed a bill in August 1942 depriving Jews in the "new territories" of Thrace and Macedonia of their Bulgarian citizenship.[46] At this time, Bulgaria seemed to be the state most ready to cooperate with Germany on Jewish matters. Italy, Romania, Hungary, and even Vichy France had raised more objections than Bulgaria had, and in conversations with Croatia and Slovakia, German representatives held up Bulgaria as a model.[47] In the winter of 1942/1943, the Main Security Service (*Reichssicherheitshauptamt*) of the SS approached Bulgaria's Commissariat for the Jewish Question, urging the transfer of the country's Jews to Germany. As a result, Bulgarian authorities deported some 11,000 Jews from Thrace and Macedonia to Nazi death camps in March 1943. But when the Commissariat drew up plans to deport Jews from Old Bulgaria that summer, it met with resistance.

Up to that point, Bulgaria's top rulers had been willing to cooperate within the limits of their own choosing, but now increasingly they would employ the machinery of state, in particular constitutional safeguards, to deceive the Germans and delay implementation of their demands.[48] This strategy applied to the war in general, and to what the Nazis called the "Final Solution of the Jewish question" in particular. When asked to send troops to the Soviet Union, King Boris argued that his country did not have the weapons for a Blitzkrieg-type attack and that Bulgarians' traditional sympathies for Russia limited any cooperation in a war against it. He would not allow even Bulgarian volunteers to fight against the Soviet Union.[49]

He also oversaw various forms of stonewalling on policies against the Jews. By late 1942, German diplomats were complaining of all manner of shortcomings: that only 20 percent of Jews had received six-pointed badges and they even refused to wear them, that the government failed to ensure that the plant making the badges had electricity, that Jews in labor battalions received normal uniforms to wear without stars.[50] The SS Main Security Office believed that this hesitation was due to pressures exerted by foreign governments: Spain, Italy, Hungary, Romania, and even Vichy France. But of more direct relevance was the unease about racial discrimination in Bulgarian society, extending into the elites, especially members of the Orthodox Synod. Church leaders cited Christian doctrine, according to which all people were equal before God.

What had made the deportations from Thrace and Macedonia take place without resistance was that the Jews there were not Bulgarian citizens. Yet the conditions of their sojourn on Bulgarian territory on the way to Poland became known and shocked the public conscience. They had had been denied food, water, and sanitation and been subject to wanton violence. Now no one doubted the meaning of further deportations: they would be the first steps to total destruction. *Subranie* Vice President Dimitar Peshev, supported by forty deputies, censured the government and a "hint from the highest quarters" followed (presumably from Boris), ordering the stop of all deportations planned from Old Bulgaria.

Yet the Germans continued to apply pressure. Foreign Minister Ribbentrop complained personally to King Boris during his visit to Berlin in April 1943 about his government's failure to honor an agreement from January to deport 6,000 Jews. Boris explained that he needed them for road building. German observers on the ground reported other methods of deception: rather than prepare Sofia's Jews for the promised deportations to Poland, Bulgarian authorities were planning to settle them in the countryside.[51] Even the fanatic Beckerle felt there was no hope in prodding the Bulgarians to further action. They had been living so long with other peoples, like the Armenians, Greeks, and Gypsies, he wrote to the Foreign Office, that Bulgarians did not see the Jews as a special enemy. Indeed, within Bulgarian society, the plans to remove Jews from Sofia was seen as a threat and an outrage, and were preceded by street demonstrations and interventions of Jews with Christian acquaintances, including members of the Orthodox Synod, as well as the Dunovist Christian sect. The Dunovists, who incorporated worship of the rising sun in their Christian beliefs, were strong at the royal court and included Princess Eudoxia, Boris's advisors, and perhaps Boris himself. One rabbi, Daniel Tsion, a mystic and student of comparative theology, managed to deliver a note to the king with what he claimed was a warning from God against persecuting Jews.[52]

Despite this unusual engagement of Bulgarian politicians and church leaders in saving their Jewish neighbors, the resistance had its limits. King Boris still thought Jews were a serious problem that had to be dealt with. In April 1943, he told members of the Orthodox Synod that Jews and their "profiteering spirit," were in large measure responsible for the present "global cataclysm."[53] Like politicians throughout the region, he was primarily interested in strengthening his nation-state, and that is why he had subjected Jews and other non-ethnic Bulgarians to a demeaning status, depriving them of civil rights. King Boris may well have approved deportations of Jews to the death camps had Germany prevailed against the Soviet Union. And if Jews had not lost their lives in virtually every other European state, Bulgaria would be remembered as a hell for Jews.

Yet Boris and other influential Bulgarians could not ignore the fact that Germany was losing the war, and they feared allied retribution.[54] When US bombers attacked the oil fields at Ploieşti in Romania, Boris rejected German requests for assistance in turning them back. He also refused to alienate the Soviets and never permitted anti-Soviet propaganda in the Bulgarian press that was routine everywhere else. The only thing that might have changed the Bulgarian position, German diplomats wrote, would be "new activation of the German war effort," that is, evidence that Germany could win. Yet as Soviet forces pushed ever closer to Berlin, anti-German forces in Bulgaria showed greater courage, carrying out attacks on right-wing leaders, like General Hristo Lukov in February 1943. The assassinations lasted into the spring, showing that the war was "coming home" to the streets of Sofia. In August, the king died of heart failure, shortly after a meeting with Hitler in East Prussia, his third of the year. Perhaps he had been poisoned, but more likely he was worn out from the stress of navigating among a plethora of competing demands.[55]

The previous month, Allied troops had landed in Sicily, placing German control of southeastern Europe in jeopardy and giving rise to speculation about further landings in the Balkans. The Italian government surrendered in September 1943, and Bulgaria, Romania, and Hungary desperately tried to switch sides and free themselves of ties to Germany. They had bound themselves to the Third Reich out of opportunism, and now opportunities were becoming liabilities.

* * *

Like Bulgaria, Romania had become closely tied to Germany through trade relations in the 1930s. Yet in 1940, thanks to German "mediation," it had lost significant territories to the Soviet Union, Hungary, and Bulgaria.[56] The losses were so humiliating that King Carol escaped for Mexico after abdicating in favor of his son Michael in September 1940. A dictatorship then took power, led by Army Chief General Ion Antonescu but with a strong presence of the Iron Guard.[57] He sided with Nazi Germany, joining the Tripartite Pact on November 23, 1940. But his government was rent by tensions from the start between radical and extreme radical nationalists, and it came apart in late January 1941, when the Guard staged a coup to protest one more sign of Antonescu's increasingly heavy-handed rule: in a semi-fascist manner, he wanted to be acknowledged as *Conducător* (leader).

The two-day uprising (January 21–23, 1941) featured a pogrom in which Guardists slaughtered some 125 Jews and went on a rampage against Jewish property, including two synagogues burned to the ground. The crimes, some of which took place in a slaughterhouse, were so gruesome that German reporters had difficulty recording them.[58] Antonescu soon gained the upper hand, and Germany gave shelter to surviving Guard leaders at a special section of the Buchenwald camp, where they were held as pawns in case Hitler needed them. For the time being, Germany prized the dependability of the semi-fascist strongman Antonescu over their own ideological cousins in the Guard. Antonescu endeavored to please Germany in order to regain the territories lost in 1940.

Antonescu was more racist than the conservative authoritarians who ruled Bulgaria or Hungary. In June 1941, within days of the attack by Germany and its allies on the Soviet Union, he gave orders to "cleanse [the Moldavian capital] Iași of its Jewish population."[59] The city bordered on Bessarabia, lands awarded to Stalin the previous year, which Romanian forces were now "reclaiming" as their part of the assult on the Soviet Union. After portraying Jews as Communist collaborators, Antonescu vowed to incapacitate anyone who might endanger the operations of Romanian soldiers fighting the Red Army. On June 25, the Romanian Special Intelligence Service spread rumors that Soviet parachutists had landed in Romania at Iași, triggering a pogrom involving local thugs, criminals, and low-lifes. Rule of law ceased, and anyone wanting to visit violence on Jews while enriching themselves had license to do so. Some of the Jews who survived the killing were placed on trains that traveled aimlessly about the countryside in the hot sun, with no water or food. The cattle cars bore inscriptions like "Communist Jews" and "Killers of German and Romanian soldiers" and stopped occasionally to offload dead bodies.[60] In all, upward of 14,000 (of about 45,000) Iași Jews died.

This was the sole case in Europe, including Germany, where a regime had ordered the open slaughter of Jews of its own nationality on its own territory. The security concerns had in fact been a cover for race war: Antonescu explicitly demanded arrests of women and children.[61] The swift advance of Nazi and Romanian armies across Soviet territory seemed to open new horizons, placing the realization of ultranationalist aims of ethnically pure territory within easy reach. Antonescu pressed for "cleansing the land" in what he called "our vital space."

He had permitted the entry of German forces into Romania in October 1940, and some took part in the Iași pogrom, according themselves the task of "molding disorganized mass violence into a controlled pattern." German officers collaborated with Romanian units dedicated to killing Jews, and the language used by the allies seemed taken from a single script. That was not coincidental. In June, Hitler had personally presented General Antonescu with "Guidelines for the Treatment of Eastern Jews."[62] By now, representatives from Heinrich Himmler's staff had also installed themselves in Bucharest as consultants on the "Jewish question." No matter what their background, Romanian politicians seemed to be loyal understudies, at least while Germany was winning.

Take Deputy Premier Mihai Antonescu (no relation to the general). In the 1930s, he was a relatively moderate member of the National Liberal Party, which condemned the far right and its anti-Semitism.[63] Yet by July 1941, he was speaking of "the ... most favorable opportunity in our history ... for cleansing our people of all those elements foreign to its soul, which have grown like weeds to darken its future."[64] His remarks were a carbon copy of statements issued in Berlin against Jews or in Zagreb against Serbs. Antonescu promised to carry the violence into recently "liberated" Bukovina and Bessarabia. He told the Cabinet on July 8:

> I am all for the forced migration of the entire Jewish element of Bessarabia and Bukovina. . . . You must be merciless. . . . I don't know how many centuries will pass before the Romanian people meet again with such total liberty of action, such opportunity for ethnic cleansing and national revision. . . . Let us use it. If necessary, shoot your machine guns. I couldn't care less if history will recall us as barbarians. . . . I take formal responsibility and tell you there is no law.[65]

The killing that ensued was in fact carefully staged. The Romanian army had formed advance teams in the recovered territories of Bessarabia and Bukovina to prepare "an unfavorable atmosphere in the villages toward Judaic elements, thereby encouraging the population to ... remove them on its own." At the arrival of the Romanian troops, the directive continued, "the feeling must already be in place and even acted upon."[66] These orders resembled those issued by the German command farther north, where during these same weeks, SS mobile killing units were following the *Wehrmacht* divisions speeding across Poland, Lithuania, and Ukraine.

In early July, the Romanian army, assisted by local populations, shot the Jewish inhabitants of villages in southern Bukovina and then extended the killing eastward. In the regional metropolis Czernowitz/Cernăuți/Chernivtsi, until recently a center of Habsburg Jewish cultural life, German regular soldiers as well as SS troops joined with Romanian forces in rounding up and murdering much of the town's Jewish population. German units claimed to be shocked by their allies' brutality, and SS mobile killing units (*Einsatzgruppe* D) received orders to entice Romanians into "a more planned procedure in this direction."[67] They objected that the Romanians failed to bury victims, took bribes, or engaged in rape and plunder (for example, taking gold from corpses).

Jews who survived were driven toward the river Dniester, where many were shot into the waters while others were kept in unspeakable conditions in newly established "ghettos" on Bessarabian territory. Next, after occupying and then annexing territory of the Ukrainian Soviet Socialist Republic on the other side of the Dniester—called "Transnistria"—the Romanians set up camps there, where unknown numbers of Jews were killed.[68] They permitted no regular food distribution, and some inmates attempted to eat grass. In the infamous camp at Bodganovka, the bakery sold bread for gold, but when the gold ran out, the commandant ordered mass shootings. Romanian forces shot some 40,000 Jews over a precipice into the Bug River, and then took a break for the Christmas holiday.[69] They had seized the regional capital Odessa after stiff resistance in October, yet after a bomb exploded killing Romanian officers, Antonescu ordered reprisals; in one of the cruelest mass murders of the Holocaust, 18,000 Jews lost their lives. By the spring of 1942, this human-made hell had consumed the lives of at least 100,000 Jews.[70]

If the Germans were shocked by the brutality of Romanian policies against Jews, they were also impressed by the apparent peace and prosperity of Ukraine under Romanian rule. After the violence against Jews subsided in the fall of 1941, the city of Odessa recovered quickly. The venal Romanian administration took its cut, but then stood back and watched as individual enterprise flourished, with new hairdressers, cafes, shops, taverns, and movie theaters. Rather than terrorize the local population, Romanian authorities allowed each village in Transnistria to vote on the language it wished to be taught to its children and set up a Ukrainian auxiliary police force.[71]

The Antonescu regime's eagerness to kill Jews in Bessarabia and Transnistria had left the Germans convinced that it would follow through with the complete destruction of Jewry in the Romanian heartlands. Indeed, Antonescu had wanted to deport the Jews there to Bessarabia, but the Germans stopped him in August 1941, afraid of overburdening SS *Einsatzgruppe* D. Romanian authorities constricted the rights of Jews in the Regat as well as Transylvania:

seizing their property, forcing them into labor brigades, and expelling them from the professions.[72] The process was called "Romaniazation." If Romania had behaved like Germany, the next step would have been mass murder, and in fact plans surfaced to transport Romanian Jews to killing camps in occupied Poland. The German railways had even set aside cars and drawn up routes.[73] Yet in the summer of 1942, Romania stopped cooperating.

Explanations vary. Radu Lecca, Romanian commissar for Jewish affairs, a man already wealthy from bribes, supposedly took offence at being snubbed during a visit to Berlin in August 1942. He and his colleagues had become tired of being treated as representatives of a second-class power and being told what to do with "their" Jews.[74] But the moment for a shift also seemed apt. The Romanian government had sent more troops to the eastern front than anyone else, and vividly sensed the coming catastrophe of the Third Reich. Two desperately undersupplied Romanian armies were just taking up positions near Stalingrad in the fall of 1942 when Antonescu requested new weapons from Hitler. This and all other requests were rebuffed.

The leadership also grew hypersensitive to warnings coming from the West about its mistreatments of Jews. President Franklin D. Roosevelt told the World Jewish Congress in New York that "punishment of countries which had persecuted Jews represented one of the aims of the war," and he promised "fearful retribution" for those who perpetrated "barbaric crimes" against civilian populations in Axis-occupied countries.[75] With the legacies of Versailles and Trianon in mind, Romanian elites knew that punishment meant loss of territory.

That same month, Romanian university professors, writers, and schoolteachers signed a memorandum to the Palace linking deportations of Jews to the postwar territorial settlement: "We must bring ourselves in line with international law and guarantee the right to life and legal protection of every Jew of the territories which we claim."[76] Ringing through this declaration was the ethnic perspective according to which human life, especially of aliens, was of secondary importance to the nation's territory. But now the fear of losing territory kindled concern for the fate of aliens, as well as some contrition. Deportations of Jews were in fact a "methodical and persistent act of extermination." The authors acknowledged that "*we* have been at the forefront of the states which persecute the Jews." "I have said it once and will go on saying it," Romanian Peasant Party leader Iuliu Maniu added in September, "we will pay dearly for the maltreatment of the Jews."[77]

Rumors of planned deportations to Poland had leaked that summer, panicking Jews in Transylvania, and Maniu and others in the Romanian Peasant

Party intervened to put a stop to them. In December, Roosevelt and now Churchill reiterated the threats. "Those responsible for these crimes," they declared, "shall not escape retribution." Warning voices also came from the Red Cross, the Turkish Government, the Orthodox Metropolitan of Transylvania, the Papal Nuncio, as well as the Romanian Jewish community (led by Alexandru Safran, the youngest chief rabbi in the world, who had worked closely with members of the royal family as well as the dictator's wife). Thanks to the insistence of several women active in social welfare, the Romanian Jewish community also mobilized to rescue some 2,000 orphans who had survived the punishing camps in Transnistria.[78]

The shift in tone of the racist Mihai Antonescu was particularly notable. In October, he admitted that the reversal came about "because of the international situation and because of the fact that in other countries the treatment of the Jews is different from that in Romania."[79] He keenly sensed the world's gaze upon his country. "I prefer to strike at the economic activity of the rich," he said in November, "rather than carry out massacres and engage in hostile acts against the poor." "The Hungarians are watching," he continued, "photographing and

FIGURE 17.4. Rescued orphans from Transnistria, with Anny (Hubner) Andermann. *Source*: United States Holocaust Memorial Museum Photo Archives #29844. Courtesy of Dr. Frederick Andermann. Copyright United States Holocaust Memorial Museum.

producing propaganda abroad about our so-called barbarism against the Jews. The abuses are not the work of the government, and I have already intervened three times to ensure that the Jews are treated in an orderly fashion. Some peripheral agencies have made mistakes."[80]

His concern about Hungary related primarily to the contest for Transylvania. After the Germans and Italians had awarded the Northern half of Transylvania to Hungary in August 1940, the two countries outdid one another in currying favor with the Germans: Hungary to acquire the south, Romania to regain the north.

* * *

Like Romania, Hungary had been drawn gradually into webs of German influence, first economic, then political and military. Had the country not fallen directly in Germany's sphere of influence, its elites would have preferred to ally with a Western power, especially Britain. (Romanian elites favored France; and regard in the Bulgarian leadership was strong for France and England). However, beyond its geographic predicament of sitting in Central Europe, Hungary felt irresistibly drawn to Hitler's Germany because of the prospect of recovering territories lost at Trianon.[81] In November 1938, Italy and Germany had granted Hungary districts of Southern Slovakia that were largely inhabited by Hungarians, causing Hungary's extreme right to proclaim adherence to the Axis as the "road leading to Hungary's resurrection." In January 1939, under right radical Prime Minister Béla Imrédy, Hungary joined the anti-Comintern pact.[82] Clearly discomfited, the more moderate Christian Right Opposition ousted Imrédy and made Count Pál Teleki prime minister in February 1939. Teleki was a respected geographer of deeply conservative inclinations from an old respected family and a man who believed in old-fashioned virtues like "honor." He had also imbibed some of the racist anti-Semitism that pervaded East European politics in this period.[83]

That maneuver tells us something important about wartime Hungary that made it different from Bulgaria and Romania: the presence of genuine opposition in parliament, including a vibrant left. The government comprised an uneasy mix of national radicals and conservatives, and the conservatives proved adept at protecting their interests, especially the holding of property. This ensured a relatively liberal atmosphere in Hungarian politics. For example, in December 1942, the anti-Nazi politician Endre Bajcsy-Zsilinszky was able to give details about atrocities committed by Hungarian troops in Serbia from the floor of parliament, resulting in the indictment of high-ranking officers before a military tribunal. "The most remarkable accomplishment of the old establishment," writes Andrew Janos, "was perhaps the preservation of a degree of political freedom and pluralism in the face of repeated attempts by the radical Right to introduce a one-party dictatorship."[84]

When Germany attacked Poland in September 1939, Hungary remained neutral, not granting German armies the right to pass through its territory and opening its borders to more than 150,000 Polish military and civilian refugees. Yet Teleki faced pressure from the Arrow Cross to inch still closer to Germany after the defeat of France in June 1940. As in the Balkan states, France's fall strengthened the hand of local politicians arguing that Germany might satisfy local territorial grievances. But there was also some ambivalence: could Germany win in the long run? Hungarians became gamblers, hoping to achieve the greatest gains in territory with the least risk.[85]

Against the worldly skepticism of the old elites—the upper nobility and grande bourgeoisie, with many writers and academics—stood the immoderate hopes of younger intellectuals, army officers, civil servants, and industrial workers, that Germany might prevail and that its social Darwinist *Lebensraum* ideology would show the way to the future. They were modernizers who hoped to break apart the country's ossified agrarian social structure while undermining the political left and Jewish bourgeoisie, making Magyar Hungary an impregnable Danubian power. In youthful, fascist exuberance, they rejected ethical and religious objections to violence as well the traditional cultural nationalism of the old Magyar elites. As a result, the government vacillated between fascism and traditionalism for the next four years, ultimately opting for neither, in the end leaving a wide opening for the extreme left, the one untried option.[86]

For the time being, politicians from right to left had their appetites whetted by territory gained at the expense of Czechoslovakia; after South Slovakia, Hungary got Ruthenia in March 1939. The next obvious target was Transylvania. The idea of splitting it into northern and southern regions seems to have been Teleki's. He proposed negotiations with Romania's government in the summer of 1940, threatening force if it did not give way. When talks failed, the Germans and Italians "arbitrated" the Vienna agreement of August 1940, granting Hungary Northern Transylvania. At this point, Romania's leader Ion Antonescu denounced British guarantees to defend Romanian sovereignty as useless, and invited German "training" troops into his country. Hungary, careful not to lag in pleasing the German hegemon, let these troops use its railways.[87]

Teleki had thus paid a price for this award. He was also expected to relieve pressure on his own country's Nazis, and therefore amnestied the charismatic Ferenc Szálasi. Meanwhile, the right-winger Imrédy had formed his own Party of Hungarian Regeneration, thus forcing Teleki to deal in parliament with a large and noisy group pressing for satisfaction of German demands. His response was to outflank them on the right by preemptively adopting the anti-Jewish legislation as well as constitutional reforms desired by the Nazis.[88] In November 1940, Teleki joined the Tripartite Pact, yet as a sign of his deeper inclinations, he also signed a treaty of eternal friendship with Yugoslavia a month later.

Soon this friction between self-assertion and self-subordination ground the prime minister down to a man without qualities. When Horthy and the right insisted that Hungary share the spoils of prostrate Yugoslavia in April 1941, Count Teleki shot himself. He refused to stand with the villains who had taken advantage of his "vacillating policy."[89] But to many Hungarians, the alliance with Germany seemed to be working: the country had recovered 80,000 square kilometers with 2 million Magyars (while adding almost 3 million non-Magyars). Yet Hungary's elites had learned nothing from their Habsburg-era predecessors' misguided nationality policies: by expropriating land from Slovaks and Romanians, they had generated opposition rather than desperately needed stability.[90]

In August 1941, the new pro-German regime of László Bárdossy expelled to German-occupied Poland some 12,000–20,000 Jews who supposedly lacked Hungarian citizenship, mostly inhabitants of Carpatho-Ruthenia, but also refugees from Poland.[91] Hungarian police abducted other foreign Jews from the streets of Budapest and pushed them over the border near Kamenets-Podolski, where they were massacred by the Nazi *Einsatzgruppe* C. The full rationale for these measures is difficult to fathom from existing accounts, but given that they coincided with the Nazi crusade on Judeo-bolshevism, perhaps they were responding to German pressure. Still, like Romania, Hungary was doing more than Germany explicitly required. Of about 18,000 deportees from Hungary, approximately 2,000 survived, some of whom made it back to tell harrowing tales of murder and mistreatment at the hands of Hungary's allies. When these stories reached the interior minister, he put an end to further deportations.[92]

Yet a few months later, in January 1942, Hungarian gendarmes themselves massacred more than 3,000 Jews and Serbs in the Bácska, lands Hungary had received from the vanquished Yugoslavia.[93] The instigator was the notorious anti-Semite General Feketehalmi-Zeisler, whom the Germans had to protect from Hungarian justice when the regime changed hands in March 1942 from the pro-Nazi Bárdossy to more circumspect Miklós Kállay. Kállay came from an old noble family and had a Habsburg-era mindset similar to Horthy's. Up to his appointment as prime minister, some 6,000 Serbs had been killed on occupied Yugoslav territory, in part as reprisals for Partisan activity.[94]

Like everywhere in the region, a noose of restrictions had slowly closed around the necks of the Jews, at a pace dictated by Hungary's desires for land as well as the shifting personalities of the prime ministers.[95] A first anti-Jewish law of May 1938 was succeeded a year later by a harsher one, and by 1941 the understanding of who was Jewish had become more stringent than in Germany. Legislators passed a further law in 1942 (public law XII) calling for expropriating Jewish landholdings, followed by an additional law excluding Jews from the regular army.[96]

Conservative elites had opposed this anti-Jewish legislation on the floors of both houses of parliament and in caucus. Even if they could not prevent the laws, they mitigated their harshness, and the results fell short of what the Hungarian Nazis desired.[97] Against the background of neighboring states, it was unusual that the Hungarian regime did not threaten Jews' lives. Until 1944, Hungary's Jews did not have to wear discriminatory insignia, faced no restrictions on freedom of movement or choice of where to live, and did not see their personal property expropriated.

The hesitation to go as far as Nazi Germany was due partly to the strong relative role of Jews among the Hungarian middle and professional classes and fears that their sudden absence would prove disruptive. Jews made up 5.1 percent of the population, yet in 1930, they constituted more than half of the country's physicians (54.5 percent), almost half the lawyers and white-collar employees in mining and industry (49.2 and about 47 percent, respectively), and almost a third of the engineers (30.4 percent). There were also concerns about economic stability. It was estimated that Jews controlled four-fifths of the country's industry.[98] The "progress" Hungary's government made in Aryanizing the economy only set off more alarm bells. Because the upper classes had an aversion to business activity, it was difficult to find ethnic Magyars to fill vacant positions, and even in 1944, German manufacturers—including some in the arms industries—remained dependent on Jewish producers. Still, the overall aim of the government was to reduce Jewish business employment by at least 50 percent.[99]

Having forbidden Jewish men to serve in regular military formations, Hungarian authorities drafted them into labor battalions, with gradually increasing maximum ages, from twenty-five in 1941 to sixty by October 1944. Military officers, some of whom were right radicals, seriously mistreated the draftees, using them for dangerous work, like construction of fortifications and roads, the clearing of minefields, and work in copper mines. Those sent to Russia did not have enough clothing for the winter. About 130,000 men served in these forces, of whom 30,000 to 40,000 lost their lives.[100] Yet the labor service turned out to be a refuge from death in the spring and summer months of 1944, when German and Hungarian officials began deporting Hungarian Jews to Auschwitz.

Until that point, successive governments had refused German demands to hand over the Jews for supposed work in the "east." Prime Minister Kállay explained the defiance in terms of "precepts of humanity which, in the course of its history, [Hungary] has always maintained in racial and religious questions." In 1943 Regent Horthy had told Hitler that one could not, after all, simply kill all the Jews. (Foreign minister Ribbentrop disagreed.)[101] As the Germans suspected, Hungarian authorities were also concerned about alienating Western powers through complicity in killing Jews. They had quietly arranged to protect downed Allied airmen, and in 1944, Kállay reached a secret agreement with the Western Allies to surrender should Anglo-American troops reach Hungarian territory. Yet that never happened, and ultimately neither he nor Horthy broke with Germany because they could not countenance the loss of territories attained by Hitler's graces.[102]

Fearing that it was about to change sides, Germany invaded Hungary on March 19, 1944. According to German propaganda, the eight German divisions arrived "at the request of the Hungarian government," though at that moment Admiral Horthy was Hitler's guest at Klessheim castle in Austria.[103] The Germans compelled Horthy to appoint a government under Lieutenant General Döme Sztójay, a man with intimate ties to the German elite, who staffed key posts with Hungarian Nazis. Now all anti-Nazi parties and organizations were dissolved, and massive arrests took place of Smallholders and Social Democrats as well as journalists, academics, and colleagues of Horthy, many of whom were sent to concentration camps in Germany. These steps telescoped the creation of total rule that had taken place in Germany after 1933.

Measures of discrimination against Jews that were introduced over several years in Germany were now squeezed into the space of a few weeks. The anti-Semitic undersecretaries in the Ministry of Interior, László Baky and László Endre, in consultation with members of a special unit (Sonderkommando) from the office of Adolf Eichmann, prepared decrees that forced Jews to wear the yellow star, forbade them from traveling, removed them from the professions, and created a Jewish council.[104] On April 7, Baky issued decrees with language similar to that which we find in Romania two years earlier: "The Hungarian Royal Government will soon cleanse the country of Jews." Following a decree of April 28, Hungarian authorities established ghettos in 185 localities; two weeks later, Hungarian police and civil authorities began preparing the first of 147 trains—mostly cattle cars of the Hungarian state railways—that would carry 437,402 Hungarian Jews to the Slovak border, where they transferred to carriages of the *Deutsche Reichsbahn* for the final leg of the journey to Auschwitz-Birkenau. The overwhelming majority was murdered just after arrival, usually more than 10,000 per day.[105]

Thanks to two young Jews who escaped Auschwitz, news of the mass murder leaked to the international press, and gave rise to appeals by the International Red Cross, the Swiss, Swedish, and American governments, as well as the Vatican.[106] Confidants of Horthy like former Prime Minister István Bethlen exerted further pressure to halt the deportations, as did his son. Horthy had attempted to wash his hands of responsibility in March, claiming that matters lay in the hands of the new government, but now he became involved, and in early July ordered a stop to further deportations, thus sparing the lives of the Budapest Jews. At a Crown Council meeting of June 26, Horthy said he would not "permit the deportations to bring further shame on the Hungarians." Baky and Endre were relieved of their tasks in the "Jewish question" on June 30.[107]

In late August, with Soviet troops already in their country, the Romanian government switched sides. King Michael invited General Antonescu for consultations and had him arrested. Now Romania fought with ferocity against the Germans and lost some 50,000 dead and wounded in the quest to recover Northern Transylvania.[108] Admiral Horthy tried to follow Michael's example. The following day (August 24), he dismissed Sztójay and placed the government in the hands of General Géza Lakatos, who established contact with the Western Allies. (They told him he must deal with the Soviets.)[109] The Red Army crossed the border on September 23, and Hungary arranged an armistice with Moscow on October 11. Yet when Horthy ordered Hungarian troops to stop fighting on October 15, the Arrow Cross and the German occupiers took countermeasures: a *Panzerdivision* occupied the Royal Palace in Budapest, and the Germans forced Horthy (by threatening to kill his son) to appoint Arrow Cross leader Ferenc Szálasi as prime minister. German troops and Arrow Cross units occupied key buildings in Budapest and encountered no resistance.[110]

Nightmare days commenced for Budapest's Jews. By December, the Soviets were surrounding the city, and the war was clearly lost for the Axis, yet the

Hungarian Nazis continued a relentless murder of Jews, assembling them in long lines along the Danube, shooting them one by one, and then throwing their bodies into the icy waters. Some 20,000 Jews are thought to have perished this way. Still, most Jews in Budapest survived, protected by foreign legations, including those of Sweden, Switzerland, Spain, Italy, and Portugal, or by the Catholic Church. The Swede Raul Wallenberg and Swiss Carl Lutz issued tens of thousands of protection papers for the Jews that the Arrow Cross honored. Wallenberg and Lutz knew about Arrow Cross plans to deport Budapest's Jews because Dr. Gerhart Feine, head of the German legation, had tipped them off. Feine and Lutz rented thirty large apartment blocks, where some 30,000 Budapest Jews found a safe haven to the end of the war.[111]

A Hungarian resistance formed under the anti-Nazi Endre Bajcsy-Zsilinszky, a major figure in the nationalist and independent smallholders party, who worked to unite right, center, and left, and crafted schemes for the postwar cooperation of the Danube states, hoping to transcend generations of hostility. Alas, Arrow Cross men captured and hanged Bajcsy-Zsilinszky in December.[112] Budapest finally fell to the Red Army on February 13, 1945. The city's Jewish population had declined from a pre-siege figure of close to 200,000 to 120,000. Of 770,000 Hungarian citizens defined as Jewish in 1944, about 250,000 survived the war.[113]

In Romania, some 290,000 Jews survived, but the Antonescu regime itself had murdered between 280,000 and 380,000.[114] Bulgaria's 48,000 Jews survived the war, but more than 11,000 Jews of Thrace and Macedonia, delivered by Bulgarian authorities to Germany, did not.[115] Only about 14,000 of the 118,000 Jews who lived in Bohemia and Moravia in 1938 lived to see the end of the war; of the 350,000 Jews of prewar Czechoslovakia, 265,000 lost their lives.[116] Of the prewar Polish community of 3.3 million Jews, about 90 percent died in the Holocaust, and most of those who survived had done so in the Soviet Union, figuring among the "uncertain elements" whom Soviet authorities transported from eastern Poland to Siberia and Central Asia in 1940/1941. The returnees mostly treated Poland as a transit stop on the way to Palestine.

* * *

In Hungary, as in Bulgaria and Romania, the first steps of killing innocent civilians involved Jews considered foreign: they lived in occupied Serbia, Thrace, and Macedonia, or Transnistria. But the murders of Jews in these places took place as momentum gathered against the "native" Jews, through the reduction

of rights, the introduction of restrictions on employment, or the issuing of separate passports, all based on supposed ancestry. Still, nowhere did East European regimes fully embrace the Nazi understanding of Jews as a race; several
made exceptions for war veterans or converts to Christianity. In each place, a
point arrived at which German authorities demanded stepping to a higher
stage beyond discrimination and restrictions, of handing "native" Jews over
for annihilation. Bulgaria and Romania stepped back from this precipice,
though additional deportations occurred from once-Austrian Bukovina to
killing camps is Transnistria in early and mid-1942. In Hungary, deportations
to death camps occurred only after Germany occupied the country, but
Hungarian officials fully cooperated. (In Eastern Europe, only Croat and
Romanian authorities had created their own death camps; in the former case,
primarily for Serbs).

In Hungary, Romania and Bulgaria, as well as the puppet regimes of Croatia
and Slovakia, an ultimate sense of justice had been transferred from human beings to *land*, that is, national territory. The bargains with Nazi Germany were
possible because of widely shared irredentism: the belief that the nation—one's
ostensible extended family—had been denied its rightful property. In effect,
the trade was territory for people: slices of Transylvania or Dobrudja were
gained in exchange for the promise to punish and kill Jews—Jews who first lost
their citizenship and then their lives.

It was shocking but logical that Operation Margarethe—the German invasion of Hungary in 1944—was preceded by German complaints that Hungarians were not fulfilling their end of the bargain. Now the devil crossed the border to claim the promised lives. In a sense, Hungary's bureaucrats recognized
the legitimacy of Germany's actions by cooperating in the initial deportations
from the provinces in the spring of 1944. Admiral Horthy closed his eyes, but
he soon found himself unable to ignore the outrage coming from many parts
of the world, stirred by the screams of the victims, his fellow Hungarian citizens, Jews loaded onto cattle cars.

If the screams were not audible to more East Central Europeans, that was
because part of the bargain involved mastering the hegemon's own language,
taking for granted that one's territory needed to be "clean"—the same words
were used by the racists in all three contexts. Everywhere, "moderate" politicians helped make the words of extremists the coin of the realm. Of course, those
words were not really foreign; they were easily translated into native versions
of ethnic nationalism, whose sources went back generations, often to the region's
most respected intellectuals.

Under conditions of war and revolution, the most extreme (but also the most consistent) nationalists could ponder one particular question undistracted by morality: why thirst for all this new territory if it was not "clean"? In the racist age, the "ultimate sense of outrage," of injured justice, made Jews, and also Roma (in Romania) and Muslims (in Bulgaria), into criminal elements, or as one German officer referred to Jewish children who had survived the first massacres in Ukraine (belaya Cercov), "scum to be exterminated." Those who pined for more land became locked into an imperial ideology but also an affective scheme; when Admiral Horthy gave orders for switching sides in October 1944, he found that his officers would not listen. "Many officers who had been trained in Germany and instilled with National Socialist values," writes Jörg Hoensch, "were not prepared to make common cause with the Soviets."[117]

In the aftermath of race war, many Jewish survivors drew conclusions from all that had happened. They could see that even in Hungary, the place Jews had survived the longest, they were the group furthest from what the sociologist Helen Fein would call the "universe of obligation"—the "circle of persons toward whom obligations are owed, to whom rules apply, and whose injuries call for amends." They remained an ultimate other, regardless of how many generations of their ancestors had devoted themselves to promoting the prosperity and cultural life of the nation, as Hungarian Jews did from the 1860s. When Jews disappeared from Bohemia, or Bosnia, or Galicia and Transylvania, locals looked on, sometimes callously, not feeling part of themselves was being removed.[118]

In a memoir written much later, the Hungarian dissident George Konrád remembered his Gentile neighbors in Berettyoujfalu, a provincial town from which the Jews had been deported in June 1944. When he and his brother, the only children to survive, returned from Budapest in the spring of 1945, their neighbors made "no comment" about the Jews no longer in their midst:

> The fact that they were loaded on to trains was met with the same indifference as news from the front or draft notices or the appearance of bombers over the town on a sunny morning: they were all so many historical events over which one had no control. It was the indifference that comes of an acceptance of fate mingled with fear and perhaps relief.[119]

That same year, the Czech Jewish survivor Heda Margolius Kovaly returned to her father's birthplace near Benešov, south of Prague, to learn of the fate of her grandmother. She had lived in the village all her 86 years and was loved by everyone. Yet when the Germans came, taking her to a horrible death, the most anyone could say was: "don't be afraid, Mrs. Bloch." Some thought the extraction of Jews from their midst was just. Now it was their turn to own the shops, the turn of their little girl to play the piano left behind. In the Czech lands there was "a place and a new owner for every head of cattle."[120] The neighbors had been envious of the status of middle-class Jews, symbolized by white gloves worn on holidays, fine homes, a remarkable facility with languages, or relatives ensconced in Budapest or, slightly farther afield, Vienna and Paris.[121] Yet it was also true that Gentiles and Jews had "lived side by side in peace until those German insanities started happening."[122]

What was true of Hungary and Bohemia was also true of Poland, Slovakia, and Romania. In 1944 and 1945, the Red Army conquered territories where Germans and their local helpers had violently made territory ethnically "clean." The "insanities" could not be undone. Encounters between Jewish survivors and ethnic locals were similar to those depicted by Konrád, revealing indifference at the Jews' disappearance and often annoyed surprise that some had returned. "I heard you were dead," was a frequent refrain.[123] The measures taken by the Nazis and their local puppets continued to find popular approbation long after Nazi rule had ended. The postwar Slovak government hanged Father Tiso but maintained the "Aryanization" of property undertaken by his regime. Neighbors simply divided Jewish jobs and property among themselves. In many villages, everyone was wearing some garment of the dead at some time in a given week, and they never dreamed of giving it back.

The nasty secret about the Holocaust in East Central Europe was that local populations despised Nazi rule, and often resisted it, but everywhere they acceded to the central aspect of it. That was how the war was forgotten, or more accurately, misremembered.

CHAPTER 18

People's Democracy: Early Postwar Eastern Europe

Eastern Europe's transformation into the Soviet Bloc might seem not to need much explanation. There was no other choice. Soviet leaders simply imposed their system on the territories their armies liberated from Nazi rule in 1944 and 1945: Romania, Bulgaria, Hungary, Poland, Czechoslovakia, and the Soviet Zone of Germany. By 1948, Communists controlled these places, and people who simply questioned the validity of Soviet models for organizing every feature of these societies' lives risked prison or worse. It would seem that the Soviet Union simply transplanted its system to the region by force.

Yet if one looks beneath the surface, satisfactory explanations for Eastern Europe's drift toward Communism become more elusive. In 1945, the Soviet leadership had no clear vision for the future and did not imagine the Eastern European states becoming Communist in the short term. That had to do with their broader vision. The workers' movement, led by the Soviet Union, had just vanquished fascism, signaling that the future of humankind belonged to the left. There was thus no need to force Communist revolution in the countries the Red Army now occupied. Instead, the Soviet leadership made certain minimal demands for its own security.

It insisted on a buffer to the west as protection from further land attacks, and thus retained the former Tsarist territories gained in the Molotov-Ribbentrop pact of 1939—the Baltic states, Bessarabia, eastern Poland. Poland, with the blessings of the Western allies, was compensated with much of Germany's eastern territories: almost all of Silesia, much of the province of Brandenburg, as well as most of Pomerania and East Prussia. The new Polish western boundary was called the "Oder-Neisse" line for the two rivers that formed it.[1] The Soviet leadership also required that the governments in Poland and Romania not be hostile to Soviet interests. This demand implied Soviet influence in these countries' internal politics but did not require the creation of the outright Soviet replica regimes that took shape in the region after 1948.[2]

For the time being, domestic factors stood against anyone dreaming of such a transformation. Eastern Europe had been the most anti-Communist territory on the continent, and to try to force Communism on it would make it more so. In the minds of most East Europeans, the Russian Revolution had inaugurated not liberation but cataclysms of suffering the likes of which Europe had never seen. For Hungarian and Polish peasants, Bolshevism evoked a system out to take their land and close their churches. In addition, many Hungarians and Poles were reared in animosity toward Imperial Russia, and encounters with Red Army units in 1944 and 1945 reinforced prejudices. In northern Serbia and central Poland, Soviet soldiers plundered, raped, and drank every drop of alcohol they could find, and in areas belonging to the Third Reich and its allies, they behaved much worse. The men and women who freed Central Europe from extreme racism thus became targets of racist beliefs: they seemed made of a different kind of human material.[3]

Moreover, in much of Eastern Europe, Communist parties were tiny, hunted entities, whose members had spent the war in exile or in prison. In 1945, there were no cadres to force Communism on the region, even had that been the Soviet plan. Romania, a country of just under 16 million, had just a thousand Communists. The situation in Hungary and Poland was similar. Part of the problem was Stalin's own doing. In the 1930s, he had ordered the arrest and murder of scores of European Communists who had sought refuge in Moscow. In 1938 he simply disbanded the Polish Communist Party after executing the top tiers of its leadership.

Still, in ways more and less evident, East European countries began advancing toward Soviet forms of rule after 1944—even if Soviet leaders themselves did not intend that outcome right away. That had to do with the Soviet political imagination, something that Western leaders understood imperfectly when they met with Soviet counterparts between 1943 and 1945 to hammer out the postwar order. The greatest misunderstanding involved the word "democracy." At the Potsdam Conference of July 1945, Soviet representatives pledged to respect democratic norms, but they did so with knowledge of their own system, where rule of "the people" meant power of the laboring classes, who were democratic by definition because they constituted the great majority of any society. In the years that followed, when Soviet officials were called to "democratize" Eastern Europe, they reflexively promoted the party that best represented the laboring classes, namely the Communists, no matter how small that party was.

An aligned stipulation of the postwar agreements between the Soviet and Western powers was to root out fascism; in Germany, the process was known as denazification. But here, too, the understandings differed. Because Communists believed fascism had been a strategy of capitalist politicians to secure hegemony over the masses—through empty promises, wars of aggression, pseudo-social policies—any politics that maintained capitalism would be insufficient to deal with fascism's legacy.

Therefore, from the start, the postwar East European states—called "people's democracies," meaning they were no longer capitalist but not yet socialist—often featured violent measures taken with scant regard for the rule of law. Among the earliest were expropriations of large landholders and capitalists, who received no compensation because they were considered fascist "collaborators." This was only logical. To grant them generous settlements for the loss of land, mines, or industrial plant would have permitted them to survive as a socially relevant force, and the economic bases of fascist rule would have survived. By contrast, giving land to peasants or transferring enterprises to state control was considered democratic because it meant putting the most vital form of power—control over the economy—in the hands of laborers and what was becoming "their" state.

In a policy that was not made official, the people's democratic regimes also retained the properties Nazi and allied regimes had seized during the war, often from Jews who had been murdered. Administrators resisted attempts even of immediate family members to reclaim these stolen assets.[4]

Yet the people's democracies were not based on the creeping application of force alone. They could also summon the acceptance and enthusiasm of hundreds of thousands, indeed millions, who saw the wealthy humbled and themselves accorded rudimentary social justice. These regimes passed long overdue legislation, granting workers health and accident insurance, security of employment, and access to free education at all levels. The last was especially attractive, because under the old systems, fewer than 5 percent of any age group qualified for higher education, and they tended to be from the middle and gentry classes. The new governments vastly expanded schooling, did away with remnants of illiteracy (see Table A.3 in the Appendix.), and streamlined educational forms so that as many children as possible could advance from primary to secondary education (previously the great majority had to leave school after six or eight years). Based on the Soviet example, they also created crash courses, so that the children of workers and peasants could get high school equivalence in one to two years.[5]

Sentiments in favor of a radical break with laissez-faire capitalism were by no means limited to one corner of Europe. From the United Kingdom through

France, Italy, into the Balkans and Poland, people felt that new governments could not simply reprise the economic mismanagement and vast social inequalities of the 1930s. In July 1945, British voters threw Winston Churchill out of office and replaced him with Clement Atlee of the Labour Party, and soon the British state was nationalizing industry, banking, health care, and transportation. In Hungary, only a small fraction of the population wanted semi-feudal conditions to continue; the vast majority favored a modern political and social structure.[6] The liberal Oscar Jászi wrote that "the road is open to really constructive experiments in socialization, since there are very few people who would shed tears for that hybrid form of capitalism which amassed enormous profits by the ruthless exploitation of monopolistic positions."[7]

Therefore much evidence justified the view that history was on the side of the Soviet Union, and the power of socialist forces would grow—provided they were not impeded by "imperialism," of which fascism was the most extreme form. Marxism found many more supporters than before the war, and not simply in the industrial regions where, according to early Marxian thinkers, the contradictions of capitalism would be most severe. Hungary was mostly rural but still provided an object lesson of Marx's teachings about the interrelatedness of economy and politics. The Horthy system had catered to the owners of huge estates, as well as the urban capitalists and financial classes. It had been propped up by the army and a bureaucracy that fed Hungarians a steady diet of irredentism while fixing elections. Most East Europeans did not reject liberal democracy in 1945 because they had never really known it.

The demand for states stonger than the old liberal regimes was also practical: the destruction and disruptions of the war required concerted and forceful governance. Budapest, for example, was in shambles after months of siege, with bridges in the Danube and a cityscape of apartment buildings gutted by shelling. Inflation had begun during the war and continued, developing its own dynamic. At the end of July 1946, the daily inflation rate was 158,486 percent, and the dollar was valued at 4,600,000 quadrillion forints. A relapse to a barter economy occurred amid a thriving black market, and Hungarians lived close to starvation; in the winter of 1944/1945, some got sustenance from horse cadavers taken from the streets. In February, orders went out to use all available land in Budapest for cultivating crops. Yet because of the weather, the wheat harvest was only one-third the prewar average. Hungarians also suffered drastic coal shortages. The privation thus encouraged demands for heavy state involvement in the economy, and in February 1946, 66 percent of workers expressed their support for nationalization of industry.[8] Authorities enacted harsh punishments for economic offenses, and, of all the parties, it was the Communists who characteristically stood for the most extreme measures.

Yet the authorities did not even call these early measures "socialist," let alone "Communist," words that might have alienated forces sympathetic to social reform but wary of anything that seemed "Soviet." Instead, the changes were called "progressive" and "necessary." Bourgeois society was a thing of the past, and people's democracy involved not one-party rule or dictatorship, but rather—another watchword of the time—"unity." All forces in favor of democratic and antifascist politics were summoned to enter government in broad coalitions, often called "National Fronts," including Communists and Social Democrats, but also peasant parties, liberals, progressive nationalists, and Catholics. By the same token, all those defined as fascist collaborators were excluded. Thus, the right-leaning Agrarians in Czechoslovakia or the National Democrats in Poland were not permitted to reorganize.

The unity concept meant that Communists did not have to worry about their small numbers. Usually they could count on the support of Social Democrats and "progressive" peasants, especially because of the mass sentiment in favor of progressive change. (As we will see below, when they could not persuade these allies, the Communists gradually corrupted or destroyed them.) Morever, Soviet patrons ensured that Communists received the most powerful portfolios in the new governments, above all the Interior Ministry. Among the progressive forces, Communists claimed to be the most democratic, because they supported the most radical transformations in the interests of the "people."

Though they supported them from behind the scenes with packages of food and supplies, Soviet authorities occasionally had to tame native Communists who wanted to move speedily to socialism. They knew that radical language or open displays of violence might alienate allies in other parties, as well as West Europeans, who looked with favor on the Soviet Union as the major force in vanquishing fascism. Following the line from Moscow, East European Communists argued that their countries might reach socialism without the disruptions of revolution. To many Czechs, local Communists seemed different, more humane than the "uncouth" easterners from Eurasia. In March 1947, Party leader Klement Gottwald said that the "system of the Soviets and of dictatorship of the proletariat" were not the only roads to socialism.[9]

Communist leaders like Gottwald also hoped to attract laborers who desired reform but tended to be moderate in their political sympathies. In rural areas, the challenges for this approach were substantial. In November 1945, the majority of Hungarian voters (57 percent) opted for the Smallholders and against the left bloc, and thus for a gradual transformation that would still feature broad property ownership, rule of law, and the institutions of parliamentary democracy. The Smallholders, as the major non-Marxist party, soon evolved into a camp for all who dissented, including conservatives, liberal intellectuals, and defenders of middle-class interests.[10] Similarly, the Polish Peasant Party was understood to be the main alternative to the Communists, and attracted the support of Poles who wanted independence and a Western-style government.

People's democracy was therefore an unstable formation, where it was both impossible to build Communism or to criticize it. The result was a half-hidden struggle, in which Communists in the government used administrative levers to marginalize opposition, to the accompaniment of an increasingly shrill polemic. What honest, well-meaning person could oppose democracy, antifascism and progress? The left—Communists as well as many Social Democrats— vilified critics as traitors. They stoked concerns about subversive activities of unredeemed cryptofascists and argued that new means were needed to root out treason. In every coalition, Communists controlled police through the interior ministries, and often they controlled the education ministries that published schoolbooks, and propaganda ministries that allotted newsprint. Communist newspapers thus got higher print runs, and all media observed a de facto ban on criticism of the National Front government and its foreign policy, including the alliance with the Soviet Union. Even in the relatively moderate Czechoslovakia, state security district commanders interpreted this to mean that criticism of Marxism was a punishable act.[11]

Societies and Nations

Communists proclaimed that true workers had healthy class instincts that made them vigilant against enemies. Thus workers, peasants, and their children were targeted in recruitment not just to higher education but also to the Communist Party, the people's army, and police forces, all of which would provide access to better grocery stores and vacation houses. The ultimate effects of this favoritism were ambivalent. At times, industrial workers took the party at its word—they were the ruling class—and were the first to express dissent in times of crisis, for example, in Czechoslovakia and East Germany in 1953.[12] Yet at other times—Czechoslovakia and Poland in 1968—industrial workers proved a bastion of support for the regime. Workers or peasants who supported people's democracy helped realize social justice while themselves becoming direct evidence that the new system kept its promises. They found career paths opened to them in state administration and the economy that their parents could not have dreamed of.

Intellectuals were generally of "bourgeois" background and destined to lose privileges in a worker and peasant state, yet many cooperated in building people's democracy. Top writers, painters, and professors supported the regime with poems, stories, plays, films, and musical scores that celebrated Soviet-style socialism. They were blissfully ignorant of the object they admired. No journalists had been permitted to investigate life in the Soviet Union, and few outside the Soviet leadership knew the extent of the misery of collectivization or party purges of the 1930s. Did tens or hundreds of thousands perish? No one could say. Left-wing critiques of Stalinism by Arthur Koestler, Victor Serge, or Boris Souvarine that checked Communist sympathies in France were deemed anti-Soviet and could not appear in Eastern Europe. Native Communists who returned from Soviet exile and knew about famine or terror first hand, kept that information to themselves, still fearful of Stalin's long reach.[13]

Yet even intellectuals who had tasted the terror and deprivations of Soviet reality often collaborated happily with the new regime. Communism found supporters among Polish writers who had seen friends arrested when the NKVD apprehended Home Army soldiers who wanted to fight alongside the Red Army. Others had survived Soviet camps or had close relatives who had not, yet they found ways to make peace with the regime.

Part of the explanation was lack of choice. When intellectuals returned to Kraków or Warsaw or Łódź in 1945 and wanted to continue their careers, they encountered a new state in the making, called "People's Poland," allied with the Soviet Union, involved in "rebuilding the country"—and not building socialism (at least not yet). What was the point of standing by idly? Did intellectuals not have a duty to Polish culture regardless of regime? Professors and teachers who had conducted classes in the underground now simply moved back into university and school buildings, for example, the critical non-Communist philologist Kazimierz Wyka, who has been likened to a practitioner of "organic work" from the late nineteenth century.[14] Simple cooperation often evolved into subtle forms of collaboration. In 1953, Wyka would write that Stalin's "genius, specifying the iron logic of dialectic assumptions . . . shows the way to understanding lasting values of literature."[15]

Still, one senses a wariness among Poles that was never far beneath the surface. Compared to Czechs or East Germans, relatively few joined the Communist Party, let alone the Secret Police, even if virtually all cooperated with the new state because it came to control most employment. Scattered units of the Home Army continued fighting in the underground after 1945, training their fire on functionaries of the Soviet-supported regime. Such units had defied orders from the central Home Army leadership in January to disband, come out into the open, and rejoin civilian life.[16]

But for many intellectuals, the issue was not simple resignation or opportunism. Their choice to work for the people's democratic regimes took place amid a general enthusiasm for Hegelian arguments of the inevitability, and therefore the legitimacy of the changes taking place. The Soviet army had moved humanity beyond capitalism and "bourgeois democracy" to a new stage, a reality that it was unreasonable to oppose. What was real was right. Dialectical visions found adherents beyond the left because they seemed to account for recent history. One historical stage emerged from the previous one, and fascism had not crushed liberal democracy, it was its product. Take Václav Lorenc, a pastor in the Hussite Czechoslovak Church writing in 1946:

> the capitalist order, which has fulfilled its historical task and is becoming a brake on further development, carried on its last struggle against the unstoppable advent of the socialist order. Fascism was consciously and intentionally summoned in order to delay the fall of capitalism. . . . We must understand the president's words about the danger the remnants of fascism still present as a call for the mobilization of all moral forces against those who are trying to turn back the wheel of history because they know that they will be removed from their privileged, exploitative and sinful positions.[17]

Here the Hegelian dialectic was mapped on a Christian salvation story, and sin equated with anticommunist resistance. The Hussite Church Assembly resolved that fascism had its origin in the internal contradictions of capitalist class society, and that there could be no security from it until socialism was established.[18]

Many East Europeans also wanted new national narratives that could absorb the humiliation, not only of defeat in 1939, but also of the occupation that followed. For Czechs, the rise of the Communist Party was part of an attempt to rewrite their nation's history, placing an emphasis on pan-Slavism and links to Russia that were foreign to T. G. Masaryk. Still, there was important continuity. As in 1918, events on the ground—the seizing of state institutions from a German regime and placing them in the hands of a Czech regime—were called "national revolution," permitting people to feel active after six years of stifling foreign rule.

Critical observers spoke of a revolutionary fetish that appealed to people try-ing to make sense of the war, people who had lost connections to stabilizing traditions.[19] The Catholic Pavel Tigrid said that young workers and students had become fanatics. But they also had a logic of national salvation on their side; if their revolution looked eastward for inspiration, that was because without armies of the east, the Czechoslovak nationality would have ceased to exist.[20] Even centrists like Edvard Beneš, who returned to Czechoslovakia as president, saw no alternative. He portrayed his country as a "bridge between East and West," with greater sympathy for the former, given the betrayal suffered at Munich in 1938.[21]

In Poland, the genocidal losses of the war made even politicians of the cen-ter and right recognize the need for closer relations with the Soviet Union. In December 1945, Poland's opposition leader, the Peasant politician Stanisław Mikołajczyk, told the Italian ambassador Eugenio Reale, that his "PSL [inde-pendent Polish Peasants' Party] believes that the basis of Polish foreign policy is the maintenance of good relations with Russia. Only Russia can effectively protect Poland from Germany and the German danger. Anyone who thinks dif-ferent is stupid or crazy, and the PSL does not have that kind of people among its members."[22] The argument was made stronger by the fact that Poland had assumed control of one-fourth of Germany's prewar territories beyond the new Oder-Neisse boundary and needed great power protection to keep them. (Ger-many did not recognize this land transfer as final until 1990.)[23]

The old heroic Polish insurgent narrative also seemed exhausted, and people asked probing questions about the catastrophic 1944 Warsaw Uprising. It was not a spontaneous act of an enslaved population, but the free act of identifiable Polish military leaders that had transformed a city inhabited by tens of thou-sands of women and children into a field of slaughter. The Catholic poets Czesław Miłosz and Jerzy Andrzejewski walked through the rubble in the spring of 1945, past countless reminders of the price of seeking independence at any cost. Miłosz recalled the lovingly tended grave of a "Lieutenant Zbyszek," one of tens of thousands who hurled themselves into combat with no "limits to the frenzies of voluntary self-sacrifice." Now their deaths seemed no more than a "gesture in the face of an indifferent world." Warsaw was so devastated that leaders weighed plans to relocate the capital to the working-class city of Łódź. (Miłosz later wrote that Andrzejewski's path to the Communist Party began on that day, as they sought traces of their dead friends in Warsaw's ruins.)[24]

Into the sense of historical inevitability mixed anger at the old elites for the disastrous policy decisions of the 1930s. With their eyes on territories in Transylvania, Hungary's rulers had moved their country into the Nazi orbit, and the consequences were horrific. Contrary to German promises, the war was not over in six weeks. In the winter of 1942/1943, thousands of Hungarian troops froze to death at Stalingrad, then in January, the survivors absorbed a Soviet offensive at Voronezh that cost 40,000 men killed and 70,000 taken prisoner. The German occupation, with heavy complicity of the Hungarian government, had cost 600,000 Hungarian Jews their lives, and the Soviet offensives of 1944/1945 had left major cities devastated. But greed for territory was not the only factor that had propelled Hungary's leaders toward Germany; as in Poland, most were united in their disdain for the Soviet Union and would gladly have sided with the West if geography had made that possible. The anti-Soviet sentiments were so strong that the Romanians repeatedly requested a Western landing in the Balkans.[25]

Despite the population's traditional sympathies for Russia, Bulgaria's predicament was little better. Here it was the alliance *between* Germany and the Soviet Union in 1939 that had made it easier to fall into the Nazis' embrace. Bulgaria's cession in March 1941 to the Tripartite Pact with Germany and Italy was not seen as anti-Russian and thus did not risk aggravating the Bulgarian public. The two totalitarian states with united power and enticements swept Bulgaria into their wake, while in Hungary and Romania, historical animosity toward Bolshevism had bound these two states even closer to Germany. This was the East European predicament, to be trapped in a geopolitical situation that impeded entry into Europe as a place of law, democracy, and commitment to social welfare.[26]

But the cultural ties to the West were relatively new for Romanian elites, dating back only a century. Before that, a rhetoric had governed of fraternal ties to Russia as a fellow Orthodox country. When in February 1947, the compliant Romanian government under Petru Groza signed the Paris peace treaty confirming the retrieval of Northern Transylvania from Hungary, the anti-Communist Constantin Rădulescu-Motru praised Groza for observing a tradition of submitting to great powers and renouncing independence in exchange for "stability and institutional continuity."[27]

Contempt for old elites derived not only from blunders of international politics, however. Beyond failing to protect their countries from the onslaught of

well-armed and rapacious neighbors, the prewar leaders had neglected grievous social problems, instead monopolizing and reproducing privilege for
themselves. They had made limited investments in modern industries and introduced few educational reforms, and therefore the overwhelming majorities
of the populations were cut off from hopes of social advancement. Now leading intellectuals sought to expiate their guilt for the rampant injustices of the
interwar regimes by siding with people's democracy, understanding that those
governing them were of lower class background and had to learn to behave "culturally" through educational advancement that only the intelligentsia could
provide.[28]

Few leaders of the interwar years remained to face the consequences. In 1945,
Admiral Miklós Horthy was a prisoner in Nuremberg, and after release went
into exile in Switzerland and Portugal. Polish foreign minister Józef Beck escaped to Romania, only to die there. Peasant Party leader Stanislaw Mikołajczyk
returned to Poland, but the rest of the London government did not. Yugoslav
King Peter had fled at war's outbreak, never to return. Boris III of Bulgaria died
in 1943 and his nine-year-old son, Simeon, went into exile in 1946. In February 1945, as the result of a decision of a Communist-controlled "people's court,"
virtually the entire surviving government of Bulgaria was executed, including
three regents, twenty-two ministers, and sixty-seven parliamentarians. The
popular King Michael of Romania was forced to abdicate at gunpoint in
December 1947 and left for exile in Switzerland the following month.[29]

The devastations of war had also weakened the governing classes, especially
in Poland. There Nazi and Soviet occupiers had acted as co-conspirators in genocide by deporting and killing Poland's national elite, most egregiously at the
forests near Katyn in early 1940, when the NKVD shot more than 22,000 reserve officers, who in civilian life were leading figures in politics, culture, and
the economy. When Soviet authorities sent four transports of more than one
million Polish citizens from eastern Poland to central Asia and Siberia in
1940/1941, they targeted persons with higher education and means; and from
the moment German armed units crossed Poland's borders, SS units followed
with lists of Polish intellectuals to kill.[30] The physical and human destruction
overlapped most dramatically in Warsaw, which had served as the political but
also as the cultural and economic locus of power. Of the city's 1.2 million inhabitants, historians estimate that 800,000 lost their lives during the war. The
municipality was still more than 80 percent ruins as late as 1948. Those elites
who survived staggered from the blows received and were unable to mount serious resistance to people's democracy.

Ethnic Revolution

Throughout Eastern Europe, the fascist enemy was not only a class enemy—the bourgeoisie—but also an ethnic other, usually German (also Hungarian in Czechoslovakia and Romania). From 1944 to 1947, East European regimes expelled some 9–10 million Germans, with the loss of all property except what they could carry, usually limited to 40 kilograms. The overwhelming majority were Germans who lived in Czechoslovakia and in the former German territories accorded to Poland, but Hungary and Yugoslavia also expelled German ethnics. Whole German families were made to bear responsibility for the crimes of the German state, and no one was exempted, not even the few surviving Czech Jews who had opted for German nationality before the war.

In Poland, both Communist and non-Communist politicians were agreed that ethnic Germans would lose citizenship and the right to remain on Polish territory. That restriction pertained even to former Polish citizens of German descent. On August 1, 1944, the day the Warsaw Uprising broke out, the new Polish government, established at Lublin by the Soviet Union, clarified who counted: those who spoke German at home, observed German habits, or raised their children in a German spirit.[31] In 1946 the new Polish state stripped citizenship from those who "after reaching eighteen years of age demonstrated German national identity through their behavior."[32] Centuries of mostly peaceful coexistence were now read as a time of constant ethnic rivalry. The real owners of Silesia or Pomerania were the Slavs who had once settled there before being displaced by German "newcomers" who had advanced onto Polish territory thanks to their "thirst for conquest."[33]

The climate of intolerance extended beyond Germans to Jews. In Poland, for example, people said in whispers that it was good that Hitler had solved Poland's Jewish problem. Ethnic Poles moved into Jewish houses and no longer faced competition from Jews for slots at universities.[34] Beginning in 1944, some 200,000 Polish Jews began returning to Poland from the Soviet Union, where they had been deported in 1940/1941, but were made to feel unwelcome.[35] Between 1944 and 1946, Polish Gentiles killed as many as 1,200 Polish Jews, mostly in small towns and villages, with the bloodiest act occurring in Kielce in July 1946, when rumors of a kidnapped Christian boy led to a pogrom in which forty-two Jews were butchered. A year after Hitler's suicide, the killers thus extended the logic of Nazi rule to Jews who had lived outside the Third Reich: they made the distinction between "Aryan" and Jew—categories known only on the extreme right before war—virtually absolute.[36] Jews now fled for

FIGURE 18.1. Germans in Prague awaiting expulsion (1945). *Source*: CTK/
Alamy Stock Photo.

their lives to Palestine via Czechoslovakia, Germany, and France, and their numbers in Poland declined from 240,000 in 1946 to about 90,000 a year later, to
60,000 in the early 1950s, and 40,000 by 1968.[37]

Poles from the territories ceded to the Soviet Union (Wolynia, Eastern Galicia, and Lithuania), had themselves been subject to a vicious war of ethnic
cleansing between Ukrainian and Polish partisan units in 1943 and 1944. Entire
villages were massacred, and up to 100,000 Poles and 20,000 Ukrainians perished.[38] The processes of ethnic purification extended into the postwar period,
when the Soviet and Polish governments exchanged populations; about 1.5 million Poles were "repatriated" from Ukraine and 500,000 Ukrainians from Poland. Poland's government also forcibly resettled 140,000 Ukrainians from

FIGURE 18.2. Pallbearers carrying the victims of the Kielce pogrom (July 1946).
Source: United States Holocaust Memorial Museum Photo Archives #14380. Courtesy of
Leah Lahav. Copyright of United States Holocaust Memorial Museum.

southeastern Poland to areas of western and northeastern Poland that had been
vacated by Germans, claiming it was quelling an insurgency.[39] The ethnic minorities that remained by the late 1940s were so small and fragmented that some
called the new state ethnically homogeneous. (See Table A.4 in the
Appendix.)

Because Jews were an urban population, Jewish survivors suffered disproportionately from nationalizing measures meant to weaken strata of the population engaged in urban pursuits, like business and commerce. In Romania,
the state with the largest post-Holocaust Jewish community (345,000), some
40 percent of Jews had been employed in commerce, which was now defined
as "speculation." The state offered to compensate those who lost their businesses
by offering them manual labor, a process known as "restratification." This, combined with other forms of hostility, caused a third of Romania's Jews to leave
for Israel by 1952.[40]

The cities of Transylvania, with 6 million inhabitants (one-third of Romania's population), were mostly Hungarian, and a half-million Germans remained
in the Banat and a strip extending from Sibiu to Brașov. At first, the official
line of the Romanian government was impartiality toward Hungarians but
denial of the Germans' civil rights. Officials therefore promoted Hungarian

cultural life and took ethnicity into account when allotting posts in the police or administration.[41] Still, the socialist state inherited its predecessor's concern for ethnic purity, and this latitude would prove temporary.

An exception to the ethnic homogenization was Yugoslavia. It also expelled Germans for supposed treason but abandoned the idea of a "Yugoslav people" in the ethnic sense. With enthusiasm for the Soviet Union at an all-time high, the Partisan leadership adopted basic elements of Soviet law, including federalism. According to the constitution of 1946, Yugoslavia was a federal state of six republics representing six *peoples*, each with a right to secession. This policy responded to concerns about Serb domination in interwar Yugoslavia. The haziness over the word "people" came back to haunt the country in the early 1990s: did the "people" of Croatia include the Serbs who lived there, or was it simply Croats? For the time being, concerns about multiethnic republics were submerged in talk of brotherhood and unity.

Only after the Soviet hold on the region was fully consolidated after 1948 did Eastern Europe become part of a socialist (Soviet-dominated) world system, governed according to the rules of "socialist internationalism." But some of the basic principles were already clear. The states that emerged were nation-states, in control of territory and acting in the name of a nominal nation. Because of the ethnic cleansings during and after World War II, the states of the nascent Soviet Bloc reflected the principles of nation-statism more than their interwar predecessors did. Czechoslovak President Beneš forcefully articulated this new spirit. His country could no longer tolerate minorities, he said, because the system of minority treaties had failed. Germans and Magyars had proved incapable of acting as loyal Czechoslovak citizens.

Thus, Europe was dividing not only between liberal capitalism and people's democracy, but also between the new internationalism in the West and nation-statism in the East, frozen beneath the power of the Soviet hegemon, which began imposing its own order on the people's democracies from late 1947.[42] Yet the state that modeled itself from the start on the Soviet Union—"federal" Yugoslavia, which claimed to transcend ethnic nationalism—was also the state that first challenged Soviet hegemony in 1948—in the name of nationalism! Dozens of show trials followed in the Soviet Bloc, in which Yugoslav leader Josip Broz Tito, a man of mixed Slovene and Croat heritage, would be made to personify the "crime" of national Communism.

* * *

Revolution, whether national or social, gave Communists a hold on state min-istries, through which they controlled vast resources and built power bases that became rooted in extensive networks of political patronage. The most striking case was the formerly German lands in western Poland, where a Communist minister of "Regained Territories" controlled the distribution of thousands of square kilometers of territory and everything on them: houses, farmlands, industrial plants, extensive administrative structures, even churches. This was a source for corruption and clientelism with few parallels in history, but a similar situation applied in the border areas of Czechoslovakia. Here the Communist-controlled Ministry of Agriculture made properties avail-able that had been confiscated from Germans and Hungarians as well as from "traitors." In all, 1.5 million hectares of agricultural land were spread among 170,000 families and a further 200,000 hectares went into pasture cooperatives. The power to distribute property lay with the local national committees, and in former German areas, the chairs in 128 of 163 of these committees were held by Communists.[43] Communist Party members thus benefited disproportion-ately from the spoils, and even those non-Communist peasants who got land tended to favor the radical left at the election box.[44]

The Communist-controlled Czechoslovak Ministry of the Interior had over-seen the expulsion of Germans and their replacement with Slavs, making avail-able not only patronage but also participation in revolutionary politics. Accord-ing to the popular postwar nationalist discourse, whose tones in public media became shriller as one moved leftward on the political spectrum, the Slavic working people had grown tired of the niceties of bourgeois justice.

The categories of "traitor" and "German" quickly became indistinguishable; not only were all Germans traitors, but traitors—all those opposing or even criticizing "revolutionary" justice—were "German." When dissident Czech lib-erals or Catholic students criticized Communist violence against Germans or Magyars, they were called "collaborators" and were suspected of close ties to German ethnity. Perhaps they had a German spouse or grandfather. In early 1946, a scandal broke out in Brno when a Czech army major, who had spent the years 1939 to 1945 in a number of Nazi camps, including Auschwitz and Nor-dhausen, praised the Czech intelligentsia for supplying the inspiration and cad-res to the tiny Czech resistance against the Nazis. Workers, by contrast, had been seduced to work overtime for extra rations of beer and cigarettes. Adolf Hitler had even praised Brno workers for bolstering the war effort. The Brno Communist newspaper demanded the lecturer be fired—and he was (as a sup-posed "fascist"). Some 200 students staged a protest supporting their teacher, and in response, Communist organizations got thousands of workers onto the streets, supported by the police, who chanted "expel fascist students" and "professors to the mines."[45]

Such was the overheated political climate of postwar Czechoslovakia, the East European state with the strongest veneer of democracy and rule of law, up to the Communist seizure of power in February 1948.[46] That triumph was not simply the story of a small minority imposing its will on a majority. The policies with which Communists were associated, like denouncing and victimizing ethnic others, had become hugely popular by 1948.[47] Communist deputies got 40 percent of the vote in the Czech lands in the May 1946 elections, but the total was 75 percent in the Sudeten areas, where authorities were handing out German property. The policy fit the overall scheme of siding with the "Slavic world" after the 1938 Munich tragedy. The choice was not only political, it was civilizational. The Czechoslovak government's postwar program (the Košice program), passed in April 1945 by all postwar Czech and Slovak parties, from Catholics to Communists, stated that:

> We will review our relationship to German and Hungarian culture by revealing its reactionary elements in all fields. A Slavic orientation will be strengthened in our cultural policy. . . . Our Slavonic Institute will be restored, as a living political and cultural institution, with close ties with the cultural institutions of others Slavic peoples and states.[48]

According to a decree of the Czechoslovak president of the summer of 1945, only "Czechs, Slovaks and persons of other Slav nations" would enjoy the active and passive right to vote.[49] This was a new kind of state, never seen before, of Slavs and for Slavs. Racism had begotten racism, and presiding over the hysteria was the same president as in 1938, T. G. Masaryk's deputy, Edvard Beneš. His foreign minister was Masaryk's oldest son Jan, who never joined a party, but supported the people's democracy regime up to his death under mysterious circumstances in March 1948.[50]

The Germans of Poland and Czechoslovakia proved excellent targets for revolutionary justice because they were people whom even liberals like Beneš—who spoke repeatedly of the need to "liquidate" Czechoslovakia's Germans—had placed outside the law. But the judicial injustice could not stop at the Germans. The Nazi occupiers had also required the assistance of many Czechs, who, as the Communist daily *Rudé Právo* warned in May 1945, still shielded themselves beneath the (Czechoslovak) tricolor of red, white, and blue. Self-appointed people's courts emerged to "uncover and arrest" former servants of the occupier. Part of the job was accomplished by Communist-controlled "workers militias" and "revolutionary guards."[51]

The Soviet Union colluded in these efforts to make Eastern Europe national, and portrayed itself as a dynamic power that could extend a shield over its new allies. It claimed to have destroyed the most aggressive imperialist regime in history, and to offer protection that the interwar arrangements had not. After helping itself to (mostly Romanian) Bessarabia, the Soviet Union guaranteed Romania's hold on Transylvania and secured for Poland new territories in the west. When West Germany rearmed in the 1950s, Moscow stepped up to defend the region from resurgent German "imperialism." Communist propagandists drove the point home by reporting on the rallies of expellee organizations in West Germany that demanded the return of Silesia and the Sudetenland.[52]

The emerging East German state—from 1945 to 1949 the Soviet Zone of Occupation, then the German Democratic Republic (GDR)—seemed to face a dilemma of asserting a national identity in less than half a nation. Yet in fact, the competition with the West made it more German. East German Communists portrayed themselves as keepers of the German classical traditions in literature and music (Goethe, Schiller, Bach: all had been at home there) and appropriated elements of the Prussian heritage.[53] In 1949 they renamed the University of Berlin "Humboldt University" after the Prussian reformers Alexander and Wilhelm von Humboldt. Then followed the rediscovery of "progressive" generals Scharnhorst and Gneisenau (1956); a recrudescence of Prussia's military rituals (1962); and, under Erich Honecker, the gradual rehabilitation of Frederick II, partitioner of Poland (1971).[54] The link to the past was about more than Prussia, however; Saxony and Thuringia were the heartlands of early agitation among the German working class, providing the meeting places for foundational programs of the Marxist social democrats, as well as the birthplace of Walter Ulbricht, the East German Stalin.

The turn to German nationalism under the Soviet aegis also faced severe challenges. Most Germans remembered the Red Army as the perpetrator of crimes, especially rapes of women (more than 100,000 in Berlin alone). For decades, this subject would remain taboo. In the meantime, the Soviet client Party in Germany acted to protect what was deeply German from Western contamination. By the late 1950s, visitors from the West began portraying the GDR as the more German state: orderly, frugal, tidy, socially conservative, and despite all the posters celebrating it as a vanguard: traditional.[55] In West Germany and West Berlin, by contrast, the effects of Americanization were impossible to ignore in glitzy town centers dominated by shops and shopping.

Poland's Communists likewise had to devise strategies to seem good nationalists among a populatoin with deeply ambivalent feelings about Russia. They portrayed themselves as good Poles by arguing that only the Soviet Union could protect Poland, not only against Germany but also against the cultural leveling of the modern world. In Czechoslovakia and Yugoslavia, by contrast, Communists were happy to stand in the Soviet shadow, as deep pro-Russian sympathies made the Soviet model seem inviting—at least until the crises of 1948 (the rift between Tito and Stalin) and 1968 (the Soviet-led crushing of the Prague Spring).

Romania's rulers also stoked ethnic resentment, at first against Germany, and much later and more daringly, against Russia. In the early postwar years, Soviet and Romanian police arrested tens of thousands of suspected German "war criminals"—both men and women—and transported them for hard labor to the Soviet Union. When they returned four and five years later, many were physically broken. Romania's land reform of March 1945 targeted Germans as well as large landholders identified as fascists. Some 800,000 Romanian peasants received 1.5 million hectares of land. Among the main beneficiaries were war widows, army veterans, and refugees from Bessarabia and Bukovina who were resettled in southern Transylvania and the Banat, places where Romanian presence was weak.[56]

In Hungary, the social discrepancies had been enormous, and the revolutionary energies released in the countryside were more class-based than ethnic. Of about 4.5 million people in the agricultural sector, 3 million had no or very little land (less than 2.8 hectares). At the opposite end, 10,000 families controlled about half the country's arable land.[57] No one in the post-Horthy political landscape objected to a proposal put forth by the National Peasant's Party in January 1945 to abolish great estates and redistribute land. Supporters of the bill made clear that the Soviets strongly desired it, and within six weeks, all estates of more than 575 hectares had been expropriated. This revolution took place under a "non-Communist" government, though it was clear that the minority Communist forces were most in favor of it.

In all, 3.222 million hectares of Hungary's 8.3 million hectares of cultivable land were expropriated (38.8 percent). Much of it (1.348 million hectares) became state property. Though increasing the number of property owners, this reform frustrated the development of a market economy because the new farmers did not receive parcels large enough to be economically viable. The Communists knew that the small plots would produce low yields, but the point was to destroy the landholding class and to make peasants grateful supporters of

FIGURE 18.3. Farmers come to claim Junker's land (September 1945). *Source*: Erich Höhne, Erich Pohl (photographers); Bundesarchiv, Bild 183-32584-0002 / CC-BY-SA 3.0.

the radical left. The new landholders, unable to produce more than required for their own needs, came to see existing farmers as enemies (in Soviet jargon, as "kulaks"): exploiters and class enemies.[58]

Yet in the meantime, Hungarians—but also Poles and East Germans—were witnessing an event of epochal significance: the destruction of the premodern caste that had kept the region backward for centuries. Before 1945, two-thirds of the Hungarian population had lived in villages under the old neofeudal elite. The liberal István Bibo, otherwise a harsh critic of socialism, wrote that this was a moment of "liberation," the first time since the codification of serfdom in 1514 that the "rigid social system started to move, and move in the direction of greater freedom."[59]

Disagreements flared over the branding of innocent people as traitors and the seizures and improper measurements of land, but the Hungarian Parliament declared the process closed in May 1946.[60] Those who argued for legality stood in the way of progress, revealing themselves as traitors or saboteurs. Communists claimed that a new nonbourgeois reality was dawning and condemned those who favored any compensation for the dying class or precise measuring of parcels. In many cases, radical peasants declared that innocent farmers were fascists or reactionaries and carved up their lands illegally. Nothing and no one could prevent them from "taking more property than the land reform had called for."[61]

Transitions to Stalinism

As with the lightning strikes of Soviet armor that had obliterated whole German divisions in June 1944, there could be no hesitation in a revolution meant to destroy forever the economic power of reaction. Communist leaders spoke of positions seized on the road forward, and they urged party members on redistribution committees to achieve their tasks "without delay even at the risk of serious errors." If they stressed the need to cooperate with other parties, that was to avoid accusations of being the sole ones responsible for inevitable abuses. Yet the revolution was not "clean." Favoritism soon crept into the redistribution of properties taken from supposed fascists. Even in cities, Communist supporters used their connections to lay hold of Švab (i.e., ethnic German) properties.[62]

The early postwar years thus created pools of accomplices for the emerging socialist order, but the accomplices needed a new language to explain what they were doing. For millions of East Europeans, acceptable vocabulary no longer permitted defense of the Hungarian Švab, the Sudeten German, or the German Silesian. Like the bourgeoisie, these were incorrigible enemies, and those who stood up for their rights defined themselves as their allies. The Hungarian Smallholders, as the sole independent political force, attracted the support of the revolution's losers, and thus brought on themselves allegations of being traitors to both ethnicity and class, which seemed to be congenital ("ascribed") conditions.[63] Germans were fascists by birth, and so were people who insisted they had rights.

Well before Eastern Europe was Stalinized after 1948, avowedly irrefutable Stalinist ideas began creeping into speech, serving to expand the power of the radical left. The Soviet word "kulak" was used in Polish as way of taking concerns about security into the realm of ongoing transformations on the land; the kulak was depicted as an ally of the "speculators" who stole the people's property whenever vigilance waned.[64] Posters demanded harsh penalties for the enemy and simply rearranged images from the war featuring Red Army soldiers and fascists.

The political and social climate left non-Communists a limited vocabulary with which to oppose the revolution under way.[65] This was especially true of

Czechoslovakia, where "socialism" or "revolution" were words clearly owned by the Communists and the call of the hour. Many years later, from Swedish exile, the Communist Arnošt Kolman, a philosopher who returned to Prague in 1945 after decades in Moscow, looked back with regret on his role in Staliniz-ing Czech culture, but he could not suppress a certain pride. He had scuffled with the most resolute and skilled liberals and Catholics in the years after the war but had "emerged victorious from all these battles of words and felt like a matador."[66]

His facility in subduing opponents had little to do with his superior intellect or his opponents' inadequate rhetorical skill: he was arguing in the spirit of time and place. All justice was by, of, and for the "people" and the Communists em-bodied the people's will. By contrast, liberalism seemed an uncoordinated set of legalistic claims that fell far short of inspiring fanatic commitment. Only in the 1950s and only in the West did liberalism receive the boost of seeming to stand against "totalitarian rule."

Still, despite the rhetorical challenges, there were opponents who stood for democracy and rule of law and favored social reform. As late as the fall of 1947, Czech students voted overwhelmingly against Communist candidates. They supported greater social equality but condemned the methods used by the far left to achieve it. A particular concern was the wanton violence employed by Communists in areas with German populations. In February 1948, some of these students—about 2,000 in number—marched to the Castle in Prague to urge President Beneš to stand fast against the Communist militias wresting control of state institutions in a sudden coup d'état.[67] The Smallholders of Hungary and the Peasants Party in Poland campaigned against Communists in free and less-than-free elections, and they tried to act as political opposition in increas-ingly dangerous conditions. In Poland, an armed underground fought against the new regime into the early 1950s.

A hallmark of this time, extending beyond 1948, was a polychromatic mix of perspectives and motives, both in and outside the Communist Party, much in contrast to the more monotone political and cultural life of the postrevolu-tionary 1960s, called "developed socialism." If former fascists entered the Com-munist movement in the immediate postwar years, there were also many who embraced Communism for its internationalism and radical promises to break with racism and chauvinism. This was the case for some Jewish survivors of the Holocaust, but also for intellectuals viscerally opposed to nationalism. Exam-ples of the latter included the eminent Polish Marxist philosopher Leszek Kołakowski, who came from a free-thinking household and detested the provincialism of Polish National Democracy, or the poet Czesław Miłosz, who had pure contempt for the small-minded, obsessive, and backward-looking nationalist mainstream he had known in prewar Wilno and Warsaw.

Yet there were also liberals who opposed the emerging totalitarian system because they saw it as a continuation of the earlier one. Against the view that capitalism had produced fascism, these observers saw Communism growing out of fascism, taking advantage of character deformations and public demoralization that were legacies of the Nazi occupation. The Czech writer and psychoanalyst Bohuslav Brouk—a onetime surrealist and one of the few Czech intellectuals to oppose Communism publically after the war—wrote that "a great many people join the Communist Party and remain in it because of their defeatist, Protectorate mentality. They came to know in the occupation the sad fate of politically unorganized people in a state with only one party . . . sadly the German tyranny cultivated chicken-heartedness in the souls of many of our people."[68]

Critics pointed to a behavioral syndrome from the occupation days, when people came passively to adapt to demands of overwhelming force. Father František Hála of the Czechoslovak Catholic People's Party likewise confirmed the spread of a "Protectorate mentality," by which the Nazis had corroded the national spirit, especially of people willing to sell their convictions for selfish reasons. These men's Communist opponents of course felt that the moral high ground was theirs. Still, across the political spectrum—from President Beneš and the Catholic Pavel Tigrid, to the Communist intellectual Zdeněk Nejedlý—critics agreed that Czechs had absorbed elements of fascism ("fascism in ourselves"). Beneš said it would take a generation before Czechs were rid of it.[69]

* * *

Officially, the people's democractic system of the early postwar years was still pluralist, and Communists shared power in multiparty governments. Yet behind the scenes, they worked to subvert the independence of non-Communist parties. The subversion occurred at differing speeds, fastest in Bulgaria and Romania, slowest in Czechoslovakia, but everywhere the tendency was the same. In retrospect, the political scientist Hugh Seton-Watson distinguished three stages in this tightening of Soviet-style rule, focusing on the evolution of the coalition governments. First came genuine coalitions, and then bogus ones, and finally monolithic rule in which non-Communist parties remained parties in name only.

The prime method of subversion was to use Soviet power to identify and compromise non-Communist politicians who maintained independence. They were branded as traitors or reactionaries. Looking back on the consolidation of power in 1950, Communist leader Mátyás Rákosi described the gradual wearing down of non-Communist forces as "salami tactics." He had cut off leaders in the other parties as one cuts off slices of salami; his knife had two edges: one was corruption, the other fear. What gave Communists the power to wield this sharp instrument was their control of the police through ministries of the interior, and their ability to rely on the Soviet occupiers, who intimidated in ways not available to the local police but also possessed stores of goods to make life pleasant in the grim early postwar years.

The process began innocently enough, under the banners of national unity, democracy, and antifascism. In December 1944, representatives of Hungary's Social Democrats, National Peasants, Democratic Party, Communists, and trade unions had come together in Szeged to form the Hungarian National Independence Front. The Front demanded democratization of public life, radical land reform, and the nationalization of major industries and banks. All parties could agree on such changes because they were broadly popular. The new government signed an armistice in Moscow on January 20, 1945, fixing borders as they existed at the end of 1937 and thus ceding Transylvania. A first major controversy arose in November 1945, when Communists won only 17 percent of the vote in free elections, while the Smallholders got 57 percent.[70] For an outsider, the results made sense: Hungary's population was overwhelmingly rural, and voters had chosen a peasant party.

But the Communist leadership did not content itself with dry sociological analysis: it embodied the people's will, whether in countryside or city.[71] Though at first speechless, Rákosi soon said reactionaries inside the Smallholders' Party were making that party seditiously oppose the workers' parties. Offering no evidence, he asserted that these enemies were acting under the "influence of the cartels, the banks and big capital." In his Leninist mindset of Kto-Kovo (which roughly translates as "who will eliminate the other"), the majority of population had thus fallen under the sway of the enemy.[72] For the time being, his party was too small to resist the hostile forces by themelves, and therefore it formed a "leftist bloc" in order to cooperate with the Social Democrats and National Peasants, both of which had already been whittled to conformity by salami tactics.

Hungary's Communists also employed their trump cards of intimidation. In late 1945 the Smallholder leadership wanted to advance the right-leaning Dezső Sulyok as their candidate for premier. Sulyok, however, gave a speech

attacking the Hungarian Soviet Republic of 1919, and leaders were told to nomi-
nate centrist Ferenc Nagy instead. They acquiesced, much to Sulyok's embit-
terment.[73] After him, other independent Smallholder leaders were cut down
by a steady drumbeat. In early 1947, Communist Interior Minister László Rajk
alleged that a conspiracy had formed among Smallholder deputies with General Secretary Béla Kovács at its head. In response, Smallholder leaders said they
were willing to suspend the parliamentary immunity of fourteen deputies, but
they would not sacrifice Kovács. The NKVD broke the impasse by simply arresting Kovács in February. Soviet diplomatic representative Georgii Pushkin
explained to Ferenc Nagy that he had repeatedly advised Kovács to purge the
party of reactionary elements, but this advice was not always heeded.[74] Kovács
wound up in Siberia and did not return until 1956.

In March 1947, the government was reshuffled, with three pliant Smallholders receiving ministerial posts while Ferenc Nagy remained head of government. During a trip he was taking to Switzerland in May, charges emerged—
based on Kovács's supposed confession—that Nagy was planning a violent
seizure of power. He received a phone call advising him not to return to Budapest, lest some misfortune occur on the drive back. Dozens of Smallholder
colleagues made telephone calls begging him to resign, supposedly in order to
save the party. Then Nagy learned that Communist security services had taken
his five-year-old son Laci into custody and would not release him until he submitted his resignation. Nagy then relented, Laci was allowed to leave Hungary,
and the Nagy family was granted asylum in the United States.

Lajos Dinnyés, a man weighed down by gambling debts, succeeded Nagy,
and the country prepared for elections in August 1947. After officials struck
hundreds of thousands from the voting lists as "fascists" and stuffed the ballot
boxes, the Communists managed to inch ahead of the Smallholders, 22.3 percent
to 15.4 percent. Nevertheless, they preferred to keep Smallholder politicians as
zombie premiers deep into the Stalinist period. By 1949, the Communists had
dissolved the other independent parties and forced a merger with the Social
Democrats—who had loyally done their bidding for three years.[75]

In Romania, the Communist position was strong from the start, even though
the party had only 1,000 members. In June 1944, as the situation at the front
deteriorated, and just before a shattering Soviet offensive, Romanian opposition parties—National Peasants (Iuliu Maniu), Liberals, Social Democrats, and
Communists—formed a National Democratic Bloc. Its plan was to leave the
Axis. On August 23, King Michael invited Ion Antonescu and foreign minister
Mihai Antonescu for a talk and had both arrested. He established a new

government under Constantin Sănătescu, an army general who had supported the coup. The new ministers came from several parties. On September 12, Romania signed an armistice with the Soviet Union and agreed to pay it reparations of 300 million dollars over six years.[76]

An Allied Control Commission under de facto Soviet control took responsibility for internal security and shifted figures within the government, making clear the benefits of belonging to the Communist Party. As a result, that party's membership rolls expanded by the tens of thousands. But the August 1944 coup was also popular, as it ended an alliance through which Romania had lost a third of its troops.[77]

Initially the government consisted of a four-party bloc, yet by October it was showing signs of strain, and thus a National Democratic Front was launched, comprising the Communists, Social Democrats, the Ploughmen's Front, the Union of Patriots, and the trade unions. Even before the war had ended, the Ploughmen's Front, though independent in the interwar period, had fallen under the direction of the Communists, who were the guiding force in the National Democratic Front. The Communists, although few in number, could rally workers for demonstrations in Bucharest, and their ability to shape events in the capital would prove decisive, given that Antonescu's dictatorship had broken up local organizations of the parties and left the countryside a political tabula rasa.[78] From the start, the Soviets observed developments from the background, and reminiscent of the Nazi legation during the war (but much more forcefully), administered "levers" in order to direct affairs in ways they found opportune.[79]

As in Bulgaria and Hungary, Romania's state administration was largely intact, and the country saw little purging at first. This was true even of the state security forces, where as late as June 1946, some 40 percent of the 8,500 officers had been appointed before 1944. The army in Romania was also less subject to purging than elsewhere. However, a radical shift occurred on December 30, 1947, with the simultaneous abolition of the monarchy and proclamation of a Romanian People's Republic. In August 1948, a new department of state security based on Soviet models replaced the old civil (internal) intelligence, bolstered with 70,000 troops, and inaugurated a fresh wave of political repression.[80]

The Bulgarian path to Communist control was smoother. The regime switched alliances a few weeks after its Romanian counterpart, and a grouping of parties that had worked together in the underground constituted a "Fatherland Front." Within the Front, the Communists held a dominant position, and in elections of November 1945 they won an overwhelming victory (the

Fatherland Front was the only option on the ballot).[81] The following year, Kimon Georgiev of the right-wing Zveno movement, who had engineered the transfer of power in 1944, was succeeded as premier by Georgi Dimitrov, head of the Bulgarian Communist Party. In Hannah Arendt's words, Dimitrov enjoyed "admiration of the whole world" for having stood up to Hermann Göring in the 1933 Reichstag fire trial in Leipzig. People used to say there was "one man left in Germany and he is Bulgarian." But now he cowered before Stalin, having survived the purge years in Moscow as Comintern General Secretary.[82] As in Romania, Communist domination of major urban centers was key to their growing control of national politics, and like everywhere, the Communists insisted on holding the interior and justice portfolios.

Dimitrov's task was to whittle away political opposition, and his first target was the sizable agrarian movement. In April 1945, its first postwar leader—G. M. Dimitrov (no relation)—was accused of spying for the British and fled the country to avoid arrest. In May, the Agrarians (BANU) divided, one faction supporting the Communists thanks to inducements and threats, and the other larger one, under Nikola Petkov (BANU-Petkov), pursuing an independent course. At the same time, the Communists were using extralegal means to split the country's Socialists.[83]

Petkov had opposed Bulgaria's alliance with Germany and had co-founded the Fatherland Front after escaping from an internment camp.[84] But he watched with disgust as the Front became a launching pad for political opportunism and a school for defiance of law. Beyond political manipulation, the government was conducting a campaign against the middle classes as supposed "war collaborators," and seizing property, including private savings, and even personal libraries. He therefore broke with the Front, demanded the return of civil liberties, and criticized the Communists for incompetence. Unemployment stood above 20 percent.[85]

In October 1946, Petkov led opposition forces and secured 101 seats against the Fatherland Front's 364. This was also a moral victory, given that fifteen socialist party leaders and thirty-five members of the Agrarian Union Presidium were languishing in prisons and concentration camps, having been arrested in the weeks leading up to the vote. The Agrarian Trifon Kunev had been incarcerated for calling the Bulgarian government "political and economic dreamers." During the war, he was among the politicians who had helped rescue Bulgaria's Jews.[86]

The Communists warned Petkov to desist. To his retort: "I am not afraid of a bullet" Communist interior Minister Yugov replied: "we shall not waste a bullet on you!" Perhaps the departure of Soviet troops from Bulgaria, a result of the peace treaty with the Allies signed in Paris in February 1947, had made Petkov optimistic. Yet in June, against all precedent, police arrested Petkov in the chambers of parliament and put him on trial for "attempting to restore fascism." Refused counsel and unable to summon witnesses, Petkov was sentenced to death, hanged, and then denied Christian burial. The Central Committee of Bulgaria's Trade Unions issued a statement read over Radio Sofia: "To a dog, a dog's death!" Before Petkov's arrest, numerous politicians and army officers were tortured to produce evidence against him. This act of terror devastated the opposition, and in the weeks that followed, the Communists disbanded all remaining parties except for the branch of the Agrarians loyal to them.[87]

The unity of the Communists versus the disunity of all other forces was symptomatic for the region. Like Petkov's wing of BANU, the Smallholders in Hungary and the Polish People's Party had come to represent opposition as such and were split among constituencies with differing preferences. Some felt that agricultural laborers were "not ready for individual farming," while others argued that peasants had been prepared for collective farming, because the large estates had operated on a collective system. Hungarian Smallholder leader Zoltán Tildy advocated the preservation of medium-sized holdings, but also a system of small landownership. The differences so confused Marxist observers that they sensed a plot: a desire to sabotage land reform as such.[88]

By contrast, the Communists were not only certain of their goal but were also consistent in their argumentation and disciplined in achieving it. As Marxists, they expected that change would unfold before their eyes. And as Leninists, they did what was necessary to make that happen, even if that meant employing tools of repression that seemed taken from the arsenal of fascist regimes. In its protest against the Petkov trial, the US government could not help noting parallels to the Reichstag fire trial in Nazi Germany in 1933, at which the Communist Dimitrov had so valiantly defended himself. "In that earlier trial," the statement read, "a Bulgarian defendant evoked world-wide admiration for his courageous defiance of the Nazi bully who participated in his prosecution. Today, that defendant has assumed another role, and it is now the courage of another Bulgarian whose steadfast opposition to the forces of oppression has evoked world-wide admiration."[89] One similarity less remarked on was this: that both fascist and Communist regimes cared little for the evident parallels in their methods before a "court of world opinion," because both thought they were reshaping history in a way that would make that court irrelevant, like some long-buried stratum of early human settlement so obscure as to have never been remembered.

Poland also had its own version of salami tactics. But given that a guerrilla war raged in the early postwar years, with state militia and the NKVD hunting down anti-Communist fighters as well as a Ukrainian insurgency, the slicing away of opponents was far more lethal. The unity government consisted of Communists (called from 1942 to 1948 the "Polish Workers' Party") and the parties they dominated—the Social Democrats, the "Democrats," and the People's Party—as well as one party they did not dominate, the Polish Peasants' Party (PSL). Its leader, Stanisław Mikołajczyk, a leader of peasant strikes in the 1930s, had belonged to the émigré London Government and unlike the great majority of his colleagues agreed to return home in 1945, though he knew that Communists would enjoy advantages thanks to Soviet tutelage.

From the start, the PSL was accused of disloyalty, yet in fact it was caught in a vise. Because it had agreed to work in a government with the Communists, the right branded the PSL as traitorous; yet because it stood up for Polish independence, the left accused it of collaboration with the pro-independence underground. As a result, its politicians fell victim to assassination by the radical nationalists of the underground, as well as to arrest and torture by the Communist-controlled security police. In one case, the PSL was charged with causing the underground to murder its own general secretary, Bolesław Ściborek. In routine vilifications, forces on the left projected the PSL as an assemblage of traitors not meriting protection of the law. The final act played out in October 1947, when Mikołajczyk, fearing for his life, was smuggled out of Warsaw in a truck by the US embassy, then taken onto a ship in Gdynia disguised as a US diplomat. The case shows how a determined minority holding vital administrative and police power can ground its rule in a hostile society: in the summer of 1946, some three-quarters of Polish voters had cast ballots against the government in a referendum, but that fact was simply suppressed.[90] Future elections would be "organized" to prevent negative votes.

* * *

As they infiltrated state offices, Communist organizations were also growing behind the scenes. If for some freshly enrolled members, conversion to the new faith was driven by conviction and idealism, for others, the move mixed enthusiasm for revolutionary social change with the knowledge that becoming Communist was a wise career move. Numbers of new cadres rose by the thousands, expanding the organization in Romania from 1,000 to 800,000 in four years.[91] In Czechoslovakia, the Communist Party grew from 47,000 in 1945 to 2.67 million by October 1948; and in Hungary, it swelled from 2,000 to 884,000 in May 1948.[92] The new members then inundated the state administration. In Hungary, the civil service had grown during the war, necessitating some reduction afterward and opening the road to a political purge, costing 60,000 their jobs. Special commissions consisting of loyal trade union representatives and fellow travelers used questionnaires to root out supposed collaborators. Then the replacements streamed in to build the new, people's democratic state.

Yugoslav Communists, not needing Soviet aid to control their country, dispensed with the two first stages of Stalinization (the "genuine" and "bogus" coalitions) and proceeded to full-scale Soviet-style rule in 1945. They "self-Sovietized" without the benefit of Soviet advisors, thus laying foundations for a severe conflict three years later with Stalin, for whom dependency was more important than loyalty. Romania had passed to stage two in a bogus coalition by March 1945, presided over by Petru Groza, a pliable prewar figure. Despite the struggle of courageous leaders like Nikola Petkov, postwar Bulgaria likewise never featured a genuine coalition government. Hungary sacrificed effective plurality in 1946, and Poland did so in 1947.

The slowest transformation occurred in Czechoslovakia, where politics seemed relatively open and democratic until the coup of February 1948. There were four political parties with independent organizations and leaders (National Socialists, People's (Catholic) Party, Social Democrats, and Communists), free elections, and civil rights that were respected. The president was Tomáš G. Masaryk's collaborator Edvard Beneš, who seemed to symbolize continuity with prewar democratic norms. Actually, as we have seen, the rule of law began eroding as early as 1945, when one class of human beings—ethnic Germans—was stripped of rights, and separate semi-legal courts were created to try "war criminals." Many Czechs had tired of "Western-style" democracy, and in May 1946, they made the Communists the strongest party with 40 percent of the vote. From that time, the Czech Stalinist Klement Gottwald held the position of prime minister, and his party occupied ministries of education, industry, propaganda, as well as the interior. But in the fall of 1947, comrades from elsewhere in Europe asked the Czech number two, Rudolf Slánský, what his party was thinking, still sharing a government with bourgeois politicians.

By that time, the Leninist parties of Eastern Europe, with their relentless and often ruthless quest for power, were revealing themselves as organizations the likes of which people in the region had never seen. Their members believed that their acts were beyond questioning, and they routinely employed violence. Soviet backing meant their supporters could take with impunity more land than was due to them and make threats with no fear of reprisals. When opponents attempted to exercise rights of free association, the party sent in toughs to break heads and furniture. In June 1947, the Hungarian independent Dezső Sulyok finally got permission to organize his "Freedom Party," and planned to assemble activists in Szeged. Yet when he did, "workers" appeared, using rubber hoses and chairs to break up the meeting. Police then completed the work, arresting Freedom Party speakers for "inciting disorder."[93]

The Communists became experts in applying pressure to several points at once: whether in the street, at mass demonstrations, or through threatening phone calls. Recruiting accomplices for noisy demonstrations or breaking heads was easy in a time of shortages and deprivation, and opponents were worn down step by step. Every demand from the far left was supposedly conclusive, cutting off one final reactionary, one last "anti-democratic" policy, one ultimate problem that supposedly bothered the Soviets. (Simply alluding to Soviet displeasure was often enough to get results.) Yet each last demand proved a prelude to further demands. The revolution proceeded at different speeds in different places, and the observer of any one moment might be deceived by temporary moderation.

But the revolution did not simply proceed, and it was not made only by Communists. Millions of East Europeans also took part, discovering as well as making opportunities for themselves. The dreams many realized were real: careers in advertising, in civil engineering, crop science, early childcare, the chemical industry, and dozens of other tasks required by a modern society. For that is what Stalinism intended to create. Communist apparatchiks not only suppressed opposition: they also worked obsessively on "campaigns" to conquer literacy, infant mortality, and alcoholism; they paved roads and inoculated against disease, and each year sent roving medical units around the countryside to x-ray people for tuberculosis. At the same time, state militia (the new word in Poland for "police") took villagers into custody who had withheld produce or failed to turn in weapons. As late as 1950, the underground was still carrying out death sentences on state functionaries.[94] Such were the realities of Poland in early Stalinism, but this mix of enlightenment, terror, and the ageless rhythms of village life was found everywhere in the region from the Baltic to the Adriatic.

The top leaders who oversaw and led this transformation did so under conditions they inherited. They had not chosen the societies they wanted to revolutionize, and the turn in 1944/1945 from proletarian internationalism to Pan-Slavism and ethnic nationalism was repugnant to many of them. Still, as Leninists, they obeyed directives. We had only this people, one old Polish Communist told me about the Poles, and they were Catholic and anti-Communist. One thing they could not anticipate or know was how far they could push the peoples of Eastern Europe, including their many collaborators, toward the socialist future, without triggering an explosion.

CHAPTER 19

The Cold War and Stalinism

The Cold War was a new kind of war. It never became "hot," that is, the opposing powers never turned weapons on each other or tried to occupy the other's territory. The occupying had been accomplished in 1944/1945, when armies from the West and East took up positions on two sides of a divide running through the center of Europe, roughly from Lübeck to Trieste, a divide that Winston Churchill soon called an "iron curtain." Over the decades, proxy wars raged from Vietnam and Korea to Angola and Nicaragua, but the two superpowers held back from assaulting each other, recognizing that wars are uncontrollable and that this one would be fought with nuclear weapons.

But beyond this revolutionary self-limiting dynamic, the Cold War was unusual for two other reasons. First, there is no consensus on who started it, and second, no one can agree on when exactly it began. In Poland, it grew out of conflicts that stretched into the war years and became a civil war between anti- and pro-Communist forces. The escalation there was gradual, as was the de-escalation, stretching into the early 1950s, when the final resistance fighters were either arrested or buried their weapons. In Romania and Hungary, Communists slowly usurped power from 1944, with no moment signaling a clear break; politics gradually dropped into a cold freeze through simple administrative measures and desultory terror. In East Germany and Poland, Soviet authorities, operating in the background, permitted no free elections, and occasionally made a "reactionary" politician disappear. Still, multiparty systems continued to exist everywhere into 1948. Until February of that year, Czech Communists shared power with a foreign minister (Jan Masaryk) and president (Edvard Beneš), whom they considered to be imperialists. Only at some point in 1949 could foreign observers agree that Churchill's Iron Curtain indeed separated two worlds, between which the only visible communication was mutual vilification.

In retrospect, the antagonism appears to have crossed a boundary from quantity to quality some time in 1947. Policymakers began seeing their diverse quarrels with the other camp as a coordinated plan of aggression and conquest by that camp. In early 1947, the Truman administration concluded that Soviet failure to permit free elections in Poland and its marginalizing of opposition in Romania, Hungary, East Germany, and Bulgaria reflected an intention to impose Communism throughout Eastern Europe, and from there to expand westward.[1] Secretary of State George Marshall had returned deeply troubled from a trip to Moscow in early 1947, during which Stalin seemed gleeful at the prospect of economic collapse in France and Italy. Such an event, Marshall knew, would have dire consequences for the US economy.[2] Washington therefore instituted countermeasures. In a speech before Congress on March 12, 1947, President Truman proclaimed the United States would "support free peoples who are resisting attempted subjugation by armed minorities or by outside pressures," and three months, later Marshall announced a massive plan of financial assistance meant to help Europe recover from the war. The aid was to be available to Western and Eastern Europe but also to the Soviet Union.

Once Marshall's plan was announced and the support offered, the Soviet Union feared a threat to its hold on Eastern Europe.[3] Marshall expected the Europeans to use aid to purchase American products, and observers on the left—not exclusively Communists—feared that the opening of Europe to American businesses would reinforce dependence on American capital. Therefore, Stalin compelled the states of East Central Europe to reject the Marshall Plan in the summer of 1947, causing Czechoslovak Foreign Minister Jan Masaryk—son of the state's founder—to lament "we are nothing but vassals!"[4] But the deeper truth was that the emerging Soviet superpower was determined not to become a vassal of the United States.

In a September 1947 address to the United Nations, Soviet Foreign Minister Andrei Vyshinskii alleged that the United States wanted to place European countries under its "economic and political control." His country now arranged self-defense. That same month, the Soviet party summoned a meeting of Europe's Communist parties at Szklarska Poręba, a mountain resort in Polish Silesia, where they formed a Communist Information Bureau—the Cominform—with the goal of coordinating the work of all "progressive" forces. Stalin's chief enforcer of ideological purity, Andrei Zhdanov, said the world had divided into two "camps," one favoring and one opposing peace. There would be no room in the center.

This message took some hammering in. The nominal host, Poland's Władysław Gomułka, thought the meeting's deliberations would be informal, and he spoke of the need for an "exchange of experiences between the Communist Parties." As de facto leader of a country hostile to Communism, he was keen to renounce the strands of internationalism in the party dating back to Rosa

Luxemburg, which had unnecessarily condemned the Polish revolutionaries to outsider status. Poland's Communists had to think of "the nation" and its needs. They had come to power in the course of a national liberation struggle by driving out the Germans, and had not needed to violently unseat the old state apparatus. Poland's path to socialism was thus different from that of Russia. It could tolerate a multi-party system, as long as the Communists' leading role was not questioned. Gomułka worried in particular that a Soviet-style collectivization of farms would sidetrack Poland, provoking needless hostility. He and his comrades were also pained by the fact that Stalin had recently—in 1938—disbanded and destroyed the Polish Communist Party, killing its top leaders. From its refounding in 1943, it was called the "Polish Workers' Party."[5]

In abandoning cooperation with a supposedly declining capitalist world, Stalin was not following a preconceived plan, but rather rejecting relations with the West that had not afforded his country the security he sought.[6] He was also responding to signs from Eastern Europe that initial support for Moscow as a liberator was shifting to resentment over repression and continued occupation. At the same time, esteem for the United States appeared to be growing among East Europeans. For a Marxist-Leninist, such facts could be explained only by a hostile imperialist conspiracy spreading lies about the motherland of socialism.[7]

The demonization went both ways, however, and gradually made conciliation impossible. To many in the West, the Soviet Union seemed a dictatorship like Nazi Germany that gradually wore away its opponents. As we have seen in Chapter 18, the Petkov trial in Bulgaria had caused the US government to note parallels with Nazi judicial practice, especially given the uncanny fact that the Bulgarian leader Dimitrov had valiantly defied a Nazi court in 1933. In September 1947, three British parties agreed that Petkov's judicial murder showed a resemblance "between Communist dictators like Dimitrov and Fascist dictators like Hitler," but they went further, insisting there was a lesson for their own time, with echoes of the Munich disaster. If Dimitrov and Stalin were Hitlers, then "there must be no appeasement of Communism. We must never again invite aggression by being weak. We must be resolute in our defense of freedom and the rule of law."[8]

The Soviet leaders were just as adamant: for them, Western "imperialism" signaled the resurgence of the dark forces they thought had been subdued in 1945. At the Cominform's founding, they urged the radical Yugoslav faction to publically humiliate French and Italian Communists for sharing government with imperialist forces, and Czechoslovak Communists understood they were implicated as well. At that time, they were sharing a coalition with Catholics, Czech National Socialists, and Social Democrats, and were gearing for parliamentary elections in 1948. On returning to Prague, Party General Secretary Rudolf Slánský informed his Politburo that the time had come for a decisive act to place the country on a direct path to socialism. That implied a rupture with existing policy: the previous year, party leader Gottwald had still been speaking of a "Czechoslovak road to socialism," without a dictatorship of the proletariat or violence on the Soviet model.[9]

In February 1948, Czech and Slovak Communists used their huge cadre base and control of the military and police to stage a rapid seizure of power. Though backed by overwhelming force, the coup was bloodless. They took advantage of an embarrassing mistake by the National Socialist and Catholic politicians, who were tiring of the sundry illegalities of their Communist coalition partners. In November 1947, Communist authorities in Prague had staged a purge of the police force. Believing the population would support them, the Catholic and National Socialist ministers resigned in protest on February 21, thinking that the president would now dissolve the government and immediately call for elections. But they miscalculated: the Communists and their Social Democratic allies still had a majority of seats in the government, and simply replaced the ministers who had resigned with politicians of their own choosing. Then they summoned party cells across the country to form "action committees" that would purge every institution in public life.

The leaders got more than they bargained for. Within a few days, mostly young and impatient Communists had ousted directors and managers from newspapers, state administration, sporting clubs, political parties, schools, and cultural institutions such as theaters. Then they began firing people the next level down. The purge was so thorough that party chief Gottwald had to restrain students, who believed that they had advanced into a new stage of history. Charles University was expecting guests from across Europe to celebrate its six-hundredth anniversary, and the young radicals had just unseated the rector, causing several Western universities to withdraw their participation and spoiling the event's propaganda value. Gottwald got on the phone to the student leader in charge and asked whether he and his comrades were thinking with their heads or "their behinds." He did not object to the purges that students were carrying out in their own ranks. Opposition leaders were simply arrested, but the rest of the student body was required to appear before "verification commissions," which expelled more than one-fifth of them. These "class enemies"

FIGURE 19.1. People's Militia on Charles Bridge, Prague (February 1948).
Source: CTK/Alamy Stock Photo.

were usually sent to do heavy labor, often in mines, and thus were erased from
Czechoslovak cultural, economic, and political life.[10]

A final stage now occurred in salami tactics. Having sliced off independent peasant, nationalist, and Catholic politicians, the Communists devoured
their Social democratic partners whole. This was a regional trend. In the summer and fall of 1948, these more moderate Marxist parties were compelled to
form "unity" parties with the Communists. The result in Hungary was the
Hungarian Workers Party and in Poland the Polish United Workers Party.
In East Germany, the Soviets had forced the merger of Communists and
Social Democrats in April 1946, producing the Socialist Unity Party of Germany. In all these cases, the joint cadre base of the new party was much larger
than when the Communists stood alone; the challenge was now to subject
Social Democrats to Leninist discipline.[11] Czechoslovakia's Communists dis-
pensed with the pretense of a new name, however, and after absorbing the

smaller Social Democratic party, they remained the Communist Party of Czechoslovakia.

Those doubting the gravity of the transformation in Eastern Europe had their illusions shattered in May 1948, when a simmering disagreement between the Soviets and their fanatic Yugoslav allies burst onto the front pages of the world's newspapers. The Cominform urged "healthy elements" in the Yugoslav party to overthrow Tito. With much chutzpa, the Stalinist mouthpiece accused him of creating a "bureaucratic regime" and squashing democracy, and "brutally repressing" the "slightest criticism." Supposedly Tito wanted to return Yugoslavia to bourgeois capitalism.[12] However, what really bothered the Soviet side was not treachery, but the failure to consult Stalin at every turn.

Especially bothersome for Moscow were Yugoslav plans to form a Balkan federation involving Bulgaria and Albania. Stalin feared that Tito might lead an independent power bloc in southeastern Europe. But there were numerous other problems as well, like Yugoslav objections to rapes by Red Army soldiers in Serbia in 1944, or complaints about spies that the Soviets had smuggled into Yugoslav organizations. According to Milovan Djilas, a Soviet film crew helping shoot the socialist realist *In the Mountains of Yugoslavia* recruited agents by luring Yugoslavs—including Tito's personal bodyguard—into orgies. When reports reached Tito, he was furious, proclaiming that a "spy network is something we will not tolerate."[13]

The international split soon had domestic consequences for Communists throughout Eastern Europe. While Tito hunted and arrested members of his own party loyal to Stalin, allegations arose that trusted cadres in Poland, Bulgaria, and Hungary had intended to follow the Yugoslav example of "national" Communism. In May 1948, Stalin ordered secret police chief Lavrentiy Beria to ferret out Titoists—national Communists—from the East European parties.[14] In Poland, the search led quickly to Party General Secretary Gomułka, who had been chiding his comrades for being out of touch with Poland's national sentiments; he even heretically claimed that Social Democrats had shown much greater wisdom than they did in the national question. But now the gloves were off, and in September, he was forced to resign his post after being pilloried by his comrades. His arrest followed in 1951.

Gomułka's case reveals the logic of the early purging when targets were "home Communists," men and women like him who had remained on native soil during the war years. Their inter-party opponents—for example, the new leader Bolesław Bierut—had spent the war under careful surveillance in Moscow, and their loyalty was beyond question. Even less reliable were Communists who had spent the war in Western exile, and supposedly come into contact with Western intelligence services. In early 1949, Soviet media identified a further class of enemy: "rootless cosmopolitans," longhand for Jews. Stalin, suspicious of the potential for subversion of certain ethnic groups, had come to think of Jews as disloyal. His obsessions culminated in the murder of thirteen members of the Jewish antifascist committee (including five Yiddish poets) in 1952, and then the fabrication of a "doctor's plot" against him supposedly funded by Zionists.

Although no one among Hungary's leaders had called for a separate path to socialism, there were dangerous rivalries at the top, and Hungary's leaders played on Soviet concerns and suspicions in order to prevail, but also to survive this very dangerous time.[15] In 1948, a clique including Rákosi, Ernő Gerő, Mihály Farkas, and József Revai decided to move against László Rajk, minister of the interior. The issue was not dedication to Stalinist-style socialism.[16] No one had outdone Rajk in securing single-party hegemony. In the summer of 1946, he had shuttered 1,500 organizations, including youth and sporting clubs as well as community service organizations and trade unions, because of their supposed reactionary spirit.[17] He had organized a show trial of Cardinal József Mindszenty and mastered techniques of repression against the Smallholder party and the Catholic Church. Yet tall and good-looking, he was also immensely popular in the party, having proved his mettle both as political commissar in the Spanish Civil War and as resistance leader in Hungary after his escape from French internment in 1941. Jealous and (with the Soviet trials of the 1930s in mind) also apprehensive, Rákosi's clique offered Rajk to the Soviets as a Hungarian Titoist.

The Soviets assented. As a top leader who had spent time in the West, Rajk could be portrayed as head of a vast conspiracy, with supposed networks running across the European continent and into other socialist countries. In May 1949, a day after lunching with Rákosi, Rajk was arrested and placed on trial for treason. In a refrain that would become familiar in the trials that followed here and elsewhere, he was accused of having entered the service of Western intelligence agencies in France. The supposed head of the spy ring was the American Noel Field, actually a Soviet agent who worked in Geneva for the Unitarian Universalist Service Committee where he assisted émigrés in need and got to know scores of Communists. Field was lured to Prague and arrested in 1949.

The Soviet show trials of the 1930s were now replayed with East European casts. Rajk voiced absurd charges against himself: that he had been an informant for the Hungarian police since 1931 and delivered fellow Communist students to police; that he had denounced Communists in Spain; and that during the war, he had aided the Gestapo in destroying the Hungarian resistance movement. That was the point at which Noel Field had supposedly recruited him. In addition, Rajk confessed to becoming a spy for Tito while on vacation in Yugoslavia in 1947. Other co-defendants, until recently the pride of the Communist movement, admitted to having secretly admired fascism from their earliest days.

Despite weeks of beatings and sleep deprivation, Rajk had held out, until threats were made to harm his family. He concluded that if the party was unanimously against him, despite his subjective certainty of his innocence, then he must die. Before going to the gallows with his "accomplices" on October 15, 1949, he called out: "Long live Stalin! Long live Rákosi!" According to witness accounts, one of the onlookers, Rajk's successor as Minister of the Interior, vomited repeatedly. He had been a friend to Rajk and his family, but also the cold

FIGURE 19.2. László Rajk clapping beneath portrait of Rákosi (1947).
Source: Pál Berkó (photographer), Foto Fortepan / CC-BY-SA 3.0.

and bullying interrogator.[18] This was János Kádár, who himself was later arrested and confessed to false charges in a show trial.

The murderous parody of justice now traveled to Bulgaria, where the party sacrificed Traicho Kostov, who like Rajk had been a high-ranking Communist. It reached a hysterical culmination in November 1952, when the Czech leadership put fourteen top cadres, including former general secretary Rudolf Slánský, on trial. He and ten supposed co-conspirators were explicitly identified as "of Jewish background," reflecting Stalin's belief that Jews represented a dark international conspiracy. Eleven of the accused were executed, and their ashes then spread on icy roads outside Prague by the Czech security police. As was the case in the Soviet Union, the trial was scripted in advance, and Soviet advisors corrected the final versions.

* * *

Explanations of why the show trials took their precise form have to be speculative because documents have yet to emerge revealing the deeper motivations of their initiators in the Kremlin. What is clear is that the hunt for nationalists stemmed from a belief that Eastern Europe could be controlled only if no citizen of a people's democracy, especially no party member, could be certain of his or her survival, let alone security. Seen in those terms, the trials were the most determined act of imperialist rule in history. Tito himself, one target of the attacks, said in 1952 that the heart of Europe had become a Soviet glacis, with countries like Poland, Romania, and Hungary transformed into the "most ordinary colonies."[19]

But there are also more conventional reasons that explain why Stalin gained collaborators for his blood purges. Party leaders believed the emerging bloc was making breakthroughs of historic dimensions, creating urban and industrial worlds as well as literate populations where none had previously existed, pointing the way forward for humankind. But they also knew of innumerable shortcomings for which ideology provided neither explanations nor excuses. According to Bolshevik interpretations of Marxism, the revolution was supposed to usher in the millennium: a transformed reality without the tensions or divisions of capitalist society. Because such a society evidently did not yet exist, there had to be scapegoats. And because these scapegoats had to bear blame for unending insufficiencies—continued rationing, food shortages, and inflation—they had to be sought at the highest levels.[20]

A loyal socialist citizen might easily imagine that purge victims, for example Czech Communist leaders like Ota Šling or Rudolf Slánský, could have given orders to cause severe damage to state and economy, making the continued success of the regime seem all the more remarkable, indeed, historically inevitable. Šling was a volunteer in Spain and head of the Brno region, who spent his wartime exile in London; Slánský a leader of the central apparatus from the 1930s with enormous influence and respect.[21] As far as records allow us to judge, few in the party cadre doubted that the charges against supposedly hidden enemies like Slánský had substance.[22] That is why the trauma would be so great for party intellectuals in 1956, when Stalin's crimes were suddenly exposed. But belief always mingled with fear, and those with doubts kept them secret while assuming that other party members—even closest friends—believed the trials were genuine.[23]

Workers, however, even Communists, often derided the absurdity of trials of people celebrated as demi-gods only a year or two before. Shortly after the former general secretary's arrest, party veterans in the Kladno areas said they could not believe that Slánský, "long-serving" co-fighter with Klement Gottwald, was capable of betrayal. Slánský was simply the "lighting rod who is blamed for all mistakes and scarcities while the guilty lot stay clean." Similarly, radical left-wing workers in the slums of Budapest who had welcomed assaults on capitalists and the Catholic Church found the charges against Rajk "very difficult to believe." The Czech author Heda Margolius Kovály heard people openly deriding the Slánský trial while she recuperated from the flu: "Who knows what they did to them? The whole thing stinks to high heaven!" A nurse recalled that in her village, "when a thief stole a goose, he denied he had done it to the end, even if he had been caught red-handed."[24]

Yet the trials helped stabilize Stalinism, at least for the time being. Whether they generated anger against scapegoats and whether the allegations were absurd or not, "show" trials were a running spectacle impossible to ignore, distracting from everyday concerns; whatever their deeper rationale, they constituted the most recent chapter in the age-old story of the high and mighty crashing to earth. By the early 1950s, the high and mighty were also widely despised: and so the party leaders, by sacrificing Slánský and other top functionaries, both appeased as well as terrorized the population.[25]

Among the allegations made, "Zionism" was the most outrageous, also the most useful, far superior to Titoism, which had involved only linear connections to the Balkans. It outdid even supposed plots of the CIA because it was simultaneously a device for provoking local ethnic nationalism as well as a fantasy of worldwide conspiracy involving agents in every place where Jews lived.[26] Among the party cadre, anti-Zionism had the utility of showing that no excuse for diluting loyalty to Soviet Union could be tolerated, not even a residual loyalty among Jews to the idea of a Jewish homeland, even after Jews had been targeted by the crime that led to the coining of the word "genocide." Zionism, a particular loyalty to one nation, now became symbolic of a universal crime: "cosmopolitanism." Ironically, this turn to anti-Semitism signaled a desperate attempt to use Europe's ultimate form of nationalist scapegoating to tame native nationalism. The Soviet Union had become the leader of a chauvinist international.

The anti-Zionist campaign became possible when Israel, a state whose founding Stalin had supported, proved unwilling to unreservedly support Soviet positions.[27] It struck most cruelly in Czechoslovakia because this was the last place where the trials were staged, and it represented the apotheosis of their logic. Because Jews were a relatively small group in the party and party leadership, they were also a group toward whom the violence could be narrowly targeted. By contrast, in Hungary or Poland, where there were more Jews in the party cadre, anti-Zionism would have led to a debilitating party purge, endangering the lives of top leaders.[28] Polish, East German, and Romanian leaders did purge top officials as "national Communists" and cosmopolitans but did not subject them to the death penalty. Why is not clear.

At the same time, friends of the Soviet Union were portrayed as the best patriots of their own countries, true nationalists. The anticosmopolitanism in Czechoslovakia coincided with a campaign of slander against T. G. Masaryk, whose policies were vilified as harmful to the ethnic nation (*protinárodní*) as well as the laboring people (*protilidové*). Masaryk, though an ethnic nationalist, had come to prominence among other things as a foe of anti-Semitism. Yet the leadership claimed it was not reviving that old heritage. In December 1952, Klement Gottwald said that "the struggle against Zionism has nothing in common with anti-Semitism." Anti-Semitism was a kind of "barbaric racism" associated with "American 'supermen,'" whereas Anti-Zionism was a defense against "American espionage." Masaryks "bourgeois" nationalism had been incapable of defending Czechs against such dangers because it lacked a healthy working-class instinct. Anti-Zionism was thus portrayed as an advanced form of class consciousness, and only two defendants in the Slánský trial were of working-class background, Karel Švab and Josef Frank. Supposedly their stay in Nazi concentration camps had contaminated them because it had brought them into contact with Jews.[29] In Hungary, János Kádár reported that "among the members of the spy network uncovered up to now there is not a single worker or working peasant."[30]

The specter of cosmopolitanism gave urgent cause for all party members, especially Jews, to examine their consciences, but if pressed too far, it could be counterproductive. The council of the Ministry of Education in Czechoslovakia stopped functioning in the early 1950s out of fears and accusations among its leading members, and the editor of the main Communist newspaper, Gustav Bareš, spent his days waiting for a knock on the door and writing denunciations of colleagues. In 1952, a special party committee had to travel to Moscow to halt the destructive self-purging of Czech students there, supposedly the party's future. On April 19, 1951, at the Hungarian Party Congress, Mátyás Rákosi criticized the work of Interior Minister Sándor Zöld—successor to Rajk and Kádár. Fearing arrest, the following day, Zöld killed his wife, mother, eight-year old son, and six-year old daughter, and then himself.[31] The more intimate knowledge one had of the Stalinist apparatus, the greater the hysteria.

Waves of purging swept the party's ranks. In Hungary, 300,000 of 1.1 million members were removed by January 1950, with former Social Democrats and trade union officials as special targets. In Poland from April 1949 to September 1953, 140,000 members were excluded, and a further 96,000 struck from party lists, and the number of party members declined from 1,443,000 (1948) to 1,298,000 (1954).[32]

* * *

While the party visited revolutionary violence on itself in the "Monster Trials" of top functionaries, tens of thousands of other East Europeans—some Communist, many not—were disappearing in prison camps for supposed political crimes.[33] The first to be targeted were those who appeared to oppose party doctrine by virtue of their alien social background, above all the middle classes, but also economically successful "bourgeois peasants," the kulaks. These people and their sons and daughters—allegedly contaminated by class background in an almost racial sense—disappeared from public institutions like universities, the police, the army, and the state administration.

Such purging of "bourgeois" elements was a relatively simple task: authorities got the appropriate "cadre file," checked class origin, and the matter was settled. Likewise, it was easy to forbid plays or movies, proscribe exhibitions of "decadent" art, close churches and monasteries, arrest priests or expunge ideologically "harmful" books from libraries. More vexing was the continued cultural domination by old elites of emerging socialist cities of Budapest, Prague, and Kraków. The upper and middle classes no longer had chauffeurs or servants, and their high salaries were a thing of the past, but they remained in their large prewar apartments and favorite spots in the coffee houses. Their poisonous attitude of social superiority had yet to be properly challenged. Thus, following Soviet examples, in the early 1950s, party functionaries expelled thousands of families identified as "bourgeois" from dwellings in Prague and Budapest and resettled them in the countryside (Operation B).[34]

Such actions belonged to a larger process of replacing old elites with new ones. Not only apartments but also positions in the state apparatus were suddenly available to functionaries, members of the secret police, shock workers, and "heroes of labor." Of all the parties, the East German proved most skilled in using social recruitment to build a politically loyal elite. It did so by requiring that worker and peasant cadres admitted to university also belonged to the party. The emerging socialist elite was thus compelled by party discipline to carry out party tasks; at the same time, they knew that they owed their elevated status—reflected in professional responsibility, access to quality goods and services, apartments and weekend houses, automobiles, and advanced education for their children—to the party. Their life histories proved that the party's line was correct. It had produced a new society administered by workers and peasants like themselves, and that involved heightened duties as well as privileges.

Everywhere Communists and their socialist allies revolutionized education systems, universalizing access to basic schooling (usually to grade 10) and opening opportunities for social groups previously denied entry to higher education. Before the war, fewer than 3 percent of university students came from manual labor backgrounds; by 1955, that figure was usually more than 50 percent and sometimes higher. This occurred within a general expansion of higher education capacity. A similar dynamic of increased opportunity took place in the expanded working class, especially in agricultural societies like Poland or Hungary. In Poland, the number of people working in industry rose from 1.8 million to 2.8 million from 1949 to 1955; in Hungary, workers in heavy industry went from 261,440 in 1949 to 405,028 in 1953.[35]

The socialist regime had thus created its own governing class, but the men and women of that class defied the regime's expectations. Part of the reason is that it attempted to transform recalcitrant realities in a very short time: new cities take decades to build, but Stalinism lasted only five or six years in Eastern Europe. It created massive construction sites in East Berlin and Warsaw, or new steel cities like Hungary's Sztálinváros and Poland's Nowa Huta with thousands of residents, but no proper restaurants or cinemas, let alone shops. It had launched a program in central Warsaw to close down private grocers, yet the regime's own alternatives were few and far between. Residents had to walk more than a mile for a loaf of bread, and when they reached the shop, they had to stand in line. Queuing became ubiquitous, robbing energy for doing much else. Young workers returned to hostels after the day's work, where they lived five to a room, and denied other outlets, they consumed prodigious amounts of alcohol and pursued other activities the party found destructive, like gambling and exploring new sexual freedoms.

And when the new apartment blocks they had worked on were finally ready, workers stood back and watched as managers and bosses moved into the larger flats, in better locations (never the ground floor) and got them more quickly than anyone else. The governing class was in fact state and party bureaucrats, and those with connections to them, and they were almost always men.[36]

The socialist state employed a rhetoric of equality between the sexes, and it went much further than any other regime in history in opening positions to females and encouraging enrollment of women in higher education.[37] Now women could work in places previously off limits—mines for instance, or heavy industry, and their overall numbers rose to well over half of the work force, far above the averages common in Western societies.[38] Many women experienced a thrill of advance, first from the countryside, then into entirely new branches; in Poland, a large percentage of those participating in socialist work competition—winners got cash bonuses and apartments—were women.[39] Because they were recruited to medical and law schools, women also entered professions in larger numbers than before, and by the late 1960s, a third of judges in Poland were women.[40]

But the basic idea of gendered work did not disappear. Party planners happily opened jobs to women—in fact, they insisted that women work outside the home—but then paid them lower wages, assuming the male "breadwinner" would provide the main income. In the workplace, in theory women could work at virtually any position, but resistance of the male crews restricted them to those that paid less. In the Hungarian oil industry, for instance, after women became truck drivers, their male colleagues made sure they were fired or transferred. In Poland, party reporters noted that when conflicts arose between men and women, the women were demoted to lower-paying positions. Sometimes, the wives of miners colluded in efforts to keep women out of positions below ground![41] And at home, women retained traditional burdens of child-rearing, cooking, and cleaning. To all that was added the new "occupation" of standing in line. In the early years of state socialism, childcare existed, but like much else was in a state of formation: crèches had to be built, and staff found and trained. And they were almost entirely female.

It was not unheard of for women to assume leading positions in the state and party bureaucracy, but they were exceptions, during and after Stalinism. All of East Central Europe featured only one prominent woman Communist leader, Romania's Ana Pauker, and she was purged in 1952; like Gomułka, she had urged moderation in the building of socialism, and opposed forced collectivization.[42]

Just as Czechoslovakia was an outlier in interwar Eastern Europe as the sole surviving democracy, from start to end Poland stood apart in how the population experienced Stalinism. Poles endured the massive social and cultural dislocation that was general to a region in the throes of a modernizing revolution, but they did not suffer as severely from *political* repression as did people elsewhere in the bloc. In September 1948, the old Comintern stalwart Bolesław Bierut succeeded Władysław Gomułka as the party's secretary-general but did not press rapid collectivization, nor thoroughly purge universities: even in law and history faculties.[43] Plans to expel "conservative" families from Kraków were drawn up but never carried out. Though scores of priests were arrested, several subjected to show trials, and Primate Stefan Cardinal Wyszyński placed under arrest at a vacated monastery, the Polish Catholic Church continued with its structures largely intact, and even carried on teaching catechism in state schools.[44] The Catholic University in Lublin had to scale down instruction but remained open. Much of what the state attempted to achieve, like removing crosses from classrooms or introducing civil wedding ceremonies, were measures any secularizing state would undertake, and internal correspondence shows that the party felt under pressure from politically active clergy in a society that considered Communism an alien and hostile force.[45]

The party appeared to compromise with Polish history and culture, printing classics of literature, rebuilding destroyed cities according to original blueprints, and supporting archeological digs to reveal "Polish" claims on territory. Even at the height of totalitarian rule, Polish Communists respected the peculiarities of Polish society and adapted their policies to its contours. (If given a different society to rule, the old Communist implied in conversation with me, they might have behaved differently.)

Polish leaders' restraint fit into a general policy of a "mild" revolution in their country. Polish Stalinism mixed different ingredients, both repelling and involving hundreds of thousands of Poles. For many peasants, workers, and women, these were years of upward mobility and new chances, though for many others, this was also a time of fear and brutalization. Prison camps filled with workers and peasants guilty of "economic crimes," like failure to deliver a few kilos of corn, killing a pig that was slightly underweight, hoarding, or trading on the black market. It is impossible to reduce this time to a single dynamic. Interviews with Polish Communists from the post-Stalinist years reveal that many never got over the shame and grief felt at the destruction of the Polish Party in 1938, and perhaps the solidarity of victimhood under Stalin before the war caused them to reject the demands of Stalin after the war to sacrifice Władysław Gomułka, the Polish Rajk.

The Stalinist World

Stalinism did more than strike fear into the hearts of enemies or craft political loyalty among new elites. More centrally, it transformed lived environments to shape human beings who would feel, see, think, and listen in new ways. It was a cultural revolution that revised the images, sounds, and thoughts in which humans lived their lives. That implied a radical change in how the creators of culture understood their tasks. In 1946, Stalin's heir apparent, Andrei Zhdanov, launched a campaign against both subjectivism and objectivism, as well as modernism and formalism in the arts. That took care of virtually everything except "realism." Invoking the writings of Lenin, he proclaimed that no art could be apolitical, and that literature should become "a part of the general cause of the proletariat, 'a small cog and a small screw' in the social democratic mechanism, one and indivisible—a mechanism set in motion by the entire conscious vanguard of the whole working class."[46]

Socialist realism was a method rather than a style, but because it was didactic, it reverted to positivist models from the nineteenth century. In 1947 and 1948, East European artists touring the Soviet Union were taken aback to discover that contemporary painting and stage sets replicated forms—like academicism—that had been current two generations earlier. What they heard in symphony halls was reminiscent of "program music" popular in the 1890s. Yet within a few years, these artists found themselves spearheading the introduction of such pieces into their own cultural landscapes.[47] How was that possible for a group whose raison d'être seemed to require artistic freedom?

The issue was more about philosophy and politics, and some would say opportunism, than the implanting of a new sensitivity: just as their countries' fates became subordinate to the avant garde political (and world historical) might of the Soviet Union, so had the fates of artists became subordinate to the demands of the *new* avant garde, the working class, toward which social elites felt a certain deference. The important question of any work was how it served to create revolutionary consciousness among workers and among society as a whole. As we have seen, a widespread philosophical temperament made adaptation to new forms seem necessary to many intellectuals. Still, they knew little about the workers they felt history had called on them to serve. Therefore, some actually treated workers as consultants. In 1950, the East German composer Ernst Hermann Meyer tried out his ideas for a musical critique of capitalism on copper miners.[48]

Socialist realism conforms to caricatures about it. The plots of novels and films became predictable, even in those that were most artistically serious. The heroine of the eminent East German author Christa Wolf's *Divided Heaven*—written well after Stalin's death and showing the continuing pull of the genre in East Germany—chooses the socialism of East Berlin over her lover in West Berlin. But it was not her doing alone: the Berlin Wall serves as a plot device resolving political and personal dilemmas that had become inseparable. Yet the protagonist, a healthy, optimistic proletarian, would have left her (bourgeois, indifferent) lover in any case, as she feels the "pull of a great historical movement." East Germany is the better Germany; what she finds in West Berlin is the absence of any principle or idea worth struggling for, and instead aimless, easy living. Polish filmmaker Andrzej Wajda's early film *A Generation* likewise mixes young love and socialism, this time amid the anti-Nazi underground in occupied Warsaw. A shiftless young man finds purpose: he falls for the young People's army resistance fighter Dorota. He loves her because she sees in him not a miscreant, but a noble proletarian. The Home Army is portrayed as a nest of collaborators.[49]

The writers and directors practicing socialist realism ranged from mediocrities to the most gifted and daring. Poets like Vítězslav Nezval, Konstanty Ildefons Gałczyński, and Johannes R. Becher, famous as expressionist poets of the far left before the war, now became tame adulators of Stalin and the Soviet Union. At the height of the movement in the early 1950s, all artistic tension found simple resolution in the creation of Soviet-style socialism. When the Italian realist film *The Bicycle Thief* was shown to Hungarian audiences in 1950, the Ministry of Culture required that a new ending be added. In the original, the hero (a worker) lost his bicycle—his sole means of subsistence—by theft. Therefore, he tried to steal one himself. Apprehended and beaten, he ultimately

FIGURE 19.3. Polish youth marching on socialist-realist style boulevard (1952).
Source: W. Sławny (photographer), Bohdan Garliński, *Architektura Polska 1950–1951*
(Warsaw, 1953). Via Wikimedia Commons.

walks into a bleak future, alone and embittered. Yet now a newsreel was added showing a mass meeting of the Italian Communist Party, at which its leader, Palmiro Togliatti, gives a rousing address. Instead of disappearing into un- certainity, the worker seems to be walking into the arms of the Communist Party.[50]

These are blatant examples of politics intruding on art, but no sphere was untouched. Modernist impulses were expunged from music and architecture as well, and composers both serious and popular devoted their energies to prais- ing Stalin as well as Soviet heroes of labor. Musical scores, apartment blocks, sculptures: all became monuments to the imaginary new socialist person. The realism was thus not "real" but reduced people to the images required by ideol- ogy.[51] Viewers were meant to feel smaller than life: surrounded and controlled by heroic and muscular figures in paintings and sculptures, or the imposing col- umns, entry ways, and other "neoclassical" forms that adorned the new social- ist housing that went up in central Warsaw or East Berlin (though not the old Habsburg metropolises of Prague or Budapest).

Because the profit motive had been abolished, workers worked for high ideals of creating socialism and making a better future for humanity. For inspiration, the party selected the most productive miners or bricklayers as hero workers, featured on giant posters, in film, and in newspapers, men and women whose enthusiasm for socialism was supposed to be contagious. These men and women had achieved productivity that amounted to many times the expected norm. For example, the East German Adolf Hennecke managed to mine 24.4 cubic meters of hard coal on October 13, 1948, 387 percent of the daily norm. He, like the model Soviet miner Stakhanov, worked for the good of themselves by working for the good of all. Whether this kind of labor competition actually contributed significantly to economic growth is another question. Much time was lost just preparing these famous shifts. What even the party press admitted was that most workers deeply resented people like Hennecke for making them work more. After his historic act, Hennecke said his workmates treated him as if he were "air." In a sense, what the hero workers produced was solidarity of the work crews against them.[52] The long-term lesson for the party was that labor competition worked dependably when it was tied to material reward for the individual worker.[53]

Though embedded in a romanticism of profound feeling, the hero laborers battled against all odds for *plan* fulfillment, thus also representing the regime's aspiration to deal scientifically with the challenges of creating a modern world. Everything of importance could be expressed in numbers and thus controlled. By counting how many bricks a worker laid or how many tons of coal a miner extracted from a pit, the state established work norms. This was not revolutionary. Henry Ford had precisely measured the time needed for each worker in a production line to complete a specific limited task. What was new was applying this principle to the economy as a whole, not simply to auto making but to every imaginable productive activity, including culture and education. Even students and professors were expected to subordinate their tasks—pages read or written—to the demands of the central state plan.

That plan was not totalitarian in the sense that central state authorities simply fashioned numbers out of whole cloth and then imposed them on unwilling workers. Instead, the huge state bureaucracy established broad guidelines favoring heavy industry, and then consulted enterprise managers who in turn consulted production units down to the factory floor. Next, preliminary plans made their way back up the hierarchy and were coordinated and finalized at the top.[54] Once formulated, however, the Plan became the highest law, and failure to fulfill it could lead to charges of sabotage.

This system had two great advantages. First, it did away with the uncertainty of capitalism. Gone were unemployment, sudden and painful price increases, and the unavailability of basic food items for the broad masses of the population. People did not need to worry about the next day or year. Just as employment was considered a basic social right, so were housing, health care, public transportation, and education, all of which had a place in the plan and—in theory and often in practice—were made available at heavily subsidized prices. Education or health care were free. In most states in the region, the prices of basic items of consumption, like bread or milk, were established at nominal prices in the 1950s and did not change much over the decades.

All branches of the economy were interrelated, so that a person studying architecture or Russian literature could be sure that employment awaited him or her on graduation. The plan reflected philosophical underpinnings: just as socialism could not tolerate unemployment or persons without health care, so, too, it could not abide consumer products that did not serve the needs of the working class. Construction involved the building of modest apartments, not villas; the clothing industry no longer produced furs but rather the durable coats and jackets "needed" by workers. And so on. The system has been aptly called "dictatorship over needs."[55]

The second advantage was the system's power to catapult societies into a kind of modernity. Until the Chinese economic revolution of the 1980s, the growth rates achieved in Soviet-type societies from the 1930s to the 1960s were unmatched. "Command" economies had unique abilities to pool resources of capital and labor and rapidly inject them into projects of enormous scale, like steel or chemical industries that had never existed before. Or they could quickly rebuild city centers that were little more than rubble in 1945. Though in our day, centrally planned economies are associated with economic dysfunctionality because of underperformance, in the early decades, they liberated economic resources in ways that market-based economies could not, forcing breakthroughs that were unthinkable under conditions of capitalist division of labor.

This revolutionary transformation required but also produced a transformation of society. Beginning in the late 1940s, thousands of peasants streamed into towns that were being stamped out of the ground. Institutions like universities, high schools, centrally located cafes and restaurants, clubs, and theaters—all preserves of the middle and upper classes—were now overwhelmed by the "governing classes," and themselves were transformed. The East German liberal student leader, Wolfgang Natonek, whose father was Jewish, publically criticized authorities for the favoritism. "In the Nazi days one needed an Aryan grandmother to be admitted to university; now one needs a prolet-Aryan." In 1949, Natonek was sentenced by a Soviet military tribunal to 25 years hard labor.[56]

Because they were the "governing class," proletarian critics by contrast felt unassailable in a way that intellectuals and even functionaries did not. Most confident were the least skilled, the concierges, technically supervisors of apartment buildings, but actually stool pigeons who caused even top party officials to shiver for fear of saying something wrong, or even littering.[57] The radical Communists in Czechoslovakia created commitees with heavy worker representation to judge the quality of intellectuals' work. If they found a certain film or theater performance too "pessimistic" or excessively "realistic," or even too "satirical" they might keep a theater director—even a famous one—from producing more plays. In every country, workers or peasants' children who were tiny minorities at universities now came to dominate them, as well as the party and trade union organizations that had ultimate say on staffing and curriculum.[58] Until the intitial enthusiasm wore off, hierarchies were reversed, with students and staff instructing professors. The new reality was also reflected in wages. For the first time in history, manual laborers earned more than white-collar workers.[59]

This is not to say that workers escaped the pervasive terror of these years. They tended to limit protest to grumbling or refusal to provide acclamation; there were occasional strikes, but much more often, feigned sickness, theft of "people's" property, and work slowdowns. Workers knew when and where to criticize, usually among family friends, or at the local pub, especially when liquor flowed freely. Soon the party recruited agents to listen in, desperately concerned to throttle labor unrest before it could erupt. Yet officials also took for granted that "occasional offhand complaints" would be made about the regime's shortcomings and deficiencies. Indeed, griping had a therapeutic effect, allowing people to make peace with the new political realties after letting off steam.[60]

Still, the long-term trend was unmistakable. By the early 1960s, one could see a new intelligentsia take charge of state bureaucracies, with a new vernacular; sense of humor; and tastes in music, food, and sport. It became not only possible but also in good taste for intellectuals to use slang or dialect in public presentations or in seminars; workers no longer felt overawed by "high society" if they went out to dinner or to inexpensive productions of classical drama or music, which themselves were adapted to mass tastes. Because it was planned, socialism was didactic and usually about enlightenment.

* * *

A prime method of funding the heavy capital investments for new industries and achieving fantastic growth in Stalin's Soviet Union was strict control of the countryside. In early capitalism, rural areas had provided labor in abundance but not foodstuffs; their prices were regulated by the market. Stalinism solved this problem of economic development by forcing peasants into collective farms and abolishing the market in the countryside, and then making food cheap.

The collectivization drives that swept Eastern Europe in the early 1950s figured among the most evident signs of Soviet imperial rule, because before 1948, even the radical left had not envisioned them. For instance, Czechoslovak Communists had not even discussed what seemed a foreign and inappropriate model for their more advanced circumstances.[61] Still, in the early postwar years, the regimes had laid foundations for this Stalinist policy by taking land away from large landholders and wealthier peasants. Although much was given to poorer and "ethnically correct" peasants, some land had gone into special funds controlled by the state, forming a prime resource for collective farms established after 1948.[62] In the early period, the authorities also disrupted market practices by compelling peasants to deliver set quantities of produce at controlled prices, yet for the most part, authorities endeavored to attract poorer peasants to socialism.

The Soviet model from the early 1930s involved using privately held land to create state farms (*Sovkhozy*) and collectives (*Kolkhozy*). On the former, peasants worked for a wage as state employees, whereas on the latter, they theoretically farmed and shared rewards in common, while selling produce to the state at fixed low prices.

Those who joined collective farms in Eastern Europe were expected to make "contributions" of land, livestock, machinery, buildings, and in the GDR even money. What was different from the Soviet Union was that land still belonged to the peasants because membership was officially voluntary. Initially, workers were credited in "work units" or "labor days," but later as a way of keeping them in countryside, workers received guaranteed wages. Collective farms in Czechoslovakia featured an appointed leadership board that was supposed to decide what to produce, but that was actually based on state plan directives. Farmers could keep some animals, usually poultry, as well as a cow or goat for their own use. They also got to keep house plots of up to a quarter hectare for personal use. All the states in the region permitted peasants to produce on private plots as well, Hungary the most openly, the others tacitly.[63]

The first years of this new system posed severe challenges for farmers working together for the first time. The change in Czechoslovakia was particularly radical, with 45 percent of agricultural land coming under collective management within two years of the 1948 revolution. The result was a drop in production and a return to the rationing of the early postwar years. In Hungary, the crisis was such that an estimated 70 percent of production came from the small private plots in the 1950s.[64] Other causes of low output included the drain of farm hands to industry and extensive soil degradation. There were also widespread reports of abuse on collective farms, involving such things as unjust distribution of income in favor of people with connections.[65]

Behind the myth of farmers voluntarily joining collective farms lay tremendous political pressure. According to the party line, socialist transformation required collectivization, which would enhance the welfare of all, anchoring the people's control of the countryside and destroying "reaction." Along with transferring land to collective use, authorities closed down church schools to shatter traditional social structures. Hold-outs were vilified as "kulaks," supposed remnants of the capitalist class who wanted to exploit the labor of their neighbors. Yet because large farms had been destroyed by this time, the number of hectares needed to qualify as kulak was low, depending on how poor the soil was, varying from ten in Bulgaria to twenty in East Germany. Ironically, the land reforms of the early postwar years had given many peasants a first taste of land ownership and had created opposition, which the party now had to break.[66]

Though the word "kulak" was a Soviet import, much less violence was used in East Central European collectivization than in the Soviet Union. Some kulaks were arrested or forcibly expelled, but there was less recourse to deportations, and none to mass starvation.[67] More often, opponents were simply subjected to steady harassment. Ostensible kulaks had to deliver more produce than others and were taxed at special rates. According to a Czechoslovak law, district authorities had the latitude to increase the land tax for particular peasants by 30 percent. In Hungary, officials summoned private farmers to council offices, or they appeared in person at gunpoint, refusing to leave until holdouts signed up for the collective farm. State radio broadcasted trials of kulaks in order to intimidate peasants still holding on to property.[68] There were violent responses to such pressures, especially in Bulgaria, Yugoslavia, and Romania, but many joined collective farms simply to have peace.

After Stalin's death, victimization was greatly reduced, and within a few years, kulaks were permitted to join collectives and in some cases become chairpersons. In most of Eastern Europe, collectivization was just getting started. By 1953, only Bulgaria had collectivized even half of its arable land; Czechoslovakia followed with 40 percent, but elsewhere, the total did not exceed a quarter.[69] Economic planners discovered the diminished returns of naked force: it drove farmers, especially young ones, into cities. Hungary witnessed a steady decrease in the percentage of total employment in the rural sector, from 52 percent in 1949 to 27 percent in 1970, and 8.5 percent in 1995. Between 1950 and 1970, one million wage earners (or 20–25 percent of employed workers) left the agricultural sector. Especially alarming was the departure of able-bodied workers in a time when the population as a whole was aging.[70]

Authorities thus gravitated toward economic incentives rather than administrative pressure, and as a sign of a new time—after Stalin's death—exhibited less ideological zeal. For example, they no longer required that all land be farmed collectively. They also promised consumer goods, such as radios and refrigerators, to those who joined collective farms and increased the number of animals that could be kept on household plots. From 1957, Czechoslovak collective farm members and their families were included in pensions and health insurance. With time, many rural inhabitants grew to appreciate the new lifestyle. They did not have to worry about hunger because of adverse weather, and they had regular working hours as well as steady incomes. By the late 1950s, the committees of collective farms were dominated by middle and large farmers, who enjoyed substantial authority among peasants.[71]

* * *

The extraordinary growth rates in the economy as a whole slowed during the 1960s. The key to success during high Stalinism had been expansive growth: adding units of production, for example, underemployed farm labor, or untapped land and natural resources. But now came challenges of intensive growth, of making each unit of production more effective. On this challenge, the socialist regimes ultimately foundered. Stalinism's extremism was the strongest argument in its favor but was also its undoing. On one hand, its achievements could be reached only by the extraordinary sacrifice of a system built on compulsion; yet on the other, compulsion cannot be sustained without engendering a response from the object to be transformed: the peoples of East Central Europe with their specific histories and national traditions.

As a form of Marxism, Stalinism recognized the economy as a base for all value; science ensured it would be rationally planned and modern. But because the model for the modern economy was Soviet, there was little concern for the special strengths and weaknesses of each East European society. Everywhere, socialism was supposed to look the same, emphasizing heavy industry over every other kind of production, and within heavy industry, the military branches were favored over those that made life enjoyable. Factories produced tanks and artillery rather than automobiles and refrigerators.[72]

This prejudice generated hardship. The housing sector suffered particular neglect, as people were told to postpone their desires to enjoy stable, comfortable home lives. Larger houses and apartments were subdivided, and often several families shared washing and cooking facilities. The situation was so dire that young couples rejoiced after receiving one room in a two-room apartment that they would share with another family.[73]

But the situation was made even worse by the inbuilt dysfunctions of the central planning system and its inability to anticipate changes in taste and style or to encourage the production of goods of high quality. For all its shortcomings, the market provides an effective means of communicating information to producers about changing tastes, and also for encouraging the diversification of supply. A state official working out a five-year plan was unable to anticipate which shades of women's shoes would seem popular in one, two, or three years' time, or the amount of several varieties of cheese that would be consumed in a particular suburb of a particular city. He or she could not anticipate the demand for seats in restaurants in out-of-the-way towns like Radom or Olomouc. Officials made rough estimates of need, and that is what East Europeans got: two types of cheese, three shades of shoe, one type of café with a standard menu offering the same choices everywhere in the country. And in that café, half the seats were permanently "reserved" because finding wait staff was difficult in the underproductive socialist economy (and waiters came to take bribes for the few available seats).

Often products fashioned in the socialist economy were durable, but their quality could not be guaranteed, because the state plan was tabulated in tons or in raw numbers, and defects were not noticed until after mass production had commenced. This system lacked the incentives as well the punishments of a market economy. Enterprises that produced popular items did not benefit. Beyond the system of labor competition discussed above, and limited experiments with wage differentiation that would come later, neither their workers nor their managers received special rewards, let alone dividends, for special achievements. The recognition tended to be of a moral sort, a medal one might affix to one's jacket, for being an "activist of the five-year plan," or member of an "outstanding youth brigade," or a "meritorious veterinarian." And those who slacked off faced weak penalties, especially after Stalin died. They lived at the same modest standard as virtually everyone else. Workers could not lose their jobs because the state guaranteed employment, and plants, even the least productive, could not be closed. An unsuccessful manager might be rotated elsewhere.

This system of limited rewards and punishments had few incentives for improvement. The pattern of production was more or less frozen, and unless a high level functionary intervened, the same product would spin off the assembly line without alteration.[74] During the 1950s, spectacular gains were made in the West in efficient nonsolid fuels (like natural gas), while the Soviet Bloc maintained a mix of coal, oil, and electric current in the same proportions, at most increasing their respective volumes. New products, like plastics, were neglected. When the East Bloc attempted to ape Western trends in economic or scientific innovation, it appeared to be "catching up"—a strange fact for societies supposedly showing humanity its future.

Much tinkering occurred over the decades as central authorities racked their brains to introduce incentives into the command economy, but these basic flaws, present at the beginning, were not overcome. Questions of efficiency were inseparable from those of quality. One could not use raw materials efficiently when the finished materials produced did not function properly. Before water or heat reached housing units, it had already been reduced by up to 30 percent due to poorly constructed boilers—boilers that began rusting before they were purchased.[75]

One little-recognized shortcoming of these early days was the wasting of resources. A case in point was the region's major source of energy, lignite (brown coal), plentifully abundant in Czechoslovakia, East Germany, and Poland. Though it is the least efficient and most polluting form of coal, lignite was used in staggering amounts to heat apartment buildings and fuel industry. The Plan left no other option; imports were too expensive. The socialist economy produced thermostats, but not pretriggered pressure regulators, and therefore thermostats quickly became defective. To regulate temperature, people would open and close windows. That too, was a partial solution, because the pollution generated by this wasteful form of energy was making the air unbreathable. Similarly, attempts to make the population use water more efficiently—for example, by increasing prices for use—failed, because the planned economy could not produce meters with which to measure the flow of water into individual housing units.

Because this inflexible and politically driven system was imported from the Soviet Union, many East Europeans saw its disadvantages in national terms. As a great power, the Soviet Union had imposed an inefficient system on its colonial empire for its own benefit. Heavy industry was favored because it could produce the arms to make the "democratic community" more secure, and reckless shifting of resources smothered local industries that had been sources of national pride. Hungary had but one iron ore mine, and no high-grade coal whatsoever, yet it now became a miniature steel-producing Soviet Union. Though it had been the breadbasket of the dual monarchy, it now had to import grain and was forced to destroy some of the best wine-producing areas in Europe to open up stone quarries. Peasants were given a liquid "wine" made from corncobs to drink.[76]

Aggravating disdain over such economic imperialism was the fact that the Soviet Union had expropriated massive amounts of material from Eastern Europe, beginning in 1944, and lasting in some cases until 1956. Hungary was again a case in point. In the early postwar years, Soviet forces had begun dismantling factories as "German," and shipping them back home. The Soviets then negotiated a reparations bill to be paid by Hungary that topped 300 million dollars that was still being paid off in the 1950s. Likewise, in Romania, Bulgaria, and East Germany, 15–22 percent of national income went to reparations.[77] Even the Poles had to pay reparations indirectly, as the Soviets dismantled and shipped formerly German industrial plant that was now on Polish territory.

Poles had perhaps the greatest reason for feeling aggrieved. Their country had lost territories in the east to the Soviet Union, despite being at war with Nazi Germany from 1939, when the Soviets were Germany's allies. After the war, the Soviets requisitioned "German" coal from Silesia, the territory Poland got as compensation. Perhaps Hungarians, whose government had been a willing participant in the war on the Soviet Union, had less to complain about. The point, however, is that in both places, people soon felt their countries were helpless colonies. To this day, economists have not figured out the precise nature of trade relations in this period, yet lacking information, East Europeans assumed that the terms of trade were stacked against them. This trend persisted after the Stalin years, when in fact the Soviets were supplying Eastern Europe with energy at well below world market prices. In a context of suppression of information and evident mendacity, people assumed the worst.

What they knew for a fact was bad enough. Workers worked long hours in shifts that extended into the night for wages that declined in real terms and bought little that made "life more beautiful" (a popular propaganda slogan). For most, life had become more brutal. Few could feel secure, let alone, relax. The early 1950s were years of intensified nationalization of small businesses, like repair shops, barbers, and cafes; of the constant purging of "bourgeois" elements from public institutions; of compulsory adoption of propaganda in art and education; of violent resettlements of thousands who had the misfortune of living in border areas and were considered politically unreliable.[78] These were stories that preceded, ran parallel with, and outlasted the party's own war against itself.

By early 1953, rumors about unrest, especially among the working classes, began circulating in the secret police. Reports of imminent dangers became more urgent in March 1953, when with no warning—he had not been ill—Radio Moscow announced that Stalin, the "greatest genius known to humankind," the source of all wisdom about statecraft, morality, and science, had died. Almost immediately, his successors in the Kremlin—a "collective leadership" that included Stalin's lieutenants—introduced measures to mollify their own working classes. But they did not react quickly enough to restrain East European comrades from continuing the painful transformation of their societies as if Stalin had not died. The first two places affected, perhaps logically enough, were those with the strongest industries, the oldest traditions of socialist organization, and the largest and most self-conscious working classes: the extreme west of Czechoslovakia and East Germany, especially Berlin and Saxony.

CHAPTER 20

Destalinization: Hungary's Revolution

At first, destalinization was a life-saving measure. When Stalin ascended to sole power in the late 1920s, he not only shunted rivals aside in the decade that followed, he also had them arrested and liquidated. When he died in March 1953, Stalin's successors agreed that those who lost political battles would no longer lose their lives. An exception was made for Lavrentiy Beria, the man to whom Stalin had entrusted his system of intimidation. Beria was executed in December 1953 after being arrested at gunpoint at a meeting of the Soviet Presidium in late June. He was accused of being a spy for Great Britain.[1]

But destalinization also involved taking terror out of the lives of Soviet Bloc citizens. By the time of Stalin's death, the bloc was on a war footing with a cataclysmic struggle against capitalism considered imminent. Indeed, fighting was raging in Korea. In the short run, a skewing of resources toward war industries had produced misery: many hours of backbreaking work in the field or the factory, little to buy in shops, little occasion to enjoy life. Five years after World War II, basic food items remained rationed even when they were available. In Warsaw, the mad drive to funnel resources into heavy industry combined with the closing of private bakeries, groceries, and cafes to produce signs of malnutrition.[2] Because of the nationalization of small businesses, nearly two-thirds of Hungary's villages had no cartwrights, blacksmiths, shoemakers, barbers, or tailors in the mid-1950s.[3]

At the same time, political terror was generating fear and large prison populations. By 1953, the Communist regime had opened legal proceedings against some 1.5 million Hungarians (the adult population comprised five–six million), and sent up to 200,000 to prison camps, many deep in the Soviet Union. Poland's Communists had punished 574,000 peasants for failing to deliver grain and were keeping some six million adults—one in three—on lists of "criminal and suspicious elements." In Czechoslovakia, 8 percent of the citizens had been personally affected by political persecution.[4] Soviet agents in Eastern Europe sent alarming reports on dissatisfaction back to Moscow, and Stalin's successors began taking countermeasures to head off anticipated upheavals.

Destalinization therefore came also to mean a less "ideological" approach to internal and external affairs. Within weeks of the dictator's death on March 5, 1953, the Soviet Politburo began relaxing the burdens of the industrialization drive and increasing investments in consumer goods and housing. It reduced taxes on peasants and paid them more for their produce; it also promoted the individual peasant plots that were producing much of the country's milk and vegetables.[5] On March 27, authorities announced an amnesty and revision of the Soviet criminal code with regard to political crimes. The belief grew that people might willingly help build socialism, less as a utopia for the unspecified future than as a better life in the present. International class struggle would continue, but it need not involve all-out war. In the summer of 1953, a cease-fire was negotiated in Korea, and as Soviet leaders sought peaceful coexistence, they transferred resources from war to consumer-oriented industries. At home, destalinization meant above all social and economic policy aimed at making life more enjoyable through higher living standards, increased income, and expanded benefits.[6]

These steps were necessary if not easy to take, but the question arose of where Stalinist distortions ended and Leninist substance began. Ironically but symptomatically, the term "collective leadership" was itself an invention of Stalin. In December 1925, he accused the "Left Opposition" (Zinoviev and Kamenev) of violating principles of collective leadership and used the phrase repeatedly in the years that followed. The idea of the "cult of personality," made famous in 1956, goes back further still, to 1902, when it was used against Lenin by the *Borba* group.[7]

If the problem of this "cult" was the license given to one man to dictate his will in a highly centralized system, was the solution to devolve power and include more people in decision making? How many? Leninism after all had prohibited "factionalism" in the party and decreed that all members must obey the directives of the center. And what about the political prisoners now walking free, arrested for things they had said? Could people begin speaking their minds without fear? Perhaps Leninism itself was the problem, at least in part, and the solution involved going back to the original Marxist inspiration. Yet Marx and his close associates had left no blueprints for how to build socialism.

Making matters still more complicated was the fact that party elites were not left to ponder these matters in peace. Beginning in 1953, they operated under pressure from their societies, sometimes expressed openly in strikes and massive street protests, most visibly by workers, but also from intellectuals and young people, at times including hundreds of thousands of Communists who felt Stalin had betrayed them.

Yugoslav Alternatives

In 1953, the question of what socialism would be after Stalin was not purely theoretical because Yugoslavia's Communists had been experimenting with new models since Stalin's break with them in 1948. The rupture was not about ideology (that is, about how to build socialism or to structure the party): it was about obedience to Stalin personally. Tito and his comrades had enraged the Soviet leader by failing to seek permission, for example, for their policies toward the other Balkan states. For the time being, references to Tito were anathema in the Soviet Bloc; as recently as December 1952, top Czech Communist leaders had gone to the gallows for association with Titoist heresies. But now Stalin's successors sought peace with Yugoslavia, leading to full restoration of relations by the summer of 1955. When the Soviet leader Nikita Khrushchev denounced Stalin the following winter in a secret speech, many Hungarian and Polish Communists, as well as workers, thought the Yugoslav way might become their way.

The best-known component of this Yugoslav path to socialism was worker self-management, enshrined in law in 1951. It grew out of a struggle of leading Yugoslav Communists for orientation after their expulsion from the Cominform. Tito had been so tightly bound to the Soviet party that he later recalled the first days of estrangement as a "nightmare."[8] Yet Yugoslav Communists had no doubt that they were in the right; their victory in the Partisan struggle, with little Soviet help, showed that history was on their side. The question was where the Soviets had gone wrong.

Yugoslav Communists located the causes of the Soviet deviation in the Communist Party itself and its untrammeled power. Tito's lieutenants Milovan Djilas and Edvard Kardelj reasoned that power in the Soviet Union lay not with workers and peasants but with bureaucrats. For example, managers and not workers controlled Soviet factories. Like capitalists, they determined what men and women on the factory floor produced, and like capitalists, they had the privileges of higher salaries. In effect, exploitation of the working class continued. This was a vital recognition and critique for a political order that claimed to embody emancipation of all human beings. Soviet reality was not socialism but "state capitalism."

Somehow Soviet leaders had failed to heed Marx's warnings about "usurpers" who might derail the revolution. Indeed, the very idea of a strong state, as the Soviet one undoubtedly was, had seemed anathema to Marx. For him, political power had been "nothing other than the organized violence of one class over another." It was true that just after toppling the bourgeoisie, the proletariat would "centralize all instruments of production" using the state apparatus, but that would be a brief transitional period, with the goal of "quickly increasing the size of productive assets." Thereafter, Marx and Engels imagined, workers would cast off all chains of domination and organize production in "free association, in which the development of each is the condition for the free development of all."[9]

Djilas and Kardelj, along with the Slovene Boris Kidrič, reread these lines from Marx's and Engels's *Communist Manifesto*, and during a chat in a limousine outside their villas in 1949, decided that this vision of workers' power held a solution to Yugoslavia's predicament of being a socialist state cut off from the socialist motherland. They suggested it to Tito, and he quickly recognized the promise, exclaiming: "Factories belonging to the workers, something that has never been achieved!"[10]

Within a year, legislation was passed, inaugurating the Yugoslav way. All larger enterprises had to elect a workers' council of between fifteen and 120 members, which in turn elected a management board charged with the daily running of the enterprise. When implemented, these steps would not immediately realize hopes for empowering the working class, because workers tended to elect people with expertise, and those individuals tended to be Communist Party members.[11] By and large the old managers survived, and they guaranteed the continued enforcement of policies decided over the workers' heads, in central bureaucracies. Still, the new style required more participation and discussion than was conceivable under Stalinism. Workers were to be persuaded rather than coerced. The party organization grew less rigid and changed its name to "League of Communists" in 1952. Its job was to stimulate and guide rather than command. After Stalin's death, and the waning of fears of a Soviet attack on Yugoslav territory, the security police were scaled back.

The party elite now took central planning out of its straight jacket and introduced some flexibility, for instance, giving firms tax breaks for better production. Though Yugoslavia was far from being a market economy, it became possible for managers to seek marketplace advantages and make higher profits. At the same time, firms were not required to act according to market rules, and bank credits became available to cushion them against budget shortfalls (that is, noncompetitive performance). After 1953, partly aided by Western credits, the Yugoslav economy—and living standards—improved markedly. One sign of this was growth in personal consumption, which went up by 45.8 percent between 1957 and 1961.[12]

A transformation took place from a "distributive model" of the early postwar years, whose aim had been to remedy deprivation, to one in which the needs and preferences of consumers guided the production of the country's enterprises. From the late 1950s, Yugoslavia thus embarked on the path to a "consumer society," and the Yugoslav economic reforms of 1965 would be the most ambitious market-oriented changes seen anywhere in the Communist world before 1989.[13]

Yet for all the heady experimentation in the economic realm, the Yugoslav way soon gave evidence of its limitations, and oddly, that involved its founding thinker, Milovan Djilas. Marx had been radical in his belief that the state must die under socialism, and so was Djilas. From October 1953 to January 1954, Djilas published articles in the party daily *Borba* attacking the power of the Yugoslav Communist bureaucracy. His views had evolved. Now the highest virtue was not Communism but the individual human spirit. Djilas advocated the "withering away" of the party, which was becoming expendable as the working people, in communes, became more experienced in handling their own affairs. The relation was dialectical. The more the party succeeded in building socialism, the less it was needed. Yet in reality, the party-state in Yugoslavia was becoming ever more entrenched.

In one of the last articles he was able to publish in socialist Yugoslavia, Djilas doubted whether that country was still in the throes of a "class struggle." The bourgeoisie had been destroyed. What then was the need for a Communist organization of any kind, no matter what it called itself? Already alarmed, Tito moved to silence his former lieutenant, proclaiming that, yes, there would be a withering of the League, but the process would be protracted, because there were still many class enemies afoot. Djilas himself was evidence of this fact.

Djilas was now removed from the Central Committee and denied permission to publish. But he continued to give interviews with Western journalists, and in 1956, he published a book arguing that the party had become a new class. For the crime of "conducting propaganda hostile to Yugoslavia," Djilas was sent to prison.

This repressive act was little noticed by Westerners, who admired Tito as a man who had defied Hitler and Stalin. Compared to the Soviet-dominated states in Eastern Europe, his country appeared liberal, and despite problems—chiefly of economic development—its "model" of worker self-management radiated the hope for freedom, equality, and justice. Yugoslavia's reputation of being much more liberal than other East European countries survived beyond Tito's death in 1980. Yugoslavia, alone among socialist states, had opened borders to the West in both directions, permitting millions of its own citizens to work abroad, chiefly in the booming economies of Germany and Austria, and millions of budget-conscious West European tourists to enjoy its seaside and mountain resorts, mostly in Croatia and Slovenia. To help maintain this non-Soviet socialist bastion, the United States injected huge inputs of cash, amounting in the 1950s to $598 million in economic and $588 million in military aid. In the period 1950–1965, foreign aid was the source of 47.5 percent of all investments in Yugoslavia, helping account for a boom in the early 1960s.[14]

A lesson that was not immediately learned from the Djilas affair, but which seems clear in retrospect, was that even under moderate Leninist rule, dissent could be managed only through coercion—by imprisoning those who attempted to air ideas that the party found dangerous. If dissent was less pronounced in Yugoslavia than elsewhere in Eastern Europe, and the ease of control greater, that was because of two things: the incomparable legitimacy of Tito and the Partisans in their society, and their ability to improve the population's living standards into the 1970s. This legitimacy also meant that Yugoslav Communists felt confident enough to extend greater cultural and artistic freedoms to the population. Djilas was the odd character who refused all compromise in matters of conviction, just as he had when he was a Stalinist (thus earning the nickname in party circles of "mad dog").

In the remaining countries, Leninism (and then Stalinism) had been imposed by force from without, and after Stalin's death, some of these societies reacted in the way an organism does to a hostile intruder: it tries to expel it. But matters were not so simple. Now it was the Soviet side that insisted on relaxation and reform, indeed, on greater local rule; yet many in the local party apparatuses, above all inside the police—"native Communists"—had sided with Stalin and staunchly resisted any change. If Stalinism was a foreign imposition, so was destalinization.

Early Upheavals

Through the decades of Communist rule, Hungary and Poland became known for frequent and sometimes spectacular resistance to Soviet rule, thanks in part to their deep histories of national self-assertion and the anti-Russian sentiments that pervaded much of their populations. But directly after Stalin's death in March 1953, the first places to produce massive, popular dissent were three countries that were later considered bastions of orthodox, Soviet-type rule: Bulgaria, Czechoslovakia, and East Germany.

In May, some 10,000 workers went on strike at the tobacco factories in Plovdiv, Bulgaria. Some had sent a letter to Sofia the previous month, warning Communist leaders that strikes would break out if they did not receive better pay, a five-day work week, and an end to being treated as seasonal labor. The mostly women workers had begun seizing control of storage rooms in the night of May 3/4 and took control of most of the factory premises. A delegation including ministers from Sofia attempted to address them and was greeted by a hail of projectiles and had to back off under militia protection. After failed attempts to restore order, local party secretary Ivan Prămov gave the order to disperse the crowds with live ammunition, certainly killing more than the official tally of three. Dozens of strikers were arrested, and the protest was quashed.[15]

A more massive act of worker protest followed in the industrialized Czech lands and was far more worrying from Moscow's perspective. On May 31, the night shift of the Škoda works (producers of automobiles and weapons) in the west Bohemian city of Plzeň went on strike. The immediate cause was a "currency reform" that would drastically reduce their savings: citizens would be permitted to exchange up to 300 crowns of the now defunct currency at a rate of 5:1, and after that 50:1. One woman had skipped lunches for years and saved 4,000 crowns, which were now worth 134 crowns. Suddenly a planned vacation with her husband—to be a surprise—was unthinkable. Multiply this woman's outrage by tens of thousands, and one gets a sense of the mood among Plzeň's workers.[16] Many said the state's actions were simple theft. They also revealed its basic mendacity; just a few days earlier, President Antonín Zápotocký had assured workers that Czechoslovak currency was sound. Earlier in the year, authorities had raised prices and increased workers' production norms by 23 percent.[17]

When the morning shift arrived, Škoda workers decided to march on the city. Soon other workers as well as college students joined them, and they set up a revolutionary committee that demanded free elections, an end to party dictatorship, and punishment for the secret police (whom they taunted as "fascists, SS men, Gestapo!"). Around midday, some 6,000 demonstrators occupied Plzeň's city hall, a six-story structure with original Renaissance façades, and threw party documents down onto the town square. This was a pattern in other antiregime workers' protests: political demands following economic grievance, then the collapse of party power, reflected in the sudden license that people took to attack hated symbols like red-lettered banners and official emblems.

Another pattern is the lightning speed at which these revolutionary energies spread. First the 17,000 men and women of a shift at one factory recognized their common outrage, but as they marched out to the city, many of their co-citizens discovered they shared the basic sense of grievance and joined in. By the evening of June 1, 1953, the fourth-largest Czech city was under crowd control, with telegraph, radio, and public administration all occupied. But then militia and army units (including some eighty tanks) arrived from Prague, and battles flared that lasted into the morning hours, leaving nine tanks destroyed and more than twenty others heavily damaged. Hundreds of citizens were arrested in the days that followed, and total casualties are estimated at about one hundred.

Yet the country was not pacified. Strikes spread eastward to factories in Ostrava—the third largest Czech city—as well as to Kladno, where 50,000 workers laid down their tools in protest of the currency reform.[18] Altogether some 360,000 Czech men and women stopped working, and perhaps a quarter million demonstrated on the streets. The workers revealed that they had not been reduced to an apathetic mass, and they indirectly established bargaining power. Though the currency reform remained, the regime retracted the price and work norm hikes and became much more attentive to the living standards of the working class. With Stalin's death, the terror had begun to abate: in contrast to its practice before 1953, the party was not quick to send in militia units to break up strikes, though it did demote functionaries who had failed to master the situation on the shop floor.[19]

Likewise deaf to popular sentiment, East Germany's leaders increased work norms on May 28, 1953. They were making up for plan targets that had proved unreachable. The norm increase meant that workers had to improve output by 10 percent to maintain the wages they were already earning. Combined with price hikes introduced at the same time, the norm amounted to a 33 percent monthly wage reduction. On Tuesday, June 16, the deputy head of the official trade union—supposedly a workers' representative—poured gasoline on the smoldering indignation by saying that critics of the work norms "deeply offended the interests of all working people," and the party had to see to it that the "enemy theory of wage reduction be smashed to bits." A group of workers decided to meet personally with officials at the State Council (*Staatsrat*) in East Berlin but found no one willing to speak to them.[20]

Soon the assembled workers swelled to more than 10,000, and a crew from a construction site commandeered a truck with a loudspeaker and began traveling about the city proclaiming a general strike. At 5:30 a.m. the following day,

FIGURE 20.1. Workers march through Brandenburg Gate, Berlin (June 17, 1953).
Source: dpa picture alliance/Alamy Stock Photo.

the US radio station in West Berlin broadcast a call by a West Berlin trade-union functionary urging Germans across the GDR to stop working: the right to strike was a right given by their own constitution, but more importantly, it was the "natural right of every oppressed human being."[21] In the course of that Wednesday, workers struck and protested from north to south in East Germany, with special vehemence in the old working-class strongholds of Saxony. First came demands to drop the production quotas, and soon thereafter calls for free elections and national unity. Workers were implicitly making a mockery of Lenin's belief that they could not recognize the link between their material conditions and the political regime that ruled them ("trade union consciousness").[22]

The government quickly rescinded the work norms, but "order" was restored only after Soviet authorities deployed the tanks that were already stationed on East German territory. A state of emergency was declared in 167 of 217 districts [*Landkreise*], and after June 18, only a few factories kept up the strike.

The ostensible "worker governments" in Prague and East Berlin accounted for protests among workers by alleging outside interference. The Czech

Communist leadership claimed that "social democratism"—the alleged inability of moderates to understand the demands of the class struggle—had infected factory labor. East German Prime Minister Otto Grotewohl, a former Social Democrat, called the June 17 uprising the handiwork of "fascist agents" smuggled in from the West, and the head of the East German writers union, Kurt Barthel, printed leaflets saying that the people had forfeited the trust of their government. The writer Bertolt Brecht, a Communist who returned from exile in the United States to live in East Berlin, replied: if Barthel is right, would it not be easier for the government to dissolve the people, and elect a new one?[23] Some 6,000 East Germans were arrested immediately, and in the following months and years, scores more were put on trial as supposed ringleaders in the pay of Western spy networks.[24] The long-term effect of the workers' protest turned out to be counterproductive because Soviet leaders confirmed the rule of the East German Stalinist Walter Ulbricht: only he seemed fit to guarantee order against chaos. Ulbricht then purged rivals who were more moderate and might have led East Germany on a course of limited reforms. The East German politburo would remain in the hands of Stalinists and neo-Stalinists all the way to 1989.

In the 1953 protests, only East German workers blatantly invoked the national question, waving huge black-red-gold flags and chanting for German unity. The speechless East German Communists clearly represented a foreign power, and only Soviet tanks kept them from being swept aside. In Bohemia, by contrast, it had been native Czechoslovak troops who upheld the repressive order, and demonstrators did not make a show of Czech pride, though they did toss busts of Stalin onto the street and destroyed other symbols of foreign rule. The actor Bohumil Vavra saw a boy in Plzeň cutting apart a Soviet flag with a knife to the cheers of the crowd, and for a brief moment, portraits of T. G. Masaryk and Edvard Beneš reappeared, as did American flags. But pro-Communist sentiment remained strong among the Czech intelligentsia; actors of the local theater retaliated against the workers by "hanging" a bronze statue of Masaryk and then having it melted down at the Škoda steelworks.[25]

As the East German crisis was unfolding in mid-June, the Soviet politburo summoned their Hungarian counterparts to the Kremlin and insisted on immediate steps to head off brewing discontent in their country.[26] Hungary's Stalinism had involved a particularly painful economic transformation; if Czechoslovakia witnessed growth of 98 percent in the years 1949–1955, in Hungary, the figure was 210 percent. The pace was pushing the Hungarian state toward bankruptcy, but the leaders seemed unconcerned. Nikita Khrushchev told Hungarian strongman Mátyás Rákosi that he and his comrades would be "chased out with pitchforks" if they did not relax the pressure. Shortly before his arrest, Soviet security chief Lavrentiy Beria charged Rákosi with having become the "Jewish king" of Hungary and wondered at the wisdom of the state pressing 1.5 million legal cases for political crimes when the overall population did not exceed 9.5 million inhabitants.[27]

Ferment and Retrenchment

The Soviets now imposed their own model of "collective leadership" on the Hungarians and demanded that Rákosi share power with Imre Nagy, an old Communist who had served as minister of agriculture and seemed reliable, because he had lived in Moscow in the 1930s and had cooperated with the NKVD while working in the Comintern.[28] At the same time, Nagy enjoyed popularity at home for opposing forced industrialization and collectivization. Nagy became the prime minister, while Rákosi maintained his post as party first secretary. In his inaugural speech to parliament, Nagy struck a new tone: as the first leader in many years, he spoke of the needs of "Hungarians" rather than of the working class. It had again become possible, Nagy was saying, to advocate the rights of a small Central European nation, if in limited fashion. At that moment, even the celebration of Hungarian national holidays was forbidden.[29]

As chairman of the Council of Ministers, Nagy now controlled the state administration yet not the party apparatus, and therefore, he was unable to alter the foundations of centralized rule. But he could undo some of Stalinism's more egregious excesses. Previously, government officials stayed in their offices past 10 p.m., fearing a phone call from Rákosi, but now they could go home right after work. Dressmakers did not have to fret about whether they were using Soviet or Western designs. Small entrepreneurs could leave collectives and reopen their shops; and barbers, pastry-makers, and opticians resumed work according to the demands of customers rather than of the central plan. Middle class Hungarians who had been banned from the capital (through Operation B) trickled back, and in the countryside, tens of thousands left collective farms, reducing their members by 37 percent.[30] Thanks to an amnesty, charges were dropped against some 750,000 persons for various political infractions, and tens of thousands began making their way home from military prisons and internment camps. Hungarians called them the "walking dead."[31] Rumors began circulating about the cruel torture many had suffered at the hands of the secret police, and gradually, consciousness spread of the injustices perpetrated under the still-mighty party boss, Mátyás Rákosi.

Liberalization in Poland proceeded with much less friction between government and party, but here, too, a general awareness spread of Stalinism's evils. Three fortuitous events explain a more gradual release of tension there than in Hungary in the years leading to the dramatic events of the fall of 1956: the spectacular defection of a Polish secret police colonel to the West in 1953; the publication in 1955 of a poem capturing in words the scorching sense of injustice that this colonel's revelations had stoked among Poles; and finally, the death in February 1956 of Poland's Stalinist Bolesław Bierut in Moscow, where he had attended Khrushchev's secret speech. This all occurred amid a Stalinism that seemed less radical than elsewhere. Poland's Communists established fewer collective farms than comrades elsewhere, and they had failed to heed Soviet demands that the "national Communist" Władysław Gomułka be executed. But to Poles, the regime seemed not moderate but nightmarish, especially as they learned more about how it operated behind the scenes.

The unraveling began on December 7, 1953, when secret police Lieutenant Colonel Józef Światło, whose job it was to spy on top party officials, suddenly slipped from the view of his comrades in West Berlin. Before the building of the Berlin Wall in the summer of 1961, it was easy to move back and forth between the Eastern and Western sectors, and the group had gone over to do some shopping. Fearing being purged as a Jew if he returned to the East, Światło now sought protection from American officials and was flown to the United States for debriefing. From the autumn of 1954, he broadcast reports from Radio Free Europe, a CIA-financed radio station in Munich, telling of the luxurious lifestyles of the working class avante garde, of the corruption and the power of secret police agents even over top party leaders, whom they humiliated and often tortured. Listeners learned that Józef Rózanski, head of the investigating department in the Polish Ministry of Public Security, had physically abused prisoners. Yet Rózanski had fallen from his post after another official, Julia Brystigierowa, began funneling accusations against him to her "lovers," Politburo members Hilary Minc and Jakub Berman. Światło had kept a vault full of statements of party leader against party leader, to be used as needed, yet ultimately, he was responsible to Moscow and had a direct phone connection to Lavrentiy Beria.[32] Productivity slackened on mornings after Światło's broadcasts, as workers whispered the revelations of the previous evening.

Światło was making a mockery of any pretense that the working class was ruling Poland, and the consequences were not long in coming. On December 7,

1954, the Ministry of Public Security was dissolved. Acting as a "collective leadership," with former socialist Józef Cyrankiewicz as prime minister, the party ramped up the production of consumer goods, curtailed pressures to join collective farms, and began releasing political prisoners. The process snowballed. Prisoners told about torture, and ferment began mounting among idealistic young party activists, but it lacked focus.

In August 1955, Adam Ważyk, until recently an enforcer of Stalinist socialist realism as the head of the Union of Polish Writers, shocked Poles by publishing his "Poem for Adults" in the journal *Nowa Kultura*. The poem was a panoramic horror show of socialist society featuring women thrown out of their homes by abusive husbands, children despised by criminal doctors, denizens of new cities who had never attended a theater, a girl raped and then driven to suicide after being expelled from art school for infractions against socialist morality, and a population forced to lie about these things and much else.[33] The poem illustrated depravations going far beyond the Party or secret police, about which, until that point, the official press had said nothing. The August edition of *Nowa Kultura* sold out immediately and was soon traded on the black market. Its editor was fired. But the transformations of mass consciousness could not be undone.

A groundswell of discontent was slowly agitating all regions, classes, and age groups of Polish society; atheists as well as Christians, men, women, teenagers, and children. Yet it took a poem by one man and the defection to West Berlin by another to channel this vague restlessness. New milieus of critical discussion emerged in the party, intelligentsia, and especially among students, who created satirical theaters and discussion clubs across Poland. Everyone read the weekly *Po Prostu*, a "revolutionary journal of youth," published in Warsaw, whose writers could not stop "meddling with all that happens around us," wanting "more things, wiser things, better things." In retrospect, people would speak of a 1956 generation, a cultural movement that drew persons just above and below age twenty into a common experience, evident in Western-inspired dress, music, leisure, and jargon—all adapted to Polish conditions. A world of frozen emotions and ideas was suddenly bursting to life, and people across the bloc spoke of a "Thaw" occurring in public life, a term coined based on the title of a novel by Soviet author Ilya Ehrenburg.

Official newspapers also built a consensus for change. Reflecting the waning of Stalinist discipline, artists began departing from the strictures of socialist realism, returning to abstract painting, contemporary music, and jazz. National heroes could be honored openly. Warsaw, for example, witnessed lavish celebrations of the centenary of Adam Mickiewicz's death.

In Hungary, too, vibrancy had been returning to intellectual milieus since late 1953, when handfuls of Budapest intellectuals formed discussion clubs, first named after Lajos Kossuth, and then, from November 1955, after the poet Sándor Petőfi.[34] Yet in these very months, Hungary's Stalinists were also reasserting claims to power. Almost from the moment Imre Nagy became prime minister, party boss Rákosi began channeling evidence of his "distortions" to supporters in Moscow. Supposedly Nagy had gone too far by claiming that everything done in the past five years was "one great error."[35] In late 1954, Rákosi convinced Kremlin leaders that his rival supported "rightist" elements in Hungary, and after being summoned to Moscow, Nagy found himself charged with endangering the "leading role of the working class" through excessive concern for agriculture. Nikita Khrushchev told him that the party had once dressed down the old Bolsheviks Zinoviev and Rykov, though they, too, had performed great services for socialism. Yes, Nagy reflected to his friends, "we all know they were shot."[36]

The following month, Nagy's Soviet patron Grigorii Malenkov lost a leadership battle to Khrushchev, and in mid-April, Nagy was removed from the Hungarian Party's Politburo. Rákosi tried to turn back the clock by forcing peasants to join collective farms and reintroducing political repression. The number of political prisoners, which had sunk to 23,000 in late 1954, climbed to 37,000. Again, the economic priorities shifted to heavy industry as the Soviet Union demanded an increase in defense expenditure of 12 percent.[37]

Yet retrenchment was not easy. Peasants resisted, refusing to work in fields managed by collectives. Writers and students had become accustomed to posing urgent questions and were no longer easily intimidated. Despite the party's best efforts to put trusted cadres in charge of the Petőfi Circle, the discussions there glided out of control, and demands spread for "independent thinking" and "socialist legality," for an end to falsifications of Hungary's history and the flawed industrial policy. Before an audience of hundreds, László Rajk's widow, Julia, said that Rákosi and his clique had murdered her husband and stolen her baby; in "Horthy's prisons," she claimed, "conditions were far better even for Communists than in Rákosi's." Across the country, Marxist believers felt remorse for participating in acts they now recognized as criminal. Writers publically asked their readers' forgiveness while in private calling Rákosi an outright murderer. The Communist László Benjamin wrote to a fellow writer "I am guilty because I believed in your guilt." Because the faith had been deep and consuming, the disillusionment produced anger and unrelenting opposition.[38]

1956

In early 1956, Moscow's pendulum swung in the opposite direction. Nikita Khrushchev, having dispensed with hated rival and fellow reformer Malenkov, now felt confident enough to take on the legacy of Stalin.[39] In February, he gave the most influential political speech of the twentieth century at a closed meeting of the Soviet Communist Party, detailing the crimes of Stalin. Listeners learned that Stalin had decapitated the Party: of 139 members of the Central Committee in 1934, ninety were murdered in the years 1937/1938. Virtually every old Bolshevik who had known Lenin personally had been liquidated, and most of the military leadership disappeared just as a mortal threat was arising from Nazi Germany. Then Stalin refused to prepare the country for war. Delegates learned that the supposedly infallible military genius had ignored numerous reports that Hitler was about to attack in 1941, and then retreated into seclusion from shock when the attack began. After recovering, he had refused permission for numerous armies to surrender, thus ensuring their destruction. He directed the conduct of war using not detailed military maps but a globe. After the war, Stalin had rent the international workers movement by provoking conflict with Tito. To objections, he had proclaimed: "I will shake my little finger and there will be no more Tito."[40]

There was a telling limit to this critique, little noticed at the time: Khrushchev did not ask what in Leninism had permitted Stalin to amass such power and promote his cult of personality.

But throughout the bloc, the effect was stunning. The speech was another "event"—after workers' protests in Plzeň and East Berlin, Józef Światło's broadcasts, Adam Ważyk's poem, and Imre Nagy's mass amnesty for camp inmates—that contributed to consciousness-raising about the hidden nature of the system, the most important event by far. Though secret, the speech's basic points were revealed within weeks, having been leaked by Polish Communists. With the blessings of highest authorities, local party organizations across Poland staged meetings at which the speech was read and discussed. Some were open to non-party people as well. By April, in Łódź alone, some 10,000 people had attended such meetings, though the meetings lasted more than six hours. They returned to their homes in a state of shock.[41]

If Khrushchev could criticize the errors of Stalinism, so could the party cadre. But where would the criticism end? If Stalin meant centralism, terror, heavy industry, and chauvinism, then was not the natural response democracy, rule of law, balanced economies, and respect for national sovereignty? And if Yugo-slavia could go its own way to socialism based on workers' self-management, what about the rest of Eastern Europe? Khrushchev had visited Tito the previ-ous year (May 1955) in a highly public step of reconciliation. Newsreels fea-tured the two party leaders with ice cream cones on the streets of Belgrade.

The trauma went deep. If one were to draw comparisons to Christianity, Khrushchev's revelations about Stalin was more like telling the Christian faith-ful of crimes of Christ—and not of any pope or bishop. Stalin had embodied the spirit of the party, and the party had claimed to have infallible knowledge of the laws of history. Where was this unerring but hopelessly divided organ-ization to go? Almost from the week Stalin died, Communists had been discuss-ing problems, yet the leadership still included scores of people implicated in Stalin's crimes. The party line, supposedly an unwavering commitment for the faithful (even Trotsky had said he could not be right against the party), had be-come a zigzag. This was perhaps true everywhere in the Soviet Bloc, but no-where more than in Hungary, where even to utter the name Tito before 1954 was to invite a long prison sentence or worse.

In the spring and summer of 1956, Moscow again told the Hungarian leader-ship to relax the course. The leadership responded by releasing some arrested Communists. Two increasingly desperate factions crystalized in the party, Stalinists and reformers, the former fearing investigations of crimes in which they were implicated, the latter fearing a return to the time of those crimes. Both sides claimed to be Marxist, one wondering whether socialism as it existed could be essentially flawed, the other insisting that socialism must be reformed so that distortions would not recur. Both were united in the belief that the party should not follow, but lead.

The Soviets' own course seemed directionless. Privately, Nikita Khrushchev was telling Marshall Tito that any unrest in Hungary would be crushed with military force. He had faith in Mátyás Rákosi to keep order. Yet Rákosi had be-come too weak to guarantee even basic stability. In July, Soviet Politburo mem-ber Anastas Mikoyan visited Budapest and decided it was time for Rákosi to go.

The sudden disappearance of the Stalinist Rákosi did more to discomfit than to reassure the Party apparatus. He at least seemed to represent stability. But for reformers, the Soviets' new choice for party leader, Ernő Gerő, was a disas-ter. Gerő was infamous as one of Rákosi's henchmen. Opposition crystalized around the once-tame monthly of the writers association (*Literary Gazette*), now a major carrier of intellectuals' call for change ("socialist renewal"), and the Petőfi Circle, where László Rajk's widow Julia called for purification of socialism, something that would be impossible so long as "murderers of my husband occupy ministers' seats."[42]

Gerő failed to channel these sentiments, and thanks to his close association with Rákosi, seemed to incorporate resistance to change. A threshold was crossed on October 6, when in a crowning act of society's self-recognition, the remains of László Rajk were reburied in Budapest amid a crowd exceeding 100,000. After years of hearing rumors, Hungarians across social strata now understood that they had been living under a regime not just of this or that misdeed, but of systematic injustice. The dictatorship of the proletariat had turned into a criminal conspiracy. And witnessing the huge crowd of like-minded people, they also knew they were not alone in their sense of outrage. Despite the growing criticism, nothing was changing to guarantee that misdeeds did not recur, however. Yet no one doubted who was guilty: the old leaders who still held on to power.

In Poland, events in mid-October generated a sudden acceleration forward. On October 18, the Polish leadership invited back its own purged Communist nationalist Władysław Gomułka with the intention of making him leader. Bringing back Gomułka was their last-ditch effort to salvage some form of control over mass discontent. In the eyes of Hungarians it seemed much more, however: Gomułka's return suggested that Poland was gripped by a revolution that the Soviets could not stop. Four days later, Hungarian students in Budapest staged a manifestation of sympathy for Poland, and the Hungarian revolution was launched.

* * *

Observers noted from the start that Hungarians drew the wrong lessons from Poland, while Poles drew appropriate lessons from Hungary. That is, Hungarians looked at Poland and were encouraged to demand more than they could have, while Poles looked at Hungary and learned not to demand more than was possible. Poland thus avoided violence, whereas Hungary stumbled into bloody upheaval. Yet several events had already occurred before Gomułka's return that reduced tensions among Poles, which, next to Hungarians, were the most brutalized society in the region, and like Hungarians, felt that a traditional enemy had deeply injured national pride. By contrast, contingent events would take Hungary into a cataclysm of violence.

The first important distinction was at the pinnacle of power. Supposedly traumatized by Khrushchev's revelations, Polish leader Bolesław Bierut had suddenly died in Moscow in February 1956. Therefore, unlike Mátyás Rákosi, Poland's top Stalinist was no longer present to forestall truth-seeking. Bierut's successor Edward Ochab was, unlike Ernő Gerő, a moderate, able to mediate between liberals and hardliners. He would prove the rare Leninist willing to part with power peacefully.

Also unlike their Hungarian comrades, Poland's new leaders could not ignore the unrest just below society's surface. In June, discontent had exploded in the industrial west Polish city of Poznań. As in East Germany and the Czech lands, it was not the poorest, most downtrodden workers who became the leading edge of protests but those working in large, advanced factories, with a high degree of class consciousness rooted in traditions dating back generations, to the beginnings of industrialization.[43] In all three countries, explosions of popular protest were preceded by workers striking at factories with the highest prestige, as recognized by the regimes. From 1953 to 1965, the Škoda factory at Plzeň was called the "Lenin Works," and from 1949 to 1956, the metalworking plant Cegielski in Poznań, from which dissent emerged, was known as the "Stalin Works." The socialist realist boulevard where workers struck in East Berlin in 1953 was Stalinallee; in 1961, it became Karl-Marx Allee.

Unrest had been percolating for years among Polish workers. Their real salaries had decreased by 36 percent from 1949 to 1955. At Poznań, workers were particularly angry because they had not received tax refunds amounting to two month's wages owed from previous years. Then, in the summer of 1956, the regime announced new production targets and work norms.[44] On June 28, work crews at Cegielski in Poznań went on strike, and marched on the center of town. Soon they were joined by thousands of other citizens from all walks of life: less-coddled workers, students, nurses, even members of the militia. Among the first banners that appeared was the simple: "we want bread." Public transport workers cooperated, and soon the entire city was shut down, with huge crowds surrounding stalled streetcars and chanting near the old city castle. Like Czech and East German leaders, Poznań's city officials refused to address a huge crowd at city center, and rioting broke out, leading to the ransacking of state and party offices. Again, busts of Stalin and portraits of leaders flew onto the streets.

That evening, authorities in Warsaw sent in 350 tanks and 10,000 soldiers to restore "order" in Poznań under the Soviet general (of Polish origin) Stanislav Poplavsky; hundreds of supposed ringleaders were arrested, and fifty-seven demonstrators lost their lives.[45] Though the soldiers were Polish, the command by the Soviet citizen Poplavsky symbolized the ultimate reality of foreign rule. The crowds chanted: "Down with Russian Democracy," "Down with

FIGURE 20.2. Workers at the Poznań demonstrations (June 1956). *Source*: ITAR-TASS News Agency/Alamy Stock Photo.

Bolsheviks," "Down with Muscovites," " Russkis, leave our city." Against intimidation, the crowds sought refuge in patriotic and religious songs, and they decorated streetcars, as well as the tanks of sympathetic soldiers, with red and white Polish flags. They entreated the police to "march with the nation," and snapshots show that some did. Workers from the northeast city of Olsztyn expressed solidarity, calling the military force sent to Poznań "armed units of a foreign red imperialism."[46]

The events shocked Party leaders, causing them to embrace "democratization" in a July Central Committee meeting. That would mean taking some issues out of the hands of the party and transferring them to nominally independent structures like the parliament, plant management (with workers involved in decision making), and the Polish Union of Youth. These changes would help relieve some of the tensions that had grown in preceding years.

Criticism focused on the centralization of power that had permitted the crimes of the police and also the pervasive lawlessness. The obvious solution—even after the self-limiting performance of Khrushchev—was some kind of "socialist democracy." On shop floors, that meant the formation of worker committees, similar to the factory-level Soviets that had emerged in Russia in 1917. Now, however, such committees would realize the ultimate goal of Marxism: to empower workers. The movement was the opposite of antisocialist. One of the best-known committees had formed at the automobile factory in Warsaw,

FIGURE 20.3. Lechosław Goździk: Communist workers' leader (1956).
Source: PAP/CAF/H. Grzęda (photographer).

FSO Żerań. It was led by the young party functionary Lechosław Goździk, a tall and gaunt James Dean, who captivated workers with impromptu speeches on democracy and socialism minus the distortions, delivered from the flatbed of a truck.[47]

But the Polish October was a mass national movement, going beyond workers or intellectuals, and it found a national hero and leader in Władysław Gomułka, the old national Communist arrested in 1951 by Józef Światło and released from prison in December 1954. As a supposedly incorruptible functionary who had stood up to Stalin and suffered for it, Gomułka could incorporate widespread grievances, but also broadly shared hopes, even for the soberest of observers, like the Catholic satirist Stefan Kisielewski, Poland's most brilliant skeptic. For the men in the Politburo, Gomułka was Poland's Tito, the only Communist who could overcome their dissension and project authority in and beyond Poland. But for Gomułka to have any success in asserting Polish independence, even his critics agreed, Poles had to tamp down their traditional anti-Sovietism. Catholic Kisielewski wrote in September 1956:

reasonable people in Poland agree that if the world is divided into blocks, then Poland's place is in the east in alliance with Russia. But within this block we would like to gain independence, the sort that Tito has gained for Yugoslavia. This is what the struggle is about right now. The Central Committee embodies Poland's raison d'etat by fighting with Russia for independence within the alliance. Unfortunately the spontaneous anti-Sovietism of society hinders this struggle for independence.[48]

Gomułka's language allowed people to dream of change. Unlike Khrushchev, he admitted that Stalinism's distortions were due not simply to Stalin, but to a "system that ruled in the Soviet Union but was transplanted to just about every Communist party." The system's essence was a "unified hierarchical ladder of cults," at the top of which stood one man. Those on the lower rungs bowed their heads to Stalin while cloaking themselves in "sovereign robes of infallibility." The system violated "democratic principles and the rule of law," it broke people's characters as well as their conscience, and reviled their honor. "Slander, lies, falsehoods, and even provocations: these were the tools of governance." Even in Poland, innocent people were sent to their deaths.

Gomułka seemed sincere in his will for change. The Polish Primate, Cardinal Stefan Wyszyński was released from detention; peasants could leave agricultural cooperatives.[49] Collectivization stopped, as did mandatory enrollment in youth organizations and automatic persecution of students of "alien" class background. Universities regained limited autonomy, and the secret police was subject to state authorities. The months that followed witnessed judicial reforms as well as a relaxation of pressures on private businesses, and Poland's parliament revived and attained seemingly independent powers.[50] Fear of speaking freely evaporated, and Polish film, music, and literature began to claim world renown. Left-wing intellectuals had been buoyed by the behavior of the working class: Poznań showed that Polish workers had stepped onto the historical stage and would remain a leading protagonist of social, political, and economic change; Communists could no longer rule without taking them into account.[51]

If such were the hopes of Poles, they were also the fears of the Soviet leaders. But they did not know what to make of Gomułka, a bald-headed Communist ascetic who stirred huge crowds while never diverging from Communist *and* nationalist rhetoric. Poland's new leader had spent a year in the Soviet Union in the early 1930s, but after that had lived in Poland, not under Moscow's control. To get a measure of the man, the Soviet Politburo, accompanied by twelve generals, flew to Warsaw uninvited on the morning of October 19, 1956. Khrushchev berated the Poles, "with coarse language," as Gomułka later admitted, shouting so that "even the chauffeurs could hear" that "we won't let pass the treacherous actions of Comrade Ochab."[52] At the same moment, two Soviet tank divisions in southwest Poland left their bases and headed toward Warsaw, while Polish units prepared defense.

The arguing continued through the night. Yet the following morning, the Soviets returned to Moscow. Military intervention seemed too costly: seventy-nine Soviet citizens served as officers in the Polish army, including twenty-eight generals, yet there were enough loyal Polish officers to ensure that the army would fight.[53] "Finding a reason for an armed conflict [with Poland] now would be very easy," Khrushchev told an expanded session of the Soviet Communist Presidium on October 24, "but finding a way to put an end to such a conflict later on would be very hard." Yet Gomułka had also impressed the Soviet leaders. Clearly possessed of iron will, he would not back down on national sovereignty, but he also reaffirmed his intent to keep Poland in the Warsaw Pact and rejected all demands that seemed anti-Soviet, for example, that Poland get back lost territories in the east.[54] Khrushchev shrewdly recognized Gomułka as a fellow Leninist who would keep order.

Such fine points did not register in Budapest. What impressed Hungarian crowds reading the headlines from Warsaw was that Gomułka was a leader whom Poland's Communists had chosen, and the Soviets had let it happen. On the morning of October 23, students in the engineering school of the University of Budapest gathered at the Petőfi monument in Budapest and marched toward the statue of József Bem, the Polish general who fought on Hungary's side in 1849. They carried Polish and Hungarian flags and chanted: "Independence! Poland shows the way!" There were Polish eagles and banners announcing "solidarity with the Polish people!"[55]

The streets filled as workers left their morning shifts, and speakers called for the reinstatement of Imre Nagy, who like Gomułka personified desires for reform. They also demanded the withdrawal from Hungary of all Soviet troops, free elections, freedom of expression, the re-establishment of political parties, and independence from the Soviet Union—things Poles had not called for even during the rioting at Poznań, and things that no Communist government could have provided.[56]

By late afternoon, some 300,000 Hungarians had gathered before parliament, eager to hear Nagy. Yet unlike Gomułka, the former Hungarian premier could not sense the mood of the crowds of 1956. Summoned from a wine harvest ceremony in the countryside, he very unwillingly appeared in front of the masses at about 6 p.m. and bumbled his way through unprepared remarks, unable to connect with (let alone channel) the popular outrage. Nagy informed his "dear comrades" that the party would continue the course ("the June way"), that is, the discredited politics dating to 1953. Fortunately or unfortunately, he had no microphone, and people could hardly hear him. Making matters worse, at 8 p.m., party chief Gerő urged "party unity" over public airwaves and railed against the "poison of chauvinism," thereby frustrating the population's hopes that he might make concessions.[57] By this time, the party he invoked had left the streets to the people.

While most demonstrators remained in front of parliament, smaller groups went off to the radio station to have their demands read over the airwaves. They found the building barricaded. Crowds grew, and the secret police and army units tried to disperse them with bayonets. Tear gas was thrown, shots fired, and more army units called in. Yet instead of "restoring order," the draftees fraternized with and armed the crowd. In Poznań, by contrast, the Polish "people's army" had loyally crushed the uprising and the Polish party never lost control. Around 9:30 p.m., the most visible symbol of oppression, the massive Stalin statue (25 meters on a pedestal), standing on the edge of a city park in Pest, was pulled down by demonstrators after metalworkers had weakened the base with blow torches. The Hungarian crowd, acting on its own cues, was dictating the pace of events, and by midnight, "revolution" was in full force.

During the night, Gerő called in Soviet units with the full support of his comrades, including Nagy, who were convinced that Hungary lacked the capacity to restore order.[58] Martial law was declared. The following day, the Central Committee appointed Nagy prime minister, yet he remained out of touch and unable to establish control. The crowds demanded freedom and national independence, while he promised "socialist legality" and an end to the "personality cult."

A second escalation occurred on the morning of October 25, when young people arrived at Parliament Square atop Soviet tanks, waving Hungarian flags. Around 11:15, bullets descended on them, apparently from the Agricultural Ministry across the square. (To this day, there is no certainty about who initiated the shooting.) The Soviets returned fire and were reinforced by tanks coming from the south toward the parliament building. In the chaos, Soviet tank crews shot down scores of peaceful demonstrators, and one American on the scene reported "a feverish desire for revenge" among the crowds as the revolution

FIGURE 20.4. Stalin standing, Budapest (1953). *Source:* Gyula Nagy (donor),
Foto Fortepan. CC-BY-SA 3.0.

FIGURE 20.5. Stalin descends to earth, Budapest (1956).
Source: Gabor B. Racz. CC-BY-SA 4.0.

evolved into "a blind, merciless war between half-armed people and the Soviet army."[59] Massive resistance spread across the country, while party and state authorities were nowhere to be seen.

Nagy was unable to return to his apartment, even for a change of clothes, and became so overwrought that he wept openly at meetings. As a Marxist, he asked whether he was witnessing counterrevolution or revolution. The workers' delegations he received insisted it was the latter. Historical time sped forward, but Nagy's work habits remained those of the scholar bureaucrat committed to methodical deliberation. The poet István Eörsi wrote that he "was an unhurried man, shaped by doubts and also by deep-rooted party discipline, who simply needed more time to make decisions than one should or could afford in a revolution. He was always two, three days behind in his decisions."[60]

On October 27, Nagy spoke of the need for political and military measures to respond to the situation, yet the following day, he proclaimed an armistice over state radio, referring to the "rebellion" as one that "embraced the entire people and was national and democratic." He announced an amnesty as well as a cease-fire, negotiations with insurgents, and the dissolution of the state security forces. The "tragic fraternal battle," he explained, was "due to the terrible mistakes and the criminal policies of the last decade." Perhaps direct contacts with the revolutionaries had changed his views. Hungarian workers were self-organizing: was that not the ultimate goal of socialism? Yet self-organization went beyond industrial workers into all social groups, and within a couple of days, virtually the entire political spectrum had reemerged. More than that, whatever their "class" or "political" background, Hungarians, in their "revolutionary unity," demanded classic liberal institutions, including parliamentary representation with several parties. They did not, however, assume that capitalism would be restored, and instead spoke of a democratic socialism that involved direct democracy.

But Nagy had still not fully captured the popular mood let alone gained control of events. Hungarians continued forming revolutionary committees across the country and insisting on an end to Communist rule. Organs of self-rule emerged in 2,804 of 3,419 communal units, with especially strong leaders in the important towns of Győr, Miskolc, and Debrecen. The Communist organization of more than 800,000 members seemed to have vanished into the late October air. Beyond Budapest, some 100 demonstrations were registered with 100,000 to 200,000 participants; later investigators counted 160 groups of armed freedom fighters as well as 2,100 workers' councils with 28,000 members, all of whom could be identified by name.[61]

FIGURE 20.6. Citizens of Budapest demonstrate (October 25, 1956). *Source*: Gyula Nagy (donor), Foto Fortepan / CC-BY-SA 3.0.

On October 30, Nagy invited the resurrected political parties into the government, thus violating Leninist principles of proletarian dictatorship. He also negotiated the departure of Soviet troops from Budapest, while establishing a National Guard consisting of revolutionaries. By now, dozens of dailies were appearing, while the party newspaper, firmly in Nagy's hands, rejected Soviet charges that Hungarian counterrevolution was instigated by "British and American imperialists."[62]

By now things had gone too far for the Soviet leadership. After heated debates and much uncertainty, a decision for decisive intervention was made on October 31, based on reports from Soviet officials on the ground that the Hungarian government had lost all ability to influence the course of events.[63] Even moderates feared the demise of Communism in Hungary; supposedly Nagy did not "know when to stop in giving concessions." Furthermore, these "liberals" in the Kremlin wanted to nip national Communism in the bud, supposedly a breeding ground for conflict with Soviet power and something also rearing its head in Poland.[64] Just as Nagy was discovering the democrat in himself, so Soviet leaders were "learning" from Hungary's revolutionaries where the boundaries lay for their tolerance of diversity. Initially, they had hesitated to use force, fearing the repercussions for their image internationally, but now they decided that Communist control within the bloc was not negotiable.

Khrushchev, who, like Nagy, could not sleep in these days, was thinking not only of the unresolved predicament in Poland but also of Romania, where there had been student demonstrations that led authorities to close their border to Hungary; he also worried about Czechoslovakia and East Germany, where the intelligentsias sensed his lack of orientation and were mobilizing. There were also reports of unrest from his own Soviet Union.[65] Khrushchev also thought in global terms, and canvassed the opinions of China's Chairman Mao Zedong and Yugoslavia's Marshall Tito. When Mao's view changed, so did that of the Soviet leadership. On October 30, the Chinese leader had still urged permitting Hungary's working class "to regain control of the situation," yet when his ambassador wired news of the lynching of secret policemen in Budapest, Mao changed his mind.

Soviet armored units now intervened to stifle the revolution, at an ultimate cost of some 22,000 Hungarian and 1,500 Soviet casualties. Yet even overwhelming force could not immediately return Hungarian public life to its prerevolutionary stasis.[66] The councils movement continued to grow, and on November 14, workers set up a Central Workers Council in the lamp factory Tungsram in Budapest. They were in close contact with opposition intellectuals and planned to implement the socialist transition program of former minister István Bibó. Their leaders, Sándor Bali and Sándor Rácz, negotiated with János Kádár—the former interior minister who replaced Gerő as party leader on October 25—in parliament. On November 23—three weeks after the Soviet assault!—a general strike was proclaimed for noon: all work stopped, and the streets emptied, except for military patrols. On December 4, several thousand women gathered at Heroes Square but were intercepted before they could reach the US Embassy. In provincial towns, independent newspapers continued to appear for several more weeks. But the Central Council was shut down on December 9, a day after it planned a general strike in protest of the shooting of miners in Salgótarján. Two days later, Bali and Rácz were arrested.[67]

Where were Hungary's leaders during these dramatic November days? When reports reached Nagy that new Soviet military divisions had entered Hungary on November 1, he declared the country's neutrality and withdrawal from the Warsaw Pact. Party leader János Kádár disappeared that same day. It later emerged that he had been flown to Moscow and agreed to form a "revolutionary government," to maintain the anti-Stalinist achievements of the revolution but also restore the leading role of the Communist Party. Imre Nagy was granted refuge in the Yugoslav embassy but then was kidnapped by Soviet troops on leaving. Because he refused to cooperate with the new Soviet-sponsored regime, he, with hundreds of other "traitors," was executed with the explicit approval of János Kádár in the summer of 1958.

* * *

What happened after that point in Hungary and Poland runs directly counter to expectations people had at the time. Kádár, traitor of the revolution and hangman of his own comrades, spent years consolidating his power, removing enemies right and left. He feared that if he did not deal decisively with revolutionaries, he might be "overtaken" on the right by hardliners. Indeed, Stalinists had maintained themselves in the leaderships of East Germany, Czechoslovakia, Bulgaria, and Romania. But in 1961, Kádár issued an amnesty that was meant to make room in public life for the revolution's supporters, and he began pursuing economic and cultural policies designed to make life more enjoyable for the masses of the population. Space emerged for private initiatives in business, and by the 1970s, with full shop windows, well-stocked cafes, relatively open borders, and a liberal approach to ideology, to outsiders, Hungary seemed to be the "happiest barracks in the bloc."

In the turbulent months of 1956, Gomułka the savior seemed to embody the nationalist passions that had radicalized the economic protests in Poznań. Unlike the prior government, he could not be portrayed as a servant of foreign interests. When he assumed power, people had already lost their fear to speak openly. "Tito was capable of opposition," said a member of the party rank and file in Bydgoszcz, "while our leadership walked on a leash." "What happened to thousands of members of Home Army, who were murdered after liberation?" asked a student at a public meeting at the Szczecin polytechnic. Demonstrators at Poznań in June had wanted "UN supervised free elections."[68]

In fact, after he was handed power, Gomułka began almost immediately to harness and then stifle such sentiments, and denounced those calling for independence as "antisocialist." Gomułka was not a Polish Tito, and he proved much less imaginative than Kádár. Like Kádár, he purged Stalinists, but even more eagerly, he purged liberals. That was a harsh disappointment to those who had hoped that he would open new realms of freedom within socialism. In 1957, he closed the most adventurous publications of the Thaw, including *Po prostu*. In the early 1960s, he closed his ears to the exciting reform ideas of Polish economists, and he maintained firm central controls over planning and continued to pursue Stalinist-style big-industry projects. But because the Polish economy stagnated, he became vulnerable to criticism from within party ranks and found himself on the defensive from criticism by nationalists on the right. He had risen and would fall as a nationalist: an increasingly doctrinaire and would-be all-knowing Leninist nationalist.

Still, he did not attempt to lead Poland back to Stalinism. He had protested the arrest of Nagy. For him and for Polish society the year 1956 was a decisive break, and liberalization endured in the countryside and in policies toward the church, higher education, and culture, which were liberal in comparison to every other place in the bloc, including Hungary. Academic disciplines like sociology were able to reestablish contacts with the West and regain international prominence, and dozens of Polish scholars visited and exchanged ideas with counterparts in Paris, London, and the United States. (The US Ford Foundation also financed stays of Western academics in Poland). Polish cinema became known for inventiveness and imagination throughout the world, through filmmakers like Andrzej Wajda and Roman Polanski. When Stalinism's spell broke, the Polish intelligentsia's flirtation with history as an all-revealing guide for politics and ethics was at an end.

CHAPTER 21

National Paths to Communism: The 1960s

Władysław Gomułka was famous as a national Communist, but nationalism was not entirely foreign to East Central Europe before 1956. For example, Poland's Stalinists gave orders to rebuild Warsaw and other cities with painstaking attention to native styles, and to uncover the "ancient Slavic" character of towns that had been German for centuries, like Wrocław and Gdansk, through elaborate archeological work. Still, nationalism had been subordinated to building socialism. For example, national culture was valuable not in itself but only insofar as it served the working class. The Polish language, according to one Polish Communist schooling pamphlet from 1948, was useful for teaching students the proper way of thinking, and the best examples of such use were party writings. But the Polish language had no independent worth. A party member belonged to the working class first, and his or her nation second.[1]

The diminution of the national had filtered into an endless array of institutions, perhaps nowhere more painfully for local sensibility than in the military. In Hungary and Poland, patterns adapted from the Red Army replaced traditional uniforms, and Soviet officers, often of Polish or Hungarian descent, rose to the top of the national hierarchies, employing terror to reorganize and to purge before introducing their own regulations, codes of service, and training manuals. Beginning in 1948, Soviet advisors "assisted" at all upper and medium-level ranks.[2]

After 1956, all of this was undone. The advisors were sent home, and local forms displaced those that had been forcibly imported. In the East German military, Soviet-style uniforms gave way to what seemed those of the Nazi Wehrmacht, with the exception of a new helmet. A similar return to local or "European" forms became evident in culture, as socialist realism retreated from music, art, film, fashion, and architecture, yielding to international styles. The Poles proved the most daring, with the recoil driven by an urgent concern to reconnect to local traditions, including the socialist heritage obliterated by

Stalin. Names of executed Communist leaders that could not be uttered for two decades suddenly adorned public places.

The Soviet Party never extended its blessings to "national Communism," but a pragmatic toleration took hold, with the basic goal of preventing outbursts like those of 1956. Twelve Communist parties passed a statement in November 1957 insisting on dictatorship of the proletariat, class struggle, the need for cooperation of the socialist community, and recognition of the Soviet Union as the first and greatest socialist power. Yet at the same time, they said it was crucial to take account of separate national characteristics and traditions, because to ignore them was to lead proletarian parties away from the masses and cripple the cause of socialism. Nationalism was not encouraged, but it was taken off the leash.[3]

As spaces opened for more national forms of socialist rule, party ideology atrophied, and a revolutionary cadre of enthusiastic and idealistic Stalin-era socialists now yielded to careerists, managers, and "young cubs interested in ruling," as one insider noted in the early 1960s.[4] Marxist principles did not disappear, but they evolved into a set of phrases that became emptier and more ritualized, a lip service used to gain other things: above all, a decent standard of living in the bloc-wide shift to consumerism that began in the weeks after Stalin's death.

No one did more to usher in the new time than Nikita Khrushchev, but few found it more unsettling. To salvage socialism, he recognized, the eclipsing of nationalism by socialism had to be abandoned. But what if anti-Soviet ideas now dominated the field? He had particular concerns about Polish comrades. "Maybe Poland would like to take over leadership of the socialist Bloc?" he taunted Gomułka in 1957. The socialist camp could do without Poland, he insisted, and added a threat: if Poland's status changed, Moscow would have to consult with East Germany about the postwar borders. There were also a lot of Soviets who "hated Poland."[5] Nationalism begat nationalism. It turned out that the bond ultimately justifying Poland's union with Russia was not the common socialist project, but Russia's neo-imperialist promise to protect Poland against ostensible West German irredentism—an irredentism that grew out of Stalin's "gift" to Poland of the Oder-Neisse border.[6]

People's Poland thus became unusually reliant on Soviet power because it was the only state on which a Western power had territorial demands. But the case of East Germany was extreme in a different way. It was born as the Soviet Zone of Occupation in Germany and constituted about a third of what was left of Germany after the cession of the lands east of the Oder-Neisse line to Poland and the Soviet Union. It was not a-national, however. Like other socialist states, East Germany placed itself in a tradition of "progressive" national forces and claimed to represent them in Germany as a whole. Yet because its ultimate reason for existence was to be socialist, it had to justify itself in terms different from those governing West Germany, where people also revered General Scharnhorst and Goethe, not to mention Frederick the Great.

That meant that when socialist realism was relaxed or forgotten in other countries, its application intensified in the GDR. No realm of culture was ever perfectly controlled by the state; even the most dreary socialist realist novel left space for individual creativity. But consider popular photography. The amateur photographic lens constantly featured a subject that was imperfect: a socialist society less than fully transformed. East German photography magazines therefore promoted doctrines of socialist realism with heightened enthusiasm *after* Stalinism, and their editors upbraided amateur photographic clubs that limited their discussions to technical matters and failed to address "ideological, aesthetic, and political questions."[7]

In the major Polish photographic magazine, by contrast, expressions like "socialist realism" or "bourgeois photography" disappeared after 1956, and authors devoted lavish attention to technical subjects or controversial issues like abstract photography. The writing was not interest-free, but it dovetailed with the interests of the Warsaw intelligentsia, who paid careful attention to international trends. Even after Gomułka had clipped the wings of Poland's more daring Marxist liberals—known as "revisionists"—his party did not return to the "Stalinist" method of dictating the content of art journals. Of special interest to the editors, whether in or outside the party, was amateur photography, the untrained, unpredictable capturing of state socialist reality, featuring whatever a person holding a lens happened to sight, including "detritus and mundane rituals of everyday life," such as "broken pots and pans in the hands of children or the odd tenderness of peasant farmers cutting each other's hair."[8] In contrast to East German counterparts, Polish intellectuals worked not toward socialism but toward Polish traditions of the past and future, some of which were socialist, and all of which were embedded in an international cultural community that included the West.

The policies toward photography were a subset of a larger campaign in the GDR. In 1957, after suppressing "revisionist" Marxists who had sympathized with Imre Nagy, the East German Communist Party (known as the Socialist Unity Party of Germany, or SED) leader Walter Ulbricht headed an ideological offensive known as the Bitterfeld way, named after a 1959 authors' conference in a town at the heart of the country's coal and chemicals industry. The point was to have writers go to factories, and for boundaries to be effaced between mental and physical labor. Workers were writers and vice versa. This aspiration was reminiscent of Marx's "realm of freedom," in which human beings were no longer "ruled by the blind forces of nature," and where communities of producers reached their full human potential every day: except that in the GDR it was achieved by force, by the loyal cadres of a state that could not afford to seem less than socialist.[9]

Given that the socialist world claimed to promote peace and brotherhood among the nations, East European Communists should have excluded all xenophobia from their efforts to build popularity on national traditions. Yet in fact, national Communism, like all nationalisms, would have been formless without a national enemy. From the start, anti-German tones could be heard in Polish or Czechoslovak propaganda, and it was no coincidence that Germany's Communists were excluded from the founding meeting of the Cominform in 1947 (though the French and Italian were included).[10] The SED, as a German organization, faced a peculiar dilemma. Given their reliance on Soviet Union for their state's very existence, East German Communists did not dare employ anti-Slavism, the standard tool of German nationalism for generations. Most of their allies in the Warsaw Pact, the military alliance of the Soviet Bloc formed in 1955, were Slavic. In a sense, East German Communists made up for it by turning up the volume of anti-imperialist propaganda to a deafening level against West Germany. Supposedly, they, in East Berlin, were the superior Germans, and the wall they built around West Berlin in August 1961 fostered German unity. The wall's real purpose was to keep highly skilled workers from fleeing to the West, thus bleeding the East German economy of labor (some 3 million Germans had fled East Germany between 1945 and 1961).[11]

Yet looking east, SED leaders also claimed to be the best Marxists, no matter how often they piously asserted that the Soviet Communist Party was their model. Behind the bland and obligatory rhetoric of "fraternal relations," leading comrades privately called Polish counterparts "Polacks" and encouraged age-old resentments in the population when party orthodoxy seemed threatened.[12] In the 1970s, the GDR also promoted the legacy of Prussia as part of its "national" past. Still, this was a muted nationalism; despite the hubristic invocations of itself as a "socialist nation," East Germany was less than half a country; unlike Romanian, Polish, Bulgarian, Czech, and Slovak counterparts, the SED was not a national party, and the longer it ruled, the more a united Germany seemed to recede into a future beyond reach.[13]

Hungary: Socialist Imagination Unleashed

Hungary's Communists understood the predicament of East German comrades. They, too, could speak for only part of the nation because millions of Hungarians lived beyond their state's borders, in Slovakia, Serbia, and Romania. Any attempt to "play" a national card could become dangerously irredentist, and it could highlight the abject failure of Hungary's Communists to secure any revision to the Trianon boundaries from their Soviet patrons after World War II. Even references to the revolutionary heritage of 1848/1849 were problematic, because Hungarian liberals of that time had insisted on Magyar rule over the enormous Hungarian kingdom, which included territories held by Warsaw Pact allies (including the Soviet Union) but also Yugoslavia and Austria. On top of this was the fact that Russian forces had crushed that revolution—like that of 1956. The difficulty of speaking about key historical events made Hungarian national consciousness profoundly pessimistic. Thus, Hungary's leaders became "internationalist" and opposed the "nationalist heresies" of their neighbors, especially Romania and Czechoslovakia, and they lectured other states to "critically examine their own chauvinism."[14]

Still, doctrinaire antinationalism would have made the Kádár regime seem even more alien than it did after being installed by Soviet tanks. Therefore, it left space for unresolved ideological conflicts, for example, in the debates of the early 1960s initiated by the Party historian Erik Molnár, where the approach to national history was moderation instead of denial.[15] Historians asked whether an economically independent Hungary would have achieved higher growth rates in the nineteenth century. The answer was no: in the economic union with Austria, advantages had outweighed disadvantages. Was the dissolution of Hungary in 1918 an inevitable result of the Compromise of 1867? Again the answer was no: that state would have collapsed in any case. Finally, in a departure from doctrinaire assessments of the Stalinist period, historians said the Horthy regime was a mixture of right-wing forces, rather than being simply fascist. These were sober compromise positions that moved beyond the dogmatic 1950s, when historians had argued that Western imperialists had destroyed the Hungarian republic of 1919 and then foisted Horthy's fascism on the Hungarian masses.[16] The new synthesis made for a more complicated reading of the past without good and evil characters or simple sequences of cause and effect. Even the history of Communism and the workers' movement appeared in an array of colors that frustrated simplistic judgments.

Such pragmatism shaped every act of Hungary's rulers. János Kádár's basic task, after suppressing the popular rising, was to restore Communist rule from top to bottom while leaving Stalinism behind. He shaved away the extremes of right and left, leaving an ideological gray zone, a suspended limbo of opportunism with doors partly open to liberalization. The Soviets could threaten to bring back Mátyás Rákosi, who was held in "exile" in the Soviet Union, and Kádár maintained basic order so that this did not happen. Moscow grew to appreciate his work. One Soviet ambassador who accused him of dragging his feet on forced collectivization was recalled to Moscow.[17] But then the wily Hungarian party leader completed the process of making agriculture socialist, giving cooperative farms three-quarters of the country's arable land, and state farms (*sovchozy*) most of the rest.[18] Kádár had succeeded where Rákosi failed. But, as we will see in greater detail, agriculture was no longer Stalinist and featured a panoply of incentives to increase production.

For those who wondered what socialism might now mean, Kádár clarified his position in 1961 and 1962. Because class struggle was largely an event in the past, discrimination against members of the middle classes, for example, in university admissions, could cease. He borrowed a formula from an émigré critic who in turn had borrowed from Luke's Gospel: "those who are not against us are with us." The punishment of supporters of the 1956 revolution would cease. Hundreds of "traitors" had been hanged, including some who were younger than eighteen when they committed their supposed crimes. Years later, Kádár told Soviet visitors that he wanted to avenge each Communist killed by the revolutionaries, and if that was true, he succeeded many times over.

If Kádár eschewed overt nationalism, he bolstered legitimacy by exploring what could be done to make socialism serve Hungarians' material interests.[19] After freeing his country from Stalinism, he determined to show that his socialism outdid anything Imre Nagy might have done. The government raised wages, liberalized the abortion law, reduced taxes on merchants and craftspeople, improved pensions, and made Christmas and Easter public holidays.[20]

Kádár's ethos of making life better had consequences for Party elites as well. Under Rákosi, they had rewarded themselves with vacation houses, special stores, and innumerable perquisites. Kádár cut those back, and now even top leaders relied on the Hungaria-Balaton Tourism and Holiday Company to get rooms in summer houses. Kádár called this policy "strengthening Communist morals." Functionaries lost the privilege of traveling with 50 percent reduction on state railways and could no longer use state automobiles and telephones for private purposes. Thus, party power was restored but there was no return to the Stalinist status quo ante. More consumer goods became available, and living standards rose by a third from 1957 to 1960. Beginning in the early 1960s, televisions, washing machines, and refrigerators became commonplace, and average wage-earners lived in much greater comfort and security than did their parents or grandparents.[21]

This non-nationalistic, consumption-oriented program also matched Hungary's specific national predicament. Kádár reckoned that after decades of being called to sacrifice for great causes—the Nazi enterprise of saving Europe and then the Soviet one of propelling humankind into a utopian future—Hungarians were ready for things more tangible. Socialist society was being built, not for the sake of ideology, he assured the population, but "because it ensures a better life for the people, and that the country and the nation will flourish."[22]

To make this strategy succeed, Hungary's Communists turned their attention to economic reform more seriously than comrades did elsewhere, over a longer period, with greater consistency and support from the top, despite objections from Moscow, and even during upheavals in other states. Socialist states had grown their economies rapidly in the early 1950s by introducing underused resources to production, especially raw materials and labor, but by the 1960s, those avenues were becoming exhausted. Now industrial growth would depend on increased productivity and technical development. The challenge of slower growth was felt keenly in the Soviet Union, given Nikita Khrushchev's bold pronouncement of October 1961 that the Soviet Communist Party would attain "over the next 20 years a living standard for the people that will be higher than that of any capitalist country." "For the first time," he said, "there will be a full and final end to the situation in which people suffer from shortage of anything."[23] (See Tables A.5 and A.6 in the Appendix.)

Hungary faced severe disequilibrium. It had mounting debts to countries outside the Soviet Bloc, going from 1,600 million forints in 1959 to 4,100 million in 1963, and its debt-servicing commitments to those countries exceeded the value of its exports to them. More than 80 percent of the growth in debt involved short-term credits that expired within three months and had to be constantly refinanced. The sum of repayment obligations was more than twice as large as the foreign exchange earnings exports could cover.[24]

Pressure for changes was strongest in agriculture, because Hungarians spent most of their money on food and because the quality of diets had dropped sharply under Stalinism. The completion of collectivization by 1961/1962 had only aggravated matters: in the following half-decade, food production barely reached the average of 1958/1959. The time of coercing people to join cooperatives was over. Now the party had to ensure that they worked effectively and conscientiously.[25]

The response was to strike out in a direction where no socialist society had gone. Perhaps stretching the truth, Kádár claimed in 1960 that Khrushchev had said each socialist country had the primary duty of satisfying its own grain requirements, and the Soviet Union would not bail them out in case of shortfalls. Two years later, Kádár told fellow party leaders that other socialist countries had taken paths of coercion that Hungarians should not follow; he was delighted that Hungary had not done "the kind of thing the Bulgarian comrades did," or for that matter, the East Germans or Czechs. Forced collectivization in East Germany had driven tens of thousands to the West. As his listeners knew, that outflow had led to the construction of the Berlin Wall, probably the greatest public embarrassment for the East Bloc in its history.[26]

The alternative to compulsion was consultation; to use directives and incentives. The ideas were not entirely new. In November 1956, the regime stopped forcing deliveries of grain, and class struggle gave way to policies of negotiated change. Rather than vilifying middle peasants as "kulaks" the regime endeavored to win them over. Those who refused to join existing collectives could form their own and assume leading positions in them. Instead of mandating the cultivation of particular crops, the state began working out what seemed fair market prices and permitting sizable private plots where farmers could also keep livestock. Beginning in 1970, there were no limits on the number of animals that farmers could raise "privately." And peasants began receiving guaranteed benefits, like health insurance. Unlike in Poland, the state actively promoted the rural sector and awarded generous subsidies for purchasing machinery.[27]

Though farmers had to work in collective farms, these did not consist solely of confiscated land. Almost three-quarters of cooperative land was privately owned, and the owners were paid rent. That touched the heart of Marxist-Leninist dogma, according to which the socialist sector must consist of property owned by the state. But Kádár was adjusting doctrine to new realities. In October 1966, he told the Central Committee that privately owned land in a cooperative could also be considered "consistent socialist property."[28] With that, the imaginative socialist was proclaiming a belated victory for the 1956 Revolution. And that was only the beginning.

Instead of being superseded like the Soviets' New Economic Policy in the 1920s, the Hungarian economic reform intensified, going beyond agriculture.

Party leader Kádár wanted to compete successfully with Western states not just for the sake of productivity, but also to make Hungary a genuine workers' state. He observed that French and Italian unions were demanding shorter hours for their workers, while Hungary was stuck with a 48-hour work week. Why? "Because work intensity is low!" "My feeling is that defeat awaits us," he told the Politburo in November 1964, "if we cannot change our ways." For him, reform was not a retreat from but a new form of state planning, based on "Marxist economic science" and greater attention to the law of value: it was in no way similar to the "market economy in a capitalist sense."[29]

That same year, the party leadership constituted twelve working committees with representatives of science, the state, and the corporate sphere; these committees produced studies that were synthesized into a Central Committee resolution the following year. After a further year's preparation, the package was introduced on January 1, 1968 as the New Economic Mechanism (NEM).[30] The major plank was to abolish disaggregation by a central plan. This meant that instead of state authorities telling enterprises what to produce, they now steered output by way of "regulators," like prices, profit, taxes, credit, and wages. State authorities still made basic decisions about economic development through plans with targets, but they no longer sent rigid, detailed directives on what to produce.

Prices increasingly reflected production costs and economic-policy intentions, but they did not float freely. A mixed system consisted of three sectors: one with fixed prices, another with prices that could move within a band set by the administration, and one with free prices. Some 70 percent of domestic raw materials and semi-finished products used in production were sold at fixed or maximized prices, but 30 percent could fluctuate. The economy remained slanted toward heavy industry—though its share decreased—but the rationale for production had shifted: for enterprises, profit became the decisive economic regulator, the yardstick of their performance and source of investment. The scope of their independent activity increased substantially. Still, enterprises could not fail because that would have produced unemployment.[31] The weaker enterprises therefore relied on state support in a way that businesses operating under market conditions could not. Hungary's firms lacked the incentive of failure to improve quality, reduce costs, or introduce new products, and these facts would ultimately set limits to the reform's ability to stimulate growth.

For the time being, however, leaders were not only optimistic but also ambitious. They began testing the waters of global competition and hoped to join the International Monetary Fund and World Bank, steps that the Soviet Union hindered, fearing hostile American influence. The third five-year plan (1966–1970) aimed at a 50 percent hike in industrial exports. Yet even intensified trade with the socialist economies exposed Hungary to the harsh winds of the global economy. Industries positioned for growth—chemicals, machine-building—required imports of part-assemblies and capital equipment that could be had only for hard currency. Take Hungary's famous export product, the Ikarus passenger buses. Some 6,000 were slotted for export for rubles to socialist countries in the 1966 plan, bringing in 1,300 million forints in foreign exchange; but production of these buses required importing from the West—for dollars—machinery worth 327 million forints. Thus, the more exports increased to Comecon countries, the more dollar imports increased as well, and without goods suitable for sale to the West, dollar debts mounted that could not be repaid.[32]

These tensions in the economic sphere threatened the progress that Hungarian leaders had made in domestic and foreign-policy consolidation.[33] Their choice was to become globally competitive or to retreat from reform and stagnate. Thus began a syndrome that would pursue Hungary to its final economic crisis of the 1980s: the money borrowed to make Hungary's industries competitive led to growing indebtedness.

But that was the macroeconomic picture. Some sectors boomed. As far as the tourist eye was concerned, Hungary—with boutiques featuring fashionable raincoats and handbags, beauty parlors, self-service restaurants, shops with sweets and citrus fruits, and well-dressed city folk speeding along in private automobiles—came to resemble a Western country. That was especially true if the tourist hailed from Poland, Romania, or the Soviet Union. In Hungary, ideology had taken a back seat, and gradually the Stalinist-era ethos of class struggle, surveillance, and ideological correctness gave way to "consumerist values, practices and patterns of behavior." Coca-Cola or blue jeans were no longer "sinful apples of western paradise," but objects people wanted because the Communists told them they should.[34]

Poland's Leninism

Poland, sometimes paired with Hungary as a special challenge to Soviet rule, went in an astonishingly different direction. If Kádár the "national traitor" pursued reform because he needed peace with society, Gomułka the "national hero" scoffed at reform because he had stood up twice to the Soviets, suffered for it, and seemed to embody the highest values of Polish sovereignty. He thought he knew more about everything than anyone else, even about the economy and agriculture, and he listened to no one, especially those who disagreed.

What he achieved by the mid-1960s, partly through misguided ideological offensives but more through contemptuous neglect, was to unite in common grievance diverse groups of Poles: peasants, churchgoers, intellectuals of all persuasions, industrial workers, and most ominously, students. By late in the decade, Gomułka faced a predicament unique in the Communist Bloc: a standoff against society in which nonstate actors disputed his claim to represent the nation. This tragedy of hubris and squandered opportunities has several acts: first, alienation of the church; then, of writers and intellectuals, students, and Jews; and finally, of workers, whom he ordered shot down in cold disregard in December 1970. Before falling from power, the ascetic know-it-all explained his reasoning to close associates: "whatever the position of the party, that will also be the position of the working class and society."[35]

The major challenge, in his view, rising to an obsession, was "revisionism," a force from within Marxism demanding the democracy, open discussion, and "free play of forces" that were common to majority socialist movements before 1918. Yet Gomułka had become a Communist in the 1930s and had absorbed Leninism's hostility to factions. By 1964, he had removed virtually everyone from the leadership associated with the liberal Puławy group, many of whom were Jewish, which had acted as a spearhead for change in 1956. Their leader, Roman Zambrowski, resigned from his position of Central Committee secretary in 1963, complaining of an absence of "regular, everyday collegial direction of party work." Gomułka did not consult him even by telephone and "ignored with irritation" every idea that differed from his own, steering the economy virtually single-handedly. Gomułka had aides bring him stacks of data on the amounts of coal mined and grain harvested, and he worked through the specifics of production and wages. He personally drew up plans to restructure scientific technical institutes. In most Communist countries, the leadership met once weekly, but in Poland, it met just once a month.[36]

Like Kádár, Gomułka was personally modest, and lived not in a villa but in a small apartment. Yet unlike Kádár, he tried to impress this characteristic on the population at large. His standard was not the growing consumer societies of Western Europe, but vivid memories of crisis-ridden Poland of the 1930s. "His" Poland would leave that past behind, giving workers basic securities and a modest but dependable standard of living. Thus for Gomułka, a good cup of coffee, something workers of his youth could hardly dream of, was a luxury for spoiled intellectuals, and he worked out how many factories might be built with the money saved by halting coffee imports. Another "luxury" was summer vacations at a warm beach, something no workers aspired to when he worked as a locksmith at refineries in southern Poland. He also imposed his Spartan standards on private dwellings, personally reducing floorplans of apartment blocks slotted for workers' use. A window in the kitchen was a frivolity.

At the same time, as a Communist who believed humankind was advancing beyond capitalism, he opposed any reform or compromise—like market mechanisms or semi-private property—that might permit the reemergence of a capitalist class and thus constitute a step backward in history. For him, economic experiments of the Hungarian type risked political instability. Socialism meant heavy industry under strict party control that would give Poland the foundations of a modern economy and reduce the advantages held by the West. Under Gomułka, planners directed investment to metallurgy, mining, and the machine-building and chemical industries at the expense of consumer and light industries.[37]

Still, in the early years of his rule, resources shifted away from military production due to the more relaxed international situation, and Poles' living standards improved markedly. In 1956/1957 real wages went up by 10 percent and by 1958, incomes had improved by more than 25 percent. Spaces opened again for small private business in cities (the number of small craftsperson's shops went up by half), and as forced collectivization ended, private initiative expanded in the countryside as well. The regime ceased compulsory deliveries of milk, and prices went up for agricultural products. By 1959, few complained of shortages of sausage or meat, and agriculture reached its highest production since the war, almost entirely due to private enterprise. As many farmers went back to private farming, the share of collectivized agriculture (area under crops) remained low: 15.0 percent (1957), 13.2 percent (1960), and 15.9 percent (1970).[38]

But these compromises were meant to be temporary. In the long run, neither Gomułka nor any other Leninist thought that private enterprise could be part of socialism. Into the mid-1980s, the Soviet Union pushed Poland toward full collectivization, and in private conversations, Communists from elsewhere never tired of impressing on Polish comrades the source of Poland's political and economic woes: it lay in private agriculture. But Poland's Communists themselves were not permanently reconciled. What happened in 1956 was not a peace treaty with the independent peasantry but a truce, permitting Gomułka to conduct a low-grade guerilla war, hoping to gain advantage through slow attrition. Though they gave up on outright compulsion, authorities never ceased

FIGURE 21.1. W. Gomułka and J. Cyrankiewicz, on eastern side of Berlin Wall (1962).
Source: Keystone Press/Alamy Stock Photo.

trying to press farmers into collectives. In 1958, they created farmer associations (*Kółki rolnicze*) that made machinery available, yet over time, the associations became tools for pressuring farmers to join the collectives by withholding machinery from the recalcitrant.[39] Similarly, pensions and insurance were introduced in the countryside, but only for those willing to join state farms.

Gomułka did nothing to promote private agriculture, and investment resources always remained skewed toward heavy industry. In the Stalinist years (1950–1955), the sum of the budget devoted to agriculture was 10 percent, but afterward that figure went up to only 17.4 (1966–1970) and 15.2 percent (1970–1975). Twice as much went to developing transportation. The state never permitted markets to develop in the countryside and remained the sole supplier of resources, as well as the monopoly purchaser of agricultural products. It kept prices of the former too high and the latter too low, stifling investment and productivity.[40] Until 1971, more ambitious farmers could not buy more than 15 hectares of land, and often they worked small plots spread over many kilometers and could not take care of them equally; much land remained uncultivated.[41] Of 19 million hectares devoted to agriculture in the state land fund (*państwowy fundusz ziemi*) in 1977, one million hectares were not farmed. And farms continued to be plagued by demands for high compulsory deliveries, which ceased only in 1972.

But the countryside had its vengeance. On the backdrop of the growing cities, life in villages seemed increasingly tedious, and young people escaped by the hundreds of thousands, leaving older farmers behind, who squeezed their parcels dry before retiring. Unproductive agriculture yielded less meat than the growing city populations desired, and Poland's state socialism had no remedy. The only mechanism the state possessed for controlling demand or increasing supply for meat was raising prices, but when it did that, industrial workers went on strike; that in turn would lead to the emergence of the popular independent trade union Solidarity in 1980. One remedy pursued was the import of agricultural products, but that worked only when Poland could export industrial goods: and since the industrial goods it produced were not competitive on world markets, grain had to be bought on credit. (See Table A.2 in the Appendix.)

Yet that strategy was anathema to Poland's Leninists. Unlike Kádár, Gomułka determined to limit any dependence on the capitalist world, and he aimed for self-sufficiency in agriculture and autarchy in industry, relying on technologies available in the socialist bloc.[42] Unlike Hungarian comrades, Poland's top leaders resisted reform and relied on central planning despite its increasingly evident problems: excessive expenditure on raw materials, ineffective use of energy, realization of growth primarily by the addition of labor (which remained plentiful), and wastefulness in the production process. Building a coal mine in Poland was twice as costly as in the West. Local party bosses had interests greater than efficient production, and once the plan was met, they considered their task fulfilled. Those who pointed out problems appeared to question these bosses' authority and themselves became problems.

Still, the Polish economy grew as cities and the working class expanded. Poland in 1965 gave evidence of an increasingly modern society, with full cafes, restaurants, and movie houses, men and women dressed in the fashions of the moment, and birth rates increasing along with life expectancy. Numbers of cars, refrigerators, and washing machines went up, and modernization began transforming the countryside. If in 1955, only 33 percent of farms had electricity, by 1970, the figure had risen to 90 percent.[43] But at the same time, queues remained a feature of everyday life, though it was not clear whether they reflected unfulfilled desires or habit. In shortage economies, people bought things as soon as they appeared in stores, and routinely got in line without asking what was for sale.

As a consumer society, Poland fell behind the West—the lights of Warsaw could not compete with those of West Berlin, let alone Paris—but in one sense, Gomułka was right. (See Table A.5 in the Appendix.) Poland of the 1960s had surpassed his 1930s ideal. The overwhelming majority of the population had little difficulty in securing the basic needs of life.[44] Still, living space was a problem never solved. Even though 3.5 million living quarters were made available from 1960 to 1970, the number of people waiting for apartments in 1970 was about one million, and that number would increase.[45]

The situation in Hungary was quite different. Technically, everything was collective, but in fact, much of collectivized agriculture made use of privately owned land, and the state permitted substantial private plots, market mechanisms, product diversification, and profit-making—all within limits. As a result, productivity gradually increased.[46] Hungarian Communists also expected the long-term decline of markets and private plots, but in the meantime were prepared for pragmatic compromise. And because technically, their market-oriented farmers were collective farmers, they had no reason to punish them.

Dissent in Poland

Over time, the underperforming Polish economy produced dissent. Economic grievances drove people onto the streets, costing Gomułka as well as his successor their jobs. But the problem was not essentially economic, because it derived from the belief among basic producers—farmers—that under no circumstances would they sacrifice the land of their fathers to the atheistic state in order to live under the "Bolshevik" system of collective farms. Perhaps if they had, Poland could at least have produced meat in sufficient supply to keep workers from striking and paralyzing the system. Punishing farmers meant punishing Poland and in turn, imperiling those who claimed to rule on Poland's behalf.

But the problem went beyond peasants to the party functionaries whose job it was to put them in collective farms. Of these functionaries, there were fewer per capita than elsewhere, and they were less fervent.[47] The fires of Marxist-Leninist faith in Poland never burned as brightly as elsewhere, and they faded more rapidly. It's hard to identify a single cause. Ultimately, Communism was about transforming the world into a place without suffering and exploitation. The revolution had happened, and such a world was nowhere to be seen. Instead, there was a clique around Gomułka who once talked about democracy but was interested in its own power; and below the elite were men and women in party and state functions interested above all in self-enrichment.

Gomułka was insensitive even to the fact that he had compromised. After eliminating challenges from the right and left in the party, he spoke confidently and menacingly about the party's task of "steering" the life of society. In 1958, he decided to cut back the one institutional competitor for influence: the Roman Catholic Church. The time had come for it to adapt to progress and renounce its hopeless struggle against socialism. The "medieval times of supremacy of church over state" had passed for good.[48]

But the challenge was more complex than the word "church" suggests. There was the hierarchy of bishops, whom he hated for their airs of social superiority, but there were also millions of churchgoers. During Stalinism, the party had not attempted to destroy Catholicism outright, though it did embed spies and informants in the clergy and interned the Primate Cardinal Wyszyński from 1954 to 1956. The state waited until 1958 for what might have seemed simple acts of secularization: removing crosses and religious instruction from state schools and keeping party members who went to church from holding offices (but not from being in the party!).[49] Now the state went on a proper offensive, withdrawing permission for the building of churches and seizing buildings that the church already held.

The almost immediate result was public confrontation. In May 1960, attempts to expel priests from a building used for religious instruction at the "Catholic House" in Zielona Góra in western Poland brought more than 5,000 demonstrators onto the streets; police were called in from as far away as Poznań and brutally dispersed crowds with truncheons. Yet women remained inside the House and around its entrance, kneeling and praying. In the end, more than 220 protesters were arrested, and 160 police were injured. Show trials followed and prison sentences of up to five years, but the church was not weakened, let alone destroyed. In southeastern Przemyśl, three days of rioting broke out in 1963 when the government closed a school for training organists.[50] Three thousand police had been summoned from as far away as Silesia in anticipation of the protests.

The largest confrontation occurred in the new socialist steel town of Nowa Huta, where the government had issued permission to build a church in 1957 but now reversed itself: socialist cities did not need churches. When workers came on April 27, 1960, to dig up a cross the faithful had planted on the building site, women passersby put their arms around the cross, while others pelted the workers with clumps of earth, forcing them to retreat. People from surrounding apartment buildings then gathered and re-anchored the cross in the earth. The crowd burgeoned as shifts emptied from the Lenin steel works, and days of rioting ensued, also involving students from nearby Kraków. In the end, 181 police were injured, and almost 500 demonstrators were arrested. Gomułka's right-hand man, Zenon Kliszko, supervised the repression, including a "path of health," which demonstrators were made to pass through as gauntlets of officers beat them with clubs.[51] Yet in the end, the cross remained.

Some have written that Gomułka needlessly provoked opposition. In these towns and beyond, he made Catholics more active churchgoers than before. But Gomułka sensed a struggle looming for the allegiance of the Polish people. Catholicism in Poland stood financially apart from the state, in a way unrivaled in the Soviet Bloc, and it possessed seminaries, newspapers, and its own university at Lublin. It was the one institution in the bloc that could contest a socialist state's claim to speak for the nation. But the church's nationalism was a tradition of recent invention: especially before 1918, its hierarchy had not shown any special interest in Polish struggles for national liberation. Rome taught that all secular power, even that of the Russian Tsar, came from God.[52]

Even so, it was Gomułka who chose the fight. He rightly believed the bishops were counting on socialism collapsing, and he wanted gestures of loyalty they did not provide. "The church is conducting a war against us," he told one Catholic intellectual in 1959. "But it will not win this war. We will win and history will sweep you aside. [Cardinal] Wyszyński is always demanding one thing or the other. He wants a reign over souls. But in this country socialism reigns over souls. Socialism reaches out for the soul, and it is here that the church has no rights!"[53]

But it was precisely there that the hierarchy would not give its assent. The struggle to build a church in Nowa Huta was about the souls of believers and the soul of Poland. The Cardinal of Kraków had just appointed as assistant bishop the dynamic thirty-eight-year-old Karol Wojtyła, a sophisticated multilingual theologian and former actor who had labored at a factory under German occupation and felt comfortable among workers. In Wojtyła's view, the state had failed the class it claimed to represent in Nowa Huta. In 1955, the journalist Ryszard Kapuściński had published an exposé depicting the new town as a place of loose living, where money was the only value. A fourteen-year-old prostitute reputed to have infected eight men with gonorrhea used language that made him want to vomit.

In the spring of 1977, now himself Cardinal of Kraków, Wojtyła blessed a church that finally was built on the site of the cross in Nowa Huta, the Church of the Ark, and proposed a new narrative: "This not a city of people who belong to no one," he said, "not a city of people, that you can do with as you wish,

FIGURE 21.2. Archbishop Karol Wojtyła (third row, second from right),
Rome (1975). *Source*: Stefanocec / CC-BY-SA 3.0.

who can be manipulated according to the rules of production and consumption. This city is a city of the children of God." Two years later, he appeared once
more in Nowa Huta, now as Pope John Paul II, and said that the defense of the
cross in Nowa Huta had strengthened the church, signaling new horizons for
Christian missionaries.[54] The following year, the new steel town became a bastion of the independent trade union Solidarity. The church's support was even
firmer in the traditional village communities from which Nowa Huta's workers
had come, villages the state was just reaching with paved roads, electricity, and
schools.

But the struggle that routed Leninism's antichurch militants was millennial:
the thousand years' celebration in 1966 of Polish statehood was also one of Polish Christianity. The Catholic Church had been preparing for years. In 1957,
Wyszyński had a duplicate of the "Black Madonna" painting from Częstochowa
blessed by Pope Pius XII. The original had been carried by Polish troops who
defeated the Swedes in 1652 when all seemed lost. King Jan Sobieski had declared

Mary "Queen of Poland." Wyszyński organized a pilgrimage for the duplicate painting around Poland, and he ordered that it be displayed in every parish after a procession. Some faithful had the honor of hosting the Virgin's image in their homes. In June 1966, officials had had enough and ordered the picture confiscated and taken back to Częstochowa. People joked that the Virgin had been arrested. But the processions continued with an empty frame where the picture had been. In the Katowice diocese, one in three inhabitants took part in the processions.[55]

These events occurred just months after the groundshaking event in twentieth-century Catholicism: the Second Vatican Council. Polish bishops in attendance had sent a letter to German counterparts, inviting them to attend the millennial celebrations in their country, but they astounded world opinion with an unexpected conclusion: "we forgive and ask for forgiveness." The time had come for Polish-German reconciliation, but as much as a gesture of Christian unity, this letter was directed against Europe's division. Against the party's claim that (West) Germans were Poland's eternal enemy, the bishops recalled centuries of good neighborly relations, and they stressed the mediating role of Germans in the Christianization of the Middle Ages, when Poland had become part of Christian Europe. Gomułka saw in this letter an attempt to reorient Poland toward the West.[56]

He also believed that the church had handed the party a golden opportunity to stage a renewed assault. In tens of thousands of meetings and dozens of articles, Communist agitators asked whether the bishops had forgotten who started World War II and how the Polish people had suffered. Poles had nothing to apologize for. The official Polish Communist press excerpted texts from German newspapers that congratulated the bishops for "surmounting" Polish nationalism. What better evidence could there be of their betrayal?[57]

In 1966 state authorities staged public gatherings, hoping to eclipse the church's millennial celebrations, and sent riot police to rough up crowds leaving masses in Warsaw. Provocateurs chanted: "down with Wyszyński!" and "Traitor!" while police arrested more than a hundred churchgoers for "disturbing the peace." Fighting also broke out in Kraków, Gdańsk, and Lublin, where hundreds more were taken into custody.[58]

Yet gradually, the antichurch campaign fell silent. In autumn 1967, authorities relented, telling Cardinal Wojtyła that a church could be built in Nowa Huta after all. The campaign had proved self-defeating. Wherever the state surged forward, the church had pushed back, and even gained new ground. Within a few years of the ban on religion in state schools, four million children were attending instruction at 20,000 "catechetical stations," that had gone up like "mushrooms after the rain."[59] Worse than that, by advancing so far against the church, the regime had courted attacks on exposed flanks from other dissenting groups in Polish society, above all the intelligentsia.

* * *

From early in the century, a large part of the Polish intelligentsia registered as "nonbelievers," and even prominent Catholic intellectuals tended to think the Polish church was comparatively backward, carried by the emotions of peasant masses.[60] Yet now writers and scholars began making common cause with the church because they worried about the survival of Polish culture. They understood the power of religious symbols to impart a language of nationhood and gravitated toward priests, especially at universities, who considered the church a protector of the nation's soul. The campaign against the church had disgusted even Marxist intellectuals, for whom Gomułka's demagoguery was just the latest chapter in a story of disappointment that stretched back to the months after he took office. Catholicism and Polish identity were causes waiting to be exploited by each other, and the antichurch campaign finally made this happen.

Gomułka's vulnerability in dealing with intellectuals, whether Marxist or not, derived from an absence of ideas. The rigid party line was gone, and by predilection, Gomułka began bringing "tough men" back into government, who favored strict centralization, for example, Julian Tokarski, a former ministry of heavy industry and a special target of workers' wrath in Poznan in 1956. Now Tokarski was quietly made deputy premier. The detested Stalinist, General Kazimierz Witaszewski, once responsible for persecuting Home Army and other non-Communist soldiers, returned from obscurity to become the most powerful man in party Central Committee.[61] People of his ilk mixed uneasily with other leaders who said that decentralization was not so bad. The party apparatus thus never knew whether to expect Gomułka to call for discipline or moderation. He cracked the whip, but then propaganda chief Edward Ochab temporized, saying, "that needs more study."[62]

A first sign of Gomułka's distaste for criticism had come in October 1957, when he closed the student weekly *Po prostu* after saying it either must follow the party's lead or disappear. Several days of rioting followed in Warsaw, with more than 500 arrested, 180 injured, and two killed. A purge of Marxist revisionists followed that removed about 16 percent of the party's members by May 1958. The government also pacified movements among students and workers that had demanded more democracy and shelved plans for "national councils" that would have permitted more grassroots representation. Gomułka had briefly considered permitting elections with more than one candidate—but then decided that free choice would endanger socialism. Censorship grew more invasive, and soon parliament was again passing resolutions unanimously. In the early 1960s, Gomułka even celebrated "socialist realism" as superior to the "destructive" trends in art and literature that Polish intellectuals were importing from the West. In October 1963, the party created an "ideological commission" led by Gomułka's right-hand man, Zenon Kliszko, a neurotic suffering from failed ambitions to be an intellectual.[63]

Yet there was no return to Stalinist controls, let alone terror. For their part, among the critical intelligentsia, no one openly questioned the existence of a socialist Poland, and years of relative stability followed. After the purge, the Communist Party grew again, from 1.15 million in 1960 to 2.3 million a decade later.[64] Yet the party's ability to inspire loyalty and sacrifice was vanishing. New party members cared above all for career advancement, while filmmakers and writers ignored the party altogether and explored questions of current interest: alienation and the vicissitudes of Polish history. Philosophers and sociologists returned to questions of interest to their disciplines internationally, like human freedom, or empirical studies of the consequences of industrialization. What was not permitted was direct defiance, a point made through several infamous cases of repression.

In 1962, the "Crooked Circle," a Warsaw club where prominent intellectuals had discussed issues freely since 1955, was forced to close its doors. In 1963, authorities shut down two major journals of the Thaw period and replaced them with Kultura, a monthly meant to battle reactionary ideologies on Polish soil.[65] Numbers of books produced fell from 85 million in 1957 to 78 million in 1962. Artists and writers began fearing the growing ambit of a chauvinist and anti-intellectual right wing in the party around Interior Minister Mieczysław Moczar.

Many in the Polish intelligentsia grew deeply concerned about the future. In 1964, thirty-four leading figures published an open letter demanding that constitutional rights of free speech be respected; they also expressed alarm at the consequences the government's anti-intellectual course spelled for Poland's national culture. Rather than discuss these concerns, the regime arrested one signatory while denying others passports and the right to publish. Several were no longer mentioned in the press. To punish Catholic editor Jerzy Turowicz, the regime reduced paper supplies for his journal Tygodnik Powszechny, forcing it to scale back from 40,000 to 30,000 copies.[66] The letter attracted international attention, because the signatories were Poland's top philosophers; its most-beloved poets; best-known literary critics; and most-influential sociologists, economists, and historians, whether popular or professional. So exclusive was the group that the writer who initiated the appeal felt it would be presumptuous to include himself. This was the incomparable multitasking Jan Józef Lipski, Catholic, Freemason, and independent socialist all in one.

The problem for the rulers was not just the reputation of these cultural figures in a nation that had been shaped by resistance to suppression of culture: it was primarily the unending diversity of their backgrounds. There were former Stalinists and Catholic émigrés, top Marxist revisionists, but also professors who taught the younger generation in ways that had nothing to do with Marxism. One official wrote in his diary that the fact that "backward" Catholic writers (Cat-Mackiewicz) teamed up with progressives (Jan Kott, Adam Ważyk) made the initiative self-defeating, but the truth was the opposite. Whatever their backgrounds, the protesters found the initiative liberating. For some it was an expiation for Stalinism, for others a chance to walk freely after years of foreign rule (wartime occupation) and what they felt to be foreign rule (Stalinism).[67]

From this time, we can date a widening rift between political elite and the intellectual class and a steady production of oppositional ideas.[68] The regime tried to demonize the thirty-four, collecting signatures in a counterresolution, but the damage was done. For Gomułka, the letter was especially unnerving, because, like the church, the signatories had contested the party's right to speak for the nation. The young dissident historian Adam Michnik wrote that the only person who might have impressed Poles more than signatory number two—the novelist Maria Dąbrowska—was the Virgin Mary.[69] What made a counter-strategy so difficult was that the intellectuals were linked by family connections that stretched back to the time of the partitions. It was impossible for anyone to know everyone else in the intelligentsia, but no one ever met anyone with whom they did not have a common acquaintance. Intellectual milieus exist in all lands, but what is striking in Poland was that they had formed and solidified in order to evade state control, once Russian and German, then Nazi, and now Communist.

Intelligentsia milieus—*środowiska*—not only intersected and overlapped, they could also coexist in a single person. Take the author Jan Józef Lipski, AK veteran and son of a patriotic engineer; from his teen years to his death in 1991, Lipski belonged to one "conspiracy" or another, beginning with wartime underground education and then the Home Army Baszta regiment, and after 1945, the "Pickwick Club," a group of skeptical neo-positivist students who cited Karl Popper or Czesław Miłosz over coffee and vodka in smoky bars just off Warsaw's central streets. Unaware that Stalinism was supposed to atomize societies, students formed innumerable and uncontrollable parallel clubs: of philologists and sociologists, Catholic devotees of Mary, but also of Marxists of various stripes, with former AK members providing a backbone. The secret police made occasional arrests but never halted the self-organizing.

After 1956, Lipski's activities went into a higher gear. He became editor at *Po Prostu* and then convener of the Crooked Circle club, while gaining and then losing positions in Polish academia. Authorities booted him from a job in 1959, when he criticized the regime for its flirtation with one-time nationalist extremists.[70] He received his salary from the Union of Polish Writers and helped organize major acts of Poland's democratic opposition. After the letter of thirty-four came the letter of fifty-nine (1975), the Committee for Protection of Workers (1976), Solidarity (1980), and an independent Social Democratic Party (1988). Throughout he belonged to the Masonic Lodge "Copernicus."

* * *

A more direct challenge to Gomułka emerged on the far left, in efforts that the non-Marxist Lipski knew about but had not organized. Similar to Tito and his comrades after their break with Stalin, Polish Communists after 1956 found themselves scouring Marxian texts to discover what had gone wrong, and to find new inspiration for building a better society. Subgroupings emerged, strongest in the philosophy and sociology departments of Warsaw University. In 1965, the young activists Jacek Kuroń and Karol Modzelewski published an "Open Letter," portraying the party as a self-serving bureaucracy that workers should oppose through their own councils. For this "heresy," the authorities locked the pair away for sentences of 3 and 3.5 years. But repression only caused the challenges to proliferate: university colleagues organized assistance for their families, and professors, lecturers, and students met to discuss the event, so that ferment grew and further divided elite party organizations.[71]

Kuroń had been a leader of leftist boy scouts and passed his enthusiasm for critical Marxism onto a younger generation, several of whom founded a "Club of Seekers of Contradictions" in 1962 under the patronage of Party philosopher Adam Schaff. Leading figures included Adam Michnik and Jan Gross. When they enrolled at the university in 1965 to study history and sociology, these argumentative freethinkers became known as "commandos" for their habit of provoking officials during party events. They stood at the center of revolutionary youth at the university, who, as Michnik later recalled, were always "mulling over what would happen next." They felt invulnerable because they believed authorities would never violate university terrain.[72]

The commandos moved onto Gomułka's radar on October 21, 1966, when Michnik invited philosophy professor Leszek Kołakowski to speak on the tenth anniversary of the Polish October. Kołakowski, once Poland's leading Marxist thinker, was now an unconventional student of religious heretics who portrayed Marxism as a faith buttressed by irrational beliefs, and in the case of Poland, one that served to justify arbitrary and ineffective rule. Whether the question was Poland's sovereignty, he proclaimed, the abolition of economic absurdities, the freedom to criticize and form associations, or the understanding that rulers were responsible to society—the promises of 1956 had been betrayed. The penal code criminalized political jokes as well as simple possession of unsanctioned literature, and the government held law in contempt. He pointed out that Poland was not only a society vexed by poverty but also one that led Europe in infant mortality. That last point particularly infuriated top leaders, and soon Kołakowski was expelled from the party. But the worst thing was not the country's poverty, Kołakowski said, but its lack of hope.[73]

Kołakowski's sense of despair ran through the leftist intellectual elite. The dissenters were a "who's who" of people whom the party had once slotted to make careers: the sociologists Zygmunt Bauman and Maria Hirszowicz; the historians Adam Kersten, Bronisław Baczko, and Bronisław Geremek; the economist Włodzimierz Brus.[74] But they were, as the Czech author Václav Havel later wrote about a dissident movement he hoped to create, the "proverbial tip of the iceberg." Ultimately it would prove insufficient to expel these lapsed and lapsing Marxists from the party: they had to be driven from any position where they might contest the party's claims to embody the will of the nation. Usually that meant forced emigration.

Yet force was not the party's only response. Seeking a new strategy of legitimation, Gomułka brought men to power who distilled a new line of attack, or perhaps more accurately, regressed to an older one: ethnic chauvinism.

Even prior to October 1956, the leadership understood its response to Stalinism as involving a "Polish way," one that was ethnically Polish, with Jews hidden from sight. The high percentage of people of Jewish background in the security services—37 percent of the directors of the Ministry of Public Security departments in 1944–1954—was considered intolerable, as were rumors that "Jews are arresting Poles."[75] In a Politburo meeting of May 1956, Józef

Cyrankiewicz, a former socialist and Auschwitz inmate, said "we know and all of us understand that we have to promote Aryan cadres." That same year, the Politburo shunted aside prominent Jewish Communists Jakub Berman and Hilary Minc who had been in charge of security, ideology, and the economy.

But the purge of people of Jewish background soon went beyond Stalinists to include liberals of the "Puławy" faction, with which Gomułka had initially sided in 1956. Replacing them were "home Communists," who had spent the war years in Poland hiding in the forests and deeply resented "Jewish Communists" like Berman and Minc, who had been catapulted to power by Soviet advisors after spending the war in Moscow. The campaign for ethnic and political correctness extended into the military, where Political Directorate chief General Wojciech Jaruzelski began easing liberals ("revisionists") and Jews out of the officer corps.[76]

One home Communist who rose quickly, General Mieczysław Moczar (1913–1986), steered ostensibly patriotic resentment into the party's own channels.[77] A one-time operative of Soviet military intelligence from a working-class family, Moczar assembled a group of nationalists who became known as the "Partisans." Not having a positive program of their own, they stoked hatred of intellectuals, liberals, Germans, and Jews. The only question was how far the Soviets would let them go. Because the economy was spluttering, Gomułka himself had become vulnerable to an attack by the right-wingers, and lacking ideas beyond discipline and frugality, he had raised the "nation" to a position of unquestioned value, making it a source of absolute judgment for everyone to measure up to.[78]

Poland remained Communist and loyal to Moscow, yet official discourse began echoing *Endek* appeals from the 1930s, including those of its fascist right-wing *falanga*. That is how Jan Józef Lipski lost his job in 1959: he had publically criticized one-time *falanga* boss Bolesław Piasecki, a high dignitary in People's Poland. Soon after the war, the emerging Communist regime had entrusted Piasecki, a pious Catholic, with running an organization that encouraged Catholics to collaborate with it as loyal Poles (for example, in helping expel Germans and populating the new Polish west). Piasecki's enterprise was called PAX, and had its own newspapers and publishing conglomerate, with the sole right to print the Bible, and to sell their very popular dishwashing liquid *Ludwik*. It was in the nature of this understanding that the binary opposition Pole-Jew once again entered public discourse.[79]

The shift to ethnic nationalism occurred with little systematic ideological preparation beyond the writings of Colonel Zbigniew Załuski, an army veteran and journalist who had achieved notoriety in 1962 by publishing a book that took aim at left-wing critics of Polish nationalism. Liberals in the party said Załuski was creating a substitute ideology, and that was true: he understood that Marxism-Leninism had lost the power to attract allegiance, and therefore fashioned a symbiosis with older ideas. In contrast to what Marx or Lenin may have taught, history did not produce complete ruptures with the past, and socialists had no alternative but to draw from the riches of a country's heritage; they had to use history to show that "we did not fall from the sky." He said nothing about the bonds of class.[80] Załuski's initiative alarmed former top functionary Adam Schaff, a philosophy professor trained in Moscow, who said the party's task was internationalism, and it needed to fight racism, which in Europe meant fighting anti-Semitism. But by the 1960s, this view grated on the leadership, and Schaff himself became a target of criticism.

In 1967 Moczar's Partisans were poised to attack Gomułka because his reign had permitted democratic ideas to spread with no effective checks inside or outside the party.[81] The party boss was in a trap from which the only exit was to surpass the nationalism even of the ultra-nationalists. He not only joined but also led a campaign against Poland's tiny Jewish community, by that time consisting of about 20,000 Holocaust survivors and their families who had stayed behind after most Polish Jews had emigrated, either because they were loyal to Poland, or to Communism, or to both.

National Communism in Southeastern Europe

To differing degrees the Communist leaderships in Bulgaria and Romania likewise used the opportunities and challenges of the post-1956 period to solidify their power through nationalist agendas. In neither case was the approach completely new. In the early postwar years, the Bulgarian regime had resettled Bulgarian Muslim villages from near the Greek border to the country's interior. In 1950, it pressured Bulgarian Turks to leave for Turkey, and by late 1951, as many as 155,000 had done so.[82]

Among the East European regimes, Bulgaria was unusual for the secure hold on power of a single individual from the Stalinist time onward. Todor Zhivkov, a leader of the wartime resistance movement, had become head of the party in 1954 as part of a campaign to promote collective leadership, but then unseated the more senior Valko Chervenkov two years later for allegedly maintaining a "cult" of personality. After that, Zhikov was not seriously challenged to the end. As in East Germany, and in Czechoslovakia until the early 1960s, there was therefore no clear break in the party leadership that had ruled in the early period of terror and heavy industrialization. The regime seemed so stable that tourists from the Soviet Union joked that they had not actually traveled abroad. Zhikov was more proud of the intimate ties to Moscow than any other European Communist leader; he said that the two countries "breathe with the same lungs, and the same blood flows in our veins" and that they were as close as "teeth to lip."[83] He even suggested that Bulgaria might be added to the Soviet Union—an idea the Soviets rebuffed.

His pro-Soviet approach was a way of appealing to local constituencies: Russia was so esteemed as a liberating power that Bulgaria's German allies had not demanded the Soviet embassy in Sofia be closed during World War II. Still, in the 1960s, Bulgaria's Communist leaders did not feel as secure as they did when Stalin was alive, so they sought new paths of legitimation. Because the economy never developed sufficiently to permit the consumerism practiced in Czechoslovakia or Hungary, they opted for asserting national identity.[84] Aggravating the regime's fears was a demographic decline beginning in the late 1960s that affected Bulgarians more than rural Turks.[85]

Soon after Khrushchev's revelations at the Twentieth Party Congress, the Bulgarian Communist Central Committee had again turned its attention to the Turks, the one significant minority on Bulgarian territory. In April 1956, the leadership pledged to fight "manifestations of nationalism and religious fanaticism" among Bulgarian Turks. Any appearance of national individuality was slated to disappear, and the Muslim population was made to seem as "Bulgarian" as possible: by making their names sound Slavic, forbidding women to wear head scarfs, and making religious practice more difficult to maintain.[86] Beginning in 1958–1959, the regime discontinued Turkish language instruction.

The campaign was titled "cultural revolution" and punctuated by meetings of the intelligentsia, at which party activists reported on progress. At one such meeting in the Roudozem municipality, they boasted that 700 of 1,100 women had stopped wearing traditional Muslim garments, and 160 people had "restored their Slavic [Bulgarian] names."[87] The revolution also involved completing collectivization of agriculture earlier than any other socialist state except the Soviet Union. The deeper conceptual drive was toward ethnic "homogenization" but also about bringing villages closer to cities. Bulgaria's Roma were forced to stop wandering and to settle in socialist settlements, where they were forced to take Bulgarian names "like everyone else."

In 1969 Turkey agreed to take more ethnic Turks from Bulgaria, leading to the emigration of more than 100,000 in next decade, about 10 percent of the total population. Campaigns to rename Bulgarian Muslims continued, and hundreds who resisted were deported to labor camps.[88] The 1974 constitution spoke of the unified Bulgarian socialist nation, and in 1977, the government proclaimed that Bulgaria "consists of one ethnic type and is heading toward complete homogeneity." A culmination of the ethno-nationalist campaign dating back to 1956 was reached in late 1984 with the "revival process," in which Turks and other Muslims were compelled to adopt Bulgarian names.

By mid-January 1985, more than 300,000 Bulgarian Turks had been renamed. The point was to push for complete assimilation. The security apparatus sealed off Muslim villages and oversaw the exchange of official documentation. Again, Turks resisted, leading to scores of casualties, for example, about forty killed in Mihaylovgrad in December 1984. Bulgarian academics colluded by producing work demonstrating the supposed Bulgarian origin of the Turkish population, which had allegedly been forced to convert during Ottoman rule. In the summer of 1989, authorities opened the border to Turkey and compelled as many to leave as possible. An estimated 370,000 did so by year's end.[89]

The state also did its best to weaken the Muslim religion, for example, by halving the number of Muslim religious officials in the late 1950s. The Bulgarian Orthodox Church colluded and developed cozy relations with state authorities, including the secret police. As late as 2013, eleven of fourteen metropolitan bishops making up the church's ruling synod had a record of cooperating with the secret police under Communism.[90]

Romanian Communists had perhaps even more profound fears and uncertainties about their claims to power. Because of abject subservience to Moscow going back to the 1930s, they worried especially about their claim to be representing the ethnic nation, which had been a prime cause of Romania's rulers at every point from the 1830s, including those imported from Germany. Stalinism was the exception. Yet after 1956, as in Hungary, Poland, and Bulgaria, Romania's Communists placed themselves in the service of the "nation." Their own peculiar approach was to meander backward, combining a fascist-seeming nationalism with Stalinist-like personality cults.

Unlike Władysław Gomułka or János Kádár, the Romanian Communist Party leader in 1956, Gheorghe Gheorghiu-Dej, had been a Stalin-worshipper, and he and other top leaders in the Romanian Communist Party were deeply unsettled by revelations of the twentieth party congress; their entire world view collapsed.[91] Gheorghiu-Dej's first reaction—echoed by the Stalinist Walter Ulbricht in East Germany—was to deny that there had been Stalinism to begin with in Romania. Supposedly the Romanian Communist Party had dealt with the problem in 1952, when it expelled "Moscovites" like Ana Pauker.[92]

Above all else, Gheorghiu-Dej and his comrades feared the costs of liberalization and decided to use their positions as supposed protectors of Romanian independence to strengthen their grip on power, basing themselves on Leninist notions of the avant garde party. As in Bulgaria and Poland, the year 1956 ushered in a more openly nationalist policy toward the domestic population and a paradigm shift in minority policy from "class dictatorship to ethnicized totalitarian regime."[93]

Up to this point, Hungarian nationalism had not been a prime concern for Romanian state security; Moscow wanted peace between Romanians and Hungarians in Transylvania, and the Romanian state encouraged integration of minority groups. Yet the Hungarian Revolution convinced Romania's leaders that this integration policy had failed and that Hungarians in Romania looked on Hungary as their homeland. State security began a focused campaign, using blackmail, to recruit informants among the ethnic Hungarian population in order to react quickly to "subversive" nationalism, whether at universities and newspapers or in factories.

By quietly raising the specter of Hungarian revisionism, Gheorghiu-Dej hoped to head off disturbances among industrial workers, precluding scenarios like Plzeň or Poznań and forestalling talk of liberalization. What previously had been projected as economic or social failings now had an ethnic dimension. The Hungarian Revolution of 1956 was interpreted not as a nation's quest for liberty worthy of imitation, but as the rising specter of a resurgent Magyar state laying claim to Transylvania.[94] Authorities alleged a Hungarian fifth column on Romanian territory consisting of old-guard bourgeoisie and landowning classes, the Catholic and Protestant faithful, students raised under socialism yet dissatisfied with Romanian rule, and finally, opponents of collectivization who liked to sing old irredentist songs at pubs. The ethnic, political, and class enemies were one.

The number of Hungarians in Romania would grow to about 1.7 million by the late 1970s, but their position in the labor market deteriorated. In the late 1950s, authorities closed the Hungarian university at Cluj/Kolozsvár as well as autonomous Hungarian language schools.[95] The resulting discontent among Hungarians seemed to confirm suspicions of their disloyalty to the Romanian state. The very sense of the subversive citizen came to rest on this ethnic other, a fact reflected in the prison population as well. If before 1956, most political prisoners were members of outlawed political movements—the Iron Guard, and peasant and liberal parties—afterward, most political prisoners were detained because of their ethnic background. Of political enemies arrested in Romania's Hungarian Autonomous Region between October 1956 and December 1965, three-quarters were Hungarian.

In July 1957, Gheorghiu-Dej eliminated his last rivals. He had earned respect in Moscow by supporting the Soviet position on the Hungarian Revolution, going so far as to provide the facilities in which Imre Nagy and his associates were held after being kidnapped in Budapest. In July 1958, Moscow rewarded Gheorghiu-Dej by ordering the departure of the last Soviet troops from Romanian territory.[96]

But the spectacle of a national revolution crushed by imperial force just beyond their western border had convinced the Romanian leaders of the necessity of standing on their own feet. As in Hungary and Poland, intensive purging took place, causing the share of the population in the Communist Party to drop to 3 percent. But then, as in Poland and Hungary, a recruitment drive followed, increasing membership by 230 percent by 1965. In charge of cadres was Nicolae Ceauşescu, an ambitious young Communist who had impressed Gheorghiu-Dej as being modest, hard-working, and utterly loyal. He had spent the war years in a variety of prisons and seemed dedicated to Leninist teaching.

Now Romania asserted itself more boldly in the international sphere. From late 1958, its trade expanded with the West and contracted with the Soviet Union. In the Soviet Bloc's equivalent to West Europe's Common Market, the Council of Mutual Economic Assistance (or COMECON), Romania opposed the plans of its allies to make it the agricultural base for their more developed economies. In the eyes of Romania's leaders, such a scheme would have condemned the country to backwardness; yet it also aggravated long-festering inferiority complexes among them toward other, better established Communist parties, but also toward their own population. The Six-Year Plan that commenced in 1960 provided for sharp increases in Romania's rate of industrialization, and Marxism-Leninism became a tool for Romanian national development.[97] In 1963 Ceauşescu accompanied Foreign Minister Ion Gheorghe Maurer on a trip to China, North Korea, and the Soviet Union, meeting with Mao, Kim Il Sung, and Khrushchev.

Ceauşescu became the party leader after Gheorghiu-Dej's death in 1965 and built his popularity on defiance of Moscow. Neither legitimation through Marxian utopianism nor recourse to crude violence was enough to stabilize rule in an intensely anticommunist population, and Ceauşescu evolved into a nationalist extremist, whose personal power increased as did his personal identification with the nation. Romania was surrounded by hostile countries, Ceaușescu claimed, and he was the only force that could protect the people. A younger generation joined him in the Romanian Communist Party leadership, and together they promoted a collective identity based on cults of Romanian historical heroes as well as anti-Russian and anti-Semitic insinuations.[98] They eschewed violent strategies of maintaining power. In the post-Stalinist period, these were not only inappropriate, they were no longer necessary. Earlier mass repression had smashed hostile social groups.[99]

Marxism-Leninism tinged with nationalism thus permitted Romania's Communists to develop a sense of their political legitimacy for the first time in their history, and also to make appeals to the population and tap "dormant social energies," among workers and among intellectuals.[100] While firming his grip on power, Ceaușescu permitted the publication of works of previously forbidden authors and fostered collusion with intellectuals that was not entirely new but was greatly intensified.[101] The turn against the Soviet Union was a rupture with previous practice, however, and endeared Ceaușescu to the West. The French leader Charles De Gaulle visited Romania in May 1968, just as workers and students were testing his own regime. He found much to admire in a country that maintained independence against the superpowers and seemed so orderly. "For

FIGURE 21.3. Queen Elizabeth and Nicolae Ceaușescu at Buckingham Palace (1978). *Source*: Trinity Mirror/Mirrorpix/Alamy Stock Photo.

you such a regime is useful because it gets people moving and gets things done,"
he told the Romanian dictator.[102] In 1969, Richard Nixon became the first US
president to visit Romania, and nine years later, Ceaușescu touched down in
Washington, DC, as neither the first nor last repressive dictator to be accorded
full state honors. What seems unusual in retrospect is that Jimmy Carter would
celebrate Ceaușescu as a champion of human rights.

* * *

Such was the topsy-turvy world of East Central Europe after Stalin, where strategies of national legitimation brought Hungary toward economic reform but
took Poland to the center of a very old and toxic nationalism, on a backdrop
of slow economic disintegration. Bulgaria as well as Romania retained important facets of Stalinist control under strong party leaders and pervasive security
apparatuses, yet one was inseparable in foreign policy from the Soviet Union,
while the other treated Moscow almost as a hostile power. East Germany behind
the Berlin Wall was modeling itself as Moscow's most loyal student, but also
building pride as the strongest economy in the East Bloc, pride that would
evolve into a kind of minor nationalism, "socialist in the colors of the GDR,"
black, red, and gold. In 1962 the Soviet Union would force Czechoslovakia to
destalinize, and after that, this country also went on its own path, toward something called "socialism with a human face," which, as it turned out, was initially
a detour back to the 1930s, connecting with native traditions of democracy and
Masaryk's idea that truth will prevail.

CHAPTER 22

1968 and the Soviet Bloc: Reform Communism

Czechoslovak Communists played the national card in the 1960s without going the route of ethnic chauvinism, but like all nationalists, they thought what they were doing had both local and global import. At the height of the country's reform movement in 1968, they said they were realizing "*our Czechoslovak* manner of constructing and developing socialism," and they insisted the reform was "our internal affair, to be decided by the sovereign will of our people."[1] Their program became famous as "socialism with a human face," showing people everywhere what Marxism could mean when practiced in an enlightened way. But their reforms were also a way back to a progressive and democratic national experiment that had been cut short decades earlier. Unfortunately for the Czechoslovak Communists, Moscow defined its policies toward the Socialist Bloc in terms of security, and what seemed progressive to many Czechs and Slovaks would appear to Soviet hardliners as counterrevolution.

Yet without the impatient prodding of Moscow, there would have been no Czechoslovak reform at all. After 1956, Czechoslovak Communists had done little to destalinize, taking at most cosmetic measures. They faced little pressure from society; quite the opposite: Communist rule had been so radical in their country, so popular among intellectuals and workers, and so successful in its nationalist propaganda, that the Hungarian philosopher Agnes Heller called it "hyper-Stalinist."[2] Czechoslovak Stalinism was also stable because having the region's most advanced economy allowed the regime to buy consent. Years after the Polish October or Hungarian Revolution, almost as a symbol of their anti-Soviet defiance, Czechoslovak Communists maintained a massive Stalin statue from a perch on the Vltava River that loomed over central Prague. Yet by 1962, Nikita Khrushchev had had enough and insisted that it must go. Then the Czechoslovak comrades were told to rehabilitate victims of Stalinism, and reluctantly, Party Secretary Antonín Novotný created a commission to investigate the Terror. Soon historians were bringing forth incredible details about arrests and murders of top figures just a decade earlier. Some of their survivors were awarded compensation.

The Czechoslovak party leadership had a special fear of questions about Stalinism because they knew questions about that period's crimes pointed directly to them. Antonín Novotný, Antonín Zápotocký, and Václav Kopecký all supported the purges and judicial murders of their comrades, and a few leaders had personally enriched themselves by taking things from the households of the comrades whom they had sent to the gallows. On festive occasions, some set their tables with the best silverware and linens of their murdered comrades. Yet the Czech Communist Party apparatus over which they presided was well rooted in factories and working-class neighborhoods, and it was able to draw on the deepest, most confident, and disciplined cadre reservoirs in Central Europe. It was not easily shaken.

The party had easily dealt with challenges from within Czechoslovak society. In 1956, after Khrushchev's revelations of Stalin's crimes, writers had demanded the lifting of censorship and freedom for authors who had been arrested. University campuses and some state ministries and party organizations were briefly transformed into hotbeds of critical discussion. The regime's response was to focus criticism on Interior Minister Alexej Čepička for fostering a cult of personality, while resisting suggestions that former leader Klement Gottwald or anyone else was guilty of misdeeds. There was no mention of Rudolf Slánský. More importantly, within days of Khrushchev's speech, party leaders took steps to improve people's living standards, especially those with low incomes.[3] The advanced Czechoslovak industrial base continued to churn out high-quality products, and so the population lived in relative affluence thanks to the sacrifices and investments made by earlier generations.

By the early 1960s, Czechoslovak industry began to wobble. Between 1949 and 1964, less than 2 percent of the value of the stock of machinery was retired, and its productivity had declined.[4] For the first time, the Czechoslovak economy registered negative growth. Though the entire Soviet Bloc was confronted with problems of growth in the early 1960s, this was the most extreme case. Some radical rethinking was necessary. In a sense, the sluggish economy combined with impatient calls for destalinization from Moscow to send Czechoslovakia on the path toward serious and wide-ranging reform.

Teams of Czech and Slovak economists led by former Mauthausen inmate Ota Šik urgently recommended taking decision making away from party bureaucrats—who calculated success in tons produced and not in terms of efficiency—and placing it in the hands of scientists, engineers, and trained managers. In line with ideas coming out of Yugoslavia and Hungary, the Šik commission stipulated that decisions on production, pricing, and wages should not be handed down from an anonymous bureaucracy, comprising about 8,500 functionaries of the national party apparatus, who were out of touch with local needs. Instead, decisions should be made locally, at the plant and community levels.[5]

They urged that market mechanisms (above all, prices) be employed, so that enterprises would gain incentives to produce things that people wanted. They would do so by retaining profit (which in the command economy went to the center), and by rewarding employees according to their contributions. Basic changes like this were meant to have far-reaching consequences, for example, creating incentives to apply modern technologies to production. They would be a way of returning Czech lands to earlier prominence. But making plants more productive would also mean letting less-productive—indeed, unneeded—workers go.

These ideas for reform represented a growing consensus among leading economists throughout the bloc, extending to the Soviet Union. The ultimate problem, everywhere, was that workers as well as large production facilities were protected from market pressures and could not be fired or closed even if radically inefficient. In the post-Stalin period, outright terror was no longer an option. But for the time being, there was optimism. In the mid-1960s, economists felt that central planning would be qualitatively improved by employment of advanced mathematical models and computerization. They thought the deeper problem lay in the crude methods used in plan calculations.[6]

As Stalinists were edged out of the leadership, younger, more enlightened figures entered the cultural bureaucracy, some of whom felt remorse and shame for the recent period of Stalinist extremism. A harbinger of new openness was an international Franz Kafka conference in Prague in 1963 under the aegis of Eduard Goldstücker, a professor of literature and former diplomat who had been condemned to death under Stalinism but had his sentence commuted for work in uranium mines. Now he was now minister of culture.[7] Kafka (1883–1924) had spent his short life almost entirely in the city's center, working in a law office during the day and writing all night after a nap. His stories evoked the disorienting anonymity of modern life, and by depicting human ciphers caught in webs of inscrutable and merciless bureaucracies, his writings seemed to foretell the fate of the region. Up to this time, Kafka had been a nonperson in Czech cultural life, and to discuss his work seemed to be a move toward waking up from the nightmares he had foreseen. Some of the hardline East German

Communists invited to Goldstücker's conference registered discomfort because they sensed that once unleashed, Kafka's challenge would act like acid on the power of the state socialist bureaucracy.[8]

In these years, Czechoslovak film developed an international reputation for combining daring humor, social criticism, and reflection on a troubled past, for example, in the gripping *Shop on Main Street* (1965), about an unlikely and ultimately fatal friendship between an elderly Jewish widow and a hapless Slovak sent to Aryanize her button shop, set against the background of the 1942 deportations of Slovak Jews to Auschwitz. The Czech production *Closely Watched Trains* (1966) followed the misadventures of an aspiring railroad clerk during Nazi occupation—in real life the pop singer Václav Neckář—who encounters vainglorious and inept Protektorat officials on the way to proving himself a man. Both won best foreign film Oscars, and in both the parallels of wartime bureaucrats to Czechoslovak Stalinists were impossible to ignore. These were only two of dozens of memorable productions in the new Czech wave. There was also the bawdy, touching humor of the early work of Miloš Forman, for example, *Loves of a Blonde*, inspired by a young woman whom he encountered lugging a heavy suitcase across a bridge in Prague, lost in the big city. She was vainly seeking an engineer who had seduced her and promised to rescue her from the dreary life of provincial Varnsdorf. In the film, the engineer morphed into a musician, but the woman was stuck with the same dilemma: how to explain her return to her old job to factory co-workers.

The energies driving reform among Czech and Slovak intellectuals, scientists, and engineers aimed not simply at undoing Stalinism but also at rejoining Czechoslovakia to Europe and the world, and making Czech and Slovak products a standard not simply in the bloc but also globally. Under Stalinism, national pride had suffered because Czechoslovak industry was reduced to processing raw materials from the Soviet Union. Due to the command economy's "extensive" approach to development, Czechoslovak industry had missed out on the revolutions in automatization that characterized production in the West.[9] In 1966, a Czech Academy of Arts and Sciences team found that the automation of the machine industry in Czechoslovakia was three to six times less advanced than in the United States and that the production of automation systems by the electronics industry was two to three times below that of Western industrial economies. In the highest form of automation, cybernetics, production in Czechoslovakia was fifty times below that of the United States.[10]

The problem was not lack of ingenuity. Czech and other East European scientists had pathbreaking ideas, but the countries in the Soviet imperial sphere

FIGURE 22.1. Film: *Loves of a Blonde* (1965, Miloš Forman), with Marie Salačová and Hana Brejchová. *Source*: United Archives GmbH/Alamy Stock Photo.

did not possess the scientific, industrial, or marketing infrastructure to develop local competitive advantages—much in contrast to small countries in Western Europe, like Denmark or the Netherlands. For example, on Christmas day 1961, the Czech chemist Otto Wichterle produced the world's first pair of soft contact lenses using a children's building kit and his son's bicycle dynamo on his kitchen table. This was a culmination of eight years of work. Within a few months, he had produced more than 5,000 lenses. Alas, without his knowledge, his employer, the Czechoslovak Academy of Sciences, sold the patent to the United States National Patent Development Corporation, and neither he nor his country profited from one of the most popular consumer goods of the late twentieth century. The Czechoslovak economy lost at least one billion dollars in foreign exchange.

In contrast to orthodox Leninists, Czechoslovak Communist reformers held that citizens of their state had a variety of interests—even after the victory of socialism. This was not a problem. Musicians, chemists, and construction workers had ideas for innovations, but also tastes, demands, and needs that central bureaucracies could not anticipate. People in one part of the country valued a cuisine that was different from that of other parts, and people of different ages liked different kinds of music. Market mechanisms would make the socialist system flexible enough to communicate the desires of specific groups, helping producers and consumers find each other and communicate perceptions of value. None of these reforms questioned socialist ownership of the means of production, but to build a consensus about tastes and desires, citizens had to speak and gather freely in the public sphere. In the view of reformers, this too was not a problem; permitting people to articulate their interests could only strengthen socialism.

Younger party cadres of this period were called "technocrats," because they possessed skills and education lacking in an older generation forged by war and revolution. But Czechoslovak reformers were also guided by idealism. For them, socialism would be a place where humans developed their full potential, much as Karl Marx had imagined in early writings concerned with the alienation that grew from the division of labor. In his utopian view, socialism was a place where no one would be reduced to a single occupation but would fully develop their human personalities in a range of pursuits.[11] Up to this time, the trend in Eastern Europe had seemed the opposite: a place where alienation had increased as a by-product of people performing ever-more minute tasks on tightly controlled assembly lines at the direction of party bureaucrats. Like Yugoslav comrades, Czechoslovak reformers wanted to activate citizens and make them learn to govern themselves, so that the party and state bureaucracy could be reduced to an increasingly distant caretaker.

Yet as specialists, led by the reform Communist Zdeněk Mlynář, worked out a program making these ideas a reality, they provoked suspicions among the party bureaucracy, which rightly saw its prerogatives threatened.[12] This was a huge group with positions of strength in all decision-making bodies. Equally seriously, economic reforms, which would permit plants to vary wages, or to release workers—both as part of market reform—threatened millions of industrial laborers whom state socialism had accustomed to wage and job security that was unprecedented in European history. They enjoyed good and cheap beer, lax labor discipline, subsidized social services and vacations, and a life in which difficult decisions could be left to the authorities.

The forces in favor of reform reached a critical mass in the summer of 1967, when fortuitously, writers, Slovaks, Communist reformers, and students all reached a tipping point in their impatience with the unreformed party leadership and began articulating insistent demands for change in public. Because the Soviet leadership believed that Czech and Slovak Communists retained ultimate control, they let the reform process move forward.

At their annual congress in June, writers attacked the Novotný regime's practice of censorship. Novelist Milan Kundera lamented the fragility of culture in a small nation. Without their language, there would be no Czechs, he said, and because censorship curtailed and suffocated language, it represented a mortal threat to Czech existence. Moreover, censorship was a throwback to forms of repressive government that Europeans—including Czechs!—had put behind them generations earlier.[13] He spoke words that might have been uttered during Central Europe's Enlightenment 200 years earlier: "Any suppression of views, even when the views that are being forcibly suppressed are erroneous, must lead away from the truth, for truth can be attained only through the interaction of views that are equal and free."[14] Indeed, the ideas of separation of powers or the legitimacy of interests in society, so attractive among reform Communists, were likewise old ideas that seemed radical only in the face of the Soviet system that Czech and Slovak Stalinists had copied, which Kundera later described as imported from a great eastern power out of touch with Central Europe's history.

Ludvík Vaculík, Pavel Kohout, and Václav Havel likewise spoke out against state control of writers, and the congress passed a final resolution calling for the "freedom of artistic questing" and defending the continuity of Czechoslovak culture. Vaculík sounded like Poland's Adam Ważyk when he said that the Communist system had not solved a single human problem. That included everything from housing and schooling to respect for manual labor, trust among people, and a general sense of fulfillment. But Czechs had also failed as a nation: "We have not contributed any original thoughts or good ideas to humanity," he wrote.[15]

Such criticism went far beyond anything functionaries in the Party Central Committee could tolerate, and in late September, they accused the writers of neglecting the dangers of anti-Communism. Their support for "abstract freedom" represented a failure to understand that freedom was based on class relations; what writers really needed to do was oppose all "bourgeois tendencies" in literature. Party leaders said that the literary journal *Literární noviny* had become a "platform of opposition political standpoints," and they attempted to purge the journal's editorial board.[16]

Slovak Communists, underrepresented in central government and mistreated during the Stalinist purges as "bourgeois nationalists," were now poised to join party intellectuals in opposition to the neo-Stalinist Novotný, who did nothing to hide his contempt for the Slovak nation. In August 1967, during centenary celebrations of the first Slovak high school at Martin in northern Slovakia, the Novotný motorcade arrived at night, refused to visit a cemetery of "national heroes," and sped through the birthplace of the poet Jan Kollár, not even waving to crowds who had waited for hours. Novotný insulted officials at the Slovak national heritage museum, rejecting the gift of a folk costume, and telling his wife: "Božena, don't take any of that stuff."[17]

A fortuitous event occurred in Prague on October 31 that generated mass awareness of the need for change, reminiscent of the Poznań events in Poland, though with much less violence. That evening, the power failed in dormitories of the Czech Technical University that had been plagued by outages for weeks. Some 1,500 students went onto the streets carrying candles and chanting "we want light!"—a literal demand that functionaries with a sore conscience understood figuratively. Public security units smothered the protest, severely beating numerous students. Reports of the injuries leaked from the emergency wards and spread across the city. Remarkably, officials did not sweep matters under the rug but held serious meetings at the university in which students threatened further protests. In early 1968, the minister of the interior and the chief of Prague's police issued apologies.[18]

This previously unthinkable gesture reflected a shift in December, when a leadership struggle was settled in favor of Slovak First Party Secretary Alexander Dubček, who combined support of reformers as well as Slovaks against Novotný and other Stalinists. Dubček had launched a challenge in October, asserting that the party was out of touch with the population and urgently needed more "socialist democracy." It needed to rely on the voluntary support of the working people.[19] Perhaps the mild-mannered Dubček did not intend to oust Novotný, but the momentum shifted in his favor. When Novotný denounced Dubček as a nationalist, other Slovaks rallied to the latter's support, even some whose enthusiasm for democracy was lukewarm, like Gustav Husák. Husák had spent nine years in Stalinist prisons for "bourgeois nationalism," resisting all admissions of guilt, despite torture, and at this point seemed to be Dubček's ally.

In December, Novotný invited Soviet leader Brezhnev to Prague, hoping for support. Yet Brezhnev, facing challenges at home and suspecting Novotný of favoring his own rivals in the Soviet Politburo, declared that this was a struggle among loyal Communists and no business of his. He thought the forty-six-year old Dubček ("Sascha") trustworthy, because like Imre Nagy, he was Soviet-trained, having lived with his parents in Russia as a child. In January, Dubček was elected the new party first secretary.[20]

Like Nagy, Dubček was open and forthright, and though a poor speaker, he quickly became popular through a new style of politics. Unlike his "infallible" predecessors, he smiled easily and had no trouble appearing before cameras as a human being, for example, in swim trunks. The affable middle-aged Slovak with his paunch and good will incorporated socialism "with a human face," but like Nagy, he had little taste for the blood sport of Communist politics and would discover that other party leaders were eager to betray him.[21]

Also like Nagy, and the later Soviet leader Mikhail Gorbachev, Dubček was the odd Leninist who rose to the top of the hierarchy only to discover a taste for consensual politics. Soon he was surprising Soviet leaders with his determination to achieve the "broadest possible democratization of the entire socio-political system" as well as the establishment of a "free, modern and profoundly humane society."[22] In March 1968, he lifted censorship, the most radical change seen in Eastern Europe since 1956. Now Czechs and Slovaks could learn from the popular press about horrors of Czechoslovak Stalinism that were previously only the subjects of internal party reports; they also read penetrating analyses of international politics, including discussions of the student and civil rights movements in the West. They learned that Tomáš G. Masaryk had been socially progressive as well as anti-Bolshevik—with no contradiction. Magazine photo layouts featured US presidential candidate Robert Kennedy, not as imperialist leader, but as a reasonable subject of interest for citizens of a modern European society. Czechs and Slovaks were finding their way back to a world they had left behind only two decades earlier. Reinforcing their sense of return to normal European existence were tens of thousands of young tourists streaming into the Czech capital, eager to experience the cultural ferment of the "Prague Spring." They came from all over the world.

In April, the Communist Party of Czechoslovakia published an "Action Program," meant to "reform the whole political system" and realize the ideas that party experts had been mooting for years, including plans to grant autonomy to social and political organizations in the "National Front." The program spoke of the need to separate and control powers, in part through regular elections, even of top party officials. It promised to break down strict economic centralism and ensure the "independence of enterprises."[23] As evidence of lessons learned from the arbitrary rule of Stalinism, it proposed that power be constrained by rule of law—constitutionalism—as a way of guaranteeing civil liberties.[24]

Yet it was also a deeply ambivalent document. While in effect dusting off an older liberal tradition, the Action Program reiterated the "leading role" of the party, thus promising to place civil liberties in a Leninist straight jacket. Would people outside the party have lower status as citizens? And could the party even continue to exist if it democratized? It was supposedly a workers' party, yet workers had serious concerns about the promised use of market mechanisms in the reform program; for many intellectuals, by contrast, the reform did not go far enough. Still, the program was deeply popular in Czechoslovak society, reaching 78 percent acceptance in a poll taken during the summer. And by saying that the party could not represent "the entire scale of social interests," it had practically invited Czechs and Slovaks to create interest groups.[25] Soon a Club of "Engaged Non-party Members" had formed, as well as a society of former political prisoners.[26] Where the self-organizing ultimately would have led is unclear.

Almost from the moment censorship lifted, Communists in neighboring countries were making threatening sounds. They were specially scandalized by the Prague reformers' plans to hold a special party congress in late summer that would choose a new Central Committee to implement the changes of the Action Program. In contrast to previous congresses, this one would feature open elections of multiple candidates, and would be, skeptics feared, a first step in the dismantling of Democratic Centralism and the destruction of the top-down Leninist organization.[27] Polish and East German Communists also worried because the Prague Spring proved deeply popular for their own young people, many of whom visited Prague. Czech media were posing dangerous questions that the tourists then asked at home: about Soviet relations to Eastern Europe, including the crushing of democratic parties after 1945, the imperialist economic exploitation, and the role of Soviet advisors in scripting Stalinist terror. But the main danger was simply the idea that socialism could be liberating.

Almost from the start, Soviet Bloc news stations, especially those in East Berlin, featured hostile reports about Prague's Spring, claiming that the gates had been opened to fascists wanting to restore capitalism. Czechoslovak leaders took umbrage because they believed they had learned the lessons of Hungary in 1956: unlike Imre Nagy, they did not threaten to leave the Warsaw Pact or restore a multiparty system or question the leading role of the Communist Party. Still, the threats multiplied from spring into summer and were backed up by movements of troops. In early August, at a summit meeting on the border to Ukraine, Soviet leader Leonid Brezhnev demanded that Czechoslovaks restore "control" of the media, and in a phone call two weeks later, he complained to Dubček that attacks on Soviet leaders had not stopped. Yet Dubček and his comrades refused to buckle under.[28] Dubček patiently explained to Brezhnev that Slovaks and Czechs had to decide certain things for themselves, and the media was one of them. That act of defiance appears to have sealed their fate.[29]

A full-scale invasion of Czechoslovakia by Warsaw Pact forces commenced in the night of August 20, 1968. After seizing Prague's airport, Soviet paratroopers rushed to the Czechoslovak Central Committee, abducted Dubček and the other leaders, and spirited them off to Moscow. A massive invasion of ground troops and armor followed. Soviet leaders expected that, like János Kádár, Czech Communists loyal to them would form a counter-government. But the traitors were few and, fearing vengeance, spent the hot daytime hours of August 21 in a Soviet personnel carrier hiding from the tens of thousands of Czechs protesting on the streets of Prague.[30] The protesters attempted to reason with the mostly frightened and exhausted tank crews, who had been told that they were sent to crush "fascism" and "counterrevolution." Such discussions seemed so subversive to the Red Army command that they quickly replaced and quarantined these first units.

Now pressure turned on the party leaders held hostage in Moscow, some of whom were ambivalent about reform.[31] Some of the Slovaks, like Husák, wanted more local rule for themselves, but cared little about civil rights let alone democracy. The Soviets dealt with them one at a time, mixing threats and promises with supposed revelations about what other comrades had already said. By August 26, with the exception of František Kriegel, an old Communist and Jew who had served as combat physician in World War II, all were ready to sign a protocol committing them to "normalizing" the situation in the country. The document required purging all cadres who "did not correspond to the needs of strengthening the leading role of the working class and the Communist Party," and reestablishing control of "the media so that it "fully serve the cause of socialism." There was also an oral agreement that leading reformers would be dismissed.[32]

In contrast to Stalinist times, the interrogators did not use torture to elicit compliance. Alexander Dubček signed because he feared that his compatriots might take any defiance on his part as a summons to active opposition, and he could not take responsibility for the resulting "bloodbath."[33] He was echoing Edvard Beneš during his capitulations to totalitarian gangsters in 1938 and 1948. Other comrades feared worse conditions would ensue for their compatriots if they did not sign and hoped that their cooperation might cause Soviet forces to leave the country (in fact, they stayed until 1991).

Whatever the reasoning, a break of broader significance had taken place in Moscow. Late in the afternoon of August 26, Alexander Dubček suddenly understood that he had been wasting his time *talking* to Soviet comrades. The dispute was not about socialism but about naked control, and in its basic structure was a replay of the Tito-Stalin standoff from 1948. Dubček had been arguing for the hundredth time that reforms would "strengthen socialism," when an exhausted Brezhnev let the mask fall. Czechoslovakia, Brezhnev said, on the verge of shouting, was "part of the Soviet security zone" gained after World War II, and that was its fate for the indefinite future. Brezhnev was especially upset that "Sascha" had not "consulted" with him about the content of speeches or planned changes in personnel.

In signing the Moscow Protocols, Dubček exchanged one cognitive frame for another: he put aside arguments about socialism and began to calculate with fellow leaders how best to weather the reassertion of imperial rule. This was something Czechs and Slovaks had been doing for many decades. But the logic that their generation would follow left no limit to compromise; every decision they took was made with the intention of avoiding something "worse."

The Soviets had gotten things started, telling Dubček that some reformers had to go. He acceded, assuming that he could still rely on other comrades who supported democracy. Then he discovered that some had already been turned. Especially egregious was Gustav Husák, the Slovak who had been imprisoned during Stalinism. In April 1969, Husák assumed leadership of the party when Dubček resigned voluntarily—again fearing that defiance might give the Soviets an excuse for a "bloodbath."[34] In fact, there had been virtually no violence by Czechs and Slovaks in their protests. But there was a grimly spectacular coda to the Czechoslovak reform experiment. In January 1969, the student Jan Palach set himself alight just below the National Museum in Prague. He was part of a small group that wanted to rouse the consciences of their compatriots, so that they might at least stand fast against censorship. Members of the group had drawn lots to see who would go first, and Palach became the first "torch." (Only one of the others followed his lead.) The viewing line at Palach's funeral stretched through Prague's old town and was among the last public manifestations for reform. Charles University's rector said Palach was a "victim at the altar of the nation."[35]

Now Husák emerged ascendant. By his side stood another man whom Dubček had considered loyal, the very popular General Ludvík Svoboda, a man of seeming integrity, and perhaps the country's greatest disappointment, who continued as president. The "normalizing" process gained rapid momentum in this wealthy, modern society, with its many amenities and institutions holding out much to gain and to lose. For those who made no trouble, life could be enjoyable, with plenty to eat and drink during long weekends in the countryside;

FIGURE 22.2. Staff of Prague delicatessen protests invasion (August 1968).
Source: CTK/Alamy Stock Photo.

FIGURE 22.3. Protesters and tank, Prague (August 1968).
Source: Paul Goldsmith. By permission.

FIGURE 22.4. Marchers display blood-soaked flag (August 1968).
Source: Paul Goldsmith. By permission.

for those who did, it could involve penury and deep doubt as to whether one
was squandering one's best years in menial labor for no evident gain. We now
know that Communism would collapse twenty years later; Czechs and Slovaks
of these years did not.

Husák remains a riddle. He pronounced fervent loyalty to the Prague Spring
ideals as late as August 20, but then quickly turned to support Brezhnev. Like
Gomułka, he revealed himself to be Leninist to the core, but also a nationalist.
A new constitution went into force in 1969 that federalized Czechoslovakia,
making the state one of "two equal fraternal nations." That change Husák had
fought for, and for many fellow Slovaks, it seemed a lasting accomplishment
of the reform process. The Soviet invasion that made Czechs feel a far western
outpost of the Soviet empire thus coincided with a milestone for Slovakia.
Husák seemed to be a local hero who had suffered for Slovak interests in the
1950s, and managed, despite humble working-class beginnings, to become the
first Slovak president of the joint state.[36] Yet Husák would also be reviled among
Slovaks as well as Czechs for the massive purging of "normalization."

In early 1970, the party apparatus set up control commissions and made each
party member write an "autobiography" describing what he or she had done

in the recent past. As a result, tens, then hundreds of thousands were stricken from the party's rolls. If the first purges of winter and spring did not catch up with those unwilling to conform, a later one would. An estimated 750,000 Czechs and Slovaks had to leave the party; with their families, that made up about two million in a country of fifteen million people. The Communist Party of Czechoslovakia shrank by about one-third.[37] The most threatened professions were in the arts and sciences, though the regime treated world-famous stars like the singer Karel Gott with greater leniency.[38] Milan Šimečka, fired from his post as lecturer in sociology at Bratislava, said that the "ruling Party of existing socialism became the vanguard of mediocrity, obedience and fear."[39]

Many Czechs had personally become accustomed to conformism under Nazism, still more under Stalinism, and they fell back on older patterns. Strangers were again potential enemies, and people shared opinions only with the closest friends and trusted relatives. Support for the Prague Spring had been massive, and therefore hundreds of thousands were suddenly vulnerable to denunciations from people beneath them on career ladders. Many tumbled into a professional abyss, denied the opportunity to practice their jobs or indeed do anything requiring higher education. Dubček was made ambassador to Turkey, then a forestry inspector in Slovakia. When not in prison, the playwright Václav Havel was a brewery worker, and hundreds of journalists, philosophers, and scientists who had supported the reform movement became chauffeurs, janitors, and "stokers" (that is, workers who fed boilers with coal). Šimečka worked in construction.

The "normalization" regime became pitiless in its destruction of human creativity, drawing on deep wells of fear and opportunism—but also on people's healthy common sense and love for their families, the bad and the good intertwined and inseparable. Why should people imperil their own comfort and welfare for utopian goals like freedom of speech or democracy? Those who stayed at their jobs discovered that their bosses had dozens of ways of exerting pressure: by refusing them raises, threatening the well-being of their children, and limiting travel opportunities essential to their work. The art world was thrust back to the dynamics of fear and opportunism from the 1950s, and Western artists and abstract works disappeared from journals, while conventional realist works dominated. The "Soviets as liberators" was again a common theme, for example, in a statue erected by Miloš Axman that depicted a group of Soviet soldiers and Czech women dancing.[40] Crushing pressures produced politically correct results across disciplines; those in charge claimed they were not returning to dogmatism (that is, Stalinism) but instead restoring art to its "social mission," something that had been suppressed in the counterrevolutionary 1960s, with the rise of abstract, and neosurrealist works—which were a "far cry from the ideals of our people."[41]

The invasion traumatized national identity because, unlike Poles and Hungarians, many Czechs thought of the Russians as liberators. A plurality had freely elected Communists in 1946. But the trauma was not limited to Czechs and Slovaks. Like Dubček, socialists everywhere felt betrayed. The Czechoslovak Communist reformers had not intended to restore capitalism; they had wanted to make socialism fit local circumstances. The Soviets had crushed them for the sake of imperial interests. In these very months, the leaders of the Polish Communist Party were waging a radically different struggle to assert their nationalist perspective: targeting Poles with Jewish origins as enemies. They, too, like Brezhnev, seemed to be underscoring the point that "socialism" was ultimately not what mattered in the Soviet-dominated sphere. When power was contested, whether by forces from within or without the party, no measures short of mass terror were unthinkable. The contrast to Stalinism was that the measures of control now employed were less violent but more effective.

March 1968 in Poland: The Death of Revisionism

Beginning in the mid-1960s, Polish Communists' appeals to workers ran thin as upward mobility slowed and the class enemy gradually vanished. There were no rich bourgeois left to dispossess and humiliate. At the same time, the policies of gender equality lost their dynamism, and women were compelled to return to traditional roles in professional hierarchies as well as maintain the burden of running households. They tended to work in "light" industry, with lower pay and privileges, in contrast to male-dominated heavy industry.[42] Therefore the rulers' legitimacy increasingly depended on appeals to the nation: either by enhancing its strength economically, or by appearing as saviors against some foreign threat. Gomułka chose the latter.

Or more accurately, he evolved in that direction because he remained wedded to unproductive heavy industry and was deaf to the ideas of reform economists. To deflect blame for the resulting stagnation by reviving antagonisms against Russia or Germany was taboo, and therefore nationalists among his comrades looked to the other group traditionally vilified by the Polish right: the Jews. Gomułka did not have the moral fiber or political imagination to resist and wound up leading the campaign himself, hoping to "outflank" rivals.[43]

In 1967 anti-Semitism suddenly became especially opportune as a political tool because the Soviet Union broke relations with Israel after its client states Egypt and Syria suffered a humiliating defeat in the Six-Day War. At a major address in June, Gomułka told Polish trade unionists that a fifth column in their country supported Israel. There is no evidence that he was taking directions from Moscow. Instead, he was concerned about sympathies for Israel that ran deep in the Polish party and population, and which might compromise Poland's solidarity with the Socialist Bloc.[44] The Interior Ministry had already concluded that Polish Jews tended to favor Israel, and now it learned that many others in the population privately celebrated the setback that Soviet power had suffered in the Middle East.

From their conspiratorial mindset, Gomułka's police officers could account for these pro-Israeli sympathies only through surreptitious activities of agents on Polish territory, and they focused their surveillance on the spread of Zionism in the intelligentsia, a group considered less reliable than workers.[45] Thus a purge began in the fall of 1967, first in the military, then in other institutions, of people supposedly sympathetic to Israel. Leaders called the campaign "anti-Zionist," but as in classical anti-Semitism, they singled out Jews for punishment because they were Jewish; and when Jews reacted by applying to emigrate to Israel, this was taken as a sign they had been disloyal to Poland and to Communism all along.

Beyond inveterate anti-Semites, the campaign appealed to party and state employees younger than forty, whose careers were blocked by older cadres, some of whom were of Jewish origin. Zygmunt Bauman, one of Poland's foremost sociologists, explained the logic to his family: there had been no purges for several years, bosses were just a few years older than their deputies, and their underlings were getting tired of waiting for promotion.[46] Many in the party and state apparatus had had enough of Gomułka's ascetic approach and wanted to "taste" the fruits of their labors. They suffered like everyone else from stagnant living standards, as well as from favoritism and corruption; they too lived in cramped apartments and were witness to pervasive misery and alcoholism.

Yet what pushed the latent tensions in Polish state and society beyond the breaking point was not material grievances in any part of the population, but controversies about a play from the 1820s. On January 30, 1968, the leadership ordered the shutting down of "Forefathers Eve" by Poland's romantic bard Adam Mickiewicz after its eleventh performance at Warsaw's National Theater. The play abounds in allusions critical of Russia, for example: "Russian rubles— very dangerous," or: "Moscow sends only villains to Poland." When such lines

were recited they elicited standing ovations from the audiences but nearly hysterical panic among party leaders. After the first performance, Gomułka's lieutenant Zenon Kliszko called the production "religious" and feared it might deliver a serious blow to Polish-Soviet friendship.[47] Giving an idea of how out of
touch Gomułka had become, his team itself had approved the production as part
of a series of events celebrating the Great Socialist October Revolution of 1917.

At the last performance, students crowded up to the stage, and as the curtain descended, began chanting: "independence without censorship!" Then
several hundred marched to the nearby Mickiewicz monument in central Warsaw carrying banners and chanting: "Down with censorship," and "We want
Mickiewicz's truth."[48] Police brutally dispersed them, arresting more than three
dozen. On orders from Gomułka, the minister of education, the historian and
former Social Democrat Henryk Jabłoński, expelled Adam Michnik and Henryk Szlajfer from the university, supposedly for keeping French journalists up
to date about what was happening. This act lacked all legal basis.

As was true in the struggle with the church, and later with workers, the party's measures of repression stoked rather than quelled unrest. On February 29,
the Writers Union released a statement calling the prohibition of "Forefathers
Eve" a "particularly glaring example" of the harm that an arbitrary policy of censorship posed for "*national* culture," inhibiting its development, distorting its
authentic character, and condemning it to sterility. Like the students, the writers, many of them Communists, rose to the challenge on a field the party really
cared about: Poland's story about itself. They called on the government to respect tolerance and freedom of creativity, "in keeping with age-old traditions."
The novelist Jerzy Andrzejewski said the rulers held the nation in contempt:
falsifying its past and lying about the present. A little more than a decade earlier,
Andrzejewski had been the party's star author, and uttering such words, he confessed, was excruciating.[49]

Historically, only Russian and German occupiers had violated the terrain of
Polish universities. Therefore, on March 8, when they staged a huge manifestation against censorship at Warsaw University, the students felt safe. State authorities had a weaker sense of national decorum than they did. Midway through
the manifestation, covered lorries rolled up before the main university gate, and
out jumped police as well as armed "workers units," swinging clubs and arresting students indiscriminately. The young people chanted "Gestapo! Gestapo!"
and also broke into Polish national hymns as well as the Internationale.[50]

Rumors began spreading that the Soviet embassy had demanded the play's
closing, and then anonymous leaflets appeared in towns and villages arguing

that no Pole could be passive while Polish students were being attacked. That language touched a nerve. In the weeks that followed, university and high school students as well as young workers came out on the streets from one end of Poland to another, marching, chanting, and streaming to Mickiewicz statues where they existed. Their outrage grew when they found themselves portrayed in newspapers as provocateurs or antisocialist elements. This was the first direct personal experience that many had with the elite's cynicism. In several towns, young demonstrators chanted to onlookers: "the newspapers lie."[51] Rioting broke out in Radom and Legnice, almost overwhelming police units, and indeed, students from Gdańsk provoked unrest in nearby Elbląg, hoping to drain the forces of order away from their own town. In some places, the government brought in the army to reinforce the police.[52]

Not until state and party archives opened in the 1990s did historians grasp the full extent of the protests, which turned out to be more massive than all other outbursts of dissent in the bloc to that time.[53] The only parallels were the workers' protests that lit up the Czech and East German political landscapes in 1953. But as in other hotspots of global 1968—Paris, Mexico City, and Prague—the demonstrators' energies gradually gave way. Weeks of mass arrests, restructurings, threats of closure, and swelling numbers of police discouraged young people, and the protests subsided. Many students were drafted into the army, and when those detained by the police were released, they returned to their homes, in Adam Michnik's words, "shattered."

Leading intellectuals did not fare much better. They likewise saw their efforts at protest wither under the officially propagated violence and cynicism. The Communist Party's resort to crude ethnic hatred scared even the former resistance fighters half to death. The Catholic satirist Stefan Kisielewski was attacked by unknown assailants in Warsaw's old town and beaten so severely that when he recovered his senses, he was in a hospital bed. Among his transgressions was to refer to the regime as a "dictatorship of morons" on his private telephone.[54] The Polish-Jewish writer Kazimierz Brandys grew so terrified that he did not venture onto the street. During the Nazi occupation, ruffians would pull down men's trousers, hoping to expose Jews in hiding (Gentiles were not circumcised), yet Brandys had not hesitated to go into the street when he needed to.

The regime kept turning up the volume of hatred until nothing else was audible. It said that the intellectuals defending Polish culture were not really Polish, and staged dozens of meetings in factories, handing workers signs proclaiming their supposed class outrage: "Zionists to Israel!" "Students to the classroom!" "Workers don't forgive provocateurs." Commentators strove to expose the origins of Jewish students whose grandparents had changed their names to defend themselves against anti-Semitism. Gomułka himself presided over a hysterical mass meeting at Warsaw's Palace of Culture on March 19 that was broadcast on live television. Sociologist Bauman and his wife Janina—both Holocaust survivors—watched from their Warsaw apartment with their three daughters and a family friend, hoping the party boss might urge moderation. Instead he said there were different kinds of Jews: those who saw themselves as Poles, those who saw themselves as citizens of the world, and a third kind, Zionists. These were:

> people whose allegiance was with Israel rather than Poland. Such people should leave our country. "At once! Now! Today!" roared the audience. "They must first apply," said Gomułka with a slight grin. There was an uproar— howls, roars, and with cries of "Down with Zionists," and "Now! Today!" the assembly turned into a raging mob. In our cozy room, in our peaceful home, we suddenly felt ourselves in mortal danger. The enraged mob would soon leave the Congress Hall and pour out onto the streets.

The Baumans blocked the door with a heavy chest and looked for sharp tools: "just in case." The night passed without a pogrom. A week later, Zygmunt and five other professors were dismissed from the university in a violation of academic tenure that neither the tsar nor Poland's Stalinists had dared perpetrate.[55] The family left for Israel as summer passed into autumn. In all, some 13,000 persons of Jewish origin applied for exit permits to Israel. The writer Henryk Grynberg later said: "they left more behind than they had."

Such was the battle for the "Polish nation" between Gomułka's ethnic version that needed fear to survive, and a much older one, represented by the heritage of Poland's best-loved poet. In his diary, the intellectual Andrzej Kijowski wrote that the Communist Party feared Mickiewicz, the "real one, the one closest to us, because he censures conservatism, servility, the collapse of the nation's hopes, the betrayal of our traditions." In prohibiting his play, authorities hoped to censor Poland. Instead, the students had written the next act. "Here on the streets, 'Forefathers Eve,' act five," composer Zygmunt Mycielski confided to his diary on March 10. "People who govern this country are clueless."[56]

Which version of Poland's story was more compelling? Among the intelligentsia, the answer was clear. If the regime got support from any writers after this point, they were second-rate. During Stalinism, top authors had vied

FIGURE 22.5. Polish workers' "spontaneous" anger at Zionism (1968). *Source*: PAP/CAF/A. Piotrowski (photographer).

to write poems that pleased the party, yet now little remained to inspire sacrifice. In the slogans held by the workers at staged meetings, the language was grotesque. Adam Schaff, the party's erstwhile top ideologist, described how his wife lost her job in Polish radio. After a warm speech complimenting her on a fine career, and lots of smiles and warm wishes, her co-workers without exception voted to fire her.[57] The powerful believed that workers, supposedly less sophisticated, stood unquestioningly behind them.

Yet because of the weak economy, Gomułka's hold on power remained tenuous. In December 1970, workers went on strike along the Baltic coast after price hikes. Rather than negotiate, Gomułka sent in militia and army units with 550 tanks to "teach workers a lesson." His regime again played the national card: political officers told the troops they were responding to an uprising of disloyal

Germans. The low point came on December 17, when militia fired salvos into crowds guilty of nothing other than arriving on time for the morning shift at the Gdynia shipyard. Some forty-five workers were killed and 1,165 wounded.[58] Many more were arrested. Still, the strikes continued to spread, and soon Gomułka resigned "for health reasons." Just as had been the case in Plzeň and East Berlin in 1953, or Poznań in 1956, workers quickly graduated from economic grievances to political demands.

Was Poland's ethnically chauvinist regime fascist? Schaff called it "communofascist."[59] The American Zbigniew Brzezinski, a frequent visitor to Poland, discerned signs of decay in Marxism-Leninism and a reversion to extreme nationalism that had little to do with the old internationalist Communist Polish Party. The Polish United Workers' Party, as Poland's Communists were known after 1948, was proudly endeavoring to create a Poland that would be nationally homogeneous, relying on Russia against Germany.[60] Yet this was a dream not of socialists but of National Democrats. In the 1950s, the Polish regime was disdained as Moscow's servant, indeed as "Moscovite." Now no one could doubt that the leaders were ethnic Poles, but the basic insecurity of their right to rule caused them to play on national feelings in a way that revived not only modern racism, but the ancient hatred of anti-Judaism.

Giving a full sense of the unpredictable dynamics of state socialism as it entered its last two decades, the one East Bloc country that refused to take part in crushing the Prague spring, Romania, did so not out of sympathy for reform, but to bolster the nationalist egomania of its own dictator. His open defiance of the Soviet Union, proclaimed on August 21, 1968, at Palace Square in Bucharest before at least 100,000 supporters, identified Nicolae Ceaușescu as a man of imagination and charisma. "Nothing," he said, "could justify the use of armed force to intervene in the internal affairs of a member country of the Warsaw Pact."[61] According to all reports, his anti-Russian rhetoric, coupled with policies of modernization that led to increasing wealth in Romanian society, were hugely popular.[62]

Brezhnev's Doctrine

In September 1968, Brezhnev put an ideological window dressing on the apparent neocolonialism of his country's invasion of Czechoslovakia. Every socialist country had the freedom to determine how it would advance, he said, as long as it did not damage the interests of socialism as a whole. However, the Communist movement could not look "with indifference" on any country that "weakened its links to the socialist world system." Czechoslovak leaders had spoken about self-determination for themselves, but by (supposedly) threatening to bring NATO forces to the Soviet borders, they had endangered the "socialist self-determination" of the European socialist countries, causing them to "discharge their internationalist duty toward the fraternal peoples of Czechoslovakia."[63] This promise of violence for any socialist state that strayed from the path dictated by the Soviet Union became known as the Brezhnev Doctrine.

In fact, Brezhnev was only lending final precision to an approach developed since the death of Stalin. As long as "Leninist" norms were respected—meaning single-party control over politics, culture, and the economy—then states could pursue separate paths. And the divergences among them had indeed become substantial.

Critics regarded the Husák regime in Czechoslovakia as neo-Stalinist, a retreat to the stifling political controls of the 1950s, featuring a bit of tinkering in the economy perhaps, but relying on centralized planning with no real reform. They likewise rated Bulgaria and East Germany as neo-Stalinist because the leaders there had never embraced destalinization. Yet the label also misleads. The atmosphere had changed since the 1950s. Communist regimes had become more sophisticated in their methods of control and did not need to employ outright terror. But the party cadre also no longer displayed the élan of Stalinism: gone were the naïve idealism and the youthful love affair with the modernization reflected in new steel cities, huge transfers of untouched resources, and mass campaigns against illiteracy and inequality.

By contrast, the 1970s were marked by conservatism, a desire to protect and preserve, to add to more units of production to extensive models of growth. More steel, more concrete. The slogans of "Forward!" remained, but they sounded empty. More accurate was the term "real existing socialism." This phrase, coined by Brezhnev, told the Western left, who had been shocked and disillusioned by the invasion of Czechoslovakia, that they were in no position to criticize. They might talk of socialism, but the Soviet Bloc actually had it.

For a few years, the East European economies continued to grow, but then in the mid-1970s, they slowed down, in part because of hikes in energy prices, in part because of the inability of the command systems to compete in new industries, like electronics. Socialist countries produced goods that increasingly no one wanted, including their own citizens. After 1975 every economy in the East Bloc witnessed reduced growth, most dramatically Poland's, which fell from 9.8 percent (1971–1975) to 1.4 percent (1976–1980).[64] (See also Table A.6 in the

Appendix.) At the same time, taking advantage of cheap credit during the oil crisis, in which the oil-producing cartel (Organization of Petroleum Exporting Countries, or OPEC) drastically raised prices and stored vast reserves of cash in Western banks, East European states began racking up huge debts, highest in Poland and Hungary, but also significant and crippling in East Germany.

Still, if neo-Stalinism is an overstatement, two countries in the region had done much more than the others to put Stalinism behind them. Poland and Hungary remained Leninist, but after 1956, the state had retreated and no longer pursued the radical transformation of the individual and society of high Stalinism. Recall János Kádár's self-confident declaration in 1961 that he who is not against us is with us. Kádár said this to applause and laughter. Those who did not attempt active opposition could pursue life and happiness (if not liberty) in relative peace. By that time, Kádár, like his Polish counterpart Gomułka, felt secure after purging rivals from the right and left.

Polish and Hungarian scholars reestablished contacts with the West, and orthodox Marxism-Leninism became all but irrelevant to the mainstream social sciences in these two countries. In film, theater, and literature there was no return to socialist realism; indeed, spaces opened for a critical view of the 1950s. For example, in 1976 the Polish filmmaker Andrzej Wajda produced a searching meditation on Stalinism in *The Man of Marble*, about the collusion of party officials and ambitious artists to exploit a well-meaning young shock-worker— and how that exploitation created a new critical consciousness among workers and young people. In East Germany, criticisms of Stalinism would have implicated the leadership and continued to be suppressed. Until 1989, East German historians portrayed the early postwar years as a heroic time of glorious and unproblematic socialist construction when the East German party leader of the present, Erich Honecker, had commanded the blue-shirted Free German Youth under Walter Ulbricht, the East German equivalent of Stalin.

Poland and Hungary also stood apart from the others in the limits to state control of the economy. Despite discouragement from the Soviet Union—and thanks to the skills of János Kádár—Hungary carried through the most extensive decentralization in the Communist Bloc; from the early 1960s, its leaders also implemented flexible and productive cooperative rather than collective farming. It was said that Hungary borrowed ideas for reform from Polish economists that could not be realized in Poland (Hungary had its own economists as well). Poland saw little effective economic reform, but due to anticipated resistance, the state never attempted to collectivize the countryside and left farming in private hands, under heavy price controls and with little access to credit. That meant that the socialist state had to exclude a major sector of the economy from the state plan.

The hardline regimes in the GDR, Bulgaria, Romania, and Czechoslovakia represented miniature Soviet Unions with the obtrusive and pervasive presence of ideology, yet there were differences: the former two were in the hold of the original Stalinist cadre from the 1940s to the 1980s, whereas the latter two had embraced partial liberalization in the 1960s. Why the Czechoslovak leadership failed to go the more moderate route of Kádár is a question that historians have not answered. Was this because the ideas of the Prague Spring were so powerful that Czechs and Slovaks needed severe treatment to be cured of them, or because they were so weakly rooted that they could be pulled up with ease? Romania's drift to its peculiar brand of cultlike national Communism was linked to the object of the cult: Nicolae Ceaușescu returned from a visit to North Korea in 1972 convinced that Leninism required strict, centralized discipline.[65]

Likewise, religious policy in Czechoslovakia returned to strict regimentation, and the state discriminated against churchgoers in ways not thinkable in Poland, where many Party members attended mass each Sunday. East German Communists were less repressive toward the churches than was the Czechoslovak regime. In fact, one prominent Catholic dissident, Tomáš Halík, traveled to Erfurt in the GDR in 1978 to be ordained in secret, because the Catholic hierarchy there was basically intact (he then returned to Czechoslovakia to work as an underground priest).[66] Still, the East German regime placed great pressure on teenagers to participate in an atheist confirmation ceremony (*Jugendweihe*, "the blessing of the young") as a rite of passage. Again, such a practice was unthinkable in Poland, where the Catholic Church was a pillar of identity, grounding Poland in the "West." Poland's Communists struggled simply to secularize their country, and not until 1960 did they make Three Kings day (January 6) or the Assumption (August 15) into regular workdays.[67] Not until 1961 did they take religion out of schools and prevent Corpus Christi parades from dominating the streets of socialist cities.

Was the Prague Spring part of the democratic mobilization that swept across Europe? Like students in Paris and West Berlin, Czechs and Slovaks rose up against the multiple alienations of modern society, challenging the presumptions of bureaucrats and administrative machines to control their lives. Though under the party's aegis, they wanted grass roots democracy and chances to make their voices heard. To that extent, they were acting along the lines of the counterculture of West Germany and France in the 1960s; in the former case, such demands became a vital impulse behind the Green Party, which entered parliament in 1983.

But Czechs and Slovaks also agitated for things the French or West Germans had come to take for granted: the right to form one's views without fear, to read and write books of one's choosing, to travel, and to be able to hold rulers accountable to the laws of their country. Such basic rights, gained by earlier generations under Habsburg rule, had been lost under the Leninist dictatorship of the proletariat imported from Moscow. This was something that Czech intellectuals increasingly recognized and regretted in the 1970s, part of a growing appreciation of "civic" and "human rights," which had been smothered and compromised in a regime that claimed to enforce social rights—the rights of the working class as the embodiment of History—above all others.

But paradoxically, it was the crushing of the Prague Spring that had cleared the way for better relations between the Leninist dictatorships and the multiparty systems of the West and opened the way for a heightened appreciation across the globe of human rights. Once the Soviet Union had "stabilized" its sphere of influence, it felt secure enough to enter negotiations with the West aimed at reducing tensions. The earliest signs were treaties with West Germany in 1970 and 1971 that recognized the inviolability of the new postwar boundaries. By 1975 detente extended to all NATO and Warsaw Pact countries and resulted in a series of agreements signed at Helsinki. In exchange for recognition of postwar political boundaries, the East acknowledged the legitimacy of "human rights," perhaps believing its own rhetoric of being the avant garde of history, and that it would never be held to account by human beings. The following year, small groups of dissidents began forming in Poland and then in Czechoslovakia, not to reform state socialism—the events of 1968 had demonstrated that this was impossible—but to hold their regimes to the language of the accords they had just signed.

CHAPTER 23

Real Existing Socialism: Life in the Soviet Bloc

Just after the unification of Germany and the removal from subsequent history of the German Democratic Republic, a historian in East Berlin and his class debated what that land—home to them all—had been. Most said it could not be counted as socialist, a word that evoked life in peace and freedom, with people realizing their worth as human beings; not simply receiving orders but deciding for themselves what to produce and what to say. Marx had wanted to place the economy in the hands of "society," meaning individuals united in control of the means of production, and Engels had warned against taking decisions on production and distribution from one ruling group and simply placing them in the hands of another. At its core, socialism meant workers ruling themselves. That evidently had not been the case in the East Germany of Erich Honecker.

But with good reason the historian sided with Honecker, and by extension, Leonid Brezhnev. Socialism in the GDR had been a reality. With other state socialist regimes, it constituted the only social formation in history to do away with the market and with exploitation based on ownership. Whatever else it was, it was not capitalist.[1] Critics called the state socialist bureaucrats a new class, but they did not possess and pass on wealth. Nor did they govern simply to govern; even the most cynical, the Rákosis and the Ulbrichts, ruled in some relation to ultimate ideals, for creating a society without distinctions. They all proudly declared themselves as workers to their dying days, and they believed that "their" class embodied a higher morality and was destined to lead humankind into the future.[2] This was the dogma to which they genuflected on special occasions, like the atheist confirmation ceremony, *Jugendweihe*, a compulsory ritual for young people in the GDR.[3] Still, they also respected the Marxian doctrine of the withering of the state: under Communism, there would be no need for it, because society would have learned the rules of socialist cohabitation.[4]

But for the time being, was the working class ready for full self-government? What would guarantee they would not make bad choices, as had German or

Hungarian workers in the 1930s? Neither Marx nor Engels had left a blueprint about how to empower workers to build socialism; both seemed to assume that a higher consciousness would emerge from improvements in the production process itself.[5] And if workers required tutelage, where should it come from if not from dedicated revolutionaries?

The state socialist regimes of Eastern Europe were thus somewhere between the world-historical break with capitalist exploitation and the dawn of tomorrow. The leaders swore there was no going back. In the early 1980s, the SED district committee of Saalfeld placed a placard near the center of town: "You have been given power such that you will never, NEVER AGAIN, let it slip from your hands."[6] More frequent in the official propaganda was the simple: Everything for the Good of the People! That was the core concern of real existing socialism, its reason for being.

As we have seen, this slogan seemed to become opportune in 1953, right after Stalin's death. His successors assumed much of the heritage of Lenin and Stalin—central planning by the party, the idea that modernity meant heavy industry, belief in the ultimate superiority of their worldview—but they rejected the willful brutalization of everyday life. Under Stalin, millions had lived in abject poverty, often near starvation. Consumers had few if any rights. None of that enforced mass misery was necessary; in fact, as events would show, it was self-destructive. The skewing of resources away from consumption had no justification outside the Stalinist doctrine of imminent war.

What followed was a bending toward reasoned moderation, independent of who was in charge. After Stalin's funeral, Western observers suspected that Georgy M. Malenkov, his personal secretary, would assume rule. Within weeks, however, Malenkov had handed the reins of party leadership to Nikita S. Khrushchev, while retaining the post of premier. (The principle, readers will recall, was collective leadership.) For two years, Malenkov and Khrushchev were rivals, competing over how best to build socialism. They had differing emphases: Malenkov favored light and Khrushchev heavy industry. Yet both understood that socialism had to appeal to *consumer interests*.[7] It meant making life more enjoyable, through higher living standards, increased income, and expanded benefits.[8]

In the years that followed, Malenkov and Khrushchev acted to increase food production, Malenkov by raising the prices the state paid for collective farm deliveries and by encouraging the cultivation of individual plots, Khrushchev by putting millions of hectares under the plow that had never been cultivated.[9] Khrushchev ruled uncontested from 1956 to 1964, when his colleagues in the

Presidium of the Communist Party of the Soviet Union (CPSU), led by Leonid Brezhnev, ousted Khrushchev for foreign policy misadventures—in particular, the fiasco of the Cuban missile crisis—and for failures to achieve the economic growth that his ambitious predictions required. He had said that socialism could overtake capitalism within a generation. Rather than being a visionary, Khrushchev seemed erratic. One lesson he inadvertently taught was to avoid precise predictions about the advent of the new society.

Brezhnev defended the purity of Marxist-Leninist teaching, the leading role of the party, and the old Stalinist commitment to heavy industry.[10] Critics would later fault him for leading his country toward stagnation. With the crushing of the Prague Spring, he signaled the limits of reform: any market mechanisms favored by reform economists would be strictly limited and controlled. The path he and the Soviet elite then chose was toward economic decline. Nevertheless, the idea survived that socialism was about improving people's lives, and the reorientation of investment resources that had started under Khrushchev continued. Capital accumulation, which had absorbed 25–35 percent of GDP in the early 1950s, dropped to about 20–25 percent from the 1960s onward.

The share of investment devoted to consumption remained high, and, in a break with Stalinist autarchy, Communist regimes adopted a more pragmatic approach to foreign trade. Between 1960 and 1975, imports to Eastern Europe rose sixfold, and exports more than sevenfold. The direction of trade shifted away from the Communist world. From 1960 to 1975, exports to developed countries increased from 19 to 22 percent of the total, while imports went from 21.8 to 33 percent.[11] To a substantial degree, the imports consisted of things meant to satisfy consumer desires, especially foodstuffs and clothing. East European and Soviet Communists purchased foreign licenses to produce Western soft drinks, tractors, and automobiles on their own territory.

This turn to consumerism was not simply a reflection of party bureaucrats' largesse, however. It was meant to ensure that mass working-class unrest did not recur after the strikes of 1953, or to use Khrushchev's image, it was about keeping workers from chasing the Communists out of town "with pitchforks." A Marxist might say that destalinization was the synthesis that emerged from the old command economy under the pressures of working-class protest. Making sure workers did not rise up again meant entering into an implicit dialogue, finding out how much privation they would tolerate, and also how to generate real support. Post-totalitarian Communism (as Václav Havel called it) became a constant negotiation between regime and society, not of two equal sides, but with a mutually recognized bargain. The regime provided a minimum of "decent" European quality of life and in return expected outward conformity.[12] People marched on May Day, joined "mass organizations," and refrained from political dissent. Those who violated the understanding risked slipping to the bottom of the social ladder and performing grinding manual labor, imperiling their own standard of living as well as that of their children.

Like all negotiations, the end-product—real existing socialism—was not something anyone could have predicted emerging at the beginning. But it solidified over the decades, through crises and past leaders, changes in fashions and generations; always a compromise between regime and society, yet always in some relation to the Marxist-Leninist project. It was never simply imposed but emerged from the state-society nexus. The regime itself was uncertain what constituted the "socialist lifestyle" and employed legions of sociologists to go into the population and find out.[13]

By the 1960s, the contours and rhythms of this lifestyle had come to constitute the most recent manifestation of the generations-old experience of living under imperial rule. After World War II, East Europeans had become subjects of the socialist world system: homo Sovieticus. People from Hungary or Poland who met each other on holiday understood without much elaboration what it meant to endure shortages, corruption, and occasional political terror; but they also knew what it was to live with social equality and security, as well as time to enjoy life with their workmates and families at an unhurried pace.

The Perils of Consumerism

If the shift to consumerism served to keep a lid on dissent, it also involved two poorly understood challenges that would erode socialism's legitimacy. First, satisfying growing consumer demand required continued economic growth, and thus surmounting the difficulties of moving from the first and second to the third industrial revolution. That was a dire challenge, given that in the early 1960s, growth began to slow (as we have seen in Czechoslovakia). But second, this growth took place in comparison not only to the capitalist past that these countries had left behind but also to the capitalist world of the present. Contrary to the predictions of Marx, that world was not declining but, despite setbacks, growing at an unprecedented pace, producing wealth that was not simply the preserve of a small elite but widely distributed among increasingly affluent societies.[14]

Because the post-Stalinist states had opened to the west—through radio and television waves, but also through tourism—the competition between the West and the Communist Bloc took place in full view of East European populations. From the early 1960s, Hungarians, Czechs, and Poles could travel to the other side of the Iron Curtain (for example, from 1966 Hungarians could visit the West as tourists once every three years, and as a guest once every two years), and at the same time, each year millions of Western tourists were visiting Prague, Budapest, East Berlin and many other East European destinations.[15]

Eastern Europe's Communists were not imitating the Soviet Union, whose citizens could not travel abroad, even to other socialist countries.[16] Instead, the East Europeans were translating the general "relaxation of tensions" into measures that fit their own histories of closer relations to the West. Huge Polish émigré communities lived in France, Britain, Argentina, and the United States, and the Polish state promoted their return to Poland on holidays or study trips. Hundreds of thousands of Hungarians and Czechs likewise lived in the West. East Germany reflected the rule so much that it became an exception to it. It was the closeness of its relation to West Germany that caused the government to put up a wall in August 1961 to keep its citizens from leaving. After that, East German males under age 65 (women under age 60) could not travel westward except in exceptional circumstances (for example, a scientific conference), and visits from the West were restricted.

When Nikita Khrushchev made his "hare-brained" predictions of the imminent victory of Communism in 1961, he directly invited competition with the West, blithely telling delegates of the twenty-second Party Congress that their country would attain a living standard within two decades that would be higher than that of any capitalist country. Part of his optimism stemmed from the belief that the command economy's problems lay not in planning but in the crude methods of plan calculation; in the view of party experts, the increased use of mathematical methods and computerization would generate improvements in quantity and quality of production.[17]

But the nature of the competition depended on what was meant by "living standard." Capitalism featured an endless array of consumer goods: dozens of types of automobiles (in new styles every year); countless varieties of cheese, or bread, or sweets, or consumer durables; fashions of clothing for every imaginable taste—as well as tastes that advertising had made imaginable. Socialism would not replicate this dazzling variety, in part because the provision of luxury goods seemed to contradict the higher proletarian morality. East German Communists called the Western race to buy goods in the latest style "consumption terror."[18] But once the distortions of suppressing the consumer sector disappeared, what exactly was the right balance between the frugal self-sacrificing ethos of Stalinism and the boundless decadence of capitalist culture? How much living space did socialist citizens require: would families have their own houses, or would they share communal apartments? Did socialist citizens drive cars or ride together in buses? Would they share meals at large common tables in cafeterias or occasionally dine in restaurants? What would those restaurants serve?

These questions were new if not revolutionary. The founders of state socialism had not considered the regime's purpose to be individual consumption of goods and services; they did not disregard consumption entirely but subordinated it to the building of Communism. State socialism was a society based on productive labor. Once it had transformed the workplace and created a set of modern industries producing wealth, distribution would take care of itself. Communism would be the bounty from which all other goods would flow. But now that Communism was fading to an ever-more distant future, functionaries found themselves focusing on distribution more than ever before. Social scientists have depicted the regimes not as "Communist" but as "centers for redistribution," and dictatorships "over needs."[19] Yet the functionaries who dictated needs through the state plan still wanted to know what people desired.

In Hungary, state functionaries began their research during the Stalinist period, when employees in the Hungarian Ministry of Internal Commerce had quietly surveyed the preferences of consumers, asking questions about specific goods whose quality they hoped to improve. East Germany's Communists studied consumption from within the Ministry of Trade and Supply, but also created an Institute for the Study of Demand in 1961, renamed the Institute for the Study of the Market in 1966.[20]

Beginning in the late 1950s, state planners throughout the bloc conceived of their populations as "shoppers," and small specialty stores gave way to supermarkets and department stores, with expanded assortments of "nonessential" goods, not only responding to, but in a sense, provoking demand. In 1963 the Luxus department store opened in downtown Budapest. It sold goods of exceptional quality, beautifully presented—often at exorbitant prices. After years of privation, window shopping was again an urban experience, and East Europeans began to differentiate products by quality, reflecting the "growing importance of consumer choice in constituting one's social identity." The state provided abundant information on how and what to consume, through advertising as well as advice magazines, whether the topic was home decoration, fashion, cooking, or cars. By 1973, advertising represented 3 percent of national expenditure.[21]

FIGURE 23.1. Strollers on the Stalinallee (East Berlin, late 1950s). *Source*: Album/
Alamy Stock Photo.

Thanks to the reorientation toward consumerism, socialist industries produced wealth that transformed people's lives. The number of Czechoslovaks
with automobiles rose from 19 percent in 1970 to 47 percent in 1985; with refrigerators, from 70.1 percent in 1970 to 96.7 percent in 1985; with color TVs, from
0.8 percent in 1976 to 26.8 percent in 1985.[22] In Hungary, the trend was similar:
television subscriptions went up twenty-fold from 1956 to 1962, car ownership
multiplied by eleven times from 1960 to 1970; and from 1960 to 1980, the number of apartments went up by 50 percent. In the 1960s, Hungary's population
as a whole "enjoyed abundant, nutritious meals for the first time in history." The
rising affluence was reflected in ever higher salaries, which in turn stimulated
increasing consumption. The Hungarian government boosted incomes by
20 percent after the 1956 revolution, and then 3–4 percent every year until the
late 1970s. In Poland, wages increased by 41 percent between 1971 and 1975; in
Czechoslovakia, they went up by almost 20 percent.[23]

Excepting some highly rewarded experts and a few "shock workers" held up
as models, Stalinism had aimed at reducing everyone to a common standard.
That time of "distortion" was over, but what would follow was not clear. People
were rewarded not according to need (though basic needs were guaranteed)
but according to the value of what they contributed. But how would a socialist

FIGURE 23.2. Healthy lunch for schoolchildren (Dillstädt, GDR, 1975). *Source*: Helmut
Schaar (photographer), Bundesarchiv, Bild 183-P1124-0029 / CC-BY-SA 3.0.

state measure value? Under capitalism, physicians might earn twenty times as
much as unskilled laborers; how much higher should their salaries be under
socialism? If physicians' salaries were too low, students might not endure the years
of tedium and hard work required for a medical degree. But if the income the
state plan budgeted for white collar workers was high, they might come to seem
a leading class in a society where class distinctions were supposedly fading.

Ultimately, the regimes in question opted against significant differentials in
income. The Gini coefficients (statistical measures of social inequality) of state
socialist societies were the lowest on earth (the Czechoslovak figure was the
lowest measured anywhere).[24] The cream of the intelligentsia and members of
the upper party bureaucracy had privileged access to goods and services, but,
as we shall see in greater detail, this was modest in comparison with the advantages in consumption enjoyed by Western elites. In the 1980s, physicians and
engineers in the Soviet Bloc had salaries not much higher than those of skilled
workers, and sometimes lower.[25] Still, gradations emerged, more strongly in Poland with its widespread unofficial or "gray" economy. The power of society
to produce and reproduce differentiations by status—if not class—was something the regime did not fully control.

Limits of Consumerism

If socialist egalitarianism remained strong, by the 1970s, it was clear that the Soviet Bloc was stagnating economically and not showing humankind the way toward greater prosperity. In the 1950s, the West had been fearful of Eastern accomplishments in science and technology, like Sputnik, but two decades later, that fear was easing. Despite impressive gains in output, socialism spelled uniformity, lack of selection, and shoddy quality. And it was incapable of producing original styles or product lines. Socialist consumerism seemed a shabby imitation of the West, where states cleverly called themselves not "capitalist" but social welfare states, often ruled by the Communists' Marxist cousins, the Social Democrats.

If product designs were usually inspired by, but not directly copied from, the West, the assortment of goods differed. Even the wealthiest society, East Germany, produced just two automobile lines, Trabant and Wartburg (with one or two models in each, and waiting lists of many years); and only one kind of refrigerator, the Kristall 140 (advertised for delivery in 1968/1969 for the equivalent of two months of wages, but often out of stock). In 1969, only some 60 percent of East German households had refrigerators.[26] In the early 1970s, with huge investment, (partly involving an enormous machine imported from Japan to produce plastic parts), the GDR began making an automatic dishwasher, but after producing 13,000 machines in 1972/1973, production ceased, in part because the state company that built apartment units failed to configure the electrical installations in kitchens to accommodate dishwashers.[27] And so East Germans washed and dried by hand. At the beginning of the 1980s, only 24 percent of East German households had a color television, but the regime was aided by its own duplicity: thousands of sets made in the GDR suddenly became available for purchase in the GDR when Western customs authorities failed to permit them to cross the border. It turned out that they violated 28 patents. Why they were headed westward is a question we will return to.[28]

Over the decades, in contrast to the West, the styles of consumer goods changed little if at all. In Poland in the 1980s, there were in general two kinds of hard cheese and two kinds of bread. Shoppers in Prague might find a half-dozen brands of wine in the supermarkets of their metropolis (and more kinds of beer). Even in high-end shops, the abundance was often quantitative and not qualitative. To make things worse, by the 1980s, shortages had developed, chronic in Poland and Romania, but aggravating and unpredictable in East Germany and Czechoslovakia. The GDR adapted its propaganda to the uncomfortable fact that scarcity had caused people to hone their do-it-yourself skills, making their own jams or their own clothing. This represented, one reporter wrote in 1976, a "meaningful use of the leisure time of our women."[29]

The most arresting shortcoming was in electronics. The technologically simple Sony Walkman entered Western markets in 1979, but not until 1988 did the GDR release its own version, at a cost of more than 300 East German marks (the average monthly salary for workers with higher education at that point was 1,477 marks).[30] But no matter one's salary, one still had to find the item in a store.[31] From the 1960s, Soviet Bloc states kept up with advances in computer technology by pirating Western designs, a fact their citizens learned from Western television stations.[32] Consumer goods had become symbols of a better, "normal" life, and as the West moved on to new technologies, the East remained stuck in products designed in earlier periods.

East European leaders knew about the problems of diversity and quality and worried about the unflattering comparisons their populations were drawing with the West. Yet because of the state's almost total responsibility for the economy, consumers interpreted such problems as reflecting evil intent on the part of state authorities. More than that, to describe the state's attitude, citizens used language harkening back to the days of the all-powerful but contemptuous colonial rulers of yesteryear. They spoke of products being "thrown" at them; for example, people on the street would tell one another: "they've thrown lemons into the grocery store." The poor quality of what was "thrown" (like inedible Cuban oranges) was taken to reflect the regime's attitude toward the people who would consume such things, no doubt grateful to receive anything at all.[33]

Often unfairly, socialist citizens simply took for granted the superiority of things from the West, supposedly representing higher quality and a freer lifestyle. Socialism had thus produced a self-destructive dynamic in the relation between desire and goods. Under capitalism, desire was rendered concrete and specific and actual goods were offered to satisfy it; socialism, by contrast, aroused vague desires with no particular focus and kept them alive through deprivation. Discontent focused on the state that had proclaimed itself the source of fulfillment of all needs. The Western state, by contrast, mediated between commercial interests and "citizen consumers," and faced much less pressure for legitimation through the satisfaction of needs because it did not pose as a dictatorship of needs.[34]

East European states additionally suffered from the fact that they provided a range of products that were free or heavily subsidized, which their citizens came to take for granted, and whose easy availability they would fully appreciate only after the Communist regimes had collapsed: food, drink, utilities, rent, education, books, culture (everyone could afford the finest symphony orchestra seats), vacation resorts, gyms, swimming pools, health spas, medical treatment, and transportation.[35] These goods and services, considered objects of individual consumption in the West, helped create affluence for which East Bloc citizens gave their regimes little credit, focusing instead on the Western style goods they lacked.

The perception of official contempt was reinforced by the practice of socialist states to contract with Western firms to produce textiles under Western license, including jeans, but also food products and electronics. Though produced in socialist factories, these goods were intended for purchase in the West. For example, the GDR Walkman was sold for a much lower price in West Germany before it became available in East Germany.[36] Western firms eagerly sold eastern products because of the low wages and high discipline of East Bloc workers. These workers in turn drew their own conclusions from the fact that their proudest manufactures went into budget department stores in the capitalist West. After the fall of Communism, reports surfaced that some products meant for Western consumption were manufactured by prison labor.[37] A double hypocrisy thus lay at the heart of the Cold War: The East reserved its best products for the class enemy, while Western capitalists undercut one another with products made, at times, by slaves of the Communist system they castigated for crushing human freedom.

Perhaps the most oppressive reflection of the socialist state's disregard for its consumer citizens was the built environment. As the anthropologist Krisztina Fehérváry notes, in the 1960s modernist apartment complexes—every structure, every apartment the same—emerged throughout the bloc. Their austerity mixed the design ideologies of architects with the production biases of economies facing challenges in maintaining growth rates. The uniform apartment complexes incorporated the regime's dedication to realizing the equality of socialist citizens living in a collective, yet over time, they seemed to incorporate the blindness of dictatorial regimes to unique human persons.[38]

Because socialist regimes were too cash-strapped to bring older apartment buildings up to date, however, many thousands happily moved into the new structures, freed from the chore of carrying coal briquettes up steps to light stoves in the frigid winters. Citizens also did their bit to break up the monotony by decorating drab interiors with wood paneling, making their spaces reminiscent of cozy homes in the village. In the meantime, the old buildings lost inhabitants, as well as windows and roof tiles, and began to deteriorate. Thus, part

of the lovely old East German city of Greifswald, untouched by wartime hostilities because its commander surrendered it without a shot in 1945—risking
execution—was torn down in the 1980s because the state could not finance
renovation of old structures. Locals twisted the peace movement slogan "Make
peace without weapons" to describe socialism: "Ruinen schaffen, ohne Waffen!"
(Make ruins without weapons).

How much did this unwinnable competition contribute to the end of state
socialism? Even behind sealed borders, guarded by elaborate systems of mines
and layers of barbed wire, East Europeans knew in great detail about Western
technological advances. Despite all attempts through socialist advertising to
steer "demand" onto desired paths, emphasizing (socialist) utility over (capitalist) conspicuous consumption, images of products streamed in from the
West and aggravated desires that socialism could not control. Western goods
seemed to embody a better world, and to argue otherwise was increasingly
futile. In 1988, finally yielding to pressures for political reform, the Polish regime
invited dissidents to negotiations. In a TV debate, independent trade union
leader Lech Wałęsa mocked his Communist opponent: the West is going into
the future by car, and we on foot. The claim went unchallenged. The following
year, his movement—called "Solidarity"—was made legal, and it won every
position for which it openly competed in Poland's first partly free elections
since the 1920s.

State Socialism in Retrospect

But that triumphal story is far from the whole story. Just a few years later these
same voters, acting in full freedom, with all ties severed between their state and
the Soviet Union (indeed, the Soviet state had collapsed), elected a former
Communist to succeed Wałęsa as president. Voters did not want to restore state
socialism, but evidently there was something about that old regime that they
had come to cherish.

If that point of view prevailed in Poland, with its deeply dysfunctional economy during late Communism, it was even more compelling in wealthier East
Germany or Czechoslovakia. In 2013, some 33 percent of Czechs said the Communist regime was better than the current one; not even a majority
(46 percent) would concede that the regime of their day was an improvement
over the old one (22 percent felt they were roughly the same).[39] Three years
earlier (and more shockingly, given the repressiveness their own late-Communist
police state), 41 percent of Romanians said they would vote for Nicolae

FIGURE 23.3. Cozy living room in socialist Schwerin, GDR. *Source*: Katscherowski (photographer), Bundesarchiv, Bild 183-N0521-0013 / CC-BY-SA 3.0.

Ceaușescu if he were running for president, and 63 percent said their lives were better under Communism.[40]

East-West competition was about more than a simple clash in consumption. We come back to the question of what Khrushchev meant by "standard of living" or what East German leaders had in mind when they spoke of the people's "welfare." That standard and that welfare were not entirely about the provision of material goods. State socialism also provided security. There was no unemployment, and little violent crime, homelessness, or drug abuse. Basic food items were affordable, and rents were protected for everyone. Women could enter the workforce in numbers that were unprecedented. In places where the welfare provisions worked best—East Germany, Czechoslovakia, and Hungary—women could pursue careers (at a slower pace than men to be sure) while having families. In the GDR, women got a paid year off after each child (the "baby year") and then guaranteed daycare until their children reached school age.

Did Western shop windows create impressions that were superficial? Fully aware that their citizens were making comparisons to the West, the Communist press began making its own beginning in the 1960s. Stories of better lives across the border, Communist writers argued, were based on hearsay and ignorance, or at best brief encounters with goods produced in the West, rather than on the actual need to live and survive there, to find work, a place to live, and food. The Czechoslovak and East German governments developed campaigns to convince citizens that existence in the West was not only insecure but also dangerous and lonely. They reprinted letters of citizens who either longed to return to the security of their homelands or had done so.

Czechoslovak returnees claimed to have lost their "illusions," and they emphasized the lack of job security and poorer social welfare in the West. A man who had lived in Canada for five years claimed that he could be fired if he felt unwell or was unable to keep up with production demands. Letters evoked a prisonlike social insecurity that people "longed to escape." In 1971 the Czech Communist daily *Rudé Právo* cited one unhappy émigré who yearned for the community of weekend cottages, volleyball games, and camping trips, all in evident contrast to the anonymous routine and solitude of his life in the West.

Return to Czechoslovakia was therefore portrayed as a return to true freedom. Some complained of the "unbelievably high speed" at which they had to work in the West. A journalist interviewing one returnee offered that the stress must have seemed strange. "It was," he admitted, "because it's a fact—let's face it—that here I made enough money and I practically didn't do any work." A Slovak who came back said he was glad he could go to bed and sleep peacefully again, not worrying that he might be fired the following day. Maybe prison was the wrong word for the West. It was more a place with no rules, a chaos of opportunities, challenges, threats, and risks, with no apparent way of calculating the future.[41] Returnees' reports evoked a warm hominess in socialism regained, only very indirectly associated with the achievements of class struggle or industrial production.

What was involved in "normalization" of life in Czechoslovakia after the Warsaw Pact intervention of 1968 was not a surrender to the West in the contest over living standards but an attempt to recalibrate the competition. Socialism was a refuge from the uncertainties and the cold lack of concern that refugees encountered the moment they left transit camps and attempted to live productive lives in the West. Socialism offered a way of living that was about more than work and involved "self-actualization."[42]

Ironically, the forces that kept socialist societies from keeping up with capitalism were the very forces that make East Europeans of our day nostalgic about socialism. The role of enterprises was to produce not profits but "social calm" or "social comfort," with management assuming that about 20 percent of the work force was not working at all. "During work hours," Czech economist Otakar Turek recalled, "it was permissible both to take care of other business and to partake of celebratory office parties; and if the management was clever, it even negotiated decent wages." No one dreamed that such behavior might lead to a factory's closing. "At the workplace," Turek concluded, "it was possible to live well."[43]

The "loosening up" of work time was greatest in factories but extended into offices. East German writer Daniela Dahn's husband worked in a research institute in Dresden in the 1970s, and every day after lunch, the scientists and engineers (including the First Party secretary) played a round of soccer on the fields along the river Elbe. The cadre secretary kept her office door open to show that she knew what was going on but did nothing to stop the afternoon recreation; the staff managed to turn their work in on time. The practice stopped only after the ministry began noticing that phones were not answered at particular times in the afternoon.[44]

In its time, even some of the regime's bitter critics appreciated the unhurried pace of life under socialism. "In global statistics of technical success we will never stand at the top," Hungarian dissident George Konrád wrote in 1982. But "we do better in less measurable things, that one might call the art of living, like care for one's home, finding pleasant ways to spend leisure time, or cordial manners." "Sitting at sunset in one's well tended garden and drinking a glass of wine with friends is worth as much as speeding along on overcrowded eight-lane highways."[45] People with a pushy, get-ahead attitude met with healthy pagan cynicism on the part of many Hungarians. What purpose was served by all that bother?

Those nostalgic for this past do not ask whether a workplace should employ people who are not really working. And even in state socialism, this kind of workplace freedom was not universal. It was strongest among self-confident industrial workers, whom historian Lutz Niethammer called "the other leading class." "The leadership of the SED respected nothing more than industrial workers," he writes. The regime felt much freer to exert pressure at universities.[46] Also ignored in fond backward glances is that the unproductive socialist economy could exist only by failing to reinvest in technology and plants, by running equipment into the ground, and by killing forests and making air unbreathable, because the state socialist economy depended on solid fuels like brown coal. Moreover, by the late 1970s, this economy was incurring huge hard-currency debts to Western creditors, which would contribute to socialism's undoing. But in the short term, the socialist "lifestyle"—an alternative to capitalism sustained by capitalism—helped stabilize dictatorship.

FIGURE 23.4. Guests enjoy a drink at the pool of a restaurant in Suhl, GDR. *Source*: Bernd
Settnik (photographer), Bundesarchiv, Bild 183-1983-0822-009 / CC-BY-SA 3.0.

Coping with the Protracted Crisis of State Socialism

There were places where a relaxed attitude toward economic and social crisis
such as George Konrád's was not possible, places where there was little good
to drink with friends, and even coming by staples like sugar or toilet paper required many hours of standing in line. There were times when things that
people desperately needed could not be had by legal methods. In Poland, the
socialist system often broke down because of its own inefficiencies, and people
crafted informal channels to obtain desired goods and services. The economic
duress that visited their country from the mid-1970s until 1989 caused Poles to
perfect such methods, producing a shadow reality that the anthropologist
Janine Wedel called the "private Poland," a place that eluded the scrutiny of
the state.

At the height of Poland's economic crisis in 1980, all that one could buy without waiting was vinegar and matches, and queues formed any time some product was "thrown" into the store, as if by some all-powerful force. The government introduced ration cards to prevent hoarding. Things people really
wanted—leather goods, or outer wear—might be displayed in shop windows
but were not freely available for sale, and clerks held them under the counter,

waiting for a customer who could give them something in return beyond money. Restaurants were open with plenty of seating and full menus, yet appearances deceived. No one could simply sit down and order. Would-be diners were told to wait in line: the empty seats, often half the restaurant, were "reserved," and on a five-page menu, only three or four items were actually available.

The point was to get to know someone who controlled access to things everyone wanted. A waiter held tables for friends or, more often, friends of friends, all links in a socialist social network. The employees of a leather shop stored a fine but scarce item, like a handbag, "under the counter," for members of their own network. If no one with connections came, the restaurant table remained empty or the handbag unavailable. Across the East Bloc, waiters gained prestige unknown in the West. "The customer is king but the waiter is emperor," went an East German saying. One writer called the GDR a "dictatorship of waiters and sales clerks."[47]

Poland was an extreme example of the shortage economy, illustrating specific aspects of the general syndrome. Each country, even the wealthiest, knew parallels of Poland's informal networks. Hungarian sociologist Elemér Hankiss spoke of a "second society," and the Czech dissident Václav Benda—with a more political idea of the world eluding state control—of a parallel polis. East Germany was the showcase socialist state where even Westerners—like US soldiers stationed in West Berlin—found things to buy (GIs liked the carpets featured in East Berlin department stores). In contrast to Poles or Romanians, East Germans got new apartments without much wait time. Yet even they spoke of connections as "Vitamin B" (*Beziehungen* = connections); they were something absolutely needed, especially if one could not do repairs on cars, plumbing, or toaster ovens, or needed spare parts that were not in shops.

One can overdo the distinction between public and private. To some extent, everyone lived in both, even toddlers who spent most of their waking hours at state-run daycare, which tended to be universal and of decent quality. The extraordinary thing was how inseparable public and private became, how a "public" place—for example, an office in city hall—might suddenly become indistinguishable from a private trading company, with public bureaucrats spending hours on the phone working out deals in their own interests. Janine Wedel met with an important historian in Warsaw and encountered a "typically Polish mixture of business and personal matters. The professor sent his secretaries scurrying to find documents necessary for my research while he chatted about family matters and thanked me again and again for the flowers."[48]

FIGURE 23.5. Line to buy meat in Poland (1986). *Source:* Wolfgang Arnold/
Alamy Stock Photo.

Wedel had brought flowers to incline this historian to help her with research.
She might have brought coffee, chocolates, or an offer to be of assistance (for
example, to help with translations of English language texts). Technically, all
of this should have been irrelevant to a state official obliged to make public documents available. One thing Wedel could not offer was US dollars, let alone
Polish zlotys. Money seemed crude because it revealed the actual nature of the
transaction. Crucial was to create a "private" relationship that obviated the need
for cash, where both sides were attentive to ways of trading access to the other:
"do you need a vacation spot," "do you need help in translating a text," "does your
child need help with physics," and so forth. This was for Wedel the etiquette of
exchange. Once a connection to Private Poland was established, one had to be
mindful of basic expectations, like remembering one's "friends" on their name
days. And when there was no option but to offer money for a special service,
the supplicant emphasized that the money was "nothing," having no resemblance to a payoff.[49] Even a friend's troublesome family members were part of
the network and had somehow to be dealt with.

The strict rules on the use of money were a way that the private protected itself from subversion, from entry beyond the socialist network. Since one could not "pay" for favors, one had to reward them in ways that seemed disinterested, and money was the very symbol of interest. The sphere of those invested with privileges of the "private" went far beyond family and friends, to constitute sub-milieus, or *środowiska*. The Polish for the one-on-one relation characterized was *swój człowiek*, a person one engaged in "intimate, intense, and usually frequent interaction."[50]

In the East German second economy, money was important, but primarily as a way of securing connections. Without ties to people who had access to desired goods or services, money had little value. "Building materials and other desirable but scarce items, like porcelain, tiles, or western clothing, could be purchased with cash," Daphne Berdahl writes, "but only if one knew where, or through whom, to find them."[51]

Currency served as a convenience, permitting prices to be attached to comparable goods and services. It was unavoidable among people who did not know each other, but when traded on the semi-legal (or "gray") market, currency tended to be Western, preferably US dollars or German marks. A pair of blue jeans might be worth fifty (West) German marks in 1980s Poland, but much depended on the cut and style. Even in rural areas, people were connoisseurs of Western brands. They got Western currency as gifts from relatives in the Polish émigré community in the West, as under-the-table wages in the West during vacations (for example, in agriculture in Norway), or through trading on the gray market (for example, a skilled mechanic would be paid in dollars for work done after hours). The situation in the medical profession was such that even in the 1960s, physicians and nurses required payments in Western currencies or other services in order to do their jobs with maximum attention to the patient. In this way, medicine became a lucrative profession under Polish socialism, and officials in the professional bureaucracy began taking "cuts"—from medical school admissions committees onward. In the 1980s, it was rumored that the admission "cost" was about the value of a small car (Polish Fiat)—not for the brilliant students, but for those who were borderline. And the bribing got more intense after doctors or nurses graduated and were called on to provide treatment in public clinics and hospitals (the situation was not so dire in the GDR or Czechoslovakia).[52]

Many things were brought into play in the gray and black markets, some invisible even to insiders. Payment might be foregone in expectation of a "favor" in the future. Of special value were connections to people with a say in student admissions, the issuing of passports, military draft deferrals, or provision of hospital beds. People could easily become unwitting participants. The mother of an acquaintance of mine was treated for a serious tumor in a hospital in Kraków. On learning that the patient was about to travel to Austria for treatment, a nurse suddenly registered a request for assistance in purchasing Western boots. After all, she had taken good care of the mother. (The boots were procured and duly sent through the socialist mails but never arrived.)

Pressures placed on family relations and friendships were pressures that could destroy and demoralize. In Poland, young people often took care of aged aunts and uncles in exchange for being made heirs to their apartments. In a country where three generations might inhabit a three-room apartment, and young people waited more than twenty years for state-provided housing, this was a reasonable strategy, but it also had the effect of making nieces and nephews look forward to the deaths of their elderly relatives.

Other strategies for coping involved stretching not just ties of family or friendship but also the boundaries of the imagination. From the 1950s to the end of the Cold War, East Europeans—especially Poles—imagined their hopeless situation was temporary, destined to end when a war might break out, promising salvation. Those who held this view (and there were many of them) did not differentiate between conventional and nuclear war. One woman encountered by Janine Wedel in 1980s Poland lamented that *in World War II, at least*, Poles had "had hope." After the imposition of martial law in December 1981, Poles Wedel met claimed to be buying their last bottle of alcohol, or eating their last piece of cake.[53] The hoped-for apocalypse would release tension, liberating Poland from its isolation.

People who despaired at the forces governing their lives—such that they either hoped for war (Poles) or deeply dreaded it (Germans)—had descended into a crisis of spirit, reflected in massive consumption of alcohol—the East German intake of pure alcohol went up from 4.1 liters in 1960 to 10.9 liters in 1989—and the erosion of "bourgeois" virtues like truth telling.[54] Wedel began routinely lying to achieve what she wanted, for example, entrance to a sold-out concert (she claimed to be the wife of an official at the US embassy). But lies were buried in layers of truth, so that the two became difficult to distinguish, even in the minds of the liars.[55] Language itself changed. The historian Timothy Garton Ash called the double-talk of Hungarian state-socialism a "language of diabolical circumlocution, of convoluted allegory, and serpentine metaphor." Intellectuals became accustomed to employing "criticisms of the authorities that are oblique, implicit, elliptical or metaphorical." He predicted that people tightly wrapped in hyper-sophisticated allusions and evasions would never find their way to the barricades.[56]

State Socialism as State Security

If there was so much activity beyond and even against the law, what did the socialist state do about it? States should be able to enforce their own rules. Perhaps the reputation of East European regimes as totalitarian was semi-fictional—certainly in the post-Stalinist period—but secret police forces bound to protect them like the East German *Stasi* (Ministry for State Security) were not.

The *Stasi* was the largest such organization in the Soviet Bloc per capita, with one operative per 180 citizens (in contrast to one per 595 in the Soviet Union, and one in 1,574 in Poland.) But even this was not enough. The East German Communist Party (SED) also had the *Stasi* recruit informal agents, whose numbers ranged from 110,000 to 180,000 in the last years of the GDR. Over the decades, about one in thirty East German citizens worked for the *Stasi* in some capacity.[57] The *Stasi* outdid other agencies not only in size but also in pervasive surveillance of society (*flächendeckende Ueberwachung*). Within East Berlin the *Stasi* could track 20,000 phone calls simultaneously and had six hundred agents opening the mail. Dozens sat and listened to conversations in the subway. The Ministry kept a library of smells, including jars with dissidents' underwear, so that dogs could connect underground literature to specific persons. It routinely summoned medical records, listened in on confessions in Catholic churches, and on booths at the Dresden state opera. Prostitutes on the Ministry's payroll seduced unsuspecting politicians and businessmen visiting from the West.[58]

How this shadow reality affected people's psyches is difficult to say. Before 1990, few suspected how large the apparatus was.[59] Ironically, it had expanded as the GDR opened to the west and became better established internationally. More tourists came in, especially to East Berlin, and as they did, concerns grew about western infiltration. And because the whole point of the *Stasi* was to remain in the background, the recruitment of ever more formal and informal agents remained hidden.

Technically, GDR citizens had nothing to fear from the paid snoopers. Freedoms of speech and conscience were guaranteed in East Germany's constitution.[60] Yet the *Stasi* was beyond public oversight and passed the information it gathered to state and party agencies that decided such things as promotions at work or school. Like other would-be total regimes, the SED regime controlled people by manipulating a virtue: concern for family and friends. When East Germans refused organizational membership, or became involved in a church or a dissident group, they knew this could well keep their children out of medical school or other paths to professional and personal fulfillment. The state also wielded concern for children as an incentive. People marched in May Day parades, joined official organizations or spoke out "in a socialist sense" at staged meetings because they knew these services were held in their favor. As in Poland, competition for spots in medical schools was intense, but the corruption state socialism generated was of a very different kind: instead of paying bribe money that disappeared into private channels, boys hoping to study medicine were expected to "volunteer" three years' service in the people's army, eighteen months more than required. This expectation was never officially stipulated but instead grew out of the encounter of the socialist state with East German society: whereas the currency offered in Poland was favors and bribes, collected unofficially by state employees for their personal benefit, in the GDR it was political subservience, offered voluntarily by citizens and collected officially by state employees; together they solidified the edifice of the most densely controlled Communist state in Eastern Europe.[61]

The relatively sophisticated levers of political control in East Germany thus reduced room for outright bribery and corruption, but at the same time, the greater abundance of consumer goods had an ambivalent effect. On one hand, the East German state's success in providing housing and medical care meant that people could get by with less frequent recourse to "private" connections; but on the other, those who refused to play along denied themselves the best fruits of an affluent society.

The Polish state failed at state security as well as social security; one could even say that one side of the failure reflected the other. It neither pervaded society with political controls, nor provided more than a primitive level of social welfare. Poles did not live homeless on the streets, but many lived two and three to a room. They did not starve but consumed a diet heavy in basic starches with few vitamins. If all East European regimes withdrew from ambitions for total control of society after Stalin's death, the Polish Communists went furthest. They staged a unique retreat from the countryside, leaving most farms in private hands, but then withdrew even further. In 1989, the private sector was responsible for 33 percent of building construction, 59.5 percent of trade, and 47.2 percent of employment. [62] The Polish state likewise left freedoms to intellectuals and artists and to the church that were unthinkable elsewhere.

If East Germany came closest to a police state, with highly developed mechanisms of control; Poland seemed relatively free. Especially after the Solidarity Revolution of 1980, people spoke their minds in public. The shelves of socialist stores were empty, but many private apartments were filled to the ceilings with underground publications, including bound books, and a vibrant intellectual and cultural life flourished beyond party purview or interest. The much smaller Polish state security had informers, but not nearly as many per capita. Could the state have shut down underground printing presses? Perhaps, but only at the cost of making oppositional energies rise to a boil.

Polish historians debate why this was so, with some claiming that Communists in Poland were a bit different, more on the side of the "nation"; others, with more documentation, arguing that society held the Communists in check. In party programs from the Stalinist years, Poland's Communists displayed the same radical intentions of comrades in other places. They wanted to collectivize and secularize, but they feared the consequences. Toward the end, the state relaxed political repression in order to satisfy the demands made by western countries and creditors: in the summer of 1986 the Polish regime freed virtually all political prisoners.[63] By that point the debt to the west had risen to thirty-one billion dollars.

The East German state dealt with a different society, where people were shocked by the brutality of the repression in 1953, but until 1961 could opt for a democratic country in the west where their own language was spoken. Those who stayed behind were those more willing to make compromises with the Communist regime, or accept it outright. East German society was thus uniquely self-selected, and the party cadre disciplined and proud of the traditions of Prussia. Ideas of a weak state were anathema. The SED and *Stasi* knew about the small but pervasive grey economy, but left it in peace, concerning themselves with overtly political challenges: actual sabotage, large-scale theft, smuggling, especially of people to West Germany. The East German state reserved to itself the right to sell people to the West, demanding up to 100,000 west German marks for each political prisoner sent across the border, thus earning hard currency and dismantling a tiny political opposition at the same time.

The point of the *Stasi* was not to know and control *everything*, but to know and control enough to keep order and frustrate political challenges. It sent agents not in search of those (illegally) using western currency to procure things unavailable in socialist stores (like battery chargers or automobile spare parts), but into churches and university study groups. The *Stasi* did worry about the economy, with its waste and low productivity, but its task was to serve state policy, and that policy accepted the existence of large swaths of private life beyond state purview.[64] After work East Germans exercised an unwritten right to escape to private apartments and weekend cottages, to the comforts of family and trusted friends, often entertained by West German television and radio

(East Germans were often more up to date on US series like "Dallas" or "Kojak" than their Western cousins).

The regime helped this "society of niches" realize ultimate consumer wishes, and occasionally "threw" western products on the market for huge prices. In 1977 the SED leadership ordered 10,000 Volkswagen Rabbits, a well-built but unglamorous vehicle, to help with unsatisfied demand for automobiles. They cost over three times the asking price for the state socialist Trabant, for which East Germans had to wait 20 years at that point.[65] East Germans could also buy this car for western marks via a state run enterprise that sold goods for Western currency (they could also receive it as a gift from relatives in the West). Characteristically, the state's purchase of Western automobiles was not mentioned in the official press. The cars came across the border in secrecy. But then they appeared on East German streets with East German license plates. The regime was careful not to order luxury cars. To drivers of the Volkswagen it was saying: you can have a limited level of affluence, a half-step above the rest perhaps, but don't be showy about it. This was the real existing socialism that the *Stasi* defended.

East German citizens knew the *Stasi* intervened either when large-scale corruption became evident or when people had attracted its attention for "political" reasons. In 1985 the *Stasi* drew a Protestant pastor into a trap. He had been coaching a theater group to play pieces critical of the arms race, suggesting that East and West were both to blame.[66] Posing as men with access to the grey economy, *Stasi* agents offered him a new heating unit for his frigid church in exchange for baroque-era statues from another church that was being torn down. After he took the bait, the pastor was arrested and tried, but then given a choice: emigration or prison. With many other dissidents and potential dissidents, he left for West Germany.[67] The *Stasi* had used the second economy to get rid of a political problem and returned the self-selected society to socialist equilibrium.

State secret services also subverted intimate relations, not hesitating to pull up the sheets and get in bed with men and women as supposed partners in marriage. In 1990, archives revealed that the husband in a prominent dissident couple had been working for the *Stasi* for years. Grainy black and white pictures show tiny GDR human rights or ecological groups, crammed into living rooms, evoking homey solidarity, wine bottles open, candles burning, a long-forgotten joke being shared. Yet interspersed on the couches and chairs are people identified after 1990 as *Stasi* "informal agents: every third or fourth "dissident" was later shown to be working for the state.[68] Whether the information provided was of any value is another question.

State versus Society: Rulers, Collaborators, and Opponents

The demoralization common in late socialist societies derived from the regimes' claims to rule in terms of a higher morality, so stratospheric that the inevitable compromises of actual rule could not help making them seeming hypocritical, even if the Gini coefficients of real socialism were the lowest on earth. Everyone knew there was a hierarchy. Those who did best were individuals close to state functionaries, those who gamed the system in their favor, or those with family in the West. People who respected official rules to the letter—waiting twenty years for an apartment or for an automobile on a legal queue—were destined to fall behind.

Women were admitted to the workforce, but not as equals. They tended to be overrepresented in branches with lower pay, according to traditional patterns. In Yugoslavia in 1970, women made up 73.7 percent of the work force in textiles, 69.7 percent in health services, but only 41.4 percent in retail and trade.[69] And if women broke through certain professional barriers (like medicine), those were areas that continued to be poorly paid. They were underrepresented in the management boards of the economy, the state, and party elites. A quiet discrimination applied against women applying for postgraduate positions, for example in medicine, because officials feared they would take the year's paid leave the state guaranteed them after each child born.

A society based on socioeconomic classes had ceased to exist, but people knew there were gradations. The competition for advantage involved not a race but a crawl to the top, measured not in yearly income but in status, reflected in better access to things that were supposedly available to all: vacations (more exclusive), apartments (larger, more comfortable), automobiles (better quality: Wartburg not Trabant; Škoda not Wartburg, and so forth), shopping at special *Delikatläden* rather than the standard *Konsum*. Once one had achieved these things, the goal became perhaps a weekend house where one could relax and plant a garden. Yet for state functionaries, the point was not simply to enjoy, but to reproduce status. From the relatively open phase of the 1940s and 1950s, a more hierarchical society had emerged with limited mobility. By the 1980s, the majority of GDR university students had grandparents from the working class but parents who had completed university studies.[70]

In Hungary, the place where the aping of Western models went furthest, functionaries openly admitted in the mid-1960s that they saw no alternative to people acquiring status goods. Take the example of private cars. Under the

FIGURE 23.6. High-end specialty store in the GDR. *Source*: Florian Schäffer (photographer) GFDL or CC-BY-SA-3.0.

Stalinist Rákosi, the number of privately owned vehicles fell below prewar levels, and those whose income might have tempted them to purchase one were held back by the likelihood that it would be confiscated. A turn took place in 1958/1959; within twelve years the number of personal cars in private hands had advanced from some 13,000 to 262,174 (which was still far behind France).[71] But those who could afford to own these cars were not the "leading" class (that is, the working class): they were the leaders in economic, cultural, and scientific life, the new socialist bourgeoisie. Party functionaries said it was not only incorrect but impossible to deny such people satisfaction of their needs. It was "no longer sinful to live the good life."[72] These were years, however, when the regimes in Bulgaria and Romania were still preaching and practicing "homogenization."

Regardless of the regime, however, at some point the struggle for outdoing one's neighbors led to the procurement of Western goods. Blue jeans were a special attraction, and East Germans with Western relatives had an unfair advantage because they could receive care packages of used (but incomparably stylish) Western clothing and occasionally also Western currency. East Germans without such connections, or without positions permitting them to obtain Western currency, often felt second-class, betrayed by socialism, and unable to keep up. Even the keepers of orthodoxy were not immune to the draw of Western products, though restrictions applied. In keeping with the maxims of the class struggle, the Politburo was chauffeured in Volvos and not Mercedes sedans. Sweden, after all, was neutral.

What struck people after the fall of the Berlin Wall was how unostentatiously these leaders lived, in solid but unglamorous two-story family houses, with printed art on the walls, mass-produced china, cutlery, and furniture; washing machines and refrigerators from state socialist production, but color televisions from the West.[73] Politburo members had access to fresh fruit and Western toothpaste and never had to wait in line. After work, Erich Honecker liked to drink West German beer from a can, and his waiter made sure that Honecker's wife, Margot (an ideologically fanatical minster of education), had a sufficient supply of West German cigarettes. Mrs. Willi Stoph (wife of the number two) became a shopaholic, appearing daily in their compound's shopping center and wanting to see something new.[74] Even rumors of these modest privileges elicited deep resentment because the leaders claimed a right to rule in the name of higher standards and yet seemed out of touch with the language they had attempted to foist on workers.

* * *

But going from such insights to actual opposition was difficult. What was opposition? Every act, even thought, directed against agenda of the state? In theory, it was every point where the would-be total state encountered limitations. It had tried, like Jeremy Bentham's panopticon, to "see and control every individual member of the society," and society's response was to draw down the shutters when possible, and when not, to protect themselves against lies by lying.[75]

Yet not every lie or evasion was opposition. Wearing jeans; slacking off at work; hoarding butter; changing money illegally (indeed, participating in any part of the gray economy)—actions that were somehow nonconformist or even subversive—were at best implicit opposition, and then only against the state as it was supposed to exist in *theory*. These acts were an adaptation to socialism as it really existed and helped stabilize it.

Intellectual dissent, however, was explicit, willed defiance by people who were self-organizing in the "underground," where they crafted ideas for an alternative political order: one that was more peaceful, less harmful to the environment, and less mendacious. Some spent years in prison for such activities. But leading dissidents recognized that the social order still depended on cooperation from all elements of society, themselves included. Hungary's George Konrád, wrote "we are all actors in the same play. . . . The performance is not first-rate, but it is tolerable."[76] Czech dissident Jiřina Šiklová spoke of an interpenetration of state and society. Just as the party pervaded every street, factory, and apartment house with its organizations, so networks of opposition spread their influence through towns and villages, often aided by "decent" conformists, who did what they could to help. Examples included the editors in state-run publishing houses who published the work of "illegal" authors under pseudonyms and then paid the honoraria.[77] State officials helped a dissident keep her head above water. As long as no one noticed.

But there was also an opposite dynamic. In the early 1980s, Šiklová was serving a prison sentence, and her daughter was studying medicine, achieving the best grade in her year. She was due to receive an award, yet the dean's office got in touch to say that her name could not appear on the school's bulletin board. They concocted another way to honor her. Since her mother was "away" and she lived with her grandmother and underage brother, they awarded the daughter the highest possible "social scholarship as well as a bonus for rent and electricity." This humane gesture, reflecting personal decency, had the effect of making the totalitarian system more bearable and therefore more possible. A gifted student had suffered unjust discrimination but could accept it without becoming angry. The solution even made her happy.[78]

A more banal experience better exemplifies the power of the regime to involve everyone in its workings. A few years earlier, this daughter had desperately wanted blue jeans, but the only place to get them was the state-run hard-currency store, Tuzex. At that time, Dr. Šiklová was working in the janitorial staff at a hospital. She succeeded in getting Western money on the black market but could not simply go and buy the jeans. There were long lines, and no time for her daughter to try a pair on. It turned out that a friend—also a demoted dissident—worked in this store, and they arranged to have the girl try on the jeans outside of normal hours. When she reached her place in line the following day, she got a pair her daughter could wear. All seemed well.

A few days later, a teacher, highly agitated, called from high school. The jeans featured a trademark with a small American flag on a back pocket. The state socialist store sold products with American flags for American currency, but they could not be worn in the state socialist school. So, even though no laws were violated, Šiklová cut off the little flag.

For Šiklová, a prominent reform Communist in 1968, this case showed the inner workings of totalitarianism. No divide separated "us" from "them." As George Konrád said, socialist society was a whole, with everyone somehow connected, pulling in the same direction, with varying levels of effort. Here it extended from the girl wanting to be a modern teenager, through her dissident mother and friends (one employed at the state hard-currency store), to a state functionary (the school principal). "What I should have done," Šiklová wrote later, "was demand to see the Comrade director (of the school), refuse to accept this nonsense, and make a scandal." No one would have arrested her for this. She should have cited the laws that were being violated (no law forbade the wearing of American flags) and demanded they be enforced. Instead she sympathized with the teacher and refused to "complicate her life."[79]

There was no "them" in this story, only "we." Even the government was not ultimately to blame. It had not stimulated the desire for jeans, only tried awkwardly to accommodate it. Where did that desire come from?

The playwright Václav Havel wrote of fellow citizens living a "lie" to secure the benefits of consumer society. He gave the example of a greengrocer putting up a sign on May Day: "Workers of the World, Unite!" The greengrocer was not expressing convictions but signaling loyalty. In return, authorities left him in peace, free to enjoy the blandishments of late socialism, like a vacation in Bulgaria. Havel did not blame state socialism for creating this world of habitual lying. "It can happen and did happen only because there is obviously in modern humanity a tendency towards the creation," he wrote, "or at least the toleration, of such a system."[80] The tendency derived not from socialism or capitalism, but from modernity itself.

The fact that Havel castigated it shows that he thought the system could change. Though they suppressed it, people retained a sense of their dignity and knew it was injured when they lived a lie. But his appeal was also a gloomy diagnosis of the infernal stability he witnessed in socialist Czechoslovakia. While he, Šiklová, and a few dozen dissident unpersons tried to arouse consciences, 17 million fellow citizens made petty but easy public compromises for the freedom to do as they liked after work—all in low-stress, relatively affluent conditions, lubricated with lots of good and cheap beer, abundantly stocked weekend houses, decent popular entertainment, and all the joys and securities of family life.

How different is that from the lifestyles millions enjoy outside socialism? How many would jeopardize the security of the home and provoke state surveillance for acts that, as far as one could see, changed nothing? Havel has struck critics as moralizing. In his view, what prevented rebellion was "the general un-willingness of consumption-oriented people to sacrifice material certainties for the sake of their own spiritual and moral integrity." Yet perhaps he was sim-ply starkly presenting the alternatives? Was not a peaceful home life for raising and educating children—something immediately endangered if a greengrocer engaged in political dissent—more than just "material certainty"? What were the standards for integrity? Were we "to employ Havel's criteria for authentic-ity and try to redo things based on his diagnosis," philosopher Petr Rezek has written, "we would have to wean the majority of citizens away from the televi-sion and other banalities."[81]

Still, people who lived under dictatorship lived in a world of fear. Not only might a word spoken "in truth" cut off a supply of consumer goods, it could, if repeated, land one in jail. Everyone knew that. Fear of political oppression may have seemed absent from people's everyday lives, but in fact it was kept at bay. One woman, an office worker in Prague, asked about "fear" by an under-ground publication in 1988, said she was afraid of being late for work. She did not worry about her adultery because she could cover that up. What about speaking her mind? "For this I am too cowardly," she responded. "Moreover, I like a comfortable life and so I don't involve myself in anything. I always stand off to the side." A coal stoker, by contrast, was not afraid to speak his mind, because he could not fall any lower.[82]

The regime was also governed by fear: it remembered August 1968 and November 1956. The dissident physicist František Janouch wrote:

> our regime today fears everything, really everything. It is afraid of the liv-
> ing . . . it is afraid of the dead and even memories of the dead. They fear fu-
> nerals and graves, they fear youth and old communists, they fear non-party
> members, intellectuals, they fear the working class. They fear scholarship,
> art, film, they fear theater, books, gramophone records.[83]

Fear of the working class and the mass unrest of 1953 explain why the East Ger-man regime monitored all complaints about the provisioning of the popula-tion with consumer goods. But it is also true that East German workers did not rise up again because they remembered the brutal repression of 1953.

More controversial than his arguments about living in truth was Havel's claim that everyone "in his own way is a victim and supporter of the system."[84] Was there not a difference between Šiklová's daughter and a high school principal who kept tabs on hundreds of teachers and pupils? Surely a gulf in culpability separated a colonel in the Stasi (in charge of a small town) from an average party member (subject to party discipline), and an even bigger difference separated them from an industrial worker who was not in any organization, or a Protestant pastor who sheltered youth groups discussing issues of environment or human rights.

One could argue that by giving alienated young people a place to meet, the pastor "integrated" them into the life of the socialist state. But this is a partial truth. The pastor's way of being "victim and supporter" differed from that of school principal: the pastor was expanding people's abilities to think critically rather than restricting them. The effects may not have been visible at once, but, like the quiet work of Hungarian and Czechoslovak dissidents or the Polish underground universities, they could be deeply destabilizing, by encouraging the sense that there was life and truth beyond the publically propagated lie.

Romania

Havel's diagnosis was all but unknown in Romania, which combined the worst features of the neo-Stalinist East German security state, the dysfunctional Polish economy, and a Latin American national-authoritarian dictatorship, and then raised them to new levels of awfulness. One leading student of Romanian socialism calls it National Stalinism. More than anywhere in the Communist Bloc, fear became part of people's daily lives. Romanians knew that those who made politically incorrect statements might disappear into prison, and after that disappear altogether. Of the half million political prisoners of the Romanian Communist regime, it is estimated that 100,000 died in prison.[85]

The terror was not always visible. The Nobel-prize-winning author Herta Müller, who left Romania at age 34 (in 1987), loved to ride her bicycle and watch as the villages and city streets appeared to stream by. One day, during an interrogation, a secret police agent told her that cyclists had accidents. Soon after, a truck knocked her off her bicycle. She sold it. She went to a hairdresser who asked whether she had come with her bicycle. "How did she know I have a bicycle," Müller wondered. When she opened the door to her apartment, she found a note from a friend on a bowl atop the refrigerator. How had she gotten in? That night her hair began falling out. "The pursuer must not be physically present to constitute a threat," Müller later reflected. "His shadow lies on things and has transferred the fear to them: to a bicycle, to hair color, perfume bottles, refrigerators. The things you own personify the pursuer. Whatever you do with your possessions in the privacy of your home, you feel the pursuer looking in your eyes and you look in his."[86]

The Hungarian author István Eörsi noted in response that the Hungarian secret police would never have used methods like staging a bicycle accident to intimidate Hungary's intellectuals. But, he added, reminiscent of Havel's critique, it did not need to. The socialist state was strong enough to avoid such methods, and that related to a bargain struck in 1956. For their agreement never to speak about the Revolution, and to acknowledge the right to rule of the men who executed Nagy and hundreds more, Hungarian intellectuals had greater freedoms to write and create than in most other places in the bloc. The collaboration became so intimate that leading figures regularly dined with members of the party establishment: their "digestive juices" could not flow unless they sat at table with a Politburo member.[87]

Romania was not an outlier from the start. Into the early 1970s, the Ceaușescu regime rewarded political compliance with a rising standard of living. Yet after that time, in part because of the regime's refusal to amass debt and under the pressure of rising energy prices, Romania's per capita income sank. Beginning in 1981, basic necessities like bread, sugar, and oil were rationed, and the consumption of other goods was severely limited. (Poland rationed various goods from 1976 to 1985, including sugar, butter, meat, rice, and flour.) The following year, prices rose drastically, and the regime began cutting off electricity without warning several times a day.[88] Romanians sat huddled in frigid, dark apartments at night and expended much of their daytime energy queuing for foodstuffs. They seemed to have reverted to premodern conditions. What did this mean for state power? Romanian psychologist Radu Clit writes, "People preoccupied with surviving are less able to involve themselves in social life."[89]

Perspectives on the good life quickly evolved and mutated in strange ways. One morning, Professor Stefan Milcu of Bucharest, a world-famous endocrinologist, got phone calls from his son and daughter telling him about things that had made them happy. The former, living in Canada, had finally managed to get the car he wanted. The daughter, living in Romania, had managed to find a store where one could buy cheese without waiting in line. She immediately bought plenty for herself and her parents.[90] People who are delighted at the prospect of buying cheese, Milcu concluded, have been successfully led to a horizon of limited expectations. Yet on most days, the thought of buying cheese—or fruit, or fish, or sweets—was a dream beyond realization.

The regime used the feared secret police—the *Securitate*—to maintain political control but offered little in return. The destitution seemed calculated to impress the rulers' supposed omnipotence on the humbled population, on a background of Ceaușescu's megalomania and chauvinism.[91] The press spouted increasingly absurd claims about the rulers' genius and beneficence, while ancient churches and priceless architectural treasures fell to the wrecking ball to make way for gargantuan socialist realist palaces bearing the leader's personal stamp.[92]

The *Securitate*, with about one in thirty adults in its employ, was among the largest in the bloc. Because of the economic calamity of the 1980s, it could recruit unofficial agents by threatening to withhold things other East Europeans took for granted, like medicine for life-threatening illnesses.[93] Or it extorted complicity from people who used the black market to obtain essentials. Herta Müller was arrested for paying "exorbitant" (that is, the going rate) prices for nuts at a "private market" in Timişoara. During confinement, she met people who had stolen candles (there was no electricity) or nails. The "mechanism" was to "criminalize as many people as possible in order to make them vulnerable to blackmail."[94] Even children were not immune.[95] The circumstances differed radically elsewhere: even in the GDR, dissidents could generally count on a warm apartment and enough income to purchase necessities. If they were arrested, they were quickly sent westward.

But as in the GDR and also in Czechoslovakia and Bulgaria, political control, if less overtly violent, was more effective than in the Stalinist period, when the state sent dissenters to prison camps and was still weaving its networks of informers. Open terror was more a sign of weakness than of confidence.[96] The GDR state had adapted its education system at all levels to the needs of political control; the higher the level of training one desired, the greater the conformity that was expected. Leadership positions, even among physicians, required party membership; and party members resembled soldiers, subjected to discipline and expected to carry out "tasks."

Women in Romania suffered acute miseries that highlighted the nationalist logic driving the regime's otherwise inexplicable sadism. If women elsewhere endured the "double burden" of profession and household chores, Romanians had one further task: to bear as many children as possible. The state wanted the Romanian ethnic element to grow. From 1966, it criminalized abortion—a procedure that had become legal elsewhere from the late 1950s to early 1970s—but also required women to appear before physicians for gynecological exams to determine whether they were pregnant. These exams were more frequent and demeaning in industrial plants than in state offices where white-collar women worked; they reflected an implicit class structure.[97]

Contraceptives were not illegal, but Romania ceased producing them, and by the 1980s, they were extremely difficult to obtain (Hungarian or Yugoslav condoms sold for high prices on the black market). To the other fears that plagued Romanians was added that of becoming pregnant. In one case, the *Securitate* promised to help a woman recover from a botched abortion but only if she revealed the name of the person who had performed the procedure. She did not and was left to die.[98] More than 9,000 women died in Romania between 1965 and 1989 from abortions performed under unsafe conditions.[99] Sometimes doctors attempted to protect women by recording abortions as miscarriages.[100] One result of this state obsession with boosting numbers of ethnic Romanians was unwanted children, thousands of whom found their way to decrepit orphanages, which horrified the world when they became open to scrutiny in 1990.

The pro-natalism was only one of the Romanian state's nationalist policies, which also included the destruction of Hungarian villages as well as an avowedly independent foreign policy. The latter led Romania to send athletes to the Los Angeles Olympics in 1984, defying the Soviet boycott, and then to resist all ideas of reform emanating from a Soviet leader who emerged the following year, Mikhail Gorbachev.

As the Ceaușescu regime descended into enforced miserliness, the secret police kept people in check—people living the lie of loving hated rulers—but also granted just enough "privileges" to keep potential sources of opposition under control, for example, in the upper ranks of the church hierarchies, which were corrupted by a mix of threats and favors. The most numerous denomination, the Romanian Orthodox Church, tended to be especially pro-regime, but the bishops and dignitaries of the smaller Hungarian Reformed Church were also reliably under control. Just behind the façades of deference, a rage over injustice was growing that far outdid what other East Europeans felt—finally exploding into violent street fighting in the fall of 1989. It would originate precisely at the place where oppression was greatest, involving a low-ranking Hungarian cleric at odds with his own hierarchy, in an ethnically Hungarian area that was a special target of harassment and disrespect.[101]

* * *

The debate sketched at this chapter's outset shows no sign of reaching a conclusion. Those who advocate socialism in our day—whatever they think it means, and for whatever reason—are likely to say that the old regime did not qualify as socialist because of its failure to advance human freedom. Yet on today's right, those who detest socialism—whatever they think it means, and for whatever reason—will portray that old regime as indeed embodying the essence of a failed idea. Like people of all times, they view the past through the lens of their own time. The fact remains that the bygone regimes called themselves socialist, and for all their shortcomings, the leaders believed they were advancing toward a better tomorrow. They did incorporate socialism at its most basic: it was not capitalism. In fact, these states represented the only time in human history when a state had largely banished markets to the edges of a society's experience. But perhaps more important than uses and misuses of the word "socialism" is popular memory, which, like all memory, dwells on the positive when it can, because the time in question was a time when the recollectors were young, a time when anything worth fondly remembering tends to happen, regardless of political system.

PART V

From Communism to Illiberalism

CHAPTER 24

The Unraveling of Communism

The East European revolutions of 1989 brought an end to complex ways of organizing and experiencing virtually everything, and even the most basic activities were suddenly new: students learned western languages instead of Russian and read books previously called "poisonous." No one cared who went to church or what was said there. Spaces opened for entrepreneurship, and within months, advertising and small shops proliferated, transforming even villages. Newsstands featured glossy entertainment, even pornography, and restaurants served "exotic" dishes like pizza or Thai noodles. Scaffolding went up around apartment buildings unpainted for decades, while below high-powered German and Italian sedans raced over streets still paved in cobblestone. In the summers, cities emptied as populations fled for the beaches, often in the west, and the divide through Europe began to fade. I remember a mother telling her child as they changed trains at Friedrichstrasse in East Berlin two days after the Wall opened: "At school you can tell everyone that you went to a different country [*ein anderes Land*] this weekend." That was an understatement. In West Berlin, the child had visited not a different country but a different world. Yet soon, downsides of the new reality also became evident: East Europeans could become unemployed. Violence, too, returned to the streets, often directed against ethnic others.

How did this radical shift occur? Television footage shows crowds filling the streets in 1989. Perhaps they were seizing power like revolutionaries of the distant past. But appearances deceived, a fact with a long tradition. "The people" did not take the reins of government in France in 1789, Petrograd in 1917, or Manila in 1986. Similarly, the crowds that formed around the Berlin Wall on November 9, 1989 did not break Communism. The party elite had lost its grip on power weeks earlier, and the border point opening—due to a misstatement on television about travel regulations by SED spokesman Günter Schabowski—confirmed, and hastened, a transfer of power that was already under way. Some two weeks later, hundreds of thousands of demonstrators began pouring into the streets of Czechoslovakia, but a few weeks after that, power traded hands behind closed doors. By the summer of 1990, a new elite was forming that revolutionaries never imagined, favoring neoliberalism and national exclusiv-ism. In Romania, revolutionaries fought and died for their cause, but when the air cleared, the "victors" saw that one set of Communist leaders had traded places with another. Still, state socialism everywhere gave way to some form of pluralism.[1]

No one had expected the old regimes to collapse, and no single act was cal-culated to bring about their end. In early 1989, it seemed that change would be limited to tinkering with the planned economy, still based on single-party rule. As late as February, an East German died trying to escape over the Berlin Wall. The democratic opposition of 1989 had initially wanted to infuse the regimes with "greater momentum," advocating respect for human rights, political plu-ralism, freedom of speech, and the right of assembly. It did not expect a transi-tion to democracy.[2] Even the seasoned revolutionaries of Poland's Solidarity trade union, permitted to field candidates in the elections of June 1989, antici-pated at first an advisory role in a liberalized Communist regime allied with the Soviet Union. East German protesters of October 1989 wanted a democratic socialism that did not exist in the West—and did not imagine their country leaving the Warsaw Pact to become part of the European Community, allied to NATO. (That happened just a year later.)

The collapse of 1989 grew out of a social and economic crisis that had been building for decades, yielding a malaise that reached deep into the Communist Party. For Communist regimes, faith was crucial. If Western modernity approxi-mated a business model of rationality, where the state acts as caretaker of eco-nomic growth and social stability, the Eastern variant was ultimately a religion with legitimacy tied to claims about ultimate truths. State publishing houses printed pamphlets answering basic questions like: why am I alive? Yet by the 1980s, Communism had become a church where people not only forgot their prayers but also scoffed at basic teachings—finding them hypocritical, fictitious, damaging, and irrelevant. In the final years, neither functionaries nor citizens thought the party had a clear right to rule, because any such right was vested in a vision of history that few continued to accept. In the late 1980s, believers among the leadership were considered naïve or worse. According to an East German joke, three attributes never went together in a party functionary: be-lief, intelligence, and honesty. Those who were honest and intelligent did not believe; those who believed and were intelligent could not be honest. Those who believed and were honest could not be intelligent.

The crisis of ideology does not mean that people were obsessed with it. As in the West, most muddled through with an indistinct and occasional awareness of the state; they ignored the omnipresent red-lettered signs proclaiming eternal friendship with the Soviet Union or the unstoppable victory of Communism. On any given day, the "ideas" upholding the system hardly seemed relevant to citizens of the Soviet Bloc because Soviet-style rule was destined to exist as long as anyone could imagine.

But even in the early 1970s, when it worked as well as it ever would, socialism was not an ideologically free space. Socialist schooling taught that governments took responsibility for a people's welfare; the absence of consumer goods was a political fact people held against the regime. The failures in the competition for material consumption that Khrushchev had unleashed gradually sapped faith in a better future. Without directly knowing the system on the other side of the Iron Curtain, East Europeans assumed that its greater wealth, military strength, and (ironically) social welfare derived from a form of government that embodied a higher morality.[3] This helps explain the almost blind leap toward market capitalism.

This gradual sapping of faith, both of cadre and people, explains why state socialism collapsed so neatly in 1989, with virtually no one trying to protect or salvage the edifice. The rotting structure was hollowed out.[4] But it does not explain why the revolutions took the courses that they did. Above all, it does not tell us why the transfer of power was peaceful. Individuals faced choices in 1989, and without thousands of small decisions— to make a particular church available for peaceful protest on one day a week in Leipzig, to cut barbed wire along one section of the "iron curtain" in Hungary, to permit trade unionists to debate the regime on live television in Warsaw, to open one gate at the Berlin Wall—the outcome would have been very different, perhaps violent.

Poland: Society versus State

Into the early 1970s, few discerned any signs at all of the ultimate denouement. The socialist economies had grown for decades. In 1971 the new East German leader Erich Honecker inherited from his predecessor Walter Ulbricht an economy almost without debt, and from Czechoslovakia to Romania, socialist citizens had become used to modest, modern comforts.[5] Romanians later looked back on the late 1960s and early 1970s as "golden years," and Poles called the early 1970s their belle époque.

But by late in the decade, East Germany, along with the other socialist economies (including the Soviet Union), were accumulating huge debts. In Czechoslovakia, despite high living standards, the population gradually became more pessimistic, and by the late 1980s, public opinion was turning "sharply critical."[6] Hungary's economy had shown growth in all sectors into the late 1970s; from 1950 to 1983, the country's national income quintupled, from an index of 100 in 1950 to 493 in 1983. In roughly the same period, the consumption index went from 100 to 323, and the country left its "former poverty stricken condition far behind."[7] But after 1980, real wages of workers fell by 6 percent in four years. Hungary was the third country in the bloc in terms of ownership of durable goods like telephones and automobiles (after Czechoslovakia and East Germany), but the gap between these leaders and Western Europe showed no signs of closing, and stood at 1:3 for telephones and 1:4 for private cars in the late 1980s.[8]

The regime's early successes had placed it in jeopardy because people took further improvements in living standards for granted. Socialism had been achieved, and there was no going back and no reason for sacrificing what had been "gained." Doctrine anticipated no future in which socialist citizens would need to make sacrifices merely because the state had accumulated hard currency deficits. After 1989, Rezső Nyers, the architect of the Hungarian reform (NEM), recalled that the party was "powerless to explain to people that necessary changes were not always going to be pleasant in the short term . . . we weren't able to be a political and social driving force and so the reform came to a dead end."[9] Even the most daring figures among the leaders were experimenters, careful mediators of the possible, managers; they were hardly recognizable as Marxists, let alone revolutionaries. The fact that the heads of state were very old men only intensified the impression of regimes not being able to learn the necessary new things.

Among the gathering signs of crisis, energy stands out as critical. In 1973, oil costs increased, and though Soviet suppliers did not immediately pass on massive price hikes, those that came strained the East European economies. For example, Hungary had to boost its exports to the Soviet Union by 600–800 million rubles above the number originally projected for 1976–1980, thus depriving it of goods for Western markets and exacerbating the convertible-currency trade balance. Austerity measures via price increases were not a socially acceptable way of dealing with this problem, even in politically stable East Germany.[10] The only solution was foreign borrowing, and that meant turning to the West, as the East either would not or could not lend. Hungary and Poland ramped up their borrowing in the mid-1970s, but they did so in the vain expectation that their own export industries would become competitive in world markets and allow the debt to be repaid.[11]

FIGURE 24.1. Workers carry the body of Zbyszek Godlewski, victim of crackdown on Baltic Coast (Gdynia, 1970). *Source*: Edmund Pelpliński. In Andrzej Wajda, "Uzupełniam swój życiorys," *Tygodnik Solidarnosc* 2:11 (July 10, 1981). Via Wikimedia Commons.

Poland found itself at the heart of socialism's woes. In December 1970, Edward Gierek had come to power after the disgraceful departure of Władysław Gomułka, whose final order was to shoot striking workers on the Baltic Coast—at Gdynia, Gdańsk, and Szczecin.[12] Gierek, a former coal miner with a populist streak, appealed to strikers to return to work. He assured them that the state would work in their common interest, and Western lenders stepped in to help him. If the oil shock of the early 1970s was a challenge to industrialized economies, it was a boon to banks flooded with money invested by wealthy oil-producing states, so-called "petrodollars." Gierek's Poland funded ambitious but ultimately uncompetitive ventures, especially in steel, ship, and automotive industries. It also used much of the loan money to import consumer goods, and Poles lived relatively well for a few years.

When time came to pay back the loans, the regime took the same first step that Gomułka had in December 1970: it raised prices on consumer goods. Sugar went up 100 percent, meat by two-thirds, and cheese and butter by about half.[13] On June 25, 1976, laborers at the General Walter metallurgy plant in Radom, a medium-sized town in central Poland, refused to work. About half their salaries were going for food, and the sudden price hikes produced immediate rage. Soon their strike spread to twenty-four other nearby factories, and by 10 a.m., some 20,000–25,000 workers had assembled in front of Radom's party headquarters. The local party secretary told the crowd he was waiting for a response from Warsaw to his request to have the price hikes withdrawn. Meanwhile, he slipped out the back door, knowing that no withdrawal was forthcoming. By noon, workers were tired of waiting and forced entry into the building. They discovered that the functionaries had fled. Yet what really made them angry was to find cans of ham stacked in the cafeteria, the likes of which none of them had seen in years. After tossing these out the window to the crowd, they set the building alight and blocked roads to keep fire crews from extinguishing the flames.

Authorities called in motorized police detachments from as far away as Lublin, Łódź, and Warsaw, and street battles lasted into the night until order could be restored. Two demonstrators lost their lives. Strikes also broke out in the truck plant Ursus near Warsaw (the workers succeeded in blocking the international train line Paris–Moscow), and in some ninety enterprises in twenty-four districts. The numbers of strikers and demonstrators were estimated at 70,000 to 80,000.[14] The regime hastily withdrew the price hikes.

Yet in a return to methods allegedly abandoned in Gierek's "contract" with Polish society, the regime sought out and punished the "ringleaders." In Radom alone, some 1,000 workers were fired, and hundreds more received prison sentences. Many were beaten.[15] During Stalinism, the poet Czesław Miłosz gave a warning to leaders who presume to hurt a simple man: "Don't feel safe, a poet remembers." In 1976, poets watched what the powerful were doing, and with other intellectuals—scholars of law, economics, and history, as well as a Catholic priest—they formed a Committee for the Defense of Workers (KOR).[16] The group, initially fourteen individuals, spanned generations (the oldest was born in 1888!), and arranged for medical and financial aid, and crucially in a country where workers did not know their rights, legal counsel. Poet Stanisław Barańczak later wrote that KOR, the beginning of the consequential story of Polish opposition that led to 1989, emerged out of an act of simple compassion. It was the brainchild of the dissident historian Adam Michnik, who attended the Ursus trials and heard workers' wives shriek as sentences were read out: one year, two years, five years, for supposed "sabotage." By the time his eyes had dried, he decided there had to be something he and his friends could do.[17]

The incidents of unrest among workers and intellectuals in the cities were only symptoms of Poland's economic problems. The ultimate cause was food policy. In the 1960s, agricultural production had risen by 2–3 percent yearly, far behind demand. After the disaster of 1970, the new leaders promised an "opening toward the village": they would increase the supply of industrial products for farms, as well as prices paid for agricultural products. In the first three years, production increased, as did the living standards of peasants, reminiscent of the first three years under Gomułka. The official language also shifted in favor of private farms. But at a certain point, Gierek, too, began favoring the small sector of socialized agriculture, despite its poorer results.[18]

In the end, ideology prevailed, and the government made no serious investment in private farms. They remained of small size, with two-thirds smaller than five hectares and had limited access to machinery or fertilizers. Farmers fled to towns when they could and held back from serious investments because they were uncertain about their futures. The amount of land left fallow increased, and agriculture's productivity remained close to stagnant.[19]

A special problem was feed-grain for livestock. Because of poor harvests in 1977/1978, 15 million tons of grain had to be imported from the West at a cost of 2 billion dollars.[20] These unspectacular facts were crucial because each major crisis—two of which cost Gomułka and later Gierek their jobs—was brought on by meat shortages, in which the government attempted to reduce demand by increasing prices. Gierek fell hostage to meat, above all, pork. If the prices were low, farmers raised fewer pigs. The only way to make pork available was to raise its price, but when the government did that, workers protested. The massive strike wave that would come in 1980 was due to an increase that affected only select cuts, like smoked bacon. One worker said: before the war we had the problem of bread, now we have the problem of what to put on bread.[21]

The party was paying for having failed to collectivize agriculture. If it could not plan production of grain, dairy products, or meat, it could not plan anything. The countryside was uncollectivized, because even during Stalinism, the party had its hands full with actual and potential resistance and did not dare moving too far forward on any of the hostile fronts it faced: the church, the intelligentsia, industrial labor, and the vast peasantry. What happened in the 1970s is that those groups finally united into a phalanx the party could not break.

* * *

The crisis that elicited such massive resistance in Poland was unique in the Soviet Bloc. In no other country did the economy contract so radically, from the good times of the early 1970s, paid for by foreign loans, to the never-ending shortages and cutbacks of the late decade. The regime introduced ration cards in 1976 and maintained them until 1989 in order to spread the dearth of even items like sugar and rice. But political mobilization did not happen automatically. The intelligentsia was deeply divided, and a chasm separated it from farmers. Required was leadership and new ideas that could unite and inspire sacrifice. Here Poland was part of a larger story. Across much of the Soviet Bloc, a movement emerged in the 1970s that advocated for civic and, above all, *human* rights. It responded to the disorientation and despair that had seized many East Europeans after the crushing of the Prague Spring in 1968 and Władysław Gomułka's proud display of ugly hypernationalism that same year.

What followed for Brezhnev and his comrades was a study in hubris. Having crushed dissent and robbed Marxist revisionists of all hope, they moved to "consolidate" their position internationally in a series of treaties about disarmament during a time of relaxation known as "detente." The crowning act came in 1975, when leaders from the NATO and the Warsaw Pact states gathered in Helsinki for a conference on Security and Cooperation in Europe. What the Soviet Union got was recognition of the boundaries of postwar Europe, including the Oder-Neisse line and the western frontier of the Soviet Union; what the West got was an accord on human rights, the so-called "Basket III."

Whether this latter affirmation represented cynicism or simple forgetful neglect is unclear. Having built a wall around West Berlin and minefields along the "Iron Curtain," the Marxist-Leninists were solemnly pledging to respect mobility; while subjecting religious believers to discrimination, they vowed to honor freedom of conscience; and though muzzling and imprisoning citizens who tried to speak freely, they were guaranteeing freedom of speech. Yet any hypocrisy was not entirely novel. In Basket III, the Soviet Union and its allies were affirming nothing that was not already contained in the 1948 Universal Declaration of Human Rights. Their willingness now publically to promise to defend human rights—yet again—with the complete text published in their newspapers, thus figured somewhere between the disingenuous and the gratuitous.[22]

But just as poets were watching abuses by the powerful at home, citizenries, above all the intelligentsias, were absorbing the message from Helsinki. The beauty of human rights was that each right implied the other. They stood together or not at all. When KOR activists stood for workers' rights to strike, they argued that what was infringed was not just social rights but also rights of association, and thus human rights. If Czech authorities suppressed religious rights, that meant that free expression—a fundamental human right—was an evident fiction in Czechoslovakia. If secular (even anticlerical) dissidents wanted

FIGURE 24.2. Helmut Schmidt, Erich Honecker, Gerald Ford, and Bruno Kreisky at Helsinki Conference (1975). *Source*: Horst Sturm (photographer), Bundesarchiv, Bild 183-P0801-026 / CC-BY-SA 3.0.

to advocate human rights, they had to stand up for religious rights. The church was not only a potential but also a necessary ally. Similarly, intellectuals and the church were bound to defend the dignity of work—a social and thus human right—when workers were denied a just income or access to adequate living space.[23]

Human rights thus provided an integrated worldview after the collapse of the Marxist worldview, available to everyone, but particularly attractive to intellectuals desperate for a cause. It was compatible with every brand of politics and every kind of faith, including none at all; it could unite various groups in East European societies like no ideology previously seen, because ultimately, human rights were also inseparable from national rights—which were also part of the 1948 United Nations catalogue.[24]

The KOR activists thus represented the breadth of Poland's intellectual opposition, of which they were only one subset. Concentrated in a few towns in the early 1970s, this opposition had consisted of former Marxist revisionists (such as Jacek Kuroń and one-time culture minister Władysław Bieńkowski) and other secular leftists; young people persecuted in 1968; and a hodge-podge of elite writers, artists, actors, and academics. Mixed in were Catholics, including priests, but also people who had been tied to the Home Army and the World War II resistance. Some of the younger people were affiliated with patriotic scouting (Antoni Macierewicz, Piotr Naimski), and some of the older ones had been victims of Stalinism. These dissidents not only "knew" their history; history was a family saga, going back generations, to earlier layers of struggle. A few had come of age before World War I and had taken part in conspiracies against Germany and Russia.[25]

What made the broader intellectual opposition actually mobilize, a year before the founding of KOR, were discussions in the Polish Party about a new constitution, updating the Stalinist one from 1952. In line with Marxist-Leninist doctrine, the drafters wrote a phrase that to them seemed commonsensical: Poland would be irrevocably connected to the Soviet Union in "fraternal bonds." This phrase caused dissidents to imagine their country in the stranglehold of its great-power neighbor for all eternity. And this at a time when peoples across the globe were breaking free from colonial domination![26] The first-line response was a series of circular protests from scores of intellectuals, the best-known being the "letter of fifty-nine" from late 1975.

The idea came from the dissident lawyer and onetime *Po Prostu* editor Jan Olszewski; he, Jacek Kuroń, and the young sociologist Jakub Karpiński served as editors; and Edward Lipiński, a world-renowned economist, delivered the letter at the chancellery of the Polish Parliament on December 5. The signatories wanted Poland's constitution to guarantee freedoms of conscience, religion, work, information, and science and education. As human rights, these freedoms were inseparable, and they intersected with civil rights: the freedom of work implied the freedom to form free associations (trade unions); freedom of education meant that universities should govern their own affairs; freedom of information necessitated freedom of expression and an end to censorship. Dozens more names were added in the weeks that followed. The deeper force driving the enterprise was fear about Poland's survival as a coherent nation. "We believe," the signatories affirmed, "that the failure to respect civic freedoms can gradually deprive a society of national consciousness and cause a rupture in its national traditions. It is a threat to the nation's existence."

Yet the cause was not just a Polish one. Respect for freedoms of conscience, religion, work, information, and education, confirmed at the Helsinki Conference, "has an international importance, because where there is no freedom, there is also no peace and no security."[27] An added beauty of "human rights" was to compel the international community—at least rhetorically—to recall the existence of places like Poland, while providing the Polish opposition an exit from the dead end of reforming socialism. Prior to that point, wrote Adam Michnik, the opposition had worked two angles: Marxist revisionist, aspiring to change the party from within, and "neo-positivist," working with authorities in an attempt to gain more freedom, as Roman Dmowski had with the Russian state. Yet 1968 had shown that the Communist Party was under the control of forces insensitive to either strategy. One historian has called human rights a last utopia, but for the Polish opposition, they were a last alternative in the catalog of efforts at national self-assertion.[28]

Because one right necessitated the other, human rights were also a perfect foil for bringing Polish society together to stand up for the nation—and against the state. A decade earlier, left-wing intellectuals and Catholic bishops would have never imagined a common cause. Now the episcopate was among the first to object to the proposed changes in the constitution. It feared that an eternal bond to the Soviet Union would make atheism a permanent force in Poland. The following year, church leaders raised their voices in defense of workers, saying workers had been compelled to fight for their bare existence as well as free expression against their own government, a government that placed production above the producer, material above human beings. The bishops ordered a collection for the sacked and arrested workers on Sunday, November 28, 1976. In a sort of reciprocation, the dissidents protested to the Polish parliament that the government's repression of religion violated UN human rights covenants.[29]

In an influential essay, Michnik called the approach "new evolutionism." As the title implied, activists were not giving up on change but simply recognizing that the effects of their efforts would be manifested only with time. For now, the point was to turn not to the powerful in the state or party, but to "give directives to the people on how to behave. . . . Nothing instructs the authorities better than pressure from below." "Every act of defiance helps us build the framework of democratic socialism," he concluded.[30]

Over time, such words would seem too left-leaning for some dissidents, but for the time being, Michnik had brilliantly combined sober analysis of what was already happening—the coming together of Poland's various social groups—with a call to action. In the second half of the 1970s, the pressure was coming from virtually every identifiable interest, spurred by an economic crisis that kept deepening. Occasionally the mass dissent became visible, but mostly it grew just beneath the surface. KOR organized "flying universities," that is, seminars on matters of public interest that would meet in different apartments each week, one step ahead of informers or the police. The tradition, as we have seen, went back to a dissident of the 1880s, the educator Jadwiga Dawidowa.[31]

Within a few years, KOR, which had grown into a nationwide social movement, and other oppositional groups (for example, a "Movement for the Defense of Human and Civic Rights") were printing hundreds of books, journals, and newspapers. By 1980, the underground publisher Nowa had printed fifty-four books of at least 200 pages each. Borders were relatively open, and many students spent summers in England, Italy, or West Germany, working in restaurants but also smuggling foreign literature back into Poland, where it would be translated. Independent networks of men and women of several generations kept unofficial news and advocacy networks alive among workers, especially on the Baltic coast. They published newspapers telling readers of "free trade unions" that were emerging in the underground.[32] There was also an unofficial movement across Poland that called itself the Student *Solidarity* Committee.

* * *

For the time being, the Polish ferment had echoes and parallels in Czechoslovakia and Hungary. In both places, from the mid-1970s small groups of writers, academics, and artists began exploring forms of organization that were uncontrolled by the state, and in both places, most of the dissident leaders were former Communists. The event that mobilized Czech and Slovak dissidents was much less dramatic than the Radom and Ursus strikes in Poland. In that same year, 1976, Czechoslovak authorities arrested a rock group called "Plastic People of the Universe" for an "organized disturbance of the peace."[33] The musicians had been playing their songs without state approval in private venues for years, yet their lyrics were not meant to be subversive. Nor was the small movement that now emerged out of outrage generated by this arrest meant to be subversive. It later became known as Charter 77. The originators were philosophers, writers, historians, and economists, united by "the will to strive individually and collectively for the respecting of civic and human rights in our own country and throughout the world." They were not an organization, but rather a "loose, informal and open association of people of various shades of opinion, faiths and professions," and their deed was simple, as was their "crime." They called on fellow Czechs and Slovaks to affix a signature to a statement demanding respect for human rights—their "Charter." The first spokespersons were playwright Václav Havel, philosopher Jan Patočka, and former foreign minister Jiří Hájek.[34]

By 1989, some 1,445 Czechoslovak citizens had signed the Charter, and Husák's regime subjected virtually all to some kind of penalty, ranging from job loss to imprisonment. Charter signatories and their families endured constant harassment, and they failed to break out of small intellectual circles with their ideas.[35] If Czechs and Slovaks came to know anything about the "Chartists," it was because official radio and television vilified them; authorities went so far as to create an "anti-charter" and demand that people affix their signatures. One who refused, the historian and writer Jan Urban, was fired from his job as teacher and spent the next twelve years working as a bricklayer, until becoming a spokesperson for Civic Forum. That was during Communism's collapse in 1989. But when he refused to condemn the dissidents as a twenty-six-year-old, he had no idea if that system would ever end.

In Poland by contrast, hundreds of citizens from all walks of life routinely supported public letters of protest with few repercussions. KOR itself was subject to surveillance and occasional active harassment. The "restraint" reflected the government's concern about its international reputation—and what a crackdown might do to its ability to attract credit abroad to manage its huge debt.

Yet in May 1977, one of KOR's student members in Kraków, Stanisław Pyjas, died after a fall in his apartment house. Police said the cause was drunkenness, his friends suspected foul play; to this day, the case has not been solved.[36] But KOR now had a martyr. Some 5,000 students, as well as workers from Nowa Huta, attended his funeral mass on May 15. Afterward a group carrying black flags marched to the house where Pyjas's body was found and observed a minute of silence. That evening at 9:00 p.m., a crowd returned to the site for a march to the Wawel castle above the Vistula, with candles and again black flags. Estimates of its size range upward of 10,000. The crowd was thick with security forces, but they hesitated to intervene, fearing a bloodbath. Students for their part did not respond to provocation. At the castle, one read a declaration announcing the formation of the Student Solidarity Committee. A minute of silence followed, the national anthem was sung, and the crowd dispersed peacefully.[37] Despite warnings from their deans, students mobilized in other cities by a similar script: memorial service followed by a march. In Wrocław, some 5,000 students were counted at a mass in the cathedral, about half of whom walked afterward to a statue of John XXIII and read a statement from Kraków. There were also reports of student activism from Łódź and Poznań; in Warsaw,

700 students signed a resolution demanding an official investigation into the violence used against workers the previous year.

That same month, authorities were turning the screws on KOR by arresting dozens of its activists, but the result was a hunger strike at a church in Warsaw involving some people who previously had no involvement in KOR. Thus the halting attempts to make KOR disappear had simply caused it to gain publicity and to grow.[38] Gierek was caught in a web of his own making. When he met with the Western statesmen he needed to impress as cultivated in order to procure credits, some of them—above all US President Jimmy Carter—reminded "Edward" of Poland's pledges to respect human rights. Additionally, KOR activist Jacek Kuroń contacted the Italian Communist leader Enrico Berlinguer to solicit his party's censure of the Gierek regime's abuse of human rights. All this imposed a certain self-restraint on Poland's ruler, from which KOR benefited. Before releasing KOR activists in July 1977 just before meeting Western leaders in Belgrade, Gierek said he did not want to be seen as a "mobster."[39] Meanwhile, some 40,000 people, mostly workers and their families who knew little of KOR, were celebrating the consecration by Kraków's Cardinal Wojtyła of their new church in Nowa Huta.[40]

Beyond Poland, dissidence was a subtle trend of at most several thousand individuals, involving tiny groups in Czechoslovakia and also Hungary. In 1979, hundreds of intellectuals in Budapest had expressed support for Charter 77, and gradually, an underground movement with samizdat took shape there as well. From the start, Hungarian dissidents had a blind spot for questions of national identity and Hungarian minorities in other countries—issues that continued to concern many of their compatriots. That left them open to allegations of being out of touch.[41] Because of the widespread underground publishing in Poland, however, and increasing unity among Poles across social milieus as the economic crisis deepened, the ideas of Czech and Hungarian dissenters, above all Václav Havel, were probably better known among Poles than among Czechs or Hungarians.

* * *

Two years later, that sense of unity in Polish society got a boost when the College of Cardinals in Rome elected the first Pole ever to the Chair of St. Peter, Cardinal Karol Wojtyła, thereafter John Paul II. Poland's government sent a report to Moscow warning that Wojtyła was a "virulent anti-Communist," but most Poles—Communists included—raised glasses to celebrate the apparent miracle. In the summer of 1979, John Paul made his first pilgrimage to his homeland, arriving just as economic crisis reached new heights, and in eight days of homilies before hundreds of thousands, convinced Poles that things could be different. He prayed that the Lord would come down and transform the earth—"this Polish earth." The crowds witnessed the contrast between the direct language of the gently self-confident man in white and the obfuscations of state officials, who squirmed in evident discomfort. One young boy said, "Now I realize that no one has ever talked to me before."[42]

The pope's visit transformed Poles' knowledge of themselves—akin to what László Rajk's reburial did to Hungarians in 1956. Amid the vast crowds, people knew for sure what they had long sensed: they were not alone in their frustration and despair. No mass organization was yet thinkable, yet here activists could sense an emerging movement, aware of its own strength. The dissident Jacek Kuroń called the moment an "awakening."[43] John Paul appealed to Poles not as consumers but as humans challenged in their dignity, a message that helped inspire transcendent self-sacrifice in the open and concealed resistance on Polish soil for the next decade.

The economic malaise continued unabated, paralyzing the party's own ranks. Criticism could be heard even at the choreographed the Polish United Workers' Party's Eighth Party Congress in February 1980. When the Congress concluded, nothing officially had changed, yet witnesses to its deliberations knew that a reform movement would find support among party members, especially in the middle levels, where career advance was blocked. Polish Communists were not especially orthodox Marxist-Leninists: more than one-fourth of them went to church regularly, and three quarters identified themselves as religious believers. In the Czech lands or East Germany, by contrast, atheism was standard even outside the party.[44]

In July 1980, Poland's leadership remade the widespread discontent into a first-class political crisis by announcing increased work norms in the machine industry as well price hikes that affected about 2 percent of the meat sold in state stores.[45] Almost immediately, work stopped at factories across Poland. The strikers' tactic was to elect a committee and then demand compensation in wages. Warsaw, fully aware of the wreckage left by worker unrest in the past, instructed management to comply with demands. Yet as news of wage hikes spread, more workers went on strike, even some who had returned to work. Underground structures like KOR ensured that news traveled from factory to factory despite an official media blackout. As numbers of striking workplaces increased—to 150 by early August—Party leader Gierek appeared on television, again

FIGURE 24.3. Crowds flock to a public mass of Pope John Paul II, carrying banner reading "God Protect the Pope and the Nation" (June 1979). *Source*: Tomasz Mickiewicz (photographer) GFDL or CC-BY-SA 3.0.

appealing to workers as a fellow Pole, arguing that Poland's economy could not afford wage increases. Yet now few believed what he said. Because the unease had gone deep into the ranks of the party apparatus, the determination to break the strike was not great. Gierek did not use force, and he left for vacation in the Crimea as the waves of strikes reached the Baltic coast.

On August 14, the morning shift at the Lenin shipyard in Gdańsk refused to work, and that afternoon, workers hoisted the electrician Lech Wałęsa over the fence. Wałęsa, a veteran of the 1970 strikes, was fired four years earlier for a provocative speech at the shipyard, and with his charisma and folksy wit, he gave new life to a strike that was on the verge of faltering. The shipyard declared an occupation strike and prepared demands, including wage increases, reinstatement of workers fired for political reasons, family allowances equal to those given to the police, and (especially important to Wałęsa) a monument to the victims of 1970.[46]

A moment of truth intervened on August 16, when the shipyard management gave in to these demands, and Wałęsa declared the strike a success. Thousands of workers started filing through the gates, returning home. But Alina Pieńkowska, a young nurse as well as editor of an underground newspaper, got on a loudspeaker and told them to go back. Had they forgotten about colleagues in other, smaller Gdańsk factories whose demands had not been met? Aided by three female colleagues from the male-dominated shipyard—Anna Walentynowicz, Henryka Krzywonos, and Ewa Ossowska—Pieńkowska intercepted dozens of workers, including her own father, and the occupation at the Gdańsk shipyard continued, in *solidarity* with workers elsewhere.[47]

The strike movement spread to nearby Gdynia, and to dozens of other factories, and the demands grew: for free access to the media; release of political prisoners; free trade unions; and, thanks to Pieńkowska, improvements in the health service. This trade union movement, the workers understood, could not simply be a workers' movement. It was the pinnacle of Poland's human rights movement: the right to form a trade union was a civic right, and it implied the rights to the freedoms of speech and publication, as well as "the availability of the mass media to representatives of all faiths."[48]

Baltic workers remembered the lessons of the tragedy ten years earlier, when they had exposed themselves to police repression—including shootings—by leaving the workplace. Now they sat tight and were supplied with food from the outside. Factory gates, meant to protect socialist property, now shielded striking workers from the socialist state.[49] Beyond offering strikers a safe harbor, this "occupation strike" had the advantages of holding valuable machinery hostage, preventing lockouts, and heightening morale among workers under siege conditions.

Soon an "interfactory strike committee" emerged to represent some 50,000 workers across the connected Baltic cities of Gdańsk, Gdynia, and Sopot. What united them emotionally was the commemoration of workers killed in 1970. On August 17, a Sunday, a large wooden cross was blessed and planted in front of the Gdańsk shipyard, where four workers had been shot in the earlier strikes. The spot became a shrine, with flowers changed daily and candles burning at night. The reverential attitude of the strikers was reflected in a ban on alcohol. If a worker was caught with a bottle, the contents were emptied and his name announced over the shipyard's loudspeakers to humiliate him.

Demands like free access to the media or independent trade unions addressed the needs of all Poles, and unlike previous strikes, this one could not be bargained away. Because of the communication among factories, authorities could not localize a hotspot and then pour money into it. By August 19, interfactory strike committees had spread to other cities. The government sent representatives to the Baltic coast, but they faced accusations of bad faith. If the war against Germany was fought for freedom, why was the government rounding up KOR activists? Why was it cutting telephone lines from Gdańsk?

Alina Pieńkowska managed to relay the strikers' demands to Warsaw through a simple ruse: asking a state employee to let her use an official telephone at the information kiosk of a rail station. When she got through, the official and everyone in the queue listened passively as she told Jacek Kuroń the details of the strike at the top of her voice.[50] In that station and much of Gdańsk, Polish Communism had gone absent without leave. The next day, the strikers' basic demands were broadcast back into Poland by Western media who had been in touch with Kuroń from his Warsaw apartment.

When government representative Mieczysław Jagielski arrived at the shipyard, he had to leave his car outside the gates and made his way to negotiations through a gauntlet of angry workers. With no live contact to Warsaw and simple instructions—"go settle this thing"—he felt humiliated and was soon apologizing. He, too, was a "good Pole" who had suffered during the war. Gradually the government gave in, restoring communications and broadcasting negotiations. On August 27, the state newspaper printed the workers' twenty-one demands.[51] That, together with the fact that the government had not used force to restore order, constituted a revolutionary development in the history of the Soviet Bloc.

Back in Warsaw, Jagielski confirmed to the leadership that the interfactory committee controlled everything in Gdańsk with the full support of "society." Workers' delegates were not interested in compromise and kept repeating a simple question: will the Communist Party permit free trade unions? The workers were not, Jagielski noted, behaving illegally, but kept to the "Geneva conventions that we have signed." He felt the government should accede but thought that the party could infiltrate a new union if it worked hard enough. By the end of August, the strikes had spread westward to Szczecin and south to Wrocław, Łódź, and the Silesian industrial centers. In all, 700,000 workers were striking in 700 factories. Jagielski was told to sign the agreement.[52] After he had done so, Wałęsa affixed his signature with an oversized souvenir pen bearing the image of John Paul II.

In early September, Edward Gierek resigned for "health reasons." The new union was called Solidarity. It had the right to represent workers, yet it also endorsed "the principle of social ownership of the means of production, constituting the foundation of Poland's socialist system." It further recognized the leading role of the Polish United Workers' Party in the state, as well as the "established system of international alliances."

Thus began fifteen months of stormy coexistence between union and party. As Jagielski's recollections later suggested, the government did not intend to

FIGURE 24.4. Anna Walentynowicz, Alina Pieńkowska and Lech Wałęsa in Kraków (1980).
Source: PAP/Maciej Sochor.

allow an independent union to flourish. Months of delay followed in registering branches, with occasional clashes, for example, in Bydgoszcz in the spring
of 1981, when union representatives were beaten and a general strike was barely
avoided. Union branches repeatedly staged warning strikes to get the agreement
respected, and they never were allowed to operate in peace. From beyond Poland's borders, the Soviet Union and its allies, above all the GDR and Czechoslovakia, threatened fraternal violence for the "enemies of socialism" in Poland.
In the winter of 1980/1981, the world held its breath as the calumnies rose to
mountainous heights. Though tanks massed at Poland's borders, no attack came.
In February 1981, Defense Minister General Wojciech Jaruzelski—a career officer of gentry background—became prime minister, and in October, he replaced Gierek's successor, Stanisław Kania, as party first secretary.

Solidarity and government blamed one another as Poland's economy sput-
tered downward. By the fall of 1981, all that could be bought in much of Poland
without ration cards or lengthy lines was matches and vinegar. An unusually
cold winter descended as Solidarity prepared for its first congress at Gdańsk.
With the union's leaders gathered in one place, General Jaruzelski pounced, declaring martial law and putting the leaders behind bars. Movement and meetings were restricted across Poland as the army took control, and police hunted
down scores more activists. At the Wujek coal mine in Katowice, workers

resisted takeover and were shot at by government forces (nine died, twenty-one were wounded).

Gorbachev: Democracy from the Stalinist Apparatus?

The chill of martial law had descended at a frosty low point of the Cold War, the first year of the presidency of Ronald Reagan. Central Europeans watched as the superpowers stationed or promised to station new generations of weapons of mass destruction astride the Iron Curtain, in West as well as East Germany. In the fall of 1982, the aged and infirm Brezhnev died, and rule passed to one (Yuri Andropov, d. 1984) and then another (Konstantin Chernenko, d. 1985) aged and infirm Soviet leader.

Out of the protracted crisis, the reformer Mikhail Gorbachev emerged in March 1985. Some have said that his coming to power was a response to protests in East Central Europe, particularly Poland, but the economic malaise across the socialist world so clearly jeopardized the Soviet Union's superpower status that deeper structural forces favored the emergence of a reformer of some kind. What is mind boggling is that the Soviet system produced *this* kind of reformer. Though surrounded by men who had survived and profited from the Stalinist and neo-Stalinist apparatus—Gorbachev's patron was Yuri Andropov, a man reviled in Hungary for his role in 1956—the new general secretary believed in the virtues of a free exchange of views. In fact, he thought that criticism would make socialism strong. In a January 1987 meeting of the Communist Party's Central Committee, he said, "we need democracy like the air we breathe."[53] At the same time, he was motivated by the original transformative faith of Marxism.

Gorbachev wanted Eastern Europe to cease being a drain on resources, whether military, political, or economic. But he did not see the satellites solely as a problem. His belief in humane socialism made him curious about the Prague Spring—he was a personal friend of reform Communist Zdeněk Mlynář from his student days in Moscow—and also about the economic reforms in Kádár's Hungary. But Gorbachev was nondoctrinaire enough to admire East Germany's Leninists, who presided over a stable state with a high standard of living, a population enjoying ready access to meat, apartment space, and health care— all in short supply in Moscow, Warsaw, and Bucharest.

Gorbachev was not alone in admiring the apparent East German economic strength. In 1987, Western economists, looking primarily at numerical data, placed East Germany ahead of the United Kingdom in per capita income, a major index of development. As late as 1988, even sober Western newspapers were describing the GDR as a powerhouse. Its deep debt, similar to that of other countries (in per capita terms) was known but was not considered an impediment to growth and continued "success." The times when East Germany's economy was lame were "long past," wrote journalist Peter Merseburger in 1987.[54] He imagined the GDR lasting far into the unspecified future, thriving as a state that had solved the problem of unemployment and social insecurity, and he praised it for low rents, ignoring the fact that they reflected low investment in housing. The data existed to draw more sobering conclusions, but few did so. The GDR was so much wealthier than Poland that no one believed it, too, might have deep problems. Per capita East German gross national product was 40 percent higher than that of the Soviet Union.[55]

The success of the GDR's economy was an illusion. The state carried an unsustainable debt and tore down centuries-old buildings in world-class architectural gems (like Greifswald, Weimar, and Brandenburg), because it was too poor renovate them. The GDR could not compete even in areas where the state made its heaviest investments, like microelectronic technology, a major focus from the late 1970s. By September 1988, some 250,000 workers at seventeen *Kombinate* and 14 billion marks of investment had yielded the production of the GDR's own 1-megabyte microchip, much celebrated in the party press, but already years behind the standard in the West. Toshiba had been mass-producing a 1-megabyte chip for two years at that point and was at work on a 4-megabyte chip.[56]

The relatively high living standards were made possible by fortuitous circumstances: a strong preexisting industrial base; heavy investments in the 1950s; rational organizational reforms in the 1970s and 1980s (*Kombinate*); and the fact that West Germany considered the GDR a part of united Germany and gave it full access to the markets of the European Union, as well as several massive loans. Still, East Germany's leaders felt that no reform was needed. Kurt Hager, East German ideology chief, said his land did not need Gorbachev's plans for greater openness and restructuring. Simply because your neighbor puts up new wallpaper does not mean that you should do the same. The GDR leader Erich Honecker even mocked Gorbachev. "The young man has been making policy for only a year, and already he wants to take on more than he can chew."[57]

Hungarian Reform

Gorbachev found greater rapport among reform-minded pragmatists in the Hungarian Communist Party, who were interested in making socialism work. To the casual observer, they seemed successful. Hungarian cities displayed such a wealth of consumer products that they struck visitors as resembling the West.

Some of the finest food in Europe was served in Budapest restaurants in the 1980s. In an important book published several years after Communism's collapse, the British historian Nigel Swain still called it "feasible socialism."[58]

The Hungarian reforms went back to Imre Nagy, who believed that Stalinist command structures inhibited rational decision making, but the Kádár regime, as we have seen in Chapter 21, launched comprehensive reform on New Year's Day 1968 as the New Economic Mechanism (NEM). NEM enhanced decision making in the enterprises, made some prices reflect value, and created incentives to stimulate productivity. The state maintained indirect control over production not through quantitative directives but by granting preferred credits, setting prices, and taxing enterprises. It also attempted to shield Hungary's industries from the world market by maintaining a monopoly over foreign trade.[59]

Agriculture was the first sector where the reform showed success, thanks to the use of flexible prices and the relatively moderate Hungarian form of collectivization, which produced not state farms but a cooperative system with a substantial role for private enterprise. By the late 1960s, Hungary's farms were exporting cereals and showing growth in producing meat, vegetables, and fruit.[60] The most important innovation—which would be echoed throughout the economy—was cooperative autonomy. Managers could run farms as they saw fit. Multiplied across the agricultural sector, that principle led to a diversification of cooperatives that were adjusted to local needs. Locals knew what grape or grain grew best in their region's soil.

Yet if the reforms made socialist agriculture more competitive, they also exposed it to grave risks. At its core, the system was committed to equality, but now differences began to emerge among farm workers. They were rewarded not according to days worked but to productivity, and holdings went to those who actually worked them, creating a class of tenant farmers.[61] And despite all the innovation, Hungarian agriculture had fallen far behind the West in productivity and efficiency.

The incipient reforms also laid bare an ideological defect. Communists believed in the dominance of state ownership, and that socialism was a society based on steel and concrete; they had adopted NEM as a set of temporary measures and had no commitment to real market relationships, producing what economist János Kornai called "soft budget constraints." Because firms could not go bankrupt, managers treated tax and price polices not as a real limitation but only as an "accounting relationship over which bargaining is possible." The state became an "insurance company taking over all the moral hazards with well-known consequences: the insured will be less careful in protecting his wealth." The soft budget constraint protected inefficient firms from constructive destruction, thus impeding innovation.[62]

Despite the glitz of shop windows in Budapest when Mikhail Gorbachev came to power in 1985, the Hungarian economic reform was therefore not a success story. Market mechanisms, including partnerships with Western firms, had failed to produce reliable economic growth, let alone make Hungary competitive with the West. The soft budget constraints had produced persistent though unpredictable shortages.[63] Traditional socialist sectors, like steel and coal, dragged down the more promising sectors, and Hungary proved unable to keep up with advances in new industries like electronics or plastics. Making matters worse was the huge, unproductive party and security apparatus. Each enterprise had full-time paid staff of party functionaries supposedly overseeing the line of the party. The dictatorship of the proletariat thus gave no hope of creating the material abundance that would free humans from the alienation of the division of labor and the rule of capital. By the 1980s, the main purpose of the dictatorship was to survive.

Yet even had the reforms that Hungary was pioneering been viable in economic terms, there was still the question of whether workers would support them. That is, the only idea for rescuing socialism seemed set against the interests of the class it was supposed to serve. From the late 1960s, workers could see their positions threatened by consumerism—including the construction of private homes—a lifestyle they could embrace only by working longer hours and seeing less of their families. Because NEM made prices reflect value, staples like meat and dairy products became more expensive. Throughout the 1970s, social differentiation grew, based on mushrooming "quasimarket" semilegal activity, and by the 1980s, workers' incomes were stagnating, privatization was spreading—even within factories— and working hours were increasing. Even unemployment made a reappearance.[64]

After 1979, the NEM was no longer a "mechanism" but a set of improvised bailing-out measures to keep Hungary from capsizing under the combined burdens of the state's external indebtedness and the party's failure to deliver on the terms of its social contract with the people (that is, that it would guarantee social security and decent living standards in exchange for political passivity). Perhaps the most self-destructive aspect of NEM for the socialist state was to involve Hungary in East–West trade, and therefore in borrowing from Western banks. The costs of buying time and maintaining political stability were the crushing short- and long-term obligations of debt servicing.[65]

Hidden from an optimistic Gorbachev peering at the abundance in Budapest's shop windows was thus the sobering truth that, rather than solve the problem of malaise, Hungary was flooding markets with it, both at home and abroad. And the future held no promises. The ideological mandates of the system (that the party retain control and not permit the reemergence of "capitalism") combined with the dictates of economic rationality (which were increasingly respected in the party) to beget an unholy mixture, a system that could neither shake off socialism nor fully embrace capitalism.

At the time, no one saw these developments as harbingers of an approaching end. Hungarian dissident author George Konrád wrote in the early 1980s that the system had become more "self-confident." It even integrated heretics, inviting them to "dialogues" and "exchanges of opinion." The regime had made itself the indispensable mediator between Hungarian society, with its specific hopes and demands, and the Soviet leadership, with its expectations of minimal orthodoxy. Pragmatic, younger functionaries did not jam Western radio broadcasts and let citizens travel and read Western newspapers.[66] To many, this leniency seemed part of a shrewd calculation signaling deeper strength. By the late 1980s, the émigré historian Miklós Molnar noticed autonomous institutions sprouting up in almost every domain, including religious communities, cultural societies, song and folklore ensembles, but also modern music groups. For him, all this social pluralism accounted for the "*stability* of the regime and the support it receives from public opinion."[67]

"The Soviet empire," Konrád concluded, "despite all of its internal difficulties, is in good shape, not headed toward collapse."[68] It was a superpower, whose conventional and nuclear forces caused great anxiety in the West, and whose Marxist ideology had legions of supporters in NATO countries. Moreover, having achieved nuclear parity with the United States, the Soviet Union competed for influence in Asia, Africa, and Central America, where populations were shaking off colonial rule. In the 1980s, one-third of the world's population was ruled by Marxist-Leninist regimes, and the number seemed likely to grow.[69] North Vietnam had just scored an impressive victory over the United States. Throughout South and Southeast Asia, the Middle East, Africa, and Central and South America, millions looked with favor on state socialism, and Soviet advisors served in Mozambique, Syria, and Nicaragua, while proxy Cuban soldiers fought in Angola. Everywhere people on the left wished Soviet leader Gorbachev success.

Among East European leaders, many of whom traced an unbroken lineage to the time of Stalin, the Soviet leader's popularity was more constrained. His only significant allies outside Hungary were Poland's leaders, including the general who had sent tanks against workers in 1981. Yet like Gorbachev, Wojciech Jaruzelski was a moderate. He eschewed the "normalization" forged by Gustav Husák in Czechoslovakia after 1969 and made modest demands on Poles for conformity. The Polish party banned open political protest but did little to curtail underground publications, which grew and flourished; by the late 1980s, some publishers were including color plates in their books. The underground newspaper from Warsaw, *Gazeta Mazowsze*, came out in 50,000 to 80,000 copies weekly, distributed by thousands of (mostly young) activists. Though its top leaders were often detained, the structures of Solidarity continued functioning in the underground, led largely by women.[70]

In an influential essay of 1978, the Czech playwright Václav Havel had encouraged fellow citizens to defy the regime's expectation that they would automatically parrot distortions of reality. He urged them to break the power of the lie.[71] Solidarity had accomplished this for Poland. People had shaken off fear, and even after the imposition of martial law, they continued to speak their opinions in restaurants, railway compartments, barbershops, and university seminars. The regime clamped down on massive public manifestations of dissent—for example, the annual commemorations of the May 3, 1791 constitution at Kraków's Wawel castle—but otherwise retreated, with little intention or ability to make Poles into loyal socialist citizens.

If Solidarity changed Poland, it also changed the Soviet Bloc. For a year and half, it proclaimed to the world that workers had achieved an independent trade union in a state that claimed to be a workers' state. Solidarity undermined the central Leninist idea that workers had one interest, represented by one vanguard party. As much as East German or Czech media tried to deny it, the truth was that Solidarity had emerged from factory floors and not from the intrigues of finance capital. Through the mere fact of the union's existence, Polish factory laborers had managed to say clearly and unmistakably, on a backdrop of empty grocery store shelves, overcrowded apartment houses, and the devastated environment, that state socialism had failed to create circumstances in which they could live dignified lives.

All the Soviet Bloc countries suffered from some combination of problems, but they took their fullest form in Poland, and it was Poland that generated the most determined opposition. By the 1980s, it had also became a mecca for dissidents and would-be dissidents from other East Central European countries, eager to find out how to undo the regime of the lie.[72] We will never know if without Poland's opposition, there would have been the Soviet reformer

Gorbachev; we do know that a bloc of controlled societies like East Germany and Czechoslovakia would have suggested nothing crucial had to change. At the same time, Kádár's Hungary, with its restless testing of the possibilities of the planned economy, revealed the fate of attempts to reform the state socialist economy: either perennial shortage, unsustainable debt, or both.

Romania: National Stalinism

Gorbachev's reign was the reverse of Stalinism. He wanted to unravel Soviet control of Eastern Europe.[73] But this was an ironic, even self-destructive enterprise, because East European leaders had based their power on Soviet support.[74] And so rather than seem liberating, beyond the Hungarian and Polish parties, Gorbachev filled Communists with fear, and when he visited Czechoslovakia, East Germany, or Romania, the visible result was embarrassed dissonance. In the spring of 1987, crowds welcomed the Soviet leader to Prague chanting "Gorbachev, Gorbachev." He later recalled the scene to fellow Politburo members. "Husák was next to me, but it was as if he wasn't there. I kept trying to push him forward, and kept using the phrase, 'Comrade Husák and I,' but the people did not respond to it." He saw a similar phenomenon in the GDR. There, too, "people are ahead of the political views and the level of their leadership."[75]

Yet if Gorbachev fretted about the leaders in Czechoslovakia or East Germany, where Romania was concerned, he worried about the regime as well as the people. "When Ceaușescu and I went out to the people," he told comrades after a visit in May 1987, "their reaction was like a wound-up music box: 'Ceaușescu-Gorbachev!' 'Ceaușescu-Peace.' It makes one's head burst." Later he was told that the criers had been shipped to the scene in buses. "Human dignity has absolutely no value," continued Gorbachev, "I was not able to have a normal conversation with people anywhere." In Ceaușescu's mind, no changes were needed because there were no problems. The Romanian leader was "unbelievably impudent. His self-assurance and self-praise are simply monumental, comparable only with his attempts to teach and admonish everybody."[76]

But Ceaușescu had experience going back to the 1960s in confounding Soviet rulers, when he refused to take part in the assault on Czechoslovakia with the rest of the Waraw Pact. His Romania was also the first Soviet Bloc state to establish diplomatic relations with West Germany (in 1967), and the only one to maintain friendly ties with China or with Israel after the Six-Day War. For this stance, the West celebrated the Romanian dictator as a maverick. Though fresh paint had been applied to every inch of the places Gorbachev toured in a carefully scripted visit, the country's decline could not be hidden from the Soviet leader. "Consumption of meat per capita is 10 kilograms per year," he reported in Moscow. "There are constant shortages of power, heat, food products and consumer goods."[77]

Ceaușescu's popularity as a nationalist had been reinforced by the country's economic success in the late 1960s. Romania seemed to be following a modernizing agenda, in many ways not so different from welfare states in the West. Even the Polish dissident Michnik thought Ceaușescu's Romania initially offered hope for a better way to socialism.[78] The point was to break the hold of backward ways of thinking and acting, and cultivate a population engaged in modern economic pursuits and living in nuclear families. In the late 1960s, Romanians were living better than their parents' generation: urban and no longer rural, with paved roads; running water; mass literacy; and modestly packaged modern comforts like refrigerators, washing machines, and automobiles. Relative affluence combined with perceived national independence to create reservoirs of goodwill for the regime, and thousands applied for membership in the Communist Party; by the 1980s, some 23 percent of Romania's adult population had party books, the highest figure anywhere in the Soviet Bloc.[79]

The Romanian Party seemed more technocratic and task oriented, interested in accomplishing goals, and no longer "ideological." But the impressions of apolitical managerism were deceiving. By the early 1970s, Ceaușescu had shunted aside his rivals—calling them "Stalinist"—and assumed a position of uncontested leadership. A 1971 visit to North Korea was a turning point. Here he encountered a purism and discipline missing in Brezhnev's Soviet Bloc, and now he began to merge ideological rigidity with a mission to the nation. Ceaușescu became a defender of Romanian values, denouncing intellectual cosmopolitanism and projecting a unity of the Romanian people on Romanian territory going back many generations.[80] According to Romanian historians, Karl Marx had "stressed the age of the Romanian people, its historical unity and continuity on the territory it had inhabited for millennia."[81]

The notion that Romania lived under a Soviet threat, implicit in the Romanian press from 1964, was strengthened under Ceaușescu, who interpreted the invasion of Czechoslovakia in 1968 as endangering Romania. His regime refashioned history to counter the popular East Bloc narrative about World War II as a battle between Germans and Latins on the one hand and Slavs (Poles, Russians, and Czechs) on the other. Instead, Romanians were portrayed as victims of Slavs and Magyars from time immemorial. Now they were standing up to

Russians as they once had to the Ottomans. This legitimation strategy built on a claim that he alone, the strongest of Romanian rulers, could protect the people; and it secured for him the allegiance even of critical intellectuals.[82] As dysfunctional and brutalizing as the Communist dictatorship in Romania seems in retrospect, in the 1970s, Nicolae Ceaușescu had achieved something that eluded other Communist leaders. If they "purchased" support among elites by promising better standards of living, he offered an attractive ideological synthesis connecting to older traditions of xenophobia.

In November 1974, Ceaușescu became president, scepter in hand, and began perfecting a personality cult as "hero of the working class and successor to the great Romanian rulers" who had defended the homeland against enemies. Until 1978, the economy grew at a rapid rate, with rapid diversification of heavy industry, but then a tipping point was reached. Excessive investments in steel and petrochemical industries were sapping away the country's natural and human resources.[83] Yet Ceaușescu's power was absolute, in a way that Edward Gierek's or even Erich Honecker's never was, and he argued that the material sacrifices he now required were necessary to protect Romania from external pressures.

Intellectuals busied themselves legitimating Ceaușescu as a "man of genius," some even writing treatises for which he took credit. Ceaușescu's wife Elena likewise found ghostwriters, and no one protested the degradation of the Romanian Academy, the dissolution of the Institute of Mathematics in 1975, or the liquidation of the Commissions of Historic Monuments two years later. Perhaps most damagingly, in 1978, the intellectual class acquiesced in the destruction of the educational system when an education law made schools a component of industrial production. Trouble was brewing, however. In August 1977, a strike of 35,000 miners broke out in the Jiu region over an extension of retirement age and frequent overtime, which ended only upon Ceaușescu's personal intervention with the strikers.[84]

By the early 1980s, the dictator's stature began to decline as it became evident that in contrast to Polish and Hungarian leaders, he was unwilling to liberalize, and that, in the name of strengthening the Romanian nation, he was committing human rights abuses, like bulldozing Hungarian villages or denying Romanian women reproductive freedom in his attempt to increase the birth rate.[85] Perhaps the most direct challenge for Ceaușescu was the rise in oil prices, whose low price Ceaușescu had relied on to achieve his unrealistic goals for the economy. In the early 1980s, Romania's dependence on expensive foreign oil for its mammoth petrochemical industry, as well as imported iron ore for the steel mills of Galați and Călărași, had produced a foreign debt that Romania was unable to repay.[86]

By 1983, that debt amounted to 10 billion dollars. This was not unusual. Hungary, Poland, East Germany, and even the Soviet Union had huge debts in foreign currency by this time. Unusual was the regime's assumption that the adoring population would absorb any sacrifice the dictator required. With no concern about resulting food shortages, Ceaușescu exported agricultural products to the West for hard currency. He reserved energy for the industrial sector (which generated goods destined for export) and starved the private sector of electricity and fuel. That accounted for the misery of a decade in which houses were cold and streets dark. In 1983 the International Monetary Fund estimated a 20 percent decrease in the standard of living from the previous year.[87] Like East Germany, Romania sold citizens to the West for hard currency.[88] This was only the beginning of the nightmare years for the Romanian population.

As Hungary and Poland liberalized, Romania's leaders turned the screws. In 1983, all typewriters had to be registered. Nicolae Ceaușescu claimed the sacrifices were necessary to defend Romania's honor and protect it from foreign interference. In a sense, he took on the world, first targeting local aliens—Transylvanian Hungarians—then Hungary itself, next the Soviet Union, which claimed Romania was in "violation" of Comecon and Warsaw Pact accords, and finally Western countries, which demanded that Romania honor its Helsinki commitments.[89] His personality cult exceeded all known cases outside Nazi Germany and Stalinist Russia, with the official media calling him the "greatest Romanian leader of all time."

But in March 1985, Ceaușescu awoke to a surprise. With the emergence of Gorbachev, Russia suddenly seemed to be a source of hope to Romanians rather than a threat. Despite the rhythmic chanting of "criers" bussed in to greet Gorbachev in May 1987, the Soviet leader was a popular figure. Though their sentiments were hidden, the population hoped for restructuring: "perestroika."[90] In his megalomania, Ceaușescu ignored a basic truth. Though he flouted the Soviets, it was the Soviets with their Brezhnev doctrine—the determination to secure Leninist rule once it has been established—that made him and his misdeeds possible. If Gorbachev withdrew that doctrine, there was nothing to protect him from Romania's citizens other than his own secret police and party. What if their loyalty should waver?

Like other Soviet Bloc leaders, Ceaușescu had received warnings as early as Konstantin Chernenko's funeral in March 1985, when freshly elected Gorbachev told them that the Soviet Union would respect their sovereignty, but that they

FIGURE 24.5. Raissa Gorbacheva, Nicolae Ceaușescu, Mikhail Gorbachev and Elena Ceaușescu (October 1988). *Source*: SPUTNIK/Alamy Stock Photo.

would bear responsibility for developments in their countries. Eastern Europe's Communist leaders would need, he added in November 1986, to earn the trust of their own peoples, because the Soviet Union would not rescue them with military intervention.[91] Two years later, Gorbachev made this line public at the United Nations, announcing that "force or the threat of force neither can nor should be instruments of foreign policy.... The principle of freedom of choice is mandatory.... To deny a nation the freedom of choice, regardless of the pretext or the verbal guise in which it is cloaked, is to upset the unstable balance that has been achieved.... Freedom of choice is a universal principle. It knows no exception." The principle applied "to both the capitalist and socialist systems."[92]

CHAPTER 25

1989

In late November 1989, revolution was under way in Czechoslovakia, and thousands of citizens streamed each day to the centers of their towns and cities to demand an end to one-party rule. On the evening of November 23, the British historian Timothy Garton Ash made a provocative prediction over drinks with the dissident writer Václav Havel, who was emerging as the revolution's leader. The overthrow of Communism had taken ten years in Poland, he said, ten months in Hungary, and ten weeks in East Germany. Maybe it would take only ten days in Czechoslovakia? It turned out that he was exaggerating, but not by much. A little over a month later, Havel was president.[1]

The revolutions of 1989 not only got shorter; they followed upon one another in what seemed to be a chain reaction. By the time Garton Ash sat down with Havel, the Berlin Wall was open in both directions, and Poland had a non-Communist government. Czechs and Slovaks knew this from television, and this knowledge spurred both leaders and people. Gustáv Husák and comrades concluded that it was better to go quietly. They were disciples of history, and as far as they could tell, the verdict had gone against them. Several leaders resigned rather than risk charges for past misdeeds and those who remained negotiated their way into oblivion with representatives of civil society. In December 1989, a Czechoslovak parliament of mostly Communist deputies unanimously chose Havel as the new president. On New Year's Day 1990, he addressed the nation from the Prague castle, and spoke words inspired by Jan Amos Comenius and T. G. Masaryk: "nation, your government has returned to you." Free elections followed later that year.

Yet when East German demonstrators commenced their ten-week revolution in September 1989, they had no idea whether their leaders would go peacefully. Erich Honecker and the gerontocratic SED leadership continued to oppose all change; one of them, the heir apparent Egon Krenz, flew to Beijing in June to congratulate Chinese Communists for crushing the pro-democracy movement at Tiananmen Square. Still, their control at home was not absolute and depended on the implicit understanding in place after the regime built the Berlin Wall in 1961: the captive population would reward the regime with political conformity in return for a decent standard of living. In the summer of 1989, however, events farther south were suggesting that East Germans were no longer a captive people.[2]

When they tuned in to Western television in June 1989, East Germans saw Austrian and Hungarian officials apply larger-than-life wire cutters to the barbed wire separating their two countries. With each snip, they were suggesting that the basic calculus of East Germans' lives had shifted. Hungary was a country they could visit without a passport, and now, it seemed, they might circumvent the Berlin Wall by escaping westward through the Hungarian-Austrian border. In June and July, tens of thousands drove south for "vacation" in Hungary, with the intention of ditching the cars and then crossing the border on foot. They knew that once they made it to the West German embassy in Vienna, they would get a passport with no questions asked, as well as a free bus ride to the Federal Republic, where they could embark on a new life in freedom. They were no longer condemned to live behind the Berlin Wall.[3]

It turned out that the Western cameras had misled the would-be refugees. Much of the border fence was still intact, and the Hungarian border guards were still apprehending escapees and sending them back to East Germany, according to an intergovernmental agreement that dated to 1969. Nevertheless, some were getting through, and in July, Hungary began honoring a different agreement: the international refugee convention, according to which East Germans had a right remain in Hungary.[4] By September, their numbers were in the hundreds of thousands, and Hungarian officials came under tremendous pressure from the West German government in Bonn to let them freely cross the border to Austria. That would involve a breach with East Germany, still an ally. Meanwhile, East Germany itself was becoming a pressure cooker, as people wondered whether their regime might close the border to Czechoslovakia, and they would find themselves trapped, just like a previous generation in August 1961, when the wall suddenly went up in Berlin. Some of the more desperate East Germans, primarily in the south, began doing something that had been unthinkable for decades: they went out on the streets and demonstrated, manifesting their desires for change.

Yet why did Hungarian officials singlehandedly open the Iron Curtain? A clue lies in Garton Ash's clocking of "ten months." The Solidarity revolution had transformed Polish society in 1980/1981. In Hungary, liberalization took place more gradually, but by 1988 had produced a similar result: a society without fear, where people could travel to the West and speak plainly at home, and where, as in Gorbachev's Soviet Union, the official press was soon filled with defiant criticisms of the government. By May 1989, the decision to open the border to Austria was not even a decision. An official of the border troops had informed a member of government that the time had come for maintenance of the border fortifications (that is, for replacing rusty sections of the fence) and upgrading mines that no longer worked. But money was tight and so the question emerged: why bother? Hungarians could travel to Austria as often as they liked—they were crowding Vienna's department stores—and the barbed wire, meant to keep people from escaping, served no purpose. Worse, replacements of stainless steel wire would have cost hard currency, because the suppliers were in the West.

The course for Hungarians to this point had been plotted in the aftermath of 1956. The Kádár regime pacified the population with decent living standards and minimal ideological pressure. Yet by the 1980s, the dynamic had run out of energy. The economy was stalled, and a huge debt had to be paid. The government attempted "capitalist" concessions, like allowing private firms up to have up to 500 employees, as well as joint ventures with Western companies, yet the reforms produced "capitalist" problems, like inflation, which ran at 17 percent in 1987 (the true rate was perhaps double that). Salaries and pensions could not keep up, and gradually the evil side effects of a bygone time reappeared: social marginalization, with 20 percent of the population living at the subsistence level.[5]

Was this still socialism? If not, what was the justification of total rule by a socialist party? The crisis loomed so large that the rulers believed they had no choice but to involve the citizenry in a search for solutions. Responsibility had to be shared for the pains of transition that were inevitable.

After Communism's collapse, Mikhail Gorbachev portrayed Janos Kádár as a man with "democratic inclinations" and "respect for people's freedom to choose their own way of life."[6] But by 1988, Kádár was a stumbling block. He could not abide Gorbachev's campaign for openness, fearing that probing questions would destroy rather than strengthen socialism. Sensing the old man's reservations, Gorbachev gently encouraged him to make way for a more energetic successor. In the spring of 1988, Kádár yielded, accepting the symbolic function of "party president," and more "technocratic" but also radical figures replaced his supporters in the Central Committee.[7]

Soon, Kádár's successor as party general secretary, Károly Grósz, found he was behind the times. In November 1988, the Party Central Committee lifted censorship and transferred most privileges incumbent on the party to the government. It accepted a multiparty political system, though socialism was supposed to be the dominant paradigm.[8] By year's end, Hungary featured two autonomous political organizations: the Hungarian Democratic Forum and the Alliance of Free Democrats, with some 10,000 members. They offered an umbrella to protect other new movements, for example, independent trade unions, and old parties like the Smallholders or Social Democrats that were reconstituting themselves.[9] In the spring, students had challenged the official youth organization by founding their own Alliance of Young Democrats. By December, there were twenty-one new political associations.[10] Not yet legal, the new organizations endured some half-hearted police harassment, yet they appeared so fragmented and diverse that few in Hungary called them an opposition.[11]

Like Poland under Jaruzelski, Hungary had maneuvered itself into a stalemate. On one hand, the regime wanted to legitimate painful reform by opening spaces for limited representation of "society." Reform, especially one that called itself democratic, could not simply be imposed top down. On the other hand, society—as represented by the new groupings—hesitated to assume the responsibilities of power.[12] Everyone knew that reforms would mean price hikes of foodstuffs that had been subsidized for generations. What would people say to unemployment? For years, party reformers had demanded change to prevent an explosion from society, but now the reform program had moved within reach, and it seemed daunting, because no one knew how society would bear the inevitable burdens of greater freedom.[13]

But in the midst of these exciting institutional changes, historical events not mentioned publically for decades suddenly moved to center stage. Before Hungarians stepped into uncharted territory, they wanted to know exactly where they had come from. Under intense scrutiny, Prime Minister Miklós Németh, a leading reformer, admitted that over 1 million peasants had been arrested or punished during the collectivization campaigns of 1945 to 1962.[14] The real bombshell involved the Hungarian Revolution, however. While Party General Secretary Grósz was traveling in Switzerland in January, reformer Imre Pozsgay called the events of 1956 a "popular uprising." For a quarter century, no official in the Soviet Bloc had called them anything but a counterrevolution.[15] It turned out that the traitorous culprit of 1956 was not Imre Nagy but the Soviets and their Hungarian allies, including Janos Kádár. A party subcommittee admitted as much in May.[16]

Now everyone who had come to power under Kádár had to acknowledge that their careers were built on the repression of a nation's revolution, as well as the attendant judicial murders and lies. Complicit were Party General

Secretary Grósz, but also his close associates János Berecz and György Fejti.[17] The problem was not just Stalinism. Kádár after all had been a victim of Stalin and became a foremost destalinizer. The problem lay deeper: in the Leninist idea that a tiny unelected group knew what was best for everyone.

Now Hungarian society could return to its own traditions, beginning with native social democratic ideas of socialism that abjured Leninism's practice of "democratic centralism." In violation of the first Soviet leader's proscription of "factions," reformers were creating their own branch of the Commumist Party in late 1988, and the following summer, the leadership oversaw a transition of the party from a Bolshevik "organizational weapon" to broad political move-ment. By September 1989, 120,000 to 200,000 party members had turned in their party books. The party retreated from the positions where it had exerted power for decades: from the military and police, but also the workplace.[18]

Precisely because it was more open, the party was increasingly on the de-fensive. In March the opposition was able to bring 150,000 people onto the streets commemorating the outbreak of the 1848 revolution; in June the regime conceded the creation of a "national round table," involving the Communists but also elements of the new public sphere (that is, opposition groups and par-ties) to discuss questions of transition.

That same month, thirty-one years after their executions, the remains of Imre Nagy and four others who died with him, along with an empty sixth casket rep-resenting all the other victims of the 1956 revolution—including some teen-agers hanged under Kádár—were reburied in a public spectacle that brought a quarter million people to central Budapest. Many more watched on television. Communist reformers such as Imre Pozsgay and Miklós Németh acted as pall-bearers, signaling a plea for national reconciliation, while one of Nagy's code-fendents, Miklós Vasarhelyi, took the podium, invoking historic justice, national unity, and the opportunity Hungarians now had for a "peaceful transition to a free and democratic society." On July 6, Nagy was officially rehabilitated. That same day, Kádár, haunted by guilt, finally succumbed to an extended illness.[19]

At Hungary's national roundtable, reformers held ascendance among the forces negotiating for the regime and proved eager to face free elections in order to relinquish responsibility for failed economic policies. In negotiations that lasted from mid-June to late September, they pledged to carry out a transition "from one-party to representative democracy." But the Hungarian population did not give their former jailers credit for their roles as avante garde socialist reformers. Guided by the local sense of propriety that had made the negotiated revolution possible, voters swept the party from power, in the March and

August 1990 elections, to the parliament and the presidency, respectively.[20] A new government was constituted by the Hungarian Democratic Forum, supported by 43 percent of the vote, in league with other center-right parties (Alliance of Free Democrats), who attained 24 percent.

Hungary, Poland, and the Fall of the Berlin Wall

Without Mikhail Gorbachev's conviction that socialism needed democracy, there would have been no revolutions in East Central Europe in 1989. But beyond Poland and Hungary, Communist leaders considered his ideas anathema, and therefore without the Hungarian and Polish reformers, perhaps Leninism would live on in Europe to this day. The fact that Poland and Hungary pushed for change, underwent months of "negotiated revolution," and ultimately forced breakthroughs to multiparty politics, made incipient democratization possible elsewhere, including in Russia.[21] The deeper reason Poland and Hungary played their pioneering roles had to do with the refusal of each to become properly Sovietized in the 1950s. That in turn had to do with national traditions that remained even after most institutions of civil society had been annihilated or subverted. As in the earlier experience of revolution in 1956, Hungarians were mimicking the Poles in 1989, but the lessons they had learned this time were to their own benefit. The idea of a round table, for example, came from Warsaw, from negotiations between Solidarity and the government in the fall of 1988.[22]

But the stimulus—the revolutionary spark that forced those negotiations—came from workers. After several years of relative peace, in the summer of 1988, strikes broke out on the Baltic coast, and Polish Interior Minister General Czesław Kiszczak contacted the leaders of Solidarity, hoping to gain their cooperation on a difficult road to reform the command economy. After months of preparation, negotiations commenced in February 1989, around a large round table in today's Presidential Palace, including members of official organizations like the non-Communist parties, and trade unions, as well as the Catholic Church. By April, participants agreed on elections in which Solidarity could compete for 35 percent of the seats in the lower house of the national legislature, and 100 percent of the seats in the resurrected upper house. An important fine point was that the other 65 percent of the lower house did automatically fall to the Communists. In fact, as noted dryly in the Soviet daily *Izvestia*, Communists would not have a majority. Instead, the seats would be divided. Thirty-eight percent (of the total) would go to them, but the rest would go to smaller parties that had been in hibernation for decades. Communists were assured the office of the president.[23]

No other country had gone as far and the sudden disjuncture with still orthodox Leninist regimes within the bloc was breathtaking. Moscow's press featured an interview with Solidarity leader Lech Wałęsa and complimented Poland's Catholic Church for efforts at finding compromise, but East Germany's government would not allow even Russian editions of reports on Poland to cross its borders. The previous fall it had forbidden the import of *Sputnik*, a Soviet-produced German-language overview of the Soviet press, in a vain attempt to keep details of Gorbachev's reforms from citizens already amply supplied by Western television reporting.

But now Solidarity had to conduct a two-month campaign using rudimentary underground structures, and even its boldest leaders did not imagine the union could assume power. At best they thought a period of shared rule would commence with the Communists, with fully free elections to take place four years in the future. Voters did not believe in radical change. A reporter overheard people saying that economic miracles are for Germany and Japan, not us. TV officials did not even bother broadcasting the final session of the round table negotiations, because they knew audiences were more interested in a soccer match against Real Madrid.[24]

To everyone's astonishment, when the polls closed on June 4, 1989, the Communists had lost every seat that was freely contested and found themselves unable to form a government. After weeks of negotiation, a compromise emerged by which a Solidarity candidate would become prime minister and form a government of Solidarity politicians as well as representatives of the non-Communist parties that suddenly awoke to new life after years of being loyal satraps to the regime. The Communists, as agreed, would continue to hold the office of president in the person of Wojciech Jaruzelski. Thus, on August 24, 1989, the first non-Communist head of state in postwar Eastern Europe, the Catholic intellectual Tadeusz Mazowieki, came to power.

Most East Germans had excellent reception of Western television and followed these developments with keen interest. None of what they saw made sense in terms of official messages of the victory of socialism, and it was that ideology that ultimately gave the Berlin Wall its power to divide Europe. How could two socialist countries in the Soviet Bloc suddenly evolve "backward," sacrificing the dictatorship of the proletariat?

Five days before the breakthrough in Poland, East Germans had been riveted to TV sets as 500 fellow East Germans attended a "pan-European picnic"

FIGURE 25.1. East Germans refugees at the West German embassy in Prague
(September 1989). *Source*: dpa picture alliance/Alamy Stock Photo.

on the Hungarian-Austrian border, and after having their fill of goulash, picked up their bags and leisurely strolled across the border, with passports obtained at the German embassy in Budapest. The Hungarian organizers were celebrating their "return to free Central Europe," and now their guests from Saxony and Brandenburg, clutching bits of barbed wire as souvenirs, boarded buses taking them to new lives. Among the organizers was Otto von Habsburg, and thus his family managed to make up for its failure 118 years earlier: this time they had a crucial role in unifying Germany.[25]

By early September, the number of East Germans in Hungary exceeded 150,000, and the Hungarian government, ignoring appeals from Erich Honecker, permitted them to leave for Austria, where they boarded trains and buses for their new homes in West Germany.[26] Instead of contemplating reform, the SED had sent hundreds of *Stasi* agents to Hungary to harass the refugees.[27] And it began denying its citizens permission to travel to Hungary.

As a result, would-be GDR refugees began seeking asylum in the countries still open to them: Poland and Czechoslovakia. By mid-September, some 4,000 sought asylum on the grounds of West Germany's embassy in Prague, creating a new humanitarian crisis and a new highly visible embarrassment for the East German regime as it sought to celebrate its 40th anniversary on October 7. A few dozen East Germans even tried to escape eastward—by swimming across the Oder River to Poland![28] In late September, West German foreign minister Hans-Dietrich Genscher, himself an émigré from East Germany negotiated a solution for the crisis of GDR citizens camping on his embassy's grounds in Prague: they could exit for West Germany. However, there was a catch. The politically insecure East German leadership insisted that the trains carrying the refugees not go directly westward, crossing the Czech-German border, but first travel north, via Dresden, Karl-Marx-Stadt, and Plauen, through East German territory, then south across the border to the West German town of Hof. That would permit GDR authorities (who fretted about international recognition of their legitimacy to rule) to "release" the refugees from GDR citizenship.[29]

Yet this gratuitous act only intensified the cauldron-like situation within the GDR. Thousands tried to board the fourteen trains as they traversed East German territory at high speed on the night of September 30. In Plauen the local police force was too small to keep locals from storming the city's train station, and dozens were injured and many more arrested. Four days later, the East German regime sealed its border to Czechoslovakia, and many feared the GDR would become a military dictatorship like Chile, or that Erich Honecker would follow Nicolae Ceaușescu's path of pure repression.

In contrast to Poland or Hungary, there was hardly an opposition in East Germany with which the government could have negotiated a way out of the crisis, had it had the mind to do so. Solidarity in Poland counted 10 million members, but the East German civil rights activists numbered in the hundreds, mostly in East Berlin and Leipzig. Small oppositional circles had emerged over the 1970s and 1980s, supported by Protestant churches—advocating for human rights, the environment, or peace—but were infiltrated and closely monitored by the secret police. Their more determined members were arrested and sent westward. For example, a small independent peace movement had emerged in the southern town of Jena in 1982, but its activists were given the choice of jail or emigration. One of its leaders, the writer Roland Jahn, refused to be intimidated. In 1982 he rode his bicycle through town with a flag proclaiming "Solidarity with the Polish people!" For this he was placed in solitary confinement and subjected to sleep deprivation. Officers threatened to put his daughter in an orphanage. Still, he refused to consent to emigration. But the state had had enough of him. In 1983 *Stasi* officers carried him into a special rail car—in chains—locked it and attached it to the Berlin–Munich express. Once he was safely out of the GDR, railway employees could open the car with keys left by *Stasi* officers and free Jahn from confinement. He settled in West Berlin, joined other dissidents from Jena, and then worked as a journalist with the local TV station, the Sender Freies Berlin. After 1989, it was discovered that *Stasi* agents had spied on him there as well, bugging a West Berlin café where he liked to spend time and tracing his daughter's way to school.[30]

Jahn's forcible deportation was a crowning hypocrisy. The refusal of the West German government to "respect" GDR citizenship was a constant complaint that East German officials had made in inter-German meetings over the decades. But when their ostensible citizens became too difficult, SED leaders simply dumped them across the border, certain that West Germany would automatically grant them its "all-German" citizenship. It was West Germany's firm insistence that only one German citizenship existed—as stipulated by a law from 1913—that ensured East Germans escaping to Austria via Hungary that they would immediately be accorded full rights in West Germany.

Though they had not intended it, the East Germans who managed to escape to the West via Hungary in 1989 gave their compatriots who stayed home the courage of desperation, above all in the southern city of Leipzig, a place of libraries and learning at the heart of an old industrial conurbation that included towns like Halle and Bitterfeld. Discontent had intensified in Leipzig due to the neglect and destruction of the urban infrastructure—buildings were falling apart—as well as decay of the environment. The region's chemical plants operated with minimal use of filters and employed heavily polluting brown coal to heat industry and private residences (this was the GDR's main native energy source).

Yet the growth of crowds in Leipzig in the fall of 1989 also depended on forces that were not deeply historical but instead related to fortuitous happenstance, as well as to the free decisions of a few identifiable human beings. In the fall of 1982, the assistant pastor Günter Johannsen mistakenly scheduled two groups for the same evening in his congregation in Probstheida, a suburb of Leipzig, one consisting of bible students in their sixties, the other of teenagers ("the young congregation"). He took advantage of the mishap to hold an impromptu conversation between the two groups. This was a time of huge fears among Central Europeans over a renewed arms race; in particular, plans to station US and Soviet nuclear missiles on German soil. Many felt helpless. The older group wanted to know why the youngsters seemed insistent on antagonizing authorities by wearing banned peace stickers (with the words "swords into ploughshares"). The younger described the militarization of their world: girls had to learn shooting at paramilitary camps, and boys feared they would not get university admission unless they succumbed to demands—which officials made from the time they were seven years old—that they volunteer three or more years of service in the "people's army."

Out of the fear and sense of helplessness came the idea of holding an evening peace prayer. Johannsen contacted the city's Protestant superintendent (equivalent to a bishop), who contacted Christian Führer, the pastor of St. Nicholas, a lovely gothic church not from Leipzig's enormous train station, and an easy walk to the university as well as world famous concert hall (the Gewandhaus, directed by Kurt Masur). They arranged for the prayer service to take place at St. Nicholas every Monday evening at 5 p.m.[31] And so an institution was born. The numbers were modest at first, but the prayers continued over the years, after Johannsen left, and after the fear of war had waned. Pastor Führer was still holding them in the late summer of 1989, when a new generation began flocking to the church with a different sense of anxiety and helplessness.

We know how many came to the prayers thanks to *Stasi* records: some 800 on September 4; then 1,000 two weeks later; 8,000 on September 25; and 20,000 on October 2. At first two groups of demonstrators could be heard leaving the church: one demanding that they be allowed to emigrate ("We want out!"), but another, which gradually overwhelmed the first, demanding reforms in East Germany ("We are staying here!").[32] Police, plain clothed and uniformed, intervened with billy clubs and dogs, and each time, dozens were arrested. Yet the numbers who attended grew as the mostly young protesters began marching in a demonstration, out to the main boulevard that wraps around the old town, and toward the train station. Tens of thousands were expected for the peace prayer and demonstration on Monday, October 9, 1989, and television audiences across the globe wondered what the police would do. A few months earlier, Chinese leaders had crushed pro-democracy forces in Beijing with little concern for casualties.

Citizens of Leipzig also knew that in East Berlin and Dresden, small groups had taken to the streets two days earlier on the national holiday of the state's founding; they had been beaten brutally. The exception to violence on that October 7 was Plauen, a manufacturing town on the border to Bavaria, where some 15,000 had marched for reforms and dispersed peacefully, thanks to the intervention of that city's Protestant Superintendent.[33] Like many citizens of southern East Germany, Plaueners had suffered poor air quality and provisioning, and they were still electrified, recalling the fourteen trainloads of fellow East German refugees from Prague that had rushed through their town on September 30, southward to freedom. But the October 7 demonstration in Plauen, the largest to that date in East Germany, would not have happened but for the act of one young man, the toolmaker Jörg Schneider. The previous week, he had distributed dozens of leaflets around town calling townspeople to a demonstration for reforms and basic rights. As a result, thousands descended on central Plauen that rainy Saturday afternoon. Authorities did nothing to stop them, because they too had called on citizens to come into town that day: for a celebration of the state's founding. The crowds had no leader, but they morphed into a demonstration when police pummeled a man who had unfurled a banner reading simply "we want reforms!" The huge crowd then marched around the city center and finally gathered at Plauen's city hall, the seat of power, where local party officials were sequestered, not knowing what to expect. Guarding them were police armed with enough ammunition to frustrate any attempt to storm the building.

Fortunately, the superintendent, Thomas Küttler, a man of peace, went through the cordon, spoke with the party secretary, a man he knew well, and elicited a pledge to receive a citizens' delegation in the coming days. He assured the crowd over a megaphone that their demands had been heard, and it dispersed peacefully. Within a few weeks, Plauen had its own round table, as did virtually every East German town.

But before that point was reached, the regime had to be openly tested in its will to use violence to maintain power, and that test occurred on Monday, October 9 in Leipzig. For reasons that are still debated, the regime backed down and let the largest demonstration to date—an estimated 70,000 people—take place without incident.[34] Honecker's heir apparent, the "youth functionary" Egon Krenz (a man famous for a big smile), later took credit, but actually decisive were three other factors: an impromptu intervention of six prominent local figures, including the SED first party secretary as well as Maestro Kurt Masur, who drafted and read a call for peace on the radio; the fact that no commander in the huge assemblage of well-armed troops and police (with ambulences at the ready) was ready to take responsibility for a bloody showdown; and the fact that the demonstration started as a peace prayer. The October 9 demonstration commenced with thousands of East Germans departing a church holding lit candles as a sign of their commitment to nonviolence.

Thanks to cameras that Roland Jahn had smuggled into the GDR, audiences in the East and West could watch on television the tens of thousands who joined them the next day. They had chanted the authorless words, "We are the people!," a phrase more daring and challenging than it sounds. For decades, authorities had claimed—in posters and other propaganda draped all over the country—to represent the people. For example, their social policies were "all for the good of the people!" Here on the streets of Leipzig, the people were in fact speaking, revealing the regime's claim as a lie. You are not the people—we are.

Without the example of a Soviet leader who sanctioned thoughts of radical change, and circumstances that desperately needed change, the demonstrations in Plauen or Leipzig would not have happened. But they also would not have happened without the courage of thousands of anonymous citizens who wanted change and believed that it would come that day or never. They marched and chanted, knowing that the police and militia might fire. After this point, the police and military seemed defanged, their ability to intimidate broken, the regime's claim to incorporate the will of a "socialist community of human beings" an obvious fiction. Within a week, more than 300,000 came for the Monday demonstration in Leipzig, and they were joined by hundreds of thousands in towns across the GDR, men, women, and children, hands often raised as a sign of peace. A little more than a week later, the leadership of mostly eighty-year-olds submitted its resignation.

In their banners and chants, the demonstrators used an eloquent German word to tell what they had come to detest in the state socialist welfare state:

FIGURE 25.2. Protesters in Leipzig (October 1989). *Source*: Bundesarchiv, B 145 Bild-00014228.

FIGURE 25.3. Monday demonstration, Leipzig (October 1989). *Source*: Friedrich Gahlbeck (photographer), Bundesarchiv, Bild 183-1989-1023-022 / CC-BY-SA 3.0.

having been treated like children. But they were "mündig," adults (literally, "people with mouths," that is, voices). One banner mocked Honecker's successor Egon Krenz, the man of the irrepressible grin, placing him in a crib above the inscription: "What big teeth you have, Grandma."

As in Hungary and Poland, organizations emerged to represent interests. Best known was the New Forum, founded by Berlin-based dissidents, but then established in regional branches from South to North, as well as civic organizations like "Democracy Now" and "Democratic Awakening," and a refounded Social Democratic Party. The moribund parties that had cooperated with the Communists, like Liberals and Christian Democrats, also stretched their atrophied limbs after decades of subservience to the SED. The future German federal chancellor Angela Merkel helped form "Democratic Awakening," which first combined with the eastern CDU and was then absorbed into the western CDU led by Helmut Kohl (in early 1990 she told friends: "I don't want anything to do with the CDU!").[35] Though for the time being led by the lackluster Egon Krenz, the Communists also attempted to speak a new language of democracy and rights, and they changed their name to Party of Democratic Socialism. (Krenz was replaced in December by the more independent Dresden party boss Hans Modrow.)

On November 9, a sensational accident intervened that robbed the revolution of its thrilling effervescence. During a free-wheeling press conference, something he was not used to, East German government spokesman Günter Schabowski fielded a question about regulations meant to give East Germans the right to travel freely. When did they go into effect, the reporter asked. With no one to consult, Schabowski said the regulations took force immediately. At this news, crowds of East Berliners gathered at border crossing points to West Berlin. Weeks earlier, groups milling near the Berlin Wall would have been taken into custody within minutes. Now security forces patrolling near the wall were nowhere to be seen. Soon, the crowd threatened to overwhelm a small unit of border troops at the border crossing point on Bornholmerstrasse, and there were no orders from above of any kind. Either they opened fire or they opened the gate to West Berlin. Harald Jäger, the ranking Stasi officer on the scene, decided on the latter, with none of his men encouraging him to do one thing or the other. The Bornholmer crossing was soon freely open in both directions for the first time in over twenty-eight years (other control points soon followed suit). In a sense, this border guard unit, the most ideologically seasoned of all East German state officials, was the first to make the transition to a new Germany. Jäger ducked out of sight to console a comrade who was crying quietly but uncontrollably. What had been the point of their work for the past quarter century? They knew that East Germany was finished.[36]

Within a few weeks, the GDR was flooded with free Western newspapers and slick Western politicians, light-years ahead of the dissident politicians of New Forum when it came to sensing and shaping the mood of a crowd. The chanting at the Leipzig Monday demonstrations took a linguistically simple but historically dramatic shift: instead of "We are the people" the crowds increasingly said "We are one people," meaning: we want unity with West Germany. Some on the left said that nationalism had hijacked the democratic revolution, but East Germans worried about the future. Many came to believe their only hope as a society, amid the ruins of 40 years of Socialism, lay in the West coming and rescuing them, above all with its currency, the deutsche mark (DM). A banner at Leipzig reflected the mood: "Either the DM comes to us, or we go to it." When Helmut Kohl made his first public speech in East Germany, at Dresden in late December, his bulky frame dwarfing the East German leader Modrow, a chant arose from the crowd "Helmut, save us!"

If anything, the numbers of émigrés increased with the passing weeks. At free elections in March 1990, East Germans in effect voted for West German political parties and selected Kohl's Christian Democratic Union, which promised political and economic unification on the speediest timetable. The native New Forum faded into insignificance, and thereafter formed an electoral alliance with the Green Party.

* * *

After the Wall opened in Berlin, attention turned to Czechoslovakia, a neo-Stalinist entity that was suddenly surrounded by democracies—Austria, West Germany, Poland—and states that were becoming democracies—Hungary and East Germany. Even its eastern neighbor, the Soviet Union, had a functioning civil society with an increasingly lively media and talk of elections. Like East German leaders, the Czechoslovak Communists, led by President Gustav Husák and First Secretary Miloš Jakeš, had claimed that Gorbachev's reforms had no relevance for them. In a speech recorded in July 1989 without his knowledge, Jakeš had complained that his country had become "the last pole in the fence."[37]

Similar to its Hungarian counterpart, the Czechoslovak regime based legitimacy on the suppression of an earlier reform movement. Indeed, an entire social order had been built out of degrading all those Czechs and Slovaks who had supported Alexander Dubček and the liberalism of 1968 and were unwilling to renounce their hopes for reform or denounce other reformers. Once eminent journalists and philosophers were now coal stokers and truck drivers. Dubček was a pipe fitter in the Slovak forestry service. But the Prague Spring had been about improving and not subverting socialism, and therefore seemed like a model to Mikhail Gorbachev and his comrades. Before accompanying Gorbachev to Czechoslovakia in March 1987, when asked what separated perestroika and glasnost from the Prague spring, Soviet foreign ministry spokesman Gennady Gerasimov said: "Nineteen years."[38]

Even Czechs whose German was rusty had been able to follow the drama of their northern neighbor via television. Citizens of Prague, however, had been direct witnesses to the unfolding story. By mid-September, the center of town resembled a camping zone of refugee East Germans, with their cars taking up virtually all parking spaces on the city's Left Bank. In early October, they were gone, but besides their tiny two-cylinder, two-stroke Trabants, they had left behind powerful images: of willingness to risk comfort for the sake of living freely. Petr Pithart, a historian and writer who worked as a gardner and night watchman after signing Charter 77, recalled his impressions:

> The distance between freedom and unfreedom could be measured in the streets of Prague's Left Bank. I stood long night hours a few hundred yards from the West German embassy, packed tightly together with other Czechs, saying nothing but watching the spectacle: that's what you do if you want to take freedom for yourself.[39]

The diminutive Czech opposition had managed to launch modest demonstrations in August and October 1988 and January 1989, all of which were suppressed, but they gave a sense of the unrest beneath the surface.[40] In light of evidence from Poland, Hungary, and now the GDR that the Soviet Union would not prop up the Leninist regimes, only a spark was needed in November 1989 to ignite a protest movement. Yet specific individuals had to act, and that took courage and ingenuity. As in East Germany, the first demonstrators took advantage of a recurring event that brought them into the streets legally. In the GDR that was a combination of the anniversary of the state's founding (October 7) and the Leipzig peace prayer (October 9); in Prague it was the yearly commemoration of November 17, 1939, when more than 1,000 Czech students protesting Nazi rule had been sent to concentration camps. Sensing the simmering unrest, party leaders had wanted to postpone the event, and the 15,000 students who assembled for the march that bone-chilling November afternoon, justified the leader's fears. The students chanted for change, sang patriotic songs, and rattled keys at the police—so that the jailers knew that they, too, could open doors. They walked with hands open to show that they bore no arms, and the police responded by brutally dispersing them, using clubs and attack dogs. A rumor spread that one student had been killed.

As in 1967, the spectacle of police injuring defenseless students mobilized tens of thousands of other Czechs to shed the uncertainty and fear that otherwise kept them indoors. Within days, crowds grew to hundreds of thousands, and students as well as professional actors staged strikes and made signs and posters. On November 19, a new civil society group, "Civic Forum," inspired by the German New Forum, was formed at the Činoherní Klub theater, and included dissidents from Charter 77, most prominently the unassuming playwright Václav Havel, who had no experience in public speaking and was embarrassed at the sound of his voice when he addressed the huge crowds.

On November 21, negotiations opened with the government at a "round table," though premier Ladislav Adamec had called Václav Havel a "zero" just weeks before.[41] On November 29, the federal parliament did away with the leading role of the Communist Party in society. Adamec's government resigned, and on December 10, a government with mostly non-Communist ministers formed under the moderate Slovak Communist Marian Čalfa. Some non-Communists were "coopted" into parliament, and on December 29, that body, whose members overwhelmingly owed their posts to sham elections, elected Václav Havel president by a vote of 323 to zero. (Some delegates had recently been calling for Havel's imprisonment).[42] The soon-to-be-defunct "lawmakers" joined diplomats and other dignitaries in congratulating Havel over champagne and snacks at the Hradčany castle. At a mass of thanksgiving across the castle courtyard in the Prague gothic cathedral, the agnostic Havel was seen to bless himself, and Prague's archbishop, once victim of a show trial, wept. So did many dissidents.[43] The Czech philharmonic concluded with Antonín Dvořák's rarely heard Te Deum played to a Native American drumbeat.

Like their East German cousins, Czechoslovakia's revolutionaries brought forth an unexpected eloquence when they rediscovered their voices that fall, and they also revealed the persistence of history; their newsletters and bulletins harked back to Masaryk's language: the most sacred word in the "symbolic system" of the revolutionaries was "humanity."[44] By the end of January, more than 200 new political organizations were legally recognized in Czechoslovakia, and Civic Forum (called "Public Against Violence" in Slovakia) got 46.6 percent of the votes in June elections. (The Communist Party of Czechoslovakia got 13.6 percent).

Like its East German counterpart, the Czechoslovak regime had discovered it lacked the will and conviction to escalate beyond truncheon and tear gas to live ammunition. Remarkably, these two well-armed hardline regimes had accepted oblivion with little protest. Except for the beatings and arrests in the early Leipzig demonstrations, those that followed in East Berlin and Dresden in early October, and the "massacre" (in which no one actually died in Prague) on November 17, the neo-Stalinist dictators departed the scene peacefully if not always gracefully. The transfer of power in Czechoslovakia became known as the Velvet Revolution.

Yet a little to the south, also in former Habsburg lands, this time in Romania, an inflexible dictator was sending militia to quell protest, and the violence he unleashed cost hundreds of lives. The situation there differed from the countries to the north in the absolute separation of the nepotistic regime from society; the extraordinary sacrifices that had been demanded for years— electricity and gas were limited to a few hours a day—and the outrage that resulted, along with revulsion and active hatred. Ceaușescu sought no understanding with groups in the party, let alone beyond the party, and, in contrast to the lands farther north, virtually no opposition groups emerged in Romania's civil society to articulate interests separate from those of the state. The dictator had regularly cleared the terrain of contenders and destroyed all loci of opposition, producing a "remarkable atomization of Romanian society, in which fear and distrust became the currency of human relations."[45] The regime and its supporters had no doubt that they would be held responsible for the injustice and misery when the inevitable accounting came, and they fought with corresponding desperation. By 1989 alienation was countrywide, and when demonstrations erupted in one place, they spread quickly, despite—but then because of—knowledge of the numbers of victims.

Protest flared in former Habsburg Transylvania because it had suffered not only privation but also the destruction of local Hungarian culture, including the bulldozing of villages and the deportation of their inhabitants to Eastern Romania. Anger crystalized in mid-December, when authorities scheduled the ejection of the popular Hungarian Reformed Pastor László Tőkés from the city of Timișoara.[46] His memoirs make clear that the Reformed church's hierarchy was colluding with the state's plans to help erase his independent voice; Tőkés had routinely acted without bothering to get approval from his superiors, for example, in organizing inter-denominational services at his church.

On December 15, protesters who had been camping near his residence marched toward the city center, where they took control of public offices and looted the well-stocked stores reserved for the *Securitate*. The following day, security forces fired on the protesters, but instead of extinguishing the embers of revolution, they caused them to spread, and even more citizens of Timișoara converged on the city center. Many were Hungarian-speakers with access to informative media broadcasts from Hungary and Yugoslavia, and word of their demonstrations was carried eastward by railway workers, troops who had rotated out of the city, and the international media. On December 18, Nicolae Ceaușescu left Romania to visit some of his last supporters, the theocratic rulers of Iran. Kept apprised of the growing unrest though his embassy in Bucharest, Soviet Foreign Minister Shevardnadze said he would welcome Ceaușescu's fall.[47]

On returning on the afternoon of December 20, Ceaușescu declared a state of emergency in Timișoara, claiming that the demonstrators were terrorists who were serving foreign espionage agencies. He then attempted to organize mass rallies in his own favor in Bucharest.[48] Until recently, individuals summoned by the party for mass spectacles could be counted on for abject expressions of adulation; now they demanded Ceaușescu's resignation. On the evening of December 21, the dictator sent in security forces to disperse the crowd and hundreds were injured. The following day, the armed forces defected to the people, and Ceaușescu and his wife Elena fled Bucharest by helicopter. Under still unexplained circumstances, they touched down in the countryside and were apprehended, placed on trial before a military tribunal, and then executed before television cameras on Christmas Eve. But the fighting between security forces and crowds, now supported by the army, lasted until December 27, spreading to other cities. In all, 1,104 Romanians lost their lives in the revolution.[49]

One explanation that has emerged for the haste in doing away with the rulers was concern that they might lead a counterrevolution against an emerging challenger, the "Front of National Salvation" that suddenly announced its existence over state radio on December 22, just as crowds were seizing the Communist Central Committee building and television station in Bucharest. The Front consisted not of leaders of civil society, let alone dissident groups— none existed—but of formerly high-placed Communists, some of whom had been disgraced by Ceaușescu. Prominent was the onetime apparatchik Ion Iliescu, who enjoyed support among top officials of the police and army. In his first speech, Iliescu called Ceaușescu a "man without a heart or soul or common sense, a feudal fanatic, who destroyed the country" and "perpetrated the worst crimes upon the people."[50]

FIGURE 25.4. Demonstrators face militia and tanks, Bucharest (December 1989).
Source: Via Wikimedia Commons.

Even in its time, this revolution seemed bizarre.[51] Beyond the chilling spectacle of the execution of the dictator and his wife before running cameras, still dressed in heavy winter clothing and looking more like ragged senior citizens than all-powerful rulers, were the sudden change of heart of the crowd facing Ceauşescu in Bucharest; the inexplicably sudden defection of the military; and the sudden rise out of nowhere of a de facto countergovernment. Even in Timişoara, pastor Tőkés had registered an uncanny shift in mood, beyond his control or anyone else's, perhaps the work of provocateurs from within the police. Was the revolution orchestrated by Ceauşescu's rivals in the party? Was it in fact staged with demonstrators acting as unwitting actors in someone else's drama? Afterward rumors spread that the secret services of the United States and the Soviet Union were informed about the activities of anti-Ceauşescu forces.

In the years since, no evidence has emerged to support claims of a wider or deeper conspiracy; what seems clear is that formerly highly placed officials wanted Ceauşescu out of the way. But they themselves were surprised and overwhelmed by the revolutionary events of those late fall days and adapted well to the events as they unfolded, posing as saviors to a deeply traumatized society.[52] The revolution had resulted from a mix of planning and spontaneity.

FIGURE 25.5. Demonstrators flee for their lives in Cluj-Napoca (December 1989).
Source: Răzvan Rotta / CC BY 2.5.

Opposition leaders emerged who, inspired by the example of Timişoara, had hoped to turn the Bucharest demonstration against the dictator. Their hopes proved justified. Many thousands arrived on December 21 in central Bucharest because they had been instructed to do so; they had no plans to oppose, much less topple the dictator. Yet once others, especially young people, began demanding the dictator's fall, they joined in, suddenly and decisively, at great personal risk, propelled by years of humiliating privation under the caprice of the "royal" couple and their entourage.[53]

Bulgaria provides the final variation on the theme of neo-Stalinist collapse: the most sudden, superficial, and ill-prepared. The Communist leadership under Todor Zhivkov had a line of succession dating back to the early 1950s, broken by no period of reform.[54] Like Ceauşescu, Zhivkov promoted members of his family to top positions in the party and state hierarchy. His daughter Lyudmila became minister of culture before dying under mysterious circumstances in 1981.

Reminiscent of the Romanian regime of the 1980s, Zhivkov's rule was characterized by an ethnic chauvinism that aroused protest even from Soviet Bloc neighbors. Starting in 1984, the leadership attempted to forcibly assimilate the Turkish minority living in the country's south and northeast. First, authorities made the Muslims' names sound Slavic, but that action elicited protests so strong that tanks had to be summoned to restore "order." It was the largest military operation seen in Bulgaria since the war. Like other ethnicizing states, the regime claimed that this minority consisted not of actual foreigners, but of natives, descendants of Bulgarians who had been forcibly converted to Islam.[55] As in Romania, the Bulgarian leadership had turned to nationalism as a way of distracting from severe economic problems, though it never equaled Ceaușescu's megalomaniacal personal cult.

Unlike Romania, the ideologically rigid dictatorship in Sofia had no history of posing as a heroic defender of local against Soviet interests. Quite the opposite: the imitation of Soviet ways was so slavish that Soviets joked that Bulgaria was a "sixteenth republic." That made the advent of Gorbachev particularly embarrassing. After claiming, like counterparts in East Berlin or Prague, that their country had reformed and did not need perestroika or glasnost, Bulgaria's rulers paid lip service to the new and confusing Soviet line, but as Gorbachev writes, "as for real democratization and glasnost, there was not a whiff of that."[56] To the end, Bulgaria's leaders maintained camps for political prisoners and a huge secret police apparatus.

Bulgarian rulers were not as homicidally repressive as their Romanian counterparts, however, and in early 1989, small opposition groups formed, some seeking to cover themselves with overtly pro-Soviet platforms, like the Discussion Club for the Support of Perestroika and Glasnost or Ecoglasnost. The fate of the oppressed Turks had given the Bulgarian intelligentsia a larger cause to rally around. In early November, the leaders of opposition groups met in Sofia, supporting a program of human rights, and associations sprouted up defending human and religious rights. Of special public concern was the country's environmental devastation: on November 3, Ecoglasnost delivered a petition to parliament signed by 12,000 people, demanding changes in leadership.[57]

Mass demonstrations had broken out in Turkish areas in the spring of 1989; the regime's response was brutal repression, but also an offer to the minority to leave. Contrary to what Zhivkov expected, some 344,000 took up his offer, so many that Turkey had to close its borders on August 22. The fiasco could not be disguised and reached the foreign press, costing Zhivkov support in Moscow. On November 10, his rivals in the party leadership engineered a coup, ousting Zhivkov after first clearing the move with Gorbachev.[58]

Now the Bulgarian streets suddenly filled with demonstrators: as early as November 18, 50,000 protested in the capital, demanding democracy and free elections. What followed—again reminiscent of Romania— was a transformation largely under the control of the old apparatus, suddenly fluent in the language of democracy. A Union of Oppositional forces was founded on December 7, almost a month after Zhivkov's fall (in contrast to the situation in Poland, Hungary, Czechoslovakia, the GDR, and even Romania, where political opposition formed while the dictator still ruled).[59] This presaged later difficulties of the transition to democracy.

The Communists' successor organization, the Bulgarian Socialist Party, won the first free elections in June 1990 (beating its main rival, the Union of Democratic Forces, with 211 seats versus 144 seats in parliament, out of a total of 400 seats).[60] Why did the "post-Communists" do so well? They were helped by strong leftist and pro-Russian traditions, extending deeply into the countryside, as well as by the cohesion of new leadership around former Foreign Minister Petar Mladenov. In contrast to "former" Communists elsewhere, they were not seen as a foreign force. And the opposition was divided, failing to produce a strong leader. Yet because the elections were fair, this was the definitive end to the Communist dictatorship in Bulgaria.[61]

* * *

The transition to something new was just beginning, and that was true in the region as a whole. People speak of the revolutions of 1989, but the process of transformation preceded that year and extended far beyond it, to our present time. The earliest revolutionary event occurred in August 1980, when Poles launched a 10-million-strong protest movement that authorities outlawed but never crushed. When strikes broke out in Poland toward the end of the decade, reform Communists called on Solidarity's leaders to negotiate the "solution" of (partly) free elections. The resonance of that event traveled beyond Poland, however, because the trade union's continued strength showed people across the Soviet Bloc that state socialism was in need of repairs that went beyond and indeed contradicted Leninism.

That is one strand of the story: how some East Europeans showed others the character of their common predicament and how to escape it. Another strand was within the Communist parties themselves, when liberals—most importantly, Mikhail Gorbachev but also Hungarian and Polish socialists—discussed and prepared for change, for example, through reforms of legal codes. Without Gorbachev, the Communist system could have continued, and perhaps transformed into something different. Reformers were absent in the GDR, Czechoslovakia, Bulgaria, and Romania, which is why the events of 1989 appeared more explosive (and revolutionary) in these places than in Hungary and

Poland. One author described the transition in Hungary as a "negotiated revolution."[62]

The "structural" argument that favored Gorbachev's reform program was economic; all the East European states registered deepening debt and thus growing dependence on banks, with no end in sight. In the 1980s, Poland was struggling simply to pay interest on its debt. The one state that opposed the reliance on Western credit, Romania, which decided in 1982 to pay all foreign debt, maneuvered itself into a position that was reminiscent of Russia in 1917: the question was not whether there would be an explosion but when. The chain-reaction character of the revolutions of 1989 ensured that when the explosion ignited in Timişoara, the subsequent denouement took place within a "discourse" of democracy, though in fact only Communists had changed places with each other.[63] An actual transition to democratic rule had to wait until later in the following decade.

Thus, when writing about chain reactions, or "avalanches" of revolution that crossed borders in 1988 and 1989, from small to huge (more like icebergs falling into the sea than a collapse of part of a glacier), historians do well to keep in mind that no one knew about the extent of change at the time. Perhaps that is because actors—the Polish dissidents and the Hungarian socialist reformers—could not discern what we now see clearly: the international dimensions of the phenomenon. The first people to make out the larger dynamic were the Czechs. After the East German trains left in early October, and the Berlin Wall fell in early November, Prague, with foreign camera crews on the scene, itself became the set for revolution, a very sudden one, where the major questions were posed and seemed to be answered in a week and a half.

There is a third level to the transnational agitation and ferment: the role of the West in the East, beginning with the work of US consular officials promoting dissenters as well as reform Communists in the 1980s, but continuing in the careful monitoring of political change in the 1990s. Next to Poland, Hungary was the front-runner. The émigré philanthropist George Soros had legally moved his Open Society Foundation to Hungary in the early 1980s, cooperating with the Hungarian Academy of Sciences, and offered technical equipment (such as copiers), stipends, and contacts with Western civil society organizations.[64] Even before Communism's collapse, Hungary was thus "networked" with pro-democracy nongovernmental organizations (NGOs). The later fall of authoritarian leaders in Slovakia and Bulgaria would be directly tied to the work of NGOs active in those counries, as well as officials of the European Union.

The region's response to a growing debt crisis, and the pressures of Western creditors, also had echoes of a deeper past. The last time peoples had mobilized en masse for freedom across Europe's borders was the spring of 1848.[65] That crisis had been preceded by a European-wide series of bad harvests, economic downturn, democratic agitation, and thus a political and intellectual ferment that went across the map. Events in France gave a signal that an opportunity had come for common aspirations to be fulfilled; and as soon as word could travel to Naples, Mannheim, or Bucharest, students, workers, and other urban revolutionaries responded. The enthusiasm was relatively short lived, as the old regime in fact was not vanquished but began reasserting itself from the summer of 1848 in northern Italy and Prague, and the revolution was crushed during the following year.

If 1848 was an attempt of urban classes to throw off the shackles of feudalism, 1989 was the effort of entire societies to shake off a modernization that came to seem counterproductive and inappropriate; from the late 1970s, the region was falling behind economically, as we know now inexorably, and outside of East Germany and the Soviet Union, even the party bureaucracy had long since abandoned commitment based on belief.

The year 1989 seemed to offer a similar script to 1848 but had a happier outcome. There was also a parallel to the Habsburg dilemma of a decade later, of the early 1860s, when perennial financial woes had forced constitutional reform on the monarchy, so that it could satisfy lenders in London and Paris. In a similar way, Polish and Hungarian governments ascended to freedom in 1990 with the immediate challenge of putting their countries back on sound financial footings to prevent their falling out of the international system of exchange. But the hyperinflation that Poland witnessed in early 1990 was a distinctly twentieth-century phenomenon, beyond anything Habsburg officials could have imagined or dealt with.

CHAPTER 26

Eastern Europe Explodes: The Wars of Yugoslav Succession

In 1989, the populations of Eastern Europe stirred to new political life. In June, millions of Poles and hundreds of thousands of Hungarians manifested their desire to live under different kinds of regimes, the former by casting votes against Communists, the latter by attending the public reburial of a slain leader. In both places, citizens were forming new political parties, newspapers, associations, and businesses. In the GDR and Czechoslovakia, much smaller—but in retrospect, revolutionary—groups were organizing independently of the state, for example in initiatives to have official elections retallied.

But easily the most boisterous crowds of 1989 were found in Yugoslavia. On June 28, more than a million Serbs descended Kosovo Polje—Kosovo's field of blackbirds, site of the 1389 battle—in the greatest mass spectacle seen in the socialist era, and perhaps at any time in Yugoslav history. In a sense, they were also demonstrating for an end to the current regime, but oddly, their hero was the leader of the Communist Party, Slobodan Milošević, a former banker and now a nationalist demagogue. They were manifesting the ostensible rights of the Serb nation to Kosovo. Thus, at a time when much of the region was moving toward peaceful reintegration with the West, forces were gathering in Yugoslavia—in Serbia, but also in Croatia and Slovenia—to drive apart a multinational state in the name of ethnic nationalism.

International media were too preoccupied with the decline of Communism farther north to take note of this very different kind of story. That was in part because it seemed very similar: what made Milošević possible, and nationalist politics elsewhere as well, was also the mobilization of civil society as an old Marxist-Leninist ideology lost its power to stir commitment. If Milošević dominated national politics in Serbia (and by extension, Montenegro, Slovenia, Bosnia, and Croatia), dozens of new civil society organizations were emerging across Yugoslavia by late 1989. But the "people" the new organizations claimed to represent—echoing the later East German chant "we are *one* people!"—was an ethnic entity. In the spring of 1991, Slovenes and Croats voted to leave the

Yugoslav Federation, and the Federation's response was violence: tanks, heavy artillery, and gunboats dispatched by Serb strongman Milošević to force compliance. By October 1991, crimes not seen in Europe for decades had become commonplace, and a new term entered popular usage to describe them: ethnic cleansing.

One author of a recent history of Europe has claimed that the forces that shook and destroyed Yugoslavia were of recent origin. Serb nationalism, he writes, emerged in "the late 1960s."[1] That is not quite right. Widespread beliefs among Serbs of a common destiny, of the inadmissibility of injuries done to Serbia, extend deep into the nineteenth century. These beliefs were a latent force, ready to be summoned by politicians pursuing their often narrow, personal interests. However, it is true that the 1960s witnessed a transformation in the quality of nationalist grievance, by no means limited to Serbia, but including the republics of Croatia and Slovenia.

In other words, the breakup of Yugoslavia cannot be explained by looking exclusively at one place, one leader, or one decade. The causes lie deeper and are more complex, going back generations, most immediately to the early 1980s, but more fundamentally, the 1960s, and beyond that, to repressed memories of earlier conflicts. The tragedy of Yugoslavia, as is true of the rest of the Soviet Bloc, was the tragedy of stalled, failed reform: first in the 1960s, and again in the 1980s.

Why the crisis of the 1980s produced a "nationalist" response in Yugoslavia has to do in part with the continued ethnic complexity of Yugoslavia, contrasting to the largely mono-ethnic states of Northeastern Central Europe. In Czechoslovakia, the two major ethnic groups were separated by a mutually recognized border, and as we see in Chapter 27, could be easily if not neatly divided. In Yugoslavia, by contrast, the major ethnic group of Serbs lived in large communities outside the Republic of Serbia. Therefore, nationalist politicians had opportunities to form a mass movement by stoking widely sensed national grievances that had been aggravated by years of grave economic uncertainty. Claims of genocide of Serbs in Kosovo had emerged before Slobodan Milošević came to power. Because the rise of this leader coincided with the dissolution of decades-old Europe-wide security structures, when the conflict broke out, it was not clear who was responsible for stopping it. Gorbachev had spoken of a common European home, but the Warsaw Pact was defunct by 1990, and NATO's purpose was unclear. The European Union had no military arm.

The horrific irony was that, Yugoslavia, the East European state that seemed most progressive and oriented toward the world up to 1989, soon became a battleground for what seemed atavistic forms of political struggle, where artillery crews began taking aim at modern urban areas, destroying the work of generations, and snipers began picking off civilians of "foreign" ethnicity. In the end, no side emerged victorious from this struggle, which threw all of Yugoslav regions backward economically. The question is: how was it possible?

* * *

The most proximate and evident causes were economic. In the mid-1960s, after years of floating atop generous provisions of Western aid, the Yugoslav economy slowed down and faced pressures to reform. That involved, as it did in Hungary, decentralization, that is, taking decision making out of the hands of central authorities who knew little of the needs and capacities of the tens of thousands of factories and farms at the "grass roots" level. The major obstacle to reform was Interior Minister Aleksandar Ranković, an original member of the Partisan leadership, thought to be next in line to succeed Josip Broz Tito. In 1966, Tito took advantage of a sensational discovery to purge Ranković: listening devices planted by Ranković's police in Tito's bedroom. On the afternoon of July 1, 1966, state radio interrupted normal broadcasts to tell Yugoslavs that Ranković had been dismissed from all his positions in party and state. The secret police had become a "state within a state." Was that not, Tito asked members of the Central Committee summoned to his island retreat at Brioni, reminiscent of Stalinism?

But Ranković was not just a policeman. He was a Serb, reputed to have stood up for Serb interests, and his removal was seen as a blow to the Serbian position in Yugoslavia. (When he died in 1983, long out of public view and expelled from the party, tens of thousands attended the funeral in Belgrade, though it had not been announced.)[2] Now younger cadres discerned new possibilities for advance, and major reform initiatives emerged in Serbia and Croatia, similar to those in the Soviet Bloc. In contrast to Hungary, however, the devolution of political and economic power in Yugoslavia would benefit explicitly ethnic entities, because the six republics had an ethnic character, even if that fact was never made clear in law (republics were considered coterminous with "peoples," but the meaning of peoples was not clarified).[3] If the powers of the Federation decreased, the republics would become proto-states.

The reform movement was strongest in Croatia, where the drive for economic liberalization became inseparable from perceived economic discrimination. Croatia took in the greatest amount of hard currency but had to remit most of it to Belgrade. Other republics felt that this was a geographic accident: Croatia attracted tourists because of its stunning coastline, and that had little to do with the hard work or other merits of its citizens. Yet Croats took this siphoning off of "their" treasure as if it were a personal affront: once again, many saw national and ethnic grievances as if they concerned their own families. As in the 1920s, amid growing nationalist grievances, awareness was lost among Croats of Yugoslavia's role of providing peace on multiethnic territory, and of protecting Croat national existence from its neighbors' irredentism. Still, economic data spoke a clear language: Yugoslavia's foreign trade and financial capital were concentrated in Belgrade, and elites there used their positions in banks and ministries to secure Serbia's preeminence in the federation by building up its economy.[4]

The Croat reform movement is known as the Croatian Spring (1970–1971), but reform impulses went beyond Croatia, animating a younger generation of reform Communists, "liberals," and "technocrats" (that is, problem-solvers) in Slovenia and Serbia as well.[5] In Croatia, the best-known figures were Miko Tripalo and Savka Dabčević-Kučar; and in Serbia, Latinka Perović and Marko Nikezić. Tripalo and Perović were professors of law, Dabčević-Kučar a professor of economics (who wrote a doctorate on John Maynard Keynes), and Nikezić a high diplomat.[6] All were a generation younger than Tito, had entered the Partisans in their youth, accepted the logic of anti-unitarianism, and favored cooperation rather than confrontation with other republics. None was considered "nationalist," but all were modernizers, popular for their youth and vigor, who could not ignore the (centrifugal) sentiments of the regions they represented—Croatia and Serbia—nor powerful (centripetal) federal institutions, like the army and the Yugoslav League of Communists. All had to pay special attention to maintain the favor of Marshall Tito, who considered it a personal mission to maintain balance and unity.

In the more liberal atmosphere after Ranković's death, grievances against central rule took on national colors. The weekly publication of the Croat cultural institution, *Matica Hrvatska*—which dated from 1842, in a sense always ready to voice national perspectives—now printed startling revelations in a mass circulation of some 100,000, for example, that 56.5 percent of the police in the Croat capital Zagreb were Serbs;[7] or that police, army, and secret police in Croatia were two-thirds Serb; or that within Croatia, Serbs held 40 percent of the posts (though they constituted only 14 percent of the population). And the Croat position in the Yugoslav state was supposedly declining: in 1918, Croats had made up 28 percent of the population, yet in 1970, only 21 percent.[8] A

FIGURE 26.1. Savka Dabčević-Kučar speaking in Zagreb (1971). *Source*: www.croatia.eu; http://croatia.eu/article.php?lang=1&id=23.

Serbo-Croat dictionary had appeared in 1967 that, according to Croat intellectuals, systematically favored the Serb variants over Croat ones in what was supposed to be a common language. Croatian writers issued a statement expressing concern over the imposition on Croats of a Serbian literary language and the weakening of Croats as a nation. After Croat scholars produced their own Croatian orthography as a means of cultural self-defense, Serbian linguists published an open letter in Belgrade expressing concern for "unprotected" Serbs in Croatia.[9]

By 1969/1970, a "mass movement" had emerged in Croatia, which the reformist leaders neither led nor condemned. Political rallies featured the waving of the Croat checkerboard flag (not seen since World War II) and the singing of nationalist songs. This opened opportunities for opponents of reform: soon the secret police were dropping hints that Croat reformers had contacts with the exiled Ustasha, and some of these insinuations made their way into the press in Serbia.

Matters escalated in the fall of 1971. After a surge on economic, cultural, and political "fronts," the Croat Central Committee of League of Communists demanded control of the republic's foreign currency reserves, and some 30,000 Croatian students went on strike in solidarity. They wanted Dabčević-Kučar to become more assertive; she begged them to return to their classes. She had lost control. Student demonstrations verged on riots, and the "mass movement" was insisting on a Croatian national state, a separate army, and a Croat seat at the United Nations. All of that raised the question of the rights of the Serb population living on Croat territory, in a would-be Croatian national state.[10]

As a Marxist, Tito, previously a strong supporter of Dabčević-Kučar, became alarmed by reports coming in from Croatia. The resurgent nationalism there seemed a phenomenon beyond reason and control. Making matters more dire, Leonid Brezhnev, who had just dealt with the Prague Spring, unnerved Tito by offering fraternal assistance in case he was unable to restore order by putting an end to the Croatian Spring. In December 1971, Tito summoned Croat leaders to his hunting lodge at Karadjordjevo in Vojvodina and demanded their resignations. A police crackdown resulted in hundreds of arrests; more than 1,000 were purged from the Communist Party, and the Matica was shut down as a supposed center of counterrevolution. The following fall, to achieve "balance," Tito purged liberals from the Serb, Macedonian, and Slovene party leaderships as well. The implicit message was that openness and tolerance— what Gorbachev later called glasnost—had opened the doors to nationalist demands that the state could not withstand. Tito demanded a return to firm party discipline and an end to the "anarcho-liberalism" of the younger functionaries. In all, some 12,000 leading personalities in political, economic, and cultural life were swept from their posts and replaced by "mediocre and practically unknown careerists," through what the Slovene historian Jože Pirjevec calls a "tidal wave of primitivism."[11]

In effect, Tito drove local nationalisms underground and made regional interests unspeakable and illegitimate. When they reemerged in the 1980s, they were no longer liberal. The legacy of the suppressed reforms was also burdensome: Serbs feared that reform and liberalization in Croatia would signal the return of the Ustasha and its crimes; and Croats resented the Serb establishment, whom they felt frustrated reform (though Tito was not a Serb). An optimist might say that a chance was squandered—a last chance, as it emerged— for Serb and Croat elites to negotiate differences under relatively open conditions, not facing the severe pressures of later times, and with Tito to provide stability. A pessimist would say the Croatian Spring showed the problems of Yugoslavia to be intractable once the country opened to liberalization and decentralization. Serb liberals had opposed the Croat demands for greater autonomy not out of chauvinism, but precisely because they were moderates, and knew that the specter of Croat nationalism would weaken their own struggle against Great Serb nationalism. Tito himself wanted to maintain balance, but he was vilified (without his name being mentioned) by those who were purged—like the important Serb author Dobrica Ćosić—as being a "Stalinist" and a "nihilist," lacking any moral compass.[12] Not surprisingly, intellectuals like Ćosić would form the crest of the nationalist wave that rose in Serbia after Tito's death in 1980.

In the meantime, Tito himself presided over a document that would energize that postmortem crisis: the 1974 constitution, the world's longest, and perhaps most complicated. It was not a return to centralized control in Belgrade, a sin known as "unitarism," but by attempting to balance center and regions while reasserting the leading role of the party, the document strengthened the role of the party in the republics and provinces. Local party bosses could rule in their own fiefdoms, unchecked by the center. Another aspect of compromise was to raise the status of Kosovo and Vojvodina in Serbia; making them quasi-republics, with their own parliaments, national banks, and police forces. Locals—in Kosovo that meant Albanians—controlled the regional party apparatus.[13] The result was that Serbs, more than 40 percent of the Yugoslav population, had nominal control in only one of its eight units. The Serb philosopher Mihailo Đurić, an expert on Nietzsche, said that this policy not only split the Serb nation into four separate states—the republics of Serbia, Montenegro, Bosnia-Herzegovina, and Croatia—but also had carved out two effectively separate states within Serbia itself.[14]

The 1974 constitution created the worst of both worlds: continued party control plus an unstable decentralization. Power devolved to Communist functionaries who were loyal to Tito in the republics, but there was no resolution of basic economic problems.

After Tito's death in May 1980, central power resided in a collective presidency that rotated each year to a different representative of the republics. Therefore, Yugoslavia had no leader, and coherent rule became impossible. To make matters worse, each republic had veto power within the federation. In March 1981, Albanian students in Kosovo, the country's poorest region, began demonstrating for better conditions. They often had to stand for hours to get a meal in the cafeteria. Soon the protests turned nationalist, with demands that Kosovo become a full-fledged republic. There were violent clashes between students and police, and the number of deaths was given at fifty-seven, though the actual figure was much higher. But the situation was not pacified, and demands escalated. Soon students were calling for unity with Albania, shouting "We are Albanians, not Yugoslavs!" Their actions call to mind the 1930s, when Germans in Bohemia overwhelmingly opted to leave the most tolerant state in Central Europe for the most repressive. These students were asking to leave the most liberal and tolerant Communist state on earth for the most doctrinaire and rigid Communist state on earth.[15]

But the Kosovar perception was of ethnic discrimination, not so different from that of Croatians in the late 1960s. In this case, the perception was fueled not by loss of status but by simple misery, keenly sensed by students who were the first generation not only to attain literacy but also higher education. (In 1981, Kosovo had the highest ratios of both students and of illiterates in Yugoslavia.)[16] Kosovo's low standard of living had worsened relative to the rest of the country from the 1950s to the 1980s; the province also featured the country's highest unemployment, and that rate was strongest among ethnic Albanians (while unemployment rose among Albanians, it fell among Serbs).[17]

The perception of discrimination was not new. In the interwar years, the Yugoslav state had refused to recognize the presence of non-Serbs in Kosovo, so that in the more tolerant conditions of postwar Yugoslavia, teachers had to be imported from Albania (in 1940, there were 252 schools in Kosovo; all were Serb-language).[18] Though Albanian was no longer suppressed, and much money was transferred to support development, the Yugoslav state did not regard Kosovars as loyal. Through the 1950s, the mostly Serb police regularly searched Kosovar villages for weapons.

Nothing the Serb administration did could halt the decline of the Serb position in Kosovo, however. The percentage of Albanians in the province increased from 48 percent in 1899 to 77 percent in 1981.[19] The number of Serbs was 264,604 in 1961 but shrank to 215,346 by 1991, a decline from 23.6 to 13.2 percent. At the same time, the Albanian population grew from 67.1 to 77.42 percent, propelled by the highest birth rate in Europe (29 per 1,000 in the late 1980s) as well as the flight of skilled Serbs to better jobs farther north. And as in a colonial situation, those Serbs who remained were overrepresented in senior positions in the professions, especially technology, medicine, and law.[20]

But Serbs felt anything but privileged. Kosovo is vital to the Serb national imagination, an ancient heartland (known as old Serbia) and site of the 1389 battle that is central to Serb historical mythology, yet reports circulated that Kosovo Serbs were being driven to extinction. In the mid-1980s, as inflation hit 1,000 percent, many Serbs (both in but especially beyond Kosovo) were willing to see malignant intent behind the economic and demographic patterns. Supposedly, Albanians victimized Serbs while police stood by, for example, in 1985, when a Serb farmer wound up in an emergency room with a broken bottle lodged in his anus. The Serb side claimed he was assaulted by two masked Albanians, engaging in a ritual method of humiliating Christians (supposedly a

"Muslim" act of sodomy to drive Serbs from the land); the Albanian side said the farmer had suffered an accident while engaging in self-gratification. Reports multiplied of rape and other acts of violence, and soon the word "genocide" was circulating in Belgrade to describe the fate of Serbs in Kosovo.

That word appeared in a "memorandum" released in 1986 by leading Serb intellectuals—including reform Communists (such as Dobrica Ćosić) and again showing the power of the national to overwhelm and smother other kinds of commitments. They wrote of "savage terror" employed by "privileged Albanian bashibazouks" before World War I to force some 150,000 Serbs from hearth and home. Such pressures had returned and intensified after World War II, the authors alleged, contrary to the facts, when "upwards of 200,000 Serbs were forced to leave." Serbia was officially a "state" within Yugoslavia, but that state was unable to "put a stop to the genocide in Kosovo and halt the exodus of Serbs from their ancestral homes." Serbia needed to become fully Serb to permit Serbs to defend themselves from "discrimination on ethnic grounds." The economic crisis was part of the problem. The economy of Serbia "has been setting aside about half its net capital savings for the underdeveloped regions, as a result of which it has been dragged down to the level of the economies of the underdeveloped republics."[21]

Such nationalist grievances had been taboo in the postwar years among the political elite, yet remarkably, a prominent Serb Communist emerged who not only refused to condemn them but made them his personal cause. This was the obscure bureaucrat Slobodan Milošević, known for prowess as a banker and as a protégé of Serb Party President Ivan Stambolić. Milošević had no previous attachment to the national cause, but at an event in April 1987, he discerned the usefulness of nationalism to aid his quest for power. Stambolić sent him to Kosovo to hear the complaints of local Serbs at the site of the 1389 battle at Kosovo Polje. While he was listening to angry speeches of the aggrieved locals in a local meeting hall, fighting broke out outside, and police responded with batons. (We now know the fight was provoked by nationalists from Serbia.) Milošević left the meeting and uttered words on which his political fortune would come to rest: "No one should dare to beat you!" The phrase was played repeatedly on Serb television, and Milošević soon became a folk hero, reputed to be the rare honest politician willing to speak the truth, no matter how politically incorrect. In December, he ousted a surprised Ivan Stambolić from the presidency.

Building on models of "people power" from the Philippines, Milošević assembled mass rallies—called "meetings of truth"—across Serbia and

Montenegro, with attendees bussed in to vent their rage against the "unresponsive" Communist bureaucracy. Soon he had taken control of the party leaderships in Vojvodina and Montenegro. In November 1988, Milošević addressed the Kosovo problem at a rally of more than 350,000 in downtown Belgrade, announcing "every nation has a love which eternally warms its heart. For Serbia it is Kosovo. That is why Kosovo will remain in Serbia."[22] The following spring, he put an end to the autonomy of Kosovo by changing the constitution of Serbia and on June 28 gathered more than 1 million supporters at Kosovo Polje for the six-hundredth anniversary of Serbia's mythic struggle for the heavenly kingdom.

This was the time when civic rights movements in other Eastern European states were turfing out Communists and proceeding toward democratic pluralism. Yet in Yugoslavia, a resurgent Communist-nationalist strongman was asserting control in four of the country's eight de facto republics. That unleashed urgent worries in Slovenia and Croatia of being overwhelmed in a Serb-dominated state. In the former, a multiparty system had emerged in 1988, and by February 1989, there were ten political organizations. Following Milošević's lead, the Slovenes changed their constitution to make Slovenia an "independent and sovereign state." The leadership claimed it wanted to stay in Yugoslavia but renegotiate the state's form. It should no longer be dominated by the League of Communists but be constituted voluntarily by democratically legitimated member states.

But what exactly would the borders of those states be? The four constitutions of socialist Yugoslavia had notoriously confused the categories of "republics" and of "peoples," assigning rights of secession to both.[23] Yet everyone knew that the Serb "people" was not delimited by the boundaries of Serbia: large communities of Serbs lived in Croatia and Bosnia-Herzegovina as well. Slovenia held a referendum in May 1990, producing a consensus for leaving the Yugoslav federation. That separation would prove relatively easy; after some skirmishes, the Yugoslav army withdrew. Croatia, however, was a different matter.

There democratization had opened roads to nationalist demagoguery, strongest in the Croatian Democratic Union (HDZ), led by Dr. Franjo Tudjman, a professional historian. Like Milošević, he had a career in the Communist movement, having joined the Partisans in 1941 and stayed in the military after the war, becoming the youngest general in the Yugoslav army by 1960. Yet he had been an outright nationalist for considerably longer than his Serb counterpart.

Living in Belgrade from 1946, Tudjman felt humiliated by Serb and Montenegrin officers who sneered at Croatia's contributions to the Partisan struggle. In 1961, he requested release from the military and became director of the Institute for the History of the Workers Movement in Zagreb, a position he used to promote Croatian views of the past. For example, he revised downward the official atrocity figures in the Independent State of Croatia. His support for the Croatian Spring was so avid that he lost his director's post and served a prison sentence in 1971 for nationalist activities (he was arrested a second time in 1981 for giving an interview to a Swedish journalist).[24]

In June 1989, with Yugoslavia coming apart, he formed his HDZ and soon began translating his ideas about history into politics. Just before the April 1990 parliamentary elections, he said that the wartime Ustasha regime of Ante Pavelić was the "expression of the historical aspirations of the Croatian nation for an independent state."[25] Once in office, Tudjman's team prepared a draft constitution calling the state of Croatia the "sovereign state of the Croatian nation." The actual constitution passed later that year demoted Serbs from constituent nation to "national minority."[26] What exactly that meant was unclear.

These facts played into the hands of the Serb nationalist leaders of the eastern areas of Croatia along the borders to Bosnia, the former Habsburg Military Frontier district—called the "Krajina," in Serbo-Croatian—with dense settlements of Orthodox Serbs, whose ancestors had settled there centuries earlier. The atrocities perpetrated against Serbs in these areas under the last "independent" Croatian regime were horrific, but now the old crimes were magnified and associated with current Croatian leaders, who had unwisely replaced the Yugoslav flag with the Croatian checkerboard flag that was associated with the Ustashas. Croatia's leaders were arming with help of Croatian émigrés, some of whom had dark pasts.[27] The majority of Croatia's Serbs—about 12 percent of the overall population—favored some kind of compromise,[28] but ultimately it was the most radical nationalists among them who secured power, as well as support from Belgrade and weapons from the stocks of the Yugoslav Federal Army (JNA), which had been left behind by the Serb commander of the Knin Corps, General Ratko Mladić.[29] By the fall of 1990, Serb militias had taken control of the Krajina, expelling Croatian police. Like Tudjman, they claimed to be realizing the desires for democratic self-determination of the local population.

* * *

War came the following year when the Slovenian and Croatian parliaments voted to secede from Yugoslavia. The JNA stormed and seized territory of these republics, claiming it was upholding the country's integrity. The fighting in Slovenia lasted only a few weeks in the summer of 1991, as the population was overwhelmingly Slovene and the state boundaries mostly coincided with ethnic boundaries. After less than two weeks of fighting, a ceasefire was arranged through the European Union, and the JNA evacuated its forces to Croatian territory. The fighting cost eighteen dead Slovenes and forty-four dead Federal troops.[30]

Once in Croatia, JNA commanders helped Serb separatists assert control over areas with heavy Serb concentrations, above all in the Krajina and eastern Slavonia. They forced non-Serbs to flee, often killing local Croat leaders—physicians and lawyers, for instance—to intimidate any holdouts. The term "ethnic cleansing" entered common parlance. Areas that would not surrender were bombed into submission. During a siege lasting eighty-seven days the baroque center of the Slavonian town of Vukovar was reduced to rubble, and the Croatian inhabitants forced to flee. Journalists visiting the city after its fall on November 18 reported that "corpses of people and animals littered the streets. Grisly skeletons of buildings still burned, barely a square inch had escaped damage. Serbian volunteers, wild-eyed, roared down the streets, their pockets full of looted treasures." Atrocities not seen since World War II suddenly became commonplace. For example, some 260 patients at the military hospital in Vukovar were summarily executed.[31] From the Croatian point of view, the defenders of Vukovar were heroes, because they blocked the JNA offensive on Zagreb and areas farther west.

Five days after Vukovar's fall, former US Secretary of State Cyrus Vance, acting as Special Envoy of the Secretary General of the UN, negotiated a ceasefire to be enforced by blue-helmeted troops.[32] It confirmed the hold of Serb nationalists on about one-third of historically Croatian territory. In a controversial move, the European Union—under pressure from a newly united Germany—recognized the independence of Slovenia and Croatia, supposedly to "internationalize" the conflict and make intervention more likely and more effective.[33] Yet this move had the unfortunate effect of isolating multiethnic Bosnia-Herzegovina within the rump Yugoslavia and raised the question of whether and how Muslims and Croats there would live in union with Milošević's Communist-nationalist Serbia.

Bosnian politics had divided ethnically, featuring Croat, Serb, and Muslim parties, and because Muslims were the largest, their candidate, lawyer Alija

Izetbegović, won the parliamentary elections in 1990 and became Bosnian president. Izetbegović had a history of activism in Bosnian politics dating back to the war, when he was a member of the "Young Muslims," and then the division the Germans formed of Muslim men in the 1943 (the SS Handschar Division); that collaboration led to a three-year prison sentence after the war. Unlike most Bosnian Muslims, he was deeply religious and wrote on the challenges of modernization for Muslim society. His "Islamic Declaration" of 1970 earned him another prison sentence—for trying to create a Muslim state—plus the reputation of being an Islamic fundamentalist among Serb nationalists. Like Tudjman, he emerged from the political underground as the Yugoslav political spectrum opened and founded his Muslim political organization in 1990.[34]

In February 1992, two months after Western countries recognized Croatia's independence, Izetbegović called for a referendum on Bosnian independence, and the result appeared to be an overwhelming victory: 99 percent in favor of secession from Yugoslavia. Yet Serbs, who constituted about a third of the population, against 44 percent Muslims, had boycotted, not wanting to become a "national minority" in the new state.[35] On April 5, Izetbegović's government declared independence nevertheless, and almost immediately, Serb militias laid siege to the capital Sarajevo and began violently cleansing as much territory as they could of non-Serb population: by forced expulsions, intimidation, and murder. For example, in April, paramilitaries from Serbia took control of the Northeast Bosnian town of Bijeljina and went about executing non-Serb men and women who fell into their hands when it pleased them. The killers were proud of their work, and the commander even invited the American photojournalist Ron Haviv, who happened to be on hand, to take pictures.

Some survivors were expelled, others sent to camps; men were mistreated, often starved, kept in stalls but treated worse than livestock. Women were systematically raped. Tales of such violence caused Muslims ahead of the fighting—on a front that was speading virtually everywhere—to flee or take up arms. By the fall, Serb forces controlled more than 70 percent of the former Yugoslav republic's territory, and an enormous refugee population had assembled in areas held by the Bosnian government and in Croatia. Fighting continued for more than three years, mostly pitting Serb against Muslim units (sometimes Croats, who made up 17 percent of the population, cooperated with Muslims; sometimes they did not).[36]

In the end, the Bosnian war cost more than 100,000, mostly Muslim, causalities. Why the fighting could not be stopped, and civilians protected, is a question that has haunted the international community since that time. NATO had

FIGURE 26.2. Serb militiaman kicks dying woman in Bijeljina (April 1992).
Source: Ron Haviv/VII/Redux.

FIGURE 26.3. Detainees in the Manjača camp, near Banja Luka (1992). *Source*: Photograph
provided courtesy of the International Criminal Tribunal for the Former Yugoslavia (ICTY).
Via Wikimedia Commons.

been spending billions for decades to maintain peace and security, yet it intervened only after three years of killing and maiming, shown almost nightly on Western television screens. In retrospect, it is hard to identify a point at which the conflict might have been avoided. Events moved forward at a steady speed, constantly putting peacemakers in situations they had not anticipated and for which they possessed no solutions.

Even before fighting broke out, the European Union and the United Nations attempted negotiation; at several times, negotiators worked out a canton-like division of Bosnia, only at the last minute to be frustrated, first by the Bosnian Muslims in February 1992, and then the Bosnian Serbs in April 1993. The canton plans now seem reasonable if imperfect compromises that might have saved lives, but at the time were criticized as "rewarding" ethnic cleansing.[37] The United Nations thought of its mission as keeping peace, but peace keepers could not take sides, even when one side, the Serb side, had launched and was responsible for most of the ethnic cleansing—which has been called "genocide" at postwar trials in the Hague. Had *that* word been applied during the fighting, the United Nations would have been obliged to do more than "keep peace."[38] As it was, UN efforts at keeping peace involved setting up "safe havens" in towns where Muslim civilians had sought shelter, like Srebrenica in eastern Bosnia. But the protection was a fiction. The Serb side used threats of force against the tiny contingents of blue-helmeted UN troops to keep US jets from threatening its own forces that were besieging the "safe havens." In the end, the havens were easily overrun. In the case of Srebrenica, the UN troops stood by and let the conquest happen; subsequently, the captured Muslim males, more than 8,000 in number, were executed in cold blood, many of them hunted from hiding places in forests.[39]

But where did support for genocide come from? Why did thousands of previously law-abiding Bosnians collaborate in running concentration camps where captured men were starved, and women were raped? Not just handfuls but tens of thousands were involved in these crimes. The riddle intensifies when one notes the high degree of acceptance of the Yugoslav state among Yugoslav citizens as late as 1990. That year, only 7 percent said that the country was likely to break up; 62 percent said that Yugoslav affiliation was very important for them. Concerning ethnonational relations at the workplace, 64 percent said they were "good" or "satisfactory." Only 6 percent claimed that they were "bad" or "very bad." Of ethnonational relations in their neighborhoods, 85 percent called them "good" or "satisfactory," and only 12 percent "bad" or "very bad."[40] The overwhelming majority of Yugoslavs were stunned by the violence that descended on them in 1991. This was true even of places that saw the greatest violence, for example, the northwest Bosnian town of Prijedor, where shortly after the Bosnian declaration of independence, the Muslim population was segregated and either killed or deported, usually to the infamous Omarska camp, where prisoners were starved and tortured. But in Prijedor, Muslims and Serbs had lived in peace, with Serbs well represented in local institutions. There was no simmering ethnic resentment among the Serb minority that suddenly "exploded" as the Yugoslav state dissolved. (Note that ethnic Muslims were also a minority.)

What happened was that violence was injected from the outside. On the night of April 29, 1992, some 1,775 well-armed Serbs seized Prijedor in a coup d'état and set up a reign of terror, removing non-Serbs from the police and municipal and factory leadership. Most of the invaders were outsiders, hardened criminals out for plunder and profit. They were led by infamous ringleaders like Arkan (Željko Ražnatović) from central Serbia, and were paid and supplied by the Serb government. Arkan had already overseen murderous takeovers in Croatia in 1991 and Bijeljina in early April. In all these places, the irregulars were supported by formations of the Yugoslav army, similar to the way the Wehrmacht supported the Nazi SS in World War II.

These forces unleashed repeated cycles of violence, much as had been the case after the first Ustasha massacres in World War II. Kinfolk of the victims—sometimes out of rage, sometimes out of desperation, sometimes because they were given no other choice—then joined armed formations of "their" ethnic groups, helped secure territory, and in some cases also perpetrated ethnic cleansing.[41] On all sides, moderates—the majority—were marginalized and vilified as "out of touch" in a time of "national crisis," when one's ethnic group "faced genocide." Vocal peacemakers attracted violence from both sides. When fighting broke out in Croatia in 1991, the Croat police chief of Osijek (Slavonia), Josip Rheil-Kir, attempted to mediate but was gunned down by an extremist of his own ethnicity. The town's moderate vice mayor had her house firebombed (one student later said it was dangerous to be seen talking to her). Before fleeing, she narrowly evaded a sniper's bullet. In Banja Luka, nonextremist Serbs soon disappeared from the town leadership. "No one wanted the coming war," one Serb later recalled, "but if I don't fight, someone from my side [Serb] will kill me, and if my Muslim friends don't fight, other Muslims will kill them." According to former Polish Prime Minister Tadeusz Mazowiecki, who served as UN special reporter, "elected authorities who were moderates and who tried to prevent acts of violence were dismissed or replaced by Serbian extremists."[42]

Thus a small minority dedicated to violence generated paroxysms of suffering, involving many bystanders in their campaigns, much resembling processes known from World War II, where small units of Ustashas, SS, and other outsiders injected violence into communities and made legions of victims into perpetrators, expanding in concentric rings to embrace community after community.

But that is not the whole story. There is also the question of how people came to their knowledge of what was happening to their own ethnic group. The answer is: they relied on disinformation coming from nationalists of their own ethnicity, which tended to fuel desires for revenge and became a main cause of atrocities. With rare exceptions, the national media tended to present distorted news of the conflict and human rights violations. "Consequently," Mazowiecki concluded, "the general public has no access to reliable, objective sources of information."[43]

A new mentality took hold of the region, supplanting that of more peaceful times. It was ethnic, ethnic to the exclusion of more complex levels of self-understanding. Even in Zagreb, the Croatian capital far from the fighting and ethnic cleansing, the journalist Slavenka Drakulić, who had fashioned an identity based on her education, profession, and personal tastes, found the environment transforming, so that only one identity counted. Her claims that she did not care whether she was Croatian were dismissed as non-sensical, indeed surreal; everyone, it seemed, had been "overcome by nationhood." Mainstream newspapers labeled her and four other critical feminists "witches" who were raping Croatia (Drakulić soon took exile in Stockholm).[44]

Drakulić was well traveled and possessed a refined critical sense. Other Yugoslavs accepted what they were told about dangers to their people propagated by authoritative news media, and fell back into habits of thought that were common during previous calamities and wars. Sociologist Anthony Oberschall says they reverted from a "normal" to a "crisis" frame of mind. The latter was grounded in memories going back generations—to the world wars, the 1875 Herzegovinian uprising, and earlier. In these wars, there had been no distinction between civilians and combatants, and no one was spared. Everyone was held responsible for their nationality; atrocities were the rule, and everyone was a potential target for revenge and reprisal.[45] The media of the early 1990s provided constant reinforcement of the crisis mind frame: ethnic cleansing may have been ghastly, but it was a "defensive" measure against resurgent Ustashas, Mujahedeen, Turks, and other enemies threatening the Serb people. In village after village, Serbs claimed that expelled Muslims had prepared "lists" of Serb leaders to be abducted. Asking for evidence was pointless. Everyone "knew" these truths.

Intellectuals were complicit in spreading the lies, even those who had traveled and should have known better. Biljana Plavšić, a professor of biology at Sarajevo University and former director of the Academy of Natural Sciences in Sarajevo, told a moderate newspaper that "rape is the war strategy of Muslims and Croats against Serbs. Islam considers this something normal."[46] Another writer maintained that international capitalism, Islam, and the Vatican had the goal of "replacing the population of Yugoslavia with Muslims from Arab countries."[47] With power over television (Serb-dominated areas of Bosnia could not get stations from Sarajevo) and news media, forces behind such messages were not subject to critical appraisal, and what they said was the only truth available.

Never has a conflict revealed so clearly the ways that ethnicity and nationalism can be fabricated and shaped. The issues at stake were power and territory, and identifiable beneficiaries were willing to use whatever arguments would bolster their positions. Slobodan Milošević cared little for nationalism until it revealed itself as a catapult to power in the Yugoslav state. In areas where violence did not serve the interests of advancing his power, like Serbia proper, Muslims continued living peacefully, in large settlements of the historic Sanjak of Novi Pazar. Similarly, thousands of Croats or Slovenes or Albanians lived without harassment in Serbia throughout the wars.[48]

If preexisting, acute ethnic tensions did not prefigure the conflict that broke out in 1991, to some extent, preexisting social tensions did. In Bosnia, Serbs tended to be rural, less educated, and more traditional, with greater consciousness of age-old divides based on religion and ethnic heritage. Denizens of Sarajevo branded newcomers from villages "Swedes," and despised them for "their rudeness, their crass tongues, their naïve ambition, and their lack of common sense."[49] City populations were more secular, mobile, and mixed, and they were less conscious of ethnicity, featuring more intermarriages and higher percentages of "Yugoslavs."[50] The "Swedes" reciprocated the condescension during the war. The leader of Bosnia's Serbs, Radovan Karadžić, who kept up a murderous siege on the capital during the war, came from a humble "Swede" background and represented that milieu's frustrations and hatreds. The American sociologist Bogdan Denitch spent time with one of the Serb gun crews that was shelling the city from the hills above and was surprised to hear a local barkeeper—an otherwise reasonable person—offer the soldiers fifty German marks for the "privilege" of firing a round into the city. When Denitch reminded him that some of the people down there were Serbs the man said: "anyone down there is not a Serb."

If many Yugoslavs lived by such prejudices, foreign observers, especially those in power, did not reveal notably sharper acumen. In 1992, authoritative reports (for example, of Mazowiecki) told of attempts to "exterminate" Muslims in Bosnia, yet the war raged for three years. Western leaders became victims of their own misconceptions, derived in part from the work of journalists, like Robert D. Kaplan's *Balkan Ghosts*. After reading it in 1993, President Bill Clinton concluded that the hatreds driving the killing were so deeply rooted that no foreign intervention could quell them.[51] "Until these folks get tired of killing each other," he told reporters, "bad things will continue to happen." The reading of Kaplan was a turning point for Clinton, who had wanted to do something but was struggling for clarity between mutually exclusive options. Now an expert had settled matters by justifying inaction. The failings did not stop at party lines. In the Bush administration, the view likewise prevailed that ethnic groups in Bosnia had been killing each other for hundreds of years. As late as July 1995, Lawrence Eagleburger, former secretary of state (charged with US policy in Yugoslavia under Bush), said "they have been killing each other with a certain amount of glee in that part of the world for some time now."[52]

Other rationalizations for nonaction included the lack of a clear US interest and signs that this was a civil war. In remarks to the House Foreign Affairs Committee in May 18, 1993, Secretary of State Warren Christopher spoke of "atrocities by all three of the major parties against each other. The level of hatred is just incredible." That made it different from the best-known case of genocide, namely the Holocaust, he said, because "I have never heard of any genocide by the Jews against the German people."[53]

US defense experts, many formed by service in Vietnam, were unsure of the goals of military action. If NATO bombed from the air, Serbs forces would simply relocate their mobile artillery pieces and fire from new positions. According to Admiral David Jeremiah, vice chairman of the Joint Chiefs, bombing would cause civilian casualties but would not lift the Serb threat. The word "quagmire" kept appearing in records of conversations of the Clinton team.[54] In any case, the United States could not act alone.

Technically, the inaction was inexcusable. According to the 1948 Convention, the United Nations was obliged to "prevent and to punish" the crime of genocide, meaning: "acts committed with intent to destroy in whole or in part a national, ethnical, racial or religious group." That criterion applied to Bosnian Muslims, a point made almost weekly by observers in the press. But which tools were appropriate to prevent the crime under way was not clear. Should not the European Union act? This was, after all, European space. But the European Union had no military arm. NATO's charter did not foresee involvement in what seemed a civil war not directly threatening its members. And the major UN policy of arms embargo starved Bosnian Muslims of weapons, while Serb forces inherited JNA stocks and received reinforcement from Serbia.[55] In May 1993, the United Nations established its seven "safe havens" for besieged populations, which the lightly armed UN blue-helmeted troops then proved unable to defend.[56]

But by 1995, the Serbs were being pushed back by Muslim and Croat forces, secretly armed by the United States in defiance of the UN embargo. The United States filtered weapons through Croatia to the Bosnian government and used Croats as proxies. In early August, a massive Croat army assault brought Croat state control into the Serb-dominated areas of Slavonia and the Krajina, causing some 200,000 Serbs to flee eastward. The United States raised no objections. Secretary of State Christopher suggested the flight "produced a new strategic situation that may be to our advantage," providing a new "basis for a negotiated settlement."[57] Bosnian Muslim and Bosnian Croat forces likewise put pressure on Serb positions in Bosnia and began to gain an advantage.

A turn came in the following month, after Serb gunners, not for the first time, bombed an open market in Sarajevo, leaving dozens dead and wounded. But this time, the attack combined with horror at the mass murder of more than 8,000 Muslim men in the fall of Srebrenica, and finally caused NATO to bomb Bosnian Serb positions from the air. The prospect of losing territory finally inclined the Serb side to relent, and all sides in the conflict met in November at Dayton, Ohio, to resolve the conflict.[58] Still, even after all the dying and the evidently diminishing returns for everyone—a centuries-old Serb presence in Croatia had just been lost—the negotiations came close to failing numerous times and required the concerted flattery and cajoling over three weeks by the US chief negotiator Richard Holbrooke, one of the most forceful, opinionated, effective, intemperate, and flawed diplomats that international politics has ever seen.[59]

The Dayton Accords provided for a relatively small contingent of NATO peace keepers (20,000 ground troops) and the division of Bosnia-Herzegovina into two areas: one Muslim/Croat (the Federation of Bosnia-Herzegovina), the other Serb (the Serb Republic), while maintaining the idea that Bosnia-Herzegovina remained a sovereign state (its independence had been recognized by the international community). The peace has endured, but the two entities have become effectively independent. The return of ethnically cleansed populations to their homes has taken place, but on a limited scale. For example, Banja Luka in the Serb Republic had a population that was 15 percent Croat, 15 percent Muslim, and 55 percent Serb in 1991; in 2006, the figures were 4 percent, 2 percent, and 92 percent, respectively.[60] In part because of continuing fragmentation and large-scale corruption, unemployment in Bosnia-Herzegovina remains high and economic growth low.

The short-term legacy of the Bosnian war was to make the West, above all the United States, less patient with ethnic cleansing. What remained of Yugoslavia was still diverse: it still consisted of multiethnic Kosovo, Macedonia, Montenegro, and Serbia, and it was still dominated by Slobodan Milošević. Kosovar Albanians still clamored for reform and autonomous status, and in 1996 and 1997 staged peaceful manifestations. At the same time, a small rebel force grew among them called the Kosovo Liberation Army. Serb army forces staged pacification operations against the rebels, and on at least two occasions, dozens of women and children were found dead in the aftermath. US secretary of State Madeleine Albright declared that the United States would not tolerate further acts of ethnic cleansing. Herself of Czech background, Albright was determined that neither Bosnia nor Munich would be repeated.[61] Given the record of the Milošević regime in fomenting ethnic cleansing, the concern seemed justified.

In late 1998, Richard Holbrooke forged an agreement with Milošević that permitted the sending of monitors to Kosovo. Following another massacre early the following year, a "Contact Group" (the Western countries plus Russia) summoned representatives of the Kosovars and Serb government to negotiations at Rambouillet in France. The result was to promise the Kosavars financial and cultural autonomy, while keeping Kosovo part of Serbia. With great reluctance, because they wanted full independence, the Kosovars agreed. The Serbs, however, refused. On March 24, 1999, a NATO bombing campaign commenced against Serbia, triggering full-scale ethnic cleansing by Serb forces in Kosovo. An estimated 10,000 Kosovars lost their lives, while some 400,000 fled. In Serbia proper, perhaps 1,000 civilians lost their lives as a result of the bombing. On April 23, a NATO missile hit the headquarters of Serb television, resulting in the deaths of sixteen employees. Richard Holbrooke welcomed news of this event, stating that TV was one of "three key pillars" of the Serb dictator's power.[62]

Milošević seemed to be playing familiar cards, defying the West and attempting to humiliate the powerful, expecting—perhaps "learning" from Hitler's triumph at Munich—to divide weak-willed Western allies. But on June 3, Milošević, recognizing that NATO was committed to a long campaign and that Russia would not support him, backed down and agreed to an international peace plan. The Yugoslav Army would leave Kosovo, and an international force led by NATO (but with non-NATO detachments as well, for example, from Ukraine) would take their place.

Milošević had overstretched one last time. In September 2000, he lost elections in Serbia and, after refusing to step down, was driven from power by street demonstrations led by the student group "Otpor" (resistance), which numbered some 30,000–40,000 activists, organized in 120 branches throughout Serbia. They suffered for their activism. Between May and September 2000, police arrested approximately 1,000 young people, some no older than thirteen. Yet the repression was the convulsive gesture of a dying regime. The fiasco of Milošević's rule was too evident. Serbia's economy had shrunk to about 40 percent of its size a decade earlier, a feat paralleled in the post-Communist world only in Georgia and Moldova.[63] Thanks to Milošević's wars, centuries of Serb presence ended in Croatia, Kosovo was severed, and Montenegrins clamored for separation.[64] Serbia was a pariah nation cut off from Europe. Yet the future held hope. The previous year, the Croatian nationalist strongman Tudjman had died in Zagreb. Both these countries now saw paths opening toward European integration.

Farther north, the quest for "return to Europe" had been the major story in countries of the former Soviet Bloc for the previous decade, but that quest also included the former Yugoslav Republic of Slovenia, which has come to be seen as an exemplary story of transition, featuring rule of law, low budget deficits, and low inflation. But it was the decision of Slovenia's political elites— responding to strong popular sentiment—that triggered the nightmare of the Yugoslav dissolution in 1991. Slovenia had deftly exchanged the protective umbrella of one federation for that of another.

CHAPTER 27

Eastern Europe Joins Europe

Democratization and Shock Therapy

If the story of post-Communist Yugoslavia was one of violent disintegration, the story elsewhere in East Central Europe was mostly of peaceful integration. Since 1989, the former Soviet Bloc countries have joined West European and North Atlantic institutions—political, cultural, economic, and military—and made transitions to pluralistic rule. Both processes are without precedent in the region's history. Yet the word "transition" suggests a journey to a new place without return, and the case of Hungary in recent times has shown that is not possible. When it entered the European Union in 2004, many observers declared the country to be in full transition to democracy. Yet beginning in 2010, a right-wing popularly elected regime under one-time student leader Viktor Orbán has been cementing what he calls "permanent" power, in effect making opposition, and thus democracy, impossible.

But equally unclear is exactly when transitions to democratic pluralism begin. To say the process begins with free elections is misleading. Elections occurred in Croatia in 1991, but the country remained years away from democracy. A transition to free-market economies occurred in Bulgaria and Romania in the late 1990s, but semi-free elections had occurred earlier and formed important preconditions. Transitions to the rule of law got started under reform Communists in Poland and Hungary in the mid-1980s with the drafting of important preparatory legislation for (what was anticipated to be) more pluralist politics. And one strand of transition to free-market practices can be traced to the gray-market activities that coaxed entrepreneurial protoclasses from late socialist Poland and Hungary. People who had surreptitiously imported computers from Western Europe or Asia now openly formed companies and increased volume. Dissident journalists emerged from underground printing presses and began publishing sleek modern newspapers full of color advertisements. Socialist universities produced legions of lawyers over the decades, with professional opportunities limited to low-paying jobs in city administration. Yet after 1989, these cadres profited, as thousands were needed to process the legal documentation of a market economy. They and other young people in urban growth industries in turn created demand for automobiles, houses, and electronics that have stimulated other secondary and service industries.

Before the rise of right-wing populism, political scientists spoke of two waves of democratization in Eastern Europe, the first involving places where native opposition movements took power in and immediately after 1989; and the second, places where native Communists managed to hold power and delay democratization into the late 1990s. Included in the first are Poland, the Czech Republic, Slovenia, and Hungary; in the second, Slovakia, Romania, Bulgaria, Croatia, and Serbia. The latter were "hybrid" regimes, with some characteristics of democracy but falling short of liberal standards.[1] The "second wave" was marked by the fall of authoritarian and illiberal rulers: Vladimir Mečiar in Slovakia (1998), Ion Iliescu in Romania (1996/2004), Zhan Videnov in Bulgaria (1997), Franjo Tudjman in Croatia (1999), and Slobodan Milošević in Serbia (2000).[2] The earlier and later transitions all witnessed increasing political diversity followed by convergence around democracy, the market, and European integration.[3]

To explain the differences between these two regions, some have pointed to underlying "civilizations." Lands closer to the historic West, or former core areas of the Habsburg Empire, tended to adapt the trappings of democracy more quickly. But such generalizing approaches are difficult to attach to specific cases. Nationalism could be as virulent in "Ottoman" Serbia as it was in "Habsburg" Croatia. Perhaps Czechs and Poles shared some deeper Western "civilization," but that can hardly account for what happened in the messy political struggle of 1989 and 1990, or later developments like asset tunneling or violence against Gypsies.[4] It is more accurate to imagine deeper traditions, like a diversified economy, and other structural factors as establishing more and less propitious circumstances for democracy. Some of the historical legacy, like the idea of separation of powers, is quite old, going back to the heritage of western Christianity and traditions of division of powers. Some is supposedly native to the region, for example, the self-rule heritage of rights of the Hungarian or Polish gentries that have left traces in their societies' political cultures.

The more recent transitions to illiberalism in Poland and Hungary show that these traces are not indelible; they are resources rather than fate; in both cases, authoritarian rulers like Orbán or Poland's Jarosław Kaczyński have ignored native traditions of pluralism, rule of law, and separation of powers; they instead harken secretly but effectively to the heritage of the Linz Program of 1882. Similar to the new right of that period, illiberal politicians of the present, above all in

Hungary, have claimed to speak in favor of an ethnic people that they portray, with some justification, as neglected by liberal elites, some in Budapest and Warsaw, and some in Brussels.

In the days before that shift to the far right, until about 2010, observers credited the relative ethnic homogeneity of Hungary, Poland, and the Czech lands as aiding in the consolidation of democracy. Democracy appears to become a viable choice only after questions of membership in the nation and state boundaries are resolved.[5] Yet now we see that even in mostly mono-ethnic societies, unscrupulous politicians, like Czech President Miloš Zeman, can drum up sentiment against a nonexistent foreign threat. Zeman portrays refugees from the Middle East as a serious danger for Czech ethnic hold on Bohemia, though the total number that his country has admitted (as of late 2018) is twelve.

Yet back in the late 1990s, when Zeman was a relatively moderate Social Democrat, what seemed to single out the first-wave "winners," like his country, Poland, and Hungary, was an opposition that could take power and thereby move beyond the Communist era.[6] Size was not crucial. The Czech lands had a tiny opposition, but it was large enough to provide the cadres to lead new political movements and take over state administration. In East Germany, Western politicians entered and essentially took control of existing institutions quickly—with legitimation attained through elections—transforming them to mirror West German counterparts. The states of the GDR then "joined" the Federal Republic of Germany in October 1990 by adopting its constitution. In Poland and Hungary, relatively large civil society movements were soon splitting into political parties. For a time, the Polish public was transfixed by a "war at the top," pitting intellectuals like Michnik against more traditional figures like Wałęsa. In retrospect, this fragmenting of a political spectrum seemed normal.

Constitutional reforms were a basic criterion for initiating a transition to democracy, because they ended the privileges of Communist parties. But in contrast to what happened in Germany, in the rest of the region this process involved revision to existing legal arrangements rather than adoption of new constitutions. Hungary, for instance, reformed elements of its Stalinist-era constitution rather than drafting a new one.[7] Poland did not adopt a new constitution until 1997; before that, lawmakers simply updated the Stalinist constitution of 1952 by, for example, proclaiming the state a "republic" rather than a "people's republic," by saying that power derives from the people (and not only the working people), and by establishing protections for private property (and not simply socialized property).[8]

There were advantages to revising constitutions under less "politicized" and divisive conditions, taking advantage of wide social approval for democratic transformation directly after 1989. Over the decades, however, even the best arrangements have not protected countries from constitutional tinkering by authoritarian and antidemocratic forces, which is the current Hungarian predicament.[9] In Poland, too, there have been discussions on the political right of a need to transcend a supposedly flawed post-Communist Third Republic in a morally regenerated Fourth Republic.[10] Kaczyński's Party of Law and Justice (PiS) has complained that the 1997 constitution had brought about neither a "Catholic state of the Polish people" nor a "strong state of order." During its hold on government between 2005 and 2007, it proposed a new constitution that would be "nation-forming" in the ethnic sense, but also in a populist vein promised that the "reason for the existence of the state is the common welfare of the citizens." Yet the project failed, because it was not able to get two-thirds of the votes in the Sejm.[11]

There would have be no politically stable Polish Third Republic to criticize if a second vital dimension of transition had not succeeded, namely, a transition to a market economy based on the rule of law. Yet because this shift of the early 1990s involved great pain in the short run, it was easier to effect in years when democratic rule was rudimentary and new regimes ruled relatively uncontested by opposition parties. Thus, poorly developed democracy proved a blessing, because more "responsible" governments could carry through reforms without concern for being thrown out of office.[12] Austerity measures were unpopular everywhere in the 1990s, yet no organized resistance emerged. Some 66 percent of the Hungarian population was outraged by an austerity package passed in 1995, for instance, but apart from some student demonstrations, no resistance emerged.[13]

Among the frontrunners—Poland, Hungary, and Czechoslovakia—transitions to a market economy took place in slightly different forms and at different speeds (fastest in Poland) and with different timing (earliest in Poland, later in Hungary and Czechoslovakia). As part of creating a market, the state withdrew from detailed regulation and planning as well as subsidization of the economy and attempted to sell state-owned industries to private investors. To stabilize the monetary system, in all three countries, the currency was pegged to a Western counterpart, and massive loans taken out to protect the currency from speculation. In all three, the transitions caused a drop in economic output and per capita GDP, partly because uncompetitive enterprises were closed. Then, from about 1993, the economies recovered. In each case, the new government teams were taken largely from the opposition movements and involved themselves in differing kinds of de-communization.

The transition in Poland was more radical and jarring than in Hungary or Czechoslovakia and is therefore called "shock therapy"; it allowed virtually no time for adjustment to the sudden withdrawal of state subsidies or to the state's refusal to guarantee prices. Instead, the government permitted goods and services to find their "true value" through floating prices. As unemployment went up and production down, prices rose to new ceilings, each boggling the imagination. Poles of every age, including young children, became adept at multiplying in their heads in this pre-smart phone time the value of goods for sale, soon by 200 times. March 1990 saw price increases of 1,395 percent (on a yearly basis), the greatest in twentieth-century Polish history. With demand seemingly uncontrolled, people bought all they could, fearing even more inflation. From 1988 to 1990, the price of a loaf of bread went from 46 to 2,000 zlotys, and of a kilogram of beef from 560 to 19,431 zlotys. A pair of stockings rose from 626 to 4,837 zlotys; a Polish Fiat from 1.1 million to 20.5 million zlotys. In contrast to previous runs on produce, the shelves kept refilling and adding much more. Yet consumers found it difficult to buy the new products. On an average monthly wage in 1988, people could buy 1,185 loaves of bread or 1,475 liters of gasoline; two years later, the total went down to 341 loaves of bread or 565 liters of gasoline.[14] As these figures indicate, salaries also rose, but not as dramatically as prices; the government also increased pension payments, though, again, not as dramatically.

Poland's production plummeted by 24 percent in 1990 as firms unable to maintain themselves under market pressures closed. The Polish economy began rebounding, however, in 1992 and has not stopped growing since. Inflation dropped steadily from 553 percent in 1990 to 15 percent in 1997, a figure that remained relatively high but not too high for continued economic growth. Unemployment reached 16.4 percent in 1993 and dropped to 10 percent by 1997.[15] By 2005, Poland was able to meet basic criteria for full membership in the European Economic and Monetary Union, measured in limits on the rate of inflation, the government budget deficit, and long-term interest rates, as well as exchange-rate stability.[16]

But in the beginning, when the Catholic dissident and writer Tadeusz Mazowiecki took power in the summer of 1989, this relative success was unimaginable. Poland had a long history of economic woe, and no end to perennial crisis seemed in sight. New and worrying questions emerged. How far would the state retreat? Was culture part of the "marketplace"? Would the state no longer support publication of books and the operation of theaters and symphony orchestras?

The revolutionaries had not anticipated taking power, and they had no immediate answers. They turned to "experts." Now that socialism had failed, the only "ideology" left appeared to be a strict form of liberalism now called "neoliberalism," which provided little guidance beyond the basic idea that markets determined value. But how much should markets be regulated? No one knew. Adam Michnik, now head of Poland's leading newspaper, *Gazeta Wyborcza*, wrote that the masses understood little about economic policy, and the best policy was to forge ahead, so that reforms could not be reversed.[17] Previously unknown economists suddenly rose to prominence. In Poland, Leszek Balcerowicz, professor at the Main School of Planning in Warsaw and a former Communist Party member, now became minister of finance and made the pains of transition seem necessary cure for the ills of socialism.[18] Though the economy's pulse sank to what seemed life-threatening levels, he did not waver, and the transition continued.

In 1991, the previously little-known econometrician Václav Klaus was elected prime minister of the Czech Republic. Unboundedly self-confident and an open admirer of Margaret Thatcher, he scoffed at talk of regulation, and went furthest in translating neoliberalism into a positive politics (more than that, into a way of life).

For all the use of the words "shock," or "transition," or even "revolution," what seemed remarkable to outside observers was how little the changes struck Poles, Czechs, or Hungarians as out of the ordinary. The author Eva Hoffman visited Poland in May 1991, wanting to know how people overturned all their institutional arrangements and dismantled a worldview that had conditioned their lives for decades—even if they had hated it. What she found was people going about business without deeper reflection. "I keep being surprised at the lack of surprise in this room," she noted after dinner with staff of *Gazeta Wyborcza*, "at how much people take this enormous tidal shift in stride, as if it were the most natural thing in the world, rather than the most amazing."[19] She attributed Poles' "stoical sobriety" to an absence of alternatives. The new reality was "normal" and the previous one "absurd," governed by the logic of scarcity and hidden connections, where people bartered for essentials like toilet paper and cotton.

The lack of alternatives became most evident when voters chose alternative parties. In 1993/1994, voters in Poland and Hungary threw out the disciples of neoliberal austerity and replaced them with members of the old Communist parties, now refashioned as Social Democrats. Hungary's got an absolute majority of seats in parliament.[20] In Poland, the Communists turned socialists (known as the Alliance of the Democratic Left, or SLD) teamed with the old peasant party, thus supposedly favoring the social groups hit hardest by transition economics: workers laboring in outmoded large factories and underproductive peasants on their tiny plots.

Yet rather than return to the past, the new leftist governments mildly adjusted the processes of transition—much in contrast to the fears stoked by their liberal opponents. In Poland, the government of Waldemar Pawlak only slightly slowed the pace of privatization. Pawlak, participant of student strikes in 1981 who ran his own farm in the 1980s after getting an engineering degree, represented Poland's revived peasant movement, which allied with the stronger SLD. He evinced a new style, communicating to the public reasons for the social costs of transformation and attempting to generate support through partnership in labor relations.[21] There was more attention now to detail, for example, to whether and how workers could get shares of privatized companies.[22] But the trend was continuity. One liberal, former finance minister Janusz Lewandowski, lauded SLD finance ministers for having "maintained a stable currency, defended private property and contracts, and pursued responsible macroeconomic policies."[23] Lewandowski felt closer to these post-Communist "capitalists" than he did to "defenders of heavy industrial working class and dwarf agricultural holdings" among the non-Communist populists, for example, in the Solidarity trade union.[24]

The return to power of "post-Communists" seemed shocking at the time, something no one would have predicted in 1989, when Communists fell from power in disgrace, saddled with the responsibility for decades of crime and mismanagement and lacking any legitimacy. They went from losing every contested seat in 1989, to forming Poland's first stable government (in coalition) in 1993 (with 20.41 percent of the vote), and then a second in 2001 (with 41.04 percent of the vote).

But in retrospect, the return makes much sense. On one hand, the old Communist parties possessed experienced reform wings. SLD leader Alexander Kwaśniewski or Hungary's prime minister Gyula Horn embodied the transition to pluralism of Communist reformers who had been seriously considering necessary changes in the legal and economic system before 1989. Part of the secret of "smooth" transformation to liberal democracy in those countries was the fact that the transformation had been happening for some years in these parties (this is in contrast to Romania and Bulgaria, which lacked not only strong opposition outside the party but also strong reform wings within).

On the other hand, the post-Communists filled spaces for left-wing politics, attracting and ostensibly representing the poor and underprivileged. Pawlak's peasant party also was a "post-Communist" organization, with cadres inherited from the old regime and an organization that had assented to everything the Communists demanded for more than four decades. From its reconstitution in 1991, Poland's post-Communist SLD focused on voters' concerns and promised to continue reform but with greater competence than the post-Solidarity camp (the period from 1989 to 1993 had seen five separate governments). Poland's voters consistently rated the SLD as the most professional and competent of Polish parties.[25]

Still, regardless whether of left, center, or right, governments showed sensitivity to the social costs of transformation. Those costs, especially unemployment, were steep. While the countrywide picture improved, and the gross domestic product grew, stubborn pockets of high unemployment remained, especially in small towns that had been dependent on single industries. For example, Radom, Olsztyn, and Koszalin were plagued by unemployment that was twice the national average, with young people and women hit hardest. Governments therefore provided unemployment benefits and maintained "work offices" (*urzędy pracy*) that helped workers find jobs and get job training. They provided aid for families with children whose incomes fell beneath certain levels and guaranteed minimum subsistence.[26] Thus "neoliberalism," harsh as it was, did not destroy social welfare, and in some cases, improved it; the governing concept was restructuring and not demolition.

Outcomes remain far from ideal. The Polish health system, a holdover from its poorly performing Communist predecessor, has continued to be plagued with corruption, and physicians as well as nurses often expect special favors for basic care but provide greatly improved services for those who can pay "on the private market." Part of the problem is the chronically low salaries of health-care workers, including physicians in outpatient clinics, whose compensation in the 1990s was lower than that of a hairdresser (as it had been under Communism).[27]

If anything, Hungary's socialists went further than their liberal predecessors in pushing austerity. Though portraying themselves as advocates of the poor, in 1995, the government under former Communist Gyula Horn—who had opened Hungary's border in September 1989—cut child-care, introduced tuition, devalued the currency (by 9 percent), and put a brake on cost-of-living adjustments for public-sector employees.[28] Yet as in Poland, after an initial drop in productivity (and a loss of 10 percent real income for wage earners and

pensioners in the first year of austerity), the economy grew steadily.[29] The reform package was the work of Finance Minister Lajos Bokros, an adherent of
the neoliberal orthodoxy of the "Chicago school" of Milton Friedman. Basic
economic facts had forced him to act: an inflation rate of 30 percent annually,
a balance of payments deficit of $4 billion, and foreign debt of $30 billion. In
1995, 70 percent of the economy was still controlled by the government. With
austerity measures and accelerated privatization, it hoped to attract investment
and make industry more competitive.[30] Horn and the Hungarian government
were pressed by the International Monetary Fund to "meet Western standards
and requirements." Thus, this post-Communist government presented its program as an "end of Kádárism," unpopular but inherently good for the economy,
and as in Poland, a harsh but necessary medicine.[31]

The story differed in Bulgaria and Romania, where Communists maintained
themselves in lightly camouflaged successor organizations, called the Bulgarian Socialist Party and the (Romanian) Front of National Salvation. Both won
free elections in 1990 and permitted the old apparatus to continue. In both
places, democratization of formal procedures was delayed, and leaders protracted the pain of transformation by subsidizing noncompetitive firms. When
this strategy burdened the state budget, they privatized by way of "manager buy-
outs," usually granting ownerships to managers directly or by way of auction.
Because of insider trading and other forms of corruption, the auctions did
not generate as much revenue as expected. As in other post-socialist countries,
new owners often used their positions to strip assets. By the late 1990s, both
countries were suffering from severe inflation. In 1997, Romania was forced to
devalue its currency by 150 percent, and Bulgaria went through a period of hyperinflation (a more than 1,000 percent devaluation).[32] The delay to privatization, marketization, and monetary stabilization proved to be worse than
shock therapy.

That fact placed the political left in a difficult position. If it had any coherence, it was in opposition to "neoliberalism," but neither then nor now has anyone identified alternatives that were substantially different as well as viable.
Decades later, the leading economist of socialism and post-socialism, János Kornai, still refused to offer "solutions." The historian Ivan T. Berend argued that
the transformation did not have to proceed so rapidly. For example, it had not
been necessary to devalue currencies so steeply. Trade liberalization could have
proceeded more slowly, so that domestic industries would have more time to
adapt to new circumstances.[33] But for Berend, too, the basic idea was to achieve
macroeconomic stability in a capitalist economy, and he agreed that some shock

was necessary, including major elements of reform: stabilization, privatization, and marketization.

And as we have seen, "neoliberalism" was never pure. If post-Communists pushed privatization, neoliberals could delay it. That was true in Western Europe (even in Thatcher's United Kingdom), but also in Balcerowicz's Poland and in the Czech Republic under libertarian Václav Klaus. Klaus and Polish counterparts delayed the sale of certain state-owned industries to cushion the pain of unemployment for thousands of workers. In Poland, governments of right and left tried to salvage large industries where jobs were at stake. The point was to prepare firms for privatization rather than release them suddenly into the gales of market competition. In August 1996, the iconic Gdańsk shipyard was declared bankrupt, but thanks to state support, it remains open despite perennial troubles, with a workforce dropping from about 20,000 to 2,000. In the Czech lands, Václav Klaus used state banks to support heavy industry in order to protect jobs, and he ran large deficits all five years of his premiership (1993–1998), heavily subsidizing energy, transportation, and rents. The strategy ran thin in 1996, when firms could no longer pay their loans. Klaus left under a cloud of scandal the following year.[34]

A potent force further diluting neoliberal purity was the continuing and pervasive public corruption, which took varying forms. The general problem was the temptation of new owners to strip plants rather than invest in them, and then transfer the assets to Western bank accounts. When Václav Klaus fell in 1997, the *Economist*, otherwise an admirer of his spirit, decried the "appalling corruption and lack of openness in business that have stained the last few years of Mr. Klaus's reign and have shriveled foreign investment." A particular problem was that political friends of Klaus had rigged privatizations to benefit their own friends. An official report of September 1997 listed 1,420 cases of privatized companies whose assets were "tunneled out" of the country by their new owners in 1996, and another 892 cases over the first half of 1997.[35] Klaus resisted creating regulatory agencies (the problem here was poorly regulated investment funds), arguing that the market could police itself.[36] "As a result," wrote the *New York Times*, "fraud and insider trading rocked Prague's stock exchange and banks accumulated huge portfolios of bad loans." Foreign investment moved from the once-popular Czech Republic to Poland and Hungary.[37]

Unwavering neoliberalism also seemed dubious in terms of basic economics, because high social welfare expenditures were positively correlated with economic growth. Though they spent much more on the unemployed and pensioners since 1989 than states in southeastern Europe or the former Soviet

Union, Poland and Hungary had much higher growth rates. And Slovakia, a place made famous by a 19 percent flat tax introduced after 1998, has seen continued growth under the more moderate Social Democrats who came to office in 2006.[38]

Nationalism

Nationalism seemed curiously dormant during this period of revolutionary transformation. Yet there was one exception in the former Soviet Bloc, namely Czechoslovakia, the old twin of Yugoslavia, also the product of intellectual musings that went back to the 1840s. In the early 1990s, the Czechoslovak Republic also came under pressures of separatism, finally splitting the country into two republics on January 1, 1993. Just as was the case in Yugoslavia, the division happened against the wishes of the overwhelming majority of the country's citizens; and just as in Yugoslavia, the new political parties opposed the holding of a countrywide referendum on the federation's future, because they knew it would reduce their powers.

Yet in Czechoslovakia as in Yugoslavia, the possibility of division grew directly out of the state structure created under Communism. In 1974, Yugoslavia became in effect a federation of eight units; and six years previously, in the fall of 1968, Czechoslovakia had divided into two republics, Czech and Slovak. This was the one lasting "reform" of the Prague Spring. The Czechoslovak Republic was a space in which the Czech and Slovak nations could exercise their rights to self-determination in a voluntary union of two republics. A two-chamber Federal Assembly was to act as the highest institution of state power. That at least was the language and intent of the reform; but it went into effect in January 1969, at time when actual self-government was impossible. In 1989, the Communist Party withdrew its monopoly of governance, and Czech and Slovak lawmakers attempted to fashion a new democratic life within the strictures of the Communist-era constitution.[39]

According to its provisions, arrangements in the joint federal assembly were such that extraordinary legislation, like constitutional amendments, declarations of war, or election of the president, required a three-fifths majority. That meant that a small minority in one of two chambers could block reforms to the constitution.[40] In the summer of 1990, newly elected president Václav Havel decided to make constitutional reform a top priority, and inadvertently took the first step in a process leading to dissolution: Czech political elites shared his sense of priority, while the Slovaks believed a state treaty must first establish equality between the Slovak and Czech republics. Attempts by Havel in early 1992 to break the deadlock by way of a constitutional reform (among other things of the antimajority principle) were blocked by the Slovak minority.

Elections in June brought to power leaderships in Slovakia and the Czech lands who did not rule out constitutional reform of a common state but had very different ideas about its shape. Slovak leader Vladimir Mečiar wanted a loose economic and defense union, and a slowing down of economic reform to mitigate its pain. A former boxer and folksy populist, he was also showing first signs of a taste for authoritarian and illiberal political practice. His Czech counterpart, Václav Klaus, argued for rapid privatization and a strong market economy. The two men's political organizations did not favor reform of the common state, because operating on a Czechoslovak stage would force compromises that would weaken each. Therefore, they initiated negotiations for dissolution, resulting in a division of the country on January 1, 1993. It was peaceful ("velvet divorce"), because there were no disputes about territories or populations.

Was the process democratic? The answer is mixed. On the one hand, polls from late 1991 showed that Czechs and Slovaks overwhelmingly desired to maintain a single state. (A referendum on this never made it through the federal legislature.) But on the other, it was up to their elected representatives to determine what unity meant. And in the June 1992 elections, Czechs and Slovaks had chosen representatives who had well-known differences on unity. The federal parliament had become dysfunctional, and in the end, the one thing lawmakers could agree on was dissolution.

"Nationalist" desires and interests, though no doubt real and potent, were never expressed in pure, unmediated fashion. (This had also been true in Yugoslavia.) Neither side directly proclaimed its intention to leave but spoke in vague terms about "sovereignty" in their half of the state and portrayed the other as the divisive and nationalistic party. Václav Klaus, for instance, camouflaged his drive for partition beneath suggestions that it was the Slovaks who desired secession. He portrayed the impending divide as the fulfillment of Slovak longings for independence, while dropping hints that his economic program would bring the Czechs success, for example, through a balanced budget in their new state.[41] Either a different set of elites or a different institutional legacy from the Communist era—for example, a unitary state—might have produced a different outcome.

As had been the case throughout the region, small groups of extremists who cared strongly about the national issue used powerful, emotionally laden rhetoric to make their points: points that may be accepted by most people in general terms, but from which these minorities drew the most radical conclusion. The great majority of Slovaks may have wanted to continue in union with Czechs, but a well-organized minority, featuring many leading intellectuals (some of whom had connections to the wartime Slovak state, as was the case in Croatia), commandeered public spaces and exploited the most dramatic tropes of ethnic nationalism, chanting slogans like "No More Czech Colonialism!" These intellectuals claimed to represent Slovak society, and no organized response from that society emerged to challenge them—precisely because the views of the majority ranged form moderate to "nationally indifferent." Who could deny that the relation with the Czechs seemed colonial? Because of its less-diversified industry, Slovakia had a much more difficult transition in the early postcommunist period, with unemployment rates several times higher than in the Czech lands. Even Slovaks who did not want division believed that Czechs looked on their less-developed land as a reservoir of cheap labor.[42]

Yet beyond Czechoslovakia and Yugoslavia, nationalism seemed to have lost its power to divide. That was not because of lack of opportunity. There was lingering potential to exploit irredentist claims, Poles against Ukrainians, for instance. Western Ukraine had been Polish before the Nazi-Soviet Pact of 1939, but thanks to the work of generations of responsible Polish intellectuals (above all, in the émigré journal *Kultura* in Paris), authoritative opinion had decided that Poland's interests were better served through cooperation with other peoples in the region.[43] Poland's political elites embraced the *Kultura* line when they became free to say so. But they did not do so in a rhetorical vacuum. There was something more interesting to Poles after 1989 than lost territory in Ukraine or Lithuania, and that was Europe. "Europe" managed a magic trick with the national question: for the first time, nationalists favored making the nation dissolve in a greater unity of nations.

Right after the collapse of state socialism, no one was sure exactly what "Europe" was, but it seemed a place of prosperity, bright colors, diversity, peace, and order, featuring new freedoms but also security. And, from what little was known, to borrow a phrase from Noel Coward at the end of a different war, in Europe, ethnic cleansing or seizing lost territory were things that "simply weren't done."[44] Poles who demanded Lwów or Wilno betrayed themselves as anti-European. At the same time, Europe—the European Union—seemed interested in uniting with Poles and other peoples from beyond the vanished iron curtain. From shortly after the fall of the old regime, the European Union and its suborganizations did much to promote liberal democracy and free-market capitalism.[45]

Exactly how former Communist states would return to Europe was not clear in the early 1990s. There was no schedule for joining the European Union, nor were there established criteria. Professed desire was not sufficient. The Romanian political establishment claimed to want to enter the European Union, but their political practices—fomenting ethnic chauvinism, bringing miners into the capital to beat protesters, widespread corruption, and the questionable conduct of parliamentary and presidential elections—gave pause to observers in Brussels, ensuring that Romania would be excluded from the first round of negotiations with the countries of Central and East European interested in upgrading relations.[46]

In 1993 the Union held a Copenhagen Council that laid out basic criteria for new members: (1) The stability of institutions guaranteeing democracy, rule of law, human rights and respect for and protection of minorities; (2) the existence of a functioning market economy, and the capacity to cope with competitive pressure and forces within the European Union; (3) the ability to take on the obligations of membership, including adherence to the aim of political, economic, and monetary union. The final condition required that a candidate accept a highly specific and technical body of EU laws and regulations.[47] Compliance to these prerequisites was linked to numerous political and socioeconomic benefits; noncompliance was linked to costs.

In the 1990s, the direct benefits of membership appeared moderate. From 1990 to 1998, the European Union invested 8.9 billion euros in ten East European countries for "economic restructuring" (above all for administrative and judicial reforms). But as candidates approached membership and entered the Union, the sums grew impressively, supporting agricultural development, road and transportation improvement, job training, and loans for businesses. In the first three years after Poland, Hungary, Slovakia, Slovenia, and the Czech Republic acceded (2004–2006), the European Union made structural investments of 15.5 billion euros for the new members; from 2007 to 2013, the totals were multiplied (in 2007, Bulgaria and Romania joined as well). By 2012, Poland received some 40 billion euros (in a similar period, foreign direct investment totaled about 50 billion euros).[48] Much of the money was invested in poorer areas desperately in need of infrastructural improvement.

This aid had the effect not only of bringing Poland and other candidate states closer to Western Europe in terms of per capita gross domestic product but also of reducing discrepancies within Eastern Europe and causing Poland and Hungary to pull far ahead of Ukraine and Belarus. Rather than increasing social inequalities within Poland or Hungary, modernization put a halt to growing

MAP 27.1. East Central Europe, 1999–present

differentiation between town and countryside, as well as between social classes. (Until 2005, the Gini coefficient climbed in the new EU states, but within two to three years after accession, it began to decline.)[49] Besides contributing to growth in East Central Europe, development in agricultural regions benefited old EU countries, which could now market more products in the east.

* * *

In the mid-1990s, when the ultimate benefits of EU membership were not known, leaders in Bulgaria, Slovakia, and Serbia attempted to steer separate "national" courses independent of or away from "Europe," in each case with disastrous results. A series of weak coalition governments first ruled Bulgaria after the 1989 upheaval, but then came a landslide victory of post-Communists (of the Bulgarian Socialist Party) in 1994 under Zhan Videnov, a young politician promoted by former members of Bulgarian State Security, known as the Orion group, who were endeavoring to become big-time capitalists.[50] Videnov projected himself as an alternative to "failed" privatization, though in fact no serious reform had been attempted.[51] Ruling with an absolute majority, Videnov promised to protect ordinary citizens from the ravages of market forces; he rejected "capitalism," the "egotism of the market," as well as the "neocolonialism" of international financial and political institutions. Videnov called his own path "socially sensible left modernization," and a "Bulgarian third way," portraying himself as a defender of the nation. He resurrected controlled prices (by the end of 1996, about half of all consumer products were subject to some form of price control), recollectivized farming, and refused to invite foreign companies to invest in and buy Bulgarian companies. That would have amounted to squandering national wealth, he said, to the advantage of "foreign influences."

Videnov's privatization scheme was meant to distribute vouchers to the public, but by the time it was implemented, most enterprises were in desperate financial straits. Though uncompetitive, they continued at full capacity, making losses in 1995 that added up to 15 percent of the country's gross national product. In 1996, the artificially supported exchange rate collapsed, in turn fueling inflation. A crisis in the banking system led to bankruptcy of one-third of all Bulgarian banks in May of that year, and the currency collapsed in November. The gross national product dropped 9 percent, and from January 1996 to January 1997, the average monthly salary fell almost tenfold, from $118 to $12. The government was not serving the nation; instead, as Tsveta Petrova writes, it had become hostage to "shadowy interests, spiraling corruption, and crony capitalism."[52]

Videnov's performance explains Bulgaria's exclusion from the first wave of EU entrants. EU agencies made clear that unless corruption and mismanagement were removed, the path to "Europe" was closed. Such messages naturally implicated the Bulgarian left. At the same time, Western NGOs on the center-right, like the Germany's Konrad Adenauer Foundation or France's Robert

Shuman Foundation, helped the opposition Union of Democratic Forces (UDF)—a diverse federation of parties that had emerged in 1989—evolve into a Christian Democratic party. Western experts advised the political campaign of the UDF presidential candidate, the anti-Communist economist Petar Stojanov, and helped it build an activist core. The German Social Democratic Friedrich Ebert Foundation made its expertise available to the Bulgarian Socialist Party (BSP), but the disappointment among Western socialists with the BSP was so great that in the 1996 presidential elections, the Socialist International supported the UDF candidate.[53]

In what was seen as a referendum on East versus West, Stoyanov won the largely ceremonial post of president in November 1996.[54] Yet the government remained in office. Propelled by the severe economic crisis, a mass movement emerged led by young people and supported by trade unions and other civic groups, bringing thousands onto the streets for weeks on end, dedicated to forcing an end to Videnov's socialist third way. The movement was aided by Western NGOs, and the International Monetary Fund made it clear that it would not negotiate a new loan with Bulgaria until a stable new government was elected.[55] Some 850,000 people observed a one-hour warning strike on June 7, 1996, and in December, almost 1 million joined a 24-hour national strike. Pressures for change reached into the ruling party, and after nineteen top BSP politicians called for a change of leadership, Videnov resigned.[56]

Stoyanov tried to form a government with the new BSP leader Nikolay Dobrev, yet wisely recognizing the need for a fresh start, Dobrev agreed to new elections. These brought to power the UDF economist Ivan Kostov, who pushed privatization of state-owned enterprises, started accession talks with the European Union, and followed a pro-NATO course. Allowing NATO to use Bulgarian airspace in the 1999 Kosovo War, his government stated that the "Republic of Bulgaria confirms its strategic civilizational choice for full membership in NATO."[57] Under Kostov, Bulgaria achieved sustained economic growth.

Bulgarian protesters had been looking across the border to Romania's liberal opposition, which had been organizing rallies in support of pro-Western candidates. They also looked to Serbia, where massive protests broke out when Slobodan Milošević attempted to deny the opposition its victories in local elections. The Bulgarian media familiarized readers with the methods developed on the streets of Belgrade, and portrayed events in Serbia as like those in Bulgaria, involving a struggle between government and people. Although Bulgaria was ahead of Serbia in its transformation to pluralism and a market economy, the street mobilization of the student-led Serb opposition to Milošević appeared as a model, and Bulgarians remade Bulgaria by thinking in terms learned from Serbia. In a stunning reciprocity, Serbs then felt inspired by the Bulgarian transition to replace their illiberal leadership with proreform elites in 2000.[58]

This transnational ferment shows how international and domestic support for democratic development could converge.[59] But it also reflected the widespread appeal of the European Union, in a movement extending across borders—of Bulgaria to Romania and Serbia—and uniting diverse populations in common aspirations.

The European Union itself did not initially intend to use its leverage to promote democracy. Into the mid-1990s, its emphasis was on keeping unqualified states out. But by the late 1990s, politicians in Brussels registered the Union's influence on aspiring members as among the most successful aspects of its foreign policy.[60] The case of Bulgaria showed how it could hold out the promise of membership to steer a country toward democracy. One scholar likened the transition in EU policy that took place from the mid- to late 1990s as from "passive to active leverage."[61] During the early 1990s, there had been no timetable for accession negotiations, yet later in the decade, the European Union began specifying conditions for accession, with precise medium-term political and economic objectives for aspiring members.[62]

The pressure that the European Union exerted in East Central Europe was not always indirect. Instead, Western actors, cooperating with local NGOs, worked on the ground to reconcile and unite opposition leaders who did not see eye to eye. They indicated which members of oppositional groupings were acceptable to "Europe." The opposition, in turn, accused ruling elites of squandering the country's chances to enter Europe. In Bulgaria, pressures from the West had simplified the domestic political spectrum by exerting a centripetal force on an unwieldy collection of anti-Communist groups, so that the UDF came to approximate a West European Christian Democratic party.

The transnational "learning" process extended to regions farther north as well. In Slovakia, the defeat of Bulgaria's Videnov inspired opposition leaders to oppose and replace Vladimir Mečiar's illiberal regime in 1998.[63] The Slovak transition had roughly three phases: democratization as part of the Czech and Slovak Federation (1989–1993); de-democratization during the first years of independence under Mečiar (1994–1998), and re-democratization under Mikuláš Dzurinda (1998–2004).

The Mečiar interlude featured backsliding in virtually every aspect of transformation: undermining the rule of law, curtailing rights of the opposition, and asserting Slovak national identity at the expense of national minorities, especially the many Hungarians. Corruption was pervasive and extended into the security services. In August 1995, the adult son of the Slovak president (and Mečiar's political rival) Michal Kováč was kidnapped by eight men, forced to drink a bottle of whiskey, and taken across the border to Austria and left in the trunk of a car. Tipped off by a telephone call, Austrian police found and arrested Kováč because of a warrant issued by a Munich prosecutor (they wanted him to testify in a fraud case involving the Slovak trade firm Technopol). When challenged about his whereabouts at the time of the kidnapping by political rival Jan Čarnogurský, Mečiar responded: "Why don't you ask your wife where I was?"[64] Suspicion fell on the Slovak Information Service, led by Mečiar ally Ivan Lexa, but the case was never resolved. A witness in the case died in a car explosion, and before leaving office, Mečiar issued an amnesty putting an end to the investigation.[65] Ultimately, Kováč Jr. was returned to Slovakia, and charges in Germany were dropped.

In 1995, the European parliament issued a rebuke to the Slovak regime: unless it fulfilled the conditions for accession, Slovakia would not enter the Union.[66] Mečiar was undeterred. Posing as a nationalist against "mondialism," he said that because of West European tariffs, Slovakia would look to Russia as its principle trading partner. "If the West does not want us," he fumed, "we will turn to the East." Soon his government was concluding agreements with Russia on military cooperation, including trade in arms.

Mečiar portrayed himself as a guarantor of social security and drew support from Slovaks fearful of transition. He introduced employee buyout privatization that favored groups close to ruling coalition and limited the flow of foreign investment.[67] Not a man of the "right," Mečiar has been compared to Serbia's Milošević: both were Communists who became nationalists. But we also see the mixture of elements of regional populism going back to the 1880s: exploitation of economic fears combined with vilification of foreigners as a threat to the nation—including "Europe." From the bunker mentality of the country's elites, the outside world seemed to consist of a conspiracy directed against Slovakia.[68]

Mečiar's final government (1994–1998) featured a coalition with the Union of Workers of Slovakia, a left-wing party proud to have hindered the privatization of the gas, energy, telecommunications, and banking industries.[69] Yet by decade's end, populist, anti-Western nationalism was losing its allure. It had nothing to promise, and ultimately these parties, similar to the HDZ in Croatia, forsook their anti-Western path and began adjusting to basic expectations of mainstream European political parties. The signs coming from Brussels were not open to conflicting interpretations.

Because of its failure to reform, Slovakia was kept out of the first round of NATO enlargement in 1997.[70] Soon a heterogeneous opposition formed to challenge Mečiar in the parliamentary elections of September 1998, consisting of Christian-Democrats, Social Democrats, and Greens (they called themselves the Slovak Democratic Coalition).[71] But decisive was a "third sector" of dozens of NGOs—supported by Western NGOs, like the US National Endowment for Democracy or Freedom House—that mobilized under the umbrella organization OK'98 ("Civic Campaign" 98) beginning in March 1998. At a meeting in Vienna a few months earlier, Western donors had introduced the leaders of Slovak NGOs to their Romanian and Bulgarian counterparts, impressing on them the need to get directly involved in the upcoming election campaign. As a result, these NGOs got out the vote.

As in Serbia and Bulgaria, young people took a central role in the mobilization, for example, in a "march across Slovakia" in which hundreds of activists went through villages and cities, distributing education materials and holding discussions as well as putting on cabaret performances.[72] In defiance of media manipulation, OK'98 used a "Rock the Vote" campaign to get out new voters, ultimately registering some 300,000 young people. Young people tended to be less happy with Mečiar's rule than the general public: 65 percent.[73] A media campaign featured radio and TV ads with foreign and domestic sport stars, actors, and rock musicians aimed at young voters. During the vote itself, the liberal opposition, with ties between opposition parties and civil society groups, expanded voter turnout and monitoring through exit poles. Mečiar's party still emerged the strongest (27 percent) from the September parliamentary 1998 elections, but because of ostracization, it failed to find a coalition partner and had to cede power to a coalition formed by the conservative economist Mikuláš Dzurinda.

Mečiar's successors now raced to make up for lost time. They reversed Mečiar's overtures to the East, canceled arms deals with Russia, and like Bulgarian counterparts, permitted NATO to use their country's airspace in 1999.[74] Prime Minister Dzurinda liberalized Slovakia in a hurry in order to catch up with the countries invited to negotiations for EU entry.[75] He and other politicians came together with main civil society actors in a "Democratic Round Table" and pledged to meet all the requirements to enter the European Union with the other first-round countries in 2004.

A similar consensus for Europe emerged in Romania, where the opposition Democratic Convention of Romania cooperated with the Hungarian Democratic Union of Romania. Western representatives of international organizations were thick on the ground, eager to provide direct input on what constituted a liberal-democratic agenda.[76] The highest stage of EU-inspired transformation in this period was that of the illiberal parties themselves, which, to improve their chances with domestic audiences, began posing as pro-European by claiming to embrace liberal democracy and economic reform; examples are the HDZ in Croatia, the BSP in Bulgaria, and the Social Democratic Party in Romania.[77] Within a few years, opposition politicians with no record of being moderate or liberal began speaking unaccustomed languages on minority rights and economic reform in order to live up to expectations of "European" style politics.

After accession to the European Union, countries scrambled to create attractive conditions for foreign investment. The Czech government, for instance, set up extensive supports, including up to $5,000 for every new job, provision of low-cost land, and infrastructure support, permitting the import of new production machinery duty-free (the requirement is at least $10 million investment within three years). Slovakia provided similar incentives and competed successfully for automobile contracts with Western countries because of lower taxes and lower labor costs.[78] Ironically, the desire for EU accession involved states in a competition over how best to aid *foreign* companies, a move that again questions the coherence of "neoliberalism."

* * *

In 2007, after the EU accession of the former Soviet Bloc countries and before the worldwide recession, there was reason to be optimistic about European unity. EU professional opinions mattered, because credit rating agencies adjusted findings in response to EU Regular Reports. Backtracking was monitored and penalized, and some said the road to the past was closed. But harsh discipline did not seem necessary: policy makers and publics had been convinced that national interests were best served through cooperation with international organizations and further integration, the incipient federation of states with the common currency, and a host of common regulations. Sacrificing national sovereignty was portrayed as being in the foremost interest of the nation. The period 1989–2007 was thus a rare time when external actors had a positive impact on democratization.[79] Given the failures of democratization after World War I, that was an achievement of historic dimensions and suggests bookends for a history of East Central Europe in the twentieth century: from the fiasco to the success of democracy-building. The story in between the bookends is a tragedy of the European nation-state.

Yet as compelling as such arguments seem, the story is not over. There is no conclusion to "democratic reform," and there is no clarity about what Europe is, what it can offer, or who belongs and why. In early 2015, Greece seemed to be on the verge of leaving; for Greek voters, it was unclear whether Europe is too painful a place to remain. Greece's finance minister was predicting that if Europe can no longer help service its debt, Greece would look to Russia or China—and would no doubt find willing creditors. Europe is about much more than economic union or cultural heritage. It is part of a geopolitical bloc. "American officials," wrote the *New York Times*, "expressed concern about the implications of any breakdown in discussions [on Greek debt] since that could propel Greece further away from Europe."[80]

In East Central Europe, that option did not end with the ousting of Vladimir Mečiar in 1998. He too had threatened to play a "Russia card" but was overwhelmed by social forces supported by Western NGOs. As Greece threatened to look eastward for assistance, the democratically elected leader of Hungary, among the earliest success stories of transition, was hosting Vladimir Putin and signing an extension of energy agreements (Hungary was obtaining 70 percent of its natural gas from Russia). Orbán has praised Russia as an "illiberal democracy." As the two men met, several thousand Hungarians demonstrated in central Budapest under banners reading: "No to Putin, Yes to Europe." One couple wore masks of Orbán and Putin and held a cross: "united in illiberalism." During their talks, Orbán made clear to Putin that Hungary needed Russia. By choosing its own path in relations to Russia, Hungary was defending its own "national interests."[81]

The development was shocking, but perhaps was also as logical as the return of post-Communists to power in 1993 in Hungary and Poland. Orbán was a leader of Hungary's struggle to free itself from Soviet influence in 1988/1989 and a proponent of a strong transition away from Communism. He spoke to the multitudes at the Imre Nagy re-burial in June 1989 and demanded the departure of Soviet troops and the holding of free elections. Yet now he seems to be propelling Hungary backward, clamping down on independent media and judiciary; placing heavy political pressures on science and education; and like other dictators, talking of a permanent regime. When pressed by Germany's Angela Merkel to explain how democracy could be illiberal, he had no answer. The best one could say is that the prospects of losing German investment appears to limit his willingness to be clearer.

What has made Hungary distinct? Neighboring countries have not embraced illiberalism. Perhaps the answer lies in deep unresolved history, in the continued fragmentation of the ethnic Hungarian nation after Trianon. In a poll of 2007, 80 percent of respondents agreed that Trianon constituted a historic injustice.[82] Hungary has the largest irredenta in East Central Europe, and it is the one place where the unresolved question of nation-state building can be made to take precedence over all other agendas, propelling it into a common front with Russia. In February 2015, Russian Foreign Minister Sergey Lavrov reminded an audience in Munich that not only Russians and Ukrainians lived in Ukraine: there was also a "Hungarian minority," whose discrimination troubled Russia, and implicitly justified Russian support of rebels in Eastern Ukraine. "Fate" had placed other nationalities in Ukraine, why should one not honor their "equal rights"? Lavrov claimed (without evidence) that more Hungarians were taken into the army than were "ethnic" Ukrainians and that election boundaries had been drawn in such a way as to hinder the dispatching of even one ethnic Hungarian to parliament in Kiev.[83]

Lavrov was echoing Viktor Orbán, who asserted on Hungarian television that "Ukraine can be neither stable nor democratic if it does not give its minorities, including Hungarians, their due." They should be granted "dual (Hungarian) citizenship, collective rights and autonomy."[84] By liberal estimates, that group is about 200,000 strong. Orbán understands these and other Hungarians in foreign countries as part of the nation he represents; during an election speech in southern Hungary in 2002, he declared a program of "national reunification that arcs over borders," that is, beyond the Trianon borders.[85] In 2010, he granted ethnic Hungarians citizenship and permitted them to vote in Hungarian national elections (expecting their support).[86]

Are Hungarians in Ukraine attracted to Orbán's "illiberal democracy" and the style of rule exemplified in Russia? Interviews show that residents of Hungarian villages in Ukraine are attracted to Hungary's prosperity, prosperity that—as they know—Hungary achieved by joining Europe. If they admire Hungary, it is because they desire life on "EU Standards."[87]

But the European Union cannot solve all problems or launch all countries on a level plane toward prosperity. For all the benefits of membership, expectations have been out of synch with possibilities. Bulgaria made its turn toward Europe in 1997, but corruption remains a problem. Members of the elite continue to plunder the country's national resources, and politicians serve at the mercy of oligarchs, for example, media-mogul Delvan Peevski, who controls large parts of the Bulgarian economy.[88] Currently, 20 percent of the population lives below the poverty level, and there are runs on supposedly well-capitalized major banks.[89] Well after Bulgaria's return to Europe, a new generation of students has taken to the streets, getting black eyes from the same old police, perhaps forgetting the work and the hopes felt among their predecessors when history "turned" in 1996/1997. They put up banners featuring important years in Bulgarian history: 1968, 2007, 2013 (the last would be the date when Bulgaria finally rid itself of the corruption that left it the European Union's poorest member).[90] They were doing exactly what their forgotten predecessors had done sixteen years earlier: marching at the center of Sofia, demanding that the socialist-backed government step down to make way for early elections. Their story has no conclusion.

Conclusion

Studies of Transylvania, Bosnia, or Western Poland show that ethnic identity matters no more to East Europeans in their everyday lives than it does to other human beings.[1] Yet for more than two centuries, from the Rhine to the gates of Russia, ethnic nationalism has acted as an ideology of unrivaled force, transforming and subverting other kinds of politics, regardless of whether national identity seems uncontroversial in normal circumstances. If the diverse space from the Baltic to the Balkans—a crossroads of religions, languages, and culinary tastes and the shatter zone of empires—has had any historical coherence, it lies here.

Yet just as ethnic nationalism has made Eastern Europe, very diverse East Europeans have made ethnic nationalism, from Czech and Hungarian dictionary writers, Serb insurgents, and Polish cadets, teachers in secret language courses, census-takers and builders of national infrastructures, collaborators with and opponents of Nazi and Soviet rule, to Slovak or Serb bureaucrats turned would-be national messiahs.

At the outset, the national patriots were almost invisible to contemporaries. František Palacký was not joking when he said one large room would have held the Czech national movement of the 1820s. Only in the 1840s did "Slavonian" nationalism become apparent to a man with obsessive passion for the subject in general, Italy's Giuseppe Mazzini, and when the outstanding Czech patriot Karel Havlíček Borovský was laid to rest a decade later, everyone knew everyone in the small group of mourners and among the elite of Czech letters.[2] Progressives outside the region, like Karl Marx or Louis Blanc, were lamenting the disappearance of Poland or the crushing of Hungary's freedoms, but a traveler conducting interviews across the Polish or Hungarian plains would have encountered puzzled faces among speakers of various dialects when they were asked about national belonging. They were Mazovians and Upper Silesian townspeople, Szeklers and literate to illiterate multilingual low- and highlanders with a decent command of several idioms, including Latin in the older generation.

Those reliably conscious of nationality before the mid-nineteenth century tended to be of the gentry, but the old world was shattering under the impact of modernization and the sale of their land. In any case, what it meant to them to be Polish or Hungarian was radically different from what it would mean later. Many in the gentry took for granted that Jews could be Poles or Magyars, and in these years of political oppression, "Poland" and "Hungary" lived as much beyond East Central Europe as within it, in the writings and arguments of émigrés who had taken refuge in Paris or New York.

Nationalists were not representative; no one had elected them to translate dictionaries and wave flags. Yet at every political "turning point," from the 1780s to the 1840s and the years after the two world wars, those wanting to make politics in East Central Europe portrayed themselves as somehow freeing "their" nations from foreign tyranny. Nationalists used all the means at their disposal—from nationalist print media, bureaucracies of nation-states, and imperial schools—to inculcate in the masses a new sense of belonging that was broad, but also narrow and exclusive, uniting the disparate populations of historic Poland or Hungary and instructing them about the aliens in their midst. This task of spreading national consciousness among often-indifferent populations absorbed the energies of generations and was completed only after World War II through bloody state-driven policies, such as population exchanges.[3]

If patriots imagined nations, the nations they ultimately helped make were not simply "artificial." Members of the Czech ethnicity had been strongly aware of their difference from German speakers centuries before people like Gelasius Dobner or Josef Jungmann lifted their pens.[4] What was very old if not ancient was a species of resentment: of people too "good" to speak your language, who seemed to have the odds stacked in their favor. Long before the mid-nineteenth century, this sense was alive among Serbs and Bohemia's Slavs, a resource for patriots, yet not infinitely elastic. One lesson from this book is that history has shown that Czechoslovaks and Yugoslavs are not peoples, contrary to the imaginings of early patriots. Ultimately, these two national ideas could not mobilize enough people to kill and die in order to keep Czechoslovakia and Yugoslavia from disappearing. The entities people could be mobilized for were Croatia and Serbia, and farther north, Romania, Hungary, and Poland. East European nationalism is about the fear of disappearance from history; it is about the fear of genocide.

This discourse, once it emerged in the late eighteenth century, changed little in its basic contours, and set itself apart from variants to the west. Nationalism is about pride and honor everywhere, but fear of disappearance from history was unknown to nationalism in England, France, Italy, Spain, Russia, Scandinavia, and the Low Countries. Not that everyone had this view at most times, but politics, especially at moments of truth (like 1849 in Transylvania,

1875 in Herzegovina, and 1919 in Eastern Galicia), was distilled to a nationalist essence. No other force could compete with it for mobilizing human energies, whether that involved calling workers to strike or paramilitaries to stage an offensive. The forces defending the Habsburg Empire when its fate hung in the balance in Hungary in 1849 were themselves not imperial but national: Croat, German, Romanian, and Serb.

A landmark in the rise of aggressive Serbian nationalism in recent times was the elicitation of genocide by the Serb Academy in its infamous Memorandum of 1986. That was linked to the supposed threat of Albanian nationalism in Kosovo. The genocide narrative continued as Serb paramilitaries "cleansed" and slaughtered Muslims in Bosnia, in turn crystalizing a sense of ethnic identity among Bosnian Muslims. Previously, "Bosnian" was in part a regional descriptor, but now it had become undoubtedly national, and Bosniaks joined the "small nations" of East Central Europe who justify claims to statehood by saying it protects them from disappearance. Nationalism was opportunistic within fixed referent points: unlike other potentially opportunistic worldviews—liberalism, socialism, Christianity—it grew when it took on new guises.

* * *

Did nationalism have to happen at all? Could East Europeans have created some other, non-national principle of belonging? This alternative hovers as a serious possibility in much recent work on East Central Europe. Yet when one surveys more than two centuries, one can imagine different shifts but not a different story. Across the region, from the Balkans northward there were perhaps a half-dozen moments when the history of nationalization might have proceeded according to a radically different scheme: had Joseph II not attempted to replace Latin with German (1784), had Gavrilo Princip not hit his target with one bullet (1914), had a US president not become an apostle of self-determination in Europe (1919), or had the many happenstances not occurred that brought Adolf Hitler to power (January 1933).[5] These were truly contingent moments, attached to individual acts, which we can imagine playing out differently, sending history along different paths.[6] Such counterfactual reasoning is crucial, because otherwise, historians face determinism.[7]

Yet beyond these cases, the plausible alternate scenarios are few. One cannot imagine away the forces of reaction that crushed the springtime of peoples in 1848/1849; nor can one rescramble the characters and events in the 1860s to construe a compromise by Habsburg elites that might have placated the Czech political class. In Poland, segments of the Polish political elites were set against every kind of rule that came from Russia, and collaborators from beginning to end were disappointed. No concessions that even the most servile Polish politicians made could reduce the intensity of Russification. It's tempting to imagine a different kind of Yugoslavia in 1918/1919—more federal—or a different outcome to the Croatian spring a half-century later, but no clear contingent moment emerges from the actual historical details of either of these events.[8]

And even if one indulges in the fantasy scenarios of any of these cases, the alternatives involve a different kind of national solution, perhaps less bloody, perhaps not. Contrary to what some scholars have written, the development of national identity was not something that may or may not have happened, but as close as human communities get to sharing a common fate. Early nationalists understood that if they did not awaken "their" group—say, Slovak speakers in northern Hungary—then that group would not continue a benign non-national existence but would become nationals of a different kind. What the analysis in this book has shown is that nationalism was not contingent, but rather situational: its strength depending above all on the level of perceived threat to a particular ethnicity.[9]

Students of nationalism stress that the intention of nineteenth-century actors creating schools or arguing for language rights fell short of demands for fully independent nation-states, but the important point is that patriots demanded national rights that could not be fulfilled within the boundaries of the empires, or even of the kingdoms of the realm. Take the early years of the Hungarian national movement in the 1830s. Hungary was not England or France. It was a patchwork of linguistic and religious groups. These "minorities" in fact made up more than half the population. Some, like the Croat elite, had their own history of rights. France also would have had extreme difficulties had it consisted of one-third Bretons and one-third Alsatians and only one-third Francophones. Thus it misses the point to say that Hungarian or later Czech liberals did not intend to upset the empire's balance: they acted in an objectively and unavoidably disruptive way, implying precedence and priority for their group and a desire to subordinate others culturally, even if that did not involve the immediate eradication of their languages.

If the discourse of nationhood seemed to move forward across the region with an implacable momentum, it also experienced a radicalization in the late

nineteenth century. In general, the greater the pessimism of a national movement, the greater its tendencies toward chauvinism. When the pessimism
eclipsed all alternative visions, the result was fascism. Pessimism was strongest
in Hungary, with its demographic panic and then the disaster of Trianon, and
that is why the reaction was extreme across social classes in Hungary in the 1930s,
yet weaker among Serbs, Poles, and Czechs.

In the late nineteenth century, ethnic ideas about nationhood also became
racialized in line with the scientific trends of the time. Czech or Polish nationalists therefore thought not simply that their peoples had come from tribes,
but that these tribes were united by blood. They knew about the absorption of
individuals into their nations through conversion or intermarriage over many
centuries. Fascists themselves were often of foreign descent, and no one held
that against them—unless it emerged that they were Jewish.

Among all the nationalisms, there was an idea that Jewishness constituted
an "otherness" unlike all others, a greater, more distinct level of difference. By
the twentieth century, the view emerged in Poland that "Jews were organically
and by definition alien to and different from Poles." Anti-Semites said this "fact"
was not as easily recognized, because Jews were "white."[10] But the view went
beyond anti-Semites: some Jews held that Jews were racially different and should
take measure to protect themselves.[11]

* * *

As an unbounded region, Eastern Europe was open to intellectual trends beyond racism and nationalism. That was especially true given that the peoples
of the region tended to live in large empires. The democratic and socialist movement in Austria-Hungary splintered by ethnicity, but ideas about liberalism
and socialism still spread with no impediment, across the realm and across Europe. The settlement after World War I fractured the map into many national
states, but the older imperial trend was revived in 1939 with Germany's conquest
of Bohemia and Poland, and the subordination of East Central Europe to its
sphere of influence. Now Eastern Europe became the heartland of something
new: two imperial systems governed by totalitarian ideologies.

Yet as was true of imperialism before 1918, to some extent the foreign rule
was domesticated. Theories and practices of genocide were imported from Nazi
Germany, but they took shape within local nationalisms. If previously the enemy
wore a different uniform, now he or she was an ethnic other, uniformed or not.

No East European society would have or could have produced a total racial war like the one Nazi Germany unleashed; but each society adjusted to this new understanding of the enemy, because it mapped onto local traditions. For the most part, Polish society accepted the segregation and removal of Jews from its midst without complaint, because Jews were seen as an alien presence. Even when it became safe to mourn the sudden absence of Jews after the war, few did so. But the same was true in the Protectorate of Bohemia and Moravia, Bosnia, and Hungary. Everywhere, Nazi occupation revealed that most Gentiles did not consider Jews to be part of their nation, and thus part of their universe of obligation.[12] Each society did, however, deeply regret the loss of its own co-ethnics.[13] To this day you can see the places where scores of Czechs fell during the brief Prague uprising of 1945; the memorials were established soon after the fighting. But only under the influence of the work of the German artist Gunter Demnig have Czechs begun commemorating, in prominent places across the republic, the incomparably greater loss of their Jewish compatriots.[14]

Concern about the safety of the local ethnos made adaptation to the second total order, the Soviet one brought in at the end of World War II, much easier. The Red Army had freed Poland and the Czech lands from German rule and was indispensable for the national future. Communists became furious nationalists. They went further than predecessors in some ways, linking social to ethnic understandings of the people. They did this to castigate the old bourgeois order, not only for failing to summon protection against the Nazi Reich, but also for failing to advance the common people. Millions of Poles and Bosnians still lived in mud villages, cut off from electricity and enlightenment, eking out an existence as their ancestors had from time immemorial. People's democracy made East Central Europe modern and European.[15]

But the basic ideas of the Leninist avant garde were foreign, even to native East European Marxian socialism. Mátyás Rákosi's extreme notion of enemy and "us," with the seemingly absolute scientific and moral certainty lying behind it—these were imports from his training in Moscow. The Central European political constellation was more of a muddle, with no party having absolute desire for control, even among the old Social Democrats. Stalin had had to purge and reshape recalcitrant Central European Communist parties when they emerged in the 1920s, the moderate Czech party proving a particular challenge. The Soviet system he represented had emerged from the extremes of political and social injustice dominant in Russia before 1917 that had led to the conviction that only complete and utter transformation was an adequate response to the injustices of bourgeois society.[16]

Nowadays, the regional narratives about the past stress ways in which East Europeans resisted the totalitarianism imported from both West and East, whether in spectacular insurgencies like Poland's 1944 Warsaw Uprising or in the more structural resistance of Hungary. János Kádár's NEM was a response to foreign domination, indeed, the fruit of the "failed" 1956 uprising, similar to the 1867 compromise that was born of the "failure" of 1848/1849. In both cases, the imperial rulers and their local servants had to adjust. The larger truth about the uprisings—of 1848/1849 in Hungary, 1953 in the GDR, 1968 in Czechoslovakia, or 1980 in Poland—is not that they were crushed, but rather that they were not supposed to recur.[17] And that meant that governments endeavored to pacify populations. With the 1867 compromise, Francis Joseph appeased the Hungarians, and a century later, Janos Kádár spent his rule of thirty years making another 1956 impossible. Yet 1956 was also impossible to forget, and that was the pain that he carried with him to his grave.

One historian has argued that the tradition of Polish resistance, especially the 1944 uprising, caused Soviet politicians to treat Poland more circumspectly.[18] Ultimately, Poland's Communists were checked and constrained by each protest, whether the early postwar anti-Communist insurgency, or the acts of workers and intellectuals in 1956, 1968, 1970, and 1976. By the 1970s, the party had ceded so much ground that the imported Leninist ideology was reduced to hollow shells of words. Then came the Solidarity revolution, which claimed not to be hostile to socialism but in fact upset its basic calculations.

Czech Communists took a different path. "Normalization" in 1969 had two goals: making sure that the Prague Spring did not recur and making sure that it was forgotten. For the next two decades, even slight demands for openness, criticism, or rational management had to be extinguished, and thus Gustav Husák's regime became the exact opposite of socialism with a human face, namely, a return to the Stalinist-style system of command, with orthodoxy dictated by a few men at the top. Normalization forced an untiring examination of conscience that left only soulless Leninism in the public sphere. At the same time, normalizers ensured and protected a high standard of living, and time and energy for people to devote to their private lives. They appealed in particular to workers—whose support for the Prague Spring had been lukewarm—by continuing the radical social leveling and by rejecting "bourgeois" expectations that higher education might translate into better access to the goods of life. That is why the Gini coefficients of Czechoslovakia were in a class by themselves.

* * *

Despite variations in regime types—liberal, fascist, Communist, or neoliberal—Eastern Europe's nationalism retained a core meaning. It was about priority and precedence. Sometimes the claim was straightforward. Sparse documentation suggested that Slavs had settled in Bohemia before Germans, and therefore Czech patriots believed unshakably that the land was theirs. Hungarian patriots had to be more inventive. They knew that Celtic and Slavic tribes had lived in Pannonia before Magyar horsemen crashed onto the scene in the 880s. A view therefore emerged that the leading strata of the Hungarian nation had precedence not simply in Pannonia, but in Eurasia as a whole. Latin was derived from Magyar. But the nobility was even more special, derived from "remnants of the royal Scythians."[19] The Polish gentry concocted a mythology of deriving from the Sarmatians, an ancient royal people.[20]

Romanian Boyar mythology was better suited to the modern age. Supposedly the Boyar class, always open to new blood from the servants of Boyar families, had anticipated the democracy of the French Revolution. This belief acted to justify Boyar holding of land and privilege as not simply hereditary. Because the Boyars had founded the Romanian principalities on the basis of institutions that were humane and egalitarian, they had nothing to fear from the ideas of the French Republic, which had swept away the nobility.[21]

Everywhere, ideas of national identity were tied to national character, a fiction that had crucial weight, because people reacted—and could be mobilized—against those who misread "their" character. Resistance to fictions can produce powerful truths, decisive in all important settings besides the academic one. Take the screen actor Curd Jürgens, who played a U-Boat captain in the film *The Enemy Below* (1957), doing his duty but out of place in the Nazis' "New Germany." "It was an important picture for me," Jürgens later remembered. "It was the first film after the war in which a German officer was not interpreted as a freak."[22] Jürgens himself was not a German officer, or soldier, or even evidently German. His mother was French, his father from Hamburg, and in the 1930s, he acted in Vienna and took Austrian citizenship. In the fall of 1944, Nazi authorities sent him to a camp for the "politically unreliable." Nevertheless, he felt implicated by criticism of the German military.[23]

* * *

There are other narratives: the social, economic, imperial. But what is interesting in each case is how nationalism insinuated itself into each and changed shape, at times anti-imperial and nation-statist, at times multiethnic

(Czechoslovakia, Yugoslavia), and at times collaborationist with one or another imperial power. For nationalists, national rights were not one species of rights—for example, of human rights—they were the right from which all others flowed; the precondition for human freedom. István Széchenyi recognized the logic in 1845, asking: "if you want to achieve liberty, on the basis of what nationality do you hope to accomplish it? Slav or German?"[24]

Széchenyi was the greatest Hungarian patriot, and he busied himself fending off even greater patriots. He and other East European nationalists were like the region itself, lacking boundaries, facing foes on shifting flanks. Their politics radicalized in anticipation of challenges. C. A. Macartney wrote that the moderates among Romanians in 1890s Transylvania were gradually worn away: "the entire national movement came under the unchallenged control of the national extremists, to all of which the government found no reply except more repression."[25] In other words, extremism in one's own ranks also anticipated radicalization on the other side. That other side in Transylvania, the Hungarian elite, had been drained of moderates like Széchenyi or the remarkable József Eötvös.[26] Theirs would be a Hungary run by Hungarians, and all other peoples enjoyed rights only at the mercy of their state apparatus.

The state builders of the late nineteenth century had arrived at a cohesive vision for Hungary's future against which no competitors could survive. The same could be said in Bohemia, where the Czech movement fought for each school, usually through private means, and those doubting that Bohemia's fate was to be Czech didn't stand a chance in the free elections made possible by the Habsburg monarchy. The German and Czech sides in Bohemia sensed it was a struggle for cultural life and death in a strictly limited space.

Nationalism's gravitational pull made extremists even of politicians who cared little for the nation. The seemingly urbane international banker and technocrat Slobodan Milošević or the idiosyncratic scientist Radovan Karadžić—both later convicted war criminals—are well-known cases. In Srebrenica, far beyond the headlines, people of different ethnicities had lived harmoniously for generations, but in the early 1990s, moderate politicians were gradually pushed aside by hardliners from their own parties.[27] Similar processes were at work elsewhere in Bosnia and in Croatia, for example, in Knin.[28] In our day, we have such "moderates" as Milorad Dodik of the Republic Srbska, of whom the savvy US diplomat Richard Holbrooke wrote: "If more leaders like Dodik . . . emerged, and survived, Bosnia would survive as a single state." That was in 1998. But now, writes Elizabeth Zerofsky, Dodik "is one of the most belligerent Serb nationalists." In June 2015, he declared Srebrenica "the greatest deception of the twentieth century." Over the decade, he has figured out what the system rewards.[29]

The dynamic is not entirely unknown in the West. For example, the German leader Helmut Kohl modified his language toward Poland before German unification in 1990, refusing to guarantee its borders, in order to compete against nationalist forces further to his right. But the issue was not, and could not be, represented as an ultimate danger; it was political opportunism in a powerful country. The more extreme argumentation was reserved for Serbs in Croatia or Bosnia; for Kosovar Albanians; or for Croats or Slovaks trying to hold on to their "own" land. Or for Poland's Tadeusz Mazowiecki, who tried unsuccessfully to relay to Kohl his own predicament as a political centrist.[30]

The fact of the threatened "people" being both social and ethnic helped make the social and ethno-national arguments inseparable and also mutually reinforcing. In the Hungary of the 1940s, the antifascist narrative—a narrative set against nationalist extremism—had to be told in terms of national liberation, with ethnic and social concerns overlapping. Here, the left argued, the real "people" were the peasantry, who had been betrayed by other classes. When the two major Christian churches attempted to legitimate themselves in the postwar order, they also did so in terms of "the people."[31] In Poland, the committee that the Soviets set up to rule the country in 1944 was called the Committee of National Liberation; farther south, the Yugoslav Communists had just set up an Antifascist Committee for the National Liberation of Yugoslavia.

In Poland, state and church competed for the more genuine representation of the national narrative in the 1950s and 1960s; both celebrated a millennium. The church's more powerful claim was evident even in a blank portrait of the Black Madonna. Across the region, there was also a rivalry among national Communists, for example, Poland's Władysław Gomułka and Hungary's János Kádár. The latter maintained power by placating the needs of the people and filling shop windows decorated in national colors on state holidays; the former failed when his policies caused students and eventually workers to emerge in opposition on the streets—singing patriotic songs and waving flags, including the powerful image of a red and white banner besmirched with blood.

* * *

In a comparative European perspective, these workers carrying national flags seem exotic and are poorly understood. Well-known treatments, even of authors from Central Europe—like Ernst Gellner or Eric Hobsbawm—whittle down the specificity of the region's nationalism beyond recognition as they shave off edges to fit it into a global definition of the term. Hobsbawm's idea of the nation was to apply to every corner of the earth, but in this book, we have paid attention to what people in one corner meant by this word. In that corner, the coordinates of the global story as told in Gellner's *Nations and Nationalism* are either irrelevant or secondary: for example, John Stuart Mills's idea that a national state had to be "feasible," or that nationalism required a particular threshold of size before it could be properly launched. Czechs or Slovenes knew nothing of such parameters and made their history without and against them. Hobsbawm's idea that language and history were not decisive criteria would have struck virtually everyone in East Central Europe as nonsensical—though it may well apply to the phenomenon of nationalism as observed from a satellite high above the earth.[32]

And one might add: a satellite in fixed orbit above Western Europe. The most influential book on nationalism supposes the vital role of "vernacular print capitalism" in propelling the spread of nationalism. Yet when the national movements arose in Hungary and Serbia or Poland, there was little if any capitalism, and into the twentieth century, the region was plagued by illiteracy. Where people could read, their vernacular was often suppressed. If nationalism arose, it was in the feelings, ideas, and violent acts of human beings we have identified, some of them priests and scholars, some of them brigands.

The author of the study in question, the anthropologist Benedict Anderson, uncovers some of those names for his readers—Dobrovský, Jungmann, and Kazinczy—but gives no inkling of the passions that fired their labors. He connects them to a genealogy of ideas of a Europe to which they did not belong, to Western imaginations preoccupied with the exploitation of America and Asia. But Dobrovský and Jungmann were concerned about their own local peoples. They were not like the scholar-historians described by Edward Said, who thirsted to witness the "different, the strange, the distant." Instead they were obsessed with ensuring that what was different and strange in Bohemia or Hungary did not disappear.[33]

They were romantics whose quiet *Sturm and Drang* struggle and lived paradox jibe poorly with the schemes of social scientists. Benedict Anderson said nothing about the hundreds of thousands who flocked to mass meetings in Transylvania or South Bohemia, not to mention the killing grounds in Serbia or Poland.[34] Neither he nor Hobsbawm takes readers into the shadow zones of empires, where the humiliation of social and national oppression coincided; they have little time for the paradox of patriots mobilizing for nationalities that did not yet exist; or of nationalists creating the new by reconfiguring the old. Modernization (though not necessarily "capitalism") was crucial, not as a nation-producing force, but as a force against which the nation emerged by reacting to it. The birth moment of 1784 was a rebellion against centralization and rationalization. Later, modernization aided the national communities, but modern nations also grew under largely premodern conditions, for example, in Serbia.

Thus capitalism did not produce nationalism in Eastern Europe; instead, it was a device that helped reshape and spread national ideas and identities that already existed.[35] What generated those ideas and identities, and the commitment to live for them, was the consuming fear of oblivion, profound resentment over condescension, and smoldering hatred of subjugation. Why these emotions emerged across the East European map in the late eighteenth century had to do with imperial powers being themselves (that is, trying to outdo one another for power and glory). Joseph II wanted to be France and Great Britain—simultaneously nation-state and vast empire—Catherine the preeminent European land power, and the sultans wanted to ensure that they were not driven from Europe altogether. Thus their dangerous acts of rooting out corruption in the Greek and Serb lands.

The first visible substance that the new nationalisms nurtured in this vast space on the edges of empires was language, and language is the most arresting blind spot in the analyses of the best-known theorists. In Anderson's scheme, the vernacular was a given that had only to be transcribed; in fact, the vernacular emerged only after decades of contentious "imagining" brought it to life despite internal dissension among patriots, and against the wishes of recalcitrant censors.[36] The Czech case again is paradigmatic: every inch of Czech newspaper space, every minute of Czech theater performance, each new Czech classroom were objects of human effort—effort for which neither Anderson, nor the other major theorists have time, because they are not universal.

Anderson imagined nationalism moving across borders in a chain reaction beginning in France. In basic outline this claim is incontrovertible. That a nation should control its destiny from within defined boundaries, was a lesson people in and beyond Europe drew from Paris. But where Eastern Europe is concerned, the reality of transfer was more paradoxical. The first to absorb the French model—Germans—simultaneously rejected it and molded their version of nationhood around things that had supposedly eluded the model nation, namely, the language and culture the French took for granted. East Europeans then formed their own ideas of nationness against Germany, while also focusing on culture and language.[37] To an outsider visiting Prague in 1860, the Czech anti-world seemed indistinguishable from the local German variant: Czechs ate the same food, wore the same clothes, loved similar music and stories, had the same local saints, and the same professional ambitions and aspirations for the good life. That was the impression one had until one began listening to what Czechs were saying in their distinct, precious, and, for the Germans, vexingly difficult vernacular.

They spoke of the fate of being a small nation, controlled like a colony, desperately in need of secure borders in a way that citizens of long-established and powerful states like Britain and France could not understand. T. G. Masaryk—an outsider who became an insider—first had to master *that* language to build the Czechoslovak nation-state. It's a message that still eludes Western observers, oddly enough, precisely for their insistence on seeing Eastern Europe simply as an extension of their own European space. (Rejoining Europe, after all, was the prime goal of the dissident movements.) In Cold War terms, what happened after 1989 appeared to be the first world embracing and absorbing the second in a concluding act of history.

Yet beginning in about 2010, we have seen that East Central Europe stubbornly carries its own past. This morning, January 4, 2019, the *New York Times* printed a letter on the injustice of Trianon![38] The fact is that East Central Europe is a place where the first, second, and third worlds persist and overlap, each making claims on the same and different pasts. After 1989, the Czech lands, for example, came under the sway of the determined neoliberal Václav Klaus, a local nationalist of sorts, but before that they were a center of the second world's anticapitalism, and before that, colonial subjects, co-inventors of the idea of national liberation struggles, going back to the late eighteenth century.

The scholar-patriots of that distant time, together with the Czech students of 1968 and 1989, Polish workers of 1956 and 1988, and Yugoslav intellectuals of the 1960s or 1980s, all intertwined three strands of struggle for liberal, social, and national rights: for responsible political representation, lives in dignity without want, protection of their national cultures. The stories of 1938, 1948, and 1968 were not a radical break but a refreshed version of older stories of self-assertion against foreign domination. In many ways the big-bang of 1919, or Budapest's 1956 and Prague's 1968, were a replay of the ferment of 1848/1849. The miraculous 1989 was a national liberation struggle, as well as an assertion of deeper traditions of local democracy, and basic civic rights, traditions going back centuries. See, for example, the Polish constitution of 1791 or the very old Hungarian traditions of local self-rule.

If there is a lesson from these stories, it is that when the demands of any of these three worlds are met with contempt, forces emerge claiming to set things right, forces that are rarely liberal. The Habsburg monarchy, under siege from many claimants, liberal and otherwise, opened the Pandora's box of representative government in the 1860s, and what came forth, especially after the liberals' failure of 1879, has been various kinds of populism, left and right, all briefly united in 1882 at Linz. The intervening generations have witnessed the temporary victories of liberal nationalism; national socialism; socialist nationalism; and most recently after the "return to Europe," yet again an intense nationalism, connected to the past—to events like Trianon—but also to a politics for which a name has yet to be found.

ACKNOWLEDGMENTS

My first debt is to the institutions that have supported my education on the East European region: Georgetown University and its School of Foreign Service, the University of Heidelberg, Jagiellonian University in Kraków and its onetime Instytut Badań Polonijnych, and then the history departments at the Universities of Michigan, at Harvard and the University of California at Berkeley. The last supported this project with a Humanities Research fellowship. I have been privileged to present my work at the Imre Kertesz Kollege at the University of Jena and at the Central European University in Budapest. That last magnificent institution shows with special poignancy how crucial universities are for sustaining our culture, yet how vulnerable they become when not protected from the forces of fear and ignorance.

I express my enduring thanks to the teachers who have helped me learn about the region, beginning with Richard Stites, James Shedel, Kurt Jankowsky, Ronald Murphy, SJ, and Jan Karski (Georgetown); then Andrzej Brożek and Władysław Miodunka (Kraków); and Bogdana Carpenter, Roman Szporluk, Zvi Gitelman, Geoff Eley, and Ron Suny (University of Michigan). Though I never enrolled in coursework at Charles University, I am especially grateful to the late Jan Havránek for his unstinting generosity. At Harvard I had the superb fortune of frequent conversations with my teachers Stanisław Barańczak, Charlie Maier, and Roman Szporluk, all three blessed with a genius for everything that is truly human. I acknowledge two Harvard institutions that provided superb conditions for reflection and engagement, Lowell House, and its generous and humane masters William and Mary Lee Bossert; as well the Center for European Studies, where Abby Collins, Guido Goldman, Stanley Hoffman, and Charlie Maier created an extraordinary climate of intellectual discovery (at a very exciting time in world history).

Over decades I have accumulated a wealth of insight on the region from friends and colleagues, of whom I mention Manuela Gretkowska, Tony Levitas, Witold Rodkiewicz, Jan-Christoph Zoels, Igor Lukes, Bärbel Baltes, Mark Pittaway, Padraic Kenney, Michael David-Fox, Katja David-Fox, Alan Taylor, Keely Stauter-Halsted, István Rév, Paul Hanebrink, Grzegorz Ekiert, Norma Feldman, Balázs Trencsényi, Iván T. Berend, Justin Jampol, Stefan Wolle, Thomas Lindenberger, Zach Shore, Christoph Klessmann, Cameron Munter, Martin Guntau, Włodek Borodziej, Evelina Janczur, Timothy Garton Ash, Ivo

Goldstain, Paweł Machcewicz, Urszula Pałłasz, Larry Wolff and David Wolff, Melissa Feinberg, Tvrtko Jakovina, Agnieszka Rudnicka, Maria Bucur, Holly Case, Anna Machcewicz, Kriszti Fehervary, Calvin Mackerron, Jim Gerlach, Artur Dmochowski, Jeff Kopstein, Piotr Hübner, Anja Machcewicz, James Felak, Peter Baldwin, Gary Cohen, Peter Haslinger, Eric Weitz, Staszek Obirek, Ralph Jessen, Jürgen Kocka, Omer Bartov, Jan Grabowski, Tim Snyder, Thomas Küttler, Steve Mull, Lutz Niethammer, Anna and Ludwik Spissowie, Michal Kopeček, Martin Putna, Małgosia Mazurek, Thomas Gertler, Peter Luban, Marci Shore, Bogdan Iacob, Vladimir Tismaneanu, Gosia Fidelis, Katherine Jolluck, Scott B. Smith, Justin Sparks, MaruškaSvašková, Bruce Berglund, Dirk Moses, Sam Moyn, Patrick Patterson, Lee Blackwood, Jeremy King, Brad Abrams, Ben Frommer, Árpád von Klimó, and Mark Keck-Szajbel.

Among the graduate students I've had the pleasure of learning from, I mention Chad Bryant, James Krapfl, Winson Chu, Edith Sheffer, Stephen Gross, Brian McCook, Michael Dean, Terry Renaud, Andrew Kornbluth, Victoria Smolkin, Nicole Eaton, Andrej Milivojevic, Sarah Cramsey, Helaine Blumenthal, Clara Leon, Elizabeth Wenger, Jacob Mikanowski, Blaze Joel, Will Jenkins, Richard Smith, Joy Neumeyer, Sara Friedman, Dan Perez, Jason Morton, Lee Hekking, Paweł Kościelny, Thom Sliwkowski, Ula Madej-Krupitski, Harrison King, Alex Soros, and Agnieszka Smełkowska.

At UC Berkeley I have also benefited from conversations with dozens of colleagues and thank those with whom I have discussed themes relevant to this book: Peggy Anderson, Vicki Bonnell, Dick Buxbaum, John Efron, Gerry Feldman, Victoria Frede, Grisha Freidin, George Breslauer, Stefan-Ludwig Hoffmann, David Hollinger, Andrew Janos, Tom Laqueur, Czesław Milosz, Eric Naiman, Vanessa Ogle, Irina Paperno, Nick Riasanovsky, Dylan Riley, Daniel Sargent, Yuri Slezkine, Ned Walker, Jason Wittenberg, Reggie Zelnik, Steve Fish, and Peter Zinoman. I also extend special thanks to Ronelle Alexander, Andrew Barshay, and David Frick, with whom I had the pleasure of co-teaching, and to Jeff Pennington, Barbara Vojtek, Louanna Curley, and Zach Kelly of the Institute for Slavic, East European, and Eurasian Studies at UC Berkeley, without whom this book would have been unthinkable.

At Princeton University Press, Eric Crahan, Pamela Weidman, and Nathan Carr all performed extraordinary labors to shepherd this book to press; Brigitta van Rheinberg suggested the book's theme and generously shared with me her wisdom about writing and about thinking.

Some colleagues very kindly shouldered the burden of reading parts of the book and offering important advice: Bill Hagen, Tessa Harvey, Konrad Jarausch,

Norman Naimark, Gyuri Peteri, Brian Proter-Szücs, Joachim von Puttkamer, Brigitta van Rheinberg, Jim Sheehan, Philipp Ther, and Jason Wittenberg. Also crucial was the careful reading given by my style and copy editors, John Palattella and Cyd Westmoreland, who improved the prose and saved me from uncounted blunders (all remaining blunders of any kind are of course my responsibility).

Special thanks to David Cox, Andrej Milivojević, and Paweł Kościelny for preparing the maps, tables, and index.

Finally, I thank my parents and brothers, as well as my wife Fiona and our children, Nico, Hugo, Charlotte, and Irena, for making and sharing a home with me.

My apologies if the foregoing resembles a list (it is): each name included here is a person whose generosity and inspiration I treasure, and to say exactly why would require another book, at least.

APPENDIX: TABLES

TABLE A.1. Population of East Central European Countries, 1870–2000 (millions)

Country	1870	1890	1910	1920	1940	1950	1960	1980	1990	2000
Germany	39.2	47.6	62.9	60.9	69.8	68.4	72.5	78.3	79.4	82.2
Austria	4.5	5.4	6.6	6.5	6.7	6.9	7.0	7.5	7.7	8.1
Poland	16.9	22.9	26.6	24.0	30.0	24.8	29.6	35.6	38.1	38.7
Czech Republic	7.6	8.6	10.0	10.0	11.2	8.9	9.7	10.3	10.3	10.3
Slovakia	2.5	2.6	2.9	3.0	—	3.5	4.0	5.0	5.3	5.4
Hungary	5.9	6.6	7.6	8.0	9.3	9.3	10.0	10.7	10.4	10.1
Croatia	2.4	2.9	3.5	3.4	3.8	3.9	4.2	4.6	4.8	4.5
Bosnia and Herzegovina	1.2	1.6	2.0	1.9	—	2.7	3.2	4.1	4.4	4.0
Serbia	—	2.2	2.9	4.8	—	6.7	7.5	9.0	9.3	10.1
Romania	9.2	10.4	11.9	12.3	15.9	16.3	18.4	22.1	22.9	22.5
Bulgaria	2.6	3.4	4.5	5.1	6.7	7.3	7.9	8.8	8.9	7.8

Source: Jonathan Fink-Jensen, "Total Population," https://clio-infra.eu/Indicators/TotalPopulation.html# (accessed June 15, 2019).

Note:—, not available.

TABLE A.2. Population Engaged in Agriculture, Forestry, and Related Activities in East Central European Countries, 1910–1990 (%)

Country	1910	1920	1930	1950	1960	1970	1980	1990
Germany	35	31	33	25	13	7	5	3
Austria	40	40	38	34	24	15	10	8
Poland		64	60	58	48	39	29	25
Czechoslovakia	40	40	33	39	26	17	13	13
Hungary	64	56	51	52	38	25	18	15
Yugoslavia	80	79	76	73	64	50	32	21
Romania	78	78	72	72	64	49	31	24
Bulgaria	78	78	75	73	57	35	18	13

Sources: For 1910: Ivan T. Berend and György Ránki, The European Periphery and Industrialization, 1780–1914 (Cambridge, 1982), 159; David Turnock, Eastern Europe: An Historical Geography, 1815–1945 (London, 1989), 104. For 1920: Derek Aldcroft and Steven Morewood, Economic Change in Eastern Europe since 1918 (Aldershot, England, 1995), 18; Dušan Miljković, ed. Jugoslavija 1918–1988: Statistički Godišnjak (Belgrade, 1989), 39. For 1930: Dudley Kirk, Europe's Population in the Interwar Years (New York, 1968), 200; Wilbert Moore, Economic Demography of Eastern and Southern Europe (Geneva, 1945), 26, 35. For 1950–1980: International Labour Office, Economically Active Population Estimates and Projections, 1950–2025, vol. 4 (Geneva, 1986), 160–170. For 1990: Alexander Klein, Max-Stephan Schulze, and Tamás Vonyó, "How Peripheral Was the Periphery? Industrialization in East Central Europe Since 1870," in The Spread of Modern Industry to the Periphery since 1871, Kevin H. O'Rourke and Jeffrey Gale, eds. (Oxford, 2017), 76. For Germany: Johan Swinnen, The Political Economy of Agricultural and Food Policies (New York, 2018), 72.

Notes: Figures for Bulgaria and Romania in 1910 and 1920 are listed as a range in the sources cited above (75% to 78%). For 1910, figures for Czechoslovakia are based on Bohemia-Moravia and Slovakia (34% and 61%, respectively), and for Yugoslavia on Serbia and Croatia-Slavonia (82% and 79%, respectively).

TABLE A.3. Illiteracy Rates in East Central European Countries, 1930s–1990s (Percentage of Population 15 years old and older)

Country	1930s	1940s	1950s	1960s	1970s	1980s	1990s
Poland	25	—	6	5	2	1	1
Czechoslovakia	4	—	3	—	—	—	—
Hungary	10	6	5	3	2	1	1
Yugoslavia	46	27	27	24	17	10	7
Romania	45	—	11	—	—	—	3
Bulgaria	34	24	16	10	—	—	2

Sources: UNESCO, Progress of Literacy in Various Countries: A Preliminary Statistical Study of Available Census Data since 1900 (Paris, 1953); UNESCO, Division of Statistics on Education, Compendium of Statistics on Illiteracy, Statistical Reports and Studies, 31 (Paris, 1990); UNESCO, Division of Statistics on Education, Compendium of Statistics on Illiteracy, Statistical reports and Studies, 35 (Paris, 1995).

Notes: Figures are for those 15 years old and above, except for Czechoslovakia in 1930 (10 years old and older); figures for Poland in 1930, 1950, and 1960, and for Romania in 1930 and 1956, are for those 14 years old and older. Figures for Yugoslavia in 1991 exclude Slovenia and Croatia, where illiteracy was below 3.3% for those 15 years old and older, according to Compendium of Statistics on Illiteracy, 1995.—, not available.

TABLE A.4. Ethnic Composition of East Central European Countries by Census Years, 1920s–2010s (%)

Era	Poland		Czech Republic		Slovakia		Hungary	
Interwar	1920 Census		1930 Census		1930 Census		1920 Census	
	Poles	83.9	Czechs	67.7	Slovaks	70.4	Hungarians	83.9
	Ukrainians	1.8	Poles	0.9	Hungarians	17.2	Slovaks	1.8
	Byelorussians	0.7	Slovaks	0.4	Ukrainians	2.7	Croats	0.7
	Germans	6.6	Germans	28.8	Germans	4.5	Germans	6.6
	Jews	6.0	Jews	1.4	Jews	2.0	Jews	6.0
Postwar	1949 Census		1950 Census		1950 Census		1949 Census	
	Poles	98.6	Czechs	93.9	Slovaks	86.6	Hungarians	98.6
	Ukrainians	0.3	Slovaks	2.9	Hungarians	10.3	Slovaks	0.3
	Germans	0.2	Germans	1.8	Ruthenes	1.4	Germans	0.2
Present	2011 Census		2011 Census		2011 Census		2011 Census	
	Poles	85.6	Czechs	64.3	Slovaks	80.7	Hungarians	85.6
	Silesians	3.2	Slovaks	1.4	Hungarians	8.5	Roma	3.2
	Germans	14.1	Not stated	26.0	Not stated	7.0	Not stated	14.1

Era	Croatia		Bosnia and Herzegovina		Serbia		Romania		Bulgaria	
Interwar	1921 Census		1921 Census		1921 Census		1930 Census		1920 Census	
	Croats	68.9	Serbs	43.5	Serbs	80.8	Romanians	77.8	Bulgarians	83.4
	Serbs	16.9	Bosniaks	30.9	Albanian	10.2	Hungarians	10.0	Turks	11.2
	Italians	6.1	Croats	21.6	Vlachs	3.9	Roma	1.7	Roma	1.3
	Germans	2.9	Germans	0.9	Germans	0.1	Germans	4.4	Germans	1.0
	Jews	0.1	Jews	0.6	Jews	0.2	Jews	3.2	Jews	0.9

Postwar	1948 Census		1948 Census		1948 Census		1949 Census		1956 Census	
	Croats	79.2	Serbs	44.3	Serbs	73.9	Romanians	85.7	Bulgarians	85.4
	Serbs	14.4	Bosniaks	30.7	Bosniaks	8.15	Hungarians	9.4	Turks	8.6
	Italians	2.0	Croats	23.9	Albanians	6.64	Germans	2.2	Germans	2.5
Present	2011 Census		2013 Census		2011 Census		2011 Census		2011 Census	
	Croats	90.4	Bosniaks	50.1	Serbs	83.3	Romanians	88.6	Bulgarians	84.8
	Serbs	4.4	Serbs	30.8	Hungarians	3.5	Hungarians	6.5	Turks	8.8
	Bosniaks	0.7	Croats	15.4	Bosniaks	2.0	Roma	3.3	Roma	4.9

Sources: Piotr Eberhardt and Jan Owsiński, Ethnic Groups and Population Changes in Twentieth-Century Central-Eastern Europe: History, Data, and Analysis (New York, 2003); Główny Urząd Statystyczny, Struktura narodowo-etniczna, językowa i wyznaniowa ludności Polski: Narodowy spis powszechny ludności i mieszkań 2011 (Warsaw, 2015); Český statistický úřad, "Obyvatelstvo podle národnosti podle výsledků sčítání lidu v letech 1921–2011," https://www.czso.cz/documents/10180/45948568/13005517016.pdf/7def9876-5651-4a16-ac13-01110eef94b?version=1.0 (Accessed June 15, 2019); Štatistický úrad Slovenskej republiky, "TAB. 115 Obyvateľstvo podľa pohlavia a národnosti, Sčítanie obyvateľov, domov a bytov 2011." https://census2011.statistics.sk/tabulky.html (accessed June 15, 2019); Központi Statisztikai Hivatal, 2011 Évi népszámlálás, vol. 3, Országos adatok (Budapest, 2013), 67; Državni zavod za statistiku Republike Hrvatske, "Popisa stanovništva, kućanstava i stanova, Stanovništvo prema državljanstvu, narodnosti, materinjem jeziku i vjeri" (Zagreb, 2012), 11; Agencija za statistiku Bosne i Hercegovine, Popis stanovništva, domaćinstava i stanova u Bosni i Hercegovini, juni 2013 (Sarajevo, 2013), 54; Bogoljub Kočović, Etnički demografski razvoj u Jugoslaviji od 1921 do 1991 godine (Paris, 1998); "Ukupno stanovništvo (građansko i vojničko, trajno i prolazno) po veroispovesti," http://pod2.stat.gov.rs/ObjavljenePublikacije/G1921/Pdf/G19214001.pdf (accessed June 15, 2019); Republički zavod za statistiku, Popis stanovništva, domaćinstava i stanova 2011 u Republici Srbiji, vol. 1 (Belgrade, 2012), 14–15; Comisia Județeană Pentru Recensământul Populației și al Locuințelor, Județul Sibiu, "Comunicat de presă 2 februarie 2012 privind rezultatele provizorii ale Recensământului Populației și Locuințelor—2011," (Bucharest, 2012, 10), http://www.recensamantromania.ro/wp-content/uploads/2012/02/Comunicat_DATE_PROVIZORII_RPL_2011.pdf (accessed June 15, 2019); Natsionalen statisticheski institute, Prebroyavane na naselenieto i zhilishtnya fond prez 2011 godina (okonchatelnidanni) (Sofia, 2012), 23.

Notes: Poland in 1931 and Slovakia in 1950: Ruthenes and Ukrainians were counted together. Yugoslavia in 1921 calculated the numbers of Jews by religion; otherwise, ethnicity was determined by mother tongue. Vojvodina, with its large Hungarian population, was not included in figures for Serbia. Bosniaks are Serbo-Croatian–speaking Muslims; Vlachs are speakers of Romanian.

TABLE A.5. National Income in East Central European Countries, 1890–2000 (gross domestic product per capita, 1990 international dollars)

Country	1890	1910	1920	1929	1950	1960	1980	1989	2000
Germany	2,428	3,348	2,796	4,051	3,881	7,705	14,114	16,558	18,944
Austria	2,443	3,290	2,412	3,699	3,706	6,519	13,759	16,360	20,962
Poland	1,284	1,690	—	2,117	2,447	3,215	5,740	5,684	7,309
Czechoslovakia	1,505	1,991	1,933	3,042	3,501	5,108	7,982	8,768	9,320
Hungary	1,473	2,000	1,709	2,476	2,480	3,649	6,306	6,903	6,772
Yugoslavia	776	973	949	1,256	1,428	2,370	6,297	6,203	4,744
Romania	1,246	1,660	—	1,152	1,182	1,844	4,135	3,941	3,047
Bulgaria	1,132	1,137	—	1,227	1,651	2,912	6,044	6,216	5,483

Sources: "Maddison Project Database 2013." https://www.rug.nl/ggdc/historicaldevelopment/maddison/releases /maddison-project-database-2013 (accessed June 15, 2019); Jutta Bolt and Jan Luiten van Zanden. "The Maddison Project: Collaborative Research on Historical National Accounts," Economic History Review 67:3 (2014), 627–651.

Notes: All figures are given in units of 1990 equivalent dollars; the 1890 and 1910 figures for Bulgaria are from 1899 and 1909; figures for Czechoslovakia and Yugoslavia before 1920 and after 1989 are for the Czech Republic and Serbia, respectively.—, not available.

TABLE A.6. Annual Rates of Growth of Net Material Product in East Central European Countries, 1956–1965 (%)

Country	1956–1960	1961–1964
East Germany	7.1	3.4
Poland	6.5	6.2
Czechoslovakia	7.0	1.9
Hungary	6.0	4.1
Yugoslavia	8.0	6.9
Romania	6.6	9.1
Bulgaria	7.0	5.8

Source: Geoffrey Swain and Nigel Swain, Eastern Europe since 1945 (New York, 1993), 127.

ABBREVIATIONS

AK	Home Army (Poland)
BANU	Bulgarian Agrarian National Union
BBWR	Non-Party Bloc for Cooperation with the Government
BSP	Bulgarian Socialist Party
CIA	Central Intelligence Agency (USA)
DM	Deutsche Mark
Endecja	National Democracy (Poland)
EU	European Union
FF	Fatherland Front (Bulgaria)
FSO	Passenger Automobile Factory (Żerań, Poland)
GDR	German Democratic Republic
GG	*Generalgouvernement* [General Government] for the Occupied Polish Territories (Nazi Germany)
HDZ	Croatian Democratic Union
IMRO	Internal Macedonian Revolutionary Organization
JNA	Yugoslav Federal Army
KOR	Committee for the Defense of Workers (Poland)
MNO	Muslim National Organization (Yugoslavia)
NATO	North Atlantic Treaty Organization
NDH	Independent State of Croatia
NEM	New Economic Mechanism (Hungary)
NGO	nongovernmental organization
NKVD	National Commissariat for Internal Affairs (Secret Police, Soviet Union)
NSDAP	National Socialist German Workers Party
OZON	Camp of National Unification (Poland)
Pětka	Committee of Five (Czechoslovakia)

PPS   Polish Socialist Party

PSL   Polish Peasants' Party

SA   Assault Division (Nazi Germany)

SDAP   Austrian Social Democratic Party

SED   Socialist Unity Party of Germany (East German Communist Party)

SLD   Alliance of the Democratic Left (Poland's post-Communist Party)

SPD   Social Democratic Party of Germany

STASI   Ministry of State Security (East Germany)

UDF   Union of Democratic Forces (Bulgaria)

NOTES

Introduction

1. The German is *völkische Flurbereinigung*.

2. According to Ernst Gellner, nationalism is "primarily a political principle, which holds that the political and national unit should be congruent." *Nations and Nationalism* (Ithaca, 2006), 1.

3. President Bill Clinton on Bosnia, February 1994. Cited in Bill Dobbs, "Pitfalls of Pendulum Diplomacy," *Washington Post*, May 16, 1999.

4. For a lucid discussion of different kinds of rationality leading to interethnic violence, see William W. Hagen, *Anti-Jewish Violence in Poland* (Cambridge, 2017), 50–54.

5. Benedict Anderson, *Imagined Communities: Reflections on the Origin and Spread of Nationalism* (New York, 1991). Historians have tended to overlook the fact that Anderson "analyzed the historical circumstances that were independent of the wishes of 'nationalists.'" For a critical discussion, see Miroslav Hroch, *European Nations: Explaining Their Formation* (London, 2015), 11–14.

6. The Kingdom of Bohemia emerged in 1198 and was part of the Holy Roman Empire until 1806. After that, it became a crown land of the Habsburg monarchy (and until 1866 was part of the German Confederation). At times the kingdom included much of Brandenburg and all of Silesia, but after 1742, it was limited to the territories of the Duchy of Bohemia (which dated from the ninth century), the Margraviate of Moravia (attached in the early eleventh century), and Austrian Silesia. At present, this territory constitutes the Czech Republic.

7. Max Schlesinger, *The War in Hungary 1848–49*, vol. 1, trans. John Edward Taylor (London, 1850), 23–24. Jonathan Sperber calls the massacres the "most violent of all the events of the mid-century revolution," *European Revolutions: 1848–1851* (New York, 1994), 137. The Greek Revolution of the 1820s had involved brutal murders and expulsions of a sizable Muslim population; more limited extrusions of Muslims occurred in the Serb uprising of 1804. Michael Schwartz, *Ethnische "Säuberungen" in der Moderne: Globale Wechselwirkungen* (Munich, 2013), 241.

8. Letter to *Magdeburger Zeitung*, April 20, 1848, in *Politische Briefe Bismarcks aus den Jahren 1849–1889* (Berlin, 1889), 2–4.

9. March 4, 1919. Joseph Rothschild, *East Central Europe between the Two World Wars* (Seattle, 1974), 79.

10. See Paul Krugman, "Why It Can't Happen Here," *New York Times*, August 27, 2018.

11. In 1941, pogroms took place in 219 of 2,304 municipalities in eastern Poland. Jason Wittenberg and Jeffrey S. Kopstein, *Intimate Violence: Anti-Jewish Pogroms on the Eve of the Holocaust* (Ithaca, 2018).

12. Karl Marx and Frederick Engels, *The German Ideology*, ed. C. J. Arthur (London, 2004), 58.

13. "It was misguided," he wrote, to think that the "Roumans of Wallachia, who never had a history, nor the energy required to have one, are of equal importance to the Italians who have a history of 2,000 years." Friedrich Engels, "What Have the Working Classes to Do with Poland,"

in Karl Marx, *Political Writings*, vol. 3, *The First International and After* (Harmondsworth, UK, 1974), 383. Marx ridiculed the idea that the insignificant Czechs, living at the heart of an economically dynamic Germany, could have a separate state. Jiří Kořalka, *Tschechen im Habsburgerreich und in Europa* (Munich, 1991), 221, fn. 61; Hans Magnus Enzensberger, ed., *Gespräche mit Marx und Engels* (Frankfurt, 1973), 709 ff.

14. "Der Magyarische Kampf," in Karl Marx and Friedrich Engels, *Werke*, Vol. 6 (Berlin, 1959), 175. Engels even took time to ridicule the Polish national anthem, according to which Poland would not perish: he wrote that the only undying characteristic of the Poles was their desire to quarrel for no apparent reason. Hubert Orlowski, *"Polnische Wirtschaft": Zum deutschen Polendiskurs der Neuzeit* (Wiesbaden, 1996), 276.

15. Kenneth Jowitt called them "geographically contiguous replica regimes." *New World Disorder: The Leninist Extinction* (Berkeley, 1993), 176.

16. Karol Goláň, ed., *Pamäti z mladších rokov života* (Bratislava, 1950).

17. Patrick Kingsley, "Safe in Hungary, Viktor Orban Pushes His Message across Europe," *New York Times*, June 5, 2018.

18. Pieter Judson, *Guardians of the Nation: Activists on the Language Frontiers of Imperial Austria* (Cambridge, MA, 2006), 257. Benedict Anderson failed to note the specificity of East European nationalism's driving concern with language and did not explore the emotional and intellectual energies driving it. Likewise, Eric Hobsbawm, adopting a mostly West European perspective, fails to appreciate the concerns about loss of identity that motivated East European nationalism. Anderson, *Imagined Communities*; Eric Hobsbawm, *Nations and Nationalism since 1780* (Cambridge, 1992), 24, 32–33.

19. Tara Zahra, "Imagined Non-Communities: National Indifference as a Category of Analysis," *Slavic Review* 69:1 (2010), 93–119. For a critical assessment of this approach, see Gerald Stourzh, "The Ethnicizing of Politics and 'National Indifference' in Late Imperial Austria," in Gerald Stourzh, *Der Umfang der österreichischen Geschichte Ausgewählte Schriften 1924–1950* (Vienna, 2011), 283–323.

20. People who spoke two or more languages "with equal proficiency was quite small" in the Habsburg monarchy, though functional bilingualism was widespread. Jakub S. Benes, *Workers and Nationalism: Czech and German Social Democracy in Habsburg Austria, 1890–1918* (Oxford, 2017), 60.

21. I therefore do not share Brian Porter-Szücs's view that what preceded modern nationalism was simply "enacted nationhood" or a "cluster of cultural practices," for example, of common cuisine, folk art, or music; there was strong ideational substance to premodern nationhood, even if it did not embrace everyone. It is also, as I will show, ahistorical to claim that any of the East European nations, Poland included, could escape ethnic nationhood, with its basic characteristic of being a "tool for demarcating 'us' and 'them.'" Brian Porter-Szücs, *When Nationalism Began to Hate* (Oxford, 2000), 7.

22. Students of national indifference have focused on areas between nations, eastern Galicia or Upper Silesia, parts of the Czech lands, or relatively short time frames.

23. Norman Davies, *God's Playground: A History of Poland*, vol. 1 (New York, 1980), 542; Karol Lutostański, *Les partages de la Pologne et la lutte pour l'indépendance* (Paris, 1918), 229.

24. Karel Havlíček-Borovský, ed., *Duch Národních novin: spis obsahujici úvodní články z Národních novin roků 1848, 1849, 1850* (Kutna Hora, Bohemia, 1851), 2; T. G. Masaryk, *Česká*

otázka (Prague, 1895), 192–193. In March 1848, the first new newspaper appearing in Vienna proclaimed that nationality was holier than freedom, because it was the first condition for freedom. In Zagreb, Croatian students were writing that freedom without nationality was like a body without a soul, and the Polish National committee in Poznań told the Prussian king's envoy "there is only one freedom for Poland: freedom within our nationality, for ethnicity [*Volkstum*] alone is the soil from which true freedom can spring forth." Nicolae Balcescu, a revolutionary leader in Ottoman controlled Wallachia (a region of Romania), proclaimed "until a people can exist as a nation, it cannot make use of liberty." R. Maršan, *Čechové a Němci r. 1848 a boj o Frankfurt* (Prague, 1898), 35; Misha Glenny, *The Balkans: Nationalism, War, and the Great Powers* (New York, 2001), 48; letter of the Polish National Committee, Poznań of April 6, 1848, to General von Willisen, *Leipziger Zeitung*, April 20, 1848 (111), 2530–2531; George Barany, "Hungary," in Peter Sugar, ed., *Nationalism in Eastern Europe* (Seattle, 1969), 268. On this conviction, see Gale Stokes, "Cognition and the Function of Nationalism," *Journal of Interdisciplinary History* 4:4 (1974), 538.

25. Franz Schuselka, *Ist Oesterreich deutsch? Eine statistische und glossirte Beantwortung dieser Frage* (Leipzig, 1843), 19, 21, 23–24. Unless otherwise noted, all translations are mine.

26. Jiří Kořalka, *Tschechen im Habsburgerreich und in Europa* (Vienna, 1991), 68–70.

27. The seminal works on national indifference document in detail the work of nationalist activists but not of activists set against nationalism, let alone favoring some other kind of "indifferent" identity. See especially Judson, *Guardians of the Nations*.

28. See Anthony Oberschall, "The Manipulation of Ethnicity: From Ethnic Cooperation to Violence and War in Yugoslavia," *Ethnic and Racial Studies* 23:6 (2000), 982–1001. The word used to inflate anxieties among Czechoslovak Germans was that they lived as "slaves" (in *Knechtschaft*). On the Nazi campaign to win sympathies for this point of view, see Hermann Graml, *Europas Weg in den Krieg: Hitler und die Mächte 1939* (Munich, 1990), 103–104.

29. Jaromír Navrátil, *The Prague Spring 1968* (Budapest, 1998), 8.

30. The synthetic literature on the region has varied in usage, mostly using "Eastern Europe" or "East Central Europe" to denote the nations of the former Soviet Bloc, but sometimes "Central Europe." For a few exemplary cases, see Antony Polonsky, *The Little Dictators: The History of Eastern Europe Since 1918* (London, 1975); Robin Okey, *Eastern Europe 1740–1985: From Feudalism to Communism* (London, 1991); Vladimir Tismaneanu, *Reinventing Politics: Eastern Europe from Stalin to Havel* (New York, 1992); R. J. Crampton, *Eastern Europe in the Twentieth Century* (London, 1994); Norman Naimark and Leonid Gibianskii, eds., *The Establishment of Communist Regimes in Eastern Europe* (Boulder, 1997); Ivan T. Berend, *Decades of Crisis: Central and Eastern Europe before WWI* (Berkeley, 1998); Andrew Janos, *East Central Europe in the Modern World* (Stanford, CA, 2000); Padraic Kenney, *The Burdens of Freedom: Eastern Europe Since 1989* (London, 2006); Joachim von Puttkamer, *Ostmitteleuropa im 19. und 20. Jahrhundert* (Munich, 2010); Irina Livezeanu and Árpád von Klimó, eds., *The Routledge History of East Central Europe since 1700* (New York, 2017).

31. If the author were not almost entirely ignorant about the history of Albania and the Albanians, they would fit very much within the subject of the book, though as outsiders to the Soviet Bloc for much of its existence, they are less central to the history of East Central Europe than the countries farther north. Greece likewise would merit inclusion for much of its history up to 1945.

32. The lament that one has become a stranger in one's own land is a complaint of voters for right-wing populism in our days. See Stephen Holmes, "How Democracies Perish," in Cass Sunstein, *Can It Happen Here? Authoritarianism in America* (New York, 2018), 327–428. Lucian Boia has written that the "past is more often invoked, and invoked in the most imperative terms, by those who want to break away from it." *History and Myth in Romanian Consciousness* (Budapest, 2001), 44.

Chapter 1: Peoples of East Central Europe

1. Paul Robert Magosci, *Historical Atlas of Central Europe*, revised edition (Seattle, 2002), 69, 77.

2. Dacians were speakers of a virtually unknown Indo-European language.

3. Traian Stoianovich, *Balkan Worlds: The First and Last Europe* (Armonk, NY, 1994), 122–124.

4. The tribes were originally multilingual, but the Megyeri tribe, a Finno-Ugric component, came to dominate. Jean W. Sedlar, *East Central Europe in the Middle Ages* (Seattle, 1994), 9.

5. Andrew Janos, *The Politics of Backwardness in Hungary* (Princeton, NJ, 1982), 3–4.

6. Reference here is to preliterate German lands. In more recent times, local dialects have receded from areas of northern and central Germany, replaced by high German, breaking the old dialect continua. There is also a continuum of western romance languages.

7. The first Polish king, Mieszko, appears to have made Poland a fief of the Holy See. Sedlar, *East Central Europe*, 142–143, 150.

8. The judgment was Leopold von Ranke's. See his *Serbische Revolution* (Berlin, 1844), 9. On the relation of the investiture controversy of the eleventh century and the later practice of division of power in the west, see Heinrich August Winkler, *Geschichte des Westens*, vol. 1 (Munich, 2009), 20, 57, 61; Hans Maier, "Canossa heute—Mythos und Symbol," in *Canossa 1077*, Christoph Stiegemann and Matthias Wernhoff, eds. (Munich, 2006), 625–630; Eckard Müller-Mertens, "Imperium und Regnum im Verhältnis zwischen Wormser Konkordat und Goldener Bulle," *Historische Zeitschrift* 284 (2007), 561–595.

9. Tim Judah, *The Serbs: History, Myth, and the Destruction of Yugoslavia* (New Haven, CT, 1997), 19–20.

10. Michael Boro Petrovich, *A History of Modern Serbia*, vol. 1 (New York, 1976), 13.

11. Veljko Vujačić, *Nationalism, Myth, and the State in Russia and Serbia* (Cambridge, 2015), 131.

12. Thomas Emmert, *Serbian Golgotha: Kosovo, 1389* (New York, 1990).

13. Laura Silber and Allan Little, *Yugoslavia: Death of a Nation* (New York, 1997), 72. Michael Sells writes that the "development of the Kosovo story in which Slavic Muslims and Serbs are ancient enemies is more recent; it was constructed by nationalist Serbs in the nineteenth century." To this the caveat should be added that nationalists took preexisting ideas and images and formed them into potent weapons for their movement, but they did not manufacture them. And of course the idea that language made a people was not a Serb idea, let alone an original idea of Vuk Karadzić, but was common to East European nationalism. See his *The Bridge Betrayed: Religion and Genocide in Bosnia* (Berkeley, 1996), 37–38. For the development of epic songs into nationalist myths, see Svetozar Koljević, *The Epic in the Making* (Oxford, 1980); Emmert, *Serbian Golgotha*, 122–129.

14. Sabrina P. Ramet, *Nihil Obstat: Religion, Politics, and Social Change in East-Central Europe and Russia* (Durham, NC, 1998), 196.

15. Cynthia Hahn, *Portrayed onto the Heart: Narrative Effect in Pictorial Lives of Saints* (Berkeley, 2001), 325; Jan Kubik, *The Power of Symbols against the Symbols of Power: The Rise of Solidarity and the Fall of State Socialism in Poland* (University Park, PA, 1994), 109 ff.

16. This consciousness formed the "most decisive criterion of proto-nationalism." Eric Hobsbawm, *Nations and Nationalism since 1780* (Cambridge, 1992), 73.

17. The growth of Islam was due also to settlement of Ottoman Muslim elements, especially in Bulgaria. Incentives to convert were high among landowners who wanted to retain their land. Beyond the periodic seizure of young boys for training in military and state administration (*devshirme*), there were also occasional forced conversions, for example, in the seventeenth century in the Rhodope Mountains. R. J. Crampton, *A Concise History of Bulgaria* (Cambridge, 1997), 33–36.

18. Charles Higounet, *Les Allemands en Europe centrale et orientale au Moyen Age* (Paris, 1989); David Frick, *Kith, Kin, and Neighbors: Communities and Confessions in Seventeenth Century Wilno* (Ithaca, NY, 2013). By the time Silesia was lost to the Polish Crown in 1348, the processes of Germanization, especially in the towns, were well advanced. Jerzy Lukowski and Hubert Zawadzki, *A Concise History of Poland* (Cambridge, 2006), 27.

19. See map 32b in Paul Robert Magocsi, *Historical Atlas of Central Europe* (Seattle, 2002), 105. The second line was more jagged than the first.

20. The city's population was about 70,000 in 1921, of whom some 10,000 were Jews. Anne Joseph, "The Secret Jewish History of Bosnia and Sarajevo," *The Forward*, January 30, 2016. Sephardim were about 40 percent of the Yugoslav Jewish population between the wars. Of some 9,000 Sarajevo Jews taken to concentration camps during the war, 1,237 survived. Ivana Vučina Simović, "The Sephardim and Ashkenazim in Sarajevo," *Transversal* 13:2 (2012), 54–57.

21. Sedlar, *East Central Europe*, 181; J. Perles, *Geschichte der Juden in Posen* (Breslau, 1863), 8–9.

22. The number of Jews in Poland-Lithuania is estimated to be between 150,000 and 170,000 in the mid-sixteenth century. Matthias Lehmann, "New Worlds, East and West," in John Efron et al., *The Jews: A History* (Upper Saddle River, NJ, 2009), 204–208.

23. Denis Bašić, "The Roots of the Religious, Ethnic and National Identity of the Bosnian-Herzegovinan Muslims" (PhD dissertation, University of Washington, 2009), 290. In the late nineteenth century, attempts were made to involve non-Muslims in military and state service, with mixed success. Carter V. Findley, "The Acid Test of Ottomanism: The Acceptance of non-Muslims in the Late Ottoman Bureaucracy," in Benjamin Braude and Bernard Lewis, eds., *Christians and Jews in the Ottoman Empire*, vol. 1 (New York, 1982), 342.

24. This blood tax (Devşirme) lasted into the seventeenth century. Noel Malcolm, *Bosnia: A Short History* (New York, 1994), 45–46.

25. Barbara Jelavich, *History of the Balkans*, vol. 1 (Cambridge, 1983), 62–126 and passim.

26. For reflections of such views, see Petrovich, *History of Modern Serbia*; Paul Lendvai, *The Hungarians: A Thousand Years of Victory in Defeat*, Ann Major, trans. (Princeton, NJ, 2003), 99 ff.

27. Petrovich, *History of Modern Serbia*.

28. Peter F. Sugar, *Southeastern Europe under Ottoman Rule 1354–1804* (Seattle, 1977), 258–261; Balázs Trencsényi and Michal Kopeček, eds., *Late Enlightenment: Emergence of Modern National*

Ideas (Budapest, 2006), 218. The Bulgarian movement was strong in South Russia, cities of the Habsburg Empire, and the autonomous principalities of Wallachia and Moldavia. Claudia Weber, *Auf der Suche nach der Nation: Erinnerungskultur in Bulgarien von 1878–1944* (Berlin, 2003), 37–38.

29. Fritz Gschnizter et al., "Volk, Nation, Nationalismus, Masse," in *Geschichtliche Grundbegriffe; historisches Lexikon zur politisch-sozialen Sprache in Deutschland*, Otto Brunner et al., eds., vol. 7 (Stuttgart, 1992), 141–431. Pieter Judson traces five distinct meanings of nation in the late eighteenth century. See *The Habsburg Empire: A New History* (Cambridge, MA, 2016), 85–87.

30. It was 0.52 percent of the French population. Jonathan Dewald, *The European Nobility* (Cambridge, 1996), 22.

31. Janusz Tazbir, "Polish National Consciousness in the Sixteenth to Eighteenth Century," *Harvard Ukrainian Studies* 10:3/4 (1986), 318. In the sixteenth century, at the height of the Polish noble republic, some one-third of the delegates to the Sejm, were non-Catholic, mostly Protestant. But over time, that group became increasingly Catholic, especially as the Catholic Church defended its privileges, so that in the seventeenth century, the idea spread that to be Polish was to be Catholic. Jerzy Topolski, "Die generellen Linien der Entwicklung der polnischen neuzeitlichen Nation," in Almut Bues and Rex Rexhauser, eds., *Mittelalterliche nations—neuzeitliche Nationen* (Wiesbaden, 1995), 145–149.

32. Tazbir, "Polish National Consciousness," 318–319. The Lithuanian nobility thought it had Roman descent. Of course, these ideas went back centuries and had an integrating function, making a diverse group more united.

33. The examples in Russian and Polish are *rab* and *cham*. The trend of using demeaning language to describe rural folk extends to Western Europe, where peasant or paysan long had the connotation of "rustic," "ignorant," "crass," and "rude." The German equivalent was synonymous with "devil," "villain," "looter," and "brigand." Marc Edelman, "What Is a Peasant, What Are Peasantries," at https://ohchr.org/Documents/HRBodies/HrCouncil/WGPeasants/Edelman.pdf (accessed October 17, 2018).

34. On the greater mobility of peasants in Western Europe and the lower propensity of labor rents there, see Markus Cerman, *Villagers and Lords in Eastern Europe, 1300–1800* (London, 2012), 134. On the contrast between England and Eastern Europe, see Mark Bailey, *The Decline of Serfdom in Late Medieval England: From Bondage to Freedom* (Woodbridge, UK, 2014), 82–83. On the failure of innovations in agriculture to reach areas of eastern and southeastern Europe, see Andrew Janos, *East Central Europe in the Modern World* (Stanford, CA, 2000), 56–57.

35. Mirjana Gross writes that the Croatian nobility as a political nation did not identify with peasants or townspeople who spoke their language. Hobsbawm, *Nations and Nationalism*, 74, fn. 50. Into the twentieth century, many Polish peasants felt alienated from the idea of "Poland," and some opposed the state's re-creation in 1918, saying "only the nobles could want a Poland so that people would work for them as they had done in feudal times." Jerzy Tomaszewski, "The National Question in Poland," in M. Teich and R. Porter, eds., *The National Question in Europe in Historical Context* (Cambridge, 1993), 296.

36. See Janusz Tazbir, "Polish National Consciousness in the Sixteenth to the Eighteenth Century," in Frank Sysyn and Ivo Banac, eds., "Concepts of Nationhood in Early Modern Eastern Europe," *Harvard Ukrainian Studies* 10:3/4 (1986), 317.

37. Hans Roos, "Die polnische Demokratie," in Hans-Erich Volkmann, *Die Krise des Parlementarismus in Ostmitteleuropa zwischen den beiden Weltkriegen* (Marburg, Germany, 1967), 15.

38. Peter Bugge, "Czech Nation-Building: National Self-Perception and Politics 1780–1914" (PhD dissertation, University of Aarhus, 1994), 18.

39. Bernd Rill, *Böhmen und Mähren* (Gernsbach, Germany, 2006), 341.

40. Keith Hitchins, *The Rumanian National Movement in Transylvania* (Cambridge, MA, 1969), 9.

41. Saxons were descendants of German settlers invited by Hungarian kings in the thirteenth century; Szeklers descended from a Bulgarian-Turkic tribe, which over the centuries became Hungarian speaking but preserved a distinct social culture. Lendvai, *The Hungarians*, 21, 24, 42. For data on language groups living in Transylvania in this period, see Valér Veres, "Adalékok Erdély 18. századi népessége etnikai összetételének kérdéséhez," *Történeti Demográfiai Évkönyv*, Központi Sztatisztikai Hivatal Népességtudományi Kutatóintézet, ed. (Budapest, 2002), 105. (Thanks to Jeff Pennington for this reference.)

42. They applied Enlightenment ideas about natural civil equality among individuals to the relations between peoples. Keith Hitchins, "Samuel Clain and the Rumanian Enlightenment in Transylvania," *Slavic Review* 23:4 (1964), 660.

43. See the discussion in Ludwig Albrecht Gebhardi, *Fortsetzung der allgemeinen Welthistorie der neueren Zeiten*, vol. 3 (Halle, 1797), 65.

44. Everywhere unflattering ideas emerged about the Germans; some called them "jokers." This from a list of stereotypes that according to one chaplain—Josef Tiso—those peoples had overcome through common service in the trenches of World War I. Roman Holec, "Die slowakische politische Elite vor 1918," in *Religion und Nation*, Martin Schulze Wessel et al., eds. (Essen, Germany, 2015), 34.

45. Nevenko Bartulin, "The Ideology of Nation and Race: The Croatian Ustasha Regime and Its Policies toward Minorities in the Independent State of Croatia, 1941–45" (PhD dissertation, University of New South Wales, Australia, 2006), 66, 72. More commonly "Vlach" is used to describe speakers of Romance languages in territories south of the Danube, but the dual usage is found even in Habsburg documents, for example, the *Statuta valachorum* (1630) regulating the rights of the Orthodox from Ottoman lands who settled in the *Miltärgrenze*.

46. Tazbir, "Polish National Consciousness," 329.

47. Edsel Walter-Stroup, "From Horea-Closca to 1867: Some Observations," in *Transylvania: The Roots of Ethnic Conflict*, John Cadzow et al., eds. (Kent, OH, 1983), 132–140.

48. Gypsies, Greeks, Armenians, Jews, and foreign merchants likewise inhabited cities. Petrovich, *History of Modern Serbia*, 9–11.

49. The example of a church is from Senj, a church in a border area of Croatia near Bosnia. Cathy Carmichael, *Ethnic Cleansing in the Balkans: Nationalism and the Destruction of Tradition* (London, 2003), 21.

50. The setting was sixteenth-century Croatian areas bordering on Bosnia. Catherine Wendy Bracewell, *The Uskoks of Senj: Piracy, Banditry and Holy War in the Sixteenth Century Adriatic* (Ithaca, NY, 1992), 33.

51. Karl Ludwig Freiher von Pöllnitz, *The Memoirs of Charles Lewis Baron de Pollnitz*, vol. 1 (London, 1739), 218, 219. Recently, historians have done much to shatter such images of peasants without agency living under unbridled seigniorial rule. See William W. Hagen, "Early Modern

Bohemia Joins Post-Communist Central Europe," review of Markus Cerman and Hermann Zeitlhofer, eds. *Soziale Strukturen in Böhmen. Ein regionaler Vergleich von Wirtschaft und Gesellschaften in Gutsherrschaften, 16.–19. Jahrhundert* (Vienna, 2002). Review is at H-German@h-net.org (accessed August 2005).

52. George Robert Gleig, *Germany, Bohemia, and Hungary, Visited in 1837*, vol. 2 (London, 1839), 330, 350–352.

53. Etienne Balibar and Immanuel Wallerstein, *Race, Nation, Class: Ambiguous Identities* (London, 1991), 89.

54. This was true of much of Bohemia, Slovakia, what became Romania, and Yugoslavia, as well as the eastern and western stretches of what became Poland; in central Poland and Hungary, landowner and people were often of the same ethnicity, though separated by worlds of difference in privilege, education, and wealth. The landowners considered themselves as a separate nation, and they behaved as such, into the twentieth century.

55. Hans Rothfels speaks of the "dappled" character [*Buntscheckigkeit*] of Eastern Europe, in contrast to Western Europe, where political boundaries more cleanly separated populations, but this did not mean that Western European states were characterized by linguistic uniformity: Hans Rothfels, *Zeitgeschichtliche Betrachtungen* (Göttingen, 1959), 102, 95.

56. For condescension in British and French opinion of the seventeenth and eighteenth century toward Serbs, see Judah, *Serbs*, 48.

57. G. Mazzini asked: "Who thought of the Slavonians ten years ago?" "The Slavonian National Movement," *Lowes Edinburgh Magazine and Protestant Educational Journal* 9 (July 1847), 182.

Chapter 2: Ethnicity on the Edge of Extinction

1. Hugo Hantsch, *Geschichte Österreichs* (Graz, Austria, 1953), 148.

2. Charles Ingrao, *The Habsburg Monarchy 1618–1815* (Cambridge, 2000), 155.

3. Hungary shifted from majority Hungarian ethnically to about 39 percent by 1787. Paul Lendvai, *The Hungarians: A Thousand Years of Victory in Defeat*, Ann Major, trans. (Princeton, NJ, 2003), 99–104; Horst Haselsteiner, "Cooperation and Confrontation," in *A History of Hungary*, Peter Sugar et al., eds. (Bloomington, IN, 1990), 147; Victor L. Tapié, *The Rise and Fall of the Habsburg Monarchy*, Stephen Hardman, trans. (New York, 1971), 184; Geza David, "Adminisration in Ottoman Europe," in *Suleyman the Magnificent and His Age: The Ottoman Empire in the Early Modern Period*, Metin Kunt and Christine Woodhead, eds. (New York, 1995), 86–89.

4. Tapié, *Rise and Fall*, 182; Jörg K. Hoensch, *Geschichte Böhmens* (Munich, 1997), 270.

5. About 185 noble families left, along with ministers, professors, and members of the urban bourgeoisie. Lonnie Smith, *Central Europe: Enemies, Neighbors, Friends* (Oxford, 1996), 89.

6. R. J. W. Evans, *The Making of the Habsburg Monarchy, 1550–1700* (Oxford, 1979), 200.

7. Though Jews continued to face legal restrictions. The crown became hereditary in Hungary in 1687 by decision of the Hungarian Diet. Henryk Wereszycki, *Historia Austrii* (Wrocław, 1972), 102–103.

8. Evans, *Making of the Habsburg Monarchy*, 200, 213. As a result of Ottoman conquest, Hungary was divided in three by the second half of the sixteenth century. A principality of Transylvania emerged in the east that was a vassal of the Ottoman state, and the largely Protestant nobility

there was protected from the Habsburg-led Counter-Reformation. In unoccupied royal Hungary, nobles protected their privileges by threatening to transfer their allegiance from the Habsburgs to the rulers of Transylvania. Most of central and southern Hungary under direct Ottoman rule was devastated, however, and the Magyar element weakened. Geza Palffy, "The Impact of Ottoman Rule on Hungary," *Hungarian Studies Review* 28:1–2 (2001), 112; Lendvai, *The Hungarians*, 98–99.

9. Jean Berénger, *History of the Habsburg Empire 1700–1918*, C. A. Simpson, trans. (London, 1997), 65–66.

10. T. C. W. Blaning, *Joseph II and Enlightened Despotism* (London, 1970), 15.

11. T. C. W. Blanning, *Joseph II* (London, 1974), 71; E. D., "Die deutsche Sprachgrenze," *Deutsche Vierteljahrsschrift* 3 (1844), 201; Corina Petersilka, *Die Zweisprachigkeit Friedrichs des Grossen: ein linguistisches Porträt* (Tübingen, 2005), 39–40.

12. R. J. W. Evans, *Austria, Hungary, and the Habsburgs* (Oxford, 2004), 136–137.

13. Ludwig Gumplowicz, *Das Recht der Nationalitäten und Sprachen in Oesterreich-Ungarn* (Innsbruck, 1879), 26; Bernard Michel, *Nations et nationalismes en Europe centrale* (Paris, 1995), 32–33.

14. Joseph Anton von Riegger, *Für Böhmen von Böhmen*, vol. 3 (Prague, 1793–1794), 2; Joseph Alexander Freiherr von Helfert, *Die österreichische Volksschule: Die Gründung der österreichischen Volksschule durch Maria Theresia* (Prague, 1860), 466.

15. He and his mother did nothing to favor German in the Austrian Netherlands or Italy. John Deak, *Forging a Multinational State: State-Making in Imperial Austria* (Stanford, CA, 2015), 25.

16. Josef Hanzal, "Nižší školství," in Josef Petráň, ed., *Počátky českého národního obrození* (Prague, 1990), 133.

17. Joseph Kalousek, *Geschichte der Königlichen Böhmischen Gesellschaft der Wissenschaften* (Prague, 1885), 23. After the *Verneuerte Landesordnung* of 1627, German was made equal to Czech, and administrative documents were issued in German, Czech, and Latin; by the time of Joseph II, German had the leading position as the administrators used German on a daily basis (they were culturally German), and therefore the shift to sole usage of German in Bohemia was the conclusion of a gradual process. Pavel Trost, "Deutsch-tschechische Zweisprachigkeit," in Bohuslav Havránek, ed., *Deutsch-tschechische Beziehungen* (Prague, 1965), 21–28; Helmut Glück, *Deutsch als Fremdsprache in Europa vom Mittelalter bis zur Barockzeit* (Berlin, 2002), 349–358.

18. Hugh Agnew, *Origins of the Czech National Renascence* (Pittsburgh, PA, 1993), 53; Miroslav Hroch, *Na prahu národní existence: touha a skutečnost* (Prague, 1999), 63. On the general spirit of enlightenment in East Central Europe, its sources and implications, see Balázs Trencsényi, Maciej Janowski, Mónika Baar et al., *A History of Modern Political Thought in East Central Europe*, vol. 1 (Oxford, 2016), 15–136.

19. Hroch, *Na prahu národní existence*, 64.

20. Evans, *Making of the Habsburg Monarchy*, 207

21. Ein Böhme [Franz Kinsky], *Erinnerung über einen wichtigen Gegenstand* (Prague, 1773), 5, 134.

22. Kinsky, *Erinnerung*, 132–134, 207–208.

23. Agnew, *Origins*, 29, 31. For the importance of institutions of the fatherland (including language) to enlightened thought in East Central Europe, see Trencsényi et al., *History of Modern Political Thought*, 16–18, 78–91. On their motivation, see Miroslav Hroch, "Why Did They Begin:

On the Transition from Cultural Reflection to Social Activism," SPIN Lecture 2010, at spinnet. humanities.uva.nl/images/2011-8/hroch-spin-lecture_-2010.pdf (accessed January 7, 2019).

24. František Martin Pelcl, *Kurzgefasste Geschichte der Böhmen* (Prague, 1774), 20; Agnew, *Origins*, 34.

25. Kalousek, *Geschichte*, 24–25; Trencsényi et al., *History of Modern Political Thought*, 58–59; František Bačkovský, *Zevrubné dějiny českého písemnictví doby nové* (Prague, 1886), 281.

26. The municipality where that woman died in 1756 was Wustrow, Lower Saxony, just north of Salzwedel, in the Wendland. Jerzy Strzelczyk, *Po tamtej stronie Odry* (Warsaw, 1968), 261. The news was reported in the local press. For Pelcl's concerns, see Thomas Capek, *Bohemia under Hapsburg Misrule* (New York, 1915), 50.

27. Cited in Eugen Lemberg, *Grundlagen des national Erwachens in Böhmen* (Reichenberg, Czechoslovakia, 1932), 82.

28. Josef Dobrovský, *Korespondence*, vol. 3, Adolf Patera, ed. (Prague, 1908), 78; Agnew, *Origins*, 29, 31.

29. Luboš Merhaut, ed., *Lexikon české literatury: osobnosti, díla, instituce*, vol. 4, part 1 (Prague, 2008), 894–896; F. V. Vykoukal, "O rodišti bratří Thámů," *Světozor* 20 (1886), 534.

30. This also bothered Kinsky, as well as Jan A. Hanke. Karel Tieftrunk, *Historie literatury české* (Prague, 1880), 95–96.

31. František Ladislav Rieger, *Slovník naučný*, vol. 9 (Prague, 1888); Karel Ignaz Tham, *Obrana jazyka českého proti zlobivým jeho utračům* (Prague, 1783).

32. This was Antonín Koniáš, himself a Bohemian. Karel Ignaz Tham, *Über den Charakter der Slawen, dann über den Ursprung, die Schicksale, Vollkommenheiten, und die Nützlichkeit und Wichtigkeit der böhmischen Sprache* (Prague, 1803), 13.

33. Karl Ignaz Tham, *Kunst in drei Monaten böhmisch lesen, schreiben und sprechen zu lernen* (Prague, 1815).

34. Josef Dobrovský, *Geschichte der böhmischen Sprache und alten Literatur* (Prague, 1792); Josef Dobrovský, *Lehrgebäude der böhmischen Sprache* (Prague, 1809); Josef Dobrovský, *Entwurf zu einem allgemeinen Etymologikon der slawischen Sprachen* (Prague, 1813).

35. Cited in Richard Pražák, *Josef Dobrovský als Hungarist und Finno-Ugrist* (Brno, Czechoslovakia, 1967), 102–103.

36. Josef Jungmann, "O jazyku českém" (1803), in *Sebrané drobné spisy*, vol. 1 (Prague, 1869), 6.

37. The feudal dues, *robot*, remained until 1848. Robin Okey, *The Habsburg Monarchy: From Enlightenment to Eclipse* (New York, 2001), 40; Blanning, *Joseph II*, 64, 73, 106.

38. R. J. W. Evans, "The Politics of Language and the Languages of Politics," in *Cultures of Power in Europe during the Long Eighteenth Century*, Hamish Scott et al., eds, (Cambridge, 2007), 203; István Gy Tóth, *Literacy and Written Culture in Early Modern Europe* (Budapest, 2000), 118–145. The names of Hungary's "nations" were given in Latin: Germani, Slavi (Slovaks), Croati, Rutheni, Illyrii (Serbs), and Valachi (Romanians). Helfert, *Österreichische Volkschule*, 467.

39. Horst Haselsteiner, "Cooperation and Confrontation between the Rulers and Noble Estates," in *A History of Hungary*, Peter Sugar et al., eds. (Bloomington, IN, 1990), 161; C. A. Macartney, *The Habsburg Empire 1790–1918* (London, 1969), 122.

40. Michael Horvath, *Geschichte der Ungarn*, vol. 2 (Pest, 1855), 492; Éva H. Balázs, *Hungary and the Habsburgs 1765–1800* (Budapest, 1997), 206, 209. The specter of Germanization awakened

fears going back generations that the Catholic Habsburgs would reduce Hungarian rights and root out native Protestantism; both "Habsburgs" and "Germans" evoked feelings of hatred among the gentry. Lendvai, *The Hungarians*, 107; László Péter, *Hungary's Long Nineteenth Century: Constitutional and Democratic Traditions in a European Perspective* (Leiden, 2012), 187.

41. Alfred Jäger, *Kaiser Joseph II. und Leopold II* (Vienna, 1867), 60.

42. Balázs, *Hungary*, 209; Horvath, *Geschichte der Ungarn*, 492.

43. From letter of May 17, 1784, to the Hungarian counties, cited in Horvath, *Geschichte der Ungarn*, 488; François Fejtö, *Józef II: Habsburg rewolucjonista*, Alojzy Kołodziej, trans. (Warsaw, 1993), 265.

44. Wereszycki, *Historia Austrii*, 143; Tapié, *Rise and Fall*, 175.

45. One sees this attitude in the questions sent for statistical information to Hungarian regions in the late 1780s, which among other things wanted to know about the spread of the German language. Balázs, *Hungary*, 241–243; Horvath, *Geschichte der Ungarn*, 492.

46. Robert J. Kerner, *Bohemia in the Eighteenth Century* (New York, 1932).

47. Eugen Lemberg, *Nationalismus* (Reinbek bei Hamburg, 1964), 135; Hoensch, *Geschichte*, 300. On the emigration of Protestant and other non-Catholic nobles and burgers following the Battle of White Mountain, as well as the rewarding of local and foreign supporters with land, see Evans, *Making of the Habsburg Monarchy*, 200–201; Hugh Agnew, *The Czechs and the Lands of the Bohemian Crown* (Stanford, CA, 2004), 93.

48. In Galicia, the estates did not protest vigorously, despite similar Germanization measures. Hungary was distinct. Gumplowicz, *Das Recht*, 28–29. Oscar Jászi identifies the attempt of Joseph to impose German on Bohemia, Hungary, and Croatia as "beginning a whole new epoch," because Joseph failed to understand "the whole psychology of national evolution." Oscar Jászi, *The Dissolution of the Habsburg Monarchy* (Chicago, 1929), 70–71.

49. Joseph was called a nationalist by Transylvanian Saxons. R. J. Evans, *Austria, Hungary, and the Habsburgs* (Oxford, 2004), 141–142. Again, to stress the paradox, he gave rise to a new sense of being by evoking a threat to something that did not yet exist.

Chapter 3: Linguistic Nationalism

1. Jean Berenger, *A History of the Habsburg Empire, 1700–1918* (White Plains, NY, 1997), 113.

2. Balázs Trencsényi and Michal Kopeček, eds., *Late Enlightenment: Emergence of the Modern National Idea* (Budapest, 2006), 100–103.

3. Alfred Meissner, *Rococo-Bilder: Nach Aufzeichnungen meines Großvaters* (Leipzig, 1876), 141; Alan Cassels, *Ideology and International Relations in the Modern World* (London, 1996), 20; Jeffrey L. Buller, "From Clementia Caesaris to Clemenza di Tito," in G. Schmeling et al., eds., *Qui Miscuit Utile Dulci* (Wauconda, IL, 1998), 83.

4. Peter Demetz, *Prague in Black and Gold: Scenes from the Life of a European City* (New York, 1997), 268; James J. Sheehan, *German History: 1770–1866* (Oxford, 1989), 277.

5. Jonathan Sperber, *Revolutionary Europe 1780–1850* (New York, 2000), 104.

6. Wolfgang Burgdorf, "Once We Were Trojans," in R. J. W. Evans and Peter Wilson, eds., *The Holy Roman Empire, 1495–1806: A European Perspective* (Leiden, 2012), 52.

7. Robert A. Kann, *A History of the Habsburg Empire, 1526–1918* (Berkeley, 1974), 221–222. Of more than forty thousand young men entering French service from Wurttemberg, only some

thirteen thousand survived in the campaigns of 1806 to 1813. Bodie A. Ashton, *The Kingdom of Wurttemberg and the Making of Germany* (London, 2017), 27.

8. Observers of the 1790s wrote that there was no desire for a German nation-state, no German patriotism with the Reich as its object. Sheehan, *German History*, 373.

9. Patricia Anne Simpson, "Visions of the Nation," in *The Enlightened Eye: Goethe and Visual Culture*, Patricia Anne Simpson et al., eds. (Amsterdam, 2007), 145–146.

10. Golo Mann, *Deutsche Geschichte des neunzehnten und zwanzigsten Jahrhunderts* (Frankfurt, 1958), 85; Thomas Rohrkrämer, *A Single Communal Faith? The German Right from Conservatism to National Socialism* (New York, 2007), 46.

11. Martin Kessler, "Herders Kirchenamt in Sachsen-Weimar," in *Johann Gottfried Herder: Aspekte eines Lebenswerkes*, Martin Kessler and Volker Leppin, eds. (Berlin, 2005), 327.

12. "This idea of uniqueness, along with a certain emotionalism, was the legacy of pietism to nationalism." Anthony Smith, *Chosen Peoples* (Oxford, 2003), 45.

13. Cited in Hugh LeCaine Agnew, *Origins of the Czech National Renascence* (Pittsburgh, PA, 1993), 64.

14. Isaiah Berlin, *The Roots of Romanticism* (Princeton, NJ, 1999), 57. On the crucial contribution of Herder to ideas of struggle among nations "as the essential process in nature and history," see Elie Kedourie, *Nationalism* (London, 1960), 47–48; on the rapid spread of the idea among Slavs (Bohemians) that statehood without nationality is worthless, see Matthias Murko, *Deutsche Einflüsse auf die Anfänge der böhmischen Romantik* (Graz, Austria, 1897), 30. He "himself constituted a turning point in the history of cognition, introducing feelings into the philosophical field as a gnosiological category." Maria Ciesla-Korytowska, "On Romantic Cognition," in Angela Esterhammer, ed., *Romanic Poetry* (Amsterdam, 2002), 40–41.

15. Thomas Nipperdey, *Deutsche Geschichte: 1800–1866* (Munich, 1983), 307.

16. Goethe's introduction to Thomas Carlyle, *Leben Schillers,* (Frankfurt am Main, 1830), ix.

17. In France, Sweden, or Britain, the "state's territory easily became national territory," and what became decisive for the shift toward "nationalism" was the "struggle for political participation and civil rights in general." Miroslav Hroch, *European Nations: Explaining Their Formation* (London, 2015), 43.

18. J. G. Herder, "Ideen zur Geschichte der Menschheit," cited in Ján Kollár, *Sláwa bohyně a půwod gména Slawůw čili Slawjanůw* (Pest, Hungary, 1839), 157.

19. Other luminaries whom students encountered to in their eight to nine hours of daily lectures included the theologians Johann Philipp Gabler, Johann Traugott Danz, and Heinrich August Schott, the philosophers Jacob Friedrich Fries and Lorenz Oken, and the classical philologist Heinrich Karl Eichstädt. Murko, *Deutsche Einflüsse*, 131.

20. John Kulamer, *The Life of John Kollár: A Biographical Sketch* (Pittsburgh, PA, 1917) 11; Konstantin Jiráček, *P.J. Šafařík mezi Jihoslovany* (Prague, 1895), 9.

21. Ferdinand Menčík, *Jan Kollár: pěvec slovanské vzájemnosti* (Prague, 1893), 21–22; Jan Kollár, *Cestopis druhý a Paměti z mladších let života* (Prague, 1863), 251–253.

22. Kollár, *Cestopis*, 276. In fact, the original Slavic settlers had been peacefully absorbed into German culture over many generations.

23. Peter Petro, *History of Slovak Literature* (Montreal, 1995), 58; Joseph Theodoor Leerssen, *National Thought in Europe: A Cultural History* (Amsterdam, 2006), 155; Otto von Leixne, *Geschichte der fremden Literaturen*, vol. 1 (Leipzig, 1899), 505; Robert Auty, "Ján Kollár, 1793–1952,"

Slavonic and East European Review 31: 76 (1952), 80–84; John Bowring, *Cheskian Anthology* (London, 1832), 225.

24. Biblical Czech was based on the language used in the first translation of the Bible into Czech in the late sixteenth century. It was popular among Slavophone Protestant pastors in Northern Hungary (today's Slovakia) and was chosen by early Slovak patriots like Kollár because it held the promise of uniting the Czech and Slovak peoples in language. Some called it "our Czechoslovak language." Tomasz Kamusella, *The Politics of Language and Nationalism in Modern Central Europe* (Basingstoke, England, 2009), 533.

25. Murko, *Deutsche Einflüsse*, 134.

26. Pavel Šafárik, *Geschichte der slawischen Sprache und Literatur nach allen Mundarten* (Prague, 1869), 52 (first edition: 1826). Cited in Tomáš Glanc, "Izobretenie Slavii," in *Inventing Slavia*, Holt Meyer and Ekaterina Vel'mezova, eds. (Prague, 2005), 13–14.

27. Milorad Pavić, "Die serbische Vorromantik und Herder," in *Vuk Karadžić im europäischen Kontext*, Wilfried Potthoff, ed. (Heidelberg, 1990), 82.

28. Johann Gottfried Herder, *Ideen zur Geschichte der Menschheit*, part 3 [1787], ed. Johann von Müller (Vienna, 1813), 10, 20. On Herder and Fichte: Wulf D. Hund, "Rassismus im Kontext: Geschlecht, Klasse, Nation, Kultur und Rasse," in *Grenzenlose Vorurteile*, Irmtrud Wojak and Susanne Meinl, eds. (Frankfurt am Main, 2002), 17–21.

29. These are Kollár's words, cited by Ľudovit Haraksim, "Slovak Slavism and Pan-Slavism," in *Slovakia in History*, Mikuláš Teich, Dušan Kováč, and Martin Brown, eds. (Cambridge, 2011), 109.

30. Nadya Nedelsky, *Defining the Sovereign Community: The Czech and Slovak Republics* (Philadelphia, 2009), 33; Peter Brock, *The Slovak National Awakening: An Essay in the Intellectual History of East Central Europe* (Toronto, 1976), 25.

31. Alfred von Skene, *Entstehen und Entwicklung der slavischen Nationalbewegung in Böhmen und Mähren* (Vienna, 1893), 97.

32. Joseph Zacek, *Palacký: The Historian as Scholar and Nationalist* (The Hague, 1970), 13. The Bohemian Brethren practiced a Czech form of Protestantism that grew out of the teachings of Jan Hus and Petr Chelčický and were forced into exile or underground after the Habsburg victory at White Mountain in 1620.

33. This exchange is from an encounter with his Slovak friends after their return from Jena in the summer of 1819. Zacek, *Palacký*, 29–30.

34. Zacek, *Palacký*, 18–19.

35. It was called the *Journal for the Society of the Patriotic Museum of the Czech Lands*. Zacek, *Palacký*, 20.

36. Peter F. Sugar, "Introduction," in *Nationalism in Eastern Europe*, Peter F. Sugar and Ivo J. Lederer, eds. (Seattle, 1969), 15; František Palacký, "History of the Czech Nation in Bohemia and Moravia," in Balázs Trencsényi and Michal Kopeček, eds., *Discourses of Collective Identity in Central and Southeast Europe*, vol. 2 (Budapest, 2007), 54–55.

37. Palacký, "History," 55; Henryk Wereszycki, *Pod berłem Habsburgów: zagadnienia narodowościowe* (Kraków, 1975), 43.

38. Michal Kopeček, "Context," in Trencsenyi and Kopeček, eds., *Discourses*, vol. 2, 52.

39. In Zacek, *Palacký*, 33.

40. Paul Joseph Šafařik and Franz Palacky, *Älteste Denkmäler der böhmischen Sprache* (Prague, 1840), 48.

41. It was demonstrated that the data were in fact available in the eighteenth century. Zacek, *Palacký*, 72–73.

42. František Palacký, "Die altböhmischen Handschriften und ihre Kritik," *Historische Zeitschrift* 2:1 (1859), 90.

43. Johann Georg Kohl, *Austria, Vienna, Prague, etc, etc.* (Philadelphia, 1844), 43. The guilty party was probably Václav Hanka. Peter Bugge, "Czech Nation-Building, National Self-Perception and Politics, 1780–1914" (PhD dissertation, University of Aarhus, 1994), 30–31.

44. Bugge, "Czech Nation-Building," 30. The patriot was Jakub Maly.

45. From a speech in the Viennese Parliament of November 1892. Roland Hoffmann, *T. G. Masaryk und die tschechische Frage* (Munich, 1988), 112.

46. "Národy ne hasnou, odkud jazyk žije." Czech female composers like Katarina Emingerova, Agnes Tyrrell, Augusta Auspitz, or Josefina Brdlíkova seemed less drawn to "patriotic" themes.

47. Josef Jungmann, "O jazyku českém" (1803), in *Sebrané drobné spisy*, vol. 1 (Prague, 1869), 6.

48. Glanc, "Izobretenie Slavii," 18; Sergio Bonazza, "Ján Kollár und das deutsche archäologische Institut in Rom," in *Schnittpunkt Slawistik*, Irina Podtergera, ed., vol. 1 (Bonn, 2012), 33–34; Glanc, "Izobretenie Slavii," 13–14.

49. Brunhild Neuland, "Die Aufnahme Herderscher Gedanken in Ján Kollárs Schrift 'Über die literarische Wechselseitigkeit zwischen den verschiedenen Stämmen und Mundarten der slawischen Nation,'" in *Deutschland und der slawische Osten*, Ulrich Steltner, ed. (Jena, Germany, 1994), 31.

50. It spread rapidly. Brock, *Slovak National Awakening*, 49.

51. Brock, *Slovak National Awakening*.

52. The need among Slovaks "to maintain close ties to the Czechs was never forgotten despite periods of friction." Brock, *Slovak National Awakening*, 36.

53. Holm Sundhaussen, *Der Einfluss der Herderschen Ideen auf die Nationsbildung bei den Völkern der Habsburger Monarchie* (Munich, 1973), 78; László Péter, *Hungary's Long Nineteenth Century: Constitutional and Democratic Traditions in a European Perspective* (Leiden, 2012), 184.

54. For example, the poet György Bessenyei was bothered by use of Latin in public life, writing in the 1770s that "every nation is primarily recognized by its own language. A nation that lacked its own language was nothing." Péter, *Hungary's Long Nineteenth Century*, 184.

55. George Barany, *Stephen Széchenyi and the Awakening of Hungarian Nationalism, 1791–1841* (Princeton, NJ, 1968), 224–225.

56. There were five in Galicia and two in Transylvania. *Neueste Länder- und Völkerkunde. Ein geographisches Lesebuch für alle Stände*, vol. 18 (Prague, 1823), 144.

57. Magyars comprised about 49 percent in the 1840s. János Varga, *A Hungarian Quo Vadis: Political Trends and Theories of the Early 1840s*, Éva D. Pálmai, trans. (Budapest, 1993), 38. In the eighteenth century, the figure was below 40 percent. Péter, *Hungary's Long Nineteenth Century*, 185. In 1846, they constituted 4,774,899 of 11,895,796 inhabitants. Alan Sked, *Metternich and Austria* (New York, 2008), 216.

58. In both cases, the German and non-German populations were more or less even around mid-century, after which Budapest rapidly gained a Magyar, and Prague a Czech appearance. See Károly Stampfel, *Deutsche Wahrheiten und magyarische Entstellungen* (Leipzig, 1882), 15; Gary Cohen, *The Politics of Ethnic Survival: Germans in Prague* (West Lafayette, IN, 2006).

59. In Hungary, "positive elements of hope and faith in progress were juxtaposed with elements of fear and hopelessness." István Deák, *The Lawful Revolution: Louis Kossuth and the Hungarians 1848–1849* (New York, 1979), 44; Julius von Farkas, *Die ungarische Romantik* (Berlin, 1931), 119

60. The friend was Johann Kis. Farkas, *Ungarische Romantik*, 118–119.

61. Sked, *Metternich*, 217.

62. Julia Pardoe, *The City of Magyar. Or Hungary and Her Institutions in 1839–40*, vol. 3 (London, 1840), 34.

63. Thus a supposed declaration of Nicholas I to the Poles. Miklos Wesselenyi, *Eine Stimme über die ungarische und slawische Nationalität* (Leipzig, 1834), 34

64. Cited from a letter to Kazinczy. Farkas, *Ungarische Romantik*, 117.

65. Cited in Farkas, *Ungarische Romantik*, 118. Sándor and Károly were brothers.

66. *Neue Leipziger Literaturzeitung* 1 (January 1808), 8.

67. Ludwig Spohr, *Geistige Grundlagen des Nationalismus in Ungarn* (Berlin, 1936), 24, marks the transition from "Hungarus" to "Rassemagyar" [racial Hungarian].

68. The genre was historical fiction. See Peter, *Hungary's Long Nineteenth Century*, 186; Józef Chlebowczyk, *Young Nations in Europe: Nation-Forming Processes in Ethnic Borderlands in East-Central Europe* (Wrocław, 1980), 120.

69. Vejas Gabriel Liulevicius writes that Herder

should be considered the father of multiculturalism, cultural relativism, and cultural nationalism in general. Paradoxically, this made him a nationalist, but an internationalist nationalist, in his central conviction that each people was endowed with a national mission which had to be brought to fruition. Herder argued that all of humanity is one, but a varied mosaic. He insisted that the problem of being human had been solved in many different ways, with all cultures worthy, contributing to a providential evolution of humanity.

The German Myth of the East (Oxford, 2009), 53–54.

70. Dóra Bobory, review of Benedek Láng, *A rohonci kód* [The Rohonc Code] (Budapest, 2011) in *Hungarian Historical Review* 2:4 (2013), 939. There was a European-wide trade in pseudo-historical sources. Nora Berend, "The Forgeries of Sámuel Literáti Nemes," in *Manufacturing a Past for the Present: Forgery and Authenticity in Medievalist Texts and Objects in Nineteenth-Century Europe*, Janos M. Bak et al., eds. (Leiden, 2015), 143.

71. Murko, *Deutsche Einflüsse*, 134.

72. Bugge, "Czech Nation-Building," 34; Milan Šarić: "Život i rad dra Ante Starčevića," *Hrvatska misao: smotra za narodno gospodarstvo, knijiževnost* 1 (1902), 133.

73. These individuals are Ljudevit Gaj (one of whose parents was also Slovak), Bishop Strossmayer, and Ante Starčević, respectively.

74. Agnew, *Origins*, 209.

75. Karl Wladislaw Zap [Karel Vladislav Zap], "Übersicht der neuern polnischen Literatur bis zum Jahre 1842," *Das Ausland: Ein Tagblatt für Kunde des geistigen und sittlichen Lebens der Völker*, 185 (July 3, 1844), 738; Eugen Lemberg, *Geschichte des Nationalismus in Europa* (Stuttgart, 1950), 183; Czesław Miłosz, *History of Polish Literature* (Berkeley, 1983), 247–249.

76. The term is Marci Shore's. See her "Can We *See* Ideas?: On Evocation, Experience, and Empathy," in Darrin M. McMahon and Samuel Moyn, eds., *Rethinking Modern Intellectual History* (Oxford, 2014), 196.

77. Alexander Maxwell, "'Hey Slovaks, Where Is My Home?' Slovak Lyrics for Non-Slovak National Songs," *Philologica Jassyensia* 2:1 (2006), 168.

78. Thus the liberal Ferenc Stuller was writing in *Pesti Hirlap* in 1842. Varga, *Hungarian Quo Vadis*, 41.

79. Given the failure of its first serious state-builder, Joseph II, it would be accurate to call the monarchy a "would-be nation-state," which attempted to standardize in a nonimperial way when possible, that is, until its diverse society stopped it. The two great instances of opposition involved the Hungarians in the 1780s and in the 1850s; the result of the latter struggle was to force the monarch to divide his lands, creating an (also flawed) Hungarian nation-state, as well as a set of territories called the lands represented in the Parliament. In 1867 the Habsburg state went from being a place that was not reconciled to difference, to one that gave up on effective sovereign rule in half its territories. For a recent definition of empire emphasizing both sovereignty and rule exercised through difference, see Ronald Suny and Valery Kivelson, *Russia's Empires* (Oxford, 2017).

Chapter 4: Nationality Struggles: From Idea to Movement

1. George Robert Gleig, *Germany, Bohemia, and Hungary, Visited in 1837*, vol. 2 (London, 1839), 330.

2. There was written Czech from the time of Rudolf II, for instance, that people still had access to. Alfred von Skene, *Entstehen und Entwicklung der slavischen Nationalbewegung in Böhmen und Mähren* (Vienna, 1893), 86.

3. László Kontler, *Millennium in Central Europe: A History of Hungary* (Budapest, 1999), 227.

4. His crime was to have possessed a copy of the "catechism of freedom" of Jean Paul. He was arrested along with other leading figures in Hungarian literary life as part of a "Jacobin" conspiracy. George Barany, *Stephen Széchenyi and the Awakening of Hungarian Nationalism, 1791–1841* (Princeton, NJ, 1968), 20.

5. Imre Szabad, *Hungary: Past and Present* (Edinburgh, 1854), 204; "Schöne Künste," *Chronik der österreichischen Literatur* 46 (June 9, 1819), 182; Alan Sked, *Metternich and Austria* (New York, 2008), 219.

6. Laszlo Péter, *Hungary's Long Nineteenth Century: Constitutional and Democratic Traditions in a European Perspective* (Leiden, 2012), 189. Later parliaments passed acts confirming the position of the vernacular in the educational system. Andrew Janos, *The Politics of Backwardness in Hungary* (Princeton, NJ, 1982), 55.

7. Sked, *Metternich*, 215–216; Péter, *Hungary's Long Nineteenth Century*, 189.

8. Alexander Szana, *Ungarn* (Suttgart, 1922), 136; Henryk Wereszycki, *Historia Austrii* (Wrocław, 1972), 156; Kontler, *Millennium*, 219. For discussions of a "missed chance" in Bohemia, see Rita Krueger, *Czech, German, and Noble: Status and National Identity in Habsburg Bohemia* (Oxford, 2009), 77–78.

9. See https://dailynewshungary.com/plcs_place/hungarian-national-museum (accessed August 24, 2018).

10. Krueger, *Czech, German, and Noble*, 185.

11. There were greater contributions to the founding of the museum itself by Bohemian nobles, but they were not comparable to the donations of Hungarian nobles. For figures, see

Stanley B. Kimball, "The Matice Česká," in *The Czech Renascence of the Nineteenth Century*, Peter Brock and Gordon Skilling, eds. (Toronto, 1970), 62.

12. Archduke Karl visited Bohemia in late 1790s and said he had never seen a land where people spoke and thought less about politics. Jörg K. Hoensch, *Geschichte Böhmens* (Munich, 1997), 312–315.

13. Ivan T. Berend, *History Derailed: Central and Eastern Europe in the Long Nineteenth Century* (Berkeley, 2003), 39.

14. Barany, *Stephen Szechenyi*, 241; C. A. Macartney, *Hungary* (London, 1934), 136.

15. Description from Julia Pardoe, *The City of the Magyar. Or Hungary and Her Institutions in 1839–40*, vol. 3 (London, 1840), 3–4. The Pest Casino was founded by Széchenyi. Alice Freifeld, *Nationalism and the Crowd in Liberal Hungary, 1848–1914* (Baltimore, 2000), 32, 199. On the creation of casinos in the Czech lands, beginning with the Catholic priest Jan Arnold in 1844, see Hoensch, *Geschichte Böhmens*, 321.

16. Robert Nemes, "Associations and Civil Society in Reform-Era Hungary," *Austrian History Yearbook* 32 (2001), 35.

17. These institutions were in place by 1866. Theodor Gettinger, *Ungarns Hauptstädte Pest-Ofen und deren Umgebungen* (Pest, 1866), 60.

18. Péter, *Hungary's Long Nineteenth Century*, 187; he wrote in the same book that "all inhabitants of Hungary must be given civil status," 190; András Gerő, *Modern Hungarian Society in the Making* (Budapest, 1995), 63.

19. János Varga, *A Hungarian Quo Vadis: Political Trends and Theories of the Early 1840s*, Éva D. Pálmai, trans. (Budapest, 1993), 2.

20. Miklós Szabó, "The Liberalism of the Hungarian Nobility," in Iván Zoltán Dénes, ed., *Liberty and the Search for Identity: Liberal Nationalisms and the Legacy of Empires* (Budapest, 2006), 207–208.

21. Robert W. B. Gray, "Land Reform and the Hungarian Peasantry" (PhD dissertation, University College, London, 2009), 50; Wereszycki, *Historia*, 186.

22. George Barany, "Hungary," in Peter Sugar, ed., *Nationalism in Eastern Europe* (Seattle, 1969), 269. Oszkár Jászi, *Dissolution of the Habsburg Monarchy* (Chicago, 1961), 305.

23. Barany, "Hungary," 200; Kontler, *Millenium*, 240.

24. He argued that emerging nationalism among Slavs and Romanians in Hungary was natural self-defense: Wereszycki, *Historia*, 156.

25. Barany, "Hungary," 270; Peter Hanák, *Ungarn in der Donaumonarchie* (Vienna, 1984), 45.

26. Kollár, Šafárik, and Palacký identified as Hungarian in 1817 when they studied in Jena. Ludwig Spohr, *Die geistigen Grundlagen des Nationalismus in Ungarn* (Berlin and Leipzig, 1936), 111, fn. 32.

27. Domaljub Dorvatovic, *Sollen Wir alle Magyaren werden?* (Karlstadt, 1833), 6–7.

28. Macartney, *Hungary*, 144.

29. Elinor Murray Despalatovic, *Ljudevit Gaj and the Illyrian Movement* (Boulder, CO, 1975), 50–51.

30. Despalatovic, *Ljudevit Gaj and the Illyrian Movement*; Marcus Tanner, *Croatia: A Nation Forged in War* (New Haven, CT, 1997), 75.

31. Josef Toužimský, "Bohuslav Šulek," *Osvěta* 26 (1896), 214.

32. Fred Singleton, *A Short History of the Yugoslav Peoples* (Cambridge, 1985), 105.

33. Slavko Goldstein, *1941: The Year That Keeps Returning*, Michael Gable, trans. (New York, 2013) 65; Giuseppe Mazzini, "On the Slavonian National Movement," *Lowe's Edinburgh Magazine*, July 1847, 189.

34. Ivo J. Lederer, "Nationalism and the Yugoslavs," in Peter F. Sugar and Ivo John Lederer, *Nationalism in Eastern Europe* (Seattle, 1994), 415–416; Henryk Wereszycki, *Pod berłem Habsburgów* (Kraków, 1986), 230.

35. J. C. Kröger, *Reise durch Sachsen nach Böhmen und Österreich*, vol. 2 (Altona, 1840), 127; Otokar Kádner, "Das böhmische Schulwesen," in *Das böhmische Volk: Wohngebiete, körperliche Tüchtigkeit, geistige und materielle Kultur*, Zdeněk Topolka, ed. (Prague, 1916), 119.

36. Miroslav Hroch, *Na prahu národní existence: touha a skutečnost* (Prague, 1999), 203; Hoensch, *Geschichte Böhmens*, 327.

37. Peter Bugge, "Czech Nation-Building, National Self-Perception and Politics, 1780–1914" (PhD dissertation, University of Aarhus, 1994), 43.

38. Matthias Murko, *Deutsche Einflüsse auf die Anfänge der böhmischen Romantik* (Graz, Austria, 1897), 96; Peter Deutschmann, *Allegorien des Politischen: Zeitgeschichtliche Implikationen des tschechischen historischen Dramas (1810–1935)* (Vienna, 2017), 136.

39. František Rieger, ed., *Slovník naučný*, vol. 9 (Prague, 1872), 139; Ondrej Hucin, "Czech Theater: A Paradoxical Prop of the National Revival," in *History of the Literary Cultures of East-Central Europe*, Marcel Cornis-Pope et al., eds., vol. 3 (Amsterdam, 2004), 155.

40. Deutschmann, *Allegorien des Politischen*, 136; Hucin, "Czech Theater," 154–155.

41. Rieger, *Slovník naučný*, 140; A. W. Ambros, "Die böhmische Oper in Prag," *Österreichisch-ungarische revue* 3:1 (1865), 179.

42. Hroch, *Na prahu*, 214–215.

43. For an eloquent disquisition on humor as a force binding the Czech nation, see Chad Bryant, *Prague in Black: Nazi Rule and Czech Nationalism* (Cambridge, MA, 2007). Gale Stokes described the linguistic nation as a community where people manipulated abstractions in a readily understandable way. Gale Stokes, "Cognition and the Function of Nationalism," *Journal of Interdisciplinary History* 4:4 (1974), 533.

44. Deutschmann, *Allegorien des Politischen*, 134, 139.

45. Karel Novotny and Miloň Dohnal, "Průmyslová výroba," in *Počátky českého národního obrození. Společnost a kultura v 70. až 90. letech 18. století*, Josef Petráň, ed. (Prague, 1990), 57, 66, 73.

46. Janos, *Politics of Backwardness*, 55.

47. Janos, *Politics of Backwardness*, 52, 56. Almost all possibilities of drawing credit were exhausted by the state, which used it to cover shortages. Wereszycki, *Historia*, 191.

48. Janos, *Politics of Backwardness*, 56; George Barany, "Age of Royal Absolutism," in *History of Hungary*, Peter Sugar, Péter Hanák, and Tibor Frank, eds. (Bloomington, IN, 1990), 202; George Barany, "Hungary," in *Nationalism in Eastern Europe*, Peter Sugar, ed. (Seattle, 1969), 270.

49. Kontler, *Millennium*, 271.

50. Hoensch, *Geschichte Böhmens*, 327; Kádner, "Das böhmische Schulwesen," 120; Joachim von Puttkamer, *Schulalltag und nationale Integration in Ungarn* (Munich, 2003), 100.

51. Wereszycki, *Historia*, 178–179. According to Ernest Gellner, agrarian societies had no room for nationalism because of cultural stratification that divided "literate urban elites from illiterate food-producing communities." See the discussion in Anthony D. Smith, *The Antiquity of Nations* (Cambridge, 2008), 36; Ernest Gellner, *Nations and Nationalism* (Ithaca, NY, 1984), 72.

52. Jiří Hochman, *Historical Dictionary of the Czech State* (Lanham, MD, 1998), 41.

53. Józef Chlebowczyk, *O prawie do bytu małych i młodych narodów* (Katowice, Poland, 1983), 157.

54. Dieter Langewiesche calls nationhood an "ultimate value:" *Nation, Nationalismus, Nationalstaat in Deutschland und Europa* (Munich, 2000), 16.

55. Rainer Schmitz, "Nationalismus als Ressource," at https://arthist.net/reviews/14442 (accessed October 21, 2017).

56. Murko, *Deutsche Einflüsse*, 28, 31.

57. Arnold Suppan, *Die österreichischen Volksgruppen: Tendenzen ihrer gesellschaftlichen Entwicklung im 20. Jahrhundert* (Munich, 1983), 23. According to figures from the Vienna City Hall, in December 1900 102,974 inhabitants of Vienna indicated Czech as their daily language of use (Umgangssprache). They did not have a single public school. Haus der Abgeordneten, Session of April 10, 1902, in *Stenographische Protokolle über die Sitzungen des Hauses der Abgeordneten des österreichischen Reichsrathes*, session 17, vol. 13 (Vienna, 1902), 11,188; Michael John und Albert Lichtblau, *Schmeltztiegel Wien: einst und jetzt: zur Geschichte und Gegenwart von Zuwanderung und Minderheiten* (Wien, 1990), 278.

58. Józef Chlebowczyk, *On Small and Young Nations: Nation-forming Processes in East Central Europe* (Wrocław, 1980), 195. For Vienna, the proportion of people born in Czech areas in 1900, was 25 percent of 350,000 people.

59. Jan Patočka, *Co jsou Češi? Malý přehled fakt a pokus o vysvětlení* (Prague, 1992), 201.

60. Gary Cohen calls the German variant "feeble." *The Politics of Ethnic Survival: Germans in Prague* (West Lafayette, IN, 2006).

61. František Adolf Šubert, *Das böhmische National-Theater* (Prague, 1892), 200; Frances Starn et al., eds., *The Czech Reader: History, Culture, Politics* (Durham, NC, 2010), 153.

62. Hroch, *Na prahu*, 258.

63. Janos, *Politics of Backwardness.*

64. But their demand was also for self-government for various peoples of Austria. Jakub Budislav Malý, "Politický obrat Rakouska," *Časopis Musea Království českého* 34 (1860), 476.

Chapter 5: Insurgent Nationalism: Serbia and Poland

1. Samuel Huntington believed that a line separated east and west due to distinctive Latin and Orthodox Christian heritages, the latter having weaker rule of law, traditions of separation of powers, and closer relations to state authorities. *The Clash of Civilizations* (New York, 1997).

2. This is the currently accepted idea of how the transition to modern nationhood occurred: through modern institutions. See, for example, Dieter Langewiesche, *Nation, Nationalismus, Nationalstaat in Deutschland und Europa* (Munich, 2000), 32.

3. In the late seventeenth century, between half and three-quarters of Polish gentry possessed the basic ability to read and write. Hans-Jürgen Bömelburg, *Frühneuzeitliche Nationen im östlichen Europa* (Wiesbaden, 2006), 107. The numbers were lower among poorer gentry.

4. Serb peasants did have traditional rights to the lands they worked as sharecroppers. They could pass these rights on to their heirs and could grow what they wanted. Barbara Jelavich, *History of the Balkans*, vol. 1 (Cambridge, 1983), 91.

5. The Serb settlers had come in waves into Habsburg territories and had built urban centers with cultural, religious, and educational infrastructures, most famously a Serb gymnasium in Sremski Karlovci (1778). Milan Kosanović, "Serbische Eliten im 19. Jahrhundert," in *Serbien in Europa*, Gabriella Schubert, ed. (Wiesbaden, 2008), 66–67; Holm Sundhaussen, *Geschichte Serbiens* (Vienna, 2007), 81.

6. Henryk Wereszycki, *Niewygasła przeszłość* (Krakow, 1987), 16–17.

7. Until 1768 the *szlachta* had the power over peasants to impose the death penalty. Michał Tymowski, Jerzy Holzer, and Jan Kieniewicz, *Historia Polski* (Warsaw, 1990), 203; Józef Andrzej Gierowski, *Historia Polski* (Warsaw, 1979), 84. The references to "Polish nation" are not limited to class or religious or cultural group. Waldemar J. Wołpiuk, "Naród jako pojęcie konstytucyjne," *Studia Iuridica Lublinensia* 22 (2014), 370–372.

8. Tadeusz Łepkowski, "Naród bez państwa," in *Polska. Losy państwa i narodu*, Henryk Samsonowicz, Janusz Tazbir, Tadeusz Łepkowski, and Tomasz Nałęcz (Warsaw, 1992), 264.

9. Gierowski, *Historia Polski*, 86.

10. Władysław Smolenski, *Ostatni rok Sejmu Wielkiego* (Kraków, 1897).

11. Łepkowski, "Naród," 266.

12. Gierowski, *Historia Polski*, 87–89; Tymowski, Holzer, and Kieniewicz, *Historia*, 204; Łepkowski, "Naród," 267.

13. Łepkowski, "Naród," 267–268; Gierowski, *Historia Polski*, 89.

14. Gierowski, *Historia Polski*, 90.

15. Andrzej Zahorski, "Powstanie kosciuszkowskie 1794," in Stefan Kienieczwicz et al., *Trzy powstania narodowe* (Warsaw, 1992), 17–36.

16. Tymowski, Holzer, and Kieniewicz, *Historia*, 205; Łepkowski, "Naród," 270.

17. Łepkowski, "Naród," 270. In Warsaw the hetmani Ozarowski and Zabiella, the Marshall of Permanent Council Ankwicz, and Bishop Kossakowski all were tried and hanged in public; others were captured by the crowds and hanged. Łepkowski, "Naród," 273.

18. "Isolated Russian patrols were hounded through the streets and cut to pieces." Norman Davies, *God's Playground*, vol. 1 (New York, 1980), 539.

19. Łepkowski, "Naród," 275.

20. Konstanty Górski, *Historia piechoty polskiej* (Kraków, 1893), 182–183.

21. Davies, *God's Playground*, vol. 1, 533.

22. Łepkowski, "Naród," 272.

23. "Original Correspondence," *The Times* (London), June 1, 1791, 3.

24. Mirosław Maciorowski, in conversation with Maciej Trąbski, "Insurekcja Kościuszki," Ale Historia, *Gazeta Wyborcza*, March 7, 2014.

25. Gierowski, *Historia*, 99; Henryk Wereszycki cited in Łepkowski, "Naród" 275; "New Partition of Poland." *The Times* (London), June 21, 1792; E. Starczewski, *Sprawa polska* (Krakow, 1912), 39–40.

26. That was the Połaniec manifesto of May 7, 1794.

27. Davies, *God's Playground*, vol. 1, 542. Karol Lutostański, *Les partages de la Pologne et la lutte pour l'indépendance* (Paris, 1918), 229.

28. Christopher Clark, *Iron Kingdom: The Rise and Downfall of Prussia, 1600–1947* (Cambridge, MA, 2006), 232; Iryna Vushko, *The Politics of Cultural Retreat: Imperial Bureaucracy in Austrian Galicia* (New Haven, CT, 2015), 37.

29. "Observations on the Dismemberment of Poland, and the Politics of the Court of Peters-
burgh," *The Times* (London), January 15, 1796, 2; *The Times* (London), Thursday, December 24,
1795; 2; "New Partition of Poland," *The Times* (London), June 21, 1792; 3.

30. From *Journal de Patriots*, as reported in "Partition of Poland," *The Times* (London), December 23, 1795, 3.

31. Davies, *God's Playground*, vol. 1, 525; Holly Case, *The Age of Questions* (Princeton, NJ, 2018),
47–50.

32. For that general perception: *Westminster Review* 24 (July and October 1863), 172.

33. Vushko, *Politics*, 241; Władysław Pobog-Malinowski, *Najnowsza historia polityczna Polski:
1864–1914*, vol. 1 (London, 1963), 143.

34. Poseł z Lechistanu jeszcze nie przybył.

35. The song continues: "march, march Dąbrowski, from Italian lands to Poland, under your
command we shall rejoin the nation." Jan Pachonski and Reuel K. Wilson, *Poland's Caribbean Tragedy: A Study of Polish Legions in the Haitian War of Independence, 1802–1803* (New York, 1986), 305.

36. Drawn up by Adam Jerzy Czartoryski and promulgated by Alexander I of Russia. R. F.
Leslie, *Polish Politics and the Revolution of 1830* (London, 1956), 45–46.

37. Harro Harring, *Poland under the Dominion of Russia* (Boston, 1834), 46.

38. Artur Hutnikiewicz, *To co najważniejsze. Trzy eseje o Polsce* (Bydgoszcz, Poland, 1996). A
further 54,000 Polish families were deported to the Caucasus Mountains and Siberia. Joachim
von Puttkamer, *Ostmitteleuropa im 19. und 20. Jahrhundert* (Munich, 2010), 26.

39. Stefan Kieniewicz, *Historyk a świadomość narodowa* (Warsaw, 1982), 60.

40. "National continuity was never seriously interrupted in Poland or Russia." Holm Sundhaussen, *Der Einfluß der Herderischen Ideen auf die Nationsbildung bei den Völkern der Habsburgermonarchie* (Munich, 1973), 100; Slawomir Gawlas, "Die mittelalterliche Nationenbildung am
Beispiel Polens," in Almut Bues and Rex Rexheuser, eds., *Mittelalterliche nationes* (Wiesbaden,
1995), 121–144; Tomasz Szumski, *Krótki rys historyi i literatury polskiey* (Berlin, 1807).

41. Ludwik Dębicki, *Widmo zdrady* (Lwów, Austria, 1876), 11–13.

42. For the calumny against Piłsudski, but also virtually every other great Pole, see Adam
Michnik, "Naganiacze i zdrajcy," *Gazeta Wyborcza*, September 28, 2006.

43. Suraiya Faroqhi, *Subjects of the Sultan: Culture and Daily Life in the Ottoman Empire* (London, 2000), 24–25; In areas with larger Muslim populations (for example, Bosnia and the Sanjak
of Novi Pazar), Muslims were also peasants, and they were often little better off than their Christian neighbors, freed from some taxes but subject to recruitment in the army. Jelavich, *History
of the Balkans*, vol. 1, 60.

44. Theologically, Ottoman conquest was presented as temporary punishment for Christian
sins. Jelavich, *History of the Balkans*, vol. 1, 52; Ivo Banac, *The National Question: Origin, History,
Politics* (Ithaca, NY, 1984), 64–65; Paul Robert Magocsi, *Historical Atlas of Central Europe* (Seattle, 2002), 44.

45. On Nicopolis: Kenneth M. Setton, *The Papacy and the Levant*, vol. 1 (Philadelphia, 1976),
355. The final loss of Serb semi-sovereignty in the despotate occurred in 1459 with the fall of the
fortress Smederovo. Tim Judah, *Serbs: History, Myth and the Destruction of Yugoslavia* (New Haven,
CT, 1997), 33.

46. The bone burning was also motivated by concerns that Muslim South Slavs would side
with rebels of the Orthodox faith in the Fifteen Years' War (1591–1606) with the Holy Roman

Empire. Remarks of Traian Stoianovich, *Actes du premier congres international des etudes balkaniques et sue-est Europeennes*, vol. 3 (Sofia, 1969), 775–776. The bone burning took place during a millenarian wave that swept across the region and was part of a jihad of the cult of Mohammed against the cult of St. Sava. Traian Stoianovich, *Balkan Worlds: The First and Last Europe* (Armonk, NY, 1994), 168–169.

47. Defacing icons in Orthodox churches was a frequent occurrence in Ottoman-controlled lands; some of the violence occurred during conquest, some because of the abhorrence among Muslims for graven images. Local communities suspected in addition a desire on the part of their rulers to expunge historical memories, for example, in the case of the queen Simonida. For cases, see Djoka Mazalić, *Slikarska umjetnost u Bosni i Hercegovini u Tursko doba, 1500–1878* (Sarajevo, 1965), 41–42 and passim; Andrei Oișteanu, *Inventing the Jew: Anti-Semitic Stereotypes in Central and East European Cultures* (Lincoln, NE and London, 2009), 398–400. It is also true that many (probably most) icons survived Ottoman rule intact. Furthermore, dozens of new icons were created over the centuries of Ottoman rule that survive to this day. For a discussion (with brilliant plates), see Svetlana Rakić, *Serbian Icons from Bosnia-Herzegovina* (New York, 2000).

48. However, the gusle tended not to be played beyond Serb lands, though the songs were known elsewhere, often sung by "blind beggars." Vuk Karadžić, *Serbische Hochzeitslieder*, E. Eugen Wesely, trans. (Pest, Hungary, 1826), 20–21. For a topography of major epic themes, overwhelmingly in Orthodox Christian areas of the Ottoman and Habsburg lands (often with mixed Muslim populations), see Svetozar Koljević, *The Epic in the Making* (Oxford, 1980), 92–93.

49. Michael Boro Petrovich, "Karadžić and Nationalism," *Serbian Studies* 4:3 (1988), 42.

50. Leopold von Ranke, *Die serbische Revolution: aus serbischen Papieren und Mitteilungen* (Berlin, 1844), 78–79.

51. Paul Schroeder, *The Transformation of European Politics 1763–1848* (Oxford, 1994), 58–59; Jelavich, *History of the Balkans*, vol. 1, 95; Michael Boro Petrovich, *A History of Modern Serbia*, vol. 1 (New York, 1976), 28; Judah, *Serbs*, 51.

52. The Janissary class had deteriorated into an "unruly riffraff of mercenaries who endangered the Sultan's throne." The sultan increasingly sided with the janissaries after 1798, and he subjected the Serb population to extreme repression as well as exorbitant taxation. Petrovich, *History of Modern Serbia*, vol. 1, 23–26.

53. Adolf Beer, *Die orientalische politik Oesterreichs seit 1774* (Prague, 1883), 184; Gunther Rothenberg, *The Military Border in Croatia* (Chicago, 1966), 102; Judah, *Serbs*, 51; Georges Castellan, *History of the Balkans: from Mohammed the Conqueror to Stalin* (New York, 1992), 235; Petrovich, *History of Modern Serbia*, 26; Charles Jelavich and Barbara Jelavich, *Establishment of the Balkan National States* (Seattle, 1977), 88–89; Dimitrije Djordjevic and Stephen Fischer-Galati, *The Balkan Revolutionary Tradition* (New York, 1981), 69–70. Some historians claim that the uprisings were not motivated by national considerations. The "mass of peasants" had traditional goals, like the reassertion of the old order. Konrad Clewing and Holm Sundhaussen, eds., *Lexikon zur Geschichte Südosteuropas* (Vienna, 2016), 145. Yet demands for independence—even if not explicitly "national"—emerged during the course of events. Otherwise, it is not clear why Serb leaders moved beyond mere requests for more equitable administration.

54. Four of its members were literate. Wayne Vucinich, ed., *War and Society in East Central Europe: The First Serbian Uprising 1804–1813* (New York, 1982), 157.

55. Thomas Emmert, *Serbian Golgotha: Kosovo 1389* (New York, 1990), 207; Jelavich, *History of the Balkans*, vol. 1, 202.

56. Vindictive because their local leader, the pasha, continued heavily repressive policies, such as executing rebels. Jelavich, *History of the Balkans*, vol. 1, 203.

57. Petrovich, *History of Modern Serbia*, 86; Sundhaussen, *Geschichte Serbiens*, 68.

58. Also known as the Sanjak of Smederevo, an administrative district that emerged in the fifteenth century.

59. Judah, *Serbs*, 53; Jelavich, *History of the Balkans*, vol. 1, 203, 207. That was in 1817.

60. Clewing and Sundhaussen, eds., *Lexikon*, 145–146.

61. Jelavich, *History of the Balkans*, vol. 1, 241; Nicolae Jorga, *Geschichte des osmanischen Reiches*, vol. 5 (Gotha, Germany 1916), 154.

62. Dietmar Müller, *Staatsbürger auf Widerruf. Juden und Muslime im rumänischen und serbischen Nationscode* (Wiesbaden, 2005), 109–110.

63. Judah, *Serbs*, 50; Hugh Seton-Watson, *Eastern Europe between the Wars* (Cambridge, 1946), 6; Michael Schwartz, *Ethnische "Säuberungen" in der Moderne: Globale Wechselwirkungen* (Munich, 2013), 239.

64. Müller, *Staatsbürger*, 110.

65. Aleksa Djilas, *The Contested Country: Yugoslav Unity and Communist Revolution, 1919–1953* (Cambridge, MA, 1991), 26.

66. Stefan Rohdewald, "Der heilige Sava und unsere Muslime," in Thede Kahl and Cay Liena, eds., *Christen und Muslime: interethnische Koexistenz in südosteuropäischen Peripheriegebieten* (Vienna, 2009), 168.

67. This from Karadžić's *Srbi svi i svuda*, cited in Sundhaussen, *Geschichte Serbiens*, 92: "All reasonable people, the Greek as well as Roman Serbs, recognize that they are one people."

68. Sundhaussen, *Geschichte Serbiens*, 92–94.

69. Karadžić did recognize late in life that Croat intellectuals did not accept this understanding and seemed resigned that they would not think of themselves as Serbs. Sundhaussen, *Geschichte Serbiens*, 93.

70. For lucid guidance, see Zofia Zielińska, *Ostatnie lata Pierwszej Rzeczypospolitej* (Warsaw, 1986); Jerzy Lukowski, *Liberty's Folly: The Polish Lithuanian Commonwealth in the Eighteenth Century* (London, 1991).

71. Cited in Roman Szporluk, *Communism and Nationalism: Karl Marx vs. Friedrich List* (Oxford, 1988), 84–85.

72. See the discussion in Brian Porter-Szücs, *When Nationalism Began to Hate: Imagining Modern Politics in Nineteenth-Century Poland* (New York, 2000), 22–27.

Chapter 6: Cursed Were the Peacemakers: 1848 in East Central Europe

1. Joseph Redlich, *Das österreichische Staats- und Reichsproblem*, vol. 1 (Leipzig, 1920), 104–105.

2. William L. Langer, *Revolutions of 1848* (New York, 1971), 33.

3. Josef Polišenský, *Aristocrats and the Crowd in the Revolutionary Year 1848*, Frederick Snider, trans. (Albany, NY, 1980), 32; Stanley Z. Pech, *The Czech Revolution of 1848* (Chapel Hill, NC, 1969), 45–46.

4. Langer, *Revolutions*, 35; Robin Okey, *The Habsburg Monarchy: From Enlightenment to Eclipse* (New York, 2001), 129.

5. Anton Füster, *Memoiren vom März 1848 bis Juli 1849. Beitrag zur Geschichte der Wiener Revolution* (Frankfurt, 1850), 58, 38.

6. Paul Lendvai, *The Hungarians: A Thousand Years of Victory in Defeat*, Ann Major, trans. (Princeton, NJ, 2003), 216–218; Alice Freifeld, *Nationalism and the Crowd in Liberal Hungary, 1848–1914* (Baltimore, 2000), 48–52; Henryk Wereszycki, *Historia Austrii* (Wrocław, 1972), 200.

7. László Kontler, *Millennium in Central Europe: A History of Hungary* (Budapest, 1999), 249; Istvan Deák, "The Revolution and the War of Independence," in *History of Hungary*, Peter Sugar et al., eds. (Bloomington, IN, 1994), 215; Wereszycki, *Historia*, 200.

8. Langer, *Revolutions*, 37.

9. Langer, *Revolutions*, 37–38; Polišenský, *Aristocrats*, 100; Wereszycki, *Historia*, 198–199. Fischhof went on to the Kremsierer Reichstag and was arrested for high treason after the revolution. R. A. Kann, "Fischhof, Adolf," in *Neue deutsche Biographie*, vol. 5 (Berlin, 1960), 214–215.

10. Polišenský, *Aristocrats*, 105; Langer, *Revolutions*, 62.

11. Josef Redlich, *Emperor Francis Joseph of Austria* (New York, 1929), 14.

12. Langer, *Revolution*, 43; A. W. Ward, "Revolution and Reaction in Germany and Austria," in *Cambridge Modern History*, vol. 11 (New York, 1918), 182.

13. Kontler, *Millennium*, 251; Langer, *Revolutions*, 39; György Spira, *The Nationality Issue in the Hungary of 1848–49* (Budapest, 1992), 106; Alice Freifeld, *Nationalism and the Crowd in Liberal Hungary* (Washington, DC, 2000), 65.

14. Marcus Tanner, *Croatia: A Nation Forged in War* (New Haven, CT, 2010), 84.

15. Baron Franz Kulmer, archconservative nobleman, head (*Obergespann*) of Zagreb county, and the Sabor's representative at court, wrote Jelačić on March 30 that Austria must reconquer Hungary, and the loyalty of the military border would be crucial. Gunther Rothenberg, *The Military Border in Croatia* (Chicago, 1966), 145; Okey, *Habsburg Monarchy*, 129; C. A. Macartney, *The Habsburg Empire 1790–1918* (London, 1969), 383–384; Michael Rapport, *1848: Year of Revolution* (New York, 2009), 247. That same month the court was preparing for conflict with Hungary in Transylvania. Edsel Walter Stroup, "From Horea-Closca to 1867," in John Cadzow et al., eds., *Transylvania: The Roots of Ethnic Conflict* (Kent State, OH, 1983), 128; Tanner, *Croatia*, 87; István Deák, *The Lawful Revolution* (New York, 1976), 130; Tomislav Markus, "Between Revolution and Legitimacy: The Croatian Political Movement of 1848/49," *Croatian Review of History* 1 (2009), 17.

16. Deák, *Lawful Revolution*, 131.

17. Deák, *Lawful Revolution*, 130; Elinor Murray Despalatovic, *Ljudevit Gaj and the Illyrian Movement*, (Boulder, CO, 1975), 192.

18. Misha Glenny, *The Balkans: Nationalism, War, and the Great Powers* (New York, 2000), 48.

19. Macartney, *Habsburg Empire*, 386–387.

20. Macartney, *Habsburg Empire*, 386–387; Karoly Kocsis and Eszter Kocsis-Hodosi, *Ethnic Geography of the Hungarian Minorities in the Carpathian Basin* (Budapest, 1998); Jovan Subbotić,

Authentische Darstellung der Ursachen, der Entstehung, der Entwicklung und Führungsart des Krieges zwischen Serben und Magyaren (Zagreb, 1849), 3–8.

21. "Triune Kingdom" refers to three historic components of the Croatian kingdom: Croatia, Slavonia, and Dalmatia, the political unification of which was a central demand of Croatian patriots. Tanner, *Croatia*, 87; Deák, *Lawful Revolution*, 128.

22. Glenny, *The Balkans*, 41.

23. Macartney, *Habsburg Empire*, 388.

24. Ward, "Revolution," 180; Heinrich Friedjung, *Österreich von 1848 bis 1860*, vol. 1 (Stuttgart, 1908), 59–60; Macartney, *Habsburg Empire*, 389.

25. The capital of the Serb insurgency in Sremski Karlovci was just inside the Military Frontier border. Macartney, *Habsburg Empire*, 388; Deák, *Lawful Revolution*, 129.

26. Freifeld, *Nationalism*, 65.

27. See the report of the Serb patriot Subbotić of an attack that supposedly took place on Sremski Karlovci, even before the Hungarian delegation had gone to Innsbruck, in which the soldiers of the Hungarian "Don Miguel Regiment" murdered and defiled defenseless inhabitants of the houses they had set on fire, vented their rage on frail women and tossed inhabitants of the town they encountered on the streets into the flames. Subbotić, *Authentische Darstellung*, 19–20. See also Johann von Adlerstein, *Archiv des Ungarischen Ministeriums und Landesverteidigungsausschusses*, 3 vols. (Altenburg, 1851).

28. Istvan Deák, "The Revolution and the War of Independence," in Peter Sugar, Péter Hanák, and Tibor Frank, eds., *History of Hungary* (Bloomington, IN, 1990), 220.

29. Pogroms also occurred in Nagyszombat, Vágujhely, Székesfehérvár, Szombathely, and Pest. Raphael Patai, *The Jews of Hungary: History, Culture, Psychology* (Detroit, 1996), 277.

30. Ignác Einhorn, *Die Revolution und Die Juden in Ungarn* (Leipzig, 1851), 83–85.

31. Einhorn, *Revolution*, 79, 85; Freifeld, *Nationalism*, 65.

32. Einhorn, *Revolution*, 87; Deák, *Lawful Revolution*, 114–115.

33. For wording: Jan Matouš Černý, *Boj za právo: sborník aktů politických u věcech státu a národa českého* (Prague, 1893), 2. A poster was also produced for citizens of the capital city of Prague. Pech, *Czech Revolution*, 47–48; Jos. J. Toužimský, *Na úsvitě nové doby: dějiny roku 1848. v zemích českých* (Prague, 1898), 47–52.

34. Peter Demetz, *Prague in Gold and Black* (New York, 1997), 290; William H. Stiles, *Austria in 1848–49*, vol. 2 (London, 1852), 356; Stanley Z. Pech, "The Czech Revolution of 1848: Some New Perspectives," *Canadian Journal of History* 4:1 (1969), 54.

35. Pech, *Czech Revolution*, 45.

36. The German for this term was *böhmisches Staatsrecht*. Jan Křen, *Die Konfliktgemeinschaft: Tschechen und Deutsche 1780–1918*, Peter Heumos, trans. (Munich, 1996), 77–79; Polišenský, *Aristocrats*, 114; Alfred Fischel, *Das österreichische Sprachenrecht: eine Quellensammlung* (Brünn, Austria, 1910), XLIX; Černý, *Boj za právo*, 3–4.

37. Introduction to Kristina Kaiserová and Jiří Rak, eds., *Nacionalizace společnosti v Čechách 1848–1914* (Ústí nad Labem, Czech Republic, 2008), 11.

38. One of these liberals was František August Brauner. Polišenský, *Aristocrats*, 110–111.

39. Franz Josef Schopf, *Wahre und ausführliche Darstellung der am 11. März 1848 zur Erlangung einer constitutionellen Regierungsverfassung in der königlichen Hauptstadt Prag begonnenen Volksbewegung* (Leitmeritz, 1848), 15; Křen, *Konfliktgemeinschaft*, 85.

40. Similar reports came from Most (Brüx), Marienbad, and Teplice. Robert Maršan, *Čechové a Němci r. 1848 a boj o Frankfurt* (Prague, 1898), 9ff, 83; Jan Havránek, "Böhmen im Frühjahr 1848," in Heiner Timmermann, ed., *1848 Revolution in Europa* (Berlin, 1999), 187.

41. Maršan, *Čechové*, 37; Schopf, *Wahre und ausführliche Darstellung*, 33; Havránek, "Böhmen," 186; Demetz, *Prague*, 293.

42. Maršan, *Čechové*, 39, 42; Havránek, "Böhmen," 184.

43. Freifeld, *Nationalism*, 63; Anton Springer, *Geschichte Österreichs seit dem Wiener Frieden 1809*, vol. 2 (Leipzig, 1865), 264; Introduction to Kaiserová and Rak, *Nacionalizace společnosti*, 12. A few Germans remained in the Prague Committee. The radical writers Alfred Meissner and Moritz Hartmann had praised Czech Hussite heroes. Demetz, *Prague*, 293. See also the recollections of Josef Alexander Helfert, later minister of state, historian, and friend of Rieger, of his trip to Vienna in the summer of 1848. *Aufzeichnungen und Erinnerungen aus jungen Jahren* (Vienna, 1904), 17.

44. Maršan, *Čechové*, 14ff; Křen, *Konfliktgemeinschaft*, 85; Gary Cohen, *The Politics of Ethnic Survival: Germans in Prague 1861–1914* (West Lafayette, IN, 2006).

45. Joseph Alexander von Helfert, *Geschichte der österreichischen Revolution*, vol. 1 (Freiburg im Breisgau, Germany, 1907), 466; Monika Baár, *Historians and Nationalism. East-Central Europe in the Nineteenth Century* (Oxford, 2010), 241.

46. Josef Kolejka, "Der Slawenkongress in Prag im Juni 1848," in Rudolf Jaworski and Robert Luft, eds., *1848/49 Revolutionen in Ostmitteleuropa* (Munich, 1996), 137.

47. Letter dated March 15–16, 1848. Černý, *Boj za právo*, 20–21; Introduction to Kaiserová and Rak, *Nacionalizace společnosti*, 12; Kořalka, *Tschechen*, 50.

48. Kořalka, *Tschechen*, 50; Peter Bugge, "Czech Nation-Building, National Self-Perception and Politics, 1780–1914" (PhD dissertation, University of Aarhus, 1994), 69.

49. Those were majority German. Bugge, "Czech Nation-Building," 68–69. Demetz, *Prague*, 294.

50. Redlich, *Francis Joseph*, 25

51. Polišenský, *Aristocrats*, 150–151; Bugge, "Czech Nation-Building," 77; Joseph Alexander von Helfert, *Der Prager Juni-Aufstand, 1848* (Prague, 1897), 4.

52. Richard Georg Plaschka, *Avantgarde des Widerstands: Modellfälle militärischer Auflehnung im 19. und 20. Jahrhundert* (Vienna, 2000), 66.

53. Polišenský counts about 10,000 soldiers. *Aristocrats*, 152.

54. František Palacký, "Manifesto of First Slavonic Congress to the Nations of Europe," *Slavonic and East European Review* 26 (1947/1948), 309–313. This manifesto was dated June 12, just when the fighting was reaching a crescendo. Demetz, *Prague*, 294–295.

55. Schopf, *Wahre und ausführliche Darstellung*, 49; Havránek, "Böhmen," 196; Pech, *Czech Revolution*, 144; Bugge, "Czech Nation-Building," 77.

56. Bertold Sutter, "Die politische und rechtliche Stellung der Deutschen in Österreich 1848," in *Die Habsburgermonarchie*, Adam Wandruszka and Peter Urbanitsch, eds., vol. 3, part 1 (Vienna, 1980), 203; Julius Ebersberg, *Vater Radetzky. Ein Charakterbild für Soldaten* (Prague, 1858), 99; Wereszycki, *Historia*, 206; Sheehan, *German History*, 697; Macartney, *Habsburg Empire*, 392–393.

57. Rapport, *1848*, 264; Richard Bassett, *For God and Kaiser: The Imperial Austrian Army, 1619–1918* (New Haven, CT, 2015), 296.

58. The Hungarian estates had accepted it in 1723. Kontler, *Millennium*, 253; Deák, "The Revolution," 216.

59. Macartney, *Habsburg Empire*, 393.

60. Deák, "The Revolution," 224; Constant von Wurzbach, ed., *Biographisches Lexikon des Kaisertums Österreich*, vol. 14 (Vienna, 1865), 40.

61. R. John Rath, *The Viennese Revolution of 1848* (Austin, 1957), 329; Rapport, *1848*, 281–282.

62. Wereszycki, *Historia*, 208–209.

63. After the National Guard had sighted the advancing Hungarians, they continued fighting. About 2,000 died on both sides. Rapport, *1848*, 286–287.

64. Rapport, *1848*, 287–288.

65. Juliusz Demel, *Historia Rumunii* (Wrocław, 1970), 300.

66. Ambrus Miskolczy, "Transylvania in the Revolution," in Zoltán Szász, ed., *History of Transylvania*, vol. 3 (New York, 2002), 243; Ștefan Pascu, *A History of Transylvania* (Detroit, 1982), 196.

67. Kontler, *Millennium*, 251; Spira, *Nationality Issue*, 124–125. The Slovak volunteers, about 5,000 in number, tended to fight in support of the imperial armies. Dušan Kováč, "The Slovak Political Program," in Teich et al., eds., *Slovakia in History*, 126–127.

68. Spira, *Nationality Issue*, 131. These constituted the most violent of all events of the 1848/1849 revolutions. Jonathan Sperber, *The European Revolutions 1848–1851* (Cambridge, 1994), 137.

69. Deák, *Lawful Revolution*, 209–210.

70. Andreas Gräser, *Stephan Ludwig Roth nach seinem Leben und Wirken dargestellt* (Kronstadt, 1852), 77; C. Edmund Maurice, *The Revolutionary Movement of 1848–49* (New York, 1887), 450; György Klapka, *Memoiren: April bis October 1849* (Leipzig, 1850), 347.

71. Demel, *Historia*, 304. For the report on Abrud: August Treboniu Laurian, *Die Romanen der österreichischen Monarchie*, vol. 2 (Vienna, 1850), 35; also: Sorin Mitu, *Die ethnische Identität der Siebenbürger Rumänen* (Vienna, 2003), 109; Wilhelm Rüstow, *Geschichte des ungarischen Insurrektionskrieges*, vol. 2 (Zurich, 1861), 12–13; "Ein nationaler Martyrer gegen dreizehn," *Die Reform* 8:41 (1869), 1294; Deák, *Lawful Revolution*, 313–314; Miskolczy, "Transylvania," 315; Ambrus Miskolczy, "Roumanian-Hungarian Attempts at Reconciliation in the Spring of 1849 in Transylvania: Ioan Dragos's Mission," *Annales Universitatis Eötvös, Historica*, 10–11 (1981), 61–81.

72. The Hungarian armies of about 170,000 had stood a chance against imperial army of 175,000, but the additional 200,000 troops tipped the balance. Paul Robert Magocsi, *With Their Backs to the Mountain: A History of Carpathian Rus and Carpatho-Rusyns* (Budapest, 2015), 119–120; Angela Jianu, *A Circle of Friends: Romanian Revolutionaries and Political Exile, 1840–1859* (Leiden, 2011), 149. Many professional officers who were Hungarian remained loyal to the crown. Deák, *Lawful Revolution*, 314, 332–334, 336. On the Vojvodina: Dimitrije Djordjevic, "Die Serben," in *Die Habsburgermonarchie*, Wandruszka and Urbanitsch, eds., vol. 3, 747.

73. Heinrich Friedjung, *Österreich von 1848 bis 1860*, vol. 1 (Stuttgart, 1908), 231; R. W. Seton-Watson, *Racial Problems in Hungary* (London, 1908), 101.

74. Maurice, *Revolutionary Moment*, 456.

75. Dieter Langewiesche, *Europa zwischen Restauration und Revolution* (Munich, 2007, 83–84); Kořalka, *Tschechen*, 91; Wereszycki, *Historia*, 199; Sperber, *European Revolutions*, 209.

76. An exception was the age's nationalist activist, Giuseppe Mazzini. See his "The Slavonian National Movement," *Lowes Edinburgh Magazine and Protestant Educational Journal* 9 (July 1847), 182–192.

77. Havránek, "Böhmen," 183; John Erickson, "The Preparatory Committee of the Slav Congress," in Brock and Skilling, eds., *Czech Renascence*, 178–179. Support for Windischgrätz's victory ran along ethnic lines. The mostly German propertied classes breathed a sigh of relief at the end of "lawlessness," when at any moment crowds might take hold of spaces at the town's center, sometimes destroying property. Polišenský, *Aristocrats*, 152.

78. Polišenský, *Aristocrats*, 167.

79. Havránek, "Böhmen," 183; Klapka, *Memoiren*, 37.

Chapter 7: The Reform That Made the Monarchy Unreformable: The 1867 Compromise

1. Henryk Wereszycki, *Historia Austrii* (Wrocław, 1972), 219–221.

2. Mobilizing the army for the Crimean War had absorbed the entire military budget of 1854 in three months. Steven Beller, *Francis Joseph* (London, 1996), 67–68.

3. Macartney, *Habsburg Empire*, 499.

4. Piotr Boyarski, "Kiedy Polacy rządzili we Wiedniu," *Gazeta Wyborcza*, June 14, 2013; Larry Wolff, *The Idea of Galicia: History and Fantasy in Habsburg Political Culture* (Stanford, CA, 2010), 199; Henryk Wereszycki, *Pod berłem Habsburgów*, 169–170.

5. Piotr Wandycz, *The Lands of Partitioned Poland, 1795–1918* (Seattle, 1974), 151–152; *Fortnightly Review* (London) vol. 6 (1866), 625; Gustav Strakosch-Grassmann, *Geschichte des österreichischen Unterrichtswesens* (Vienna, 1905), 240.

6. Macartney, *Habsburg Empire*, 503; Stanisław Estreicher, "Galicia in the Period of Autonomy and Self-Government," in W. Reddaway et al., eds., *Cambridge History of Poland* (Cambridge, 1941), 440.

7. Louis Eisenmann, "Austria-Hungary," in A. W. Ward et al., eds., *Cambridge Modern History*, vol. 12 (Cambridge, 1910), 176–177. Bohemia's Count Clam-Martinic made common cause with Count Anton Szécsen and also with Count Thun. Robert Kann, *Multinational Empire: Nationalism and National Reform in the Habsburg Monarchy*, vol. 1 (New York, 1950), 179.

8. "Mailath, Georg," in *Biographisches Lexikon des Kaiserthums Oesterreich*, Constant von Wurzbach, ed., vol. 16 (Vienna, 1867), 297–299; Macartney, *Habsburg Empire*, 506; Albert Sturm, *Culturbilder aus Budapest* (Leipzig, 1876), 46; K. M. Kertbeny, *Silhoutten und Reliquien*, vol. 2 (Prague, 1863), 29.

9. Eisenmann, "Austria-Hungary," 177; Lothar Höbelt, *Franz Joseph I.: der Kaiser und sein Reich: eine politische Geschichte* (Vienna, 2009), 47–48; Macartney, *Habsburg Empire*, 499, 503; Alexander Matlekovits, *Das Königreich Ungarn*, vol. 1 (Leipzig, 1900), vi–vii.

10. Gejza von Ferdinandy, *Staats- und Verwaltungsrecht des Königreichs Ungarn und seiner Nebenländer*, Heinrich Schiller, trans. (Hannover, 1909), 17; C. A. Macartney, *Hungary: A Short History* (Chicago, 1962), 167. The tavernicus was a royal appointee in charge of towns, a kind of minister of the interior. Jean W. Sedlar, *East Central Europe in the Middle Ages* (Seattle, 1994), 329.

11. *London Review*, September 7, 1861, 287.

12. Eisenmann, "Austria-Hungary," 178.

13. Robert C. Binkley, *Realism and Nationalism 1852–1871* (New York, 1935), 237.

14. Robin Okey, *The Habsburg Monarchy: From Enlightenment to Eclipse* (New York, 2001), 184; Eisenmann, "Austria-Hungary," 179.

15. Schmerling's gerrymandering made German constituencies in towns and country much smaller than Czech constituencies. Bugge, "Czech Nation-Building," 109.

16. Levente T. Szabo, "Patterns, Ideologies and Networks of Memory," *Berliner Beiträge zur Hungarologie* 19 (2016), 35, 38; http://geroandras.hu/en/blog/2016/03/24/march-15-the-birthday -of-the-nation/ (accessed September 26, 2018).

17. *New Hungarian Quarterly* 33 (1992), 116; András Gerő, *Emperor Francis Joseph*, James Paterson, trans. (Boulder, 2001), 101; Peter Hanák, *Ungarn in der Donaumonarchie* (Vienna, 1984), 71; Wereszycki, *Historia*, 225; Eisenmann, "Austria-Hungary," 180.

18. Thanks to Joachim von Puttkamer for this formulation. The Hungarian diet convened in April but was disbanded in August when Francis could not come to terms with it. Eisenmann, "Austria-Hungary," 179; Wereszycki, *Historia*, 224.

19. Hanák, *Ungarn*, 72–73, 75. For a revealing contemporary analysis of Austria's limited options, see "The Hungarian Ultimatum," *The Spectator*, May 25, 1861, 553–556.

20. Macartney, *Hungary*, 168; Eisenmann, "Austria-Hungary," 182.

21. Macartney, *Habsburg Empire*, 537.

22. Gerő, *Emperor Francis Joseph*, 94.

23. Critics wrote that one could not apply "Solomon's judgment" to the Habsburg lands and still use the word "empire" to describe them. See the Catholic conservative opinion in "Zeitläufe," *Historisch-politische Blätter für das katholische Deutschland* 56 (1865), 648.

24. Hanák, *Ungarn*, 86.

25. Binkley, *Realism*, 275; Macartney, *Habsburg Empire*, 538; Hanák, *Ungarn*, 84.

26. Eisenmann, "Austria-Hungary," 182.

27. This was the "September manifesto" of September 20, 1865. The name of the party went back to 1861, when Deák had wanted to address the crown directly, but his opponents insisted on a parliamentary resolution (thus "Resolutionists"). See "Recent Hungarian Politics," in *Saturday Review*, November 17, 1866, 607–608.

28. The historian Heinrich von Treitschke wrote in 1859 that only when Austria had been expelled from the German Confederation would it be possible to imagine that this "unholy mixed state could find a purpose to exist through its cultural mission in the Slavic east." Sheehan, *German History*, 866.

29. Prussia had spent almost twice as much on each man under arms. Peter J. Katzenstein, *Disjoined Partners: Austria and Germany Since 1815* (Berkeley, 1976), 87–89.

30. Macartney, *Habsburg Empire*, 546; John Deak, *Forging a Multinational State: State-Making in Imperial Austria* (Stanford, CA, 2015), 151ff.

31. According to this reasoning, it was in these tribes' own interests to assist in spreading German culture, because it was the essential intellectual leaven [*Bildungsferment*] for their own development. *Die Aufgaben Österreichs* (Leipzig, 1860), 19–20, 27; Ian Reifowitz, "Threads Intertwined: German National Egoism and Liberalism," *Nationalities Papers* 29:3 (2001), 446; Carl E. Schorske, *Fin-de-Siècle Vienna: Politics and Culture* (New York, 1980), 117.

32. Johann Ritter von Perthaler, *Hans von Perthaler's auserlesene Schriften*, vol. 2 (Vienna, 1883), 47; Selma Krasa-Florian, *Die Allegorie der Austria* (Vienna, 2007), 177. For biography: "Johann Ritter von Perthaler," *Biographisches Lexikon*, Wurzbach, ed., vol. 22 (Vienna, 1870), 39.

33. Friedrich von Hellweld, *Die Welt der Slawen* (Berlin, 1890), 139.

34. Viktor Bibl, *Der Zerfall Österreichs*, vol. 2 (Vienna, 1924), 312.

35. Okey, *Habsburg Monarchy*, 187; Macartney, *Habsburg Empire*, 547. On Polish accession to the Compromise with Hungary in return for autonomy in Galicia: Jonathan Kwan, *Liberalism and the Habsburg Monarchy* (Basingstoke, UK, 2013), 53. The situation of Croatia was much better than the Ukrainian one in Galicia (which was more like the Serb, Slovak, or Romanian situations).

36. In February 1867, *Die Neue Freie Presse* wrote that German liberals could choose between "the Slavs and Hungary." Kwan, *Liberalism*, 54. In the early 1860s, of 261 members of the Bohemian diet, 70 were great landowners; the number of Germans was inflated. Kann, *Multinational Empire*, vol. 1, 401.

37. He spoke of the "artificial preponderence" of Slavs. *Die Presse* (Vienna), Abendblatt 241, September 3, 1866.

38. Eduard von Wertheimer, *Graf Julius Andrássy: sein Leben und seine Zeit*, vol. 2 (Stuttgart, 1912), 224.

39. "If Austria does not at this moment develop its own internal forces, it will be expelled not only from the German Confederation, but from civilized Europe." Von Wertheimer, *Graf Julius Andrássy*, 226.

40. Pieter Judson, *Exclusive Revolutionaries: Liberal Politics, Social Experience, and National Identity in the Austrian Empire* (Ann Arbor, MI, 1996), 108; Kwan, *Liberalism*, 55.

41. Macartney, *Habsburg Empire*, 548. See the recollections of Moritz Kaiserfeld and the reporting from the *Neue Freie Presse*, June 1867, in Kwan, *Liberalism*, 55–56.

42. Josef Redlich, *Das österreichische Staats- und Reichsproblem*, vol. 2 (Leipzig, 1920), 523; Stefan Pfurtscheller, *Die Epoche Maria-Theresiens bis zum Ausgleich Österreich-Ungarns aus französischer Perspektive* (Innsbruck, 2013), 93.

43. Eisenmann, "Austria-Hungary," 183; Redlich, *Das österreichische Staats- und Reichsproblem*, vol. 2, 561; Macartney, *Habsburg Empire*, 549, 568.

44. Viktor Bibl, *Der Zerfall Österreichs*, vol. 2 (Vienna, 1924), 313; Brigitte Hamann, *Elisabeth: Kaiserin wider Willen* (Munich, 1998), 259; Katzenstein, *Disjoined Partners*, 87–89; Hanák, *Ungarn*, 88; Deak, *Forging a Multinational State*, 147.

45. Macartney, *Habsburg Empire*, 227.

46. Only if Francis Joseph completely trusted Andrássy, she wrote him, could the empire be salvaged. Hamann, *Elisabeth*, 241.

47. Eisenmann, "Austria-Hungary," 184; Hamann, *Elisabeth*, 253, 258.

48. Macartney, *Habsburg Empire*, 555; Hanák, *Ungarn*, 94. The data are from between 1911 and 1913. In 1897 an irate Austrian delegation demanded a 42–58 division of expenditures, but they had to settle for 32.5–67.5, thanks to Hungarian assertiveness. Janos, *Politics of Backwardness*, 123.

49. Okey, *Habsburg Monarchy*, 188; Eisenmann, "Austria-Hungary," 184.

50. Bugge, "Czech Nation-Building," 115. Censorship had already been relaxed under Schmerling, and confessional tolerance enhanced. Wereszycki, *Historia*, 231.

51. Redlich, *Österreichisches Staatsproblem*, vol. 2, 580; Hanák, *Ungarn*, 93; Alexander Maxwell, *Choosing Slovakia: Slavic Hungary, the Czechoslovak Language and Accidental Nationalism* (London, 2009), 25.

52. Victor L. Tapié, *Rise and Fall of the Habsburg Monarchy* (London, 1971), 305.

53. Maxwell, *Choosing Slovakia*, 26.

54. This right pertained in cases where the nationality could claim to speak a "Landesprache" in a given area, as the Czechs could in Bohemia, but not in Austria. Pieter Judson, *Guardians of the Nation: Activists on the Language Frontiers of Imperial Austria* (Cambridge, MA, 2006), 24; Bugge, "Czech Nation-Building," 115–116; Kwan, *Liberalism*, 60. The Czechs had to catch up in secondary and higher education,but did so impressively beginning in the late 1880s. Jiri Kořalka and R. J. Crampton, "Die Tschechen," in *Habsburgermonarchie*, Wandruszka and Urbanitsch, eds., vol. 3, 510–512; Gary B. Cohen "Education and Czech Social Structure in the Late Nineteenth Century," in *Bildungsgeschichte, Bevölkerungsgeschichte, Gesellschaftsgeschichte in den böhmischen Ländern und in Europa*, Hans Lemberg et al., eds. (Vienna, 1977), 32–45.

55. These were called *tábory*. Bugge, "Czech Nation-Building," 116–119; Otto Orban, "Der tschechische Austroslawismus," in Andreas Moritsch, *Der Austroslawismus: ein verfrühtes Konzept zur politischen Neugestaltung Europas* (Vienna, 1996), 59; Stanley Z. Pech, "Passive Resistance of the Czechs, 1863–1879," *Slavonic and East European Review* 36 (1958), 443.

Chapter 8: The 1878 Berlin Congress: Europe's New Ethno-Nation-States

1. The most prominent recent case of such usage is Christopher Clark, *Sleepwalkers: How Europe Went to War in 1914* (New York, 2013).

2. Tibor Frank, "Hungary and the Dual Monarchy," in Sugar et al., eds., *History of Hungary*, 254–256; Okey, *Habsburg Monarchy*, 325 (on Romanians and Serbs); Rebekah Klein- Pejšová, *Mapping Jewish Loyalties in Interwar Slovakia* (Bloomington, IN, 2015), 10–12 (on Slovaks). The Magyarization policies intensified beginning in 1875, with the Liberal Party rule under Kálmán Tisza. In 1873 the government ceased publishing the Slovak edition of the official gazette, and in 1874, it closed down Slovak secondary education. The state administration was fully Magyar, and even when officials used the local languages as the law stipulated before 1875, their intention was to Maygarize. Still, forced Magyarization dated only from the early 1880s. Robert A. Kann and Zdeněk V. David, *Peoples of the Eastern Habsburg Lands* (Seattle, 1984), 380; Macartney, *Hungary*, 182–183.

3. James J. Reid, *Crisis of the Ottoman Empire: Prelude to Collapse* (Stuttgart, 2000), 309; Fred Singleton, *A Short History of the Yugoslav Peoples* (Cambridge, 1985), 102. The percentage of non-Muslim tax farmers varied over time, but by the nineteenth century, they tended to be a minority in the European territories, because the taxing authority had passed to former military men, who were almost entirely Muslim. But historians register an uptick in numbers of Christians in the late nineteenth century, for example, in Bulgaria. Svetla Ianeva, "The Non-Muslim Tax-Farmers," in *Religion, Ethnicity, and Contested Nationhood in the Former Ottoman Space*, Jorgen Nielsen, ed. (Leiden, 2012), 48–52.

4. Martha M. Čupić-Amrein, *Die Opposition gegen die österreichisch-ungarische Herrschaft in Bosnien-Hercegovina* (Bern, 1987), 14. Initially the event had involved five villages. "The

Herzegovina," *The Times* (London), July 19, 1875, 5; Arthur Evans, *Through Bosnia and Herzegovina on Foot during the Insurrection* (London, 1876), 338.

5. Evans, *Through Bosnia*, 333, 336.

6. For example, through military service. Francine Friedman, *Bosnian Muslims: Denial of a Nation* (Boulder, 1996), 44.

7. This incident was at Konjica. Josef Koetschet, *Aus Bosniens letzter Türkenzeit* (Vienna, 1905), 18. When the authorities moved to introduce conscription in the nineteenth century, they excluded Christians, fearing that Christian soldiers would damage morale, which was to a high degree based on religious fervor. Erik Jan Zürcher, "The Ottoman Conscription System," *International Review of Social History* 43 (1998), 445–447.

8. Evans, *Through Bosnia*, 338–342; "Christian Populations in Turkey," *London Quarterly Review* 46 (April 1876), 82–83; Hannes Grandits, "Violent Social Disintegration: A Nation-Building Strategy in Late Ottoman Herzegovina," in *Conflicting Loyalties in the Balkans: The Great Powers, the Ottoman Empire, and Nation-Building*, Hannes Grandits et al., eds. (London, 2011), 112–113.

9. Evans, *Through Bosnia*, 331.

10. Evans, *Through Bosnia*, 340.

11. Evans, *Through Bosnia*, 340; Koetschet, *Aus Bosniens*, 5. Koetschet was a Swiss physician in Turkish state service who had access to the most powerful figures in the Ottoman Empire. He acted as that state's representative, for example, to the Prince of Montenegro. Grandits, "Violent Social Disintegration," 114.

12. Singleton, *Short History*, 102; Čupić-Amrein, *Opposition*, 21.

13. These Bosnian Serbs called themselves "Bosniaks" and appealed to Bosnian Muslims for support of the rebellion, promising to respect their religion and property. Marko Attila Hoare, *The History of Bosnia* (London, 2007), 61–64.

14. Grandits, "Violent Social Disintegration," 121, 133; "The Herzegovina," *The Times* (London), July 19, 1875, 5; "The Herzegovina and Turkestan," *The Times* (London), August 12, 1875, 10.

15. Noel Malcolm, *Bosnia: A Short History* (New York, 1994), 132; *The Times* (London), August 5, 1875, 8. On the religious, anti-Muslim character of the war, see also Kemal H. Karpat, "Foundations of Nationalism in South East Europe," in *Der Berliner Kongress von 1878: Die Politik der Grossmächte*, Ralph Melville and Hans-Jürgen Schröder, eds. (Wiesbaden, 1982), 385–410.

16. Malcolm, *Bosnia*, 133. Christians had put land around Mostar under the plough, and after the harvest were forced to cede it to local *begs* under punishment of imprisonment. Koetschet, *Aus Bosniens*, 22; Friedman, *Bosnian Muslims*, 44. Christian villagers were not permitted to remain neutral: "If a village refused to throw its lot in with the rebels, they first burnt one house and one maize plot, and then another." Evans, *Through Bosnia*, 329–330.

17. Singleton, *Short History*, 101.

18. From January 1875. Horst Haselsteiner, "Zur Haltung der Donaumonarchie in der Orientalischen Frage," in *Berliner Kongress*, Melville, ed., 230.

19. Singleton, *Short History*, 103.

20. Serbia, Austria, and Greece were unhappy about the San Stefano treaty. Barbara Jelavich and Charles Jelavich, *The Establishment of the Balkan National States* (Seattle, 1977), 153.

21. Hoare, *History of Bosnia*, 67.

22. Jared Manasek, "Empire Displaced: Ottoman-Habsburg Forced Migration and the Near Eastern Crisis 1875–78," (PhD thesis, Columbia University, 2013), 224–225.

23. The Congress was originally Andrássy's idea, and Berlin was deemed an acceptable meeting place, as Germany was thought to have no direct interests in the Balkans. Jelavich and Jelavich, *Establishment*, 155; Theodore S. Hamerow, *The Age of Bismarck* (New York, 1973), 263–272; Mihailo D. Stojanovich, *The Great Powers and the Balkans 1875–1878* (Cambridge, 1939).

24. Bulgaria kept 37.5 percent of the San Stefano territories. R. J. Crampton, *A Short History of Modern Bulgaria* (Cambridge, 1987), 85.

25. Historically those areas, mostly Romanian ethnically, had belonged to the principality of Moldavia, but were seized by Russia at the conclusion of hostilities with Turkey in 1812 and were lost against in 1856. The reacquisition was thought to compensate Russia for Austria's gains in Bosnia and the Sanjak of Novi Pazar. In the process, the Turkish possessions on the peninsula continued to shrink, from 82 percent (1830s) to 44 percent (1878) to 5 percent (1913). Holm Sundhaussen, *Geschichte Serbiens* (Vienna, 2007), 132. For the Salisbury statement: Piotr S. Wandycz, *Die Grossmächte und Ostmitteleuropa vom Berliner Kongress bis zum Fall der Mauer* (Leipzig, 2007), 17.

26. Crampton, *Short History*, 85.

27. Robert Donia, "The Proximate Colony," in Clemens Ruthner et al., eds., *Wechselwirkungen: Austria-Hungary, Bosnia-Herzegovina and the Western Balkans* (New York, 2015), 67, 79.

28. Singleton, *Short History*, 104.

29. Robin Okey, *Taming Balkan Nationalism* (Oxford, 2007), 57, 64.

30. Malcolm, *Bosnia*, 149. The Austro-Hungarians estimated the rebel army at 93,000. Hoare, *History of Bosnia*, 69.

31. Jovana Mihajlović Trbovc, "Forging Identity through Negotiation: The Case of the Contemporary Bosniak Nation" (MA thesis, Central European University, 2008). Based on the work of Ivan Franjo Jukić, *Zemljopis i poviestnica Bosne* (Zagreb, 1851).

32. Benjamin Kállay, *Geschichte der Serben* (Vienna, 1878). Contrary to rumor, he did not ban his own book. Okey, *Taming*, 63.

33. Okey, *Taming*, 60, 254; Andrea Feldman, "Kállay's Dilemma on the Challenge of Creating a Manageable Identity in Bosnia and Herzegovina," *Review of Croatian History* 13:1 (2017), 117.

34. Mihajlović Trbovc, "Forging Identity," 12. That church's actual teachings and history are enveloped in the fogs of nineteenth-century myth-making. What seems clear is that a western-oriented Bosnian church was cut off from effective control by Rome in the early thirteenth century and developed rituals and teachings that diverged from orthodoxy (and may have been related to the poorly understood group of Bogumil heretics). Perhaps it fostered theological dualism. That relatively independent church declined in the fifteenth century when Franciscans reasserted Rome's authority. The Orthodox are known in Bosnia only after the Turkish conquest, that is, from the late fifteenth century. Malcolm, *Bosnia*, 27–42; 70–71.

35. "The idea of a single Bosnian national identity never gained support beyond the small circle of youthful pro-regime Muslim intellectuals." Donia, "Proximate Colony," 71.

36. Hoare, *History of Bosnia*, 74–75.

37. Mihajlović Trbovc, "Forging Identity," 10.

38. Okey, *Taming*, 51–52. Serbs were also vigilant concerning attempts by Croat authorities to dissolve Serb identity in Croat civil society through schooling. The Serb society was set up in 1863. Mihajlović Trbovc, "Forging Identity," 8, citing: Mustafa Imamović "Integracione nacionane ideologije i Bosna," *Godišnjak Pravnog fakulteta u Sarajevu* 39 (1996), 115.

39. The number of parochial schools dropped by 13 percent. Okey, *Taming*, 52; Dimitrije Djordjević, "Die Serben," in *Habsburgermonarchie*, Wandruszka and Urbanitsch, eds., vol. 3, 768.

40. Donia, "Proximate Colony," 72; Feldman, "Kállay's Dilemma," 108; Jelavich, *History of Balkans*, vol. 2, 60; Malcolm, *Bosnia*, 145.

41. Of 11,264 officials in 1902, only 1,217 were natives. Hoare, *History of Bosnia*, 72; Clemens Ruthner, "Bosnia-Herzegovina: Post-colonial?" in Ruthner et al., *Wechselwirkungen*, 9. In 1904, 26.5 percent of officials were natives; 3 percent were Serbs and 5 percent Muslims. Newspaper article from 1890, cited in Okey, *Taming*, 52.

42. Donia, "Proximate Colony," 69.

43. Aydin Babuna, "Nationalism and the Bosnian Muslims," *East European Quarterly* 33:2 (June 1999), 204. In that budget, £5,667 went to primary education, and £125,974 to the gendarmerie: Okey, *Taming*, 65–67. Various communities responded differently: 64 percent of Jewish children attended school, and 22 percent of Catholic, but only 13 percent of Orthodox children and 6 percent of Muslim. Malcolm, *Bosnia*, 144–145; Feldman, "Kállay's Dilemma," 109; Donia, "Proximate Colony," 74.

44. Non-Muslim landholders (with kmets, that is, tenants with specific rights under Ottoman law) were 8.85 percent of the whole in 1910. Babuna, "Nationalism," 211.

45. The regulation of the Narenta from Metković to the Adriatic greatly increased the amount of farmland. Between 1907 and 1909, landowners brought 56,000 complaints into courts against peasants who were not making full payments. Despite provision for peasants attaining partial ownership rights, by 1910 only 10.8 percent of kmet land had been purchased in this manner. Djordjević, "Die Serben," 765; Babuna, "Nationalism," 212; Friedrich Hauptmann, *Die österreichisch-ungarische Herrschaft in Bosnien* (Graz, 1983), 194.

46. Kállay was "retaining the ancient traditions of the land, vivified and purified by modern ideas." Donia, "Proximate Colony," 68–69. Changes in the planting regime had to be agreed on by peasant and landlord; peasants could not undertake any bettering of their property, nor could they be forced to do so. The rights pertained to families and existed as long as the family did; the landlord had no right to use peasants' holdings for his own sake. Karel Kadlec, "Die Agrarverfassung," in *Österreichisches Staatswörterbuch: Handbuch des gesamten österreichischen öffentlichen Rechts*, Ernst Mischler and Josef Ulbrich, eds., vol. 1 (Vienna, 1905), 113–116.

47. In 1910, Muslims constituted 91.15 percent of the landowners with kmets, but only 4.58 percent of kmets; 73.92 percent of kmets were Serbs, and 21.49 percent were Croat. Babuna, "Nationalism," 211; Djordjević, "Die Serben," 769.

48. Hoare, *History of Bosnia*, 72; Babuna, "Nationalism," 201; Djordjević, "Die Serben," 771.

49. Malcolm, *Bosnia*, 145.

50. Contentions and contradictions arose, writes Robert Donia, "not only between colonizers and colony, but among major actors within the colony, contributing to the ultimate demise of the Dual Monarchy itself." As in other colonial situations, "development heightened social inequalities and ethnic divisions rather than attenuated them." Donia, "Proximate Colony," 67, 69.

51. Article one of the agreement with Bulgaria, Treaty of Berlin; Edward Hertslet, *The Map of Europe by Treaty*, vol. 4 (London, 1891), 2766; http://www.zeit.de/zeit-geschichte/2014/04 /otto-von-bismarck-juden (accessed August 30, 2018).

52. In the London Protocol number 3 of February 3, 1830, Greece had to promise, at the request of France, to allow free Roman Catholic worship and respect of Catholic ownership of

property; Greek citizens without regard to religion would be admitted to all offices, functions, and honors, and in all church, civic, and political relations would be treated according to the principle of complete equality. Ernst Flachbarth, *System des internationalen Minderheitenschutzes* (Budapest, 1937), 12. The Berlin Congress represented an expansion in quantity and quality from the international protections established at earlier times, for example, in 1815 at Vienna for Poles, or in 1830 for Greece. Rainer Hofmann, "Menschenrechte und der Schutz nationaler Minderheiten," in *Zeitschrift für ausländisches öffentliches Recht und Völkerrecht* 65 (2005), 589.

53. Dan Diner, *Das Jahrhundert verstehen* (Munich, 1999), 30–31; Davide Rodogno, *Against Massacre: Humanitarian Interventions in the Ottoman Empire* (Princeton, NJ, 2012), 145.

54. The language was identical, though only in Bulgaria was it stated explicitly that the new government would be Christian. Flachbarth, *System*, 14. Turkey also had to agree to respect religious liberty. Articles four and five, Hertslet, *Map of Europe by Treaty*, 2769–2770; Manasek, "Empire Displaced," 236.

55. Cathie Carmichael, *A Concise History of Bosnia* (Cambridge, 2012), 43. An agreement was signed in 1862 to displace the remaining Muslim population from Belgrade. Michael Schwartz, *Ethnische Säuberungen in der Moderne: globale Wechselwirkungen nationalistischer und rassistischer Gewaltpolitik im 19. und 20. Jahrhundert* (Munich, 2013), 240–241; Karpat, "Foundations," 404.

56. Manasek, "Empire Displaced," 226–227.

57. This is the impression of the author Emily Gerard in "Transylvanian Peoples," *The Living Age* 58 (April 1887), 135. Contrast the much clearer sense—as expressed by western observers—of the origins of the Bulgarians, based on a history of settlement and early statehood, as producing a bounded ethnicity, a "Bulgarian race." Review of Mr. and Mrs. John Eliah Blunt, *The People of Turkey* (London, 1878), *London Quarterly Review* 51 (1879), 415.

58. All nations are built on a combination of mythology and identifiable social and political interest, but in some cases, the mythology is of more recent origin and less rooted in popular consciousness and therefore requires more conscious work to seem credible. In Romania and Bulgaria, the national movements emerged comparatively late, but in the latter, the movement had the easier task of creating statehood in an area widely understood to have been an empire that was subdued by Ottoman rule, as had been Serbia and Byzantium. In the case of Romania, patriots claimed to be returning a state that had existed for one year, had not even borne the name "Romania," and went across boundaries of empire as well as religions. They of course "solved" this problem, bequeathing fascinating gyrations on the basic questions of national unity. For a lively discussion, see Lucian Boia, *History and Myth in Romanian Consciousness* (Budapest, 2001). On Bulgaria, see Roumen Daskalov, *The Making of a Nation in the Balkans* (Budapest, 2004); Claudia Weber, *Auf der Suche nach der Nation: Erinnerungskultur in Bulgarien* (Berlin, 2006). On the Bulgarian national movement and its concerns for culture, education, and above all, its struggle for a separate church, see R. J. Crampton, *A Concise History of Bulgaria* (Cambridge, 1997), 46–76.

59. Some of the family names are: Cuza, Golescu, Rosetti, Bratianu, Balcescu, and Kogalniceanu. Jelavich and Jelavich, *Establishment*, 95.

60. Russia held a protectorate. Keith Hitchins, *A Concise History of Romania* (Cambridge, 2014), 95–96. Also: Ioan Stanomir, "The Temptation of the West: The Romanian Constitutional Tradition," in *Moral, Legal and Political Values in Romanian Culture*, Michaela Czobor-Lupp and J. Stefan Lupp, eds. (Washington, DC, 2002).

61. R. W. Seton-Watson, *History of the Roumanians* (Cambridge, 1934), 230, 266–268.

62. This result was largely a farce, given the prevailing illiteracy, but it was also secured by coercion. Jelavich, *History of the Balkans*, vol. 1, 293; Seton-Watson, *History of the Roumanians*, 301–309.

63. Hitchins, *Concise History*, x; Seton-Watson, *History of the Roumanians*, 310.

64. Jelavich and Jelavich, *Establishment*, 120; Jelavich, *History of the Balkans*, vol. 1, 294.

65. Frederick Kellogg, *The Road to Romanian Independence* (West Lafayette, IN, 1995), 13.

66. Jelavich and Jelavich, *Establishment*, 122–123.

67. All Jews not "engaging an any useful occupation may be removed" and no longer enter Moldavia. This was Article 94 of Chapter III of the Organic Law of Moldavia. Carol Iancu, *Jews in Romania 1866–1919: From Exclusion to Emancipation*, Carvel de Bussy, trans. (New York, 1996), 25. Article 7 of the 1866 constitution stated that naturalization would be given only to foreigners belonging to the Christian faith. Jelavich and Jelavich, *Establishment*, 178. It built on the Organic Statutes from the mid-1830s, according to which only Christians had counted as citizens.

68. "In 1878, a total of 218,304 Jews were recorded, and in 1899 there were 269,015—4.5 percent of the population." Leon Volovici, "Romania," in *YIVO Encyclopedia of Jews in Eastern Europe*, 2010, at http://www.yivoencyclopedia.org/article.aspx/Romania (accessed March 24, 2016); Isidore Singer, ed., *Jewish Encyclopedia* (New York, 1906), vol. 7, 77; vol. 3, 413; Jelavich and Jelavich, *Establishment*, 178.

69. Kellogg, *Road to Romanian Independence*, 45–46, 53.

70. Stephen Fischer-Galati, "Romanian Nationalism," in *Nationalism in Eastern Europe*, Peter Sugar and Ivo Lederer, eds. (Seattle, 1969), 385–386; Carole Fink, *Defending the Rights of Others: The Great Powers, the Jews, and International Minority Protection, 1878–1938* (Cambridge, 2004), 14.

71. Seton-Watson, *History of the Roumanians*, 349; Kellogg, *Road to Romanian Independence*, 49, 58.

72. From an article of February 1879 cited in Dieter Müller, *Staatsbürger auf Widerruf: Juden und Muslime als Alteritätspartner im rumänischen und serbischen Nationscode* (Wiesbaden, 2005), 67.

73. Kellogg, *Road to Romanian Independence*, 44, 49. The exception that proves the rule was the liberal politician Petre P. Carp.

74. Ioan Slavici writing in 1878 and Eminescu writing in 1879. Müller, *Staatsbürger*, 68, 70–71; Kellogg, *Road to Romanian Independence*, 44.

75. He was the father of Ion I. C. Brătianu (d. 1927) and grandfather of Gheorghe I. Brătianu (d. 1953). Radu Ioanid, *The Sword of the Archangel: Fascist Ideology in Romania* (New York, 1990), 31, 33; Müller, *Staatsbürger*, 66–67. For additional luminaries who promoted anti-Semitism, see International Commission on the Holocaust in Romania, *Final Report* (Bucharest, 2004), 24–25, at https://www.ushmm.org/m/pdfs/20080226-romania-commission-holocaust-history.pdf (accessed October 26, 2016).

76. Among Romanian intellectuals of the late nineteenth century, there was "a negative evaluation of everything foreign with the exception of France." Emanuel Turczynski, "The Background of Romanian Fascism," in *Native Fascism in the Successor States*, Peter Sugar, ed. (Santa Barbara, CA, 1971); 106. Albert S. Lindemann, *Esau's Tears: Modern Anti-Semitism and the Rise of the Jews, 1870–1933* (New York, 1997), 307, 312.

77. Bismarck's banker Gerson Bleichröder and other investors wanted to be compensated by the Romanian government. Müller, *Staatsbürger*, 61; On Bleichröder's personal interest: William O. Oldson, *A Providential Anti-Semitism* (Philadelphia, 1991), 32. Also: Jelavich and Jelavich, *Establishment*, 155–157, 178; Seton-Watson, *History of the Roumanians*, 352; Müller, *Staatsbürger*, 74, 81–82. On number of Jews: "Romania," in *Jewish Encyclopedia*, Singer, ed., vol. 9 (New York, 1909), 512–516.

78. "Die Judenfrage in Rumänien," *Das Ausland* 52:2 (1879), 610.

79. Ioanid, *Sword*, 31; Müller, *Staatsbürger*, 71–72.

80. "Romania," in *Jewish Encyclopedia*, Singer, ed., 512–516.

81. Carol Iancu, "The Struggle for the Emancipation of Romanian Jewry," in *The History of Jews in Romania*, Liviu Rotman and Carol Iancu, eds., vol. 2 (Tel Aviv, 2005), 136–137.

82. Josef Perwolf, *Die slavisch-orientalische Frage: eine historische Studie* (Prague, 1878). The respect did not extend to tolerance of Polish demands for nationality rights. See William W. Hagen, *Germans, Poles, and Jews: The Nationality Conflict in the Prussian East* (Chicago, 1980).

83. Leopold Kammerhofer and Walter Prenner, "Liberalismus und Außenpolitik," in *Studien zum Deutschliberalismus in Zisleithanien 1873–79*, Leopold Kammerhofer, ed. (Vienna, 1992), 219.

84. There was nothing new about treaties mandating protection of religious practice in sovereign entities, what was new was to say that religious practice—being Christian in Serbia, Bulgarian, Montenegro, or Romania—was a source of sovereignty. Eric D. Weitz, "From the Vienna to the Paris System: International Politics and the Entangled Histories of Human Rights, Forced Deportations, and Civilizing Missions" *American Historical Review* 113:5 (2008), 1317.

85. Hoare, *History of Bosnia*, 64.

86. Malcolm, *Bosnia*, 149.

87. Helmut Rumpler, *Eine Chance für Mitteleuropa: bürgerliche Emanzipation und Staatsverfall in der Habsburgermonarchie* (Vienna, 1997), 450.

88. "The vote of 112 liberals against the Berlin treaty, six months after Imperial troops had entered Bosnia-Herzegovina, was a symbol of protest against the executive's abuse of the constitution . . . Liberal opposition and disunity . . . made Francis Joseph regard them as an unreliable support for his government." Kwan, *Liberalism*, 98.

Chapter 9: The Origins of National Socialism: Fin de Siècle Hungary and Bohemia

1. Zdeněk David and Robert Kann, *Peoples of the Eastern Habsburg Lands* (Seattle, 1984), 303; C. A. Macartney, *The Habsburg Empire 1790–1918* (London, 1969), 554, 583–584; Wereszycki, *Historia*, 238.

2. Nicknamed "first cavalier of the Reich." Macartney, *Habsburg Empire*, 571.

3. The "more they came to resemble Germans in lifestyle, education and culture, the more hostile and denouncing the depiction of them became in the German media." Peter Bugge, "Czech Nation-Building, National Self-Perception and Politics, 1780–1914" (PhD dissertation, University of Aarhus, 1994), 165; Macartney, *Habsburg Empire*, 612. For details on electoral manipulation in Bohemia and Moravia, see Kwan, *Liberalism*, 79.

4. As stated by Fischhof in 1882. Kwan, *Liberalism*, 133.

5. R. Charmatz, *Adolf Fischhof. Das Lebensbild eines österreichischen Politikers* (Berlin and Stuttgart, 1910), 320ff.

6. Hugo Hantsch, *Geschichte Österreichs* (Graz, Austria, 1953), 438; Macartney, *Habsburg Empire*, 612; A. J. P. Taylor, *The Habsburg Monarchy: 1809–1918* (Chicago, 1976), 157.

7. Bugge, "Czech Nation-Building," 158ff; David and Kann, *Peoples*, 305.

8. Bugge, "Czech Nation-Building," 161, 163.

9. His government also let pass school legislation that led to the closing of Czech secondary schools supposedly because of overproduction of students; it also failed to consider Czech economic interests in the renegotiation of the compromise in 1886–1887. Bugge, "Czech Nation-Building," 163.

10. Bugge, "Czech Nation-Building," 164; Hantsch, *Geschichte Österreichs*, 443. The "right," consisting of clericals and large landholders, as well as Poles, Czechs, and other Slavic groups, grew to 190 deputies, whereas the German liberal "left" declined to 136. Macartney, *Habsburg Empire*, 614. The Young Czechs emerged with the Czech National Party in the 1860s as a more democratic alternative to the Old Czechs, and constituted themselves as a separate party in 1874.

11. Kwan, *Liberalism*, 166.

12. Formulation of Helmut Rumpler, cited in Piotr Majewski, *Sudetští Němci: dějiny jednoho nacionalismu* (Brno, 2014), 78; Hoensch, *Geschichte Böhmens*, 368. For a contemporary German perspective ["Damit drang die tschechische Sprache auch in rein deutsche Bezirke"], Theodor Lindner, *Weltgeschichte seit der Völkerwanderung*, vol. 10 (Stuttgart, 1921), 168.

13. A two-volume study was printed detailing the retreat of German wealth and population in Bohemia: Heinrich Rauchberg, *Der nationale Besitzstand in Böhmen* (Leipzig, 1905). See also Bugge, "Czech Nation-Building," 166; Křen, *Konfliktgemeinschaft*, 175 (on "fearful anxiety").

14. Catherine Albrecht, "Rural Banks and Czech Nationalism in Bohemia," *Agricultural History* 78:3 (2004), 317, 322. In the Most/Brüx area of northwest Bohemia, which had been overwhelmingly German, the increase of Germans in the late nineteenth century was 60 percent, but of Czechs 300 percent. Mark Cornwall, "The Struggle on the Czech-German Language Border," *English Historical Review* 109:433 (1994), 218. A decline of the German industrial working class took place in north Bohemian towns. Markus Krzoska, "Frieden durch Trennung?" in *Die Destruktion des Dialogs*, Dieter Bingen et al., eds., (Wiesbaden, 2007), 90–91.

15. Křen, *Konfliktgemeinschaft*, 177.

16. Helmut Rumpler, *Eine Chance für Mitteleuropa* (Vienna, 1997), 452–453.

17. Between 1873 and 1882, only 6 percent of the males over twenty-four could vote.

18. Carl Schorske, *Fin de Siècle Vienna: Politics and Culture* (New York, 1981), 126–127; Peter Pulzer, *The Rise of Political Anti-Semitism in Germany and Austria* (Cambridge, MA, 1964), 147.

19. Schorske, *Fin de Siècle Vienna*, 126. See also: Bugge, "Czech Nation-Building," 164, 213; Macartney, *Habsburg Empire*, 653; Georg von Schönerer, "Aufruf zur Gründung einer deutschnationalen Partei," (1881) in *Österreichische Parteiprogramme 1868–1966*, Klaus Berchtold, ed. (Vienna, 1967), 192; "Das Friedjung-Programm," in Berchtold, *Österreichische Parteiprogramme*, 191.

20. Andrew Whiteside, *The Socialism of Fools: Georg Ritter von Schönerer and Austrian Pan-Germanism* (Berkeley, 1967), 97.

21. On Austria's Christian Socialism, see John W. Boyer, *Political Radicalism in Late Imperial Vienna: The Origins of the Christian Social Movement* (Chicago, 1981).

22. He wanted to build on the support of Czechs, Poles, Slovene/Serbs/Croats/Ukrainians, the Catholic center, and the Catholic People's Party. Johann Albrecht von Reiswitz, "Kasimir Graf von Badeni," *Neue Deutsche Biographie*, vol. 1 (Berlin, 1953), 511. The Young Czechs held a majority from 1889, and in 1891 won all seats in the Czech districts, extruding the Old Czechs from the Czech Club in Vienna.

23. Douglas Dion, *Turning the Legislative Thumbscrew: Minority Rights and Procedural Change in Legislative Politics* (Ann Arbor, MI, 2001), 241–242; Michael John, "Vielfalt und Heterogenität," in *Migration und Innovation um 1900: Perspektiven auf das Wien der Jahrhundertwende*, Elisabeth Röhrich, ed. (Vienna, 2016), 45–46; "Rioters Killed in Prague," *New York Times*, December 3, 1897; Stefan Zweig, *The World of Yesterday* (Lincoln, NE, and London, 1964), 65.

24. Martial law had been in existence from 1893. Reiswitz, "Kasimir Graf von Badeni," 511; "Race Riots in Bohemia," *New York Times*, December 2, 1897.

25. In 1900, Jews constituted 1.82 percent of the population in Moravia, and 1.47 percent in Bohemia. Arthur Ruppin, *Die Juden in Österreich* (Berlin, 1900), 7.

26. Reiswitz, "Kasimir Graf von Badeni," 511; Hantsch, *Geschichte Österreichs*, 469.

27. In fact, there was a provision according to which officials in employ until 1901 were grandfathered in. John Boyer, "Badeni and the Revolution of 1897," in *Bananen, Cola, Zeitgeschichte: Oliver Rathkolb und das lange 20. Jahrhundert*, Lucille Dreidemy et al., eds. (Vienna, 2015), 74. Silesian Polish deputy Jan Michejda (1853–1927) argued: you cannot hate a nation whose literature you know. Remarks of February 5, 1898, in *Offizielle stenographische Berichte über die Verhandlungen des schlesischen Landtags*, thirty-fifth session (Troppau, 1898), 427.

28. *Neue Freie Presse*, October 31, 1897, cited in Hugh LeCaine Agnew, *Czechs and the Lands of the Bohemian Crown* (Stanford, CA, 2004), 149; *Stenografické zprávy sněmu království Českého*, January 22, 1898 (Prague, 1898), 1583. Other German delegates (Glöckner, Wolf, and Eppinger) likewise projected as inconceivable the notion that Czech might be considered equal to German. For Wolf's comment: John, "Vielfalt," 45–46.

29. Jiří Kořalka, *Tschechen im Habsburgerreich und in Europa 1815–1914* (Vienna, 1991), 112.

30. Meeting of Bohemian parliament, in *Stenografické zprávy sněmu království Českého*, January 22, 1898, 1580.

31. Speech of Koldinský, in *Stenografické zprávy sněmu království Českého*, January 22, 1898, 1582.

32. See the remarks of the Silesian Pole Jan Michejda to German deputies: "You have the power, the possessions, the schools; you have the offices and courts thanks to the exclusive use of German. You have all of politics in your hand and oppose any reform that might lessen your hold." Remarks of February 5, 1898, *Offizielle stenographische Berichte über die Verhandlungen des schlesischen Landtags*, thirty-fifth session (Troppau, 1898), 424. See also the thoughts of the Young Czech Edvard Grégr, *Naše politika: otevřený list panu dr. Fr. L. Riegrovi* (Prague, 1876), 1–6. For an important study of the battles in Bohemia for the national adherence of school children, see Tara Zahra, *Kidnapped Souls: National Indifference and the Battle for Children in the Bohemian Lands, 1900–1948* (Ithaca, NY, 2008).

33. Macartney, *Habsburg Empire*, 664–665: *Historia*, 249. Harold Frederic, "Germans or Czechs," *New York Times*, December 5, 1897; Maurice Baumfeld, "The Crisis in Austria-Hungary," *American Monthly Review of Reviews* 31 (January–June 1905), 446.

34. Nancy Wingfield, *Flag Wars and Stone Saints: How the Bohemian Lands Became Czech* (Cambridge, MA, 2007), 76.

35. Michael Wladika, *Hitlers Vätergeneration: Die Ursprünge des Nationalsozialismus in der k.u.k. Monarchie* (Vienna, 2005), 631.

36. Comments of Friedrich von Wieser in Robert A. Kann, *Multinational Empire*, vol. 1 (New York, 1950), 51–52; Peter Pulzer, *The Rise of Political Anti-Semitism in Germany and Austria* (Cambridge, MA, 1988), 142–155 and passim.

37. Zweig, *World of Yesterday*, 64.

38. Schorske, *Fin-de-siècle Vienna*, 117.

39. Kořalka, *Tschechen*, 114.

40. For a lucid discussion of Marsaryk's policy of small steps (*drobné práce*) in the context of Central European phenomenology, see Michael Gubser, *The Far Reaches: Phenomenology, Ethics and Social Renewal in Central Europe* (Stanford, CA, 2014), 143.

41. By 1884 they had "by natural growth" achieved majorities in the chambers in Plzeň and České Budějovice, but they were still working on Prague. Josef Jakub Toužimský, "Rozhledy v dějinách současných," *Osvěta* 14:1 (1884) 474–475; Catherine Albrecht, "Nationalism and Municipal Savings Banks in Bohemia," *Slovene Studies* 11:1/2 (1989), 57–64; Bugge, "Czech Nation-Building," 39.

42. On the tendency of commercial and economic interest group associations to become ethnic in Bohemia, see Peter Heumos, "Interessensolidarität gegen Nationalgemeinschaft: deutsche und tschechische Bauern in Böhmen, 1848–1918," in *Die Chance der Verständigung: Absichten und Ansätze zu übernationaler Zusammenarbeit in den böhmischen Ländern, 1848–1918*, Ferdinand Seibt, ed. (Munich, 1987), 87–99. Thus the opposite of Peter Bugge's statement is also true: "from the moment modern constitutional politics was introduced in Austria in 1848, any formulation of Czech national aspirations had to obtain political dimensions." That is, any attempt to organize political interests had to have national dimensions. Bugge, "Czech Nation-Building," 10.

43. Ivan T. Berend, *History Derailed: Central and Eastern Europe in the Long Nineteenth Century* (Berkeley, 2003), 184.

44. Big estates constituted 40 percent of the land in Bohemia and 35 percent in Poland. Berend, *History Derailed*, 184

45. That is the number with their families. László Kontler, "The Enlightenment in Central Europe," in *Discourses of Collective Identity*, Balázs Trencsényi and Michal Kopeček, eds., vol. 1 (Budapest, 2006), 39; Janos M. Bak, "Nobilities in Central and Eastern Europe," *History and Society in Central Europe*, 2 (1994), 164; Oszkár Jászi, *Dissolution of the Habsburg Monarchy* (Chicago, 1961), 299.

46. Janos Tisza "was in charge of the period's most controversial institution, the electoral system, tied to extremely high property qualifications for voters. Elections were characterized by corruption and, on occasion by the government's hardly disguised intervention." Tibor Frank, "Hungary and the Dual Monarchy," in *History of Hungary*, Sugar et al., eds., 263; Laszlo Katus, "Die Magyaren," in *Die Habsburgermonarchie*, Adam Wandruszka and Peter Urbanitsch, eds., vol. 3 (Vienna, 1980), 470–472.

47. Janos, *Politics of Backwardness*, 130.

48. These great families formed the "nucleus of an agrarian pressure group whose aim was to subvert the forces of the market and restore the institutional supports of traditional land ownership." Members of the agrarian middle class, the gentry and lower nobility, left their farms and sought refuge in the bureaucracy. Janos, *Politics of Backwardness*, 121, 130–132.

49. The electorate was 56.2 percent Hungarian and 11.2 percent Romanian, whereas the figures for the population as a whole were 54.5 and 16.1 percent, respectively. András Gerö, *Modern Hungarian Society in the Making* (Budapest, 1995), 172–174, 177–179.

50. Between 1899 and 1913, the horsepower capacity of industry increased more than threefold. Janos, *Politics of Backwardness*, 132–136, 149–155.

51. Magyarized Jews were "often more loyalist than Apponyi, more chauvinistic than Ugron; they composed Magyar songs, wrote romantic poems, and when they founded new factories they did so 'for the benefit of the fatherland.'" Janos, *Politics*, 117, 131.

52. Janos, *Politics of Backwardness*, 115; Katus, "Die Magyaren," 465; Paul Lendvai, *The Hungarians: A Thousand Years of Victory in Defeat*, Ann Major, trans. (Princeton, NJ, 2003), 339.

53. Janos, *Politics of Backwardness*, 126.

54. Henry L. Roberts, *Rumania: Political Problems of an Agrarian State* (New Haven, CT, 1951), 6; Diana Mishkova, "The Uses of Tradition and National Identity in the Balkans," in *Balkan Identities: Nation and Memory*, Maria Todorova, ed. (New York, 2004), 272.

55. Gale Stokes, "The Social Origins of East European Politics," *East European Politics and Societies* 1:1 (1986), 56.

56. Whereas only 13.7 percent of the ethnic Romanian workforce was employed in industry, trade, and credit, 79.1 percent of the Romanian Jewish workforce was employed in those areas. Stokes, "Social Origins," 57.

57. Stokes, "Social Origins," 55; Daniel Chirot and Charles Ragin, "The Market, Tradition and Peasant Rebellion: The Case of Romania in 1907," *American Sociological Review* 40 (1975), 431.

58. Berend, *History Derailed*, 186–187. "By a law of 1884 he structured his voting system to emphasize the strength of the urban professionals that his policy of modernization and state formation was creating, rather than the mass of subjugated peasants that his developmental plan ignored." Stokes, "Social Origins," 56.

59. Chirot and Ragin, "The Market," 434; Juliusz Demel, *Historia Rumunii* (Wrocław, 1970), 355.

60. The phrase is David Mitrany's. Roberts, *Rumania*, 21; Demel, *Historia*, 356; Keith Hitchins, *Rumania: 1866–1945* (Oxford, 1994), 170, 172, 176, 180.

61. Where there was great violence, in Wallachia, the percentage of non-Romanian ethnics in charge of land was much lower than in Moldavia. Chirot and Ragin, "The Market," 433; Raul Carstocea, "Anti-Semitism in Romania," European Centre for Minority Issues, ECMI Working Paper 81 (October 2014), 7; Demel, *Historia*, 355–356.

62. Stephan Fischer-Galati, *Twentieth Century Rumania* (New York, 1991), 22.

63. Mishkova, "Uses of Tradition and National Identity," 270–272; Ivan Bičík, "Land Use Changes in Czechia," in *Land Use Changes in the Czech Republic*, Ivan Bičík et al., eds. (Cham, Switzerland, 2015), 110.

64. Stokes, "Social Origins," 61.

65. Stokes, "Social Origins," 63; Sundhaussen, *Geschichte*, 200.

66. Before war broke out in 1914, the state had constructed only three agricultural schools training 222 students. Stokes, "Social Origins," 64.

67. Stokes, "Social Origins," 64, 66.

68. Stokes, "Social Origins," 62–63.

69. Barbara Černič, "The Role of Dr. Janez Evangelist Krek in the Slovene Cooperative Movement," *Slovene Studies* 11:1/2 (1989), 75–81. On the agrarian politics of Radić, see Mark Biondich, *Stjepan Radić, the Croat Peasant Party, and the Politics of Mass Mobilization* (Toronto, 2000), 246.

70. Janko Pleterski, "Die Slowenen," in *Habsburgermonarchie*, Wandruszka and Urbanitsch, eds., vol. 3, 831.

71. Seventeen were German and twelve Hungarian. But elsewhere, the relations differed: in the military frontier area, for example, there was much more independent as well as communal farmer ownership. Arnold Suppan, "Die Kroaten," in *Habsburgermonarchie*, Wandruszka and Urbanitsch, eds., vol. 3, 668–671. Going down the scale to smaller holdings, the percentage of Magyars owning landed properties in Hungary decreased. Katus, "Die Magyaren," 480.

Chapter 10: Liberalism's Heirs and Enemies: Socialism versus Nationalism

1. William O. McCagg, Jr., *A History of the Habsburg Jews 1670–1918* (Bloomington, IN, 1989), 198–199.

2. R. J. Crampton, *A Concise History of Bulgaria* (Cambridge, 1997), 124–127; Diana Mishkova, "The Interesting Anomaly of Balkan Liberalism," in *Liberty and the Search for Identity*, Iván Zoltán Dénes, ed. (Budapest, 2006), 401.

3. Carl E. Schorske, *Fin-de-Siècle Vienna: Politics and Culture* (New York, 1980), 116–120, 144.

4. R. R. Palmer and Joel Colton, *A History of the Modern World*, sixth edition (New York, 1984), 606–607.

5. Jonathan Kwan, *Liberalism and the Habsburg Monarchy* (Basingstoke, UK, 2013), 206.

6. Socialism also took in nonsocialist ideas for reform if they served the cause of progress. See the comments of Kazimierz Kelles-Kraus in Micińska, *Inteligencja na rozdrożach 1864–1918* (Warsaw, 2008), 121. On the ideal of "general, equal, secret and direct" elections, see Wereszycki, *Pod berłem Habsburgów*, 260.

7. Schorske, *Fin-de-siècle Vienna*, 119.

8. Jakub Beneš, "Social Democracy, František Soukup, and the Habsburg Austrian Suffrage Campaign 1897–1907," *Centre. Journal for Interdisciplinary Studies of Central Europe in the 19th and 20th Centuries* 2 (2012), 14.

9. Karl Marx and Frederick Engels, *The German Ideology*, C. J. Arthur., ed. (London, 2004), 58. Some socialists, like Jean Jaurès, regretted the line from the *Communist Manifesto* according to which "workers have no fatherland," thinking it might have been meant sarcastically, but neither Marx nor Engels attempted a correction, though Engels wrote introductions to many reprints. Marek Waldenberg, *Kwestie narodowe w Europie Środkowo-Wschodniej: dzieje, idee* (Warsaw, 1992), 186–187.

10. Friedrich Engels, "Der magyarische Kampf," *Neue Rheinische Zeitung*, January 13, 1849, in Karl Marx and Friedrich Engels, *Werke*, vol. 6 (Berlin, 1959), 165–176; Kořalka, *Tschechen*, 221–223; Hans Magnus Enzensberger, ed., *Gespräche mit Marx und Engels* (Frankfurt, 1973), 709ff.

11. Engels, "magyarische Kampf," 175; Friedrich Engels, "What Have the Working Classes to Do with Poland," in Karl Marx, *Political Writings*, vol. 3 (Harmondsworth, UK, 1974), 383. On Poland: Hubert Orlowski, *"Polnische Wirtschaft": Zum deutschen Polendiskurs der Neuzeit* (Wiesbaden, 1996), 276.

12. From February 1869. Kořalka, *Tschechen*, 224.

13. The Polish socialist Józef Piłsudski attempted to have a resolution about Polish independence placed on the agenda. Waldenberg, *Kwestie narodowe*, 166; Eduard Bernstein, *Die heutige Sozialdemokratie in Theorie und Praxis* (Munich, 1905), 42.

14. František Modráček, "K národnostní otázce," *Revue socialistická Akademie* 3 (1899), 337–344.

15. Kořalka, *Tschechen*, 224; Józef Chlebowczyk, *O prawie do bytu małych i młodych narodów* (Katowice, Poland, 1983), 377, n. 14; Pech, *Czech Revolution*, 300.

16. Emphasis added. Kořalka, *Tschechen*, 244–245.

17. Waldenberg, *Kwestie narodowe*, 168. In the 1907 elections, the Czech party got 389,497 votes, the Polish 77,131, the Italian 21,370, the Ruthenian, 29,957, and the Slovene 5,310. Kořalka, *Tschechen*, 235.

18. Waldenberg, *Kwestie narodowe*, 168–169. The founders of the Austrian Social-Democratic party claimed to represent all workers on Austrian territory, and they pledged to struggle for the economic and political rights of the "people without regard for nation, race or sex." From the Hainfeld Programm, January 1889. Berchtold, *Österreichische Parteiprogramme*; Wingfield, *Flag Wars and Stone Saints*, 66; Hantsch, *Geschichte Österreichs*, 471–472.

19. Okey, *Habsburg Monarchy*, 309. This was an idea with numerous authors, from the Hungarian liberal József Eötvös to the Slovene Social Democrat Etbin Kristanm, but it is most strongly associated with the Austrian German Karl Renner. Waldenberg, *Kwestie narodowe*, 170.

20. Antonín Němec, "Die tschecho-slawische sozialdemokratische Arbeiterpartei in Österreich," in *Die sozialistische Arbeiter-Internationale: Berichte der sozialdemokratischen Organisationen Europas, Australiens, und Amerikas an dem internationalen Sozialistenkongress zu Stuttgart* (Berlin, 1907), 165.

21. Okey, *Habsburg Monarchy*, 309; Otto Bauer, *Nationalitätenfrage und die Sozialdemokratie* (Vienna, 1907), 452; Jakub S. Beneš, *Workers and Nationalism: Czech and German Social Democracy in Habsburg Austria, 1890–1918* (Oxford, 2016), 202–204.

22. That was the official number based on "language of common use," though Czech advocates put the number above 250,000 based on place of origin. Maureen Healy, *Vienna and the Fall of the Habsburg Empire* (Cambridge, 2004), 151–152; Hans Mommsen, "Otto Bauer, Karl Renner, und die sozialdemokratische Nationalitätenpolitik in Österreich von 1905 bis 1914," in *Studies in East European Social History*, Keith Hitchins, ed., vol. 1 (Leiden, 1977), 22.

23. Hans Mommsen, *Arbeiterbewegung und nationale Frage* (Göttingen, 1979), 72, 76-78.

24. Czechs were 63 percent but brought in about 45 percent of tax receipts. Hoensch, *Geschichte Böhmens*, 395–396; Waldenberg, *Kwestie narodowe*, 172.

25. Kořalka, *Tschechen*, 235; Waldenberg, *Kwestie narodowe*, 173; Hans Mommsen, *Arbeiterbewegung und nationale Frage*, 209; Mommsen, "Otto Bauer, Karl Renner," 21. In the Czech party, the Catholic Anton Dermota opposed anticlericalism and urged a proactive stance on the national question. Trencsényi et al., *History of Modern Political Thought*, 453.

26. But in a sense the Marxist schemes were also native to the region, as German publishing houses worked in such diverse places as Lodz, Zagreb, Budapest, and Sarajevo. František Modráček, "Odpověď Prof. Masarykovi," *Akademie revue socialistická* 3 (1899), 390.

27. Wereszycki, *Pod berłem Habsburgów*, 258.

28. Otto Urban, *Česká společnost 1848–1918* (Prague, 1982), 540–541; Beneš, *Workers and Nationalism*, 226.

29. Kann, "Zur Problematik der Nationalitätenfrage," in Wandruszka and Urbanitsch, eds., *Habsburgermonarchie*, vol. 3, 1324, 1330.

30. Wereszycki, *Pod berłem Habsburgów*, 272–273; Kořalka, *Tschechen*, 171.

31. Brian Porter-Szücs, *When Nationalism Began to Hate* (Oxford, 2000), 79; Leonard Szymański, *Zarys polityki caratu wobec szkolnictwa ogólnokształcącego w Królestwie Polskim w latach 1815–1915* (Wrocław, 1983), 47; Piotr Paszkiewicz, *Pod berłem Romanowów: sztuka rosyjska w Warszawie 1815–1915* (Warsaw, 1991).

32. Tadeusz Łepkowski, "Naród bez państwa," 414–416; Danuta Waniek, *Kobiety lewicy w polskim doświadczeniu politycznym* (Poznań, 2010), 34.

33. Szymański, *Zarys polityki*, 60–61; Jerzy Jedlicki, *A Suburb of Europe: Nineteenth-Century Approaches to Westwern Civilization* (Budapest, 1999), 236–237.

34. On the cities, see Łepkowski, "Naród bez państwa," 410. On the libraries and self-help associations, see William W. Hagen, *Germans, Poles, and Jews: The Nationality Conflict in the Prussian East, 1772–1914* (Chicago, 1980), 142; Patrice M. Dabrowski, *Commemorations and the Shaping of Modern Poland* (Bloomington, IN, 2004), 160. The Polish language could be used in lower grades until the time that children could supposedly learn entirely in German. Wandycz, *Lands of Partitioned Poland*, 234–235;

35. The journal was *Głos* (*The Voice*), on which the nationalist Zygmunt Balicki later worked, and later socialist Bolesław Limanowski. As in Austria, the later fierce opponents on the left and right initially shared many demands, like suffrage and nationality rights, and continued to cooperate even after the split began to emerge. Porter-Szücs, *When Nationalism Began to Hate*, 135–143. To be clear, *Endecja*, refers to National Democracy as a movement; *Endeks* to individual National Democratic party members.

36. Yet still the movement grew along with the population, from 5 million in 1863 to 9.4 million in 1897. The leader of the first movement ("Proletariat"), Ludwik Waryński, was arrested in 1883 and died in 1889. Four early leaders were hanged in January 1886. R. F. Leslie, ed., *The History of Poland since 1863* (Cambridge, 1983), 45, 52–53.

37. Łepkowski, "Naród bez państwa," 400; Leslie, *History of Poland*, 57; Adam Ciołkosz, *Róża Luksemburg a rewolucja rosyjska* (Paris, 1961), 103.

38. Joshua D. Zimmerman, *Poles, Jews, and the Politics of Nationality* (Madison, WI, 2004), 206. The Bund was created in 1897 in Wilno as the General Jewish Workers Union in Lithuania, Poland, and Russia and had 30,000 members. There were other Zionist socialist organizations as well. Waldenberg, *Kwestie narodowe*, 177.

39. This was the Bezdany raid. Davies, *God's Playground*, vol. 2, 54–55; Wandycz, *Lands of Partitioned Poland*, 326–327; Józef Krzyk, "Socjalista i terrorysta; lata Piłsudskiego w PPS," *Gazeta Wyborcza*, May 11, 2015. He wrote before the Bezdany raid: "I am unable to live in an outhouse . . . it humiliates me, as it would any man who has dignity that is not [a] slave's." Adam Michnik, *Letters from Prison* (Berkeley, 1985), 209–211. Piłsudski converted to Protestantism in 1899 in order to wed a woman who had been divorced, but he returned to Catholicism in 1916.

40. M. B. B. Biskupski, *Independence Day: Myth, Symbol, and the Creation of Modern Poland* (Oxford, 2012), 6–7. He formed his legions in August 1914 from the Polish Rifleman's

Association. See Andrew Michta, *Red Eagle: The Army in Polish Politics, 1944–1988* (Stanford, CA, 1990), 26.

41. Leslie, *History of Poland*, 59.

42. M. K. Dziewanowski, "The Making of a Federalist," *Jahrbücher für die Geschichte Osteuropas* 11:4 (1963), 551; Michal Śliwa, *Obcy czy swoi* (Kraków, 1997), 70.

43. The National Democratic party was founded in 1897 and had grown out of the National League founded, under Roman Dmowski's leadership, in 1893. Leslie, *History of Poland*, 54–56.

44. Brian Porter-Szücs, *When Nationalism Began to Hate* (Oxford, 2000), 155.

45. Piotr Wandycz, *The Price of Freedom: A History of East Central Europe from the Middle Ages to the Present* (London, 2001), 173; Bogumił Grott, *Dylematy polskiego nacjonalizmu: Powrot do tradycji czy przebudowa narodowego ducha* (Warsaw, 2014), 87.

46. Leslie, *History of Poland*, 71.

47. This is Peter Fritzsche's summary of the predicament as seen on the German right. Peter Fritzsche and Jochen Hellbeck, "The New Man in Stalinist Russia and Nazi Germany," in *Beyond Totalitarianism: Stalinism and Nazism Compared*, Michael Geyer and Sheila Fitzpatrick, eds. (Cambridge, 2008), 314.

48. For the shift in German nationalist writing, see Christhard Hoffmann, *Juden und Judentum im Werk deutscher Althistoriker des 19. und 20. Jahrhunderts* (Leiden, 1988), 68.

49. Wandycz, *Price of Freedom*, 173.

50. On the origin of the family: *Neue Deutsche Biographie*, vol. 3 (Berlin, 1957), 152. On his conversion: Joseph Marcus, *Social and Political History of the Jews in Poland 1919–1939* (Berlin, 1983), 211; Kathrin Krogner-Kornalik, *Tod in der Stadt: Religion, Alltag und Festkultur in Krakau 1869–1914* (Göttingen, 2015), 122.

51. Andrzej Żbikowski, *Żydzi* (Wrocław, 1997), 92–93; Danuta Zamojska-Hutchins, "Form and Substance in Norwid's Poetry," *Polish Review* 28:4 (1983), 39. For copious examples of anti-Jewish statements in the Polish press before that time, see Alix Landgrebe, *"Wenn es Polen nicht gäbe, dann müsste es erfunden werden"* (Wiesbaden, 2003), 255–268.

52. Leopold Caro, *Nowe drogi z przedmowa X. Arcybiskupa Teodorowicza* (Poznan, 1908), 1–2; Leopold Caro, "Idea gospodarcza Polski," *Przegląd Powszecny* 180 (1928), 163; Leopold Caro, *Die Judenfrage: eine ethische Frage* (Leipzig, 1892), 10–14.

53. Andrzej Brożek, "Die Nationalbewegung in den Teilungsgebieten," in *Die Entstehung der Nationalbewegung in Europa 1750–1849*, Heiner Timmermann, ed. (Berlin, 1993), 85, 87–88; František Graus, *Die Nationbildung der Slawen im Mittelalter* (Sigmaringen, West Germany, 1980), 64; Tadeusz Łepkowski, *Polska—narodziny nowoczesnego narodu, 1764–1870* (Warsaw, 1967), 508–509.

54. "Podiven" (Peter Pithart, Milan Otáhal, Peter Příhoda), *Češi v dějinách nové doby—pokus o zrcadlo* (Prague, 1991).

55. Keely Stauter-Halsted, "Jews as Middleman Minorities in Rural Poland: Understanding the Galician Pogroms of 1898," in *Anti-Semitism and Its Responses*, Robert Blobaum, ed. (Ithaca, NY, 2005), 39–59; Keely Stauter-Halsted, *The Nation in the Village* (Ithaca, NY, 2001), 134; Włodzimierz Borodziej, *Geschichte Polens im 20. Jahrhundert* (Munich, 2010), 16.

56. Stauter-Halsted, *Nation in the Village*, 1, 4, 245.

57. Śliwa, *Obcy czy swoi*, 33.

58. See the complaint of the co-founder of the Croatian Peasant Party, Ante Radić, in a piece from 1903, cited in Božidar Murgić, ed., *Život, rad i misli Dra Ante Radića* (Zagreb, 1937), 83.

59. Fischer-Galati, "Romanian Nationalism," 386.

60. From 1905, cited in Grott, *Dylematy*, 54. On Ledóchowski, see Wandycz, *Lands of Partitioned Poland*, 234.

61. Leslie, *History of Poland*, 72.

62. Grott, *Dylematy*, 57–58; David Nirenberg, *Anti-Judaism: The Western Tradition* (New York, 2013).

63. They made up a significant share of reserve officers (about 18 percent of the total) in the Austro-Hungarian army, though few were in the German army. Erwin A. Schmidl, *Habsburgs jüdische Soldaten* (Vienna, 2014).

64. Even after that rejection, he remained decidedly "German," and hoped that Zionism would cause Jews to love Germany even more. Jacqueline Rose, *The Question of Zion* (Princeton, NJ, 2005), 110.

65. Karlheinz Rossbacher, *Literatur und Bürgertum: fünf Wiener jüdische Familien von der liberalen Ära* (Vienna, 2003), 297–300.

66. John Efron, "The Politics of Being Jewish," in *The Jews: A History*, John Efron, Steven Weitzman, and Matthias Lehmann (London, 2008), 319–322.

67. Max Brod, *Streitbares Leben: Autobiographie* (Munich, 1960), 42–45.

68. On the Czech movement, see Michael W. Dean, "'What the Heart Unites, the Sea Shall Not Divide,' Claiming Overseas Czechs for the Nation" (PhD dissertation, University of California, Berkeley, 2014). The deal that the Ottoman side refused was for Herzl to organize relief for Ottoman debt through a Jewish syndicate, in return for permission for Jews to settle in Ottoman territories. The Ottoman state was willing to grant Jews permission to settle anywhere on their territories except Palestine. Isaiah Friedman, *Germany, Turkey, and Zionism 1897–1918* (New Brunswick, NJ, 1998), 100–102; Efron, "Politics of Being Jewish," 324.

69. Francis L. Carsten says that Stöcker, who founded a Christian Socialist party in Berlin in 1878, "discovered anti-Semitism" as a weapon only after failing miserably against Social Democrats. Francis L. Carsten, *The Rise of Fascism* (London, 1967), 23. According to Peter Pulzer, Lueger gave no evidence of sincere conversion to anti-Semitism, and supposedly had waited to see whether the Democratic or anti-Semitic movement grew stronger. Peter Pulzer, *The Rise of Political Anti-Semitism in Germany and Austria* (New York, 1964), 160–161.

70. Pulzer, *Rise of Political Anti-Semitism*, 162.

71. Kořalka, *Tschechen*, 199.

72. Bugge, "Czech Nation-Building," 270.

Chapter 11: Peasant Utopias: Villages of Yesterday and Societies of Tomorrow

1. Johan Eelend, "Agrarianism and Modernization in Interwar Eastern Europe," in *Societal Change and Ideological Formation among the Rural Population of the Baltic Area 1880–1939*, Piotr Wawrzeniuk, ed., *Studia Baltica* 2 (2008), 35–56. The general argument that follows owes much to Hugh Seton-Watson, *East Central Europe Between the World Wars* (Cambridge, 1945).

2. For a lucid discussion of the rise of charismatic personalities in politics, see Derek J. Penslar, "Theodor Herzl: Charisma and Leadership," in *The Individual in History*, ChaeRan Yoo Freeze et al., eds. (Waltham, MA, 2015), 13–27.

3. Bruce Berglund, *Castle and Cathedral in Modern Prague: Longing for the Sacred in a Skeptical Age* (Budapest, 2017), 50–51; T. G. Masaryk, *Der Selbstmord als sociale Massenerscheinung der modernen Civilisation* (Vienna, 1881).

4. For citations and analysis of Hitler: Thomas Schirrmacher, *Hitlers Kriegsreligion*, vol. 1 (Bonn, 2007), 239–240.

5. Milan Hauner, "The Meaning of Czech History: Masaryk vs. Pekař," in *T. G. Masaryk (1850–1937)*, Harry Hanak, ed., vol. 3: *Statesman and Cultural Force* (Basingstoke, UK, 1989), 24–42.

6. Masaryk, *Selbstmord*, 156.

7. He and Charlotte translated Hume into German. Roman Szporluk, *The Political Thought of T. G. Masaryk* (New York, 1981), 32–33.

8. H. Gordon Skilling, *T. G. Masaryk: Against the Current* (University Park, PA, 1994), 82.

9. Skilling, *T. G. Masaryk*, 84.

10. Skilling, *T. G. Masaryk*, 86-88, 93.

11. Skilling, *T. G. Masaryk*, 90, 92. He did believe Jews would still remain a separate group in Czech society even when they became Czech culturally.

12. Industrialization was advancing, but so was a stratum of medium-sized farmers. Masaryk stood with the revisionist Marxists Vollmar and David, and against the authoritative Kautsky. See T. G. Masaryk, *Die philosophischen und sociologischen Grundlagen des Marxismus* (Vienna, 1899), 304–305.

13. This finding, based on the work of Peter Heumos, is developed in my book: J. Connelly, *Captive University* (Chapel Hill, NC, 2000), 271.

14. Karel Čapek, *Talks with T. G. Masaryk*, Dora Round, trans. (North Haven, CT, 1995), 175.

15. Bruce Garver, "Masaryk and Czech Politics," in *T. G. Masaryk*, Stanley B. Winters, ed., vol. 1 (London, 1990), 225–239; Szporluk, *Political Thought*, 111–119.

16. In July, Austria-Hungary closed its borders to all meat products, whether for import or sending elsewhere, and imposed the highest tariffs on Serb products. Sundhaussen, *Geschichte Serbiens*, 210; Macartney, *Habsburg Empire*, 773.

17. T. G. Masaryk, *Der Agramer Hochverratsprozess und die Annexion von Bosnien und Herzegowina* (Vienna, 1909), vii–ix.

18. In the sense of its historic nobility.

19. Ante Starčević, *Politički spisi* (Zagreb, 1971), 30.

20. Mark Biondich, *Stjepan Radić, the Croat Peasant Party, and the Politics of Mass Mobilization, 1904–1928* (Toronto, 2000), 48.

21. Biondich, *Stjepan Radić*, 45, 33–34. "The peasants could no longer be neglected while the old patriots sang odes to the homeland."

22. Written in the late 1890s. Biondich, *Stjepan Radić*, 44, 50.

23. Biondich, *Stjepan Radić*, 58.

24. Biondich, *Stjepan Radić*, 45–46, 48.

25. Biondich, *Stjepan Radić*, 59.

26. Biondich, *Stjepan Radić*, 59.

27. John D. Bell, *Peasants in Power: Aleksander Stamboliski and the Bulgarian Agrarian Union 1899–1924* (Princeton, NJ, 1977), 69.

28. The term is Barrington Moore's, cited in Bell, *Peasants*, 52. A charter myth "provides an explanation of what is wrong with the current state of affairs and what should be done to fix it."

29. Bell, *Peasants*, 59.

30. In one village, the mayor performed "civil functions only for heads of families who would send their sons to schools, for the teachers were his enemies." Bell, *Peasants*, 9.

31. Bell, *Peasants*, 60, 65.

32. Bell, *Peasants*, 83. They also objected to his wearing the crown while the deputies sat bare headed.

33. Bell, *Peasants*, 57.

34. Bell, *Peasants*, 94, 98.

35. Steven Constant, *Foxy Ferdinand, Tsar of Bulgaria* (London, 1979), 292.

36. David G. Winter, *Roots of War: Wanting Power, Seeing Threat, Justifying Force* (Oxford, 2018), 109–110.

37. Okey, *Habsburg Monarchy*, 376.

38. Gołuchowski said of Serbia in 1901: "Politically in complete disorder, financially on the verge of bankruptcy, militarily quite insignificant and weak, this country lies so much within our power that it will always be dependent on us." Okey, *Habsburg Monarchy*, 362. Heinrich Kanner wrote of a campaign of hatred against a Serb "Zwergstaat" (gnome state) that left Austria itself a "Krüppelstaat" (crippled state). Heinrich Kanner, *Kaiserliche Katastrophenpolitik: Ein Stück zeitgenössischer Geschichte* (Leipzig, 1922), 58. See also Hans Hautmann, "K.u.k. Mordbrenner," *Junge Welt* (Berlin), July 28, 2014.

39. Igor Despot, "Croatian Public Opinion toward Bulgaria during the Balkan Wars," *Études Balkaniques* 46:4 (2010), 147–148.

40. Joachim Remak, *Sarajevo: The Story of a Political Murder* (New York, 1959), 65.

41. Gale Stokes called this "politics without development." John Lampe, *Yugoslavia as History: Twice There Was a Country* (Cambridge, 1996), 55.

42. Hoensch, *Geschichte Böhmens*, 400.

43. Pavlina Bobič, *War and Faith: The Catholic Church in Slovenia, 1914–1918* (Leiden, 2012), 12–14.

44. Charles Arthur Ginever, *The Hungarian Question: From a Historical, Economical and Ethnographical Point of View*, Ilona De Györy Ginever, trans. (London, 1908), 45.

45. Solomon Wank, "The Nationalities Question in Habsburg Empire," Working paper 93-3, Center for Austrian Studies, University of Minnesota, April 1993, 3. On the obstruction of Croats after 1907 due to language laws, see Robert A. Kann, *A History of the Habsburg Empire, 1526–1918* (Berkeley, 1974), 448.

46. Macartney, *Habsburg Empire*, 792, 799. Jan Křen, *Integration oder Ausgrenzung: Deutsche und Tschechen* (Bremen, 1986), 17.

47. He was not yet twenty years old. Those over twenty years old were hanged. Cathie Carmichael, *Concise History of Bosnia* (Cambridge, 2015), 55–56.

48. William Carr, *History of Germany, 1815–1945* (New York, 1979), 219. As Robin Okey writes, "the perception of Pan Slavism as a restlessly aggressive foe besieging a too passive monarchy helped propel the latter to war." Okey, *Habsburg Monarchy*, 378–379.

49. Victor Mamatey, "The Establishment of the Republic," in *A History of the Czechoslovak Republic 1918–1948*, Victor Mamatey and Radomir Luža, eds. (Princeton, NJ, 1973), 10–11.

50. The vengeance was all the more furious given the Habsburg forces' inability to take the tiny Serb territory and reminds one of imperial misadventures elsewhere in the world. Hans Hautmann, "k.u.k. Mordbrenner"; *Krvavi trag Velikog rata. Zlocini Austrougarske i njenih savenznika 1914–1918*, Hans Hautmann and Milos Kazimirovic, eds. (Novi Sad, Serbia, 2015).

51. While they professed loyalty to the House of Habsburg, they also spoke of "self-rule." On the national liberal political elite of the late century, see Otto Urban, "Czech Liberalism," in *Liberty and the Search for Identity*, Ivan Zoltan Denes, ed. (Budapest, 2006), 304.

52. McCagg, *History of Habsburg Jews*, 163.

Chapter 12: 1919: A New Europe and Its Old Problems

1. In the Constituent Assembly, elected in November 1917, there were 370 Socialist Revolutionaries, 40 Left Socialist Revolutionaries, 170 Bolsheviks, 34 Mensheviks, and not quite 100 deputies of other parties. Nicholas V. Riasanovsky, *A History of Russia* (New York, 1993), 476–477; Scott B. Smith, *Captives of Revolution: The Socialist Revolutionaries and the Bolshevik Dictatorship* (Pittsburgh, PA, 2011).

2. For an approach to the postwar mobilization suggesting four strands of revolution—pacifist, socialist (meaning Communist), nationalist, and peasant—all of which came together most successfully in Russia, see Tibor Hajdu, "Socialist Revolution in Central Europe," in *Revolution in History*, Roy Porter and Mikuláš Teich, eds., (Cambridge, 1986), 101–118.

3. If socialists failed to stand up for the rights of oppressed nationalities, then these nationalities, including their working classes, would succumb to the trickery of bourgeois calls for patriotism, and oppose socialist revolution. V. I. Lenin, "The Socialist Revolution and the Right of Nations to Self-Determination," February 1916, in *Collected Works*, vol. 5 (New York, 1935), 272.

4. Statement of December 29, 1917, in Derek Heater, *National Self-Determination: Woodrow Wilson and His Legacy* (New York, 1994), 36–37.

5. "A League for Peace." Address to the US Senate of January 22, 1917, in 64 Congress, 2 Session, Senate Document no. 685 (Washington, DC, 1918).

6. On May 18, 1918, Wilson took up the cause of "oppressed and helpless peoples all over the world" who longed for liberty. Ray Stannard Baker, ed., *Woodrow Wilson and World*, vol. 1 (New York, 1923), 16. For his work on the Habsburg state, see Woodrow Wilson, *The State: Elements of Historical and Practical Politics* (Boston, 1889), 334–365.

7. August Schwan, "Permanent Peace," *The Survey*, March 6, 1915, 623; *Supplement to the Messages and Papers of the Presidents Covering the Second Term of Woodrow Wilson* (New York, 1921), 8667.

8. "Reply of President Wilson to the Austrian Proposal," October 18, 1918, in *Official Statements of War Aims and Peace Proposals*, James Brown Scott, ed. (Washington, DC, 1921), 427–428.

9. Ivo Banac, *The National Question in Yugoslavia: Origins, History, Politics* (Ithaca, NY, 1984), 98. Supilo died of a stroke in a sanatorium in London, having left the committee in 1916 over quarrels about Serb centralism. Ahmet Ersoy et al., eds., *Modernism: The Creation of Nation-States*, vol. 1 (Budapest, 2007), 250.

10. Alan Sharp, *The Versailles Settlement* (New York, 1991), 130–131.

11. Z. A. B. Zeman, *The Break-Up of the Habsburg Empire* (New York, 1961), 113; Macartney, *Habsburg Empire*, 829.

12. István Deák, *Beyond Nationalism: A Social and Political History of the Habsburg Officer Corps* (Oxford, 1990), 201. The casualty figures were also above average for Germans and Hungarians, as the army command also used them more often in dangerous sectors.

13. Włodzimierz Borodziej, *Geschichte Polens im 20. Jahrhundert* (Munich, 2010), 87.

14. Zeman, *Break-Up of the Habsburg Empire*, 169. On the flood of denunciations based on deeply rooted anti-Slavic stereotypes, see Martin Moll, "Mentale Kriegsvorbereitung," in *Die Habsburgermonarchie und der erste Weltkrieg*, Helmut Rumpler, ed., vol. 11, part 1 (Vienna, 2016), 196; Jürgen Angelow, "Der Erste Weltkrieg auf dem Balkan," in *Durchhalten: Krieg und Gesellschaft im Vergleich*, Arnd Bauerkämper et al., eds. (Göttingen, 2010), 183. A group of Czechs taken for basic training to Hungary saw their sergeant condemned to death for insubordination. They had been singing "The Sixth of July," a song commemorating the martyrdom of Jan Hus. "Story of a Czechoslovak Private," *Czechoslovak Review*, December 1918, 206.

15. Zeman, *Break-Up of the Habsburg Empire*, 126, 128. The demand for the natural rights of nations had been a program point of Masaryk's Progressive Party.

16. Otto Bauer, *Die österreichische Revolution* (Vienna, 1923), 110; Zeman, *Break-Up of the Habsburg Empire*, 145.

17. According to Emil Strauss, this was the first time revolutionary tones were struck in that area. Emil Strauss, *Die Entstehung der tschechoslowakischen Republik* (Prague, 1934), 229–230; Bogumil Vosnjak, "Jugoslavia: A Commonwealth in the Making," *The Nation*, July 13, 1918, 36; Edward James Woodhouse, *Italy and the Jugoslavs* (Boston, 1920), 147.

18. Mutinies occurred on May 13 at Judenburg and Murau, May 20 in Pécs, May 21 in Rumburg, May 23 in Radkersberg, June 2 in Kragujevac (where forty-four soldiers were executed), June 16 in Kraków, July 2 in Wörgl, and July 4 in Zamość. Jaroslav Pánek, *A History of the Czech Lands* (Prague, 2009), 389; Robert Foltin, *Herbst 1918* (Vienna, 2013), 171; Manfred Scheuch, *Historischer Atlas Österreich* (Vienna, 2008), 212; Wolfdieter Bihl, *Der Weg zum Zusammenbruch. Österreich-Ungarn unter Karl I.(IV.)*, in *Österreich 1918–1938. Geschichte der Ersten Republik*, Erika Weinzierl and Kurt Skalnik, eds., vol. 1 (Vienna, 1983), 35; Borodziej, *Geschichte*, 88; Strauss, *Die Entstehung*, 229–230.

19. This was part of the Haller affair. Peter Broucek, "Seidler von Feuchtenegg, Ernst," in *Österreichisches biographisches Lexikon 1815–1950*, vol. 12 (Vienna, 2001–2005), 131–132.

20. Okey, *Habsburg Monarchy*, 392, 394.

21. Socialists had formed their own Polish government the previous week.

22. More than 100,000 people supposedly took part in the meeting. Keith Hitchins, *Rumania 1866–1947* (Oxford, 1994), 283.

23. Karel Zmrhal, *Armáda ducha druhé mile* (Chicago, 1918).

24. Derek Sayer, *The Coasts of Bohemia: A Czech History* (Princeton, NJ, 1998), 86; Josef Harna and Rudolf Fišer, *Dějiny českých zemi*, vol. 2 (Prague, 1995), 136; *Pilsner Tagblatt*, October 29, 1918, 1.

25. Zdeněk Kárník, *České země v éře první republiky*, vol. 1 (Prague, 2000), 37.

26. Stanisław Kutrzeba, *Polska odrodzona* (Kraków, 1988), 74, 77, 78; Borodziej, *Geschichte*, 91; Davies, *God's Playground*, vol. 2, 289.

27. Davies, *God's Playground*, vol. 2, 391.

28. The statement was by Oskar Jaszi. Lendvai, *Hungarians*, 367; Tibor Hajdú and Zsuzsa Nagy, "Revolution, Counterrevolution, Consolidation," in *History of Hungary*, Sugar et al., eds., 303.

29. Ivan T. Berend, *Decades of Crisis: Central and Eastern Europe before World War II* (Berkeley, 1998), 127.

30. But at the same time, his government introduced social legislation, for example, unemployment compensation and the forty-eight-hour work week. Berend, *Decades of Crisis*, 128.

31. The ordinance was issued July 17, 1919, two weeks before the republic collapsed. György Borsányi, *The Life of a Communist Revolutionary: Béla Kun*, Mario Fenyo, trans. (New York, 1993), 198.

32. Raphael Patai, *The Jews of Hungary: History, Culture, Psychology* (Detroit, 1996), 468.

33. Kun and thirty-two of his forty-five commissars were Jewish. Robert Paxton, *The Anatomy of Fascism* (New York, 2004), 25.

34. The lowest estimate of Jews killed in Poland was 400, the highest 532. William W. Hagen, *Anti-Jewish Violence in Poland, 1914–1920* (Cambridge, 2018), 512. In the context of the Russian civil war, more than 1,500 pogroms took place in Ukraine alone. Most victims died in areas under control of White or Ukrainian forces, but all forces, including the Red Army, victimized Jews. Oleg Budnitskii, *Russian Jews between the Reds and the Whites* (Philadelphia, 2012), 1, 216–217, 367–369.

35. Ezra Mendelsohn, *The Jews of East Central Europe between the World Wars* (Bloomington, IN, 1987), 98–99.

36. Reflections of Ján Smrek, *Sborník mladej slovenskej literatúry*, Ján Smrek, ed. (Bratislava, 1924), 298.

37. Kerner memorandum of March 25, 1918. Lawrence E. Gelfand, *The Inquiry: American Preparations for Peace* (New Haven, CT, 1963), 219. A Hungarian geographer, Ferenc Fodor (1887–1962), at the same time insisted that Slovaks and Czechs were not of the same stock, and that Magyar victories in the ethnic contest with Slovaks gave them a natural right to the Carpathian range. Ferenc Fodor, *The Geographical Impossibility of the Czech State* (Budapest, 1920), 7–8.

38. James Felak, "The Slovak Question," in *The Czech and Slovak Experience*, John Morison, ed. (London, 1992), 141; Brent Mueggenberg, *The Czecho-Slovak Struggle for Independence* (Jefferson, NC, 2014), 243; Stephen Bonsal, *Suitors and Suppliants: The Little Nations at Versailles* (New York, 1946), 160. The total for Hlinka's People's Party in 1925 was 489,111, which translated to 34.4 percent of the vote in Slovakia, making it the largest party there. Joseph Rothschild, *East Central Europe between the Two World Wars* (Seattle, 1974), 110.

39. Marcus Tanner, *Croatia: A Nation Forged in War* (New Haven, CT, 1997), 120.

40. Carol Skalnik Leff, *National Conflict in Czechoslovakia* (Princeton, NJ, 1988), 135–136.

41. Samuel Ronsin, "Police, Republic, and Nation: The Czechoslovak State Police," in *Policing Interwar Europe: Continuity Change and Crisis*, G. Blaney, ed. (New York, 2007), 154. Václav Beneš, "Czechoslovak Democracy and Its Problems," in *History of the Czechoslovak Republic*, Mamatey and Luža, eds., 77.

42. Leff, *National Conflict*, 138.

43. On the promise of autonomy, see David and Kann, *Peoples of the Eastern Habsburg Lands*, 324.

44. Rothschild, *East Central Europe*, 89; "Summary," in *History of the Czechoslovak Republic*, Mamatey and Luža, eds., 462. Šrobár selected half of the Slovak delegates to the National

Assembly from the Protestant minority (about 12 percent of the total), as well as seven Czechs. Beneš, "Czechoslovak Democracy," 57, 92–94.

45. Lucian Boia, *History and Myth in Romanian Consciousness* (Budapest, 2001), 43; Katherine Verdery, *Transylvanian Villagers: Three Centuries of Poltical, Economic, and Ethnic Change* (Berkeley, 1983), 273, 278.

46. Stephen Fischer-Galati, *Twentieth Century Rumania* (New York, 1991), 27; Caius Dobrescu, "Conflict and Diversity in East European Nationalism," *East European Politics and Societies* 17:3 (2003), 398.

47. Rothschild, *East Central Europe*, 287. By 1931, eleven officials from the kingdom and three locals sat in the Transylvanian Court of Appeal; in the district attorney's office, there were no Transylvanians at all. The situation was similar among police, education, and customs authorities. Florian Kührer-Wielach, *Siebenbürgen ohne Siebenbürger? Zentralstaatliche Integration und politischer Regionalismus nach dem Ersten Weltkrieg* (Munich, 2014), 241–249.

48. Banac, *National Question*, 233.

49. This is a complaint of voters for right-wing populists in our day as well. See Stephen Holmes, "How Democracies Perish," in Cass Sunstein, *Can It Happen Here? Authoritarianism in America* (New York, 2018), 327–428.

50. Sherman Spector, *Rumania at the Paris Peace Conference* (New York, 1962), 234.

51. John Maynard Keynes, *Economic Consequences of the Peace* (New York, 1920), 52, 249.

52. Jeremy King, *Budweisers into Czechs and Germans: A Local History of Bohemian Politics, 1848–1948* (Princeton, NJ, 2002), 157.

53. Bonsal, *Suitors and Suppliants*, 150–151, Detlev Brandes, "Die Tschechoslowakei," in *Versailles 1919: Ziele, Wirkung, Wahrnehmung*, Gerd Krumeich, ed. (Essen, Germany, 2001), 177. When a Dutch correspondent asked him why he was including 3 million Germans in his state against their will, Masaryk replied: "A nation of seventy million like the Germans can much more easily lose three million souls than a nation of ten million can lose half a million; and this consideration here is the only right one." Roman Szporluk, *The Political Thought of Tomáš G. Masaryk* (New York, 1981), 136. On the shootings, see Rothschild, *East Central Europe*, 79.

54. This is a diary entry from December 20, 1918, cited in D. Perman, *The Shaping of the Czechoslovak State: A Diplomatic History of the Boundaries of Czechoslovakia* (Leiden, 1962), 139.

55. Perman, *Shaping*, 139; "Big Fleet to Meet Wilson," *New York Times*, December 4, 1918, 3.

56. His colleagues complained of Kerner's pro-Slavic bias, but his linguistic skills were so unusual that House kept him. Gelfand, *Inquiry*, 45, 58, 131. The figure of Germans given in the Inquiry's tentative report of January 1919 was 250,000. Gelfand, *Inquiry*, 204

57. Other experienced diplomats also served on the Commission. Perman, *Shaping*, 133.

58. Perman, *Shaping*, 134–135.

59. Hugh Seton-Watson, *Eastern Europe between the Wars* (Cambridge, 1945), 198; Rothschild, *East Central Europe*, 89.

60. See the map in Paul Robert Magosci, *Historical Atlas of Central Europe* (Seattle, 2002), 149.

61. Zsuzsa L. Nagy, "Revolution, Counterrevolution, Consolidation," in *History of Hungary*, Sugar et al., eds., 314.

62. Margaret Macmillan, *Paris 1919: Six Months That Changed the World* (New York, 2003), 260; Hitchins, *Rumania*, 284.

63. There were demands, especially by Americans, that plebiscites be held in Transylvania and Bessarabia, but the Romanians strongly objected; the same was true of the Poles in Galicia. On the former, see Spector, *Rumania at the Paris Peace Conference.*

64. This was the year when Frederick William revoked Polish sovereignty in East Prussia. A smaller area, Warmia and Ermland, including Allenstein/Olsztyn, was in Poland until 1772. Robert I. Frost, *After the Deluge States: Poland-Lithuania and the Second Northern War* (Cambridge, 2004), 97–98.

65. Piotr Wandycz, *The United States and Poland* (Cambridge, MA, 1980), 142–143.

66. Davies, *God's Playground*, vol. 2, 398–399.

67. Wandycz calls it a National Democratic peace: *The United States and Poland*, 156.

68. Andrzej Micewski, *Roman Dmowski* (Warsaw, 1971), 296.

69. Żeligowski's act was presented as a mutiny, supposedly out of Piłsudski's control; in fact, the latter had organized it. Antony Polonsky, "The Emergence of an Independent Polish State," in *History of Poland*, Leslie, ed., 138. The promises were made by Władysław Grabski at Spa. Borodziej, *Geschichte*, 119.

70. Suggestions for a more "ethnic" Poland running along a line set by British Foreign Secretary Lord George Curzon still excluded millions of Poles and was rejected by all Polish parties. Borodziej, *Geschichte*, 119. This "Curzon line" was held by British public opinion to represent a fair delimitation of Polish ethnicity. See the views of R. W. Seton-Watson in Hugh and Christopher Seton-Watson, *The Making of a New Europe* (London, 1981), 407.

71. Wandycz, *The United States and Poland*, 157.

72. He was cleared of all charges after an investigation of the Polish parliament. Alina Cała, *Ostatnie pokolenie: autobiografie polskiej młodzieży żydowskiej okresu międzywojennego* (Warsaw, 2003), 137; Agnieszka Knyt, ed., *The Year 1920: The War between Poland and Bolshevik Russia* (Warsaw, 2005).

73. After an international outcry, the camp was closed, but the discrimination against Jewish soldiers continued. Tomasz Stanczyk, "Internowani w Jabłonnie," *Rzeczpospolita* (Warsaw), July 28, 2008. On the support of Jews for the Polish cause, see Janusz Szczepański, *Społeczeństwo Polski w walce z najazdem bolszewickim 1920 roku* (Warsaw, 2000), 242–247. Especially Zionist and Orthodox communities called on their members to "fulfill their patriotic duties" for "the independence of the Polish state." Yet there were also many Jews, especially in the east, who did not identify with Polish statehood. Szczepański, *Społeczeństwo Polski*, 243, 246. Andrzej Krzysztof Kunert, *Polacy—Żydzi 1939–45: wybór źródeł* (Warsaw, 2006), 9.

74. It was held by Polish troops after fierce fighting (that also involved several pogroms, the worst of which in Lwów in November 1918, claimed 150 lives). William W. Hagen, "The Moral Economy of Popular Violence: The Pogrom in Lwów, November 1918," in *Antisemitism and Its Opponents in Modern Poland*, Robert Blobaum, ed. (Ithaca, NY, 2005) 129.

75. March 18, 2014.

76. Paul Robert Magocsi, *Historical Atlas of Central Europe* (Seattle, 2002), 140.

77. J. W. Bruegel, *Czechoslovakia before Munich* (Cambridge, 1973), 60; King, *Budweisers into Czechs and Germans*, 169.

78. Daniel Stone, ed., *The Polish Memoirs of William John Rose* (Toronto and Buffalo, NY, 1975), 104.

79. King, *Budweisers into Czechs and Germans*, 160; Szporluk, *Political Thought*, 135. Masaryk said that "humanity and nationality require each other." H. Gordon Skilling, *T. G. Masaryk: Against the Current, 1882–1914* (University Park, PA, 1994), 147.

80. Robin Okey, *Eastern Europe, 1740–1985: Feudalism to Communism* (Minneapolis, MN, 1982), 165.

81. Austen Chamberlain: "The object of the Minorities Treaties, and of the Council in discharging its duties under them, was to secure for the minorities that measure of protection and justice which would gradually prepare them to be merged in a national community to which they belong." Hans Rothfels, *Bismarck, der Osten , und das Reich* (Darmstadt, 1960), 16; C. A. Macartney, *National States and National Minorities* (London, 1934), 275, 277.

82. Helke Stadtland, "Sakralisierte Nation und Säkularisierte Religion," in *Beyond the Balkans: Toward an Inclusive History of Southeastern Europe*, Sabine Rutar, ed. (Vienna, 2014), 190; and with many sources: Nikolaus Barbian, *Auswärtige Kulturpolitik und Auslandsdeutsche in Lateinamerika* (Osnabrück, 2013), 67; Matthias Lienert, *Zur Geschichte des DAI* (Berlin 1989), 7.

Chapter 13: The Failure of National Self-Determination

1. British Scholar James Bryce wrote in his important 1921 book *Modern Democracies* of the "universal acceptance of democracy as the normal and natural form of government." Cited in Mark Mazower, *Dark Continent: Europe's Twentieth Century* (New York, 1999), 4.

2. The Corfu Declaration therefore proclaimed the new state would be a "constitutional, democratic, and parliamentary monarchy." Nikola Pašić, an avowed democrat, assumed that the democratic spirit that animated the Serbs would also find a home among Slovenes and Croats. Alex N. Dragnich, *The First Yugoslavia: The Search for a Viable Political System* (Stanford, CA, 1983), 7–8.

3. Stone, *Polish Memoirs*, 77.

4. This was an aspiration of one Pole he talked to during the war who had refused to become German. William John Rose, "A New Idealism in Europe," *New Europe*, December 12, 1918, 197.

5. Carlton Hayes, *A Brief History of the Great War* (New York, 1920), 388, 395; G. K. Chesterton, "Edward Benes—Central Europe's Peacemaker," *Current History* 16 (1922), 575. "In general, the postwar public discourse was dominated by enthusiastic interpretations . . . universal suffrage seemed to hold the curative power of a panacea." Sorin Radu, "Peasant Democracy," in *Politics and Peasants in Interwar Romania* (Newcastle upon Tyne, UK, 2017), 30–34.

6. Rose, "New Idealism," 198–199.

7. The franchise fell to 29.5 percent in 1922. In four general elections between 1922 and 1935, the government party won 628 of 980 available seats (64.1 percent), 578 of them in constituencies where the open ballot was in effect. Andrew Janos, *The Politics of Backwardness in Hungary* (Princeton, NJ, 1982), 212–213.

8. David Mitrany, *Rumania: Her History and Politics* (London, 1915), 29–30.

9. In Mitrany's idea of Greater Romania, there was no sense that Magyars belonged in Transylvania; it was presented as a Romanian land. David Mitrany, *Greater Rumania: A Study in National Ideals* (London, 1917), 15, 20. For his later views, see David Mitrany, "Human Rights and International Organization," *India Quarterly* 3 (1947), 402–430.

10. Romania followed in 1929, Yugoslavia after World War II.

11. Emperor Charles died in exile in 1922.

12. Hajdú and Nagy, "Revolution, Counterrevolution, Consolidation," 312–313.

13. C. A. Macartney, *Hungary: A Short History* (Edinburgh, 1962), 211.

14. From the declaration of the government of April 19, 1921. Margit Szöllösi-Janze, *Die Pfeilkreuzlerbewegung in Ungarn* (Munich, 1989), 78. On Bethlen's approach to democracy, see Janos, *Politics of Backwardness*, 210–211.

15. Mária Ormos, "The Early Interwar Years," in *History*, Sugar, ed., 320; Zsolt Nagy, *Great Expectations and Interwar Realities: Hungarian Cultural Diplomacy 1918–1941* (Budapest, 2017), 48–49.

16. This was a step backward from 1919/1920, when 58.4 percent of the population could vote. Paul A. Hanebrink, *In Defense of Christian Hungary: Religion, Nationalism, and Anti-Semitism* (Ithaca, NY, 2006), 109.

17. Macartney, *Hungary*, 213, 218. There were some 298,000 beneficiaries.

18. Seton-Watson, *Eastern Europe between the Wars*, 190.

19. Ormos, "Early Interwar Years," 321, 324.

20. The opposition consisted of Social Democrats, Christian Socialists, and members of bourgeois parties; Ormos, "Early Interwar Years," 320.

21. The agreement, the Bethlen-Peyer pact, was reached in 1921. Janos, *Politics of Backwardness*, 234–235; Dylan Riley, *The Civic Foundations of Fascism in Europe* (Baltimore, 2010), 176.

22. Seton-Watson, *Eastern Europe between the Wars*, 191.

23. Rothschild, *East Central Europe*, 297.

24. The reason was that the king first appointed a government, and then entrusted it with "making" elections with the aid of the administrative apparatus, now under its control. Henry L. Roberts, *Rumania: Political Problems of an Agrarian State* (New Haven, CT, 1951), 102; Stephen Fischer-Galati, *Twentieth Century Rumania* (New York, 1991), 35.

25. Fischer-Galati, *Twentieth Century Rumania*, 35–36; Rothschild, *East Central Europe*, 297. They did much better in land reform than the Hungarians did, but the reform was exclusively political.

26. Roberts, *Rumania*, 100–101.

27. Rothschild, *East Central Europe*, 301.

28. Rothschild, *East Central Europe*, 306–308; Rebecca Haynes, "Reluctant Allies? Iuliu Maniu and Corneliu Zelea Codreanu against King Carol II of Romania, *The Slavonic and East European Review* 85:1 (2007), 109; "Rumania: Its People Await Hitler's Drive," *Life*, January 9, 1939, 49.

29. Roberts, *Rumania*, 134; Hitchins, *Romania*, 415.

30. Rothschild, *East Central Europe*, 332, 336; Seton-Watson, *Eastern Europe between the Wars*, 243.

31. Richard Busch-Zantner, *Bulgarien* (Leipzig, 1943), 136.

32. R. J. Crampton, *A Concise History of Bulgaria* (Cambridge, 1997), 151; Misha Glenny, *The Balkans: Nationalism, War, and the Great Powers* (New York, 2000) 397.

33. Crampton, *Concise History*, 154; Rothschild, *East Central Europe*, 337.

34. Alan Palmer, *The Lands Between: A History of Eastern Europe* (London, 1970), 179.

35. Lawyers were forbidden from sitting in parliament or on local councils and in other public offices. Crampton, *Concise History*, 152.

36. Rothschild, *East Central Europe*, 334–335; Seton-Watson, *Eastern Europe between the Wars*, 243; Crampton, *Concise History*, 154; Glenny, *The Balkans*, 398.

37. This agreement was the Niš convention. Crampton, *Concise History*, 155.

38. IMRO was founded in 1893 to liberate territory from Ottoman rule and became a terrorist network as well as a guerrilla army in the interwar years, cooperating with the Croatian Ustashas. Seton-Watson, *Eastern Europe between the Wars*, 244; Busch-Zantner, *Bulgarien*, 139.

39. Crampton, *Concise History*, 155; Seton-Watson, *Eastern Europe between the Wars*, 245.

40. Crampton, *Concise History*, 156; C. A. Macartney and A. W. Palmer, *Independent Eastern Europe: A History* (London, 1962), 227.

41. Frederick B. Chary, *History of Bulgaria* (Santa Barbara, CA, 2011), 71–72; Busch-Zantner, *Bulgarien*, 141; Seton-Watson, *Eastern Europe between the Wars*, 246; Crampton, *Concise History*, 157.

42. Paul Robert Magocsi, *Historical Atlas of Central Europe* (Seattle, 2002), 141; Rothschild, *East Central Europe*, 202.

43. Rothschild, *East Central Europe*, 82.

44. This at a congress refounding the Slovak People's Party. James Mace Ward, *Priest, Politician, Collaborator: Josef Tiso and the Making of Fascist Slovakia* (Ithaca, NY, 2012).

45. Cited in Ante Cuvalo, "Stjepan Radić: His Life, His Party, His Politics," *American Croatian Review* 5:3–4 (1998), 36–40.

46. He allied his party to a front for the Communist International, the Peasants International, in 1924, and was arrested with the entire Peasant Party leadership in 1925. Markus Tanner, *Croatia: A Nation Forged in War* (New Haven, CT, 1997), 121.

47. Tim Judah, *The Serbs: History, Myth, and the Destruction of Yugoslavia*, second edition (New Haven, CT, 2000), 110. The king sent his offer via Svetozar Pribićević: "Since we cannot live together it is better to separate in peace like Sweden and Norway."

48. That party did have some prominent Croat figures as well. The coalition was called the "Peasant Democratic Coalition." Dejan Djokić, *Elusive Compromise: A History of Interwar Yugoslavia* (New York, 2007), 65–68.

49. In a proclamation of January 6, 1929, he stated: "Blind political passions have begun to misuse the parliamentary system . . . to such an extent that it has become a hindrance to any fruitful work in the state." Snežana Trifunovska, *Yugoslavia through Documents: From Its Creation to Its Dissolution* (Dordrecht, 1994), 191.

50. See Peter Haslinger, "The Nation, the Enemy, and Imagined Territories: Slovak and Hungarian Elements in the Emergence and Decline of a Czechoslovak National Narrative 1890–1938," in *Creating the Other. The Causes and Dynamics of Nationalism, Ethnic Enmity, and Racism in Eastern Europe*, Nancy Wingfield, ed. (Providence, RI, 2003), 169–182.

51. The *Pětka* emerged in the fall of 1920 shortly after this incident. Zdeněk Kárník, *České země v éře První republiky, 1918–1938* (Prague, 2000), 140–142; Victor S. Mamatey, "The Development of Czechoslovak Democracy," in *History of the Czechoslovak Republic, 1918–1948*, Victor S. Mamatey and Radomir Luza, eds. (Princeton, NJ, 1973), 108.

52. Antony Polonsky, *The Little Dictators: A History of Eastern Europe since 1918* (Abington-on-Thames, UK, 1975), 120; Mamatey, "Development," 127. The new church had some 800,000 members within a few years. It celebrated the liturgy in Czech and attempted to shape its own rituals according to Hussite practices. Martin Schulze Wessel, "Die Konfesionalisierung der

tschechischen Nation, in Heinz-Gerhard Haupt and Dieter Langewiesche, eds., *Nation und Religion in Europa* (Frankfurt, 2004), 146.

53. Polonsky, *Little Dictators*, 120

54. British Prime Minister David Lloyd George could not say where or what Těšín was. Stone, *Polish Memoirs*, ix; R. H. Bruce Lockhart, *Retreat from Glory* (London, 1934). For the reduction of trade throughout East European states, see Ivan T. Berend, *Decades of Crisis* (Berkeley, 1998), 241–242.

55. The Serbs were from Serbia, Bosnia, and Austria-Hungary; Poles from Germany, Austria, and Russia.

56. Supposedly he was prepared to sell Poland to his old Russian comrades. Borodziej, *Geschichte*, 117; Adam Michnik, "Naganiacze i zdrajcy," *Gazeta Wyborcza*, September 28, 2006.

57. The złoty replaced the mark in 1924 and was tied to gold. It depreciated from 1925 but then stabilized in late 1926 at about 72 percent of its value in 1924. "Zloty Will Replace Polish Mark," *New York Times*, May 19, 1924; Barry Eichengreen, *Monetary Regime Transformations* (Aldershot, UK, 1992), 161.

58. Piotr Wróbel, "The Rise and Fall of Parliamentary Democracy in Interwar Poland," in *The Origins of Modern Polish Democracy*, M. B. B. Biskupski et al., eds. (Athens, OH, 2010), 135. The number of Jews at Polish universities dropped from 25 percent in 1925 to about 8.2 percent in 1937/1938. Yfaat Weiss, *Deutsche und polnische Juden vor dem Holocaust* (Munich, 200), 113. Under the Habsburgs, there were 2,612 Ukrainian elementary schools in East Galicia; by 1928 there were only 700 of them. Wenzel Jaksch, *Europe's Road to Potsdam* (New York, 1964), 255.

59. The entire press seemed to be calling for an alternative to the pre-1926 political system, as is well described in Borodziej, *Geschichte*, 144–145.

60. Borodziej, *Geschichte*, 145.

61. Andrzej Garlicki, *Przewrót majowy* (Warsaw, 1979), 388; Antony Polonsky, "The Emergence of an Independent Polish State," in Leslie, ed., *History*, 155.

62. "Gave a Cue for Revolt: Pilsudski Began Movement through Democratic Newspapers," *New York Times*, May 15, 1926. An interesting, revealing, and confusing mix of metaphors ensued from left and right. See Rothschild, *East Central Europe*, 53–55.

63. Rothschild, *East Central Europe*, 57.

64. Ferdynand Zweig, *Poland between Two Wars* (London, 1944), 13.

65. Andrzej Jezierski, *Historia Gospodarcza Polski* (Warsaw, 2010), 253.

66. Jezierski, *Historia*, 253.

67. From a speech of the early postwar period cited in Radu, "Peasant Democracy," 32.

68. Roberts, *Rumania*, 134–136, 174–175.

69. "Rumanian Revolt Hinted," *New York Times*, June 30, 1935, 13.

70. The list would include BANU of Stamboliiski, Radić's Croatian Peasant Party, the Romanian national peasant party of Maniu, and the Piast and Wyzwolenie Party in Poland. Palmer, *The Lands Between*, 178. The historian is Hans Lemberg. Thanks to Joachim von Puttkamer for the reference.

71. George Orwell, *Homage to Catalonia* (Boston, 2015), 69.

72. About 29.9 percent of the Hungarian holdings were larger that 575 hectares. The drawn-out process did not increase by much the number of self-sufficient landowners: "the structure of society remained practically unchanged." The "structure of land distribution remained

unhealthily polarized between big estates and dwarf holdings." Nagy, "Revolution," 317; Rothschild, *East Central Europe*, 190. In Romania, the reform was more successful in taking land from Hungarian large landowners.

73. Rothschild, *East Central Europe*, 300–301.

Chapter 14: Fascism Takes Root: Iron Guard and Arrow Cross

1. Ernst Nolte, *Der Faschismus in seiner Epoche* (Munich, 1963); Geoff Eley, "What Produces Fascism," *Politics and Society* 12:53 (1983), 77. For a definition of fascism that stresses the role of paramilitaries, the revolutionary agenda of transcendence, and creating a purified ethnic society without contradictions, see Michael Mann, *Fascists* (Cambridge, 2000).

2. The state was not mature enough to fall back on a consensus that liberal democracy was the "sole valid basis for a healthy society." Roger Griffin, *The Nature of Fascism* (New York, 1991), 211.

3. Robert Paxton, "The Five Stages of Fascism," *Journal of Modern History* 70:1 (1998), 14.

4. Eugen Weber, *The Hollow Years: France in the 1930s* (New York, 1994), 119.

5. Paxton, "Five Stages," 17

6. Charles S. Maier, *The Unmasterable Past: History, Holocaust, and National Memory* (Cambridge, MA 1988), 112.

7. A law restricting Jewish enrollments at university had been passed in 1920, but the government under Bethlen somewhat blunted the impact, so that numbers of Jewish students, which had dipped to about 5 percent, rose to close to 10 percent by 1930 (still far lower than the more than 30 percent during the war years). The Jewish business community became wealthier than ever before. Janos, *Politics of Backwardness*, 225–226.

8. Janos, *Politics of Backwardness*, 177.

9. Jaff Schatz mentions a more general factor at work: "given a certain level of literacy, education, and exposure to the injustices of society, members of discriminated minorities are more likely than others to join radical movements for change." Jaff Schatz, "Jews and the Communist Movement in Interwar Poland," in *Dark Times, Dire Decisions*, Jonathan Frankel, ed. (Oxford, 2004), 32. The percentage of Jews in the interwar Polish Communist Party reached a peak of 35 percent in 1930. Archie Brown, *The Rise and Fall of Communism* (New York, 2009), 129–130.

10. Alexander F. C. Webster, *The Romanian Legionary Movement: An Orthodox Christian Assessment of Anti-Semitism*, Carl Beck Papers No. 502 (Pittsburgh, PA, 1986), 43–44, 52; Corneliu Zelea Codreanu, *For My Legionaries* (London, 2015), 51. Thanks to Marina Cuneo for this reference.

11. Paul A. Shapiro, "The German Protestant Church and Its Judenmission, 1945–1950," in *Anti-Semitism, Christian Ambivalence, and the Holocaust*, Keven Spicer, ed. (Bloomington, IN, 2007), 139.

12. He formed a political party in 1934: Tutul Pentru Tara (Everything for the Country). Stephen Fischer-Galati, *Twentieth Century Rumania* (New York, 1991), 53. He also won a seat in parliament in 1931.

13. Nicholas M. Nagy-Talavera, *The Green Shirts and the Others* (Portland, OR, 2001), 77.

14. Hungary lost about 72 percent of its territory (from 325,411 square kilometers to 93,073 square kilometers) and dropped from 18 million to 8 million inhabitants. Arpad von Klimo, "Trianon und der Diskurs über nationale Identität in 'Rumpf-Ungarn,'" in *Die geteilte Nation: Nationale Verluste und Identitäten im 20. Jahrhundert*, Andreas Hilger and Oliver Wrochem, eds. (Munich, 2013), 15; Raphael Vago, "Eastern Europe," in *The Social Basis of European Fascist Movements*, Detlef Mühlberger, ed. (London, 1987), 297–298.

15. Marcin Kula, *Narodowe i rewolucyjne* (Warsaw, 1991); Francis Carsten, "Interpretations of Fascism," in *Fascism: A Reader's Guide*, Walter Laqueur, ed. (London, 1976), 418; Vago, "Eastern Europe," 294.

16. Juan Linz notes a strong presence of white-collar employees, professionals, and public servants in fascist parties in general, but he emphasizes the prominent place of students in Romania. "Comparative Study of Fascism," in Laqueur, *Fascism*, 63, 70; Radu Ioanid, *The Sword of the Archangel: Fascist Ideology in Romania*, Peter Heinegg, trans. (Boulder, CO, 1990), 27.

17. Vago, "Eastern Europe," 288–289.

18. In Romania, such demands, put forth in the 1930s by peasant politician Vaida and others, failed to gain political support. The term used was "Romanianization," and the problem was that these demands infringed on the minority protections agreement, and minorities could protest. Keith Hitchins, *Rumania, 1866–1947* (Oxford, 1994), 417; Dietmar Müller, *Staatsbürger auf Widerruf: Juden und Muslime als Alteritätspartner im rumänischen und serbischen Nationscode* (Wiesbaden, 2005), 404–405.

19. Henry Eaton, *The Origins and Onset of the Romanian Holocaust* (Detroit, 2013), 24. The number of Jews in the medical faculty at Iași was 43.3 percent from 1923 to 1930, and 39.6 percent from 1930 to 1936. The number of Jewish students in Iași was 26.7 percent from 1923 to 1930 and 23.1 percent from 1930 to 1936; and in Cernăuți, it was 31.1 percent from 1923 to 1930 and 29.6 percent from 1930 to 1936. Lucian Nastasa, "Anti-Semitism at Universities in Romania," in *The Numerus Clausus in Hungary*, Victor Karady and Peter Tibor Nagy, eds. (Budapest, 2012), 222–223. The relatively high number of Jews at universities in Moldavia, Bessarabia, and Bukovina was connected to high numbers of Jews among the literate urban population of those areas. In 1930, 44.2 percent of the population in Moldavia and Wallachia could not read or write, and the areas with high illiteracy were those that "voted more heavily for fascist organizations." Ioanid, *Sword*, 40, 64. In Romania as a whole, 57.1 percent of those older than seven were literate. Rothschild, *East Central Europe*, 285.

20. Z. Barbu, "Rumania," in *Fascism Reader*, Aristotle Kallis, ed. (London, 2003), 199. "Most of its members were climbing up the ladder of social hierarchy in the direction of the middle class. But the point is they had not yet arrived." Vago, "Eastern Europe," 256.

21. István Deák, "Hungary," in *The European Right*, Hans Rogger and Eugen Weber, eds. (Berkeley, 1965), 389. Codreanu's father was Ion Zelinski, a teacher. Vago, "Eastern Europe," 287; Barbu, "Rumania," 200.

22. Stanley Payne, *A History of Fascism* (Madison, WI, 1995), 276; Vago, "Eastern Europe," 293–294.

23. Hitchins, *Rumania*, 368–370; Rothschild, *East Central Europe*, 300.

24. That was in 1934. Hitchins, *Rumania*, 418.

25. István Deák, "Hungary," in Kallis, ed., *Fascism Reader*, 202–203; Jörg K. Hoensch, *A History of Modern Hungary: 1867–1994* (London, 1995), 126.

26. Deák, "Hungary," in Kallis, ed., *Fascism Reader*, 203; Hoensch, *Hungary*, 128.

27. He did so essentially through control of state apparatus. Deák, "Hungary," in Kallis, ed., *Fascism Reader*, 205. He was of German, Slovak, and Armenian heritage. Paul Lendvai, *The Hungarians: A Thousand Years of Victory in Defeat*, Ann Major, trans. (Princeton, NJ, 2003), 415.

28. Hoensch, *Hungary*, 129.

29. Andrew C. Janos, *East Central Europe in the Modern World* (Stanford, CA, 2000), 288–291; Hoensch, *Hungary*, 127, 129; Deák, "Hungary," in *The European Right*, Rogger and Weber, eds., 380, 391; George Barany, "The Dragon's Teeth," in *Native Fascism in the Successor States, 1918–1945*, Peter Sugar, ed. (Santa Barbara, CA, 1971), 79.

30. Hoensch, *Hungary*, 131.

31. J. B. Hoptner, *Yugoslavia in Crisis, 1934–1941* (New York, 1962), 157; Frederick B. Chary, *The History of Bulgaria* (Santa Barbara, CA, 2011), 83–84; Rothschild, *East Central Europe*, 256; Marshall Lee Miller, *Bulgaria during the Second World War*, (Stanford, CA, 1975), 7.

32. Chary, *History of Bulgaria*, 89.

33. Janos, *Politics of Backwardness*, 302–303.

34. Janos, *East Central Europe*, 290. Those words are Janos's, not Horthy's.

35. "In 1938 over 10,000 sq. kilometers of cultivable land was still owned by only eighty magnate families; a further 16,000 sq. kilometers was in the possession of 1,000 smaller estate-owners." Hoensch, *Hungary*, 131.

36. Stephen Fischer-Galati, "Fascism," in Sugar, *Native Fascism*, 118; Rothschild, *East Central Europe*, 294.

37. Payne, *History of Fascism*, 275. See also Margit Szölösi-Janze, *Die Pfeilkreuzlerbewegung in Ungarn* (Munich, 1989), 134–147; Nagy-Talavera, *Green Shirts*, 94–155; Janos, *Politics of Backwardness*, 270–271; Deák, "Hungary," 380, 392.

38. Rothschild, *East Central Europe*, 296. Of ninety-three Legionnaires executed in 1939 whose professions could be ascertained, thirty-three were students. Almost all the rest were from the middle classes, including fourteen lawyers. Payne, *History of Fascism*, 287.

39. Rothschild, *East Central Europe*, 310; Fischer-Galati, *Twentieth Century Rumania*, 56–57; Eugen Weber, "Romania," in *European Right*, Weber and Rogger, eds., 549; Radu Ioanid, "The Sacralised Politics of the Romanian Iron Guard," *Totalitarian Movements and Political Religions* 5:3 (2004): 419–453.

40. Radu Ioanid, "The Sacralised Politics of the Romanian Iron Guard," in *Fascism, Totalitarianism and Political Religion*, Roger Griffin, ed. (New York, 2005), 155; Deák, "Hungary," 392.

41. Cited in Deák, "Hungary," 392.

42. Deák, "Hungary," 388–394.

43. Constantin Iordachi, "Fascism in Southeastern Europe," in *Entangled Histories of the Balkans*, Roumen Daskalov and Diana Mishkova, eds., vol. 2 (Leiden, 2014), 382; Mircea Platon, "The Iron Guard and the Modern State, Iron Guard Leaders Vasile Marin and Ion I. Mota, and the 'New European Order,'" *Fascism: Journal of Comparative Fascist Studies* 1 (2012): 67.

44. This from a letter of Eugéne Ionescu to Tudor Vianu. Marta Petreu, *An Infamous Past: E. M. Cioran and the Rise of Fascism in Romania*, Bogdan Aldea, trans. (Chicago, 2005), 58–59. The group of young intellectuals was called the "Criterion" group: including Cioran, Eliade, Haig

Acterian, Marietta Sadova, Dan Botta, and others. Petreu, *Infamous Past*, 60. See also Matei Calinescu, "Romania's 1930s Revisited," *Salmagundi* 97 (1993): 133–151.

45. Petreu, *Infamous Past*, 67. "In the Aryan world of self-reliance," George Mosse writes, "liberty and self-reliance in the national community were deemed essential." *Toward the Final Solution: A History of European Racism* (New York, 1978), 49.

46. Emile Cioran, *On the Heights of Despair* (1934), Ilinca Zarifapol-Johnston, trans. (Chicago, 2003), 6.

47. Petreu, *Infamous Past*, 60, 63; Barbara Jelavich, *History of the Balkans*, vol. 2 (Cambridge, 1983), 205. Men predominated in the Iron Guard (Legionaries were males carrying out "men's tasks"), but the Guard also created "nests" and "fortresses" for women and young people, which had the function of supporting the Legion "in every way possible." Roland Clark, *Holy Legionary Youth: Fascist Activism in Interwar Romania* (Ithaca, NY, 2015), 115.

48. Alfred Läpple, *Kirche und Nationalsozialismus in Deutschland und Österreich* (Aschaffenburg, Germany, 1980), 32.

49. Ioanid, *Sword*, 141. In addition, a Maria Rusu began speaking to the Holy Virgin, and people flocked to her to be healed.

50. Goergetta Pana, "Religious Anti-Semitism in Romanian Fascist Propaganda," *Occasional Papers on Religion in Eastern Europe* 26:2 (2006), 3; Deák, "Hungary," 394; Weber, "Romania," 535. On Mussolini: Denis Mack Smith, *Mussolini* (New York, 1982), 8, 15.

51. Webster, *Romanian Legionary Movement*, 38–39; Petreu, *Infamous Past*, 63–64.

52. Z. Barbu, "Rumania," 200; Ioanid, *Sword*, 140, 142.

53. Emphasis added. Weber, "Romania," 542, 545.

54. Clark, *Holy Legionary Youth*, 157.

55. From the journal *Libertatea*, April 1936, cited in Clark, *Holy Legionary Youth*, 156.

56. Estimates vary, but Armin Heinen claims the number of camps grew from four in 1934 to fifty in 1936, with another 500 smaller camps. Clark, *Holy Legionary Youth*, 156.

57. Clark, *Holy Legionary Youth*, 163–164.

58. Platon, "Iron Guard," 69.

59. Vago, "Eastern Europe," 290; William Totok: "Meister des Todes. Über die Wiederbelebungsversuche des Kultes von Moța und Marin/Maeștrii morții. Despre încercarea de reînviere a cultului Moța și Marin," *Apoziția* 7 (2007), 396–422; Ioanid, *Sword*, 89.

60. Barany, "Dragon's Teeth," 77.

61. They won 15.58 percent of the vote. Clark, *Holy Legionary Youth*, 216.

62. Payne, *History of Fascism*, 284; Deák, "Hungary," 391; Fischer-Galati, *Twentieth Century Rumania*, 55, 57.

Chapter 15: Eastern Europe's Antifascism

1. Piotr Wilczek, Letters to the Editor, *New York Times*, August 31, 2018; responding to Paul Krugman, "It Can Happen Here," *New York Times*, August 27, 2018.

2. Michael Mann, *Fascists* (Cambridge, 2004), 13.

3. Antony Polonsky, *The Little Dictators: A History of Eastern Europe since 1918* (Abington-on-Thames, UK, 1975), 120–121; Andrea Orzoff, *Battle for the Castle: The Myth of Czechoslovakia in Europe* (Oxford, 2009).

4. Joseph Zacek, "Czechoslovak Fascisms," in Sugar, *Native Fascism*, 61.

5. He was the only major political leader to use such language. The bureaucracy, however, behaved as if the state had been created for the Czechs. J. W. Bruegel, *Czechoslovakia before Munich* (Cambridge, 1973), 62. His party achieved 6.25 percent of the votes in the 1920 parliamentary elections and declined thereafter. In 1926 he praised Italian fascism for its ability to keep order, and he advocated the disbanding the parliament if it harmed the state. Hans Lemberg, "Gefahrenmomente für die demokratische Staatsform der Ersten Tschechoslowakischen Republik," in *Die Krise des Parlamentarismus is Ostmitteleuropa zwischen den beiden Weltkriegen*, Han-Erich Volkmann, ed. (Marburg, 1967), 115. The fascist "Community" got 2 percent, and the National Democrats 5.6 percent of the vote in 1935. Jaroslav Krejčí, *Czechoslovakia at the Crossroads* (New York, 1990), 150.

6. Rothschild, *East Central Europe*, 125. The leaders worried that Gajda might use a summer Sokol meeting in Prague to stage a fascist putsch. Orzoff, *Battle*, 101–102; Lemberg, "Gefahrenmomente," 116.

7. Zacek, "Czechoslovak Fascisms," 61.

8. H. Gordon Skilling, "Gottwald and the Bolshevization of the Communist Party of Czechoslovakia," *Slavic Review* 20:4 (1961), 650.

9. This was a formulation of Comintern functionary Georgi Dimitrov from 1924. A certain sobering set in after the coming to power of the Nazis in Germany in 1933. Jacques Rupnik, *Histoire du parti communiste tchécoslovaque: des origines à la prise du pouvoir* (Paris, 1981), 89–90, 98.

10. Ladislav Cabada, *Intellectuals and the Communist Idea: The Search for a New Way*, Zdeněk Benedikt, trans. (Lanham, MD, 2010), 153. Support was also strong in outlying areas of Prague, with relatively large groups of unemployed and seasonal laborers. Zdenek Kárník, "KSČ—úspěchy a neúspěchy," in *Bolševismus, komunismus a radikální socialismus v Československu*, Zdeněk Kárník and Michal Kopeček, eds., vol. 1 (Prague, 2003), 77–79; Josef Harna, *Krize evropské demokracie a Československo 30. let 20. století* (Prague, 2006), 115–117.

11. Lemberg, "Gefahrenmomente," 120; Jan Křen, *Bila místa v našich dějinách?* (Prague, 1990), 76–77.

12. The prime ministerships of František Udržal (1929–1932) and Jan Malypetr (1932–1935) saw frequent strikes and other actions of dissatisfied workers and rural laborers, and sometimes witnessed police brutality leading to loss of life and provoking criticism by intellectuals but also by the president. See also Harna, *Krize*, 118.

13. Also Polish: see Lucian Leustean, "Economy and Foreign Relations in Europe in the Early Inter-War Period—The Case of Hungary's Financial Reconstruction," *Eastern Journal of European Studies* 4:1 (June 2013), 45; Lemberg, "Gefahrenmomente," 119.

14. See Cynthia Paces, *Prague Panoramas: National Memory and Sacred Space* (Pittsburgh, PA, 2009).

15. Mamatey, "Development," 146; Věra Olivová, *Doomed Democracy: Czechoslovakia in a Disrupted Europe, 1914-38* (London, 1972), 184.

16. Olivová, Doomed Democracy, 185–186; Mamatey, "Development," 146–147.

17. Eugen Steiner, *The Slovak Dilemma* (Cambridge, 1973), 30–31.

18. Among the Social Democrats was Otto Bauer. Von Horvath lived in Vienna and then Paris, but had his plays premiered in Prague and Ostrava. Bohumil Černý, *Most k novému životu: Německá emigrace v ČSR v letech 1933–1939* (Prague, 1967), 159–177.

19. Mamatey, "Development," 154; Rene Küpper, *Karl Hermann Frank: politische Biographie eines sudetendeutschen Nationalsozialisten* (Munich, 2010), Emil Hruška, *Boj o pohraničí: sudetoněmecký freikorps v roce 1938* (Prague, 2013). In the relatively free Danzig elections of 1935, the Nazis got 59 percent of the vote. Ernst Sodeikat, "Der Nationalsozialismus und die Danziger Opposition," *Vierteljahrshefte für Zeitgeschichte* 12:2 (1966), 139–174.

20. Havránek, "Fascism in Czechoslovakia," in Sugar, *Native Fascism*. Konrad Henlein was made an honorary SS officer. Küpper, *Karl Hermann Frank*, 116; Mamatey, "Development," 154.

21. Blanka Soukupová, "Modern Anti-Semitism in the Czech Lands between the Years 1895–1989," *Lidé města = Urban People* (Prague) 13:2 (2011), 242, 244.

22. Within *Sanacja*, important segments opposed creating a fully authoritarian state. Jerzy Borejsza, "East European Perceptions of Italian Fascism," in *Who Were the Fascists: Social Roots of European Fascism*, Stein Larsen et al., eds. (Bergen, Norway, 1980), 354.

23. For sources, see Zbigniew Karpus et al., eds., *Zamach stanu Józefa Piłsudskiego i jego konsekwencje w interpretacjach polskiej myśli politycznej XX wieku* (Toruń, Poland, 2008), 154. Piłsudski said that he intended to maintain "parliamentarism," though his respect for politicians was virtually nonexistent. Polonsky, *Little Dictators*, 37. He also said that the role of parliamentarians should be reduced to "lifting their hands" in assent. Andrzej Chojnowski, *Piłsudczycy u władzy. Dzieje Bezpartyjnego Bloku Współpracy z Rządem* (Warsaw, 1986), 11.

24. "Polish fascism went against the long tradition of Polish ideals of freedom, individualism, and toleration." Piotr S. Wandycz, "Fascism in Poland," in Sugar, *Native Fascism*, 97.

25. Tommasini wrote (sometime before 1923): "if anyone sought such an analogy in Poland he would have to look for it among the followers of Piłsudski, a born leader, an extraordinarily courageous man, prepared to accept violent changes in politics." Borjesza, "East European Perceptions," 355.

26. Polonsky, *Little Dictators*, 38–39.

27. Polonsky, *Little Dictators*, 59; Borjesza, "East European Perceptions," 358.

28. Borjesza, "East European Perceptions," 356.

29. Antony Polonsky, "The Emergence of an Independent Polish State," in *The History of Poland since 1863*, R. F. Leslie, ed. (Cambridge, 1983), 178.

30. In all, sixty-four politicians from the Bloc were detained, along with several thousand suspected sympathizers. When these stories emerged the following year, revulsion set in even among *Sanacja's* supporters. Polonsky, "Emergence," 174. Some 3,000 people were being held at Bereza before the outbreak of war. Andrzej Garlicki, "Bereza, Polski obóz koncentracyjny," *Gazeta Wyborcza*, April 4, 2008; Polonsky in Leslie, History, 178, 180.

31. Despite the repression a strong Ukrainian intelligentsia developed along with a vibrant Ukrainian cooperative movement. Rothschild, *East Central Europe*, 42–43.

32. Henryk Wereszycki, *Niewygasła Przeszłość* (Kraków, 1987), 401 ff.

33. Polonsky, "Emergence," 176.

34. Rothschild, *East Central Europe*, 60: "Given his reluctance to shake the nation into genuine confidence and political partnership, Piłsudski might have done better to establish an explicit dictatorship on the morrow of the coup rather than lead the country through a demoralizing pseudo-parliamentary charade."

35. The Camp imitated the Italy's fascist party. Borejsza, "East European Perceptions," 356.

36. Jerzy Holzer, "Polish Political Parties and Antisemitism," in *Jews in Independent Poland, 1918–1939*, Antony Polonsky, Ezra Mendelsohn, and Jerzy Tomaszewski, eds. (London, 2004), 199; see the description from a conversation with an *Endek* in Alfred Döblin, *Reise in Polen* (Freiburg im Breisgau, 1968), 336.

37. This was their "green program." Holzer, "Polish Political Parties," 200.

38. Andrzej Garlicki, *Z dziejów Drugiej Rzeczypospolitej* (Warsaw, 1986), 244; Elżbieta Janicka, *Sztuka czy naród? Monografia pisarska Andrzeja Trzebińskiego* (Kraków, 2006), 36–38; Włodzimierz Borodziej, *Geschichte Polens im 20. Jahrhundert* (Munich, 2010), 176.

39. Borjesza, "East European Perceptions," 355.

40. The article is in *Przegląd Wszechpolski*, May 1926, 396, and is cited in Krzysztof Kawalec, "Narodowa Demokracja wobec przewrotu majowego," in Z. Karpus et al., *Zamach Stanu*, 159.

41. Borejsza, "East European Perceptions," 355.

42. BBWR dissolved in late 1935. Borodziej, *Geschichte*, 183; Holzer, "Polish Political Parties," 203.

43. A program for emigration was worked out in the Ministry of Foreign Affairs. Jolanta Żyndul, *Zajścia antyżydowskie w Polsce w latach 1935–1937* (Warsaw, 1994), 87.

44. Holzer, "Polish Political Parties," 203–205.

45. Borodziej, *Geschichte*, 179–180. For the text of Hlond's 1936 pastoral letter, see Ronald Modras, *The Catholic Church and Antisemitism: Poland, 1933–1939* (Chur, Switzerland, 1994), 346. He said it is good to avoid Jewish stores and stalls, to love one's own nation more; that the "Jewish problem" will continue as long as Jews remain Jews.

46. If in 1921 most Polish parties rejected anti-Semitism, by 1939 a majority openly endorsed it. Holzer, "Polish Political Parties," 205.

47. Andrzej Micewski, *Polityka staje się historią* (Warsaw, 1986), 114.

48. Andrzej Friszke, *Adam Ciołkosz : portret polskiego socjalisty* (Warsaw, 2011), 161–165. Czeslaw Brzoza, *Kraków miedzy wojnami* (Kraków, 1998), 319; Stanisław Piech, *W cieniu kościołów i synagog: życie religijne międzywojennego Krakowa 1918–1939* (Kraków, 1999), 136.

49. Włodzimierz Kalicki, "29 czerwca 1936 r.: General zmyka przed ludem," *Gazeta Wyborcza*, July 2, 2010; Zbigniew Moszumański, "Historia mało znana : Nowosielce 1936," *Gazeta : Dziennik Polonii w Kanadzie*, December 1, 2006. Śmigły-Rydz is a controversial figure; he died in the underground conspiracy in 1941 after returning to Poland in secret, but was himself was a supporter of OZON, which brought Poland closer to fascism, and he orchestrated the taking of Těšín from Czechoslovakia in 1938.

50. Stephanie Zloch, *Polnischer Nationalismus: Politik und Gesellschaft zwischen den beiden Weltkriegen* (Cologne, 2010), 437; Andrzej Garlicki, *Piękne lata trzydzieste* (Warsaw, 2008).

51. With 500 getting prison sentences: Micewski, *Polityka*, 115. Polonsky, "Establishment," 195.

52. Emanuel Melzer, *No Way Out: The Politics of Polish Jewry, 1935–1939* (Cincinnati, OH, 1997), 98; Michael Marrus, ed., *The Nazi Holocaust*, Part Five: *Public Opinion and Relations to the Jews in Nazi Europe* (Westport, CT, 1989), 263; Polonsky, "Establishment," 198.

53. Serb Democrats were the major Serb party in former Habsburg areas. Rothschild, *East Central Europe*, 258.

54. Rothschild, *East Central Europe*, 202, 238; Holm Sundhaussen, *Geschichte Serbiens* (Vienna, 2007), 266.

55. Of 909 senior permanent functionaries in the Yugoslav government (ministries of interior, foreign affairs, education, justice, transportation, the state mortgage bank, and the office of the premier), 813 were Serbs. Rothschild, *East Central Europe*, 278–279.

56. Sundhaussen, *Geschichte*, 267; Tihomir Cipek, "Die kroatischen Eliten und die Königsdiktatur in Jugoslawien," in *Autoritäre Regime in Ostmittel- und Südosteuropa*, Erwin Oberländer, ed. (Paderborn, Germany, 2017), 547. Other victims of assassination were the Croatian Peasant Party politician Josip Predavec and historian Ivo Pilar. Branimir Anzulović, *Heavenly Serbia: From Myth to Genocide* (New York, 1999), 199. See the coverage in the *New York Times*, February 20, 21, 1931; *The Nation* 132 (1931), 544; *The New Outlook* 158 (1931), 72; and *Current History* 34 (1931), 468.

57. The Serb Svetovar Pribićević, a founder of the state from former Habsburg areas, was arrested in 1929, but then permitted to emigrate after intervention by T. G. Masaryk. Sundhaussen, *Geschichte*, 266.

58. In January 1929.

59. Alex N. Dragnich, *The First Yugoslavia* (Stanford, CA, 1983), 103.

60. Jovan Byford, "Willing Bystanders: Dimitrije Ljotić, Shield Collaboration, and the Destruction of Serbia's Jews," in *In the Shadow of Hitler: Personalities of the Right in Central and Eastern Europe*, Rebecca Haynes and Martyn Rady, eds. (London, 2011), 297–298. Integral nationalism was the idea that pursuit of a nation's interests, with violence if necessary, was an end in itself. Louis Snyder, *The New Nationalism* (Ithaca, NY, 1968), 52.

61. Supporters were mostly from German areas and tended to be doctors, lawyers, judges, civil servants, teachers, traders, students, priests, and army officers. Byford, "Willing Bystanders," 297, 299.

62. Avakumović, "Yugoslavia's Fascist Movements," in Sugar, *Native Fascism*; Byford, "Willing Bystanders," 299. He and his followers did intervene with Nazi authorities to reduce retaliation against ethnic Serbs. However, they showed no concern for getting the release of Jews. Byford, "Willing Bystanders," 305–306.

63. Rothschild, *East Central Europe*, 254; Dejan Djokić, "'Leader' or 'Devil'? Milan Stojadinović, Prime Minister of Yugoslavia (1935–39), and His Ideology," in Haynes and Rady, *Shadow of Hitler*, 153; Avakumović, "Yugoslavia's Fascist Movements," 136.

64. Djokić, "'Leader' or 'Devil'?," 157.

65. John Lampe, *Yugoslavia as History: Twice There Was a Country* (Cambridge, 1996), 182.

66. Paul was worried about Stojadinović's dictatorial measures. Hoptner, *Yugoslavia*, 128.

67. Marcus Tanner, *Croatia: A Nation Forged in War* (New Haven, CT, 1997), 130. Nineteen percent of the population was Orthodox, 3.8 percent Muslim. Veljko Vujačić, *Nationalism, Myth and the State in Russia and Serbia* (New York, 2015), 209.

68. For a description of this terror in Dalmatia, see Hugh Seton-Watson, *Eastern Europe between the Wars* (Hamden, CT, 1962), 236.

69. "So much for the notion that irreconcilable antagonisms had closed off all options for Serb-Croat reconciliation." Lampe, *Yugoslavia*, 180.

70. It had achieved only 0.1 percent of the vote in the 1925 Yugoslav elections. *Statistika izbora narodnih poslanika Kraljevine SHS održanih 8. februara 1925* (Belgrade, 1925).

71. Rothschild, *East Central Europe*, 246.

72. R. J. Crampton, *A Concise History of Bulgaria* (Cambridge, 1997), 158–159.

73. Barbara Jelavich, *History of the Balkans*, vol. 2 (Cambridge, 1983), 207–208. *Zveno* was formed in 1927 and included some Social Democrats and some military people. Chary, *History of Bulgaria*, 76–77.

74. Chary, *History of Bulgaria*, 77. This was the edition of May 28, 1934.

75. Its orientation was liberal. Alexander Velinov, "*Religiöse Identität im Zeitalter des Nationalismus*," (Phd dissertation, Cologne, 2001), 133.

76. Jelavich, *History*, vol. 2, 208; Chary, *History of Bulgaria*, 77, 87–89.

77. The military government was in place from May 1934 to January 1935.

78. Chary, *History of Bulgaria*, 81, 89.

79. Mary Neuburger, *Balkan Smoke: Tobacco and the Making of Modern Bulgaria* (Ithaca, NY, 2013), 131–132.

80. Mobilization is an outcome of modernization; because when they gain "rudimentary skills of social communication," people "become available for sustained, systematic, and organized political action." Janos, *East Central Europe*, 140.

81. See Armin Heinen, "Die Notwendigkeit einer gesamteuropäischen Perspektive auf den südosteuropäischen Faschismus," *East Central Europe* 37 (2010), 367–371.

82. Ian Kershaw, "Working toward the Führer: Reflections on the Nature of the Hitler Dictatorship," *Contemporary European History* 2:2 (1993), 103–118.

Chapter 16: Hitler's War and Its East European Enemies

1. W. D. Smith, "Friedrich Ratzel and the Origins of Lebensraum," *German Studies Review* 3:1 (1980), 51–68; Gerhard Weinberg, *The Foreign Policy of Hitler's Germany*, vol. 1 (Chicago, 1970); Ian Kershaw, *Hitler*, vol. 1 (New York, 1998), 247–249.

2. This was the communal election of May 1938. Piotr M. Majewski, *Sudetští Němci1848–1949: Dějiny jednoho nacionalismu* (Brno, 2014), 356; Jörg Osterloh, *Nationalsozialistische Judenverfolgung im Reichsgau Sudetenland 1938–1945* (Munich, 2006), 150.

3. For this argument, as well as details on German grievances about language use in Czechoslovakia, see Maria Dowling, *Czechoslovakia* (London, 2002), 47-49; on the Nazi propaganda campaign against Czechoslovakia aiming at audiences in and beyond Germany, see Katja Gesche, *Kultur als Instrument der Aussenpolitik totalitärer Staaten: Das Deutsche Ausland-Institut 1933-1945* (Vienna, 2006), 110-112. For an eloquent argument about the power of nationalists to stimulate national feeling, see Pieter Judson, *Guardians of the Nation* (Cambridge, MA, 2006).

4. Igor Lukes, *Czechoslovakia between Stalin and Hitler: The Diplomacy of Edvard Beneš in the 1930s* (Oxford, 1996), 82–83. On at least two occasions, Lord Halifax said no one in London expected that the "world could stay as it is forever."

5. See https://www.gettyimages.com/detail/video/news-footage/mr_00011324 (accessed January 1, 2019).

6. Petr Bednařík, "Antisemitismus v českém tisku v období druhé republiky," in *Židé v Čechách*, V. Hamáčková et al., eds. (Prague, 2007), 32–45; Zacek, "Czechoslovak Fascisms," 61. Hitler's threat was made to the new foreign minister František Chvalkovský. Theodor Prochazka, "The Second Republic," in Mamatey and Luža, eds., *History*, 263–264.

7. Jaroslav Čechura, *Historie českých spiknutí* (Prague, 2000), 156; Livia Rothkirchen, "The Protectorate Government and the 'Jewish Question,'" *Yad Vashem Studies* 27 (1999), 331–362.

8. Vojtěch Mastný, *The Czechs under Nazi Rule: The Failure of National Resistance* (New York, 1970); Chad Bryant, *Prague in Black: Nazi Rule and Czech Nationalism* (Cambridge, MA, 2007). Of the students arrested, 1,185 were sent to Sachsenhausen, and nine were shot. John Connelly, *Captive University: The Sovietization of East German, Czech, and Polish Higher Education* (Chapel Hill, NC, 2001), 84.

9. Leni Yahil, *The Holocaust: The Fate of European Jewry, 1932–1945* (Oxford, 1990), 354.

10. *Ilustrowana Republika* (Łódź), June 14, 1934; Stefan Martens, *Hermann Göring; erster Paladin des Führers* (Paderborn, 1985), 60–61. The two countries also involved themselves in an intensive cultural exchange, for example, via the German-Poland Institute in Berlin. Karina Pryt, *Befohlene Freundschaft: die deutsch-polnischen Kulturbeziehungen, 1934–1939* (Osnabrück, Germany, 2010). On Poland's foreign policy in the 1930s, see Henry L. Roberts, *Eastern Europe: Politics, Revolution, and Diplomacy* (New York, 1970), 138–177.

11. Ian Kershaw, *Hitler*, vol. 2 (New York, 2000), 155.

12. That number is from Gerd Ueberschär, *Wojskowe elity III Rzeszy* (Warsaw, 2004), 41. Also: Alexander Rossini, *Hitler Strikes Poland* (Lawrence, KS, 2004).

13. In the west, the Nazis created the district *Wartheland*, which consisted entirely of Polish territory, as well as Danzig West Prussia, some of which had belonged to German East Prussia. Added to Upper Silesia was Katowice.

14. The "Pacification Action" (*Befriedungsaktion*) involved about 60,000 victims, some of whom were drawn from the GG. The number shot in the annexed areas was about 16,000. Some 400,000 Poles were deported to the GG. Andrzej Paczkowski, *Pół wieku dziejów Polski: 1939–1989* (Warsaw, 1996), 31–32; Phillip T. Rutherford, *Prelude to the Final Solution* (Lawrence, KS, 2007), 42–43; Rossini, *Hitler Strikes*, 58 ff.

15. Peter Longerich, *Heinrich Himmer: A Life*, Jeremy Noakes and Lesley Sharpe, trans. (Oxford, 2012), 451, 456–457; Paczkowski, *Pół wieku*, 35.

16. Paczkowski, *Pół wieku*, 34. On German women who worked in the GG administration, see Elizabeth Harvey, *Women and the Nazi East: Agents and Witnesses of Germanization* (New Haven, CT, 2003).

17. Norman M. Naimark, *Stalin's Genocides* (Princeton, NJ, 2011), 90–92; Timothy Snyder, *Bloodlands: Europe between Hitler and Stalin* (New York, 2011), 149–151.

18. Estimates of the deported range from 320,000 to 350,000. The first transport contained 139,794 people, of whom 15,000 died. Snyder, *Bloodlands*, 129; Aleksander Wat, *My Century: The Odyssey of a Polish Intellectual*, transl. Richard Lourie (Berkeley, 1988), 104.

19. Stanisław Ciesielski, Wojciech Materski, and Andrzej Paczkowski, *Represje sowieckie wobec Polaków i obywateli polskich* (Warsaw, 2002).

20. Mark Mazower, *Hitler's Empire: How the Nazis Ruled Europe* (New York, 2008), 214. The difficulties in finding Germans to settle vast areas of Eastern Europe were evident to SS planners, however. John Connelly, "Nazis and Slavs," *Central European History* 32:1 (1999), 29–30.

21. Alexander Werth, "Russland im Krieg," *Der Spiegel*, July 7, 1965.

22. Helmut Greiner, ed., *Kriegstagebuch des Oberkommandos der Wehrmacht*, vol. 1 (Frankfurt, 1965), 176.

23. Britain had made guarantees to Greece after Mussolini's occupation of Albania in the spring of 1939; Peter Calvocoressi and Guy Wint, *Total War: Causes and Consequences of the Second World*

War (London, 1972), 84. Eager to please Germany, Romania and Hungary in fact vied for who would be first to sign. C. A. Macartney, *Hungary* (New York, 1956), 230.

24. Igor-Philip Matic, *Edmund Veesenmayer. Agent und Diplomat der nationalsozialistischen Expansionspolitik* (Munich, 2002), 125ff; Hoptner, *Yugoslavia*, 241.

25. That had been the German hope for some years. See Martin Van Crefeld, *Hitler's Strategy 1940–41: The Balkan Clue* (Cambridge, 1973), 7.

26. Hoptner, *Yugoslavia*, 236

27. Hoptner, *Yugoslavia*, 255.

28. Aleksa Djilas, *Contested Country: Yugoslav Unity and Communist Revolution: 1919–1953* (Cambridge, MA, 1991), 137; Hoptner, *Yugoslavia*, 259.

29. Jozo Tomasevich, *The Chetniks* (Stanford, CA, 1975), 45.

30. Germany, Auswärtiges Amt, *Documents on German Foreign Policy* (Washington, DC, 1962) Series D, vol. 12, docs. 219, 383; Hoptner, *Yugoslavia*, 258–259; Branko Petranović, *Srbija u Drugom svetskom ratu, 1939–1945* (Belgrade, 1992), 94ff.

31. Germany, Auswärtiges Amt, *Documents on German Foreign Policy*, vol. 12, docs. 217, 373.

32. Tomasevich, *Chetniks*, 87; Germany, Auswärtiges Amt, *Documents on German Foreign Policy*, vol. 12, docs. 217, 373.

33. The civilian casualties in Belgrade from the bombings of April 6 and April 7 amounted to about 2,300. Lampe, *Yugoslavia*, 199–200.

34. Djilas, *Contested Country*, 140; Arnold Suppan, *Hitler, Beneš, Tito: Konflikt, Krieg, und Völkermord in Ostmittel- und Südosteuropa* (Vienna, 2014), 939; Ladislaus Hory and Martin Broszat, *Der kroatische Ustascha-Staat* (Stuttgart, 1964), 52–53; Tomasevich, *Chetniks*, 109. Nedić called his regime the Government of National Salvation. It was permeated by members of the Chetnik movement.

35. Djilas, *Contested Country*, 137. For an internal analysis of the Croatian regular armed forces, the "Home Guard," (Domobran), and their members' self-defense against allegations of being servants or opportunists, see Nikica Barić, "Domobranstvo Nezavisne Države Hrvatske," in *Nezavisne Države Hrvatske 1941–1945*, Sabrina P. Ramet, ed. (Zagreb, 2009), 67–86. Supposedly only Germany was willing to guarantee Croatian independence and its "place in the sun."

36. For an argument that the Germans' unrestrained terror gave Poles little reason to abstain from resistance, see Jan T. Gross, *Polish Society under German Occupation: The Generalgouvernement* (Princeton, NJ, 1978).

37. Alexander Prusin, *Serbia under the Swastika: A World War II Occupation* (Champaign, IL, 2017), 97; Tim Judah, *The Serbs: History, Myth, and the Destruction of Yugoslavia* (New Haven, CT, 1997), 101; Mark Cornwall, "Introduction," in Andrej Mitrovic, *Serbia's Great War* (West Lafayette, IN, 2007), vii.

38. The Serb population on the territory of the Independent State of Croatia was 1.9 of 6.3 million. Noel Malcolm, *Bosnia: A Short History* (New York, 1994), 176. The unwritten plan was indeed to convert one-third of the Serbs, expel another third, and kill the remainder. Ivo Goldstein, *Croatia: A History* (London, 1999), 137. The number murdered comes from the US Holocaust Memorial Museum: http://www.ushmm.org/wlc/en/article.php?ModuleId=10005449. The conversion number is in Stevan K. Pavlowitch, *Hitler's New Disorder: The Second World War in Yugoslavia* (New York, 2008), 135–36.

39. Slavko Goldstein, *1941: The Year That Keeps Returning* (New York, 2013), 88.

40. Goldstein, *1941*, 177.

41. "Virtually nothing is left of the enthusiasm of the Croatian people that greeted our army," a German intelligence officer wrote; "deep distrust of Germany reigns in this country because it is supporting a regime that has no right to exist in either a moral or a political sense." "This was not the independent Croatia we imagined" is a common refrain of recollections written by Croats after the war. Goldstein, *1941*, 178.

42. For the number 700: Tanner, *Croatia*; Jozo Tomasevich, *War and Revolution in Yugoslavia* (Stanford, CA, 2001), 337. The Ustashas thought they had about 40,000 sympathizers.

43. The recourse to race was also urgent, because other Europeans saw Croats not as state builders but rather as a regional group destined to disappear into the larger whole of Yugoslavia. See John Connelly, "Language and Blood," *The Nation*, September 9, 2014.

44. Stevan K. Pavlowitch, *Hitler's New Disorder: The Second World War in Yugoslavia* (New York, 2008), 133.

45. This "Handschar Division" ultimately numbered some 21,000 troops and was composed in large part of men forcibly transferred from other NDH units. Parts of the Muslim elite initially thought the unit could be used to achieve their own national goals, but they were disappointed when the soldiers were trained outside Bosnia-Herzegovina and could not defend Muslim villages. Some members of the division mutinied when deployed to southern France; others were deployed under German orders on Yugoslav territory (from February 1944), engaging in atrocities against Serbs. Late in the war some defected to the Partisans, along with other NDH units. Emily Greble, *Sarajevo 1941–1945. Muslims, Christians, and Jews in Hitler's Europe* (Ithaca, NY, 2011), 149–178; Marko Attila Hoare, *Bosnian Muslims in the Second World War* (Oxford, 2014), 53–54, 117, 194. On Ustasha ideas about race, see Nevenko Bartulin, *The Racial Idea in the Independent State of Croatia* (Leiden, 2014).

46. These "cleansing actions" were justified by "aggressive actions of the Moslems who had attacked Serbian villages and killed Serbian people." Tomasevich, *Chetniks*, 258. Noel Malcolm gives the number of 8,000 elderly people, women, and children massacred in August 1942 under the leadership of Zaharija Ostojić, a top Chetnik commander. Malcolm, *Bosnia*, 188.

47. Malcolm, *Bosnia*, 178; Vujačić, *Nationalism*, 221.

48. Some observers argue for an important distinction between Ustasha policies of extermination versus Chetnik reprisals. Vujačić, *Nationalism*, 218–220.

49. There were four more cities with populations of more than 50,000. Rothschild, *East Central Europe*, 204.

50. Rothschild, *East Central Europe*, 213.

51. The number of women is estimated at 100,000, about one-sixth of the full strength. Jelena Batinić, *Women and Yugoslav Partisans: A History of World War II Resistance* (Cambridge, 2015), 2. The Partisans did have strong early support in eastern Bosnia, but had to flee Foča in March 1942 to evade the joint German-Italian offensive "Operation Trio." Kenneth Morrison, *Nationalism, Identity and Statehood in Post-Yugoslav Montenegro* (London, 2018), 15.

52. Official Communist Yugoslav historiography acted as though there had been no contacts at all between the Partisans and Germans, but at least one high-ranking delegation, including Milovan Djilas, did treat with German officials (in 1943), mainly to arrange a prisoner exchange. See Milovan Djilas, *Wartime* (New York, 1980), 229–245; Walter R. Roberts, *Tito, Mihailović, and*

the Allies, 1941–1945 (New Brunswick, NJ, 1973), 106–113. The latter cites German documents according to which the Partisans proposed a cease-fire with Germany in order to focus on the Chetniks, an idea supported by German authorities in Croatia but ultimately rebuffed by the foreign ministry in Berlin.

53. That was half the total cadre of doctors. F. W. D. Deakin, *The Embattled Mountain* (London, 1971), 38, 42, 50.

54. For example, Italians during the fifth offensive. Djilas, *Wartime*, 268.

55. Djilas, *Wartime*, 340, 355. The movement highjacked the word "people," and villagers or townspeople were not told that Communists were behind the actions. Franklin Lindsay, *Beacons in the Night: With the OSS and Tito's Partisans in Wartime Yugoslavia* (Stanford, CA, 1993), 110.

56. Vujačić, *Nationalism*, 228; Djilas, *Wartime*, 321.

57. Djilas, *Wartime*, 165–166.

58. "Those few days I spent with them reassured me that the legendary Montenegrin heroism still lived." Djilas, *Wartime*, 170; Vujačić, *Nationalism*, 224.

59. "For a private, the transfer from one side to the another is far simpler than the ideologized mind can comprehend." Djilas, *Wartime*, 251, 305.

60. Progress was slower in ethnically solid Croatia, though people there did not accept the Ustasha regime either. Djilas, *Wartime*, 310–313, 323.

61. As described by Timothy Snyder, *Black Earth: The Holocaust as History and Warning* (New York, 2015), 47; Deakin, *Embattled*, 80.

62. Paczkowski, *Pół wieku*, 84; Norman Davies, *Rising '44: The Battle for Warsaw* (London, 2003), 183. In total, the Communist People's Army had about 20,000 fighters in the spring of 1944, whereas the AK had some 400,000.

63. Piotr Stachiewicz, *"Akcja Koppe" : Krakowska akcja Parasola"* (Warsaw, 1982); Paczkowski, *Pół wieku*, 89.

64. Some 110,000 Poles were removed from the region (the plans called for removal of 408,000); between 9,000 and 12,000 Germans were settled. Włodzimierz Borodziej, *Der Warschauer Aufstand* (Frankurt, 2001), 64; Joseph Poprzeczny, *Odilo Globocnik: Hitler's Man in the East* (London, 2004), 190, 251. Some 30,000 children were taken from their parents; an estimated 10,000 did not survive. Agnieszka Jaczyńska, *Sonderlaboratorium SS Zamojszczyzna* (Lublin, 2012); Werner Röhr, "Speerspitze der Volkstumspolitik," *Junge Welt*, November 28, 2002.

65. Borodziej, *Geschichte*, 233. The departments included those for foreign policy, planning for postwar, and social services. "Secret state" was a phrase used by the underground courier Jan Karski. See his *The Secret State* (New York, 1944).

66. Krystyna Kersten, *The Establishment of Communist Rule in Poland*, John Micgiel and Michael Bernhard, trans. (Berkeley, 1991), 50–51.

67. This was part of "Operation Storm." Poles managed to send up a Polish flag at the castle, which was then taken down and replaced by a red flag.

68. Borodziej, *Warschauer Aufstand*, 120–123.

69. Paczkowski, *Pół wieku*, 90.

70. Borodziej, *Geschichte*, 234.

71. Twelve percent was booked as lost in transfer. Borodziej, *Geschichte*, 233.

72. Borodziej, *Geschichte*, 234, "explicable only by the constant threats to which Poles were subject."

73. Paczkowski, *Pół wieku*, 92.

74. Kilian Kirchgessner, "Ende des Verdrängens," *Jüdische Allgemeine*, January 26, 2017.

75. This is the distinction made by Raul Hilberg, *The Destruction of the European Jews* (Chicago, 1961), 474. For further sources on Nazi-instigated killing policies in Eastern Europe, see Peter Longerich, *Holocaust: The Nazi Persecution and Murder of the Jews* (Oxford, 2010), 313ff; Mazower, *Hitler's Empire*, 368ff; Saul Friedländer, *The Years of Extermination* (New York, 2007).

Chapter 17: What Dante Did Not See: The Holocaust in Eastern Europe

1. John Connelly, "Nazis and Slavs," *Central European History* 32:1 (1999), 1–33. For a contrasting approach: Jerzy W. Borejsza, "Racisme et antislavisme chez Hitler," in *La politique nazie d'extermination*, François Bédarida, ed. (Paris, 1989), 57–84; Jerzy W. Borejsza, *Antyslawizm Adolfa Hitlera* (Warsaw, 1988).

2. An exception was Kraków because the Soviet offensive of January 1945 happened so rapidly that German forces did not have time to destroy the city. World War II cost the lives of some 6 million Polish citizens, of these, about 3 million were Jews.

3. The major exception was the decision in 1943 to spare the lives of Jewish men who had married "Aryan" women, after hundreds of those women staged a public protest. See Nathan Stolzfus, *Resistance of the Heart* (New York, 1996).

4. John Lukacs, *The Hitler of History* (New York, 1997), 123; Saul Friedländer, *Nazi Germany and the Jews*, vol. 1 (New York, 1997), 95–104; Eberhard Jäckel, *Hitler's World View* (Cambridge, MA, 1981), 47–66; Gerhard Weinberg, *The Foreign Policy of Hitler's Germany* (Chicago, 1970), 1–25.

5. Hilberg, *Destruction*, 32 and passim.

6. Jean Ancel, "The German Romanian Relationship and the Final Solution," *Holocaust and Genocide Studies* 19:1 (2005), 252.

7. Pavelić's deputy Dido Kvaternik doubted as early as July 1941 whether Germany would win the war and became all the more determined to create facts on the ground that could not be nullified. Tomasevich, *War and Revolution*, 408.

8. Hannah Arendt, *Elemente und Ursprünge totalitärer Herrschaft* (Munich, 2006), 624.

9. Janina Bauman, *Winter in the Morning: A Young Girl's Life in the Warsaw Ghetto and Beyond* (New York, 1986).

10. The total deaths in the ghettos has been estimated at half a million. Longerich, *Holocaust*, 160–161, 167; Friedländer, *Years of Extermination*, 38; Alon Confino, *A World without Jews: The Nazi Imagination from Persecution to Genocide* (New Haven, CT, 2014), 167.

11. Christopher Browning with contributions by Jürgen Matthäus, *The Origins of the Final Solution: The Evolution of Nazi Jewish Policy, September 1939–March 1942* (Lincoln, NE, 2004); Paul Hanebrink, *A Spectre Haunting Europe: The Myth of Judeo-Bolshevism* (Cambridge, MA, 2018).

12. Jan T. Gross, *Neighbors: The Destruction of the Jewish Community in Jedwabne, Poland* (Princeton, NJ, 2000); Dieter Pohl, *Nationalsozialistische Judenverfolgung in Ostgalizien 1941–1944: Organisation und Durchführung eines staatlichen Massenverbrechens* (Munich, 1997). In more than twenty other places, Polish populations joined in the killing, encouraged but not forced by the Germans. K. Persak and P. Machcewicz, eds., *Wokół Jedwabnego* (Warsaw, 2002). The SS General Walter Stahlecker had issued a directive to initiate "self-cleansing operations" to make it seem that

that local populations were doing the killing of their "own initiative, without German orders becoming visibile." *Trial of the Major War Criminals before the International Military Tribunal*, vol. 37 (Nuremberg, 1949), 682.

13. In the days that followed, SS mobile killing units aided by Ukrainian militia executed an estimated 4,000 more Jews. Hannes Heer, "Blutige Ouvertüre. Lemberg, 30. Juni 1941: Mit dem Einmarsch der Wehrmachttruppen beginnt der Judenmord," *Die Zeit*, June 21, 2001, 90.

14. Longerich, *Holocaust*, 255.

15. Reviel Netz, *Barbed Wire: An Ecology of Modernity* (Middletown, CT, 2004), 225. Only Majdanek and Auschwitz used Zyklon B; the other camps used carbon monoxide gas. The Nazis used one further camp at Chełmno in annexed Polish territory (Warthegau) from late 1941 to kill Jews from Łódź, through transport in "gas vans." Longerich, *Holocaust*, 290.

16. Christopher Browning, cited in Inga Clendinnen, *Reading the Holocaust* (Cambridge, 1998), 131.

17. Zygmunt Klukowski, *Diary from the Years of Occupation*, George Klukowski, trans. (Urbana, IL, 1993), 195–196.

18. The survivors are estimated at 50,000–60,000. Numbers are from Barbara Engelking, cited in Jarosław Kurski, "Życie w polskich rękach," *Gazeta Wyborcza*, January 9, 2011. "Hunting" was the word used at the time: Judenjagd. See Jan Grabowski, *Hunt for the Jews* (Bloomington, IN, 2013). See also Barbara Engelking, *Jest taki piękny słoneczny dzień: losy Zydow szukających ratunku na wsi polskiej* (Warsaw, 2011).

19. Some of their neighbors then proceeded to murder the twenty-four Jews they had been sheltering. Grabowski, *Hunt*, 152–153.

20. A major voice in promoting new questions and perspectives is Jan T. Gross. For the line of reasoning cited here, see his "A Tangled Web: Confronting Stereotypes Concerning Relations between Poles, Germans, Jews, and Communists," in *The Politics of Retribution in Europe*, István Deák, Jan T. Gross, Tony Judt., eds., (Princeton, NJ, 2000), 80–87. For the case cited here, see Joanna Beata Michlic, *Poland's Threatening Other: The Image of the Jew from 1880 to the Present* (Lincoln, NE, 2006), 190. The man is Emanuel Tanay, and his recollection is in Marian Turski, ed., *Losy żydowskie : świadectwo żywych* (Warsaw, 1996–1999), 66.

21. Bauman, *Winter in the Morning*, 141.

22. Gross, *Neighbors*, 161.

23. Thus the memoir of the Slovak Jew Jozef Lánik, *Co Dante neviděl* [What Dante Did Not See] (Bratislava, 1964).

24. This was Eli Goldsztejn. Barbara Engelking et al., eds., *Sny chociaż mamy wspaniale: okupacyjne dzienniki z okolic Mińska Mazowieckiego* (Warsaw, 2016).

25. Some of these articles include: Stanislav Nikolau, "Židovská otázka," *Národní Politika*, November 20, 1938; Dr. Karel Strejček, "Nove Úkoly, Odstraňovat Kazy," *Venkov*, December 22, 1938; Jaroslav Arnošt Trpák, "Evropě asi nezbude než vytvořit svaz států na ochranu proti židovstvu," *Večer*, December 28, 1938; Miloš Krejza: "Udělejme si pořádek!" *Lidové listy*, October 12, 1938. Other authors include: Václav Kubásek, Rudolf Halik, Antonin Pimper, and Dr. Vladimir Mandel. On the British promises of aid: Miroslav Kárný, *Konečné řešení: Genocida českých židů v německé protektorátní politice* (Prague, 1991), 22–24. On the poisonous atmosphere for Jews among the Czech political elites coming to terms with Munich: Livia Rothkirchen, *The Jews of Bohemia and Moravia: Facing the Holocaust* (Lincoln, NE, 2005),

83–85; Wolf Gruner, *Die Judenverfolgung im Protektorat Böhmen und Mähren* (Göttingen, 2016), 23–33.

26. Jan Láníček, *Czechs, Slovaks, and the Jews* (London, 2013), 28. On personal attacks on Jewish writers, actors, and intellectuals in late 1938, see Rothkirchen, *The Jews*, 90.

27. Kárný, *Konečné řešení*, 26–33.

28. Kárný, *Konečné řešení*, 12; Jan Gebhart and Jan Kuklík, *Velké dějiny zemí Koruny české*, vol. 15 (Prague, 2007), 198.

29. Láníček, *Czechs*, 30.

30. Called the Zentralstelle für jüdische Auswanderung [Central Office for Jewish Emigration].

31. James Mace Ward, *Priest, Politician, Collaborator: Jozef Tiso and the Making of Fascist Slovakia* (Ithaca, NY, 2013).

32. Jean-Marc Drefes and Eduard Nižňanský, "Aryanization: France and the Slovak State," in *Facing the Catastrophe: Jews and Non-Jews in Europe during WWII*, Beata Kosmala et al., eds. (Oxford, 2011), 20–21.

33. Christian Gerlach, *The Extermination of the European Jews* (Cambridge, 2016), 94; Longerich, *Holocaust*, 294.

34. Gerlach, *Extermination*, 94; Ivan Kamenec, "The Slovak State, 1939–1945," in *Slovakia in History*, Mikuláš Teich et al., eds. (Cambridge, 2011), 188–191.

35. Longerich, *Holocaust*, 365; Ivo Goldstain and Slavko Goldstain, *The Holocaust in Croatia* (Pittsburgh, PA, 2016).

36. Longerich, *Holocaust*, 300–301; Lucy Dawidowicz, *The War Against the Jews: 1933–1945* (New York, 1975), 392.

37. Hilberg, *Destruction*, 32 and passim.

38. Frederick B. Chary, *The History of Bulgaria* (Santa Barbara, CA, 2011), 83–84. The imports to Bulgaria from Germany went from 25.9 (1932) to 65.5 percent (1939).

39. The Balkan Entente was signed in 1934 by Greece, Turkey, Romania, and Yugoslavia, and it aimed to preserve the territorial status quo. In July 1938, the Entente agreed to permit Bulgaria to rearm, in contradiction of the Treaty of Neuilly-sur-Seine. Dennis P. Hupchick, *The Balkans: From Constantinople to Communism* (New York 2002), 349.

40. Crampton, *Concise History*, 169.

41. In Germany, the rule was that one Jewish grandparent made one a "Mischling" [hybrid] of the second degree, and two a "Mischling" of the first degree, with corresponding limits on one's rights. Karl A. Schleunes, *The Twisted Road to Auschwitz: Nazi Policy toward German Jews* (Urbana, IL, 1990), 128–130; Hilberg, *Destruction*, 476; James Frusetta, "The Final Solution in Southeastern Europe: Between Nazi Catalysts and Local Motivations," in *The Routledge History of the Holocaust*, Jonathan C. Friedman, ed. (New York, 2011), 271; Crampton, *Concise History*, 170.

42. As the Ministry of Finance explained, Jews owed a debt to Bulgaria for "over sixty years of exploitation." It amounted to 20 percent on property worth more than 200,000 leva ($2,430), 25 percent on that worth more than three million. Frederick B. Chary, *The Bulgarian Jews and the Final Solution, 1940–1944* (Pittsburgh, PA, 1972), 43.

43. Jews were now barred from the armed forces but could wear regular Bulgarian uniforms in these battalions until German observers complained. Restrictions were also introduced on the rights of the Roma population. Hilberg, *Destruction*, 478.

44. Crampton, *Concise History*, 171.

45. Hilberg, *Destruction*, 480; Frusetta, "Final Solution," 271.

46. "It was a decision which was to cost most of those Jews their lives." Crampton, *Concise History*, 176. In June 1942, an ordinance went into effect for acquiring citizenship in new provinces that was inapplicable to Jews. Hilberg, *Destruction*, 482.

47. Chary, *Bulgarian Jews*, 51.

48. "It was vital to them that the back door be open and the escape route be clear. They wanted . . . to play the game in such a way that there was chance of gain but no risk of loss." Hilberg, *Destruction*, 474–475.

49. He initially agreed that fifteen Bulgarian pilots trained in Germany could serve for Germany, but only in North Africa. But soon that permission was revoked. Crampton, *Concise History*, 175; Marshall Lee Miller, *Bulgaria during Second World War* (Stanford, CA, 1975), 73.

50. By October 1942, only 20 percent of Bulgarian Jews had been given stars, the smallest number in Eastern Europe. Neuburger, *Balkan Smoke*, 149; Hilberg, *Destruction*, 478, 482.

51. This involved some 20,000 Jews who would live with Jewish families in the countryside. Hilberg, *Destruction*, 483–484.

52. Chary, *History of Bulgaria*, 145–148. As a result of this intervention, a communication reached the rabbi from Boris that Jews would not be sent outside the borders of Bulgaria. When Jews learned of plans to expel them from Sofia, they assumed that this might mean deportation beyond the country's borders.

53. Tzvetan Todorov, *The Fragility of Goodness: Why Bulgaria's Jews Survived the Holocaust* (Princeton, NJ, 2001), 104–105.

54. Two nations would be victors in his view: the United States and the Soviet Union. Chary, *Bulgarian Jews*, 46.

55. Chary, *Bulgarian Jews*, 139–140, 158; Hilberg, *Destruction*, 484.

56. In June it lost Bessarabia and north Bukovina; in August/September, north Transylvania and south Dobrudja.

57. September 6, 1940 to January 23, 1941. Antonescu was named prime minister two days before Carol's abdication.

58. International Commission on the Holocaust in Romania (Wiesel Commission), *Final Report* (Bucharest, 2004), 114.

59. June 27. International Commission, *Final Report*, 121.

60. Hilberg, *Destruction*, 491; International Commission, *Final Report*, 124, 126; Christopher Browning, *The Origins of the Final Solution: The Evolution of Nazi Policy*, with contributions by Jürgen Matthäus (Lincoln, NE, 2004), 276–277; Edward Zuckerman, "God Was on Vacation," *New York Times*, October 4, 2018.

61. From his order to Colonel Constantin Lupu, June 27, 1941: "The evacuation of the Jewish population from Iaşi is essential, and shall be carried out in full, including women and children." International Commission, *Final Report*, 121.

62. Browning, *Origins*, 277; International Commission, *Final Report*, 122.

63. Victoria Gruber, *Partidul National Liberal (Gheorghe Brataniu)* (PhD dissertation, Universitatea "Lucian Blaga" din Sibiu, 2006), chapter six.

64. International Commission, *Final Report*, 127.

65. International Commission, *Final Report*, 128.

66. International Commission, *Final Report*, 128.

67. "Preventing further executions carried out by the Romanians in an unprofessional and sadistic manner" was one of the tasks of Einsatzgruppe D until the formal Romanian takeover of Bukovina, Bessarabia, and Transnistria, following the Tighina agreement of August 30, 1941. Browning, *Origins*, 277; International Commission, *Final Report*, 129, 133–134.

68. The deportations from Bessarabia/Bukovina to this region took place in fall 1941. Raul Hilberg speaks of 185,000 total deported to camps in Transnistria: Hilberg, *Destruction*, 495; International Commission, *Final Report*, 137, 140 (about 150,000).

69. Hilberg, *Destruction*, 496; Christian Hartmann et al., eds., *Verbrechen der Wehrmacht: Bilanz einer Debatte* (Munich, 2005), 95.

70. Some estimates go as high as 250,000–410,000. Hartmann et al., *Verbrechen der Wehrmacht*, 95; Mark Mazower, *Hitler's Empire: How the Nazis Ruled Europe* (New York, 2008), 337–338.

71. Mazower, *Hitler's Empire*, 332–333.

72. Hilberg, *Destruction*, 493, 498.

73. International Commission, *Final Report*, 170.

74. Hilberg, *Destruction*, 501–502; International Commission, *Final Report*, 172. When apprehended in 1944, Lecca was in possession of 2,000 gold pieces and sixty gold watches. Radu Ioanid, *The Holocaust in Romania: The Destruction of Jews and Gypsies under the Antonescu Regime* (Chicago, 2000), 285.

75. Dennis Deletant, *Hitler's Forgotten Ally: Ion Antonescu and His Regime, Romania 1940–44* (New York, 2006), 208; AP report of August 21, 1942, *Lawrence (Kansas) Journal-World*, 3.

76. Deletant, *Forgotten Ally*, 207; Holly Case, *Between States: The Transylvanian Question and the European Idea during World War II*, (Stanford, CA, 2009), 188.

77. Deletant, *Forgotten Ally*, 207–208.

78. A leader was Anny Andermann, who in the 1930s served as president of the Romanian branch of the Oeuvre de secours aux Enfants (the Jewish children's welfare organization). When information became available about the plight of Jewish orphans stranded in Transnistria, Andermann organized a campaign with other women calling for their repatriation. Once they were safely on Romanian territory, the women endeavored to have them sent to Palestine. Anca Ciuciu, "Kinder des Holocaust: Die Waisen von Transnistrien," in *Holocaust an der Peripherie: Judenpolitik und Judenmord in Rumänien und Transnistrien 1940–1944*, Wolfgang Benz et al., eds. (Berlin, 2009), 187–193; Jon Meacham, *Franklin and Winston: an Intimate Portrait of an Epic Friendship* (New York, 2004), 192; Richard J. Evans, *The Third Reich at War* (New York, 2009), 393; International Commission, *Final Report*, 170–171; Obituary, *The Independent* (London), July 31, 2006.

79. Case, *Between States*, 188.

80. Ronit Fischer, "Transnistria" in Friedman, *Routledge History of the Holocaust*, 286.

81. Janos, *Politics of Backwardness*, 301.

82. Loránd Tilkovszky, "Late Interwar Years," in *A History of Hungary*, Peter Sugar et al., eds. (Bloomington, IN, 1990), 340.

83. On this complex personality, see András Bán, *Hungarian-British Diplomacy 1938–1941: The Attempt to Maintain Relations* (London, 2004), 56–59, 141–142; Browning, *Origins*, 209.

84. Janos, *Politics of Backwardness*, 306.

85. Frederick B. Chary, *The History of Modern Bulgaria* (Santa Barbara, CA 2011), 91; Jörg Hoensch, *A History of Modern Hungary* (London, 1988), 146–148.

86. Hoensch, *History*, 147.

87. That was the second Vienna arbitration; the first took place in November 1938, awarding south Slovakia to Hungary. Tilkovszky, "Late Interwar Years," 342–343.

88. Hoensch, *History*, 149; Tilkovszky, "Late Interwar Years," 343.

89. Hoensch, *History*, 150. Hoensch uses the quote marks.

90. Hoensch, *History*, 150–151.

91. Rudolf Braham, *The Politics of Genocide: The Holocaust in Hungary* (Detroit, 1981), 33.

92. Browning, *Origins*, 291; Braham, *Politics of Genocide*, 34.

93. Arpad von Klimo, *Remembering Cold Days: The 1942 Massacre in Novi Sad* (Pittsburgh, PA, 2018).

94. Hilberg, *Destruction*, 521. Feketahalmi-Zeisler escaped to Germany before the trial could take place.

95. Béla Imrédy was pro-German; Pal Teleki was not; László Bárdossy was pro-German; Miklós Kállay was not; Döme Sztójay was pro-German; Géza Lakatos was not. Finally in 1944, the Germans imposed their own prime minister, the Arrow Cross leader Ferenc Szálasi.

96. Janos, *Politics of Backwardness*, 302.

97. Large estates were hardly touched, and even less affected were the industrial concerns in Jewish hands; some met quotas of the second anti-Jewish law by adding Gentiles to their boards of directors. "Through such expedients, the largest industrial plants remained under the effective control of their Jewish owners, and during the war continued to function as before, often making substantial contributions to the war effort of the Axis powers." Janos, *Politics of Backwardness*, 303, 305.

98. Rothschild, *East Central Europe*, 196; Hilberg, *Destruction*, 514–515.

99. Jews had been pushed out of many branches of commerce almost entirely, for example, from the cement trade, restaurants, the eggs and milk trade, and the fats and hogs trade. Hilberg, *Destruction*, 516.

100. Braham, *Politics of Genocide*, 42, 49; Hilberg, *Destruction*, 517–518.

101. After the Nazis ousted him in 1944, Horthy told the Hungarian Crown Council that he had been charged with "not permitting the Jews to be massacred, according to Hitler's wishes." Hilberg, *Destruction*, 524, 527.

102. István Deák, *Essays on Hitler's Europe* (Lincoln, NE, 2001), 156.

103. Hoensch, *History*, 156. Janos speaks of eleven divisions. *Politics of Backwardness*, 308.

104. The council created by decree of April 22, 1944. Kinga Frojimovics, "The Special Characteristics of the Holocaust in Hungary," in Friedman, *Routledge History of the Holocaust*, 255.

105. Frojimovics, "Special Characteristics," 256–257; Christian Gerlach and Götz Aly, *Das letzte Kapitel: Der Mord an den ungarischen Juden* (Stuttgart, 2002), 274; Lendvai, *Hungarians*, 422.

106. The "Vrba report" was written by the Slovak Jew Rudolf Vrba, who had escaped the camp and was excerpted in Swiss newspapers from June 1944 (though prepared in April). Pius XII addressed a personal plea on June 25; Roosevelt on June 26; the king of Sweden on June 30. The US president demanded an immediate end to the deportations and a cessation of all anti-Jewish measures, threatening reprisals. US planes raided Budapest on July 2. Braham, *Politics of Genocide*, 161.

107. Braham, *Politics of Genocide*, 161.

108. Keith Hitchins, *Rumania 1866–1947* (Oxford, 1994).

109. Macartney, *Hungary*, 234.

110. Hoensch, *History*, 157.

111. Feine did so behind the backs of the German Army and the SS. Heinrich August Winkler, *The Age of Catastrophe: A History of the West* (New Haven, CT, 2015) 835; Heidi Eisenhut, "Im Leben etwas Grosses vollbringen," *Appenzellische Jahrbücher* 140 (213), 44–65.

112. Tilkovszky, "Late Interwar Years," 353.

113. Zoltán Vági et al., eds., *The Holocaust in Hungary: Evolution of a Genocide* (Lanham, MD, 2013), 330.

114. The prewar population of Jews in Romania was about 757,000. International Commission, *Final Report*, 179.

115. Figures are available at www.yadvashem.org (accessed October 6, 2018).

116. Estimates are of 80,000 killed. Gruner, *Judenverfolgung*, 289.

117. Browning, *Origins*, 291; Hoensch, *History*, 157.

118. Helen Fein, *Accounting for Genocide* (New York, 1979), 33. During the war, the citizens of Sarajevo banded together to protect one another: Muslims, Catholic Croats, and Orthodox Serbs. However, the city's 10,000 Jews perished almost entirely. Emily Greble, *Sarajevo, 1941–1945: Muslims, Christians and Jews in Hitler's Europe* (Ithaca, NY, 2011), 114–115.

119. George Konrád, *A Guest in My Own Country: A Hungarian Life* (New York, 2007), 103.

120. Heda Margolius Kovaly, *Under A Cruel Star: A Life in Prague* (New York, 1986), 66; Gruner, *Judenverfolgung*, 260–263.

121. This is stressed by István Deák in his excellent review of Konrád in *The New Republic*, April 2, 2007.

122. Konrád, *Guest*, 113–114.

123. For Poland, see Jan T. Gross, *Fear: Anti-Semitism in Poland after Auschwitz* (New York, 2006); Celia Stopnicka Heller, *On the Edge of Destruction: Jews of Poland between the Two World Wars* (Detroit, 1994), 296; Anna Bikont, *The Crime and the Silence* (New York, 2015), 442; Anna Cichopek-Gajraj, *Beyond Violence: Jewish Survivors in Poland and Slovakia in 1944–1948* (Cambridge, 2014); Yehoshua Büchler, "Slovaks and Jews after World War II," in *The Jews are Coming Back: The Return of Jews to Their Countries of Origin after WWII*, David Banker, ed., (Jerusalem, 2005), 257–276. For attitudes about returning Jews among Czechs: Hana Kubátová and Jan Láníček, *The Jew in Czech and Slovak Imagination 1938–89* (Leiden, 2018), 115.

Chapter 18: People's Democracy: Early Postwar Eastern Europe

1. The Soviet Union also took part of East Prussia, including the city of Königsberg (now Kaliningrad) as well as the eastern part of Czechoslovakia, subcarpathian Ruthenia, many of whose inhabitants feel a cultural unity with Ukraine.

2. "Replica regimes" is a formula of Kenneth Jowitt. See *New World Disorder: The Leninist Extinction* (Berkeley, 1991), xvii, 250.

3. Soviet soldiers raped an estimated 10,000 to 20,000 women in Czechoslovakia and 40,000 in Poland. Anna Cichopek-Gajraj, *Beyond Violence: Jewish Survivors in Poland and Slovakia,*

1944–1948 (Cambridge, 2014), 48. In Budapest alone, some 50,000 women were raped. James Mark, "Remembering Rape: Divided Social Memory and the Red Army in Hungary," *Past and Present* 188 (2005), 133. On the shift of sentiment from relief to dread and anxiety, see Marcin Zaremba, *Wielka trwoga: Polska 1944–1947. Ludowa reakcja na kryzys* (Kraków, 2012), 153–154. For popular perception of Soviet soldiers in Hungary: Sándor Márai, *Memoir of Hungary 1944–48*, Albert Tezla, trans. (Budapest, 1996); on the Soviet Zone in Germany, see Norman M. Naimark, *The Russians in Germany* (Cambridge, MA, 1996).

4. Cichopek-Gajraj, *Beyond Violence*, chapters 2–3; Samuel Herman, "War Damage and Nationalization in Eastern Europe," *Law and Contemporary Problems* 16: 3 (Summer 1951), 507.

5. In Poland, the reform replaced a system of seven classes of general education dating from 1919 with a two-step system (from 1948/1949) of seven years primary and four years secondary schooling for everyone. Jerzy Wyrozumski, *Pińczów i jego szkoły w dziejach* (Kraków, 1979), 221. For discussion of those crash courses and of higher education reform, see John Connelly, *Captive University: The Sovietization of East German, Czech, and Polish Higher Education* (Chapel Hill, NC, 2000).

6. Jörg Hoensch, *A History of Modern Hungary* (London, 1988), 160.

7. From 1946. Norman Naimark, "Revolution and Counterrevolution" in *The Crisis of Socialism in Europe*, Christiane Lemke and Gary Marks, eds. (Durham, NC, 1992), 67.

8. Peter Kenez, *Hungary from the Nazis to the Soviets: The Establishment of the Communist Regime in Hungary, 1944–1948* (Cambridge and New York, 2006), 120–124.

9. President Beneš added that the Soviet Union did not want to "Bolshevize other countries." Igor Lukes, *On the Edge of the Cold War* (Oxford, 2012), 30, 40, 166.

10. Mark Pittaway, "The Politics of Legitimacy and Hungary's Postwar Transition," *Contemporary European History* 13:4 (2004), 466.

11. Bradley F. Abrams, *The Struggle for the Soul of the Nation: Czech Culture and the Rise of Communism* (Lanham, MD, 2004), 316, note 62.

12. On the forms and consequences worker dissent, see Andrew Port, *Conflict and Stability in the German Democratic Republic* (Cambridge, 2007); Padraic Kenney, *Rebuilding Poland: Workers and Communists* (Ithaca, NY, 1997); Jeffrey Kopstein, *The Politics of Economic Decline in East Germany* (Chapel Hill, NC, 1997); Adrian Grama, *Laboring Along: Industrial Workers and the Making of Postwar Romania* (Berlin, 2019); Mark Pittaway, *The Workers' State: Industrial Labor and the Making of Socialist Hungary* (Pittsburgh, PA, 2012). See also the overview in Peter Heumos, "Workers under Communist Rule," *International Review of Social History* 55:1 (2010), 83–115.

13. See, for example, the recollections of Heda Margolius Kovaly, *Under a Cruel Star: A Life in Prague, 1941–1968* (New York, 1997).

14. Adam Michnik said that in 1945, on emerging from the anti-Nazi underground conspiracy, Wyka never had a moment to think about embracing or rejecting the new regime, he simply continued his work. "Polski rachunek sumienia," *Gazeta Wyborcza*, April 12, 2010. For a discussion of organic work, see Chapter 10.

15. Sebastian Drabik, "Komuniści i społeczeństwo PRL wobec śmierci Stalina," *Arcana*, March 5, 2011, at http://www.portal.arcana.pl/Komunisci-i-spoleczenstwo-prl-wobec-smierci -stalina,845.html (accessed December 19, 2018).

16. Marta Markowska, *Wyklęci. Podziemie zbrojne 1944–1963* (Warsaw, 2013). For data on the strength of the Communist parties, see chapter 21, note 47.

17. Abrams, *Struggle*, 116. In Poland, the popularity of dialectics came to be known as the Hegelian sting. See, for instance, Jan Kott, *Theater of Essence* (Evanston, IL, 1984), 203.

18. Abrams, *Struggle*, 116.

19. Bradley Abrams cited in E. A. Rees, "Intellectuals and Communism," *Contemporary European History* 16:1 (2007), 145.

20. This was the view of Josef Macůrek: Rees, "Intellectuals," 145.

21. Lukes, *On the Edge*, 30–31.

22. Eugenio Reale, *Raporty. Polska 1945–1946*, Paweł Zdiechowski, trans. (Paris, 1968), 104. From December 1945.

23. East Germany recognized the Oder-Neisse border in 1950, and West Germany recognized it as "inviolable" in 1970 but remained open to alteration in the case of a peace treaty. Dieter Blumenwitz, "Oder-Neisse Linie," in *Handbuch zur deutschen Einheit*, Werner Weidenfeld and Karl-Rudolf Korte, eds. (Frankfurt, 1999), 586–597.

24. Czesław Miłosz, *The Captive Mind*, Jane Zielonko, trans. (New York, 1955), 98; Adam Michnik, *Polskie pytania* (Warsaw, 1993), 96.

25. For Romanian requests: Henry L. Roberts, *Rumania: Political Problems of an Agrarian State* (New Haven, CT, 1951), 259.

26. This was former German foreign minister Joschka Fischer's definition of socialism: Steven Erlanger, "What's a Socialist," *New York Times*, July 1, 2012.

27. Stefano Bottoni, "Reassessing the Communist Takeover in Romania: Violence, Institutional Continuity, and Ethnic Conflict Management," *East European Politics and Societies* 24:1 (2010), 65.

28. The author Maria Dąbrowska was representative of this trend of thought. Jacek Kuroń and Jacek Żakowski, *PRL dla początkujących* (Wrocław, 1996), 42–43.

29. Peter Gosztony, *Miklós von Horthy: Admiral und Reichsverweser* (Göttingen, 1973), 114. The precise numbers of those summarily executed in Bulgaria after the September 1944 coup are unknown but are in the thousands, including generals, publishers of newspapers, lawyers, and officers. Poliã Meshkova and Diniũ Sharlanov, *Bŭlgarskata gilotina : taĭnite mekhanizmi na Narodniia sŭd* (Sofia, 1994), cited in Maria Slavtscheva, *Auf der Suche nach dem Modernen: Eine komparatistische Verortung ausgewählter bulgarischer Lyriker* (Stuttgart, 2018), 115.

30. See Chapter 18; the total killed by direct execution amounted to some 60,000. One of the operations was dubbed "Intelligenzaktion." See Snyder, *Bloodlands*, 149–151; Maria Wardzyńska, *Był rok 1939: Operacja niemieckiej policji bezpieczeństwa w Polsce. Intelligenzaktion* (Warsaw, 2009).

31. "Rozporządzenie z dnia 1 sierpnia 1944 r. Krajowej Rady Ministrów o utracie obywatelstwa przez Niemców," *Dziennik Ustaw Rzeczpospolitej Polski*, August 2, 1944, part 3, position 7, 17.

32. "Dekret z dnia 13 września 1946 r. o wyłączeniu ze społeczeństwa polskiego osób narodowości niemieckiej," *Dziennik Ustaw Rzeczpospolitej Polski*, November 8, 1946, no. 55, position 310, 632.

33. Speeches of Wacław Barcikowski and Władysław Gomułka. *Wiadomości Mazurskie* (Olsztyn, Poland), November 12, 1946, 2.

34. Jan Błoński, *Między literaturą a światem* (Kraków, 2003), 238; Stanisław Krajewski, *Tajemnica Israela a tajemnica kościoła* (Kraków, 2007), 67; Teresa Torańska, *Śmierć spóźnia się o minutę* (Warsaw, 2010), 150. On Gentile Poles taking Jewish property: Jan Gross and Irena Grudzińska-Gross, *Golden Harvest: Events at the Periphery of the Holocaust* (New York, 2012).

35. Of a prewar population of more than 3.1 million, some 145,000 Polish Jews survived on Polish territory; 232,000 in the Soviet Union, and 40,000 elsewhere. Cichopek-Gajraj, *Beyond Violence*, 10, 44.

36. For this point, see Cichopek-Gajraj, *Beyond Violence*, 145. Estimates of the total number of Jewish victims in Poland between 1944 and 1946 range from 650 to 1,200: Cichopek-Gajraj, *Beyond Violence*, 117. On the pogrom, see Jan T. Gross, *Fear: Anti-Semitism in Poland after Auschwitz* (New York, 2006).

37. See http://www.yivoencyclopedia.org/article.aspx/poland/poland_since_1939. The peak number of Jews in postwar Poland was 240,489 in June 1946. Cichopek-Gajraj, *Beyond Violence*, 44.

38. Bernhard Chiari, "Limits to German Rule: Conditions for and Results of the Occupation of the Soviet Union," in *Germany and the Second World War*, Jörg Echternkamp, vol. 9/2 (Oxford, 2014), 964.

39. Helga Hirsch, "Nach dem Hass das Schweigen," *Die Zeit*, April 16, 1993; Jerzy Lukowski and Hubert Zawadzki, *Concise History of Poland* (Cambridge, 2006), 279.

40. Bottoni, "Reassessing," 74. Between 1948 and 1952, 130,000 left for Israel.

41. Germans' civil rights were restored in 1948. Starting in 1945, a university with Hungarian as the main language of education (named Bolyai János University) was operating in Cluj, giving support to a network of hundreds of high schools, popular colleges, and other vocational institutions. Bottoni, "Reassessing," 72–73.

42. The new internationalism that flourished in the West originated from specialists on Eastern Europe, inspired by the conflicts of the region, for example, over Trieste. Their ideas could not be implemented in their home region until much later. Glenda Sluga, *Internationalism in the Age of Nationalism* (Philadelphia, 2013), 81–85.

43. Zdeněk Radvanovsky, "The Social and Economic Consequences of Resettling Czechs into Northwestern Bohemia, 1945–1947," in *Redrawing Nations: Ethnic Cleansing in East-Central Europe, 1944–1948*, Philipp Ther and Ana Siljak, eds. (New York, 2001), 243, 251. The number of women in leading positions remained low in the Communist apparatus and decreased as one rose to the top. Sharon Wolchik, "The Status of Women in a Socialist Order: Czechoslovakia 1948-1978," *Slavic Review* 38:4 (1979), 583–602.

44. Josef Korbel, *The Communist Subversion of Czechoslovakia, 1938–1948: The Failure of Coexistence* (Princeton, NJ, 1959), 161–162.

45. Connelly, *Captive University*, 108–109.

46. In this regard, see the reports of the Czech National Socialist Party from the postwar years, describing the constant, violent pressure of Czech Communist organizations against all those who dared to oppose the "power of the people." Authors' Collective, *Tři roky : přehledy a dokumenty k československé politice v letech 1945 až 1948*, 2 vols. (Prague, 1991).

47. Communist minister Václav Kopecký was most the radical in demanding full expulsion of Germans and Hungarians and the taking of territories in Lusatia, arguing that Slavs had settled the Berlin areas. Karel Kaplan, *Mocní a bezmocní* (Toronto, 1989), 184. In June 1945, Klement Gottwald said that "hostile elements" had to be eliminated from the border areas forever. This was atonement for White Mountain (1620) and also a correction of the mistakes of Czech kings who had invited German colonists to Bohemia. Tomáš Staněk, *Odsun Němců z Československa, 1945–1947* (Prague, 1991), 60.

48. František Čapka, *Sborník dokumentů ke studiu nejnovějších českých dějin* (Brno, 2002), 120–122.

49. From Sarah A. Cramsey, "Uncertain Citizenship: Jewish Belonging and the Ethnic Revolution in Poland and Czechoslovakia, 1938–1948" (PhD dissertation, University of Califoirnia, Berkeley, 2014), chapter two.

50. The exceptions were the liberals Pavel Tigrid, Ferdinand Peroutka, and Václav Černý. The Roman Catholics generally stood up better than other non-Communists in opposition to racism and in support for Western values. Abrams, *Struggle*, 163–167, 174.

51. Tomáš Staněk, *Persekuce* (Prague, 1996), 72.

52. Contrary to the historical record, the Soviets claimed to have offered assistance to Eastern Europe when it faced Nazi aggression in the 1930s. Igor Lukes, *Between Stalin and Hitler: The Diplomacy of Edvard Beneš in the 1930s* (Oxford, 1996). On the predominantly Romanian ethnic character of Bessarabia: Henry L. Roberts, *Rumania: Political Problems of an Agrarian State* (New Haven, 1951), 32–33.

53. Elaine Kelly, *Composing the Canon in the GDR* (Oxford, 2014).

54. The National People's Army uniform, designed in 1955, was modeled on the uniform of the Wehrmacht. Rüdiger Wenzke, *Ulbrichts Soldaten: die Nationale Volksarmee 1956 bis 1971* (Berlin, 2013), 87–88, 96, 407. On Frederick, see Christoph Dieckmann, "Der König der DDR," *Die Zeit*, November 22, 2011.

55. Peter Fritzsche, *The Turbulent World of Franz Göll: An Ordinary Berliner Writes the Twentieth Century* (Cambridge, MA, 2011), 210; Günter Gaus, *Wo Deutschland liegt: Eine Ortsbestimmung* (Munich, 1986).

56. The point was to generate mass support. Stephen Fischer-Galati, *Twentieth Century Rumania* (New York, 1991), 92. The number of Romanian Germans deported to the Soviet Union was between 75,000 and 80,000. Most had been released by 1949/1950, but some were kept longer. Anneli Ute Gabanyi, *Die Deutschen in Rümanien* (Bonn, 1988), 34; Bottoni, "Reassessing," 79–80. The recipients amounted to three-quarters of those who had requested plots.

57. One thousand had a quarter of all land, and the Catholic Church had 500,000 hectares.

58. Hoensch, *History*, 169–170; N. G. Papp, "The Political Context of the Hungarian Land Reform of 1945: A Reassessment," *Historian* 46:3 (May 1984), 385–387, 395.

59. Kenez, *Hungary*, 107.

60. Papp, "Political Context," 392. Retroactive to January 1, 1946. That is, there could be no appeals on lands distributed before that date.

61. Kenez, *Hungary*, 112; Papp, "Political Context," 388.

62. Papp, "Political Context," 388–389.

63. In the fall of 1945, the Smallholders campaigned against abuses of land reform, especially by Communist-dominated land-distribution committees. Papp, "Political Context," 391.

64. See the images in Andrzej Paczkowski, *Zdobycie władzy: 1945–1947* (Warsaw, 1993), 30.

65. Abrams, *Struggle*, passim.

66. Connelly, *Captive University*, 75.

67. Unfortunately, the street on which they marched, Nerudová, was narrow, and it was easy for the police to trap and keep them from reaching the castle. Peter Demetz, *Prague in Gold and Black: The History of a City* (London, 1998), 367; Zdeněk Pousta, "Smuteční pochod za

demokracii," in *Stránkami soudobých dějin. Sborník stadií k pětašedesátinám historika Karla Ka-plana*, Karel Jech, ed. (Prague, 1993), 198–207.

68. Abrams, *Struggle*, 115.

69. Abrams, *Struggle*.

70. János M. Rainer, *Imre Nagy: Vom Parteisoldaten zum Märtyrer des ungarischen Volks-aufstandes. Eine politische Biographie 1896–1958*, Anne Nass, trans. (Paderborn, Germany, 2006), 65.

71. See the records of Mátyás Rákosi's talk to the Communist Party Central Committee in May 1946, in Csaba Békés et al, eds., *Soviet Occupation of Romania, Hungary, and Austria 1944/45–1948/49* (Budapest, 2015), 185ff.

72. Mark Pittaway, "Politics," 470–471; Kenez, *Hungary*, 128–129.

73. He accused them of abetting Sovietization Kenez, *Hungary*, 130.

74. Alfred Rieber, *Salami Tactics Revisited: Hungarian Communists on the Road to Power*, Trond-heim Studies on East European Cultures and Societies no. 33 (Trondheim, 2013), 85.

75. The politically lifeless figure succeeding Lajos Dinnyés was István Dobi. After hollowing out the Smallholders, the Communists closed down two small independent parties in late 1948. Hugh Seton-Watson, *The East European Revolution* (London, 1956), 198–202; "Zwei Kilo Gold," *Der Spiegel*, June 14, 1947; László Borhi, *Dealing with Dictators: The United States, Hungary and East Central Europe* (Bloomington, IN, 2016), 72; Anne Applebaum, *Iron Curtain: The Crushing of Eastern Europe* (New York, 2012), 210–211; Jason Wittenberg, *Crucibles of Political Loyalty* (Cambridge, 2006), 56–57.

76. Keith Hitchins, *Rumania 1866–1947* (Oxford, 1994), 500; Roberts, *Rumania*, 259.

77. Bottoni, "Reassessing," 64.

78. Roberts, *Rumania*, 261.

79. This is Andrew Janos's term in regard to Nazi power in Hungary: he speaks of triple lever-age. Janos, *Politics of Backwardness*, 301.

80. Bottoni, "Reassessing," 67–68.

81. Crampton, *Concise History*, 187.

82. Hannah Arendt, *Eichmann in Jerusalem: A Report on the Evil of Banality* (New York, 1976), 188; Wilfried F. Schoeller, "Georgi Dimitroff: Held und Schurke," *Der Tagesspiegel*, March 11, 2001.

83. The technique involved seizing the newspaper, then the organization. Seton-Watson, *Revo-lution*, 213–217.

84. *Sydney Morning Herald*, September 25, 1947.

85. Chary, *History of Bulgaria*, 127.

86. Crampton, *Concise History*, 188; Seton-Watson, *Revolution*, 216; Harold Segel, *The Walls behind the Curtain: East European Prison Literature, 1945–1990* (Pittsburgh, PA, 2012), 11–12; Mi-chael Bar-Zohar, *Beyond Hitler's Grasp: The Heroic Rescue of Bulgaria's Jews* (Holbrook, MA, 1998), 146; Khaim Oliver, *We Were Saved: How the Jews in Bulgaria Were Kept from the Death Camps* (Sofia, 1978), 65.

87. Michael Padev, *Dimitrov Wastes No Bullets. Nikola Petkov: The Test Case* (London, 1948); Chary, *History of Bulgaria*, 127; "Petkov's Death Shocks West," *Sydney Morning Herald*, Septem-ber 25, 1947; Seton-Watson, *Revolution*, 217; Crampton, *Concise History*, 186.

88. Papp, "Political Context," 385.

89. "US Excoriates Bulgaria," *New York Times*, September 24, 1947.

90. In January 1946, Mikołajczyk compiled a list of eighteen activists arrested in Wrocław, as well as eighty more in Łódź. Applebaum, *Iron Curtain*, 198–199. Reale, *Raporty*, 103; "Die Memoiren Mikolajczyks," *Der Spiegel*, March 13, 1948, 48–49; Paczkowski, *Pół wieku*, 192.

91. Cătălin Augustin Stoica, "Once Upon a Time There Was a Big Party: The Social Bases of the Romanian Communist Party," *East European Politics and Societies* 19:4 (2005), 694.

92. Samuel L. Sharp, *Industry and Agriculture in Eastern Europe* (New York, 1951), 184.

93. "Free Speech: Reds Turn Assembly into a Brawl," *Life*, June 30, 1947, 30–31.

94. Krystyna Badurka, "Stalinizm w mojej pamięci," January 17, 2017, at https://obserwatorpolityczny.pl/?p=45317 (accessed October 23, 2018).

Chapter 19: The Cold War and Stalinism

1. Daniel Yergin, *Shattered Peace: The Origins of the Cold War and the National Security State* (New York, 1977), 312–313; Vojtech Mastny, *The Cold War and Soviet Insecurity* (Oxford, 1996); Norman M. Naimark, "The Sovietization of Eastern Europe, 1944–1953," in *The Cambridge History of the Cold War*, Melvyn P. Leffler and Odd Arne Westad, eds., vol. 1 (Cambridge, 2010), 175–197. See also the papers in Francesca Gori and Silvio Pons., eds., *The Soviet Union and Europe in the Cold War, 1943–53* (London, 1996); and Norman M. Naimark and Leonid Gibianskii., eds., *The Establishment of Communist Regimes in Eastern Europe 1944–1949* (Boulder, CO, 1997).

2. Scott D. Parrish, "The Turn toward Confrontation: The Soviet Reaction to the Marshall Plan, 1947," Cold War International History Project Working Paper 9 (Washington, DC, 1994), 14.

3. Parrish, "Turn toward Confrontation," 3.

4. Hubert Ripka, *Czechoslovakia Enslaved: The Story of the Communist Coup d'Etat* (London, 1950), 70.

5. W. Gomułka, *Artykuły i przemówienia*, vol. 1 (Warsaw, 1962), 295 (from June 1945); Krystyna Kersten, *Narodziny systemu władzy, Polska 1943–1948* (Warsaw, 1990), 239–240; Jerzy Jagiełło, *O polską drogę do socjalizmu* (Warsaw, 1983), 134; Jan Ciechanowski, "Postwar Poland," in *The History of Poland since 1863*, R. F. Leslie, ed. (Cambridge, 1983), 296–297.

6. The correlation of forces in favor of "socialism" was not working to Moscow's advantage in the way that Stalin had hoped. This had become evident by mid-1947. Mastny, *Cold War*, 25.

7. Ted Hopf, *Reconstructing the Cold War* (Oxford, 2012), 84–85.

8. *Sydney Morning Herald*, September 25, 1947. The statement is by Clement Davies (Liberal), Lord Vansittart (Conservative), and A. R. Blackburn (Labour).

9. Mastny, *Cold War*, 33; Jiří Pernes, "Specifická cesta KSČ k socialismu," *Soudobé dějiny* 1–2 (2016), 11–53.

10. Connelly, *Captive University*, 127–132, 250–251.

11. This was an extended process that lasted into the 1950s, and in every case involved purging hundreds of thousands of Social Democrats. See Joachim von Puttkamer, *Ostmitteleuropa im 19. und 20. Jahrhundert* (Munich, 2010), 117–119.

12. See the June 28 resolution at http://www.fordham.edu/halsall/mod/1948cominform-yugo1.html (accessed November 23, 2016).

13. Richard West, *Tito and the Rise and Fall of Yugoslavia* (New York, 1995), 220–221.

14. Georg Hodos, *Schauprozesse: stalinistische Säuberungen in Osteuropa 1948–54* (Frankfurt am Main, 1988), 68–69.

15. Hopf, *Reconstructing*, 84–85.

16. Two of the four (Ernő Gerő and Mihály Farkas) were themselves KGB agents. In May 1948, Rákosi was in Moscow to prepare the show trial of Rajk with Secret Police chief Beria.

17. Applebaum, *Iron Curtain*, 164–165.

18. Roger Gough, *A Good Comrade: János Kádár, Communism and Hungary* (London, 2006), 43–44, 46.

19. Geoffrey Swain, *Tito: A Biography* (London, 2011), 103; Andrzej Leder, *Prześniona rewolucja* (Warsaw, 2014), 155.

20. On problems even in Czechoslovakia: Kevin McDermott, "A Polyphony of Voices? Czech Popular Opinion and the Slánský Affair," *Slavic Review* 67:4 (2008), 859; Jiří Pernes, *Krize komunistického režimu v Československu v 50. letech 20. století* (Brno, 2008), 41-56.

21. Thanks to Dylan Brooks for making this point. Šling was a Spanish volunteer, a wartime exile in London, and had contacts at the highest levels of the Communist Party of Czechoslovakia. Karel Kaplan, *Report on the Murder of the General Secretary*, Karl Kovanda, trans. (London, 1990), 86.

22. For an example of the view of young metalworker from a Communist family in North Hungary, see Sándor Kopácsi, *In the Name of the Working Class* (New York, 1986), 33–34.

23. There was a story of two Communist Hungarian sisters, who both became disenchanted during the trials, but each refused to confide to the other, assuming that she still believed. Applebaum, *Iron Curtain*, 292.

24. Kevin McDermott, *Communist Czechoslovakia 1945–89* (London, 2015), 70; Mark Pittaway, *The Workers' State: Industrial Labor and the Making of Socialist Hungary* (Pittsburgh, PA, 2012), 101–102; Kovaly, *Under a Cruel Star*, 140.

25. Marián Lóži, "A Case Study of Power Practices: The Czechoslovak Stalinist Elite at the Local Level," in *Perceptions of Society in Communist Europe: Regime Archives and Popular Opinion*, Muriel Blaive, ed. (London, 2019), 49-64; McDermott, *Communist Czechoslovakia*, 70.

26. Hana Kubátová and Jan Láníček, *The Jew in Czech and Slovak Imagination 1938–89* (Leiden, 2018), 169–211; Bożena Szaynok, "The Anti-Jewish Policies of the USSR in the Last Decade of Stalin's Rule and Its Impact on East European Countries," *Russian History* 29:2–4 (2002), 301–315. For a deeper history of hatred against Jews, with special consideration of continutities over many centuries, see David Nirenberg, *Anti-Judaism: The Western Tradition* (New York, 2013).

27. Kaplan, *Report*, 242.

28. For example, Hilary Minc and Jakub Berman in Poland, or Mátyás Rákosi and József Révai in Hungary.

29. František Nečásek et al., eds., *Dokumenty o protilidové a protinárodní politice T. G. Masaryka* (Prague, 1953); McDermott, "Polyphony," 856; Martin Wein, *A History of Czechs and Jews: A Slavic Jerusalem* (New York, 2015), 162.

30. This from his report to the Central Committee of June 1, 1949. Gough, *Good Comrade*, 45.

31. István Rev, *Retroactive Justice: A Prehistory of Postcommunism* (Stanford, CA, 2005), 120–121; Bennett Kovrig, *Communism in Hungary* (Stanford, CA, 1979), 245.

32. Kuroń and Żakowski, *PRL*, 74; Jörg K. Hoensch, *A History of Modern Hungary, 1867–1994* (London, 1996), 192.

33. The name "monster trials" was in circulation even in World War I to denote unfair show trials. See Vladimir Nosek, *Independent Bohemia: An Account of the Czechoslovak Struggle for Liberty* (London, 1918), 53.

34. "B" stood for "bourgeois." The number in the Czech case was approximately 15,000. For the Soviet precursor, see Sheila Fitzpatrick, *Education and Social Mobility in the Soviet Union 1921–1934* (Cambridge, 1979), 76–77.

35. Dariusz Jarosz, *Polacy a stalinizm 1948–1956* (Warsaw, 2000), 64; Pittaway, *Workers' State*, 145.

36. Sharon Wolchik, "The Status of Women in a Socialist Order: Czechoslovakia 1948–1978," *Slavic Review* 38:4 (1979), 583–602; Isabel Marcus, "Wife Beating: Ideology and Practice in State Socialism," in *Gender Politics and Everyday Life in State Socialist Eastern Europe*, Shana Penn and Jill Massino, eds., (New York, 2009), 120.

37. The number of women approached a third in Poland and East Germany, a quarter in the Czech lands in the mid-1950s. The goal in the former two was 40 percent. Connelly, *Captive University*, 267.

38. For example, in Romania in 1970, 74.9 percent of women were employed outside the home, compared to just over half in France or the United Kingdom. Jill Massino, "Workers under Construction," in *Gender Politics*, Massino and Penn, eds., 16–17.

39. In the first half of 1951, half the workers in taking part in labor competition in the Żyrardów textile factory were women. Małgorzata Fidelis, *Women, Communism and Industrialization in Postwar Poland* (Cambridge, 2010), 80.

40. In Poland before World War II, women began entering law school but had not made a dent in the judiciary. The first woman judge was appointed in 1929. As a result of relative equality of opportunity in People's Poland, the number of women judges went from 33.2 percent in 1968 to 61.6 percent in 1990. Małgorzata Fuszara, "Women Lawyers in Poland," in *Women in the World's Legal Professions*, Ulrike Schultz and Gisela Shaw, eds. (Oxford, 2003), 375.

41. The number of women being trained for mining in 1956 was 7.63 percent; for light industry, 61.06 percent. Jarosz, *Polacy*, 127–129; Pittaway, *Workers' State*, 155. On average, women earned 25 to 35 percent less than men did. Lynne Haney, "After the Fall. East European Women since the Collapse of State Socialism," *Contexts* (Fall 2002), 29.

42. Robert Levy, *Ana Pauker: Rise and Fall of a Jewish Communist* (Berkeley, 2001), 108–109, 126; Norman Naimark, review of Levy, *Ana Pauker*, *Slavic Review* 61:2 (2002), 389–390. On the Soviet role in targeting her, see Vladimir Tismaneanu, *Stalinism for all Seasons: A Political History of Romanian Communism* (Berkeley, 2003), 128–129.

43. By 1955, only about 9 percent of agriculturally useful land was included in collective farms. Włodzimierz Borodziej, *Geschichte Polens im 20. Jahrhundert* (Munich, 2010), 288.

44. Catechism in state schools was successively reduced, from about 47 percent of the total in 1952/1953 to 26 percent in 1955/1956. Jarosz, *Polacy*, 195–196. But in December 1956, state and church reached an agreement that returned religious instruction to state schools (in 1961, the state finally laicized state schools). Paweł Załęcki, "Roman Catholic Church," in *Europe since 1945*, Bernard A. Cook, ed., vol. 2 (New York, 2001), 1011–1012. By 1950, the state had arrested some one

hundred priests. Andrzej Paczkowski, *Pół wieku dziejów Polski : 1939–1989* (Warsaw, 1996), 277; Andrzej Friszke, *Polska: Losy Panstwa i narodu* (Warsaw, 2003), 200–201.

45. That explains why the arrest of Wyszyński and the show trial of Kielce Bishop Kaczmarek took place after Stalin's death: the party felt weak in a hostile society, and functionaries feared that suppressed aspirations would burst through the surface. Krystyna Kersten, "The Terror, 1949–1956," in *Stalinism in Poland, 1944–1956*, A. Kemp-Welch, ed. (London, 1999), 87.

46. See the summary of how Zhdanov's ideas made their way into music in Eastern Europe in 1947–1949 in Steven Stucky, *Lutosławski and His Music* (Cambridge and New York, 1981), 35–36; Robert V. Daniels, *A Documentary History of Communism in Russia* (Hanover, NH, 1993), 236.

47. For the eager self-adaptation of musicians to socialist realism, see David G. Tompkins, *Composing the Party Line: Music and Politics in Early Cold War Poland and East Germany* (West Lafayette, IN, 2013).

48. He was accompanied by the author Stephan Hermlin. The result was the seven-part Mansfelder Oratorium. Tompkins, *Composing the Party Line*, 55.

49. Janina Falkowska, *Andrzej Wajda: History, Politics, and Nostalgia in Polish Cinema* (New York, 2007), 36–38. On Wolf see Anna Chiarloni, "Nachdenken über Christa Wolf," in *Rückblicke auf die Literatur der DDR*, Hans-Christian Stillmark, ed. (Amsterdam, 2002), 117–118; Hermann Kurzke, "Warum 'Der geteilte Himmel' ein Klassiker ist," *Die Welt*, December 30, 2006.

50. Tamás Aczél and Tibor Merry, *The Revolt of the Mind; A Case History of Intellectual Resistance Behind the Iron Curtain* (New York, 1959), 122.

51. The basic demand, in a Soviet formuation, was the artists "depict reality in its revolutionary development." But there was constant debate about exactly how to do this, and in music especially, it proved impossible to identify what kind of compositional trend would prevail. What was clear was that more experimental, "difficult" modern music was not in favor. See Tompkins, *Composing the Party Line*, 19 and passim.

52. It is not clear by what method one could measure their contribution in general, and assessments vary. For a more skeptical take, see Jeffrey Kopstein, *The Politics of Economic Decline in East Germany* (Chapel Hill, NC, 1997), 33; for one more positive (and the Hennecke story), see Christoph Klessmann, *Arbeiter im Arbeiterstaat DDR* (Bonn, 2007), 216–218.

53. Mark Pittaway, *The Workers' State*, 104–105.

54. Nigel Swain, *The Rise and Fall of Feasible Socialism* (London, 1992), 55.

55. Ferenc Fehér, Agnes Heller, and György Markus, *Dictatorship over Needs* (Oxford, 1983).

56. He was released in 1956 and went to West Germany to become a teacher. His father was the writer Hans Natonek. Ilko-Sascha Kowalczuk, *Geist im Dienste der Macht: Hochschulpolitik in der SBZ/DDR 1945 bis 1961* (Berlin, 2003), 503–504.

57. Kovaly, *Under a Cruel Star*, 70; Hanna Świda-Ziemba, "Stalinizm i społeczeństwo polskie," in *Stalinizm*, Jacek Kurczewski, ed. (Warsaw, 1989), 49.

58. This was the fate of the well-known Czech director František Čáp in the early 1950s. Jiří Knapík, "Arbeiter versus Künstler: Gewerkschaft und neue Elemente in der tschechoslowakischen Kulturpolitik," *Sozialgeschichtliche Kommunismusforschung*, Peter Heumos and Christiane Brenner, eds. (Munich, 2005), 243–260.

59. In Czechoslovakia the difference between salaries and wages was abolished in 1953; by 1955 the average earnings for white-collar employees was 14.9 percent lower than those of industrial workers. Alice Teichová, *Wirtschaftsgeschichte der Tschechoslowakei 1918–1980* (Vienna, 1988), 93.

60. McDermott, *Communist Czechoslovakia*, 82; Andrew Port, *Conflict and Stability in the German Democratic Republic* (Cambridge, 2008), 102–103. For examples of crimes that sent workers and peasants to penal camps, see Kopácsi, *In the Name*, 43.

61. Jan Rychlík, "Collectivization in Czechoslovakia in Comparative Perspective," in *The Collectivization of Agriculture in Communist Eastern Europe*, Constantin Iordachi and Arnd Bauerkämper, eds. (Budapest, 2014), 213.

62. Sometimes they benefited at the expense of ethnic minorities. Nigel Swain, "Eastern European Collectivization Campaigns Compared," in Iordachi and Bauerkämper, *Collectivization*, 582, 585.

63. Swain, "Eastern European Collectivization," 577, 603; Rychlík, "Collectivization in Czechoslovakia," 217.

64. In the 1960s, that figure dropped to 50 percent. József Ö. Kovács, "The Forced Collectivization of Agriculture in Hungary," in Iordachi and Bauerkämper, *Collectivization*, 249.

65. The leadership "frequently violated the most fundamental rights of the members, expelled them, usually without the approval of their council and without justification. There were thousands of legitimate grievances concerning the unjustified distribution of income and the illegal retention of earned dividends." From an internal report of 1955, cited in Kovács, "Forced Collectivization," 252.

66. Kovács, "Forced Collectivization," 245–247; Swain, "Eastern European Collectivization," 588.

67. One such case occurred in Czechoslovakia, where 1,421 kulak families were "resettled" to border regions between September 1951 and August 1953 and made into laborers on state farms. Swain, "Eastern European Collectivization," 572; Rychlík, "Collectivization in Czechoslovakia," 225.

68. Rychlík, "Collectivization in Czechoslovakia," 223; Swain, "Eastern European Collectivization," 595–596, 593.

69. By 1953, only Bulgaria had topped 50 percent collectivization of arable land; the Czechoslovak total was 40 percent; Hungary 26 percent; Poland and Romania 7 and 8 percent, respectively. East Germany was just getting started (3.3 percent). Both the Hungarian and Polish totals would drop after 1953, and again after 1956; the Polish government ultimately gave up on the project. Ben Fowkes, *Rise and Fall of Communism in Eastern Europe* (New York, 1993), 58, 199.

70. Kovács, "Forced Collectivization," 245; Swain, "Eastern European Collectivization," 575, 601.

71. Rychlík, "Collectivization in Czechoslovakia," 228; Swain, "Eastern European Collectivization," 596.

72. For discussion of the benefits and costs of central state planning, see Judy Batt, *Economic Reform and Political Change in Eastern Europe* (New York, 1988), 56–61; Teichova, *Wirtschaftsgeschichte*, 112–115; Ivan T. Berend, *The Hungarian Economic Reforms 1953–1988* (Cambridge, 1990), 1–14; Janusz Kalinski and Zbigniew Landau, *Gospodarka polska w XX wieku* (Warsaw, 1999), 233–240.

73. Świda-Ziemba, "Stalinizm," 53–54.

74. Alec Nove, *An Economic History of the USSR* (New York, 1982), 316. For studies of other socialist economies: Nigel Swain, *The Rise and Fall of Feasible Socialism* (London, 1992); Andre

Steiner, *The Plans That Failed: An Economic History of the GDR*, Ewald Osers, trans. (New York, 2010).

75. Oskar Schwarzer, *Sozialistische Zentralplanwirtschaft in der SBZ/DDR: Ergebnisse eines ord-nungspolitischen Experiments (1945–1989)* (Stuttgart, 1999), 61–62.

76. Támas Aczél and Tibor Méray, *Revolt of the Mind: A Case History of Intellectual Resistance behind the Iron Curtain* (New York, 1960), 195; Batt, *Economic Reform*, 56–67.

77. Robert Frucht, *Eastern Europe: An Introduction to the People, Lands, and Culture* (Santa Barbara, CA, 2005), 363; Kenez, *Hungary*, 77.

78. For the East German case, called "Action Vermin," see Edith Sheffer, *Burned Bridge: How East and West Germans Made the Iron Curtain* (Oxford, 2008), 102–117.

Chapter 20: Destalinization: Hungary's Revolution

1. The arrest took place on June 26. The plotters included his rivals Nikita Khrushchev and Georgy Malenkov, who feared that Beria was planning a coup d'etat. William Taubman, *Khrushchev: The Man and His Era* (New York, 2003), 250–257.

2. Reports multiplied in 1951 of passengers on public transportation lacking the strength to get on the proper tramlines. They had not had breakfast. Błażej Brzostek, *Robotnicy Warszawy. Konflikty codzienne (1950–1954)* (Warsaw, 2002), 133. The number of private shops went from 130,000 in 1948 to 14,000 in 1955; the number of private cafes and restaurants from 14,000 to fewer than 500. Borodziej, *Geschichte*, 289.

3. This from a report from a Party economic weekly in 1956. Judy Batt, *Economic Reform and Political Change in Eastern Europe* (New York, 1988), 62.

4. That was one Polish adult in three. Police in Hungary had meted out punishment in 850,000 cases. László Borhi, *Hungary in the Cold War, 1945–1956* (Budapest, 2004); Peter Heumos, *"Vyhrňme si rukávy, než se kola zastaví!" Dělníci a státní socialismus v Československu 1945–1968* (Prague, 2006), 17; Dariusz Jarosz, *Polacy a stalinizm* (Warsaw, 2000), 236–237; Applebaum, *Iron Curtain*, 110–111.

5. These changes were associated with Georgy Malenkov. Taubman, *Khrushchev*, 260.

6. Jan Foitzik, "Ostmitteleuropa zwischen 1953 und 1956," in *Entstalinisierung in Ostmitteleuropa: Vom 17. Juni bis zum ungarischen Volksaufstand*, Jan Foitzik, ed. (Paderborn, Germany, 2001), 30–31, and passim; Steffen Plaggenborg, introduction to Galina Ivanova, *Entstalinisierung als Wohlfahrt: Sozialpolitik in der Sowjetunion, 1953–1970* (New York and Frankfurt, 2015), 8–9.

7. The *Borba* group consisted of left-wing writers living in Paris. Jan Plamper and Klaus Heller, *Personality Cults in Stalinism* (Göttingen, 2004), 28–29.

8. Dennison Rusinow, *The Yugoslav Experiment 1948–1974* (Berkeley, 1977), 33.

9. These quotes are from the *Communist Manifesto*. Cited in Pavel Câmpeanu, *Exit: Toward Post-Stalinism* (London, 1990), 52.

10. Rusinow, *Yugoslav Experiment*, 51.

11. Patrick Hyder Patterson, *Bought and Sold: Living and Losing the Good Life in Socialist Yugoslavia* (Ithaca, NY, 2011), 25.

12. That was the second five-year plan. Between 1952 and 1960, per capita GDP increased by 54 percent, and consumption rates grew at 4.8 percent. Real personal income increased from 1960 to 1965 at an astounding rate of 9 percent yearly. Patterson, *Bought and Sold*, 30–31, 33.

13. Patterson, *Bought and Sold*, 34–35.

14. Novak Janković, "The Changing Role of the U.S.A. in Financing Yugoslav Economic Development Since 1945," in *Economic and Strategic Issues in U.S. Foreign Policy*, Carl-Ludwig Holt-frerich, ed. (Berlin and New York, 1989), 266.

15. Marian Gyaurski, "Die Unversöhnlichen-Widerstand gegen den Kommunismus in Bulgarien," in *Texte zum Kommunismus in Bulgarien. KAS e.V. Bulgarien*, Konrad-Adenauer Stiftung, ed., November 26, 2014, 6–7; available at http://www.kas.de/wf/doc/kas_39743-1522-1-30.pdf ?141208085543 (accessed November 24, 2016).

16. Seymour Freidin, *The Forgotten People* (New York, 1962), 151–159. On Zápotocký: Alena Zemančíková, "Plzeň 1953 a Masaryk se smyčkou na krku," *Denik Referendum Domov*, March 7, 2016, available at

http://denikreferendum.cz/clanek/tisk/22492-plzen-1953-a-masaryk-se-smyckou-na-krku (accessed December 19, 2018).

17. That reform meant that workers had to produce approximately a quarter more for the same wage. Ivan Pfaff, "Weg mit der Partei," *Die Zeit*, May 22, 2003, 76; Keven McDermott, *Communist Czechoslovakia 1945–1989: A Political and Social History* (London, 2015); Jakub Šlouf, *Spřízněni měnou : genealogie plzeňské revolty 1. června 1953* (Prague, 2016).

18. Pfaff, "Weg mit der Partei."

19. Heumos, "Vyhrňme si rukávy," 72.

20. Jeffrey Kopstein, "Chipping Away at the State: Workers' Resistance and the Demise of East Germany," *World Politics* 48:3 (1996), 412. The official was Otto Lehmann. His article was "Zu einigen schädlichen Erscheinungen bei der Erhöung der Arbeitsnormen," in *Tribüne*, June 16, 1953, reprinted in Ernst Deuerlein, ed., *DDR* (Munich, 1966), 133.

21. The West Berlin functionary was Ernst Scharnowski. Ilko-Sascha Kowalczuk, *17. Juni 1953* (Munich, 2013), 43. For the text of Scharnowski's call ("Naturrecht jedes bedrückten Menschen"), see Gerhard Beier, *Wir wollen freie Menschen Sein: Die Bauarbeiter gingen voran* (Cologne, 1993), 104.

22. "We have said that *there could not have been* Social-Democratic consciousness among the workers. It would have to be brought to them from without. The history of all countries shows that the working class, exclusively by its own effort, is able to develop only trade union consciousness." V. I. Lenin, "What Is to Be Done" (1902), in *Essential Works of Lenin*, Henry Christman, ed. (New York, 1966), 74.

23. Tony Judt, *Postwar: A History of Europe since 1945* (New York, 2005), 177.

24. By July 3, 10,506 persons had been arrested for supposed crimes committed on June 17, of whom more than half (6,529) were released. Others stood trial. "Chronologie des Aufstandes," *Die Tageszeitung*, June 14, 2003.

25. Zemančíková, "Plzeň 1953"; Memoirs of Bohumil Vávra, *Dnes* (Plzeň), October 14, 2014. For the US flags: Čestmír Císař, *Paměti* (Prague, 2005), 412–417.

26. They were at the Kremlin on June 13–16, 1953. György T. Varga, "Zur Vorgeschichte der ungarischen Revolution von 1956," in Foitzik, *Entstalinisierungskrise*, 64.

27. Charles Gati, *Failed Illusions: Moscow, Washington, Budapest, and the 1956 Hungarian Revolt* (Stanford, CA, 2006), 32; János M. Rainer, "Der 'Neue Kurs' in Ungarn 1953," in *1953: Krisenjahr des Kalten Krieges in Europa*, Christoph Klessmann, Bernd Stöver, eds., 77, 79; George Paloczi-Horvath, *Khrushchev: The Making of a Dictator* (Boston, 1960), 225.

28. Gati, *Failed Illusions*, 40.

29. Nagy's speech is cited in Rainer, "Der 'Neue Kurs,'" 89.

30. The overall number of collectives dropped by 14 percent in a year. It had stood at 26 percent, a mammoth increase since 1950. The 1953 total was not reached again until 1959. Samuel Baum, *The Labor Force in Hungary* (Washington, DC, 1962), 20–22; Ben Fowkes, *The Rise and Fall of Communism in Eastern Europe* (New York, 1993) 58, 199.

31. László Varga, "Der Fall Ungarn Revolution, Intervention, Kádárismus," in *Kommunismus in der Krise*, Roger Engelmann et al., eds. (Göttingen, 2008), 129. Internment camps holding more than 40,000 prisoners were dissolved, and more than 15,000 people were released from military and civilian prisons. István Vida, "Vorgeschichte," in *Ungarn 1956: Zur Geschichte einer gescheiterten Volkserhebung*, Rüdiger Kipke, ed. (Wiesbaden, 2007), 16; Lendvai, *Hungarians*, 446.

32. L. K. Gluchowski, "The Defection of Józef Światło and the Search for Jewish Scapegoats in The Polish United Workers' Party, 1953–1954," *Intermarium* 3:2 (1999); George Błażyński, ed., *Mówi Józef Światło: Za kulisami bezpieki i partii 1940–1955* (London, 1986), 12.

33. Adam Ważyk, "Poemat dla dorosłych," [Poem for Adults] *Nowa Kultura*, August 21, 1955.

34. William E. Griffith, "The Petőfi Circle: Forum for Ferment in the Hungarian Thaw," *Hungarian Quarterly*, January 1962, 15–16.

35. This was Revai's argument to Rákosi from 1953: Varga, "Zur Vorgeschichte," 64. Árpád von Klimó and Alexander M. Kunst, "Krisenmanagement und Krisenerfahrung. Die ungarische Parteiführung und die Systemkrisen 1953, 1956 und 1968," in *Aufstände im Ostblock. Zur Krisengeschichte des realen Sozialismus*, Henrik Bispinck et al., eds. (Berlin 2004), 287–308.

36. Varga, "Zur Vorgeschichte," 76.

37. Klimó and Kunst, "Krisenmanagement," 292; Jörg Hoensch, *A History of Modern Hungary* (London, 1988), 212–213.

38. Hoensch, *History*, 212; Griffith, "Petőfi Circle," 19–20; Charles Gati, "From Liberation to Revolution, 1945–1956," in Sugar et al., *History*, 377–378; Varga, "Fall Ungarn," 129.

39. On the sources of their mutual antipathy despite shared hopes for reform, see Taubman, *Khrushchev*, 258–261.

40. T. H. Rigby, *The Stalin Dictatorship: Khrushchev's "Secret Speech" and Other Documents* (Sydney, 1968), 37–66.

41. Paweł Machcewicz, *Rebellious Satellite: Poland 1956* (Stanford, CA, 2009), 21–22.

42. Gati, "From Liberation," 378; Andrea Petö, "Julia Rajk or the Power of Mourning," *Clio* 41 (2015), 147.

43. Machcewicz, *Rebellious Satellite*, 87, 92, 95.

44. Neal Ascherson, *The Polish August: The Self-Limiting Revolution* (New York, 1982), 71; Janusz Karwat, "Powstanie poznańskiego Czerwca 1956," in *1956: Poznań, Budapest*, Janusz Karwat and Janos Tischler (Poznań, 2006), 19.

45. Łukasz Jastrząb, "Rozstrzelano moje serce w Poznaniu," in *Poznański Czerwiec 1956 r.— straty osobowe i ich analiza* (Poznań, 2006), 152, 178; Johanna Granville, "Poland and Hungary, 1956. A Comparative Essay Based on New Archival Findings," in *Revolution and Resistance in Eastern Europe: Challenges to Communist Rule*, Kevin McDermott and Matthew Stibbe, eds. (New York, 2006), 57–77.

46. Machcewicz, *Rebellious Satellite*, 101, 132; Karwat, "Powstanie, 33.

47. Maria Jarosz, *Bearing Witness: A Personal Perspective on Sixty Years of Polish History*, Steven Stoltenberg, trans. (London, 2009), 64–65.

48. Krzysztof Pomian, *W kręgu Giedroycia* (Warsaw, 2000), 95.

49. Their total area declined from 11.2 percent of all agricultural land in 1955 to 1.2 percent in 1960. Jerzy Kostrowicki et al., *Przemiany struktury przestrzennej rolnictwa Polski, 1950–1970* (Wrocław, 1978), 39.

50. This summarizes things mentioned by Stefan Kisielewski in September 1956, as cited in Pomian, *W kręgu Giedroycia*, 95.

51. Pomian, *W kręgu Giedroycia*, 97.

52. He meant bringing Gomułka back into Politburo meetings without Soviet permission. Mark Kramer, "Soviet-Polish Relations," in Engelmann et al., *Kommunismus in der Krise*, 118; Borodziej, *Geschichte*, 299.

53. Kramer, "Soviet-Polish Relations," 120, note 223.

54. He called for stronger political and military ties to the Soviet Union and condemned those who tried to steer Poland away from the Warsaw Pact. Kramer, "Soviet-Polish Relations," 122–123.

55. Granville, "Poland and Hungary," 61; János Tischler, "Polska wobec powstania węgierskiego 1956 roku," in Karwat and Tischler, *1956*, 192–193.

56. The first demonstration, according to the regime's estimates (collected during studies by State Security in 1959–1960) included some 250,000 (starting with 10,000–20,000 students). Janos M. Rainer, "A Progress of Ideas: The Hungarian Revolution of 1956," in *The Ideas of the Hungarian Revolution, Suppressed and Victorious, 1956–1999*, Lee Congdon and Béla K. Király, eds. (New York, 2002), 24; Granville, "Poland and Hungary," 61.

57. Paul E. Zinner, *Revolution in Hungary* (New York, 1962), 253.

58. Granville, "Poland and Hungary," 62.

59. As many as 200 demonstrators were killed. Paul Lendvai, *One Day That Shook the Communist World: The 1956 Hungarian Uprising and Its Legacy* (Princeton, NJ, 2008), 77–78; Varga, "Fall Ungarn," 132.

60. Lendvai, *One Day*, 67.

61. The party had fallen "utterly to pieces." Ferenc Donáth, reform Communist, cited in Lendvai, *One Day*, 86–87. Rainer, "Progress of Ideas," 24.

62. The charges were made in *Pravda*.

63. The reports were from Serov, Mikoyan, and Suslov. Lendvai, *One Day*, 88.

64. János M. Rainer and Bernd-Rainer Barth, "Ungarische Revolution: Aufstand—Zerfall der Partei—Invasion," in *Satelliten nach Stalins Tod*, András B. Hegedüs and Manfred Wilke, eds. (Berlin, 2000), 250–251; János M. Rainer, "The Yeltsin Dossier: Soviet Documents on Hungary, 1956," *CWIHP* 5 (Spring 1995), 25.

65. Vladislav M. Zubok, *A Failed Empire: The Soviet Union in the Cold War from Stalin to Gorbachev* (Chapel Hill, NC, 2007), 117.

66. Taubman, *Khrushchev*, 299. On the Hungarian side, there were 2,700 officially registered dead. Lendvai, *Hungarians*, 453; Soviet authorities counted 669 dead among their troops. Joanna Granville, "In the Line of Fire: The Soviet Crackdown on Hungary 1956–57," in *Hungary 1956—Forty Years On*, Terry Cox, ed. (London, 1997), 82.

67. Rainer and Barth, "Ungarische Revolution," 279–281.

68. Machcewicz, *Rebellious Satellite*, 30, 101, 237.

Chapter 21: National Paths to Communism: The 1960s

1. Marcin Zaremba, *Komunizm, legitymizacja, nacjonalizm: Nacjonalistyczna legitymizacja władzy komunistycznej w Polsce* (Warsaw, 2001), 179.

2. Zoltan D. Barany, *Soldiers and Politics in Eastern Europe: The Case of Hungary* (New York, 1993), 47.

3. Zaremba, *Komunizm*, 270; Peter Zwick, *National Communism* (Boulder, CO, 1983), 88.

4. Zaremba, *Komunizm*, 272. This was Mieczysław F. Rakowski.

5. Zaremba, *Komunizm*, 267.

6. "Ostensible" because, though there were expellee organizations in the Federal Republic of Germany, the state was also bound to the West and to NATO.

7. David Crowley, "Socialist Recreation? Amateur Film and Photography in the People's Republic of Poland and East Germany," in *Sovietization of Eastern Europe*, E. A. Rees et al., eds. (Washington, DC, 2008), 104.

8. Crowley, "Socialist Recreation?" 108.

9. Marx described the realm of freedom in *Das Kapital*: "The realm of freedom actually begins only where labor which is determined by necessity and mundane considerations ceases. . . . Freedom in this field can only consist in socialized man, the associated producers, rationally regulating their interchange with Nature, bringing it under common control, instead of being ruled by it as by the blind forces of Nature." Cited in Crowley, "Socialist Recreation?" 97.

10. The Cominform was dissolved in April 1956.

11. "Der Fakt," *Der Spiegel*, January 2, 1967, 37. The number was 200,000 in 1960.

12. See the contributions in Wolf Oschlies and Hellmuth G. Bütow in *Die Rolle der DDR in Osteuropa*, Gert Leptin, ed. (Berlin, 1974); and Erwin Weit, *Ostblock intern* (Hamburg, 1970).

13. "Die SED unterscheidet zwischen Nation und Nationalität," *Die Zeit*, February 21, 1975.

14. François Fejtö, *A History of the Peoples Democracies: Eastern Europe since Stalin* (London, 1971), 188–189.

15. Molnar was a Central Committee member and chairman of the Hungarian Historical Society. Balázs Trencsényi, "Afterlife or Reinvention? 'National Essentialism' in Romania and Hungary after 1945," in *Hungary and Romania Beyond National Narratives: Comparisons and Entanglements*, Anders Blomqvist et al., eds. (Frankfurt, 2013), 540.

16. L. Péter, "A Debate on the History of Hungary between 1790 and 1945," *Slavonic and East European Review* 50:120 (1972), 443–444.

17. György Péteri, "Demand Side Abundance: On the Post-1956 Social Contract in Hungary," *East Central Europe* 43 (2016), 315–343; Gough, *Good Comrade*, 127.

18. This was done by February 1961.

19. Thanks to György Péteri for this formula.

20. Péteri, "Demand Side," 322; Tibor Valuch, "After the Revolution," in *Hungary under Soviet Domination*, Tibor Valuch and Gyorgy Gyarmati (New York, 2009), 315. Thanks to Lydia Maher for the reference.

21. Péteri, "Demand Side," 325, 329; Derek H. Aldcroft and Steven Morewood, *Economic Change in Eastern Europe since 1918* (Aldershot, UK, 1995), 112.

22. Gough, *Good Comrade*, 135, 141.

23. Iván T. Berend, The Hungarian Economic Reforms 1953–1988 (Cambridge, 1990), 113; Zsuzsanna Varga, "Reshaping the Socialist Economy: The Hungarian Case," in Österreich und Ungarn im Kalten Krieg, István Majoros, Zoltán Maruzsa, and Oliver Rathkolb, eds. (Vienna, 2010), 407.

24. Berend, Hungarian Economic Reforms, 114.

25. Zsusanna Varga, "Questioning the Soviet Economic Model," in Muddling Through in the Long 1960s: Ideas and Everyday Life in High Politics and the Lower Classes of Communist Hungary, János M. Rainer and György Péteri, eds. (Trondheim, 2005), 113, 115.

26. Varga, "Questioning," 115.

27. Nigel Swain, Hungary: The Rise and Fall of Feasible Socialism (London, 1992), 123; Aldcroft and Morewood, Economic Change, 123.

28. Varga, "Questioning," 125.

29. Varga, "Reshaping," 415; Gough, Good Comrade, 152–153.

30. Varga, "Reshaping," 415.

31. A levy was imposed on enterprise profits that was redistributed centrally to loss-making factories. Varga, "Reshaping," 415–416.

32. Varga, "Questioning," 126; Berend, Hungarian Economic Reforms, 117–118.

33. Varga, "Reshaping," 409.

34. Péteri, "Demand Side," 327.

35. Roman Laba, The Roots of Solidarity: A Political Sociology of Poland's Working-Class Democratization (Princeton, NJ, 1991), 18–19.

36. Paweł Machcewicz, Władysław Gomułka (Warsaw, 1995), 56. Only eight of eighty-five Central Committee members elected for the Fourth Polish United Workers Party congress in 1964 belonged to liberal Puławy group. Andrzej Friszke, Polska: losy państwa i narodu (Warsaw, 2003), 250.

37. Friszke, Polska, 250–251, 262; Machcewicz, Gomułka, 57.

38. Zbigniew Landau and Jerzy Tomaszewski, The Polish Economy in the Twentieth Century (London, 1985), 266.

39. Kuroń and Żakowski, PRL, 127.

40. Nails and tools were expensive. Wiesław P. Kęcik, "The Lack of Food in Poland," in Poland: Genesis of a Revolution, Abraham Brumberg, ed. (New York, 1983).

41. After 1971, they could increase their holdings to a maximum of 30 hectares; farmers were also included in national health care. George Blazynski, Flashpoint Poland (New York, 1979), 190.

42. Friszke, Polska, 263.

43. By 1970, 45 percent of Polish families had a television. Friszke, Polska, 265.

44. Borodziej, Geschichte, 319. From the memoir of a French diplomat.

45. Friszke, Polska, 264.

46. The same was true for Bulgaria. Andrzej Jezierski and Cecylia Leszczyńska, Historia Gospordarcza Polski (Warsaw, 1999), 504.

47. The party apparatus was about the same size in Hungary, the Czech lands, and Poland in the mid- to late 1960s (7,000; 8,700; 8,000), but the Polish population was about three times larger (in 1970: 32.6 million versus 10.3 million [Hungary] and 9.9 million [Czech lands]). The Polish party was smaller during the formative years of Stalinism than counterparts elsewhere, always below 6 percent of the population, while the Czech, Hungarian, and East German totals

in the mid-1950s were 13 percent, 8.8 percent, and 9 percent, respectively. Anna M. Grzymała-Busse, *Redeeming the Communist Past: The Regeneration of Communist Parties in East Central Europe* (Cambridge, 2002), 32, 43, 52; John Connelly, *Captive University* (Chapel Hill, NC, 2000), 351, note 18.

48. Machcewicz, *Gomułka*, 54, 58.

49. Paczkowski, *Pół wieku*, 342.

50. Sheldon Anderson, *A Cold War in the East Bloc: Polish–East German Relations* (Boulder, CO, 2001), 227–228. Other places witnessing confrontation included Kraśnik, Głuchołazy, Gliwice, and Toruń. Paczkowski, *Pół wieku*, 343.

51. Machcewicz, *Gomułka*, 59.

52. Brian Porter-Szűcs, *Faith and Fatherland: Catholicism, Modernity, and Poland* (Oxford, 2011), 208 and passim.

53. Robert Jarocki, *Czterdzieści pięć lat w opozycji* (Kraków, 1990), 205.

54. Pope John Paul II, *Wybór kazań nowohuckich oraz homilie Jan Pawła II w Krakowie-Nowej Hucie* (Kraków, 2013), 134, 222; Monika Golonka-Czajkowska, *Nowe miasto nowych ludzi: Mitologie nowohuckie* (Kraków, 2013), 341.

55. Karol Sauerland, "Die Verhaftung der Schwarzen Madonna," *Frankfurter Allgemeine Zeitung*, August 17, 2010.

56. He said this in January 1966 to the National Unity Front. Robert Żurek, "Der Briefwechsel der katholischen Bischöfe von 1965," in *Versöhnung und Politik*, Friedhelm Boll et al., eds. (Bonn, 2009), 70–71.

57. Borodziej, *Geschichte*, 310; *Życie Warszawy*, December 10, 1965, cited in Andrzej Micewski, *Kościół i państwo* (Warsaw, 1994), 45.

58. Sauerland, "Verhaftung."

59. Paczkowski, *Pół wieku*, 343.

60. Comments of Tadeusz Mazowiecki, cited in Stefan Bratkowski, ed., *Październik 1956: Pierwszy wyłom w systemie* (Warsaw, 1996), 220–221; Paczkowski, *Pół wieku*, 346. In 1914, 77 percent of students raised in the Russian partition considered themselves "nonbelievers." Porter-Szűcs, *Faith*, 217.

61. He was called General "gas pipe" for saying that the party would defend itself with that instrument if need be. Paulina Codogni, *Rok 1956* (Warsaw, 2006), 159. On Tokarski, see Hansjakob Stehle, *Nachbar Polen* (Frankfurt, 1968), 67–69.

62. A. M. Rosenthal, "Polish Reds Turn Bitter over Rule," *New York Times*, December 1, 1959.

63. Borodziej, *Geschichte*, 304; Paczkowski, *Pół wieku*, 317; Andrzej Werblan, "Władysław Gomułka and the Dilemma of Polish Communism," *International Political Science Review* 9:2 (1988), 154; Friszke, *Polska*, 248–249; Adam Leszczyński, "Najsłynniejszy list Peerelu," *Gazeta Wyborcza*, March 17, 2014.

64. Paczkowski, *Pół wieku*, 318; Borodziej, *Geschichte*, 307.

65. The journals were *Nowa kultura* and *Przegląd kulturalny*. Paczkowski, *Pół wieku*, 328.

66. Arrested was art historian Karol Estreicher. For a full list of penalties, see Aleksandra Ziółkowska-Boehm, *Melchior Wankowicz: Poland's Master of the Written Word* (Lanham, MD, 2013), 31–33.

67. The official was Mieczysław Jastrun. Cited in Joanna Szczęsna and Anna Bikont, *Lawina i kamienie: pisarze wobec komunizmu* (Warsaw, 2006), 323–324.

68. Paczkowski, *Pół wieku*, 329.

69. This from his diary, June 17, 1964. Cited in Szczęsna, and Bikont, *Lawina*, 328.

70. That was in the Catholic front organization PAX, headed by former fascist Bolesław Piasecki. See Mikołaj Kunicki, *Between the Brown and the Red* (Athens, OH, 2012).

71. Machcewicz, *Gomułka*, 60; Friszke, *Polska*, 292–293.

72. Maryjane Osa, *Solidarity and Contention* (Minneapolis, MN, 2003), 92–93.

73. Szczęsna and Bikont, *Lawina*, 341–342.

74. Paczkowski, *Pół wieku*, 329.

75. Krzysztof Szwagrzyk, ed., *Aparat Bezpieczenstwa w Polsce*, vol. 3 (Warsaw, 2008) 59. The latter was the view of Zenon Nowak. Zaremba, *Komunizm*, 237–238.

76. Włodzimierz Rozenbaum, "The March Events: Targeting the Jews," *POLIN: A Journal of Polish-Jewish Studies* 21 (2008), 64.

77. Other examples include Generals Kazimierz Witaszewski and Grzegorz Korczyński. Rozenbaum, "March Events."

78. People who did not vote, for example, were enemies, standing against a nation understood in terms of "tribal connections, mythology of blood and soil." Zaremba, *Komunizm*, 301; Borodziej, *Geschichte*, 309.

79. Zaremba, *Komunizm*, 301. The analysis is based on the work of Michał Głowiński.

80. Tomasz Leszkowicz, "Zbigniew Załuski: niepokorny pisarz reżimowy," Histmag.org, May 3, 2013, at http://histmag.org/Zbigniew-Zaluski-niepokorny-pisarz-rezimowy-7681 (accessed December 19, 2018). Other critics included Kazimierz Koźniewski, Dariusz Fikus, Professor Bogusław Leśnodorski, and Stefan Kisielewski. Zbigniew Brzezinski, *Alternative to Partition* (New York, 1965), 32; Dariusz Stola, *Kampania antysyjonistyczna w Polsce 1967–1968* (Warsaw, 2000), 22.

81. The Gomułka regime had been unusually passive toward the rising challenge from the "Partisans," probably because its energies were devoted to combating the church. Borodziej, *Geschichte*, 309.

82. The original threat was to move 250,000. Mark Biondich, *The Balkans: Revolution, War, and Political Violence since 1878* (Oxford, 2011), 172.

83. David Binder, "Todor Zhivkov Dies at 86," *New York Times*, August 7, 1998.

84. R. J. Crampton, *A Concise History of Bulgaria* (Cambridge, 1997), 203.

85. Biondich, *Balkans*, 175.

86. Biondich, *Balkans*, 173.

87. Bulgarian Helsinki Committee, *The Human Rights of Muslims in Bulgaria in Law and in Politics since 1878* (Sofia, 2003), 56.

88. Biondich, *Balkans*, 173.

89. Involved was the imposition of new identity cards and birth and marriage certificates. Biondich, *Balkans*, 174. National chauvinism was even a kind of defense against reform: it increased with advent of the Soviet reformer Mikhail Gorbachev. Vladimir Tismaneanu, "What Was National Stalinism," in *The Oxford Handbook of Postwar European History*, Dan Stone, ed. (Oxford, 2012), 473.

90. Matthew Brunwasser, "Bulgaria's Unholy Alliances," *New York Times*, March 7, 2013; Bulgarian Helsinki Committee, *Human Rights*, 52.

91. Vladimir Tismaneanu, *Stalinism for All Seasons* (Berkeley, 2003), 144.

92. And Vasile Luca and Teohari Georgescu. Tismaneanu, *Stalinism*, 175. Walter Ulbricht spread the idea that it was discussion of "problems" that had made the protests of June 17, 1953, possible, and he relied on Soviet help, as well as a coherent cadre, tested under Nazism, to band together against all criticism of the party. Supposedly the events of 1956 had only confirmed the error of pursuing destalinization. See Catherine Epstein, *The Last Revolutionaries* (Cambridge, MA, 2003), 167–184.

93. Stefano Bottoni, "Nation-Building through Judiciary Repression: The Impact of the 1956 Revolution on Romanian Minority Policy," in *State and Minority in Transylvania, 1918–1989: Studies on the History of the Hungarian Community*, Attila Hunyadi, ed. (Boulder, CO, 2012), 415.

94. Bottoni, "Nation-Building," 421.

95. Bottoni, "Nation-Building," 415.

96. Bottoni, "Nation-Building," 404, 409.

97. Tismaneanu, *Stalinism*, 179; Zbigniew K. Brzezinski, *The Soviet Bloc: Unity and Conflict* (Cambridge, MA, 1957), 383–384.

98. "This policy was the underpinning of the nationalist Communism developed beginning in 1971." Caius Dobrescu, "Conflict and Diversity in East European Nationalism, on the Basis of a Romanian Case Study," *East European Politics and Societies* 17:3 (2003), 404.

99. Stefano Bottoni, "Find the Enemy: Ethnicized State Violence and Population Control in Ceauşescu's Romania," *Journal of Cold War Studies* 19:4 (2017), 4.

100. Tismaneanu, *Stalinism*, 183. The term is Zbigniew Brzezinski's.

101. The internationalist leadership of the early years, including Ana Pauker, had revealed a Great Romanian understanding of their country. (Personal communication of Bogdan Iacob, July 2013.) For example, in 1944, in conversations with Stalin, Romanian Communists "based their plea for Transylvania by insisting on the history of the region, from the Roman conquest onwards." In the 1960s, they published "scholarly work, arguing for the incorporation of Bessarabia, based in Marx." Dragoş Petrescu, "The Alluring Facet of Ceauşescuism: Nation-Building and Identity Politics in Communist Romania, 1965–1989," *New Europe College Yearbook* 11 (2003/2004), 249–250.

102. Judt, *Postwar*, 431.

Chapter 22: 1968 and the Soviet Bloc: Reform Communism

1. Peter Zwick, *National Communism*, 108. Emphasis added.

2. Cited in Pavel Kolář, "Post-Stalinist Reformism and the Prague Spring," in *The Cambridge History of Communism*, Norman Naimark, Silvio Pons, and Sophie Quinn-Judge, eds., vol. 2 (Cambridge, 2017), 170–172.

3. The leading student of the challenges of 1956 in Czechoslovakia, Muriel Blaive, argues that many people hoped for a return of more democratic forms of rule and resented specific party leaders, but were too attached to their comfortable lifestyle to take risks. See her "Perceptions of Society in Czechoslovak Secret Police Archives: How a 'Czechoslovak 1956' was Thwarted," in *Perceptions of Society in Communist Europe*, Muriel Blaive, ed. (London, 2019), 101–122.

4. John N. Stevens, *Czechoslovakia at the Crossroads: The Economic Dilemmas of Communism in Postwar Czechoslovakia* (New York, 1985), 306.

5. About 750 ran the party center. Kieran Williams, *The Prague Spring and Its Aftermath* (Cambridge, 1997), 14.

6. Varga, "Reshaping," 408.

7. Stalinists Bruno Koehler, Josef Urválek, and Karol Bacílek left, while reformers Čestmír Císař and Alexander Dubček advanced in this early period. Galia Golan, *The Czechoslovak Reform Movement: Communism in Crisis 1962–68* (Cambridge, 1971), 27, 32–34.

8. The initiator of the idea for a conference had been Jean-Paul Sartre, who challenged writers in East and West to consider Kafka a "test case" for Cold War rivalry. Goldstücker, an old Communist, had taken up the challenge. The East German cultural functionaries, led by Alfred Kurella, were bothered by the political challenge: the idea that they might be led to agree that socialism had not done away with capitalist alienation. Martina Langermann, "'Nicht tabu, aber erledigt.' Zur Geschichte der Kafka-Debatte aus der Sicht Alfred Kurellas," *Zeitschrift für Germanistik* 4:3 (1994), 606–621. On the naps: Antje Schmelcher, "Onkel Franz Geht Spazieren," *Die Welt*, June 14, 2000.

9. Extensive production had involved increasing quantities of workers and raw materials and machines; intensive production aimed at making all elements of the production process function more effectively, and therefore competitively on world markets.

10. This report was titled "Civilization at the Crossroads." Zbyněk A. B. Zeman, *Prague Spring: A Report on Czechoslovakia 1968* (Harmondsworth, UK, 1969), 89 and passim.

11. A person would "hunt in the morning, fish in the afternoon, rear cattle in the evening, criticize after dinner . . . without ever becoming hunter, fisherman, herdsman or critic." Karl Marx and Frederick Engels, *German Ideology*, C. J. Arthur, ed. (London, 1970), 53.

12. For a gripping narrative of the reform process told from the inside, see Mlynář's memoir of the period, *Nightfrost in Prague: The End of Humane Socialism* (London, 1980).

13. His words: "Was the cultural worth of the Czechs great enough to justify their existence as a nation?"

14. Jaromír Navrátil, *The Prague Spring 1968* (New York, 1998), 8.

15. H. Gordon Skilling, *Czechoslovakia's Interrupted Revolution* (Princeton, NJ, 1976), 70; Navrátil, *Prague Spring*, 10.

16. Skilling, *Interrupted Revolution*, 71.

17. Dušan Hamšík, *Spisovatelé a moc* (Prague, 1969), 190.

18. Maria Dowling, *Czechoslovakia* (London, 2002), 104–105.

19. Eugen Steiner, *The Slovak Dilemma* (Cambridge, 1973), 154–159.

20. Frank Magill, *The Twentieth Century, Dictionary of World Biography*, vol. 7 (Pasadena, CA, 2008), 968.

21. For example, he states in his memoir that he had no desire to be included among those called to play cards with Novotný. Alexander Dubček, *Hope Dies Last*, Jiří Hochman, trans. (New York, 1993), 83.

22. Richard Severo, "Alexander Dubcek, 70, Dies in Prague," *New York Times*, November 9, 1992. The former statement was made on February 22, 1968, with Leonid Brezhnev present.

23. Dubček, *Hope Dies Last*, 302–303, 313.

24. Williams, *Prague Spring*, 15.

25. On the ambivalence as well as popularity of the reform program (as well as a slow backlash in the party itself beginning in June 1968), see Kolář, "Post-Stalinist Reformism," 176–178.

26. "Action Program of the Communist Party of Czechoslovak Communist Party," *Marxism Today*, July 1968, 205–213. On these groups, see Skilling, *Interrupted Revolution*, 264–266.

27. That principle, going back to the 1920s, had involved above all strict control of cadres and appointment of party functionaries by the leadership rather than by their election from the base.

28. That was in part due to their conviction that they should be able pursue their own course, in part due to the inability of the Czechoslovak reformers and conservatives to decide for or against decisive intervention in the media. Karen Dawisha, *The Kremlin and the Prague Spring* (Berkeley, 1984), 260–269; Williams, *Prague Spring*, 104–105; Jiří Valenta, *Soviet Intervention in Czechoslovakia, 1968: Anatomy of a Decision* (Baltimore, 1979), 84.

29. There was a lengthy and emotional phone call on August 13, during which Brezhnev accused Dubček of deceit and sabotage—because of supposed anti-Soviet slander. Jaromir Navratil, ed., *The Prague Spring 1968. A National Security Archives Document Reader* (Budapest, 1998), 345–348; Valenta, *Soviet Intervention*, 172.

30. They were Vasil Biľak, Alois Indra, and Drahomír Kolder, who along with Oldřich Švestka and Antonín Kapek had written Leonid Brezhnev in August to request aid against the "counterrevolution." For the text, see F. Janáček and M. Michálková, "Příběh zvacího dopisu," *Soudobé dějiny* 1 (1993), 92–93.

31. Valenta, *Soviet Intervention*, 174.

32. Dubček, *Hope Dies Last*, 213.

33. Dubček, *Hope Dies Last*, 209.

34. Dubček, *Hope Dies Last*, 239. This was right after the hockey games in which the Soviet Union had staged a provocation in Prague, placing a huge pile of stones in front of the Aeroflot (the Soviet airline) office and encouraging people to throw them; the Soviets sent in more troops at that point.

35. Sabine Stach, *Vermächtnispolitik. Jan Palach und Oskar Brüsewitz als politische Märtyrer* (Göttingen, 2016), 87.

36. That occurred in 1975. See http://www.radio.cz/en/section/czech-history/president -gustav-husak-the-face-of-czechoslovakias-normalisation (accessed November 25, 2016).

37. About 500,000 were removed, of about 1,500,000. Jiří Vykoukal, Bohuslav Litera, and Miroslav Tejchman, *Východ: vznik, vývoj a rozpad sovětského bloku, 1944–1989* (Prague, 2000), 575–576.

38. Vykoukal et al., *Východ: vznik*, 575. There were decisions to check party cards in the plenum of January 1970, and because that check was judged too benevolent, then again in April.

39. Cited in Maruška Svašek, "Styles, Struggles, and Careers: An Ethnography of the Czech Art World, 1948–1992" (PhD dissertation, University of Amsterdam, 1996), 114.

40. Svašek, "Styles," 120. In 1975.

41. Svašek, "Styles," 122.

42. Małgorzata Fidelis, *Women, Communism, and Industrialization in Postwar Poland* (Cambridge, 2010), 203–230; Małgorzata Mazurek, *Społeczeństwo kolejki. O doświadczeniach niedoboru 1945–1989* (Warsaw, 2010), 153–154.

43. Authors agree that neither Gomułka nor other top figures in leadership were "personally" anti-Semitic, but instead they used the issue for its potential to form constituencies in support of his policies. Adam Schaff, *Moje spotkania z nauką polską* (Warsaw, 1997), 107 and passim.

44. Gomułka reacted when the interests of the Soviet Union seemed threatened. Zaremba, *Komunizm*, 334.

45. Zaremba, *Komunizm*, 336.

46. Janina Bauman, *A Dream of Belonging: My Years in Postwar Poland* (London, 1988), 177.

47. Jacek Kuroń and Jacek Żakowski, *PRL dla początkujących* (Wrocław, 1996), 137; Adam Michnik, "Rana na czole Adama Mickiewicza," *Gazeta Wyborcza*, November 4, 2005; Harold B. Segel, "Introduction," in *Polish Romantic Drama: Three Plays in English Translation* (Ithaca, NY, 1977), 42; Jerzy Eisler, *Polskie miesiące: czyli Kryzys(y) w PRL* (Warsaw, 2008), 180; Zaremba, *Komunizm*, 340.

48. Eisler, *Polskie miesiące*, 31.

49. Eisler, *Marzec 1968: geneza, przebieg, konsekwencje* (Warsaw, 1991), 158; Szczęsna and Bikont, *Lawina*, 356.

50. Bauman, *Dream*, 185–186.

51. Comments of Andrzej Chojonowski, who was a student in 1968. Barbara Polak, "Pytania, które należy postawić," *Biuletyn IPN* 3:86 (2008), 9.

52. Andrzej Friszke, "Miejsce marca 1968 wśród innych polskich miesięcy," in *Oblicza marca 1968*, Konrad Rokicki and Sławomir Stępień, eds. (Warsaw, 2004), 17; comments of Paweł Tomasik in Polak, "Pytania, które należy postawić," 2.

53. Protests took place in Warsaw, Gdańsk, Gliwice, Katowice, Kraków, Lublin, Łódź, Poznań, Szczecin, Bielsko-Biała, Legnice, Radom, Tarnów, Cieszyn, Przemyśl, and Opole; public meetings with resolutions took place in Wrocław, Białystok, Bydgoszcz, Olsztyn, and Toruń. Eisler, *Polskie miesiące*, 32–33.

54. In Polish: "dyktatura ciemniaków." Kisielewski claimed he was referring only to the censors.

55. Bauman, *Dream*, 189–191.

56. Michnik, "Rana."

57. Schaff, *Moje Spotkania*, 115.

58. Zaremba, *Komunizm*, 354–355; Edward Jan Nalepa, *Wojsko polskie w grudniu 1970* (Warsaw, 1990), 7.

59. Schaff, *Moje Spotkania*, 113; Michał Głowiński ("Communism turned out to be fascism, that is total and left-wing, but also right-wing.") cited in Szczęsna and Bikont, *Lawina*, 372.

60. Cited in Włodzimierz Rozenbaum, "The March Events: Targeting the Jews," *Polin* 21 (2009), 63.

61. Stephen D. Roper, *Romania: The Unfinished Revolution* (Amsterdam, 2000), 49.

62. Petrescu, "Alluring Facet," 251.

63. Bernard Wheaton and Zdeněk Kavan, *The Velvet Revolution: Czechoslovakia, 1988–1991* (Boulder, CO, 1992), 14–15; Robert V. Daniels, *A Documentary History of Communism*, vol. 2 (London, 1985), 338.

64. Czechoslovakia went from 5.5 to 3.7 percent; Bulgaria from 7.9 to 6.1 percent; Hungary from 6.5 to 3.5 percent; East Germany from 5.4 to 4.1 percent; Romania from 9.1 to 7.2 percent; and the Soviet Union from 5.6 to 4.3 percent. Vykoukal et al., *Východ: vznik*, 475.

65. Florin Abraham, *Romania since the Second World War* (London, 2017), 51.

66. His "day job" was as psychotherapist. For more on the secret ordinations, also of bishops, see David Doellinger, *Turning Prayers into Protests: Religious-Based Activism and Its Challenge to State Power* in Slovakia and East Germany (Budapest, 2013), 41.

67. Article two of a law on education (July 15, 1961) proclaimed that schools were secular. "Ustawa z dnia 15 lipca 1961 r. o rozwoju systemu oświaty i wychowania," *Dziennik Ustaw* 1961, no. 32, position 160.

Chapter 23: Real Existing Socialism: Life in the Soviet Bloc

1. This was also the baseline self-understanding of Soviet Stalinism. Stephen Kotkin, *Magnetic Mountain: Stalinism as a Civilization* (Berkeley, 1995), 360.

2. Erich Honecker was a roofer, Władysław Gomułka an oil field mechanic, Janos Kádár a typewriter mechanic, Antonin Novotný a metal worker, Todor Zhivkov a printer, Gheorghe Gheorgiu Dej a railway electrician, Josip Broz Tito a machinist, and so on. Ghiţa Ionescu, *Communism in Rumania, 1944–1962* (New York, 1964), 45; Jozo Tomasevich, "Yugoslavia during the Second World War," in *Contemporary Yugoslavia*, Wayne Vucinich and Jozo Tomasevich, eds. (Berkeley, 1969), 84; Obituary (Zhivkov), *New York Times*, August 7, 1998; on Kádár, see John Moody, "Hungary Building Freedoms out of Defeat," *Time*, August 11, 1986.

3. In a book presented to East German teenagers at their atheist confirmation ritual in the late 1970s, the Soviet philosopher G. I. Gleserman described Socialism and Communism as two phases of the *same* economic and social order, featuring social ownership of the means of production, aiming not for profit, but to "satisfy the growing needs of the population." Communism would feature a higher material-technical base, including the automation of production processes, the electrification of all branches of the economy, and the exploitation of new, more efficient energy resources. The cultural and technical level of workers would rise, and all boundaries disappear between the intelligentsia and workers and peasants. G. I. Gleserman, "Auf dem Weg zur kommunistischen Zukunft," in *Der Sozialismus: Deine Welt*, Heinrich Gemkow et al., eds. (Berlin, 1975), 290.

4. Real existing socialism was not a "brief stop on the way to Communism," warned Gleserman, and it was harmful to announce utopia's arrival before its time. That future would feature not only a new society but also new human beings. "The transition to Communism," he wrote, "is tied to the continued strengthening of social order and discipline, to achieving a level of development of society such that people are used to keeping the rules of socialist cohabitation and no longer require force. Gleserman, "Auf dem Weg," 296.

5. Engels was not clear exactly how workers would be inclined to govern their own lives, but he had basic faith in technological progress to generate a change in consciousness. Karl Marx and Friedrich Engels, *Werke*, vol. 38 (Berlin, 1968), 64. (A letter of March 1891 to Max Oppenheim).

6. The words were written in 1950 by the Communist poet Johannes R. Becher. Michael Brie and Dieter Klein, *Der Engel der Geschichte: befreiende Erfahrungen einer Niederlage* (Berlin, 1993), 267.

7. Alec Nove has written that given Stalinism's extremism, a return to some more moderate course seemed politically expedient to everyone. Alec Nove, *Stalinism and After* (London, 1975),

120. "Around 1981," Martin McCauley writes, "Communism meant almost entirely food and consumer goods. The material was again the master." *The Soviet Union 1917–1991* (London, 1993), 219.

8. Steffen Plaggenborg, introduction to Galina Ivanova, *Entstalinisierung als Wohlfahrt: Sozialpolitik in der Sowjetunion, 1953–1970* (New York and Frankfurt, 2015), 8–9.

9. William Taubman, *Khrushchev: The Man and His Era* (New York, 2003), 260.

10. Stephen E. Hanson, *Time and Revolution: Marxism and the Design of Soviet Institutions* (Chapel Hill, NC, 1997), 172. Khrushchev was associated with "revolutionary denial of time constraints," but Brezhnev was a centrist, who attacked deviations of right and left and upheld the purity of Marxist-Leninist doctrine, the leading role of the party, and the Stalinist socioeconomic status quo.

11. Ivan T. Berend, *Central and Eastern Europe 1944–93: Detour from the Periphery to the Periphery* (Cambridge, 1998), 162; Vernon Aspaturian, "Eastern Europe in World Perspective," in *Communism in Eastern Europe*, Teresa Rakowska-Harmstone, ed. (Bloomington, IN, 1984), 22–23.

12. John Keane, ed., *The Power of the Powerless: Citizens against the State in Central–Eastern Europe* (Armonk, NY, 1985), 45.

13. Małgorzata Mazurek, "Keeping It Close to Home: Resourcefulness and Scarcity in Late Socialist Poland," in *Communism Unwrapped: Consumption in Cold War Eastern Europe*, Paulina Bren and Mary Neuburger, eds. (Oxford, 2012), 300–302; Paul Betts, *Within Walls: Private Life in the German Democratic Republic* (Oxford, 2012), 180.

14. Gábor Kovács, "Revolution, Lifestyle," in Rainer and Péteri, *Muddling Through*, 29.

15. Janos Rainer, "The Sixties in Hungary," in Rainer and Péteri, *Muddling Through*, 16, note 57.

16. Rainer, "The Sixties in Hungary," 13.

17. Varga, "Questioning," 110–111.

18. Annette Kaminsky, *Illustrierte Konsumgeschichte der DDR* (Erfurt, 1999), 51.

19. Mark Pittaway, *The Workers' State: Industrial Labor and the Making of Socialist Hungary* (Pittsburgh, PA, 2012), 6–7; Katherine Verdery, *What Was Socialism, and What Comes Next?* (Princeton, NJ, 1996).

20. Mark Pittaway, *Eastern Europe, 1939–2000* (London, 2004), 122; Kaminsky, *Illustrierte Konsumgeschichte*, 31.

21. T. Dombos and L. Pellandini-Simányi, "Kids, Cars, or Cashews?: Debating and Remembering Consumption in Socialist Hungary," in Bren and Neuburger, *Communism Unwrapped*, 325–326.

22. Bradley Abrams, "Buying Time: Consumption and Political Legitimization in Late Communist Czechoslovakia," in *The End and the Beginning: The Revolutions of 1989 and the Resurgence of History*, Vladimir Tismaneanu with Bogdan C. Iacob, eds. (Budapest, 2012), 405.

23. Abrams, "Buying Time," 401; Dombos and Pellandini-Simányi, "Kids, Cars," 326.

24. A Gini coefficient of 0 indicates perfect equality, of 1 perfect inequality. The Czechoslovak figure was .22; GDR was .28; Cuba, .27; and Poland, .31. K. Griffin, *Alternative Strategies for Economic Development* (New York, 1999), 219. The US figure has been rising, from .37 in 1986, to .38 in 1991 to .40 in 1994. World Bank, "GINI Index for the United States," retrieved from Federal Reserve Bank of St. Louis, https://fred.stlouisfed.org/series/SIPOVGINUSA (accessed November 9, 2018).

The West European figures were over .5: France was .68, FRG .78.

25. The engineer Dieter Mosemann, for instance, earned less than a worker. http://www
.spiegel.de/wissenschaft/technik/patente-der-letzte-erfinder-der-ddr-a-702108.html (accessed
November 25, 2016).

26. The refrigerator had a capacity of 140 liters, with 7 liters for the freezer. Kaminsky, *Illustrierte
Konsumgeschichte*, 42. In the United States, household ownership of refrigerators went from
56 percent in 1940 to 80 percent in 1960, and to close to 100 percent by the mid-1960s. In France,
the total reached 80 percent by 1970, and rose to more than 100 percent by the 1980s. Vaclav
Smil, *Transforming the Twentieth Century: Technological Innovations and Their Consequences*
(Oxford, 2006), 42.

27. Heike Hüchtmann, "Küchen-Schätzchen entdeckt," In *Südthüringen.de*, July 30, 2011, at
http://www.insuedthueringen.de/lokal/suhl_zellamehlis/suhl/Kuechen-Schaetzchen
-entdeckt;art83456,1710085 (accessed November 25, 2016).

28. Kaminsky, *Illustrierte Konsumgeschichte*, 93.

29. Kaminsky, *Illustrierte Konsumgeschichte*, 95.

30. See http://doku.iab.de/mittab/1990/1990_4_mittab_stephan_wiedemann.pdf, 552 (accessed November 25, 2016).

31. Bernd Stöver, *Der Kalte Krieg, 1947–1991: Geschichte eines radikalen Zeitalters* (Munich,
2007), 304.

32. Stöver, *Der Kalte Krieg*, 303–304. Stöver claims this was true for personal computers and
the microchip.

33. Krisztina Fehérváry, "Goods and States: The Political Logic of State Socialist Material Culture," *Comparative Studies in Society and History* 51:2 (2009), 444, 446.

34. Fehérváry, "Goods and States," 430–431; Verdery, *What Was Socialism*, 28; John Borne-
man, *After the Wall: East Meets West in the New Berlin* (New York, 1991), 17–18.

35. I owe this point to Krisztina Fehérváry.

36. According to Mike Burkhardt, it sold for DM 59. See http://www.geschichte-entdecken
.com/Meine_DDR/ (accessed November 26, 2016).

37. Tobias Wunschik, *Knastware für den Klassenfeind* (Göttingen, 2014).

38. Fehérváry, "Goods and States," 448.

39. See http://www.b92.net/eng/news/world.php?yyyy=2013&mm=01&dd=31&nav_id
=84442 (accessed November 26, 2016).

40. See http://www.balkanalysis.com/romania/2011/12/27/in-romania-opinion-polls-show
-nostalgia-for-communism/#_edn1 (accessed November 26, 2016). That survey is from July 2010.
On the phenomenon in general, see the essays in Maria Todorova and Zsuzsa Gille, eds., *Post-
communist Nostalgia* (New York, 2010).

41. Paulina Bren, "Mirror, Mirror on the Wall, Is the West the Fairest of Them All. Czechoslovak Normalization and Its (Dis)contents," *Kritika* 9:4 (2008), 842, 844.

42. Bren, "Mirror, Mirror," 846.

43. Cited in Bren, "Mirror, Mirror," 846.

44. Daniela Dahn, "Wir wollten doch auch noch leben oder Die Legende vom faulen Ossi,"
in *Ein Land genannt die DDR*, Ulrich Plenzdorf and Rüdiger Dammann, eds. (Frankfurt am Main,
2005), 117.

45. György Konrad, "Wir schauspielern alle in ein und demselben Stück," in *Ungarn: Ein kommunistisches Wunderland?* István Futaky, ed. (Reinbek bei Hamburg, 1983), 29.

46. Cited in Dahn, "Wir wollten," 139.

47. Monika Maron cited in Kaminsky, *Illustrierte Konsumgeschichte*, 92.

48. Given because she discovered it was his birthday. Janine R. Wedel, *The Private Poland* (New York, 1986), 23.

49. Wedel, *Private Poland*, 45–47.

50. Wedel, *Private Poland*, 26.

51. Daphne Berdahl, *Where the World Ended: Re-unification and Identity in the German Borderland* (Berkeley, 1999), 120–121.

52. Berdahl, *Where the World Ended*, 12, 120. In 1979, it was estimated that one-third of all maintenance of houses and apartments in Hungary was accomplished by people working in the gray economy. Pittaway, *Eastern Europe*, 129. Friends of mine in a small Polish town "paid" the equivalent of a house to keep their father alive, who had a chronic illness requiring special care and Western medicines.

53. Wedel, *Private Poland*, 12.

54. That amounts to 146 liters of beer and 15.5 liters of hard alcohol. Kaminsky, *Illustrierte Konsumgeschichte*, 89.

55. "Dishonesty had become so ingrained in my approach to bureaucracy and formal relations," she wrote, "that when I returned to the United States several friends complained that I lied too much." Wedel, *Private Poland*, 17.

56. Timothy Garton Ash, *The Uses of Adversity: Essays on the Fate of Central Europe* (New York, 1989), 133.

57. Paul Betts, *Within Walls: Private Life in the German Democratic Republic* (Oxford, New York, 2010), 24–25.

58. Jens Gieseke, *Die Stasi: 1945–1990* (Munich, 2011), 163; Betts, *Within Walls*, 22, 39.

59. Betts, *Within Walls*, 24–34.

60. Harald Schultze, *Berichte der Magdeburger Kirchenleitung zu den Tagungen der Provinzialsynode* (Göttingen, 2005), 238.

61. The term developed for this kind of "negotiation" of state and society was *vorauseilender Gehorsam* (anticipatory compliance). See Stefan Wolle, *DDR: eine kurze Geschichte* (Frankfurt, 2004), 18 and passim; Jürgen Kocka, "Eine durchherrschte Gesellschaft," in *Sozialgeschichte der DDR*, Jürgen Kocka and Hartmut Kaelble, eds., (Stuttgart, 1994), 547–553.

62. That last figure was 31.1 percent if private agriculture was excluded. Simon Commander and Fabrizio Coricelli, *Output Decline in Poland and Hungary in 1990–91* (Washington, DC, 1992), 27. By 1984 there were approximately 470,000 private non-agricultural enterprises. Wedel, *Private Poland*, 37, 53.

63. Interior Minister Kiszczak personally ordered the release of the final 225 prisoners in September 1986. Kuroń and Żakowski, *PRL*, 254.

64. Its leaders believed that the Party had irresponsibly permitted a huge trade deficit to develop by the early 1980s. Jonathan R. Zatlin, *The Currency of Socialism: Money and Political Culture in East Germany* (Cambridge, 2007), 191.

65. This is a Westdeutscher Rundfunk story from November 30, 1977. At: http://www1.wdr.de/themen/archiv/stichtag/stichtag7126.html (accessed 26 November 2016). The official Trabant price was 7,850 East German marks. The VW Golf was between 27,000 and 36,000 East German marks.

66. Bruno Schrep, "Kinder der Schande," *Der Spiegel* 28 (1995), 60.

67. There was a wave of some 30,000 emigrants in 1984, as the regime attempted to "let off steam." Helge Heidmeyer, "Antifaschisticher Schutzwall oder Bankrotterklärung des Ulbricht-Regimes?" in *Das doppelte Deutschland*, Udo Wengst et al., eds. (Berlin, 2008), 94.

68. And in the more troublesome southern districts of the GDR, about every fourth informal agent was working against the opposition. Helmut Müller-Enberg, ed. *Inoffizielle Mitarbeiter des Ministeriums für Staatssicherheit: Statistiken*, vol. 3, (Berlin, 2008), 52; Irena Kukutz and Katja Havemann, *Geschützte Quelle : Gespräche mit Monika H., alias Karin Lenz, mit Faksimiles, Dokumenten und Fotos* (Berlin, 1990).

69. Pittaway, *Eastern Europe*, 128.

70. That coincided with a stagnation in the growth of this stratum. In 1982, 61 percent of university (Hochschule) students in the GDR had a father with university education, but only 20 percent had grandparents who had been educated as skilled workers. Doris Köhler, *Professionelle Pädagogen? Zur Rekonstruktion beruflicher Orientierungs- und Handlungsmuster von ostdeutschen Lehrern der Kriegsgeneration* (Münster and London, 2000), 75.

71. The number of cars per 1,000 inhabitants was 267 in France and 33 in Hungary. György Péteri, "Streetcars of Desire: Cars and Automobilism in Communist Hungary (1958–70)," *Social History* 34:1 (2009), 2–3.

72. Péteri, "Streetcars of Desire," 13; György Péteri, "Demand Side Abundance: On the Post-1956 Social Contract in Hungary," *East Central Europe* 43 (2016).

73. Gerd Schmidt, *Ich war Butler beim Politbüro : Protokoll der Wahrheit über die Waldsiedlung Wandlitz* (Schkeuditz, 1999), 59–60.

74. Schmidt, *Ich war Butler*, 43; Lothar Herzog, *Honecker Privat: Ein Personenschützer berichtet* (Berlin, 2012).

75. Panoptikon refers to a form of incarceration permitting wardens to have the most effective possible central control, in part by being able to monitor all inmates from a single "all-seeing" place. Elemér Hankiss, *East European Alternatives* (Oxford, 1990), 94.

76. Konrad, "Wir schauspielern." Other dissidents who thought the state involved everyone in upholding socialism included Adam Michnik, Václav Havel, and Roland Jahn. See Jahn's *Wir Angepassten* (Munich, 2014).

77. Šiklová gives the example of an editor at the daily newspaper *Mlada Fronta*, Jan Halada. Jan Hron, ed., *Věčné časy: československé totalitní roky* (Prague, 2009), 18.

78. Hron, *Věčné časy*, 20.

79. Hron, *Věčné časy*, 17.

80. Keane, *Power of the Powerless*, 38.

81. Caleb Crain, "Havel's Specter?" *The Nation*, April 9, 2012; The Rezek quote is from Paulina Bren, *The Greengrocer and His TV: The Culture of Communism after the 1968 Prague Spring* (Ithaca, NY 2010), 206.

82. Bren, *The Greengrocer*, 204.

83. Quoted in Bren, *The Greengrocer*, 204.

84. Keane, *Power of the Powerless*, 37.

85. Vladimir Tismaneanu, "Understanding National Stalinism: Reflections on Ceauşescu's Socialism," *Communist and Post-Communist Studies* 32:2 (1999), 155–173; "The Fate of Half a Million Political Prisoners," *The Economist*, August 5, 2013.

86. The Müller quotes are in *Die Erblast von Stasi und Securitate: eine Debatte mit deutschen, rumänischen und ungarischen Antworten: Simposium, 6–8.06.2001* (Bucharest, 2002), 116.

87. *Erblast von Stasi und Securitate,* 117–119.

88. Adrian Neculau, ed., *La vie quotidienne en Roumanie sous le communisme* (Paris, 2008), 163.

89. Neculau, *La vie quotidienne,* 60.

90. Neculau, *La vie quotidienne,* 65.

91. The program was announced in March 1988 and involved the destruction of half of some 13,000 villages; the inhabitants would be moved to 558 "agro-industrial towns." Dennis Deletant, *Ceaușescu and the Securitate: Coercion and Dissent in Romania, 1965–1989* (Armonk, NY, 1995), 134–135.

92. This is based on the observation of Radu Clit, in Neculau, *La vie,* 57.

93. The number of recruits is cited by Oana Lungescu, "Romania Securitate Legacy 20 Years after Revolution," BBC, December 10, 2009, available at http://news.bbc.co.uk/2/hi/europe/8401915.stm (accessed June 21, 2019). See also, for Sibiu county, Deletant, *Ceaușescu,* 394.

94. Herta Müller in *Erblast von Stasi und Securitate,* 151.

95. This claim made in the BBC article of Lungescu, "Romania Securitate."

96. Neculau, *La vie,* 57.

97. Decree 770 of October 1, 1966. Jill M. Massino, *Engendering Socialism: A History of Women and Everyday Life in Socialist Romania* (Bloomington, IN, 2007), 165, 210.

98. Massino, *Engendering Socialism,* 165, 190.

99. Ann Furedi, "On Abortion, We Should Study Romanian History," *The Guardian,* January 15, 2013.

100. Massino, *Engendering Socialism,* 191.

101. The pastor was László Tokes. See Chapter 25.

Chapter 24: The Unraveling of Communism

1. It was a "sudden rupture in the normal and familiar practices of politics and society." Padraic Kenney, *Carnival of Revolution: Central Europe 1989* (Princeton, NJ, 2002), 305.

2. Miklós Molnar, *From Béla Kun to János Kádár: Seventy Years of Hungarian Communism,* Arnold J. Pomerans, trans. (New York, 1990), 200.

3. Krisztina Fehérváry, "Goods and States."

4. Vladimir Tismaneanu, ed., *The Revolutions of 1989* (New York, 1989); Charles Maier, *Dissolution: The Crisis of Communism and the End of East Germany* (Princeton, NJ, 1997); Tony Judt, *Postwar: A History of Europe since 1945* (New York, 2005); Stephen Kotkin with Jan T. Gross, *Uncivil Society: 1989 and the Implosion of the Communist Establishment* (New York, 2009); Timothy Garton Ash, *The Magic Lantern* (New York, 1990); Konrad Jarausch, *Out of Ashes: A New History of Europe in the Twentieth Century* (Princeton, NJ, 2015). On the building of dissent in Central Europe in the 1980s, see Kenney, *Carnival.*

5. Dahn, "Wir wollten auch doch leben," 132.

6. Only 32 percent thought their standard of living would improve in the next five years; one-fourth anticipated a decline. Twenty-nine percent said their standard of living had risen over the previous five years (in contrast to 46 percent in 1985), while 36 percent believed it had fallen (22 percent in 1985). Abrams, "Buying Time," 408, 417, 420.

7. The consumption of meat per inhabitant more than doubled. All these numbers are based on official statistics in Molnar, *From Bela*, 189.

8. Molnar, *From Bela*, 190–191.

9. Roger Gough, *A Good Comrade: János Kádár, Communism and Hungary* (London, 2006), 176. Nyers looking back from 1998.

10. Against a consensus in the leadership in 1979 that price increases on consumer goods were the only way out to avoid a spiraling debt, Erich Honecker said: if we do that, the entire Politburo might as well resign. Hans-Hermann Hertle, *Der Fall der Mauer: Die unbeabsichtigte Selbstauflösung des SED-Staates* (Opladen, Germany, 1996), 41–42.

11. Kádár came up with the formulation: "we would really like to borrow from the east, but we couldn't, because they simply did not make it possible." Gough, *Good Comrade*, 192, 200.

12. Some forty-five were killed and more than 1,100 injured. Jerzy Eisler and Tomasz Szarota, eds., *Polska 1944/45–1989. Studia i materiały*, vol. 7 (Warsaw, 2006), 310. See also Roman Laba, *The Roots of Solidarity* (Princeton, NJ, 1991).

13. Włodzimierz Borodziej, *Geschichte Polens im 20. Jahrhundert* (Munich, 2010), 353.

14. Jerzy Eisler, *Polskie Miesiące, czyli kryzysy w PRL* (Warsaw, 2008), 46–48.

15. Borodziej speaks of *Prügelorgien* [orgies of beating], *Geschichte*, 353.

16. Jerzy Andrzejewski, Andrzej Szczypiorski, Stanisław Barańczak, Jan Józef Lipski.

17. Stanisław Barańczak, *Breathing under Water and Other East European Essays* (Cambridge, MA, 1990), 46.

18. In 1972, obligatory deliveries were entirely repealed. Zbigniew Landau and Jerzy Tomaszewski, *The Polish Economy in the Twentieth Century* (London, 1985), 306.

19. It rose only about 2–3 percent yearly. Andrzej Friszke, *Polska: losy państwa i narodu* (Warsaw, 2003), 265.

20. Zbigniew Pełczyński, "Poland under Gierek," in *History of Poland since 1863*, R. F. Leslie., ed., (Cambridge, 1980), 439.

21. "Polish Workers Protest Increase in Meat Prices," *Washington Post*, July 4, 1980; Kuroń and Żakowski, *PRL*, 131.

22. Basket I was about security, Basket II about cooperation in technology.

23. See the analysis of Adam Michnik, "Unbeugsame Verteidigung der Menschenrechte: was die Polen von dem neuen Papst erwarten," *Der Spiegel*, October 23, 1978, 26–27.

24. Andrzej Brzeziecki, *Tadeusz Mazowiecki: Biografia naszego premiera* (Kraków, 2015), 270.

25. Andrzej Friszke, *Opozycja polityczna w PRL 1945–1980* (London, 1994), 300–302; Adam Zagajewski, *Polen: Staat im Schatten der Sowjetunion* (Reinbek bei Hamburg, 1981), 159–160. The milieus were concentrated in a few places: Warsaw, Kraków, Łódź, and the Catholic University in Lublin. Andrzej Paczkowski, *Pół wieku dziejów Polski : 1939–1989* (Warsaw, 1996), 428–429.

26. Jacques Rupnik, "Dissent in Poland, 1968–78," in *Opposition in Eastern Europe*, Rudolf L. Tőkés, ed., (Baltimore, 1979), 78–79.

27. Friszke, *Opozycja*, 326.

28. Samuel Moyn, *The Last Utopia: Human Rights in History* (Cambridge, MA, 2010).

29. Frischke, *Opozycja*, 362–363; Rupnik, "Dissent," 90–91.

30. Adam Michnik, *Letters from Prison and Other Essays*, Maya Latynski, transl. (Berkeley, 1985), 144.

31. See Chapter 10.

32. Neal Ascherson, *The Polish August: The Self-Limiting Revolution* (New York, 1982), 115; Michael H. Bernhard, *The Origins of Democratization in Poland: Workers, Intellectuals and Oppositional Politics* (New York, 1993), 185, 196–197; Justyna Błażejowska, *Papierowa rewolucja : z dziejów drugiego obiegu wydawniczego w Polsce 1976–1989/1990* (Warsaw, 2010).

33. According to dissident and political scientist Jan Šabata, of the original 242 signatories of Czechoslovakia's Charter 77, 140 were former Communists. Henry Kamm, "Evolution in Europe," *New York Times*, April 17, 1990; Jan Bažant, Nina Bažantová, and Frances Starn, *The Czech Reader: History, Culture, Politics* (Durham, NC, 2010), 392.

34. Judt, *Postwar*, 569.

35. That number was as of December 1988; there were other signatories who preferred that their names not be known. Vilém Prečan, *Charta 77, 1977–1989* (Prague, 1990), 358.

36. Paczkowski, *Pół wieku*, 430–431; Andrzej Romanowski, "Stansiław Pyjas nie został zamordowany ani pobity," *Ale Historia, Gazeta Wyborcza*, May 4, 2017.

37. Rupnik, "Dissent," 93; Bernhard, *Origins*, 114–115.

38. That was why the government was careful not to employ too much repression. Paczkowski, *Pół wieku*, 430–431. In May, 118 detentions and twenty apartment searches were recorded. Bernhard, *Origins*, 117.

39. See Adam Michnik's recollections in *Letters from Freedom: Post-Cold War Realities and Perspectives* (Berkeley, 1998), 57. The Belgrade Conference was monitoring compliance with the Helsinki Accord, and was attended by representatives of the signatory countries. Though at the time considered "moralizing," Carter's insistence on East European states abiding by human rights pledges did much to support the position of dissidents. He also explicitly linked US credits for food to Poland's relative respect for human rights. P. G. Vaughan, "Brzezinski and the Helsinki Final Act," in *The Crisis of Détente in Europe*, Leopoldo Nuti, ed. (London, 2009), 19–23. On Berlinguer, see Robert Brier, "Broadening the Cultural History of the Cold War: The Emergence of the Polish Workers' Defense Committee and Human Rights," *Journal of Cold War Studies* 15:4 (2013), 104–127.

40. Peter Osnos, "Current Unrest in Poland Reveals Rising Influence of Populace," *Washington Post*, June 3, 1977.

41. Máté Szábo, "Hungary," in *Dissent and Opposition in Communist Eastern Europe*, Detlef Pollack and Jan Wielgohs, eds. (Aldershot, UK, 2004), 58–59. A statement of solidarity with Charter 77 from 1979 had 250 signatories.

42. Patrizia Hey, *Die sowjetische Polenpolitik Anfang der 8oer Jahre* (Berlin, 2010), 137; Ascherson, *Polish August*.

43. Kuroń and Żakowski, *PRL*, 209. See also the discussion of opposition and the papal visit in Brian Porter-Szűcs, *Poland in the Modern World: Beyond Martyrdom* (Hoboken, NJ, 2014), 286–296.

44. Borodziej, *Geschichte*, 356.

45. Kuroń and Żakowski, *PRL*, 209.

46. According to Ascherson, *Polish August*, 14–15.

47. Barbara Szczepuła, *Alina, Miłość w cieniu polityki* (Warsaw, 2013).

48. From the twenty-one demands of the workers: this demand went into the final accord.

49. In 1936 almost two-thirds of a million Polish workers had been engaged in such strikes. Roman Laba, *The Roots of Solidarity* (Princeton, NJ, 1989), 154.

50. "Alina Pieńkowska," *Gazeta Wyborcza*, August 8, 2005.

51. Borodziej, *Geschichte*, 362.

52. Borodziej, *Geschichte*, 362; Maciej Sandecki, "Mieczysław Jagielski: Musimy wyrazić zgodę," Gazeta Wyborcza, August 18, 2005.

53. Richard Sakwa, *Soviet Politics in Perspective* (London, 1998), 180.

54. "Die Zeiten, in denen die DDR in die Reihe der wirtschaftlich Lahmen und Fusskranken gehörte, sind längst vorbei." Merseburger was a top West German journalist accredited to East Berlin (he lived there from 1982 to 1987). See Peter Merseburger, *Grenzgänger: Innenansichten der DDR* (Munich, 1988), 44, 47. For the generally positive assessment of the GDR economy of this time, see also "It's a Long Way from Prussia to Russia," *The Economist*, February 22, 1986; Roy Vogt, "Prospects for Improvement in the Standard of Living of the German Democratic Republic, *Canadian Slavonic Papers* 29:1 (1987), 63–80.

55. Bennett Kovrig, *Of Walls and Bridges: The United States and Eastern Europe* (New York, 1991), 267.

56. Susanne Wesch, "Mit den Krümeln vom Kuchen," *Handelsblatt*, September 15, 2006.

57. Cited in Angela Stent, *Russia and Germany Reborn: Unification, the Soviet Collapse, and the New Europe* (Princeton, NJ, 1999), 55.

58. In a thought-provoking analysis, he writes: "History has turned its back on an attractive and plausible real-world option." Nigel Swain, *Hungary: The Rise and Fall of Feasible Socialism* (London, 1992), 2.

59. Pittaway, *Eastern Europe*, 76–77.

60. Gough, *Good Comrade*, 152, 160–161; Ivan T. Berend, "Veränderungen waren notwendig" in *Ungarn: Ein kommunistisches Wunderland?* István Futaky, ed. (Reinbek bei Hamburg, 1983), 121.

61. "The state far from trying to stop them, tends to encourage diversity and diversification ... rural Hungary has become an immense agricultural producer with a flourishing market." Molnar, *From Bela*, 194.

62. János Kornai, "The Soft Budget Constraint," *Kyklos* 39:1 (1986), 10.

63. Swain, *Hungary*, 124.

64. Gough, *Good Comrade*, 154; Mark Pittaway, *The Workers' State: Industrial Labor and the Making of Socialist Hungary, 1944–1958* (Pittsburgh, PA, 2012), 270.

65. Rudolf L. Tökés, *Hungary's Negotiated Revolution: Economic Reform, Social Change, and Political Succession, 1957–1990* (New York, 1996), 115.

66. George Konrád, "Wir schauspielern alle in ein und demselben Stück," in *Ungarn: Ein kommunistisches Wunderland?* István Futaky, ed. (Reinbek bei Hamburg, 1983), 25–26.

67. Emphasis added. Molnar, *From Bela*, 202.

68. Konrád, "Wir schauspielern," 12.

69. About 1.6 billion people. Minxin Pei, *From Reform to Revolution: The Demise of Communism in China and the Soviet Union* (Cambridge, MA, 1994), 1.

70. Paweł Wierzbicki, "Tygodnik Mazowsze, cudowne dziecko drugiego obiegu," *Dzieje najnowsze* 44:4 (2012), 68; Shana Penn, *Solidarity's Secret: The Women Who Defeated Communism in Poland* (Ann Arbor, MI, 2006).

71. Václav Havel, *Power of the Powerless*, John Keane, ed. (New York, 1985).

72. Padraic Kenney, "Borders Breached: The Transnational in Eastern Europe since Solidarity," *Journal of Modern European History* 8:2 (2010), 187. There were even organized convocations

in Poland of East European oppositionists, in Warsaw in 1987, Kraków in 1988, and Wrocław in 1989.

73. The term "national Stalinism" is Vladimir Tismaneanu's. It means the systematic effort to reject reform through nationalism.

74. "Openness Vital, Gorbachev tells Romania," *Los Angeles Times*, May 27, 1987.

75. "Notes from CC CPSU Politburo Session, April 16, 1987," in *Masterpieces of History: The Peaceful End of the Cold War in Eastern Europe*, Svetlana Savranskaya et al., eds. (Budapest, 2010), 247–248.

76. "Notes from CC CPSU Politburo Session, June 4, 1987," in Savranskaya et al., *Masterpieces of History*, 253–254.

77. *Milwaukee Journal*, May 25, 1987; "Notes from CC CPSU Politburo Session, June 4, 1987," in Savranskaya et al., *Masterpieces of History*, 253.

78. Adam Michnik, *Letters from Prison and Other Essays*, Maya Latynski, trans. (Berkeley, 1985), 204.

79. That was 3.7 million. The percentages in the 1980s in Hungary and Poland were 10.3 percent and 8.1 percent, respectively, of the adult populations. Peter Siani-Davies, *The Romanian Revolution of December 1989* (Ithaca, NY, 2005), 21; Stephen Kotkin, *Uncivil Society* (New York, 2010), 77. The total in Czechoslovakia was about 17 percent in the 1960s, and in the GDR about 17 percent in the 1980s. Muriel Blaive, "The Czechs and Their Communism, Past and Present," in *Inquiries into Past and Present*, D. Gard et al., eds., vol. 17 (Vienna, 2005); Rusanna Gaber, *Politische Gemeinschaft in Deutschland und Polen* (Wiesbaden, 2007), 105.

80. Stephen Fischer-Galati, *Twentieth Century Rumania* (New York, 1991), 186; Stephen Roper, *Romania: The Unfinished Revolution* (New York, 2000), 51.

81. From 1983, cited in Petrescu, "Alluring Facet," 250.

82. Petrescu, "Alluring Facet," 251, 253.

83. Economic self-sufficiency would help "fulfill the country's historic destiny of living well and free in Communist Romania." Fischer-Galati, *Twentieth Century Rumania*, 190, 188.

84. He spoke for more than five hours to them; the strike broke up after his departure. Fischer-Galati, *Twentieth Century Rumania*, 190–191. Despite promises that the strikers would not be punished, some 4,000 were removed from the Jiu Valley. Dennis Deletant, *Ceauşescu and the Securitate: Coercion and Dissent in Romania* (Armonk, NY, 1995), 246.

85. For details, see Chapter 24.

86. Connected to the fall of the Shah of Iran, with whom Ceauşescu had good relations. Fischer-Galati, *Twentieth Century Rumania*, 193.

87. Fischer-Galati, *Twentieth Century Rumania*, 195.

88. This from 1982 onward; the price was the equivalent in Western currency of expenditures the Romanian state had made on a person's college degree.

89. Fischer-Galati, *Twentieth Century Rumania*, 195–196.

90. Petrescu, "Alluring Facet."

91. Archie Brown, "The Gorbachev Era," in *The Cambridge History of Russia*, Ronald Suny, ed., vol. 3 (Cambridge, 2006), 336. In public (for example, at the July 1986 Polish Party congress), Gorbachev still spoke of the paramount need for the unity of the Soviet Bloc and said that

"socialist gains are irreversible." Mark Kramer, "The Demise of the Soviet Bloc," in *The End of the Beginning: The Revolutions of 1989 and the Resurgence of History*, Vladimir Tismaneanu and Bogdan Iacob, eds. (Budapest, 2012), 181.

92. Martin Walker, *The Cold War: A History* (New York, 1994), 309.

Chapter 25: 1989

1. Timothy Garton Ash, *The Magic Lantern: Revolution Witnessed in Warsaw, Budapest, Berlin and Prague* (New York, 1990), 78.

2. On Krenz: Wolfgang Leonhard, *Meine Geschichte der DDR* (Berlin, 2007), 216. On the situation in East Germany following the construction of the wall, see Roland Jahn, *Wir Angepassten: Überleben in der DDR* (Munich, 2014); Peter C. Caldwell and Karrin Hanshew, *Germany since 1945: Politics, Culture, and Society* (London, 2018); Patrick Major, *Behind the Berlin Wall: East Germany and the Frontiers of Power* (Oxford, 2010), 156–159.

3. The determination of some East Germans to escape, and the regime's determination to stop them, is reflected in the case of Bulgaria, a state that East Germans could visit on holiday. A few dozen tried making it across the forbidding frontier to Greece, either to be apprehended or die. Nevertheless, the East German government sent *Stasi* agents to Bulgaria to inspect the fortifications there and make sure they were as impenetrable as possible. Christopher Nehring, *Tödliche Fluchten über Bulgarien: Die Zusammenarbeit von bulgarischer und DDR-Staatssicherheit zur Verhinderung von Fluchtversuchen* (Berlin, 2017).

4. Mary Elise Sarotte, *The Collapse: The Accidental Opening of the Berlin Wall* (New York, 2014), 22–29.

5. George Barany, "Epilogue," in *History of Hungary*, Peter Sugar Tibor Frank and Péter Hának, eds. (Bloomington, 1990), 401.

6. M. S. Gorbachev, *Memoirs* (New York, 1996), 468.

7. Gough, *Good Comrade*, 239.

8. That was in February 1989. Nigel Swain, "Negotiated Revolution in Poland and Hungary, 1989," in *Revolution and Resistance in Eastern Europe: Challenges to Communist Rule*, Kevin McDermott and Matthew Stibbe, eds. (New York, 2006), 147.

9. The democratic forum was founded in September 1987 by writer Sándor Lezsak. The Scientific Workers Democratic Union was formed in May 1988, the first independent union in Eastern Europe since Solidarity. Pittaway, *Eastern Europe*, 189.

10. Tőkés, *Hungary's Negotiated Revolution*, 308.

11. David Stark and László Bruszt, "Remaking the Political Field in Hungary: From the Politics of Confrontation to the Politics of Competition," in *Eastern Europe in Revolution*, Ivo Banac, ed. (Ithaca, NY, 1992), 30.

12. Though insisting that the state place limits on itself and "institutionalize the right of society to have its own autonomous representative organizations." Stark and Bruszt, "Remaking the Political Field," 26.

13. Stark and Bruszt, "Remaking the Political Field," 26.

14. This was in February. Barany, "Epilogue," 402.

15. Pittaway, *Eastern Europe*, 190.

16. Tőkés, *Hungary's Negotiated Revolution*, 329.

17. Berecz was the party's former hardline ideological chief. Henry Kamm, "Party's Hardliners Form Party to Toe the Old Line," *New York Times*, October 13, 1989.

18. Now its offices were supposed to be in neighborhoods, like those of "normal" political parties. Tökés, *Hungary's Negotiated Revolution*, 296, 332.

19. Tökés, *Hungary's Negotiated Revolution*, 330. Kádár gave a valedictory to the Central Committee in April 1989 that was long-winded and embarrassing, in which he returned, yet again, to the haunting presence of the men he had ordered executed in 1958: "what is my responsibility? . . . the doctor said that my problem is that I am forever thinking about my responsibility . . . day and night. . . . my head spins as to what my responsibility is." Gough, *Good Comrade*, 244.

20. Tökés, *Hungary's Negotiated Revolution*, 33, 349. The refounded socialist party received 10.89 percent of the vote. Swain, *Hungary: The Rise and Fall of Feasible Socialism*, 31.

21. Ákos Róna-Tas, *The Great Surprise of the Small Transformation: The Demise of Communism and the Rise of the Private Sector in Hungary* (Ann Arbor, MI, 1997) 167.

22. Poland was the only model for peaceful transition at that moment. András Bozóki, "Hungary's Road to Systemic Change. The Opposition Roundtable," in *Lawful Revolution in Hungary, 1989–94*, Béla K. Király, ed. (Boulder, CO, 1995), 65.

23. This included the Peasant Party, which had supported every move the Communists made since 1947, but now began taking advantage of the new freedoms. Francis X. Clines, "Isvestia Reports Poland's Changes in Detail and Straightforwardly," *New York Times*, April 7, 1989.

24. Anna Machcewicz, "Historia sentymentalna," *Więź* 37:7 (1995), 135; John Tagliabue, "For Many the Accords Seem a Non-event," *New York Times*, April 7, 1989. The underground had done a poll showing that 85 percent of workers wanted fully free elections.

25. István Rev, *Retroactive Justice: Pre-history of Postcommunism* (Stanford, CA, 2005), 304.

26. Thanks to Grósz, Németh, Pozsgay, and Foreign Minister Horn. Norman Naimark, "'Ich will hier raus,' Emigration and Collapse of the German Democratic Republic," in Banac, *Eastern Europe*, 84; Robert J. Macartney, "Bonn, Budapest Discuss East German Escapees," *Washington Post*, August 26, 1989.

27. "Und wenn sie die ganze Stasi schicken," *Der Spiegel*, August 21, 1989, 30–31.

28. Some 6,000 East German citizens had collected in Warsaw before they were permitted to travel to West Germany in early October. http://www.tagesschau.de/ddrfluechtlinge-warschau-101.html (accessed December 20, 2018).

29. Bonn had never recognized this citizenship but insisted there was one German citizenship. The number in the embassy was estimated at 4,000, but many more waited outside. Karel Vodicka, *Die Prager Botschaftsflüchtlinge 1989* (Göttingen, 2014).

30. "Gift für die Stasi," *Tageszeitung*, March 12, 2011.

31. Günter Johannsen, "Ironie der Geschichte oder wunderbare Fügung: Die Wurzeln des Montagsfriedensgebetes in Leipzig," http://www.gesellschaft-zeitgeschichte.de/geschichte /friedensgebete/ironie-der-geschichte/ (accessed June 19, 2019); Charles S. Maier, *Dissolution: The Crisis of Communism and the End of East Germany* (Princeton, 1995), 139.

32. "Demonstrationen und Kundgebungen in Leipzig," http://www.archiv-buergerbewegung .de/index.php/demonstrationen?bezirk_ddr=Leipzig&ort=Leipzig (accessed June 19, 2019).

33. Thomas Küttler, *Die Wende in Plauen. Eine Dokumentation* (Plauen, Germany, 1991). The historian Ilko-Sascha Kowalczuk said this was the first victory over the state power that fall. "Die unbemerkten Helden," *Der Spiegel*, July 20, 2009.

34. Sarotte, *Collapse*, 190.

35. Merkel apparently never signed papers indicating a desire to join the CDU, west or east. Ewald König, "'Mit der CDU will ich nichts zu tun haben,'" *Die Zeit*, June 18, 2015.

36. Sarotte, *Collapse*, 147; Kerstin Völlig, "Uns war klar, das war's mit der DDR," *Bergedorfer Zeitung*, November 28, 2014.

37. "Václav Havel: Living in Truth," *The Economist*, December 31, 2011.

38. Daniel Shanahan, "20 Years Too Late for Czechs: In Time of Glasnost, Restraint Still the Rule," *Los Angeles Times*, August 13, 1988. In his March 1987 visit to Prague, Gorbachev, still a centrist in the Soviet leadership, refused openly to show sympathy with the Prague Spring or to support reformers like Lubomír Štrougal in the Czechoslovak leadership. Jacques Levesque, *The Enigma of 1989* (Berkeley, 1997), 62–63.

39. Cited in Jürgen Danyel, "Abschied von der DDR," in *ZeitRäume: Potsdamer Almanach des Zentrums für Zeithistorische Forschung 2009*, Martin Sabrow, ed. (Göttingen, 2010), 43–46.

40. An estimated 10,000 demonstrated in Prague on August 21, 1988, and several thousand gathered on January 15, 1989 to commemorate the self-immolation of Jan Palach; see Milenko Petrovic, *The Democratic Transition of Post-Communist Europe* (New York, 2013), 106.

41. That was while visiting Austria on October 25. Jiří Vykoukal, Bohuslav Litera, and Miroslav Tejchman, *Východ: vznik, vývoj a rozpad sovětského bloku, 1944–1989* (Prague, 2000), 722.

42. Vykoukal et al., *Východ*, 726; Adam Michnik, "Wielka Historia Vaclava Havla," *Gazeta Wyborcza*, April 27, 2012.

43. Jonathan C. Randal, "Prague Names Havel President," *Washington Post*, December 30, 1989.

44. James Krapfl, *Revolution with a Human Face* (Ithaca, NY, 2013), 104.

45. Katherine Verdery and Gail Kligman, "Romania," in Banac, *Eastern Europe*, 118.

46. On December 15. Stephen D. Roper, *Romania: The Unfinished Revolution* (Amsterdam, 2000), 58. Denis Deletant, *Romania under Communist Rule* (Portland, 1999), 135.

47. Verdery and Kligman, "Romania," 120; Vykoukal et al., *Východ*, 733.

48. Vykoukal et al., *Východ*, 733.

49. György Dalos, *Der Vorhang geht auf: das Ende der Diktaturen in Osteuropa* (Munich, 2009), 236. The toll in Cluj-Napoca was twenty-six. The shooting into crowds at the city center by army units in the early afternoon only hardened the resolve of others to take part in the protests. Siani-Davies, *Romanian Revolution*, 79–80.

50. Vykoukal et al., *Východ*, 732–734.

51. The overwhelming majority of deaths, 942 of 1,104, occured after Ceauşescu lost his grip on power on December 22. Dalos, *Vorhang*, 236.

52. There is no evidence that the revolution was the result of a conspiracy. Siani-Davies, *Romanian Revolution*, 175–176; Fischer-Galati, *Twentieth Century Rumania*, 200–205.

53. Vykoukal et al., *Východ*, 734–736.

54. He became head of party in March 1954.

55. R. J. Crampton, *A Concise History of Bulgaria* (Cambridge, 1997), 209. This was part of a broader attack on Islam, which had included outlawing circumcision some years earlier and making it hard to journey to Mecca.

56. Gorbachev, *Memoirs*, 485.

57. Crampton, *Concise History*, 214; Vykoukal et al., *Východ*, 729.

58. With Petar Mladenov at the head, who had been minister of foreign affairs since 1971.

59. Dalos, *Vorhang*, 169.

60. Crampton, *Concise History*, 219; Vykoukal et al., *Východ*, 731.

61. Vykoukal et al., *Východ*, 731–732.

62. Tökés, *Hungary's Negotiated Revolution*.

63. For the shift in rhetoric in the new government, from talk of perestroika-like reform of socialism to (a still somewhat ambivalent) invocation of democracy, under the pressure from the international community, but also "local counsel," see John Gledhill, "Three Days in Bucharest: Making Sense of Romania's Transitional Violence, Twenty Years On," in *Reflections on 1989 in Eastern Europe*, Terry Cox, ed. (London, 2013), 116–117.

64. Máté Szabó, 'Hungary' in *Dissent and Opposition in Communist Eastern Europe*, Detlev Pollack and Jan Wielgohs, eds. (Burlington VT, 2004), 62–63. US consular officials in Warsaw actively encouraged the work of the Polish underground in the 1980s.

65. Charles Maier, *Dissolution*.

Chapter 26: Eastern Europe Explodes: The Wars of Yugoslav Succession

1. Dan Stone, *Goodbye to All That: The Story of Europe since 1945* (Oxford, 2014), 252.

2. John Lampe, *Yugoslavia as History: Twice There Was a Country* (Cambridge, 1996), 284–286; Sabrina P. Ramet, *The Three Yugoslavias: State-Building and Legitimation* (Washington, DC, 2006), 335; Robert Donia and John V. A. Fine, *Bosnia-Herzegovina: A Tradition Betrayed* (New York, 1994), 180.

3. Audrey Helfant Budding, "Nation/People/Republic: Self-Determination in Socialist Yugoslavia," in *State Collapse in South-Eastern Europe*, Lenard J. Cohen and Jasna Dragović-Soso, eds. (West Lafayette, IN, 2008), 91–130.

4. The concentration of foreign-trade firms in Belgrade gave Serbia 56 percent of Yugoslav foreign trade, versus Croatia's 18 percent; Belgrade banks held more than 70 percent of Yugoslav financial capital. Branka Magaš, *Croatia through History: The Making of a European State* (London, 2007), 624.

5. Jill Irvine, "The Croatian Spring and the Dissolution of Yugoslavia," in Cohen and Dragović-Soso, *State Collapse*, 149–178.

6. Savka Dabčević-Kučar, *John Maynard Keynes: teoretičar državnog kapitalizma* (Zagreb, 1957).

7. Misha Glenny, *The Balkans: Nationalism, War, and the Great Powers, 1804–1999* (New York, 2000), 591. And 40.8 percent of the city police force were Croats. The data are from 1971.

8. There were also complaints of the relative weakening of the Croat economy: Croatia's share in the Yugoslav industrial product had declined from 35 percent in 1925 to 19 percent in 1965. And the demographic decline was due both to a high birthrate in republics farther south and the fact that Croats were disproportionately represented among Yugoslav workers who went abroad. Marcus Tanner, *Croatia: A Nation Forged in War* (New Haven, CT, 1997), 196–197; Andrej Milivojević, "Almost a Revolution: 1960s Liberal Reforms in Slovenia, Croatia, and Serbia" (PhD dissertation, UC Berkeley, 2013).

9. That was in 1971. Ronelle Alexander, *Bosnian, Croatian, Serbian: A Grammar with Sociolinguistic Commentary* (Madison, WI, 2006); Lampe, *Yugoslavia*, 299; Tanner, *Croatia*, 190–191.

10. Holm Sundhaussen, *Geschichte Serbiens* (Vienna, 2007), 374–375.

11. Jože Pirjevec, *Tito and His Comrades* (Madison, WI, 2018), 388–389. Also: Tim Judah, *Serbs: History, Myth, and the Destruction of Yugoslavia* (New Haven, CT, 1997), 147; Tanner, *Croatia*, 202; Sundhaussen, *Geschichte Serbiens*, 375; Milivojević, "Almost a Revolution," 137–138.

12. Tanner, *Croatia*, 202; Magaš, *Croatia through History*, 629. Tito likewise was not so much concerned about Croat nationalism per se, but about how it might unleash a response among Serbs: it was a "child's toy" compared to that. Tanner, *Croatia*, 199.

13. Aleksandar Pavković, *The Fragmentation of Yugoslavia: Nationalism and War in the Balkans* (New York, 2000), 70; Marc Weller, *Contested Statehood: Kosovo's Struggle for Independence* (Oxford, 2009), 35; Tim Judah, *Kosovo: What Everyone Needs to Know* (New York, 2008), 57. A constitution had been in the works from the 1960s.

14. The driving force intellectually was the Slovene Edvard Kardelj. Aleksandar Pavković, "The Role of Serbia in the Process of the Disintegration of Yugoslavia," in *Serbien und Montenegro: Raum und Bevölkerung, Geschichte, Sprache*, Walter Lukan, ed. (Berlin and Vienna, 2006), 336–337.

15. For superb histories of Albanian communism, see Daniel I. Perez, "Between Tito and Stalin: Enver Hoxha, Albanian Communists and the Assertion of Albanian National Sovereignty," (PhD dissertation, Stanford University, 2017); Elidor Mëhilli, *From Stalin to Mao: Albania and the Socialist World* (Ithaca, NY, 2017).

16. In 1948, 73 percent of Albanians in Kosovo were illiterate; by 1979, that number had dropped to 31.5 percent—still the highest in Yugoslavia. Judah, *Kosovo*, 58; Julie Mertus, *Kosovo: How Myths and Truths Started a War* (Berkeley, 1999), 29.

17. In 1952, Kosovo's per capita social product was 44 percent that of Yugoslavia, but in 1988, it was 27 percent. The decrease was due in part to high birth rates. Momčilo Pavlović, "Kosovo under Autonomy, 1974–1990," in *Confronting the Yugoslav Controversies: A Scholars' Initiative*, Charles Ingrao and Thomas Emmert, eds. (West Lafayette, IN, 2013), 54. The unemployment rate was 27.5 percent in Kosovo in the early 1980s, the highest in Yugoslavia. In Slovenia, it was 2 percent. Mertus, *Kosovo*, 23.

18. Serbs claimed that Albanians did not want schools. Kristaq Prifti, *The Truth on Kosovo* (Tirana, 1993), 136. The number 252 is also given in Radošin Rajović, *Autonomija Kosova: istorijsko pravna studija* (Belgrade, 1985).

19. The exact numbers: 47.88 percent and 77.42 percent.

20. Mertus, *Kosovo*, 25.

21. Kosta Mihailović and Vasilije Krestić, eds., *Memorandum of the Serbian Academy of Sciences and Arts: Answers to Criticisms* (Belgrade, 1995), 124, 139.

22. Gale Stokes, *The Walls Came Tumbling Down: The Collapse of Communism in Eastern Europe* (Oxford, 1993), 235; Laura Silber and Allan Little, *Yugoslavia: Death of a Nation* (New York, 1997), 63; Robert J. Donia, *Radovan Karadžić: Architect of the Bosnian Genocide* (Cambridge, 2015), 44; Sabrina P. Ramet, *Nationalism and Federalism in Yugoslavia* (Bloomington, IN, 1992), 226–234.

23. For guidance, see Budding, "Nation/People/Republic," 91–130.

24. The numbers killed at Jasenovac were thought to be in the hundreds of thousands, and Tudjman claimed they were fewer than 100,000. Ejub Štitkovac, "Croatia: The First War," in *Burn This House: The Making and Unmaking of Yugoslavia*, Jasmina Udovicki, ed. (Durham, NC, 2000), 155. He was closer to the truth than official Yugoslav historians. On Jasenovac, see: http://www

.ushmm.org/wlc/en/article.php?ModuleId=10005449 (accessed November 29, 2016). For his biography: Branka Magaš, "Obituary: Franjo Tudjman," *The Independent*, December 13, 1999.

25. Cited in Stokes, *Walls*, 242. The elections were in April, his speech in February.

26. He took office as president of Croatia in May 1990. Štitkovac, "Croatia: The First War," 156.

27. On the role of Croatian émigrés in financing extremism, see Paul Hockenos, *Homeland Calling: Exile Patriotism and the Balkan Wars* (Ithaca, NY, 2003), 100–102.

28. A point made in Silber and Little, *Yugoslavia*, 97, tracing the rise of Milan Babić, the nationalist extremist who took hold of the Serb Republic of Krajina. Many of the Serb-populated areas "were interested in dialogue with Zagreb, and were far from hostile to the new government. In these areas Babić used force to impose his authority."

29. Štitkovac, "Croatia: The First War," 155.

30. Thomas Roser, "Als mitten in Europa wieder der Krieg ausbrach," *Die Presse*, June 24, 2016; James Gow and Cathie Carmichael, *Slovenia and the Slovenes* (Bloomington, IN, 2000), 174–202.

31. Silber and Little, *Yugoslavia*, 180; Dunja Melčić, *Der Jugoslawien-Krieg: Handbuch zu Vorgeschichte, Verlauf und Konsequenzen* (Wiesbaden, 2007), 555. Estimates of the dead in the Croatian population of East Slavonia range between 2,000 and 5,000. Brendan O'Shea, *Perception and Reality in the Modern Yugoslav Conflict* (London, 2001), 20; Central Intelligence Agency, Office of Russian and European Analysis, *Balkan Battlegrounds: A Military History of the Yugoslav Conflict*, vol. 1 (Washington, DC, 2002), 101.

32. Fighting had commenced in August. The accord was signed by Tudjman and Milošević in Geneva on November 23, 1991; the cease-fire took full effect in early January.

33. Other arguments in favor: Yugoslavia was already dead; and one should not penalize a state trying to realize its independence separate from Communism. For a critical discussion, see Glenny, *Balkans*, 637–638. German unification occurred on October 3, 1990.

34. David Binder, "Alija Izetbegović, Muslim Who Led Bosnia, Dies at 78," *New York Times*, October 20, 2003; Cathie Carmichael, *A Concise History of Bosnia* (Cambridge, 2015), 106. The Young Muslims aspired to unity of Muslims of the whole world, and the establishment of a "great Muslim state." Marko Attila Hoare, *The History of Bosnia* (New York, 2007), 135. On Izetbegović's promotion of Islam as a "spiritual and intellectual synthesis which includes the values of Western Europe," see Noel Malcolm, *Bosnia: A Short History* (New York, 1994), 219–221. On the Handschar Division, see Chapter 16, note 45.

35. On the numbers, see Sundhaussen, *Geschichte Serbiens*, 424.

36. On the rapes and mistreatment of civilians, see Norman Naimark, *Fires of Hatred: Ethnic Cleansing in the Twentieth Century* (Cambridge, MA, 2001), 163–171; on Bijeljina, see Eric D. Weitz, *A Century of Genocide: Utopias of Race and Nation* (Princeton, NJ, 2015), 215.

37. The first was the Carrington-Cutileiro plan; the second the Vance-Owen plan. Who would enforce the canton boundaries? That was a concern of the Muslims. For the concerns in the Clinton administration, see John W. Young and John Kent, *International Relations since 1945* (Oxford, 2013), 465; for a critique of these "realist" plans for failing to permit "right of return," see Gearoid O'Tuathail and Carl Dahlman, "The Clash of Governmentalities," in *Global Governmentality: Governing International Spaces*, Wendy Larner and William Walters, eds. (London, 2004), 143.

38. On the very high threshold for applying the term "genocide," and the consequent difficulty of punishing human rights abuses that seem to fall short of it, see A. Dirk Moses, "Raphael

Lemkin, Culture, and the Concept of Genocide," in *Oxford Handbook of Genocide Studies*, A. Dirk Moses and Donald Bloxham, eds. (Oxford, 2013).

39. After NATO F-16 jets destroyed a Bosnian Serb tank, Radko Mladić threatened to execute the Dutch peacekeepers, and brought further strikes to a halt (ordered to stop by UN Special Representative Yasushi Akashi). Sabrina Ramet, *The Three Yugoslavias: State-Building and Legitimation* (Bloomington, IN, 2006), 460.

40. From a national sample of 4,232 Yugoslavs. Anthony Oberschall, "The Manipulation of Ethnicity: From Ethnic Cooperation to Violence and War in Yugoslavia," *Ethnic and Racial Studies* 23:6 (November 2000), 988.

41. In the beginning, some Serbs and Croats served in the Bosnian army, but with time their numbers declined.

42. Cited in Oberschall, "Manipulation," 996. Mazowiecki was using the case of Bosanska Dubica to generalize on the situation in Bosnia, on methods used to achieve ethnic cleansing. Tadeusz Mazowiecki, *Report on the Situation of Human Rights in the Territory of the Former Yugoslavia* (New York, 1992), 4, available at: http://repository.un.org/bitstream/handle/11176/54365/A_47_418-EN.pdf?sequence=3&isAllowed=y (accessed January 5, 2015).

43. Mazowiecki, *Report*, 12.

44. Tatjana Pavlović, "Women in Croatia: Feminists, Nationalists, and Homosexuals," in *Gender Politics in the Western Balkans: Women and Society in Yugoslavia*, Sabrina P. Ramet, ed. (University Park, PA, 1999), 136.

45. Oberschall, "Manipulation," 989.

46. This was from the Sarajevo edition of the Belgrade paper, which was moderate. Oberschall, "Manipulation," 991. Also see Ivan Turov, "The Resistance in Serbia," in *Burn This House: The Making and Unmaking of Yugoslavia*, Jasminka Udovicki and James Ridgeway, eds. (Durham, NC, 2001), 250; Roger Cohen, *Hearts Grown Brutal* (New York, 1998), 222; Michael Sells, "Islam in Serbian Religious Mythology and Its Consequences," in *Islam and Bosnia*, Maya Shatzmiller, ed. (Montreal, 2002), 58.

47. "What under peaceful circumstances were totally implausible events," Oberschall concludes, like "young women becoming sexual slaves in harems for breeding janissaries; a fifteenth- and sixteenth-century style Turkish/Islamic invasion of Europe—become credible narratives of ethnic annihilation and domination within the crisis frame." Oberschall, "Manipulation," 991–992.

48. See the essays in Cohen and Dragović-Soso, *State Collapse*.

49. Chuck Sudetic, *Blood and Vengeance: One Family's Story of the War in Bosnia* (New York, 1999), 52.

50. In Sarajevo, the number of marriages between members of different ethnic groups was just over 10 percent (the category no longer exists in the census).

51. Elizabeth Drew, *On the Edge: The Clinton Presidency* (New York, 1995), 157. He read the book at the point where he had to decide on the "lift and strike," that is, to lift the weapons embargo and arm the Bosnian side. Facing heavy pressure to decline it, because he lacked support in Western Europe and had tepid support at home, Kaplan's book gave Clinton a "vision" to apologize for nonintervention, that is, it helped him rationalize a choice he was very hesitant to make. This was a clear turning point. Defense Secretary Les Aspin, hearing Clinton speak of Kaplan's view, said: "Holy S..t, he's going south on lift and strike." Drew, *On the Edge*, 150. See also: Michael Kaufman, "The Dangers of Letting a President Read," *New York Times*, May 22, 1999.

52. In an interview with Charlie Rose, July 13. Cited in Michael Sells, *The Bridge Betrayed: Religion and Genocide in Bosnia* (Berkeley, 1996), 204.

53. Arne Johan Vetlesen, *Evil and Human Agency: Understanding Collective Evil-Doing* (Cambridge, 2005), 247.

54. When the subject of using force came up, Colin Powell always asked what precise effect was expected. "What is the end point?" he asked. "Any US military intervention should involve massive force and a clearly defined objective." Drew, *On the Edge*, 149, 154.

55. This UN policy was stated in resolution 713 of the UN Security Council of September 25, 1991. The council "Decides, under *Chapter VII* of the Charter of the United Nations, that all States shall, for the purposes of establishing peace and stability in Yugoslavia, immediately implement a general and complete embargo on all deliveries of weapons and military equipment to Yugoslavia."

56. Fear of endangering their own forces explains why the French and British opposed the "lift [embargo] and strike" option in 1993. Drew, *On the Edge*, 155.

57. Cited in Mark Danner, "Operation Storm," *New York Review of Books*, October 22, 1998.

58. Estimates of the dead from the market bombing range from 37 to 38. By May 2003, the bodies of more than 5,000 victims of the Srebrenica massacre had been exhumed. Ramet, *Three Yugoslavias*, 460, 703.

59. George Packer, *Our Man: Richard Holbrook and the End of the American Century* (New York, 2019).

60. Dabibor Bjelitsa, ed., *Prostorni plan Republike Srpske do 2015* (Banja Luka, 2008), 67, 69.

61. Principle enunciated in June 1999 by Bill Clinton: "we ought to prevent the slaughter of innocent civilians and the wholesale uprooting of them because of their race, their ethnic background or the way they worship God." Interview with Jim Lehrer, June 11, 1999, available at http://clinton6.nara.gov/1999/06/1999-06-11-pbs-interview-of-the-president.html (accessed November 30, 2016).

62. The other pillars were the security forces and the secret police. Thomas E. Ricks, "Clinton Edges Closer to Supporting the Use of Ground Troops in Kosovo," *Wall Street Journal*, April 23, 1999.

63. Valerie Bunce and Sharon Wolchik, "Defining and Domesticating the Electoral Model: A Comparison of Slovakia," in *Democracy and Authoritarianism in the Post-Communist World*, Valerie Bunce, Michael McFaul, and Katyhryn Stoner-Weiss, eds. (Cambridge, 2010), 139–140, 141, 146.

64. The Milošević opponent Miro Djukanović was elected president of Montenegro in 1997 and quickly began loosening ties to Serbia. Raymond Detrez, "The Right to Self-determination and Secession in Yugoslavia," in *Contextualizing Secession*, Bruno Coppieters and Richard Sakwa, eds. (Oxford, 2003), 127.

Chapter 27: Eastern Europe Joins Europe

1. These regimes were also known as competitive authoritarian, or semi-authoritarian regimes. Ukraine also fell into this category.

2. Padraic Kenney, *The Burdens of Freedom: Eastern Europe since 1989* (London, 2006), 114–122; Sharon L. Wolchik and Jane L. Curry, "Democracy, the Market, and the Return to Europe:

From Communism to the European Union and NATO," in *Central and East European Politics from Communism to Democracy*, Sharon L. Wolchik and Jane L. Curry, eds. (New York, 2011), 5–6. For a description of "democratization in stages," see Valerie Bunce, "The Political Transition," in Wolchik and Curry, *Central and East European Politics*, 33–35.

3. Bunce, "The Political Transition," 40–41; Grzegorz Ekiert, "Patterns of Postcommunist Transformation in Central and Eastern Europe," in *Capitalism and Democracy in Central and Eastern Europe: Assessing the Legacy of Communist Rule*, Grzegorz Ekiert and Stephen Hanson, eds. (Cambridge, 2003), 89–119; Kenney, *Burdens of Freedom*.

4. Asset tunneling became possible in the privatization adopted in the Czech lands, in which unscrupulous new owners could monetize assets and "tunnel" them to foreign bank accounts; the Czech lands were also known for hostility to Sinti and Roma populations, especially in the city Ústí nad Labem, where authorities acted to wall in the local Gypsy population.

5. Dankwart Rustow's views, as summarized by Bunce, "The Political Transition," 38.

6. "At least in Central and Eastern Europe," writes Valerie Bunce, "rapid progress toward democracy seems to have depended upon a dynamic wherein the development of a strong opposition during communism translated, with the end of the party's monopoly, into an unusually strong political showing in the first elections—which augured well for the quality of democratic governance." Bunce, "The Political Transition," 42.

7. Some argued that this failure reduced the legitimacy of the constitution as well as the post-Communist governmental system. See András Körösényi, *Government and Politics in Hungary* (Budapest, 1999), 145.

8. The revisions of April and December 1989 also removed the installation of the Polish United Workers' Party as the "leading political force in society," which had been article three of the 1952 variant. See "Konstytucja Polskiej Rzeczypospolitej Ludowej uchwalona przez Sejm Ustawodawczy w dniu 22 lipca 1952 r." and "Ustawa z dnia 29 grudnia 1989 r. o zmianie Konstytucji Polskiej Rzeczypospolitej Ludowej," available at http://isap.sejm.gov.pl (accessed November 29, 2016).

9. After 2010 Viktor Orbán's Alliance of Young Democrats produced a new constitution favoring their hold on power. As Allison Stanger wrote of Hungary, which seemed a successful case of forming a "newly democratic political system," long before this denouement could be anticipated: "The critical question is how durable such a system might be when prosperity fades or when the international system in which a given state is embedded undergoes profound change." Allison Stanger, "Leninist Legacies and Legacies of State Socialism in Postcommunist Central Europe's Constitutional Development," in Ekiert and Hanson, *Capitalism and Democracy*, 204.

10. See Robert Brier, "The Roots of the 'Fourth Republic': Solidarity's Cultural Legacy to Polish Politics," *East European Politics and Societies* 23:1 (February 2009), 63–85.

11. By contrast, Victor Orbán's Alliance of Young Democrats has had a majority, enabling a rewriting of the constitution. The Party of Law and Justice had only 33.7 percent of the popular vote for the parliament in 2005, and with its allies could not reach the two-thirds necessary for changes to the constitution. Andrzej Chwalba, *Kurze Geschichte der Dritten Republik Polen 1989 bis 2005*, Andreas Hoffmann, transl. (Wiesbaden, 2010) 198–200.

12. Philipp Ther, *Die neue Ordnung auf dem alten Kontinent: Eine Geschichte des neoliberalen Europa* (Berlin, 2014), 93.

13. This was the Bokros austerity package, named after the finance minister of that time. See below. László Andor, *Hungary on the Road to the European Union* (Westport, CT, 2000), 63.

14. Agnieszka Stawariarska, "21 lat temu dopiero były podwyżki," *Gazeta Lubelska*, March 14, 2011; "Obwieszczenie prezesa głównego urzędu statystycznego z dnia 7 lutego 1990 r. w sprawie przeciętnego wynagrodzenia miesięcznego w gospodarce uspołecznionej w 1989 r.," *Monitor Polski* 5 (1990), 40, 44.

15. Ther, *Neue Ordnung*, 91; Frances Millard, *Polish Politics and Society* (London, 1999), 152, 155.

16. These are the Maastricht criteria for states wanting to enter the third stage of the European Economic and Monetary Union and adopt the Euro as the country's currency. Millard, *Polish Politics*, 153.

17. Ther, *Neue Ordnung*, 93.

18. He had worked at the Institute of Marxism-Leninism and left the Polish United Workers' Party in 1981 after the imposition of martial law. For critiques of the government's economic policy, see Tadeusz Kowalik, *From Solidarity to Sellout: The Restoration of Capitalism in Poland*, Eliza Lewandowska, trans. (New York, 2011); David Ost, *The Defeat of Solidarity* (Ithaca, NY, 2005).

19. Eva Hoffman, *Exit into History: A Journey through the New Eastern Europe* (New York, 1993) xv, 67.

20. Anna Grzymala-Busse, *Redeeming the Communist Past: The Regeneration of Communist Parties in East Central Europe* (Cambridge, 2002); Ther, *Neue Ordnung*, 91. That majority was 54.1 percent; still, they decided to enter a coalition with the Free Democrats.

21. This was done under the new finance minister, Grzegorz Kołodko. Millard, *Polish Politics*, 153. The SLD had some 20 percent of the vote, Pawlak's People's Party had 15 percent.

22. For example, the workers at the Gdańsk shipyards got 40 percent of free shares; those at Wedel Chocolate 10 percent. There was a lot of negotiation and deal-making of various actors— SLD, PSL, opposition, and within parties—in advance of the commercialization law of 1997. Workers of course hoped to benefit from holding shares. Millard, *Polish Politics*, 154.

23. Lewandowski was born in 1951. He became European Commissioner for Financial Programming and the Budget, 2010–2014.

24. Cited in Millard, *Polish Politics*, 155. Still, he lambasted the government for delays in privatization.

25. The SLD was formed from an alliance of center-left parties, including the old official trade union. Grzymala-Busse, "Redeeming the Communist Past," 157–181.

26. The minimum was calculated based on things like household income and number of children. Millard, *Polish Politics*, 157.

27. In 1998, it was estimated that a starting hairdresser earned more than a doctor in an outpatients' clinic. Millard, *Polish Politics*, 157.

28. As a response to a severe balance-of-payments deficit of $3 billion, and made Hungarian products more attractive, foreign ones more expensive.

29. After 1997. Andor, *Hungary on the Road*, 65.

30. Donald Blinken, "Privatization Helps: The Hungarian Example," *Huffington Post*, July 31, 2011. Available at http://www.huffingtonpost.com/donald-blinken/privatization-helps-the-h_b_914383.html (accessed December 20, 2018).

31. Andor, *Hungary on the Road*, 62–64.

32. Ther, *Neue Ordnung*, 100–101, 120.

33. One World Bank survey claimed that the initial devaluation in Poland and Czechoslovakia was four times larger than that necessary to maintain purchasing power parity for Polish and

Czech goods. Ivan T. Berend, *From the Soviet Bloc to the European Union: The Economic and Social Transformation of Central and Eastern Europe since 1973* (Cambridge, UK, 2009), 67.

34. "Unfinished Czech Reforms," *New York Times*, December 2, 1997; Ther, *Neue Ordnung*, 99. As late as 1999, 60 percent of the labor force in "coddled industries" had not changed jobs since 1989. "Little to Cheer About," *Time*, November 29, 1999.

35. The fall was accompanied by stagnant growth, rising unemployment, and steep devaluation of the currency. *The Economist*, December 4, 1997. One of the simpler methods of "tunneling" was for management of one publically owned company to sell assets to a second company at an unreasonably low price; the shareholders for the first company typically owned the second company. Jonathan Stein, "Between Stagnation and Integration," in *Holding the Course: Annual Survey of Eastern Europe and the Soviet Union*, Peter Rutland, ed. (Armonk, NY, 1999), 74.

36. "Most of the asset tunneling was carried out by poorly regulated investment funds established to concentrate ownership of the nominal shares distributed to the more than 6 million adult citizens who participated in the 'voucher' privatization completed in 1994." Stein, "Between Stagnation and Integration," 75.

37. "Unfinished Czech Reforms," *New York Times*, December 2, 1997.

38. Ther, *Neue Ordnung*, 172–173.

39. The act of federation of October 1968 was an amendment to the constitution of 1960. Josef Žatkuliak, "Slovakia's Position within the Czecho-Slovak Federation," in *Slovakia in History*, Mikuláš Teich et al., eds. (Cambridge, 2011), 324–326.

40. Citing Cutler and Schwartz, Alison Stanger writes: "There was no democratic government anywhere else in the world 'in which comparable minorities of legislative bodies [had] as much blocking power.'" Stanger, "Leninist Legacies," 199.

41. Abby Innes, *Czechoslovakia: The Short Goodbye* (New Haven, CT, 2001), 209.

42. "'Wir haben die Nase voll von Prag!' und 'Fort mit dem tschechischen Kolonialismus!'" *Der Spiegel*, September 30, 1991. The economy featured more heavy industry, much of it military, that was not competitive. That of course exacerbated the belief that Slovaks were exploited. Foreign direct investment also lagged; Bunce and Wolchik, "Defining and Domesticating," 139–140.

43. It helped that few Poles lived in Ukraine. Timothy Snyder, *The Reconstruction of Nations: Poland, Ukraine, Lithuania, Belarus, 1569–1999* (New Haven, CT, 2003), 220–231.

44. See his song, "Don't Let's Be Beastly to the Germans," in *The Noel Coward Reader*, Barry Day, ed. (New York, 2011), 440.

45. Milada Vachudova, "Democratization in Postcommunist Europe: Illiberal Regimes and the Leverage of International Actors," *Center for European Studies Working Paper Series* 139 (Cambridge, MA, 2006), 5.

46. The National Salvation Front had issued a statement on December 22, 1989, stating a desire to "join in the process of building a united Europe, a common home of all the peoples on the continent." Dimitris Papadimitriou and David Phinnemore, *Romania and the European Union: From Marginalization to Membership* (London, 2008), 66. In June 1990, President Ion Iliescu summoned miners to Bucharest to quell what he called a fascist rebellion, namely, students and opposition party rallies. The 7,000 miners ransacked opposition headquarters and beat passersby indiscriminately; police also intervened to crush demonstrations, killing at least four. *New York*

Times, June 15, 1990; Dennis Deletant, *Ceaușescu and the Securitate: Coercion and Dissent in Romania* (Armonk, NY, 1997), 397.

47. Laid out in Lenka Fedorová, *The Effectiveness and Limits of EU Conditionality: Changing Domestic Policies in Slovakia (1989–2004)* (Berlin, 2011), 40.

48. Ther, *Neue Ordnung,* 156–159.

49. Ther, *Neue Ordnung,* 163–164.

50. Videnov, a graduate of the Plovdiv English language school, was thirty-five at the time of his election. The Orion group founded a Bulgarian Agricultural and Industrial Bank after Videnov's accession, which wound up defrauding farmers of their savings. Orion members left the country for a comfortable retirement in South Africa. Venelin I. Ganev, *Preying on the State: The Transformation of Bulgaria after 1989* (Ithaca, NY, 2007), 78.

51. Milenko Petrovic, *The Democratic Transition of Post-Communist Europe: In the Shadow of Communist Differences and Uneven Europeanization* (New York, 2013), 27.

52. Tsveta Petrova, "A Post Communist Transition in Two Acts," in *Democracy and Authoritarianism in the Postcommunist World,* Valerie Bunce et al., eds. (Cambridge, 2009), 113–115.

53. Crampton, *Concise History,* 234; Petrova, "A Post-Communist Transition," 127.

54. Though the prime minister has real power, this election was presented as a referendum by the UDF versus socialists and their third way. Petrova, "A Post-Communist Transition," 119.

55. Petrova, "A Post-Communist Transition," 124: only 15 percent of people had a negative view regarding the events.

56. Petrova, "A Post-Communist Transition," 117, 119; Crampton, *Concise History,* 234.

57. Ekaterina Balabanova, *Media, Wars, and Politics: Comparing the Incomparable in Western and Eastern* (Aldershot, UK, 2013), 99–101.

58. Petrova, "A Post-Communist Transition," 108, 120.

59. Bunce and Wolchik, "Defining and Domesticating," 134.

60. In 1999, the European Union, in the "Stability Pact for Southeastern Europe," made the prospect of joining the Union a "cornerstone" of its foreign policy toward the western Balkans. Vachudova, "Democratization," 8.

61. Fedorová, "Effectiveness," 40. The term "passive leverage" is Milada Vachudova's, defined as "the traction that the EU has on the domestic politics of credible candidate states merely by virtue of its existence and its usual conduct." Milada Vachudova, *Europe Undivided: Democracy, Leverage, and Integration after Communism* (Oxford, 2005), 65.

62. Fedorová, "Effectiveness," 42.

63. Petrova, "A Post-Communist Transition," 108.

64. Young Kováč was suspected of fraud by German authorities. The investigator of this incident found his car fire-bombed. Bunce and Wolchik, "Defining and Domesticating," 143. For the Čarnogurský anecdote: Marci Shore, *The Taste of Ashes: The Afterlife of Totalitarianism in Eastern Europe* (New York, 2013), 99.

65. The kidnapping was supposed to help discredit Kováč, whom Mečiar hoped to unseat. Sharon Fisher, "Slovakia Heads toward International Isolation," in *Transition* 3:2 (1997), 23.

66. Federova, "Effectiveness," 47–48.

67. Marián Leško, *Mečiar a mečiarizmus: politik bez škrupúl', politika bez zábran* (Bratislava, 1996), 56. His popularity peaked at 90 percent in March 1991.

68. Bunce and Wolchik, "Defining and Domesticating," 138.

69. He also allied with the nationalist Slovak National Party: http://www.zrs.zvolen.szm.com (accessed February 20, 2015).

70. Yet Mečiar also feared that compliance with EU and NATO demands would destroy his government. Ivo Samson, "Slovakia: Misreading the Western Message," in *Democratic Consolidation in Eastern Europe*, Jan Zielonka and Alex Pravda, eds., vol. 2 (Oxford, 2001), 363–382.

71. Stephen R. Grand, *Understanding Tahrir Square: What Transitions Elsewhere Can Teach Us about the Prospects for Arab Democracy* (Washington, DC, 2014), 43.

72. Rodger Potocki, "Slovakia's Election: Outcomes and Consequences," available at http://www.wilsoncenter.org/publication/167-slovakias-elections-outcomes-and-consequences (accessed December 3, 2016).

73. This and other actions, like OK'98 (Citizens' Campaign 98) resulted in an 80 percent turnout rate for first-time voters. Bunce and Wolchik, "Defining and Domesticating," 146.

74. The cooperation with Russia stopped in 1999 under the government of Dzurinda. Rüdiger Kipke, "Das politische System der Slowakei," in *Die politischen Systeme Osteuropas*, Wolfgang Ismayr, ed., second ed., (Opladen, 2004), 315.

75. Fedorová, "Effectiveness," 52.

76. Vachudova, "Democratization," 18–19.

77. The Social Democratic Party in Romania was founded by Ion Iliescu in 1992, as a splinter of the National Salvation Front. Vachudová, "Democratization," 25.

78. In 2002, Spain attempted to delay Slovakia's accession to the European Union over charges that the Slovak state was providing too much state aid, in the form of a ten-year tax holiday to Volkswagon. Spain recalled its veto 20 minutes before the Accession Conference of October 24, 2002. Mikael Lönnborg, Mikael Olsson, and Michael Rafferty, "The Race for Inward FDI in the Baltic States," in *European Union and the Race for Foreign Direct Investment in Europe*, Lars Oxelheim and Pervez Ghauri, eds. (Amsterdam, 2004), 338.

79. Vachudová, "Democratization," 5, 24. The exception was democratization on the European continent, where joining the European Union was credited with supporting transition and consolidation in Portugal, Spain, and Greece.

80. "Meeting on Greek Debt Produces an Ultimatum," *New York Times*, February 17, 2015.

81. "Putin Offers Hungary Natural Gas Deal," *Wall Street Journal*, February 17, 2015; http://www.tagesschau.de/ausland/putin-ungarn-101.html (accessed December 3, 2016).

82. Árpád von Klimó, "Trianon und der Diskurs über nationale Identität in Rumpf-Ungarn," in *Die geteilte Nation. Nationale Verluste und Identitäten im 20. Jahrhundert*, Andreas Hilger and Oliver von Wrochem, eds. (Munich, 2013), 11.

83. Speech of February 7, 2015, at the fifty-first Munich Conference on Security Policy, Munich. Lavrov spoke of "Kiev's supposed mistreatment of ethnic Hungarian minorities, which the Russians have cited as causes for them to support the rebels." Alison Smale, "Crisis in Ukraine Underscores Opposing Lessons of Cold War," *New York Times*, February 9, 2015.

84. Speech of May 16, 2014, available at http://www.reuters.com/article/2014/05/17/us-ukraine-crisis-hungary-autonomy-idUSBREA4G04520140517 (accessed December 3, 2016).

85. Speech of March 23, 2002, available at http://2001-2006.orbanviktor.hu/angol/hir.php?aktmenu=0&id=384 (accessed December 3, 2016).

86. "Four More Years," *The Economist*, April 5, 2014, available at http://www.economist.com /news/europe/21600169-viktor-orban-heads-third-termand-wants-centralise-power-four -more-years.

87. See http://www.rferl.org/content/ukraine-hungarian-minority-autonomy/25412593.html (accessed December 3, 2016).

88. Frances Coppola, "The Bulgarian Game of Thrones," *Forbes*, July 15, 2014.

89. See http://seekingalpha.com/article/2296535-bulgarias-strange-bank-run (accessed 3 December 2016).

90. Max Rivlin-Nadler, "Think the E.U. Is Great for Eastern Europe," *New Republic*, December 16, 2013.

Conclusion

1. "Nationalism may have stirred up passions in group situations . . . but its centrality often faded once an event had ended and more quotidian concerns took over." Judson, *Habsburg Empire*, 10; Rogers Brubaker et al., *Nationalist Politics and Everyday Ethnicity in a Transylvanian Town* (Princeton, NJ, 2006). On the contingency of nationality in Bohemia, see Jeremy King, "The Nationalization of East Central Europe: Ethnicism, Ethnicity, and Beyond," in *Staging the Past: The Politics of Commemoration in Habsburg Central Europe, 1848 to the Present*, Nancy Wingfield and Maria Bucur, eds. (West Lafayette, IN, 2001), 112–152. For the argument that nationalism began to "hate" only in the late nineteenth century, see Brian Porter, *When Nationalism Began to Hate* (Oxford, 2000), 7. For the argument that national indifference constituted a potential alternative to national identity, see Tara Zahra, "Imagined Non-Communities: National Indifference as a Category of Analysis," *Slavic Review* 69:1 (2010), 93–119.

2. Giuseppe Mazzini, "On the Slavonian National Movement," *Lowe's Edinburgh Magazine*, July 1847, 189.

3. Chad Bryant, *Prague in Black: Nazi Rule and Czech Nationalism* (Cambridge, MA, 2009). For superb studies of efforts to convert the nationally indifferent to an awareness of national identity, see Peter Judson, *Guardians of the Nation: Activists on the Language Frontiers of Imperial Austria* (Cambridge, MA, 2006); Jeremy King, *Budweisers into Czechs and Germans: A Local History of Bohemian Politics* (Princeton, NJ, 2002); Tara Zahra, *Kidnapped Souls: National Indifference and the Battle for Children in the Bohemian Lands* (Ithaca, NY, 2008).

4. Miroslav Hroch, *Na prahu národní existence: touha a skutečnost* (Prague, 1999), 59. František Graus and others would date this from much earlier. *Die Nationenbildung der Westslawen im Mittelalter* (Sigmaringen, 1980).

5. On the last point, see Henry Ashby Turner, *Hitler's Thirty Days to Power* (New York, 1996).

6. But they are not without objections. For example, the fact that a half-dozen assassins trained their weapons on Archduke Franz Ferdinand made it likely that one would succeed; and Joseph had been gathering data and ideas for years before ascending the throne.

7. Max Weber, "The Logic of Historical Explanation," in *Weber: Selections in Translation*, W. G. Runciman, ed. (Cambridge, 1978), 118.

8. That is, a moment when history might have taken a different course.

9. For the argument that nations and national identities are "contingent" phenomena, see Judson, *Guardians,* 176; Ernest Gellner, *Encounters with Nationalism* (Oxford, 1994), 60.

10. A good list of sources on this topic is in Bruce S. Hall, *A History of Race in Muslim West Africa* (Cambridge, 2012), 12.

11. John Efron, *Defenders of the Race: Jewish Doctors and Race Science in Fin-de-Siècle Europe* (New Haven, CT, 1994); Aleksander Hertz, *The Jews in Polish Culture* (Evanston, IL, 1988), 15–17.

12. This is a conclusion I have drawn from reading thousands of pages of postwar correspondence of all kinds in Polish higher education and also the Polish press. But the same was true of other places in Eastern Europe where Jewish co-citizens were suddenly absent.

13. For attitudes among Czechs, who began expressing concern during the war that Jews might return, see Hana Kubátová and Jan Láníček, *The Jew in Czech and Slovak Imagination 1938–89* (Leiden, 2018), 115. This did not imply any support for the German position in the war, however; the comments are also full of anti-German hostility.

14. German artist Gunter Demnig's *Stolpersteine,* memorials in bronze in the pavements before houses where Jews once lived, have been transported to the Czech Republic; and there are now local groups supporting this initiative.

15. Both the Nazis and the Communists appealed to East Europeans in terms of a discourse on Europe. East German media liked to inform listeners that two-thirds of Europe was socialist; and Gorbachev spoke of a common European home.

16. Yuri Slezkine, *The House of Government: A Saga of the Russian Revolution* (Princeton, NJ, 2017).

17. For an elegant statement of this view regarding the GDR, see Jeffrey Kopstein, *The Politics of Economic Decline in East Germany* (Chapel Hill, NC, 1997).

18. Maria Turlejska, as recalled by Jerzy Holzer. Joanna Szymoniczek and Eugeniusz Cezary Król, eds., *Rok 1956 w Polsce i jego rezonans w Europie* (Warsaw, 2009), 311.

19. István Zimonyi, *Muslim Sources on the Magyars in the Second Half of the Ninth Century* (Leiden, 2016), 185; Theodore Duka, "The Ugor Branch of the Ural-Altaic Family of Languages," *Journal of the Royal Asiatic Society of Great Britain and Ireland* 21 (1889), 627.

20. The situation was similar in Sahel: "There was a widespread reconfiguration of genealogies by Sahelian intellectuals that served to justify noble social status by reference to foreign origins." Hall, *History of Race,* 40.

21. Lucian Boia, *History and Myth in Romanian Consciousness* (Budapest, 2001), 43.

22. "Playing the Last Hour in the Life of Hemingway," *San Francisco Examiner,* August 21, 1977.

23. This was for making jokes about a group of Nazis, including Robert Kaltenbrunner and Otto Skorzeny. Heike Specht, *Curd Jürgens: General und Gentleman: Die Biographie* (Berlin, 2015).

24. George Barany, *Stephen Széchenyi and the Awakening of Hungarian Nationalism* (Princeton, NJ, 1968), 225.

25. C. A. Macartney, *The Habsburg Empire 1790–1918* (London, 1969), 732. For the concept of flanking as applied to Yugoslav territories, see Robert Hislope, "Intra-ethnic Conflict in Croatia and Serbia: Flanking and the Consequences for Democracy," *East European Quarterly* 30:4

(Winter 1996), 471–494. Jeremy King notes this phenomenon in 1890s Bohemia, where the Old and Young Czechs became successively more anti-German by trying to demonstrate their Czechness. Jeremy King, *Budweisers into Czechs and Germans: A Local History of Bohemian Politics, 1848–1948* (Princeton, NJ, 2002), 86. For a general evocation of this principle, see also Judson, *Guardians*, 9, with copious references.

26. Yet even the enlightened Eötvös had extended cultural rights to minorities in the Hungarian kingdom as a way of lessening their opposition: he did not doubt that the ultimate fate of every citizen of the kingdom was to become culturally Magyar; they would ultimately find its attractions irresistible. Andreas Moritsch, *Ein verfrühtes Konzept zur politischen Neugestaltung Mitteleuropas* (Vienna, 1996), 94.

27. Christian Braun, *Vom schwierigen Umgang mit Massengewalt* (Wiesbaden, 2016), 95–96.

28. See Hislope, *Interethnic Conflict*; Nina Caspersen, *Contested Nationalism: Serb Elite Rivalry in Croatia and Bosnia in the 1990s* (New York, 2010); Ivan Grdešić et al., *Hrvatska U Izborima '90* (Zagreb, 1991). Thanks to Andrej Milivojević for these references.

29. That is the estimation of Jasmin Mujanović of York University. Elizabeth Zerofsky, "The Counterparty: Can Bosnia Escape the Stranglehold of Ethnic Politics?" *Harpers*, December 2015.

30. Kohl's maneuvering ruined years of careful work for German-Polish understanding, lending credibility to the idea that Germans cannot be trusted. Helga Hirsch, "Geprägt von Krieg und Geschichte," *Die Zeit*, April 6, 1990.

31. Árpád von Klimó, "Nation, Konfession, Geschichte," 293–294 and passim.

32. Eric Hobsbawm, *Nations and Nationalism since 1780* (Cambridge, 1992), 24, 32–33. On why language attracts people to national communities more strongly than to competing options for self-identification, see Gale Stokes, "Cognition and the Function of Nationalism," *Journal of Interdisciplinary History* 4:4 (1974), 536–538.

33. Edward W. Said, *Orientalism* (New York, 1977), 137.

34. Yet it was not missing from the main work that Anderson used for his understanding of East Central Europe: Oscar Jászi's *The Dissolution of the Habsburg Monarchy*, who speaks of the 1780s as a new epoch (70), because Joseph II misunderstood the psychology of national evolution. How was he to do so if it did not yet exist?

35. On Bohemia, see Eugen Lemberg, *Nationalismus*, vol. 1 (Reinbek, 1964), 136. On the absence of a clear correlation between nationalism and industrialization, see Miroslav Hroch, *European Nations: Explaining Their Formation* (London, 2015), 95.

36. Anderson writes that "print capitalism gave a new fixity to language" and that it created "languages of power different from the older administrative vernaculars." Benedict Anderson, *Imagined Communities: Reflections on the Origin and Spread of Nationalism* (New York, 1991), 44–45. What happened in fact was that independent of capitalism, administrators introduced official languages, against which patriots mobilized. He writes that the fixing of print languages was largely an "unselfconscious process." The fact was the opposite. As Geoff Eley has written, "language is less a prior determinant of nationality, than part of a complex process of cultural innovation." "Nationalism and Social History," *Social History* 6:1 (1981), 91.

37. Without being overawed by the heritage of antiquity. Anderson, *Imagined Communities*, 68–69. For the way that universal Enlightenment ideas became predictably national across the

East European map, see Balázs Trencsényi et al., *A History of Modern Political Thought in East Central Europe*, vol. 1, (Oxford, 2016), 143 and passim.

38. This insight is a variation on a claim made by the literary historian Kristin Ross, who, in her work on 1968, placed France in the broader focus of those three "worlds" by treating that year as a convergence of national liberation struggles of Cuba and Indochina, the antibureaucratic struggles in Hungary and Czechoslovakia, and the anticapitalist, antiauthoritarian struggles of the imperial metropoles of Europe and North America: Kristin Ross, *May '68 and Its Afterlives* (Chicago, 2002), 19. For the letter to the editor, see Béla Liptak, "Hungary's Plight," *New York Times*, January 4, 2019.

INDEX